TEACHER'S MANUAL
to
TORTS AND COMPENSATION
PERSONAL ACCOUNTABILITY AND SOCIAL RESPONSIBILITY FOR INJURY

Sixth Standard Edition and Concise Edition

■ ■ ■

By

Dan B. Dobbs
Regents Professor and
Rosenstiel Distinguished Professor of Law Emeritus
University of Arizona

Paul T. Hayden
Professor of Law and Jacob J. Becker Fellow
Loyola Law School, Los Angeles

Ellen M. Bublick
Dan B. Dobbs Professor of Law
University of Arizona

AMERICAN CASEBOOK SERIES®

WEST®
A Thomson Reuters business

Mat #40657553

© West, a Thomson business, 2001, 2005
© 2009 Thomson Reuters
    610 Opperman Drive
    St. Paul, MN 55123
    1–800–313–9378
Printed in the United States of America

ISBN: 978–0–314–18493–1

 TEXT IS PRINTED ON 10% POST CONSUMER RECYCLED PAPER

Acknowledgements

Special thanks to Carol Ward, Judith Parker, Lynda Koepfer, Diane Hayden, and Dorothy Hayden for expert assistance in the preparation of this Teacher's Manual.

Using this Manual

▶**Note to Users of the Fifth Edition:** Each chapter contains a note on changes introduced in this edition, both additions and deletions. We have updated this edition with new cases throughout, and we've also shortened the length of the book to under 1,000 pages. Obviously that has necessitated the deletion of some material, including some main cases. Sometimes we have reduced a case that was formerly a main case to a shorter case abstract; most of the time when we have deleted a case abstract it is at least cited in a Note following a main case. We have not usually indicated specifically when we've changed the order of Notes, or when we've added or deleted particular Notes. By all means, check the note on changes in each chapter, but it does without saying that you need to look at the materials themselves to see in detail what has been revised.

▶**Note to Users of the Concise Edition.** There is no separate Teacher's Manual for the Concise Edition; rather, this Manual covers both books. Please see the segments at the end of this "Using this Manual" section titled Using the Concise Edition and Using this Manual with the Concise Edition.■

You may not need this Teacher's Manual at all. If you use it, selective use is probably best. Here is basic information you may need to use this manual effectively.

1. This manual contains a few generalized suggestions about teaching the casebook, and about possible omissions. These appear in the short segment, Using the Casebook, just below.

2. General organization is summarized in the segment below, Aims and Directions.

3. Most of this manual is keyed to particular materials in the casebook. You don't need to read all of this manual's coverage of a section assigned for class. Instead, you can scan the relevant segment of the manual, or turn to the manual only when you come to matters that puzzle you or to matters that require increased attention or detail.

To use the manual selectively, you need to recognize the main types of materials it contains. These are:

Changes in this Edition. This brief note at the beginning of each chapter alerts teachers who used the Fifth Edition to the general changes, such as cases added and omitted.

Scheduling Omissions. Few, if any, teachers can teach the entire standard edition of the casebook. This manual suggests possible omissions and sometimes mentions the disadvantages of omissions.

Preliminary Notes. Some chapters or sections contain a Preliminary Note. Such notes attempt to explain the general direction in which that part of the casebook is heading, or how it might relate to other materials or broader ideas.

Outlines. Many of the chapters (especially the longer ones) begin with an outline of materials to be covered in the casebook. This gives you a little more detail than the topic headings in the casebook and may explain why one case comes before another. You can get an overview before you start reading the casebook cases, or you can refer back to the outline after you've read material if you are not clear about our organization.

Summary. Many chapters or sections contain brief summaries of the cases and topical notes. These can refresh recollection or provide a quick survey before you read the cases yourself. Most of them would not suffice as detailed case briefs, but they should remind you of the main facts and issues if, for example, you are reviewing before class.

Comments. The bulk of this Teacher's Manual is found in the materials labeled as Comment. Most of the book's primary cases get a separate comment. Longer comments may contain several different types of material.

Comments vary in scope, but they often include these kinds of materials: (1) a comment upon or suggested analysis of the main or abstract case, perhaps indicating explicitly why the case is included; (2) references to related materials in the course; (3) tentative suggestions about how the case can be taught in class; (4) explanation of questions asked in the notes; (5) a statement of the courts' holdings in cases cited in the notes; (6) something more about "the law" on the topic raised by the main case; (7) suggestions about expected classroom problems or teaching opportunities, such as distinctions you may need to emphasize, or issues you may need to handle with care; (8) limited references to sources for further investigation of the topic.

You may find some of the comment useful, some not. If you know how you want to teach the material, you can skip the comments unless you are looking for related materials or additional analysis. The presence of this material is NOT an implied suggestion that you teach all or indeed any of it. In some instances the material includes so many issues, cases, and ideas that no one could possibly teach it all. The point is to use any portion of it you find useful, but certainly not that you could use it all. Skip the details of this kind if you have planned a full class with your own preferred material and you are satisfied with your plan.

■**FYI Notes.** Notes labeled FYI and boxed material embedded in comments take up a related point or to provide background information you might want to have in mind before teaching but one that you probably would not use in class unless student questions raised the matter. These are separately labeled or boxed so you can easily spot and skip them if you wish.■

Locating material. This manual is not indexed, but we provide a Table of Contents that tells you where each Section of each Chapter begins. The headers at the top of each page indicate the Chapter you are in.

Using the Casebook

This casebook attempts to cover all the main rules of tort law with materials that challenge students to develop skills in analysis and synthesis, to understand and evaluate judicial reasoning, and to grapple with issues of justice, policy, process, and fact. The book attempts also to get students to think about how rules affect people, so it includes a number of rather specific rules or issues that bear on the actual working of a rule. That might include the strategies it induces.

The materials in the casebook take one of the following five forms:

(1) **Main cases.** These are edited versions of cases that appear in the reporters.

(2) **Case abstracts.** These are summaries of facts, holding and reasoning of cases as they bear on the issue at hand. A case abstract may be used to establish a point of law, a line of reasoning, or a set of facts that will not be otherwise covered. Or it may be used for comparison or contrast other cases. A case abstract should not be considered unimportant merely because it appears in the shortened, summary form. A case may appear in that form because the case, although establishing an important point or providing a dramatic example, is nevertheless unsuitable for editing as a main case. A case may also be presented as a case abstract because such a presentation sharpens the point and facilitates comparison with other cases around it.

(3) **Notes.** "Notes" is of course a conventional word that includes "questions." Notes following a main or note case elaborate on the case or ideas in it or on related materials. Sometimes the notes contain additional information or explanation so that, having read the explanation, the students are prepared to proceed with a discussion of the logic, policy, or justice of the case. Perhaps more often the notes will start right off with questions intended to get the student to think about the case before coming to class. If you regularly discuss questions raised in the notes, students soon learn that the questions are advance notice about topics worth their consideration.

(4) **Topical Text Notes.** Textual notes have often been given titles. Topical Notes are thus formally treated like cases. How you cover them in class is another matter. Textual Notes segments usually give legal information about cases, or about some point of law. They almost always raise discussable issues about the information.

(5) **Problems.** Problems are scattered throughout the book, but are not a major portion part of the teaching equipment. Problems state a set of facts. Discussion asks the student to apply the known legal rules, principles, or attitudes to the solution or

argumentation of the problem. Problems are essentially more detailed hypotheticals. None rises to the complexity or detail of an actual case that might be on the law office's docket.

Teaching the main cases. Although some teachers have told us they teach by working through the notes, we suspect that most teachers treat the main case as the anchor most discussion. There is nothing special about the main cases in this book except that they might sometimes reflect contemporary and often sensitive problems. We think you can teach them in whatever style you prefer Socratically, by lecture, by hypothetical, or by some combination.

Teaching the case abstracts. You can try to give at least some class time to most note cases to get the students to recognize that their length is not an index of their significance. You might summarize the facts of the note case or merely indicate its general factual context. "Smith v. Jones is essentially the same set of facts as the main case, Perez v. Garcia" might be the ploy. "Why did the court reach a different result?" Sometimes you might be surprised to find that the student did not see the similarity between the two cases and failed to see that they were contrary. Or it might be that the student really can distinguish apparently contrary cases. It's wonderful when you get a chance to give the student credit for that kind of ability.

When the note cases differ from the main case or other note cases, students sooner or later seem to assume that the main case is the "majority rule," because its name is in bigger type. If they don't so assume, then they often ask how to know which case represents "the rule." This is a good chance to remind them that rules tell us about what to argue and what kind of evidence to look for and invite them to recognize that knowing a majority rule is not much help to the lawyer who practices in Maryland, if Maryland follows some other approach. You can truthfully add that on many issues, no majority rule can be confidently stated, and in any event, judicial decision-making is not political– we aren't voting in a kind of judicial electoral college. Sooner or later this line of discussion (which may be repeated in some classes) leads to a discussion about what you will be looking for on the exam. The "majority rule"? If not, then what? That's a good opportunity to clarify the goals of legal teaching and the skills you want the students to have, which are not likely to emphasize the memorization of majority rules.

Teaching the notes. Some teachers feel they must take class time with every item in an assignment. Others approach the written materials selectively, trying to discuss issues the students have trouble with or ask questions about. If you feel that the information notes are sufficiently self explanatory, you can put the burden on the students to ask questions about them if they have any, otherwise use class time for more difficult matters such as analysis, application, comparisons, and synthesis. Explicitly putting the burden on the students to ask questions about material can be part of the effort to move students from the role of passive recipients of information to the role of active participants who take some responsibility for their own development. A good lawyer skill.

Provocative notes, as distinguished from information notes, ask questions or give hypotheticals. They are intended to give the student a chance to think about important issues *before* going to class. First-year students are initially unlikely to consider issues in any very sophisticated way. Teachers can appear very knowledgeable and threatening with those classroom questions that to students seem to be pulled out of nowhere. Provocative notes aim to give the student a chance to consider the case or its issues ahead of time, so that classroom questions and discussion are not wholly a surprise. (Plenty of surprise seems to remain, however.) Particular notes that ask questions or give examples may be covered by the ordinary coverage of the case.

You may sometimes want to begin case coverage by asking a student's answer to a question in the notes, a ploy that can often lead into a series of questions to clarify the student's understanding of facts or reasoning of the main case. Similarly, if a note poses a set of facts, you can begin by asking the student to apply the rule in the main case to that set of facts. Your own more demanding or complex hypotheticals for which the student was *not* prepared by the notes might then follow. Again, the student's answer to the note hypothetical may well take you into a full-blown discussion of the main case.

At other times questions or hypotheticals posed in the notes may not come up in the discussion of the case. In that case, you can turn to the notes as a discrete part of the discussion after the case discussion is completed.

You have plenty of room for a flexible, varied approach to the notes. The book was written on the assumption that assignments would include notes and all. If for any reason you prefer to do so, you can of course exclude all notes from the assignment.

Teaching the text. Many Socratic teachers once felt uncertain about teaching text. It turns out, however, that teaching text is no problem at all. You can teach text in at least three distinct ways, depending on time available, class abilities, subject matter and the other usual variables affecting teaching modes.

(a) *Assign text but do not explicitly cover it in class.* If you choose this route you can invite the class to ask any questions they may have from reading it.

(b) *Cover text with a dialog, using questions and hypotheticals.* Most of the text material in the casebook presents at least one issue of policy, the application of a rule, or synthesis of a rule. If nothing else, you can invite the students' opinions on that issue.

(c) *Cover the text with lecture.* You can summarize the text's points and illustrate with materials of your own. You can tie the text to other themes you have covered.

A fourth possibility is to exclude texts from your assignment. This may not be wise in the case of some short textual notes, but omitting some text might be the best choice for a particular class in a particular years.

Teaching the problems. Teaching problems is easiest of all. Ask for the result the court should get or the argument a student would give. The rest is like a dialog about a case. Students may apply some rules correctly but miss other rules altogether or misapply them. Encouragement and discussion work best. You can ask students to imagine that they are discussing the issue as equal partners in a small firm, or with a lawyer-friend over a cup of coffee. If you can break the ice with students and remove their fear, problems become an excellent method of review, application, and issue-analysis.

Omissions

Suggestions for omissions appear almost every chapter or section. Here are some general ideas about omissions. If you have as much as five hours to teach torts, you may be able to cover all of the personal injury materials in Chapter 1 through Chapter 31 without substantial omission. That includes the alternatives to tort law. However, you may find you'd like a much slower pace, so that even with five hours to teach, you might selectively omit some materials. (One of us, teaching a five-hour course, has routinely covered Chapters 1-31 without substantial omissions, then lectures for two hours on the economic and dignitary torts.)

If you have the luxury of six hours, you can probably teach the entire book without omissions, but again, you might want to make selective omissions so as not to drive the class too hard.

Pressed for time, we'd consider omitting (1) all the economic and dignitary tort materials, especially if some of them are available in advanced courses; (2) the tort law alternatives, workers' compensation, social security, and no-fault insurance (Chapters 28-31). If we had to omit the alternatives, we'd cover some main points in a lecture at the end or raise the alternatives and some of their main characteristics from time to time as you consider cases in the course. If products liability law is taught as a separate advanced course in your school and is commonly taken by many students, you could consider omitting (3) Chapter 24 on products. But even if that is the case, something of products "strict liability" probably is needed to give a fair picture of tort law and even to introduce the basic concepts. Every bulk omission of this kind has substantial disadvantages. You could consider omitting (4) Chapter 22 on vicarious liability, for example, but if you do, students will have a significantly reduced appreciation of how tort law actually works and also some of the basic thought behind enterprise and strict liability. Some teachers do little with immunities, but as legislatures have increasingly protected special defendants from accountability under tort law, immunity is a serious topic we think should not be omitted in bulk. Consequently, we do NOT suggest omission of the entire chapter 15 on governmental and official liability (mostly a matter of immunity).

We suggest you check out selective omissions before you opt for bulk omissions.

Aims and Directions:
Where the Casebook Goes and How It Gets There

This note is not about the intellectual skills the book attempts to foster, nor about the specific information it contains. It is instead about the general organization and direction of the casebook.

The casebook is mainly about physical injury, or at least the danger of physical injury. For several reasons, we treat emotional harms as belonging in this category. Physical injury may be either to persons or to property as long as it is associated with physical harm or the risk of physical harm. Economic or commercial harms (those without physical harm) are associated with such torts as interference with contract and fraud. They are relegated to four short chapters at the end of the book. Non-trespassory dignitary torts not involving physical action or violence are associated with such torts as libel and privacy invasion. These are likewise covered in the last chapters of the book.

The focus on physical harm corresponds to the needs of first-year students and to the time limits commonly imposed. However, the main reason for emphasizing physical harms is different. That emphasis allows us to concern ourselves with an important public issue. What systems should we adopt for dealing with injuries? We can use a fault-based tort system, a strict liability tort system, or any one of several non-tort systems. The casebook aims to provide students with a basis for beginning to evaluate the alternatives, including the "tort reform" alternatives within the fault system. If you examine the table of contents or the notes in this manual for Chapters 38-31, you will see both the practical and policy importance of this material.

Using the Concise Edition

The Concise Edition attempts to present core materials of tort law in personal injury and property damages cases in a short form that makes it possible to teach the central materials in a four hour course. However, we are not cops of the tort canon, and many teachers may have different ideas about what constitutes the core materials. Consequently, teachers using the Concise Edition will still have some choices to include this but omit that.

Cuts in the material have taken several different forms and some of them affect teaching.

1) We eliminate many citations and examples. The teacher can find them in the standard edition and/or this Manual. These cuts should not affect classroom reading and teaching, although the teacher can find the omitted citations and examples in the standard edition.

(2) We have eliminated some main cases and some case abstracts. In many instances, in cutting the main cases, we retained the underlying topic by presenting a case abstract or a note. These changes may affect the balance between main case material, case abstracts, and note material and to some extent the actual teaching. As with the standard edition, the teacher's flexibility and ability to teach from diverse material such as case abstracts will be important. On the other hand, reducing the number of main cases may free the teacher to spend time on ideas (found in case abstracts or notes) and less time forcing students to state facts. Similarly, the idea content may profitably outweigh the emphasis that otherwise might be given to supposed majority and supposed minority rules.

(3) In a few instances we have cut whole chapters or whole sections, but in most of those, if not all, we have written a short statement about some of the issues covered. We've usually renamed these sections or chapters by adding "Being Aware of....." at the beginning of the section or chapter name so that teachers and students can know immediately that only a little information is provided. Some teachers may find it useful to omit these sections and chapters altogether, although they are exceedingly brief. Other may wish to assign such "awareness" materials and add a point or two in lecture or hypothetical.

Using this Manual with the Concise Edition

► At the beginning of each Chapter of this Manual, you will find a shaded paragraph that begins, "The **Concise Edition** . . ." that tells you what has been changed from the standard edition. We note only the major revisions (deletions of cases or abstracts, sections or blocks of notes) as opposed to minor deletions, which typically occur dozens of times in each Chapter.■

Chapter numbers in the Concise and Standard editions. The chapter numbers in the Concise Edition correspond exactly with the Chapter numbers in the standard edition in the first 28 chapters. However, Chapters 28-31 in the standard edition are combined in a single chapter 28 in the concise edition, and chapters 32-33 are combined into a single Chapter 29 in the Concise edition.

Users of the concise edition will therefore be able to use this manual without adjustment for all chapters up to chapter 28. For materials in the Concise Edition Chapter 28, however, users will turn to Chapter 28, 29, 30 or 31 in this manual for materials on workers' compensation, social security and other public support for injured people, for no-fault private insurance plans, and for evaluative materials respectively.

Likewise users of the Concise Edition Chapter 29 can turn in this manual to Chapter 32 or 33 for materials on dignitary torts and economic torts respectively.

Section numbers in the Concise and standard editions. In the core chapters, we omitted some entire sections, but when we did so, we inserted a brief text to alert the readers to the general content and to give the teacher a basis for adding comments or illustrations if wished. The result is that the section numbers in core sections remain the same in both the standard and the Concise Editions.

Note numbers in the Concise and standard editions. We've deleted some numbered notes, then renumbered notes to keep them consecutive. We have not indicated such changes in this Manual to avoid cluttering it, although you should have no trouble figuring out which Notes are omitted.

Because some text, references and examples have been cut from the Concise Edition notes, the discussion of any given note in this Manual may address points that do not appear in the Concise Edition note. These points may or may not add materials you'll want to raise in your class.

Using the Full Edition for reference. In a number of instances, to achieve brevity, we've stated a rule in a note, but cut out case references or examples. In most of these, if you want references or examples, you can check the corresponding note in the full edition. In those few cases in which the Concise Edition omits notes and renumbers those that remain, you can look up omitted references by checking the standard edition to determine the original note number. It will ordinarily have the same black-letter name as the renumbered note in the Concise Edition.

In some ways the Concise Edition should be easier to teach. Some issues that appeared in notes or in cases where some text that has been removed simply won't be involved unless the teacher raises them. At other times, however, we eliminated notes that were inserted in the standard edition to reinforce or emphasize an issue or holding, which may sometimes mean that the point will elude some students unless the teacher makes such in class discussion that students have grasped it.

TEACHER'S MANUAL
TABLE OF CONTENTS

Part 3. Limiting or Expanding the Duty of Care According to Context or Relationship

TOPIC A: LIMITING DUTIES ACCORDING TO CLASS OR STATUS OF THE PARTIES

PART 1

A FIRST LOOK AT TORTS

CHAPTER 1

TORT LAW: AIMS, APPROACHES, AND PROCESSES

▶**Changes in the Sixth Edition:** The main change in this chapter is the deletion of the *Estevez* case (which has now been reduced to a Note), and the addition of a Florida statute that authorizes payment of the personal injury claim of Brian Daiagi.

▶The **Concise Edition** omits the Florida statute on Brian Diaigi and its Notes.■

Overview. After a one-page introduction, this chapter introduces major tort goals with a brief discussion of justice vs. policy, deterrence, compensation, and process values. We begin with some excerpts from Dan B. Dobbs, The Law of Torts (2000) (DOBBS ON TORTS), followed by a hypothetical case demonstrating different judicial styles of reasoning about justice and policy. The last section presents a statute authorizing compensation and a case about damages. These two scenarios permit students to gauge plaintiff recoveries against the tort-law goals mentioned. The new statute is designed to facilitate discussion of justice and policy factors in a liability context, not only in the context of damages.

Objectives. (1) This chapter was previously added based on our experience and the recommendation of some teachers who suggested that a little material on the aims or theories of tort law was needed up front as a basis for exploration. Section 2 distinguishes between rules grounded in justice or fairness on the one hand and those grounded in policy or utilitarian aims on the other. A little discussion identifies one particular policy, deterrence of wrongdoing. The material is intentionally brief. It sets some themes about goals that you can raise throughout the course as you see fit. (2) A number of students in recent years have begun the course with strong views – you can see some of this on the web – that tort law is merely a matter of greedy plaintiffs seeking to get something for nothing. Such plaintiffs exist, but this view of all injured humans and this view of tort law is not only off base, it has made it difficult for some of our students to understand rules and principles, not to mention the realities. There are many ways to approach that problem. We wanted to avoid loading statistics about tort claims at the beginning of the course. We chose instead to include a statute and a case to let students see a legislature and a court trying to figure appropriate compensation for injury (not something for nothing). We think these materials will also allow you to refocus students on the aims of tort law.

Scheduling omissions. You have a lot of options about omissions. We think this chapter will be a good beginning, but you can omit it entirely if you wish. In that case, you can begin with Chapter 2, which introduces some elementary procedures found in the cases, or you can omit that as well and go straight into Chapter 3 on intentional torts. If you want to assign only part of the present chapter, that's easy, too. It may pay to keep the tiny § 1 to give students some idea of what the course is about before they get to class, but you could omit § 2 entirely or either of its subsections if, for example, you wanted to introduce the ideas there in your lecture but thought both subsections would take too much time. Another approach would be to keep the first part of § 2 but rather than discuss the Daiagi statute, give students a newspaper article about a recent wrongful injury, such as harm to a child caused by melamine-tainted baby milk. Section 3 has a case that is not good for briefing, only some thoughtful discussion about the function of tort damages.

§ 1. WHAT IS TORT LAW?

This little section should require only limited discussion, but some students may profit by an opportunity to clarify the distinction between criminal and tort law. If you want to extend discussion, DOBBS ON TORTS §§ 1-5 (2000), defines torts and compares crime, contract, property and regulatory controls. Tort law includes injuries besides personal injury, and personal injuries may be redressed outside tort law by workers' compensation or other systems. *See* Id. § 6. You might want to mention those systems at this point. *See* Chapters 28-30.

§ 2. THE AIMS AND APPROACHES IN TORT LAW – JUSTICE AND POLICY, COMPENSATION AND DETERRENCE

A. Some Broad (and Conflicting) Aims

We don't expect most students to fully grasp these concepts right away. Rather, the point is to give a fair introduction to ideas to that recur as you interpret cases and to foreshadow many specific discussions to come.

We hope the simple readings are self-explanatory to teachers, but students may need discussion and questions. The readings raise ideas about the distinction between justice and policy, liability based upon fault and strict liability, compensation and risk distribution. They introduce the idea of economic analysis as one form of pursuing policy or utility (but without technical material of any kind). This includes ideas of deterring some (but not all) activities that cause harm. Finally, they introduce the idea of process values, but again without analysis of all the values that might be involved.

Your discussion can use an example of a tort issue in the news or examples from the readings (anticipating *Surroco's* spreading fire problem perhaps). Society at large may benefit from activities that are known to cause harms. Thus society may want people to use motor vehicles, as this increases trade and other exchanges among people. Yet the activity of motoring is costly in lives and injuries. If society perceives motoring to be a social good, then maybe society generally should foot the bill, including the bill for the injuries that are inevitable. Or should we say that individuals also gain from their use of automobiles and should pay the costs of their driving activities, including the inevitable costs of injuries they cause, even innocently?

Justice and policy (or deterrence) can be in conflict as abstract goals, but they often coincide. Professor Gary Schwartz argues for a "mixed" theory that accommodates both. *See* Gary T. Schwartz, *Mixed Theories of Tort Law: Affirming Both Deterrence and Corrective Justice*, 75 TEX. L. REV. 1801 (1997). If you are teaching torts for the first time, this article can provide some very helpful background about the development of tort theory. The actual structure of the mixed theory might have to be developed by torts thinkers over time. Schwartz suggests some possibilities: (1) tort law assigns liability for deterrence reasons, subject to overriding constraints imposed by corrective justice criteria; or conversely, (2) liability is assigned by corrective justice criteria, subject to overriding constraints dictated by deterrence policies. The Simons article provides a more recent view of these mixed theories as well as a number of provocative hypotheticals that illustrate the tradeoffs.

The Kaplow & Shavell article cited here was already a book-length work, but was turned into a book of the same title (with some revisions, of course) in 2002. Kaplow and Shavell's argument is that notions of fairness or justice are never correctly considered by legal decision-makers independently of the overriding interest in "welfare," which they describe basically as the satisfaction of individual preferences. Yale professor Jules Coleman calls this a "radical claim" which is not only unsupported but logically and empirically unsupportable. Jules Coleman, *The Grounds of Welfare*, 112 YALE L.J. 1511, 1538 (2003). Coleman concludes his book review by asserting that "whatever it is about persons that ultimately warrants concern for human welfare warrants the view that justice must regulate affairs between persons. It is not that justice is a constituent of welfare or welfare a constituent of justice. Rather, both are important and distinct reflections of the dignity and importance of persons. Any theory of the law that would direct us to evaluate our practices by considering only welfare or justice and not the other could do so only by impoverishing the idea of the person."

Some writers want to discard theories and go straight to compensation for injured people without regard to fault or deterrence when a person is injured by an enterprise. Nolan and Ursin have repeatedly urged the risk distribution idea propounded by James in the depression era. A recent example of their writings is Virginia E. Nolan & Edmund Ursin, *The Deacademification of Tort Theory*, 48 U. KAN. L. REV. 59 (1999). This risk distribution idea —enterprises will pass their tort liability costs on to customers— may be an expensive way to deal with injury costs even if you regard it as fair. For this reason, you might want to redress the social problems of uncompensated injury through other non-tort mechanisms. In fact, some who focus on the needs of injured people despair of the tort system and propose a welfare system. *See* STEPHEN SUGARMAN, DOING AWAY WITH PERSONAL INJURY LAW (1989). In Chapters 28-30, this book takes a brief look at some alternative ways of dealing with injury outside the tort system, mainly workers' compensation and the social security welfare system.

If you want to discuss the reading on its own, questions can readily include these and many others:

Justice, Policy, and Process Aims of Tort Law. (1) How does a justice approach to tort decision-making differ from a policy or utilitarian approach? (2) Are those two approaches or goals in conflict with one another?

Ideas of Corrective Justice. (3) If you take a justice (or "corrective justice") approach rather than a policy approach to tort decision, does that mean that you'd impose liability *only* for fault? (4) Correspondingly, would you *always* impose liability for fault that causes harm?

Compensation, Risk Distribution, Fault. (5) Do you favor liability of a person who harms another on the ground that the harm-causer is a good risk-distributor? How is that different from merely imposing liability upon people who have money?

Fostering Freedom, Deterring Unsafe Conduct. (6) Would a policy approach to torts based upon economic analysis favor deterrence of all harm-causing activity? (You may encounter the view that individuals engaged in activities like driving too fast are unlikely to be deterred by the potential for tort liability. True enough. However, enterprises and institutions engaged in economic activity will have economic motives to respond to the potential for liability and at least some institutions are likely to do so.)

Process values in tort law. (7) What is meant by "process values?" (8) Do you favor tightly formulated legal rules governing tort law? What is the advantage of that? (9) Are rules of tort law made exclusively to guide people's conduct?

B. Applying Some Approaches

PROSSER v. KEETON, 143 Unrep. Case 1113 [a fictitious case].

If you think your class has enough grasp of different approaches to tort without further discussion, you can readily skip the material in this subsection. But the material works well on the first day of class to help students recognize and apply different goals of tort law.

The facts present an innocent purchaser of a converted article, a watch. Some students will take this as a case about the substantive rules. But our point is that these three opinions (all hypothetical, of course) present radically different ways of thinking about the problem.

Conceptual postulates. Judge Allen begins with a purely conceptual statement, not clearly grounded in either considerations of justice or considerations of policy. Hooray for the students who recognize that whatever this approach is, it is not one of articulated policy or justice concerns. The thief did not gain title. This is "conceptual" at least in the sense that this is how we think about or conceive or conceptualize the situation that exists after the theft. It is a statement about how the situation is perceived "in the eyes of the law." As with many forms of reasoning that we are likely to recognize as "conceptual," it uses a reifying locution. That is, it treats title as a thing (the thief does not have it). (You may have to explain that you can acquire legal title to a watch, though not a car, without a piece of paper.) By treating title as a thing, Allen may lead the reader to think that the absence of title is a fact and thus indisputable, not an opinion, value judgment, or merely a way of thinking about the situation. Yet the statement that the thief does not have title is *not* an empirical statement, and the value judgment behind it is quite hidden by the watertight conception. It is the pivot for Allen's argument, which then follows, more or less logically.

Justice. Bateman, J. has a different approach. Bateman begins by appeals to justice. In general, watch owners are in the best position to guard against theft, so it is more just to make the owner bear the loss than to make the innocent purchaser do so. We don't learn very much about Bateman's standards of justice, but real world human relations are a part of the justice ideal. It is not enough for Bateman to posit a conception and work it out logically; Bateman wants to make law work justly in the world as Bateman understands it to be. Bateman works with an empirical premise.

Notice, however, that Bateman has no empirical evidence for the empirical premise; we are not really sure that watch owners are better able to guard against theft than buyers are to guard against thieving sellers. Furthermore, Bateman does not explain why the fact that owners can *generally* protect themselves better should make any difference on the justice issue. Perhaps in this particular case Keeton was better able to protect himself, or there was no real difference in the ability to provide protection against the wiles of the thief. These two criticisms of Bateman's opinion suggest that some people

5

might not accept the opinion, or might like to see it more fully developed. (Perhaps Bateman means that watch owners are cheaper cost avoiders when she says that watch owners are in a "better position to guard against theft than purchasers are to discover it." This seems less about justice than it is about efficiency.) But the class should not lose sight of the point that the thrust of the opinion is a claim that justice should be done, and that this stands in great contrast to the thrust of the Allen opinion, however defective Bateman's demonstration of justice might be.

Policy. Compton, J., is not much concerned about either legal conceptions or about justice. She turns instead to social policy. There is a distressing problem about "policy" arguments. Some law teachers use "policy" as synonymous with "argument," and thus find themselves offering redundancies about "policy arguments." Students, on the other hand, seem often to think that "policy" means the same as "gut reaction" or "intuition." Compton's opinion demonstrates something of the difference between policy and justice arguments. The policy argument is a social good argument. It may not entail actual injustice, but it turns on the general good, not on the exact relationships of the very parties before the court. Thus Compton believes that policy requires relatively unfettered movement of goods in commerce; to get this, she would make a rule that the buyer gets title. Justice between individuals is explicitly *not* her criterion where social policy is more important.

You might have the feeling that Compton could be brutally quick to decide that social policy is whatever Compton thought it should be. Certainly this judge is very much a realist, and an outspoken one, too, on the issue of legal conceptions: the law can give the purchaser title if it wants to, and you suspect Compton knows very well that by "the law," is meant "the majority of the court." Some people might yearn to ask Compton whether this reasoning would permit execution of an innocent woman or holding seven people liable on the ground that one of them was probably guilty if it would be for the "transcendent" social good. As with Bateman, you find you can make criticisms, but again, the class should not lose sight of the nature of the argument and the contrast it forms with the other two.

You can ask a student which opinion he or she thinks is best. Why? What characteristics do you like? Questions lead to some of the difficulties with any given opinion, along the lines sketched above, or, alternatively, you will find that other members of the class will choose a different opinion as a favorite and you have a ready-made discussion on your hands.

Note 4. Justice entails a judgment about rights, not about the value of the thing in dispute or the social costs of deciding disputes. If justice is your guiding star, you cannot dismiss a claim because you don't regard the stake as high enough. What about social policy, however? Would it be good policy to dismiss disputes the parties care about but that judges think are insignificant? One policy is revealed by asking: If disputes are not to be resolved by courts and by law, then by whom and by what standards? You can also notice that in the common law system, the judges' resolution of small disputes contributes to the jurisprudence and may make rules that govern future large disputes.

FLORIDA 2008 SESSION LAW SERVICE, Twentieth legislature, Second Regular Session, Chapter 2008-269, C.S.H.B. 787, Personal Injuries—Negligence—Brian Daiagi.

Although this is a slightly unconventional text to include in a casebook, we found this Florida statute useful to the question of justice and policy reasons for awarding compensation. As mentioned in note 1, Florida law limits claims against the government to $200,000 in the absence of specific legislation. Accordingly, the state did not have to pay the multi-million dollar judgment against it in the Daiagi case. Yet sixteen years after Mr. Daiagi was injured, it ultimately decided to do so. Why afford Mr. Daiagi recovery for his injuries? Does payment of the claim meet goals of accountability, deterrence, compensation? Because the statute fleshes out Mr. Daiagi's legal claim, you can use this example to help students apply policy and justice rationales to an actual case.

Note 1. Florida permits the legislature to grant recovery of damages in excess of the $200,000 statutory cap. The Florida legislation allows the legislature to authorize the additional recovery after a judgment has been issued. This statue appears to be a fairly unusual provision. However, a few other states have similar laws. Colorado permits a governing body to increase by resolution the maximum amount of liability for a type of injury. However, the resolution can have prospective application only. *See* Colo. Rev. Stat. § 24-10-114(2). Two other state statutes permit the legislature to allow recovery of tort damages in excess of a statutory cap if the legislature increases the limits prior to the commencement of an action seeking greater damages. *See* Me. Rev. Stat. title 14 § 8105(3) and R.I. Gen. Laws § 9-31-4.

Note 2. This question gives teachers an opportunity to begin addressing the major goals of tort law. In terms of accountability, was the Water Management District's conduct wrongful (you may want to introduce students to the term "negligent")? Factors that suggest that harms were likely or easily avoided might suggest wrongful conduct. However, factors that would make it unlikely that someone would be hurt might make the District's action seem less wrongful. As for deterrence, if the District has to pay damages, might it use more care in the future? Why do you think it didn't fence the area in the first place? Might cost have been a factor? Finally, what of Mr. Daiagi's need for compensation? Should it matter if he has needs for nursing or other types of healthcare?

Note 3. These questions are designed to show not only what we know about the case from the description in the statute, but also what we don't know. Whether Daiagi was authorized to be on the land might impact the landowner's obligation to use reasonable care for him. If there had been a similar accident six months earlier that might put the landowner on notice of the danger. The employee email might further establish the notice of danger and foreseeability of injury. Although students will not have discussed these concepts in a formal way, they can start to see the relevance of these sorts of issues. If Daiagi was not wearing a helmet, the issue of his own fault also may be at issue. Of course, if even a working helmet would not have prevented the injury, perhaps Daiagi's failure to wear a helmet would be irrelevant. The case calls on students' intuition to foreshadow some of the concepts that become important in permitting or rejecting tort actions. In terms of accountability, even if you don't yet introduce the issue of negligence, students may care a lot about whether the South Florida Water Management's conduct was wrongful. Some of the specific issues mentioned in note 3 relate to this question. A similar prior accident might afford notice of a potential hazard and an opportunity to cure it. A note in the file might demonstrate awareness of the risk.

§ 3. IMPLEMENTING TORT LAW PURPOSES WITH DAMAGES AWARDS

We hope this section can provide some information that will be useful throughout the course and also serve to give us a chance to apply ideas about tort goals to specific cases. Restatement Second § 901 specifically identifies the purposes of tort law as the basis for measuring damages. It identifies the purpose to provide compensation, to determine rights, to punish and deter, and (by providing appropriate redress for wrongs) to deter retaliation.

HOLDEN v. WAL-MART STORES, INC., 608 N.W.2d 187 (Neb. 2000).

The plaintiff, who had a disability permit because of difficulties with knees and feet, fell in a hole in the defendant's parking lot. She eventually underwent a complete knee replacement costing her over $25,000 in medical expense. Other operations would be needed in the future. The jury awarded only $6,000 as damages, a sum reduced to $3600 because they attributed 40% of the fault to the plaintiff. (Issues other than those about damages are edited out of the casebook version.) On appeal, the court affirmed. The court recognizes that a jury award should not be set aside by judges unless the award is so excessive or inadequate that it betrays passion or prejudice. If some of the evidence in the record supports the award, the judge must respect it. In this case, the jury could have found that the fall caused only a small portion of the damages, seemingly because Holden would need a knee operation soon anyway. Similarly, a jury might properly exclude damages for pain that resulted from earlier accidents. *See Davis v. Mullen,* 773 A.2d 764 (Pa. 2001).

An annual trickle of appellate cases deal with jury verdicts that find liability but reject all damages or reject damages for pain and suffering. Some years juries seem more prone to these zero awards than others. A number of recent appellate cases reflect zero awards (or zero awards for pain) that had to be corrected as well as some that did not. *E.g.,Schroeder v. Triangulum Assocs.,* 789 A.2d 459 (Conn 2002); *Amalfitano v. Baker,* 794 A.2d 575 (Del.Supr. 2001); *Gainza v. Stearns,* 785 So.2d 683 (Fla. Dist. Ct. App. 2001) (no damages at all awarded); *Russell v. Neumann-Steadman,* 759 N.E.2d 234 (Ind. Ct. App. 2001); *Hobbs v. Ryce,* 769 A.2d 469 (Pa. Super. Ct. 2001) (no pain award). Sometimes these zero awards are justified, as in *Holden* and *Davis,* but at other times it looks as if the jury decided against pain damages on extra legal grounds. Perhaps the jury disliked the plaintiff or perhaps it made a political decision to minimize the plaintiff's recovery out of supposed self-interest, that is, a fear that insurance premiums might rise; perhaps the defendant's counsel found a way to communicate the limits of the defendant's insurance coverage. Sometimes we get a hint about the jury's attitude; in *Gainza,* supra, the jury asked questions about the plaintiff's insurance coverage. Mostly, however, appellate cases leave us nothing but speculation about the jury's motives. Still, the potential for illicit motives suggests that courts are right to exercise a degree of control. When the jury finds liability but awards nothing for pain, the court cannot usually merely determine the pain damages for itself; it must order a new trial so that a jury makes the determination. *Russell v. Neumann-Steadman, supra.*

We wouldn't call for briefs on this case, but discussion may helpfully suggest a few things students should be looking for. In this case, it may be useful to ask students to try to identify the issue being addressed by the court and to notice that some other issues that might have been raised have either been excluded in the editing or have disappeared in the litigation process.

Our main objective is to let students express judgments about awards and their relationship to the purposes of tort law. We'd like to caution those students with strong opinions that they don't have detailed facts and hence have little basis for judgment. Still, it does not seem to us that anyone could say that the *Holden* jury overcompensated the plaintiff. Some students may not get past their feeling that the defendant should not be liable at all. But that viewpoint, even more clearly than viewpoints about the damages award, can hardly have a basis in fact, since we don't even have the court's recitation of factual details, much less the actual testimony. If you have students who take this stance, you have an opportunity to help them begin to acquire a more professional, fact-respecting attitude. This is one of the themes that is likely to recur throughout the course. In fact, it is one of the questions about judicial process on which we end the coverage of personal injury tort law in Chapter 28.

If we can't form firm opinions about whether the damages award was too low or too high, we can at least begin to see that in making such decisions, we must have reasonable respect for the judgment of others. The appeals judges are saying something like that. The jury's decision, if supported by evidence, is not lightly to be rejected merely because the judge would have awarded a different sum. This describes a little bit about the relationship between judge and jury; judges make rules of law and review evidence to determine that the jury's decision is within a reasonable range. In a social world we must all inhabit, there are few points on which there is only one acceptable answer. There is a little more on judge, jury, and community values in DOBBS ON TORTS § 18 (*not* cited in the casebook). If students can absorb more, you can point out that the judge-jury relationship is not the only one that impacts our evaluation of judicial decisions. Some questions of law can should perhaps be allocated to the legislature (or, once so allocated, delegated to administrative agencies.)

The notes following *Holden* sketch some of the points just made, then go on to outline compensatory and punitive damages. These points are related back to the general goals of tort law by questions.

Note 4. Some students believe that there are no checks whatsoever on "runaway juries" who give overly-large awards. The case cited in this note, *Advocat, Inc. v. Sauer*, a 2003 Arkansas Supreme Court case, exemplifies the court's power to remit awards that "shock the conscience." This power is referenced in the block quote at the top of page 16 in *Holden*. Does even the remitted amount sound outrageously high?

Note 5 & 6. Some students don't get the distinction between compensatory and punitive damages, so you may have to highlight these two notes. It can be helpful to put the categories of legally-cognizable compensatory damages on the board.

Note 8. More to come on this when we attempt to evaluate the tort system. *See* Chapter 27. That chapter also contains a little more data on injuries. In the meantime, here are a few quick points: (1) Products liability plaintiffs recovered in only about 20% of the cases, or one in five. (2) The number of such claims filed has not increased. (3) The amounts awarded have not increased. (4) In medical malpractice cases, plaintiffs lost more than two-thirds of the cases going to jury trial. These points are from Deborah Jones Merritt & Kathryn Ann Barry, *Is the Tort System in Crisis? New Empirical Evidence*, 60 OHIO ST. L.J. 315, 334, 350, 352 (1999) (hereafter Merritt & Barry), based on an intensive twelve-year study in the Columbus, Ohio area. The numbers of claims in various categories are shown in the chart on the next page. Incidentally, the average economic (not human) cost of death from injury is $980,000 and the average economic cost of incapacitating injury (still not human costs like pain) is $44,000 per person. NATIONAL SAFETY COUNCIL, INJURY FACTS 83 (1999). A 2008 Bureau of Justice Statistics report estimates that the average tort award was only $24,000, lower than the value of the median contract claims. BUREAU OF JUSTICE STATISTICS BULLETIN 1 (October 2008). Consider this chart:

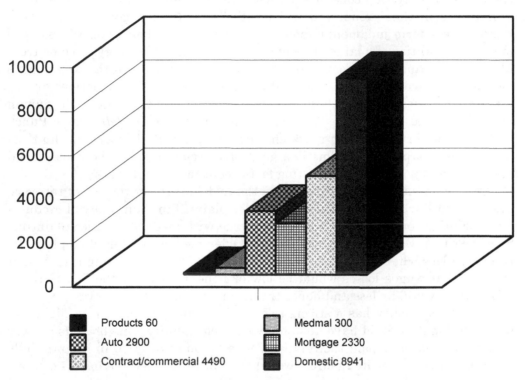

Annual filings by type of case in Franklin County.
Based on Deborah Jones Merritt & Kathryn Ann Barry, *Is the Tort System in Crisis? New Empirical Evidence,* 60 OHIO ST. L.J. 315, 381-82 (1999)

Students must remember that most tort cases are settled, not tried. Most do not even get as far as a filing in court. However, to get a little perspective on the "tort system," it may be useful to recognize that in litigation itself, tort cases represent only a fraction. (If we consider criminal litigation, the fraction becomes very small indeed. The chart above uses the figures from Merritt and Barry about the annual filings of claims in Franklin County, Ohio. Although figures differ from county to county and in federal courts, and classifications of cases can be more or less detailed, this chart shows that in general, tort law plays a limited role in litigation and that the big cases–products and medical malpractice–play a tiny role in the overall picture.

Note 9. McDonald's coffee. This note is part of a chain formed with succeeding notes, which verbalize the difficulty of fixing pain and suffering damages. But the note and the case have other lessons. Many people demonstrate two complementary reactions to the case. On the one hand, they are willing to generalize about the "tort system" from a few anecdotes or cases like the coffee case. (If you condemn a whole ethnic group because of misdeeds of individuals in that group, you will rightly be called a bigot.) On the other hand, others form judgments about individual human beings on the basis of supposed qualities of a large class of persons, "plaintiffs" so they have no trouble in concluding that because plaintiffs are greedy, so was the McDonald's victim. (This is also bigotry if applied to ethnic groups.) Both reactions are intellectually unsound and both will lead us to false pictures of human individuals and of systems. A lawsuit is not a *commedia dell'arte* or Punch and Judy performance with stock characters. It is full of individual humans and specific corporations. This is a good place re-emphasize the professional and human importance of respecting facts about individual cases.

On the possible bigotry reflected in the "old woman" criticisms of the case, Merritt and Barry found *no* successful elder plaintiff in their study of products liability litigation, although this was not true with medical practice plaintiffs. See Merritt & Barry, *supra* at 337, 356. Older medical malpractice plaintiffs recovered less when they recovered at all, *id.* at 358, but that might represent the fact that wages losses would be low or nonexistent and the fact that life expectancy would be less and hence the duration of pain less as well.

Deterrence policy has a strong role in discussing the case. You might ask what McDonald's could have done to avoid such liability. One obvious answer is that it could have paid the relatively small sum of $11,000 in hospital bills it necessitated. It (or its insurer) would then have avoided paying its own attorneys, would have avoided pain and suffering damages, and most of all would have avoided punitive damages. What else could it have done? It could have provided ordinary hot coffee, but not hot enough to burn to the bone in a few seconds. It could have responded positively to the reports of serious burns by reducing the heat. That's what we presumably want it to do. Like many children, some tortfeasors learn the hard way, by sad experience. Punitive damages may be the experience needed to get through to tortfeasors who shrug off ordinary information like the burn reports.

Why didn't McDonald's settle when it could have done so by paying hospital bills alone? One answer may be that sober professional analysis could have led to different evaluations of the case. We have no facts before us to allow exploration of this idea, but you might want to keep in mind that defendants' lawyers accurately estimate jury verdicts better than plaintiffs' lawyers. That is to say, plaintiffs often reject offers that turn out to have been better than the jury's verdict.

A quite different answer is suggested in the Merritt and Barry article, su-pra. Those authors found that major repeat player defendants frequently reject settlement at any price even in cases that plaintiffs ultimately win. Combine this information with the fact that major defendants such as product manufacturers and medical malpractice defendants win by far most of the cases they try, and you can see that these defendants can afford to take a hard line, losing a few cases but winning many more. In this situation, the authors suggest that the risk of punitive awards serves to encourage repeat players to come to the bargaining table.

A third possible reason is related and offers a warning to new students. If you don't try to see the case from the other's point of view or from the public point of view, you may misjudge it entirely. The word for this is arrogance and it is costly to professionals. In the Merritt and Barry study, among the medi-cal malpractice cases won by the plaintiff, the defendants had offered nothing in settlement. Merritt & Barry at 372. Defendants often refused the plaintiffs' favorable offer and went on to lose big as a result. We aren't saying that these defendants were arrogant; that depends upon the facts it knew or should have known, upon strategic considerations we cannot judge, and upon the integrity of the juries. Still, students can see that a defendant in McDonald's position should take facts seriously and try to see whether other points of view than their own might have some validity.

Greenlee's article is both fascinating and useful. You might want to know, however, that he veers off to conclude his article in religious terms.

Note 12. In *Estevez v. United States,* cited here, the defendant (the United States) was responsible for harm inflicted when a postal truck collided with the Estevez vehicle. The opinion addresses appropriate damages for harms to one member of the family, two-year-old Joseph. The court awarded nearly two million dollars, but not in a haphazard way. Instead the court catalogued each injury, the cost of past and future medical care, reduced work-life expec-tancy, and intangibles like pain and suffering. If the numbers assigned for various injuries don't quite add to the total award, it is in part because we've edited out the court's notation that New York's no-fault insurance law paid the first $50,000 of this amount and the City of New York has a lien for $88,000 based on its contribution of Medicaid payments. The *Estevez* award illustrates the fact that large sums of money can represent real losses and, that the courts working through the facts and the elements of damages care-fully. Of course, many of the specific awards rest on the best projection the court can make. Some students will think the pain awards, which comprise the bulk of the total ($1,250,000) are too high. Given time, we would let stu-dents express opinions pro and con. With uncertainties like pain, there is enormous room for different opinions. We might differ with many awards without thinking that the "system" has gone haywire or that Joseph is trying to get something for nothing.

Note 13. *Norfolk Beverage Co., Inc. v. Cho,* cited here, affirmed jury verdicts for Mr. and Mrs. Cho in the sums of $160,000 and $310,000 respectively. Although these damages are nominally compensatory, it is hard to believe the award was not influenced by Buckner's egregious behavior.

CHAPTER 2

READING TORTS CASES:
TRIAL PROCEDURES

▶**Changes in the Sixth Edition.** We've rewritten and rearranged materials in this chapter. The discussion in § 1 has been arranged to track the format of a case brief. The discussion in § 2 now lists trial procedures in the order in which they are likely to arise at trial. In addition, this discussion now explains some additional aspects of litigation, such as discovery.

▶The **Concise Edition** cuts a few sentences from the trial procedures discussion and omits *Appendix: A Narrative Case with Procedural Rulings*, which appears at the very end of this Chapter.■

Coverage options. The materials in § 1 are often helpful for teaching first-semester first-year students who have not previously briefed a case. If you are teaching second-semester students, you might skip these. Section 2 provides a brief description of trial procedures that students can look back upon to check the significance of a motion to dismiss, summary judgment, and other procedures that raise legal issues. You can assign § 2 without assigning § 3 and its narrative of a trial (or vice versa). Although all of us assign these materials, one assigns this chapter without classroom discussion (until procedural issues arise in subsequent cases), another invites student to ask questions, and the third briefly reviews the material by placing a diagram on the board that reflects the progression of the case toward trial.

§1. LOOKING FOR FACTS, RULES, AND REASONS

This text emphasizes case reading skills. Students should look for the judge's reasoning and interpret it in context, not necessarily literally. They should know the facts of the case and understand how facts and rules can be focused by understanding the legal issue.

Learning to read cases in a sophisticated way requires students to recognize that they are not merely collecting rules but learning how legal rules or principles may be used in developing arguments that in turn might lead to still other rules. At the very end, the text asserts a related point: rules point to evidence you need and arguments you can make (not necessarily to certain outcomes).

The background information in this section requires little explanation.

§ 2. PROCEDURES RAISING LEGAL ISSUES

The procedures in this section are now organized in the order in which they generally appear in the case. Procedures that frequently raise legal issues are no longer placed in a separate list, but are instead included in the general list and marked with an asterisk.

One way to discuss this material is to draw a line of boxes that lists each necessary step in the trial process—complaint, answer, discovery, pretrial matters, trial. Then use stop signs at the various junctures at which motions might end the case—motion to dismiss, motion for summary judgment, and so forth. These sorts of motions threaten to disrupt the flow of the case. You might also talk about what happens if one of these motions is granted and later reversed. It is helpful for students to see that the case resumes where it left off. The plaintiff may ultimately win the case, but this is by no means guaranteed.

A different way to begin discussion of the procedures is to ask why a procedure you name might have been adopted by the law. You can also ask or observe the effects of each procedural step on the allocation of power between judge and jury. If the judge grants a motion to dismiss or general demurrer, the case ends at the earliest possible moment and thus saves expense to the defendant and the public. It would also eliminate any role for the jury. That would be justified only if there were clearly no claim stated in the complaint. (The last point ties very well to the idea that in tort cases, we listen to each individual's story.) You may need to explain that the plaintiff is usually allowed to amend the complaint if she did not get it right to begin with. The same kind of discussion can take place as to motion for summary judgment and directed verdict.

Objections to evidence are a little different and involve a recognition that the jury should not even hear evidence that is legally irrelevant and possibly prejudicial. This kind of discussion can lead to a little discussion about the role of juries in tort cases. The same can be said about directed verdicts. If reasonable people could differ about the facts, the jury should be allowed to work its will.

However you cover this material, it should be obvious to the students that it is not presented at the technical level that will be required in procedure courses, but that, all the same, it is an accurate and important way of understanding the issue-raising devices that will appear in the cases.

A note to teachers: A Motion for Directed Verdict and a Judgment N.O.V., or judgment notwithstanding the verdict, is now called a J.M.L, or a judgment as a matter of law, in federal court. The text is updated to reflect that change.

FYI: The procedures at trial segment summarizes the trial structure in courts of general jurisdiction, usually called circuit, superior, or district courts depending upon the state. New York's trial court of general jurisdiction is the Supreme Court; Pennsylvania's the Court of Common Pleas. Lower courts are not courts of general jurisdiction and usually not courts of record. These would often try small cases and offer no jury trial, but their judgments may be appealed with a trial de novo in a court where juries are available. Most of states use 12-person juries, but a substantial number, around 20, use six or eight jurors. The states differ about whether a unanimous verdict is required, or whether something like 5/6 or 3/4 will suffice. Unless students are confused (maybe some have been in a justice or municipal court), they do not necessarily need this information here. However, the unanimous verdict vs. the 3/4 verdict point has strategic importance. If a unanimous verdict is required, the plaintiff will lose if a single juror opposes a verdict for the plaintiff. Lawyers would presumably estimate the value of their cases in the light of that possibility. The unanimity issue might also affect how you structure empirical studies or how you evaluate them. The Ohio sample reported in Deborah Jones Merritt & Kathryn Ann Barry, *Is the Tort System in Crisis? New Empirical Evidence,* 60 OHIO ST. L.J. 315 (1999), and discussed in Chapter 1, was made in a state that does not require a unanimous verdict. So when the study finds a relatively small success rate for plaintiffs, it has greater significance than if it had drawn its sample in a unanimous verdict state. ∎

Appendix. A Narrative Case with Procedural Rulings

We hope this effort to act out the procedural rules in a simple case will help students who have conscientiously read the material in § 3, but we doubt that this requires classroom discussion.

PART 2

FAULT-BASED LIABILITY FOR PHYSICAL HARMS TO PERSONS AND PROPERTY

TOPIC A. DIRECT INTENTIONAL WRONGS

CHAPTER 3

ESTABLISHING A CLAIM FOR INTENTIONAL TORT TO PERSON OR PROPERTY

▶**Changes in the Sixth Edition:** We have made several changes here both to update the chapter and to highlight some aspects of intent. In § 1 (battery), we have cut *Hall v. McBryde* and reduced to a note *Leichtman v. WLW Jacor Communications Inc. and Polmatier v. Russ*. In that section we have added *Mullins v. Parkview Hospital Inc.* (a case about intent to harm or offend), *Wagner v. State* (a single intent case) and two transferred intent cases: *Stoshak v. East Baton Rouge Parish School*, and *Baska v. Scherzer*. In § 2 (assault) we have eliminated *Koffman v. Garnett*. In § 4 (property torts) a number of new note cases have been added. Finally, we have reorganized § 5 (civil rights) with some new note cases. Specifically, *Brown v. Muhelenberg Township* has been converted into a note case.

▶The **Concise Edition** reduces the length of this Chapter by over 25% by trimming materials throughout. Major changes include the cutting of *Wagner v. State* (substituting a Note about it); *Baska v. Sherzer*; and the whole section on § 1983 claims (substituting a short textual overview). Minor changes include edits within *Van Camp v. McAfoos* and *Garrett v. Dailey*, and the deletion of a few Notes.■

Overview. This chapter discusses the prima facie case requirements of a number of common-law intentional torts as well as the federal statutory civil rights claim under § 1983. Students explore the contours of the prima facie cases of **Battery** (§1); **Assault** (§2); **False Imprisonment** (§3); **Torts to Property**, including Trespass to Land, Conversion of Chattels, and Trespass to Chattels (§4); and **Forcible Harms as Civil Rights Violations** [§1983] (§5).

In the first two sections of this chapter, we use the cases to illustrate various procedural concepts that students will see throughout law school, and which they must grasp early to understand the cases they are reading. Issue-raising procedures appear in the cases as follows: (1) **Complaint and Motion to Dismiss**: *Van Camp v. McAfoos, Cohen v. Smith, Wagner v. State*; (2) **Summary Judgment**: *Mullins v. Parkview Hospital Inc., Cullison v. Medley*. (3) **Motion for Directed Verdict**: *Snyder v. Turk*; (4) **Bench trial**: *Garratt v. Dailey*; *Polmatier v. Russ*; (5) **Jury instructions**: *White v. Muniz.*

Objectives in Chapter 3. This chapter aims to accomplish several minor goals and these major ones:

1. To provide basic information or rule content about the basic intentional torts (those based on the writ of trespass), plus one contemporary development in analogous areas—the § 1983 civil rights claims for physical invasions.

2. To provide a challenging but not overwhelming first experience with law which will assist in developing skills and elementary knowledge necessary to move forward.

3. To begin introducing skills, including (a) analysis and case briefing, (b) synthesis of cases, and relatedly, inductive reasoning from cases, (c) the construction of arguments or opinions using two or more rules.

4. To provide a limited amount of collateral information about the legal system–the writ system, the modern procedural system as applied in tort cases, and a little about the common law versus the civil law.

The material can spark some ideas it does not address directly. You should have opportunities to advise students along these lines: (1) Expect change and learn how to forecast and understand it. (2) Rules and principles are important, not merely results in a case. Learn how to see the rules or principles embedded in a case. (3) Rules do not necessarily determine or predict cases, but they do tell lawyers something about the kinds of arguments that must be made and the kinds of evidence to obtain. (4) Rules may be thought of narrowly in terms of technical doctrine, as by defining battery in terms of touching; but interpreting the rules and applying them in particular cases may be easier if we try to see the underlying purpose or principle (the autonomy-protecting purpose in battery cases, for example).

Suggested Omissions. Coverage of property torts is already minimized, but if you are severely pushed for time and your students are sure to get good coverage of trespass, conversion, and trespass to chattels in a property course, you might omit all of § 4, covering the high spots by lecture. It is possible to omit § 5 on civil rights, perhaps on a theory that it is too early to introduce a statutory claim, or that what students really need to learn here are the common law torts. We have found, however, that covering § 5 helps our students understand that identical facts do not lead to recovery if the underlying legal standards are not identical—for example, that just because a plaintiff has a good claim for battery does not mean that he or she will also succeed in a civil rights suit. Also although civil rights claims are a substantial part of the federal docket, we have found that only a portion of our students take an upper-level civil rights course. .

§ 1. BATTERY

OUTLINE

A.   Requiring fault. Van Camp v. McAfoos

B.   Elements of battery
   [1] Intent and interests protected. Snyder v. Turk; Cohen v. Smith; Mullins v. Parkview
   [2] What damages are available. A.R.B. v. Elkin

C.   Refocusing on Intent
   [1] Intent as Purpose or certainty. Garratt v. Dailey
   [2] Dual v. single intent. Capacity to commit torts. White v. Muniz; Wagner v. State; Polmatier v. Russ.
   [3] Transferred intent. Stoshak v. East Baton Rouge Parish School; Baska v. Scherzer.

SUMMARY

VAN CAMP V. MCAFOOS. The defendant, a three-year-old child on a tricycle, ran into the plaintiff. The plaintiff did not allege fault, (possibly because at the child's age fault would be impossible to prove). The trial court sustained a motion to dismiss the complaint. *Held*, affirmed. The case introduces the idea that injury may occur without fault, the idea that fault is generally required to establish tort liability, and the idea that a deficient complaint may be dismissed without a jury trial, via the motion to dismiss. The special policy considerations involved in holding a child or parent liable are postponed for development in connection with *Garrett v. Dailey* and *Hall v. McBryde* (and notes that follow those cases), though they could be introduced here briefly.

SNYDER V. TURK. The defendant, a surgeon, became annoyed with a nurse in the course of a surgical operation; apparently believing she was providing inappropriate instruments, he pulled her face close to the surgical opening, saying, "Can't you see where I'm working?. . . I need long instruments." The trial court granted a directed verdict for the defendant. *Held,* reversed. The defendant must intend either harmful or offensive contact, but intent to harm is not required.

COHEN V. SMITH. The plaintiff, a female, held religious convictions against being seen unclothed by a male. She communicated these feelings to medical personnel when she was about to undergo a Cesarean section. Nevertheless, the defendant Smith, a male nurse, saw and touched the plaintiff's unclothed body during a cesarean section required by the plaintiff. The plaintiff sued the nurse and the hospital for battery. The trial court granted the defendant's motion to dismiss. *Held,* reversed. The plaintiff has a right to refuse a touching, including one for medical treatment, and, by implication, a touching against her known wishes, even for medical treatment, is an offensive-type battery.

MULLINS V. PARKVIEW HOSPITAL. The plaintiff had asked for assurance that the anesthesiologist would personally handle her anesthesia. As soon as the plaintiff was unconscious, the anesthesiologist told an EMT student who had never intubated a patient before to intubated the patient. The student lacerated the patient's esophagus. The plaintiff sued several defendants including the EMT student. The Indiana Supreme Court upheld the trial court's grant of summary judgment on behalf of the EMT student. There was no evidence that the student knew the plaintiff had objected to the participation of students and no indication that the student intended to harm the patient.

A.R.B. V. ELKIN. A trial judge awarded a plaintiff $100 in "nominal" damages because he had been physically harmed by the defendant's touching, but awarded nothing to a second plaintiff because she was merely offended, not physically injured. The trial judge believed that damages for emotional injury in a battery case could be recovered only where there was some medical evidence that proved such injury. This was held to be error; where a battery or an assault is proved, a plaintiff is entitled to recover nominal damages plus compensatory damages for pain, humiliation, mental anguish, and any other kind of injury that occurs as a natural consequence of the tortious conduct. Notes after this note case discuss some more damages issues, and distinguish parasitic emotional distress damages from a stand-alone claim of intentional infliction of emotional distress, a tort we do not see until Chapter 19.

GARRATT V. DAILEY. The defendant, a six-year-old boy, moves a chair as the elderly plaintiff is about to sit in it. The plaintiff falls to the ground. The trier ultimately found that the boy had no purpose to cause a bodily touching, but the reviewing court concluded that one could have an intent to touch if one acted with substantial certainty that a touching would occur, even if purpose was lacking. This is the classic case. It establishes a general concept of intent to be carried over to other sections. It resembles extreme forms of negligence. That resemblance is confronted head-on in the notes and the cases following.

WHITE V. MUNIZ. A resident in a long-term care facility has substantial mental deterioration. She struck one of the facility's staff, the plaintiff, while the plaintiff was attempting to change her adult diaper. In the plaintiff's suit for "assault and battery," the trial judge charged that liability for battery would be imposed only if the defendant "appreciated the offensiveness of her conduct." [Presumably this rather informal instruction is equivalent to saying that the defendant must intend harm or offense as well as the touching itself.] The jury found for the defendant but the intermediate court reversed. *Held,* jury verdict reinstated. Although insane persons are liable for their torts, there is no tort of battery unless the defendant intends to touch and intends as well that the touch will be harmful or offense. The instruction is thus correct in telling the jury in effect that the insane defendant is not liable unless she intended offense [or harm].

WAGNER V. STATE. A customer in a department store was attacked by a mentally-disabled man who had been brought to the store as a part of a state treatment program. The state would not be liable for harm to the plaintiff if the patient's conduct "arose out of battery." The Utah Supreme Court dismissed the case against the state on the basis that the intent required for battery is only the intent to make contact not the intent to harm or offend. This single-intent decision provides a contrast to *White v. Muniz.*

STOSHAK V. EAST BATON ROUGE PARISH SCHOOL. A teacher who tried to break up a fight was punched and injured in the process. The boys did not punch him deliberately, but rather were trying to injure each other. Under Louisiana's "assault pay" provision, the teacher was entitled to braoder disability benefits if the injury resulted from an assault or battery by a student. The trial court held this was not an assault or battery. *Held,* reversed. Under the doctrine of transferred intent, this was a battery which entitled the teacher to assault pay.

BASKA V. SCHERZER. A mother tried to break up a fight between two young men during her daughter's party. The mother was hit and injured. Neither defendant intended to strike the mother. If the conduct qualified as a battery, it was subject to a one-year statute of limitations. *Held,* under the doctrine of transferred intent the cause of action was for battery not for negligence. As such, a one-year statute of limitations applied and the trial court correctly granted defendant's motion for summary judgment.

COMMENTS

A. Requiring Fault

Experienced teachers will recognize that this section is intended to do double duty. It provides the basic rules of battery and serves also to define the concepts of intent as they will apply to other torts. This seems to work better than providing a section on intent before battery is defined, or considering intent after all the torts have been covered.

VAN CAMP V. MCAFOOS, 156 N.W.2d 878 (Iowa 1968).

This is a simple case and easy for students to identify with. A three-year old boy on a trike ran into the plaintiff, who was lawfully using the sidewalk. She suffered injury, but she did not allege either intent or negligence, and the trial court granted a motion to dismiss. This was affirmed on appeal. The court's discussion emphasizes three main points: (1) Some kind of fault is required to show a tort in most instances, including this one. (2) The complaint ("petition" as it is called here) must contain ultimate facts which would be sufficient to justify a recovery if they are proven at trial. (3) A child may be liable for a tort, but of course he is not liable for mere injury without tort any more than the adult is. All these points may be dragged out in discussion and given significance by questioning whether the rules they represent are necessarily sound.

The case introduces (1) the requirement of fault, as contrasted with strict liability based on causation alone, (2) the distinction between causing harm and being faulty, and (3) procedural information about the complaint and the motion to dismiss. The second point is only implicit, but as fundamental as the distinction is for tort lawyers, the distinction is difficult for some students, so the point may be worth verbalizing. The other two points are the main ones, but deep discussion is not necessary.

Discussion: procedure. You can get the student to identify the kind of information that ought to be in a complaint – the basic facts, but not much in the way of conclusions of law and not much in the way of specific evidence. Was there any statement that Mark intended to harm or even touch Van Camp? Was there any statement of any *fact* that would lead you to think such an intent was probable? Was there any *fact* that would make you think he was careless? The defendant wants to argue that if there are no such facts, the law does not recognize the plaintiff's claim as a good one. Procedurally he does this by filing a motion to dismiss on the ground that the claim is not legally a good one. When the judge decides such a motion, either way, we can know whether the claim is good or not.

Under modern pleading, the pleader is not usually required to allege conclusions such as "fault." Is the court violating this rule? Perhaps not. The plaintiff has made it clear he asserts a claim *not* based on fault. And the facts are such that fault seems less likely than accident.

You might raise an ethics point here with the class. Should a lawyer allege a fact that the lawyer believes cannot be proved, just to defeat a motion to dismiss? Most cases settle, after all, and the case is unlikely to be tried. (Sometimes a student suggests this.) To allege facts when you don't have a good faith belief that they can be proved after discovery is improper, and sanctionable. If you raise this point it can reinforce in students' minds that pleading is not simply a game of chess between lawyers – it involves real people and real, provable facts.

Discussion: the substantive rule or principle. What different allegations in the complaint would have led the judge to overrule the defendant's motion to dismiss? This question takes us to the substantive issue and at the same time shows the connection between procedural rulings and substantive legal rules. The motion to dismiss should have been granted because of a substantive legal rule that tells us some kind of fault is required. Since no fault was alleged in the complaint, either in so many words or by alleging facts that would show fault, and since fault is required, the plaintiff must lose. Procedurally, this is a "dismissal" of the complaint. The term, you might note, is a term of art; the complaint is kept on file in the clerk's office, along with a judge's order saying it is "dismissed." This is merely a formal way of saying that the plaintiff loses.

This is not to say that the plaintiff must use the word fault or intent in the complaint, but that she must at least allege some fact from which the jury could infer intent. For example, suppose the complaint alleged that the defendant was angry with the plaintiff and pushed his tricycle into her. We might then think that the facts alleged showed intent. Cf. *O'Hayre v. Bd. Of Educ. For Jefferson County Sch. Dist.-1,* 109 F.Supp.2d 1284 (D. Colo. 2000) (word intent not required where the plaintiff alleged an angry adult slammed him into a locker).

The case is not too difficult for students to grasp, and yet it is one that does not lend itself to the approach of the student who wants to find "the holding" in a given sentence. Students cannot simply highlight the magic words. Interpretation is required. (Students may need to hear that interpretation may be required even when a court says "we hold that. . . .").

Discussion: evaluation. Maybe most discussions of cases should involve some kind of evaluation: (1) Is the rule right? We've been introduced to some criteria for judgment–justice, public policies such as deterrence, compensation due for fault-caused harm. (2) If the rule is right, is it rightly applied to the facts? Answers during the course develop skills in application of rules and fact-sensitivity.

Evaluation of *Van Camp* need not be complicated. You can ask whether Mark should be liable even though he is not at fault. If his age is a problem to the student, pose the case of an older child or an adult who is not at fault. (You might have to alter facts a little to get this; imagine a bike rider stung by a bee; he loses control and hits Mrs. Van Camp.) Most of the discussion is unsophisticated. But someone is likely to say that, after all, Mark caused the injury even if he was not at fault. Or "Mrs. Van Camp certainly wasn't at fault." If the class doesn't take this view, you can suggest it yourself to promote further evaluation.

The idea that Mrs. Van Camp is not at fault is not irrelevant. It is an elliptical way of saying that if neither is at fault, someone will still have to bear the loss caused by the injury. It is not utterly foolish to say that if someone must bear the loss, then the person who causes the loss should bear it, not the victim. But, except for some very specific kinds of cases, that is not the law. Instead, as *Van Camp* suggests, we impose liability for fault, not cause. The argument will arise again soon in *Polmatier*, so you can terminate discussion on the schedule you've planned without trying to come to a final closure.

Omitted portions of the opinion. In omitted portions of the opinion the court rejected a separate claim against Mark's parents. The court may have felt that the plaintiff conceded an absence of fault; or it may have felt that the word "negligence" or at least "fault" would be required in the complaint; or it may have felt that the parents, even if negligent, could not be liable unless Mark was at fault. Here again, you can postpone discussions of parental liability until you reach *Garratt*, *Hall*, and the notes that follow *Hall*.

Note 2. The rules today. This note tests the students' grasp of the historical structure and the rule in *Van Camp*. The answer to the question in this note is that the court in *Van Camp* does *not* follow the historical rule. If it had done so, it would have held Mark liable for the direct harm (in the absence of a defense based on his incapacity). More on the trespass-case distinction and its history in Chapter 23. Also you might mention here that fault is not required in all cases, and we will see that later (especially in Chapters 22 through 24).

Note 3. What is fault? It is sometimes helpful for students to talk about what would show fault. Running into Van Camp on purpose to see her get angry would be intended harm—a form of fault. If there were a rule against riding bikes on the sidewalk, or conduct like riding with hands in the air, this might be some evidence of another form of fault—negligence. But the accident might well have happened without fault. The young child may have tried to control the bike but not been able to do so. To prevail in a battery action, the plaintiff would have to show the fault required for a battery action—intent to contact and perhaps also intent to harm or offend.

Note 4. Tort law and the states. The Van Camp case comes from Iowa, which you can see from the case citation. Tort law is generally state law. Just because Iowa has a particular rule does not mean Illinois has to follow suit. We will see some differences in the dual-intent single-intent divide shown by *White* and *Wagner*. However, there are also many similarities in the common law of different states, in part because of the influence of national norms provided by treatises and the Restatement. This book endeavors to track common law rules that are not idiosyncratic to one state, but more broadly relevant to the law of man jurisdictions.

Note 6. Grasping a principle. You must generalize a rule so that it applies to something other than the very set of facts that generated the rule. If the rule in *Van Camp* applies only to Mark and Mrs. Van Camp, it is not a *rule* at all. And it is not very much of a rule if it applies only to tricycle cases. Unless it has generality, it is only an "isolated doom," an adjudication that has no ancestry in principle and no posterity in practice. This point is made here by using hypotheticals on different facts. You can even discuss the use of hypotheticals in law school: we use hypotheticals in law not simply to aggravate the student but to test the application or limits of a rule or principle, or to test whether we have stated the rule adequately.

The first hypothetical. The husband is indeed guilty of a battery. Nothing in *Van Camp excludes* liability, although the case does not go so far as to explain what kind of fault would count as a tort.

We want to include this hypothetical not only to focus upon the use of principle in new cases, but also to let students see some ugly and physical sides of battery. We don't want to develop the point here, though. An unhappy number of sexual and domestic batteries will appear in this book. Development here would blur the focus.

The second hypothetical. The second hypothetical has a tree on the defendant's land fall on the plaintiff. Louisiana imposed liability under its Civil Code on similar facts, even though the defendant might not be at fault. Does *Van Camp* tell us anything about what Iowa would do on these different facts? It surely tells us that fault will have to be shown against the tree-owner, doesn't it? We may have to argue about whether the falling tree shows that fault, but it seems clear that the principle in *Van Camp's* requirement of fault should apply as well to tree-falling cases. Getting the *principle* is important. As here, the principle at least tells what kind of evidence to adduce at trial and what kind of arguments we'll have with counsel on the other side. We can see here, for example, that the Iowa plaintiff injured by the tree would probably have to argue that the landowner was at fault. Once we see that such an argument must be made, we know that we must look for evidence of fault. (For example, did the landowner know of the danger?)

Note 7. Procedure. *Van Camp* was decided on a motion to dismiss. Students should understand that (a) procedure conditions most of the cases we read, so they should pay attention to it; (b) a motion to dismiss attacks the plaintiff's complaint, not the adequacy or admissibility of evidence, or the propriety of instructions. This plaintiff never got to present her case to a jury because she lost on a motion to dismiss.

B. Elements of Battery

SNYDER V. TURK, 627 N.E.2d 1053 (Ohio Ct. App. 1993)

Procedure: Directed verdict. This differs from the motion to dismiss that appeared in *Van Camp* and will appear again in *Cohen*. You may wish to spend a few moments helping students visualize a litigation, with a motion to dismiss based on the written complaint and a motion for directed verdict based on evidence adduced by the plaintiff at trial. The trial court in *Snyder* granted the defendant's motion for directed verdict, but the appellate court reverses, holding that the plaintiff can get to the jury.

Substantively, *Synder* introduces the main rules of battery. In holding that the plaintiff should get to the jury, the court states the tort rules that show the plaintiff has a case. You may want to discuss it, or some of the points raised below, only after you have also elicited the facts and holding in *Cohen*. The casebook's notes following *Cohen* support discussion of both cases.

The *Snyder* court broadly defines battery as an intentional, unconsented-to contact with another. The rule statement is rather informal, but you can piece together the requirement of a touching (contact) and an intent to either harm or offend. The either/or formulation means that intent to harm is not required, as the court specifically holds. The court goes on to define offense as an affront to a reasonable sense of personal dignity. This terminology parallels that of the Restatement.

You can't quite get all the elements of battery from this case. For that reason and because students are not accustomed at this point to a radical distinction between intent and result, you might want to do some chalkboard work to spell out the rules and so segregate the intent and result rules. The defendant must intend a touching and a touching must result. The defendant must intend either harm or offense and either harm or offense must result.

INTENT REQUIRED	RESULT REQUIRED
Touching and	Touching and
One of these:	*One of these*:
Harm or	Harm or
Offense	Offense

One line in the court's opinion is most inartful. "A person is subject to liability for battery when he acts intending to cause a harmful or offensive contact, and when a harmful contact results." To be complete, the statement should have said ". . . and when a harmful *or offensive* contact results."

The statement is not literally wrong because it says only that intent to harm or offense coupled with actual harm is *sufficient;* it does not say that actual harm is *necessary.* (Necessary/sufficient distinctions can start right now.) Perhaps students will read this as meaning that harm is required because the court does not go on to say that offense is sufficient. But the outcome of the case is that the plaintiff will be allowed to get to the jury, and no physical harm is mentioned in the case. So you can lead students to see that the court is not requiring proof of physical harm. Consequently you can write on the board the two columns above to summarize discussion.

If you wish, you can make explicit the implication that intent to touch in an offensive way followed a touching that was actually harmful rather than merely offensive would suffice, and vice versa. If you have already put the two columns above on the board, you can make this clear by drawing a line from offense in the intent column to harm in the result column, or similarly from harm to offense.

As all this implies, the conception of harm involved in these rules is one of physical harm. You could just as well structure the rule to say that harm is always required but that harm includes the kind of mental or emotional harm called offense.

COHEN V. SMITH, 648 N.E.2d 329 (Ill. App. Ct. 1995)

Read-ahead. We suggest you will want to read *White v. Muniz*, and *Wagner v. State* the last case in this section, before you teach *Cohen, Mullins* and *Snyder* so you'll see how the intent issue will be revisited there.

Procedure: The trial court sustained a motion to dismiss. If you worked on the directed verdict procedure in *Synder,* you might want to begin by drawing the distinction between directed verdict and motion to dismiss.

What makes touching offensive? As far as we can tell, the touching would have been medically appropriate and was only actionable if the defendant allegedly knew that it was objectionable to the plaintiff. As in *Synder,* the court first quotes a rule about a harmful battery, then proceeds to make a holding about offensive battery. What makes the touching offensive? That the defendant knows the touching to be unconsented to. The fact that most people would accept the touching as medically desirable does not matter. It is the plaintiff's body and her decision to make. If the defendant has affirmative reason to believe that the touching is unacceptable, he becomes liable for the touching, harmful or helpful.

Anger and duels. Earlier battery cases often emphasized violence or anger. See the quotation from *Cole v. Turner* at the head of this subsection. Because that is the model judges most often have in mind–a punch in the nose–they sometimes still inaccurately suggest that battery or assault entail violence. *See, e.g., Bollaert v. Witter,* 792 P.2d 465, 466 (Or. Ct. App. 1990) (defining assault as an attempt to do violence). The *Cohen* court characterizes the battery rules a little differently, as attempts to substitute a legal claim for private acts of revenge such as duels. From this the court segues into the idea that battery rules protect personal "integrity," meaning not physical integrity but personal autonomy. Drawing on a note in an earlier edition of Richard Epstein's casebook on torts, the court tells us about a case in which the defendant struck the cane of the French Ambassador. This was thought to be a battery and because it was "within the definition" but also because it would help prevent dueling.

Autonomy. A duel between Patricia Cohen and Nurse Roger Smith seems unlikely. The real reason for liability in cases like *Cohen* is the protection of personal autonomy, the right of each person to decide what touchings to accept. *Snyder* might conceivably fit the court's concept in *Cole v. Turner,* but the medical touching in *Cohen* does not. The subtext of our lesson is that law changes. That may seem too simple to mention, but many first year students expect law to be a stable refuge in a changing world. It's not.

Cohen and *Synder* together give us a picture of battery rules (and also a picture of the rather casual and informal way courts sometimes state rules.)

Violent batteries. Because we've begun with the more subtle forms of battery, you may want to remind students of the spouse abuse hypothetical following

Van Camp to emphasize that the most common batteries are simply intended violence. Spousal beatings, rape, an unconsented-to attack in a bar, a shooting all obviously fit the definition of battery. We would not raise this statute here, but some students may know about it and raise it. The statute, 42 U.S.C.A. § 13981(c), created a federal tort claim for victims of gender-based violence. In *United States v. Morrison,* 529 U.S. 598 (2000), the Supreme Court held that Congress has no constitutional authority to create the federal tort claim. Criminal violence within a state has too tenuous a connection with interstate commerce to rely upon the power of Congress to regulate interstate commerce. And although Congress has the power to enforce the 14th Amendment which forbids discriminatory state action, the civil remedy in this statue is not addressed to state action or state officials but only to the criminal. Consequently the 14th Amendment provides no basis for Congressional power either. If you use any of this, you may have to emphasize that common law battery claims under state law are unaffected by this decision.

MULLINS V. PARKVIEW HOSPITAL, INC., 865 N.E.2d 608 (Ind. 2007)

Procedure: Summary judgment. The EMT student's motion for summary judgment is granted by the trial court, reversed by the appellate court, and then reversed again by the Indiana Supreme Court. The ultimate grant of the motion for summary judgment here reveals an important point that many students miss in *Cohen.* When the plaintiff in *Cohen* is allowed to proceed with her claim, she still has to produce some evidence that the male nurse knew the touching would be offensive (for example, that it was unconsented to) in order to prevail. If there is no evidence that the actor knew that consent had not been given, summary judgment should be granted with respect to the battery case, as it was in *Mullins.*

Note 1. We hope that reading this note will help prepare students for the discussion of the *Snyder, Cohen* and *Mullins* cases. If you have not already done so, you might put the two-column list of elements on the board now. We use a dual-intent formulation here and revisit the intent issue later with *White* and *Wagner.*

Note 2. No, intent to harm is not required, because an intent *either* to harm *or* to offend will suffice for this element. Liability does not depend upon actual harm resulting, either. Again, offense is sufficient. That seems quite apparent if you compare facts and results of both *Snyder* and *Cohen,* although the words used by the court in both cases are somewhat inadequate. You may notice that *Mullins* addressed only intent to harm not intent to harm or offend. This may be because Indiana has a narrower battery rule, but it may also be because there was no evidence of intent to offend either, so a discussion of the possibility was unnecessary.

Note 3. *Whitley v. Andersen,* cited here, holds that LeGault would be subject to liability for the shove even though she intended no harm and no harm was done. Why? Touching with an intent to offend and resulting offense suffices.

Caudle v. Betts, cited in paragraph b, also imposed liability. If the defendant knew that the touching was unconsented to, he knew it was offensive and he becomes liable for harm actually resulting. You might need to distinguish horseplay in which the plaintiff takes part; that would be an implicit consent, as in a game of tag.

Although not in the note itself, you make be interested in *Johnson v. Ramsey County*, 424 N.W.2d 800 (Minn. Ct. App. 1988), which holds that of course an unwanted kiss is a battery. Every potential kisser should assume no consent and hence offense unless the kisser has reason to think otherwise. If domestic partners normally exchange kisses and other touchings, they expect no offense and intend none by a normal kiss. The judge's case is different. He cannot assume that the kiss will be unoffensive and must have some reason to think it is accepted if he is to avoid liability. His case is especially bad because he is an employer, so that what he does to an employee along these lines may count as sexual harassment. Some offensive battery cases as well as some cases of overt violence, involve sexual touching which may also be subject to legal prohibitions against harassment.

Note 4. *Motive versus intent.* Intent is determinative, not motive. So a good motive battery is still a battery. This result can be derived from the rules requiring only intent to touch in a harmful or offensive way coupled actual touching and actual harm or offense. This good motive may well have been what was at issue in *Mullins*. The anesthesiologist may only have wanted the EMT student to get appropriate medical training. Regardless of this benign motive, once the doctor knew that the patient had not consented to the student contact, ordering the student to go ahead looks like an intent to engage in unconsented-to contact, which is offensive.

Note 5. Procedure: Motion to dismiss. This topic has been addressed in the procedure section of the *Mullins* case. In *Cohen*, the court overturned a motion to dismiss. This means that Ms. Cohen's case can go forward to discovery. It does not mean that Ms. Cohen will necessarily win the case. If Ms. Cohen cannot produce adequate evidence to support the claim she may well lose on a motion for summary judgment, as did the plaintiff in *Mullins*.

Note 6. Procedure: Motion for summary judgment. You can ask the student to distinguish the summary judgment motion from the motion to dismiss and motion for directed verdict seen in § 2. One difference is the time. The motion to dismiss attacks the *allegations* of the complaint and is usually made first. The motion for directed verdict attacks the *evidence* at trial and hence is not made until the trial, or at least the plaintiff's presentation of evidence at trial, is over. The summary judgment motion asserts that on the non-disputed facts, there is no legally sound claim (or defense). The "facts" here are gleaned from discovery and affidavits. If the relevant "facts" are in dispute, the case goes to trial. If not, the judge can decide whether the law permits recovery on the undisputed facts. You may wish to refer back to the Introduction Chapter for review of the summary judgment motion or coordinate with civil procedure teachers.

Analysis of the motion for summary judgment might very well have been different if VanHoey had been told that Ms. Mullins did not want a student performing the procedures. In this situation, Van Hoey would know that the contact was unconsented to and there might well have been a genuine issue of material fact regarding her intent to engage in harmful or offensive contact.

Note 7. Bodily contact. The extended personality rule discussed in this note is an old standard and is anticipated by the case of the French Ambassador's cane discussed in *Cohen.* It is obviously a matter of degree. Touching the plaintiff's gigantic Lincoln Town Car is probably not equivalent to touching the plaintiff personally, even though touching a plate or a camera held by the plaintiff is. See *Picard v. Barry Pontiac-Buick, Inc.,* 654 A.2d 690 (R.I. 1995) (finger on the plaintiff's camera in offensive manner is actionable under extended personality rule). The anesthesiologist who directed the student to touch Mullins might well be guilty of a battery, despite the fact that the anesthesiologist was not the one to lacerate Mullins' esophagus. See *Holleman v. Aiken,* 668 S.E.2d 579 (N.C. Ct. App. 2008). In *Holleman v. Aiken* the author of book about a celebrity singer stated battery claim against the singer when the singer's bodyguard offensively touched the author without her consent. The case proceeded under a theory of vicarious liability. The singer, as the bodyguard's employer, had a right to control the manner in which the bodyguard performed details of his job, within the scope of his employment in furtherance of the singer's business and as a means or method of performing his job duties.

Liability of one who aids, or abets or conspires with another to commit a tort is joint. That is a concept we'll see later, but the "aiding and abetting" idea seems to be prevalent enough in the culture to permit you merely to take note of it as a general rule and go on.

Note 8-9. What counts as a touching? *Leichtman* used to be a full case in this section, but now it has been reduced to mentions in these two Notes. In that case, the Ohio court specifically recognized that "particulate matter" (smoke) is capable of causing the "touching" required for a battery. Yet the court is troubled enough about liability to say that it rejects a slightly different kind of smoking battery, one based on substantial certainty that someone will be touched by exhaled smoke. The court's concept of substantial certainty need not be developed here; you can come back to this case after covering *Garratt v. Dailey* if you wish. But it is clear that the court is not willing to say that a smoker is liable merely because he knows his smoke will necessarily "touch" others. Perhaps this is the modern equivalent of the idea that people will have to expect some jostling in a crowd.

In *Swope,* the Fifth Circuit case cited in this Note, the plaintiff claimed illness resulting from repeated exposure to ozone fumes caused by the defendant with substantial certainty that harm would result. The court held that a battery claim might be stated on these facts, without addressing the issue of whether the contact element in a battery claim requires some tangible-object touching. In a similar vein see *Field v. Philadelphia Elec. Co.*, 565 A.2d 1170, 1178 (Pa. Super. Ct. 1989) (plaintiff alleged that the defendant, to keep its nuclear reactor operating, intentionally vented radioactive gases or steam into a tunnel where it knew the plaintiff was working) and *Bulot v. Intracoastal Tubular Servs., Inc.*, 730 So.2d 1012 (La. Ct. App. 1999) (defendant's exposure of the plaintiff to radioactive material was not actionable because no intent to harm or offend was alleged; the court did not discuss the question of tangible substances).

A.R.B. v. ELKIN, 98 S.W.3d 99 (Mo. Ct. App. 2003)

The trial judge sitting as trier of fact finds a battery claim established by each of two plaintiffs (brother and sister) against their abusive father. But the judge rejects even nominal damages for the girl because she had not been physically harmed, and produced no evidence of medically-diagnosable emotional injury. The judge awards the boy $100 in "nominal damages" since he was physically injured, but rejects anything else for lack of proof. This is, of course, not a correct application of the law and the appeals court reverses. The note case is a good one to illustrate the kind of damages that may be awarded in a battery case, and that there are no rigid rules to constrict the jury's ultimate award. The goal is simply fair and reasonable for the interest that has been invaded by the intentional tort.

Elkin and the two Notes that follow it drive home the rule that trespassory torts–those based on direct use of physical action–permit the award of damages even when no physical or economic harm is done. *See, e.g., Johnson v. Pankratz*, 2 P.3d 1266 (Ariz. Ct. App. 2000) (battery). Nominal damages are always recoverable for such torts as battery, assault, false imprisonment, trespass to land and trespass to chattels. Courts sometimes allow substantial actual damages as well. In most unusual circumstances, the court in *Anderson v. St. Francis-St. George Hospital, Inc.*, 671 N.E.2d 225 (Ohio 1996), held that only nominal damages could be recovered for a non-harmful battery.

Note 2. You probably don't need to make much of this note at this point; we will see the stand-alone claims for negligent and intentional infliction of emotional distress in Chapter 19.

C. Re-focusing on Intent

GARRATT V. DAILEY, 279 P.2d 1091 (Wash. 1955)

The classic case defining intent to include either (a) purpose to obtain the invasive result or (b) substantial certainty that the invasive result will follow. Procedurally, the case was tried by a judge without a jury.

Note 2. Defining intent. Purpose or desire to do something suffices as one form of intent. This note poses a hypothetical involving desire and act coupled with an unexpected success. Its point is to contrast purpose with substantial certainty. *Garratt* does not say that substantial certainty of a touching is *necessary* for intent, but that it is *sufficient*. Purpose is also sufficient and purpose does not entail even risk, much less certainty, that the touching will occur. *But cf. Gouger v. Hardtke*, 482 N.W.2d 84 (Wis. 1992) (seemingly assuming that substantial certainty was the only test of intent).

Note 3. Intent and Negligence. The substantial certainty test in *Garratt* is in one sense simple realism, but it does cause problems. Can we distinguish this from negligence? The operative word here is certainty. Risk or chance, the operative ideas in negligence, are not enough to show intent.

In Taneff v. Hoehn, 190 B.R. 501 (W.D.N.Y. 1996), the court emphasized that even a high probability of harm is not enough, saying that drunk driving that caused injury (and death) was not intentional infliction of harm. The argument for finding substantial certainty intent was that drunk driving was like shooting a gun in a dark room full of people. The court held that substantial certainty was not shown, but veered away from direct comment on this analogy.

Note 4. Recklessness, wantonness and wilfulness. Recklessness and wilful and wanton misconduct are verbally distinguishable from ordinary negligence and from intent. Conscious indifference to consequences or something similar is characteristic of recklessness but that falls short of purpose and substantial certainty. As to this and as to cases in which recklessness is important, *see* DOBBS ON TORTS § 27 (2000). We quote the definition of recklessness given in a comment in the new Restatement Third of Torts: Liability for Physical Harms; note the ALI's stress on "known" risks – as opposed to the "should have known" negligence standard we will encounter throughout the course, starting with Chapter 5.

Some courts have thrown up their hands in trying to draw distinctions between wilful, wanton and reckless, but have no trouble distinguishing those things from negligence. For example, in *Craig v. Driscoll*, 813 A.2d 1003 (Conn. 2003), the court said this: "While we have attempted to draw definitional distinctions between the terms willful, wanton or reckless, in practice the three terms have been treated as meaning the same thing. The result is that willful, wanton, or reckless conduct tends to take on the aspect of highly unreasonable conduct, involving an extreme departure from ordinary care, in a situation where a high degree of danger is apparent. . . . It is at least clear . . . that such aggravated negligence must be more than any mere mistake resulting from inexperience, excitement, or confusion, and more than mere thoughtlessness or inadvertence, or merely inattention."

FYI: Gross negligence. Since the class has not considered the concept of negligence, it seems inappropriate to raise the idea of gross negligence at this point. Gross negligence is usually what norm--but in most cases courts have no need to distinguish gross from ordinary negligence, although statutes sometimes limit liability to cases of gross negligence. Traditionally, at least, gross negligence did not imply any bad state of mind such as conscious indifference to the rights of others. The gross negligence term in the sense of great negligence is thus seldom relevant and we make nothing of it in this casebook.■

Note 5. The object of intent. This note sets up the dual-intent, single-intent problem that will be addressed next in *White* and *Wagner*. You may want to ask the question at the beginning and then explore the courts' different answers.

WHITE V. MUNIZ, 999 P.2d 814 (Colo. 2000)

White v. Muniz approved an instruction that allowed the jury to exculpate the insane defendant. Although there is no blanket exclusion of liability for insane persons, *McGuire v. Almy*, 8 N.E.2d 760 (Mass. 1937), they are liable for battery only when they have the requisite tortious intent. *White v. Muniz* then spells out the tortious intent required to establish a battery: the insane defendant must intend to harm or offend, or in the language of the instruction, must "appreciate" that his touching will be offensive. Thus the fact that the defendant suffers from dementia does not dispense with the intent requirement. White makes it clear that the intent is not merely an intent to touch but an intent to harm or offend by touching. Suppose the defendant insanely believes he is alone when he fires his gun, but in fact he is firing at and hits the plaintiff? Cf. RESTATEMENT (SECOND) OF TORTS, § 895J, *Ill. 1.*

White v. Muniz is one of the few cases that has explicitly identified a split among the states on the issue of whether a defendant in a battery case must intend both to touch and to offend or harm ("dual intent"), or whether a mere intent to touch will suffice ("single intent"). One reason, perhaps, is that in the typical punch-in-the-nose battery case, there is simply no need to choose. The Colorado court asserts, we believe correctly, that the so-called "dual intent" rule is the one followed by most states, although it cites no cases for this point.

WAGNER V. STATE, 122 P.3d 599 (Utah 2005)

Wagner v. State takes the minority view. According to *Wagner*, only "intent to make contact" is required, "the actor need not intend his contact to be harmful or offensive." The court raises the concern that a person who causes harm or offense, as with an unpetitioned-for kiss, might not be liable on a single-intent rule if the intent was not to harm or offend.

Note 1. Single versus dual intent. Of course the plaintiff's burden in a single-intent jurisdiction is much easier. The plaintiff only needs to establish intent to contact, not intent to harm or offend as well.

Where a plaintiff must prove that a defendant intended merely to touch, and that harm or offense resulted, then even the "insane" would often be subject to liability. But where the plaintiff must prove that the defendant also intended to harm or offend by touching, liability will perhaps be more difficult to establish. This is not because insanity is a defense in a civil case, but because the fact of "insanity" means that the defendant may not have formed the requisite intent to be found liable in the particular case.

A similar case can be made with children. If a child must be proved to have the intent to harm or offend as well as to touch (the White v. Muniz "dual intent" rule), then liability will not be as easy to establish as it would if the court were to use a "single intent" rule requiring merely the intent to touch. The younger the child, presumably the more difficult the intent will be to prove – even where age itself is not a categorical defense.

Not only would it be easier to hold insane people and children liable, the single-intent rule should make it easier to hold anyone liable for battery (think of the EMT student in *Mullins*).

Note 2. Making a choice. We feel that intent to touch without intent to harm or offend should not be sufficient to establish a battery. One who intends neither harm nor offense by a touching is not at fault. Indeed, far from meeting the demands of an intentional tort, the language in some single-intent cases suggests a kind of strict liability for innocent touchings. *See* Osborne M. Reynolds, Jr., *Tortious Battery: Is "I Didn't Mean any Harm"Relevant?,* 37 OKLA. L. REV. 717 (1984) ("intent to harm or offend is not necessary").

We don't believe that such a broad view of the battery action is required. Think of the unpetioned-for kiss that *Wagner* provides as a case that justifies its broad view. A dual-intent standard might still render that conduct a battery. If you agree that offense is intended when the defendant intends to touch knowing that the plaintiff has not consented to it, a jury could easily conclude that despite the defendant's stated lack of intent to offend, intent to offend nevertheless existed. Consent and intent are two sides of the same coin. Liability is imposed when the defendant intends a harm or knows that the touching is not consented to, since intent to engage in unconsented-to conduct will always count as offense. If the defendant reasonably believes from the plaintiff's behavior that consent has been given, then he is protected by the apparent consent, as we'll see in the next chapter. If he does not believe that, he knows that the intended touching will be offensive and thus intends offense under the substantial certainty rule. (Certain intended touchings, such as the jostling in the subway, will be privileged and not actionable for that reason.)

We don't read the cases as providing much support for the single-intent view. We'll give a couple of examples.

Masters v. Becker, 254 N.Y.S.2d 633 (App. Div. 1964), is a case containing language suggesting that intent to touch is by itself enough. When you read *Masters's* language in the context of the facts and the issues, however, it become clear that it does not adopt such a strict liability approach. A six-year-old fell when a nine-year-old pried her fingers off the tailgate of a standing truck. The trial judge instructed that the nine-year-old had committed no battery unless she intended to injure the plaintiff. This was plainly wrong under the Restatement test, since he would be liable if he intended offense and either harm or offense occurred. The instruction error was compounded when the judge instructed that the intended injury must be the very same one suffered. On appeal, the court held this to be error. No argument was raised suggesting that intent to touch would by itself be sufficient for liability. The plaintiff in fact argued on the contrary assumption. She requested the court to instruct the jury that "plaintiffs were required to establish only that 'the act was done with intent to inflict an offensive bodily contact.'" So neither the plain holding nor the issue presented suggests that liability can be imposed merely because the plaintiff intended a touch.

Yet two very short passages, if read without regard to the issues in the case, might be thought to support a kind of strict liability for intended touchings. In the first passage, the court tells us that

> A plaintiff in an action to recover damages for an assault [meaning battery] founded on bodily contact must prove only that there was bodily contact; that such contact was offensive; and that the defendant intended to make the contact.

This passage standing alone and read like a statute might be thought to support the view that only an intent to touch is required. The next sentence, however, shows that the court's point is more limited and one addressed to the issues in the case:

> The plaintiff is not required to prove that defendant intended physically to injure him.

To say that the first quoted sentence establishes strict liability based upon intent to touch standing alone is to ignore the issue in the case, the court's actual holding, and the court's own idea of the point as expressed in the very next sentence. As Judge Posner has warned, "it is a disservice to courts, as well as a common source of erroneous predictions concerning the scope and direction of the law, to treat a judicial opinion as if it were a statute, every clause of which was Law." *All-Tech Telecom, Inc. v. Amway Corp.*, 174 F.3d 862, 866 (7th Cir. 1999). That is surely so in spades when the judicial text makes us doubt that the court even had the issue in mind at all.

We think cases like *Masters* with odd or inadequate formulations of rules, should be read as all cases should be read–with due attention to the issue at hand and to the actual result in the case. So read, we don't think they support strict liability for touchings that are intended to be neither offensive nor harmful. We think the cases right, too.

A strong statement that only an intent to touch is required is embedded in the reasoning in *Vitale v. Henchey*, 24 S.W.3d 651 (Ky. 2000). But, first, this was seemingly a case in which the defendant knew the touching was not consented to, so liability is quite appropriate under the intent to harm or offend standard. Second, the court in *Vitale* lumped motive and intent together. The defendant argued that he had no intent to harm and thus would not be liable. This was rejected, as it would it under the intent to harm or offend standard and as it would be under the rule that good motive for a touching intended to be harmful or offensive does not relieve the defendant of liability. In this light look at the court's statement:

The intent necessary for battery "is not necessarily a hostile intent, or a desire to do any harm." Rather, it is an intent to make contact with the person, not the intent to cause harm. Accordingly, the surgeon's lack of intent to harm the patient is no bar to an action for battery. . . .

What the court is asserting, in response to the defendant's argument, is that intent to harm is not required. This is plainly right. Does it mean that offense is not required when it says that "intent to make contact" is sufficient? The remainder of the sentence accurately shows that the court is merely trying to say that intent to harm is unnecessary. The same point can be made by noticing that intent to make contact in this context means intent to make an unconsented to contact–in other words, an intent to make offensive contact.

There seems to be no reason to impose strict liability for a touching that reasonably seems to be permitted and non-harmful. Strict liability is not needed to protect the plaintiff's autonomy. That is fully protected by saying that an offensive touching is intended whenever the defendant knows that his touching is unwelcome or unconsented to. More on that with consent. If you want to pursue this further, *see* DOBBS ON TORTS § 30 (2000).

Note 3. Single-intent outside the context of defendant incapacity. There are actually cases like this in which someone means no harm, but ends up causing injury. Liability for battery in a case like this would be liability without fault, essentially strict liability. This is in a way what happened in *Mulins*. The EMT student meant to contact the patient but not to harm or offend her. If intent to contact is all that is required, it seems as though *Mullins* would have to be decided the other way. This, even though there is no evidence of wrongdoing on the part of the student.

Note 4. Insanity. What are the reasons for holding insane persons liable for intentional torts? *Polmatier*, cited here, suggests these:

(a) Where one of two innocent persons must bear the loss, it must be borne by the person who occasioned it.
(b) Enforcement of liability will encourage relatives and others to restrain the insane person.
(c) Liability forestalls the possibility that sane persons will pretend insanity to avoid liability.
(d) "If he was not liable there would be no redress for injuries, and we might have the anomaly of an insane person having abundant wealth depriving another of his rights without compensation."

McGuire v. Almy, supra, gave another:
(e) Policy, including practical needs of courts, may require a rule that in the abstract, the court might hesitate to adopt. The complications of judging

insanity that have appeared in criminal cases might make the court unwilling to adopt similar rules for tort cases.

How sound are these reasons? The one-of-two-innocent-persons argument seems to mean that one who physically moves is treated as more morally responsible than one who sits still. Can that be right? And in any event, don't we know that the argument is generally if implicitly rejected under the principle requiring fault? In fact, didn't *Van Camp* implicitly reject it? You might also consider whether we really want to force relatives to constantly supervise insane persons. If you did, you might hold the relatives liable, not the insane person.

Second, are reasons for the rule about justice, about policy, or about process values? Do they argue that it is *right* to impose liability upon insane persons? Or only that it is expedient? One kind of expediency or policy is to provide appropriate incentives –to deter injury, to encourage control by relatives. This kind of argument assumes that law becomes known and that people react and react appropriately to it. A very different policy reason invokes process values: you must make legal rules that can be administered by courts with at least a degree of practical fairness and efficiency. The argument [(e) above] is that rules requiring us to distinguish sane from insane asks too much of us. Notice how different this kind of argument is from the other policy argument which seeks to impose social controls by getting good reactions to legal rules. And notice how both differ from arguments of justice.

Note 5. Civil law. The term civil law is routinely used in contrast to criminal law, but the term can also refer to the legal system that governs most developed countries. In that sense, civil law contrasts with common law. Civil law influence in the United States appears notably in Louisiana, but some southwestern and western states have been influenced on certain legal issues by the Spanish-Mexican heritage.

The note refers to "traditional" civil law because France and some other countries, including Mexico, impose some duties to compensate even upon insane persons, much in line with the common law rule. *See Torts—Liability for One's Own Act* § 215, in XI INT. ENCYC. COMP. L. (A. TUNC, ed., 1979). Some other civil law countries continue to follow the classical Roman view that infants and persons of unsound mind are like a force of nature and cannot be at fault and cannot be liable. *See* GERMAN CIVIL CODE § 827 (I. Forrester, S. Goren & H. Ilgen 1975). This material is a fulcrum on which to balance discussion of the underlying issue, not an invitation to plumb the civil law.

In *Yancy v. Maestri,* 155 So. 509 (La. Ct. App. 1934), the court, after reviewing the arguments for the common law rule, offered this justification for the traditional civil law:

[S]ince an insane person is not a rational being, he is incapable of appreciating right from wrong or distinguishing carefulness from carelessness, and therefore, his acts are looked upon as inevitable accidents. The common law considers the effect of the insane person's act, while the civil law regards the cause of it.

Note 6. Options. Professor Charlene Smith's article lists the statutes and the main literature on crime victims' compensation. Although protection of citizens might be regarded as one of the basic purposes of the state, these statutes do not accept responsibility for the state's failure to protect. They are rather more like welfare statutes, providing limited aid to a limited group with special need.

Punitive damages against children and insane persons. Punitive damages may be awarded for egregious misconduct coupled with a bad state of mind. The bad state of mind is variously and not very helpfully defined as "malicious" or sometimes "wanton" or even reckless. *See* 1 DAN DOBBS, THE LAW OF REMEDIES § 3.11 (2d ed. 1993). Should either a child or an insane person be held for punitive damages in a battery case? It seems clear that either kind of incapacity could indicate a lack of malice or recklessness; the actor who is a small child might formulate an intent to harm or offend without, however, any real understanding of the significance of the action and the reasons why social restraint is required. Similarly with an insane person. Some authorities state generally that insane persons may not be held liable for punitive damages, though these are old and may not be assumed to have contemporary notions of insanity in mind in making these statements. *See* Annotation, 49 A.L.R.3d at 202 (1973).

Some children are capable of entertaining malicious or other outrageous states of mind and may be held for punitive damages when this is proved to be the case. See *Angelo v. Savignac*, 342 N.W.2d 440 (Wis. 1983).

NOTE: CHILD LIABILITY

We have now seen several cases in which children are held liable for intentional torts. Is *Van Camp* contrary to the general rule? No – the child in that case was not alleged to be at fault in any way, either negligent or intentional. Again, you might take the opportunity to reinforce an ethical consideration that the lawyer in *Van Camp* was correct not to seek to amend to add an allegation of intentional tort (or even negligence) if he did not believe that such an allegation could be proved at trial. Some states immunize children below a certain age from liability for intentional torts, or from all torts, as Note 8 references. Note 9 presents some other solutions to the problem of child liability for intentional torts. You might mention that courts have a great deal of flexibility in crafting common-law rules that basically compromise between two opposing yes-or-no positions.

You may choose to raise the topic of child liability together with the liability of insane persons, discussed in the next case. If subjective moral fault is the only basis for liability, many children will not be liable for the harms they cause. This will preserve the strong sense of many persons that "wrong" is the only basis for liability here.

NOTE: PARENTAL LIABILITY FOR THE TORTS OF THEIR MINOR CHILDREN

While this can be a difficult doctrinal topic for students to grasp at this point, the Note is designed here to lay out the basic law (including the typical statutory scheme) without much explanation from the teacher. It also attempts to answer commonly-asked questions about why someone would ever sue a child since children don't have money; the answer is that children are generally listed as "insured persons" on a homeowner's insurance policy.

That being said, discussions on this topic can be quite interesting since students so readily grasp the factual problem.

The common law says that parents are not liable vicariously (just by being parents) for the torts of their children. But statutes in most states abrogate that common law standard in part, often by making parents liable where the child commits an act "wilfully or wantonly." These statutes often cap damages at a relatively low amount. You can point out that in a suit against parents under one of these statutes, the issue will NOT be whether the parents are at fault, or whether the child committed an intentional tort. The issue will be whether the parents are liable under the statute – which means, as in the cited case of *Walker v. Kelley*, whether the child committed the act wilfully. As with the civil rights material in § 5, this makes students realize that a change in the applicable law compels a completely different analysis than what they've seen so far on the same facts – a basic legal reasoning lesson.

You might raise *respondeat superior*. Students should distinguish vicarious liability of parents from the parents' liability for their own negligence in failing to control a child known to create risks to others. That is covered in Chapter 18. This said, we can get to the policy issue: Should parents be responsible for the intentional torts of their children in the absence of specific parental fault? All torts? Wilful torts? What will happen to children whose parents are held liable for a childish escapade? Will this, for example, encourage child abuse?

STOSHAK V. EAST BATON ROUGE PARISH SCHOOL, 959 So. 2d 996 (La. Ct. App. 2007)
BASKA V. SCHERZER, 156 P.3d 617 (2007)

This pair of cases illustrates the transferred intent rules in similar circumstances but with very different effect. The transferred intent rules can be broken down into two kinds of rules: (1) where the defendant intends an intentional tort (such as battery) towards A but winds up hitting B instead, the intent towards A "transfers" to B, allowing B to sue the defendant for battery. (2) where the defendant intends one intentional tort (such as assault) but winds up committing a different tort (like battery, or false imprisonment), then the intent to commit the inchoate tort "transfers" to the tort that was actually accomplished. In answer to note 1, you might note that in both *Stoshak* and *Baska*, the transferred intent rules follow pattern (1).

Note 3. Accepting or rejecting the rule in light of policy considerations. Do we need transferred intent at all? A more direct method of stating the result would be to say that, given a consciously tortious trespassory act, the defendant is liable for all the damages that he actually inflicts, even if those damages represent harm different from the harm he intended.

Osborne M. Reynolds, Jr., *Transferred Intent: Should its "Curious Survival" Continue?,* 50 OKLA. L. REV. 529 (1997), suggests that the doctrine–we'd call it the terminology–of transferred intent can be abolished. We agree that the terminology is misleading. We are more cautious, however, about his proposed rule that "liability for an intentional tort extends to all direct consequences, and extends to remote, indirect consequences where the tort of trespass to land is concerned, so long as there is some chain of causation." We aren't sure that it would be helpful to state the rule that broadly when it comes to, say, intentional interference with contract or business opportunity or misrepresentation. In addition, see the limitations suggested in the materials on trespass to land below.

The transferred intent rule might be employed to extend liability but not to limit it. Another way to address the problem in *Baska*—that the plaintiff has a shorter time in which to file her suit when the misconduct is labeled intentional rather than negligent, would be to change the short statute of limitations for intentional torts.

Vincent Johnson's article, *Transferred Intent in American Tort Law*, 87 MARQ. L.REV. 903 (2004), is well worth reading.

On the transferred intent/extended liability rule (explained in Note 5), *see* DOBBS ON TORTS §§ 40 & 41 (2000).

"Transfer" of Non-tortious Intent. A defendant who has no wrongful intent whatever causes harm when his aim goes awry. Is he liable under the transferred intent doctrine? Of course not. But students sometimes have a problem with such situations. If the actor could have carried out his act without liability, then it seems plain that he cannot be held for an intentional tort merely because the act miscarries. If he took unreasonable risks in such a case, he would be liable for negligence, but if he is not negligent and has no tortious intent, then he is not liable.

Suppose a defendant threw a rock at a target, such as a discarded beer bottle he has found. The stone goes wild and strikes the plaintiff. Unless the defendant is negligent, creating a risk to the plaintiff that is unreasonable in the circumstances, there is no reason to impose liability.

To carry out the metaphor involved in "transferred intent," we can say there is "no intent to transfer." If the intent would not have sufficed for liability had it been carried out, it should not suffice for liability when it miscarries.

Note 4. The effects of classifying a tort as intentional. Transferred intent often looks like negligence or recklessness, and in some cases a plaintiff will be better off suing for negligence rather than battery accomplished by way of transferred intent or extended liability. This is so because insurance may cover negligence but not intentional torts. A plaintiff might prefer a negligence claim to take advantage of a longer statute of limitations, also. In *Lynn v. Burnette,* 531 S.E.2d 275 (N.C. Ct. App. 2000), the court said that although battery and negligence are discrete concepts, some sets of facts might warrant a suit on either theory at the plaintiff's choice. In that case, the defendant fired a pistol, intending to strike the tire, but unintentionally pulled the trigger before her aim was complete. The bullet struck the plaintiff in his neck. The defendant argued that this was a battery and that the one-year statute of limitations had run. The court held that the plaintiff could assert a negligence claim on their facts and that suit was timely under the three-year statute for negligence.

§ 2. ASSAULT

Related materials. Assault can be compared and contrasted with intentional infliction of emotional distress. We deal with emotional distress as a separate topic in Chapter 19. You can import § 1 from that chapter if you wish to develop the comparison here, although we find that an exploration of the intentional infliction of emotional distress cases works best when considered with negligent infliction cases, in Chapter 19.

You can continue raising the procedural issues attendant to summary judgment in *Cullison v. Medley.*

SUMMARY

CULLISON V. MEDLEY. The plaintiff is menaced by the defendants, one of whom has a gun in his holster and grabs for it while telling the plaintiff to leave his teenage daughter alone; another defendant (the girl's mother) keeps her hand in her pocket, leading the plaintiff to believe that she, too, has a gun. The plaintiff is never touched but suffers rather severe psychological damage as a result of this incident. Reversing a summary judgment for the defendants, the court holds that the plaintiff's alllegations and testimony could support a jury verdict in his favor on an assault claim. It is for the jury to decide, says the court, whether his apprehension of imminent battery was reasonable.

COMMENTS

Preliminary Note: You can move faster in this section than in the battery section, especially since assault relates so closely to battery and you will probably have explored a number of common issues already. The concepts of intent are the difficult ones here. Students should be able to glean the elements of assault from the primary case.

CULLISON V. MEDLEY, 570 N.E.2d 27 (Ind. 1991)

Plaintiff Cullison made the mistake of socializing with the 16-year-old Sandy Medley. Some hours after what appears to be a rather innocent meeting between

Sandy and Cullison, she showed up at the door of his mobile home accompanied by her father, her mother, a brother and a brother-in-law. The father, Ernest, had a gun in a holster; the mother kepts her hand in her pocket, "convincing Cullison that she was also carrying a pistol." According to Cullison, Ernest grabbed for his gun a few times and threatened him with bodily harm if he did not leave Sandy alone. Cullison was never touched by anyone. Immediately afterward Cullison suffered from chest pains. Shortly after this Cullison learned that Ernest had once shot a man. Two months later, Ernest (again armed with a weapon) glared at Cullison in a restaurant and stood about a foot from him. Cullison went to a psychologist shortly after this, and was in therapy for 18 months. He also saw a psychiatrist and was prescribed drugs that prevented him from operating power tools or driving, injuring him in his sole-proprietorship construction business. He also testified to sleep disorders, depression, nervousness, and impotency, all allegedly caused by the Medleys.

Cullison sued the Medleys for assault. The trial court granted summary judgment for defendants, and this was affirmed by the intermediate appeals court. *Held*, reversed. The facts alleged and testified to could allow a jury to find the defendants liable for assault. Last paragraph: "It is for the jury to determine whether Cullison's apprehension of being shot or otherwise injured was one which would normally be aroused in the mind of a reasonable person."

Was the plaintiff reasonable in believing that he was threatened with an imminent harmful touching? He could not know that the defendant had the present ability to shoot him, because the gun might not have been loaded. But the plaintiff knew that the defendant had the *apparent* present ability. See *Allen v. Hannaford*, 138 Wash. 423, 244 P. 700 (1926). In any event, whether his apprehension of imminent contact was reasonable was a jury question that could not be resolved on summary judgment.

Does Cullison have a battery claim? No, because he was not touched. But he does state a claim for assault, and a jury might find for him on the facts adduced thus far – the defendants intentionally placed him, arguably, in reasonable apprehension of imminent contact that would be battery if completed. This was, here, quite purposeful – although even if they knew that the plaintiff's apprehension of harmful contact was only substantially certain to occur, that would suffice as well.

Note 1. Applying Cullison. The *Raess* court held that the plaintiff did have a claim. In fact, it upheld a judgment of $325,000 for the plaintiff.

Note 2. Assault and battery. Not every battery gives rise to an assault. This is so because the interests protected by each respective tort are different. Battery protects autonomy and the person's freedom from unwanted harmful or offensive touching. Assault protects the interest in being free from the mental perception that such a touching is imminent.

Assault and battery do not always go hand in hand – liability for assault requires a "reasonable apprehension of imminent conduct that would be battery if completed" – an awareness, in other words, of what appears to be an imminent battery. So one could be hit on the head while asleep and not have a good claim for assault.

The sleeping plaintiff case and *Koffman* [which was a full case in the previous edition] illustrate that a plaintiff who did not apprehend the harmful or offensive contact will not have a cause of action that sounds in assault. Specifically, in Koffman the court reasons that because Koffman had "no warning of an imminent forceful tackle," he lacked one necessary element of assault, i.e., he was never placed in reasonable apprehension of an imminent contact. Essentially everything happened too fast – by the time he had an awareness of anything, he was already being battered.

Note 3. Apprehension. It is awareness of imminent contact that is required, not "fear," although fear is often present as a matter of fact in assault cases.

Note 4. "Words alone." "Mere words, no matter how violent, do not amount to an assault." *Bollaert v. Witter*, 792 P.2d 465 (Or. Ct. App. 1990). The words-alone rule is probably a rule about reasonableness of apprehension. Probably there is no such thing as words alone. Even the masked person acted to put on a mask, albeit outside the plaintiff's presence. The words-alone rule points in the right direction most of the time, but should not be taken literally.

Note 5. Words negating intent to effect immediate touching. Words can negate the threat, or, more subtly, can indicate that the threat is really a threat about future action and that although harmful or offensive touching is threatened, the touching is not imminent. It is a matter of reasonable interpretation, isn't it? Some words might formally assert a threat, yet connote a present unwillingness to carry it out. In *Allen v. Walker*, 569 So.2d 350 (Ala. 1990) co-workers engaged in a confrontive argument. The male shook his finger in the female's face and said he would "whip [her] ass anytime, anywhere," a statement repeated the next day in another confrontation. Should these words be taken to mean that the male is going to carry out the threat right away or that he definitely is NOT going to do so? The Alabama Court thought the facts sufficient to get the plaintiff to the jury. But don't the quoted words sound like the words a man might use when he is NOT going to fight or attack?

Note 6. Words offering a choice of tortious alternatives. Words are used in these cases, but they are in a sense an accidental feature. The defendant has no right to make you choose between an intact face and your basketball tickets. If you intend immediately to give up your tickets, maybe there is no apprehension of an imminent touching, only a conversion of your tickets, a tort to be seen soon. If, however, you decided to exercise your privilege to defend yourself rather than give up the tickets, the threat seems like an assault.

Note 7. Imminent Apprehension. The idea that battery must appear imminent for an assault claim to succeed is an easy one to play with. It is a question of degree and judgment, as a few hypotheticals can show. A telephone threat, even to someone next door, does not seem imminent enough. You can vary the facts until you reach a point that touching has become imminent. For example, suppose the defendant starts down the stairs, in full view of his next-door neighbor; he reaches the front porch; he starts across the lawn. . . .

These kinds of cases present questions of degree. The question of degree is unanswerable except by making a judgment call. When that is the case, you can best leave all debatable cases to the jury or other trier of fact. As soon as the class can see that point, the hypothetical is *functus officio*. You can consider whether the imminent touching rule is workable, since it will necessarily invoke questions of degree and judgment. But of course it is workable, given the small number of borderline cases and the ability of the jury to bring a common sense judgment to bear on the issue. What is not workable is an effort to state in advance exactly where the line should be drawn as a matter of law. If you take up this point, you can once again point out that rules may be chiefly useful in pointing lawyers to the kind of evidence and argument they need to make, not in guiding us to an indisputable solution to the case.

If your students are taking criminal law concurrently with torts, you might want to note that threats of future harm may be criminal even though they form no basis for civil action. That depends upon the criminal statute. See, e.g., holding a threat of future harm sufficient under a criminal statute, *Commonwealth v. Sholley*, 739 N.E.2d 236 (Mass. 2000). From a deterrence point of view, criminal liability might be right (if we thought the threat were serious). Since civil (tort) law has deterrence purposes, too, why not allow the assault claim for future threats, too? We seem to be unwilling to permit private citizens to pursue the deterrence purpose unless the private citizen himself has a recognizable injury. That, at least is the effect of the assault rule's requirement of imminent battery.

Dickens v. Puryear, discussed here, was a primary case in the last edition. The court held that although the threats of castration were assaults and barred by a one-year statute of limitations, the threat to kill him later – unless the plaintiff departed what early settlers called the "goodliest land under the Cope of Heaven" – was not an assault. This is so because assault requires apprehension of imminent harmful or offensive bodily contact. Thus mere words are not sufficient; overt action is required to show imminence. Although there was plenty of overt action here, it did not relate to this particular threat, which lay in the future. (The court held that this might be an intentional infliction of emotional distress.)

Note 8. Revisiting transferred intent. Now we have the second meaning of transferred intent—the defendant intends one type of intentional tort but instead commits another. Instead of speaking of transferred intent, we could state the second part of the transferred intent rule this way: the defendant is subject to liability for battery whenever, without apparent consent, he intends to touch or to create an apprehension of imminent touching and a touching results. The Restatement Second, structures assault and battery rules along these lines.

Damages. The traditional rule makes defendants liable for substantial (not merely nominal) damages for trespassory torts, at least when the trespass occurred to the person rather than to property. This means that Cullison would be entitled to substantial damages even if he had not shown all the medical evidence and the evidence of lost business opportunity. Discussion of recoverable damages in assault cases usually starts with the famous *I. de S. and wife v. W. de S.*, 22 Lib. Ass. f. 99, pl. 60 (1348) where the defendant "struck at" but did not hit the plaintiff and where the trier was expected to award damages. Judge Morris Arnold refers to some other early cases and gives the presumed damages rationale. MORRIS ARNOLD, SELECT CASES OF TRESPASS FROM THE KING'S COURTS 1307-1399 xxxiii (1985). You can look at the recovery of substantial damages in several different ways:

(1) the plaintiff's right is valuable in itself even if it is not sold on the market; (2) damage can be "presumed;" (3) the substantial damages recovery is "really" a punitive recovery under another name; (4) it is "really" a mental distress damages under another name; (5) it is "really" a means of providing funds from which an attorney's contingent fee is paid, thus providing incentive to keep the peace through tort suits.

Modern cases may show a tendency to limit such recoveries, and certainly there is in some such tendency in civil rights cases. Still, some courts have allowed substantial damage recovery in § 1983 cases where there was a trespassory, physical invasion. In a state tort-law case involving an assault, *Campbell v. Jenkins*, 608 P.2d 363 (Colo. Ct. App. 1980), however, the Colorado Court of Appeals limited recovery for an assault to $1 nominal damages. The defendant had driven a car toward a boy playing in a sandpile, screeching to a stop very close to him. Although this was an assault, the damages were limited.

NOTE: RELATED STATUTORY CLAIMS

This Note briefly discusses two areas where statutes have entered to add to (or sometimes supplant) common law assault claims. You may not need to discuss this in class, but it's a good idea to let students know that the law of assault is not the only law around that might give an aggrieved person a cause of action on "apprehension of imminent battery" facts. Further, common law assault has some limiting rules but those rules may be avoided by making some different kind of claim. While torts is largely a common-law course, statutes are important in tort law, as elsewhere. Some students may even need to learn that statutes are different from the common law. In the *Planned Parenthood* case cited here, the court upheld an award of damages for the abortion providers, holding that the defendants' actions were "threats of force" within the FACE statute's prohibitions. Because the defendants' speech threatened force, their speech was not protected by the First Amendment.

The FACE statute has non-tort provisions we see no need to mention. Defendants who violate its terms may be subjected to government litigation seeking injunction, criminal, and civil penalties, and statutory damages with joint and several liability. See *United States v. Gregg*, 226 F.3d 253 (3d Cir. 2000). Although this would be significant in civil rights course and remedies courses, our focus here is on the assault comparison, so we mention it solely as background information for the teacher.

Stalkers. As mentioned here, several states have stalking statutes, all relatively new. Wyoming's statute, WY.ST. § 6-2-506, was applied in *Veile v. Martinson,* 258 F.3d 1180 (10th Cir. 2001) (upholding a jury verdict against a male who stalked his business competitor). Most of these statutes provide for both punitive and compensatory damages. The statutes often make actionable conduct that does not ordinarily fit the requirements necessary to show assault. Stalking statutes are not identical. Notice that the California statute requires a credible threat. Some others, not requiring a credible threat, nevertheless require some kind of objective, definable action. The California criminal version of the stalking statute, Cal.Penal Code §646.9, was upheld in *People v. Borrelli,* 91 Cal.Rptr.2d 851 (Ct. App. 2000). Kansas revised its stalking statute, K.S.A. 60-31a01 *et seq.,* after it was held to be unconstitutionally vague in *State v. Bryan,* 910 P.2d 212 (Kan. 1996). The new version was upheld against a constitutional vagueness challenge in *Smith v. Martens,* 106 P.3d 28 (Kan. 2005).

Even in the absence of a stalking statute, victims of such conduct might be able to claim intentional infliction of emotional distress or invasion of privacy. See *Bristow v. Drake Street Inc.,* 41 F.3d 345 (7th Cir. 1995); *Troncalli v. Jones,* 514 S.E.2d 478 (Ga. Ct. App. 1999) (privacy invasion and intentional infliction of emotional distress). The intentional infliction tort was itself generated in part to allow some claims that would be dismissed under the assault rules. It is considered in Chapter 19, § 1 and the stalker issue could be postponed for consideration there, too, if you wish.

Clinical descriptions of stalking may be legally difficult because they emphasize the subjective reaction of the victim rather than acts that can be judged objectively. Stacy Casper Martinez, *Utilizing the Tools: Successfully Implementing the Stalking Statutes,* 35 LAND & WATER L. REV. 521 (2000) succinctly summarizes clinical views and a number of other points.

REVIEW, TUTORIALS AND PRACTICE EXAMS

If your school does not provide a program of tutorials or the like, you can provide essay exam questions with sample answers without much time investment, adding a discussion of answers if your time permits. You can also provide multiple choice questions, the answers to which may be informative. Short of those techniques, you might simply provide questions for review.

Here are some simple examples of rule statements that can also serve as review. They are not always linguistically precise but perhaps good enough to help students see that the material is manageable.

1. A battery requires a touching.
2. A battery requires an intent to touch.
3. A battery requires either harm or offense as a result of the touching.

4. A battery requires an intent to harm or offend through the intended touching.

5. Intent to do a thing can be shown by showing that an actor had a purpose to do it.

6. Intent to do a thing can also be shown by showing that the actor, though having no purpose to do it, knew with (substantial) certainty that the thing would result from his action.

7. If an actor intends acts that would constitute a tort to one person, but his acts miscarry and a second person is injured, the second person has a tort action.

8. If an actor intends one tort, but his acts miscarry so that another kind of tort is committed instead, he is liable for that other tort.[1]

9. A minor is generally liable for his or her torts, but some minors may be so young that they cannot formulate the required intent. A few jurisdictions may excuse minors under 7 years of age.

10. An insane person may be liable for his or her torts, provided the person has the kind of intent required to establish the tort under the ordinary legal rules.

11. An actor who intentionally puts another in reasonable apprehension of imminent bodily contact of the kind that, if carried out, would amount to a battery, is liable for assault.

12. There is no assault unless the victim reasonably believes that an unpermitted touching is imminent.

13. Mere words cannot ordinarily create an apprehension of immediate bodily touching and are not ordinarily enough.

14. A conditional threat of touching may be a threat of imminent bodily touching if the condition is one the actor has no right to impose, as where he says "I will beat you unless you give me your purse this instant."

REFERENCES:
DOBBS ON TORTS §§ 33-35 (assault) & §§ 40-41 (transferred intent); RESTATEMENT SECOND OF TORTS §§ 21-34 (1965); DIGESTS, *Assault and Battery*.

§ 3. FALSE IMPRISONMENT

MCCANN V. WAL-MART STORES, INC., 210 F.3d 51 (1st Cir. 2000)

The plaintiffs, mother and children, were stopped by two of the defendant's security guards as they were leaving a Wal-Mart store. The guard asserted that one of the children had previously stolen items from the store and was not permitted there, then asserted that the family must remain as police were being called.

---

1. This is put in question-begging form purely for convenience. The question is whether it is a tort to intend an assault but accomplish a touching that was never intended. But everyone will understand quickly what is meant, which is not the case if you write the rule with precision.

While the family waited, the guard refused to let one boy go to the bathroom and refused to examine proffered identification. The guards, both female, called their superior, not the police. When the superior arrived, she told the guards they were mistaken and the family left. The chief issue is whether all this counted as a confinement that would support the family's claim for false imprisonment.

Such cases are inherently difficult, since the confinement is not physical but results, if at all, from the plaintiff's state of mind as created by threats, express or implied. In this case the difficulty is a little greater because Maine, whose law controls in this diversity case, had said there actual physical restraint was required to establish confinement. The federal court in *McCann* rejects a literal reading of that statement, looks at context, and concludes it was only a way of saying that confinement was required, not that confinement must always be by physical constraint. Accordingly, it upholds a jury verdict for the plaintiffs.

The case summarizes basic elements of false imprisonment, establishing the softer meanings of confinement, and provides a discussion of literal and non-literal reading of precedent. The last point as well as the more routine rule statements make this case worth attention.

You can use the case to launch various scenarios that demonstrate the need for judgment in applying the confinement rules to cases of explicit and implicit threats and demands. You can start with the *McCann-Knowlton* factual differences and then consider scenarios in Note 4 if you like.

A Wal-Mart argument not included in the edited version was that the jury should have been instructed that there would be no false imprisonment if the security guards had only told the plaintiffs that they were under a moral obligation to stay. The court thought that might indeed be a permissible or even required instruction if properly offered. But Wal-Mart's offered instruction on this point was combined with an erroneous instruction that an actual physical restraint was required. So it was not error to refuse this instruction, part of which was wrong. We would love to have included this cautionary segment of the case and omitted it only because of space constraints.

Note 1. Elements. Brevity of confinement is relevant to damages but the fact that it is brief does not deprive the plaintiff of a claim. As to on awareness of confinement below, see materials on Note 7 below.

Note 2. Exclusion and public accommodation. Exclusion from a place of public accommodations may give the plaintiff some kind of claim NOT based on false imprisonment -- for instance, a claim under federal or state public accommodations statutes. (This is not a damages claim but only an injunctive claim under federal law.) Disability law takes this further by requiring businesses affirmatively to provide certain access. You can alert students to these potential claims without engaging in extended discussion.

Shen v. Leo A. Daly Co., cited here, held no false imprisonment. The stated ground was that "the country of Taiwan is clearly too great an area within which to be falsely imprisoned." Taiwan has more than 12,000 square miles of land.

Rhode Island, about 1200 square miles. Could you be imprisoned by being confined to the state of Rhode Island?

Note 3. Confinement by physical barrier or force. Students should be able to say that as a matter of definition, the plaintiff is confined when she is locked in a room and knows it, but that she is not when she knows she can leave by a safe and reasonable means. The moving car example reflects confinement that is imposed by making it unsafe to leave.

Note 4. Confinement by threats or duress. *(a) Threats and demands.* In *Hardy v. LaBelle's Distributing Co.,* 661 P.2d 35 (Mont. 1983), a store employee asked to the manager's office where she found several store officials and two police officers. She was accused of theft. She denied it. The discussion continued 45 minutes. Eventually the store conceded it was in error. The jury found no false imprisonment. The employee admitted she wanted to clear up the matter, although she also felt coerced. If she stayed because she was compelled to, she was confined. If she was not compelled to but stayed because she wanted to clear the charge, she was not. The jury found not and the court affirmed the judgment for the defendant. What if she had started to leave and the manager had said in a loud void, "sit down," or the police officer had moved to the door? That was *Dupler v. Seubert,* 230 N.W.2d 626 (Wis. 1975). The implicit assertion of force is clearer and the plaintiff recovered. The point that factual details are significant can also be made by comparing *McCann* to *Knowlton,* the Maine case the *McCann* court does not follow. The defendant's threat to act in the future is comparable to future threats in assault cases–it will not suffice to create present confinement. *(b) Submission to the assertion of colorable legal authority.* This is enough. You can see elements of this in *McCann* itself. *(c) Duress of goods.* This seems to be one specific kind of threat: I'll keep your wallet until I'm ready for you to leave. See Restatement Second § 40A, Ill. 2. As in all these cases, confinement is largely a matter of degree; it might not count as confinement if instead of a wallet the defendant merely hold's the plaintiff's pencil. These and other situations are summarized in DOBBS ON TORTS § 37 (2000).

Note 6. Asking the police to confine. Yes, a defendant who "procures" the arrest of another may be liable for false imprisonment, but of course that procurement must itself be more than just a request to arrest, and must itself be wrongful. For example, in the *Wal-Mart v. Rodriguez* case cited here, the Texas Supreme Court said that a defendant who commands a police officer to arrest the plaintiff – as by saying, "Arrest this man" – can be liable for false imprisonment if the defendant knowingly gives false information to the police, such as would occur if the defendant wilfully identifies the wrong man in order to have him arrested. In the case, however, Wal-Mart was found not liable because there was no evidence that it had knowingly provided false information to procure the plaintiff's arrest for passing a bad check. This was true even though Wal-Mart did not tell the police that its check-verification system was subject to error, and that very system is what made Wal-Mart believe (wrongfully, it turns out) that the plaintiff had passed a bad check. In the *Alvarez-Machain* panel opinion cited here, the defendant U.S. government was held liable when it had a Mexican national arrested in Mexico. This opinion was reversed by the U.S. Supreme Court in *Sosa v. Alvarez-Machain*, described briefly in the Casebook on page 78, on the grounds that the government was immune from suit under the Federal Tort Claims Act since the wrongful act took place in a foreign country, and could not be sued under the Alien Tort Statute either, for reasons explained on Casebook page 78.

Note 7. Damages. This note reiterates the rule stated in connection with battery and assault, that substantial damages may be recovered for invasion of the right itself. In *Phillips v. District of Columbia*, 458 A.2d 722 (D.C. App. 1983), officers stopped the plaintiff as he was leaving a bank, thinking he may have been involved in a grand larceny. Plaintiff thought the plainclothes officers were robbers and he offered resistance. He ended up in jail and sued for false arrest. The jury awarded $10,000 on the false arrest claim, but the trial judge ordered a remittitur to $260.65, representing his wage loss and legal expense. On appeal this was remanded for reconsideration. "[T]he single fact of imprisonment, the deprivation of one's right to move about, is compensable," and compensation is not limited to the out of pocket losses.

Punitive damages may also be assessed if the false imprisonment is "malicious." E.g., *Smith's Food & Drug Centers, Inc. v. Bellegarde,* 958 P.2d 1208 (Nev. 1998) (affirming an award that assessed no punitive damages against the employees but $65,000 against the employer).

Awareness of confinement. The victim's knowledge of confinement is an element of the tort of false imprisonment, but in *Creek v. State,* 588 N.E.2d 1319 (Ind. Ct. App. 1992), the court held that such knowledge was not required for a *criminal* conviction. In that case the criminal defendant was convicted of kidnaping after he held a sleeping child hostage. Notice that if the victim suffers actual harm, she may recover even if she was not aware of confinement at the time. So the rule might be rephrased to say that damages will not be presumed in the absence of the victim's awareness of confinement.

Should the awareness rule apply when the defendant's conduct not only causes confinement but also destroys the plaintiff's awareness of it? That is seemingly the case of the secretly sedated nursing home patient.

In *Parvi v. City of Kingston,* 362 N.E.2d 960 (N.Y. 1977), police officers placed plaintiff, a drunk, in a squad car. Plaintiff had no place to go, so the officers transported him to an abandoned golf course outside the city, leaving him to dry out. The plaintiff was struck by a car as he tried to find his way home. He sued the officers, claiming a false imprisonment in the police car. There was no privilege to run the plaintiff out of town, though there may have been a privilege to arrest him for the purpose of taking him to jail or a place of safety. Absent the privilege to run him out of town, there was an improper confinement in the car. The plaintiff, however, was drunk, and he admitted he had no recollection of being detained in the car. The court said:

[F]alse imprisonment, as a dignitary tort, is not suffered unless its victim knows of the dignitary invasion . . . .
However . . . [courts must] distinguish between a later recollection of consciousness and the existence of that consciousness at the time when the imprisonment itself took place . . . . [W]hile it may well be that the alcohol Parvi had imbibed . . . had the effect of wiping out his recollection of being in the police car against his will, that is a far cry from saying he was not conscious of his confinement at the time. . . . . "

Since the plaintiff's negligence claim was also held sufficient to get to the jury, the court did not have to reach the issue whether the false imprisonment would justify recovery for the later injury under the extended consequences rule.

The awareness rule and other torts. The more interesting question is whether you can justify the Restatement rule requiring awareness of confinement. Would an unknown battery be possible? If the battery is physically harmful, it would be analogous to actual harm in the false imprisonment case. What if the battery were merely offensive and unknown at the time? It is hard to believe that one could justify sexual contact with a stranger on the ground that the stranger was asleep and only heard about it later. Even though "no harm is done," this is an invasion of personal autonomy. Is it any less so with false imprisonment?

Note 8. Privileges; false arrest. False arrest is merely a descriptive term for false imprisonment committed by an officer or one claiming legal authority. The ultimate resolution of false imprisonment cases may turn on defenses or privileges to be encountered in the next chapter. The note indicates one such privilege–the officer's privilege to arrest–to forestall all those "what if" questions from the class and leave the issue for the next chapter.

Note 9. Duration of privilege. In *Dett* the officer could not detain the arrestee after he had information suggesting she was not the person sought by the warrant. Similarly, a jailer is under a duty to release his prisoner when the prisoner's sentence is served. *Bennett v. Ohio Dept. of Rehab. and Correction*, 573 N.E.2d 633 (Ohio 1991). In *Whittaker v. Sandford*, 85 A. 399 (Me. 1912), the defendant, leader of a religious sect, induced the plaintiff to go to the sect's colony in Syria. When she decided to leave the sect, the defendant offered her transport home on his yacht, the Kingdom, but back in American waters he would not provide a small boat to take her ashore. This was held as false imprisonment. Since defendant had put the plaintiff in the position in the first place (and had given assurances she would be transported), it is an easy case to impose a duty release the confined passenger.

We don't take up malicious prosecution here. It is covered briefly in Chapter 32. In some ways malicious prosecution is more akin to a libel action than a false imprisonment action. It is not a trespassory tort; the interference with free movement is indirect, taking place through legal process, and in some cases there is no restraint at all. The gist of the malicious prosecution claim is improper prosecution, not confinement. In fact, it may be necessary to bring both false imprisonment and malicious prosecution claims to vindicate all the plaintiff's rights. Thus a detention will entitle the plaintiff to damages for false imprisonment, but only until such time as the detention becomes justified by a warrant and prosecution. One important difference in the two actions is that if there is a confinement of the plaintiff, the burden of justifying that confinement is upon the defendant in a false imprisonment claim. But in the malicious prosecution action the burden is on the plaintiff to show that the defendant wholly lacked probable cause for prosecution. This difference in the burdens is at times significant. Several other differences can be found as well.

REVIEW HYPOTHETICALS, MINI-EXAMS

1. Plaintiff, a 38-year-old woman, was admitted to the defendant's private hospital for surgery. She made some arrangements about payment, but there were complications and her bill was higher than anticipated. She was unable to pay it at the time. A hospital official, a man, entered her room the day before she was to be discharged. He said: "You can't leave until you pay your bill. Don't try it." He then walked out. The plaintiff remained the next day after the doctor had discharged her, trying to get the hospital officials to agree she could go. After two days, she dressed and walked out. Has she a claim for false imprisonment?

2. Without any kind of commitment procedures, McBryde took his uncle to a nursing home and arranged for him to stay there. The uncle objected fiercely, but was old and weak and unable to resist as McBryde took him in. The attendants there told him he could not leave, but after many weeks, he walked out and no one ever tried to stop him. He sued his nephew and the nursing home for false imprisonment. Has he an action?

Cf. Pounders v. Trinity Court Nursing Home, 576 S.W.2d 934, 4 A.L.R.4th 442 (Ark. 1979). In that case the plaintiff went without protest, so there was no claim against the person who took her to the nursing home. "There is no imprisonment when one agrees to surrender her freedom of motions . . . . [N]o force or threats were used, and there was actually consent." As to the claim against the nursing home, she could have left any time except that the nursing home had her shoes and she did not want to leave in bedroom slippers. And an aide told her "they'd get you before you'd get anywhere and they would just bring you back." There was no threat of force and this was no false imprisonment. The decision provoked two dissents, however. The decision is critized in Cathrael Kazin, *"Nowhere to Go and Chose to Stay" Using the Tort of False Imprisonment to Redress Involuntary Confinement of the Elderly in Nursing Homes and Hospitals*, 137 U. PA. L. REV. 903, 904 (1989) for failing to recognize the non-physical ways in which an older person may be imprisoned by a nursing home's aggressive policy.

3. Steven, a six-year-old boy, was throwing eggs at cars passing by his house. One hit Drawback's car. Drawback stopped, got out, ran toward Steven and told him to get in his car, they were going to the police. Steven got in, crying. At the

police station Drawback delivered Steven and reported the incident. The police called Steven's parents who came for him. Suit was then filed in Steven's name.

(a) This is not a false imprisonment since Drawback had no intent to imprison but rather to report the incident to the police.

(b) There is no confinement, since Steven appears to have entered the car without protest; certainly he entered it by his own movements.

(c) This is not a false imprisonment because Steven asked for it by throwing eggs.

(d) This is a false imprisonment, and possibly another tort (assault) as well. [There is no doubt sufficient force implied here to warrant a finding of confinement with a small boy. In *Drabek v. Sabley*, 142 N.W.2d 798, 20 A.L.R.3d 1435 (Wis. 1966) on similar facts a false imprisonment could be found as to a ten year old. At fifteen the force or threat might have to be somewhat stronger. This point will tie in well with the material on intentional infliction of mental distress as to vulnerable persons.

§ 4. TORTS TO PROPERTY

Preliminary Note: This section covers the traditional trespassory torts to property in a textual summary. Nuisance is touched upon in Chapter 23, as is strict liability for abnormally dangerous activities. Injuries to intangible property – economic interests, trademarks and the like – are covered principally in Chapter 33. You can effectively cover the materials in this section with discussion of a few hypotheticals. Comparisons to nuisance, negligence and strict liability are possible but likely to be inefficient because they can be drawn more readily when the materials are reached in the ordinary course of development.

SUMMARY

A. Trespass to Land

1. One who directly enters or causes an entry upon the land of another is liable if the entry is intentional. This includes entries above and below the surface.

2. Intent is required. This may be any of the intents we have already seen, including transferred intent and *Garratt v. Dailey* intent.

3. Damage: at least nominal damages are recoverable even where there is no actual harm. Actual and parasitic damages are also recoverable. As to extended liability, see ¶ 5.

4. Trespass is an interference with possessory interests and possessors may sue as well as fee owners. But non-possessors who merely have a right to use the land, may not sue for trespass.

5. Hypothetical: if entry is substantially certain, the requisite intent is shown.

6. Hypothetical: an accidental entry is not a trespass.

B. Conversion of Chattels — Trover

1. Intent: Intent to exercise dominion is required.

2. Modes of converting an object: anything that shows "dominion," such as taking, using substantially, altering, destroying, selling, or buying will suffice.

3. What may be converted: tangible personal property.

4. Serial conversations: There may be several converters of P's goods, one buying from another. Each is liable.

5. Bona fide purchasers. A bona fide purchaser from a thief does not get good title; he is a converter. However, if A by fraud gets good title from P, A's transfer of the goods to B who is a bona fide purchaser for value will transfer good title to B. B is not a converter, though A is.

6. The UCC: special rules for those who entrust goods to a merchant who deals in such goods. The entruster takes a risk that the merchant will sell the goods as his own. A bona fide purchaser from such a merchant takes good title and is not a converter.

7. Remedies: damages for the value of the goods at the time of conversion is the normal rule, varied somewhat with property having fluctuating value. Replevin or actual recovery of the chattel is often also available.

C. Trespass to chattels

A trespass to chattels may occur when the defendant's conduct falls short of a conversion. However there can be a recovery for this tort only if there is either dispossession or actual damage. Damages recovered are not the value of the chattel, but for the actual damage or dispossession only.

COMMENTS

A. Trespass to land

Trespass terminology: direct and indirect injuries. The term "trespass" is used in at least two distinct senses. In the first, it refers simply to an entry upon land, its airspace, or its subsurface. In this rather loose sense, the term trespass refers to the factual context and you could have a negligent trespass or even a wholly innocent one.

In a second sense, trespass traditionally referred to wrongs that were accomplished by direct application of physical force. In this sense, trespass refers at least in part to the old writ of Trespass. Trespass to land, trespass to chattels, battery, assault, and false imprisonment all used forms of the writ of "trespass" all were trespassory torts. Trespass in this second sense was quite different from nuisance, which could involve indirect injuries without tangible force (polluting smoke and smells for example, often even flooding by water). Nuisance is touched upon in Chapter 23. If you are interested in the nuisance-trespass contrast, see the FYI note below.

Teaching procedure. This is a good section to teach simply and quickly, beginning with the hypothetical cases provided in ¶8 or your own preferred hypotheticals. Discussion of these, with appropriate corrections of student errors and mini-lectures seems to work very well.

¶ **2. Intent**. You can review what we know of intent rules and at the same time be sure that the class understands the object of the intent in trespass cases. The object does not have to be "harm," or even "interference" or even "entry on the land of another." It is enough if the defendant intends to enter where he does enter, and if the place he enters is in fact and in law the land of the plaintiff. Students may tend to generalize the basic rule here by saying "intent is not required." This is incorrect. Intent to *harm* is not required and intent to assume the character of a trespasser is not required. But intent to *enter* land is required. The defendant who is carried on the land while he is drugged is not a trespasser for this purpose, though he may be for purposes of landowners' liability rules. Put differently, the defendant who mistakenly believes he is entering his own land, but does intend to enter the land, is a trespasser if the land lawfully belongs to the plaintiff. He has intent to enter and that is enough. Students do have trouble with this so maybe it bears some emphasis and repetition to work on analytical skills if nothing else.   Accidental entry is not intentional entry. If defendant falls onto the land, or staggers, or negligently drives his car so that it is out of control and it enters the land, he might be negligent and liable for any actual damages. But for mere negligence, he would not be liable for damages unless harm was done. He is not a trespasser in the second and historical sense. In *Amarals* the court seems to embrace a substantial certainty argument. After 1800 stray balls in 5 years, the golf club, even if it did not have a purpose to enter the plaintiff's land, must have been substantially certain of entry. Accordingly, a case of trespass had been stated.

Child trespassers. Can a child be a trespasser? Previously covered materials can be used to answer this question. The student might reason that children can be liable for their torts, as recognized in *Garratt v. Dailey*; and that, except in jurisdictions still following the view that children under seven are incapable of torts, the question becomes whether the child was capable of and did in fact entertain the requisite intent. Since the intent required in trespass actions is quite narrow–to be on the land or in the airspace–even a small child might have this intent. Combining this rule with the extended liability rule, a child could even be liable for substantial unintended harm. See *Brown v. Dellinger*, 355 S.W.2d 742 (Tex. Civ. App. 1962) (7-8 year old boys liable for trespass which unintentionally caused $28,000 in harm to house and contents). The landowner's liability to a child on the land is a different matter, covered in Chapter 12 § 2.

¶ **3. Trespass and nuisance.** Although you need not fully differentiate the two torts, this paragraph gives students a sense of the differences between the two torts.

Nuisance law, like trespass law, protects interests in land. But nuisance protects use and enjoyment, not possessory interests. The approach in nuisance cases is not to assert categorical rights of the landowner against even trivial, but to weigh the landowner's interests and the interests of the putative tortfeasor, and to insist at the very least that the invasion must be substantial. A trivial invasion–cigarette smoke blowing across the plaintiff's lawn, maybe–would not be actionable as a nuisance. (Compare *Leichtman*, § 1 supra.) This approach is vastly different from the categorical approach to trespassory torts. *See* DOBBS ON TORTS § 50 (Regimes of rights vs. regimes of accommodation). "To classify a problem as nuisance rather than trespass is to invoke a regime of reasonable accommodation between conflicting uses and to reject absolute rights associated with trespass." Id., § 462.

A rational means for selecting which regime should govern a particular case (or which set of rules to apply) has perhaps never developed to any serious degree. Traditionally the trespass rules were invoked where (1) injury was direct *and* (2) injury involved visible forces, something big enough to see when it enters the land. The second requirement is thought of as a part of the rule that, after all, trespass was intended to protect *possession*. If the force entering the land were small, like a molecule of gas, it could hardly be said to interfere with possession. If it were smelly or dangerous it could interfere with use and enjoyment–the buzz words for nuisance. Thus the choice of trespass analysis instead of nuisance analysis was made if the injury were direct and involved some forces large enough to permit people to think of "dispossession" rather than "use and enjoyment."

There has been a feeling, largely inarticulate, that the choice between these two kinds of analysis ought to be made on more considered grounds than the directness or indirectness of injury or the size of the invasion force. Accordingly, some courts have disdained any distinction they feel technical or fictional as to directness or the size of the invading force. This permits one to bring a suit for trespass when there has been a pollution of the kind once considered only a nuisance. *See Borland v. Sanders Lead Co.*, 369 So. 2d 523, 2 A.L.R.4th 1042 (Ala. 1979) (discussing some leading decisions). Cf. *Stevenson v. E.I. duPont de Nemours & Co.*, 327 F.3d 400 (5th Cir. 2003) (under Texas law, airborne metallic particles going onto a plaitniff's property constitutes a trespass, discussing requirement that trespass requires a physical entry of some "thing" onto the land).

We have miles to go before we put this issue to sleep. In *Borland,* the court discarded the direct and visible force rule, but retained the rule that trespass occurs only when possession is interfered with. This is the principle upon which the visible force rule was built, since possession is seldom interfered with by smoke, noise, barking dogs and the like. Those are all cases of interference with use and enjoyment. The court in *Borland* thought that if the invasion were trivial enough it would not, after all, be a trespass case. So maybe *Borland* does not really arrive at any basic way of deciding whether to apply categorical rules of trespass or the weighing of interests rules of nuisance.

If you applied privileges flexibly in trespass cases or abolished weighing of interests in nuisance cases, see Bramwell, B. in *Bamford*, Casebook Chapter 23; DOBBS ON TORTS § 465, at 1329 (2000), the two torts would look more alike. As it is, the difference are fascinating and potentially enlightening to students, as is the economic analysis that can accompany nuisance cases. Yet, we think it is too much too soon, so we have not included the nuisance cases for comparison. We think that if you are so minded, you can use a brief lecture to introduce the idea of intangible invasions in nuisance cases and the idea that harm must be substantial in those cases. The contrast with trespass cases will be easy to demonstrate.

¶ **4. Damages without harm**. The damages rules are usually straightforward. Nominal damages are always available, even if no harm is done. Compensatory damages might be based upon cost of repair or diminished value of the land, or on some more complicated measure if the defendant has severed timber or minerals and taken them. In *Robert v. Scarlata* the diminished value from use of the plaintiff's land for many years was quite low.

¶ **5. Punitive damages without harm.** Not every trespass warrants an award of punitive damages, but a malicious, oppressive trespass, or repeated trespasses might. The trouble is that a traditional rule bars recovery of punitive damages when no compensatory damages are awarded or actual harm done. See, criticizing this rule as a misstatement, 1 DAN B. DOBBS, THE LAW OF REMEDIES § 3.11 (10) (2d ed. 1993). In *Jacque v. Steenberg Homes, Inc.*, 563 N.W.2d 154 (Wis. 1997) the court said that in trespass cases, even nominal damage could support a punitive award that was otherwise justified, since in trespass cases nominal damages reflect a recognition that invasion of the plaintiff's rights was in itself an actual harm.

¶ **6. Extended liability.** Since trespassers are often relatively innocent – sometimes entirely innocent – should the extended liability rule apply to hold them liable for all harms done? In line with the fault principle, should we redefine trespass to require something more than an intent to enter?

¶ **7. Limiting extended liability. (Covert investigations.)** This note suggests that extended liability should apply only to harms of the same general type the tort rules were attempting to redress in the first place. (Experienced teachers will recognize this as a forecast of similar ideas about proximate cause to be encountered in Chapter 8.) In trespass to land cases, that would be harms related to security of possession, integrity of the land itself, and possibly its use and enjoyment. So for damages resulting from publications, you might want to say that the plaintiff must establish a claim under the rules for defamation or privacy invasion.

Food Lion, Inc., v. Capital Cities/ABC, Inc., cited here, actually turned on First Amendment protections for publication, although the court recognized a technical trespass and upheld a $1 award against each trespassing journalist. The murder hypothetical here and its no-liability answer could be explained on similar grounds – a privilege to report crimes. Exclusive possession of land serves to protect privacy interests, so damages from the trespasser's publication of private matters he discovers while trespassing might well be awarded, either directly on a trespass theory or as an invasion of privacy. Even so, in the absence of privilege or constitutional free speech right, you can strongly suspect that damages will not be awarded unless they in some measure relate to the landowner's right of exclusive possession.

In *Desnick v. American Broadcasting Companies, Inc.*, 44 F.3d 1345 (7th Cir. 1994), like *Food Lion*, an investigative reporter case that turned in part on the fraudulently secured consent of the landowner, the claim was trespass but the damages sought were those resulting from publication of information gained. Judge Posner rejected liability, saying "There was no invasion . . . of any of the specific interests that the tort of trespass seeks to protect." *American Transmission, Inc. v. Channel 7 of Detroit, Inc.*, 609 N.W.2d 607 (Mich. Ct. App. 2000), made the same analysis. Both *Desnick* and *American Transmissions* emphasized that the trespass occurred in space open to the public and involved no disruption of activities.

¶¶ **8 & 9. Hypotheticals.** It is easy to use these instead of lecture and to add variations and lecture as discussion develops. *The cat*: Durfee might be privileged to defend his sleep from the cat, under the rules that sometimes permit self-help in nuisance cases, but if so, that is nothing the class knows. If there is no privilege, Durfee is liable. His purpose is cat-damage, but it is substantially certain that there will be an entry on the plaintiff's land next door. The rule stated in paragraph 1 says that entry above ground is sufficient and another rule in the same paragraph says that causing an object to enter is sufficient. The rule of nominal damages allows at least a minimal $1 recovery. If the class thinks this is silly, it is a good sign. Many students will be so buried in these technical rules they may forget that there is a real world. Why would Plunkett sue? Harassment?

The hang-glider: This is really quite similar to the cat problem in the rules it invokes. It does permit introduction of some additional rules if you wish. Navigable airspace is protected for navigation by federal law. Even low levels of airspace are protected for takeoff and landing. (14 C.F.R. § 1.1 defines navigable airspace to mean "airspace at and above the minimum flight altitudes prescribed by or under this chapter, including airspace needed for safe takeoff and landing." 14 C.F.R. § 77.23 sets standards for obstructions in airspace, including "mobile obstructions.") In the actual landing area of an airport, any thing above the surface is an obstruction. What if a commercial airliner flies above plaintiff's land, but in the "navigable airspace?" It appears to be protected. If, on the other hand, the plane flies at an altitude under the navigable airspace, it might be a trespass, and federal law would have no objection to so holding. Yet if the flight is above the level of interference with any actual or immediately potential land uses, might we expect the courts to qualify the common law rule by saying that an invasion of airspace is actionable only when it reaches very low levels or levels of actual use?

RESTATEMENT SECOND OF TORTS § 159 (1965) provides in subparagraph (2) that aircraft entries above the land constitute a trespass only if the entries are "into the immediate reaches of the airspace" and this interferes substantially with the possessor's use and enjoyment. This moves the law of trespass very close to the ideas of nuisance law when it comes to aircraft in airspace. Why not leave it to nuisance law, with its usual balancing, then? *See* DOBBS ON TORTS § 54 (2000).

The hang-glider, however, is probably not a licensed aircraft. In any event it is probably below the navigable airspace as defined in the CFR. The class can discuss whether this is, or should be, a trespass while it is in the air.

The landing of the hang-glider. This may be intentional in a statistical sense–that is, Dangle must land somewhere and there is a high chance at least in some localities that he will land on private property, though he may not intend the property of any specific person. If this is the case, transferred intent doctrines might allow Burger to recover. However, some student should respond by saying that he did not intend to land when he did, and that his entry was purely the result of accident (as far, at least, as he was concerned.) (Another possibility, to be investigated with the *Ploof* case, Chapter 4, is the privilege of necessity. But if Dangle knows to a certainty that, having taken off from the mountain, he will almost inevitably land somewhere on private property, should we recognize any privilege defense? You can usually avoid getting into any discussion of privilege here, but it is good to come back to when you get to *Ploof*. The statistical nature of the supposed "certainty" of landing on someone's land is very similar also to the issue raised in the *Brown v. Stiel* Problem, Chapter 6. ■

Related material: privilege. Some questions that can come up in class turn on privilege, not on the elements of trespass. The landowner may have a privilege to eject a trespasser, or to remove a trespassing object, for instance. A counter privilege may allow one to enter another's land under some circumstances, chiefly out of dire necessity. Consent, implied or express, may operate to permit an entry until the consent is revoked. Privileges come in Chapter 4. You need not go into these. If you get some questions, the best answer may be "there may be a privilege as to that, but in the absence of a privilege, this is a trespass."

B. Conversion of Chattels

The hypothetical case introduces the tort of conversion of chattels. Notes lay out the basic law and provide hypotheticals for class use. Students seem to like playing with this little segment of materials. Illustrations are easy and most of them fun.

Note 1. Intent. The court in *LaForce* says that even if the defendants thought they were returning the pub and its contents to its rightful owner, this is no defense because they intentionally exercised dominion over the plaintiff's property (as it turns out), thus intentionally depriving him of it. The point is that the intent for conversion need not be evil: the actor who decides to burn his torts casebook, but who burns the plaintiff's by mistake, is liable for conversion: he has had his fun and now he must pay for it. In this kind of case we might observe that the actor is frequently no worse off for the liability. He simply sells his own book (the one he intended to burn) and the proceeds will pay the damages if the two books are worth about the same. However, it may be that the two books were worth different amounts, plaintiff's being worth more for its better condition, or because Page Keeton had written a letter to John Wade on the flyleaf. In this case, defendant's mistake is costly to him: he intended to burn his own relatively worthless copy of the casebook, but he must pay for the plaintiff's relatively valuable copy. Mistake is no defense.

In *Wiseman v. Schaffer,* 768 P.2d 800 (Idaho 1989), "an imposter, identifying himself as Larry Wiseman, telephoned Schaffer and asked him to tow the Ford pickup at the Husky Truck Stop to the yard of a local welding shop. The imposter told Schaffer that $30 for the towing charge had been left on top of the sunvisor in the pickup. Schaffer located the pickup and the cash. He then towed the pickup to the welding shop as directed. Sometime later, the pickup was stolen." The court held that a jury's finding of no conversion was inconsistent with the law.

What is a case of non-intent? This question is necessary lest the student generalize this tort as one in which intent is not required. Suppose the actor, without intent to touch the book that is lying on a table near the fireplace, backs into the table while talking, knocking it over and knocking the book into the fire. This may be negligence and if so, there is liability for negligence, not conversion. But it may not be negligence at all: the actor may be retreating in an emergency from the vicious attack of the plaintiff's house cat. If there is no negligence, there is no liability on these facts, since there is clearly no intent to affect the book.

Dominion. It is likewise possible to affect the chattel intentionally but to lack an intent to affect it in any substantial way. The actor picks up the plaintiff's casebook, thumbs through it, and puts it down. This is not a conversion. Since there is neither dispossession nor damage, it is not a trespass to chattels either. Dominion must be some act that tends to show the defendant is treating the chattel as his own, as by selling it or buying it. (Students should not understand this as a requirement to deprive another of his interest in the chattel; one might treat a book as his own because he reasonably and honestly believes it is. The point is that the conduct must be such that an observer might well think, "Oh, there is the owner of the book."

Dominion by controlling access. Dominion when the defendant controls the means of access to the chattel would include: (a) Defendant locks the plaintiff's valuable painting in a garage so the plaintiff cannot get it. (b) Defendant takes the certificate without which the plaintiff cannot claim his shares of stock in the X Corporation. (c) Defendant takes the keys to the plaintiff's car. (d) Defendant takes the keys to the plaintiff's bank deposit box, which contains his stamp collection. The defendant has converted the painting, the share of stock, the car and the stamp collection.

Note 3. New forms of property. What types of property may be converted. The *Kremen* case is quite fascinating. The court proceeds through an analysis of why the plaintiff did not only have an economic interest in the domain name but a property interest as well. The domain name that is wrongfully disposed of by the defendant was held to constitute a conversion in *Kremen v. Cohen*, 325 F.3d 1035 (9th Cir. 2003). The court decided that intangible property can be converted under California law even if not "merged into a document," as some prior law indicated. The court cited with approval an 1880 case that held that shares in a corporation, as opposed to the share certificates themselves, could be converted.

In *Unruh* the court recognized a property interest in a woman's egg. Is this because an egg is different from blood to the extent that one person's possession of it deprives the other of its use? It is difficult to know whether the court thought the situation different from *Moore v. Regents of the University of California*, 793 P.2d 479 (Cal. 1990). Although *Unruh* was an appellate court decision, it did not mention the state Supreme Court opinion in *Moore*.

In *Moore* it is important to recognize that the court does recognize potential liability based on the doctors' duty to inform his patient. (The casebook considers informed consent primarily in Chapter 13, § 3). The court's rejection of the conversion theory is almost certainly based upon a desire to limit the plaintiff's damages so that he does not participate by way of royalty or otherwise in the profits earned by the cells taken from his body. The case is complicated. Only brief comments on it seem advisable in spite of the case's intrinsic interest.

The plaintiff's cells overproduced some useful material, but the material they produced was material present in all persons and in no way unique to the plaintiff. What was unique or special was that his cells were especially good producers and that the useful materials, hard to locate in many cells, were relatively easy to find and use in his. His cells were thus like machines that produced useful items when they were installed in a factory and properly operated and managed. The plaintiff's machines were unusually efficient and therefore more valuable than some others.

One of the court's reasons for refusing to find a conversion was that the goods manufactured by the plaintiff's "machine"–his cells and their progeny–were not themselves part of the plaintiff's body and never had been, so the plaintiff could not claim to own the manufactured goods and thus could not claim damages that might approximate their net commercial value.

This analysis might miss something important. Suppose the defendants HAD taken the plaintiff's factory machinery (and not just his cells). Suppose they used the machinery to produce goods that could not be so efficiently produced otherwise. They would not be converters of the goods produced, as the court seems to say. Yet they would surely be converters of the *machines*. As converters of the machines they would be liable for their market value. The market value of the machines would be quite high because of their unusual and more or less unique capacity. So the court's focus on "ownership" of the *product* seems misleading.

Another argument advanced by the court was that liability would inhibit good research and development because the conversion theory would "impose a tort duty on scientists to investigate the consensual pedigree of each human cell sample used in research." That might indeed be a concern; the liability of bona fide purchasers is indeed a bad rule for many situations. But the court could have limited the conversion liability to those who intentionally and secretively take the plaintiff's body parts for commercial purposes; instead it presented a concern about *some* defendants as a ground to immunizing *all* defendants.

Notes 5 & 6. Serial conversions and bona fide purchasers. These notes are meant to be straightforward. If you want to read more, *see* DOBBS ON TORTS §§ 65-66.

Hypotheticals:

1. Dameron takes the keys to Pelton's car. Pelton has no other keys. Dameron does not move the car, but does throw the keys into the Charles River. Conversion? What if there were another set of keys easily accessible to Pelton? What if Dameron took the keys to a lock box in which Pelton kept a coin collection worth $100,000?

2. Damon Deptford stole a watch belonging to his twin brother, Robertson. The watch was engraved "Deptford." Damon sold the watch to Tribble. Damon then fled the jurisdiction. Is Tribble a converter? Suppose: (a) she thought Damon was Robertson and the watch was Robertson's; (b) she thought Damon was Damon and that the watch was his.

C. Trespass to Chattels

The computer age has breathed some new life into the trespass to chattels claim, as the cases in the first and the last paragraphs in this subsection indicate. Courts continue to sort out how this ancient tort applies in the modern age. The New York court in *School of Visual Arts* took a broad view but the California Supreme Court in *Hamidi* read things quite narrowly in holding that no trespass to chattels action could lie unless the "computer system itself" was damaged by the spam emails; evidence in the case showed many lost man-hours of labor in dealing with the massive influx of spam.

Examples. *Petting the dog*: unless there is some extended personality possible, this is not a tort, since there is neither dispossession nor harm. *Leaning on the car*: the same rule. *Joyriding*: this may be a dispossession, especially if it had previously been forbidden. Since there is a dispossession of the car and perhaps the dog, there is a trespass to chattels. Damages would presumably be the rental value for the time, plus any special damages (such as lost wages because the plaintiff cannot get to work without the car), plus any parasitic damages. In the absence of proven damages, nominal damages would be proper. *Pushing the car over the cliff*: This is a conversion of the car, and the kick to the dog presumably causes "harm," so that there is a trespass to chattels claim as to that. If vicious enough, it may be an intentional infliction of mental anguish to the dog's owner.

Poff v. Hayes, 763 So.2d 234 (Ala. 2000), is an interesting case. The law clerk "dispossessed" Hayes of some documents (although he returned them after making copies). For this reason, in the absence of some other factor, he would be liable for nominal damages for trespass to chattels. On the other hand, this did not interfere with the plaintiff's possessory rights in any substantial degree, so he's not liable for conversion. The court went on to hold that as to some of the copied documents, the firm was the owner, so that Hayes did not have exclusive right of possession; as to these, the plaintiff could not maintain the trespass to chattels action.

REFERENCES:

> DOBBS ON TORTS §§ 50-58 (trespass to land); § 463 (nuisance vs. trespass); §§ 59-67 (interference with chattels); HARPER, JAMES & GRAY §§ 1.1–1.8 (trespass to land); §§2.1–2.38 (interference with chattels).

§ 5. FORCIBLE HARMS AS CIVIL RIGHTS VIOLATIONS

Preliminary Note: Civil rights torts *are* torts. Those introduced in this section are always batteries, assaults, false imprisonment, or property torts. What the civil rights claim adds is a new theory of relief based on federal law. The new theory brings in its train some new jurisdictional and procedural rules, and a different set of rules about defenses and immunities that concern us only in a limited fashion. The physical injury civil rights torts analogous to the common law trespassory torts usually arise from the Fourth Amendment's prohibition against unreasonable searches and seizures, the Eighth's Amendment's prohibition of cruel and unusual punishment, or the Fourteenth Amendment's requirement of (substantive) due process. The cases in this section illustrate each of those claims. Other kinds of governmental attacks on constitutional rights, such as the sustained attack on free speech rights seen in *White v. Lee,* 227 F.3d 1214 (9th Cir. 2000), are non-physical and not covered here, although some are covered in Chapter 32.

SUMMARY

A. The § 1983 Claim

42 U.S.C.A. § 1983. This is the "basic" civil rights statute and the one most directly concerned with conduct that might also count as a traditional trespassory tort. It provides that those who deprive the plaintiff of federal rights by acting in some manner "under color of state law," may be held liable under the statute. The statute does not list the federal rights, which are found primarily in the constitution. Instead it creates a federal cause of action for their violation. The first two cases here illustrate the basic workings of the statute.

YANG V. HARDIN. One police officer steals the plaintiff's goods in the course of investigating a break-in; he attempts to drive away with the plaintiff gamely hanging on the car; another points a pistol at the plaintiff to drive him away. The other officer neither says nor does anything to stop the first officer's shameful behavior. *Held*, the affirmative acts are violations of the Fourteenth Amendment, depriving Yang of his "liberty"; and the silent officer's failure to stop these violations is also a violation.

B. Exemplars of Constitutional Violations

The case abstracts illustrate the three most commonly-invoked constitutional provisions in §1983 cases: (1) Fourteenth Amendment due process clause; (2) Fourth Amendment search and seizure; and (3) Eighth Amendment cruel and unusual punishment. The main point of these materials is to get students to understand that the Constitution itself forms the basis of a § 1983 claim, and that each particular constitutional provision has its own key provisions, taken either literally from the words of the Constitution or as interpreted by the Supreme Court, or both.

MEALS V. CITY OF MEMPHIS and ALEXANDER V. DEANGELO – Fourteenth Amendment due process clause.

BROWN V. MUHELENBERG and GRAHAM V. CONNOR – Fourth Amendment.

HUDSON V. MCMILLAN – Eighth Amendment.

COMMENTS

A. The § 1983 Claim

42 U.S.C.A. § 1983

If you agree that it is none too soon to ask students to begin the tough job of reading statutes, you can parse this one with the class. It sounds silly, but you may need to be sure first that everyone understands the difference between the state and federal levels of government and the difference between common law torts, created by state judges, and federal statutory torts, created by the Constitution directly or by federal statutes.

The elements of the claim. The syntax of § 1983 is not contemporary but once the reader goes through it and gets the basic structure, it is easy to "reform" the statute to a different structure:

Every person . . . shall be liable to the party injured under the following circumstances: (1) when that person deprives the party of any rights, privileges, or immunities secured by the Constitution and (federal) laws, and (2) does so under color of state or other local law.

This is a paraphrase and as such omits details and problems. But a first approximation to help the reader get to the essence is helpful.

Once the student has perceived the elements –deprivation of federal rights under "color of" state law, you may want to spend a minute clearing up that "color of" phrase. The idea is that the defendant is using state authority or the appearance of such authority, even if he uses it wrongly and in violation of the written words of state law. A uniformed officer who stops a citizen on the street is acting under color of law. Private persons who use or join with public officials are also acting under color of law, but there is no particular point in developing this unless the class raises the question. More of this appears in **Note 2** after *Brown*, and you can jump to that Note during an introduction if you find it helpful.

Note that the conduct that amounts to a constitutional tort based on the Fourth and Eighth Amendment (as incorporated in and applied to the states by the Fourteenth Amendment) is often the same conduct that counts as a prima facie battery, a false imprisonment, an assault, or possibly a conversion, although the elements of the torts are stated differently according to whether the claim is under the common law or under the constitution. Examples that parallel common law torts are cited in DOBBS ON TORTS § 44 (2000).

The civil rights torts here are federal statutory torts, the term statutory of course including constitutional. So although conduct may be conduct that counts as a common law tort, the source of law, the system of legal rules, and the court systems may all be different according to whether you sue under a common law or under a § 1983 theory. However, federal civil rights claims are among those that can be brought in *either* state *or* federal courts. Wherever they are brought, federal *law* governs them. It also happens that in many instances, the state common law claims like the assault claim in *Yang* can be brought in the federal court as a kind of tag-along with the federal civil rights claim, provided it arises from the same set of facts. In such a case, the state-law tort claims are governed by state legal rules, even though they are tried in the federal court.

Note on damages: The history that shaped common law damages rules does not apply to civil rights claims under the constitution, so the "presumed damages" rule for, say, a common law battery, does not apply. *See Carey v. Piphus*, 435 U.S. 247(1978).

Selective incorporation. This is a topic you can probably avoid dealing with, but if some students recognize that the first en amendments or the Bill of Rights apply only to the federal government, you may need to explain that the Fourteenth Amendment, which applies to the states, has been understood as selectively incorporating some of the specific rules from the Bill of Rights, including the Fourth Amendment and the Eighth Amendment. Some of the thinking on that topic is summarized in *Duncan v. Louisiana,* 391 U.S. 145 (1968). Thus the claim that a state agent was guilty of unreasonable search and seizure is technically a claim that he violated the Fourteenth Amendment. But the specific rule applicable in determining whether due process was violated is nonetheless derived from the Fourth Amendment and its terms control, as we will see.

YANG V. HARDIN, 37 F.3d 282 (7th Cir. 1994)

Investigating a break-in of the plaintiff's shoe store, one officer, Brown, attempted to steal a pair of shorts. Confronted by the plaintiff-owner, he first denied the attempted theft, then threw the shorts at the plaintiff and got in the police car. The plaintiff held the door open to prevent his leaving, but he drove off anyway, in a zig-zag pattern seemingly intended to throw the plaintiff off the car. Brown's officer-partner, Hardin, did nothing. When bystanders stopped the zig-zagging police car, Brown got out and knocked the plaintiff to the ground. Hardin finally acted: he pulled a gun. The plaintiff froze and the police officers drove off. The plaintiff sued under § 1983 and also for state common law false imprisonment and assault. The trial judge found for the plaintiff against Brown, the violent thief, but found in favor of Hardin, who seems to have been the strong silent type. Since Yang is appealing here (not Brown), students should be able to see that only Hardin's liability is in issue on appeal, where the court holds that Hardin, too, is subject to liability under § 1983 and also for common law torts.

The most central thing in introducing § 1983 and civil rights torts is to get students to recognize the bases of liability–action under color of law and violation of a federal, usually a constitutional right. The court's focus on Hardin's liability is his responsibility for failing to intervene in the violation of the plaintiff's rights by Brown, but Hardin would also be violating the plaintiff's rights by an unreasonable search or seizure and "seizure" occurs when an officer subjects the plaintiff to a restraint by either physical force (the gun) or show of authority.

Other courts support liability for failure to intervene. *E.g., Priester v. City of Riviera Beach, Florida,* 208 F.3d 919 (11th Cir. 2000) (citing other cases). You can reconsider this when you discuss nonfeasance, especially nonfeasance of officials in connection with *DeShaney*, Chapter 16.

Harris v. Roderick, 126 F.3d 1189 (9th Cir. 1997), involved the shootout at Ruby Ridge. With complications not useful to recount here, the court held that the FBI's rules of engagement authorizing killing a person who was no threat, were unconstitutional as a violation of the Fourth Amendment. As shown in *Graham* (below) and notes following, excessive force, including killing, violates the Fourth Amendment's prohibitions.

Note 2. Color of state law. We don't develop this statutory requirement in any detail, either in cases or notes, so you probably won't be required to make much of an issue about it in class. (See our comment on this, just above.) The point is that a private citizen with an insufficient nexus to the state simply won't be liable under § 1983 because a required element of liability is missing. But you might need to emphasize that color of law does not require actions of an officer in uniform. Not surprisingly, cases sometimes turn on this issue. *See, e.g., Rayburn v. Hogue,* 241 F.3d 1341 (11th Cir. 2001) (foster parents who care for children on behalf of the state are not acting under color of state law); *Chapman v. Higbee Co.,* 319 F.3d 825 (6th Cir. 2003)(en banc) (off-duty sheriff, in uniform and wearing his badge and sidearm but working as a private security guard held be to acting under color of state law).

Note 3. Liability of public entities. This note provides some key information about who can be sued. Liability of governmental entities (and some more on officers as well) is covered in detail in Chapter 15. If you are asked questions about this note, you should know that (1) Public entities might be liable under individual *state* constitutional provisions. *See Katzberg v. Regents of University of California,* 29 Cal.4th 300 (2002); *DeGrassi v. Cook,* 29 Cal.4th 333 (2002); *Dorwart v. Caraway,* 58 P.3d 128 (Mont. 2002); *Brown v. State,* 674 N.E.2d 1129 (N.Y. 1996); *cf. Binette v. Sabo,* 710 A.2d 688 (Conn. 1998) (on analogy to *Bivens,* officers' are liable where state legislation neither forbids a remedy nor provides a meaningful statutory alternative remedy for constitutional violations but not all constitutional violations will be actionable). (2) Section 1983 does *not* cover federal officers acting under color of *federal* law. However, a plaintiff can sue federal officers directly for violating the constitution under the Supreme Court's decision in *Bivens v. Six Unknown Named Agents of the Federal Bureau of Narcotics,* 403 U.S. 388 (1971). As to liability of public entities and the privileges of officers, *see* DOBBS ON TORTS § 277 (2000).

NOTE: INTERNATIONAL CIVIL RIGHTS

While we don't feel that we have the room to develop international materials fully, in the area of civil rights violations involving forcible harms we do see some similar problems arising under international law. For example, Radovan Karadzic, the Bosnian Serb "President," has been sued in tort in the United States. In *Kadic v. Radovan Karadzic,* 70 F.3d 232 (2nd Cir. 1995), the plaintiffs were Croats and Muslims claiming that Karadzic was liable under international law for some of the genocide, rape, and other tortures inflicted by the Serbs in Bosnia. They claim that he acted (a) as a state actor–more or less under color of "law"– or (b) as a private person, and/or (c) in concert with the rump state of Yugoslavia-Serbia. Under various international rules, torture unconnected with genocide or war crimes was actionable only against state actors. The plaintiffs' "allegations entitle them to prove that Karadzic's regime satisfies the criteria for a state. . . .[I]t is likely that the state action concept, where applicable for some violations like 'official' torture, requires merely the semblance of official authority." In 2000, at least two verdicts against Karadzic (a convicted war criminal) were reported in the press, one in August for $745 million on behalf of a small group Muslim women who survived his regime of rapes, tortures, and killings, and another, in September, for a total of $4.5 million on behalf of another group of plaintiffs.

The first case cited in this Note, *Mehinovic,* was brought by Bosnian Muslim victims of torture and other human rights violations against a Serbian who now lives in Georgia. The court awarded compensatory and punitive damages totaling $140 million to the four plaintiffs.

We also mention here the Alien Tort Statute, which gives United States courts jurisdiction over cases where an alien (non-U.S. citizen) sues for a tort in violation of "the law of nations or a treaty of the United States." The statute, largely dormant for a very long time, was given a narrow construction by the Supreme Court in the *Sosa* case cited here. Time will tell whether the Court's construction will essentially re-establish the statute's dormancy. For deeper coverage of the Alien Tort Statute, *see* JULIE A. DAVIES & PAUL T. HAYDEN, GLOBAL ISSUES IN TORT LAW, Chapter 3 (2008).

B. Exemplars of Constitutional Violations

The three main theories of § 1983 liability are listed here, and the cases that follow give examples. The point is that to succeed on a § 1983 claim has nothing to do with the ability to prove a common law intentional tort. Rather, the plaintiff must show that a federal right (usually a constitutional right) was violated by a defendant acting under color of state law. The Fourteenth Amendment rights are very general and in a sense incorporate some more specific ones; thus we see in *Alexander* the court relying not so much on particular language in the text of the Amendment but rather interpreting what the Amendment's guarantees mean. The other two Amendments provide very specific rights with specific constitutional language – "unreasonable" search and seizure in the Fourth Amendment, and "cruel and unusual" punishment in the Eighth.

[1. Fourteenth Amendment Due Process Clause]

MEALS V. CITY OF MEMPHIS, 493 F. 3d 720 (6th Cir. 2007). In this case involving a high-speed police chase the court makes clear that only conduct which "shocks the conscience" is actionable under the 14th amendment. Reckless conduct is not enough.

ALEXANDER V. DEANGELO, 329 F.3d 912 (7th Cir. 2003). Police coerce a woman into posing as a prostitute and providing oral sex to a sting target. They tell her that if she does not cooperate that they will arrest her and she will serve 40 years in prison, even though they are fully aware that she would not possibly be sentenced to such a long term. She goes along with the scheme until the sting target's trial, at which point she refuses to testify and sues under § 1983. Judge Posner concludes that she was basically raped by the police, and that rape is a "serious battery" that constitutes a deprivation of due process under the Fourteenth Amendment. Notice that a "normal battery" would explicitly NOT be such a deprivation, according to the court.

Note 1. Common law torts and § 1983. This note explains the basics and probably needs little explanation from the teacher.

Note 2. Practical value of § 1983. Connections to the world to litigation are not easy for most students; this is a useful paragraph to help get them started connecting rules to strategic or tactical results.

Note 3. Qualified immunity. Although defenses to intentional torts don't come up centrally until the next chapter, you have probably already assigned part of that chapter and may well have raised the possibility of particular defenses to common-law intentional torts already. A key defense in a § 1983 case is that the state actor is immune from suit because his conduct did not violate "clearly established statutory or constitutional rights of which a reasonable person would have been aware." *See generally* DOBBS ON TORTS § 276 (2000).

Note 4. Corporal punishment as a civil right violation. In the Kirkland case cited here, the court said these facts do state a claim under § 1983, finding the corporal punishment shocking to the conscience. For an excellent summary of corporal punishment and the constitutional issues it raises, *see* Deana A. Pollard, *Banning Corporal Punishment: A Constitutional Analysis*, 52 Am. U. L. Rev. 447 (2002) (arguing for abolition of child corporal punishment).

[2. Fourth Amendment – unreasonable search and seizure]

BROWN V. MUHLENBERG TOWNSHIP, 269 F.3d 205 (3d Cir. 2001). A policeman shoots the plaintiffs' pet Rottweiler without provocation, and without being threatened by the dog. The court holds that this act (clearly under color of state law) may constitute a violation of the plaintiffs' right to be free of an unreasonable seizure of their property under the Fourth Amendment. Thus this does state a good § 1983 claim. While a state actor can perhaps destroy a pet in the owner's presence where "there is reason to believe the pet poses an imminent danger" without violating the Fourth Amendment, those facts were not present here. So a summary judgment for the defendant was reversed. Again, students should recognize that the issue is NOT whether the officer committed a common law tort; the issue is whether his action violated a constitutional right of the plaintiff, in this case the right to be free from "unreasonable" seizures of property.

GRAHAM V. CONNOR, 490 U.S. 386 (1989). Here you get a glimpse of the Court focusing on the specific language of the Fourth Amendment – reasonableness – and rejecting tests that have no textual basis in the Constitution. The officer's good faith is no part of the issue because the constitutional language is reasonableness, not good faith.

Excessive force and the 4th Amendment. The Fourth Amendment prohibits not only an unwarranted arrest but excessive force in making an appropriate arrest. In *Gardner v. Buerger,* 82 F.3d 248 (8th Cir. 1996), the plaintiff claimed that a police officer had shot her husband in the back of his head, and that the husband died as a result. Judge Richard Arnold summarized some of the leading ideas about the scope of Fourth Amendment protection this way [most citations omitted]:

The Fourth Amendment forbids "unreasonable searches and seizures" by police officers. This prohibition protects not only our privacy and property;

the Fourth Amendment is also a "primary source of constitutional protection against physically abusive government conduct." For Fourth Amendment purposes, a police officer "seizes" a person when he, by physical force or show of authority, limits that person's liberty. Terms like "seizure" and "intrusive governmental conduct," cannot capture the facts of this case; it is an unavoidable understatement to observe that the shooting was a seizure. Tennessee v. Garner, 471 U.S. 1 (1985) ("The intrusiveness of a seizure by means of deadly force is unmatched."). But even if the translation is imperfect, we use the Fourth Amendment's objective-reasonableness standard to analyze excessive-force claims.

Curley v. Klem, discussed briefly in the Note after *Graham*, is an excessive force case. That the officer *subjectively* believed he was shooting at a dangerous suspect was irrelevant unless his belief was reasonable. The court was able to find on the facts that the officer's seizure of the person (by shooting him) was unreasonable because the shooting victim was wearing a standard police uniform and not behaving in any way like a criminal suspect. But whether the defendant's subjective belief was reasonable was a contested issue of fact that went to the existence of a qualified privilege – that is, to whether it would have been clear to a reasonable officer that his actions were unlawful in the situation he confronted.

Another example of an excessive force claim is *Priester v. City of Riviera Beach, Florida*, 208 F.3d 919 (11th Cir. 2000) (allegations that police officers loosed dog on a suspect who was not resisting; proof of such allegation would prove excessive force and no immunity attached).

[3. Eighth Amendment – cruel and unusual punishment]

HUDSON V. McMILLIAN, 503 U.S. 1 (1992). The Court again focuses on the text of the Constitution, this time the Eighth Amendment. Here the court rejects the minor injury test because, again, the Constitution uses entirely different language. Furthermore, under the Eighth Amendment, the reasonableness test we just saw under the Fourth Amendment is definitely not the test for the same reason. The constitutional language is cruel and unusual and the Court insists on that.

Failure to attend health needs of a prisoner may be a violation of the Eighth Amendment if it results from deliberate indifference to his medical condition. On this basis the court in *Herron v. Campbell*, 198 F.3d 245 (6th Cir. 1999) (unpublished) held that a prisoner had stated a claim when he alleged that with knowledge of his serious condition, officials subjected him repeatedly to second hand smoke. And in *Olson v. Bloomberg*, 339 F.3d 730 (8th Cir. 2003), the court held that a prison guard who saw an inmate threaten suicide and tie a rope around his neck could be liable under § 1983 if he was "deliberately indifferent" to the threat. The man hanged himself just 30 minutes after the guard left him.

If you cover civil rights in one day, some students may have difficulty absorbing it all. If you think that's the case, you might summarize the three Constitutional claims we've looked at in columns on the board, perhaps asking students to help you fill in the blanks as you go. A simple example:

Constitution	Case	Test of violation
4th Amendment	Brown v. Muhlenberg Graham v. Connor	"unreasonable," "search," "seizure"
14th Amendment	Meals v. City of Memphis Alexander v. DeAngelo	shocks the conscience (in custody, deliberate indifference may suffice)
8th Amendment	Hudson v. McMillian	"cruel," " unusual" and "punishment"

Mini-Problem
DOUGHERTY V. HART

Cindy Dougherty and Fairchild Ferraro were two young women in Hart's public high school history class. They began a shouting match during class. Hart asked them to sit down and be quiet, but they approached each other yelling obscenities and offering threats of bodily harm. Hart stepped between them but still had difficulties separating them. He took Cindy's wrist and began to lead her out of the classroom. At the door she stomped out, slamming the door. Cindy's parents brought suit on her behalf against Hart and the school district. Consider whether Hart or the district would be liable for (a) any common law tort and/or (b) a constitutional violation.

This mini-problem asks the student to fit the claim to the terms of the different amendments. The Fourth is the best bet for a formal fit, but on similar facts *Wallace v. Batavia School District 101*, 68 F.3d 1010 (1995), held the seizure not uneasonable. A brief discussion should do the job with this little problem and make students feel more at home trying to construct a constitutional argument.
The most likely common law claim would be battery (possibly false imprisonment as well). What would common law judges say? They would NOT say "no battery because the wrist seizure was reasonable." Battery law does not judge reasonableness on the prima facie case. But it does judge reasonableness when a privilege is invoked. So the common law process would probably come out the same way, but by a different route. Prima facie, Cindy established a battery. But Hart can show the discipline privilege if he was, guess what, "reasonable."

CHAPTER 4

DEFENSES TO INTENTIONAL TORTS — PRIVILEGES

►**Changes in the Sixth Edition:** In § 1 we have added *Peters v. Menard, Inc.* and deleted (reduced to a Note) *Great Atlantic and Pacific Tea Co. v. Paul.* We have also shortened the *Brown v. Martinez* abstract. In § 2 we added *Robins v. Harris* on the issue of consent, deleted *Reavis v. Slominski,* and reorganized some of the Notes. In §3 we shortened *Wagner* substantially and added a Note on Coase.

►The **Concise Edition** omits some materials on Self-Defense; virtually all of the materials on Defense of Third Persons; the *Peters v. Menard* case; the section on Discipline; and the *Payton v. Donner* Problem.■

Preliminary Note:

This chapter surveys the traditional privileges to intentional trespassory torts. It does not include the "immunities" covered in Chapters 14 and 15.

Our short treatment of most privileges is justified first because many of them can appropriately be considered in the criminal law course and because it is important to get students to the negligence materials as soon as possible. More extensive development is justified or required where the privilege seemed to throw added light on the prima facie case. False imprisonment is better understood when one understands the Restatement's privilege to detain for investigation. And a case like *Brown v. Martinez* adds depths to our understanding of "transferred intent."

We begin this chapter with cases in which the burden of proof is indisputably upon the defendant. This is the point that distinguishes the "defense" from the prima facie case. In contrast, in the case of battery, manifested consent operates to negate the existence of tortious intent. In such cases it is not an affirmative defense at all. Consent cases, then, are postponed. On the other hand, to end with consent cases has the effect of segregating the necessity privilege from the next chapter, which begins negligence. Given that necessity ought to end the chapter and that "true affirmative defenses" ought to begin it, consent must fall in the middle, and that is where it is here.

§ 1. PROTECTING AGAINST THE APPARENT MISCONDUCT OF THE PLAINTIFF

SUMMARY

A. Self-Defense

One may use force, threat of force, or imprisonment in self-defense. This is true only if there is a reasonably apparent need for self-defense and the force, threat, or imprisonment used is reasonable in degree and responsive to the apparent threat.

B. Defense of third persons

One may also defend third persons from attack in the same way one may defend one's self. There is some division in the cases whether this privilege turns on a "reasonably apparent" test, or whether the defendant takes the risk of mistake.

C. Arrest and detention

PETERS V. MENARD INC. A security officer saw a customer walk out of the store with an item he hadn't paid for. When confronted by the officer, the customer began to run. The chase lasted for some distance and ended when the customer jumped into a flooded river and in which he drowned. The court compares the state's rule affording merchants a privilege of reasonable detention for investigation with the Restatement rule. It adopts a view of the state rule that merchants can pursue suspects off of the premises if the pursuit meets reasonableness criteria.

D. Defense and Repossession of Property

KATKO V. BRINEY. Defendants rigged a shotgun in an empty house they owned. A trespasser had much of his leg blown away when he entered and tripped the wire to the trigger. He was allowed to recover on the ground that defendants were not justified in using deadly force to defend an unoccupied building, though such force might be permissible if the trespasser was committing a felony of violence or one punishable by death.

BROWN V. MARTINEZ. Boys were stealing watermelons from defendant's patch. The defendant fired in the opposite direction from the noise, hoping to scare them off. The shot struck one boy who had gone in the opposite direction. This is treated in the same way as *Katko*, even though here the landowner merely meant to frighten, not to injure.

E. Discipline

TEXT. Parents and those in loco parentis, including teachers, are privileged to discipline children. A military privilege was once recognized to chastise subordinates, but the Code of Military Justice now appears to control such matters.

F. Observing Privileges

TEXT. When privilege is invoked, courts depart from the categorical rules of the prima facie case and adopt reasonableness rules, or at least rules about degree and extent rather than about category and definition. This foreshadows negligence a little bit.

COMMENTS

A. Self-Defense

Burden of Proof. You can set up a prima facie case in a hypothetical. Analysis of tort cases probably should first consider the prima facie case, then turn to affirmative defenses. Instead of starting with self-defense, then, you might begin by getting a student to work through the elements of battery in a realistic setting. P files a complaint stating that at a certain time and place D shot P in the arm with a .38 pistol. This states a claim good against a demurrer or motion to dismiss. Then suppose the defendant files an answer saying he did indeed shoot P but that on the occasion in question P and D were in a bar, that P started a fight and broke a glass bottle, that P was lunging at D with the jagged bottle, and that D fired the shot in self-defense. Now we can see that the defense comes in only when the complaint (or proof) makes out a prima facie case.

In this instance, the prima facie case is one for battery. The plaintiff will get to the jury on these pleadings no matter what. If the jury believes the plaintiff, the plaintiff will win. The defendant will have the burden of convincing the jury by a preponderance of the evidence that this is a self-defense case under the rules stated (e.g., that there was reasonable ground for believing he was attacked, that the force used was reasonable). If the jury thinks this might be so, but is not convinced, the plaintiff will still win. The judge will instruct the jury that the burden in on the defendant.

Role of factual analysis. *Hypo A.* A and B, though the best of friends, get into a vehement argument. A, angrier and angrier, doubles up a fist and, to make a point, strikes B on the shoulder. B, feeling himself attacked, pulls a knife and slashes A's arm as he pulls it back from the blow.

Hypo B. X is in a dangerous part of town, late at night. Walking warily and in some fear for his safety, he suddenly feels two arms around his neck. In fact this is Y, an old friend, who has often surprised X in this fashion, but never before in dangerous circumstances. X, thinking he is attacked, probably with a deadly weapon, goes into a judo defense and throws Y over his shoulder. Y hits the ground and suffers serious and permanent back injury.

You might emphasize the inferences to be drawn from the facts (B deals with a known friend in the first case, but X deals with a seeming attacker in the second). Maybe these cases turn less on rules than on jury arguments. It is not too soon to try to help students understand when to look for rules and when to look for arguments and evidence.

Complications in the evidence. It is often very hard to get the kind of detail that makes it possible to judge who was the aggressor and whether the force used was reasonable. The shifting fortunes and attacks of a really good fight, to say nothing of a barroom brawl, can render rational assessment almost impossible. This can be fun to talk about but if students grasp the idea that factual detail governs most outcomes, further discussion may not represent the best use of limited time.

1. Rule. The privilege is based on reasonable appearance, not on objective actuality. In other words, the defendant's reasonable mistake that he is attacked is good enough to justify a reasonable response. Privilege issues often turn on reasonableness. They are thus structured quite differently from the categorical rules of the prima facie case. The prima facie case turns on intent, for example, not on the reasonableness of intent or even on the motive for the intent. But the privileges very often turn on matters of degree and reasonableness. They thus move us gradually toward the flexible analysis of the negligence action.

2. Deadly force and commensurability. *The response, whether force, assault, or imprisonment, must be commensurate with the reasonably perceived attack.* As a rule, deadly force cannot be used except to counter the threat of deadly force. Nor can the force go beyond defense. *Denson* is an interesting case. The defendant had evicted the tenant, but the tenant later reentered the building. The defendant, a 67-year-old man, felt threatened in a later confrontation and shot the tenant. The court upheld the verdict for the defendant after examining a multi-factor test.

3. Retreat. Some courts hold you must retreat in the face of deadly force rather than defendant yourself with similar force. The authorities are divided. Most cases actually involve criminal prosecutions.

4. Excessive force. Excessive force is more than is reasonable in the light of the reasonably apparent threat. That means that the greater the reasonably apparent threat, the greater the amount of force can be and still be considered reasonable. But where a person's belief about the nature of the threat (or how to subdue it) is unreasonable, and where that unreasonable belief motivates an unreasonable amount of force, clearly the privilege is lost. The characterization of unprivileged excessive force as negligence makes a difference with respect to insurance coverage.

5. Provocation. Students should understand that provocation is not an attack. It is usually a communicative act such as an insult. Legions of criminal cases deal with defendants who have been provoked when someone "flips the bird" or "gave me the finger." These defendants pull guns, beat the bird man, or run him down with their trucks. E.g., *State v. Garner,* 800 S.W.2d 785 (Mo. Ct. App. 1990).

Provocation traditionally did not provide a defense but could be considered as grounds for reducing punitive damages. Some states even allow provocation to be considered in determining the amount of compensatory damages. In some cases, provocation might also help convince the jury that the defendant reasonably thought he was attacked thus generating the self-defense argument. In Chapters 9 & 25 we raise the possibility that comparative fault rules might apply to intentional torts. If so, provocation might be regarded as a species of comparative fault that reduces the plaintiff's recovery, though we think this shift of responsibility for the intentional tort away from the intentional tortfeasor is generally undesirable.

6. Assault and imprisonment in self-defense. One might defend oneself by an imprisonment of the attacker. Jones, pursued from the depths of the cave by Amazons with poison-tipped arrows, reaches the entrance and causes an avalanche that blocks the cave so that the Amazons cannot get out. The Amazons have no false imprisonment claim; Jones is privileged. Possibly one could imagine hypotheticals that do not sound like a movie. The view of the Restatement is that one could commit an assault in self defense, e.g., by pulling a gun and threatening to shoot if the attacker comes closer. The question posed is intended to raise an issue to which you can return in discussing *Brown v. Martinez*–whether one is privileged to threaten an act one would not actually be privileged to carry out.

B. Defense of Third Persons

Under the Restatement rule, you may defend third persons under about the same circumstances as you may defend yourself. But some cases have held otherwise by insisting that the "defender" must take the risk of a reasonable mistake. If he "defends" the attacker, even though he acts in good faith and under a reasonable mistake, he has no privilege. Criminal statutes have changed this rule and may have tort side-effects. *See* DOBBS ON TORTS § 74 (2000).

C. Arrest and Detention

PETERS V. MENARD, 589 N.W.2d 395 (Wis. 1999)

This case introduces the merchant's privilege to detain for investigation. The facts begin with a fairly typical of the problem – a shop security guard discovers a shoplifter and confronts him. What results, a chase that ends with the man drowning in the swollen Lacrosse River is more than a bit surprising however. Under a Wisconsin statute, the merchant has a privilege to detain if the merchant is reasonable essentially with respect to the need for detention, the manner of detention and the length of the detention. If the shopkeeper behaves reasonably and merely seeks to investigate, the detention for a short period is privileged under the Restatement view and that of a number of cases and statutes. The Restatement Second expresses "no opinion" about a privilege to detain one who has left the premises. However, the Wisconsin Supreme Court holds that its state statute provides such a privilege as long as the various reasonableness requirements have been met.

Note 2. The policy of a broad privilege to detain. Look at the court's reasons for allowing off premises pursuit—failure to catch shoplifters will result in increased prices, lack of pursuit will encourage more shoplifter flight. Think back to the *Prosser v. Keeton* case in chapter 1. This looks like policy-based reasoning doesn't it? How persuasive the reasoning is may depend on whether the judges policy rationales are correct. Suppose research shows that shoplifters are less likely to flee in states where off-premises pursuit is banned. This seems like it would undermine the court's judgment.

Note 3. Rules v. standards. This question raises the issue of whether rules like pursuing "within 50 feet of the property" are better than standards such as pursuit for "a reasonable distance." With a rule, it is difficult to take account of particular circumstances. Might it be reasonable to pursue for a longer distance someone who stole expensive merchandise rather than an inexpensive item? Might it be more reasonable to pursue off premises a person whose license plate number or drivers license the security officer had not already obtained? A set guideline—"pursue for 50 feet"—doesn't give the security guards flexibility to act in different way as the circumstances dictate. Under a standard like reasonableness though, it may be very difficult for a merchant to know in advance what distance of off-premises pursuit would be reasonable. As such, it might be harder for the merchant to conform his or her conduct to the legal requirement. Although the reasonableness issue was decided by the court in *Peters*—the decedent's conduct would have been greater than half the negligence in the case so that recovery would not be allowed—reasonableness determinations are generally for the trier of fact.

Note 4. Mistake. It is difficult to know if the shopkeeper in *Great Atlantic* would have fared any better under a reasonableness standard. The shopkeeper's conduct might have been considered unreasonable on several dimensions. The Maryland court concludes, correctly, it would seem, that the Restatement privilege would not apply in that case.The Restatement's privilege depends on (1) reasonable belief by the defendant (2) that the plaintiff has taken goods or services without paying, and (3) a reasonable detention for investigation. Probably none of these elements is present. The belief that the plaintiff in the case took the tick spray is strained at best; and the plaintiff did not appear in any event to have removed the spray from the premises; and the detention was not reasonable in manner or degree.

How would a reasonableness query have come out in *Peters?* Any time a jury decision is involved, there is some degree of uncertainty.

Comparing recapture of chattels. Some teachers will want to compare recapture of the chattel to the privileged detention. The storekeeper in *Paul* could have used force in a hot pursuit recapture of the tick spray if Mr. Paul had actually taken it. But that privilege of recapture would make no allowance for mistake.

The storekeeper here wants to assert a privilege to detain even if he is mistaken, and the Restatement § 120A recognizes that privilege. If there is no room for mistake, there is no effective privilege in these situations.

Peter's focuses on the privilege to detain. It can provide a nice lead in to the recapture of chattels materials at the end of the next section too though. Why wouldn't that case be a recapture of chattels case? Could it be because Peters left the chattel in the truck when he took off?

D. Defense of Property and Recapture of Chattels

KATKO V. BRINEY, 183 N.W.2d 657 (Iowa 1971)

This is the modern classic case of defense of property. Before discussion: First, as *Katko* clearly implies but does not spell out, the defendant has a general privilege to defend his property by the use of reasonable force. *Katko* deals with what force is reasonable under the circumstances. Second, the privilege applies only when defense appears reasonably necessary. The first point states the basic rule on which all the discussion is built; the second states a point that reminds the class of the risk of mistake issue that comes up in so many of these cases. It is also important in the critique of the rule that you can do by a spring gun what you can do in person.

You may want to add a third point: the privilege belongs to the possessor of land, not merely the title holder. The student who lives in a rented apartment or is otherwise in possession of the premises has the privilege. Even the squatter in possession may have this privilege.

A question can quickly establish that the building in *Katko* was empty and no human beings were threatened. Does that matter, we ask in **Note 1**? In *Graves*, cited in that Note, the decedent forcibly entered a home and shot the occupant in the leg. The occupant returned fire, killing the decedent. The decedent's estate sued. The court held the occupant entitled to partial summary judgment on the ground that "he was justified in using deadly force to protect himself and the other person in the dwelling." Other courts might well permit the use of deadly force in the case of a burglar in the bedroom. *See* DOBBS ON TORTS §76, p. 172 (2000) (deadly force) & § 77 (spring guns). In terms of the instruction approved in *Katko*, this would depend on whether the burglar in the bedroom was committing a "felony of violence or a felony punishable by death, or . . . was endangering human life . . . ." Burglary as such is not punishable by death, so the rule stated in the instruction might not permit the use of the defense even there, so long as unalloyed burglary was involved.

However, burglary may result in a confrontation with persons actually present. As soon as this happens, there may be reasons for the land possessor to defend his or her person, so that the law of self-defense is invoked rather than the law of property defense. If the person is attacked, reasonable force, including where necessary deadly force, may be used, as we have seen. *Cf. Graves*, cited in Note 1 after *Katko* and discussed above.

Katko repeats the Restatement's idea, that one may not do by a mechanical device that which he would not be privileged to do in person. This seems to mean that if you could personally shoot the intruder, you can arrange to do so by a spring gun. Is the position sound? See criticisms in DOBBS ON TORTS § 77, at 175.

One solution in these cases would be to allow a recovery, but not of punitive damages. Any punishment of the spring gun user could be left to the criminal law. Another would be to deny recovery altogether, on the same hope that the criminal law would punish the landowner. The hope that criminal punishment will adequately take care of most crimes has long since ceased to be very bright, however. If criminal law would prosecute the offending landowner, would either of these solutions be attractive to the class?

The classic English case. The English case that has influenced American law is *Bird v. Holbrook*, 4 Bing. 628, 130 Eng. Repr. 911 (C.P. 1828), a case decided by an English court in 1828. The defendant set a spring gun in his walled garden because he had previously suffered theft of some of the tulips he raised there. A neighbor's peahen escaped and got into the garden. The plaintiff offered to get it. The plaintiff climbed the wall and called out for the occupant, but, getting no answer, jumped into the garden to retrieve the hen. The spring gun was triggered and the plaintiff was seriously wounded.

The *Bird v. Holbrook* court imposed liability upon the defendant. Distinguishing earlier authority, one of the judges emphasized that the defendant had not only failed to give notice that the gun was there but had tried to keep it secret in order to wound the tulip thief. Another judge emphasized that if the spring gun were justified, it would be justified only at night when the thief might come. *Bird* is clear about the defendant's liability on the facts, but uncertain about the defendant's potential liability to an actual burglar.

American tort decisions. Most of the direct law on this subject is criminal law, embodied in statutes or criminal prosecutions. There are not many tort decisions. Criminal statutes aside, some states seem to permit the defendant to protect his dwelling place by deadly traps against intruders who are in fact entering or attempting to enter in the course of a felony or attempted felony, provided deadly traps are otherwise reasonable. In some states, this privilege may even be extended to permit protection of other buildings against serious depredation.

Risk of error. Courts would probably agree that even if the possessor enjoys a privilege to use a spring gun against some intruder, the possessor does so at his peril. If the spring gun harms or kills a straying child who is not in fact attempting felonious entry, the privilege would be no protection. See *Allison v. Fiscus, supra* ("[O]ne who sets a spring gun or trap does so at his peril"); Restatement § 85, cmt. *d.* Put differently, actuality, not reasonable appearances would control.

FYI: Suing for one's own wrong. Courts sometimes announce a principle, supposedly distinct from contributory negligence and assumed risk, to the effect that one cannot sue for his own wrong, or that one cannot found a claim in tort on the basis of his own criminal conduct. So long as his injury can be seen to result from his "own wrong", the criminal forfeits his civil rights in this respect. The casebook considers this idea briefly in connection with comparative negligence rules. *See* Chapter 9; *see also* DOBBS ON TORTS § 208. The idea is also relevant to, or gets mixed up with, the question of consent to an illegal act discussed in the next section.

Perhaps the principle is applied selectively. Cases allowing recovery for injuries or death resulting from a deadly trap seem to be contrary to the "own wrong" rule. See *McKinsey v. Wade,* 220 S.E.2d 30 (Ga. Ct. App. 1975). In *Oden v. Pepsi Cola Bottling Co. of Decatur,* Inc., 621 So.2d 953 (Ala. 1993) the court reiterated its principle that one "cannot maintain a cause of action if, in order to establish it, he must rely in whole or part on an illegal or immoral act or transaction to which he is a party", but added that this principle "does not foreclose a trespasser's action against a landowner who willfully or wantonly injures him, unless the injuries incurred are a direct result of an injured party's knowing and intentional participation in a crime of moral turpitude." In Iowa, where *Katko* was decided, a court has perhaps suggested that liability would not have been imposed if the defendant had invoked the forfeiture principle. *Pappas v. Clark,* 494 N.W.2d 245 (Iowa Ct. App. 1992). Iowa had advanced the forfeiture or "own wrong" rule in *Cole v. Taylor,* 301 N.W.2d 766 (Iowa 1981), a completely different setting. In *Cole* the plaintiff sued her therapist for failing to prevent her from murdering her husband. The claim was denied, the court giving the "own wrong" rule as one reason. The *Pappas* court, wishing to distinguish *Katko,* observed that the "own wrong" rule had not been raised there, an observation that presumably is meant to suggest that *Katko* would go the other way if the rule were raised. That seems improbable, especially in light of the Iowa statutes. Time adds wrinkles to rules as well as to faces.

Note 3. Defense of property v. crime prevention. At times, state statutes permit much broader uses of force in protection of property through crime prevention defenses. Defense of property statutes might not permit killing someone who was stealing items of small value such as $5 folding chairs. However, if the chairs were stolen from a fenced yard and the theft therefore considered a burglary, crime prevention defenses might permit such force to be used. In a case like this, an Arizona court was able to avoid the question because the act was not a burglary given that the yard was not fully fenced. *See State v. Barr,* 565 P.2d 526 (Ariz. Ct. App. 1977).■

BROWN V. MARTINEZ, 361 P.2d 152 (N.M. 1961)

Many students favor the plaintiff and oppose the landowner here. The facts require careful attention. The landowner, at least on his story, did not attempt to shoot any of the boys. Nor, it would seem, did he take any unreasonable risk. He fired in exactly the opposite direction of the boys. (If this was an unreasonable risk, then he should be liable for negligence, but not for battery.) On the landowner's story, at least, the intent is an intent to assault, not one to batter.

If the class accepts this last point, you can ask why, then, the defendant should be liable for a battery, since he intended none. Students will almost certainly answer, "transferred intent." Yet would the defendant not be privileged to threaten an assault that he would not be privileged to carry out? See the discussion above in § 1. That seems to be what he intended to do – threaten, not harm. If the act was privileged as an intended and non-negligent threat, it does not become tortious by way of transferred intent. If there is policy behind the transferred intent metaphor, it is that one guilty of actionable intent and conduct should not escape merely because the harm he produces is different from that intended. To answer the metaphor of transferred intent with another metaphor, you can't transfer an intent that does not exist. If the defendant's intent is not tortious, there is no intent to transfer.

The argument just stated finds support in the rule that A is privileged to shoot B in self-defense and does so but accidentally injures C in the process, he is not liable to C in the absence of negligence. *See* DOBBS ON TORTS § 75 (2000).

An interesting speculation but one that could take the class far too long to deal with, is whether B, who attacks A, would be liable to C who is injured when A's self-defense miscarries. B provoked A's defense, which in turn caused injury to C. B might be liable for negligence if this was within the scope of the risks he took in attacking. If he is not negligent, but intends injury to B, he would be liable under ordinary transferred intent rules if he himself accidentally injured C. Can we extend this to say that he is liable if, intending injury to B, he provokes B's defense, which in turn causes injury to C? The analogous doctrine of felony murder would not, seemingly, apply to hold B criminally liable for C's death. *See* Annotations, 56 A.L.R.3d 239 (1974).

Note 2-3. Recapture of chattels. Defending possession for force is entirely different from regaining possession by force. The recapture privilege deals with cases in which the chattel has in fact been taken; it does not deal with cases of mistaken attempts to recapture. The privilege of forcible recapture is quite limited to more or less immediate recapture–cases that are comparable to the use of force in defending possession in the first place. Once the status quo has changed and another person has taken a chattel and reduced it to his possession, it is time to resort to law if the chattel cannot be peaceably recaptured. This is another version of the "escalation" problem raised before, for example, in connection with resistance to unlawful arrest. *Grier*, discussed here, is a memorable example of rather extreme escalation; clearly the defense of recapture of chattels would not have worked any better for the defendant than did the assertion of self-defense.

Repossession by sellers. Sellers who sell goods "on time," may be entitled to repossess the property when payments are not made. The Uniform Commercial Code permits peaceful repossession but not possession that results in a "breach of the peace." "Breach of the peace" seems to include a good deal besides actual violence. Perhaps it includes anything that amounts to a trespassory tort or an unconsented-to taking. So the repossessor could not enter the buyer's home to repossess unless the buyer consents. The repossession problem is usually covered in courses on the UCC or secured transactions. *See* JAMES WHITE & ROBERT SUMMERS, UNIFORM COMMERCIAL CODE § 27-6 (3d ed. 1988).

Note 4. Repossession of land. "A large group of courts, usually said to be the majority, permit the wrongful possessor to recover from the owner who violates the statute by using force to reenter, even though the amount of force used is no more than made necessary by the possessor's resistance." DOBBS ON TORTS § 80, at 183 (2000). Some statutes regulating landlords forbid any self-help to gain repossession, even self-help without anything you would ordinarily call force. This would mean the landlord could not lock out the tenant who fails to pay rent. The forcible entry statutes inflict penalties for use of force but also offer the landowner a palliative–he can get a relatively speedy, summary trial to get immediate possession.

E. Discipline

The parents' privilege. Parental immunity may protect some parents from some tort suits brought by their minor children. If it does not, the specific privilege to discipline children may do so. We wish to respect the right of families to follow their own perceptions about discipline, but we also wish to protect children from brutal parents. What is discipline and what is mere brutality? One component is the force used; another is the occasion for discipline. Does a child's talking too much warrant a bruise? The difficulty of this problem and the parallel problem that arises when state protection for children is in issue is discussed in DOBBS ON TORTS § 94 (2000). In the *DeShaney* case in Chapter 16 we'll see a case of undoubted brutality and the state's failure to protect the child.

The cases of school officials' response to the behavioral problems of special education students are taken from a recent newspaper article. Some lawsuits have arisen from those sorts of responses. *See* Benedict Carey, *Calm Down or Else*, N.Y. Times, July 15, 2008, at F1.

A number of thoughtful scholars have argued over the past several years that it is never reasonable to spank a child. *See, e.g.,* Deana Pollard, *Banning Child Corporal Punishment*, 77 TUL. L. REV. 575 (2003) (pointing out that most other countries have banned corporal punishment of children, even in private homes, and that the policies thought to support spanking – that it is beneficial to children and helps them become better citizens – is belied by all competent studies); Deana Pollard, *Banning Corporal Punishment: A Constitutional Analysis*, 52 AM.U.L.REV. 447 (2002); Patricia E. Weidler, *Parental Physical Discipline in Maine and New Hampshire: An Analysis of Two States' Approaches to Protecting Children from Parental Violence*, 3 WHITTIER J. CHILD & FAM. ADVOC. 77 (2003); David Orentlicher, *Spanking and Other Corporal Punishment of Children by Parents: Overvaluing Pain, Undervaluing Children*, 35 HOUS. L.REV. 174 (1998). See also 8 VA. J. SOC. POL'Y & L 1 et seq. (2000) (symposium issue).

Standing in the parents' shoes–loco parentis. The teacher's privilege is said to derive from the parent's privilege. Does this mean that the parent could forbid the teacher to administer corporal punishment? In *Ingraham v. Wright*, 430 U.S. 651 (1977), the Supreme Court commented:

> Although the early cases viewed the authority of the teacher as deriving from the parents, the concept of parental delegation has been replaced by the view–more consonant with compulsory educational laws–that the State itself may impose such corporal punishment as is reasonably necessary. . . .

One would hardly expect that the parent could forbid the punishment under these views. The RESTATEMENT (SECOND) OF TORTS § 153 states the rule that the parent can restrict the privilege to punish to those to whom the parent delegates control of the child, except that a "public officer" such as a teacher may not be so restricted.

A number of other people may be in loco parentis, that is, standing in the position of the parents. The grandparents or other persons with whom the child lives would be in this category. What about the babysitter? Would punishment reasonable for a parent be equally reasonable for a babysitter?

For an example of a teacher's claim of privilege see *Thomas v. Bedford,* 389 So.2d 405 (La. Ct. App. 1980).

Civil rights. The Supreme Court has held that corporal punishment in the schools is not a violation of due process rights when administered without a hearing. This is partly due to the common law privilege, which the Court accepted as a kind of norm, and partly because the process of a hearing was not thought required in the light of other protections, such as the common law tort suit. *Ingraham v. Wright, supra.*

Denying the privilege. In *Rodriguez v. Johnson*, 504 N.Y.S.2d 379 (City Court 1986) a school bus matron slapped Eric, who was one of a number of children being noisy and troublesome but not otherwise doing wrong. The slap was not "because of maliciousness, but rather [was] a result of frustration and anger. Further, the court does not find that the slap itself was an excessive use of force." The child's age is not given. The court first discussed the fact that "historically. . . only men moved about freely without fear" and said that women and children were viewed as property of husbands and fathers. Punishment of wives was considered appropriate and "Indeed, only during the past fifteen years have [sic] there been significant changes. . . ." The court found a battery and gave judgment for $250 in favor of the child. The opinion opposed any degree of corporal punishment.

F. Observing Privileges

This short text permits a certain amount of review and synthesis. Privilege, with its burden on the defendant, is really an important part of our understanding of the whole lawsuit. When we do understand that the privilege issue differs from the prima facie case issue, some things become clearer. The prima facie case for trespassory torts is structured as a set of categorical rules. It is rights oriented. Once privileges are invoked, however, we see that the rigid rights of the prima facie case are ultimately treated with more flexibility as we consider issues of reasonableness and excessiveness of force, for example. When we come to negligence, we see that it is possible to introduce the flexibility in the prima facie case itself. Indeed, a claim of excessive force (in an arrest, say) looks very much like a negligence claim, even though we our theory says it is a battery coupled with the assertion of a privilege defense. When we consider whether comparative fault should apply to intentional tort claims, this will be something to have in mind.

§ 2. THE SPECIAL CASE OF CONSENT

Preliminary Note: *The Restatement: consent vs. effective consent.* The Restatement differentiates between consent and effective consent. Consent is the real thing, a subjective willingness. Effective consent is based upon appearances that would be reasonably understood as consent by an observer. This section goes directly to the idea that the defendant is entitled to rely upon reasonable appearances created by the plaintiff.

Sensitive issues. This book does not shy away from sensitive issues, even those that may be divisive (temporarily, we can hope). If you are uncomfortable in dealing with sexual battery cases like *Robins v. Harris,* you can drop that case and use the much easier *Payton v. Donner* problem. None of the authors of this book has had difficulty with such sensitive material. In presenting other potentially polarizing materials, we have told our classes in advance that lawyers must expect to differ but that differences should be explored professionally, with courtesy, and with genuine respect for opposing views. We think that students are glad to have some guidelines of that kind and we try to conduct ourselves accordingly. A teacher's model in accepting the speaker even while challenging the speaker's views is important. On the other side of the coin, we are aware that a torts class cannot fully explore all this material and in a sense that the material is too brief. But we hope it strikes a reasonable balance for teachers who want to teach a whole course in torts.

SUMMARY

INTRODUCTORY HYPOTHETICAL AND QUESTIONS. In a setting where a kiss is often expected, A kisses and caresses B. Unexpectedly, a neckbone is broken. Discussion along common sense lines develops the point that a consent may be manifested non-verbally, that a consent to an act bars recovery for harm resulting even though the harm itself was not consented to, and that the appearance of consent negates an intent to offend.

NOTE: RELATIONSHIP OF THE PARTIES. Relationship matters in determining what consent you can infer either from conduct or words.

ROBINS V. HARRIS. The plaintiff performed oral sex on a corrections officer. She claimed it was a battery. The officer asserted that she consented. Given the obvious inequality of the parties, consent would not be a defense available to the officer under the criminal law. Should it be a defense in this tort action? The court of appeals said no, as does a strong dissent from Justice Sullivan of the Indiana Supreme Court. However, a majority of the Indiana Supreme Court takes the view that consent is a proper defense in the tort action.

ASHCRAFT V. KING. A patient who consents to transfusions only with family-donated blood has a battery action against a doctor responsible for transfusing with other blood.

KENNEDY V. PARROTT. In the course of an operation, the doctor discovered a condition as to which no consent had been given. He dealt surgically with that condition. This was held not a battery, though it was outside the scope of the formal consent. The rationale seems to be that the patient impliedly consented to any medically desirable operation.
Notes briefly allude to informed consent, substituted consent, and the consent of minors, including consents to abortions and crimes.

DOE V. JOHNSON. A species of informed consent: The plaintiff agrees to sexual intercourse with the defendant, and as a result contracts a serious venereal disease. The defendant knew he was at risk but did not inform the plaintiff. He is liable on a battery, not merely on a negligence theory, for her consent was, as he knew, based on a false assumption about the degree of risk.

PROBLEM: PAYTON V. DONNER. A woman who is addicted to drugs expresses "consent" to engage in a sexual relationship with a doctor in exchange for a continuing supply of drugs. Is it consent at all? Is it consent but one that will not be given legal effect? A chance to review rules, principles and attitudes.

COMMENTS

A CANDLELIGHT DINNER:
Introductory Hypothetical and Questions

Teaching from this hypothetical is unorthodox but seems to work very well. Class discussion has always elicited a very quick recognition of the common sense of the situation, and the students have no difficulty in accepting the legal rules we erect on that sense. (We have never had a claim that this is a sexist illustration, and it is not; the gender of the parties cannot be determined by name or conduct.)

The hypothetical is a gentler beginning than the cases because the parties are not concrete beings and we have no judicial language that can cause a reaction.

(1) Manifestation of consent by conduct. Your date, spouse, or domestic partner, having passed a few romantic words on a moonlit evening leans toward you as if to give you a kiss. You make no move. Does it seem as if you are in fact consenting? Does it seem that way to the other person? Students agree that this probably reflects an inner consent and also a manifestation. You can express consent in ways other than words.

Date rape issues are near the surface of this hypothetical, as students are often quick to recognize. Consent is NOT manifested in the hypothetical if Berwyn says "Don't touch me," or struggles to prevent the impending caress. If Berwyn says "no," Austin cannot infer consent. No one should think that manifestation of consent in this hypothetical means any more than what is says.

Sometimes conduct is not so easy to interpret. Maybe if you knew more facts you would think that Berwyn's conduct is NOT consent. If you knew that Berwyn had been fraudulently led to sit beside Austin or required to submit to avoid serious harm, Berwyn's acts would not look like consent at all.

Hypotheticals: *A more neutral hypothetical*: I hold out my hand to shake hands with a person to whom I have just been introduced. In fact, he hates contact, especially handshakes and becomes somewhat physically ill when such a contact occurs. Nevertheless he holds out his hand, I shake it. He then becomes ill and claims I have battered him. Apparent consent or no?

Silence as consent hypothetical: Carrying a nightstick upraised as if to strike, I run at a man. He does not move, but looks at me directly in the eyes, smiling slightly. I hit him. Apparent consent or no?

"No means no" hypotheticals: (a) Defendant is man who has a date with the plaintiff, a woman. After a nice evening, he parks the car in a lonely spot and the two move close together and began to engage in physical touchings of various kinds. After a while the man begins to go further and the woman says "no, stop." He doesn't stop but proceeds to engage in sexual intercourse with her.

(b) A patient is about to have blood drawn by the lab technician. He has consented to this procedure, but when the needle appears, he decides he cannot stand the idea and says, "no don't touch me." The tech stabs him with the needle anyway.

In the last two hypotheticals, you can't infer consent when the plaintiff says "no." This does not mean that verbal behavior trumps nonverbal behavior: sometimes a verbal "yes"cannot be relied upon as consent, as we'll soon see. The lab technician hypothetical makes these additional points: (A) Motive, which we can assume to have been the best, is no part of the consent issue; that is, a good motive does not authorize the tech to override the consent. (B) Consent as well as blood can be withdrawn.

(2) Legal effect of manifested consent. The Candlelight Dinner facts given might reflect paralyzed horror, not actual consent. But if there are no facts to suggest that, then the date or spouse is likely to believe, reasonably, that consent is given. If the kissee testifies that there was really no consent and if the jury believed it, would this eliminate consent and permit the battery claim? Drawing on the rule about appearances in self-defense, the class can usually recognize that one will be permitted to act on the reasonable appearance of consent in these cases. That is indeed the rule, so long as the appearance of consent was not itself induced by misrepresentation or by a basic mistake of which the defendant was aware. Fraud vitiates consent, as all courts clearly hold.

A well-known case, used in some casebooks, is *O'Brien v. Cunard Steamship Co.*, 28 N.E. 266 (Mass. 1891). Passengers on a ship had to have a vaccination before entering the United States unless they were willing to sit out a two-week quarantine. The ship provided a vaccination for them before docking. They lined up and held up their arms. One of them was the plaintiff. She held up her arm, was examined and vaccinated. She may not have understood what was happening. Or she may have understood but objected, because she claimed to have been vaccinated before, although it left no mark. But the court thought that in lining up and holding up her arm, she gave the appearance of consent and this was held sufficient.

The actual facts of the case, interpreted from other perspectives might yield a different conclusion. You may not wish to develop different factual inferences possible at this point. If you do want to explore different viewpoints about *O'Brien*, by all means consult the articles in the Symposium, *Five Approaches to Legal Reasoning in the Classroom: Contrasting Perspectives on O'Brien v. Cunard S.S. Co. Ltd.*, 57 MO. L. REV. 346 (1992).

Both words and conduct are subject to interpretation. Conceivably, the social customs in the community might suggest other interpretations of the scene in the casebook hypothetical. To work with a different hypothetical, suppose a homeowner does not post a sign excluding door-to-door salespersons. May such persons take it they at least have consent to enter the land and knock on the door? What about a car driver who uses your driveway to turn around–has the landowner consented by not posting a sign? Community custom dictates much of how we interpret such situations.

Consent genuine but not manifested. Should a consent not manifested but subjectively real bar recovery if it can be proven? In that case, the defendant looks like a tortfeasor for he necessarily believes that his act is not permitted. The reason for protecting the defendant in that case is different: the plaintiff has suffered no injury. While manifested consent negates the intent element of the plaintiff's case, unmanifested consent does not. See paragraph (4) below. Unmanifested consent thus looks like a true affirmative defense. See DOBBS ON TORTS § 97 (2000).

(3) Consent to the act, not the result. In the hypothetical, Berwyn did not consent in any way to the injury. Is consent to the act a bar to the claim, at least if one knows the nature of the act? The answer is "Yes." In *Hellriegel v. Tholl*, 417 P.2d 362 (Wash. 1966), boys were horseplaying. Several of them picked up one of the group, the plaintiff, and threw him into the water. The tacit agreement to horseplay easily covered this kind of act. However, when the plaintiff was picked up, something snapped and he was paralyzed. The consent to horseplay barred his recovery. In the hypothetical here, consent to the kiss and caress would bar recovery for unintended and non-negligent results of the acts consented to.

Although the broken vertebrae example seems unlikely, there are actual cases in which a small touch inadvertently results in significant harm. For example, in *White v. University of Idaho,* 797 P.2d 108 (Idaho 1990), a piano professor was staying at Mrs. White's home. "Unanticipated by Mrs. White, Professor Neher walked up behind her and touched her back with both of his hands in a movement later described as one a pianist would make in striking and lifting the fingers from a keyboard. The resulting contact generated unexpectedly harmful injuries, according to the Whites.... Mrs. White suffered thoracic outlet syndrome on the right side of her body, requiring the removal of the first rib on the right side. She also experienced scarring of the brachial plexus nerve which necessitated the severing of the scalenus anterior muscles.

(4) Consent as negating the *prima facie* case. If Berwyn proves only the facts given in this hypothetical, she has not proved tortious intent. The defendant has no reason to think that a kiss or caress will break a bone, so we cannot infer intent to harm. An actor might have an intent to offend by a kiss or caress if a stranger is involved; but we cannot infer an intent to offend when consent is apparent. When it reasonably appears to the defendant from the plaintiff's own conduct that the plaintiff will not be offended by a touch, the defendant cannot have intended to offend by that touch. The appearance of consent in this case seems to have negated the intent necessary to show the battery.

In this kind of situation, consent is not an affirmative defense so much as it is a datum from which the intent of the defendant may be inferred. It negates the prima facie case. The judge should not instruct the jury that the plaintiff has shown a battery and then leave it to the defendant to shoulder the burden of proving consent. The judge should instead instruct the jury that there is no battery unless the plaintiff proves intent to harm or offend.

Two qualifications: (a) In the case of property torts like trespass to land, consent seems to be a true affirmative defense. That is because the plaintiff in a trespass to land case makes out her claim by showing an intentional entry upon land she possessed. She need not show an intent to cause harm or offense. Consent does not negate that intent. It is rather a plea that the plaintiff has a suffered no harm because she willed the entry upon her land.

(b) As noted in paragraph (3) above, actual but unmanifested consent also represents a true affirmative defense. If the defendant touches her in spite of her manifest opposition, he has the requisite intent to offend or perhaps to harm. Thus the prima facie case of battery is made out. Here is an example.

Paar believes it is wrong to accept a blood transfusion and carries a card on her person so stating and explicitly denying permission to give a transfusion. Dr. Day knows of all this, but, facing an emergency in which Paar, who appears unconscious, will die unless a transfusion is administered, Day orders a transfusion anyway, believing that Paar objects. Paar, though she appears unconscious, is in fact aware of what was going on and makes no objection. She admits this later.

In a case of this kind, the defendant intends to do an act that is offensive, although he intends it for Paar's own good. (It is offensive because forbidden. This is the autonomy interest.) Since Dr. Day has the requisite intent, there is a prima facie case of battery. The consent, if there is consent and if it is legally effective at all, is effective only in a purely defensive way; it does not negate intent.

NOTE: RELATIONSHIP OF THE PARTIES.

In the model presented by the scenario, Berwyn and Austin are given no identities: they have no stated gender, no stated culture, race, or ethnic background. They have no known relationship; they are "new acquaintances." The note on relationship of parties raises the possibility that Berwyn lacked capacity and that Austin knew it; or that Berwyn's apparent consent might be tempered by the fact that Austin was Berwyn's employer, teacher, doctor, or lawyer. This note allows you to fill in factual details hypothetically or ask the class what factors would be relevant. You can also bypass discussion of it right now and let it serve only to lead to the *Robbinsi* case and to foreshadow the *Payton v. Donner* Problem.

ROBINS V. HARRIS, 769 N.E.2d 586 (Ind. 2002)

The procedural posture of this case is a bit tricky. The court of appeals held that plaintiffs battery claim was viableagainst the corrections officer and that consent to sexual contact provided no defense to the claim. Although the case was subsequently resolved, so that no state supreme court decision was required at all, the Indiana Supreme Court chose to affirm except as to the availability (really nonavailability) of the consent defense. No majority opinion was issued, but Justice Sullivan issued a dissent.

Note 1. Power relationships. If ever there was a power imbalance, the situation of jailer and prisoner would be it. Should the plaintiff's consent act as a defense or does consent in that circumstance necessarily lack indicia of voluntariness given the inmate's lack of autonomy. In the criminal context, the state's public policy recognizes that the jailer is in the best position to avoid inappropriate sexual contact. Is the public policy different once the plaintiff is suing for damages rather than pursuing a criminal sanction against the officer?

Other power relationships besides jailer and prisoner raise the implied duress issue. Some states have enacted statutes that permit the patient to recover, at least under some circumstances, for injury suffered as a result of sexual contact with a mental health professional, regardless of consent. *E.g.,* CAL.CIV.CODE

§ 43.93 (b) (if there is therapeutic deception); ILL. STAT. ch. 70 ¶ 802 § 2 (if the patient was emotionally dependent or the therapist practiced deception); On the kinds of harm inflicted by therapists who inflict sexual contacts upon patients and on the special power exercised by therapists, *see* Linda Jorgenson, Rebecca Randles, & Larry Strassburger, *The Furor over Psychotherapist-Patient Sexual Contact: New Solutions to an Old Problem*, 32 WM. & MARY L. REV. 645 (1991). The setting also implicates statute of limitations and professional malpractice issues. *See* Chapters 11 & 13.

Note 2. Employers. The power relationship problem arises in the context of employers as well. We might worry that an employee who is dependent on a particular job can't freely reject some sexual advances. Some students may raise the economic duress issue. In part of the *Reavis* case in the note, a plurality of the Nebraska court holds (by way of an approved instruction) that the employment relationship does not itself count as an implicit job threat that vitiates an otherwise apparent consent. Why not? It is easy to imagine that an employer's demand for sexual contact can put an employee under severe constraints. No employee, surely, should be forced to choose between a job, raise, or promotion on the one hand and having an adulterous affair on the other. Yet, how would you construct a reliable rule? Could you construct one that allowed full play to the actual desires of both parties, so that if both parties really did want to engage in a sexual relationship, they could do so? For those who believe that sexual relationships are wrong, period, this would not be a legitimate objective. But suppose instead of sexual contact it is a very chaste avowal of love and proposal of marriage. The constraints on the employee may be similar: a rejection may jeopardize the job or prospects for advancement. Should we have a per se rule that the employment relationship forbids the human relationship? A little later, (or now if you have assigned the *Payton v. Donner* Problem for coverage here), we can see a variations on this idea. A couple of pros and cons are suggested in connection with notes on that problem.

In addition to the consent issue, the problem might also involve statutes exist against sexual harassment. It seems appropriate to acknowledge the existence of statutes and to observe that the employer's conduct may well count as sexual harassment and hence discrimination under Title VII (and some state statutes).

FYI: welcome vs. voluntary: Title VII. Under Title VII, issues somewhat similar to issues of consent might arise, but the terminology and perhaps the substantive concepts are different. In a Title VII sexual harassment case in which the plaintiff employee claimed that she had sexual intercourse with her supervisor on numerous occasions, the Supreme Court recognized that the supervisor or employer might have a defense if the sexual advances were "welcome." At the same time, however, it said that "the fact that sex-related conduct was 'voluntary,' in the sense that the complainant was not forced to participate against her will, is not a defense to a sexual harassment suit brought under Title VII." *Meritor Savings Bank, FSB v. Vinson,* 477 U.S. 57 (1986).■

Notes 5-6. Minors. Some minors have a right to some abortions. The abortion decisions of the Supreme Court are grounded in "privacy," a non-constitutional word that seems in these cases to mean something very much like "self-determination," at least in the sexual sphere.

In evaluating the issue of consent to intercourse, the class might consider: (a) Some minors may fail to appreciate the moral, emotional or physical risks of sexual acts. (b) Regardless whether he is liable in tort, an unwed father is liable on a non-tort remedy for support of any child that results from intercourse. (c) If a minor who is a mature female can consent to abortion, and this is in fact a constitutional right of self-determination, why cannot a minor of either sex consent to intercourse for the same reason? One important difference between the intercourse situation and the abortion situation is that the minor's consent serves a very different legal function in the two cases. In the tort context involving consent to intercourse, the consent serves to relieve a tort liability of another person; in the abortion context, the minor's consent serves to achieve a goal of the minor herself.

Note 7. Incapacity to consent: adults. People who are incapable of handling their own business, taking care of themselves, paying bills and the like, may lack legal capacity for certain consensual transactions. In other cases, courts test capacity by asking whether the plaintiff could understand the nature and character of the act in question. *See* DOBBS ON TORTS § 98, pp. 225-226 (2000). The issues in the case may depend a great deal on the plaintiff's specific capacity and so may present issues of fact for the jury as in *Mallory*.

Where tort claim is equivalent to a contract rescission. Some cases of incapacity may call for a different answer. Those are cases in which tort liability is more or less equivalent to contract rescission. You might be justified in rescinding a deal and returning the parties to the status quo ante but not justified in imposing a loss on the defendant who has acted reasonably. Suppose the plaintiff is mentally incompetent but does not appear so. She contracts to and does sell her goods to the defendant. Under the normal rules of restitution, an incompetent person may avoid or rescind her purported contracts, even though the defendant was unaware of the incompetence at the time of contracting. On the facts supposed, it is possible that the plaintiff would sue in tort for conversion of the goods. The defendant would be liable for the value of the goods less the price he paid. Any why not? Financially speaking, the result described is the same result as avoidance of the contract. The defendant does not make his expected profit on the deal, but, transaction costs aside, he loses nothing. In this situation, it makes sense to hold that the plaintiff's consent is ineffective even though the plaintiff's incompetence is unknown to the defendant and undiscoverable by him. The formal tort liability is functionally merely a rescission.

ASHCRAFT V. KING, 278 Cal. Rptr. 900 (Ct. App. 1991)

Similar cases have proceeded on non-battery theories of informed consent or medical malpractice. *See Jeanne v. Hawkes Hospital of Mt. Carmel*, 598 N.E.2d 1174 (Ohio Ct. App.), *appeal dism'd*, 579 N.E.2d 210 (Ohio 1991). *See* Note 1 following *Kennedy*, infra.

The opinion does not explore the respective roles of doctor and hospital in providing or monitoring the blood, but seems instead to assume that the doctor, not the hospital, was responsible. What if the doctor had made arrangements with the hospital, which negligently provided the wrong blood? Would the doctor then be guilty of a battery?

If the doctor rather than the hospital is the responsible party, still another question arises. Does it matter *why* the patient wanted family-donated blood? The operation occurred at an unspecified date in 1983. At that time AIDS was well-known, but not everyone had drawn the connection between AIDS and blood. What if the patient had insisted on family-donated blood only because she had a a bizarre belief that blood of other donors would cause her to take on their physical characteristics? If the wrong-blood operation was a battery, it would surely still be one even if the patient's reasons for wanting family blood were ignorant or foolish. But it is not so clear that liability should extend to cover harms from AIDS if AIDS was not part of the harm the plaintiff sought to avoid by limiting her consent. Is there any place in the consent cases for a limitation on liability to reflect the limits of the plaintiff's demands? This point foreshadows the scope of risk or proximate cause issue covered in Chapter 8.

In *Ashcraft* itself, the defendant's argument was couched as an argument that conditions about "collateral matters" are irrelevant, or at least that their violation does not turn the operation into a battery. What if the patient said, "I consent to the operation only on condition that you wear a bow in your hair when you perform it." If the doctor did not wear a bow in her hair during the operation would the operation be a battery? Clearly enough the family blood condition is not collateral if it was imposed to make the operation safer from AIDS.

Exceeding the scope of conditional consent. The *Duncan v. Scottsdale Medical Imaging* holding reinforces for students the decision in *Ashcraft* on slightly different facts – in both cases, the plaintiff had expressly consented only to Procedure A, and the doctors performed Procedure B. This exceeds the scope of consent and is therefore a battery where other elements of that tort are established. *Peters* held that the uninformed consent was not effective to bar the claim.

KENNEDY V. PARROTT, 90 S.E.2d 754 (N.C. 1956)

The plaintiff consented to an appendectomy, nothing more. While she was on the operating table, the doctor discovered ovarian cysts, which he then dealt with in a medically proper way. Unfortunately, he cut a blood vessel and there were blood clots and complications. But the plaintiff showed no negligence and the claim here is for battery. The argument is that the consent did not extend to the cysts. The court takes the view that the surgeon should proceed to do what is medically best, in this case to puncture the cysts. The court thought that since new problems may be encountered in the operative field and the patient knows it, the patient has impliedly consented to the doctor's handling those problems. "[T]he consent . . . will be construed as general in nature and the surgeon may extend the operation to remedy any abnormal or diseased condition in the area of the original incision. . . ."

This raises a host of questions, perhaps more than you'll have time to pursue. Does the patient really understand she is consenting to any other operation? Does the doctor think the patient is impliedly consenting to such an extension? And suppose the doctor should foresee that cysts might be discovered. If personal autonomy is the basis for battery law, should the doctor not be required to secure consent for any likely extension of the operation? Is *Kennedy* contrary to *Ashcraft*? If *Kennedy* is right in principle, why doesn't the implied consent extend to whatever the doctor finds, whether in the area of incision or not? How did the patient manifest her implied consent in *Kennedy*–merely by agreeing to have an appendectomy? Do most women who consent to removal of an appendix would think they are consenting to sterilization. Might a doctor reasonably think they are consenting to his best medical judgment, whatever that is, including sterilization.

The central thread is personal autonomy. But justice to the doctor is an issue, too. If a doctor reasonably believes that consent is "general," should the doctor not be protected? One problem is that patients are likely to be different. An emotionally strong patient may want to decide for herself; an ill-educated and dependent person may wish the doctor to decide. Some patients will consider the possibilities, some not. Perhaps the best solution is to require the doctor to give as much information about prospective extension of the operation as possible. This leads into the informed consent issue.

Note 1. Emergencies. The court in *Miller* held that in an emergency situation, such as the one presented, a doctor does not commit a battery in giving treatment without parental consent or court intervention. This is an exception, the court said, to the usual rule that unconsented medical treatment is a battery. Surely policy concerns played a role here, don't you think?

In *Shine v. Vega,* 709 N.E.2d 58 (Mass. 1999), the defendant, an emergency room doctor, forcibly restrained and intubated a patient who was undergoing an asthma attack although she objected vigorously and her father, a doctor, begged him not to do so. The patient even tried to escape. She was traumatized by her treatment. The doctor, supported by a trial judge's instructions to the jury, argued that given an emergency, he had the right to override the patient's wishes. The Supreme Judicial Court of Massachusetts held the instructions to be erroneous and upheld the right of the patient to reject life saving treatment.

Note 2. Is *Kennedy v. Parrott* correct? The informed consent problem differs from *Kennedy*. In the informed consent case the patient consents to the very operation given, but consents without knowledge that it entails certain risks or that alternative safer procedures were available. This topic is considered in Chapter 13 (medical malpractice), and need not be developed in any detail here. However, one can argue that the risk of extending an operation because of new-found conditions is a "risk" of which the patient should be advised. Thus informed consent law might hold that a doctor who fails to advise a female patient that an appendectomy might lead to an operation on the ovaries would be liable for a battery, or at least for the harm done.

On the issue of having a different doctor perform a procedure see *Perna v. Pirozzi*, 457 A.2d 431 (N.J. 1983). This case involved a group medical practice. The doctors regarded the group itself as "the physician" and accordingly the doctor interviewed by the patient might not be the doctor who performed the operation. The patient, however, did not realize this. The court considered the operation to be a battery by the physician who actually performed the operation, since he was not authorized. The physician the patient had interviewed and thought would perform the operation might be liable on other grounds, but, since he did not touch the plaintiff, not on battery grounds.

Notes 3 & 4. Substituted consent. In *Harvey*, cited here, the court held it was a jury question whether the plaintiff had impliedly consented to allow his mother to give substituted consent on those facts. The doctor's testimony that the patient said in advance he might consider a transfusion was enough to create a contested issue of fact.

Grimes v. Kennedy Krieger Institute, Inc., also cited here, tells quite an unbelievable tale. Researchers (most connected with a research institution affiliated with Johns Hopkins) developed a study in which children would be exposed to different levels of lead dust to test its effects, although the researchers were fully aware that lead-bearing dust is particularly dangerous to children. The idea was to test different levels of lead abatement in low-cost rental housing to determine whether less (and hence cheaper) abatement would be sufficiently safe. Families recruited to rent lead-contaminated houses agreed in "consent" forms to allow periodic testing of the premises for lead and periodic testing of their children's blood for lead. In return, the families were paid small sums and received the lead reports. The children in the "study" had no preexisting medical conditions, but it was foreseeable that some of them would suffer from elevated lead in their blood. The study involved no medical treatment whatsoever; it was purely an experiment on human subjects. Two children who suffered elevated lead levels sued the researchers. The trial judge granted summary judgment to the defendants on "no duty" grounds, but the Maryland high court reversed and remanded, finding a duty of care. With respect to informed consent, the court held among other things that parents cannot effectively consent to experiments that may put their healthy children at risk. Furthermore, the consent in this case was not fully informed.

Note 5. Incompetence to give or withhold consent. Although doctors generally must act in accordance with an adult's desire to refuse treatment, there are some situations in which perhaps a doctor can disregard that refusal, as were the person is incompetent to make that decision.

DOE V. JOHNSON, 817 F.Supp. 1382 (W.D. Mich. 1993)

Can the plaintiff demonstrate intent to harm or offend, or is this only a negligence case? Some sexual disease cases have been pursued under a negligence theory. E.g., *S.A.V. v. K.G.V.*, 708 S.W.2d 651 (Mo. 1986) (spousal immunity abolished as to wife's claim against husband for negligently communicating sexual disease).

The plaintiff's best claim may be an that defendant intended an offensive touching, not a harmful one. The argument would be that the plaintiff did not consent and that the defendant knew it. The argument is based on the idea that the *nature* of the act was different from the one she consented it. To say this, you must say that intercourse with an HIV infected person, or with one who knows or suspects that he is infected, is essentially a different act from intercourse with a person who is not infected with that virus. Platonists in the class may find this easy; literal lawyers may not.

However, if the plaintiff did not give the appearance of consent (because Johnson knew she did not know his risky HIV status), then it seems right to find an intent to offend. The logic of saying that the claim is one for battery rather than one for negligence is that the plaintiff would be permitted to recover even if she were not infected. The consent having been vitiated by the fraud or basic mistake, the touching itself becomes an actionable battery.

Whether courts would actually so hold is another matter. When they perceived that this might be the result of the medical informed consent cases, they began to treat them in terms of negligence. Likewise, the female partner's representations of sterility or the like has not relieved the male of liability for child support because of the fraud. *See Welzenbach v. Powers,* 660 A.2d 1133 (N.H. 1995).

The judge seems to have focused, not on intent to commit an offensive touching but intent to commit a harmful one. That seems harder to support. It is not clear that the defendant knew he was infected. You can't find intent to harm based upon the argument that the defendant should have known the risk. But even assuming that defendant knew he had HIV, does that support an inference that he intended harm? Nothing indicates a purpose to harm. The judge suggested substantial certainty intent would take care of the problem, but the weakness of that idea is revealed in the judge's own language–the plaintiffs alleged, he said, that "defendant knew with 'substantial certainty' that he could transmit the HIV virus to Ms. Doe." The statement that he *could* do so is a statement that there was a risk. No matter how certain you are that a risk exists, it remains only a risk, not a certainty. The claim of intended offense, in spite of its peculiar structure, might be better than the claim of intended harm.

However, newspaper stories might fill in some of the blanks in the Magic Johnson case. Johnson claimed to have had sexual intercourse with thousands of women, making the substantial certainty issue a stronger possibility. See Robert Lipsyte, *Celebrate Magic, but There's More Work to Be Done*, N.Y. Times, Feb. 16, 1992, at §8, p.11. Other reports cite him as saying that those encounters were unprotected.

Note 4. Consent to crime. Courts use two distinct and opposite rules: (1) your consent to a crime is ineffective so that you can sue in spite of the consent; and (2) you can never found a claim on your own participation in an illegal act, i.e., your "consent" or participation bars your recovery. Both rules may be partly superseded by more precise analysis as to what counts as consent and by a recognition that the defendant may sometimes owe the plaintiff a duty of protection in spite of consent. Though the Restatement generally makes consent effective to bar the tort claim, it also recognizes an exception where plaintiff consents to acts that have been made criminal mainly to protect the plaintiff from her own consent. The note gives examples.

Coming back to autonomy: The principle behind battery and consent rules seems to be a principle of respect for each competent individual's right of bodily self-determination. If this idea has been lost in the forest of rules and situations, it may be worth while to reinject it. Suppose a woman will die unless her diseased leg is amputated. Suppose she is competent mentally, but refuses the amputation nonetheless. Could a court order the operation? Or appoint a guardian to consent? The principles we have discussed in terms of battery and consent answer this question if those principles are predicated upon a respect for personal self-determination. *See Lane v. Candura*, 376 N.E.2d 1232, 93 A.L.R.3d 59 (Mass. Ct. App. 1978) (competent patient can reject life-saving operation).

Connections: (a) The idea that the defendant might be obliged to protect people in spite of their consent surfaces again almost immediately in the *Payton v. Donner* Problem below. The idea is also the core idea behind *Bexiga* and related cases, where courts hold the defendant to a duty to protect the plaintiff from his own (contributory) negligence. See Chapter 9, § 5. (b) Related to the consent to crime issue, the idea that one cannot found a claim on his own wrongdoing arises in Chapter 9 § 3, Casebook 288-89.

PROBLEM: PAYTON V. DONNER

Connections forward: Sexual abuse by clergy acting as counselors is often pursued as a negligence claim (perhaps with insurance coverage or respondeat superior liability in mind). We'll see some of those situations in Chapter 13 on professional malpractice, and Chapter 19 on emotional harm.

The *Payton* problem presents a chance to review the rules and perhaps to draw some distinctions among three similar setting represented by Austin and Berwyn's candlelight dinner, by *Reavis v. Slominski,* and by *Payton* itself. It furnishes a chance to see if the student will be able to apply (or consciously reject) the consent-to-crime rule. You might ask students if, as lawyers, they would attempt to ascertain Lisa's age, a point that could raise the consent of minors rules. The doctor cannot very well claim apparent consent if he knows that the consent is coerced or if he knows that Lisa acts under an incapacity. More broadly, it may be that courts will refuse to permit the doctor to extract a consent against the patient's interest.

And what about those statutes giving a patient a claim against a psychotherapist for sexual contact injury? If they had no application at all in the employer case, do they nevertheless reflect a general policy from which the plaintiff could reason by analogy in the doctor case? Or do they have a negative impact because by allowing the claim in one setting they are implying that no claim exists against ordinary physicians or other people who abuse their power?

Payton raises some similar but perhaps not quite identical questions. In *Payton*, the doctor presumably knows that the patient's ability to withhold consent is compromised or nonexistent and must at least suspect that there is no real consent at all. In addition, in *Payton*, if we think of the parties as being in a doctor-patient relationship, then the doctor has undertaken to act in the plaintiff's best interests–something no one seems to claim about employers. If the professional undertakes to act in the client's best interest, he should not put himself in a conflict of interest position. So *Payton* might be a much easier case for liability in the eyes of a moderate judge.

But a cluster of common issues underlies *Payton v. Donner*, even if you end up resolving that issue differently in the two cases. One is whether the relationship itself is such that NO manifestation of consent should suffice to exculpate the dominant person. Put differently, should we hold that the activity itself is simply prohibited even if both parties wish to engage in it? The broader issue is whether we wish to (or can) protect the autonomy of individuals to choose for themselves. The right to choose is central to individual autonomy and personal development. Is that right compromised or diminished if we hold that an employee or patient cannot effectively consent to an act with an employer or a doctor? A vast gulf lies between the view that people of either gender must have the right to choose for themselves and the view that sex of employers and employees is inherently exploitive rather than potentially mutually fulfilling.

One problem in the discussion may be that it is usually specifically about sexual activity, a topic that apparently can generate mind-numbing chemicals. If sex gets in the way of good discussion, you might want to try the issues with hypotheticals in which the employer or the doctor seeks marriage, not immediate sexual activity. Or in which the employer or doctor seeks to purchase the employee's or patient's property.

Payton v. Donner is based on a decision of the Supreme Court of Canada in *Norberg v. Wynrib*, 92 D.L.R. 4th 449 (Can. 1992). The decision provides much more in the way of detailed facts that the problem does, but the problem is analytically very close to the case. If you or your class find it uncomfortable to discuss, you can simply report to the class the result or the result and the reasoning. The

Canadian Justices were divided about reasons for liability, but they agreed that liability was appropriate.

Consent and other torts. You may need to point out that consent would defeat other intentional tort claims, not only those based on battery theories. This could be developed by hypothetical if you preferred. Adam operates a "meditation therapy" business in which the client is locked in a dark room and floats on salt water of exactly body temperature. The idea is sensory deprivation. Bell, the patient, understands all this and is duly locked in. The attendant goes away and comes back at the end of the hour to find Adam clawing at the door. Adam has discovered he is claustrophobic. He has no claim for false imprisonment, having consented to the confinement. If you don't like fanciful hypotheticals, here is a simple one: A and B are on a yacht moored in the harbor. The yacht is out of fuel. A, who owns it, with B's agreement, takes the only boat and rows to land for gas, leaving B unable to get off. If B had agreed, there is no false imprisonment.

Deprogramming. Parents are concerned because their adult child has been, in their view, "indoctrinated" by a "cult." Does the child's consent or apparent consent to the cult's ways, preclude a claim by the child herself if she later "escapes"? Would parents have a privilege to "deprogram" the child against her will on the ground that her consent was void due to incapacity or fraud? *See Peterson v. Sorlien*, 299 N.W.2d 123, 11 A.L.R.4th 208 (1980) (parents have a privilege to detain their adult child for a deprogramming effort after she had been "indoctrinated" by a "cult").

§ 3. PRIVILEGES NOT BASED ON PLAINTIFF'S CONDUCT

SUMMARY

SUROCCO V. GEARY. The public official known as the Alcalde, in an effort to prevent the spread of fire throughout the city of San Francisco, blew up the plaintiff's house. The house would have burned in any event, but without the Alcalde's intervention, the plaintiff could have saved his goods. *Held*, as a matter of "natural law" the public officer must be permitted to act for public benefit without liability.

WEGNER V. MILWAUKEE MUT. INS. CO. In a case shortened for this edition of the casebook, a suspected felon entered the plaintiff's house. The police staked it out and attempted to persuade the man to surrender. Eventually the ERU or SWAT team fired chemical munitions into the house. This inflicted great damage to the plaintiff's house. *Held*, the public entity is liable for the damage done under a constitutional provision; public necessity is not defense.

PLOOF V. PUTNAM. The plaintiffs docked on the defendant's property to escape a serious storm, but defendant allegedly pushed the plaintiffs off, and the plaintiffs and their property were injured in the storm. The normal rule that gives the defendant a privilege to defend his property is suspended here because of the private necessity — which seems to have been entirely apparent to the defendant. And since the defendant was unprivileged, he was liable for the tort of casting the plaintiffs out.

VINCENT V. LAKE ERIE TRANSP. CO. The steamship had docked at the plaintiff's dock, apparently by agreement, but had completed its unloading. It did not leave, however, because of a storm that made leaving dangerous. Instead, it renewed the lines to the dock. This was justified because to do otherwise would have endangered ship and seamen, but it had the effect of dashing the ship against the dock repeatedly, with damage to the dock. Although the steamship was privileged because of the same necessity involved in *Ploof v. Putnam*, there was actual damage done and the court held that it had to be paid for.

COMMENTS

Necessity bears some resemblance to self-defense or defense of others but it differs enormously in one respect. If A attacks B, B's right to defend himself is self-defense, not necessity and it arises from appearances that A himself has some part in creating. In necessity cases, the A is *not* culpable in creating the danger to B; B claims a privilege to harm A's property interests by reason of events for which A is not responsible. Accordingly it is much more difficult in necessity cases to say that B should be privileged in any sense to harm A or A's property. Cases using "necessity" to refer to self-defense or defense of others are thus obscuring an important value. See *McMillan v. City of Jackson*, 701 So.2d 1105 (Miss. 1997) (discussing the case in terms of necessity but holding that abortion protestor had no privilege of necessity to trespass in the absence of an ongoing and illegal abortion).

SUROCCO V. GEARY, 3 Cal. 69 (1853).

A city official blows up the plaintiff's property in a well-meant effort to prevent the spread of a serious fire. Is the official liable? Because the casebook includes *Wegner*, which deals with liability of the public entity, you might postpone the discussion of public entity liability until you reach that case.

The plaintiff's house would have been destroyed by fire in any event, but the Alcalde's decision to blow it up prevented removal of the plaintiff's goods. Did the Alcalde intend to destroy them? Evidently so, at least under the substantial certainty definition of intent. Non-liability, then, turns on a privilege, not a failure in the prima facie case.

General rules. The general rule now accepted is that individuals are privileged to damage or destroy private property when public necessity demands. Public necessity differs from private necessity illustrated in *Vincent*. In the case of public necessity the privilege protects the actor even if actual harm is done, as it was in *Surocco*. The privilege would not be limited to official actors, as long as it is exercised for the public benefits. *See* RESTATEMENT (SECOND) OF TORTS § 196, cmt. *e.* The actor, whoever he is, must be reasonable in believing that the action was needed and the action he takes must be in reasonable response to the necessity. As with self defense, the privilege arises upon reasonable belief and thus protects the actor even though it later appears that no action was needed.

What aggregation of people could count as "the public" for this purpose can easily be considered in connection with the note on the school bus driver's dilemma following *Vincent*. The court's illustrations contains one that is suggestive: a tempest justifies throwing goods overboard to save the ship that carries them. Suppose an airline captain, during a flight, reasonably concludes that there is a bomb on board, probably in the luggage compartment and that he somehow has the ability to dump all luggage. If he dumps it and no contract provision controls, will he or the airline be liable to all passengers for the value of their luggage (up to the limits specified by the tariff)?

You can state these rules for the class or you can draw some of them out Socratically. If the case is an exemplar (and it is), then what does the necessity privilege look like? Who is the person benefitted? (The city. This is a public necessity case.) Did the defendant's destruction of the property do any good? (No; yet he still has the privilege. Perhaps in a sense there was no necessity for this action, since it proved useless. But reasonable mistake works in self-defense, and it seems to work here). What if the Alcalde had destroyed $ 1 million in property to save a city shed worth no more than $5,000? Most of the court's illustrations appear to contemplate a very substantial interest in the public, or a substantial group of people. The one example of private necessity (appropriation of a plank in a shipwreck, "though the life of another be sacrificed" is a case in which the actor has at least equal value at stake. So maybe the class could generate the idea that it would be unreasonable action to protect a $5,000 shed at the expense of $1 million of the plaintiff's property.

Natural law. The court reasons to the privilege by adverting to the "natural rights of man" and later to "natural law," which it says is adopted by the common law. Where is this to be found if you want to argue a case? Not in any text, of course. A traditional natural law idea is that one can perceive the nature of human beings, or the universe, and can deduce those "laws" which must accord with that nature. One idea is that people have basic desires to pursue perfection, and hence desires to exist. Preservation of existence is thus basic, and natural law will recognize this. These remote premises–or premises somewhat similar –seem to be what the court has in mind in *Surocco*. A natural law theorist might similarly deduce that there is a "natural law" against suicide (existence is required, suicide must be evil). The development of legal ideas from extremely remote and large premises probably does not characterize much judicial decision-making today. Perhaps one should notice that "natural law" is not merely an equivalent of "justice" or of "principled decision-making."

Three observations about the natural law premises: (1) The natural law premises just sketched do support the idea that you must be permitted to preserve existence, but why does the court think that you are free to do so without paying for the harm done? (2) Having justified the defendant on natural law grounds, the court then suggests toward the end of the opinion that the legislature should provide some mode of compensation–a rather clear recognition that "natural law" and "justice" need not be the same thing! (3) Mexico ceded California to the United States by the Treaty of Guadalupe Hidalgo. As it happened, that was nine days after gold was discovered in California. California became a state on September 9, 1850. The fire in *Surocco* occurred almost a year earlier, on Christmas Eve, 1849. What law should be applied? Perhaps it is not surprising in this political vacuum that the court urged natural law grounds for its decision and at the same time suggested that the new state should pass legislation.

WEGNER V. MILWAUKEE MUT. INS. CO., 479 N.W.2d 38 (Minn. 1992).

We have shortened this case substantially for this edition. The main effort in editing was to focus on the necessity issue rather than the question of a taking. Police engage in a shootout with fleeing felons who have holed up in the innocent plaintiffs' house. The plaintiffs sue the police for damages to their property, and win. The result is the exact opposite of the result in *Surocco*. Is that because judicial attitudes have changed and courts are no longer willing to make the individual suffer for the good of the community? Or is it because there is a specific legal text to aid the plaintiff, namely the Minnesota Constitution's taking clause? (When *Surocco* was decided, the Fourteenth Amendment's due process clause did not exist; when the events there occurred, the land was part of Mexico.)

Will any act of police count as a taking? Minnesota courts had held previously that the police might act in a proper way to destroy the *wrongdoer's* property without incurring liability for a taking. *See McGovern v. City of Minneapolis*, 480 N.W.2d 121 (Minn. App. 1992). Apart from that, taking might require either purpose or substantial certainty that property would be harmed and that the property be specifically identified. That would be the substantial certainty rule and although "taking" is theoretically quite different from the commission of a tort, the two in fact do not much differ. If some kind of substantial certainty or purposeful intent were required, maybe a collision that inflicts harm on an innocent person's car in the course of a high speed police chase would still not result in any liability. *See Cairl v. City of St. Paul*, 268 N.W.2d 908, 100 A.L.R.3d 807 (Minn. 1978).

Taking vs. destruction. Minnesota's constitution specifically requires payment for destruction as well as taking of property (see the Constitutional provision quoted in *Wegner*). The United States Constitution is not identical. In the well-known *Caltex* decision from the U.S. Supreme Court, the plaintiff's oil refinery in Manila was destroyed by the army to prevent its falling into the hands of the advancing enemy army. The plaintiff claimed compensation under the takings clause of the Fifth Amendment to the U.S. Constitution. The Court appeared to distinguish a taking for use and a mere destruction. The property "was destroyed, not appropriated for subsequent use." And its destruction was one of the "necessities of the war." *United States v. Caltex, Inc.*, 344 U.S. 149 (1952). Hence compensation, required for "takings," was denied.

In a slightly different context, Professor Christie supports the distinction between destruction and use. George Christie, *The Defense of Necessity Considered from the Legal and Moral Points of View,* 48 DUKE L.J. 975, 1007 (1999). Yet if you destroy something because it is advantageous to you that it be destroyed, destruction has utility or use-value for you. In this respect, use and destruction seem more alike than different. See *Thayer v. Boston*, 36 Mass. (19 Pick.) 511 (1837), which emphasizes "lawful benefit or advantage rather than "use."

Caltex's denial of compensation might be justified on other grounds. Had the facilities not been destroyed, the enemy army would have seized them and, would probably have destroyed the facilities when the fortunes of war were reversed to prevent the facilities returning to the United States. Thus the decision might be a sound one on grounds quite different from those given by the Court.

Professor Christie, drawing a radical distinction between private and public necessity, argues that public officials (not just anyone acting for the public benefit) "are charged with promoting common good" and have the authority to decide that some lives are more important than others and to sacrifice some of the lesser lives to save a larger number of others. Christie, supra, at 1027-28. Would that justify the government's nonpayment?

Note 2. Who pays as a policy matter? A number of courts have now aligned themselves with California's *Customer Company v. City of Sacramento,* cited here. It would be nice if a bright student recognizes the possibility that the constitutions of California and Minnesota might word their taking clauses differently. But in fact the California constitution, like Minnesota's, specified compensation for *damage to*, as well as *taking* of property. The California Court thought the provision should be limited to public improvements or public works. The rules of necessity ("the emergency exception") were thought to reinforce this conclusion. The opposite conclusions of the Minnesota and California courts suggests a basic difference in their conception of justice or grounds for a policy that overrides justice.

With some help from the teacher, students should be able to discuss these different approaches. One idea is that the defendant-governmental entity or the public it represents did benefit from the destruction. Why should the plaintiff bear all the costs of producing a benefit for the public?

Do students accept the idea that no individual should be singled out and forced to buy something of value for the public as a whole? If the answer is yes, then perhaps the *Caltex* and *Customer Company* decisions do not seem to represent just results, because it would not matter for this purpose whether the public's benefit was gained by destruction or taking.

Note 3. Scope of principle. At least to some readers, this note will suggest a practical reason not to extend liability as far as *Wegner* did. If we wish to make the public pay for benefits it takes by imposing losses upon private individuals, we will need to define benefit with caution.

Note 4. Insurance. The suggestion in this note that fire insurance might solve the problem is not unrelated to the discussion. Fire insurance is a form of loss sharing–large numbers of people contribute premiums, just as large numbers of people contribute taxes. In an ordinary city, most property will be insured for fire; the premiums will come from property owners, and, indirectly, from tenants. So government payment and fire insurance payments are both means of loss-sharing. But payment on tort principles, and after litigation, is more expensive than payment without litigation–which is the normal mode in cases of fire insurance. A fire insurance program might simply let every person insure his or her own property and ban all tort suits except for fires set maliciously. This solution would reach the same result as reached in *Surocco*.

PLOOF V. PUTNAM, 71 A. 188 (Vt. 1908)

The landowner's servant repels the plaintiff who attempts to land at the dock to escape a storm. The plaintiff and his family are injured as a result of being cast into the stormy waters. The landowner would ordinarily be privileged to use reasonable force to repel a trespasser. But this privilege is lost in the face of the plaintiff's superior privilege of necessity. This is "private necessity" without actual harm to the landowner. It will contrast with *Vincent,* a case of private necessity that inflicts actual harm.

VINCENT V. LAKE ERIE TRANSPORTATION CO., 124 N.W. 221 (Minn. 1910)

The defendant's vessel is tied to the plaintiff's dock pursuant to a proper agreement. When the cargo is unloaded, the normal course would be for the ship to cast off into Duluth harbor on Lake Superior. But a storm was rising and ordinary care dictated that the captain keep the ship at dock. He took active steps to do so, by renewing the lashings as they frayed. The wind cast the ship against the dock repeatedly, damaging the dock. The captain was not negligent, because his decision was reasonable with respect to all the risk–it would have been extremely dangerous to move into the storm. The easiest and most orthodox explanation for the liability imposed is that this was an intentional trespass to the dock, since the captain must have known to a substantial certainty that damage was being done. Although the court does not characterize the case as one of "trespass," it fits that mold under the substantial certainty test.

Another way to express the result in *Vincent* is to say the ship had a privilege based upon private necessity. That privilege allowed the ship to remain at the dock even though damage was certain. However, the privilege only functioned to protect against liability for technical, non-harmful trespass and (reading *Vincent* with *Ploof*) to eliminate the landowner's privilege to forcefully remove the ship.

This might be a good place to ask the class to outline the functions or effects that a private necessity privilege could conceivably have:

> 1. The defendant under a necessity may enter and remain without liability for a technical trespass that causes no physical harm. The landowner temporarily loses his purely possessory interests.
> 2. The landowner confronting a defendant who enters out of necessity loses his privilege to oust the trespasser.
> 3. The defendant is not liable even for actual harm. *Vincent* rejects this effect of a privilege. The *Vincent* privilege embodies the first two effects but not the third.

Professor Christie would distinguish life-saving from property saving in various ways, one of which would add a fourth privilege effect:

> 4. The defendant who destroys property to save human life does NOT owe compensation. *Vincent's* rule of liability would not apply to property-for-life cases. Christie, *supra* at 980.

Should the defendant be required to pay for the physical harm to the dockowner's property? The answer would be yes if this is a case of no privilege; the ship captain intentionally caused harm and that more than meets the usual test of liability for trespass. The answer would be yes also if there is a privilege but it has only the first two or *Ploof*-type effects. That privilege tells the dockowner that he may not resist and cast the ship adrift and also that he has no complaint if no physical harm is done, but that he may insist upon compensation for actual harm.

Aside from the argument that no privilege should be recognized at all, two major arguments might be advanced for imposing liability under a limited privilege. First, the *Vincent* court suggests an unjust enrichment rationale, that the ship was preserved at the expense of the dock, so that the ship should be liable regardless of intent or negligence. Second, Epstein has argued that one who chooses to engage in conduct gets the rewards of that conduct and must equally pay for the harms he does.

Unjust enrichment. If the defendant preserved the ship at the expense of the dock as the court suggests, liability for unjust enrichment (not fault) is appropriate. Unjust enrichment would be measured by the defendant's gains, not the plaintiff's losses. At least the plaintiff's gains would set an upper limit on liability.

If unjust enrichment really is the reason for liability, we must be sure what the defendant gained by damaging the dock. We cannot say that the defendant saved the value of the ship because we do not know that it would have been lost had the lines not been renewed. We know only that the defendant avoided a risk or chance of losing the ship. If you can quantify the risk, say one chance in 500 that the ship would go down if cast into the harbor, the value would be 1/500 the total value of the ship. That would be the enrichment gained from renewing the lines. You can imagine potential ship buyers lined up on the dock, bidding for the ship in the first case with knowledge it will be held fast to the dock and in the second with knowledge it will be put out in the harbor. The difference in the two bids will reflect the market value of minimizing the risk. Since we have no numbers suggesting that this enrichment approximates the $500 damage, it is hard to believe that unjust enrichment is really a basis for the liability imposed in *Vincent*.

Epstein: taking the sour with the sweet. Richard Epstein's way of thinking about *Vincent* seems more satisfying. He asserts that the defendant should "bear the costs of those injuries that he inflicts upon others as though they were injuries that he suffered himself." (This idea can be raised again with *Carroll Towing,* Chapter 6.) One who makes a decision to act will ordinarily enjoy the benefits of the decision, and should equally bear all the costs that decision imposes. *See* Richard Epstein, *A Theory of Strict Liability*, 2 J. LEG. STUDIES 151, 157-160 (1973). You could say that the problem of protecting a ship in a storm was the shipowner's problem not the dock owner's problem; whatever decision the shipowner makes about that problem, whether he benefits or not, should bring the shipowner both the benefits and the costs of the decision. This rationale would work even if, after damaging the dock, the ship were somehow to sink anyway. The unjust enrichment rationale, depending upon "preservation of the ship," or the value of the chance of preserving the ship at the expense of the dock, would leave us most uncomfortable in that setting. But Epstein's rationale would be comfortable here–it was the shipowner's problem, the shipowner's decision, the shipowner's potential benefit, and the shipowner's cost.

This suggests that there are at least some cases in which, after all, fault in the ordinary sense is not required. The captain did what was best, both socially speaking and for the shipowner. No matter how wise and right the captain's decision, it was his decision, and it is morally right that he (or the ship) should be strictly liable.

It may be true that those who intend to cause direct harm should be liable regardless of fault, but that does not necessarily mean they should be liable when they intend only to cause risks. Suppose that at the time the ship first docked, there was a storm brewing that might hit the area and might foreseeably lead to the damages done in *Vincent*. Mere risk of harm is not intent, even under the substantial certainty definition. Thus if the captain decided to dock knowing that a storm might strike, the ship would not automatically be liable for any damage done as a result of the decision to tie up. It might, as in *Vincent* itself, be liable for damages caused by later decisions to renew the lines, but if he did not renew them, liability would be judged by asking whether he was negligent in docking in the first place, not by saying he made a choice and must pay for all its consequences.

Note 1. *Vincent* and other cases. Is *Vincent* contrary to *Ploof*? No. The issue of the trespasser's liability did not arise in *Ploof*. It only recognized that the trespasser would be privileged in the sense that the landowner could not exercise his normal privilege of defending his possession. Perhaps *Ploof* assumed as well the privilege to enter without liability when no harm is done.

Is *Vincent* contrary to *Surocco*? Not if you accept the public-private necessity distinction, with liability in the latter case, not in the former. If the *Vincent* rationale is right, why would you accept a distinction between public and private necessity–at least in cases where the plaintiff sues the public entity? In either case, one person is made to bear the costs of a decision made by another. But see Christie's argument referenced above in the paragraph on Taking vs. Destruction.

Is *Vincent* contrary to *Van Camp v. McAfoos*? *Van Camp* told us that liability would not be imposed without fault; yet the captain by all accounts did the right thing in not allowing the ship to drift out into the storm. The simplest answer of all is that his motive was good and his heart was pure but he nevertheless intentionally damaged the dock and is thus a trespasser. Another answer (subject to doubt raised above) is that *Van Camp* was not addressing unjust enrichment and we will redress unjust enrichment (if any) regardless of fault. (Students can see this easily: if you pick up my book by a reasonable mistake and you are not at fault, you still must not be allowed to keep or sell my book; you must give it back or pay for it).

Note 2. The school bus driver's dilemma. Discussion of the school bus case is a good place to end. You can look at it as either a public or private necessity case and you can discuss it on both bases. It also helps tie the whole necessity doctrine to the emergency situation in negligence cases.

The Note 2 hypothetical is a horrible case that boggles the mind if you try to carry over ordinary legal rules. The bus driver is forced to choose which group of people she will kill (or "let die"). She herself is one of those saved by choosing to run into the two children waiting, so you could look at this very readily as a private necessity case, since the decision-maker gains from the decision. In this respect it differs from *Surocco*, where the Alcalde might not have gained personally in any identifiable way. Looking at the fact that there is a bus load of school children saved, however, it looks more like public necessity, which, according to *Surocco* is a no-liability situation.

Should the necessity rules even apply to life-saving, death-dealing situations like this? What would have happened if the driver had made the opposite decision and the bus full of children had been killed? Their parents might have had claims against the driver's estate or the school district. Would the two children "saved" by this action be liable? Notice that in this variation of the hypothetical, the saved children did not participate in the decision. Although their lives are saved because the choice is to run off the cliff instead of into the children, they did not make the choice. Nor could the driver be said to be their agent for making such a decision in the way the Alcalde might have been the agent for the city of San Francisco.

Philosophers have worked over variations on similar facts at great length. Christie, supra, reviews some other philosophers. Relying heavily on a nonfeasance-misfeasance or "killing and letting die" distinction, he concludes that a private person has no privilege to kill some in order to save a larger number.

With limited time you might have to have very limited expectations is discussing this problem. When you are finished, you can inject the question whether the driver would be negligent in any of the choices she might make? This will take you directly into the negligence chapter and very soon to the emergency doctrine.

Note 3. Contractual rights. The parties are free to allocate their respective duties by contract. If the parties want to, they can bargain around the legal rule. For example, if the parties agreed that the dock owner would bear the costs of damage to the dock, the dock owner might agree to indemnify the ship owner for any damages incurred. The baseline rule only applies absent a valid contract displacing it.

Florida, which has many marinas, boats, and hurricanes in a turbulent mix, actually has a statute providing a privilege to boat owners to remain tied up in a marina after a hurricane notice, even if the marina owner asks them to depart. This has been interpreted by one court as eliminating any duty to remove the boats and hence as eliminating any liability for damages to the docks and equipment resulting when a hurricane strikes. *Burklow & Assocs., Inc. v. Belcher,* 719 So.2d 31(Fla. 1998). The statute does not specifically address the question of renewing the lines.

Note 4. An economic perspective. Consistent with **Note 3**, this a good case for talking about parties bargaining around the legal rule. With which rule—dock owner pays or ship owner pays—will the parties reach the efficient result. With bargaining, the parties might well reach the efficient result regardless of the legal rule. However, the legal rule might matter to the distribution of wealth between the parties. In addition, bargaining to reach the efficient result may not be possible if transaction and information costs are too high.

CHAPTER 5

DUTY

▶**Changes in the Sixth Edition:** We've added two new primary cases, *Bjorndal v. Weitman* (in §3), and *O'Guin v. Bingham County* (in §4), and Notes contain over a dozen new citations to recent cases. We've also changed slightly the order of presentation of some material in §3, as further explained below.

To make way for new material, and to streamline coverage, we've deleted four primary cases that appeared in the Fifth Edition: *Wilson v. Sibert* in § 2 (for which *Bjorndal* substitutes on the emergency doctrine); *Roman v. Estate of Gobbo* in §3 (now covered in a Note); and *Rains v. Bend in the River* and *Wright v. Brown* in §4 on negligence per se (their essential points being covered by *O'Guin* and new Notes).

▶The **Concise Edition** contains a number of cuts, as follows: In § 1, we edited the Holmes excerpt in several places. In § 2 we cut subpart B, Assessing Responsibility. In § 3 we edited the *Stewart v. Motts* case (it is still there, but shorter); cut Note 1 after *Shepherd* and renumbered the Notes; and cut Notes 5 and 7 after *Creasy v. Rusk*. In § 4 we edited portions of the *O'Guin* case and some of the materials in Notes; and we cut the *Lind v. Maigret* Problem.∎

Subchapter A. The Fault Basis of Liability

§1. NEGLIGENCE AND FAULT

OLIVER WENDELL HOLMES, THE COMMON LAW

This short passage is an introduction intended to propel us into negligence law. It is not intended as a piece for extended discussion.

If fault is the basis for liability, then people who are not faulty should not be liable for the harms they cause. We are back to *Van Camp v. McAfoos*, the first case in the book. But now we can use the idea to foreshadow things to come. If fault is the basis of liability, should liability always be imposed for fault?

One idea in the Holmes passage, one he rejects, is a social response to injury. If the defendant causes injury without fault, he should not be liable; but does that mean that a social response is equally inappropriate? Could society not agree (through legislation) that innocently caused injuries would be compensated through an injury fund to which we all contribute? Or should we think of injury innocently inflicted by a person as no different from an injury inflicted through a force of nature? You can let the class comment on these ideas or merely raise them as questions that will recur from time to time.

You can also use these questions and ideas either to foreshadow alternative compensation systems if you intend to cover Chapters 28-30, or to bring in an example here if you are not going to cover that material. Maybe the least time-consuming examples would be the Vaccine Act and the September 11 Compensation scheme. On both of these, see Casebook 953-956.

§ 2. INSTITUTIONS AND ELEMENTS OF NEGLIGENCE

A. Some Institutions of Negligence Practice

This is a short text but an important one. We must evaluate what we encounter in negligence law in the light of three practical institutions –the contingent fee, which is necessary if all injured people are to have representation, liability insurance with its policy limits, and settlement as the predominant means of resolution of tort disputes. We emphasize that in reaching a settlement amount, lawyers must evaluate legal rules and how they would apply. Memorization of rules will help not at all.

B. Assessing Responsibility

Overviews usually don't work very well, but the text of this subsection may at least help students realize that what comes next requires analysis and care. The overview here is also the foundation for a statement of the elements of the negligence case in the next subsection.

C. The General Formula for Negligence Cases

We put these elements on the board for emphasis. We don't want to encourage students to be naive and mechanical. To know these elements is not to resolve cases. The elements are rather guideposts about where we are in the journey through analysis of a negligence cases. They remind us of the issue we are trying to decide and the kind of evidence we need. Sometimes they carry warnings, too. If an issue is about duty rather than breach or negligence, judges, not juries, will make the governing decisions.

Our experience is that students have not learned to judge rules and statements in context of legal issues. Consequently frequent recurrence to the duty-breach-cause elements is desirable as a means of forcing students to recognize what is in issue in any given discussion. We come back to this list repeatedly, just as we remind students of the section's name or topic when they lose track.

Subchapter B. Duty and Breach

§ 3. THE GENERAL DUTY OF CARE

Scheduling omissions: If you must omit materials, you might try dropping *Creasy v. Rusk*. (Instead of case discussion, use hypotheticals, compare *Robinson*, and hark back to parallel materials on the liability of the mentally infirm in Chapter 3.)

Preliminary Note:

Standard and duty. "Standard of care" is a way of referring to the nature or extent of duty owed. With exceptions we'll see in special situations (landowners, for example), the duty is to behave as a reasonable and prudent person with respect to risks of harm to others. The duty is also expressed as a duty to use ordinary care or due care or reasonable care, all meaning the same. The duty of reasonable care requires one to recognize risks or dangers a reasonable person would recognize and to act to minimize those risks in the way a reasonable and prudent person would act. To recognize a risk now is to foresee possible harm in the future, so the language of risk and the language of foreseeability deal with the same problem.

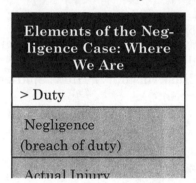

Perception and action on risk. The standard of care formula compares the actor to the reasonable and prudent person in two ways. First it asks whether the reasonable person would have recognized a risk of harm. Second it asks what a reasonable person would have done to avoid or minimize the risk. The actor's conduct is judged against that of the hypothetical reasonable person on both counts, perceiving risk and acting upon it.

Adjudication of particular facts vs. rules of law. Law must have rules but must also be flexible enough to deal with the peculiar realities of particular cases. The reasonable person standard is "objective" –it does not purport to take into account the personal or subjective foolishness of the actor, for example. Yet no legal system will work without some adaptability to circumstances. The rule, then, is "reasonable person under the circumstances," and the cases explore what we mean by "circumstances."

The first case, *Stewart v. Motts*, sets up the standard of care as a constant standard. The standard remains the same regardless of danger, but in referring to that standard we can see that it may call for greater care when danger is greater. The second case, *Bjorndal v. Weitman*, arises in an emergency context but its main point is again that the standard of care does not change with circumstances – the standard itself already takes circumstances into account. In this case, the circumstances are external to the actor. The next cases deal with "circumstances" that are more difficult– those arising because of special characteristics of the actor himself– physical characteristics (*Shepherd*), insanity (*Creasy*), special ability or experience (*Hill*), and childhood (*Robinson* and *Hudson-Connor*). These cases show considerable flexibility–enough that you may wonder whether there really is an "objective" or reasonable person standard.

SUMMARY

§ 3. THE GENERAL DUTY OF CARE: THE PRUDENT PERSON STANDARD

STEWART V. MOTTS. Motts was working with gasoline in repairing a car's fuel tank and directing the plaintiff, who was assisting him. An explosion occurred and the plaintiff suffered severe gasoline burns. The plaintiff requested an instruction on the special care required in working with flammable or especially dangerous substances. The judge rejected any such instruction and the jury found for the defendant. *Held,* affirmed. The standard of care remains the same even when danger is great. At the same time, the defendant must exercise a degree of care that is commensurate with the high danger.

BJORNDAL V. WEITMAN. Defendant caused an auto accident in which plaintiff was injured. Defendant claimed that the accident was caused by plaintiff's sudden deceleration; at trial Defendant sought and the jury was given an "emergency instruction." After a defense verdict, plaintiff appealed, claiming that giving the instruction was error. The court held that the emergency instruction "as used in ordinary vehicle negligence cases, is an inaccurate and confusing supplement to the instructions on the law of negligence, and, therefore, should not be given." The case allows the class to draw important points about the roles of judge and jury in negligence cases and helps flesh out what "taking into account external circumstances" might mean in the basic standard of care.

SHEPHERD V. GARDNER WHOLESALE, INC. This case shows how the reasonable and prudent person standard takes account of the physical limitations of the actual actor in the case. In *Shepherd*, the actor has cataracts. The case sets up an opportunity to compare the law's treatment of physical limitations (which are taken into account) with mental limitations (which are not), as discussed in the next case.

CREASY V. RUSK. An agitated and combative Alzheimer's patient kicked and hurt the nursing assistant working with him. She sued him. The trial judge granted summary judgment for the defendant but the intermediate court reversed, saying that mental capacity had to be "factored in." *Held,* a person with mental disability is generally subject to the same standard of care as a reasonable person under the circumstances; but in this case, the caretaker had no claim, for the duty runs from caretaker to patient, not the other way around.

HILL V. SPARKS. A machinery operator who knew more about machinery than ordinary persons was held liable for negligent operation, partly because, given his expert knowledge, a jury could find he failed to exercise ordinary care. An actor is held to the standard of care of a reasonable person with any actual, superior knowledge or training that the actor actually has, on a theory that a reasonable person would use all of the knowledge and training they possess. The standard of care does not change, but the higher knowledge is taken into account.

ROBINSON V. LINDSAY. What is the standard for minors? The general rule is that a child is held to the standard of care of a reasonably careful child of the same age, intelligence, and experience. This may be seen as a separate standard of care rather than merely a "circumstances" conception. The case discusses the basic child standard and a major exception, adopting the rule that a minor is held to the adult standard of care when the minor is operating "powerful mechanized vehicles."

HUDSON-CONNOR V. PUTNEY. A golf cart with a maximum speed of 12 m.p.h. is not inherently dangerous, and no evidence showed it required adult skills or was an adult activity. The adult standard is therefore rejected.

COMMENTS

§ 3. THE GENERAL DUTY OF DUE CARE: THE PRUDENT PERSON STANDARD

Dobbs on Torts. This quote states the duty owed in the vast majority of cases: the duty of reasonable care, defined as the care a reasonable person would exercise under the same or similar circumstances. It also connects the reasonable person standard to foreseeability. Teachers know that foreseeability might be part of the analysis of duty, part of the analysis of negligence, or part of the analysis of proximate cause. But students don't need to encounter proximate cause or duty issues beyond the duty of reasonable care yet, so we can postpone the confusions resulting from this multiple use of foreseeability.

Other problems with foreseeability may require explanations, however. Holmes told us correctly that the defendant is liable only if a reasonable person in the circumstances would have foreseen harm resulting from his acts. But foreseeability of harm is not enough for liability. The defendant is not liable unless a reasonable person would have foreseen harm and would also have conducted himself more safely in light of that foreseeable harm.

This idea deserves a little expansion because foreseeability language can lead to errors in analysis. In a sense all harms are foreseeable if you think about them enough, but courts seem to mean that a harm or risk is unforeseeable if it is "too unusual, too uncertain, too unreckonable to make it feasible or worthwhile to take precautions against. . . ." *Edwards v. Honeywell, Inc.*, 50 F.3d 484, 491 (7th Cir. 1995). This means that some harms might be literally foreseeable but still so unlikely to come about that reasonable people would not take precautions. The legal standard demands that the defendant take precautions about foreseeable harms only when reasonable persons would do so.

Sometimes judges speak of one thing as more foreseeable than another, as if foreseeability were a murky analysis of some cognitive psychology. But that isn't the point at all. "To say that an injury is not 'foreseeable' is simply to say that the probability of loss is low. . ." *Reardon v. Peoria & Pekin Union Railway Co.*, 26 F.3d 52 (7th Cir. 1994). In other words, forseeability is sometimes a way of speaking of risk. A judge who says that X is more or less foreseeable is saying that the risk a reasonable person would perceive is greater or smaller.

You may or may not want to add a caution at this point–there are other standards besides the reasonable person or ordinary care standard. Sometimes defendants owe no duty at all. But these are special cases. For cases like ordinary auto accidents, we can confidently say that the ordinary care standard is the one to be applied.

[1] Circumstances External to Actor

STEWART V. MOTTS, 654 A.2d 535 (Pa. 1995)

Teaching goals. We would use this case to: (1) emphasize the unchanging standard of care; (2) show that circumstances, including increased danger, count in determining negligence, even though the standard remains constant; (3) pursue briefly the technical side–the offer of an erroneous instruction (that was also badly written); (4) point out that courts sometimes reconstruct or reinterpret precedent as the court did here; and (5) note the jury's role by discussing the trial judge's correct instruction to the jury: "It is for you to determine how a reasonably prudent person would act in those circumstances." The case also sets up the discussion in the next case.

The unchanging standard and commensurate care. Unfortunately, we don't know exactly what the plaintiff claims as the negligent act in this case. Perhaps he claimed that the defendant turned the key while the plaintiff was still pouring gasoline. Students should not get sidetracked on this point. It is not the issue. The court takes the case as the lawyers present it. The defendant, having won below, is of course not arguing about the sufficiency of the evidence and neither should we.

The main point of this case is that the standard of the reasonable person remains the same whether danger is great or small. On the other hand, the defendant must exercise a greater degree of care when danger is greater. Many students find these two statements puzzling or contradictory. But they can be sensibly understood if you carefully segregate the *standard* of care from the *degree* of care. The standard is like a yardstick. Suppose you measure the space available for a new desk. Using the yardstick, you find you have exactly 30 inches available. You then measure the desk you hope to buy and find it is 34 inches. You used the same yardstick, but that yardstick reports different numbers depending of what you are measuring. Similarly, you use the same standard of care, but the amount of care required will vary just as the yardstick's measurements vary.

A good judicial statement is this one from *First Assembly of God, Inc. v. Texas Utilities Elec. Co.,* 52 S.W.3d 482 (Tex. App. 2001): "[A] public utility has a duty to exercise ordinary and reasonable care, but the degree of care required must be commensurate with the danger. This 'commensurate with the danger' standard does not impose a higher duty of care; rather, it more fully defines what is ordinary care under the facts presented."

Another way to approach this if students have difficulty is to ask them to identify some standard different from the reasonable person standard. Consider this pair:

Reasonable person (who exercises a reasonable amount of care)
An extraordinarily cautious person (who exercises more care than is reasonable, say the utmost care)

When we say the standard remains the same, we are rejecting variations like "extraordinarily cautious" as well as lesser standards. But in rejecting a *standard* of extraordinary caution we are only choosing the yardstick, not performing the measurement. Once we have selected reasonable person as the yardstick, we still have to ask what that reasonable person would do under the circumstances. Would he provide 30 inches of care or 34 inches of care in the dangerous circumstances? The reasonable person would ordinarily provide more care when danger increases, but that does not change the standard; we still judge by what the reasonable person would do when confronted with that particular danger.

Many ordinary decisions in life are similar, though they are not about danger. You eat vegetables each week. You could buy whatever you felt like at the moment you shop, or always buy yellow squash, or you could set a kind of rule or standard:

Standard	Application
buy whatever vegetable is freshest	Week 1: buy broccoli (it is freshest)
	Week 2: buy peas (they are freshest)

If you use the "freshest" standard, that *standard* does not change merely because the grocer has a lot of squash. But, to finish the analogy, although you adhere to your freshest standard, you will still have to estimate freshness, just as, under the reasonable person standard, we must estimate what a reasonable person would do to avoid injury to others. If vegetables are too domestic for your class, try music CDs with a plan to buy one a month, say, whichever is tops on the charts that you don't already have. If your students do computer programming, you can try explaining standards as variables, which always requires the input of other information for their application–freshest, tops in the charts, or in the case of negligence, "circumstances."

The instruction. The technical side of this case is that the plaintiff asked the judge to instruct the jury on the effect of high danger and the judge refused. When the jury found for the defendant, the plaintiff appealed, in effect saying that the jury might have found for the plaintiff if it had been given the requested instruction. This raises the question whether the instruction was a correct statement of law. The jury could have understood it to say that once the defendant knows the danger, he is obliged to use a high degree of care. That, we learn, is an incorrect statement of law and thus erroneous. Hence the judge was correct in refusing to give the instruction.

Contributory negligence. As the *Stewart* court mentions application of the same principle in contributory negligence cases, you may wish to make a statement to the effect that negligence of a plaintiff is "contributory negligence," that contributory negligence might bar the plaintiff or reduce her damages, and that, in general, negligence of a plaintiff is judged by the same standards as those used to judge a defendant's negligence. Other places to raise this point might be with your coverage of *Shepherd* or *Robinson* below.

FYI: Instructions: formulating the standard. The simplest statement of the standard is that it requires conduct of a reasonable and prudent person or a "reasonably prudent person" under the same or similar circumstances. E.g., *Mansfield v. Circle K Corp.*, 877 P.2d. 1130 (Okla. 1994). An older locution is derived from *Blyth v. Birmingham Waterworks Co.*, 11 Ex. 781, 156 Eng. Rep. 1047 (1856): "Negligence is the omission to do something which a reasonable man, guided upon those considerations which ordinarily regulate the conduct of human affairs, would do, or doing something which a prudent and reasonable man would not do." A contemporary example of that form is found in *Hearon v. May*, 540 N.W.2d. 124 (Neb. 1995). This kind of language is often combined with both the reasonable person, due care, or ordinary care language in a single instruction. E.g., *Caliri v. State Dept. of Transportation*, 620 A.2d 1028 (N.H. 1993) (quoting New Hampshire's standard negligence instruction).

Sometimes instructions speak of the "*ordinarily* prudent person" rather than the *ordinary* prudent person. A large number of courts have actually used this phrase. As to the courts' general failure to instruct in terms of the *Carroll Towing* risk-utility formula, see the notes to *Carroll Towing*, § 3 below. ■

Precedent. Pennsylvania precedent is largely omitted here, but we do learn that the court had previously referred to a higher degree of care in special danger cases. That sounds as if it had accepted a standard of "high care" or something of the kind in those cases. Yet it rejects such a rule here and accounts for its precedent by saying:

> When we referred to a "higher degree of care" in these cases, we were not creating a second tier of "extraordinary care" over and above ordinary or reasonable care. Instead, we were simply recognizing the general principle that under the reasonable care standard, the level of care must be proportionate to the danger involved.

Does the class think this case offers lessons in the use of precedent?

Note 1 simply restates the basic rule before the Notes that follow raise some complications.

Notes 2 & 3. Orthodoxy and departures from it. Note 2 asks students to be sure they understand the distinction between the invariant standard and the variable circumstances. If they fail to grasp the distinction, Note 3 will add confusion, so feedback and careful navigation may be required of the teacher here.

Purtle v. Shelton reinforces the single standard approach, but adds the possibility that counsel can argue to the jury the amount of care (not the standard). Counsel can argue, consistent with the *Stewart-Purtle* single standard, that the reasonable person would use extraordinary caution in handling firearms, but cannot properly argue that the standard itself is anything but the reasonable person standard.

In *Whaley v. White Consolidated Ind., Inc.*, 548 S.E.2d 177 (N.C. App. 2001), the defendant negligently caused high voltage burns to the plaintiff. The defendant argued contributory fault as a defense and asked the judge to instruct the jury that the plaintiff was under a "heightened standard of care" requiring "utmost diligence." The trial judge rejected this instruction and told the jury that "[a] person is under a duty to use ordinary care to protect himself and others from injury. Ordinary care means that degree of care which a reasonable and prudent person would use under the same or similar circumstances to protect himself and others from injury." The jury found for the plaintiff and the defendant attacked the instruction on appeal. The court held that the instruction was not error, saying that "the standard of care does not vary. The standard is *always* the rule of the prudent man, or the care which a prudent man ought to use under like circumstances. What reasonable care is, of course, varies in different cases and in the presence of different conditions. The standard is due care, and due care means commensurate care under the circumstances.'"

We wish cases like *Wood* did not exist, but as they do, we think they must learn to cope with decisions that depart from the theory, that use confusing shorthand expressions, and that are sometimes even confused. Courts like the *Wood v. Groh* court are in fact departing from the theory advanced in *Stewart*. *Wood* is not alone, of course. "When the defendant confronts heightened danger, it is easier to say that he must exercise the highest care than to explain the full meaning of the reasonable person standard. Perhaps for this reason, courts have often said they required the utmost care, or extraordinary care, or the highest care when it comes to handling a firearm, or supplying gas or electricity. Opinions that speak in such language probably mean only what has already been said, that the defendant must act as a reasonable person under the circumstances and that a reasonable person will normally conduct himself in accordance with the dangers reasonably to be perceived." DOBBS ON TORTS § 128, at 303 (2000).

Note 4. Judge and jury. This note anticipates a major issue presented by the next set of materials: Why does it matter whether the standard itself changes as the danger (or the situation) changes, as opposed to leaving it to the jury to decide whether the defendant behaved reasonably after being instructed more generally on the standard of care? Students should begin to notice that the reasonable person standard in fact has little or no detailed content. If reasonable people can differ, then the jury must decide what is reasonable care under the circumstances. The judge may overstep her bounds in highlighting particular circumstances that should be considered (as with "emergency" instructions), let alone in changing the very standard itself from the general reasonable person standard.

BJORNDAL V. WEITMAN, 184 P.3d 1115 (Or. 2008)

Defendant caused an auto accident in which plaintiff was injured. Defendant claimed that the accident was caused by plaintiff's sudden deceleration; at trial Defendant sought and the jury was given an "emergency instruction," quoted in the case. After a defense verdict, plaintiff appealed, claiming that giving the instruction was prejudicial error. The court held that the emergency instruction "as used in ordinary vehicle negligence cases, is an inaccurate and confusing supplement to the instructions on the law of negligence, and, therefore, should not be given." The case allows the class to draw important points about the roles of judge and jury in negligence cases and helps flesh out what "taking into account external circumstances" might mean in the basic standard of care.

The emergency is merely one instance of "circumstances" in which an actor's care is evaluated. The main idea to be derived from the case is the wider principle that everyone is ordinarily held to the *same* standard– the care of the reasonable prudent person under similar circumstances, often called the "due care," or the "reasonable person" standard.

The objective or "rigid" standard illustrated. The standard is objective. This implies the rule, recognized since *Vaughan v. Menlove*, 3 Bing. (N.C.) 467, 132 Eng. Rep. 490 (C.P. 1837), that if a defendant were hasty, awkward and nervous, not very smart or quick, these qualities would not change the kind of care we would demand of him. You can present *Vaughan* by some simple hypothetical – a not-so-bright person who stores rags, gasoline and paint thinner in his garage and who thus unwittingly causes a fire. Students believe he is held to the same standard and you can affirm it and move right along.

The flexible standard seen through the emergency rule. You can begin with the "flexible" side of the standard, exemplified here by the emergency rule. Emergency can be found either when some unforeseeable event arguably occurs to create a new risk, as in *Bjorndal*, or when the actor himself suddenly becomes incapacitated. The standard is that of the reasonable person, but with the qualification – "under the circumstances." Emergency, not created by the actor, is one of the circumstances. A reasonable person may act with less perception, less balance, less foresight, when she is thrust into an emergent situation than when there is time to think. The standard, however, remains that of the reasonable person, although it is the reasonable person whose judgment is diminished by the circumstance of emergency.

Connection forward: internal emergency of sudden incapacity. Note 6 on page 116 (after *Shepherd*), deals with a sudden physical incapacity; the rule there is that a person who causes an accident due to an unforeseeable physical incapacitation, such as a heart attack, should not be liable. You could mention that Note here, or save it in connection with the physical characteristics materials coming up next.

Notes 1 & 2. Ideally, the emergency doctrine is consistent with the reasonable care rule; it merely recognizes that emergency is one of the circumstances and requires reasonable care in the light of those circumstances. *See Caristo v.*

Sanzone, 750 N.E.2d 36 (N.Y. 2001). This is the usual understanding: emergency is merely a fact to be considered along with others in determining negligence. *Kreidt v. Burlington Northern R.R.,* 615 N.W.2d 153 (N.D. 2000). However, some courts may hold a different view or may be quite loose with language. In *Hargrove v. McGinley,* 766 A.2d 587 (Me. 2001), the court said that under Maine's emergency doctrine, the defendant is not held to the same *standard* of care. (The plaintiff objected to the instruction, but not on the ground that the rule was erroneously expressed.)

Other conceptions sometimes crop up, but the dominant view is clearly the one set forth in *Bjorndal. See, e.g., Totsky v. Riteway Bus Serv., Inc.,* 607 N.W.2d 637 (Wis. 2000) (speaking of emergency as an "excuse" for negligence already established).

The fact of emergency remains relevant, then, to a case and could be used in the ways suggested in **Note 2**, even in a state that has disapproved separate jury instructions. In those states, the judge still instructs that the standard is reasonable care under the circumstances. The defendant can still argue to the jury that he exercised reasonable care under the circumstances, that is, reasonable care in light of the emergency.

Notes 3 & 4. Rejecting emergency instructions. Several courts have rejected the emergency instruction or have expressed concerns about its use. *See* DOBBS ON TORTS § 131 (2000). These courts typically reiterate that the general reasonable person standard adequately allows a jury to take account of the external circumstances, including an "emergency," and that separate instructions are redundant, confusing and unduly prejudicial to plaintiffs. *Willis* was an automobile crash case in which the plaintiff was rear-ended at a stop light; the court expressly rejected the notion that "sudden emergency" was an affirmative defense.

Note 5. Defining emergency. Cases usually define "emergency" much as the *Herr* court here does. Note that it is never an "emergency" if it's a situation that is either foreseeable or created by the party seeking the instruction. The court in *Willis,* cited in Note 4 above, said that a party seeking a sudden emergency instruction must show (1) that he did not create the emergency through this own negligence; (2) that the danger was so imminent as to leave no time for deliberation, and (3) that the party's perception of the danger was reasonable. In *Herr v. Wheeler,* cited here, the defendant's car "hydroplaned" during a rainstorm, crossed the center line of the highway and crashed into plaintiff's car. The defendant sought to rely on the "defense of sudden emergency." The trial judge gave a sudden emergency instruction and the jury found for defendant. Reversing, the Virginia Supreme Court held the instruction was error because "the occurrence of standing water on a roadway during a heavy rainstorm" is not an "unexpected happening." Rather, it is a foreseeable circumstance that a person "must anticipate and exercise reasonable care to avoid." Furthermore, the court said, the real issue in the case for the jury was whether the defendant "exercised reasonable care under the circumstances," not whether the event was some "unexpected happening." Thus the instruction was both unnecessary and prejudicial.

Similarly, if you have encountered a patch of ice on the road, you cannot very well claim that you faced an unforeseeable condition (an emergency) when you encounter ice again a few minutes later. *See Caristo v. Sanzone,* 750 N.E.2d 36 (N.Y. 2001). Beyond this, some dangers are foreseeable even if you have no specific notice that they are imminent. *Beyer v. Todd,* 601 N.W.2d 35 (Iowa 1999), held that although "Todd was forced to take immediate action in response to the vehicles stopping in front of him, . . . such an event does not qualify as an emergency" because the need for sudden stops in traffic is foreseeable, the very thing drivers should be on guard about. However, although you might think that sudden stops are foreseeable, *Hargrove v. McGinley,* 766 A.2d 587 (Me. 2001), approved use of the emergency instruction favoring the last driver in a line of cars; she failed to stop when the car ahead suddenly stopped. *Hargrove* gives no reason why the need to stop quickly would not always be foreseeable, but you can imagine that need for a sudden stop might be precipitated by a series of events that create an emergency, as perhaps was the case in *Bettis v. Thornton,* 662 So.2d 256 (Ala. 1995), in which an unknown driver changed lanes to come immediately in front of the plaintiff, then went back to his original lane, revealing the plaintiff's stopping car immediate ahead.

Note 6. Unavoidable accident instructions. The unavoidable accident instruction is comparable to the emergency instruction in that it, too, emphasizes a particular instance of the reasonable care standard and does so from the defendant's viewpoint. Here again, courts and pattern jury instructions seem increasingly to disapprove or counsel caution in giving such instructions. *See* George Blum, Annotation, *Instructions on "Unavoidable Accident," . . . in Motor Vehicle Cases — Modern Cases,* 21 A.L.R.5th 82 (1994). In *Fry v. Carter,* the Maryland court considered the issue extensively. It held that the unavoidable accident instruction was confusing, because it was merely another way of requiring a finding that the defendant was causally negligent, because it overemphasized the defendant's side of the case by repeating in a new form the ideas already covered with the basic negligence instruction, and because it might be misleading to the jury by leaving the impression that there was an issue besides negligence and causation. The court also noted that almost half the states had abolished use of the instruction. A similar instruction, tells the jury that the mere happening of an accident or the suffering of an injury does not prove negligence, or, in its worst form, that the mere happening of an accident is not even evidence of negligence. This instruction, too, is beginning to meet with disfavor. E.g., *Kennelly v. Burgess,* 654 A.2d 1335 (Md. 1995).

Note 7 gives the students a chance to apply the rules just discussed to a simple fact pattern. The standard of care is that of a reasonable and prudent person under the same or similar circumstances. The circumstances include the children who are playing soccer adjacent to the road. Whether a reasonable person in defendant's position, given the circumstances, would have slowed down, is a jury issue if reasonable people can differ. Is this an "emergency?" We think not. This seems as foreseeable a situation as one could imagine – a child running after a ball. And did Allen create the "emergency" by not slowing down? Even if this was an "emergency," should the judge give a separate instruction? Discussing what might be wrong with that (using the materials above) should nail the points down for the class.

[2] "Circumstances" in the Actor's Own Characteristics

[A] Physical limitations of the actor

SHEPHERD V. GARDNER WHOLESALE, INC., 256 So.2d 877 (Ala. 1972)

The standard of care takes physical disabilities of the actor into account. Put that way, we can see that the approach in mental disability cases (coming up) is different.

The positive effects of the rule: freedom for those with disabilities. If physical limitations were not taken into account, perhaps some persons with impairments could not go into the world without risking liability. The rule that one must act as a reasonable person with a like disability thus has a positive or freedom-enhancing effect. One is not held liable merely because, say, blindness, is one of the causal factors in an injury, even though most people are not in fact blind. Thus one is not negligent merely because he is not physically up to any kind of average standard.

The constraining effects of the rule: duties of those with disabilities. The constraining effect of the standard however, is that one is not free to disregard his disability; he must take it into account and avoid activities which, normal for most people, would be dangerous when performed by a person with such a disability. If he knows he is subject to seizures, he must use care to take his anti-seizure medicine before he drives. If he cannot reach the brake pedals, he must use care to provide himself with other means of braking the car. If a blackout is a substantial and foreseeable possibility, then perhaps driving itself is negligent. *See, e.g., Storjohn v. Fay*, 519 N.W.2d 521 (Neb. 1994).

Note 1 quotes the new Restatement on physical disabilities, which is in line with *Shepherd*. See the above text for some answers to the question asked here.

Note 2. Effect of the rule. See above text, addressing the first few questions here. The new Restatement comment cited here says that disability is neither a "justification" nor an "excuse" for otherwise negligent conduct; rather, the reasonableness of the actor's conduct is "evaluated in light of the individual's disability. . . . With physical disabilities, then – just as with childhood – the law tailors the negligence standard to acknowledge the individual situation of the actor." The comment goes on to say that "persons with particular disabilities can appreciate that some conduct on their part will foreseeably entail a greater risk than the same conduct engaged in by able-bodied persons. Able to foresee this, an actor can be found negligent for not adopting special precautions that can reasonably reduce the special dangers that the actor's conduct involves." *Roberts*, cited here, is an interesting example. A blind man operated a concession stand in the lobby of a post office, and had done so for over three years. He had special mobility training and good mobility skills. He went to the restroom without using his cane, and ran into the plaintiff, injuring him. One might think that a reasonable blind person would be negligent for not using a cane; that was plaintiff's argument. But testimony came in that blind people routinely and safely use other techniques, other than canes, when moving around in familiar surroundings. One expert testified that it was in fact more dangerous to use a cane in a crowded, familiar area. The court affirmed the trial judge's judgment for the defendant, on the ground that he was not negligent.

Note 3. Old age. The Restatement (Third) § 11, cmt. *c* (Proposed Final Draft No. 1, 2005), explains that while old age as such is not taken into account," where physical disabilities are caused by old age, those disabilities are taken into account just as those caused by anything else would be: "Thus an 80-year-old actor who is no longer able to run will not be found negligent in failing to run as a hazard approaces."

Note 4. Exceptional physical ability. Superior physical abilities are presumably to be treated in the same way as disabilities: you must act reasonably and a reasonable person will act in the light of his own abilities, taking extra precautions where that is required by a disability, and performing feats of unusual skill to save a life where he possesses that skill.

Note 5. Intoxication. If the answer here is not the same as that given with other physical disabilities, is it because intoxication is partly a mental disability, to which the answer is usually different? Or is it that one is negligent in getting drunk in the first place? One who sets out to do an evening of drinking, knowing that he will also be driving, probably is negligent in putting himself in such a position: he runs the risk of bad and drunken driving, and if that risk comes to fruition, he should no doubt be held liable. What if, however, one voluntarily drinks at home, with no intention of going out, then is forced by some emergency to drive a short distance? There may have been no unreasonable risks in drinking in such a case. Would driving the best a drunk can under the circumstances be negligent? Would the mental decision to drive be negligent? Necessarily?

Note 6. Sudden incapacitation. The first part of this Note is designed to be self-explanatory. In Roman, cited here, Gobbo suffered an unforeseeable heart attack while driving. It killed him and his car veered this way and that, striking two other cars. Occupants of all cars were killed or injured. Suits were brought against Gobbo's estate by occupants of the other cars or their estates. The trial judge instructed the jury that the defendant had the burden of proving an unforeseeable medical emergency that made it impossible for Gobbo to control his car, but that if such proof was made, it was a good defense. So instructed, the jury found for the defendant. On appeal, the court held that one who unforeseeably loses consciousness and control while driving is not chargeable with negligence. This is the rule by the great weight of authority; the court also said that the burden of proof was on the defendant to prove that the sudden physical incapacitation was unforeseeable. The court also pointed out that Gobbo did know he had heart problems, though the risk of a deadly heart attack while driving was not "foreseeable." Operating with knowledge of medical problem is not sufficient to impose liability. If the heart attack was not foreseeable or not very likely, the driver would not be negligent in choosing to drive. If, once the attack struck, he did as well as a reasonable person suffering from such an attack, he would not be negligent then, either. *See, e.g., Goodrich v. Blair*, 646 P.2d 890 (Ariz. Ct. App. 1982); cf. *Knoxville Optical Supply, Inc. v. Thomas*, 1993 WL 574 (Tenn. Ct. App. 1993) (epileptic seizure, no medical testimony to show that defendant's failure to take her anti-seizure medicine was a cause of the seizure and ensuing accident, held for defendant).

[B] Mental capacity of the actor

CREASY V. RUSK, 730 N.E.2d 659 (Ind. 2000)

The point is that we use an objective standard of care– the reasonable person standard. *Creasy* makes it clear that mental disabilities are not "circumstances" to be considered; rather, the mentally disabled are held to the reasonable person standard. In reaching that conclusion, the court reviews some of the traditional policy reasons and adds a new one– that current policy to integrate mentally disabled into the community means a policy to treat those persons like all others.

We would emphasize the objective standard, perhaps in connection with Note 2. Perhaps process considerations dominate here. All disabled persons are not always incapable of exercising any degree of care. If we do not use the reasonable person standard, what standard can we use? A subjective standard, based upon the care the mentally disabled person was capable of seems almost impossible.

To keep focus on the objective standard and the use of individuating circumstances, you might discuss the last twist in the case first. The caretaker's duty to protect the patient precludes liability of the patient. This idea is worth repeated exploration, and we'll consider it in several places, notably in Chapter 10 with "assumed risk" and with cases like *Bexiga* in Chapter 9. Here we'd treat the idea in passing as an idea that foreshadows things to come rather than as a basis for extended discussion. If you discuss the twist first, you'll end discussion with focus on the standard of care and that will lead right into the next materials.

Note 1. Other cases. *Berberian* holds that "mentally incompetent patients owe no duty of care to protect paid caregivers from injuries suffered while caring for those patients." The plaintiff there was the head nurse in a dementia unit, and the defendant was an institutionalized patient suffering from Alzheimer's. The case discusses the history of the objective standard of care for those with mental disabilities, but ultimately bases its non-liability decision not on a subjective standard literally, but rather on a "no duty to caregivers" ground. *Arias*, also cited here, involved an inmate who died in a prison due to an intentional suicide by prescription drug overdose. His estate sued the State (which ran the prison and employed its doctors); defendant claimed contributory negligence. The court said "The standard of care which a mentally ill patient must exercise to protect himself is not based upon the objective standards of a reasonable person, but rather it is based upon the capacity of the patient and his perception of danger, considering the degree of her illness." The court granted partial summary judgment for plaintiff (unusual, as the court noted), stressing the duty that the prison owed to protect the decedent from his own self-destructive tendencies, where it knew of those tendencies. The case turns, then, on the idea we will see recur in *Bexiga* and *McNamara* in the next chapter, than on any "subjective" standard of care for the mentally infirm.

Hofflander, cited at the end of this Note, does hold that a mentally disabled person is held to a subjective standard of care when under the protective custody and control of another; the court recognizes, however, that this is an exception to the usual rule that the mentally-disabled are held to the same standard as a person of normal mental capacity. *Hofflander* involved a negligence claim by a mental-health patient against the hospital in which she was a patient, after she fell from a third-floor window in an escape attempt. Reversing a summary judgment for defendant, the court held that fact issues remained on whether the hospital knew of the risk that the patient would try to escape, and on whether the patient was contributorily negligent, under a standard that must take into account the patient's mental capacity.

Notes 2 & 3 should be self-explanatory and should not require class discussion.

Note 4. Contributory negligence. Some of the disability cases arise when the disabled person is herself injured (as in *Shepherd*, above), so that the issue is contributory negligence. For present purposes we might just assume that the standard of care for one's own safety is at least approximately the same as the standard of care for others. As *Creasy* and the cases in Note 1 show, many of the cases on this topic are contributory negligence cases that may even entail some obligation of the defendant to care for the plaintiff who is unable to care for herself.

Distinguish the duty owed *to* persons with an impairment. In *Payne v. North Carolina Dept. of Human Resources*, 382 S.E.2d 449 (N.C. Ct. App. 1989) a teacher in the state's school for the deaf was allegedly negligent in failing to instruct or supervise a student, who, as a result, suffered injury while working on a hydraulic lift. The plaintiff argued that the teacher owed a "greater than normal" duty of care because of the student's hearing impairment. The court held that the standard "remains that of the exercise of ordinary prudence," although it agreed that the "amount of care due a student increases with the student's immaturity, inexperience, and relevant physical limitations." One perhaps sees similar reasoning in the caretaker cases, discussed in Note 1 above.

Notes 5 & 6. Considering rationales, and the consistency question.
Now that students have seen both the physical disability rule (in Shepherd) and
the mental disability rule, what do they think of them? Are they consistent? We
have found this an interesting topic for class discussion, often producing passion-
ate arguments on both sides. The new Restatement, in Comments to § 11,
highlights "convenience of administration" in taking the position that disabilities
must be "susceptible to objective verification" in order to be considered by courts.
Might this distinguish physical from mental disability? Comment *e* explains that
minor mental disabilities are usually disregarded because of "problems of admin-
istrability that would be encountered in attempting to identify them and assess
their significance," and that disregard of serious disorders may be based on similar administrative concerns. Perhaps the most compelling difference, however,
between mental and physical disability is context-specific. We are dealing here
with liability for negligent conduct and focusing on whether a particular actor's
conduct should be deemed unreasonably risky. A person with physical disability
has unimpaired judgment in terms of risk. By contrast, a person with mental or
emotional disability has impaired judgment with respect to choices about safe
conduct. Does this reasoning change, then, if the mental impairment is clearly
due to a physical cause? The court in *Burch*, cited here, held that the answer is
no. A mentally-retarded child drove a truck and caused injuries. The court applied the reasonable (and adult) standard of care, without much discussion.

Note 7 is a lead-in to the next case and its Notes.

HILL V. SPARKS, 546 S.W.2d 473 (Mo. Ct. App. 1976)

Where Mr. Rusk in *Creasy* had diminished capacity, the actor in *Hill* has
added capacity (from his experience). *Hill* tells us that the actor's special knowl-
edge-experience can be considered in judging the sufficiency of the evidence. And
here, quite differently from *Creasy,* his experience/knowledge is treated as a circumstance to be considered. The reasonable person, in other words, will use all
the knowledge and experience he actually has, not merely some part of it. This is
not a decision about the *standard* of care. The court is not saying that an experienced and knowledgeable person must use more care than a reasonable person.
The court is saying instead that the jury can consider how a reasonable person
would behave if he knew of the dangers known to the defendant. You can promote
this discussion and thereby test the students' mastery of the reasonable care
standard by asking whether this case is contrary to *Stewart v. Motts*. The answer
is no for the reasons just given.

Note 1. In *Cerny,* a high school football coach allowed a student to play and
work out after the student was injured, although the student said he had dizzi-
ness, headache, and disorientation. The student allegedly suffered serious harm
as a result. The coach had a state certificate for coaching, based upon special
training. Experts said that coaches with such training should not permit a stu-

dent to play or workout again until he had medical clearance. In a bench trial, the judge rejected this testimony on the ground that the experts were *too* expert to set a standard for local coaches. The Nebraska Supreme Court reversed, holding that certified coaches were expected to use the special knowledge and skill they acquired in their training. The court expressed this by saying that the standard of care was the standard of the reasonable person with the certificate and training that led to it. The standard was not local and the experts correctly stated the standard.

Maybe there are some advantages in clarity if, instead of saying that the standard is that of a certified coach, you say it is the standard of the reasonable person, and that the reasonable person would ordinarily use the special skill or knowledge he actually has. Either way, however, the special skill must be taken into account. On remand in *Cerny*, there was a second bench trial. The judge gave weight to expert testimony of the defense and found that the coaches had met the standard of conduct required of a person with the special training. On appeal after remand, this was affirmed, since the weight given to expert testimony was a matter for the trier of fact.

Note 2. What knowledge does the reasonable person have? You might want to discuss this topic without actually revealing all the details in *LePage,* cited here, some of which can be raised when you come to risk-utility weighing under *Carroll Towing.* The *LePage* court was unwilling to say that a daycare center operator would know the risk of stomach-sleeping babies in December, 1998, although it had been the subject of a national "back to sleep" campaign and had been known to many people for years. That led the court to think expert testimony would be required to show "the standard," seemingly meaning what knowledge the daycare center should have. That holding might be arguable but not controversial except for the fact that the defendant admitted she knew of the recommendation of the Pediatric Academy that babies should sleep on their backs and also knew of the reason for it– that stomach sleeping was associated with SIDS. In an unrevealing passage, Justice Katz said that admission was not good enough because she admitted only "that she was aware that the prone position was recommended because it is *associated* with a risk of SIDS." There are sometimes reasons for putting a baby on her stomach, as where there is a special risk that the baby on her back would spit up and aspirate the material into her lungs. But Justice Katz' opinion suggests no reason whatever for taking the known risk in this case. Given the defendant's knowledge of the risk of death associated with prone sleeping and the absence of any utility in allowing a baby to sleep in that position, it is hard to see why a jury should not be allowed to find negligence. In fact, the defendant's explanation was that she originally placed the baby on her side, and when she later saw the baby on her stomach, "she did not think of SIDS."

Note 3. In *Jackson v. Axelrad,* the court held that the plaintiff's skill and experience as a physician had to be taken into account in judging the reasonableness of his disclosures to his treating doctor. This seems entirely consistent with *Hill.*

[C] The child standard of care

ROBINSON V. LINDSAY, 598 P.2d 392 (Wash. 1979)

Robinson recognizes the traditional child standard of care as an exception to the general reasonable person standard; then it creates an exception to that exception for cases in which the minor is engaged in an "inherently dangerous activity."

The subjective standard, based on the characteristics of a child exactly like the child before the court, is supported by many authorities. See , e.g., Restatement (Third) § 10 (Proposed Final Draft No. 1, 2005); Restatement (Second) § 283A; *Camerlinck v. Thomas*, 312 N.W.2d 260 (Neb. 1981) ("an ordinary prudent child of the same capacity to appreciate and avoid danger," also "age, intelligence and experience"). It is probably fair to regard the child standard as essentially subjective or perhaps just meaningless. It tells us to hold the child to the standard of care of a person who has all the child's own relevant characteristics–his age, experience, intelligence and so on. Maybe juries invest the standard with sense by applying this standard as if it said the child should be held to the standard of reasonable children of similar age. On application of the child standard, see DOBBS ON TORTS § 127.

The Washington Court concludes in *Robinson* that an exception is required when children engage in inherently dangerous activities. It regards snowmobiling and perhaps all motorized activity as included in that category.

The opinion begins with conclusion, not reasons. Two critical conclusions are: (1) an adult standard is sometimes required and (2) the trigger for the adult standard is inherently dangerous activity rather than "adult" activity. In the paragraph beginning "Courts in other jurisdictions have created an exception...." the court seems to conclude that, under some circumstances, it would be unjust if a child could "defend" by using the child standard. At the end of the same paragraph, the court concludes that the adult activity basis for the adult standard is the wrong one; "a better rationale" is that the child should be held to the adult standard when engaged in inherently dangerous activities. In this paragraph, the court gives no hint of a reason for either the conclusion that the child standard is sometimes "unjust" or the conclusion that "inherent danger" rather than "adult activity" is the proper test.

The next paragraph vaguely suggests some possible reasoning along these lines: First, the child standard is applied generally to allow children to be children. Second, they should not be allowed to be children when engaged in certain activities, but instead should be discouraged from engaging in especially dangerous activities. (Will a rule of law, which most adults in the class never heard of, be uppermost in the mind of children, so that, after all, the 13-year-old won't operate a snowmobile?) This also explains why the court prefers the inherent danger test rather than the adult activity test. Unless the activity is especially dangerous, a child should be free to be a child. Although even in childish activities the child might inflict some harm, the danger is not so grave.

HUDSON-CONNOR V. PUTNEY, 86 P.3d 106 (Or. Ct. App. 2004)

In contrast to *Robinson*, the court adopts an "adult activity" rather than "inherent danger" test. Yet inherent danger is one element of the two-part adult activity test, so maybe the Oregon court will get about the same results that Washington courts will get. Note the two-part test under *Hudson-Connor:* the activity must be (1) one that requires adult skills *and* (2) is normally engaged in only by adults. On the first point, skills, the degree of danger presented by the activity is relevant because that will affect the degree of skill required. A golf cart that moves at a maximum of 12 miles per hour is not inherently dangerous and does not require adult skills. As to negligent entrustment, students are not likely to pursue this idea separately, but if they do, you can suggest that this topic be postponed and considered in Chapter 18.

Note 1. See discussion above.

Note 2. Tests and policies for the adult standard. The *Robinson* court's idea of inherent danger really seems to mean grave danger or danger of serious harm. Is the exception for "inherently dangerous" instrumentalities correct, workable or accurately stated? Might it be, for instance, that if an adult is the plaintiff, and if the adult knows he is dealing with a child, he can only expect a child's level of care? Professor Seidelson's article, *Reasonable Expectations and Subjective Standards in Negligence Law: The Minor, The Mentally Impaired, and the Mentally Incompetent*, 50 GEO. WASH. L. REV. 17 (1981) advances a kind of reasonable expectation test.

Conversely, suppose the adult does not know he is dealing with a child, as where a child drives an auto on the highway and the adult is merely a pedestrian. If the child is liable, is it because he is doing something inherently dangerous? Because he is carrying on an adult activity? Or because the adult has every reason and right to expect that unidentifiable drivers meet a minimum standard? These questions may properly induce some skepticism about judicial formulations of rules. Restatement of the Law Third, Torts: Liability for Physical Harm § 10, cmt. f (Tentative Draft, 2001) uses the "adult activities" standard, yet seems to say that the point is to hold the child responsible when others could not recognize that they are dealing with children. At best, the adult activities and inherent danger tests only coincidentally command a result in accord with this reason. Why not restate the rule to align with the policy or justice said to support it?

Is the *Hudson-Connor* test any better? The inherent danger and adult activity tests seem almost perverse in one respect. Under that rule, as under the traditional rule, older minors are not expected to meet the adult standard even when engaged in activities like bicycling, at which they are generally competent. Since bicycling creates an interaction with adults and others (car drivers), and since a 17-year-old minor is normally more competent to handle a bicycle safely than to handle a car safely, it seems strange to impose the higher standard in the case of the car but not the bike.

Note 3. Application of the adult standard. Many of the cases involve motorized vehicles, as noted here. Use of firearms is another common example. For more cases, *see* Restatement (Third) § 10, cmt. *f*, Reporter's Note, at 144-47 (Proposed Final Draft No. 1, 2005).

Note 4. The rule of sevens. For more on this, *see* DOBBS ON TORTS § 126 (2000) and *Savage v. Martin*, 628 N.E.2d 606 (Ill. App. 1993). *Penn Harris* holds the 17-year-old to an adult standard using a mechanical rule: children over 14 are held to that standard. The court noted that the child standard would probably have made no difference anyway if it had applied, since the "child" was almost an adult in terms of intelligence and experience.

Note 5. Trial problems. The lawyer's role. Maybe students can begin to recognize that as lawyers they must take initiative and must keep up with new ideas. What would make a lawyer raise the issue the lawyers raised in *Robinson* unless she kept up with legal ideas or researched materials that did not seem to need researching? After all, Washington law had been settled.

A plaintiff's strategy on the Robinson instruction. Strategy is involved in every case. To what extent does the outcome depend upon adjudication of fault and to what extent upon strategic moves? The plaintiff in a case like this will probably have a strategy something like this: (1) Ask the judge for an adult-standard instruction (which is not the law of the state at the time of trial); (2) make no argument for such an instruction and hope the judge refuses to give it. If the jury's sympathy is for the plaintiff, the instruction will not be likely to matter to the verdict, but the failure to give it will provide the plaintiff a ground for appeal in the event the jury finds for the defendant for any reason at all.

A judge's strategy on the Robinson instruction. The judge's strategy may have been: (1) refuse the instruction (it is not the law as it then stood); and (2) hope the jury finds for the plaintiff anyway, since in that case the plaintiff will have no ground for appealing and reversing the judge. Since the judge would have been uncertain whether an instruction such as that requested would be upheld, this seems to have been a wise course, though in fact it did not work out as a judge in this circumstance might predict. The judge could hardly have given an instruction that matched the court's decision, by the way, since the "inherent danger" compromise is not the one the judge would have found in decisions from other jurisdictions. Do we, in practice, lose sight of the effort for accountability in the thicket of tactics?

Note 6. Very young children. Some courts use other more or less conventional ages for immunizing children from liability. See *Thompson v. Wooten,* 650 S.W.2d 499 (Tex. Ct. App. 1983) (children under six). Georgia, by construction of a statute, has immunized all children under the age of 13 years. *Horton v. Hinely,* 413 S.E.2d 199 (Ga. 1992) (two nine-year-olds poured gasoline on a seven-year-old and set him afire, no liability). As noted here, the new Restatement takes the position that children under the age of five are "incapable of negligence." Comment *d* to section 10 reasons that careless conduct by children under five is neither subject to moral criticism nor effectively deterred by tort liability.

The mini-problem at the end of this Note allows for synthesis, although you can leave it for students to work through on their own if you wish. In a state that says children under age 7 are incapable of negligence, the issue would not come before the jury at all. If there was a presumption of non-negligence, or simply the application of the child standard, the jury would have to determine whether the child was, in fact, negligent. Would running like this trigger the "adult" exception? Unlikely. So a jury would determine whether a child of the same age, intelligence and experience as the actual chilled here would have behaved any differently. We would probably need additional facts to make an ultimate judgment, of course, in terms of breach of duty; that is the subject of the next chapter.

§ 4. SPECIFICATION OF PARTICULAR STANDARDS OR DUTIES

OUTLINE OF SECTION 4

[1] Judicial treatment of specific duties
    [A] General duty is specified to a particular requirement of action. Marshall v. Southern Ry. Co.
    [B] Specification of general duty rejected and jury role restored. Chaffin v. Brame.
[2] Legislative treatment of specific duties
    [A] Legislative specification accepted as tort standard. Martin v. Herzog.
    [B] Limitations on use of the negligence per se rule– class of persons and scope of risk rules. O'Guin v. Bingham County
    [C] Limitations on use of the negligence per se rule–excuses. Impson v. Structural Metals, Inc.

Problem: Lind v. Maigret

SUMMARY

MARSHALL V. SOUTHERN RY. CO. The court holds that a plaintiff driving at night should be able to stop within the range of his headlights and that if he runs into an obstruction, he is necessarily guilty of contributory negligence. The effect is to state, not a general duty of due care which the jury applies in its best judgment, but a specific duty to drive within the range of one's lights.

CHAFFIN V. BRAME. On very similar facts, the same court a year later rejects this specification of duties as too rigid, and leaves the question of ordinary care to the jury.

MARTIN V. HERZOG. A driver at night, in violation of statute, fails to light his buggy. This is held to be negligence per se. The effect is that the duty is to drive with lights–not to drive with ordinary care whatever that may be, and the jury thus has no role in the decision. Martin does under statute what Marshall did without it.

O'GUIN V. BINGHAM COUNTY. A violation of statute is negligence per se only if the plaintiff is within the class the statute intends to protect and only if the harm sued for is the kind the statute seeks to avoid. Trespassing children were killed playing at a county landfill, and sued the county on a negligence per se theory, pointing to the county's violation of state statutes and federal regulations governing landfills. The court explains the court's power to adopt or reject non-tort statutes and then applies the class of persons, type of harm test for statutory applicability. The court holds that these tests were met, so that the statutory standard "replaces the common law duty of landowners" in the case.

IMPSON V. STRUCTURAL METALS, INC. Another attempt to avoid the rigidity of the negligence per se doctrine is seen in the doctrine that some violations are "excused." In this case, an attempt to pass at an intersection was not, however, excused, since it did not fit the Restatement's list of cases for excuse.

PROBLEM: LIND V. MAIGRET.

COMMENTS

In § 4 we begin to look at efforts to specify required conduct with particularity. In the first group of cases, this was done by judges with rules such as the rule that it is always negligence not to be able to stop within the range of vision (*Marshall*). One effect of this is to limit the jury's role; judges decide for themselves that what the specific standard or duty requires. In real life, however, these rules have often come to seem too rigid. Judges have often moved away from specific duties assigned by judges for each case, to a general standard of the reasonable person (*Chaffin*). One important effect of this is to expand the jury's role; juries, not judges, decide whether the general, reasonable person standard was breached in the particular case.

In the second group of cases you can examine the same phenomenon as it developed under the doctrine of negligence per se. The per se rule is stated in *Martin*, and elaborated upon in *O'Guin*. A statute will apply to a case only if the statute's purpose is to protect the class of which the plaintiff is a member and to protect against the kind of risk or harm which came about. Even this, however, is subject to either debate or vagaries in application. It is possible to treat the actor's violation of statute as evidence of negligence only, either as a general preference, or because for some reason it fails to meet the rules for a "per se" application. Then in *Impson* we see the rule that a violation of statute may be "excused" in some cases.

Is the per se doctrine too rigid in the same way the rule in *Marshall* was too rigid? Or, conversely, do we need specific rules in place of vague general standards like the reasonable person standard? Or does the flexibility of negligence per se, starting with the "class of persons, type of harm" requirement, and including the possibility of "excuses," render elusive any surface precision?

In the course of developing these basic ideas quite a few important questions arise. What are the limits of specific rules? What are the relative roles of three major legal institutions, judge, jury and legislature? How should we balance the conflict between hard-and-fast rules, which serve to protect against caprice and unfairness, and the need for enough flexibility to adjudicate the rights of individuals justly?

MARSHALL V. SOUTHERN RY. CO., 62 S.E.2d 489 (N.C. 1950)
CHAFFIN V. BRAME, 64 S.E.2d 276 (N.C. 1951)

In *Marshall*, the trial judge granted a nonsuit (similar to a directed verdict) on the ground that in outrunning his headlights, the plaintiff was guilty of contributory negligence as a matter of law. A year later, in *Chaffin*, the same court seems to reject the rule as too rigid. The conflict between rules, with their certainty and rigidity, and ad hoc decisions, with their flexibility and uncertainty, is staked out.

The judge who directs a verdict for the defendant will often express the view that there is "no negligence," or, as here, there is contributory negligence "as a matter of law." This means only that reasonable people could not differ in evaluating the conduct. However, in cases like *Marshall*, the judge is going further, because the judge is not merely assessing evidence in the particular case. Instead, the judge is holding *anyone* outrunning the range of visions will *always* be guilty of contributory negligence (or negligence). He is enunciating a rule of law.

Other examples of courts creating or rejecting duties more specific than the reasonable care duty. West Virginia once suggested that a pedestrian was guilty of contributory negligence as a matter of law if he was struck near the curb by an oncoming automobile, but that contributory negligence was a jury question if he was struck when he was further into the street. This analysis was repudiated in *Sydenstriker v. Vannoy*, 150 S.E.2d 905 (W.Va. 1966) much as *Chaffin* repudiated *Marshall*. Although the creation of specific duties seems an outdated way of taking cases from the jury, you can still find cases that take such an approach. Pennsylvania requires that when the plaintiff falls on ice for which the defendant is putatively responsible, the plaintiff must show that the icy condition is not generally prevailing in the community and/or that the ice had hills or ridges. See *Wilson v. Howard Johnson Restaurant*, 219 A.2d 676 (Pa. 1966). Some states have enacted an assured clear distance ahead rule similar to the common law rule imposed in *Marshall*. See *Pond v. Leslein*, 647 N.E.2d 477 (Ohio 1995).

The jury's role. The underlying problem is to allocate decision-making power between judge and jury. The jury is to decide pure facts ("Was the stop light red?"). It is also to make certain value judgments ("Did this amount to negligence?"). It also determines credibility of witnesses. (More on all these functions in Chapter 6.)

The judge's role. In contrast, the judge's role is to declare the law and make the decisions conform to that. Thus judge and jury are institutional expressions of the conflict with which we began: rule of law versus adjudication of individual disputes. The judge appears as a rule maker in *Marshall*, and that is an appropriate role. The only real questions in our system is whether the judge should have created any rule of law at all or whether, instead, the judge should have left the issue for the jury's factual-evaluative determination under the general rule that invokes the reasonable prudent person standard.

Besides creating rules imposing specific duties, judges often control the outcome without help from the jury by declaring that a defendant owes no duty at all. Without a duty, the defendant has no obligation to exercise reasonable care. Where a landowner or city fails to trim bushes, leaving an intersection obscured and leading to traffic accidents, courts have often said the defendant had no duty to trim. Such cases are parallel to *Marshall* in sidetracking any judgment about reasonable care from the jury. Other cases in this setting are like *Chaffin,* leaving it to the jury to determine whether the defendant exercised reasonable care or not. See *Coburn v. City of Tucson,* 691 P.2d 1078 (Ariz. 1984) ("[T]he duty remains constant, while the conduct necessary to fulfill it varies with the circumstances... . The city has a duty to keep the streets reasonably safe... the details of conduct necessary to meet those duties will vary from case to case, depending upon the foreseeability of harm. . . ."); *Donaca v. Curry County,* 734 P.2d 1339 (Or. 1987) (emphasizing that circumstances such as the degree of danger and the ease with which it can be avoided will vary).

MARTIN V. HERZOG, 126 N.E. 814 (N.Y. 1920)

This case parallels *Marshall*, but it involves a legislature-made, not a judge-made rule of law about specific conduct required. Violation of the statute requiring lights on the buggy was not merely evidence of negligence as the Appellate Division had held. Cardozo holds that "[t]he unexcused omission of the statutory signals is more than some evidence of negligence. It is negligence in itself."

Where we are headed. The remainder of the materials on violation of statute deal with some of the ways courts have backed down from the negligence per se rule, or, if you prefer, the ways courts have qualified it. Martin merely states the general rule but does not offer qualifiers (perhaps other than the term "unexcused," which becomes the focus of *Impson* below.

Note 1. Kinds of statutes covered. Students sometimes have trouble understanding the difference between a statute that creates tort liability directly and the kind of statute (a "non-tort" statute, if you will) that is involved in negligence per se. This Note is designed to forestall some of that confusion, but you may need to spend some class time on it. The kinds of statutes mentioned in this Note are not the kinds that are at issue with negligence per se. Many students seem to have only the most shaky understanding that criminal law is not civil or tort law, but we can usually convince them that a statute that says "if violation, impose criminal punishment" is not like a statute that says, "if violation, hold defendant liable to the victim." In the second category, the legislature has created a cause of action. That cause of action may have other qualities that differentiate it from common law tort claims, for example, special conditions or defenses. Or, as in the case of the FELA, it may remove defenses. But it's a tort statute, and not the kind of thing we are dealing with in negligence per se.

Note 2. Effect on duty of care. This Note is designed just to answer a common question clearly; the *O'Guin* case coming up says the same basic thing in slightly different language. You can wait for *O'Guin* to raise the point.

Note 3. Jurisdictional variations. While most states follow the *Herzog* rule (with the qualifications coming up in *O'Guin* and *Impson*), some do not. Some follow the *evidence of negligence* rule, either generally or for particular statute violations. Some follow this approach by statute, as noted; others have adopted the rule as a matter of common law. In *Kalata v. Anheuser-Busch Companies, Inc.*, 581 N.E.2d 656 (Ill. 1991), cited here, the court said that when the plaintiff shows violation of statute, the defendant could nevertheless "prevail by showing that he acted reasonably under the circumstances." Illinois labels this as a prima facie evidence of negligence rule.

A few states express a rule that seems like the per se rule but they name it differently. They say that violation of statute creates a *presumption of negligence*. As with negligence per se, negligence is shown unless the defendant can justify or excuse his violation. *See* CAL. EVID. CODE § 669; *Ramirez v. Plough, Inc.*, 863 P.2d 167 (Cal. 1993); *Zeni v. Anderson*, 243 N.W.2d 270 (Mich. 1976). Sometimes judges specifically equate "presumption" with "prima facie," as in *Kizer v. Harper*, 561 S.E.2d 368 (W.Va. 2001). So the difference between negligence per se jurisdictions and presumption jurisdictions lies mainly in the language (unless the court means to use a "bursting bubble" presumption, a concept that surely must be avoided in first year classes).

Note 4. Statutory instruments covered by the rule. Ordinances and administrative regulations are treated as statutes for the purpose of the negligence per se rules. RESTATEMENT (SECOND) § 286, cmt. *a*. Some states treat most ordinances and administrative regulations as merely evidence of negligence, as indicated here.

O'GUIN V. BINGHAM COUNTY, 122 P.3d 308 (Idaho 2005)

Children trespassing in a county landfill die when a section of the pit they are playing in collapses. Their parents sue the county on a negligence per se theory. They rely on both state statutes and federal regulations.

The court gives a basic foundational rule in the fourth paragraph: "Negligence per se, which results from the violation of a specific requirement of law or ordinance, is a question of law, over which this Court exercises free review." Note that the court refers to a "specific requirement" that the statute must embody, a requirement picked up again in **Note 6** following the case. Where a statute or ordinance does not set out a clear standard or requirement, it cannot be given negligence per se effect. This is logical, of course, since giving a statute per se effect allows the statutory standard to substitute for the usual common law standard.

Most cases involve the substitution of the statutory standard for the general reasonable and prudent person standard, but in this case the court allows the statutes to "replace the common law duty of landowners to trespassers." Since the class will not have studied the landowner duties yet (Chapter 12), you can't really go into detail on that standard here. But it's useful to note that negligence per se operates to displace the common law standard, whatever it is in the particular case.

The court's analysis of why the statutes and regulations here set the standard of care is worth going through with the class; you can jump back and forth between Notes as needed. First, as noted briefly above, the court says that the statute must clearly define the required standard of conduct (see also **Note 6**). Second, the statute must "have been intended to prevent the type of harm the defendant's act or omission caused." Third, "the plaintiff must be a member of the class of persons the statute or regulation was designed to protect." These requirements are further explored in **Notes 1-5** after the case. Finally, the court adds a "proximate cause" requirement. The court's discussion of this requirement indicates that it means "cause in fact" in this context: The court says that the question is "whether the violation of the statute and regulations resulted in the O'Guin children's deaths." We see variations on what courts mean when they say "proximate cause" in upcoming Chapters.

Notes 1 & 2. Class of persons, type of harm tests. As *O'Guin* states, the violation of a statute does not operate as negligence per se unless both the plaintiff and the type of harm or occurrence are within the scope of the statute's intended protection. If the legislature intended the statute to protect against Risk A, but the plaintiff is injured as a result of Risk B, the defendant's violation of statute is not negligence per se. The same principle applies if the legislature intended the statute to protect persons in Class X but the plaintiff is in Class Y.

Note 3. Statues intended to protect the public at large. Sometimes a court will determine that a statute that is designed to protect the general public is therefore designed to protect the plaintiff, as a member of that broad class. This was the holding of *Wright v. Brown*, 356 A.2d 176 (Conn. 1975), which appeared in the Fifth Edition as a primary case. There, the court found that a dog-quarantine statute "was intended to protect the general public," and that "plaintiff, as a member of the general public, is within that class." As noted here, however, other courts have held that where a statute protects the general public, it cannot be given per se effect at all. In the *Pehle* case cited here, the court held that Wyoming's statutes requiring laboratories to report communicable diseases "were primarily intended to protect the general public, not HIV victims" such as the plaintiffs in the case. The inquiry in negligence per se, said the court, is whether the statutory duty "runs to individuals, or rather to the public at large"; when it's the latter, the statute cannot be given per se effect. This position may be a cousin of the "public duty" doctrine we see later in Chapter 15 § 3; the idea there is that where a state owes a duty to the public at large, an individual within the state cannot claim that a duty is owed to her individually.

Note 4. Making the determination. How does a court decide whether a statute fulfills the class of persons and type of harm requirements?

– *Scope of risk*. Suppose the statute requires impoundment of dogs who have bitten someone. Warden Wally impounds a dog named Dan but then violates the statute by authorizing parole of the dog before his sentence is up. Dan immediately runs in front of a pedestrian, causing her to fall. This does not look like a risk the legislature sought to protect against, so Wally's violation does not in itself impose liability.

– *Class of persons*. Suppose a city ordinance requires that in-ground home swimming pools be surrounded by a fence 6 feet high. It requires that handles for opening gates be at least five feet off the ground and that the gate be locked when the owner is not present. The defendant's pool, in violation, is not fenced. The defendant's 22-year-old nephew, who was visiting the defendant, went for a swim alone at night and drowned. His estate sued the defendant, claiming negligence per se. If the fencing requirement is only instituted to protect small children, the grown nephew would not be within the class of persons the ordinance was meant to protect.

– *Class of interest*. The scope of protection analysis can be broken down even further, but we are going to suggest that such a further analysis is only useful for illustrative purposes, not essential to decision-making. In particular, the statute might be intended to protect against one type of interest but not another and that violation of the statute is negligence per se only if the type of interest invaded is the type the statute was intended to protect. Suppose the dog Dan, illegally released, takes a long nap in the plaintiff's flower bed, destroying her freshly planted petunias. If you think the statute requiring impoundment was to protect safety of persons, not property, you would say the plaintiff cannot get the benefit of the negligence per se rule for her petunia claims.

Further classifications and why they are not necessary. You can keep going with this type of analysis. The Restatement Second wanted us to consider (1) kind of harm, (2) class of person, (3) the type of interest, and (4) the particular hazard. *See* RESTATEMENT SECOND OF TORTS §§ 286, 288 (1965). But if you allow any reasonable latitude in describing the risk or "accident," you can cover the scope of the intended protection very well. Put differently, when you describe the risk that is covered you may also implicitly say something about the class of persons covered. If there were no class of person rule, we would almost certainly say in the swimming pool case that the risk the ordinance was intended to avoid was not the one that came about. The risk the ordinance was intended to avoid was a risk to small children who might not be able to understand the water risk and to protect themselves. That is not the risk that eventuated. Class of person and type of interest are not so much independent rules as categories of risk that might not be within the scope of the statute's protection.

Note 5. Judicial adoption theories. If a court is enforcing a statute that creates a tort cause of action – or regulates the tort cause of action in any way– the court will be obliged to enforce all the statutory directives, expressed and implied. But given that a penal statute does not direct the court to do anything about tort liability, the court can reject or adopt the statutory standard as a matter of its common law powers. Then why should a court limit the tort law effects of a statute according to the intent of the legislature that was not addressing tort law in the first place? Is this just a confusion of penal statutes with statutes creating a cause of action? A confusion about why the penal standard is used? And what about the fact that even if we know the legislature's intended scope of protection, the legislature intended that scope only for the purpose of limiting *criminal* responsibility?

Besides the materials in this Note, consider *Kernan v. American Dredging Co.*, 355 U.S. 426 (1958). In that case, a regulation required lights on river scows no less than eight feet above the water. The purpose was to make the light visible at a distance. The defendant had a light only three feet above the water and it was a kerosene lantern. It ignited vapors from river pollution and a worker lost his life. Given the navigation purpose of the 8-foot regulation, the class of risk rules would normally exclude liability, but the Supreme Court applied the statutory standard.

Note 6. "Defining the standard of conduct." See discussion in *O'Guin* above. The *Hurst* case cited here was overruled on other grounds in *Wallace v. Ohio Dept. of Commerce*, 773 N.E.2d 108 (Ohio 2002).

Obscure or irrational statutes, as well as statutes that set no precise standard, can also readily be rejected as inappropriate for setting standards. When statutes have been formulated in terms of "reasonable" conduct rather than in terms of precise actions, a number of courts have refused to give them any special effect and the jury is instructed instead only in terms of the prudent person standard. See *Kimberlin v. PM Transport,* 563 S.E.2d 665 (Va. 2002): *Chadbourne, III v. Kappaz*, 779 A.2d 293 (D.C. App. 2001); *Osborne v. Russell*, 669 P.2d 550 (Alaska 1983) *; Deering v. Carter*, 376 P.2d 857 (Ariz. 1962). Some courts, however, have given effect to statutes that are fairly abstract. *See, e.g., Lozoya v. Sanchez,* 66 P.3d 948 (N.M. 2003) (evidence that vehicle behind collided with rear of forward vehicle as a matter of law showed negligence per se in violating the statute against following too closely).

Note 7. Rejecting statutory standards imposing new duties. Negligence per se rules are most likely to be applied when the defendant is already under a duty to use care for the plaintiff's benefit. If the statute imposes a duty to report child abuse and prescribes a criminal penalty for failure to do so, the court must of course enforce the statute in a criminal prosecution. But very likely it will not consider the statute at all in a civil case because there is no common law duty to report suspected abuse. In contrast, there is a common law duty to drive with reasonable care, and a statute setting a speed limit creates no new duty but merely describes what will count as a breach of that duty. We will have a chance to review this point when we come to the problem, *Paton v. Missouri & Atlantic Railway*, at the end of Chapter 12.

Note 8. The "causation" requirement. As mentioned above, the *O'Guin* court's "proximate cause" requirement appears to be nothing more than a "cause in fact" rule. Some courts do appear to add on a "scope of risk" requirement; this seems redundant of the basic class of persons/type of harm test for applicability of the statute itself. You probably need not bring this up in class unless you are asked, since students will not have read about either cause in fact or proximate cause yet.

Note 9. Licensing statutes. This note resumes the question, what statutes should courts adopt or reject as setting a specific standard?

Sometimes it is said that violation of licensing statutes is not negligence per se. In *Talley v. Danek Medical, Inc.*, 179 F.3d 154 (4th Cir. 1999), the defendant manufactured a medical device without obtaining required approval of the Food and Drug Administration. A surgeon used the device on the plaintiff's spine, allegedly to her injury. The court held that the defendant's failure to obtain required approval before marketing a medical device would not be negligence per se. Cf. *Buckman Co. v. Plaintiffs' Legal Committee,* 121 S.Ct. 1012 (2001) (claim that medical product injured the plaintiffs and that defendant secured FDA approval for marketing the product by fraud was preempted; if defendant's alleged fraud violated federal regulations, FDA could seize the product or impose penalties, but not to the benefit of the plaintiffs).

Perhaps the most famous case on this topic is *Brown v. Shyne*, cited here. If negligence per se is the right approach in other cases, why not here? Professor Gregory concluded that the decision in *Brown v. Shyne* was correct because the licensing statute established no standard of conduct at all, that is, it did not prescribe any particular act to be done in any prescribed way. He contrasted the licensing statute with a hypothetical statute making it a misdemeanor for a doctor to use a hypodermic needle that had not been sterilized in a certain way. Such a statute prescribes a course of conduct and its violation would be negligence per se. Charles Gregory, *Breach of Criminal Licensing Statutes in Civil Litigation*, 36 CORNELL L. REV. 622 (1951).

The rule against treating violation of a licensing statute as negligence per se is thin or ragged in places.

In *Kizer v. Harper*, also cited here, an electrician's work was prima facie negligent because the electrician did not have the license required by statute. The result was that the plaintiff, who fell from a utility pole because of some electrical defect not explained in the case, recovered almost $1.3 million dollars.

In *Duty v. East Coast Tender Service, Inc.*, 660 F.2d 933 (4th Cir. 1981) the majority held that federal law governing the case made it negligence per se to operate a motor vessel without a licensed operator as required by Coast Guard regulation. The court thought the cases did not in fact create a licensing exception. "Instead they hold largely that, despite the violation of a licensing statute by defendants, plaintiffs may not recover where they have proved no causal connection between the failure to possess a license and the injury suffered." In *Corgan v. Muehling,* 574 N.E.2d 602 (Ill. 1991), the plaintiff had been a patient of a psychologist who was not registered. His failure to register violated a statute which declared that it was a nuisance for anyone to represent himself as a psychologist without a current registration. The plaintiff alleged that the psychologist had engaged in sexual intercourse with her during treatment and had thus caused harm. This stated a cause of action for negligent malpractice, but the court then went on to say that the registration statute created a private right of action as well.

Klanseck v. Anderson Sales & Service, Inc., 393 N.W.2d 356 (Mich. 1986) involved a motorcyclist who was injured when the cycle began to fishtail right after he bought it. He sued the seller and manufacturer and established a defect in the cycle. The defendants were allowed to show that the plaintiff had not secured a motorcycle endorsement on his driver's license as required by statute. The court held that the violation of this licensing statute could be used as evidence of negligence (not as negligence per se) where its relevance is "specifically established." Here it was relevant as tending to show that the motorcycle user was incompetent, where the issue of his incompetence or inexperience had been properly raised by other evidence.

FYI: Workplace safety statutes. Workplace safety has long been a problem and long been the subject of statutory regulation. The Federal Safety Appliance Act (now in new form), the FELA, the Jones Act, federal and state OSHA statutes, and scaffolding acts are all examples. These statutes tend to make special provisions that alter the effect of violation. See generally DOBBS ON TORTS § 133 (2000).

In some jurisdictions "scaffolding acts" or "structural work acts" may set standards for a variety of work related equipment. The Illinois Structural Work Act is one that has drawn a good deal of attention. See ILL. REV. STAT. Ch. 48, ¶ 60 et seq. The scope of the statutes may be subject to considerable litigation. Some statutes approach, or achieve, strict liability to workers injured by violation. Cf. *Mydlarz v. Palmer/Duncan Const. Co.,* 682 P.2d 695 (Mont. 1984) ("absolute duty"). The statutes may be given liberal interpretation so that any risk from "elevation differentials" is covered. In *Gordon v. Eastern Railway Supply, Inc.,* 626 N.E.2d 912 (N.Y. 1993), the plaintiff fell from an improper scaffold, but was not injured by the fall. He was injured because of a defective machine he was using. Nevertheless, the scaffolding act applied. ■

Note 10 reminds students that if a court holds a statute inapplicable to a case, it does not mean that the defendant wins outright – simply that the standard of care reverts to the common-law standard. If you stress this point here, it might drive home to some students that we are not dealing here with some kind of exclusive "statutory liability or nothing" situation.

IMPSON V. STRUCTURAL METALS, INC., 487 S.W. 2d 694 (Tex. 1972)

Impson elaborates on the idea of excused violation. It is not a rejection of the negligence per se notion; indeed in *Martin v. Herzog* Cardozo said that the "unexcused" violation of a statute was negligence per se. The Restatement effort to describe excuses, valiant perhaps, still seems almost meaningless. Instead of the *Restatement's* formulae for excuse, why not the California approach based on a statute and stated in *Alarid*, **Note 3**? See the similar formulation in *Chadbourne v. Kappaz,* 779 A.2d 293 (D.C. Ct. App. 2001) ("[i]f the violator demonstrates that she did everything a reasonably prudent person would have done to comply with the law, then her violation merely constitutes evidence of negligence rather than negligence *per se*").

The excuses enumerated by the quoted portions of the *Restatement* sometimes seem to overlap. Excuse (b) and excuse (c) could readily apply to the same situation. Sometimes the whole idea of an excused violation is vague. In *Hall v. Warren,* 632 P.2d 848 (Utah 1981), the court said: "Such a violation may be subject to justification or excuse if the defendant's conduct could nevertheless be reasonably said to fall within the standard of reasonable care under the circumstances." This is very broad and may in effect reject the per se rule. Conceivably, a single jurisdiction would treat violation of some statutes as evidence of negligence only, violation of others as negligence per se subject to excuses, and violation of still others as grounds for strict liability. That is the position taken in *Sikora v. Wenzel,* 727 N.E.2d 1277 (Ohio 2000).

Note 2. The Third Restatement, raised here, seems to attempt a simpler statement of excuses, but still comes up with five categories. It eliminates separate reference to emergency, apparently because emergency would be covered under a separate rule, which excuses the actor when compliance would entail greater risk. The Restatement Second excused one who neither knows nor should know of occasion for compliance; this is broken down into two parts in the newer Restatement. It recognizes excuse when the actor neither knows nor should know the factual circumstances that make the statute applicable (c), and also when the actor violates the statute because of the confusing way in which the statute's requirements are presented to the public (d). These seem to correspond roughly to mistake of fact and mistake of law. Note that the Third Restatement explicitly provides that where one of these excuses is made out, not only is the statute irrelevant, the actor's conduct is not negligent.

Note 3. Why not a rule in the form of a principle rather than a list like the list of excuses? That's what *Alarid* gives us. Would that be too uncertain for judges to apply? One reason for detailed rules is to provide illustrations that might not otherwise occur to lawyers or judges. The difficulty is that you might not capture all the good excuses in your list.

What excuse, if any, applies to this example. A building is constructed or maintained so as to violate a building code's safety provisions because stairs have no handrails or stair risers are uneven. Some courts have said this is not negligence per se unless the owner knew or should have known of the code violation. *Bills v. Willow Run I Apartments,* 547 N.W.2d 693 (Minn. 1996); *Lamm v. Bissette Realty,* Inc., 395 S.E.2d 112 (N.C. 1990). Neither of these cases involved transient conditions like a spill that makes a surface slippery. Instead, they both involved construction that failed to meet the code requirements for handrails and steps.

Note 4. The child standard. Many courts have held that the child standard "trumps" the negligence per se standard; others use the "infancy/ incapacity" excuse. If you get into this Note, you might use it as an example of a situation where two policies collide, in this case the policies behind the child standard (let children be children) versus the policies behind the negligence per se rule. Many courts believe that giving a statute negligence per se effect against a child actor would improperly erase the child standard in a situation where the policies behind the child standard are fully extant.

Note 5. Non-excuses. The cited Restatement comment says simply, "nor is it an excuse if there is a custom to depart from the statutory requirement." *See, e.g., Johnson v. Garnand,* 501 P.3d 32 (Ariz. Ct. App. 1972); *Smith v. Aaron,* 508 S.W.2d 320 (Ark. 1974).

PROBLEM. LIND V. MAIGRET

Maigret slowed when he hit a fog bank, but a boulder rolled down the hill and struck his car. Maigret went into shock, closing his eyes. His engine stalled when he came to a stop and he could not start it. The car was projecting across a lane of traffic and fog was thick. He was struck by Lind. The statute provided "no person shall stop" etc. on the highway.

Negligence per se. Statutory construction. Maybe Maigret did not "stop" within the meaning of the statute. His car was struck by a boulder and "came to a stop," but that doesn't mean that Maigret stopped it. Maybe you need more factual detail, but it seems probable that Maigret did not violate the statute by stopping, which implies some volition or "act" by the driver.

Excuses for violation. (1) Is this an emergency not of Maigret's own making? Would emergency doctrine apply? (2) Or is this better characterized as a case in which the defendant is unable after reasonable diligence to comply? Any other recognized excuse? (3) The *Alarid* formula: doing what a reasonable person would do with a desire to comply with the law. Maigret tried to start the car and could not.

Class of risk. Is the no-stopping/standing statute aimed at providing safety from or to other drivers, or only aimed at moving traffic?

Common law negligence claims. Don't overlook this.

Claims against truck driver. The range of lights cases like *Marshall* and *Chaffin* can be generalized to mean that it is negligence or at least evidence of negligence if you are unable to stop within the range of your vision. Applied to the truck driver in the fog, that would mean he is at least arguably guilty of common law negligence (a jury question under *Chaffin,* a rule of law under *Marshall*).

CHAPTER 6

NEGLIGENCE: BREACH OF DUTY

▶**Changes in the Sixth Edition:** We've cut this chapter down pretty dramatically by moving ten former case abstracts (or just their main points) into Notes. We have added one new primary case, and there are two dozen new cases cited in Notes to keep everything current.

Specifically: In § 1, we have dropped four case abstracts: *Lee, Fintzi, Giant Food*, and *Parsons*. We have added a new primary case up front, right after the Brown v. Stiel Problem, *Pipher v. Parsell*, which sets out the basic idea of foreseeability in judging negligent conduct. In § 3, we've dropped three case abstracts: *D.C. v. Shannon, Hammons v. Poletis*, and *McComish v. DeSoi*; we've also turned the *Wal-Mart Stores v. Wright* case into a shorter case abstract. In § 4, on res ipsa, we've greatly streamlined the coverage by dropping the *Widmyer* case, and three case abstracts: *Valley Properties, Eaton v. Eaton*, and *Lambrecht v. Estate of Kaczmarczyk*. We've also reversed the order of subsections 4(b) and (c) on res ipsa.

▶The **Concise Edition** omits the *Upchurch v. Rottenberry* case in § 3; cuts Note 2 after *Duncan v. Corbetta* and renumbers the Notes; and omits the *Chang* problem at the end of the Chapter.■

Scheduling omissions. This chapter develops core ideas about negligence, so cuts must be judicious, especially given our lean presentation here. For *maximum* omissions consider these. *Section 1*: Omit the *Brown v. Stiel* problem (but this one is a matter of teaching style). *Bernier* might be omitted if the class can get the ideas of risks and costs without it. *Section 3 a*: If you are willing to develop ideas in lecture or discussion, you may be able to drop all of this subsection except *either Santiago* or *Upchurch*. Against dropping the whole subsection: you'd be dropping the distinction opinion evidence and factual evidence as well as the distinction between fact and value judgment, essential to understanding. *Section 3 b:*

This is the more difficult material about how to evaluate conduct once it is proven. There are no obvious omissions if you decide to teach it at all. *Section 4:* Omissions in this section do not seem advisable. You could perhaps drop *Collins* and its Notes at the end, simply lecturing briefly on the idea that res ipsa has traditionally not been used with multiple actors, but there might be some exceptions. On balance, however, it's probably faster to allow students to read the material for themselves since the Notes are pretty straightforward.

OUTLINE

§ 1. BREACH: ASSESSING REASONABLE CARE BY ASSESSING RISKS AND COSTS

[a]   Where we are in the analytical structure (one-paragraph text)

[b]   Negligence is conduct, not state of mind (one-paragraph text)

[c]   Risks and utilities introduced. Problem: Brown v. Stiel.

[d]   Forseeability. Pipher v. Parsell

[e]   Cases exemplifying the risk-utility analysis without discussing it in words: an inductive exercise. Indiana Consol. Ins. Co. v. Mathew (low risks, high utilities); Stinnett v. Buchele (low risk in light of plaintiff's ability to protect himself); Bernier v. Boston Edison Co., (costs of safety in dollars and in other risks).

[e]   A formula or model that can explain the cases? The risk-utility balance. United States v. Carroll Towing Co.; Note: Applying the Risk-Utility Formula; Note Evaluating the Risk-Utility Assessment

§ 2. ASSESSING RESPONSIBILITY WHEN MORE THAN ONE PERSON IS NEGLIGENT

The structure of apportionment – comparative fault reductions in damages, joint and several liability with contribution, and several liability. Four-page text and diagrams.

§ 3. PROVING AND EVALUATING CONDUCT

A. Proving Conduct

[i] Direct Proof

[A] Sufficiency of proof – the requirement of specific conduct. Santiago v. First Student, Inc.

[B] Conflicting evidence – credibility, experts and the process of determining facts. Upchurch v. Rotenberry

[ii] Circumstantial evidence – inferences of fact

[A] Permissible inferences of fact. Forsyth v. Joseph.

[B] Opinion evidence bearing on factual inferences. Note: Witness' Opinions as to Facts and Factual Inferences

SUMMARY AND COMMENTS

Preliminary Note. The previous chapter introduced the basic duty in negligence cases – the duty of reasonable care. Later on, we'll consider more about particular duty issues, but first we march through the other elements of the plaintiff's case. This chapter deals with the second element, breach of duty. You might write the elements on the board and highlight the breach element. In ordinary negligence cases, you breach the duty of reasonable care by negligence. What counts as negligence and who decides?

The two-paragraph text preceding the *Brown v. Stiel* problem attempts to emphasize some key points that usually require repeated attention. (1) The key idea of negligence is unreasonable risk. (2) Negligence is conduct (either an act or an omission to act when there is a duty to do so). A state of mind by itself is not negligence. (3) Negligence and intentional torts are contrasting ideas. (4) Nevertheless, students need to recognize that many intentional *acts* merely create unreasonable risks and thus are merely negligent act, not intentional harms. In the speeding example, which will lead us to the first of the questions following the *Brown* problem, anyone struck and injured by the speeder could show an intentional tort– battery– only by showing an intent to strike the victim. Intent might take the form of purpose to strike with the car, or it might take the form of substantial certainty that striking would occur. See, explicating the intentional tort/negligence distinction, DOBBS ON TORTS § 116 (2000). The idea of substantial certainty versus the idea of high risk is reprised in the Brown problem and its notes.

PROBLEM: BROWN V. STIEL

A builder chooses to build a structure with steel because the same size building with concrete would be more expensive. But, the problem says, use of steel in this way creates greater likelihood of injury or death. On the average, three people will be killed in constructing a steel building like this, but only one for a concrete building. When two injuries in fact occur in a collapse of steel beams, can you say the builder is negligent? The problem introduces a discussion on risks, costs, risk-utility balancing and alternative "moral" and insurance approaches.

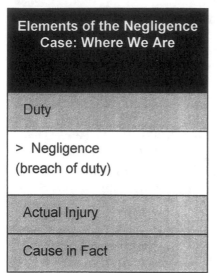

Issues. (1) Was the builder guilty of a *Garratt v. Dailey* intent, since he knew of the risk? (2) Was the builder negligent, considering the risks he took and the value of building such structures? (3) Should alternatives to negligence have a place in our system of law? Should a workers' compensation scheme apply to provide compensation not only for the injured worker but also for anyone injured on the job site?

§ 1. ASSESSING REASONABLE CARE BY ASSESSING FORESEEABLE RISKS AND COSTS

Intentional torts: *Garratt v. Dailey*. Some students think that whatever the analysis of negligence shows, the builder is guilty of an intentional tort. He has intentionally built a steel building when knew that its construction would statistically kill more people than an alternative, concrete building. Explicitly or implicitly, a discussant suggests that this is intentional in the sense of *Garratt v. Dailey*. But it is not. The certainty here is statistical certainty–it is "certain" that someone will be injured only in the sense that given many such buildings, an average number of persons will be killed in the construction. This is quite unlike the mechanical certainty in *Garratt* and it is quite unlike *Garratt's* focus on an identified individual victim or small class of victims. Either difference takes us away from a substantial certainty kind of intent. The substantial certainty rule is a here and now rule. It you could take an infinite time frame, all injuries would be certain. There would be no negligence law, only a spurious kind of intent that would amount to strict liability. In our problem, the builder knows the risk, but it is still a risk, not a substantial certainty. We can thus mark the fact that we have moved to a new concept, quite different from the intentional tort concept. On the limits to the substantial certainty concept *see* RESTATEMENT (THIRD) OF TORTS: LIABILITY FOR PHYSICAL HARMS § 1, cmt. e (Proposed Final Draft No. 1, 2005).

Breach of duty: unreasonable risk. To state the standard or duty, as we did in the last chapter, is not to decide whether that standard has been breached. On the issue of breach, unreasonable risk becomes the central topic. What makes a risk unreasonable? You don't need to introduce the terminology we eventually arrive at. It comes naturally for discussants to assert that the builder took a risk that was greater than the alternatives and for others to point out that there were nevertheless good reasons to take it. After all, any activity carries *some* risks. We don't want to eliminate all risks, only those that are unreasonably large. You can use driving as an example. Statistically, driving will predictably produce a much greater number of injuries, but we have not yet said that driving carefully is negligent. The Restatement of Physical Harms comments that large activities– like driving vehicles, operating railroads or supplying electricity or constructing buildings– will seldom count at negligence in themselves. Instead, the plaintiff will need to prove that the activity was carried out in some unreasonably dangerous way. *See* RESTATEMENT (THIRD) OF TORTS: LIABILITY FOR PHYSICAL HARMS § 3, cmt. *j*. Constructing buildings, including the imaginary steel building here, is useful enough that we might we willing to accept the risks of careful building. Even if not, we'd want to know more about the advantages and disadvantages– those things we'll come to call risks and utilities.

Discussion can explore the question whether a risk-utility balance is a desirable way of judging fault. For instance, you could judge fault in *Brown* by considering community standards or the reasonable expectations of the injured people. The discussion of risk will be untutored and unstructured, but this need not be troubling. At the end of the subsection we'll come to the Learned Hand formulation in *Carroll Towing*, and we'll find that much of our discussion of this problem is recapitulated by the Hand-Posner analysis.

The problem becomes a constant example. It is a small example of a big idea in negligence law. We can recur to the problem periodically throughout the course. Risks must be taken in life if you act at all. Not all risks are condemned.

Alternative compensation systems. The problem also looks forward and helps establish and reiterate the theme– should the injury problem be dealt with through a system of personal accountability for fault? Might one want to deal with it through a system of insurance, such as that involved in workers' compensation? Or even through other forms of strict liability, in which the business is regarded as the source of the problem and expected to bear its costs? It is not too soon to tell the students that such alternatives exist and ought to be kept in mind.

PIPHER V. PARSELL, 930 A.2d 890 (Del. 2007)

The case introduces a key concept about negligence that was set out initially on the first page of this chapter: that negligence is conduct that creates unreasonable risks, and one main component of judging that is whether a reasonable person would foresee that harm might result from his actions. While judging foreseeability may be a complex matter, in some cases it may simply come down to asking whether something similar has happened before. And where reasonable people could conclude that harm was foreseeable, this is an issue that should be left to the jury.

Three teenagers were sitting in the front seat of a pickup truck being driven by Parsell. As they were going 55 miles per hour down the highway, Beisel suddenly grabbed the wheel without warning, causing the truck to swerve onto the shoulder. About 30 seconds later Beisel did the same thing, causing the truck to slide down an embankment into a tree, injuring the plaintiff, Pipher.

Pipher sued Parsell for negligence, claiming he should have done something to prevent Beisel's actions. Pipher pointed to the fact that Parsell should have been on notice that Beisel was a risk after the first incident 30 seconds before. Pipher also claimed that because Parsell "laughed it off" the first time, Parsell actually encouraged Beisel to do it again.

In order to establish negligence, the plaintiff must point to some alternative conduct that the defendant should have engaged in. Pipher's lawyer got Parsell to admit at trial that he could have done several things differently: (1) he could have admonished Beisel not to do that again; (2) he could have pulled over and ordered Beisel into the back seat; and (3) he could have warned Beisel that he would kick her out of the truck if she did that again.

But would a reasonable and prudent person in Parsell's position have done any of those things? The trial court held that no was the answer, as a matter of law, because it was not reasonably foreseeable that Beisel would grab the wheel again. That is, the trial judge believed that reasonable people could not differ on whether Parsell's conduct created a foreseeable risk of harm to Pipher.

The court here agrees that "where the actions of a passenger that cause an accident are not foreseeable, there is no negligence attributable to the driver." But here, the court said, reasonable people could believe that Beisel's second grab was foreseeable since Beisel had grabbed the wheel once before. Thus summary judgment was improper and a jury should be allowed to decide whether Parsell breached a duty of reasonable care.

Note 1 ties right in. Would the trial judge have been correct if the accident was caused when Beisel suddenly grabbed the wheel the first time? *Brown v. Mobley* is such a case (albeit with a twist), holding that a passenger's sudden grabbing of the steering wheel was unforeseeable as a matter of law. The twist is that the passenger in Brown was drunk and his grabbing the steering wheel was in reponse to another passenger's refusing to give him a bottle of liquor. The court characterized the passenger's action as "criminal conduct" and based its opinion in part on the idea that an intervening criminal act is unforeseeable, breaking the causal chain – a kind of proximate cause reasoning we see in Chapter 8. But the court clearly says in *Brown* that there was no evidence that the driver "should have anticipated" the passenger's actions. The court noted that the driver had driven this person home drunk before without incident.

Note 2 invites the class to begin thinking about what kinds of facts might tend to show breach of duty, with a focus on foreseeable risks. Remind the class that the court in *Pipher* reversed and remanded because the facts produced an issue on which reasonable people could differ; it did not decide whether Parsell breached a duty. What might the plaintiff argue to the jury? Perhaps: (1) Parsell knew or should have known that Beisel posed a risk because of Beisel's initial actions 30 seconds before. That is, it was foreseeable to a reasonable and prudent person in Parsell's position (driving a car at high speed) that there was a risk of injury presented by Beisel. (2) A reasonable person would also have foreseen that this risk of harm was fairly great, both in terms of its likelihood (i.e., the odds that Beisel would try it again) and its potential severity (given the speed of the car). Given that, it was foreseeable that something like this would happen, so a reasonable person would have done something other than just forge ahead. Look back at the case for the various suggestions of alternative conduct that the plaintiff raised. What might the defendant say in response? (1) The trial judge, remember, thought it was clear that a reasonable person would NOT have expected Beisel to do this again, so the defendant could build on that. Would a reasonable person in Parsell's position have thought that Beisel would be very unlikely to do this again, given that they had run off the road the first time? Would a reasonable person have believed this was likely to happen again? If not, this would cut strongly against negligence. What about the laughing and joking around? The plaintiff argued that the laughing actually encouraged Beisel to grab the wheel again, but might you see it as creating the opposite reaction in a person – that the joke is over, we had a close call, now let's forget about it?

One thing will almost certainly emerge if you get the class going in a discussion like this: We need to know a lot more information about the situation, these relationships, what kinds of things may or may not have happened in the past, and so on. We can't really judge "foreseeability" without knowing a lot more about what a reasonable person in the defendant's position would reasonably anticipate, and that would be influenced by a number of things. For example, what if we learned that Beisel was Parsell's girlfriend, but that Parsell had just made a pass "in jest" at Pipher? What if Beisel was known for doing crazy, unexpected things? Wouldn't that influence how a reasonable person would predict her actions in this instance?

You might, if you want to anticipate the kind of analysis at the heart of the next case, even get into the assessment of the proposed alternative conduct in *Pipher*. If you think the risks of harm in the case were present at least to some degree, were these risks sufficiently great to warrant, for example, stopping the car and admonishing Beisel? Would that have possibly made things even worse (creating an even greater risk that Beisel would do something crazy)? If the proposed alternatives are either riskier than the conduct actually engaged in, or unreasonably burdensome when compared to the gravity of the foreseeable risks, then a reasonable person would not have done the alternative conduct – and thus would not have breached a duty of reasonable care by doing whatever was done. To assess this, would we again want to know more information about Beisel and what Parsell knew about her? If Beisel was the kind of person known to get quietly angry and lash out violently, then perhaps a verbal dressing-down is that last thing a reasonable person with such knowledge would do before putting her back into a moving car next to the driver. On the other hand, if she was the kind of person who rarely did stupid things and always admitted error, and this was known to Parsell, then perhaps the admonishment would have been a reasonable thing to have done. Would it have avoided the harm entirely for Parsell to have stopped the car and thrown the keys into a nearby river, causing them all to walk home? Yes, but that "alternative" conduct would be overkill, would it not? A reasonable person does not have to take every conceivable measure to avoid harm in order to be found non-negligent. This is raised centrally, and rather humorously, in the *Mathew* case coming up.

Note 3. This Note points out briefly that foreseeability of harm has many roles in a negligence case. You probably don't need to address it now at all. It will unfold as we continue looking at the other elements of the prima facie case. Sometimes foreseeability may be shorthand for policy judgments not much related to probability, judgments usually reserved for discussions of limited duty. This duty-connected use of foreseeability can wait until we reach the special-duty chapters, however. At this juncture, what seems most important is to get students settled in the notion that foreseeability means probability, sufficiently high and/or severe enough that ordinary care requires some precaution.

NOTE: ASSESSING THE *LANGUAGE* OF FORESEEABILITY AND RISK

Hopefully starting off with *Pipher* does not suggest that foreseeability is simply based on what has happened before. Certainly something can be foreseeable even when it happens for the first time; we will see some cases like that in this and later chapters. But *Pipher* makes the point that where something has happened before, it will likely create a jury issue, at a minimum, as to whether that prior occurrence makes a repeat occurrence reasonably foreseeable. To make sense of foreseeability talk you have to realize that, however vague or contradictory opinions might be, foreseeability makes sense as a value loaded term referring to probability. "Unforeseeable" has become a lawyer's way of saying that something was so improbable that reasonable people would not need to take precautions against it. It's absurd to think that the court in *Romine* meant anything different from that.

Another case that seems to make this clear is *A.H. v. Rockingham Pub. Co., Inc.*, 495 S.E.2d 482 (Va. 1998). There, a young teen paper boy was sexually assaulted in early morning hours while delivering papers. His employer, the newspaper, knew of three other similar sexual assaults on its carriers in a town of only 30,000. Yet the court said that such assaults were unforeseeable. It seems unlikely that "unforeseeable" is a literal psychological description. It seems to mean instead to mean that in the court's judgment the risk or probability was small enough to justify the newspaper's failure to protect the boy, even by a warning.

INDIANA CONSOLIDATED INS. CO. V. MATHEW, 402 N.E.2d 1000 (Ind. Ct. App. 1980).

The defendant starts a riding lawnmower in his brother's garage, it catches fire, and the garage burns. The insurer of the garage sues him for negligently causing the fire, which required it to pay off. Should he have pushed the mower outside before starting? The risk was very low. Should he have moved it after the fire started? The risk of losing the garage was high, but the risk to himself was more important. Weighing risks and utilities is very much in the court's mind, though not so much in its words. Before you begin substantive analysis, you may need to explain subrogation, although experience indicates that students have no difficulty with this idea.

Very few rules are stated in this case and those that immediately follow. The teacher must guide the student in the art of interpretation and induction. What factors might the courts have in mind in making these judgments?

The first specification of negligence. It may be useful to parse out the three claims of negligence. The first, that defendant spilled gasoline, is the least interesting. There was no proof that he did.

The second specification of negligence and the meaning of foreseeability. The second argues that he should not have started the machine in the garage. To this contention– which involves no dispute about the underlying facts at all– the court makes two responses. The first is that the garage was large and suited to starting cars and mowers. The second is that fire was "unforeseeable." Both these responses come to much the same thing –risk of fire was so low that a reasonable person would not have felt it necessary to move the mower, at least when that risk is balanced against the inconvenience of pushing the heavy mower out. See *Wotiz v. Gruny,* 667 N.E.2d 102 (Ill. Ct. App. 1996) ("[N]o one is expected to guard against harm from events which are not reasonably anticipated at all or are so unlikely to occur that the risk, although recognizable, would commonly be disregarded").

The third specification of negligence. The third argument is that the defendant was negligent in not pushing the mower to a position of safety after the fire started. This, however, involved a greater risk, that is, a risk of greater harm (not greater probability, but greater harm). Thus while in the second argument we were concerned with probabilities, here we are concerned with the extent of harm that may result if the risk becomes reality. The risk to person is of such a serious nature that the balance requires no action.

Specific alternative conduct compared. You may want to point out (because the facts lend themselves to this observation) that the court is comparing the defendant's actual conduct with some very specific alternative sets of conduct. This important idea will come up more directly a little later.

Emergency doctrine. The court's language suggests this is an emergency doctrine case, but it is not. That doctrine will be involved only if we think the actor made a wrong choice, one that a reasonable person would not make in sangfroid but might make in the heat of emergency. But here a comparison of the risks suggests that we do not need to resort to the emergency doctrine–the actor made the right choice, given the harm that could have resulted if he pushed the mower.

Seeing the case as a weighing of risks and utilities. You need not anticipate the *Carroll Towing* case in your classroom discussion. But if the class has difficulty with the probability and seriousness of threatened harm, you can imagine these probabilities hypothetically:

Risk of injury to garage if mower is not moved: .90 (i.e., highly probable)

Risk of injury to D if mower is moved: .20 (i.e., not very probable)

Does this suggest defendant should be liable? No, because the injury if it occurred to defendant would be, either in human or economic terms, much worse. It might have been death or permanent and painful injury. We could put figures on this to make the comparison explicit. We could imagine that garages could be rebuilt for $10,000 but that defendant, if burned, would probably have $100,000 or more in injury. Multiplying the $10,000 garage injury by the probability, we find that the risk on that side is $9,000. Multiplying the defendant's potential injury by .20 we come to $20,000. The weight is clearly on the side of the defendant.

	Garage	Person
Risk	.90 (very likely)	.20 (unlikely)
Dollar harm threatened	10,000	100,000
The multiplication	.90 x 10,000	.20 x 100,000
The risk-utility "score" or stake	$9,000	$20,000

This table shows, a la *Carroll Towing*, that the defendant has the higher net stake, or put otherwise, more social good comes from protecting the defendant than from protecting the garage. This is not to say that judges, juries or lawyers go through such figures, or that the figures could be found empirically. The numbers arc only illustrative. A jury will reach a conclusion without being able to verbalize it in most instances, but the result is no less sound. If you want to avoid being this explicit until you've covered *Carroll Towing*, that works well.

Seeing the case in other terms. *(1) Life versus property.* You can present students with at least two other ways to think about *Mathew.* Indeed, students are likely to present one of them. They frequently cast the problem as a balancing problem, but one that simply balances human life (or injury) against property. This simple balancing is far removed from what we'll see in *Carroll Towing*, but it is not foolish. Quite arguably, the law cannot really expect to do anything in a fine-tuned way, much less do a quantified weighing of risks and utilities. Still, you can encourage students to see that the idea of weighing is not necessarily limited to cases of life-vs-property. Suppose Mathew decided he had time to take out and save one of his brother's two motorcycles and chose his favorite, worth $1,000, rather than a classic Harley worth $50,000. The jury might forgive him because of the emergency but if emergency does not permit such a lapse in judgment, then isn't he clearly making a bad choice? If he had a duty of care (because, after all, he is the cause of the fire, albeit an innocent one) then he would surely be negligent. This is property vs. more valuable property, not life vs. property. If students will agree, they are accepting a balance of value in this step.

(2) Treating others as you would treated yourself. A second way to think of *Mathew* will be helpful when you evaluate *Carroll Towing.* If you think that the defendant in *Mathew* behaved as he would have behaved had he owned the garage, then it is hard to find fault with his conduct. Is this perhaps a way to judge reasonableness of risks?

Note 1. See discussion above.

Note 2. In *Fintzi*, cited here, the court held there was no negligence in allowing children to play on wet grass at a camp. To impose liability would "so sterilize camping . . . as to render it sedentary." Thus part of the court's reasoning was that holding the defendant negligent here would change the nature of camping (for everyone) in a socially undesirable way. One might see this as simply balancing the "utility" of the conduct engaged in again the foreseeable risks of the same conduct, a point we will see in more detail later. See also **Note 3** below on the "burdens to third parties" point.

Note 3. In *Barnes*, cited here, the court affirmed. The court concluded: "The facts presented suggest nothing more than a possibility that a passenger might fall while attempting to remove her shoes. However, this mere possibility does not rise to a level of foreseeability suggesting negligence on the part of the TSA." There was no evidence in the case that anyone had ever fallen before. The court also stressed that the burden of providing a chair, while seemingly small, was still great compared to the foreseeability of a fall (since foreseeability was negligible), and was in fact not as small as it seemed at first glance. If we hold that this was negligent not to provide a chair, the court reasoned, then all airports would have to provide chairs, and even "mosques and temples, and entrances to homes" would have to have chairs; "anytime footwear is removed," the court thought, people in all kinds of walks of life would have to provide chairs. "The possibility of an occasional fall does not warrant the widespread precautionary provision of chairs." Would the court's reasoning be entirely different if there had been evidence that passengers were falling right and left when removing their shoes at TSA security checkpoints? Of course. But the evidence did not show that.

STINNETT V. BUCHELE, 598 S.W.2d 469 (Ky. Ct. App. 1980).

An employee (not covered by workers' compensation, explained briefly in **Note 1**) falls off the employer's roof. The employer has provided no protection against a fall. Yet the employer may not be negligent, given the fact that the employee was also in a good position to prevent harm, by providing himself with protection or by demanding it from the employer. The specific idea is not contributory negligence of the employee, but that the employer is not negligent if he reasonably relies on the employee to protect himself.

The broader idea, the one we want to emphasize, is that the likelihood that the risk will come to fruition seems small. There is a risk of falling to the ground and causing, one thinks, quite severe harm– death or serious paralysis would not be out of the picture. Yet the risk may be so small that an employer could reasonably take that risk. Is this the explanation? Perhaps so, if we add that the employer might assess the risk as a small one because he reasonably relies on the employee to protect himself from obvious risks, a point emphasized in *Halek*, **Note 4.** As Judge Posner said before he wrote the opinion in *Halek*, "an obvious danger is no danger to a reasonably careful person." *Pomer v. Schoolman*, 875 F.2d 1262 (7th Cir. 1989).

The trier judging fault might ask who is in the best position, psychologically or otherwise, to provide the necessary safety precaution. The person on the scene is Mr. Stinnett. He is also the person whose interest is most implicated in the safety– he is the one whose body may be broken or life lost. Maybe we could expect people to be most motivated by immediate physical danger and least aware of danger that is only an abstract proposition. Dr. Buchele might never think of danger on the roof except in the most abstract way; Mr. Stinnett can look down and see that a fall might easily occur. In this rather narrow sense, Mr. Stinnett might be thought to be psychologically the best safety provider, especially if the cost of safety is equal for both him and Buchele.

If this is right, the most effective allocation of responsibility would be to hold Stinnett responsible for his own safety. In fact, if we diffused or eliminated Stinnett's responsibility for himself by holding Buchele liable, the world might become riskier for everyone. The Bucheles of the world, confronted only remotely with danger are apt not to recognize it and not to provide safety, even though they are held liable later. The Stinnetts, knowing that a fall is their problem, will take a rope with them to the vertiginous heights. Responsibility and fault are complex matters.

The term "best safety provider" is sometimes used in a quite different way, to mean the actor who can most cheaply purchase safety. This is a complex idea in itself and not one that goes particularly well with this case.

The obvious danger rule. Experienced tort teachers will recognize *Stinnett* as a variation on the obvious danger rule. We don't' take that rule up here, but in the chapters on landowners and products. Our point here is about probability of injury, although probability is judged in this case in a way more subtle than many students are prepared for.

You might think the Kentucky court applied the legal principle wrongly because Buchele should have foreseen that Stinnett would not provide his own safety equipment. In *Lee Lewis Construction, Inc. v. Harrison,* 70 S.W.3d 778 (Tex. 2001), the court held that a general contractor was liable for failing to insist that its subcontractors supply an independent lifeline to workers outside the 10th story. But even if *Stinnett* misapplied the principle, it is the principle more than its application that we want our students to see here– negligence entails an unreasonable risk of harm, and assessments of the risk include assessments of what the plaintiff himself might do to avoid it. If the court had permitted a finding of negligence against Buchele, the issue of contributory fault would still arise and might defeat or reduce Stinnett's recovery.

Note 1. Workers' comp. This should be self-explanatory. We also saw a brief mention of workers' comp in the notes after the Brown v. Stiel problem at the beginning of this chapter. Workers' compensation is the focus of Chapter 28.

Note 2. Social vs. individual responsibility. Although we might agree that Buchele should not be liable if he is not negligent, uncompensated injury is nevertheless sometimes a social problem. Let's assume it is. That does not change Buchele's liability. A social problem caused by no one's fault may be resolved by social means– welfare, public insurance, social security or other systems. Individual responsibility in damages is not justified merely because a social problem exists. You can recall Holmes' comments in Chapter 5. The point is to emphasize the vast difference between social responsibility– the liability of all of us through taxes and governmental action or through insurance– and individual responsibility– the liability of a particular individual for another's misfortune. If you pick an individual to bear the loss for no particular reason, you have simply taken a hostage or extorted money. This point also takes us back to ideas advanced in connection with *Surocco, Wegner,* and *Vincent.*

If you have time to remind the class of the lawyer's responsibility, you can ask whether the lawyer should do anything further for Stinnett.

Note 3. Expecting the plaintiff to care for himself. The *Stinnett* court does not make an apportionment or comparative fault decision here. The court does not bar Stinnett because he was negligent or more negligent than the defendant. Instead, the court bars Stinnett because Buchele was not (in the court's view) negligent at all.

How does the court come to the view that Buchele is not negligent? The court believes that Buchele would not have reasonably foreseen danger for a very specific reason– because Buchele would have reasonably expected Stinnett to protect himself (perhaps by asking for safety equipment if he had none). This is a bit more subtle than many students are expecting.

Compare *Stinnett* to *Lowery,* cited here. In that case, the court also affirmed a no-negligence finding when the plaintiff fell off a roof, suggesting that it was the plaintiff who had the greater understanding of the particular danger than the defendant, and that the defendant was not unreasonable in assuming that the plaintiff could watch out for herself.

The exact converse would be true if the defendant has reason to believe the plaintiff would NOT protect himself. In *Daniels v. Senior Care, Inc.,* cited here, the defendant had been hired to take care of Ingram, an older person suffering dementia. One risk recognized was that the Ingram might forgetfully start a fire. Yet the caregiver took no steps when Ingram piled magazines on a heating element. A fire started resulting in Ingram's death and suit was brought against the caregiver. The court observed that the caregiver should take into account Ingram's incapacity in determining what safety steps were needed and went on to hold that the caregiver was subject to liability. The "ability of the person injured to take care of his personal safety" turned out to be controlling –exactly as it was in *Stinnett*. The result was different in the two cases because the injured person in Stinnett's case would foreseeably care for himself, but could not do so in *Daniels.*

Note 4. The obviousness of the danger. Perhaps the clearest situation in which a person can justifiably rely on the plaintiff to protect himself is where the danger is obvious to everyone, as the cases in this Note suggest. The open and obvious danger conception will arise several times in the course, in the landowners chapter and elsewhere. *Accord,* that only if the risk remains unreasonable despite its obviousness would the defendant be negligent. *Perkoviq v. Delcor Homes-Lake Shore Pointe, Ltd.,* 643 N.W.2d 212 (Mich. 2002) (another fall-from-a roof case). Open and obvious danger is, however, merely a factual element in some cases; the principle is much larger, involving as it does the concept of a low probability (risk) of harm, and specifically a low probability due to the fact that the plaintiff can care for herself.

Note 5. Expecting care by third persons. Essentially the same principle applies when the defendant, instead of expecting that the plaintiff will make conditions safe for himself, expects that some third person will do so. If parents are caring for a child, others might reasonably think the parents will take appropriate steps to avoid injury. But not when the others know the parents are distracted. *Herron* holds it may be reasonable for the host to expect parents to protect the child in swimming pool cases. *Perri* deals with the case in which the risk is greater because the host knows of parental distraction or ignorance of the risk. *Perri* is not a swimming pool case. It involved a Chinese restaurant where hot tea was set on a lazy susan at a large table as adults were being seated. The waitress knew there were small children there but did not alert the adults to the presence of the tea on the turntable. One small child spun the turntable; hot tea spilled on an infant. The court held that a jury could find risk to a child foreseeable because adults were still being seated and knew nothing of the tea or its unstable location. The court also emphasized that a warning by the waitress would not be burdensome. *Foss,* cited here, held that the homeowner could rely upon the parent to protect a child from harm from ordinary household hazards, a clear distinction from the finding made in *Perri.*

BERNIER V. BOSTON EDISON CO., 403 N.E.2d 391 (Mass. 1980).

This is another case that seems to be engaging in some kind of risk-utility analysis without explicitly discussing the *Carroll Towing* formula. Ramsdell, pulling out of a parking place, collided with Boireau's car. Ramsdell then lost control of her car, went around Boireau's car with her foot on the gas, and proceeded along a sidewalk, hitting a camera store, leveling a parking meter, damaging a Chevelle, and finally knocking down a light pole, which struck still another car and came down across Bernier's legs and apparently injured Kasputys, too. Should the pole have been structured so that it would not fall in case a driver took to the sidewalk and weaved into it? The court holds that the designer-owner of the pole can be found negligent for failing to provide a stronger pole.

Some students are troubled by holding Boston Edison liable when it was, they think, Ramsdell who knocked the pole down. The next section deals (albeit briefly) with the idea of multiple tortfeasors and apportionment of responsibility. Here we try to get students to focus on the question of negligence rather than causation or apportionment. How does one weigh the costs of a stronger pole against the risk to pedestrians?

The company actually seems to have argued that the social utility of falling poles was high (that is, benefits were high in relation to costs) because poles that stood on impact would harm motorists, presumably a more numerous group than the pedestrians likely to be injured by the falling poles. This does not involve either costs or benefits to the defendant, but rather benefit (*social* utility) to others.

Suppose we added the (hypothetical) fact that stronger poles would also cost $100 more per pole. Is the increase in safety resulting from strong poles worth this cost?

Actually, the added investment would almost certainly mean a rate increase, so that the public itself would pay. That may make the company a good risk distributor; the loss can be absorbed by citizens of the area as a whole, almost in the same way it would be absorbed if the injury were compensated from tax monies. This would mean that no one would feel the blow very heavily, and that is to the good. Is this a good enough reason to impose liability? How many taxpayers would vote to have this increased safety on the public streets if it meant even a small rate increase?

Both kinds of cost-benefit assessments– the benefit of safer streets for drivers and the cost of safer poles– seem involved here. Yet it is striking that we have almost no picture at all about either the benefits (how much safer is it for drivers to have tear-away poles?) or costs (how much more will it really cost to install solid poles?). If this cost-benefit analysis really is part of fault assessment, don't we need to know a good deal more than we do here? One answer is that we must pursue law in a practical world. We have no laboratories. We must not commit real life issues to 20 years of academic study. We must make decisions at the end of the trial and must expect to act upon judgment as well as fact. Here the court seems to assume that there is enough evidence, at least when coupled with the general experience of juries, to permit a finding of fact about risk. Is this right?

Note 1. See above.

Note 2. See above. On the question whether these polycentric-task cases are suitable for adjudication within the tort system, consider some arguments made by one of the great legal thinkers of our time, the late Lon Fuller. In *Adjudication and The Rule of Law*, [1960] PROC. AM. SOC'Y INT'L L. 1, Fuller contrasted polycentric decisions with decisions suited for adjudication. The latter can be formulated in terms of issues to which proofs and arguments can be directed, and (one thinks) there is one best solution or at any rate a manageable number of suitable solutions. Polycentric tasks, however, involve situations in which many appropriate solutions can be reached and the parts to solutions are interlocking. A sequence of decisions must be made, and each slot in the sequence could be resolved by one of several acceptable decisions. Yet each decision in sequence will affect the appropriate decisions at later points in the sequence. Suppose you are the manager of the co-op grocery and you're planning the work schedules for all the clerks for the month of November. Susie wants Thursday afternoons off because she has no child-care then. Brad does not want to work Thursdays at all because he is devastated by Wednesday night's group therapy. Jennie will work Thursdays happily, but if so, she must switch her regular bowling team and will not work Friday nights. If you start by switching Jennie, you must find someone for Friday nights. If you start by requiring Brad to work Thursdays in order to help Susie, you don't have to worry about Friday night. Whatever you decide first will determine something about all other decisions. Although each worker has an argument of sorts, the problem is not readily reduced to a series of rules which tells you which decision to make first. You can imagine administrators or managers dealing with the problem, but it is hard to imagine judicial decisions setting up general rules of duty and breach to cope with such cases. (This example, incidentally, tells you why the deans never schedule your classes for the times you wish.)

If Fuller was right that evaluation of polycentric tasks is not appropriate for adjudication, and if it is also true that the risk-utility analysis is polycentric, then negligence law is not suitable for adjudication. That's a pretty extreme conclusion. It might be more helpful to suggest that when a defendant is faced with such decisions, the defendant ought to be permitted more leeway in decision-making than Boston Edison was given. The argument was hard for Boston Edison to make, however, since it seems to have made no conscious choices at all.

Note 3 anticipates Chapter 9 on contributory and comparative fault. You can begin to kick these ideas around here in class, before the students have studied the doctrines, or you can simply plant the seed by having students read this but not raising it in class.

Note 4. We saw in some earlier materials that the social utility of a defendant's conduct might be important in assessing negligence. That is, where the utility of the conduct outweighs the foreseeable risks created by the conduct, many would conclude that the conduct is simply not negligent. The three cases discussed here all make that basic point. They help set the stage for the notes after *Carroll Towing*.

UNITED STATES V. CARROLL TOWING CO., 159 F.2d 169 (2d Cir. 1947)

"[A] conclusion that the burden of precautions would substantially exceed the loss such precautions could prevent forecloses the possibility of recovery." *Reardon v. Peoria & Pekin Union Railway Co.*, 26 F.3d 52 (7th Cir. 1994) (Easterbrook, J.).

The Grace Line employees, operating the Carroll Towing tug boat, negligently ran into a barge and broke a hole in her bottom. The barge would not have sunk if a bargee had been on board to activate the pumps, but he was not and the barge sank. Was it negligence not to have a bargee on board so that the barge owner's recovery should be reduced under Admiralty comparative fault rules?

A portion of what Judge Hand says should be familiar. In saying that there is no general rule requiring a bargee's presence or forgiving a bargee's absence, he is saying that Admiralty law's attitude is like the attitude in *Chaffin v. Brame* and *Pokora v. Wabash Railway* (range of vision rule and the stop, look, and listen rule, mentioned in Chapter 5). Hand makes the point that risks and other factors differ with circumstances so that a "rule" is really not justly possible.

Hand got more specific about why no general rule requiring a bargee can be announced. We have said circumstances differ; Hand now analyzes circumstances that matter and classifies them. One's "duty" (meaning, probably, the decision that one is negligent) is a function of three variables: (1) probability of harm, (2) magnitude or gravity of harm, and (3) burden of adequate precautions. He then reduces this to an "algebraic" formula, imposing liability when B<PL (when the burden of precaution is less than the probability of harm times its magnitude). On the facts of the case, the risk of harm was high enough to require the defendant to bear the burden of having a bargee on board.

Note 1. *Carroll Towing* and mainstream analysis. Courts routinely weigh risks against utilities in some fashion to determine whether the evidence of negligence is sufficient. The cases we've just covered were balancing or weighing risks and utilities, but evidently not with any explicit standards or formulas in mind. In *Indiana Conslidated Ins. Co. v. Mathew,* in *Stinnett,* and in *Bernier,* the courts considered probability of harm, extent of harm, social utilities and burdens of avoiding injury. In none of the cases did the court explicitly adopt the *Carroll Towing* formula, but in each the court considered one or more of the elements in that formula that were salient on the facts. Some courts expressly follow the *Carroll Towing* formula on the negligence issue. E.g., *Rice v. Sabir*, 979 S.W.2d 305 (Tenn. 1998). Others do so in discussing issues they identify as "duty" issues. *See* DOBBS ON TORTS § 229 (2000).

The explicit formulas along *Carroll Towing* lines tighten up the ideas about how risks and utilities should be weighed against one another. Hand introduced a system or model that describes rather precisely how the factors are to be weighed. Although this more rigorous approach may offer clarity and discipline, it does not really depend upon the algebraic formula, much less upon any quantification of risks or utilities. The "algebra" illustrates the idea, but the plaintiff is not required to actual figures for B, or P or even L. Instead, the triers of fact normally use their experience to make estimates.

Note 2. The alternative conduct was having a bargee on board at all times, as is developed further in the upcoming notes.

Notes 3-5. Toward student understanding. You might first need to go over Notes 3 and 4 to see how the formula would work in a case where it *is* possible to quantify the terms. In the hypothetical used in Note 3, the barge will (statistically speaking) break loose once a year, doing an average of $25,000 in damage. This could be prevented by spending $30,000 to have a full-time bargee, but that would be economically foolish (inefficient). Hence, Judge Posner thinks, the law of negligence should not force that expenditure by assessing damages against the barge owner. But as Note 4 points out, if the barge would foreseeably break loose twice a year, with an average of $50,000 in damages per year, the expenditure of $30,000 for the bargee would make economic sense, and the barge owner who failed to get a bargee under those circumstances would definitely be negligent.

Note 5. Once this idea is demonstrated, you can apply this type of analysis in reviewing the preceding cases and also the *Brown v. Stiel* problem. In those applications of the idea, we will have no figures for probability, amount of harm, or burden. But once again, you can apply the idea even when you cannot quantify it. You can reconsider the *Mathew* case to see how the idea of *Carroll Towing* was applied even though no figures were available to tell us exactly how probable the harm might have been if the lawnmower twin had pushed the mower out of the garage.

Burden of adequate precaution. The "adequate precaution" is not just any adequate precaution. It is the precaution the plaintiff claims should have been taken but was not. Except in *res ipsa loquitur* cases, the claimant always has the burden of identifying the ways in which the defendant could have proceeded more safely. In *Carroll Towing*, the claim was that the barge owner should have had a bargee on board.

Precaution that diminishes social utility. There is an element in the burden of adequate precaution that may be concealed from many students until it is discussed. This is the idea that there are social utilities in many risky activities (driving cars, for example). The burden of adequate precaution requires us to assess costs such as the cost of paying for stronger poles in *Bernier*. But it also requires us to consider costs to others if stronger poles are used, specifically, the injury costs to occupants of cars that strike rigid poles. (Note that Judge Kaplan *did* consider that cost in *Bernier*, though arguably he did not give it enough weight.) So we can say that part of the burden or precaution or the cost of changing conduct is the loss of social utility or the imposition of social costs.

Thus "social utility" is a feature of the Hand formula. This means that a defendant might create a serious risk to the plaintiff that is "justified" if at all only by reason of the fact that the defendant himself and/or the public gets something good out of risky behavior. For example, in the *Brown v. Stiel* problem, the builder creates serious risks, even if he builds the safer, more expensive concrete building. Yet it is certain that courts will not find him negligent merely because he builds a building, since the social utility of buildings generally is very great (and maybe because it is impossible to rate the utility and disutility of such large activities as "building" in general). Put in terms of burden of precaution, the burden is great because the utilities would be lost if the defendant changed his conduct.

Determining social utility by dollar value. How do you determine the social utility of an activity? You might judge social utility by dollar value. The argument would be that an activity that produces a high income is more socially valuable than an activity that produces a low income. This is regarded as a true social value because people only pay money for an activity like hauling goods by barges because it is worth that much money or more to them. The shipper's willingness to pay for carriage of goods by barge is thus one measure–a dollar measure–of the social value to the community at large. If liability is imposed on barge operators, barge customers will have to pay higher prices and their customers will have to pay and so on. So the dollar measurement of utility and costs is arguably a good measure and it has one especially strong advantage: it reduces the risks and utilities on both sides to a common denominator. This will provoke discussion in most classes, especially if you tie it back explicitly to *Brown v. Stiel*, where the dollar valuation seems to disregard non-dollar values in human life and limb.

Bearing the burden of social utility. Some bright student, having gone this far, may suddenly say, "But, at least as applied to *Brown v. Stiel*, the *Carroll Towing* formula asserts the very position that seemed unacceptable when we talked about *Surocco*." We suggested in discussing *Surocco* that if a public agent destroys the plaintiff's property to save the property of other citizens, that it would be unjust to make one citizen, the plaintiff, suffer for the public good, though there might be reason to ask the whole public to share in the costs, since it is getting the benefits.

If the argument was valid in connection with *Surocco*, isn't it also valid in connection with *Carroll Towing*'s formula? If the public benefits from buildings in the *Brown v. Stiel* problem, but the plaintiff suffers the harm, the plaintiff has been sacrificed to the public needs, and neither the defendant nor the public is required to pay. The fathers eat grapes and the sons' teeth are set on edge; the builder and the public take the benefits, the plaintiff takes the burden without compensation. The plaintiff's burden is "justified" by defendant's benefit! If you want to consider this kind of argument, take a look at *Bamford v. Turnley,* 3 B. & S. 67, 122 Eng. Rep. 27 (Exch. Ch. 1862), Chapter 23. If you want to pursue this at length here, you can import the excerpts from Bramwell's judgment. Before any such discussion, you will also want to consider the argument that the Hand formula is really a moral requirement that the defendant treat the plaintiff's property as he would treat his own.

Excluding some social costs from the calculus. A point to have in mind rather than a point to discuss: Suppose that a bargee's full-time presence helps reduce crime in the dock area. The crime that would be prevented has an annual cost of $15,000. Should we consider those costs as well as damages to ships and docks in calculating the social costs of not having a bargee on board?

We can exclude all unforeseeable costs under the reasonable person test. They would not affect the conduct under Hand's formula or under a "moral" version of the test for liability. But suppose the barge owner knows of the crime and that it would be prevented by having a bargee there. In that case, the crime and its costs are foreseeable. Nevertheless, should we exclude the crime costs if the defendant owes no duty to prevent crime in the neighborhood or, what may be about the same thing, because those costs are not part of the reason we think he should have a bargee on board in the first place?

If you *do* wish to talk about this problem in class, you can connect it back to the type of risk, class of person rules we saw in the last chapter on negligence per se. Equally, you can shape your discussion bearing in mind the scope of risk or proximate cause materials in Chapter 8.

Activity. Any system of judging utility will depend in part on how you characterize the activity. Suppose that a teen-aged male drives to a convenience store for cigarettes at midnight and has a collision on the way. Suppose that the store was only two blocks away and the young man could have walked. The social utility of cigarettes must be very low indeed if you subtract the costs of death and addiction from the dollar gains that cigarettes produce for the sellers. The utility of driving must also be very low if the driver could walk safely. Driving cars in general is very useful, but driving cars when you could walk and driving them to purchase a toxic substance is not very useful. The same point applies to risk. The activity is not too risky if you think the activity is "driving cars." If you think the activity is "teen-aged male driving" or "night driving" then it becomes riskier. This is a puzzling difficulty, recognized by the Restatement discussed above in connection with the Brown v. Stiel problem. See RESTATEMENT (THIRD) OF TORTS: LIABILITY FOR PHYSICAL HARMS § 3, cmt. j (Tent. Draft. 2001). The problem may be dealt with indirectly by a proximate or legal cause analysis, where courts may characterize the risks of conduct and thus implicitly characterize the "activity" they are addressing.

Note 6. Hand uses the term "duty" but seems to mean what we have been calling "negligence," the breach of duty of reasonable care. Expect students to be baffled about "duty" for a long time. They are in a grand tradition of confusion, shared by judges, professors, and practicing lawyers.

NOTE: APPLYING THE RISK-UTILITY FORMULA

This note lets students work through other applications of the Hand formula. Paragraphs 1 and 2 specifically recognize that in no version of it do courts expect the plaintiff to fill in dollar amounts. Instead, the formula is a model for thinking about what counts as negligence and for making appropriate estimates.

¶ ¶ 2-6. These paragraphs let you explore the possibility that the formula works well in some cases but not in others. When the claim is that the defendant did not remember or that he lacked sufficient information, it may be very difficult to apply the formula in a sensible way. Does it really seem appropriate to estimate the cost of schooling oneself to remember something affecting risks? *See Wassell v. Adams*, Chapter 9. Or to develop back up systems for failed memory? (¶ 5).

¶ 7. When Judge Posner (and our notes based on his analysis) worked with average costs over a period of time, it was easy to visualize the formula's application. But lawyers figuring the probable outcome of a trial will probably find it difficult to conceptualize and estimate averages. Taking *Mathew* as an example, the lawyer may estimate that some jurors would find a 90% of fire damage to the garage of $10,000, and a 5% probability of a $100,000 loss, a 4% probability of a million dollar loss and so on. This is a double-layered problem. On the first layer, can the jury really estimate an "average" loss and if so, would the estimate be meaningful? On the second layer, can lawyers might guess or estimate that some jurors would come up with figures like that but that other jurors would have quite different figures. So the lawyer attempt to reach a settlement figure would be required to average her estimate of the juror's averages. Is this becoming useless as a model? Or is the business of lawyer's estimates of settlement value simply not one of the functions of the *Carroll Towing* model? Perhaps our every day estimates are formed on the *Carroll Towing* model, but we don't expect to have finely tuned estimates. If you or your class wish to do numbers based on the hypothetical, it will be easier to simplify it. Suppose a .90 chance that damages will be about $10,000 and a 10% chance that damages will be about $100,000. Discounting the first by probability gives you $9,000; discounting the second gives you $10,000. The average is $9,500. The discount for probability has already been applied to weight the average. PL is $9,500.

FYI: leading the jury by the Hand: Negligence instructions As trial lawyers know, instructions to the jury on the standard of care do not usually match the terminology of risk-utility balancing we see in *Carroll Towing*. Learned Hand's formula in *Carroll Towing* was used by Hand and is used by other courts in evaluating the evidence to determine whether the case should have been submitted to the jury, but almost never mentioned explicitly in jury instructions, except in product liability cases where judges may instruct on the reasonable alternative design rule, which incorporates a risk-utility balance. The risk-utility idea leads to instructions on foreseeability and to instructions that emphasize particular risks or costs in particular cases, but otherwise juries are largely left to figure out on their own whether the defendant acted with the care of a reasonable prudent person. However, lawyers are free to argue to the jury about what counts as reasonable care. They can argue (and jurors may argue among themselves) costs and benefits or risks and utilities. In the light of this, should we think that the reasonable person standard is in conflict with the *Carroll Towing* risk-utility balance? Stephen G. Gilles, *The Invisible Hand Formula*, 80 VA. L. REV. 1015 (1994), says not, but thinks that some version of the risk-utility formula should be submitted to the jury and that the Hand formula is under-enforced. Whether you agree may depend in part on the values you attach to individualized adjudication as opposed to "ex ante" rules. Should judges lead the jury by the Hand? A view that is only partly different from Gilles' might be that the reasonable person instruction and the Hand formula are not inconsistent, but that the reasonable person formula is a broader one that allows jurors, when not constrained by judicial control, to decide on grounds other than the risk-utility balance, for example, on the basis of community custom. ∎

NOTE: EVALUATING THE RISK-UTILITY ASSESSMENT

¶ 2. Gregory C. Keating, *Reasonableness and Rationality in Negligence Theory*, 48 STAN. L. REV. 311 (1996), cited here, develops complex arguments for a "social contract" rather than an economic interpretation of the Hand formula. He does not oppose weighing of risks and costs, but thinks they must be weighed with the notion that reasonable people assign great value to security, that they cooperate on fair terms with others, and not prefer their own interests to others, nor make demands upon others they would not honor themselves. See Id. at 373-74. This leads him to the position stated in the note, that you must not offset "losses of liberty with increases in wealth." Id. at 383. Remember that utility is not necessarily the same as dollars.

¶ 3. Alternatives to the risk-utility formula? This paragraph offers a series of alternatives to the Hand formula, ranging from raw intuition to custom to a revised reason for the Hand formula. A discussion of this note, or some parts of it, can foreshadow things to come (custom) and can even illuminate the effects of the Hand formula itself. The main possibilities, in brief:

(a) Jury intuition. Juries can actually do this and do it very well. We trust them to do so in many kinds of cases in which there is no evidence whatever quantifying the degree of risk or the costs of avoiding it. But while juries can do the intuitive job, appellate review without having in mind some model like the risk utility assessment will be impossible. Look back at the reasoning in the cases that precede *Carroll Towing.* Didn't the judges in those cases apply some relevant parts of the risk utility assessment in determining whether the plaintiff could get to the jury?

(b) A moral version of the Hand formula. Maybe the Hand formula only means that you must act with the same care toward others that you would devote to your own interests. *See* Stephen G. Gilles, *The Invisible Hand Formula,* 80 VA. L. REV. 1015, 1032-36 (1994) (the "single-owner heuristic"); Kenneth W. Simons, *De-*

ontology, Negligence, Tort, and Crime, 76 B.U. L. REV. 273 (1996). If you owned all the ships and docks at risk when you have no bargee, and a bargee would cost you $30,000 annually to save you $40,000 in costs to your ships when the barge breaks lose, you'd hire a bargee. Hand's formula says you must do the same when you don't own all the ships and docks, a kind of variation on the Golden Rule: treat the property of others with the same respect you'd treat your own.

But this variation on the Golden Rule is not good enough if you think that the defendant's willingness to impose risks on himself is a bad measure of his responsibility to others. I might happily tolerate serious risks but you might want even more than average security from harm. Courts would have little basis for saying that your extreme desire for security should restrain my freedom to act. And vice versa: courts would have little basis for saying that if I am a risk-taker by nature, I have the right to impose big risks on you. One solution to this is to say that we must reduce all risks to a common denominator, even though you might want a great deal more security. That is what the economic interpretation of the Hand formula does.

Richard Wright, *The Standards of Care in Negligence Law,* in PHILOSOPHICAL FOUNDATIONS OF TORT LAW 249 (David G. Owen, ed. 1995), thinks that morally speaking, you need not treat others as yourself and in fact a rule requiring you to do so treats no one as a distinct person with her own life to lead.

(c) Custom or community standards. Custom or community standards might better reflect efficiencies than some estimate of dollar/market values. Alternatively, community standards, inarticulate or not, might reflect the community's moral values. Even if there is no specific custom in the community, the jury process might represent or embody the community's unexpressed standards or ideals. We could leave the negligence question to the jury with only an instruction to judge reasonable care. That is in fact the instruction. Maybe we don't need risk-utility analysis. See Catharine Pierce Wells, *Tort Law as Corrective Justice: A Pragmatic Justification for Jury Adjudication,* 88 MICH. L. REV. 2348 (1990); cf. Michael Wells, *Scientific Policymaking and the Torts Revolution: The Revenge of the Ordinary Observer,* 26 GA. L. REV. 725 (1992); Patrick J. Kelley, *Who Decides? Community Safety Conventions at the Heart of Tort Liability,* 38 CLEV. STATE L. REV. 315 (1990). But what about malignant community customs like segregation or discrimination?

FYI: When the issue is whether to impose a duty to use care rather than whether care was exercised, judges may at times do their own risk-utility assessment, excluding the jury from this operation (see DOBBS ON TORTS § 229), but at other times they may invoke open-ended formulas based upon "existing social values, customs, and considerations of policy." That's the Massachusetts Court in *Luoni v. Berube,* 729 N.E.2d 1108 (Mass. 2000)– the same court that performed some sort of risk-utility assessment in *Bernier.* The issue is conceived differently in the two cases– whether there was evidence of negligence in *Bernier,* whether the defendant under a duty to use care in *Luoni.* Still, if custom and "existing social values" are good enough guides for judges on the duty issue, would those factors suffice as guides for the jury on the breach issue? ■

Opposing negligence-based liability altogether. Some thinkers oppose the Hand formula in *Carroll Towing* on moral grounds, preferring strict liability for those who impose risks upon others, at least when they do so by affirmative acts or when the risks imposed are non-reciprocal. *See* George P. Fletcher, *Fairness and Utility in Tort Theory,* 85 HARV. L. REV. 537 (1972); George P. Fletcher, *Corrective Justice for Moderns,* 106 HARV. L. REV. 1658 (1993). Others oppose the Hand formula, at least for certain cases, because they favor strict liability on economic grounds. *See* M. POLINSKY, AN INTRODUCTION TO LAW AND ECONOMICS 37-49 and 65-71 (1983); Thomas C. Galligan, Jr., *Strict Liability in Action: The Truncated Learned Hand Formula,* 52 LA. L. REV. 323 (1991). Or because they favor a loss-spreading theory of liability for enterprises. *E.g.,* Virgina E. Nolan and Edmund Ursin, *Enterprise Liability and the Economic Analysis of Tort Law,* 57 OHIO ST. L. J. 835 (1996).

Guido Calabresi and Jon T. Hirschoff, *Toward a Test for Strict Liability in Torts,* 81 YALE L. J. 1055 (1972), start with the idea that you ought to attempt to minimize the sum of accident costs and accident cost avoidance. A reverse Hand formula would do that. The reversed Hand test would impose the costs of an accident on the injurer unless the victim could have avoided injury at a cost less than the accident costs. Id. at 1059. That would make the injurer always liable without fault unless the victim were negligent. If both were negligent, the injurer would be liable. This approach changes the distribution of losses, but not the way of determining negligence. However, the authors propose something else: strict liability based on determining which party can best make the risk-utility analysis. That person becomes the "cheapest cost avoider" and upon that person falls the loss, regardless of fault.

Eclectic or varied standards of care. Richard Wright, *The Standards of Care in Negligence Law,* in PHILOSOPHICAL FOUNDATIONS OF TORT LAW 249 (David G. Owen, ed. 1995), a strong opponent of the Hand formula, thinks that you can see different standards operating in different circumstances. In his first pattern, (1) defendants' treat others as means to the defendants' own ends, putting the plaintiff at risk to benefit the defendants although the plaintiff is not seeking benefits directly from the activity. He believes that in this pattern, courts generally find the defendant to be negligent if he "created a foreseeable significant unaccepted risk of injury" even though he might not be negligent under the risk-utility balance. *See id.* at 261-63. But surprisingly, he cites only *Brown v. Kendall* and *Depue v. Flateau.* In Wright's second pattern, (2) the defendant is carrying on a socially (not merely personally) useful activity. Here social interests are appropriately taken into consideration, although he denies that this is a utilitarian balance. A third pattern (3) involves cases in which, after all, the defendant's own interests are taken into account, as where the defendant is a landowner and the plaintiff an entrant upon land. The third pattern might explain cases, but it might also undermine the claim that defendant's own interests are not to be considered in the first pattern, unless you happen to think that interests in land are materially different from interests, say, in earning a living by engaging in the shipping business. Wright discusses five other patterns: (4) Plaintiffs who voluntarily seek to benefit from the defendant's risky activities. (5) Defendants who paternalistically seeks to act for the plaintiff's benefit, but without the plaintiff's consent or voluntarily participation. (6) Plaintiffs who engage in self-interested conduct. (7) Plaintiffs who engage in self-sacrificing conduct. And (8) defendants who fail to aid or rescue.

The RRC & the MMI. Professor Howard Latin offered two models of accident causing behavior. The first he called the Rational Risk Calculator (RRC). This model assumes that people are rational and will weigh risks and utilities of their conduct. (He is thinking in the context of plaintiff rather than defendant behavior.) A plaintiff who minimized expenses by purchasing a lower-cost but riskier product, has simply made a decision to take the risk in exchange for the gain in cost saving. The second model he calls the Mistake and Momentary Inattention (MMI) model. In this model, people are assumed (or known) to have "severe restrictions on cognitive capacity and attention span" and cannot rationally evaluate all their choices. Injuries result from miscalculations and mistakes, not rational choice. Accidents are truly accidents, not rational gambles that didn't work. Howard Latin, *"Good" Warnings, Bad Products, and Cognitive Limitations,* 41 U.C.L.A. L. REV. 1193 (1994). Latin was writing in the context of products liability warnings, a specialized topic, but his models of behavior may be of interest in connection with *Carroll Towing.* Latin believes that behavioral research shows the second model to be the correct one. He emphasizes his view that we "need to ground legal doctrines on realistic behavioral assessments." Id. at 1295. If normative rules should follow realistic behavioral assessments, would that mean that *Carroll Towing* and all risk-utility balancing is wrong? Is it true that normative rules must demand of people only what they can give? Does the jury fit into this picture somewhere?

References: You do not need a background in economics to teach *Carroll Towing.* However, if you know nothing of that subject and want to get a little feel for it, consult Richard Posner, Economic Analysis of Law (4th ed. 1992); A.M. POLINSKY, AN INTRODUCTION TO LAW AND ECONOMICS (1983), and C. GOETZ, LAW AND ECONOMICS (1984) (especially pp. 292 ff. where *Carroll Towing* is discussed). Two succinct paperback books might also be helpful to both teacher and student: DAVID BARNES & LYNN A. STOUT, THE ECONOMIC ANALYSIS OF TORT LAW (1992) (part of West's American Casebook Series); and ROBIN PAUL MALLOY, LAW AND ECONOMICS: A COMPARATIVE APPROACH TO THEORY AND PRACTICE (1990) (which helpfully compares and explains various "camps" within the law and economics universe).

§ 2. ASSESSING RESPONSIBILITY WHEN MORE THAN ONE PERSON IS NEGLIGENT

This section is a product of our concerns that students mis-evaluate tort cases and rules because they fail to remember that more than one tortfeasor may be liable and that apportionment of some kind is required. Accordingly, we created this short section and pushed it as far forward in the course as we thought feasible. (We actually tried it out in Chapter 1, but found that was too early.) Our second concern was that when the topic was introduced with causation, to which it is intensely relevant, some students confused the issue of causation with the issue of joint and several liability.

The text of this section briefly explains comparative fault. That does no harm, even though we will look at the subject more systematically in Chapter 9. The comparative fault material here requires no special knowledge and a little familiarity with it may actually save time and avoid confusion.

The text then turns to apportionment of liability among tortfeasors. It explains joint and several liability, contribution, and the alternative several liability system. Some students do not readily make the mental shift from plaintiff-defendant apportionment to defendant-defendant apportionment. A few minutes working through the diagrams and examples should make the systems clear, but you may have to remind students several times later on how to apply the rules.

The diagrams are probably unnecessary, but we hope they will serve as flags to indicate that the subject, though not developed in cases, it worth their attention.

We would elicit the students' first reactions to the systems by reference to the second diagram. When B cannot pay his share, is it better that the other tortfeasor pay the plaintiff's damages or that the plaintiff go uncompensated? The joint and several system makes the tortfeasor pay more than his share rather than make the plaintiff pick up the tab. It thus fosters the compensation and deterrence goals. The several liability system puts the loss on the plaintiff.

Most students readily join the assumption that both tortfeasors have caused the harm. At the same time, students cannot fully consider some layers of the problem until they know the causal rules and more about comparative fault. Partly for this reason, we would resist temptations to explore the apportionment rules in depth. Quite a bit more on apportionment appears in Chapter 7 on causation, in Chapter 9 on comparative fault, and in Chapter 25 on settlement, apportionment, and damages.

A few extreme students may reject the fundamental ideas that more than one person can be at fault and that more than one person can be a cause of the plaintiff's harm. This viewpoint is counter to both systems of apportionment and rejects the notions of causal responsibility to be developed in Chapters 7 and 8. We would respond to such students by saying that we'll have opportunities later to consider causal responsibility and that this section deals only with apportionment once fault has been assigned by judge or jury to more than one person.

§ 3. PROVING AND EVALUATING CONDUCT

A. Proving Conduct

[i] Direct Proof

This subsection deals wholly with the problem of finding out and proving what the actors actually did. The next subsection deals with the quite distinct problem of evaluating the conduct once it is established. The two subsections together form the basis for moving into *res ipsa loquitur*, which, by contrast, does not require us to know the defendant's precise actions. The emphasis in the present subsection, then, is on establishing conduct that can be evaluated. This requires first of all, evidence of specific conduct. It is not enough to say the defendant should, in some unspecified way, have avoided injury. The materials then establish several means of proving conduct, including direct, eyewitness testimony, the use of circumstantial evidence, and the use of opinion evidence. Larger concerns that lurk in this material include: (1) the judge-jury role, and even the judge-jury-expert role; (2) procedural means by which some of these issues are raised, e.g., directed verdict motions; (3) the role of the lawyer as investigator and effective presenter of evidence and inference; and (4) the ability of any system to deal with conflicts of testimony and inference and uncertainties demonstrated in some of the cases.

[a.] Sufficiency of proof — the requirement of specific conduct

SANTIAGO V. FIRST STUDENT, INC., 839 A.2d 550 (R.I. 2004)

The court does *not* say it disbelieves the plaintiff. It is saying that her evidence does not show negligence. It shows there was some kind of collision between the school bus and the other vehicle and that she was injured. It does not show what the school bus driver should have done differently, mainly because we don't know what he actually did. Except in res ipsa loquitur cases, you'll have to prove unreasonable risk, commonly by proving the risk-utility balance. But you cannot prove a risk-utility balance or any form of unreasonable risk without proving facts, and not only general facts, but very specific conduct. This is the problem in *Santiago*, and in *Gift*, cited in **Note 1**; we then highlight this issue in **Note 2**. "Driving" is not negligent because driving is socially useful. The Restatement (Third) of Torts, Liability for Physical Harms, § 3, cmt. *j*, observes that claims of negligence based on an "entire activity" – perhaps an activity such as "driving"– are uncommon and almost impossible to prove. You'll have to go further and prove something like "driving without a lookout," or "driving too fast." Only when the plaintiff can show the defendant's specific conduct can we compare the utility of his conduct with the alternative, safer conduct. The plaintiff in *Santiago* provided no basis for inferring what the driver actually did and hence no basis for a decision about what he should have done instead. On the specific conduct requirement see DOBBS ON TORTS § 153 (2000).

[b.] Conflicting evidence

UPCHURCH V. ROTENBERRY, 761 So.2d 199 (Miss. 2000)

With no outside eyewitnesses, Rotenberry's car went off the road and struck a tree, killing her passenger, Upchurch. In a suit for his death, the jury found for the defendant. Rotenberry herself claimed to have no memory, but later said she was trying to evade a large animal in the road. Other witnesses testified as to tire marks, impact speed, and possible alcohol use by Rottenberry. All four of the witnesses were contradicted by their own later testimony or by other witnesses or both. Here is a table of the main contradictions:

Witness	Statement	Contradicted by
Rotenberry (D)	no memory of events	self; describes animal
Guyton (D)	D admitted drinking	self
Guyton (D)	D's memory	self
Rosenhan (P)	no skid marks	Schaeffer
Rosenhan (P)	P's drinking	self (on redirect)
Schaeffer (D)	skid marks	Rosenhan
Schaeffer (D)	impact speed	self, Rosenhan

The court affirmed the trial judge's denial of the plaintiff's motion JNOV on the ground that credibility of witnesses is a jury question in which the court will not intrude. It notes that the jury may accept some of a witness's testimony without accepting all of it. It supports this rule by reference to the witnesses' demeanor, which can be evaluated by the jury but not by a reviewing court looking only at the record.

Notice that the holding in *Rottenberry* implies that the jury may accept portions of the party's testimony favorable to that party, while rejecting the same party's admissions or unfavorable testimony.

The process of determining fault. **Notes 1-3** suggest reasons why it is difficult to determine the facts, and hence to determine fault, in many tort cases. The small human failures emphasized in Note 1 are important in lawyering tort cases, as are the problems of witness perception in Note 2. However, the first point here is not so much to work on the lawyering problems as it is to raise the fundamental policy question: can we adequately get the "facts" necessary to make just adjudications of accountability?

Impeaching the witness. The notes do not talk about evidence offered to impeach a witness, that is, to show the witness is lying. This is important evidence when credibility is an issue and it would be useful to discuss it to show the limits of getting at the truth. Because impeaching testimony raises many other issues and we lack world enough and time to pursue this subject, we do nothing with that topic in the casebook. If you want to look at this and some related reasons why getting at the truth is extremely difficult, check out *Washington Metro. Area Transit Auth. v. Cross,* 849 A.2d 1021 (D.C. Ct. App. 2004). The plaintiff there boarded the defendant's bus. She said it suddenly "took off" before she was seated, then suddenly braked, throwing her off balance and causing her to hit her head on the fare box. The driver said that on the contrary, the plaintiff, regarded as a frail and elderly woman, got up from her seat while the bus was accelerating. The plaintiff offered evidence to impeach the driver's testimony: that the driver had said nothing about the plaintiff's getting up when the driver made her accident report. That led the driver in turn to explain "her accident report statement by saying that although she herself had not seen it, passengers on the bus told her after the accident that [the plaintiff] 'had gotten up from her seat to move to another seat.' The jury was admonished to consider this hearsay only for the purpose of evaluating Carswell's credibility and not for the truth of the matter asserted." Although we think this clearly demonstrates some problems with impeaching testimony– pursuing collateral inquiries too far, introducing hearsay, trying to limit the impact of inadmissible hearsay– we also think it is too much work to make a point that we hope is already obvious, namely, that we cannot be completely confident of getting the truth.

In Chapter 1 we briefly considered the argument that Americans litigate too much and we'll see it again in Chapter 27. As a matter of fact, a fair amount of scholarly study has long indicated that asserting tort claims for injury is "a statistically *unusual* behavior." DEBORAH HENSLER, SUSAN MARQUIS, ALLAN ABRAHAMSE, SANDRA BERRY, PATRICIA EBENER, ELIZABETH LEWIS, ALLAN LIND, ROBERT MACCOUN, WILLARD MANNING, JEANNETTE ROGOWSKI & MARY VAIANA, COMPENSATION FOR ACCIDENTAL INJURIES IN THE UNITED STATES 142 (Rand Corporation 1991). But that is NOT the question we are raising here. Our question here is whether *any* dispute-resolving process can work on *any* amount of litigation in cases such as routine auto accidents. If accidents occur because of reactions times or diminished peripheral vision, tort liability will not improve safety. And the moral basis for tort liability in such cases is doubtful.

Note 2. Accuracy of testimony. Witnesses are not generally reliable. At least that is so when the witness is called upon to testify about sudden, dramatic events such as auto accidents or personal attacks. This is a very different reason why it is difficult or impossible to get the facts necessary to an assessment of fault. Is that assessment so difficult that the system becomes a mere lottery? Notice that the negligence per se doctrine may relieve us of any need to evaluate conduct, but does not relieve us of the need to find out what that conduct is. Hence, the witness-reliability problem remains even in per se cases.

ELIZABETH LOFTUS, EYEWITNESS TESTIMONY (1979), cited here, collects much interesting data and is quite easy to read. She deals both with the problem of perception of events and the problem of memory and its distortions. In Chapter 3, Perceiving Events, (pp. 20-51) she collects a number of studies and anecdotes, beginning with the famous classroom demonstration in which a violent event occurs before an entire class, whose reports on what they saw contained 26 to 80 per cent erroneous information. She then deals with a number of factors that seem to affect perception, classifying them as event factors and witness factors. Event factors include (1) exposure time; (2) frequency; (3) detail salience (the tendency of some details to stand out in complex events, and the tendency of others to become submerged); (4) type of fact (showing a constant tendency to overestimate time, a critical feature in legal reconstruction of a sudden event); and (5) violence of the event. Witness factors include (1) stress; (2) expectations (the hunter who expects to see a deer, though in fact to everyone else it would clearly be a human being in a bright red coat). The latter includes cultural expectations, expectations from past experience, expectations built on personal prejudice and "temporary biases." There is a great deal more to the book. Much of this information has now been put in a lawyer's book, ELIZABETH LOFTUS & JAMES DOYLE, EYEWITNESS TESTIMONY: CIVIL AND CRIMINAL (1987). See also BRUCE SALES, THE TRIAL PROCESS (1981) (among other things reviewing the literature, dealing with a number of topics that reveal the difficulty of processing information to a conclusion in a trial, including, for example, the jury selection or voir dire); ELIZABETH LOFTUS, MEMORY (1980).

Note 4. Changing safety environments. If facts are hard to get and fault is very difficult to evaluate, tort law will not be effective in deterring unsafe conduct. Maybe we should put more effort into getting safety by other means. *Educational promotions.* One approach is to use promotional efforts to increase safety when human factors play a leading role in death or injury. For instance, a pilot school and television program using animated characters was aimed at dealing with the problem of children darting out into traffic. This program may have reduced injuries to child pedestrians under 15 years of age by 20% in the locality where it was used. See LEON ROBERTSON, INJURY EPIDEMIOLOGY 198-200 (1992). For other injury data, broken down by cause of injury or death, see SUSAN BAKER, BRIAN O'NEILL, & MARVIN GINSBURG, GUOHUA LI, THE INJURY FACT BOOK (1984).

Building safer roads and cars. In the 1960s reformers thought we could force the auto industry to develop a safer technology, so the NHTSA was erected to pass regulations. The Mashaw-Harfst book, THE STRUGGLE FOR AUTO SAFETY, describes the whole thing and concludes it has been a failure. Early attempts to regulate were usually thwarted and the agency has relied mostly in recent years on recalls of products, which has been expensive without promoting mass improvements in safety. See book reviews, Michael J. Trebilcock, *Requiem for Regulators: The Passing of a Counter-Culture?*, 8 YALE J. REG. 497 (1991); Stephen D.

Sugarman, *Nader's Failures?*, 80 CALIF. L. REV. 289 (1992). Better engineered roads, however, have probably mattered a good deal. These approaches may or may not increase safety, but either way they were not used to displace personal responsibility in tort when individuals drove unsafely.

Note 5. Jury role. Credibility determinations are for the jury, and standard instructions tell the jury that. You can probably find your own state's standard instruction on Westlaw and give it to your class if you want to emphasize this point. These instructions are addressed to juries but speak to lawyers. They suggest some of the things lawyers may do in dealing with witness' testimony. The class may want to discuss how a credibility instruction can guide the lawyer's efforts, for example, in cross-examination. "Where were you standing?" raises ability to perceive. "How long ago did this happen?" tests memory, etc. But appearance and demeanor may be more important. See the discussion of Note 6 below.

Note 6. Lawyers' roles. *Witness' appearance; ethics of lawyers' "packaging" a witness.* What can a lawyer do about a witness who does not make a good impression, or one who may be telling the truth but who is likely to seem untruthful because of nervous mannerisms or poor dressing habits? Should the lawyer try to be an image maker, package his witnesses and clients to make them desirable products?

Lawyers often do tell witnesses, particularly clients, how to dress, with the idea that credibility depends in part on how the speaker looks. This is troubling. To the extent that this creates a false impression of the witness, it is surely image-making, not a search for truth. Yet, juries are more likely to believe someone who seems more or less in accord with their ideas of truth-tellers, often someone like themselves. The problem of credibility, which lies at the heart of most trials, raises ethical concerns and doubts about our ability to resolve conflicts of testimony in suitable ways.

Demeanor. Demeanor, of which appearance is a part, is important in judging credibility, and appellate courts almost always recognize that they are not in a position, reading a cold transcript, to judge what the jury saw in demeanor. Self-contradictions which seem like lies to a reader may seem to be only confusion to one who is present, and instead of poisoning the whole testimony of the witness, the confusion may suggest its truthfulness. As *Rotenberry* implies, the mere fact of self-contradiction, then, is no ground for a directed verdict. See also *Gilliam v. Waltsons Corp.*, 201 A.2d 107 (N.H. 1964). But researchers indicate that demeanor is a treacherous guide for determining facts. Olin Guy Wellborn, III, *Demeanor*, 76 CORNELL L. REV. 1075 (1991), reviews the research and concludes that it consistently demonstrates that people are not able to judge truthfulness or accuracy by non-verbal cues summarized as demeanor.

"Power speech." One interesting anthropological study of courtroom speech distinguished witnesses who used "powerful" speech from those who used "powerless speech." Experiments strongly suggested that "powerful" styles of speech

made the witness more convincing to jurors. If this is so, much depends on the speech style of the witness, not the underlying facts. See Conley, O'Barr & Lind, *The Power of Language: Presentational Style in the Courtroom*, (1978) DUKE L.J. 1375.

A well-packaged, well-coached witness; a witness with "good" demeanor; a witness who uses power speech; a witness who lies, a witness who misperceives or mis-recalls the events. These problems make it easy to understand conflicts in testimony and hard to believe that the fault can be assessed with supreme confidence.

Note 7. Directed verdicts. The jury may reject testimony even if it is not contradicted and may interpret the meaning of testimony. This explains the cases cited here. As to credibility generally, see DOBBS ON TORTS § 148 (2000).

[ii] Circumstantial evidence — inference of fact

Professional language often refers to "inferences" in at least two distinct senses. In one sense, the facts are known or established and the trier is allowed to "infer" negligence. This is very loose usage, and in reality seems to mean only that the jury is free to characterize the particular facts as "negligence." This kind of evaluation of conduct is considered in the next subsection. Here we are concerned with inferences of fact, inferences in the more ordinary sense of the word. Skid marks 600 feet long permit an inference that the vehicle was probably exceeding the 30 m.p.h. speed limit. In other words, one fact implies another, or permits one to infer the other. On circumstantial evidence, see DOBBS ON TORTS § 151 (2000).

[a.] Permissible inferences of fact to be drawn or rejected by the trier

FORSYTH V. JOSEPH, 450 P.2d 627 (N.M. Ct. App. 1968)

The physical facts, including skid marks and post-impact travel, permit an inference that defendant was speeding. This cooperative defendant helped a great deal by admitting he was traveling at the speed limit even after he skidded 129 feet. Discussion can emphasize that the New Mexico Court is approving an inference of fact drawn by the trier of fact. It is not *requiring* such an inference. Whether to draw the inference or not is itself a "fact question" for the jury.

Might a jury differ here? It conceivably could interpret Villa's speed statement as referring to the time he first saw the other car in danger rather than the "moment of impact." The suggestion in **Note 2** is meant to raise this possibility and also to emphasize the need for lawyer's vigilance on such details. Villa's lawyer should go over this with him many times and be sure what he intends; if Villa means 55 m.p.h. at the time he first saw the other car, not "point of impact," his lawyer should be quick on re-direct examination to get this cleared up. But even without this, the jury has room for interpretation of the statement and if the statement is viewed in Villa's favor, the jury or trier might find in his favor. The other Notes after the case drive home this point.

[b.] Opinion evidence

NOTE: WITNESSES' OPINIONS AS TO FACTS AND FACTUAL INFERENCES

1. *Non-expert opinion on "ultimate issues."* Witnesses usually are not permitted to give opinions on ultimate issues to be decided. Testimony as to legal conclusions–the defendant was negligent, the defendant violated the statute–would normally be inadmissible. "Each courtroom comes equipped with a 'legal expert,' called a judge, and it is his or her province alone to instruct the jury on the relevant legal standards." *Burkhart v. Washington Metropolitan Area Transit Authority*, 112 F.3d 1207, 1213 (D.C. Cir. 1997). If skid marks are 100 feet long, we are not asking the expert in this segment to tell us that the defendant was driving "too fast," or "negligently," but to say that the skid marks indicate a speed of 40 m.p.h.

2. *Expert opinion.* Experts can give opinions in the field of their expertise, but even this does not normally permit experts to say "in my opinion the defendant was negligent." What is the jury to do when experts have different opinions on critical facts? Do jurors rely too heavily on experts or not enough? Jurors do rely heavily on some expert opinion. Raitz, Green, Goodman & Loftus, *Determining Damages: The Influence of Expert Testimony on Jurors' Decision Making*, 14 LAW AND HUMAN BEHAVIOR 385 (1990), reports a study that found that in many cases the jurors matched damages figures in an economic claim in the exact amounts suggested by expert testimony for the plaintiff. Champagne, Shuman & Whitaker, *An Empirical Examination of the Use of Expert Witnesses in American Courts*, 31 JURIMETRICS 375 (1991), concluded that experts testified in most cases, but usually only on one side, so that the battle of experts issue was overrated. This article also concluded that although lawyers comparison shopped for favorable experts, most of the experts really were experts, not professional witnesses. (There is a bit more in our Casebook on expert opinion, in Chapter 24 in connection with proof in products liability cases.)

Note. We don't wish to induce despair, only a realistic expectation that legal systems, like those who work in it, face limitations. This note does not suggest that we should give up. Only human beings can decide disputes, so we must do our best to do so conscientiously and fairly. At the same time, we must play the hand we are dealt.

B. Evaluating Conduct

[i] Evaluation of Known Conduct Generally

PROBLEM: KIBLER V. MADDUX

If you are uncomfortable with problems, omit this. You can let students work this out in their own words. The question is not to determine the facts but to determine whether those facts constitute "negligence." We know the defendant's speed. We need to judge whether 20 m.p.h. is "too" fast for safety? It is for the jury to say on the basis of its understanding of the community's standard. This is quite different from determining historical facts, but this, too, is part of the jury's role. *See* DOBBS ON TORTS § 148 (2000).

The lawyer's task here is not to discover and present facts so much as to persuade jurors that they should characterize the defendant's conduct as negligence. The lawyer must also identify conduct that should have been changed. What should Ms. Maddux have done differently? Speed does not seem very high here. Should she have realized that small children might run out in front of her? And if so, should she have reduced her speed? Alternatively, should she have sounded the horn? These questions point to the need (1) to identify specific conduct you wish to argue as negligence, and (2) to persuade. In none of these questions will any form of proof be likely to assist. The lawyer must be sure to identify all the acts (including omissions) of negligence and to argue those that can be effective with the judge or jury.

Some of the facts in *Kibler* were suggested by *Hieber v. Watt*, 165 S.E.2d 899 (Ga. Ct. App. 1969), where a jury verdict for the defendant was upheld, the court saying the issues were for the jury. A number of cases involving motorists' liabilities to children on or near streets are collected in Annotation, 30 A.L.R.2d 5 (1953).

Note 2. Summary judgment. The courts' reluctance to grant summary judgment "even when the facts underlying the issue of negligence are undisputed" serves to emphasize that pure factual proof is only the first step. Even when there is no dispute about historical facts, parties may dispute how those facts are evaluated, judged or characterized. If some reasonable persons would say those facts add up to negligence and others not, the question will be one for the jury. At this point we can see rather clearly that the professional language, "fact question for the jury" or "question of fact," is artful rather than literal–the jury not only decides historical facts, but, where reasonable persons can differ, evaluates them, too. When there is room for evaluation, summary judgment is inappropriate.

THOMA V. CRACKER BARREL OLD COUNTRY STORE, INC., 649 So.2d 277 (Fla. Dist. Ct. App. 1995).

> Almost 40 per cent of all injuries in the United States are from slips and falls.

Thoma raises the question of evaluation of conduct. As in *Hammons*, that question is embedded in a factual inference issue. Plaintiff slipped and fell on a patch of clear liquid on the floor of defendant's restaurant. No one saw anyone drop anything on the floor. Can an inference be drawn that one of defendant's employees spilled the liquid? Alternatively, can we infer that allowing the liquid to remain on the floor was negligent?

The court here states the law succinctly: the plaintiff must show either that the defendant created the condition, or had actual or constructive knowledge of it. How can that be shown? The court explains that circumstantial evidence may lead to an inference that the substance had been on the floor for a sufficient length of time that a reasonable proprietor would have seen it and cleaned it up. Unless the defendant created the condition, or at least an unreasonable risk of the condition, courts' evaluations turn almost exclusively on the question how long the dangerous condition has existed. If it has existed a short time, the defendant is not negligent. If it has been there a long time, then the jury is permitted to believe that the defendant should have discovered and removed the condition in the exercise of ordinary care. Courts often discuss the issue as one of "constructive notice," but this is a shorthand phrase; the issue is one of reasonable care.

Two inferences of fact the plaintiff might urge: (a) that an employee spilled the liquid and/or (b) an employee saw the liquid spilled by someone else, but did nothing to clean it up. If the jury draws either inference, evaluation of the conduct will present virtually no problem because it will be easy to characterize both spillage and failure to clean up a known hazard as negligence. Perhaps these are not so improbable in the light of the fact that only employees were usually carrying food or drink in the area and the further fact that they traversed the area "regularly."

The third possible argument for the plaintiff raises the evaluation question. It is that, if the defendant's employees did not cause the spill and did not know of it, they nevertheless *should have* discovered it and made the premises safe. So the court says that if the jury were to believe Thoma's testimony about the size of the spill, then an inference could be drawn that defendant should have noticed it. Is this true no matter how long it was there?

In any event, how is the jury to decide that waitpersons *should* have seen the spill? We almost never see cost data in these or similar cases, nor any data about risks or their magnitude. Are courts or juries really using the *Carroll Towing* test for evaluating conduct? The reasoning of these slip-and-fall cases seems stylized. A number of cases deal with claims like that in the plaintiff's third argument. If the jury can reasonably infer that the condition had been present for a long time, it might draw that inference and then evaluate the defendant's failure to deal with a long-existing situation as negligence. *E.g., Sokolowski v. Medi Mart, Inc.,* 587 A.2d 1056 (Conn. Ct. App. 1991). But we get no guidance in determining how long is "too long." Resolution is by more by convention, or the jury's personal judgment and less by the facts.

Nevertheless, as we will see, courts refuse to apply res ipsa in slip and fall cases, on the grounds that such accidents do normally occur in the absence of negligence, or that the accident cannot be attributed to the defendant's conduct as opposed to someone else's. Where no evidence at all supports an inference that the condition had been present for any substantial period of time, the jury has no basis for concluding that the defendant's failure to correct it amounted to negligence and the defendant will be entitled to a summary judgment or a directed verdict. *E.g., Gulycz v. Stop and Shop Cos., Inc.,* 615 A.2d 1087 (Conn. Ct. App. 1992).

Note 1. Three common theories of liability. We have been look at *Thoma* with the idea in mind that the defendant either created the risk (as by spilling the liquid) or that the defendant should have discovered the spill and cleaned it up. A third possibility is the defendant the defendant somehow creates a risk that a customer will cause a spill. This could happen if the defendant's method of operation makes it likely that customers will drop or spill slippery substances, as where customers picking over green beans in a grocery may knock some on to the floor. As noted in the last paragraph of this Note, this theory has grown in popularity and almost half the states have now adopted it in some form. In *Kelly v. Stop and Shop*, cited here, the court explained the "mode of operation" rule as "a rule of premises liability pursuant to which a business invitee who is injured by a dangerous condition on the premises may recover without proof that the business had actual or constructive notice of that condition if the business' chosen mode of operation creates a foreseeable risk that the condition regularly will occur and the business fails to take reasonable measures to discover and remove it." The plaintiff in *Kelly* slipped on a piece of lettuce that had fallen on the floor from a self-service salad bar in defendant's supermarket. In *Sheehan*, also cited here, the Massachusetts high court adopted this "mode of operation" theory for the first time in a case in which the plaintiff slipped and fell on a grape in defendant's grocery store. The court noted that the "modification of the traditional premises liability approach" to slip and fall cases "is, in large part, based on the change in grocery stores from individualized clerk-assisted to self-service operations and focuses on the reasonable foreseeability of a patron's carelessness in the circumstances, instead of on constructive or actual notice."

Note 2. Evidence that the defendant should have discovered. Where the defendant did not himself create the dangerous condition or dangerously design the premises, the plaintiff must show that the substance has been on the floor long enough that a reasonable store operator would have found it and removed it and without such proof the plaintiff simply loses. This was plaintiff's problem in Spates, cited here.

One type of evidence attempts to bracket the time. A witness saw a substance on the floor an hour earlier. Or the store owner mopped the location only two minutes before. But even that evidence might permit different inferences. See *Winn-Dixie Stores, Inc. v. Parker*, 396 S.E.2d 649 (Va. 1990) (rejecting the inference that the employee mopped poorly and instead inferring that the foreign matter had been on the floor for no more than the two-minute period after the mopping).

Note 3. Evaluating reasonableness. Since we cannot ordinarily estimate risks and utilities in these slip and fall cases, maybe courts are really groping toward a kind of consumer expectation standard, an idea that not only foreshadows the consumer expectation test in products liability cases but also closely relates to custom, which comes up next.

In *Jones v. Brookshire Grocery Co.*, cited here, the court, describing the obligations of the merchant in general terms, noted: "[T]he degree of vigilance must be commensurate with the risk involved, as determined by the overall volume of business, the time of day, the section of the store and other relevant considerations." In other words, the volume of traffic bears on the degree of risk (more volume, more risk, risk being a statistical notion). More risk means a reasonable person would exercise more care. The standard of care is the same—reasonable care—but the acts required to meet that standard might be greater.

Note 4. Judicial help for the plaintiff. This Note mentions several approaches that appear to lessen the plaintiff's burden; some relate to the "mode of operation" theory or some variant on it. In *Edenshaw*, cited here, the Alaska Supreme Court rejected the exclusive use of any particular "test" in such cases in answering a certified question from the federal district court. Under Alaska law, the court held, the plaintiff in a slip-and-fall case does not have to meet any special "elements" beyond duty, breach of duty, causation and actual harm. "We continue to trust that factfinders can best ascertain whether the proprieter of a grocery store acted reasonably in maintaining the store's premises considering all of the circumstances. We see no reason to tilt the contest between plaintiffs and defendants at the outset of a case." Thus the court expressly rejected the adoption of an actual or constructive notice test (which it characterized as "a maze of legal rules and exceptions"). The court rejected the adoption of a "mode of operation" rule as well, on the ground that it is not needed in a state that does not make "notice" a required element; the "mode of operation" rule is, thought the court, useful only as an "exception to the requirement of actual or constructive notice or as a type of constructive notice." Evidence of a grocery store owner's knowledge of a hazard "would bolster a plaintiff's case," the court said, but such evidence is not a required element in all cases.

[ii] Evidence to Assist Evaluation: Defendant's Own Rules

WAL-MART STORES, INC. V. WRIGHT.

As a slip-and-fall case, *Wal-Mart v. Wright* adds to the methods of proof that might be available to evaluate the storekeeper's conducts and hence relates back to *Thoma* and its notes. As a case on using the storekeeper's own rules or policies as a standard for evaluating his conduct, *Wal-Mart v. Wright* leads right in to the similar but distinct issue of custom as a standard raised in the cases that follow. The cases of course hold that neither the defendant's rules nor general custom is a standard, but that both are evidence the jury may consider in evaluating conduct.

Note. The idea here is that if internal safety rules were given the force of law, they would either be watered-down (to avoid liability for their violation) or not adopted at all. (We see a similar concern with the ABA's and the states' approach to lawyer ethics rules — that they should not be given negligence per se effect or create a cause of action, in order to promote rules that are more aspirational in character.)

[iii] Evidence to Assist Evaluation– Custom

[a.] Admissibility and sufficiency of custom evidence for the plaintiff: custom as a sword.

DUNCAN V. CORBETTA, 577 N.Y.S.2d 129 (App. Div. 1991)

Duncan states the general rule which is then reiterated in **Note 1**. Notice that the custom may require acts that are not required by statute or ordinance.

Note 2. Customary statute violations. A number of cases have held that the statute must take precedence. *See, also, e.g., Smith v. Aaron*, 508 S.W.2d 320 (Ark. 1974) (custom not to provide warning signs required by statute could not be admitted in evidence). This point is also made in the Casebook in the negligence per se materials.

Note 3. What custom proves. If custom is not in itself the standard of care, what exactly does custom prove? Lawyers do not always present their best arguments. At the very least, a strong custom to protect against an identifiable risk would tend to prove that a risk is recognized and harm is foreseeable and also that protection is feasible. Might custom itself be some evidence of a risk-utility balance struck by the community that is just as strong as market or cost-based evidence? If a community always uses crossing guards for school children, even at great cost, maybe the community's evaluation of the risk to children or the value of their lives ought to be more persuasive than evidence about the number of injuries at unguarded crossings or the costs of keeping the crossing guard on duty. Or should we say that community custom, far from being evidence of a risk-utility balance, is a way of judging negligence that it entirely opposed to the *Carroll Towing* formula?

Note 4. Custom other than safety custom. The idea expressed in Levine, and widely held, is that some custom is not relevant to proving negligence. We are focused here on proving that the defendant fell below the standard of care, not simply on what the custom in an industry is, as if we were anthropologists rather than lawyers.

Note 5. Safety manuals. This note summarizes material that was addressed at greater length in the prior edition. You may not need to raise it in class at all. We have tried to make the note self-explanatory: safety manuals are usually relevant to show "custom," and of course they relate to safety (as referenced in the Note above). Further, if the safety codes prepared by an industry have been adopted as the law, then such provisions could even be given negligence per se effect.

[b.] Compliance with custom: custom as a shield

Connections: More on custom appears in the Casebook in the specific setting of medical or other "professional" malpractice, where the rules may be quite different. Custom is also closely related to the "state of the art" arguments in products liability and at bottom perhaps to the consumer expectation test as well.

THE T.J. HOOPER , 60 F.2d 737 (2d Cir. 1932)

The defendant failed to have a radio receiver on board the tug. Had there been one, the captain could have avoided a storm that sunk the barges in tow, for which the barge owner claims. The defense, put in its best light, is that it was a custom of the industry not to have radios, or, in other words, that there was no custom to have them. This is held to be an interesting and relevant fact, but not a determinative one. One may be in compliance with custom and still negligent.

In the preceding materials on custom, we saw that custom was usually admissible and that it was often sufficient to get the plaintiff to the jury. *T.J. Hooper*, however, is different from the earlier materials. In those materials the plaintiff sought to use custom as a sword. The claim was that the defendant's failure to comply with custom was negligence. Now in *T.J. Hooper* the defendant seeks to show compliance, or that there was no custom, and seeks to draw from that proof the conclusion that it could not be at fault. *T.J. Hooper*, like almost every modern case, takes the position that although defendant may introduce such evidence and may argue it, the trier is not bound to believe that current custom reflects due care.

Custom, in short, does not set the standard of care.

Note 1. *Elkerson v. North Jersey Blood Center,* cited here, held that the trial court's instruction was error. The reasonable person standard should have been used instead. The trial judge apparently felt that the case was analogous to a medical malpractice case. (We will see in Chapter 13 that custom or something like it is often the standard of care in medical malpractice cases, but there is no need to embark on that topic here.)

We phrased the question in this note to push students toward a recognition that cases establish rules or principles that can then be asserted in argument. This one is especially clear. In one form of words or another, your main argument in the brief is that the trial judge erred in instructing that custom was the standard because the standard is the reasonable person standard.

Note 2. See DOBBS ON TORTS §164 (2000). In *Jones v. Jitney Jungle Stores of America, Inc.,* 730 So.2d 555 (1998), a father left a small boy on a "ride" outside a supermarket while the father deposited groceries. The boy got off, stepped into the parking lot, and was promptly struck and killed by a car. The wrongful death plaintiff sought to introduce photographic evidence that other Jitney Jungle stores used speed humps, stop signs, and pedestrian crossings to deter speeding. The trial judge rejected this. Considering the evidence to be evidence of custom, the Supreme Court of Mississippi upheld the decision with the observation that although evidence of custom could be relevant, admission "is disfavored and recognized as dangerous. The danger is that a jury will define negligence simply by a departure from custom."

Note 3. Custom, if it really is community custom, does the same work a jury should do: it reflects what the community (or sub-community) itself holds to be reasonable care. That is not necessarily the same as the most dollar-efficient result, although no doubt it very often is. Sword and shield customs together make a possible system for evaluating negligence.

§ 4. PROVING UNSPECIFIED NEGLIGENCE: THE SPECIAL CASE OF RES IPSA LOQUITUR

Planning to teach this subsection: Medical malpractice *res ipsa loquitur* is considered separately in Chapter 13, where it can reinforce what is learned here, provide review, and introduce the "smoking out" version of *res ipsa* in the *Ybarra* case. If you want to teach *Ybarra* in this subsection, you'll need to import it by assigning it with this section. It would fit right after *Giles*.

Reading legal materials, including rules, requires discernment, not highlighters. That is a theme that no doubt runs through all law school courses, more or less. In Section 4, that theme prominently weaves through some of the materials and is one many teachers will wish to work with. It is at the surface in comparing the rule formulations in the various cases here. Discernment, interpretation, and judgment may become large elements in discussion of this section. Students who still read literally, without testing the logic or context of what they read, will have a difficult time with this section if you pursue this theme. But those are the students who stand most to gain from more sophisticated reading.

"Some circumstantial evidence is very strong, as when you find a trout in the milk." Maybe Thoreau means the milk has acquired a strong fishy smell– hence the evidence is "strong." And if you tasted the milk, it would provide strong circumstantial evidence that the trout had been there. Perhaps the best interpretation envisions a bucket of milk diluted by a dairy farmer who waters the milk, pouring water from a bucket dipped in the river. The saying seems to be an old one known in England.

The first portion of this material introduces the origins and basic features of the res ipsa doctrine– that is, the grounds for applying the doctrine, the procedural effect as an inference in most states, and the distinction between the doctrine of *res ipsa loquitur* and other cases of circumstantial evidence. The second portion asks how and when you can infer unspecified fault. How can we know you are negligent yet know not how or why we think so? Maybe res ipsa is a primitive form of strict liability. These materials mainly take the doctrine at face value and let it speak for itself. It is, or purports to be, a straightforward inference of negligence, a decision about probabilities. How does one decide? Are the rules properly stated? Does one ever really consider the accident alone, or is there always other circumstantial evidence? What effect should the parties' access to other evidence have on the inference? The final portion of this section examines the problem of drawing an inference that the defendant, rather than others, was at fault in the case. It addresses the putative control rule, the idea that plaintiff's contribution or fault must be eliminated, and the question of multiple actors.

A. Origins and Basic Features

BYRNE V. BOADLE , 2 H. & C. 722, 159 Eng. Rep. 299 (Exch. 1863)

The classic case. A barrel of flour falls on the passing plaintiff from the defendant's warehouse or shop. The Barons thought this was sufficient proof of negligence, even though no one could identify specific acts of negligence.

More or less the original *res ipsa loquitur* case, this furnishes a good, typical set of facts–the falling object pattern of facts–with which to begin, and on which the doctrine can be readily understood.

The argument in court is a good one for the students to see. Charles Russell's speech is edited here, but students should see his grasp of the authorities and his ability to use them effectively in argument. This, ladies and gentlemen, is what class discussion is supposed to look like! Page Keeton used to say, "If the thing speaks for itself, why doesn't it speak in English?" Actually in a sense *Byrne v. Boadle* speaks to us more in English than in Latin– the homey common sense of the Barons comes through so strongly in *Byrne v. Boadle* that we may miss the complications that are readily if mysteriously suggested by the Latin phrase. If the last portion of this material is to be omitted, you may wish to drag out the implications and ambiguities in the *Byrne* case: Is this the kind of accident that is more probably than not the result of negligence? Is control by the defendant important?

Most fundamentally, *Byrne* offers a first opportunity to contrast the inference of specific negligence we have already seen with the inference in *res ipsa* cases of some unspecified fault. Long skid marks might justify an inference of speed, but

Byrne's inference is not of any particular conduct or fault. We might infer fault somewhere in the background, but we do not know whether the defendant handled the barrel improperly, stored it improperly, or perhaps dropped it because a hoisting rope was defective. In short, we do not know the facts of defendant's conduct any more than we knew them in *Santiago v. First Student.* And, not knowing the facts, we cannot evaluate the conduct. Yet, somehow, we conclude that there must be some unknown conduct and that it can be evaluated as negligent. The radical distinction we have tried to draw between proof of conduct and evaluation of conduct now assumes its full significance in understanding *res ipsa loquitur*: the jury is permitted to evaluate unknown conduct!

Note 1. A challenge. This note broaches the topic considered immediately above. Students must recognize that although res ipsa loquitur is sometimes identified with circumstantial evidence, its distinctive quality lies in the fact that the plaintiff can get to the jury without identifying any particular conduct that should have been carried out more safely.

Note 2. This note gives students a chance to see whether, initially, they feel the doctrine points to an answer. The wheel is actually a good deal like the flour barrel, isn't it? Although the action here is in the horizontal rather than the vertical plane, the case otherwise looks a good deal like *Byrne,* and the Florida Court in *McDougald v. Perry,* cited here, holds that res ipsa applies because by common experience and general knowledge, such things do ordinarily not occur without negligence. *Ex parte Crabtree Industrial Waste, Inc.,* 728 So.2d 155 (Ala. 1998), not cited in the casebook, goes the other way on similar facts because the court thought that a third person's recent repair suggested that he, not the driver, might have been at fault.

Note 3. This Note sets out the "traditional" and Restatement tests for res ipsa; the real challenge is in applying these rules, not in discerning the doctrine itself. We ask whether the "traditional" and Restatement Second tests are materially different from each other. The requirement that the event must be of a kind that ordinarily does not occur absent negligence is a common element in these formulations. The Restatement's requirement that other responsible causes be eliminated can be seen as a more general (or just plain better) statement of the second and third requirements used in the traditional test (as reported from *Eaton*). As we will see in *Giles,* the second and third elements in the Restatement Second test have not usually been read too rigidly by modern courts.

It behooves us to interpret rules rationally. Different words may mean the same thing and different legal rule formulations may likewise. Maybe in some cases the different rule formulations we quoted in this Note will yield different answers. But maybe they come down to much the same thing. That does not mean the formulations are equally good; one of them may tend to mislead or overemphasize, potentially misleading lawyers or judges who tend to read without interpretation.

There are some clear differences in language and perhaps scope to the formulations. The Restatement Second's formulation tells us that when res ipsa applies, causation as well as negligence can be inferred. ("It may be inferred that harm suffered by the plaintiff is caused by the negligence of the defendant. . . .") Causation has not yet been addressed in these materials, so unless the class raises the causal issue, you might avoid discussion of it until you reach the section on causation. If you do discuss causation, you might have to observe the Restatement's causal inference would apply only in certain limited ways. We could infer that the *Byrne v. Boadle* defendant's negligence caused the barrel to fall and we already know that the barrel caused the plaintiff's harm. But would not think that res ipsa justified an inference that the barrel caused the plaintiff's prostrate cancer or ingrown toenail.

The Restatement Second's formula also says that the indicated negligence must be within the scope of the defendant's duty. This has puzzled some students; it appears that this deals with the situation in in which the negligence inferred from res ipsa loquitur does not show a breach of the defendant's *limited* duty. We have not seen any "limited duty" cases yet but you can tell students that we will do so in upcoming Chapters (beginning with Chapter 12).

NOTE: PROCEDURAL INCIDENTS AND EFFECTS OF RES IPSA LOQUITUR

¶ ¶ 1 & 2. **Sufficiency and instructions on res ipsa.** These notes first answer questions that procedurally-minded students frequently ask. The judge first determines as a matter of law whether the plaintiff has made a sufficient showing on each requirement of res ipsa. If no such showing is made, then the res ipsa instruction is not given and indeed the judge may direct a verdict for the defendant unless the plaintiff has some evidence of specific negligence. If, on the other hand, the judge rules that a sufficient showing has been made, then the jury may be given an instruction stating that an inference of negligence is permitted (not required) if the jury finds that an instrumentality of the defendant's caused harm to the plaintiff that does not ordinarily occur without negligence. You can see an example in *Mireles v. Broderick,* 872 P.2d 863 (N.M. 1994).

Are instructions on res ipsa desirable? Is an instruction on res ipsa loquitur necessary or desirable? One option would be for the judge to say nothing to the jury, and simply instruct that the defendant will be liable if the plaintiff proves by a preponderance of evidence that the defendant was negligent. Circumstantial evidence and all the inferences reasonably to be drawn therefrom may be considered. Would this be sufficient? Perhaps if the plaintiff also introduces evidence of specific conduct, some distinction would be required. If instructions are to be given, is there any reason to tell the jury that there is a doctrine or that it is called res ipsa loquitur as New Mexico does? (See *Mirales,* supra.) The judge could simply tell the jury that if it found negligence to be more likely than not and that it was also more likely than not that the negligence was the defendant's, it should bring in a verdict for the plaintiff. Some courts have said in at least some cases, the instruction need not be given. *Grajales-Romero v. American Airlines, Inc.,* 194 F.3d 288 (1st Cir. 1999); *Mobil Chemical Co. v. Bell,* 517 S.W.2d 245 (Tex. 1974); see *Dover Elevator Co. v. Swann,* 638 A.2d 762 (Md. 1994).

¶ ¶ **3 & 4. Permissible inference effect and beyond**. The inference rule is followed in the great majority of cases. What did the *Byrne* court think it was doing procedurally? Pollock's "prima facie" case references suggest an inference rule: it gets the plaintiff to the jury, i.e., makes a prima facie case. This would ordinarily imply that the jury could accept or reject the inference. But Pollock also used the term "presumption." Probably he did not use this in any rigorous sense, but quite loosely, as equivalent to the prima facie case.

In rare cases, the permissible inference may become a mandatory inference, provided the predicate facts are undisputed or the plaintiff's testimony is accepted by the trier as credible. By far the most common assessment of the evidence is that it permits but does not require an inference of negligence.

¶ **5. Presumption effect**. A presumption would presumably have the effect of requiring the defendant to put on some evidence and directing a verdict against him if he failed to do so. Sometimes, however, a presumption does not merely require "some evidence" but instead requires the defendant to prove his innocence by a preponderance of the evidence. See *Boudreaux v. American Ins. Co.*, 264 So.2d 621 (La. 1972), (burden shifting, but based on stringent showing that negligence is the *only* reasonable conclusion). For first-year students, the main thing is to grasp the permissible inference approach and to see that a presumption approach would be far more radical.

¶ **6. Rebuttal by defendant.** What happens if the defendant presents evidence tending to show he is not at fault? There are two situations.

(a) Defendant presents evidence that, if believed, will show how the accident happened and show lack of fault on his part. In this situation, the only question is whether the jury accepts the defendant's testimony. If it does, it will work its will, presumably by finding for the defendant. If it does not credit the defendant's testimony, the inference of negligence still stands and may even be strengthened as a practical matter, since if the jury not only suspects negligence but believes defendant lied about it, it will very likely draw the *res ipsa* inference.

(b) Quite distinct is the situation in which the defendant offers testimony that tends to show he was not at fault but still falls short of showing how the injury did come about. Even if the jury believes such testimony, it might still conclude that in some unknown way the defendant was at fault. In *Goldstein v. Levy*, 132 N.Y.S. 373 (App. Term. 1911), a case used in many editions of the Prosser casebook, a part of a light fixture in a music hall fell and injured the plaintiff. Defendant showed that she had the fixtures checked every week for safety by an electrician, but did not show how the accident happened. Even though the defendant's testimony is fully believed, she has not explained how the injury did occur and the jury is permitted to draw the inference of negligence in spite of belief in her testimony.

B. Is Negligence More Probable Than Not?

Res ipsa does not apply unless it can be said that, given the facts (and attending circumstances) negligence is more likely than not the explanation for the injury. This is a much more central question than the much-debated "control" or attribution issue, which is covered in the next subsection. But it is an intractable question that does not lend itself to rules; there are not even any bad rules to debunk as in the case of the old "control" rule, discussed in the *Giles* case in the next subsection.

Do we really have any basis for concluding that negligence is more likely than not when something happens and a plaintiff is injured? Is it important that there is, or is not, any supporting evidence that would tend to prove specific fault? Does the access of one party or another bear on our willingness to draw adverse conclusions on the negligence issue? And how, exactly, should we formulate and apply the test of *res ipsa*?

KOCH V. NORRIS PUB. POWER DIST., 632 N.W.2d 391 (Neb. App. 2001)
COSGROVE V. COMMONWEALTH EDISON CO., 734 N.E.2d 155 (Ill. App. Ct. 2000)

Both the *Koch* and *Cosgrove* courts are attempting to estimate probability that negligence is a reasonably probable explanation when an electrical line falls and a fire follows. *Koch* says it is, *Cosgrove* says not. Neither court has data on the topic. Both believe they have sufficient experience to enter a pronouncement about probability ex cathedra, from their chairs, not from the field. Not too surprising; there really is no field where data can be gleaned in most res ipsa cases. But does that mean that res ipsa is forever irrational, a matter of each judge's sense of probability?

You can let students try factual distinctions between the two cases if you like, though there is a risk that such an exercise will bury the more difficult issue just raised. The factual distinctions may not be entirely convincing. In *Cosgrove,* there were stormy conditions, but power lines should be constructed to withstand foreseeable storms, so if the line fell only because of the storm, you might think the power company was negligent in constructing a line that would fall under such predictable conditions.

The gas leak was presumably not foreseeable to the electric company, but that goes only to the issues of damages and scope of risk/proximate cause, not to the question whether the electrical company was negligent. So why not permit the trier to find both the electrical and the gas company negligent and hold them jointly and severally liable? Students probably cannot get very far with this idea because they have not yet covered causation and scope of risk. Still, they may be able to see that there is nothing new to us about the idea that two people could be negligent and both liable for some share of the damages.

Finally, in *Cosgrove,* the court emphasized (a) superior knowledge and (b) duty to the community as grounds why res ipsa loquitur should be applied in the claim against the gas company. Does this mean that more-probable-than-not is really not all there is to res ipsa loquitur?

Note 1. Judging probabilities. As this Note points out, judging the probability of something occurring in the absence of negligence is virtually always a matter of common-sense and common experience, although expert testimony might be admitted in some cases (as noted in Note 7 following *Warren v. Jeffries*, coming up). In *Eversole*, cited here, the planitiff's car was destroyed by fire four days after the defendant performed maintenance work on it. Plaintiff sued in both tort and warranty, and on the former theory relied on res ipsa. A plaintiff's verdict was affirmed. The court stressed "common life experience" in concluding that a fuel fire in a three-year old car ordinarily does not occur absent negligence, in this case some "intervening act of manipulation" such as "some negligence [by defendant] in performing the repair work." The court brushed off the defendant's argument on appeal that the plaintiff had produced "no evidence" on this first element of res ipsa, saying plaintiff did not have to: "Whether a given event is an unusual occurrence ordinarily resulting from negligence 'is a judicial decision which is arrived at by judges applying their common experience in life to the event." (Quoting *City of Kennett v. Akers*, 564 S.W.2d 41 (Mo. 1978).)

Courts state the probability rule in different ways. Sometimes a single case will use more than one formula. In *Newing v. Cheatham*, 540 P.2d 33 (Cal. 1975), where a private plane crashed and all aboard were killed, the court stated the Restatement formula that the accident must be of the kind that ordinarily does not occur without negligence. But the *Newing* court also states that "the accident [must be] of such a nature that it can be said, in the light of past experience, that it probably was the result of negligence by someone . . . ."

Courts probably do not think of these as different tests. Both are aimed at reaching a sense of probability that defendant was guilty of some unspecified negligence. In other words, the courts do not intend to authorize an inference of negligence from the mere fact of rarity, but rather from the fact (or general belief) that, however often the accident occurs, it results from negligence more often than not. But as Professor David Kaye has pointed out in *Probability Theory Meets Res Ipsa Loquitur*, 77 MICH. L. REV. 1456 (1979), it is possible to indulge a different line of reasoning. It is possible to reason that air crashes (for example) occur rarely because in most instances pilots and others exercise reasonable care, and that when one of these rare events does occur, it must have been the result of negligence. Professor Kaye actually cites cases that might be interpreted to reason in some such way. He then proceeds to show that this is inappropriate reasoning. That injury is rare if due care is exercised tells us nothing about the probability that injury when it occurs is due to negligence. What we really want to know in a *res ipsa* case is that given injury, the probability is that defendant was negligent.

Note 2. Common knowledge. If judges think juries cannot rationally estimate the probability of negligence from their common knowledge, judges will direct a verdict. In *Scott v. James,* cited here for this proposition, the plaintiff had a burning sensation, then pinpricks, then hair that fell out after a hair relaxer treatment. She sued the beauty salon (not the manufacturer of the chemical). Although there are surely cases that have applied res ipsa loquitur to various burns other ill-effects of hair styling, the majority in *Scott* thought jurors generally would not know the chemistry involved and hence could not say as a matter of common knowledge that the injury was probably caused by stylist negligence rather than chemical reactions.

Note 3. "Ordinary accidents." Students reading a casebook don't have the luxury of surveying hundreds of opinions on particular points. This Note points out that when you look at a lot of decided cases, it becomes pretty clear that courts do not use res ipsa in "ordinary" cases, usually because, as stated by the Louisiana case cited here, that in such cases one cannot conclude that these accidents normally do not occur in the absence of negligence. Of course we see some variation; this is not as much a rule as a rule of thumb.

Many courts have said, apropos of this notion, that res ipsa is inappropriate in slip and fall cases because the fact that a substance is on the floor does not show that the defendant is more likely than not negligent. See *Brown v. Poway Unified School District*, 843 P.2d 624 (Cal. 1993).

Note 4. Rear-end collisions. This Note gives students another chance to think about res ipsa and ordinary inferences of negligence. You can emphasize the need for fact-sensitivity, the importance of avoiding over-generalizations, and the procedural effect.

Terms of analysis. When the forward car is properly stopped to make a left-turn, brake lights showing and left-turn signal blinking, the driver of the car behind is probably negligent, but is that res ipsa loquitur or merely an inference that he failed to keep a proper lookout, followed too closely, or drove too fast? Courts that do not use res ipsa terminology may often have in mind an inference of specific negligence rather than res ipsa's general inference of unknown negligence. *Garnot v. Johnson,* cited here, is in this category, analyzing the problem in terms of following too closely. *Mercer v. Perez,* 436 P.2d 315 (Cal. 1968) specifically recognized similar alternative inferences of specific negligence– "he either was driving at too high a rate of speed, or that he was following too closely"– but then said that the rear-end collision warranted a res ipsa loquitur inference of negligence. Courts can also view the claim as a violation of statute, again in terms of following too closely, or failing to have adequate brakes.

Generalizations and rebuttal. Some rear-enders warrant an inference of negligence, but not all; if the defendant drives into the plaintiff's car when the plaintiff makes a sudden and unsignalled lane change, swerving in front of the defendant's car, negligence does not look so likely.

Procedural effect. In some courts, the plaintiff will be entitled to a directed verdict or summary judgment on the issue of negligence (not damages) unless the rear-ending defendant comes forward with sufficiently exculpating evidence. *Hunter v. Ward,* 812 So.2d 601 (Fla. Dist. Ct. App. 2002) (directed verdict for plaintiff); *Bustillo v. Matturro,* 2002 WL 464707 (N.Y.A.D.) (summary judgment for the plaintiff). If you take the view that a rear-ender creates a permissible inference of negligence, you drop all the talk of res ipsa, presumption, and prima facie negligence, and simply let the case go to the jury, who figure out whether the rearward driver was negligent or not. See *Sheltra v. Rochefort,* 667 A.2d 868 (Me. 1995).

Fact sensitivity. In *Clampitt v. D.J. Spencer Sales,* cited here, the court held that a sudden stop by the forward car did not tend to disprove negligence of the rearward driver–sudden stops being one of the things that requires reasonable care from the driver behind. The year before, however, the same court in *Eppler v. Tarmac America, Inc.,* also cited here, held that the driver of the car in the rear rebutted what Florida calls the rebuttable presumption of negligence by showing that the forward car stopped arbitrarily for no reason while it and others were accelerating.

General anti-res ipsa rule on moving vehicles. Courts have generally held that res ipsa loquitur is not warranted when two moving vehicles are involved. In rear-enders, the forward vehicle is often stopped. New York cases state the formula for dealing with rear-enders by saying that "a rear-end collision with a stopped vehicle creates a prima facie case" (emphasis added). See *Bustillo v. Matturro,* 292 A.D.2d 554, 740 N.Y.S.2d 360 (2002). But sometimes the forward vehicle comes to a stop only moments before impact and sometimes it is not stopped at all. Perhaps forward movement should make no difference, since, stopped or not, the inference of defendant-negligence seems to remain in the absence of explanation. However, in *Sheltra v. Rochefort,* 667 A.2d 868 (Me. 1995) the court that the two-vehicle rule applied to bar use of res ipsa in a rear-end collision.

WARREN V. JEFFRIES , 139 S.E.2d 718 (N.C. 1965)

A parked car starts rolling while children are in ittestimony shows that the children did not tamper with the car. One of the children, trying to escape from the moving car, falls under its wheels and is killed. This is virtually all the evidence. Is the owner-driver, who had parked the car a little earlier, negligent? The court holds that *res ipsa* cannot be applied. On the fact situation, *see* Annotation, 55 A.L.R.3d 1260 (1974) (cars accidentally starting).

Why is res ipsa not applied? If the jury accepts the testimony of the children that they did not tamper with the car, the most likely conclusion is that the driver negligently failed to set proper brakes or otherwise secure car on the incline. Professor Robert G. Byrd wrote of this case: "It is difficult to find more than two inferences as to the cause of the car rolling down the incline which have any degree of probability at all. One possible cause is mechanical defect. As there was no evidence that defendant had knowledge of any such defect and as plaintiff's intestate should probably be considered a licensee, the defendant would have no responsibility to the intestate for the condition of the car. The other possible cause of the accident was the negligence of the defendant in failing to take proper precautions in parking the car. It should be remembered that plaintiff's evidence negated any tampering with the car from the time it was parked by defendant until the accident happened. Of these two possible causes, the negligence of the defendant would seem to have by far the greater probability. The probability of any combination of either the brakes or gears, or both, being defective, unknown to the defendant, or failing at the same time seems slight." Robert G. Byrd & Dan B. Dobbs, *Torts*, 43 N.C. L. REV. 906, 916 (1965).

Before we go on, let's clear some underbrush. Many students tend to think that the children were lying and that this is simply a case in which the children did, after all, tamper with the car. The students did not see the children or hear their testimony; they have not even read the actual trial transcript. So their easy belief that the children were lying may reveal some bias. Beyond that, you may have to remind the class forcefully of two points: (1) the issue of credibility is for the jury and (2) the issue before the Supreme Court of North Carolina is only whether to let the case get to the jury, not whether the defendant will ultimately be liable.

That said, consider whether there is any explanation at all for the *Warren* decision. It may be that the plaintiff did not produce evidence that was at one time available. A post-accident car inspection, or even evidence that the defendant was able to continue to use the car without repair of brakes or gears, would have eliminated the alternative. "Ironically," says Professor Byrd, "plaintiff's, rather than defendant's, apparent opportunity to give a fuller account of the accident than that presented by this evidence may have had a greater impact on the North Carolina decision." Robert C. Byrd, *Proof of Negligence in North Carolina*, (Part I), 48 N.C. L. REV. 452, 456 (1970).

Although a reasonable assessment of the probabilities seems to be that negligent parking must be the answer if one credits the children's testimony, you might revise this estimate of probabilities in light of the plaintiff's failure to produce post-accident inspection proof. The factfinder "also knows the plaintiff has relied on the *res ipsa* doctrine and has not brought forward independent, direct evidence of defendant's negligence. Unless this failure to produce direct evidence of negligence is explained or explicable, the factfinder would seem justified in revising his estimate of the probability that defendant's negligence caused plaintiff's injuries." David Kaye, *Probability Theory Meets Res Ipsa Loquitur*, 77 MICH L. REV. 1456, 1476 (1979).

That seems entirely correct, but why is it not the *jury* in *Warren* that revises its estimates of probability rather than the appellate judges? Is there no room for weighing the inference and could reasonable persons not differ on so uncertain a matter?

Note 1. *Porterfield v. Brinegar*, 719 S.W.2d 558 (Tex. 1986), holds that *res ipsa loquitur* can apply in a car-going-off-the-road case. The driver was killed and the passenger was asleep. But there was no evidence that the driver encountered any special conditions or had any mechanical trouble for which he was not responsible. The possibility of other causes of the injury do not have to be completely eliminated; it is enough if "their likelihood [is] so reduced that the jury can reasonably find by a preponderance of the evidence that the negligence, if any, lies at the defendant's door."

Compare *McDonald v. Smitty's Super Valu, Inc.*, 757 P.2d 120 (Ariz. Ct. App. 1988), where the plaintiff was injured when a stool collapsed. The defendant argued that the plaintiff should be required to show an inability to produce direct evidence and that since the plaintiff had not shown that she could not have inspected the stool and its pole after the injury, she could not use the *res ipsa loquitur* inference. The court agreed in part. "Invocation of res ipsa loquitur is no substitute for reasonable investigation and discovery. The doctrine may benefit a plaintiff unable directly to prove negligence; it does not relieve a plaintiff too uninquisitive to undertake available proof." However, the court refused to entertain the argument unless the defendant first gave assurance that the defendant had preserved the stool and pole in their post-accident condition for the plaintiff's inspection.

Note 2. Inferences from plaintiff's failure to offer available proof? When the plaintiff seems to have access to evidence but doesn't produce it, the inference may be that the missing evidence would be detrimental to the plaintiff's case. Some courts go far beyond analysis of the facts in the particular case to lay it down as a rule of law that res ipsa loquitur simply does not apply when the plaintiff has access to evidence. See *Lowrey v. Montgomery Kone, Inc.,* 42 P.3d 621 (Ariz. Ct. App. 2002) ("the plaintiff must not be in a position to show the particular circumstances that caused the offending agency or instrumentality to operate to her injury"). Is the North Carolina court in *Warren* thinking along those lines, or that the plaintiff had access to evidence she did not produce? **Note 4** tells us that when the shoe is on the other foot, courts may be similarly skeptical about defendants who fail to produce evidence in their possession. In that case, the court may specifically permit the trier to draw an inference that the defendant failed to produce it because it was adverse and to render a verdict on that basis.

Spoliation of evidence. You may want to have in mind the fact that some courts have recognized a tort for interference with or spoliation of evidence. This is neither a personal injury nor property damage tort and there are complications and issues, so it is probably not appropriate for development here. One idea in cases of spoliation by a party litigant relates closely to ideas we advanced with *Warren v. Jeffries*, namely, that adverse inferences or estimates of probability may be drawn against the responsible party. Suppose a patient sues a hospital for medical malpractice, then tries to obtain relevant records, but they hospital has "accidentally" destroyed the records. If the jury could find on the facts that the hospital deliberately destroyed the records, it could infer that they tended to prove the plaintiff's case against the hospital. No separate tort action would be needed; the plaintiff could get to the jury on the inference resulting from the defendant's spoliation of evidence. *See Cedars-Sinai Med. Center v. Superior Court,* 954 P.2d 511 (Cal. 1998). In *Verchot v. General Motors Corp.,* 812 So.2d 296 (Ala. 2001), the plaintiff's brakes failed and he sued the car's manufacturer, but not until he had disposed of the car. The manufacturer's inability to defend by examining the brakes was enough to warrant dismissal of the plaintiff's claim. More of the duties and rules in spoliation cases in DOBBS ON TORTS § 451, at 1280-82 (2000). ■

Note 3. Judge Posner's bus example. We hope this note and the next push students to see the points we've made above– that failure to produce available evidence may make you revise your estimate of probabilities. *Howard v. Wal-Mart Stores, Inc.,* discussed here, was a slip and fall case with rather weak evidence. The court thought there was a slight probability by a "hair's breadth" that the defendant had spilled liquid soap on the floor, causing the plaintiff's injury. Judge Posner then used the bus hypothetical to discuss whether the slight probability of negligence was enough and ended up finding for the plaintiff. In the material quoted in this note, he makes the point that the absence of evidence alters your estimate of probability.

Note 4. See discussion of **Note 2**, above, and **Note 5**, below.

Note 5. Defendant's superior knowledge. Some writers have argued and some courts have stated or implied that *res ipsa* applies only when the defendant has superior knowledge of or access to the facts explaining how the accident happened. One form of the implication is that res ipsa loquitur "permits the inference of negligence on the basis that the evidence of the cause of the injury is practically accessible to the defendant but inaccessible to the injured person." *Pacheco v. Ames,* cited here, is an interesting example because although the court tells us that the defendant's superior knowledge/accessibility is the "basis" of the doctrine, yet when it comes to state the elements required to establish a res ipsa loquitur case, it lists the usual elements and says nothing whatever of superior knowledge. You have to wonder how serious the superior knowledge point is if superior knowledge is the "basis," but not necessary to the doctrine. In *De Bussher*, cited here and in Note 4 as well, a woman was injured when a portable basketball goal on display in a Sam's Club unexpectedly fell on her. This occurred just after one of her small children had said, "There's nothing in it," presumably meaning that the base of the goal was not filled with anything heavy (as it would be when used, to prevent it from falling over). In its recitation of facts, the court noted "The goal in question was taken off the display floor after the accident and has subsequently been either lost or destroyed." In its later analysis the court said, "evidence of the true explanation for the accident was more readily accessible to Sam's East than to DeBusscher. The store maintained exclusive possession of the basketball goal both before and after the accident, removed it from the display floor after it fell on DeBusscher, and sent it to the Claims Department."

1 DOBBS ON TORTS § 160 (2000 & Supps.) suggests that superior knowledge is often a shorthand statement of other rules. It may be just another way of stating the control rule, for example, since some courts may think control is equivalent to superior knowledge, if not in the particular case, then at least as a general model.

If we take superior knowledge to be a meaningful demand and one that is distinct from other rules, however, the requirement is not on its face consistent with the idea that res ipsa loquitur simply permits rational, probabilistic inferences. It is rather facially consistent with the idea that res ipsa loquitur is used to smoke out the defendant who knows the truth but won't tell it. Courts have not explored this topic very well, but have tended to repeat rules or supposed rules by rote.

Inference that known but unrevealed facts are unfavorable. The parties' relative knowledge or access to knowledge is, however, highly relevant in one way we've discussed already– because if you fail to produce evidence available to you the inference may be that it is unfavorable to you. Alternatively, the plaintiff's failure to produce available evidence reduces the probability that the defendant was negligent in some way.

Note 6. Specific evidence of negligence. *(a) Under a rational inference view. (i) Incomplete explanation.* If you view *res ipsa* as merely a rational rule, authorizing an inference where rational people would draw it based on probabilities, you'd let the plaintiff introduce evidence of specific negligence and also rely on *res ipsa loquitur,* so long as the specific negligence falls short of explaining the accident. Thus specific evidence of negligence might tend to add weight to the *res ipsa* inference, just as other "surrounding circumstances" might. In a plane-crash case, then (such as *Widmyer,* cited here), what if there was evidence that the defendant was irregular in required maintenance and repair of the plane? This would strengthen, not eliminate, the *res ipsa* inference.

(ii) Full explanation rejected by trier. Consider the possibility that the plaintiff can introduce evidence of specific negligence but that the jury rejects it. Should the plaintiff be permitted to use res ipsa loquitur theory as a backup, so that the jury could reject the specific evidence but still conclude that in some mysterious way the defendant was negligent? In *Peplinski v. Fobe's Roofing, Inc.,* 531 N.W.2d 597 (Wis. 1995), the plaintiff was installing a toilet at a construction site. A large cast iron pipe fell on his hand. The pipe had been supported on the rafters above, extending up through the roof. The plaintiff's main theory was that the defendant roofer, using a heavy cart on the roof, had struck the upright pipe, knocking it off the rafters below and allowing it to fall on the plaintiff. The plaintiff supported this theory of the case with testimony of an expert, who basically said that it was negligent to drive the cart as close to the pipe as the roofer had done and that a blow from the cart would have caused the pipe to fall. The plaintiff attempted to support the theory also by cross-examination of the roofer, who flatly denied that he struck the pipe, but admitted that he alone drove the cart. The trial court refused to submit a res ipsa instruction. The jury found for the defendant roofer. On appeal, the court upheld the trial judge's refusal to charge on res ipsa. "The proffered evidence, including both the cross-examination testimony of Slaughter and the expert testimony of Hagberg, offered a complete explanation of the incident and, therefore, an instruction on res ipsa loquitur would have been superfluous."

Could the jury have properly found for the plaintiff under a res ipsa loquitur theory even though it rejected the plaintiff's specific proof? A general verdict is an enemy of the plaintiff in this kind of case, because a jury that renders a general verdict on such facts might have done so on the ground that the defendant did indeed strike the pipe but that it was not negligent to do so because it would not foreseeably cause harm. If the jury believed that, to give the jury a res ipsa instruction would be to invite it to hold for the plaintiff even though the facts as found affirmatively supported the defendant. If the jury accepted the invitation, injustice would be done; if it rejected the invitation, the invitation would be superfluous.

But suppose that the plaintiff had for some reason secured a special verdict in which the jury found in effect that the defendant did not strike the pipe at all. Would res ipsa loquitur be ruled out by *that* finding? Maybe so, on some sets of facts, but perhaps not here because, although not emphasized, there was another contractor who had worked in the pipe area and the inference might then be that he was negligent.

(b) Under a smoking out theory. If you feel that *res ipsa* is based on the defendant's superior knowledge, as discussed in Note 5 above, you might feel that use of specific evidence of negligence destroys the very basis of *res ipsa*, since if the plaintiff can introduce evidence, the superior knowledge of the defendant may disappear. Similarly, if you think of *res ipsa* as a "smoking out" device, a deliberate policy adopted to force the defendant to come forward with evidence, as in *Ybarra,* Chapter 13, specific evidence offered by the plaintiff may eliminate the need for any such policy.

Note 7. Res ipsa, probability, and experts. This Note simply makes the point that expert testimony is not considered inappropriate in res ipsa cases, at least where that issue is posed that a jury, applying common knowledge, cannot determine.

C. Attributing the Fault to Defendant Rather Than Others

This subsection focuses on two supposed "rules" of the *res ipsa* module. (1) the plaintiff must exclude her own fault and (2) the plaintiff must show defendant was in exclusive control of the harm-causing instrumentality.

GILES V. CITY OF NEW HAVEN , 636 A.2d 1335 (Conn. 1994)

It will not be either fair or rational to infer negligence on the part of the defendant unless the facts show that he, not others, was the probable wrongdoer. A simple case to make the point parallels *Byrne v. Boadle*. The plaintiff, preparing for golf at the defendant's golf club, was struck on the head and suffered brain damage when a pull-type golf cart falls on his head. As similar as this is to *Byrne,* the court rejected res ipsa because the golf cart, never identified, could just as well have been rented to and in the possession of a golfer, not the defendant. *Holst v. Countryside Enterprises, Inc.,* 14 F.3d 1319 (8th Cir. 1994) (Iowa law). You could imagine a different result with a little more evidence. If the layout of the premises suggested that the cart was probably one of those not yet rented out to golfers, the answer should be different. But the evidence seems scanty and it is easy to understand why the court thought it inadequate to trigger res ipsa: someone was at fault, but you can't feel any confidence that it was the defendant.

Many res ipsa cases involve runaway elevators. In *Giles,* the plaintiff is a long-time operator in an office building in the "Elm City." The 65-year old elevator suddenly begins to shudder and shake as it approaches a high floor; the plaintiff panics and leaps out onto the eleventh floor, suffering injuries. Testimony reveals that the elevator acted in this manner because the compensation chain had become slack and had hooked on another part of the elevator. The defendant produced testimony that the problem could only have been caused by the kind of mis-operation of the elevator that occurs when the operator reverses direction too rapidly.

The parties agreed that the first requirement of res ipsa was met– that this was not the kind of accident that would normally occur absent negligence. They just disagreed about *whose* negligence was the likely cause. Thus the court faced both the "defendant's exclusive control" and "no plaintiff contribution" tests of res ipsa.

This court is in the mainstream in rejecting literal readings of those tests. On "exclusive control," it stresses that the point of the test is merely to show that defendant's negligence, not someone else's, was the likely cause of the injury. Quoting Prosser, the court says it is the "right or power of control, and the opportunity to exercise it" that is sufficient, and that plaintiff's *use* of some instrumentality does not mean that it is outside of defendant's "exclusive control."

On the "no contribution by plaintiff" rule, the court basically eliminates it, on the ground that if it adds anything at all to the "exclusive control" rule, it is at odds with comparative negligence. (Students should remember the damages-reduction rules of comparative fault, summarized briefly in § 2 above. Full treatment comes in Chapter 9.) This is a case that gets results in line with the Restatement Second's formulation of res ipsa loquitur, as described in the first subsection above. The case should serve to explain the way courts use these sub-rules as a flexible means to get at the attribution question.

Note 1. Verbal obeisance to the control rule. This Note advises students that the control rule is routinely stated. But it contains a warning– that the verbal obeisance to the rule does not necessarily mean the court will actually apply the rule rigorously.

That opens the possibility of discussing broader topics– Should we say that meaningful legal rules are reflections or paraphrases of the *words* courts use, as when courts say exclusive control is required? Or should we say that legal rules are reflections of what courts actually do? And relatedly, should any given issue be governed by hard and fast rules or only by principles that point the way to the court's on-the-spot analysis? More in **Note 2**, below.

Courts often waffle when they assert the control rule, or sometimes perhaps state the rule but apply it so liberally that it is eviscerated. An example of waffling: In *Allen v. Thompson Overhead Door Co.,* 3 A.D.3d 462, 771 N.Y.S.2d 521 (2004), a firehouse garage door fell on a firefighter. The court said: "The trial court properly gave a res ipsa loquitur charge since the plaintiff established that the control of the garage door by the City . . . was of "sufficient exclusivity to fairly rule out the chance that the defect was caused by some agency other than [the City's] negligence." *Sufficient exclusivity.* That phrase must mean that exclusive doesn't mean exclusive– it mean exclusive *enough*. So in practice "exclusive control" has become "some control." See the next note.

Note 2. Contemporary view of control rule. This note nudges students to see *Giles* as a departure from a rigid control rule. In our experience, some students continue to state the exclusive control rule throughout the course as though *Giles* didn't exist. Should we restate the rule to recognize the outcomes courts get? (Formalist-minded students might prefer to keep the rule intact and add definitions of "control," as some courts do, but we hope most will want to recognize that the rule can be realistically restated.) If we restate the rule to be in accord with Giles and the outcomes most courts get, how would we stated it? If your students cannot respond to that question you might see if this think something like this would be right:

> The defendant's exclusive control is not a rule or a requirement but a piece of evidence pointing to the person responsible.

For some students, this is a tenuous idea; some just don't readily grasp the distinction between rules of law and evidence to be considered in adjudicating the outcome. Some don't understand that that there may be many kinds of evidence on a given point. Some students will also have difficulty with the idea that a "rule" should state what courts actually do rather than the words they use but then ignore.

In *Harder v. F.C. Clinton, Inc.*, cited here, a nursing home resident somehow ingested an overdose of a medicine that was not prescribed. This led to a coma and eventually amputation of a leg. The nursing home denied that it had provided the medicine, had any stock of such medicine, or knew where it came from. The court allowed the resident's guardian to proceed on a res ipsa loquitur theory even though there was no evidence that the nursing home had physical control of the medicine causing the harm; it was enough that it was in charge of medicines generally (and of course had a duty to protect the resident). The control rule only "denotes no more than elimination, within reason, of all explanations for the genesis of the injurious event other than the defendant's negligence."

Note 3. Absurd control arguments? *Kilgore*, discussed here, is a good illustration of a rigid application of the control rule. On facts similar to those in *Kilgore*, the New Mexico Court in *Trujeque* (also cited here) thought *Kilgore* was both artificial and ridiculous. The key question was whether it is "unreasonable to infer that the maintainer of an instrumentality was responsible for a danger in its use." The defendant's ownership and maintenance of the chair satisfied the control rule. The classic California case is *Rose v. Melody Lane of Wilshire*, 247 P.2d 335 (Cal. 1952), where the court said in part: "Once it has been established that the accident was more probably than not the result of negligence, it need only be determined that defendant is the sole person who could have been guilty of that negligence. Here it was the condition of the stool, not the use made of it, that was responsible for the fall." *Res ipsa* thus applied. But cf. *Rivera-Emerling v. M. Fortunoff of Westbury Corp.*, 721 N.Y.S.2d 653 (App. Div. 2001), where the court rejected res ipsa loquitur, not because the victim of the collapsing chair was in control but because "the chair was on an open sales floor to which innumerable shoppers had access. Hence, there was no basis for concluding that defendant had exclusive control of the chair."

So much for the law of stools and chairs. *Aldana v. School City of East Chicago,* cited in the second paragraph of this Note, gives us another absurd control argument of the same family, this time that a driver is not in control the roadway's surface, so res ipsa loquitur cannot be applied when he inexplicably goes off the road on a clear, dry day without other vehicular involvement. The court rejected the argument, saying, among other things, that it was enough that "any reasonably probable causes for the injury were under the control of the defendant."

When negligence is a failure to exercise control. In some cases, the defendant is not in exclusive control but, in the exercise of ordinary care, should have been. In that kind of case, the fault lies in his failure to control, so he does not escape liability on the ground that he lacked exclusive control.

In *Cogan Kibler, Inc. v. Vito,* 695 A.2d 191 (Md. 1997), the defendant applied a paint primer in an office building near a number of employees. The primer carried serious warnings about dangers of inhaling fumes and requiring adequate ventilation. Unfortunately, the primer was odorless. After the defendant had worked for a time, 10% of the office workers on the other side of a plastic sheet became ill. Some passed out. Ambulances took some of the hospital. The defendant argued that res ipsa loquitur was not made out because defendant did not have exclusive control of the ventilation system that might have carried the fumes. One response is that "[i]f . . . a defendant spilled a toxic chemical in the out-of-doors, and the fumes were borne by ambient air to a plaintiff who inhaled the fumes and was harmed, the defendant's lack of control over the ambient air would not insulate the defendant from liability. In the instant matter, where the chemical was exposed indoors, the fact that the atmosphere may be artificially created does not alter the result. C-K had the duty to use care in releasing the fumes, and the indoor atmosphere was one of the circumstances to be taken into consideration in executing that duty." (We might add that the *Cogan* case does not depend upon res ipsa loquitur anyway because the jury could infer specific negligence.)

Note 4. Instrumentalities accessible to the public. This should be self-explanatory; a literal reading of the "control" rule would exclude res ipsa from use whenever the public has access to the instrumentality. But the vast majority of courts would not engage in such a reading, as shown by *Giles.*

Note 5. Exploding bottles; the liberal formula. The *Escola* case illustrates the possibility of excluding other causes. This formula is the one used by the Restatement § 328D—the plaintiff need not prove exclusive control, but must instead "sufficiently eliminate" other causes. See DOBBS ON TORTS § 157 (2000).

Notes 6 & 7. Eliminating plaintiff's fault; Effect of comparative fault systems. As stated in some courts, the supposed rule excludes res ipsa unless the plaintiff proves she did not participate in or contribute to the events causing injury. E.g., *Bunn v. Urban Shelters and Health Care Systems, Inc.,* 672 A.2d 1056

(D.C. App. 1996). The plaintiff "participation" version is broader than the plaintiff "fault" version of the supposed rule. Neither version seems logically grounded in contributory negligence. Rather, they are corollaries of the control rule: If the plaintiff participated, then the defendant was not in exclusive control. As indicated in Note 7, some courts have interpreted the rule as a rule about contributory negligence. But if you interpret it that way, it is a strange rule indeed, because it puts the burden upon the plaintiff to prove that she is *not* guilty of contributory negligence, reversing the normal burden of proof for no stated reason. Still, this strange interpretation of the rule has paid off for plaintiffs in a number of cases, because courts have used the adoption of comparative fault systems as a ground for dropping the plaintiff participation rule.

Incidentally, some cases never discuss the plaintiff fault rule at all. See *Khirieh v. State Farm Mut. Auto. Ins. Co.*, 594 So.2d 1220 (Ala. 1992); *Sheltra v. Rochefort*, 667 A.2d 868 (Me. 1995).

COLLINS V. SUPERIOR AIR-GROUND AMBULANCE SERV., INC., 789 N.E.2d 394 (Ill. App. Ct. 2003).

Collins permits res ipsa against two defendants who had control over the patient at different times. The problem is that if we do not know when injury occurred, we do not know which of the two defendants was in control at the time of injury. Control at some other time would be irrelevant. Yet the court permits the inference.

Note 1. The special problem of multiple actors. This paragraph states the general rule that *res ipsa loquitur* is not ordinarily applicable to multiple actors. In *Novak Heating*, cited here, the plaintiff purchased a rooftop air conditioning and heating unit for its building. It was shipped by the manufacturer via Yellow Freight. When unpacked, it had serious damage. Plaintiff sued Yellow Freight and the manufacturer together. Although the trial judge permitted a res ipsa inference of negligence against both defendants, but the Iowa Supreme Court reversed. It held that res ipsa could apply to multiple defendants only if joint control is established. Here the control was consecutive, not joint.

Note 2. The vehicular collision example. (a) *Unexplained collision between A and B injures one or both parties.* (i) *Moving cars generally.* A and B, each driving a car, collide. Neither can claim *res ipsa loquitur* against the other. Of course the point is not limited to car collisions. See *Dillworth v. Gambardella*, 970 F.2d 1113 (2d Cir. 1992) (skiers collide, explanation might be inherent risks of skiing).

(ii) *Moving car and stationary car.* When the defendant collides with a stationary car in the lane ahead of him, the inference is usually permissible that the defendant was negligent. Such a case seems to be a version of the assured clear distance rule we first saw in *Marshall v. Southern Ry*. You don't need to call it a *res ipsa* rule. Perhaps the inference is not unknown negligence but rather an alternative inference of either specific negligence in the defendant's failure to keep a proper lookout or excessive speed.

(b) Unexplained collision between A and B injures third person. A and B each driving a car collide and injure P, an innocent bystander. The answer is the same. Since P is innocent, this is a sympathetic case. Probably we would be willing to conclude that most auto accidents are the result of the fault of at least one person. In some cases it will be the fault of both. This has not been enough, however, to induce the courts to let P recover. The principle, of course, is not one about vehicles, but about any two actors where known probabilities do not indicate only one of them at fault. Thus if two persons are moving furniture down the stairs when the load is dropped and one is injured, there is no reason to conclude that the injured person was innocent of fault and the other guilty. *Hancock v. Safeco Ins. Co.*, 368 So.2d 1162 (La. Ct. App. 1979).

Note 3. Questioning *Collins*. Res ipsa works, as the Restatement Third recognizes, if multiple parties have "shared responsibility" (perhaps joint control) over some activity. In such a case both may be held liable even where negligence is established against only one. In *Southern Indiana Gas & Elec. Co. v. Indiana Ins. Co.*, 383 N.E.2d 387 (Ind. Ct. App. 1978), the water lines of one defendant crossed the gas lines of another so that there was actual physical contact. This created a risk of gas leakage, and the plaintiff's home was damaged in a gas explosion. Since both the gas company and the city water authorities had "assumed the duty to inspect," and since each had control over the danger because each could have rearranged the pipes, *res ipsa loquitur* was held properly invoked. *Foster v. Keyser*, 501 S.E.2d 165 (W.Va. 1997), also contemplated that res ipsa might be invoked in a gas explosion case with multiple actors. See also *Corcoran v. Banner Super Market, Inc.*, 227 N.E.2d 304 (N.Y. 1967).

Southern Indiana Gas makes sense if one imagines that the pipes were installed under a single plan, or at the same time. But suppose the gas company installed its lines and that at some later date the water authorities installed their pipes in a way that touched the gas lines underground. Would the gas company have any duty to discover this situation or to remedy it if it were discovered?

Distinguish alternative liability. In *Pitre v. Bourgeois*, 371 So.2d 330 (La. Ct. App. 1979), plaintiff was injured when the wheels came off a road sweeper. Goodyear had installed new tires two weeks earlier, but there was some evidence that the owner of the machine had removed them since then. The court imposed *res ipsa loquitur* liability on the owner because it could not eliminate its own handling of the wheels, and in accord with that let Goodyear off. Accessibility of evidence to the owner must surely have played a significant part in the decision that the owner must exclude its own negligence rather than that Goodyear must exclude its fault.

There may well be situations not involving joint control in which, nevertheless, one might conclude that two actors were both probably negligent. There are very few cases and most have involved some special element. One of the cases, however, is famous–*Ybarra v. Spangard*, in Chapter 13 (with the medical malpractice materials). It can be assigned here if you prefer, but for several reasons it will work better later and most especially after we have covered *Summers v. Tice*

(Chapter 7), with which it must be contrasted.

PROBLEM: CHANG V. GREY'S DEPARTMENT STORES, INC.

This problem is based on *Cox v. May Department Store Co.*, 903 P.2d 1119 (Ariz. Ct. App. 1995). In that case, the court reversed a summary judgment for defendants and held that the requirements of res ipsa loquitur were met.

This problem should allow students to test their understanding of how all of the requirements and various "rules" of res ipsa apply. It seems especially good on the "exclusive control" and "no plaintiff contribution" issues.

In *Barretta v. Otis Elavator Co.*, 698 A.2d 810 (Conn. 1997), where the escalator suddenly stopped for no known reason and the plaintiff fell the court said: "We . . . are not persuaded that, in the ordinary course of events, this escalator would not have stopped but for negligent inspection or maintenance by the defendant."

In *Holzhauer v. Saks & Co.*, 697 A.2d 89 (Md. 1997), a similar escalator-stop-and-fall case, the court rejected res ipsa loquitur for a combination of reasons. Negligence was not more likely than not because there were emergency stop buttons at each end of the escalator that someone could have pressed. The pushed-button hypothesis was just as likely an explanation as the defendant's negligence. Further, even without buttons, the court thought common knowledge insufficient to permit an inference of negligence where there had been no problem before and none afterwards. Third, the court thought the defendant was not sufficiently in control of the escalator's movements in the light of the stop buttons' presence.

In *Crenshaw v. Washington Metropolitan Area Transit Authority,* 731 A.2d 381 (1999), the escalator gave a sudden, violent jerk. But res ipsa did not apply because the court could not "see how a jury, in the absence of expert testimony or some other evidence of a violation of an established standard of care, can conclude that the jerking motion in this case . . . is the result of negligence on the part of Appellees."

As to elevators, *see* Annotations, 64 A.L.R.3d 950 (1976); 64 A.L.R.3d 1005 (1976), 63 A.L.R.3d 893 (1975); and escalators, 66 A.L.R.2d 496 (1959).

CHAPTER 7

HARM AND CAUSATION IN FACT

▶**Changes in the Sixth Edition:** In § 1 we replaced the Connecticut Superior Court case *Preston v. Cestaro* with a new Connecticut Supreme Court case on the same topic—*Right v. Breen.* In § 2.A we added *Hale v. Ostrow* to introduce the but-for test and address the possibility of multiple causes. In § 2.C we cut *Dillon v. Twin States Gas and Elec. Co.* (which remains quoted in text) and *Doe v. Baxter Healthcare Corp.* Throughout the chapter many Notes have been updated, rewritten and reorganized.

One particularly interesting new Note is about *Williams v. Manchester,* in Note 1 after *Dillon v. Evanston Hospital* in § 2.C. The case involved a negligent tortfeasor who caused a car accident with a pregnant woman. The woman had planned to continue her pregnancy but the accident posed huge health risks to her and to her fetus if she continued the pregnancy. Faced with that situation, she elected to terminate the pregnancy. The case follows the increased risk line of cases, but also makes for an interesting adjunct to *Salinetro*. Was the tortfeasor who caused the car crash an actual cause of the terminated pregnancy? If the pregnant woman had chosen not to terminate the pregnancy, would the tortfeasor have been an actual cause of the likely subsequent injuries to mother and child?

▶The **Concise Edition** reflects edits to the *Right v. Breen* case in places (§ 1), reduces the *Landers* case (§ 2.B) to a shorter case abstract, and trims some note material.■

Scheduling omissions. If you must cut coverage of this chapter, the easiest material to drop is probably all of § 1 on the actual harm requirement. You can simply state the rule that the plaintiff must show actual harm in order to have a negligence claim. You'll need to contrast that rule of harm in negligence cases with the different rule for intentional, trespassory torts. The latter cases permit a substantial or at least a nominal damages recovery without any proven harm. We would teach both *Landers* and *Anderson*, but you could drop one of them if you must, retaining the notes. The problem, *Tillo v.*

Eagle should reinforce learning and check for gaps, but that problem can also be omitted. In our opinion, the remainder of the material is too central to omit, even under pressure.

§ 1. ACTUAL HARM

COMMENTS

Note to the Teacher: This section is designed to make the straightforward point that actual harm is required as an element of the prima facie case. Notes present modest opportunities for critical analysis.

The actual harm requirement is one of the things that distinguishes negligence claims from trespassory tort claims. (If you skipped trespassory torts entirely, you may need to explain the presumed damages rules for those torts if this chapter is to make sense to students.) The actual damage requirement affects the statute of limitations in some instances and simply eliminates a potential claim in others. It is hand-in-glove with the causation rules seen in the next section: legally recognizable harm is the thing that must be caused in fact.

Elements of the Negligence Case: Where We Are
Duty
Negligence (breach of duty)
> Actual Injury
> Cause in Fact
Proximate Cause

This is probably not the place to explore what counts as legally cognizable harm, but if students ask, you might explain that in some instances neither pure economic harm without physical injury nor pure emotional harm without physical injury is sufficient. In the very next section, we see that loss of a chance is sometimes regarded as actual harm and sometimes not.

Although the focus here is upon the actual harm requirement in the negligence case, other non-trespassory torts might fall under the same rule. Some intentional and non-trespassory constitutional torts, for example, require actual harm, however that required harm may be constitutionally defined. See *Carey v. Piphus,* 435 U.S. 247, 98 S.Ct. 1042, 55 L.Ed.2d 252 (1978).

RIGHT V. BREEN, 890 A.2d 1287 (Conn. 2006)

The plaintiff here stopped at a red light and was hit by another vehicle. The plaintiff sued for injuries resulting from the collision, but the defendant presented evidence that the injuries stemmed from previous accidents (5 previous accidents to be exact, which makes us wonder if this rear-end accident claim was legitimate at all). But the jury concluded that the plaintiff suffered no damage. However, the plaintiff moved to recover nominal damages at least because he had suffered "a technical legal injury that admittedly had been caused by the defendant." The court held that plaintiff could not. Without proof of actual damages, the plaintiff could not prevail on the negligence claim.

The reason for "no" lies partly in history and partly in contemporary policy. Where the writ of *Trespass* was used at common law, as in battery, assault, false imprisonment and trespass to land, the plaintiff was not required to prove damages. The invasion of the plaintiff's interest *was* damage in itself. Plaintiff could recover at least nominal damages and perhaps sometimes substantial damages as well.

Where the writ of *Case* was used, the plaintiff was required to prove actual damages. Negligence claims were initially based upon the writ of *Case*, and the requirement of actual damage has continued to apply, no doubt because it is good policy to filters out relatively minor claims negligence claims. (On the *Trespass-Case* distinction and the development of negligence law, see Dobbs on Torts §§ 14, 42, 110 & 111 (2000)).

The requirement of actual harm in negligence cases can be expressed by saying actual harm is one of the elements the plaintiff must prove to establish actionable negligence.

One value of this case for a casebook is that it distinguishes trespassory torts from negligence. Another value is that the case recounts how one state's courts may have strayed from the traditional rule—or maybe have not—and requires students to consider just how uncertain the law may be when judges slip into ill-considered dicta or seek a procedural solution for a substantive issue. The steps in this legal process matter are these:

(1) The Connecticut court decisions first recognized that damages can be recovered in a trespassory tort case even though no actual harm has been done, but then, generalized the idea too broadly. The original case was a battery case and thus fell under the rule that allows damages without actual harm.

(2) Still, the language might turn out to be pernicious in the hands of judges who read local precedent without knowing traditional rules. And in later cases, Connecticut authority seemed to say in a dictum that the plaintiff, having established negligence, can recover at least nominal damages.

(3) But this statement seems to be dictum and in fact in a couple of cases the court took a procedural out to avoid awarding nominal damages. This was done by holding that it was not reversible error NOT to award such damages.

In *Right v. Breen,* the Connecticut Supreme Court finally finds its way out of the cconfusion. A judge or jury cannot award nominal damages in a negligence case in which no actual damages have been incurred.

Note 1. Nominal damages. Such damages are literally $1 in most states. Lawyers seldom sue for nominal damages. The "market" in legal services keeps many undesirable claims out of the courts, including claims for trivial or nominal awards. Because lawyers must eat and provide for their families, they will routinely accept cases only if they estimate they will be paid by winning a recovery large enough to provide appropriate compensation for the time and money invested. We want to make this point several times in this book because students and critics of the "torts system" should recognize some of the built-in constraints on plaintiff-abuse. (This market effect will not exclude bad claims brought by lawyers who are over-optimistic about the merits of their clients' claims, but that only proves that we still need judges.)

–*Pro bono or legal aid lawyers.* What about pro bono work or legal aid– might they sue for nominal damages since they are not being paid out of the recovery? Lawyers are unlikely to use their pro bono time to sue for $1 on behalf of someone who was not in fact injured. The same is true with legal aid lawyers. These lawyers have plenty of serious work to do for clients who seem deserving.

Nominal damages claims in personal injury cases, then, usually arise because the plaintiff has tried to prove a substantial damages claim and failed. In most jurisdictions physical injury to the car would be enough to support a tort claim for damages. However, Connecticut's no-fault insurance statute may make take these compensated damages out of the picture.

Practical effects of nominal damages awards. (1) In a few cases, but seldom if ever personal injury cases, lawyers might assert nominal damages claims to establish a right, such as boundary to land in a trespass action, or a constitutional right to free speech. (2) If the plaintiff basically loses his claim but recovers nominal damages, he is the prevailing party and can at least recover statutory costs. Where attorney fees are recoverable as "costs," as in civil rights actions, the prevailing party who recovers only nominal damages may recover an award for reasonable attorney fees in addition to the statutory court costs. (3) If punitive damages are warranted by the defendant's egregious misconduct, the nominal damage award may support a punitive recovery, although this is unlikely in routine negligence cases, since negligence alone is an insufficient basis for a punitive award.

Note 2. What counts as legally cognizable harm? *Causing impermanent bodily changes without pain.* In *Dailey v. Methodist Med. Center,* 790 So.2d 903 (Miss. Ct. App. 2001), Ron was admitted to the defendant's hospital to build up fluid levels. He was placed on a sodium chloride drip at 150 to 200 ml/hour; it was supposed to be reduced to 50 ml/hour but it wasn't reduced. When he suffered chills, no blankets were available; indeed no nurse was on duty on the floor at all. When he fell the next day, his drip began leaking and he could not get up. An hour and a half later, a family member found him. No treatment was given and he was never able to walk again. But all this is prologue to the negligence we're concerned with. A nurse erroneously installed Pitocin, a labor inducing drug in Ron's IV, and administered it at 150 ml/hour–the wrong drug for a male cancer patient and three times the rate ordered for the correct drug. In fact this act may have caused some serious medical problems, but the hospital defendant claimed otherwise and the trial judge granted summary judgment to the hospital and the nurse, apparently in part on the ground that no harm to Ron was shown sufficiently to make a question of fact for the jury. The drug may have changed the plaintiff's heart rate, blood pressure; it did cause swelling; possibly it caused other effects. The hospital argued that none of the named effects counted as damages. It is not clear whether the court rejected this argument, because it seemed to go off on the fact that the trial court granted defendant's summary judgment on the basis of unsworn documents.

Searfoss v. Johnson & Johnson Co., 2004 WL 792789 (Pa. Super. 2004) (unreported), however, is quite clear. It holds that change in the heart's reset time for the next heartbeat is not in itself actionable harm. In this respect, it follows the attitude in connection with the physical injury required to sustain emotional harm claims.

For another set of interesting cases on this issue, you might be interested to see cases about altering an animal. *Ponder v. Angel Animal Hospital, Inc.*, 762 S.W.2d 846 (Mo. Ct. App. 1988) may anger some animal lovers. Viewing a dog as property, the court thinks no "actual harm" is shown unless market value has been diminished by the dog's castration. The court seems to hold at least implicitly that neither the owner's feelings nor the dog's hedonic losses qualify as actual damages. Accord in denying emotional harm recovery for the shooting of a companion dog, *Rabideau v. City of Racine*, 627 N.W.2d 795 (Wis. 2001). You might want to be sure the class understands that if the defendant had caused a loss in the pet's value on the market, or had inflicted wounds that required medical expense, the plaintiff would recover for those items of economic loss. In addition, if the pet is actually destroyed and has no market value, the plaintiff might recover "value to the owner," which excludes "sentimental value," but allows an indeterminate measured that might include replacement cost and investment in the pet's training or shots. See the excellent summary in *Mitchell v. Heinrichs*, 27 P.3d 309 (Alaska 2001). We have much more on emotional harm in Chapter 19.

Note 3. Damages recoverable in a personal injury case. If you skipped Chapter 1, this note lists the general damages categories. It also establishes that there is no cause of action as such for punitive damages. The plaintiff must prove a cause of action (for example, a cause of action for extreme negligent misconduct). Proving the negligence action requires proof of actual or legally cognizable harm, so punitives are out unless actual harm is shown. Some cases say that punitive damages may not be awarded if the plaintiff recovers only nominal damages; a preferred rule might be that the plaintiff can recover punitive damages if she establishes a cause of action for negligence and the conduct is otherwise the kind that would justify punitive damages. *See* DAN DOBBS, THE LAW OF REMEDIES § 3.11(10) (2d ed. 1993).

One caveat on nominal damages in negligence actions: In specific cases, nominal damages may be recoverable in a negligence action when the amount of actual damages cannot be established to the satisfaction of the jury, but only if some actual harm has been inflicted. The death of the child was easily actual harm under the wrongful death statute, so a zero verdict was out of line. Some students may think that death, like trespass, is harm in itself. It may be, too, but death damages generally require proof of amounts (such as the amount the child was contributing to the family coffers). *See* Chapter 21. When no such proof permits the jury to calculate a sum of money, the plaintiff may be thrown back on nominal damages.

Note 4. Statutory offer of judgment or compromise. The Connecticut statute is quite straightforward. We feel that these statutes are now prevalent enough that it makes sense for students to me aware of their purpose and operation.

§ 2. CAUSE IN FACT

Preliminary Note:

Confusing cause in fact with others issues. This chapter is important, not only because it is basic in itself but because students and judges can easily confuse causation in fact issues with other issues in the negligence case. This is the place to get a clear conception of cause in fact if that is possible.

Besides confusing causation in fact with proximate cause (fairly serious problem discussed below), causation can also be confused with negligence or fault itself, especially when the issue is apportionment of responsibility among multiple actors. See *Degener v. Hall Contracting Corp.,* 27 S.W.3d 775, 779 (Ky. 2000) ("apportionment of causation" seemingly identified with "comparative negligence"). In addition, both students and courts can easily misapply the but-for test of causation. See *Lamp v. Reynolds,* 645 N.W.2d 311 (Mich. Ct. App. 2002) (stating the but-for rule but then seemingly reasoning that since plaintiff's injury arose from an unforeseeable concealed danger, plaintiff's conduct was not a cause in fact).

Two locutions. You can separate the cause in fact issues from issues of policy or principle about the scope of risk associated with the term "proximate cause." Many judges who agree that cause in fact issues differ in important respects from legal or proximate cause issues will still use a locution that subsumes both under the rubric of proximate cause. They will say that the plaintiff must prove duty, breach, actual harm, and proximate cause, the last of which consists of (a) cause in fact and (b) legal cause. This locution is common and it recognizes the difference between cause in fact and legal cause even while it suggests a common parentage. This book originally used the terms legal cause and proximate cause as referring to principle and policy decisions about the scope or extent of liability; in this edition, we have tried to be more direct in many instances by using the term scope of risk rather than proximate cause.

Fact and policy in cause-in-fact issues. Sometimes people say that cause in fact issues are true issues of fact, while scope of risk or proximate cause issues are matters of policy (or justice). But there are several kinds of cause in fact issues (see Comments below) and some of them depend heavily upon concepts or definitions. Causation is not factual in the sense that the tree in your backyard is a fact. Policy will become involved at least when we must decide whether to demand proof of causation or whether the plaintiff can recover in some cases when causation is not in fact proven. But if policy is involved in cause in fact issues, it is *not* the policy about scope of risk involved in the "proximate cause" issue.

Related issues considered elsewhere. We postpone some issues related to causation, mainly market-share liability and some issues of apportionment. *If you are a first-time torts teacher* you may wish to check Chapter 25 on apportionment or, as to market-share, DOBBS ON TORTS § 176 (2000).

OUTLINE

The rule stated.
a. The But-for Test of Causation. *Hale v. Ostrow, Salinetro v. Nystrom.*
b. Problems With and Alternatives to But-for Tests.
Causation and Apportionment. Note: Liability of Two or More Persons
Indivisible injury caused by two actors. *Landers v. East Texas Salt Water Disposal Co.* Duplicative causation: Each of two causes is sufficient to cause the harm. *Anderson v. Minneapolis, St. Paul & S.M. Ry.*
c. Proof: *What* Was Caused?
(1) Causing the loss of causal evidence or certainty. *Summers v. Tice.*
(2) Causing the loss of a chance. *Lord v. Lovett; Alexander v. Scheid; Dillon v. Evanston Hospital.*

COMMENTS

Types of causal issues. DOBBS ON TORTS § 166 (2000), summarizes four forms of cause in fact issues somewhat along these lines:

Type 1 causation problem: scientific connection. One kind of cause in fact problem centers on scientific doubt, or at least on lay ignorance about the connection between the defendant's acts and the plaintiff's injury, frequently a problem in toxic tort cases. The plaintiff gets skin cancer after she is in an auto accident. Did the accident cause it? This can be conceived as a question whether auto accidents have the capacity to cause cancer; courts sometimes call it a question of "general causation."

Type 2 causation problem: who is the cause? The plaintiff is definitely injured by someone or something but cannot produce evidence to indicate which person among many was the injurer.

Type 3 causation problem: would safe behavior have avoided injury? This is the but-for question that generates much academic writing. The defendant fails to keep a proper lookout, but as it happens a lookout would not have avoided the injury. This kind of cause in fact question turns heavily, not on scientific or medical causation but upon estimates about what would have happened if the defendant had behaved more carefully and upon the legal tests or standards for judging causation.

Type 4 causation problem: what harm was caused? A final cause in fact problem is to determine *what* harm was caused by the defendant's negligent conduct. In some instances it is appropriate to apportion harm to causes, that is, to hold a defendant liable for a portion of the plaintiff's harm but not all of it. That is most obviously the case when one defendant breaks the plaintiff's arm and another defendant, acting independently, breaks the plaintiff's leg. Apportionment problems turn both on proof of facts—who caused what?—and also on several kinds of legal policy.

Expert testimony. This chapter mainly addresses the Type 3 and Type 4 kind of causation, without probing questions of proof and evidence. *If* expert testimony is required, a number of contemporary cases demand much of the expert. We'll see a little of that on proof of scientific causation in Chapter 24 on products liability. *Expert testimony not required.* But of course expert testimony is *not* required to establish causation at all in a vast number of cases because causal inferences can be drawn as a matter of common knowledge. The Iowa court made this helpful observation: "Expert testimony may be helpful in establishing causation, but we do not indiscriminately impose a requirement for expert testimony in order to establish an element for tort recovery. Even if expert testimony would clearly be helpful to fact finders ... it is not a condition precedent. Furthermore, it is unnecessary to present expert testimony on causation in those situations in which the subject is within the common experience of laypersons. . . . . In fact, the use of expert testimony on this issue in this case would likely have created confusion of the issues . . . . Expert testimony on causation and the predictability and probability of the actions of a mental health patient was unnecessary in this case." [internal quotations and punctuation omitted.] *Long v. Broadlawns Med. Ctr.,* 656 N.W.2d 71, 83 (Iowa 2002).

Conduct vs. "negligent aspect" as causal. In some cases, the defendant's conduct causes harm in the sense that harm would not have occurred if the defendant had not engaged in wrongful conduct. Yet the feeling may persist that the "negligent aspect" of the defendant's conduct was unrelated to the harm. Defendant is negligent in failing to check his rear view mirror before backing up. Had he looked, he could not have seen a small child by the rear bumper. Defendant's conduct in backing is a cause in fact of the child's harm but his failure to check his mirror was not. Some writers would like to say that the negligent aspect or segment of his conduct was not a cause in fact of the harm that is, so liability is inappropriate. See generally Robert N. Strassfeld, *If...: Counterfactuals in the Law,* 60 GEO. WASH. L. REV. 339 (1992) and Richard W. Wright, *Causation in Tort Law,* 73 CAL. L. REV. 1735 (1985). Others might prefer to say that his *conduct* was a cause in fact but the injury was not within the scope of the risk (next chapter).

Henderson and Twerski favor the "negligent aspect" approach and have used the term "but-for proximate cause" to describe this issue. James A. Henderson, Jr. and Aaron D. Twerski, *Intuition and Technology in Product Design Litigation: an Essay on Proximate Causation,* 88 GEO. L.J. 659 (2000). (In another view, it is meaningless to talk of "negligence" as causing anything— only conduct causes harms. Negligence, in this view, is merely the a noun with adjectival qualities with which we characterize conduct. See, debating some of this, Wayne Thode, *The Indefensible Use of the Hypothetical Case to Determine Cause in Fact*, 46 TEX. L. REV. 423 (1968); James Henderson, *A Defense of the Use of the Hypothetical Case to Resolve the Causation Issue—The Need for an Expanded, Rather than a Contracted, Analysis*, 47 TEX. L. REV. 183 (1969); Thode, *A Reply to the Defense of the Use of the Hypothetical Case to Resolve the Causation Issue*, 47 TEX. L. REV. 1344 (1969). We are not much concerned with which form of expression is used. Sometimes it is handy to look at the case as a but-for case. In other instances, scope of risk is in the forefront.

Alternative analyses. Some cases perceived to raise cause in fact difficulties for the plaintiff might be analyzed, not as cause in fact issues at all, but quite differently as cases that should turn on issues of duty, breach, or scope of risk.

For example, although loss of a mere chance of a better outcome is often conceived as an issue about causal proof, you might resolve the question by asking whether the defendant had a duty to maximize the plaintiff's chances of safety or survival rather than a duty merely to avoid inflicting harm. See § 2 subsec. c., below.

A. The But-for Test of Causation

First-time teachers may want to read the introductory comments to the proximate cause materials before teaching this section.

HALE V. OSTROW, 166 S.W.3d 713 (Tenn. 2005)

The defendant had bushes that had overgrown and obstructed the sidewalk. The plaintiff had to leave the sidewalk and enter the street to avoid the protruding bushes. En route, she tripped over a chunk of concrete and crushed her hip. She sued the neighboring property owners—the one whose bushes obstructed the sidewalk and the one that had the crumbled concrete where she fell. The trial court granted a motion for summary judgment in favor of the landowner whose bushes obstructed the sidewalk, and the appellate court agreed. The lower courts were persuaded by the argument that the "injury was caused by the defective sidewalk, not by the overgrown bushes." At the Tennessee Supreme Court, however, the grant of summary judgment was reversed. There is not necessarily *a* cause of an injury, there can be more than one cause. Cause in fact is judged by the but-for test. The court applies the test to the facts of the case and finds that but for the overgrown bushes, the might not have left the sidewalk and tripped on the concrete. At a minimum, it is a fact issue for the jury.

This case seems particularly useful to us in stating the but-for standard, applying it to a set of facts, and noting that an injury may have more than one actual cause. This idea may bother students at first, but notes later in the chapter should help them understand that saying there is more than one actual cause does not necessarily mean that each cause will be assigned full liability. There are still proximate cause limits to be discussed, as well as various forms of apportionment of damages.

SALINETRO V. NYSTROM, 341 So.2d 1059 (Fla. Dist. Ct. App. 1977)

The defendant X-rayed the plaintiff without asking whether she was pregnant. She later discovered that she was in fact pregnant. Danger from the X-rays necessitated a termination of the pregnancy. *Held*, if the defendant was negligent in failing to ask about pregnancy or to explain X-ray dangers for any possible fetus, the plaintiff still cannot win because the defendant's fault is not causal. If asked about pregnancy, the plaintiff would have answered that she was not pregnant and that the defendant would have proceeded with the X-rays. If the defendant had not been negligent, nothing would have changed, so negligence is not a cause of the harm.

Salinetro does not require an understanding of the special medical standard of care.

Basic analysis in *Salinetro*. What could the defendant have done to avoid being negligent? He could have inquired whether the plaintiff was pregnant or not. If he had done this, would that have avoided the injury? The court thinks not. Its hypothetical alternative scenario is that the plaintiff would have answered, "No, I'm not pregnant," that the doctor would then have properly proceeded with the X-ray. The court does not state the "but-for" phrase, but clearly applies the test. We *cannot* say that "but-for the defendant's conduct, the injury would have been avoided." This demonstrates that there is no cause in fact. If the class can work through this discussion it can proceed to a more difficult level.

Going deeper. The reasoning the court seems to employ—very ordinary actual cause reasoning—illustrates that causation is not simply a "fact" question. Causation is a concept about the relation between two events. Under the but-for test, causation involves comparing a real-world, past-fact situation with a hypothetical, possible alternative. If anyone doubts this, we have only to review the *Salinetro* case itself. What would have happened if the defendant had behaved non-negligently? The question entails imagining something that did *not* happen. This leads to some specific problems.

(a) First, we must be sure what it is that the defendant should have done differently. If the defendant's negligence is failure to ask about pregnancy, the court's reasoning may be correct. But suppose the plaintiff were to prove that the doctor should have *tested* for pregnancy and that he was negligent in failing to do so? If that was the negligent conduct, failing to test, then cause-in-fact is established! Identifying specific negligent acts is a key element in getting the cause in fact issue right.

(b) Second, the hypothetical world envisioned by the court may be wholly inaccurate. At best it is unprovable. If the doctor had said to the plaintiff, "are you pregnant?" she might have said "no," but she might then have added, "but come to think of it, my period is late. Does it matter?" The conversation thus begun might have led her to recognize the risk and to prefer a

pregnancy test. The truth is that none of us– including the plaintiff herself– can say with confidence exactly what would have happened. Does that make the test unworkable?

(c) In some cases there are many ways to avoid being tortious, not merely one. Some of those ways of complying with the law might have led to the same result and some might not. For example, you could imagine that the doctor in *Salinetro* might have exercised due care *either* by (a) providing a written notice to all female patients that x-rays could harm a fetus *or* (b) by actually speaking to the patient about that risk. You could also imagine that upon being questioned about that topic, the plaintiff would have refused the x-ray but that the plaintiff would have ignored the written warning.

A another version: Suppose D might have avoided being negligent *either* by using a simple clinical diagnosis for pregnancy *or* by a pathological test in a lab. Then suppose that the lab test would have shown pregnancy and the X-ray would not have been given. This would lead to the conclusion that cause-in-fact exists here, since non-negligent conduct would have avoided the injury. But suppose that the clinical diagnosis that would also have been non-negligent would *not* have revealed the pregnancy, and that if a clinical test had been chosen, the X-rays would have proceeded. This supposition would lead to the conclusion that failure to test was not a cause in fact. Since either form of test would be non-negligent, which form should we assume for the purpose of applying the hypothetical but-for test? – the *most likely* conduct of a doctor if he was not going to be negligent? – the *least costly* conduct? This kind of analysis indicates that the test is not a sound one in inviting us to consider possibilities we cannot really assess.

Alternatives to the but-for test. But-for is the standard beginning place, but there are alternative ways of dealing with the causal issue. (1) *Substantial factor*. With multiple tortfeasors, we must often give up on the but for test in favor of the vague substantial factor test or a rule that treats the acts of multiple tortfeasors as causal even when each act alone would have sufficed to cause the plaintiff's harm. This and the reasons for it come up in subsection c. (2) *Proportional causation/value of the chance*. We'll see other possible ways for the plaintiff to dodge the but-for bullet by recovering for the value of a lost chance. (3) *Risk equals cause*. In addition, when the harm that befalls the plaintiff is identical to the harm risked by the defendant, you might simply count that as cause or infer causation. See Note on Increased Risk Showing Causation. (4) *Rules for particular situations*. Still another possibility is to prescribe by rule situations or models in which causation is found (or not required). Professor Richard Epstein constructed a causal approach based upon a series of models or paradigmatic cases. The first paradigm is "A hit B." If a case is analogous to this, causation is shown. As you can imagine, the going gets tougher with cases of omissions, nonfeasance, and passive conditions on land. *See* Epstein, *A Theory of Strict Liability*, 2 J. LEG. STUD. 151 (1973), *reprinted in* RICHARD EPSTEIN, A THEORY OF STRICT LIABILITY (1980). (5) *De-emphasizing causation*. Finally, you can de-emphasize the causal analysis significantly. One could, with Leon Green, simply refuse to analyze cause at all, on the ground that analysis is meaningless: "cause" itself asks for a judgment that has no component parts. Leon Green, *The Causal Relation Issue in Negligence Law*, 60 MICH. L. REV. 543 (1962).

Plaintiff as cause. There is a good chance that a student will suggest that the plaintiff was the cause in fact of the harm because she obtained an abortion. Such a comment assumes that the fetus was not injured by the X-ray and would have survived had there been no abortion. This may not be the fact, but taking that as true for the moment, then we can say that, yes, indeed, the plaintiff is a cause in fact of the harm. Does that establish that the defendant was not? Certainly not. There are always many causes of harm. If the plaintiff's action is legally permissible, she is a cause, but is not guilty of tort or crime and there is no reason to deny her recovery on causal grounds alone, so long as defendant is *also* a cause.

Application of the but-for test to negligent failure to act. *Salinetro* involves negligent action (negligent X-ray use), but the specific negligence is an omission. The but-for test does, then, apply to omissions that are negligent as well as to acts. But this creates some fairly absurd situations.

A leaves his car at his usual garage with instructions to repair the brakes and an agreement that he will pick it up after the garage has closed. The garage leaves the car as promised, indicating that the brakes are sound, and A drives it out of the lot. A does not apply the brakes as he should have done while driving and he crashes into P. P sues A, who by now has discovered that the brakes were not repaired. "I was negligent," A says, "but my negligence was not a cause, since if I had put on the brakes, they would not have worked." P, losing on the but-for test, then sues B, the garage owner. his response is to admit negligence, but to deny cause: "I failed to repair the brakes," he says, "but, after all, A did not attempt to use them anyway, so the but-for test lets me off."

Note 1. But-for as a hypothetical or counterfactual test. It is always difficult to imagine what might have happened in a scenario that didn't. *Salinetro* illustrates this problem well. Would the patient have said, "No, I'm not pregnant," or might she have said, "I don't know, but I'm trying"? The problem is that the jury has to make a determination about what would have happened even though there is no way to be certain about this.

Note 2. The alternate scenarios in *Hale* and *Salinetro*. If Ms. Hale would have tripped even absent the overgrown bush there would be no actual cause and that property owner would be entitled to summary judgment. But for the overgrown bush, the plaintiff would still have suffered the actual harm (the fall and the broken hip).

If the defendant in *Jordan v. Jordan*, cited here, had looked in her rear view mirror, the injury would not have been avoided, since she could not have seen anyone there.

As noted in the broader discussion of *Salinetro*, there are certainly scenarios under which the patient might have said something that made the doctor aware that pregnancy was a possibility. If the patient had argued that failure to test for pregnancy was the negligence, that might have been an actual cause of the x-ray. For any of this negligent conduct to be the actual cause not just of the x-ray being taken but of the fetus' death, we would have to show that the x-ray caused the harm to the fetus, another tricky issue of causation.

Note 3. Actual and proximate cause. The *Hale* opinion actually has a very fine discussion and application of the differences between actual and proximate cause. However, we chose not to include the proximate cause portion of the case on the theory that a full discussion of actual cause and then a full discussion of proximate cause might best convey the differences. This Note does flag the subsequent issue.

Note 4. Res ipsa loquitur and cause in fact. The Restatement Second's version of res ipsa loquitur explicitly states that if the three requirements for applying res ipsa are met, then "it may be inferred that harm suffered by the plaintiff is caused by negligence of the defendant." *See* Chapter 6. Res ipsa loquitur may allow a plaintiff to "finesse" the causal issue in many situations, simply because if we do not know what the defendant's conduct is (having only the injury to show that there is negligence), then we can hardly apply a but-for test to find out whether a change in the conduct would have avoided harm. But this note shows that res ipsa cannot always provide causal assistance, let alone a causal inference. Res ipsa loquitur might warrant an inference that someone is negligent when the sponge appears in the abdomen and that the negligence caused the plaintiff pain and perhaps caused a second operation to remove the sponge. But when we get to the additional claim of stomach cancer, we have a second causal issue. Res ipsa almost certainly will not assist the plaintiff in proving the scientific connection involved in the Type 1 causal issue –that the stomach cancer was a result of the sponge. Cf. *Barnes v. Bovenmyer*, 122 N.W.2d 312 (Iowa 1963).

B. Problems with and Alternatives to But-for Tests

NOTE: LIABILITY OF TWO OR MORE PERSONS

These notes attempts to put emphasis on the but-for issue and to help distinguish it from the issue of fault apportionment. The short of it is that when tortfeasors cause divisible or separate injuries, the amount of their respective liability is determined by causal rules; each is liable for what he causes, no more, no less. A caused the broken arm and he is liable for that, but he is not a but-for cause of the broken leg and he is not liable for that in the absence of conspiracy or concert of action.

Conversely, when two or more tortfeasors are but for causes of a single indivisible injury, causal apportionment is impossible—that's what it means to say the injury is indivisible. Therefore, the respective responsibility of each tortfeasor must be determined by some form of fault apportionment, not by apportioning damages to separate causes.

To round out the picture, this note goes on to indicate that some actors are liable vicariously without respect to whether their fault was a but for cause. This point is covered primarily in Chapter 22 and is included here only to avoid presenting a picture that is too distorted.

This note builds on information in Chapter 6, § 2 about joint and several liability and proportionate liability. If you did not cover that material in the sequence presented in the book, you will need to use it here. The advantage of using the material on joint and several and several liability earlier is now apparent; you can more readily separate the but-for issue.

LANDERS V. EAST TEXAS SALT WATER DISPOSAL CO., 248 S.W.2d 731 (Tex. 1952)

Two polluters, each presumably dumping sufficient pollution to cause the harm, have ruined the plaintiff's lake, killing fish. They are held jointly and severally liable, largely because the plaintiff cannot distinguish how much damage each one caused.

The important phrase is indivisible injury. When two or more tortfeasors cause a single injury, or one that cannot practically be apportioned, the courts traditionally applied fault apportionment in the form of joint and several liability.

Two different kinds of issue arise with *Landers* and *Anderson*. First, how does fault apportionment (in this case joint and several liability) compare with causal apportionment? Second, how do these cases fit with the but-for causation rules we've just seen? You can introduce both issues beginning with *Landers,* but it may be easier to postpone the second until you get to *Anderson*. We'll comment on the second issue there.

The idea in *Landers* is that when no basis for causal apportionment can be found, then a fault apportionment system will apply. That sounds more complicated than it is. Suppose we somehow knew that the first polluter killed only 10% of the fish and that the damages effects of its pollution were then exhausted. And we knew that the second similarly killed 90% of the fish. Armed with that knowledge, we would apportion responsibility causally, holding the first tortfeasor liable for the fish he killed and no more, the second for the fish he killed and no more. This is causal apportionment. It may be easier to see if you imagine that A negligently runs over the plaintiff's dog and B negligently runs over his cat. Clearly enough, A caused harm to the dog but not to the cat and A is liable only for harm to the dog. That is the harm he caused, hence we speak of causal apportionment.

Causal apportionment is nothing at all like fault apportionment, but students often have difficulty learning, remembering, and applying the difference. To see the difference, you can use *Landers*. The court there was unable to apportion responsibility between the defendants according to separate harms they caused, so it approved joint and several liability. That is, as we know from the brief encounter in Chapter 6, § 2, one form of fault apportionment. Each defendant would end up (through contribution or otherwise) paying 50% of the plaintiff's damages under the older rules, or a percentage equal to its comparative fault share under the newer rules. To make things simple, you might suppose that the comparative fault of each is the same, so each bears 50% of the responsibility under either calculation. If we could apportion causally, however, the relative responsibility might be quite different. Suppose the pollution was not salt water but a chemical and that the first polluter's chemical killed 10% of the fish, after which its potential for harm was totally exhausted. In that case, instead of liability for 50% of the total harm, the first polluter would be liable only for 10%.

ANDERSON V. MINNEAPOLIS, ST. PAUL & SAULT STE. MARIE RY., 179 N.W. 45 (Minn. 1920)

Two fires combined and spread to the plaintiff's property. One fire was negligently set by the defendant. The other may have been an innocent fire set by lightning. The defendant argued the but-for rule–that the innocent fire would have destroyed the plaintiff's property even if the defendant had set no fire at all. The court in effect rejects the but-for rule for this situation and adopts a "substantial factor" test.

The but-for test would have relieved the defendant of liability if the other fire would have burned the plaintiff's place even in the absence of the defendant's fire. We could not say that "but for" the defendant's negligence, the plaintiff's place would not have suffered damage. If liability is to be imposed, the but-for rule must be rejected, at least on the facts, and the substantial factor rule used instead. At one time courts (like *Cook*, cited in *Anderson*) associated joint and several liability with concerted action. *Landers* associates joint and several liability with indivisible injury instead. *Anderson* does the same, arguably in a more extreme case, one in which there is only one tortfeasor, who is held responsible for an indivisible injury to which innocent forces also contributed.

In a way, *Landers* is probably also rejecting but-for causation, at least as a measure of liability. If you assume that either defendant's pollution would have been sufficient to kill all the fish, each defendant could say that he was not a but-for cause–the other pollution would have killed all the fish anyway. When a court applies any fault apportionment system to impose liability upon such tortfeasors, it cannot be applying the but-for rule.

Notes 1 & 2. The but-for test applied to *Landers* and *Anderson*. If one of the pollutants reached the lake first, it is the cause of the fishes death and the other pollutant isn't (assuming the pollutants killed the fish on contact). If both entered the lake at the same time, we would get the unacceptable answer that neither of the pollutants caused the fishes' death. How can that be when the fish are all dead? This is a failure of the but-for test in cases in which there are two sufficient but not necessary causes. In cases like these courts might use the substantial factor test in note 5. The same problem is true of *Anderson*.

Note 3. Duplicative causation. Although *Anderson* does not pass the but-for test, you can notice that both fires combined. It was not a case of one fire burning the property and then another fire racing over the same property. This is Wright's case of duplicative causation. Where the duplicative causes are both tortious, the courts pretty much agree with the result in *Anderson* on some theory or another.

Note 4. "Preemptive" causation. Now imagine that *Landers* is different because one body of pollution reached the lake before the other. If we treat pollution as the harm and not the death of each individual fish, then the first body of salt water to reach the lake polluted the lake. The second caused no harm because the harm was already done. Assume that, as with the two fires in *Anderson*, the second pollution would have sufficed to destroy the lake even without the first. If we know that the second body of salt water arrived after the pollution was complete from the first, this is a case of Wright's preemptive causation. (The court recognizes this point in its last paragraph.) In Wright's view the first would be a cause but the second would not; you cannot cause the death of a person who is already dead, and similarly you cannot pollute a lake already dead from another's pollution. Landers is only like this preempted cause case if one of the bodies of salt water arrived first.

Wright's test. Wright's test is difficult to go into either in a casebook or in a torts class. He calls it the NESS test, short for Necessary Element of a Sufficient Set. You will need to read Wright's work if you want to discuss it in class. The idea is something like this: You first identify a set of facts or conditions that would be *sufficient* to cause the harm under discussion. The defendant's conduct must be one of these facts or conditions. Second, you determine whether the defendant's conduct was a necessary element in that set in order to get the consequent harm. If so, you have causation. In the two-fire cases, you describe the set as including a fire, combustibles, wind, and other such conditions as actually existed. The set of conditions–fire, wind, etc.–is sufficient to cause the burning. The wind alone would not burn, however; the fire is a *necessary* element to the burning. So the fire is causal under the NESS test because it is a "necessary element of a sufficient set." Do you have the feeling something has slipped by you? The *set* is *any* set of facts that meets two criteria: (a) the facts must be the actual facts in the case, and (b) they must, taken together, be sufficient to cause the harm in question. But notice the set does NOT have to include all the facts of the case. In this instance, the set does not have to include the second fire. This is a complex and maybe elegant way of saying that you can ignore duplicative causes, (those outside a set or group of facts that are sufficient to cause the harm). Indeed, that is the purpose of constructing this test.

In the preemptive cause case– the victim who is about to drink a deadly poison is first shot to death– the first cause is the only cause. The putative "second" cause is no cause at all under the NESS test. The set of conditions sufficient to cause death must include a living person; you can't kill one who is already dead. No set of conditions from the real case can be described that will allow you to kill a dead person, so in preemptive cause cases the NESS test points to the first act or condition as a cause and excludes the second.

Notes 5-8. Substantial factor. As in *Busta*, courts tend to use either but for or substantial factor as its test of cause in fact, depending on the facts of the case at hand. The Restatement Second of Torts, §§ 431-33, also adopts the substantial factor test. Courts don't need to use this test for every case in which there are multiple defendants. It is not a problem for the but-for test to determine that there is more than one actual cause of a harm (as previously discussed in connection with *Hale*). The but-for test only fails in a smaller subset of multiple actor cases—those with 2 sufficient causes. In those cases only, although we know that both actors caused the harm, the but-for test asked separately would lead to the anomalous result that neither of the two actors caused it.

Does substantial factor mean anything? *See* David W. Robertson, *The Common Sense of Cause in Fact,* 75 TEX. L. REV. 1765, 1780 (1997); DOBBS ON TORTS § 171 (2000). Why not just say that in the case of concurrent tortfeasors either of which alone would have been sufficient to cause the plaintiff's harm but-for causation is not required? Or that we aggregate the conduct of concurring tortfeasors and apply the but-for test to the aggregate? As mentioned in note 8, the newer Physical Harms Restatement avoids the substantial factor term by simply providing that when each of the negligent conduct concurrent tortfeasors would be sufficient to cause the harm, both are treated as causes.

▶**FYI:** *Substantial factor as a test of proximate cause.* Sometimes the substantial factor test seems related more to the proximate cause or "remoteness" problem covered in the next chapter. See *Scoggins v. Wal-Mart Stores, Inc.,* 560 N.W.2d 564 (Iowa 1997).You can see why if you translate "substantial factor" as "significant cause."At the same time, it serves to bypass the but for test. Because it allows the plaintiff to get to the jury without but for cause, you could regard it as a different test of causation, or alternatively as a policy decision that causation is not required.■

Note 9. Indivisible injury. *Bockrath v. Aldrich Chem. Co., Inc.,* 980 P.2d 398 (Cal. 1999), allowed the plaintiff to join 55 alleged polluters. Accord: *James v. Bessemer Processing Co., Inc.,* 714 A.2d 898 (N.J. 1998), in effect noting, however, that the injury might be apportioned less to defendants whose products were less carcinogenic. The plaintiff must still of course prove the fact of causation against each of the 55, as well negligence or grounds for strict liability.

Note 10. Indivisible injury in a several liability system. This hypothetical is an opportunity for students to distinguish divisible vs. indivisible injuries and fault vs. causal apportionment. As we've couched the hypothetical, students can be led to see that causal apportionment is readily possible in the case of the injury to the grass, so respective fault does not come into play at all. If the grass is harmed only by one defendant, we can have only that defendant pay for that harm.

With respect to the damage to the lake, in which causal apportionment is not possible, fault apportionment is required. The fault apportionment may be done under a joint and several liability system with contribution or a several, proportionate liability system. In the latter system, damages resulting from an indivisible injury are directly apportioned according to fault. How wrongful the conduct was that led to the release of saltwater might be a factor to consider in terms of the percentages of fault to assign to each party.

The more difficult question arises when one body of salt water is twice the amount as the other. Would the bodies of water actually cause different amounts of harm proportioned to their respective volumes? Even if we feel uncertain about that, might we apportion responsibility two-to-one rather than as a percentage of fault?

NOTE: INCREASED RISK SHOWING CAUSATION

Before we reach the loss of chance cases coming up soon, we wanted to give prominence to the idea in *Zuchowicz* that when the defendant creates a risk of a particular type of harm and that harm in fact follows in expected temporal sequence, an inference of causation may be justified. These cases are distinguishable from the loss of chance cases, but they bear some resemblance and deserve to be singled out as we attempt to do in this Note.

Zuchowicz is maybe the best case explication of the idea. It was quoted and followed in an interesting toxic exposure case, *Alder v. Bayer Corp., AGFA Div.,* 61 P.3d 1068 (Utah 2002).

The *Zuchowicz* analysis does not apply unless we know (from common experience or from evidence adduced in the case) that the defendant's conduct *can* cause the type of harm the plaintiff suffered. The plaintiff who has cancer cannot use the *Zuchowicz* approach to show that she got cancer because the defendant negligently caused an intersection collision, since we don't know that collisions are generally capable of causing cancer. It would be otherwise if admissible testimony showed collisions were capable of causing cancer. But even in that case, the *Zuchowicz* approach is not likely to aid the plaintiff, because the defendant must be negligent and the harm must be harm of the general kind that he should have foreseen and avoided (as we see in the next chapter).

Perhaps the principle would only be accepted when the harm is not merely within the scope of the risk but represents the very core of risk unreasonably created by the defendant. In the lifeguard case, the failure to have a lifeguard risks drowning; perhaps it also risks some peripheral harms in some settings, say, a child choking on the beach sand, but maybe the principle would apply only to the core risk of drowning. Perhaps also courts will ignore the principle when they are already skeptical about liability for policy reasons. In *Saelzler v. Advanced Group 400,* 23 P.3d 1143 (Cal. 2001), the plaintiff went to the defendant's place of business to deliver a package. She was brutally attacked by three unknown persons. Her claim that the defendant was negligent in failing to provide better security was dismissed because, although better security would make the premises safer, they might still have been unsafe for this particular plaintiff. The court did not explicitly address the *Zuchowicz* principle.

The synthesis of cases that supports the *Zuchowicz* approach was done and done beautifully by the late Wex Malone in *Ruminations on Cause in Fact,* 9 STAN. L. REV. 60 (1958). More recently, David Fischer has skillfully summarized this part of Malone's long article in *Tort Recovery for Loss of a Chance,* 36 WAKE FOREST L. REV. 605 at 650-51 (2001).

What is the danger of leaving a pool unlocked or of children playing with flames? The *McQuire* and *Yount* cases seem reasonable in their inferences of causation.

Problem

TILLO V. EAGLE

This is an easy problem except for the fact that the initiative is put upon the student to seek evidence. (The class need not understand what the meaning of the two medical terms, hyperbilirubinemia and high hematocrit levels. It is a given that those conditions could cause brain damage and retardation if not properly treated and that is the important point.

If the obstetrician's negligence had caused all the brain damage that Desiree ever suffered, then the pediatrician, Dr. Eagle, could not have caused brain damage at all under the preempted cause argument. In that case Eagle may avoid liability for brain damage (although he might still be liable for separable injuries such as pain or other physical harm resulting from the jaundice). If we cannot know whether all the damage had been done and cannot know how much was caused by each defendant, then the single indivisible injury rule would presumably apply. Students might think of *Landers*. This is a very simple analysis which tells you to ask experts (1) was all the brain damage caused and irreversible upon delivery (or at any time before Eagle took over)? (2) If not, can you state what additional harm (if any) was probably caused by Dr. Eagle's conduct?

If you want to act this out, let the student ask you whatever she likes and see why she thinks the questions she asks are relevant and what rule makes them so. You can answer if you like in the voice of two different witnesses, or assign those roles to class members. *Witness A:* (1) "I cannot say whether or not all the brain damage was caused or irreversible at the time of delivery; some of it may have resulted from acts of Dr. Eagle." (2) "I cannot be sure how much of the brain damage resulted from Dr. Eagle's acts." *Witness B:* (1) "I believe that all the brain damage was done or at least irreversibly begun by the time Dr. Eagle first saw Desiree." (2) "If it is possible that Dr. Eagle's act caused some of the brain damage, it could not have caused more than 10%, measured by degree of retardation."

The basic facts (but not the imagined testimony suggested above) are derived from *Ravo v. Rogatnick*, 514 N.E.2d 1104 (N.Y. 1987). Although the case statements are not as precise as you might want, evidence there indicated that the experts could not determine how much, if any, of the brain damage was due to the pediatrician's negligence. Consequently, he was held jointly and severally liable.

C. Proof: What Was Caused?

This subsection's title emphasizes the connection between *Dillon*, *Summers* and the value of the chance cases by treating them all together as cases in which the defendant has caused something deleterious, but perhaps not the main injury. In *Dillon* now just a few-sentences-long example for teachers who want to address it, the defendant causes the loss of a life that is already devalued by the immediate prospect of almost certain death; in *Summers* the defendant whose shot does not strike the plaintiff causes a critical loss of evidence; in *Lord*, the defendant causes loss of a chance at life, even though the chance is relatively small. These cases can be viewed as going to the damages issue, that is, to the question of WHAT was caused.

DILLON V. TWIN STATES GAS & ELEC. CO., 163 A. 111 (N.H. 1932). We've taken out most of the *Dillon* case, but left in a few lines for teachers who want to tackle it. It is such an unusual case and something of an exception to the normal rule that the one who caused the death first (remember the poison and the shooting) is liable.

A boy is falling off a bridge and will (it may be hypothetically assumed) certainly die when he hits the rocks below. Before this happens, however, he grabs at the defendant's electric wire to save himself. This does not save him at all; it electrocutes him. The defendant is liable on this supposition only for the remaining split second of his life before he hit the ground. If it is hypothetically assumed that the boy would have lived, but in a seriously injured condition with less earning power, then the defendant's liability would be limited to liability based on that lessened earning power, "as though he had already been crippled" when he was electrocuted.

Accord: *Follett v. Jones*, 481 S.W.2d 713 (Ark. 1972) (decedent killed in an auto accident had terminal cancer and would have died in a few weeks in any event; the defendant is liable for causing the death, but damages are based on the decedent's limited life expectancy).

If you go very far with the *Dillon* idea, you'll undermine the normal allocation rules. *See* DOBBS ON TORTS § 177 (2000). Imagine that A blows up the plaintiff's house, which stands in the path of B's fire. By the time B's fire sweeps over the property fifteen minutes later, the house is already in rubble from A's demolition. A argues under *Dillon* that he is liable for no more than rental value of the house for 15 minutes–its life expectancy. B argues "preemptive cause"– that he caused no loss at all, as the house was already destroyed. If you accept both the *Dillon* argument and the preemptive cause arument, you give the plaintiff essentially nothing (the value of 15 minutes of property ownership).

Hypotheticals and cases. The defendant negligently injures the plaintiff's leg, causing both pain and a permanent loss of earning capacity. Just before trial of the plaintiff's claim, a robber shot the plaintiff in the injured leg. Amputation was required as a result. Can the defendant now argue he has not caused permanent loss of earning capacity, since we now know that the plaintiff would have lost his left leg in any event? The House of Lords rejected this argument in *Baker v. Willoughby*, 3 All E.R. 1528 (H.L. 1969). A very similar case with the same result is *Spose v. Ragu Foods, Inc.*, 537 N.Y.S.2d 739 (Sup.Ct. 1989). A later decision of the House of Lords in *Jobling v. Associated Dairies Ltd.*, 2 All E.R. 752 (H.L. 1981), casts doubt on *Baker.* Both the English cases are discussed in W.V.H. ROGERS, WINFIELD & JOLOWICZ ON TORT 215-17 (16th ed. 2002). *Dillon* does not support the defendant's argument in *Baker,* does it? At most it suggests that conditions existing at the time of the tort could be considered in valuing what lost was caused.

SUMMERS V. TICE , 199 P.2d 1 (Cal. 1948)

A and B both negligently fire guns in the direction of the plaintiff. A shot from one of the guns strikes and injures the plaintiff, but there is no way to tell which one. One of the defendants is definitely *not* a cause and his act would not have been sufficient to cause the harm. For these reasons the case is different from the others we have seen. Yet both are held liable.

Tice's shot might not have touched Summers at all, and if not, the presence or absence of Simonson makes no difference. It is this fact –doubt that Tice had any part at all in the harm–that distinguishes cases like *Landers*. To make *Landers* parallel to *Summers*, you would have to imagine that one body of salt water ran off in a different direction without entering the lake at all and that we don't know which body of water entered the lake.

Concert of action. Summers mentions the concerted action theory used in some cases for the same result. You can explain briefly that concert of action implies agreement to act for a common purpose and that this is a traditional basis for joint and several liability where the goal or agreed-upon acts are tortious. But an agreement to hunt probably is not an agreement to fire negligently, so concert of action seems fictional here. If both are held liable on the ground that they have tacitly agreed to hunt together, Tice would be liable even if he had not fired at all. The concert theory would also logically reject liability in the case of two independent hunters who never knew of each others' presence and certainly did not act in concert, while *Summers* itself would presumably impose liability in such a case.

Defendants' knowledge. The *Summers* court suggested that the hunters might know whose shot caused the harm and that the threat of liability might force one of them to reveal the other's culpability. But it is hard to believe that this motivated the court, first because it seems inherently unlikely that the hunters knew any more than the plaintiff and second because the court did not require evidence that the hunters knew more.

Tortiously obscuring cause in fact. What was caused? One defendant caused the injury. The other defendant caused loss of evidence about causation. You can see this by imagining that Tice had acted carefully and thus had not fired. In such a case the plaintiff would either be uninjured (because it was in fact Tice's shot that injured him) *or* the plaintiff would have good proof against Simonson (because he was the only person who fired.) Tice's firing the gun thus either injured the plaintiff or obscured his case against Simonson. Either way, something can be said for holding Tice liable. The same analysis works as to Simonson. *See* DOBBS ON TORTS § 175 (2000).

Plaintiff's participation in confusing the causal issue. In the *Summers v. Tice* pattern of cases, the plaintiff is free of any fault that confuses the causal issue. But suppose that the plaintiff and both defendants were all negligently firing at a wall and shot from one of the guns struck the plaintiff because it ricocheted. In that case, if we do not know who fired the ricochet shot, the plaintiff's moral ground for recovery is quite weak, not because she is negligent but because she has also participated in confusing the causal issue. In that case the moral strengths of *Summers* become soggy uncertainties and the rule probably should not apply. But in some other cases of plaintiff fault the plaintiff does not confuse the cause issue and should not be barred on causal grounds. Suppose the plaintiff is a deer hunter dressed in such effective camouflage that she is negligently exposing herself to hunters' shots. And in fact the hunters mistake her for a deer and one shot strikes her. In that case the plaintiff may be negligent in being there and should suffer a comparative fault reduction in liability, but she has not confused the causal issue, so the rule of *Summers v. Tice* should continue to apply, subject only comparative fault reduction in damages.

Note 1. The harm caused. This is intended to prompt students to recognize that the tort of each tortfeasor made it impossible for the plaintiff to present evidence of causation. *Hellums* took a different tack however. In that case the court saw the harm caused by the other hunter as an encouragement to shot in that direction.

Note 2. Harm by one of seven. *State v. CTL Distribution, Inc.,* 715 So.2d 262 (Fla. Dist. Ct. App. 1998): The court said that if you were to compare the *Summers* case, the CTL case was "like having seven hunters in the forest with weapons, only one of whom (CTL) was known to have fired his weapon. Following our analogy, though the other six hunters were carrying weapons, there was no evidence here that any of them fired his weapon. The wrongdoing is firing the weapon—spilling the hazardous substance—not carrying the weapon–transporting the hazardous substance." See also *Peck v. Serio*, 801 N.E.2d 890 (Ohio App. 2003) ("[T]hey must all be wrongdoers before the burden shifts to them to disprove causation."). This note is preparation for distinguishing *Ybarra* in Chapter 13, where a number of people were involved in a surgery but there was no reason to think all were chargeable with negligence.

Note 3. Aggravation of an existing injury. *Canada v. McCarthy,* 567 N.W.2d 496 (Minn. 1997): the trial court held that apportionment between preexisting lead injury and new exposure caused by the defendant was possible but that the defendant had the burden of proving appropriate apportionment. The Supreme Court of Minnesota affirmed this holding.

Connections. *Summers* has two important connections. First, it is important in distinguishing *Ybarra* v. *Spangard*, considered in the medical malpractice materials, Casebook Chapter 13. Second, it is background to or basis for elaboration of the market share type of liability represented in *Hymowitz v. Eli Lilly & Co.*, Casebook Chapter 25.

LORD V. LOVETT, 770 A.2d 1103 (N.H. 2001)

The plaintiff's neck was broken in an automobile accident. She claims that had the health care providers failed to diagnose her injury and consequently failed to immobilize her and provide steroid therapy. Had they done so, she claims, she would have had a substantially better recovery, although she cannot say how much so.

The court outlines three approaches to the problem of lost opportunity for a better outcome. The first, preponderance of the evidence approach, makes it clear why there is a problem. "[A] patient whose injury is negligently misdiagnosed, but who would have had only a fifty percent chance of full recovery from her condition with proper diagnosis, could not recover damages because she would be unable to prove that, absent the physician's negligence, her chance of a better recovery was at least fifty-one percent." (The court should have said 50+%.)

A different approach is to junk the preponderance rule and allow the plaintiff to recover in full for her injury, even though a substantial portion of it would have been incurred even had the defendants exercise perfect care.

"The third approach permits plaintiffs to recover for the loss of an opportunity for a better outcome, an interest that we agree should be compensable, while providing for the proper valuation of such an interest."

The court opts, without a lot of explanation, for the third approach: "[A] plaintiff may recover for a loss of opportunity injury in medical malpractice cases when the defendant's alleged negligence aggravates the plaintiff's preexisting injury such that it deprives the plaintiff of a *substantially* better outcome. . . ." Its main reason is that loss of a chance is itself an injury (and therefore worth whatever the chance was worth).

In so holding, the court rejects the argument that the injury is too difficult to calculate on the ground that the defendant's negligence caused the difficulty. The plaintiff must, however, provide some basis for identifying "that portion of her injury caused by the defendant's negligence from the portion resulting from the underlying injury."

On the main issue, whether the court should adopt a rule permitting recovery for lost chance, the court's holding for the plaintiff is in line with substantial contemporary authority. But shouldn't the plaintiff be required to offer evidence about the nature or size of the chance? When the plaintiff conceded (Casebook 226, top) that she could not prove how much of a chance she lost, why doesn't that put her out of court? To answer that question well, students will need to distinguish –

(a) The plaintiff suffers paralysis of her right leg, but proper diagnosis and treatment probably would not have avoided this outcome. On the preponderance test, her evidence is insufficient.

(b) The plaintiff suffers paralysis of her right leg, and the plaintiff lost a 40% chance of avoiding paralysis because the health care providers failed to provide proper care.

(c) The plaintiff suffers paralysis of her right leg. Although proper care would have improved her chances of avoiding paralysis, no one can say how much. This is the plaintiff's case here after the concession, Casebook 226.

Although the court takes the plaintiff-favorable view of this case, that loss of a chance is recoverable, presumably in example (b) above, that presumably does not mean the plaintiff can recover any percentage of her damages the jury might wish to assign. She presumably still must prove that she in fact lost a chance by a preponderance of the evidence and possibly something about the size of that chance. Students will probably need to work through the case and the notes to get these distinctions. Notes 4-6 and Note 8 are particularly relevant to the issue just posed.

Note 2. Relaxed causation. How could you justify this approach? We could say that the health care provider's negligence concurred with a preexisting condition (the patient's illness or disease) and produced a single indivisible injury, death. A tortfeasor whose negligence causes a single indivisible injury is liable for the entire injury. Is the class convinced that this is sound?

Notes 4 & 5. Quantified value of the chance and items of damages proved by a preponderance. Once the class grasps the idea that you simply discount full damages by the chance or probability, you can go on to recognize that the plaintiff may have proved some elements of damages by a preponderance of the evidence, like the pain in Note 4. In that example, should the plaintiff recover 100% of the pain damages that were proven by a preponderance of the evidence, plus 40% of the damages otherwise allowable for the death itself?

Note 6. What *must* be proved by a preponderance of the evidence. Maybe if you require quantification of the chance, you think that the quantification numbers must be proved by a preponderance of the evidence. Put otherwise, suppose the plaintiff proves she had a chance of recovery but cannot prove how much of a chance. Unless the facts permit common knowledge or lay inferences about how big the chance was, it seems doubtful that the jury should be permitted to award any damages in a range of zero to 50%. (But see Note 8.) Distinguish this from cases in which some experts say the change is 35% and some say 45%. Perhaps in that case juries might be allowed to fix the chance at any number from 35 to 45%, as juries are allowed to do with different expert valuations in eminent domain cases. *Alphonse v. Acadian Ambulance Servs., Inc.,* 844 So.2d 294 (La. Ct. App. 2003) holds the plaintiff must prove loss of chance and its value by a preponderance; *Alberts v. Schultz,* 975 P.2d 1279 (N.M. 1999) is roughly in accord.

Verdicchio v. Ricca, 843 A.2d 1042 (N.J. 2004), presents a complicated variation on the problem. It was also a malpractice-wrongful death case. Evidence supported a finding that the defendant physician was negligent in failing to examine the patient's leg, that an examination could have revealed cancer, and that *if* the cancer was localized at that time, the patient had an 85% chance of five years' survival, though if the cancer had metastasized, the chance of five years' survival was only 20-30%. The problem was that no one knew whether the cancer had metastasized at that time. The trial court ruled that no increased risk or value of the chance recovery was permissible without proof that the cancer had not metastasized at the time the defendant could have discovered it. The court held this ruling error. "Even if it had metastasized, his survival rate was, according to the evidence, 20-30% or higher." So far, so good. But in the absence of evidence that the cancer had *not* metastasized, shouldn't the plaintiff's recovery be limited to no more than 30% of the total damages? The court did not directly discuss that possibility, although the jury found that the defendant was responsible for only 55%, a percentage that looks like a compromise not based on evidence. Although we cannot be sure, it looks like a case in which the defense went for the jugular and thus missed its best defense— that the plaintiff should be required to prove the predicate for a quantified lost chance by a preponderance of the evidence.

Jorgenson v. Vener, 640 N.W.2d 485 (S.D. 2002) involved a man who shattered his leg. He alleged that this doctor negligently failed to get him to a specialist quickly and as a result, his chance of saving the leg was reduced by 15%. In fact, though, he had accepted amputation with a 60% chance of saving it and testified that he would still have accepted amputation had the chance been as high at 75%. That would mean that he lost a chance that he would not have accepted. The court said he could get to the jury on his lost chance claim. Comment: He DID lose the chance. But could a chance that the plaintiff would not accept have any value?

Relating back to *Zuchowicz*/Increased Risk. You can reconsider or review the material in the note on increased here if you think your class is not exhausted. Suppose the plaintiff was exposed to asbestos fibers by two different tortfeasors at different times and suffers a deadly cancer, mesothelioma, as a result of one of the exposures. Medical knowledge (so far) indicates that a single fiber of asbestos could cause the cancer, but that knowledge also indicates that the more fibers to which the victim is exposed, the more risk of cancer. So a cancer cell could have been caused to develop by the first exposure or the second, but quite possibly not by both, although both increased the risk. In *Rutherford v. Owens-Illinois*, 941 P.2d 1203 (Cal. 1997) the California Supreme Court held that on similar facts it would not shift the burden of proof as it had done in *Summers v. Tice*, but would allow the plaintiff to recover without showing "which fiber" triggered the cancer. *Fairchild v. Glenhaven Funeral Servs.*, [2002] 3 All E.R. 305, [2002] 3 All. E.R. 305, 2002 WL 820081 (H.L. 2002) the English House of Lords tackled such a set of facts. Surveying the law of many European and other countries, the one of the judgments in *Fairchild* observed that many other countries had confronted similar problems and variously used one of four different approaches: (1) an increase in risk is equivalent to a material contribution or substantial factor; (2) the burden is on the defendant to disprove causation; (3) the tortfeasors are treated as if they had been acting in concert; and (4) policy or justice simply requires that the plaintiff be permitted to recover. Under one or the other of these approaches, most European countries "would, it seems, afford a remedy to the plaintiff."

Note 7. Reducing damages under quantified approach to reflect probability where plaintiff proves causation is actually more likely than not. If valuing the chance furnishes the best, most just, or most policy-right approach when the chance is less than 50+%, should we not value the chance when it exceeds the magic preponderance level as well? That would mean a plaintiff who proves injury was caused by the defendant to a 95% probability would still not collect 5% of her damages. Right or wrong?

Note 8. Recent cases. The Massachusetts Supreme Court case has an excellent discussion of recent developments in the area. It also provides a thoughtful discussion of the issues.

Note 9. Deterrence. This Note raises some considerations that may be significant in determining whether to adopt the lost chance approach. Might repeat players (like doctors, for example) be woefully underdeterred under the traditional rule. The table says it all, but you might have to work through it with the class. What it says is that, on our hypothetical of repeated negligence and a plaintiff with a 33% chance of survival, the physician will escape liability for his negligence in all cases, even though the right amount of liability would be full liability for one-third of the cases. The value of the chance rule gets that right amount where the damages are approximately equal for each patient. It distributes those damages to all three patients, instead of to the one patient who (if we could but know it) would have been saved. But that's no concern of the defendant's; he pays the same as he would pay if we knew which patient would have lived. Thus, on our hypothetical, deterrence requires a lost chance approach. But of course our hypothetical is not the only one. If damages are wildly different for different patients, it won't average out so neatly. Still, it is the best estimate we can make, isn't it?

A case emphasizing deterrence is *Holton v. Memorial Hospital,* 679 N.E.2d 1202 (Ill. 1997), where the court said:

> We . . . reject the reasoning of cases which hold, as a matter of law, that plaintiffs may not recover for medical malpractice injuries if they are unable to prove that they would have enjoyed a greater than 50% chance of survival or recovery absent the alleged malpractice of the defendant. To hold otherwise would free health care providers from legal responsibility for even the grossest acts of negligence, as long as the patient upon whom the malpractice was performed already suffered an illness or injury that could be quantified by experts as affording that patient less than a 50% chance of recovering his or her health.
>
> Disallowing tort recovery in medical malpractice actions on the theory that a patient was already too ill to survive or recover may operate as a disincentive on the part of health care providers to administer quality medical care to critically ill or injured patients. Moreover, it has been noted that '[i]t is impossible to divine who would fall into one category [survivor] or the other [nonsurvivor]. Not allowing such a case to be decided by a jury means that statistical proof of a less than 50% chance would be dispositive, even though no expert in the world could prospectively state who would survive and who would die. That is why doctors treat all patients, not just those with better than even odds.

Note 10. Limits on lost chance liability? One obstacle for value of the chance arguments may lie in the fear that endless liabilities would result. After all, you diminish a person's *chances* of survival every time you drive negligently, even if nothing untoward happens. However, the value of the chance rule is flexible because its formulation is adaptable to a duty analysis. Although we have not yet reached the major duty portions of the casebook, we can plausibly tell students now that sometimes a defendant is under a duty to maximize the plaintiff's chances, but that at other times the defendant's duty is only to use due care to avoid actual injury. This was apparently the court's view in *Gardner* (Note 3), with a ship captain and a crew member who had gone overboard. The Michigan Court seemed to be saying something like this, also, in *Falcon v. Memorial Hospital,* 462 N.W.2d 44 (Mich. 1990), although its actual formulation was a little narrower and it has been rejected by legislation in Michigan. See MCL 600.2912a(2) & MSA 72A.2912(a)(2).

ALEXANDER V. SCHEID, 726 N.E.2d 272 (Ind. 2000)

A delay-in-diagnosis case in which a living person sues. Loss of chance of survival (or increased risk of harm) is viewed, not as a substitute for causation, but as itself the injury. Growth of a tumor is injury, so the question whether some injury must accompany lost-chance claims does not arise. Insubstantial loss of chance: the market will prevent such claims from being brought, but if they are, additional limits may be imposed.

With *Alexander* and *Dillon* (next case), we move from potential limits on lost chance recovery to potential and actual expansions. Notice that this case differs from the death cases; we know that death actually occurred and that we can never know in the future any more than we know now. In *Alexander*, however, the patient has not suffered an early death and may actually outlive her anticipated life span. So lost chance here is being used even though later on we'd have more accurate information whether the plaintiff suffered the loss in life expectancy.

DILLON V. EVANSTON HOSPITAL, 771 N.E.2d 357 (Ill. 2002)

Dillon reinforces *Alexander* on facts that may be more dramatic. The Illinois Court distinguishes what it calls increased risk from lost chance, but says both kinds of cases share a similar basis.

Michigan once judicially recognized a lost chance recovery, but the legislature squelched that by statute, although the statute by its terms only covers health care providers. MICH. COMP. LAWS ANN. § 600.2912a (2). In *Wickens v. Oakwood Healthcare Sys.*, 631 N.W.2d 686, 691 (Mich. 2001), the court held that a living plaintiff whose ten-year life expectancy had been reduced from at least 55% to 15% could claim under the statute only for "present injury" and had no claim for loss of survival opportunity, but that she could claim for "present injuries" that included pain and also "emotional trauma attributable to her unnecessarily worsened physical condition." The judges all interpreted the statute to mean that malpractice plaintiffs can only recover for present injuries, "injuries that have already been suffered." What if you followed the rule that the defendant takes the plaintiff as he finds her? He finds here with a 55% survival chance and leaves her with a 15% survival chance. The thing to which she was entitled was 100% of her existing chance. Her existing chance was reduce by more than 70%. Does that matter?

Note 1. Present injury. *Williams* is a fascinating case. He fetus had a substantially increased risk of injury. However, in the individual fetus it was unknown whether the x-rays would cause any injury at all or quite severe injury. The court found this case unlike Dillon, where there was some injury for certain—the catheter in the heart—even if the severity of that injury was still unknown.

Note 2. Small risks. If you accept "increased risk" as well as "lost chance" and also expand the recoveries to defendant who have not undertaken to maximize chance (as doctors have), then toxic torts might become a fertile field for the proportional recoveries. Value of the chance or "proportional causation" measurement of damages is especially adapted to some kinds of mass toxic tort cases.

One kind of toxic, mass tort results from distribution of a commercial product such as a prescription drug that may cause harm to users. Whether the drug has capacity to cause harm is often difficult to prove, perhaps impossible. Yet corporate behavior in marketing drugs without adequate research persists. Margaret A. Berger, *Eliminating General Causation: Notes Towards a New Theory of Justice and Toxic Torts*, 97 COLUM. L. REV. 2117 (1997), proposes to drop the requirement of "general causation," and to impose liability upon a manufacturer for failing to research and disseminate information about risks. The manufacturer could still shoulder the burden of proving the absence of causation in the plaintiff's specific claim, for instance on the ground that the harm was caused by genetic defect rather than by the product. She accepts the idea that damages might be limited in such a regime, perhaps even scheduled. One basis for this proposal is the argument that causation requirements, at least in that setting, are unrelated to the moral responsibility of the defendant, which turns on negligence and interference with individual autonomy, not on causation itself. In this respect, the proposed claim bears some resemblance to medical claims based on lack of informed consent. Would some students prefer this to a proportional or lost chance approach? What about suits against polluters whose pollution exposes all of us to increased cancer risks?

An End Note

Would students accept the proposal to eliminate a requirement of causal proof where the other elements are present? Would such a radical rule even change the result in *Landers, Anderson*, or *Summers*? Instead of a rule, what about simply recognizing that the jury may be permitted to infer causation when the above factors are shown and a strong causal link is suggested by the testimony?

The End Note has two valences. One reaches directly into the next section on proximate cause by emphasizing that a class of harm and class of person rule could be used in lieu of causation.

The other connection is more basic. Is causation part of the normative structure of tort law? Would we violate ideals of justice to ignore it under the conditions outlined? On this a number of writers in the Symposium in 63 CHI-KENT L. REV. 397 (1987), address their thoughts. You might recall for the class that although in criminal law some acts are crimes only if harm is done,(homicide, for example), statutes may make some acts criminal even when no harm has been done. Possession of a unregistered sawed-off shotgun has high potential for criminal use and almost no potential for any other use, so it is a crime calling for serious punishment. Attempts (including attempted harms of which the intended victim knows nothing about it) also represent a potential but unrealized harm. The same statements could be made about tortious conduct that has not demonstrably caused harm. You could think that there are moral reasons for requiring injury to the plaintiff and wrongdoing by the defendant, but we do not need to connect the two when causation is difficult or impossible to determine, provided the injury to the plaintiff is one risked by the defendant's negligent conduct.

CHAPTER 8

NEGLIGENCE: THE SCOPE OF RISK OR "PROXIMATE CAUSE" ELEMENT

▶**Changes in the Sixth Edition:** We have added one new primary case to this chapter, *Delaney v. Reynolds*, in § 2, dealing with self-inflicted injury or suicide as a superseding cause. There are also over a dozen new cases cited or discussed in Notes. To make way for new material, and to streamline our presentation somewhat, we have cut three case abstracts (*Mellon, Austermiller* and *Anaya*) and one primary case, *Sheehan*.

First-time users. We take up emotional harm and failure to protect the plaintiff from third persons as duty issues and accordingly consider those topics in later chapters.

▶The **Concise Edition** omits ¶ (c) of Note 3 after *Abrams*; a paragraph of the Note on the Rescue Doctrine; a portion of the *Hughes* case; Note 2 after *Doughty* (which necessitates renumbering) and Note 6 after *Derdiarian*. ■

Preliminary Note:

General scope. This section deals with the problems that arise when the plaintiff's injury, or the way it came about, is unexpected or fortuitous. Proximate cause arises as an issue only when something out of the ordinary has allegedly occurred. As the court said in *Goldberg v. Florida Power & Light Co.*, 899 So.2d 1105 (Fla. 2005), "harm is 'proximate' in a legal sense if prudent human foresight would lead one to expect that similar harm is likely to be substantially caused by the specific act or omission in question. . . . The law does not impose liability for freak injuries that were utterly unpredictable in light of common human experience." This may overstate the case a bit, since many cases addressing proximate cause involve more ordinary kinds of conduct and injuries, where there are a number of contributing causes.

The traditional language expresses the problem as one of proximate or "legal" cause, but some courts deal with the problem as a "duty" issue. Either way, and in spite of clumsy and opaque language, the issue is usually about the scope of the risk unreasonably created by the defendant. If the defendant's act produces results that are outside the risks he unreasonably created, courts may say that the defendant's conduct is not a proximate cause of the harm and if it is not, the defendant is not liable.

Excluded cases; the alternative duty analysis. There are many, many other cases in which the defendant is relieved of liability for quite different reasons, even when he is negligent and his negligence is a "cause in fact" of harm. For example, many persons who serve alcohol to a dangerously drunk person or to one who is likely to become drunk and drive, were traditionally held not liable for injuries later caused by the drinker. *See* Casebook Chapter 18. But this cannot be because injuries that result are unexpected; it can only be because the court does not wish to impose responsibility upon the server of alcohol.

Although a duty analysis often considers "foreseeability," duty analysis also considers other reasons why a negligent defendant might be relieved of liability. In considering many factors other than foreseeability/scope of risk, cases that limit liability by appeal to the duty concept somewhat resemble Andrews' approach to "proximate cause"– foreseeability is to be considered, but it is not the only consideration. This continues today under the label of "policy factors" in Wisconsin.

The present chapter does not deal with duty cases, or with any of the others that involve highly foreseeable injury, as where a child is injured before birth or someone is subjected to emotional injury without physical harm. Though all these questions can be discussed in terms of proximate cause, especially where there is a second actor who ought to take sole responsibility, they do not involve unexpected or unforeseeable harm. Partly for this reason, we do not think it helpful to consider such cases here, although they are important and we definitely consider them later.

Proximate and legal cause terminology and the "duty" debate. This book attempts to use the term scope of risk when feasible, to denote a consideration that limits liability separate and apart from some other policy limitations. It also uses the terms "proximate cause" and "legal cause," because these are the terms of the profession for the scope of risk problems described in this chapter. Use of these terms does not foreclose debate on whether the language of duty might be more appropriate (or whether proximate cause should be dropped and scope or risk substituted). Indeed, it may be hard to avoid the "duty" and "proximate cause" debate entirely. You can certainly see the scope of risk issues in this chapters as scope-of-duty questions. But they differ from duty questions that turn on judicial policies unrelated to foreseeability and they differ also in that no-duty rules usually deal with a whole category of liability, not the facts of particular cases. Finally, the "proximate cause" issues are usually issues for the jury where reasonable people can differ, while duty issues are determined by the judges. These distinctions mean that whatever the terminology we adopt, duty or proximate cause, we must recognize that scope of risk issues are quite different from some of the duty issues we consider largely in Chapter 18. Probably the best time for discussing the choice of language will be in teaching Chapter 18 or other chapters in Part III. For now, we'll try to use the term scope of risk from time to time to avoid too much emphasis on the duty vs. proximate cause debate.

Scope of risk terminology. The essential thrust of the problem considered in this chapter is best understood as a problem about the scope of the risk created by the defendant's negligence, not as a problem about any kind of causation, remote, attenuated, or otherwise. Courts agree that the problem is a scope of risk problem and say so both directly and indirectly by making foreseeability of harm the test. On the other hand, courts also talk the talk of causation and frequently emphasize vague concepts like remoteness or broken causal chains. This metaphorical, almost mystic talk is an old professional habit and we must recognize it even though we think it hides the issue.

Foreseeability and risk. Courts adopt the scope of risk idea when they say that liability is limited to foreseeable types of harms, risks, or classes of persons. However, professionals get confused by the foreseeability term. Not every foreseeable harm is within the scope of the risk negligently created. Some harms are foreseeable but so unlikely or so minor that reasonable people would not spend time or money to avoid them. Happily, the risk of falling in the bathtub does not persuade most of us to avoid bathing. So foreseeability is shorthand and while it reflects the scope of risk point, we must be alert to avoid saying that foreseeable harms necessarily import liability. See DOBBS ON TORTS § 181 (2000).

We think that if students can keep causal language in mind and at the same time recognize the scope of risk logic, these things will appear easier and quite straightforward once it is given that the defendant has a duty of care:

1. The Scope of Risk Principle

(a) A defendant is subject to liability for all harm he causes within the scope of the risks he negligently created.

(b) A defendant is not liable for any harm he causes that is not within the risks he negligently created.

2. Types of Harm and Class of Persons Outside the Risk

A harm or risk is not within the scope of the risks negligently created by the defendant in any of the following circumstances:

(a) if a reasonable person in similar circumstances would not have foreseen harm or risk of the same general type.

(b) if a reasonable person should have foreseen the general type of harm but would not have taken greater precautions to avoid it than the defendant took (a case of no negligence or breach of duty).

(c) if a reasonable person would not have foreseen harm of the same general type to the a general class of persons that includes the plaintiff.

3. Manner of occurrence and extent of harm

A harm or risk of the general kind that would have been foreseeable to a reasonable person is within the scope of the risk even though neither the exact harm nor its extent, nor the exact manner of its occurrence was or could have been foreseen.

4. Risks of Specific Type of Force

(a) A harm or risk is not of the same general kind that the defendant should have foreseen if he risked harm that would occur only through a specific force or class of forces and the harm that resulted was caused by a radically different force or class of forces.

(b) Unless the defendant created a risk that foreseeably would result in harm only through specific forces, the fact that harm is most immediately caused by acts of another person that constitute crime or negligence does not in itself mean that the harm is outside the scope of the risk created by the defendant.

5. Exclusion of Liability on Policy Grounds

A defendant whose unreasonably risky acts in fact cause harm within the scope of the risks he created may be absolved from liability on grounds unrelated to scope of risk considerations. [Usually under the rubric of duty. Part III of the Casebook.]

OUTLINE

SUMMARY

§ 1. THE PRINCIPLE: SCOPE OF RISK

MEDCALF V. WASHINGTON HEIGHTS CONDOMINIUM ASS'N, INC. The plaintiff buzzed her friend to permit entrance into the friend's condo. The buzzer, for which defendants were responsible, did not work. The plaintiff was thus left standing outside the building while her friend came downstairs to let her in. While she was waiting, she was attacked and injured. She is now suing the condo association and the property manager for negligently failing to have a working buzzer. Held, the trial court should have directed a verdict for defendants. The plaintiff must prove proximate cause, that is, that the harm suffered was the "same general nature as the foreseeable risk created by the defendant's negligence." Although proximate cause is a question of fact for the jury where reasonable minds could differ, the defendants here could not have foreseen that a malfunction might create a risk of attack from the outside.

ABRAMS V. CITY OF CHICAGO. When the defendant failed to provide an ambulance to take the plaintiff to the hospital for delivery of her baby, a friend took her. The friend collided with Jones, who was driving 75 m.p.h. The plaintiff suffered injury and her child died. *Held,* the city could not have foreseen that refusal to send an ambulance when labor pains were 10 minutes apart would result in injuries from a traffic accident. This is not the kind of harm that was foreseeable.

PALSGRAF V. LONG ISLAND RY. CO. The defendant, it is assumed, was negligent in pushing a man who was boarding a moving train. This knocked a package from his arms. The package unforeseeably contained fireworks, the detonation of which allegedly caused scales some distance away to fall and injure the plaintiff. *Majority*: Harm to the plaintiff was not one of the things that defendant might have foreseen. The risk to her was not part of what made the defendant negligent. As to her, the Cardozo opinion for the majority says, the defendant was not negligent at all. The defendant is thus not liable.

This is a rejection for negligence cases of the rule applied in intentional tort cases under the name of "transferred intent." *Dissent*: Judge Andrews, dissenting, does not embrace the concept of the "foreseeable plaintiff;" he thinks the case turns on proximate cause, not negligence (duty and breach). His description of "proximate cause" mixes both foreseeability and practical policies.

NOTE: THE RESCUE DOCTRINE. When the defendant creates a risk to A and B is injured in attempting A's rescue, courts treat B, the rescuer, as being within the class of persons to whom the defendant created a risk.

NOTE: VIOLATION OF STATUTE AND "PROXIMATE CAUSE." *Medcalf* and *Palsgraf* together pursue rules similar to those used in negligence per se cases, limiting liability to certain classes of harm and certain classes of persons in these cases, to classes of harm or person foreseeability of which made the defendant negligent.

§ 2. ASSESSING THE SCOPE OF THE RISK

A. Is Harm Outside the Scope of the Risk Because of the Manner in Which It Occurs?

HUGHES V. LORD ADVOCATE. Workers negligently left a "manhole" open while they were away and some boys climbed down in it. They got back up without difficulty, but then knocked a kerosene lamp down into the hole. The kerosene, unforeseeably, vaporized. This permitted an explosion and a fire. One boy fell into the hole as a result of the explosion. The Law Lords take the view that fire was foreseeable and that explosion, though not foreseeable, was a mere variant of the fire so that the defendant is liable. The scope of risk rule does not require foreseeability of the precise harm, only the general type of harm or instrument of harm.

DOUGHTY V. TURNER MFG. CO., LTD. A worker negligently knocked a lid into a vat of molten liquid maintained at 800 degrees C. This created a risk of a splash of the liquid which might have injured others. However, the lid did not splash, but a moment later chemical interactions of the lid and the liquid caused an eruption of the liquid which injured the plaintiff. This was thought unforeseeable and not a mere variant on the foreseeable splash.

B. Is Harm Outside the Scope of the Risk Because Its Extent Is Unforeseeable?

HAMMERSTEIN V. JEAN DEVELOPMENT WEST. A guest in defendant's hotel, known by defendant to have diabetes, is put in a fourth-floor room. A faulty fire alarm goes off, and the elevators are locked. He turns his ankle and gets a blister walking down the stairs, a condition which later becomes quite serious. While the extent of this harm might not have been foreseeable, the type of harm that resulted, and the class of persons to whom it happened, was foreseeable from negligently failing to have a properly-working fire alarm.

As Notes point out, the "thin skull" rule is that you take the plaintiff as you find him. If you can reasonably foresee harm that a reasonable person would have avoided, you are liable for the damages inflicted even if the plaintiff suffers some condition that makes her damages worse than they would be to a normal person.

C. Is Harm Outside the Scope of the Risk Because It Results Most Directly from an Act of an Intervening Person or Force?

1. Introduction: Scope of Risk and Natural and Continuous Sequence.

We quote in text some typical continuous sequence language in intervening cause cases and then attempt to explain how some intervening causes are part of the risks negligently created by the defendant and some are not. When courts use continuous sequence or intervening cause language are they nonetheless carrying out the scope of risk principle?

2. Intentional or Criminal Intervening Acts

WATSON V. KENTUCKY & INDIANA BRIDGE & R.R. Defendant negligently overturns a car of gasoline. A third person causes it to take fire and explode and the plaintiff is injured. If the third person acted purposefully, the defendant is relieved of liability.

DELANEY V. REYNOLDS. Plaintiff and defendant live together. Defendant, a police officer, keeps a gun in the house. Defendant knows that plaintiff is a drug abuser and is depressed, and also knows that plaintiff knows where his gun is. Plaintiff tries to kill herself and sues defendant for negligence. Rejecting the traditional view that suicide (or attempted suicide) cannot be reasonably foreseeable as a matter of law, the court holds that plaintiff should be allowed to prove to a jury that the risk she would use defendant's gun to harm herself was reasonably foreseeable, making defendant's failure to secure his weapon a proximate cause of her harm.

3. Negligent Intervening Acts

DERDIARIAN V. FELIX CONTRACTING CORP. The defendant inadequately protected workers installing a gas main in a street excavation. One Dickens failed to take medicine he needed, suffered a seizure and lost control of his car. It ran into a vat of boiling liquid enamel at the excavation and the plaintiff, a worker there, was splattered. His body ignited into a fireball. Was Dickens an intervening cause such that would relieve the defendant of liability for failing to provide protection of the plaintiff? "That the driver was negligent, or even reckless, does not insulate [the defendant] from liability."

VENTRICELLI V. KINNEY SYSTEM RENT A CAR, INC. Defendant furnished plaintiff a car with a defective trunk lid. Plaintiff was parked in a parking space attempting to fix the lid when Maldonado's car went out of control and ran into the plaintiff. The defendant is not liable, since plaintiff was in no riskier a position than if he had been loading a suitcase in the trunk.

MARSHALL V. NUGENT. The car in which Marshall was a passenger was forced off an icy road by a negligently driven oil company truck. The truck stopped, however, to provide help in getting the car back on the road. While this was going on, Marshall walked up hill to flag any approaching cars to prevent further collisions; but he was not in time and one of the approaching cars struck him. *Held,* the truck driver and his employer are liable for this injury and the negligence of the other driver is not an intervening cause that relieves them. The "risks created [by defendant] were not all over . . . ."

PROBLEM: WOLFE V. GRAMLICH, INC. A chance to apply what you've discussed.

AN END NOTE: THE FUTURE OF PROXIMATE CAUSE OR SCOPE OF RISK ANALYSIS. Proximate cause rules are all or nothing rules; comparative fault, which apportions responsibility, may tend to minimize proximate cause/scope of risk analysis.

COMMENTS

§ 1. THE PRINCIPLE: SCOPE OF RISK

MEDCALF V. WASHINGTON HEIGHTS CONDOMINIUM ASS'N, INC., 747 A.2d 532 (Conn. App. Ct. 2000)

Principle. The language of the cases often obscures proximate cause issues, but this case states the principle straightforwardly. If we think you are negligent only because you created Risk A, say a risk of fire, you are subject to liability for all the harms that fall within risk A but you are not liable for every other harm caused in fact by your act. For instance, if you negligently made matches available to an 8-year-old with known pyromanical tendencies, you risk arson but maybe

Elements of the Negligence Case: Where We Are
Duty
Negligence (breach of duty)
Actual Injury
Cause in Fact
> Proximate Cause

you don't risk his use of the match heads to concoct a poison for a classmate. If the risk of poisoning is not the reason we think you should have kept control of the matches, you are not negligent about that, only about arson, and your liability is limited accordingly.

Reasons for the principle. Why do we have such limits on liability? Since Andrews' dissent in *Palsgraf* (next) courts and lawyers have been prone to say that the reasons are purely pragmatic. However, at least to some extent the reasons seems principled. If you are liable for negligence and only for negligence, you *should not* be liable for harm as to which you would not negligent at all.

Extended liability/transferred intent. These simple principles can be contrasted to the rule of extended liability seen in trespassory torts. Once you are guilty of battery, you are liable for all kinds of unintended harm, including harm to others. This is the meaning of "transferred intent" or extended liability.

Rationale or principle: No negligence as to unforeseeable harms. With negligence cases, by contrast, we depart from the extended liability rule used with many intentional torts. Instead, we say that you are liable only for foreseeable harms that a reasonable person would have avoided. *See* DOBBS ON TORTS § 181 (2000). As to other harms, those that are unforeseeable and also distinct from the foreseeable harms, the defendant simply is not negligent. This rationale is reflected in the formulation of the principle in the Basic Principles Restatement quoted in **Note 1.**

"Foreseeability." The foreseeability or scope of risk rule actually means two different things. (a) You are not liable for harms that are not foreseeable in general; and (b) you are not liable for foreseeable harms that a reasonable person would not have taken precautions to avoid. (Recall that under a risk-utility analysis or just about any other imaginable scheme of negligence assessment, the reasonable person might ignore some foreseeable risks because they are small or benefits of taking those risks are great.) Courts and lawyers tend to conflate the two ideas expressed in clauses (a) and (b), which frequently leads them to assert that a stated harm is not foreseeable when they mean only that, though it was foreseeable, reasonable care did not require the defendant to protect against it. Perhaps that is so in the *Medcalf* case.

Jury role. The principles seems clear and seem entirely justified, but application is another matter. If reasonable people can differ–which is most cases–the issue of proximate cause is for the jury to decide. When, as the *Medcalf* court thinks is the case on its facts, reasonable people cannot differ, courts take over and declare as a matter of law that the general type of harm suffered by the plaintiff reflected a risk the defendant did not unreasonably inflict–that it was unforeseeable or at least a type of harm a reasonable person would not have tried to protect against. In technical cases and those involving professional judgments, the plaintiff may need to produce testimony specifically addressed to the foreseeability issue. If the plaintiff's point is to prove that his therapist should have acted to prevent the plaintiff from murdering people, the plaintiff may need expert testimony to prove that the defendant should have foreseen the plaintiff's violence. *Williamson v. Liptzin,* 539 S.E.2d 313 (N.C. Ct. App. 2000) held on similar facts that foreseeability of the plaintiff's violence had not been shown by experts and that the trial judge should have directed a verdict for the defendant. The result may be right, but unfortunately it seems to have turned on the therapeutic mantra that violence cannot be foreseen, a view that uses a concept of foreseeability that seems markedly unlike the law's attempt to ask whether harm was probable enough to warrant the effort to prevent it.

Solving Medcalf *under a no-duty approach.* Later, in Chapter 18, we consider whether a defendant is under a duty to protect the plaintiff from attacks by third persons. The *Medcalf* court could have dealt with its facts by declaring that the property manager was under no duty to protect the plaintiff from an attacker. Many courts have said that. But a no-duty rule is broad and general; it categorically excludes many cases without regard to their individual facts. A proximate cause approach, even if it operates in this case to protect the defendant, is different. It is a based upon the facts of the particular case. It says the defendant was not negligent in respect of an attacker in this case, but he might be in another. The scope of risk/proximate cause rules are, then, less categorical, less rigid, and less radical, than the rules excluding duty altogether. (Recall that proximate cause, unlike duty, is for the jury in all but extreme cases.) *See* Dobbs on Torts § 182 (2000).

Direct harm tests. At one time, some courts made defendants liable for all harms directly caused (not the case in *Medcalf*) and, more often, excluded liability if an intervening cause appeared. *See* DOBBS ON TORTS § 185 (2000). We'll be addressing the intervening cause form of analysis in § 2.

Notes 2 & 3. These ask students to be able to state the principle in *Medcalf*, to distinguish cause in fact, and to be alert for ambiguities when cause in fact and scope of risk rules are conflated. Sometimes courts unpack the conflated version: "Proximate cause has two components: (1) the defendant's conduct must have in fact caused the damages; and (2) the policy of the law must require the defendant to be legally responsible for them." *Bellman v. City of Cedar Falls,* 617 N.W.2d 11 (Iowa 2000).

Even so, the ideas may collapse upon themselves again. In *Bellman*, the court, having separated cause in fact from the "policy" issue, almost immediately began to treat foreseeability and proximity as a cause in fact issue. In *Lamp v. Reynolds,* 645 N.W.2d 311 (Mich. Ct. App. 2002), the plaintiff, riding in a motocross race on defendant's track, followed the usual practice or riding in the weeds just off the track itself. In doing so, he struck a stump, which, in the light of the known practice of racers to ride in the area, should have been removed, marked, or warned of. The defendant put the plaintiff's fault in issue to reduce damages, but the court held that damages should not be reduced because the plaintiff's negligence was not a cause in fact of his harm. Apparently what the court had in mind was not a but for test– although it had recited that– but something else altogether. It said: "Here, plaintiff's alleged at-fault conduct consisted of him racing his motocross bike just off the outside edge of the racetrack, through the weeds. However, it is uncontested that plaintiff's injuries arose solely as a consequence of him hitting an unknown, unexpected, and concealed tree stump; therefore, defendants have failed to prove that plaintiff's conduct was a cause in fact of his damages." The court's reasoning, of course, does not suggest an absence of cause in fact, but perhaps it suggests an absence of proximate cause (or maybe a lack of comparative negligence), and the court later in fact turned to proximate cause/scope of risk reasoning.

It may be worth your while to deal specifically with these notes in class to clear the mental underbrush.

Note 4. Formulations of the principle. This is a reinforcer. Both statements seem to be ways of stating the principle, although neither is fine-tuned.

Note 5. Applying the rule in *Medcalf*. If you have not already discussed application of the principle in *Medcalf*, you can do it here. *Benaquista,* cited here, is much like *Medcalf* except that the tenant is injured walking downstairs when the intercom didn't work. This is the kind of case that shows the inadequacy of the foreseeability shorthand, for surely a jury could find it foreseeable that tenants walking down stairs might sooner or later suffer an injury. Yet if the stairs were not themselves dangerous or the tenants especially vulnerable, the risk of falling would not be an unreasonable one. What the defendant risked (and maybe risked unreasonably) was inconvenience to the tenants and economic harm in the sense that their lease rights were worth less as a result of that inconvenience. As the Appellate Division in *Benaquista* said, "the intercom and door buzzer system was neither designed nor intended to prevent tenants from falling down the stairs."

Although the point will not aid students at this juncture, first-time torts teachers may wish to be aware now that some courts approach the same problem in the conclusory language of precedent. *Harpster v. Hetherington,* 512 N.W.2d 585 (Minn. 1994), is much like *Benaquista*. The court asserted that the defendant only provided the condition, not the cause of the harm, as if that were a reason rather than a conclusion and also struggled through some arguments based on "no duty." Although courts may appeal to various precedents and various locutions such as the cause-condition distinction, the straightforward logic of *Medcalf* predicts and explains a large bulk of the cases.

ABRAMS V. CITY OF CHICAGO, 811 N.E.2d 670 (Ill. 2004)

There is a duty question lurking behind the proximate cause issue in this case, because it may be that the city had no duty to send ambulances. But we hope it can be sidestepped for now by assuming (as the court did) that the city had a duty to provide an ambulance. There is some basis for that; the city did provide this service on a regular basis, but dispatchers here thought 10 minute contractions were not close enough and refused to send help. Given duty and breach by negligence, it seems clear that the core unreasonable risks would be medical risks of birth without medical attention. Expressed in terms of foreseeability, the risks the defendant would recognize (foresee) would be those medical risks. If those are the only risks, then injury in the car accident simply was not one of them; the plaintiff's injury was outside the scope of the risks, creation of which made us say the defendant was negligent. Put succinctly, the defendant's failure to send an ambulance did not create an unreasonable risk of a car accident, even though it may have created some other and quite different unreasonable risk.

Cases like *Medcalf* and *Abrams* help establish what the question is, even if the language courts use is not always adroit. (*Abrams* doesn't quite use the scope of risk terminology.) Some people seem to have trouble with this simple proposition because they confuse the question with the answer. What is the scope of the risk is the question, but we might differ about the proper answer, as **Note 2** tries to point out.

Note 3. Other examples. (a) *Wagon Mound*, the classic case we used in the first three editions, announced a rule like the one in *Medcalf* and relieved the defendant of liability because the risk of polluting the docks was quite different from the risk of burning them. (b) A made up case with made up diseases. The facts of this problem are derived from claims asserted and lost for want of an appropriate expert witness in *United Blood Services v. Longoria*, 938 S.W.2d 29 (Tex. 1997). To say that the supplier should be liable for Disease B that was an unforeseeable result of its failure to screen for Disease A seems opposed to the scope of risk principle. Judge Posner, in *Rhone-Poulenc Rorer Inc.*, 51 F.3d 1293 (7th Cir. 1995), believed that at least some states would reject liability on similar facts. (c) *Lodge v. Arett Sales Corp.*, cited here, holds for the defendant. Expressing itself in terms of duty rather than proximate cause, the court observes that literal foreseeability is not the test. Our paraphrase is that this is because many things are foreseeable that are nevertheless outside the scope of the risk.

You might enjoy presenting the facts in *DiPonzio v. Riordan*, 679 N.E.2d 616 (N.Y. 1997), to your students. A customer at a self-service gas station pumped gas without turning off his car's engine. The station had rules against allowing customers to pump gas while the engine was running and also the means of cutting off the pump if a customer attempted to do so, but the station did not enforce the rule. When the customer went into to pay for the gas, his car began rolling. The rolling car pinned the plaintiff against his own car, breaking his leg. The plaintiff sued both the driver and the gas station. Against the station, the plaintiff argued it should not have permitted the customer to pump with the engine running. Although the court approached the case in terms of duty rather than proximate cause, it applied the scope of risk rule. The court said that if the occurrence is within the class of foreseeable hazards that the duty of care exists to prevent, the defendant can be held liable even though the harm may have been brought about in an unexpected way; but if the hazard is not one risked by the breach of duty, there is no liability. That was the case here.

PALSGRAF V. LONG ISLAND RAILWAY COMPANY, 162 N.E. 99 (N.Y. 1928)

In *Palsgraf*, Cardozo adopts a variation on the risk rule. The scope of risk problem in *Palsgraf* does not turn on "type of harm" as in *Medcalf* but on "class of person." The unforeseeable plaintiff is not within the risk unreasonably created by the defendant, so as to her the defendant is not liable. Cardozo specifically holds that the extended liability imposed by the transferred intent doctrine in intentional tort cases has no place in negligence law.

Cardozo casts the problem in terms of duty and negligence rather than proximate cause. Since harm to the plaintiff was not within the risk reasonably to be perceived, the defendant was not negligent toward Mrs. Palsgraf. "Relatively to her it was not negligence at all." The same point was expressed in terms of duty. "The risk reasonably to be perceived defines the duty to be obeyed. . . ."

Although this reasoning proceeds without reference to proximate cause, which Cardozo regards as "foreign to the case before us," he is only limiting liability to the scope of risk. He is not making a categorical no-duty rule that excludes liability for a class of cases that can be determined in advance. On the contrary, the rule he calls a no-duty or no-negligence rule depends entirely upon adjudication of the particular facts rather than rule-making. It is thus by no means a no-duty rule like the traditional rule that landowners owe no duty of care to trespassers.

Andrews, dissenting, does not agree that liability is limited by any logical or moral principle, much less by the principle that limits the scope of liability to the scope of the risk. For him, the limitation on liability is the result of balancing many factors, the practical politics of decision making. If you drop the issue of terminology (duty vs. proximate cause), the conflict between Cardozo and Andrews is about how to limit liability, by a foreseeability principle or by what might be called a more or less intuitive application of an array of factors of no particular weight.

Unfortunately for students struggling to master or even to grasp proximate cause materials, the debate over how liability is to be limited must share attention with a vastly different kind of issue about how the language of discourse is to be structured. Cardozo chooses the language of duty/negligence while Andrews insists that the appropriate language is the language of proximate cause. Many people have been interested in *Palsgraf* primarily because of this dispute over the conceptual structure. Almost no students have a basis for choosing between the negligence/duty terminology and the proximate cause terminology at this point. If you conduct a wide-open discussion on this point, you may risk losing clarity on the central idea that courts will limit liability to the kinds of harms or events or persons negligently put at risk.

If you decide to emphasize both issues, you may want to glance at Part III of the Casebook on duty limitations. As we will see there, courts often limit the duties owed by defendants on grounds other than scope of risk grounds.

The notes to *Palsgraf* are highly structured in hopes that they will aid students in recognizing separate issues and facilitate classroom analysis.

Note 1. Integrating *Palsgraf* and *Medcalf*. Note 1 synthesizes *Medcalf* and *Palsgraf* on the scope of risk point; both are scope of risk rules and of course perfectly consistent with each other.

Note 2. Jury role. This note is multifarious, but it points to the basic role of the jury as the decision maker on scope of risk issues. That is to say, we usually don't make category-wide rules against liability on scope of risk grounds, although we do so under the rubric of duty when other considerations come into play. On proximate cause or scope of risk issue, the inquiry is fact-sensitive and doesn't lend itself to a rule of law. Why didn't the jury get to decide in *Palsgraf*? Not because of a rule of law about scales, railways, or fireworks, but because on the facts, reasonable people could not differ whether the plaintiff was at risk when the defendant's guards pushed another person some distance away.

Note 3. What is the class of persons? There is no authoritative master list of classes of persons. Judges characterize the class of person at risk just as they characterize the risks themselves. But class discussion about how to describe the group of people at risk from the defendant's actions demystifies this issue. Sometimes it is commonsensical even if it is also indeterminate. In *Mellon Mortgage Co. v. Holder,* cited here, a police officer stopped a woman for an alleged traffic violation, led her into the defendant's parking garage, and sexually assaulted her. The garage was so maintained that it either invited or failed to minimize foreseeable crime. The court held for the defendant, reasoning that while crime in the garage may have been foreseeable, the plaintiff was not a member of the class of persons foreseeably at risk, since she was pulled over blocks from the garage.

Notes 4-7. Negligence, duty, or proximate cause? Expect confusion about the role of foreseeability on the negligence issue, the proximate cause issue, and (later) the duty issue. If a reasonable person would foresee no harm at all, or no risk worth minimizing, then the defendant is not negligent. You may have to work this through for some students as both lawyers and judges confuse the negligence and proximate cause issue, often assuming that if foreseeability is the issue, then they are discussing proximate cause. Here is the thought students must understand: If a reasonable person would have recognized ("foreseen") a risk of harm and would have sought to avoid it, then the defendant who fails to do so is negligent. A foreseeability question may remain, however: should the defendant have foreseen a harm of the same general kind that occurred to a class of persons that included the plaintiff?

Most courts, like Andrews, seem to use proximate cause language; but, like Cardozo, they seem to emphasize foreseeability as the governing limitation. If you are going to discuss the terminology issue with your class, you might help students recognize the difficulty of proximate cause language: it sounds as if it is about causation (not scope of risk) and may therefore mislead us subliminally. (It also leads to conclusory assertions such as the statement that the defendant's conduct was a condition, not a cause and to an undue emphasis on continuous sequence of events rather than to scope of risk.) What about the duty language? The disadvantage is not easy for students to see yet, but the duty language suggests that the decision is (a) for the judge rather than jury, (b) and categorical, excluding a whole class of claims. We might drop both terms and refer to the issue as the scope-of-risk issue instead.

Note 8. Cardozo and Andrews differed not only on the language of discourse but also on the basis for determining liability. For Cardozo, you could exclude liability if the plaintiff was not within the class of persons put at unreasonable risk. For Andrews, the fact that the plaintiff was not within the risk was a factor to consider, no more. A jury could allow an unforeseeable plaintiff to recover if other more or like intuitive factors supported recovery. Logically, the same view would seem to apply in a *Medcalf* scope of risk case. Most courts seem to use Andrews' language but Cardozo's limiting principle, although a few say they are willing to impose liability for directly caused unforeseeable harms. See DOBBS ON TORTS § 185 (2000).

Wisconsin is a court that continues to follow something like the Andrews' views. There is a duty of reasonable care to all, but liability is limited by considering a series of "policy factors," of which foreseeability is only one. These factors are vague and invoke enormous judicial discretion. They may also impose limits that differ from scope-of-risk limits on liability, because they invite consideration of issues besides foreseeability. Wisconsin doesn't want to say it is considering proximate cause, but admits that what it now calls policy factors is equated with what it used to call proximate cause. The upshot is that under the policy factors approach, Wisconsin limits liability not merely by scope of risk but by conceptions of public policy unrelated to scope of risk considerations. In *Fandrey v. American Family Mut. Ins. Co.*, cited here, which walks through the equation of proximate cause/duty with policy factors, the court refused to permit liability under a dog bite statute because it considered that liability would be "out of proportion with the culpability" of the defendants and for other similar reasons.

Note 9. Duty, breach, or proximate cause? As noted above, this is a very confusing issue for many people, not just students. The reality is that some courts use "no duty" when they mean an injury, or a plaintiff, is unforeseeable, while others use that locution for entirely different reasons. This Note is really just meant to tell students that this complex issue is developed more fully in later chapters; you probably don't want to wade in very deeply at this point.

Note 10. Perhaps. If the defendant did not foresee any kind of harm occurring to anyone from his push of the passenger with the package, then he would not be negligent. Perhaps, however, Cardozo thought he was negligent towards the man he pushed, and perhaps towards others in the immediate vicinity who might have been hurt because the man (or his package) flew into them.

NOTE: THE RESCUE DOCTRINE

In *Wagner,* discussed here, the defendant created a risk of harm to A, but it was B who was harmed in attempting a rescue. On the surface, *Palsgraf* would seem to require a decision for the defendant. *Palsgraf* and *Wagner* were both decided by Cardozo. Are they contrary? If so, should we regard the rescue doctrine as a simple fiat, addressed to one exceptional situation? You could reconcile the two cases if you thought rescue itself was one of the foreseeable risks as to which the defendant was negligent, but then you must explain Cardozo's statement that the defendant is liable even if he did not foresee the rescue. Another possibility is that *Palsgraf* implicitly overruled *Wagner,* but the courts evidently do not think so.

Clinkscales and *Sears*, cited just after *Wagner*, both apply the *Wagner* rule to potentially allow recovery by a rescuer against the person who caused the need for rescue. In *Clinkscales*, the plaintiff was a patron in defendant's bar when a gas grill ignited a grease fire, endangering patrons. Plaintiff was burned trying to turn off the propane tanks. The court quoted *Wagner* extensively, holding that a summary judgment for the defendant was improper. The rescue doctrine, the court said, "involves heroic people doing heroic things. . . . Those who negligently imperil life or property may not only be liable to their victims, but also to the rescuers." The court noted that it had applied the rescue doctrine "consistently and liberally" for over a century.

Both *Lambert* and *Snellenberger*, cited here in he final paragraph, excluded recovery not by rejecting the rule itself, but rather by defining the terms rescue or rescuer so that those terms definitionally excluded the plaintiff. *Lambert v. Parrish* concluded that "Rev. Lambert did not attempt to rescue his wife. His only attempt was to reach the scene of the accident." *Snellenberger v. Rodriguez*, 760 S.W.2d 237 (Tex. 1988), where the police officer collapsed at the scene of the child's injury, the intermediate court reasoned that the rescue doctrine had no application because "no perilous situation existed to invite rescue. The negligent act . . . had already occurred . . . ." The Supreme Court did not pass on this reasoning but instead held that the heart attack was "unforeseeable" and that foreseeability was required (as to the type of harm?) even in rescue cases.

Should the rescue doctrine apply to assist the claims of professional rescuers like firefighters? See *Daigle v. Phillips Petroleum Co.*, 893 S.W.2d 121 (Tex. Ct. App. 1995) (yes); *Heck v. Robey*, 659 N.E.2d 498 (Ind. 1995) (no). The court applied the "Fireman's Rule" instead. As to that rule, see Chapter 10, § 3. The branch of "rescue doctrine" that deals with contributory fault is considered in Chapter 9.

NOTE: VIOLATION OF STATUTE AND "PROXIMATE CAUSE"

We know that a violation of statute is not negligence per se unless the statute was designed to protect against the kind of harm that occurred, the class of persons of which the plaintiff is a member and the kind of interest involved in the claim. These rules parallel the principles embraced in *Medcalf* and *Palsgraf*.

"Interests" classification. You can inject a discussion of the type of interest classification which we pretermitted in our discussion of negligence per se. Cardozo mentions this at the end of the opinion in *Palsgraf* and his point is that the negligence in *Palsgraf* seems to have created a risk not only to a different person but also to a different "interest." What he means is that one's interest in bodily security is in some important way to be distinguished from one's interest in the security of property. In fact, this interest analysis has never really caught on in these cases so far as the distinction between personal injury and property damage is concerned.

The boy in the box. Suppose the defendant negligently runs over a box that appears to be abandoned, belonging to no one. That is presumably no tort, even if appearances were deceiving and the box was actually owned by the plaintiff. But change the supposition to imagine that the defendant should have recognized that the box was the property of someone. He would be liable to the owner for damage to the box. Finally, suppose a small boy is playing in the box and that his presence is wholly unforeseeable. The interest analysis might say that there is no liability to the boy since only property appeared to be at risk. Would *Palsgraf* itself foreclose liability unless the boy was the owner of the box? On essentially similar facts, the court in *Barker v. City of Philadelphia,* 134 F.Supp. 231 (E.D. Pa. 1955) thought the boy's presence was foreseeable and that the driver should be liable. Alternatively, it said that if the boy's presence were not foreseeable, the driver would be liable because he would still be negligent and it would not matter that he could not foresee the particular harm. (If the box belonged to no one, in what way was he negligent?) Similar facts appear in *Railway Express Agency v. Brabham,* 62 So.2d 713 (Fla. 1952), but the court dodged the difficult issue by saying that the driver could have foreseen that the box "contained animate objects in the form of the two little boys."

As we noted in discussing violation of statute, the different interest language is mainly useful as a way of pointing potentially different kinds of harm or risk. You don't really need a separate rule about different interests; judges can decide whether the unforeseen harm to the boy in the box is outside the scope of the risk created by negligent driving or whether it is not that different from damage to the box itself.

Although you might reject the division between interests in the security of property and interests in the security of person, you might easily think that purely economic interests, divorced from physical harms, are entirely different. For example, it is usually said that there is no liability for negligent interference with contract. The purely economic harm cases that is harms without physical injury to person or property are excluded from this section; but anyone minded to do so can raise such issues by extending a discussion of the interest analysis. *See Kinsman II,* 388 F.2d 821 (2d Cir. 1968).

The main point of the note is that the statute violations rules, which usually seem to disturb no one when they are initially covered, are really only expressions of the risk rules seen in *Medcalf* and *Palsgraf.* Conversely, the risk rule under statutes is often expressed, not in terms of classes of risk, but in terms of proximate cause.

Preliminary evaluation of the scope of risk principle. The risk rule seems to derive from orthodox negligence analysis. Under *Carroll Towing* or any of the softer variations on it, you are negligent only if the pool of all foreseeable costs exceeds the pool of all utilities. Risks of harm are costs to be evaluated in this risk-utility balance. But, clearly enough, you cannot balance risks that cannot be foreseen by a reasonable person. Since they cannot go into the negligence calculus, they cannot be part of the liability either.

On the other hand, even small foreseeable risks might be aggregated even though no one of them standing alone would be sufficient to justify liability. See Mark F. Grady, *Proximate Cause and the Law of Negligence,* 69 IOWA L. REV. 363, 382 ff. (1984). That is one reason that large forces are important; if you drive on the highway, the small risks of oddball but serious injury are quite numerous. Speeding does not ordinarily create a risk that the car and driver will crash into the plaintiff's living room, but that is one of the many small risks that go into making high speed unreasonable.

§ 2. ASSESSING THE SCOPE OF THE RISK

A. Is Harm Outside the Scope of the Risk Because of the Manner in Which it Occurs?

HUGHES V. LORD ADVOCATE, [1963] A.C. 837 (H.L.)
DOUGHTY V. TURNER MFG CO. , [1964] 1 Q.B. 518 (C.A. 1963)

It is often said, as it is in *Hughes,* that the plaintiff is entitled to recover for damage caused by the defendant's negligence even though a reasonable person in the defendant's shoes could not have foreseen the manner in which the injury came about. *See* Dobbs on Torts § 189 (2000). The hindsight test invoked in a few cases seems to be less about hindsight than about the idea that you need only foresee the general character of the injury, not its details or manner of occurrence. *See Woollen v. State,* 593 N.W.2d 729 (Neb. 1999) ("The test of causation is not that the particular injury could be anticipated but whether, after the occurrence, the injury appears to be the reasonable and probable consequence of the acts or omissions.").

Is the manner of harm rule consistent with the scope of risk principle? The answer depends on how you envision describing the risk. *Hughes* helps make it clear that risks can be thought of in quite different ways. One of the claims in *Hughes* is that fire and explosion should be treated as different general kinds of harm. The court dismisses this on the belief that they are different mechanisms rather than different kinds of harm. It regards the explosion as a "variant" on a fire. If you describe the risk in terms of kind of harm or general type of harm, then the *Hughes* rule is entirely consistent with the scope of risk principle.

But you could describe the risk by describing the forces or mechanisms that result in harm, such as a risk of burning by the flame. If that were the proper way to describe the risk, the *Hughes* rule would be a deviation from, or substantial qualification of, the risk principle. Are there cases in which you should describe the risk narrowly to include the forces that cause harm as well as the harm itself?

Doughty warns us that sometimes you must describe the risk narrowly to include its mechanisms. Whether it is right on its facts or not, it is certainly true that when the risk is a narrow risk of specific manner of harm, the defendant is not liable when the same type of personal injury results through a different mechanism. In *Doughty*, the unreasonable risk was a risk of splashing as a result of mechanical forces–the lid falling into the vat. The harm occurred differently, through chemical forces or interactions after the lid was in the vat. If the *Doughty* facts do not make it clear that manner of harm is sometimes important, imagine a variation in which an airplane crashes into the factory and splashes the molten substance onto the plaintiff. The injury is the same as risked, but the defendant did not risk airplane-caused splashing and would not be liable for it.

This said, it may be necessary to return to the central rule: the question is what was risked by the defendant's negligence; in stating that risk, the manner of harm is often unimportant.

The class of persons analog and large forces. The scope of risk principle includes the class of persons issue as well as type of risk. You must state the class of persons generally just as you must describe the type of risk in general rather than specific terms. In *Kinsman I*, 338 F.2d 708 (2d Cir. 1964), the defendants negligently permitted a ship to break loose its moorings in a river and it drifted downstream. Damage to downstream ships and riverine property was easily foreseeable. But the ship hit others and knocked them loose. They struck a bridge and blocked it, effectively damming the river. It flooded *up*stream owners. Mechanically speaking, upstream damage might seem unforeseeable. But given the very large force at work, damage to the class of persons on or near the river might better describe the class of persons at risk. The court imposed liability. Consider: A defendant negligently throws a baseball that might strike bystanders in front of him. After the ball is in the air, someone moves a large truck into the path of the ball. The ball strikes the truck's side and bounces back, striking someone behind the defendant. Would *Palsgraf* exclude liability on the ground that foreseeable harm was limited to harms in front of the pitcher? We think not. The telling fact in *Palsgraf* was that the guard was NOT launching a force of general power with potential environmental impact. He did not break loose a ship, start a train, operate an automobile or even throw a baseball. The force he launched was quite narrow and specific. Large forces foreseeably entail risks that are unforeseeable in detail.

Note 1. *Hughes* echoes the generally-held conception that the precise manner of harm need not be foreseeable in order to hold a defendant liable, if the general type of harm was. *See,e.g., Baggerly v. CSX Transportation, Inc.,* 635 S.E.2d 97 (S.C. 2006) ("[T]he plaintiff need not prove that the defendant should have contemplated the particular event which occurred.") Is this really a separate rule, or does it follow from the notion that liability can extend only to those harms that are within the risks created by the defendant's negligent conduct? That is, is the manner of harm truly irrelevant to determining whether the harm is outside the proper scope of liability? Perhaps not. *See* RESTATEMENT (THIRD) § 29, comment *o* (calling the manner of harm rule a "helpful guideline," but noting situations where the manner of harm might be relevant). Perhaps when the Hughes court used the word "precise" to modify "manner," it was serious. The "precise manner of harm" need not be foreseeable, but at some point, if the manner of the harm is truly bizarre, that might indeed be a relevant consideration in judging foreseeability.

Notes 2 & 3. *Darby*, discussed in Note 2, is an interesting example that might reinforce the point made just above. If the risk created by the defendant was death, and the harm that occurred was death, then that would seem to be that. But the court drew a distinction between "death by drowning" and "death from Weils disease." Perhaps this is beyond the "precise manner" being unforeseeable; it's an entirely unforeseeable manner of death that occurred, and on that ground liability should be limited. In any event both *Doughty* and *Darby* demonstrate that the "manner of harm" rule is not entirely straightforward in application, thus meaning there is a good deal of play in the doctrine for skillful advocates to make use of. *Morguson*, cited in Note 3, is a domestic example.

B. Is Harm Outside the Scope of the Risk Because Its Extent is Unforeseeable?

HAMMERSTEIN V. JEAN DEVELOPMENT WEST, 907 P.2d 975 (Nev. 1995)

Hammerstein has diabetes, and defendant, in whose hotel he is a guest, knows it. Defendant's fire alarm system is faulty, and it knows that, too. When the fire alarm sounds in the night, Hammerstein has to walk down from his fourth floor room since the elevator is locked. He winds up getting gangrene as a result of the unwanted hike down the stairs. Can the defendant's negligence in maintaining the fire alarm be a proximate cause of Hammerstein's serious injuries? The court says yes, that the extent of the harm was not foreseeable but the type of harm was.

Really? What types of harm would your class foresee from an alarm that, far from failing, goes off too often? One is the risk of injury in a panicked crowd, but surely the aggravated blister is not in that category. Is the blister aggravation foreseeable only because the hotel actually knew of the blister and the diabetes? If so the decision should be noncontroversial. Gangrene itself might be unforeseeable, but it would be merely a matter of extent of harm if some kind of blister injury was foreseeable.

Notes 1-3. The thin skull rule; Nuances; A broader principle. The thin skull rule seems to be plain and generally accepted. However, the generalization that one takes the plaintiff as he finds her may not be its most illuminating expression. It is perhaps better to recognize that the thin skull rule is a rule that the extent of harm need not be foreseeable in order to impose liability. For emotional harm more extensive than foreseeable, see Chapter 19.

Reconciling or accommodating the risk principle. Does the extent of harm rule deviate from the risk principle? If the risk rule is expressed as a rule about "kind" of harm, and we regard the thin skull cases as cases involving "extent" of harm, the two are entirely reconcilable. Some may have doubted whether it was so easy as all that. It is certainly possible to think of a broken leg as a very different injury in kind from delirium tremens. What the courts seem to have felt, however, is that the relevant "kind" of harm is "personal injury." Arguably that violates the risk rule in extreme cases such as *McCahill*, discussed in **Note 1**. If so, the thin skull rule can still be well justified on grounds of judicial convenience. A little imagination suggests the difficulties that would be encountered trying to determine whether a broken foot was an injury different in kind from an amputated leg.

The Dillon-McCahill discount. The reference in **Note 2** to *Dillon v. Twin States Elec. Co.*: the court held in *Dillon* that since the defendant was responsible for death of the boy only moments before he was certain to die or be injured anyway, it would be liable only for those few moments of life. Applied to *McCahill*, this idea suggests that although you are liable for injuries that are greater than you might have foreseen, damages should be discounted because the plaintiff's condition was such that delirium tremens was definitely in the cards for the plaintiff in the foreseeable future anyway. That is, the defendant only hastened the moment of the delirium. Accordingly, he should be liable for damages for the amount of increased time that the plaintiff suffered that disease. This was in fact recognized in *McCahill* itself.

Contrast cases of no negligence. The extent of harm rule and the thin skull rule only address cases in which the defendant was negligent and created some kind of risk of physical harm to the plaintiff. If the defendant is not negligent at all, he is not liable unless you can invoke some strict liability regime.

C. Is Harm Outside the Scope of the Risk Because It Results Most Directly from an Act of an Intervening Person or Force?

1. Introduction: Scope of Risk and Natural and Continuous Sequence

We are about to see a series of cases in which courts emphasize the presence or absence of intervening causes in determining "proximate cause." This may be consistent with the scope of risk approach in a great many cases, although the talk of superseding causes often obscures that point as well as others. It is consistent with the risk rule when the court recognizes that foreseeable intervening causes do not supersede the first tortfeasor's responsibility. In such cases, we are left with joint and several liability or perhaps with proportionate liability. Almost all courts do recognize the ultimate rule of foreseeability in the intervening cause cases when they are forced to do so. However, courts often imply that the mechanism of harm must be foreseeable—that is, the intervening act itself.

You may wish to be aware that the emphasis on intervening causes at one time had both a limiting effect in protecting defendants and an affirmative effect in aiding plaintiffs. This was because some courts held that the negligent defendant was liable even for unforeseeable harms if they came about directly, without an intervening cause. This was the rule in *Arbitration Between Polemis and Furness, Withy & Co., Limited*, [1921] 3 K.B. 560 (C.A. 1921), finally disapproved in *Overseas Tankship (U.K.) Limited v. Morts Dock & Engineering Co., Limited (The Wagon Mound)*, [1961] A.C. 388 (Privy Council 1961). Some American cases might stand for the same proposition or might merely mean that the defendant could be liable in accord with *Hughes* even if the manner or details of harm were not foreseeable. See *Christianson v. Chicago, St. P.M. & O. Ry.*, 68 N.W. 640 (Minn. 1896), or might be trying to state the thin skull rule. See *David v. DeLeon*, 547 N.W.2d 726 (Neb. 1996). See DOBBS ON TORTS § 185 (2000).

The limiting side of the intervening cause emphasis has been more prevalent in contemporary cases. The defendant escapes liability because a second actor or force is the most direct cause of the plaintiff's harm and is said to supersede the defendant's responsibility. Where courts treat foreseeability broadly, this should work out to the same result as the risk rule. However, courts are apt to lose focus on foreseeability and emphasize the new cause, or to apply foreseeability tests narrowly when they began to speak in the arcane language of superseding acts. Even if superseding cause analysis reaches the same outcome as scope of risk, the scope of risk question is more direct and certainly we don't need to approach the problem twice, once by talking about scope of risk/foreseeability and then again by talking about possible superseding causes. Among the recent cases recognizing that the superseding cause talk is duplicative and potentially misleading to the jury are *Barry v. Quality Steel Products, Inc.*, 820 A.2d 258 (Conn. 2003), *Control Techniques, Inc. v. Johnson*, 762 N.E.2d 104 (Ind. 2002), and *Torres v. El Paso Elec. Co.*, 127 N.M. 729, 987 P.2d 386 (1999).

2. Intentional or Criminal Intervening Acts

WATSON V. KY. & INDIANA BRIDGE AND R.R., 126 S.W. 146 (Ky. 1910)

Tortfeasor A negligently causes a gasoline leak. Tortfeasor B intentionally causes an explosion, causing the plaintiff injury. The court treats the intentional criminal wrongdoer's act as unforeseeable as a matter of law. The court seems to be say, not that criminal acts are unforeseeable to a reasonable person, but that the defendant is not obliged or "bound" to do so. The underlying idea seems to emphasize that a deliberate choice has been made by a "moral being."

If the court had instead used a simple scope of risk rule, it might have said that the defendant negligently risked a fire and explosion when it negligently caused the gasoline leak; the fact that the fire or explosion was triggered by a criminal act is only one of the several ways it could have come about. Given this line of thought, foreseeability of the criminal intervention would be unimportant because the risk of fire was foreseeable. Notably that is not what the court did. This line of thought can be continued in discussing *Wiener,* **Note 3**. See below.

Note 2. *Craig v. Driscoll,* cited here, states the general principle and places intervening acts, intentional or criminal, within that principle. The test is scope of risk, and the risk may include intervening acts, intentional and criminal intervening acts. If the defendant creates a risk that someone will criminally intervene to trigger harm, the defendant's doesn't escape liability merely because someone did so. Why in the world should he?

Note 3. The courts requiring heightened foreseeability of criminal intervention are presumably saying that the risk of the crime must be especially probable. Sometimes the issue will be conceived of as a duty rather than a scope of risk issue, but even so, scope of risk may be the major factor, as it was in *Wiener v. Southcoast Childcare Ctrs., Inc.,* cited here.

In the *Wiener* case, children at the defendant's day care center were injured and killed when Abrams deliberately drove his Cadillac through the 4-foot chain-link fence and into the children playing there. It was a busy corner; there had been another, accidental incursion by a motor vehicle, though no one was hurt in that instance. According to the plaintiffs, the defendants, which included the landlord as well as the daycare center itself, were aware the chain link fence in front of the property provided inadequate protection against intrusion. The fence was only three to four feet from the busy roadway and could have been higher or stronger. The Court of Appeals thought that liability was appropriate because intrusion by a motor vehicle was foreseeable, even if a deliberate criminal murder was not. That was in line with a type of risk/type of harm analysis– the risk was not crime but intrusion, and intrusion is what came about.

That analysis was rejected in the Supreme Court of California. The Supreme Court insisted that, even if the type of harm or risk was foreseeable. "It is true that in an ordinary negligence action, the precise details of the third party's actions are not overly significant. But ours is not an ordinary negligence action. . . . [T]the courts look to a higher level of foreseeability of crime in a particular location, as might be indicated by prior similar incidents. . . our cases analyze third party criminal acts differently from ordinary negligence, and require us to apply a heightened sense of foreseeability before we can hold a defendant liable for the criminal acts of third parties." In other words, the criminality as well as the intrusion had to be foreseeable. Indeed it had to be foreseeable at a "higher level," presumably meaning especially probable.

Some older cases obtained similar results when an intentional or criminal tortfeasor triggered the harm, without necessarily making a rule of law out of it. More modern cases tend to hold that if criminal acts are reasonably foreseeable risks of the defendant's negligence, then the negligent defendant does not escape liability. *See* DOBBS ON TORTS § 190 (2000). But of course, some criminal acts are unforeseeable and where that is the case, maybe the type of harm is unforeseeable, too, so that the plaintiff in such a case would lose under the ordinary scope of risk rules.

On the other hand, where the risk is general, is there reason to shelter the defendant from responsibility merely because the foreseeable injury comes about through a crime? *Wiener* is not a case of a foreseeable criminal intrusion into the play yard. If the only foreseeable intrusion was the tiny possibility of a deliberate murder of the school children, the risk would be too small to require precautions. But arguably, the risk the defendants foreseeably created was of such generality that it included particular intrusions that were not themselves specifically foreseeable– for instance, intrusions by an unarmored Humvee or a 1948 Nash automobile or by a person who forgot to take his medicine. The defendants risk was not focused on the nature of the automobile or the state of mind of the actor; it was focused defensively on the kind of protection provided. Doesn't that suggest that the criminal mind of the intruder should be ignored? *Derdiarian,* below, will be of great interest in considering questions like this.

Note 4. If we say the defendant was negligent partly because we think it risked criminal attack by a third person, then there is no new independent cause and the defendant remains liable. *Wiener* can be contrasted. The defendants there did not unreasonably risk criminal action; what they risked was intrusion of some kind, but they did not create a specific likelihood of criminal intrusion.

Notes 5 & 6. Both *Tenney* and *Linder Construction* deal with criminal, sexual attacks on female residents of residential complexes. The results are markedly different. We don't juxtapose the cases because we think the issue debatable. We think *Linder* is flatly wrong in every way. That case purported to apply the central rule that if the criminal act was a reasonably foreseeable risk that made the defendant negligent, then the negligent actor will not escape liability; conversely, if the criminal act was not reasonably foreseeable, then it will be a superseding cause, relieving the negligent defendant from liability. But *Linder* then declared rape would not be foreseeable if you made keys available to a random group of workmen at a job site. Even if you thought that the particular crime of rape (not, say, burglary) had to be foreseen, that seems foreseeable enough if newspapers, television, legal cases, and books tell us anything. The *Linder* majority found as uncontroverted the "fact" that the defendants who left the woman's key available had "no warning" of the criminal acts. This looks like a decision that is definitely NOT based upon foreseeability but some kind of preference of the majority for insulating the defendant.

DELANEY V. REYNOLDS, 825 N.E.2d 554 (Mass. App. Ct. 2005)

Plaintiff and defendant live together. Defendant, a police officer, keeps a gun in the house. Defendant knows that plaintiff is a drug abuser and is depressed, and also knows that plaintiff knows where his gun is. Plaintiff tries to kill herself and sues defendant for negligence. Rejecting the traditional view that suicide (or attempted suicide) cannot be reasonably foreseeable as a matter of law, the court holds that plaintiff should be allowed to prove to a jury that the risk she would use defendant's gun to harm herself was reasonably foreseeable, making defendant's failure to secure his weapon a proximate cause of her harm.

Notes 1 & 2. Suicide. The traditional rule treated suicide (whether attempted or successful) as a superseding cause that relieved the defendant of liability. Gradually, exceptions were recognized when the person committing suicide was insane (although sometimes that did not matter unless the defendant's own actions induced the insanity) and when the defendant owed a duty arising from a special relationship to prevent suicide. See DOBBS ON TORTS § 195 (2000). The jailer-custodian is such a relationship. In *Hickey v. Zezulka,* 487 N.W.2d 106 (Mich. 1992,) the court held that the deceased's own behavior was not a superseding cause that relieved the jailer of liability. *Murdock v. City of Keene,* 623 A.2d 755 (N.H. 1993), held similarly, but insisted that liability would not be imposed unless the jailer knew of the prisoner's propensity for suicide. *Murdock* is a reminder that the plaintiff must prove negligence as well as foreseeability. *See also Johnson v. City of Detroit,* 579 N.W.2d 895 (Mich. 1998) (detainee was not apparently suicidal, no negligence; dissents wanted more factual development on this issue). What if the defendant is definitely negligent in risking harm, but knows nothing to suggest that the victim might be at risk for suicide? In that case, foreseeability issues will related to proximate cause or scope of risk rather than to negligence. Relationships creating duties are considered mainly in Chapter 18.

Plaintiff's own act as a superseding cause. We take up the problem of the plaintiff's own conduct as a superseding cause when we consider the scope of comparative fault rules in Chapter 9, below.

3. Negligent Intervening Acts

DERDIARIAN V. FELIX CONTRACTING CORP., 414 N.E.2d 666 (N.Y. 1980)

In *Derdiarian* there is a most surprising reason for the intervening act. Yet the result is easily within the risk and the court imposes liability upon the negligent contractor who set the plaintiff in the position of peril. The case says with *Hughes* that the defendant does not escape liability merely because the peculiar manner in which the harm came about was unforeseen. At the same time it will help illustrate why some new intervening acts cause harms not-within the original risks. On both points, it can be played as a rebound off the *Wiener* case discussed above.

Notes 1 & 2. Suppose a pedestrian walks up and pushes over the kettle, causing the same burning. Or a plane crashes into the excavation, causing the same burning injury. A placement of the kettle in a different location, we might suppose, would have avoided both those events; yet we are likely to say that the contractor is not liable. It is not, then, solely a question of "type of harm." We almost always build in *some* description of the forces when we describe the risk. It is interesting to note that *Wagon Mound*, discussed briefly in Note 3 after *Medcalf*, viewed the type of harm as "harm by fire," a description which builds in the nature of the force as well as describing the type of harm.

In *Derdiarian*, though, Mr. Dickens' crash is not a superseding cause even if an airplane crash would be. His seizures and his failure to medicate himself might be unforeseeable, but the forces he unleashed were not. A reason for moving Derdiarian to the far end of the excavation included all the variations on road traffic crashes even though it included no airplanes at all. Why not say the same about the road traffic crash that killed the children in *Wiener*, cited in Note 3 after *Watson* and discussed above? This discussion puts a new emphasis on the force or mechanisms by which the result came about. Should that be done? Is it consistent with *Hughes'* rule?

Notes 3 & 4. *Malolepszy*, discussed here, may provide an interesting comparison to *Derdiarian*. The Nebraska court's focus is clearly on the foreseeability of the intervening act itself (which one might say is a species of "manner" of harm), rather than on merely the foreseeability of the general type of harm. The court said "The question is whether the State should have foreseen the possibility that Atkins [the second driver] would fail to look and would execute a dangerous driving maneuver from the shoulder onto the roadway in front of James' [Malolepszy's] vehicle." The second driver, the court said, "totally and unreasonably" disregarded the "obvious danger inherent in vehicular travel into a visually obstructed intersection," and the State could not have foreseen that. Thus "even if the design of the construction zone was negligent, the evidence shows that the State's actions were not the proximate cause of the collision."

Summy, cited in Note 4, was a suit by a golfer against the city, which owned the golf course, after he was hit in the eye by a golf ball hit by another golfer. The court held that the city was liable to the plaintiff where it was foreseeable that he could be hit by errant shots by other golfers, and failed to take reasonable care to protect him from such acts.

Another New York case presents an interesting comparison with Derderian, also. In *Cruz v. City of New York*, 630 N.Y.S.2d 523 (App. Div. 1995), the plaintiff, a motorist, struck a large hole on FDR Drive, rendering his car immobile in the right traffic lane. The plaintiff got out to inspect the car and was struck by a second vehicle driven by a drunk driver. The trial court granted summary judgment for the City on the ground that the drunk driver's conduct was a superseding cause. The appeals court reversed, saying "a fact-finder could conclude that defects in a heavily traveled roadway might cause a motorist to break down in a traffic lane (since the highway has no shoulder), creating the hazard of a collision with another vehicle traveling at a high rate of speed. It is also foreseeable that the highway might be used by someone driving while intoxicated."

Notes 5 & 6. If you are negligent in risking X result, which comes about through third-person action, then that means the third person's action was foreseeable. And if it is foreseeable, it cannot be a superseding cause. That's the point of the quote from Broadlawns here, and it should reinforce the Derderian rule along with other Notes. *Fuhrman v. State,* 655 N.W.2d 866 (Neb. 2003), not cited in the casebook, is another recent case clearly affirming the *Broadlawns* point.

We want students to recognize that a finding of negligence in the *September 11* and *Heck* cases, cited here, would seem to rule out any superseding cause argument; negligence in each case would seem to encompass the harm that occurred and even the way it occurred. In *Heck,* parents, knowing their adult son (a fleeing felon) was seeking to avoid apprehension, knowing he had the keys to their home, and knowing he had stolen from them before, left a gun in their home where he could get it. He got it and shot it, killing Officer Heck as the officer tried to apprehend him. The estate sued the parents, alleging they were negligent in failing to better secure the gun. The defendant argued "no duty," but lost on that, then argued that the son was a superseding cause. This court was not confused. It said: "Reasonably foreseeable intervening acts therefore do not break the chain of causation and the original wrongful act will be treated as a proximate cause. In this case, a gun owner's duty to safely store and keep his/her firearm protects against the very result the trial court ruled was an intervening act– that a third party would obtain the firearm and use it in the commission of a crime. Denying recovery because the very act protected against occurred would make the duty a nullity." We would add: likewise it would make a finding of negligence a nullity, since such a finding would be based on the foreseeability of harm by a thief.

In *In re September 11 Litigation,* the court determined that the airlines owed a duty of care in controlling cockpit access because terrorist acts were foreseeable; yet it said or implied that superseding cause issues remained to be determined.

Note 6 adds the *Charles* case to the mix if you want some more facts to kick around in class. Perhaps the message is that how the court characterizes what must be foreseeable – the risk of harm described more generally, or the particular manner in which the intervening act caused the harm – may well be determinative of the outcome.

VENTRICELLI V. KINNEY SYSTEM RENT-A-CAR, INC., 383 N.E.2d 1149, *modified* 386 N.E.2d 263 (N.Y. 1978)

The defendant provided a car with a defective trunk lid. It is not clear from the opinions whether or not the lid popped open while the plaintiff was driving or whether he was attempting to avoid the problem with the lid before he set out. Later we see cases in which the plaintiff is injured in coping which actual harm caused by the defendant's negligence, but here we see a plaintiff injured in seeking to minimize a *risk* created by the defendant.

We ask in **Note 1** why this is a case the plaintiff does not win. Is the intervening fault of Mr. Maldonado somehow less foreseeable than the intervening act of Mr. Dickens in the *Derdiarian* case? And in any event, should the plaintiff not get the benefit of a rule analogous to the rescue doctrine?

The majority's conception of the facts seems to be that although the defendant was negligent in supplying the defective vehicle, and although its conduct in fact caused the plaintiff to be in what in a position of danger, nevertheless the position in which the plaintiff found himself was in no way abnormally risky. The plaintiff and his companion might have stood in just such a position to remove baggage from the car, to await the passage of traffic in order to cross the street, or even simply to hold a conversation. If they are in a position that, statistically speaking, seems safe, there is a fortuitous element if they are allowed to blame the defendant for the injury. This conception also distinguishes *Ventricelli* from *Cruz*, cited in our discussion above following *Derdiarian,* where the defendant's negligence left plaintiff standing behind his car in a traffic lane on FDR Drive —an obvious "position of danger."

If this captures or at least hints at the majority's conception when it said "he might well have been there independent of any negligence," then the majority can be relieved of a charge of inconsistency with *Derdiarian*. This is so because, although we may not distinguish the foreseeability of the intervening acts of the two cases, we can distinguish them on the ground that this case involves a "position of danger" problem not involved in *Derdiarian*.

Note 2. This might lead us to think that the position of risk approach, which seems to be taken or rejected without a complete articulation, is enormously different from an emphasis on the foreseeability of the intervening cause. The position of risk analysis has a great deal in common with, and may in fact be a special case of, the risk rule. In fact all this might be sufficient basis for a hypothesis: all "intervening cause" cases can be adequately analyzed by using the risk rule and dropping the special language of intervening cause. This is perhaps easier to see in *Marshall,* coming up next.

Note 3. This Note relates the rule that a defendant who negligently injures a plaintiff will be liable for any "enhanced harm" caused by subsequent negligent medical treatment. The rule is well established, and has been expanded in some states to include harms beyond medical treatment (such as the helicopter transport to the hospital involved in *Anaya,* cited here). If the scope of risk when a defendant negligently injures someone is that they will be further injured while seeking medical treatment, then these cases are consistent with a basic risk rule.

Under traditional rules, the initial tortfeasor and the negligent doctor would be jointly and severally liable or for the doctor's aggravation of injury, but under causal apportionment rules the initial tortfeasor alone would be liable for the injury that existed before the doctor's aggravation. *See, e.g., Underwood-Gary v. Mathews,* 785 A.2d 708 (Md. 2001). Where joint and several liability has been abolished it may be that courts will divide responsibility for the aggravation according to comparative fault of the tortfeasors. Some states seem to have gone further, holding that the first defendant is no longer liable for injuries resulting from medical malpractice in treating the injury. *Dumas v. State,* 828 So.2d 530 (La. 2002)*; Haff v. Hettich,* 593 N.W.2d 383 (N.D. 1999). On second injury cases see DOBBS ON TORTS § 192 (2000).

MARSHALL V. NUGENT, 222 F.2d 604 (1st Cir. 1955)

We look at Judge Magruder's words and conceptions of proximate cause and then at the facts and comparisons to or contrasts with other cases.

Scope of risk reasoning. Judge Magruder is very clear that, although this is in intervening cause factual situation, you can go straight to the heart of the issue without the added language about the intervening cause and causal chains. It is a matter of confining the liability to a negligent actor to "consequences which result from the operation of . . . a risk, the foreseeability of which rendered the defendant's conduct negligent." We hope students recognize this point, but if not, we would hope to lead them to do so.

Foreseeable risks that bespeak negligence. Magruder's formulation is careful. He does not merely say the risk must be foreseeable; it must also be a risk that a reasonable person would have avoided by exercising care. That is the meaning of the phrase "the forseeability of which rendered the defendant's conduct negligent." Many risks are reasonable even when foreseeable.

As in *Ventricelli,* the plaintiff is attempting to cope with the defendant's conduct and is injured in the process. However, in *Marshall,* one incident or accident has already occurred. The plaintiff is attempting to minimize the risk resulting from the position on the highway and is injured in the process. So described, the case seems a great deal like *Ventricelli;* yet here Judge Magruder is willing to impose liability. What is the distinction? In *Marshall* the defendant initially subjected the plaintiff to a wide variety of risks of injury on the highway including the risk of second or even third or fourth collision injuries. The risk of even post-accident injuries may be a risk in much the same way that rescue is a risk. As in the rescue cases, we can see the post-accident injury cases as involving a second-stage injury which is either foreseeable or so closely related to the first-stage injury that it ought to be compensable; and where, as in *Marshall,* the plaintiff is in a greater position of risk from the forces which cause him harm, there should be no difficulty in imposing liability. Does this also sufficiently distinguish *Ventricelli?*

A recent case for comparison is *Staelens v. Dobert,* 318 F.3d 77 (1st Cir. 2003). Dobert negligently ran into a gasoline tanker driven by the plaintiff. Dobert was injured and taken away. The plaintiff was not. The Department of

Transportation investigated. Several hours after the impact, the DOT representative, having inspected the tanker's lights, told the plaintiff he could turn them off. Moving to do so, the plaintiff stepped on a wheeled flat board (a creeper) used for under-vehicle inspections. He was thrown to the ground and suffered injury. *Held*, summary judgment for Dobert affirmed. "[N]o jury could conclude that it was reasonably foreseeable that, three to five hours after the collision, Staelens would trip over a piece of equipment brought to the scene sometime after the accident by a state employee inspecting the tanker. Staelens suffered no injury from the collision itself nor from any risk of harm resulting therefrom; *e.g.*, he did not slip on fluids or trip over debris from the vehicles involved in the accident. Instead, Staelens's injury resulted from an independent agency. . . ." The court did not discuss any other post-impact scope of risk cases.

Notes 1 – 3. Termination of Risk. The idea that a risk once created by the defendant's negligent conduct might "terminate" as suggested by Judge Magruder in *Marshall*, is, of course, a part of the risk rule approach of these cases. *Pittsburg Reduction Co. v. Horton* is a leading example but not necessarily a defensible one. The defendant negligently left dynamite caps where children might find them. The mother of one of the children actually took possession of the caps. Anyone would probably say that once the boy's mother knew of the dynamite caps, one might expect a great deal more safety, but that is still not as much safety as one would expect if the caps had been carefully handled in the first place. *Horton* is a case in which there might be apparent safety, but not actual.

Actually, even the words "appearance" and "apparent safety" are peculiar in the context of the *Horton* case. If the defendant had been aware that the mother had picked up the dynamite caps so that there was "appearance" to him, there are adequate reasons to suggest that this should terminate his liability. If he seeks assurances of safety from the mother and gets them, there are even better reasons for terminating any liability. But the "appearance" in some of these cases is not an appearance to the defendant at all: in *Horton* there was no evidence that defendant knew where the caps were at all. Perhaps this so-called "appearance" of safety should have no effect at all, as distinct from a real reduction of the risk and the achievement of genuine safety.

Prosser and the Restatement have recognized a concept similar to termination of the risk. They call it "shifting responsibility" and in some ways it is distinct from the termination of risk idea. If the foreman for the Pittsburg Reduction Company had discovered that caps had gotten out and then called Mrs. Copple and received her assurance that she would return any caps she found, then it is reasonable to talk not merely about "termination of risk" but also about the power of a negligent party to shift responsibility to another person. This involves a consensual transaction and the effect of it is to shift a duty of care from one person to another unless courts believe that such a shift violates public policy. See DOBBS ON TORTS § 194 (2000). The idea comes up again in discussing contracts and torts, Chapter 17.

Note 4. Keys in the car. See Dobbs on Torts §§ 190 (2000). In *Kozicki v. Dragon,* 255 Neb. 248, 583 N.W.2d 336 (1998) the court thought a duty of care was created by a statute that prohibited leaving keys in an unattended vehicle. There was evidence that theft was predictable at the time and place, that car thieves are not responsible drivers, and that theft was encouraged by leaving the keys in the car. This made foreseeability a jury question. The court was addressing a proximate cause argument, but the same reasoning shows why the defendant could be accounted negligent. Some of the cases raise what might be thought of as termination of the risk issues, as where the thief reaches a point of safety and is no longer fleeing or joyriding. The cases have divided on a number of lines, some permitting liability. See Annotation, 45 A.L.R.3d 787 (1972). More on car key cases in Chapter 16 on duty.

Note 5. Courts often present the condition-not-a-cause proposition without analysis as if it were a reason. E.g., *Quirke v. City of Harvey,* 639 N.E.2d 1355 (Ill. Ct. App. 1994); *Harpster v. Hetherington,* 512 N.W.2d 585 (Minn. 1994); *Gaige v. Kepler,* 756 N.Y.S.2d 644 (App. Div. 2003).

Judge Magruder delivered a succinct comment on the condition-cause rule in his decision in *Marshall.* We see condition-cause language, at the very best, as bumper-sticker law that takes the eye off the central issue of foreseeability and find it either useless or misleading. If students need a bit more than Magruder's comments, this Note should serve that purpose. This Note, then, is another note that is more about language or concepts used rather than about outcomes.

(1) If the cliche is meant to imply that condition and causation are mutually exclusive, it is flatly wrong. Conditions in the sense of a physical state such as a hole in the ground, may risk harm and may cause it. Conditions in the more abstract sense of anything that is a prerequisite to something else are likewise perfectly compatible with the notion of proximate cause. (2) It looks, then, as if the cliche is only one other way of saying that the defendant's conduct in creating the condition is not a proximate cause of the harm and that the author of the superseding cause is the only one to be held liable. You can glean this from *Dirickson v. Mings,* 910 P.2d 1015, 1019 (Okla. 1996) where the court explains that

> A condition also begins with the breachj of a duty of care. With a condition, however, the subsequent injury was neither foreseeable nor reasonably anticipated as the probable result of the breach.

In other words, the condition-not-a-cause statement merely appears to the foreseeability test. That being so, it is wholly unnecessary; we can go straight to the foreseeability without adding or passing through the layer created by the condition-cause cliche. The condition-cause cliche is literally meaningless except as an expression of the judge's conclusion. Unfortunately it is presented as a reason and reasoning usually stops when the cliche is trundled out.

The casebook note suggests that the condition-conduct cliche is unsound and reflects the notion that condition-cause language could be profitably dropped, leaving courts to pursue the central foreseeability question. *First Springfield Bank & Trust v. Galman,* 720 N.E.2d 1068 (Ill. 1999) seems to support this idea. It treats the question as one of foreseeability. (It held for the defendant trucking company on ordinary foreseeability or scope of risk grounds: "Nothing in [the truck driver's] conduct increased the likelihood that a pedestrian would forgo an open crosswalk in favor of an obstructed and unlawful mid-block crossing."

■**FYI: Intervening forces of nature.** Sometimes an "unforeseeable Act of God" intervenes and is held to bar the liability of an allegedly negligent tortfeasor.

In many such cases an unforeseeable force of nature merely shows that the defendant could not have foreseen any harm at all and is thus not negligent. Some cases may discuss "Act of God" as negating negligence and at the same time may discuss the whole matter in terms of causation.

Cases also speak of a "defense," but, as a matter of logic at least, this is clearly wrong as well. If the issue is negligence, the plaintiff must prove fault; if the issue is legal cause, the plaintiff must prove that as well. The issue is one of "defense" only in the sense that although the defendant has no burden of proof on the issue, he is free to argue it. In *Tel Oil Co. v. City of Schenectady,* 757 N.Y.S.2d 121 (App. Div. 2003), the defendants had notice of a hillside problem. Perhaps they should have known that the "crib" shoring up the hillside was inadequate. But that was not the source of the problem; unforeseeable natural forces caused a large avalanche that killed one man and injured the plaintiff. Perhaps the defendant was not negligent. Or perhaps the defendant was negligent but only with respect to the different risk. The plaintiff would have the burden of proving negligence and also harm within the scope of the risk; yet the court insisted that "By asserting the act of God defense, the burden now fell upon defendants to show that those losses and injuries [were] occasioned exclusively by natural causes, such as could not be prevented by human care, skill and foresight." The court had precedent, but isn't it strange to say the plaintiff has the burden of proving negligence and proximate cause and then turn around and say that the defendant has the burden of proving no foreseeability? The effect is not clear. Maybe the defendant is shouldering a burden he need not shoulder. Or maybe this is one of those cases in which courts allow the defendant to present the same argument twice, once as no negligence/no proximate cause and then again in the guise of a defense. If courts instruct the jury on both, the effect will be that the Robes emphasize the defendant's viewpoint. ■

PROBLEM:

WOLFE V. GRAMLICH, INC.

The problem is based on *Hartsock v. Forsgren Inc.*, 365 S.W.2d 117 (Ark. 1963). In that case, the court held that as a matter of law the defendant was not liable, in part because "the overflow of the tar did not lead in a natural and continuous sequence, unbroken by any efficient intervening cause, to the accidental igniting of gasoline fumes in the Hartsock's back yard."

The words-are-everything approach of some courts, perhaps the Arkansas Court in *Forsgren*, tends to make the judges resistant to the lawyers' analysis. But suppose the lawyer had persuaded the Arkansas Court to consider foreseeability of the general type of harm under the *Medcalf* approach instead of simply reciting the proximate cause mantra.

Some students may want to make an analogy to *Hughes*. Or to the now-overruled *Watson v. Kentucky & Indiana Bridge & Railroad* case. Might you convince a court that new harm resulting from efforts to undo the harm or risk caused by the defendant is always within the risk? We have some cases in that general pattern: *Marshall v. Nugent* and maybe *Anaya*.

In the *Hartsock* case itself, the court relied on *Pittsburg Reduction Co. v. Horton*. It thought *Horton* was a stronger case for liability because it focused on the acts of the intervening cause, the mother in *Horton*. The mother's intervening conduct, it said, was passive, while here the parents actively introduced a new dangerous substance. The court also emphasized that tar was an innocuous substance, while dynamite was not. Reasoning that *Hartsock* was a weaker case than *Horton,* the court naturally found it easy to hold for the defendant in *Hartsock* on demurrer.

The cases printed in this section, although they do suggest some "rules," have been selected mainly to permit analysis and argumentation. With this problem, the student has a chance to attempt to put it together. You can craft arguments based on principle or policy; here, that the injury to the plaintiff is (or is not) within the scope of risks created by defendant's original negligence. You could also craft arguments from fact-pattern rules, comparing the case to factually-similar ones. Note that the "similarity" of facts is also a matter of argumentation and skillful grouping of cases rather than being some preordained or mechanical exercise. The lawyer adept at finding and describing cases often finds "rules" in her favor, not in the language of courts but in their composite results. Another use of facts in cases that requires skill is the argument from analogy or disanalogy.

AND END NOTE: THE FUTURE OF PROXIMATE CAUSE OR SCOPE OF RISK ANALYSIS

As to the use of proximate cause when comparative responsibility can do the job of apportionment, see Michael D. Green, *The Unanticipated Ripples of Comparative Negligence: Superseding Cause In Products Liability and Beyond*, 53 S.C. L. REV. 1103 (2002).

The cases cited here are recent examples of courts that have concluded that special "intervening cause" rules are more trouble than they are worth, and that cases can be resolved sensibly using the basic foreseeability/scope of risk rule. Time will tell whether this is a genuine trend.

Subtopic 2. Defenses

_____

CHAPTER 9

CONTRIBUTORY/COMPARATIVE FAULT

▶**Changes in the Sixth Edition:** Much of this chapter has been re-organized. In particular, the traditional exceptions to the contributory negligence bar now end the chapter as §5. It was previously §3. In addition, causation and scope of risk in comparative fault were previously § 4, but are now § 3. We think that the structure flows more smoothly from the history of contributory negligence to the current rules of comparative fault, to the relationship of those rules to other doctrines, limits on the defences and then the former limits. Teachers who want to cut materials from this section can easily skip the last section of the chapter, which is now more historical in nature.

In terms of deletions, *Sollin v. Wangler* and *Mercer v. Vanderbilt* have been reduced from full cases to case abstracts. As for additions, *Royal v. Christensen School District No. 160,* has been added.

▶The **Concise Edition** shortens this Chapter by over 25%. We have substituted a short case abstract, *Crownover v. City of Shreveport,* for *Wassell v. Adams;* omitted the commentary to the Restatement of Apportionment; and cut *Bexiga v. Havir* (along with its Notes 1 & 2), substituting a short case abstract of *McNamara v. Honeyman.*■

Scheduling Omissions. Perhaps the easiest material to omit is the very last section. You can also omit either *Bexiga* or *Royal* if you want to give briefer coverage to the limits on comparative fault defenses. Cases to omit are two new ones— *Sollin v. Wangler,* and *Mercer v. Vanderbilt University.*

COMMENTS

INTRODUCTORY TEXT

The introductory text emphasizes three points: (1) This chapter address *affirmative* defenses, those in which the burden of proof falls upon the defendant. Some arguments for the defense side of the case are not really *defenses* at all. To argue that the plaintiff has not proved proximate cause is not to raise an affirmative defense. It is to say that the plaintiff's proof has failed.

(2) Specific statutory defenses are not covered. Students should be aware that in practice they must examine statutes more or less constantly. For example, California provides that a vehicle owner cannot recover pain and suffering damages for injuries he sustains in an accident with his vehicle if that vehicle is uninsured. CAL. CIV. CODE § § 3333.4. Specific partial or complete statutory defenses of this kind are not covered in the present chapter, even though such defenses do require litigation. *See Horwich v. Superior Court*, 980 P.2d 927 (Cal. 1999) (held that a wrongful death plaintiff could recover for loss of care, comfort and society of the deceased uninsured operator of a vehicle in spite of statute above).

(3) Other impediments to suit include limited duty rules and procedural obstacles. We see some limited duty rules soon, in Chapter 12, and some procedural obstacles in Chapter 13. The point is that students should not assume that the defendant will lose merely because he has no defenses to his harmful negligent conduct.

§ 1. CONTRIBUTORY NEGLIGENCE: THE COMMON LAW RULE

BUTTERFIELD V. FORRESTER, 11 East. 59, 103 Eng. Rep. 926 (1809).

Defendant left a pole across a part of the road. The plaintiff, riding his horse hard, ran into it, though there was room to pass freely on the other side. The trial judge told the jury that if the plaintiff could reasonably have avoided the obstruction by ordinary care, they should find for the defendant. Reviewing this instruction on a rule, the judges here hold that the instruction was correct.

Butterfield is said to establish the rule of contributory negligence as a complete bar to the plaintiff's claim, though the reasons given by the judges are obscure. Bayley, J., saying that the accident happened entirely from the plaintiff's fault, might be asserting that the plaintiff in this particular instance is a superseding cause of his own harm. A different reading might suggest that the defendant is not at fault at all–perhaps because he could expect that the plaintiff would take care of himself. A third view, perhaps the one followed by Lord Ellenborough, is that contributory negligence of the plaintiff is a ground for denying recovery, independent of either the superseding cause or no-fault arguments.

It is especially important for the student to see that contributory negligence of the plaintiff and negligence (or duty) of the defendant are correlative in a number of ways. What appears on first study to be a case of contributory negligence, may turn out on analysis to be a case of no negligence on the defendant's part. This might in fact be *Butterfield* itself, an idea you can developed from Note 2 (c).

Why is the distinction important if the plaintiff loses either way? The quickest way to show the importance is to notice that with the coming of comparative fault systems, a finding of contributory fault might only reduce damages without barring the claim entirely. A finding of no negligence or no proximate cause would mean that the plaintiff had not proved an element of her case and that she would recover nothing.

Note 2. *(a) The fault principle.* The fault principle does seem to compel some judicial reaction to the plaintiff's fault, if it is a cause in fact and a legal cause of his own harm. But the fault principle does *not* seem to compel a dismissal of the plaintiff's claim. Liability for fault may well be thought to be justified best when liability is not only limited to the fault in question (the risk theory of proximate cause) but also when it is proportionate to fault. A scheme of comparative negligence might well comport better with the fault principle than the complete defense. Are there counter arguments?

(b) Proximate (intervening) cause. The proximate cause analysis might be the basis for dismissing the plaintiff's claim in some cases, but it could never explain the general rule of contributory fault, which dismisses *all* claims of negligent plaintiffs. That is so because even if the plaintiff's fault is the "sole proximate cause" in some cases, there are many other cases in which the plaintiff's fault would be deemed concurrent. Thus in many courts today, the negligence of both plaintiff and defendant would be actionable. To answer the note's question, they would be jointly and severally (or proportionately) liable to the child injured. To say so is to say that both are proximate causes. So the proximate cause analysis does not explain the rule that contributory negligence is *always* a defense so long as the contributory negligence itself is causal.

(c) Negligence. It may be possible to assert that the defendant was not negligent. (A proximate cause/scope of risk version of this idea is that the defendant was not negligent with respect to the risk of harm to the plaintiff, only negligent in risking an inconvenient detour.) The defendant might not be negligent at all because no harm was reasonably foreseeable. Why should the defendant foresee that someone would run into the open and obvious obstruction? But a defendant may often reasonably expect the plaintiff to take care of himself. See *Stinnett v. Buchele* (Chapter 6, §1) and hence may foresee no harm from an open danger.

One might raise pragmatic arguments for a complete bar, but these comments suggest that in principle it is quite unjustified as an across-the-board rule. That takes us to comparative fault systems.

§ 2. CONTRIBUTORY NEGLIGENCE: ADOPTING COMPARATIVE FAULT RULES

> ### How to Say It
>
> (1) In traditional terminology, one who fails to exercise reasonable care for her own safety is guilty of contributory negligence. The *legal effect* of the plaintiff's contributory negligence (or "contributory fault") under the traditional rule was that the plaintiff guilty of such fault was barred completely. The *legal effect* of contributory fault is now changed in almost all states under comparative negligence systems. It remains possible to describe the plaintiff's *conduct* as contributory negligence, even though the legal *effect* of contributory negligence or fault is now different because it only reduces the recoverable damages.
>
> (2) Contemporary professionals tend to speak of comparative *fault* or comparative *responsibility*. Those terms are more capacious than comparative *negligence*. They imply, for example, that the plaintiff might suffer a reduction in damage for her own negligence even in a claim based upon the defendant's non-negligent strict liability, that is that you can compare both negligence and breach of a strict duty.
>
> (3) Comparative *responsibility* is the term adopted by the Restatement of Apportionment to indicate that, in apportioning responsibility among two or more persons, the trier (under the Restatement's rule) can consider not only traditional fault or risk but also matters such as closeness of causal connection. More on that in connection with Restatement of Apportionment § 8 (printed following *Wassell*.)

NEW YORK MCKINNEY'S CIV. PRAC. LAW § 1411
WISCONSIN STAT. ANN. 895.045

New York's is a "pure" comparative negligence statute. In "any" action, the plaintiff's fault shall not bar recovery, but damages are reduced. Wisconsin's is a "modified" comparative fault statute. It bars the plaintiff completely unless his fault is "not greater than the negligence of the person against whom recovery is sought." Some modified statutes require that the plaintiff's fault be *less* than the defendant's, but Wisconsin allows the recover so long as it is "not greater than."

Note 4. Applying the rules. For purposes of this problem, think of P as party "A." We structured this note to give you an option. You can use it simply to make sure the class understands the basic calculation and skip the ramifications that can be added. Or you can add a fact to the hypothetical to raise two issues about the modified statutes.

The simple calculation. The question only asks what P recovers. P is chargeable with 5% of the negligence and therefore entitled to recover 95% of his damages. In a joint and several jurisdiction, he could recover $95,000 against any one of the others, or against all. In a proportionate share jurisdiction, he can recover $10,000 from B, $40,000 from C, and $45,000 from D. "Recover" of course means he can recover a judgment, not that he can actually collect. That will depend upon assets or insurance of the defendants.

The additional problems. To raise the additional problems that arise when tortfeasors are also claimants, and especially those in jurisdictions following the modified plan of comparative fault you need only extend the hypothetical as follows:

B, C, and D also suffer damages of $100,000 each.

This will allow you to work out what recoveries the New York, Wisconsin and North Dakota statutes will yield. It will also raise two specific issues. First, in determining whether the claimant's fault is equal to or greater than the fault of others, do we aggregate all the fault of others? Or must the claimant lose as to any defendant whose personal fault is less than the claimants? Second, do we set off awards (mostly a problem in pure, New York type jurisdictions). Other issues about comparing fault, including the problem of fault of non-parties, appear in Chapter 25. Here, we first outline the two issues, then show the workout in a table.

(1) *Aggregation of fault to meet the equal to or greater than test.* This issue can be simplified by recognizing that all parties could recover from all others in a pure jurisdiction, then working only on D's claim to show the aggregation issue. D's negligence is 45% of the whole, more than any other single party. Under a plain "equal to" or a plain "greater than" modified system, D seems to be barred. That in fact is the rule in Wisconsin, announced in *Walker v. Kroger Groc. & Baking Co.,* 252 N.W. 721(Wis. 1934). However, *Sollin* gives us a glimpse of the North Dakota statute, which denies recovery to a negligent actor only when his fault is "'as great as the combined fault of all other persons' who contributed to the injury." That permits the claimant like D to compare his fault with the aggregate fault of all others. In a system like that, D recovers against all the other actors, much as he would in a pure comparative negligence jurisdiction. Some states have reached that result without a specific statutory provision. See *Graci v. Damon,* 374 N.E.2d 311 (Mass. App. 1978), aff'd, *Graci* v. *Damon,* 383 N.E. 842 (Mass. 1978).

(2) *Set-off.* This problem arises in any cases, even a simple two-party case, in which each party can recover against the other. In a two-party case that will necessarily be in a pure comparative fault jurisdiction, but as shown above, in an modified comparative fault with aggregation it will be possible for

multiple parties to recover against each other. We can illustrate the problem by looking at the recovery of P alone in a pure comparative jurisdiction and supposing a joint and several rule. P, with 5% of the fault, can recover $95,000 against B. B, with 10% of the fault, can recover $90,000 against P. Since these claims will be tried together because B's claim will be a compulsory counter-claim, do we simply setoff B's judgment off against P's, leaving P with a net $5,000 recovery? *Jess v. Herrman*, 604 P.2d 208 (Cal. 1979), held not, so long as both parties were covered by liability insurance. That means that P's liability insurer would pay all of B's $90,000 judgment and B's insurer would pay all of P's $95,000 judgment. The insurer has been paid a premium to shoulder the liability of its insured; it is not entitled to reduce its liability because of the very fact that its insured also has his own claim against another person. So no mandatory set off. That result also makes each party should the burden of his own fault. B, with 10% of the fault, recovers damages less than 10%. A set off rule, giving the insurer the benefit, would mean that B's recovery would be reduced, not in proportion to his fault, but in fact reduced to nothing.

Tabulating the recoveries. We reiterate the assumption that each party has damages of $100,000 and that we are in a joint and several liability jurisdiction. We also assume a no-set-off rule.

Recovery of the Parties

Pure comparative fault	Wisconsin "greater than" bars; no aggregation	North Dakota "equal to" bars; aggregation permitted
P (5%): $95,000 vs. all	P: $95,000	P: $95,000 vs. all
B (10%): $90,000 vs. all	B: $90,000 vs. C and D	B: $90,000 vs. all
C (40%): $60,000 vs. all	C: $60,000 v. D	C: $60,000 vs. all
D (45%): $55,000 vs. all	D: $0	D: $55,000 vs. all

To put the North Dakota column in perspective, you may need to go back to the two party case in *Sollin* to remind the class that where aggregation is not possible (it never is in a two-party case), North Dakota's statute is far more stringent than Wisconsin's because it will bar a plaintiff whose fault is 50%.

Note 5. Information to the jury. Should the practical effects of the verdict be explained to the jury? *Sollin* considers whether to blindfold the jury about the effect of their fault assignments. The blindfold issue lends weight to the distinctions among the different types of comparative fault. Of course a jury would not know of different effects in different jurisdictions if it is not instructed about the ramifications.

Note 6. Two types of modified comparative fault systems. Students need to make two distinctions–first between pure and modified statutes, and second between the modified statutes. Wisconsin allows the plaintiff to recover so long as his fault is not "greater than" the defendant's, so a 50-50 fault case would theoretically allow each party to recover from the other. The other kind of modified statute is North Dakota's seen in *Sollin*. Under that kind of statute the plaintiff is barred unless his fault is actually less than the defendant's. There is another difference – whether the fault of multiple parties is figured in making this calculation as developed from of the hypothetical in Note 4.

WASSELL V. ADAMS, 865 F.2d 849 (7th Cir. 1989)

The plaintiff, a guest in defendant's motel, was raped by an intruder. She is here suing the defendant motel-owner, but the jury assessed 97% of the negligence against the plaintiff, who stayed in a motel in a very dangerous part of town and in addition opened the door to the stranger's knock and suffered a rape. Notice that the *jury* made the fault assessment. This is NOT a case in which the judge bars the claim or even reduces damages. Judge Posner only held that the jury's assessment could not be overturned. If that ruling is emotionally difficult for some observers, it is nevertheless a ruling in line with the usual view that the jury's evaluative findings must be upheld in disputable cases.

Later we'll consider whether the plaintiff's freedom or entitlements should preclude charging her with contributory fault. Here we can explore different issues. One of the less obvious themes of this case and the two case abstracts that follow is reflected in the question: How do you determine or compare fault or responsibility?

Comparative negligence is comparative. One point you can see in *Wassell* is that comparative negligence is comparative. It is not that the plaintiff did anything particularly awful. The 97% is *not* 97% of the most negligent thing one could do. It is rather a reflection of the jury's estimate that her negligence was more than 30 times as bad as the defendant's negligence. So, except as to states like Maine (**Note 9** following *Wassell*), you always have to talk about *both* parties' negligence in a comparative negligence suit. The claim that the defendant should have provided security anticipates or foreshadows the claims we see in Chapter 16, that some defendants owe us protection from third persons.

Notes 2-5. *Risk-utility issues.* The fault alleged by the motel owners was failing to have a security guard or a phone in the room or failing to warn. The fault alleged on Wassell's part was opening the door late at night without looking to see who was there. How do we compare these very different acts? Does the *Carroll Towing* cost-benefit type of analysis really work in cases like this? In Chapter 6 following *Carroll Towing* we mentioned Howard Latin's idea that most negligence was not a matter of rational risk calculation but of mistake and momentary inattention. Howard Latin, *"Good" Warnings, Bad Products, and Cognitive Limitations,* 41 U.C.L.A. L. REV. 1193 (1994). The plaintiff negligence in *Wassell* looks like the latter. Should we drop all attempt to apply *Carroll Towing* to cases in that category?

-**Comparative costs**. Judge Posner suggests that comparative costs of avoiding injury would be one way to measure the comparative negligence of the parties. Perhaps he did not mean that as a complete formula. Would comparative unjustified risk be closer to the mark? Defendant and plaintiff both drive negligently by driving too fast. Defendant's excessive speed is ten miles per hour, the plaintiff's is five. If risks are increased in exact proportion to the increase in speed, then why not say that defendant's negligence is twice that of the plaintiff's so that the comparative responsibility should be 66.66 while the plaintiff's is 33.33? Comparative costs might lead you to think that a 50-50 apportionment would be appropriate if each could reduce speed at the same cost.

-**Allocation of fault by custom and expectation.** What is reasonably expected is in part a function of custom or culture or social habits. In Posner's example in Note 5, the pedestrian is not expected to wear a helmet to guard against a car driver's negligence. Maybe that would be the right result even if wearing helmets would overall avoid more injury at a cost less than the costs of minimizing driving errors. If you believe customs and expectations of society are important in allocating the responsibility to drivers rather than to pedestrians in the first place, you might believe that the same expectations take comparative costs out of the picture. Latin's mistake and momentary inattention might be especially significant in cases of intensely personal and emotional risks.

-**Warnings: costs and cause.** The idea that the defendants should be liable for failure to warn the plaintiff of dangers in the neighborhood draws two responses. The determinative one is simple: the warning would not have saved the plaintiff because it would have been a warning not to walk in the neighborhood, not a warning against opening the door to strangers. (The latter would not be required by due care because, a la *Stinnett*, the Adams could expect the plaintiff to care for herself on that point). You can reprise causal issues here if you are so minded.

More interesting is the response to the Adams' argument against counting a failure to warn as fault because warning would have caused the Adams to lose paying customers. Judge Posner says this argument is absurd because "The loss of business from telling the truth is not a social loss, it is a social gain." Is he suggesting that the warning would be a social gain because in spite of the costs in reduced income, the value of increased safety would be even more? The statement seems much broader than that because it does not suggest that he has actually estimated costs or increased safety. Perhaps the social gain in truthful warnings is not only any increased safety but also increased ability of consumers to decide for themselves what they regard as important, whether or not that results in greater safety.

Simons' Corporate vs. Individual Conduct

Beyond the difficulty of using the *Carroll Towing* risk-utility balance in cases that turn on information or memory, maybe you could think that the risk-utility balance is unsuited to judgment of individual actions generally, as opposed to "corporate" conduct. See, suggesting that there might be differences in the analyses appropriate in the two kinds of cases, Kenneth W. Simons, *Deontology, Negligence, Tort, and Crime*, 76 B.U. L. REV. 273 (1996). Another possibility is to say that *Carroll Towing* best works with repeated conduct, not with isolated acts. Both these ideas correlate to some extent with Latin's mistake and momentary inattention model.

-**Measuring costs; memory**. What would the plaintiff's cost be as compared to the Adams' proposed cost of $20,000 for a guard? How could you measure or even estimate the plaintiff's costs? Posner speaks of the costs of schooling oneself. Perhaps it is possible to imagine that you could school yourself to remember everything you need to when you are awakened from a deep sleep, but it seems preposterous to suggest that anyone in the world does that except, maybe, James Bond.

-**What is the relevant cost comparision?** Posner suggests that the motel's annual costs for security of all guests should be compared to the costs of Wassell in schooling herself in greater vigilance. But perhaps the appropriate comparison would be the cost per room/night for the motel to provide security and the cost per room/night for the guest to be more vigilant. Based on evidence in the record in the case, if this comparison were made the jury would be asked to compare $5 per room per night with the plaintiff's costs—possibly a very different calculation.

Note 5. Optimal risks. Judge Posner is surely right in *Greycas, Inc. v. Proud*. We don't want to double the appropriate precaution merely because there are two actors. This idea is also reflected in the frequent if overstated instruction that "[e]very person using ordinary care has a right to assume, until the contrary is, or reasonably should be apparent, that every other person will use ordinary care and obey the law. To act on that assumption is not negligence." *Haynes v. Bee-Line Trucking Co.*, 80 F.3d 1235 (8th Cir. 1996).

But how can we all make an efficiency analysis to determine which actor should bear the burden of achieving the safety? Perhaps as pedestrians we know we need not wear helmets because we know that social custom has allocated the safety burden to the driver. But analysis of easy cases does not always help resolve hard ones. Could the plaintiff in *Wassell* decide that she did not need to engage in self-protective measures because she thought the motel would protect her?

Wassell was tried under the old pure system Illinois had judicially adopted. For cases filed after 1986, Ill. Rev. Stat. ch. 110, ¶ 2-1116 applies a modified comparative negligence rule, barring plaintiffs whose fault "is more than 50%" of the cause of harm.

Note 6. Harms to self versus harm to others. The defendants might have created risks to the plaintiff, but the plaintiff did not create risks to the defendants. The risks were "non-reciprocal." That is often the case with contributory fault but never the case with the defendant's own negligence. Does that matter in weighing the plaintiff's fault? The Restatement decided that it does not. Does that mean that failure to take omega 3s or eat a reasonable healthy diet could count as contributory negligence? Conduct that poses risk to self might be a much wider category than conduct that poses risks to others. The treatment of nonreciprocal risks foreshadows *Bexiga's* discussion.

Note 7. Different standards of care. Maybe under *Arguallo* the jury will compare deviations from the separate standards, and maybe that's the same as comparing all the relevant fault. At this place in the course, perhaps the best you can hope for from this note is to forecast limited duties once again and to suggest that comparing fault or responsibility may be more a matter of rough estimates or even intuition than a truly precise mental operation. We would probably not take this note up in class but instead might come back to it after duty and immunity are covered.

How would the *Arguallo* test work if the state has a guest statute that holds defendants liable only for gross negligence? The defendant drives 90 m.p.h., at least 30 m.p.h. over a safe speed, but the state says speed alone is not gross negligence. In addition, the defendant looks at passengers in the back seat while telling a joke. The combination of speed plus inattention to the road might count as gross negligence. Must the jury try to disregard damages resulting from the high speed? Or do we think that once we know that a defendant is grossly negligent, he is liable for all his negligence? We might speculate that you could come up with different answers in different contexts.

Note 8. Apportioning in res ipsa cases. *See* DOBBS ON TORTS § 159 (2001). How can we compare known, specific negligence of the plaintiff with unknown negligence of the defendant? This isn't just comparing apples to oranges; it's comparing apples to a dream of oranges. We know that juries can do anything; that is not the problem. The problem is that no one, not even juries, can make principled decisions if there is no principle, nor factual decisions if there are no facts. Nor can appellate courts bring appropriate review to bear. We have no answer that satisfies us.

Note 9. Equitable and just apportionment. Maine's free-wheeling approach to comparative fault invites jurors to apportion according to some unidentified kind of feelings unrelated to their assessment of comparative fault. This should lead discussion directly to the Restatement of Apportionment § 8, which arguably runs the same risks of unreviewable and biased judgments.

▶Concise Edition insert:

CROWNOVER V. CITY OF SHREVEPORT, 996 So.2d 315 (La. Ct. App. 2008)

This simple case abstract substitutes for *Wassell* in the Concise Edition, with a new Note 1 (which cites *Wassell*). Note 2 after *Crownover* is Note 5 after the state statutes, standard edition p. 255; Note 3 after *Crownover* is Note 6 on the same page; and Note 4 after *Crownover* is Note 9 after Wassell. You should be able to use the case and the Restatement section that follows to make many of the same points discussed above (and below) on how the basic allocation works, focusing on what a jury is to take into account in fixing percentages.

RESTATEMENT THIRD OF TORTS, APPORTIONMENT OF LIABILITY § 8

If you think the Restatement is too hard or requires too much class time, you might consider omitting it or its comments. Section 8 gives us a number of concerns.

Both Restatement § 8 and the Maine statute seem to create a basis for apportioning liability that is quite different from the standard used to impose liability in the first place. For instance, in addition to the legal standard of care, each person's personal abilities and disabilities are considered. See Restatement cmt. *c.* Liability is thus apportioned on grounds that would not be considered in determining whether liability exists.

To reinforce this, the Restatement calls for apportionment, not on the basis of negligence or fault, but upon the basis of a word that has no specific legal meaning –responsibility. The trier is to consider the state of mind, not merely the unjustified risks created. Although state of mind may be bad enough to warrant punitive damages, importing that consideration into comparative fault or responsibility determinations is a different matter because it is likely to affect the ability of the plaintiff to recover for actual harm done where joint and several liability has been abolished. (See Chapter 23).

We worry, too, about the risk that the trier is invited by § 8 to vent bias, both because objective bases for liability are removed and because the trier is specifically directed to consider state of mind. This is especially true since Comment c specifically says that state of mind for which responsibility may be allocated need not be causal.

Finally, the opaque "responsibility" erects a screen that may make intelligible review well-nigh impossible as well. We will say a little more about the "strength of causal connection" later.

§ 3. ALL OR NOTHING JUDGMENTS AFTER COMPARATIVE FAULT

¶1. *No plaintiff negligence.* This point is fairly simple. If there is no plaintiff negligence, the comparative negligence issue is not raised. The plaintiff-fault defense should be stricken.

¶2. *Plaintiff negligence that is not an actual cause of injury.* Again, a simple point. In order for the plaintiff's negligent conduct to have any comparative effect, that conduct must be an actual cause of the plaintiff's harm. If not, it is not taken into account at all.

The same is true of the defendant, of course. The ordinary rules of causation tell us that a faulty defendant is not liable if his faulty conduct caused no harm; that principle remains unchanged under comparative fault rules.

In making a fault apportionment, we are only interested in fault that is a cause in fact of the injury. We are not interest in the parties' lifetime accumulation of fault. The only fault to be apportioned is fault that is a but-for cause of the injury. If a faulty act causes no harm, it is no more to be considered after adoption of comparative fault than before.

¶3. *Plaintiff injury that is not within the scope of the risk.* How does comparative fault relate to proximate or scope-of-risk cause? Proximate cause rules sometimes exclude liability of the defendant altogether. (They could also be applied to the plaintiff so that no reduction in recovery would be made if the plaintiff was at fault only with respect to risks that did *not* eventuate in her harm.) The question here is whether the law should handle all cases under comparative fault or responsibility rules, leaving no role for proximate cause. The houseguest example aptly illustrates the problem. The risk of going out by the pool at night is a risk that the person might trip or fall. It is not a risk of a car crash.

¶**4.** *No defendant negligence.* Of course all-or-nothing rules also operate on the defendant's side. If the defendant is not negligent, the defendant has no liability. The issue will not be left for comparative percentages.

¶**5.** *Sorting claims.* When the rule was contributory negligence, all issues in the case were all-or-nothing issues. Now with comparative fault, apportionment issues can be decided in percentages. Meanwhile, other issues in the case such as actual and proximate cause are still all-or-nothing issues. As early as *Palsgraf* we saw disputes about whether an issue was one of duty or proximate cause. Those disputes take on even more importance once the characterization of the issue determines whether the issue will be decided on a percentage basis or an all-or-nothing basis.

¶**6.** *Reasonable care by the defendant in light of plaintiff fault?* In *Juchniewcz* the plaintiff argued that the defendant had essentially made a case of plaintiff comparative fault without formally presenting that defense to the jury. However, the court ruled that the jury could have found the doctor non-negligent given the information plaintiff had told him.

¶**7.** *Plaintiff's fault as a superceding case of the harm.* *Exxon Company, U.S.A. v. Sofec, Inc.*, cited here, is another matter. The Court accepted the argument that the plaintiff's contributory negligence was also a superseding cause. Notice that the case is a reverse last clear chance case: the *plaintiff* had the last clear chance to avoid harm. By the time the vessel was in a position of safety, there was nothing the defendant could do. Recall that although last clear chance is no longer determinative in most comparative negligence regimes, the trier might still think that the party with the last chance was more negligent in some cases. *Eichelberg v. National Railroad Passenger Corp.*, 57 F.3d 1179 (2d Cir. 1995) ("The factors pertinent to the last clear chance doctrine remain relevant in assessing the comparative fault of the plaintiff and the defendant."); RESTATEMENT OF APPORTIONMENT § 8.

Would you prefer to resolve the *Exxon v. Sofec* case by allowing some recovery under comparative fault principles? If you emphasize the plaintiff's negligent conduct as a superseding cause you run the risk of diluting the comparative fault regime. But the point seems less impressive if instead of focusing on the plaintiff's conduct as a superseding cause you examine the risks created by the defendant in the first place. Look at *Exxon v. Sofec*. Although the Supreme Court used familiar superseding cause language, we know that such language may mask scope of risk considerations. Did the defendant in *Exxon* create a risk of captain error at a point when the emergency was over? Had the risks terminated? Did the vessel achieve a position of safety at least as good as other vessels? With the focus on the risks created by the defendant, rather than on the plaintiff's foolish conduct, maybe the use of proximate cause reasoning does not seem so contradictory to the system of comparative fault.

But proximate cause analysis does seem wrong in cases like *Wright v. New York City Transit Auth.*, also cited here, for reasons explained in the casebook. Those who dislike New York's pure comparative fault system might find a proximate cause/scope of risk argument congenial as a mechanism for circumventing liability to a seriously negligent plaintiff. *See* Paul T. Hayden, *Butterfield Rides Again: Plaintiff's Negligence as Superseding or Sole Proximate cause in Systems of Pure Comparative Responsibility,* 33 LOY. L.A. L. REV. 887 (2000).

One place for change in response to comparative fault: What if courts were more or less consciously helping the plaintiff out under the old regime by finding that his contributory negligence was not "proximate?" Comparative negligence is certainly a ground for changing *that* practice, isn't it? *Brisboy v. Fibreboard Corp.*, 418 N.W.2d 650 (Mich. 1988) (deceased died of lung cancer resulting from exposure to asbestos and from deceased's own cigarette smoking; jury's comparative fault finding upheld; the plaintiff's smoking created no risk of danger from asbestos, but it created a general risk of lung cancer).

¶8. *Causal apportionment of separate injuries.* If the defendant is not a cause in fact of some distinct item of harm, he is not legally responsible for that item. If we can show which part of the harm was caused by the plaintiff and which by the defendant, causal apportionment can apply here, just as it did in a multiple defendant case.

However, if causal apportionment cannot be determined, fault-based apportionment will be undertaken. See *Owens Corning Fiberglas Corp. v. Parrish,* 58 S.W.3d 467 (Ky. 2001), since no evidence was introduced to show what part of the injury was caused by each party, the trial court properly invoked comparative fault. The jury then assessed each of the two plaintiffs with 50% of the fault.

¶9. *The mitigation of damages rule.* The process of excluding recovery for specific items of harm usually goes under the name of the avoidable consequences rule, or minimizing or mitigating damages. *See generally* 1 DAN DOBBS, THE LAW OF REMEDIES §§ 3.9 & 8.7(4) (2d ed. 1993) (the latter section covering seat belt cases). It can be based upon the conclusion that the defendant was a but-for cause of the harmful event and some of the harm that followed but not a but-for cause of some particular items of harm. For those he is not liable at all.

Alternatively and quite differently, the latter process could be based upon a scope of risk or proximate cause rationale. That rationale would be that the defendant was a but-for cause of all the harms the plaintiff suffered, but that some discrete items of harm were not within the scope of the risks negligently created. The avoidable consequences or minimizing damages rules have operated on one or both of these rationales to reduce damages for the specific item of harm. With the advent of comparative fault, the legal system has choices: (1) we could simply treat all of the plaintiff's failure to minimize damages as a form of comparative fault and give up trying to separate discrete items of harm; or (2) we could maintain both systems of damages reduction, one for the plaintiff's fault and another to exclude all recovery for items of harm outside the scope of the risk created by the negligent defendant.

Seat belt cases. The seat belt cases adopt different rules. The older rule, still followed in some recent cases, ignores the plaintiff's failure to use a restraint and allows a full recovery. Other cases have said that failure to wear a seat belt could at least reduce damages attributable to the failure. This is an avoidable consequences or causal apportionment rule applied to pre-injury conduct. Its application would raise a difficult question if the injuries from failure to wear a seat belt could not be separated from the other injuries. *See* DOBBS ON TORTS § 205 (2001).

Examples for discussion or lecture:

(1) The defendant doctor negligently fails to diagnose or treat the plaintiff's condition. This creates the risk that it will be necessary to amputate the plaintiff's leg. To minimize this risk the doctor tells the plaintiff not to smoke. The plaintiff smokes anyway. A day later the condition worsens dramatically and the leg is amputated. If the plaintiff's smoking for one day did not cause the condition to worsen, her contributory negligence is not a cause in fact of the harm and she may fully recover.

(2) Same facts except that the amputation is not required for months and the plaintiff's smoking has the effect of hastening an inevitable loss. The *Dillon v. Twin States Electric* case (discussed briefly at Casebook p. 208) might apply to this topsy-turvy, contributory negligence case so that the plaintiff still recovers for loss of the leg, but only from the time it would have been lost without her smoking. The key element here is that the plaintiff's fault only hastened the loss, as the electric company's fault only hastened the death in *Dillon.*

(3) Same facts except that before the doctor is negligent at all, he advises the plaintiff to quit smoking because smoking compromises her already-poor blood circulation in her feet. She negligently continues to smoke. Thereafter the doctor negligently prescribes the wrong drug for her condition, which becomes much worse and causes loss of the leg. Even if the plaintiff's smoking is one of the causes in fact of her harm, a jury might be permitted to find that the doctor's subsequent negligence was a superseding cause. If so, the plaintiff would recover fully. Some of the facts were suggested by *Ostrowski v. Azzara*, 545 A.2d 148 (N.J. 1988).

§ 4. ALLOCATING FULL RESPONSIBILITY TO THE DEFENDANT IN THE INTERESTS OF POLICY OR JUSTICE

BEXIGA V. HAVIR. MFG. CORP., 290 A.2d 281 (N.J. 1972).

In *Bexiga,* the plaintiff negligently operated a power press in such a way as to put his hand in the machine as it came down. The hand was crushed. The manufacturer could have designed a safety feature to protect against workers' hand injuries. The court imposes a duty upon the manufacturer to provide a machine that will protect against foreseeable contributory negligence. Hence the contributory negligence is no bar.

The principle. The principle becomes more obvious in cases like *McNamara v. Honeyman* in **Note 2** (a case abstract in the Concise Edition, substituting for *Bexiga*). It seems in some cases that the defendant has a duty to use care to protect the plaintiff from the plaintiff's own contributory fault— and that when such a duty exists, the plaintiff's contributory fault is no defense.[2] This principle is a kind of common law version of what we see in some of the statute cases, **Note 4.** It runs counter to a great deal of the individualism of the common law to hold that A must protect B from B's own fault or stupidity. But if there are situations in which A as a reasonable person should nevertheless do so— caretaker situations, for example— then the *Bexiga* result is understandable in the same way that the statutory duties are understandable.

As backside to the rule applied when the plaintiff can care for himself. In one sense the *Bexiga* duty and the corollary rule that the plaintiff is not barred by his own fault is the backside of the rule that holds a defendant free to create risks which he reasonably believes the plaintiff can easily avoid for himself. The defendant, free to create risks the plaintiff is likely to avoid for himself, is not free to create risks the plaintiff is likely to encounter without self-protection. In a sense, then, *Bexiga* is the complement of *Stinnett v. Buchele* and, if *Butterfield* is a case of no negligence, then it is the complement of *Butterfield,* too.

---

2. *Hobart v. Shin*, 705 N.E.2d 907 (Ill. 1998), allowed a suicidal patient's contributory negligence as a defense to a claim that the physician was negligent, but in that case the patient seemed to have fully recovered; the better analysis might be that the physician was not negligent as the risk had been eliminated. Unfortunately, however, the case is likely to lead to reduction in a physician's duty of care by the introduction of contributory negligence.

Creating the *Bexiga* duty out of community custom. The *Bexiga* principle may strike some as creating an awesome vacuum– when should courts create a duty to care for another and to protect that other against his own fault? That is, when should courts assign all the risks or duties to the defendant? One of the merits of the foreseeability test is that it permits the community of persons to whom the law applies very largely to create the standards that will govern that community. If it is foreseeable to the defendant in *Butterfield* that the plaintiff will be able to avoid the obstruction and will thus not be injured, this is merely to say that the community generally behaves that way in similar situations and that how the community behaves is a very good test of the defendant's liability. And, by the same token, if it is foreseeable in *Bexiga* that the users of the machine will use it so often, or under such repetitive circumstances, that their care will fall short, this is to say that the community of users behaves that way and that this community of manufacturers would reasonably take this into account. Unless it is fictional to say self protection is foreseeable in *Butterfield* and not in *Bexiga*, the communities of real-life people have largely defined the rules for themselves in both cases. In addition, at least some limited guidelines are possible for constricting the *Bexiga* duty. See **Notes 5 & 6** below.

Note 1. *Bexiga* and comparative fault. The principle does not seem grounded in the old harsh rule that barred the negligent plaintiff entirely but in a special duty of the defendant to protect the plaintiff from the plaintiff's own fault. Consequently, adoption of comparative fault should not affect the principle. See, applying *Bexiga* after comparative fault, *Suter v. San Angelo Foundry & Mach. Co.,* 406 A.2d 140 (N.J. 1979) (now subject to a products liability statute).

Note 2 Defendant's undertaking to protect the plaintiff. *See also Hickey v. Zezulka,* 487 N.W.2d 106 (Mich. 1992); *Saunders v. County of Steuben,* 693 N.E.2d 16 (Ind. 1998) (to treat suicide as contributory fault would be to eliminate the custodian's duty to protect).

In *Reeves v. Commissioner of Police,* [2000] 1 A.C. 360, [1999] 3 All E.R. 897, [1999] 3 W.L.R. 363 (H.L. 1999) a prisoner, found to be of sound mind, committed suicide in his cell. The police had recognized that he was suicidal (two prior attempts while in custody) but negligently left the means for suicide available to him. The House of Lords held that, since the prisoner was of sound mind, his own decision to commit suicide would be counted and recovery for his death reduced 50 per cent. That sounds like a rejection of a *Bexiga* duty that would protect the prisoner from his own fault, but maybe not entirely. There was a strong argument for apportioning all of the fault to the prisoner. Rejecting that apportionment, Lord Hoffmann said:

But whatever views one may have about suicide in general, a 100 per cent. apportionment of responsibility to Mr. Lynch gives no weight at all to the policy of the law in imposing a duty of care upon the police. It is another different way of saying that the police should not have owed Mr. Lynch a duty of care. The law of torts is not just a matter of simple morality but contains many strands of policy, not all of them consistent with each other, which reflect the complexity of life. . . . The apportionment must recognise that a purpose of the duty accepted by the commissioner in this case is to demonstrate publicly that the police do have a responsibility for taking reasonable care to prevent prisoners from committing suicide. On the other hand, respect must be paid to the finding of fact that Mr. Lynch was "of sound mind." . . . I therefore think it would be wrong to attribute no responsibility to Mr. Lynch and compensate the plaintiff as if the police had simply killed him.

Note 3. Plaintiff negligence that occasioned the need for treatment. *Mercer* held that patients who have negligently injured themselves are nevertheless entitled to non-negligent medical attention.

The outcome here probably could not be dictated by causal apportionment rules. The plaintiff is a but-for cause of all his injuries, including the aggravation, even though the defendant is also a but-for cause of the aggravation. However, there is a causal apportionment to be made here. The defendant cannot be held liable for injuries already inflicted, only for the injuries he himself caused. The question whether damages are reduced for the plaintiff's fault is an entirely different question.

What does your class think of this argument: The defendant's negligence was not foreseeable to Qualls at the time Qualls was negligent; therefore, the defendant's aggravation of his injury by medical malpractice was not within the risk Qualls created by his negligence. Consequently, as to harm resulting from the medical malpractice, Qualls' negligence is not, in the traditional language, a proximate cause of that harm.

The trouble with the proximate cause argument is that it turns its back on the usual foreseeability rule. It is usually held that when injury is foreseeable, medical negligence in treating it is also foreseeable. *See* RESTATEMENT (THIRD) OF TORTS: APPORTIONMENT OF LIABILITY § 7. If applied to the plaintiff's negligence as well as to the negligence of a defendant who causes the initial collision, that would mean that Qualls, driving with an extremely high blood alcohol content, should have foreseen not only his own injury, but the risk that it would be treated negligently. Consequently the Restatement thinks scope of risk or "proximate cause" reasoning won't do in these antecedent negligence cases, where the plaintiff's own negligence caused the very condition the defendant undertook to treat. It concludes that the defendant's liability should not be reduced simply because "it would be unfair to allow the doctor to complain about that negligence" he undertook to treat. (Reporters' Notes to cmt. *m*.) And that might fit our sense of fairness in analogous cases, too. Restatement, supra, recognizes, the same rule would apply to antecedent negligence of a plaintiff who damages his own car, then is injured when the defendant negligently repairs it, causing further injury. The plaintiff's antecedent negligence in such a case is not weighed under comparative fault statutes.

Maybe the outcome in *Mercer* is justified by the defendant's undertaking as a physician, which is to use standard medical care without regard to why the medical care was needed. This is perhaps more closely related to the idea of shifted responsibility than to the idea of scope of risk. When the plaintiff obtains an agreement (often implicit) to receive medical care and the defendant undertakes to provide it, responsibility is shifted by agreement to the defendant. To be sure, the defendant may disclaim some responsibility in the care as it goes forward by demanding that the plaintiff take prescribed medicines, for example. But so far as he accepts responsibility he's paid to accept, the legal rules shifts it to him and there is no occasion to worry about antecedent negligence of the plaintiff. A review of shifted responsibility materials seems to warrant this analysis.

We can also test this out by asking how the reverse kind of case should come out. Suppose a landowner negligently allows his building to fall into serious disrepair (or negligently damages it). The landowner then hires a worker to repair the building. The worker attempts to do so, but the *worker* is injured because of the building's damaged condition, perhaps because a joist breaks and fall on him. You may well agree with cases that the parties have implicitly or explicitly shifted responsibility for the dangerous condition to the worker. Consequently, he has no complaint for the antecedent negligence of the landowner. In *Mercer* the shoe is on the other foot because the one undertaking a service in *Mercer* is not the person suffering harm; but the shift in responsibility to one undertaking the service is the same. We should expect the *Mercer* case and the reverse case to have similar outcomes and they do. *See* DOBBS ON TORTS § 284 (2001).

Note 4. Statutes to protect vulnerable plaintiffs. Examples of statutes construed to avoid the contributory negligence defense, even after the adoption of comparative fault include:

(1) Workplace protections statutes, such as scaffolding acts or structural work statutes. See, e.g., *Gordon v. Eastern Ry. Supply, Inc.*, 626 N.E.2d 912 (N.Y. 1993).

(2) Regulation of sales of dangerous articles. See *Zerby v. Warren*, 210 N.W.2d 58 (Minn. 1973)(defendant sold glue in violation of statute and it was used by a minor for "sniffing" with deadly results); *Tamiami Gun Shop v. Klein*, 116 So.2d 421 (Fla. 1959) (gun); but see *Crown v. Raymond*, 764 P.2d

1146 (Ariz. Ct. App. 1988) (gun dealer selling to minor with a clearly forged driver's license used to establish age, minor's contributory negligence could be invoked in a suit for the minor's suicide).

(3) Child labor laws forbidding employment of minors in certain work or occupations. E.g., *Strain v. Christians,* 483 N.W.2d 783 (S.D. 1992). *See generally* RESTATEMENT (SECOND) OF TORTS § 483. As to alcohol sales, see Chapter 18.

Notes 5 & 6. Reciprocity and risks to others. The contemporary view treats plaintiff and defendant negligence alike in many ways. *See* RESTATEMENT OF APPORTIONMENT § 3, cmt. *a.* But all contributory negligence is not alike; sometimes it creates no risk at all to anyone else. That is surely so in cases like *McNamara* and *Bexiga.* In the caretaker situation in *McNamara,* it is easy enough for most people to feel that the caretaker is under a duty to protect the ward from her own incapacity. From the other end of the telescope, the rule is that the beneficiary of care is not only not contributorily negligent in doing what the caretaker is hired to deal with, but not liable either. That's the *Creasy v. Rusk* case, **Note 1**. But *Bexiga* is not a caretaker case. In what cases should courts recognize a duty of the defendant to protect the plaintiff so that her own fault does not count against her?

The hypothetical cases in **Note 6** work through the permutations of two variables that might be relevant in answering that question. We'll be raising reciprocity again in less neutral examples when we come to the alleged contributory fault of a rape victim below. The first variable here relates to the question whether those dealing with the actor knew or should have known of the plaintiff's limited capacity. The other relates to the question whether the actor created a risk only to himself or whether he created a risk also to the defendant.

In matrix form:

Risk To		
	Self Only	Defendant

| Others' Knowledge | Others either know or should know actor's disability | Case 1

The mentally limited adult working for the farmer who knows the disability | Case 2

The 12-year-old driver, inflicting risks upon others, but whose age is known |
| | Others neither know nor should know actor's disability | Case 3

The mentally limited adult walking in the dark | Case 4

Speeders inflicting risks on each other, but seemingly unknown to each other |

Case 1. This is the most appealing case for allowing plaintiff to recover. The plaintiff, if judged by the prudent person standard, would have to lose this case unless we apply a *Bexiga* rule. And we should. The defendant knows of the plaintiff's special disability and the special need it entails. (An added factor makes this esspecially important. The defendant in this case has at least tacitly agreed to work with and guide the plaintiff; he is not a stranger whose problem is none of the defendant's concern. He is, in fact, in a caretaker role.) The other factor here also works in the plaintiff's favor—he has not created any risk of physical harm to others by sticking his hand in the grinder. (That is also the case in *Bexiga*, you might observe.) The facts of Case 1 are similar to those in *Lynch v. Rosenthal*, 396 S.W.2d 272 (Mo. Ct. App. 1965) where the court allowed the plaintiff to recover on the ground that he did not realize or appreciate the danger. Lynch's reasoning, however, requires you to depart from the normal standard of care for mentally limited persons. It seems much easier to maintain the normal standard but to apply *Bexiga*—the

defendant knew of the plaintiff's likely dangerous conduct and should have used reasonable care to protect against it?

The case could just as well have been put in terms of a child. The traditional analysis of such a case would first ask the age, and if the child were very young, say under 4 (7 in some states), there could be no contributory negligence at all. Older children would be judged by the standard of children of like age, intelligence and experience. But the *Bexiga* principle would equally take care of this situation. *See* Oscar S. Gray, *The Standard of Care for Children Revisited*, 45 MO. L. REV. 597, 602 (1980) (observing that there is an objective benchmark, but in the conduct of the adults not in other children).

It should be no surprise that the defendant who knows or should know of the plaintiff's disability or special danger is held liable without regard to the plaintiff's fault. This is the *Bexiga* element in many last clear chance cases.

Case 2. This changes one of the factors. Kincheloe was known to be a dangerous driver and a minor. Davis recognized this, yet he did not slow down. But Kincheloe is not so attractive a case for the plaintiff. Possibly there are several reasons for this, one of which might be that he is perhaps a conscious wrongdoer. That factor could be eliminated by imagining that all this took place on private land, where the statutes did not prohibit a child-driver. The more significant factors are different. (1) Kincheloe was creating risks not only to himself but to others. The case in which the minor or mentally disabled plaintiff creates risks to others as well as himself may test our willingness to apply a subjective standard of care. If someone is injured, liability may be preferable and that is certainly most consistent with an objective prudent person standard. If so, you might equally want to charge the plaintiff with contributory fault and bar the claim or reduce the damages. (2) Although not reflected in the two-factor matrix, you might think that before Davis is obliged to protect Kincheloe from Kincheloe's own fault, something more than mere knowledge would have to be shown. Davis knows he deals with a minor, but Davis is on a public road where he has a right to be; he has not asked to deal with a law-breaking, reckless child, nor has he tacitly agreed to do so. Nor is it a case of an emergency. This is not an appealing case to relieve Kincheloe from the consequences of his own fault.

Case 3. In walking on the wrong side of the road in dark clothes the plaintiff creates a risk to himself, but very little risk to others. The case is like Case 1 and *Bexiga* in that respect. (It is possible that a driver might cause a collision with others in an effort to avoid the plaintiff, but this is probably not one of the risks that makes us think the pedestrian is negligent in the first place.) Case 3 differs from Case 1 in that the defendant has no basis for knowing that he will have to deal with a person of diminished capacity. If defendant should win this case it may well be because of this factor. There is no need to see any duty of care beyond that required towards normal persons unless the defendant knows or should know of the diminished capacity, or should know that normal persons are likely to be negligent in the same way.

In *Dorais v. Paquin*, 304 A.2d 369 (N.H. 1972) the facts were similar, except that the plaintiff was an older minor. The court resolved the case by holding that an older child should be held to an adult standard. It seems simpler to say the plaintiff is subject to such an objective standard of care and to explain defendant's liability only when the defendant should have known of some need to provide protections against the plaintiff's contributory negligence. *Fox v. City and County of San Francisco*, 120 Cal. Rptr. 779 (Ct. App. 1975) is in line with this analysis.

Case 4. This illustrates the fourth position. The plaintiff is under an incapacity as a minor, but the defendant does not know it and the plaintiff's conduct creates a risk not only to himself but to others as well. This is the least attractive case for the plaintiff. Malone goes so far as to say that in cases of this kind "the decision as to who should bear the cost will unavoidably be arbitrary," and suggests that this kind of case may be the best for comparative negligence.

Recall the cases holding a minor to an adult standard when the minor is engaged in adult activity or inherently dangerous activity. Perhaps they have not captured the significant idea. If the child creates risks to others, he is not to be relieved under the *Bexiga* principle unless the others know or should know of his incapacity and fail to care for themselves. Correlatively, if he is not to escape the consequences of his own contributory fault, he should be subject to liability when he creates risks to others who cannot reasonably recognize his incapacity. If this is right, then the "adult activity" cases have not captured the principle.

Bexiga and the Negligent Child or Incompetent. The notes to the four case examples imply that the objective standard of care of the reasonable person should apply alike to older children and to mentally disabled adults, and that they should be relieved of responsibility for their fault, not by adopting a subjective standard of care, but by determining whether the defendant was negligent in the light of the disabilities of which the defendant should have known. Almost all our formulations of legal rules are subject to review and reformation. We almost never "get it right" the first time, even if what is "right" remains the same indefinitely.

Note 6. Policy factors. Are there policy factors that underlie court limitations on comparative fault defenses? This article in this note attempts to articulate those.

CHRISTENSEN V. ROYAL SCHOOL DIST. NO. 160, 124 P.3d 283 (Wash. 2005).

Can contributory fault be assessed against a 13-year-old victim of sexual abuse for her participation in the relationship with her teacher? This was the question asked by the *Christensen* court. The court's answer was that the girl had no duty to protect herself from sexual assault and thus a contributory negligence defense could not be maintained.

Why not? As the dissent rather pointedly argued, children of that age can be charged with all sorts of comparative fault?

The policy reasons against a comparative fault claim may be multiple. We might not expect children to know what to do when confronted with age-inappropriate situations. Given the differential in maturity and experience we might think that the defendant can best be charged with ensuring safety. We might also be concerned about process values. Litigating the case in terms of child fault might traumatize the victim. There is some evidence that victim blame contributes greatly to victim post traumatic stress disorder. If we can litigate cases without raising the issue of victim blame and simply focus on whether or not the school district should have taken further action, we might be able to avoid revictimizing victims in the tort context.

Note 1. Plaintiff "no duty." The plaintiff "no duty" language may be surprising to some seasoned teachers. This is new language from the Restatement of Apportionment. The concept is fairly simple though—just as there are reasons of principle or policy that might limit claims against defendants, so too might there be reasons of principle or policy for limiting plaintiff fault defenses.

Note 2. No duty to guard against sexual abuse. In a case like *Robinson v. Lindsey* we said that children engaged in dangerous or adult activities that risk others might be subject to an adult standard of care in order to ensure safety. These cases may be something of a corollary. When child safety is at risk, others may have a greater duty of care to ensure their protection.

Note 3. Failure to disclose sexual contact. If a child is held to the standard of a reasonable child of the same age, maturity and experience, this "no duty" case may simply be a "no negligence" case. Evidence suggests that children do not reveal sexual abuse, particularly to strangers like the school officials. So the lie that the dissent makes so much of may simply be what a reasonable child (or at least the typical child) would do.

Note 4. Effect of no-duty rules. Remember that the effect of a plaintiff no-duty rule is simply to convert the case back to an all-or-nothing proposition. The plaintiff may indeed recover nothing. In *Christensen* the plaintiff's attorney moved to have evidence of plaintiff fault excluded. In part this may reflect concern that the evidence would hurt plaintiff's case. A stipulation that the girl did not tell the school of the abuse might be more a more favorable posture for the plaintiff. In part the move to exclude may also be based on a concern about the harm that might be caused to the victim in a trial that focuses on blaming her for the abuse. In one case, the case of a young boy sexually assaulted by a priest, in a symposium panel the lawyer for the victim announced that he was glad the defendant had raised a child-fault defense because the lawyer thought the defense would help him turn the jury against the defendant and award punitive damages to the victim.

LEROY FIBRE CO. V. CHICAGO, M. & ST. P. RY., 232 U.S. 340 (1914)

When the defendant railroad created a risk of fire, the abutting landowner was not obliged to limit the use of his own land to minimize the risk of fire loss, so the claim of contributory negligence did not defeat the landowner's claim for fire loss.

LeRoy like *Christensen* reflects an entitlement rather than an individualized judgment about the plaintiff's fault. The Court thought the plaintiff entitled not only to assume reasonable care by the defendant but to take obvious risks with his own property in what is perhaps an unreasonable reliance on that assumption.

The alternative to such a holding seems very bad, indeed. The defendant who could defeat the plaintiff's claim because of the plaintiff's contributory negligence would get for free the right to continue its negligent firesetting.

Worse: fire spreads, so that if the defendant avoids all responsibility to the plaintiff it may be encouraged to continue its negligent(presumably cheaper) practices to the occasional detriment of others farther away whose property is burned when fire spreads. The plaintiff's contributory negligence might even have been deemed a superseding cause in such a case, in which case the flax owner might be liable to neighbors to whose property the fire spread while the firesetting railroad would not be. The risks to others as well as the plaintiff may be a reason to think this is not merely a case of an especially sensitive use by the plaintiff that would defeat a claim founded upon nuisance or abnormally dangerous types of strict liability.

Conversely, if nonliability in *LeRoy* did not encourage the railroad to continue its negligence, and it chose to behave reasonably for fear of liability for distant landowners, it would cost the railroad nothing more to behave reasonably for the benefit of near neighbors like the plaintiff. Either way, liability of the railroad for negligence seems like a good policy.

Note 1. Trying the shoe on the other foot. Note 1 turns the analysis above on its head by asking students to think about the *plaintiff's* responsibility to others. If a plaintiff used her land so that others' properties might be burned, that might be negligence. If her objectively described conduct is negligence, why is it not also contributory negligence? Is there really a difference? You can either discuss or avoid the question of reciprocity of risk and risks to others that we covered in the matrix above. The flax owner does not seem to threaten physical harm to the railroad by using his land as he does, so risks are not reciprocal. However, he may well be threatening *others*, because a foreseeable fire communicated to his land is all too likely to spread to others' property. In terms of the matrix used following *Bexiga*, this is neither the best nor the worst case for invoking contributory fault.

Although we favor the result in *LeRoy Fibre*, this note raises doubts about constructing anything like a rule of law or an entitlement. In some cases the plaintiff's conduct might be too extreme, the cost in his free use of his land too little, to warrant that. If he stored Napalm or dynamite next to the track, even if for some reason that created no risk to the trains, that might be going too far. Perhaps that kind of case should be resolved under nuisance rules, which might conceivably require the plaintiff to move his dynamite or Napalm storage facilities further from the railroad.

A plaintiff entitlement, like a defendant no-duty rule, must be capable of generalized advance statement. When we start looking at the facts of particular cases for reasonableness (flax vs. Napalm), we are not working with an entitlement but with adjudication of contributory negligence on the facts. Maybe the principle should be: judge contributory fault in the light of the plaintiff's rights, entitlements, and interests, but do not award broad entitlements that are free from the censorship of negligence analysis. The Powers article cited in **Note 2** is extremely helpful, but his metaphors point in a direction different from this suggestion; in his view, negligence law should take a back seat. To stay with an automotive metaphor, we think maybe negligence law should not be the driver but definitely should be the governor. But this is a difficult topic and one we hope scholars will develop.

Notes 3-4. Once we say plaintiffs have some entitlements—a plaintiff has no duty not to breathe air—we must define when a plaintiff has an enetitlement and when she does not. What about an entitlement to report crime to the police even if it's risky? Could there be an entitlement to wear expensive jewelry in a poor neighborhood? What about no duty for a woman to shape her conduct around fear of rape?

The reciprocity idea might be an appealing but quite incomplete principle for judging contributory fault or for granting entitlements. (See the matrix following *Bexiga* and the notes to *LeRoy Fibre* above). Surely it is harder to say that the plaintiff is chargeable with contributory fault when her fault risks no physical harm to anyone. That is the case with provocative clothing or demeanor, late night shopping, chatting with strange men in a bar, even with yelling obscenities and imprecations.

Lynch v. Scheininger, 744 A.2d 113 (N.J. 2000), poses an example of entitlement removed both from the property analysis in cases like *LeRoy* and the rape setting upon which Bublick focuses. A woman's right to have children is surely an appealing one. Must she forego the chance to have a child because the doctor's negligence makes it likely that the child will suffer abnormalities? We expect people to differ about this. The issue was not raised in *Lynch*, which discussed the possibility that the mother's knowledgeable choice was a superseding cause or that it was a failure to minimize damages resulting from the doctor's negligence.

In *Brandon v. County of Richardson*, 624 N.W.2d 604 (Neb. 2001), the trial judge concluded that the rape victim was chargeable with comparative negligence, but didn't say why. On appeal, the defense argued that Brandon's negligence was in failing to keep the sheriff aware of his whereabouts (but this did not affect the sheriff's plan for protection; he had no protection plan at all). The defense also argued that the victim was negligent in giving an inconsistent story, but in fact his story was consistent. The Nebraska court held that as a matter of law the victim was not chargeable with comparative fault in this case. The case thus did not actually decide the issue raised in the casebook note, but we suspect that few people would think that a plaintiff could be charged with fault for reporting rape, even though the report would put the victim at further risk.

Although plaintiff entitlements seem like they would generally be favorable to plaintiffs, the ultimate effects are more ambiguous. If a court had extended a plaintiff no-duty to *Wassell*, would the plaintiff in that case have recovered in full or recovered nothing at all?

Note 9. Entitlements vs. case-by-case adjudication of plaintiff fault. Here we pose the idea that courts could handle these cases by making an ordinary contributory negligence analysis case by case, a view reflecting the idea we suggested about *LeRoy Fibre*. Such an analysis would take into account the plaintiff's rights and interests. However, traditionally, the thought was that comparative fault defenses involved no duty. Accordingly, judges saw their role in limiting duties for defendants much more clearly than they saw their role in cases involving plaintiffs. Also, if you believe that a plaintiff should have a right to report crime for example, should that right necessarily rely on what a jury thinks is reasonable in a given case?

§ 5. TRADITIONAL EXCEPTIONS TO THE CONTRIBUTORY NEGLIGENCE BAR

A. The Rescue Doctrine

The risks entailed in a rescue attempt may be worthwhile under *Carroll Towing*, since rescue may save a life or minimize another's suffering. Even if the risk is unjustified, the hoped-for gains might count when it comes to assigning comparative responsibility. Notice that the rescuer-plaintiff is not inflicting risks upon others in most cases, although she did unintentionally put the defendant at risk in *Ouellette*. The Rhode Island Court in *Ouellette* was unwilling to use ordinary comparative fault rules, saying they did not fully protect the policy of promoting rescue. Can this be right? *Govich* takes the opposite view; comparative fault allocations would surely take rescue into account, but no rule of law covering all rescue cases prevents the trier from assigning fault to the plaintiff. Notice that this view still leaves it open to the judge to say that in the particular case, reasonable people cannot find fault in the rescuer.

Note. *Hutton v. Logan,* 566 S.E.2d 782 (N.C. Ct. App. 2002), on facts like those stated in the casebook, held that the rescue doctrine did not apply in an action against a third person. The court did not conceive of the rescue doctrine as an application of the risk-utility assessment, with rescue counting as a strong utility that warranted risk-taking. Had it held such a conception, the rescue would be highly relevant in any action, including one against a third person. The court saw the rescue doctrine as an independent rule barring the contributory negligence defense entirely unless the plaintiff's fault reached the level of recklessness. The rule was not tethered to negligence analysis, so the court was felt free to apply it only as between the original tortfeasor (unknown in this case) and the plaintiff, not between the plaintiff and a new tortfeasor who did not cause need for rescue. If you took the milder, *Govich* view, that the rescue doctrine is merely an instance of the risk-utility assessment, presumably that assessment would apply against third persons as well. Note that North Carolina is a state that still uses the complete defense of contributory negligence.

Collateral consequences of the untethered rescue doctrine. The core idea of rescue[1] here is that rescue status relieves plaintiffs of the effects of their own contributory negligence, or that rescue status is at least one of the circumstances that tends to show they were not at fault given the utility of rescue.

B. Last Clear Chance/Discovered Peril

The last clear chance doctrine has almost disappeared under the impact of comparative fault. It remains important in the few jurisdictions that apply the traditional complete bar of contributory negligence and its ghosts may haunt

---

1. Sometimes referred to as Good Samaritan doctrine. But so is the idea that a volunteer may be undertaking a duty of care. So is the immunity under Good Samaritan statutes covered in Chapter 13. So we stick to the "rescue" terminology here, but "rescue" must be construed broadly.

bar exam questions for some years. We think it is enough to clear students to the main model and move on.

However, the last two questions allow students to apply what they've learned about comparative fault and apportionment or to show that their knowledge is incomplete. On these: (1) There seems no support in the cases for applying last clear chance to assist a plaintiff whose negligence is equal to or greater than the defendant's and who is barred entirely under a modified comparative fault scheme. (2) If you covered Restatement § 8, students can probably suggest that last clear chance is still a factor relevant in assigning percentages of fault. Section 8 (b) specifically mentions the strength of the causal connection, presumably having in mind sequential torts where courts have tended (in intervening cause cases) to emphasize the fault of the last wrongdoer and often to relieve the first. Comment c specifically mentions "timing" of the conduct.

C. Defendant's Reckless or Intentional Misconduct

Under the pre-comparative fault rules, the plaintiff's fault was ignored when the defendant was guilty of heightened fault such as intent or reckless-ness. In that case, the plaintiff recovered 100% of her damages. With the adoption of comparative fault rules, you could (1) retain this old rule and al-low full recovery against a reckless defendant; (2) Treat reckless conduct as a species of negligence and apply comparative fault rules to that, but continue to allow a contributorily negligent plaintiff to recover full damages from an in-tentional tortfeasor. (3) Apply comparative fault rules even to intentional torts.

The issue here is whether the plaintiff's recovery will be reduced against an intentional tortfeasor because of the plaintiff's negligence. Chapter 25 con-siders the different question of how to apportion responsibility between intentional and negligent tortfeasors and revisits the plaintiff-defendant ap-portionment as well.

The only two points about intentional tortfeasor-defendants we would pur-sue with the class are (1) the difference between plaintiff-defendant apportionment on the one hand and defendant-defendant apportionment on the other (although both apportionments can hurt the plaintiff); and (2) the fact that not all intentional torts are alike, so that some might warrant com-parative fault apportionment while others do not.

The first point is made by the two hypothetical cases at the end of this subsection. Apportionment in either case will present problems, but it seems outrageous in the first. Apportionment in the first would mean that if the rap-ist in *Wassel* were found and the victim sued him, the plaintiff's recovery would be reduced because she negligently opened the door to a stranger.

The second point turns on the fact that some "intentional" torts look a great deal like negligent torts. For example, when the plaintiff makes a prima facie case of an intentional tort such as battery, the defendant may advance a privilege such as self-defense. When self-defense becomes the central issue, it is the reasonableness of the defense that determines liability. The reasonableness of self-defensive acts raises a question that looks much like negligence, so courts could apply a coherent system of comparative fault to such a case. The rape case is entirely different. It is very difficult to find a common denominator when defendant A commits a rape as a result of defendant B's failure to maintain adequate security.

The Restatement Third of Torts, Apportionment of Liability seems to favor a very broad application of comparative fault, so that, as between two defendants, the intentional tort of one would be compared with the negligence of the other. In a several liability jurisdiction, this makes the negligent tortfeasor responsible only for his comparative fault share, usually to the plaintiff's loss, as we will see in Chapter 25. On the other hand, the Restatement denies the intentional tortfeasor the benefit of comparative fault apportionment; he is jointly and severally liable, even in a several liability jurisdiction. RESTATEMENT OF APPORTIONMENT § 12. Doesn't the logic of that provision imply that the intentional tortfeasor could not reduce his liability to his intended victim by pointing to her negligence?

Two minor points. (1) Comparative fault statutes may by their terms compel comparison of recklessness or intent or both. Under the UNIFORM COMPARATIVE FAULT ACT, § (b), the fault to be compared includes any acts or omissions that are "in any measure negligent or reckless...." The Indiana statute defines the fault to be compared to include "any act or omission that is negligent, willful, wanton, reckless, or intentional toward the person or property of others." IND. CIV. CODE § 34-4-33-2(a)(1) (1996). (2) Particular states may work out variations or complications. In *Poole v. City of Rolling Meadows*, 656 N.E.2d 768 (Ill. 1995), the court explained Illinois' evolving conception this way: "a plaintiff's contributory negligence may be compared to a defendant's willful and wanton misconduct, if that willful and wanton misconduct was committed recklessly, rather than intentionally." But if the defendant's "willful and wanton misconduct was intentional," the plaintiff's comparative fault would not reduce damages.

D. Plaintiff's Illegal Activity

BARKER V. KALLASH, 468 N.E.2d 39 (N.Y. 1984)

This section points out the rule barring the plaintiff's action when it is based in whole or part on the plaintiff's criminal or immoral conduct. The scope of the rule, and its appropriate use after the adoption of comparative fault, remain in doubt. Should the rule be dropped altogether in favor of comparative fault damages reductions? Maybe some students would be more comfortable with that solution in modified comparative fault states. If the criminal-immoral plaintiff is barred entirely, students should remember that the negligent defendant will entirely escape liability. If a terrorist hires fifteen-year-olds to make pipe bombs and one of the teenagers is injured or killed in an explosion of a bomb she is making, is there really any reason to protect the terrorist's treasury from a tort suit?

You might want to take a look at the summary of *McCummings v. New York City Transit Auth.*, Casebook p. 291, ¶ 1 in the Note: Beyond the Sports Context. In that case a mugger recovered against the police officer who shot him while he was trying to escape.

Levels of case evaluation. *Barker* easily produces a reaction in many students that the outcome is right. The reaction may be so strong that students fail to examine the policy, principle, and application dangers. With that in mind, you can remind them of the levels of analysis or evaluation that are important and urge them not to mistake an outcome that might be right for the principle that might be doubtful:

Reacting to outcome of the particular case
Developing of policy-justice considerations and making policy-justice choices
Developing and evaluating a principle expressing the policy or justice choices
Wording the principle and its qualifications
Applying the principle

Flanagan v. Baker, 621 N.E.2d 1190 (Mass. App. Ct. 1993) was another case of boys making pipe bombs from powder obtained from firecrackers; but this is less sinister than it might sounds to innocent elders. They were exploding the "bombs" in the air or on the ground in the same way they might have exploded firecrackers themselves. The plaintiff was injured and sued his friend and co-bomb-maker and his friends parents. Recovery might be denied for other reasons, but the court refused to rule out recovery on the basis of *Barker*. First, to rule out liability on this ground would also rule out liability of the person who sold the boys the illegal firecrackers and that would be against public policy. Second, the statutory provisions violated here "can be fairly read as intending to protect the general public, which includes the violator, by preventing dangerous situations." Hence the court refused to apply *Barker's* all or nothing rule.

In *Alami v. Volkswagen of America, Inc.*, 766 N.E.2d 574 (N.Y. 2002), the intoxicated driver crashed his car. As a result of defective design, the car crumpled up and killed him. In a suit against the manufacturer for the driver's death, *held,* the rule in *Barker* does not bar recovery. This is not a case in which the plaintiff must assert that the manufacturer's duty arose out of the driver's intoxication; it was a duty owed to all. The New York court limited the *Barker* rules.

Note 2. If we retain the illegal-immoral activity rule that bars the plaintiff completely, what is its appropriate scope? You might not be surprised to learn that a court was far more concerned about the fraud in *Price* than it was bout the illegal riding in *Winschel*. What about violation of a criminal fornication statute? In *Doe v. Roe*, 841 F. Supp. 444 (D.D.C. 1994), Judge John Pratt roundly criticized a decision applying the illegal activity rule to that context, calling the prior case's logic "flawed" and saying that its holding, coupled with Virginia's failure to enforce its criminal fornication statute, "essentially immunizes from all possible liability those who consciously or unconsciously spread infectious and incurable disease." Note that Virginia makes contributory fault a complete bar, so proportional recovery was not a choice here.

Note 3. Commentary. Are we really going to let plaintiffs guilty of misconduct try their luck with a jury? A number of cases and statutes make this look unlikely. For example, a California statute immunizes landowners for injuries to persons committing a felony. *See* CAL. CIV. CODE § 847. In *Calvillo-Silva v. Home Grocery*, 968 P.2d 65 (Cal. 1998) this was construed to protect the landowner who actively inflicts harm so long as it is not wilful or wanton.

CHAPTER 10

ASSUMPTION OF THE RISK

▶**Changes in the Sixth Edition:** We have added one new primary case in this chapter (*Avila*, in § 2), and 19 new case citations in Notes. Nonetheless, we have reduced the length of this Chapter by about a quarter, by cutting the *Crews* and *Turcotte* cases (discussing both of them in long Notes), and the case abstracts of *Siragusa, Sunday, Bjork,* and *Gauvin.* The Chapter now has only two main sections rather than four, which should speed coverage. These cuts and simpler organization leave the chapter quite lean, but there remains plenty of room for analytical work with the class, especially in § 2.

▶The **Concise Edition** reflects no revisions in this Chapter.■

§ 1. CONTRACTUAL OR EXPRESS ASSUMPTION OF THE RISK

BOYLE V. REVICI , 961 F.2d 1060 (2d Cir. 1992)
TUNKL V. REGENTS OF UNIVERSITY OF CALIFORNIA, 383 P.2d 441 (Cal. 1963)

This section deals with what was traditionally called express assumed risk. The Restatement of Apportionment § 2 refers to it as a contractual limitation on liability, terminology that helps separate it from comparative fault.

You can contractually assume a risk unless in the particular case public policy voids such an agreement. The "contract" may be express or implied, so long as reasonable persons would really understand that the responsibility is shifted to the plaintiff. "Contract" is the Restatement's word. But we've known since *Stinnett v. Buchele* that the defendant's own reasonable expectation that the plaintiff will avoid harm by caring for himself is enough to allow us to say that the defendant is not negligent. So the emphasis should be on genuine understandings of the parties rather than formal contract elements. The most important point is that contractually shifted responsibility or assumed risk is a complete bar (because the contract, express or implied, says so). It is definitely *not* a matter of judging fault.

Boyle: A patient consented to unorthodox cancer treatment; it did not work and she died. The defendant was negligent by normal medical standards, but her express assumption of the risk barred recovery completely. The case furnishes an occasion at the outset to make the points that (1) assumed risk was traditionally a complete bar, as was contributory negligence; and (2) if an express assumed risk is valid, it still is. It ties back to consent materials in Chapter 4.

The quotation from the Restatement of Apportionment § 2, cmt. *b,* in the short note following *Boyle,* serves mainly to emphasize the contractual nature of assumed risk, an idea that some students have difficulty with when we reach the "implied assumed risk version." The note also makes it clear that there is no occasion to reduce damages if the "contract" bars the claim.

Although the result in *Boyle v. Revici* sounds rational and supports the right of patients to make a choice, Revici himself was in fact a problem that New York should have dealt with long before. An unsympathetic view of Revici, his history and his "work," is presented in a popular book by a writer who is also one of the authors of a treatise on medical malpractice in HARVEY F. WACHSMAN, LETHAL MEDICINE 78 ff (1993).

Tunkl: A consent form, signed in advance, purported to absolve the hospital from liability for negligence in medical treatment. *Held,* this release is not valid. Although one may voluntarily assume a risk the law places on another person, when one is compelled to assume a risk to obtain essential medical treatment, the assumption is not voluntary and the release is not valid.

In *Tunkl,* the consent is informed but not valid, because it was in effect extorted. The court emphasizes interdependence. Although not spelled out in this summary, the *Tunkl* court emphasized several factors: (1) the business is of a type generally thought suitable for public regulation; (2) the defendant's service is of "great importance to the public," and perhaps a practical necessity; (3) the defendant is holding himself out as performing the service generally for the public; (4) the need for the service and the economic setting give the defendant "decisive advantage of bargaining strength." The Restatement (Third): Apportionment of Liability § 2, cmt. *e,* summarizes broad principles that guide judicial decisions in determining whether an advance release is enforceable.

In *Eelbode v. Chec Med. Cntrs, Inc.,* 984 P.2d 436 (Wash. App. Ct. 1999), Norbert Eelbode was required to undergo a pre-employment physical exam. He signed a document that provided in part: "To the fullest extent permitted by law, I hereby release Chec and the Washington Readicare Medical Group and its physicians from all liability arising from any injury to me resulting from my participation in the exam . . . ." Chec allegedly required the plaintiff to perform a medically improper back stress test that injured his back. *Held,* the release is ineffective because it violates public policy.

Note 1. Do students recognize that the answer turns on whether *Tunkl* and *Boyle* are distinguishable? They are, aren't they, and students are usually able to describe some distinctions. Notice that although contractual assumed risk is a bar in *Revici* and not in *Tunkl,* the cases are consistent in that both support the patient's right of choice. In *Tunkl,* if hospitals could avoid liability simply by refusing necessary services to those who would not give up their rights, they undoubtedly would do so and *Tunkl* would have to do without medical care or take it at the price of subjecting himself of hospital negligence. But *Boyle* had a choice of *Revici's* approach to cancer and the standard medical approach. New York treats her choice as valid and California insists that *Tunkl* must be given a choice. More succinctly, you could say that California's *Tunkl* decision does not impose liability on "health care" practitioners merely because they hold themselves out as practicing an unorthodox form of treatment. So a little analysis shows that the two care are not contrary. Authority might suggest the same thing. *Ash,* cited here, holds in accord with *Tunkl,* discussing *Tunkl* and a number of other cases.

Note 2. A chance to consider potential application of public policy. *Gavin v. YMCA of Metropolitan Los Angeles,* cited here, held that the release was void under *Tunkl.* The court emphasized the difficulty of parents in getting child care, the imperative need for it among families with two working parents, and the short supply. The real need for the service plus the restricted availability of service, would mean that parents would be likely to have little choice. Perhaps the thinking is that if the supply far exceeded demand, the parents would have more bargaining power and more choice and probably would be able to reject demands for releases if they thought about it. (We might be doubtful about this release even in the oversupply case, first because people are not likely to think of and bargain about release terms and second because locality is so important in child care for working parents— child care still won't be competitive unless there is competition in the same neighborhood offering full responsibility child care. The question whether two pre-schoolers playing "penis in the mouth" is harmful or lawsuit-worthy is of course irrelevant, as the *Gavin* court noted. That question goes to issues of duty and breach, not the validity of the contract.

MOORE V. HARTLEY MOTORS, 36 P.2d 628 (Alaska 2001)

The plaintiff signed a release-in-advance exculpating the teacher of an ATV safety course, then was injured in the safety course when her ATV hit a hidden rock. The defendants pleaded the release and the court upheld it against the plaintiff's argument that it was against public policy and void. The safety course was not an essential service. The plaintiff could have chosen not to take it on the conditions offered, that is, subject to the release. From that, the court concludes that the defendant had no decisive advantage in bargaining. All told, that left the release standing.

The scope of the release is another matter. Although some language has the plaintiff agreeing to release the defendant from liability for injury, it mentioned to unavoidable and inherent risks, so the court thinks the document released the defendants only from inherent risks and "ordinary negligence associated with those inherent risks." There was an implied "presumption" that the training course was not itself unreasonably dangerous. A dangerous course layout with hidden rocks may be represent a risk that is not necessary or inherent in a training course (even if hidden rocks are an inherent danger in some other ATV use). Consequently, summary judgment was error.

There is a puzzling passage in which the court may seems to say that the plaintiff also assumed risk, not only of inherent or unavoidable risks, but also some kinds of "ordinary" negligence "associated" with inherent risks. We're not sure why the court said that or what it had in mind.

Note 1. *Moore's* construction of the release. One of Moore's points, once the basic enforceability of these releases is taken as a given, is that the court must determine whether the scope of the release covers what happened. At one level, it is a matter of construing the release language. But we liked having the case here because it begins to introduce the idea that becomes critical in the implied assumed risk cases– the idea that you really only assumed inherent risks. That turns out to mean, as the *Moore* court said, necessary risks. Necessary or inherent risks are those that cannot be reasonably avoided. That comes down to saying you never impliedly assume the risk of negligence, which by definition entails an unnecessary and unreasonable risk, not an inherent risk at all. That is a hard idea for many students to grasp, so *Moore's* introduction of the idea in a much more limited context may be a useful wedge. There is no need to get into implied assumed risk in discussing *Moore's* construction of the release, but if you cover *Moore's* reasoning about the scope of the release, that should give students a conceptual background that will prove useful very soon.

Note 2. *Moore* represents one more entry on the question of public policy limitations on contractually assumed risk, suggesting, perhaps, that contractual assumed risk clauses are valid with all non-essential services.

If you take that view, you will need to develop a rather precise concept of what services count as essential. In these Notes, we see cases in which students might be excluded for school-related sports activity if they or their parents don't give up the right to ordinary care. Sports are not essential in the way that, say, a cancer operation is, but they are important, sometimes terribly important to students. In addition, you might say that a demand for a release that allows a public school to be negligent is repugnant to ideas about the way government treats citizens and to ideals of equality, as well.

Hojnowski, cited here, is another recent decision holding that a parent cannot release a child's potential cause of action in advance. Accord, *Cooper v. Aspen Skiing Co.,*48 P.3d 1229 (Colo. 2002); *Hawkins v. Peart,* 37 P.3d 1062

(Utah 2001); *Scott v. Pacific West Mountain Resort*, 834 P.2d 6 (Wash. 1992). Contra, *Sharon v. City of Newton*, 769 N.E.2d 738 (Mass. 2002) (reasoning that allowing such releases encourage athletics); *Zivich v. Mentor Soccer Club, Inc.*, 696 N.E.2d 201 (Ohio 1998) (same).

Note 3. Does it offend public policy for a release to purport to bar claims where the defendant's act is reckless or worse? As this Note points out, many courts have so held. In *City of Santa Barbara v. Superior Court*, cited here, the California Supreme Court faced a case in which parents of a 14-year old developmentally disabled child sued the city after the child drowned while participating in a city recreational program. The city defended on grounds that a release signed by the mother barred the claim. The court held the release invalid to the extent that it purported to waive liability for "gross negligence," which the court defined as "a want of even scant care or an extreme departure from the ordinary standard of conduct." The court said its conclusion rested on a different ground from the "public interest" focus in *Tunkl*, although its conclusion was fully consonant with that opinion. In this situation, the court said, the focus is on "the degree or extent of the misconduct at issue, in order to discourage (or at least not to facilitate) aggravated wrongs." The court found no public policy arguments that would favor enforcing a "gross negligence" waiver. In *Moore*, cited at the end of this Note, the court held that the contract was valid. The court noted that it had in previous cases recognized that waivers are invalid "to the extent that they limited a party's liability for gross negligence, recklessness and intentional torts," and that in this case the plaintiff alleged reckless conduct by the defendant. But the plaintiff failed to produce evidence of recklessness or gross misconduct by the defendant in opposition to the defendant's summary judgment motion, meaning that the broad waiver did not run afoul at all of the "gross misconduct" rule.

Note 4. The court in *Hanks*, cited here, invalidated an exculpatory agreement on public policy grounds that purported to release ski resort operators from liability for negligently-caused injury. The court said that a waiver covering only "inherent risks" would be enforceable, but not "risks over which operators would have control." Such exculpatory provisions, said the court "undermine the policy considerations governing our tort system," namely, the deterrence of wrongful conduct. The court discussed *Tunkl* at length, and also stressed the expectations of patrons that the defendants would operate the ski resort in a "reasonably safe" manner. *Reardon*, from the same court, reached the same result, relying on *Hanks*. The release in *Reardon* was signed by the plaintiff, indemnifying the defendants, who ran a horse-riding facility, from any action brought in negligence. Plaintiff was injured while taking a horse riding class, and sued for negligence. The court found the release unambiguous (as had the court in *Hanks*) but nonetheless unenforceable. As in Hanks, the court said, defendant's facility was open to the public and available to patrons of all skill levels, invoking the "societal expectation that family oriented activities will be reasonably safe." Further, there is an "illogic in relieving the party with greater expertise and information concerning the dangers associated with the activity from the burden of proper maintenance." The court also characterized the release as a "classic contract of adhesion," not something that the plaintiff could bargain about.

Note 5. This note can be used to generate discussion. The cases upholding the athletic releases rely heavily on the supposed "policy" of encouraging athletics by relieving athletic sponsors of liability, or at least by allowing them to do so. Athletics are good (in some ways, at least), but why should courts take on the job of subsidizing them by permitting sponsors to be negligent without accountability? Would courts treat other "good" activities the same way? Consider whether courts would say, "we want to encourage economic activity, so retailers, hospitals, carriers, and other businesses can exact releases as a condition of providing services." You might think that businesses might have more incentive avoid injuring customers for economic reasons. If school districts and other non-profits are relieved of liability, do they have adequate incentive for safety? The Massachusetts Court in *Sharon* said, maybe somewhat oddly, that schools districts are "accountable," even while it was holding that they are not accountable in money for the harms they do. Presumably, the court meant that voters could eventually exert political pressure. But that is hardly like the opportunity customers have to switch to different suppliers, who may even be able to provide goods more cheaply because they are safer and have less liability costs attached to them. Another question is whether liability for negligence really would discourage athletic programs. If the harm they do in broken necks outweighs their value, they *should* be discouraged, at least according to basic ideas of negligence law. If the harm they do does NOT outweigh their value, the programs can continue to be pursued for the value they have; they would only pay their way– or be run more with reasonable safety. On another note, if you wanted to encourage athletics wouldn't you recognize that it is important, and especially to high school students, and in that sense, for them, "essential"? Finally, is there something economically discriminatory about these releases? Imagine that your teenaged daughter wants desperately to be accepted, has a talent for jumping up and down and screaming and is invited to be on the cheerleading squad. You are presented with the release as a condition for her acceptance. But you don't work for a large, responsible corporation or a university; you work for the gas station at the corner and there is no health insurance. Daughters and sons of well-insured parents might only worry about life-threatening injuries; but you, as an uninsured, might have to worry about a simple broken wrist. Maybe you should say "no." Isn't that discriminatory? Does it encourage athletic activity? We wonder what your students think of those questions.

§ 2. IMPLIED ASSUMPTION OF THE RISK

Assumption of the risk is a term that seems to mean either contractual agreement to shift responsibility to the plaintiff, or contributory fault of the plaintiff, or, for policy or mixed reasons, no duty on the part of the defendant.

DAN B. DOBBS, THE LAW OF TORTS § 214

Actions (or maybe customary expectations) often implicitly convey informal agreements, so an implied assumed risk might be as "contractual" as those seen in the § 1. But courts were off-base in assuming that every confrontation of a risk conveyed an implicit contract to accept the risk. A confrontation of a known risk might instead often look like ordinary contributory negligence and subject to the comparative fault rules.

BETTS V. CRAWFORD, 965 P.2d 680 (Wyo. 1998).

The point made in the Dobbs quotation is acted out in *Betts*. The household employee might have been negligent in tripping on items someone left on the stairs, but she had not conveyed any consent to accept all negligently created risks merely by work in the household. The court's use of comparative fault instead is in line with many broad statements about the scope comparative fault in statutes or otherwise.

Note 1. Traditional rules of assumed risk, barred the plaintiff who was not contributorily negligent and who had not consented to shoulder responsibility for the defendant's negligence, even when there was no reason in policy to relieve the defendant of a duty to use reasonable care. That result was obtained because courts often treated voluntary confrontation of a known risk as if it were equivalent to an agreement to accept responsibility for another's negligence. Few states follow this approach now, but it is not entirely dead, as these citations demonstrate. *Crews v. Hollenbach*, cited here, was a primary case in the prior edition of this book. In that case the court barred a gas company foreman from recovery against people who struck a gas line and caused a leak that was later ignited by a spark. The court rested its no-recovery result on the idea that plaintiff freely consented to such conduct, as shown by intentional and voluntary exposure to a known danger, one he "appreciated." The equation of consent with intentional exposure to known danger is the trick to the traditional forms of this defense. If that were true, Prosser's jaywalker (in the Dobbs quote) would be assuming the risk.

How can you be barred every time you confront a known danger? Prosser's jaywalker shows quickly why this won't work. There are risks in everything, not only in jaywalking but in crossing with the light. But courts have not yet barred all tort suits whatever. So it cannot be right to say that, even in the absence of fault on the plaintiff's part, voluntary confrontation with a known danger always bars her claim

As sensible as Prosser was on this point, many courts have in fact equated known voluntary exposure with consent. The *Crews* court did not require the plaintiff's actual consent (contract). Nor did the court focus upon the objective manifestation of consent to the defendant. We don't even know if the defendants ever saw the plaintiff. The defendant's negligent act occurred in fact before the plaintiff arrived at the scene, and it is hard to imagine that the defendants acted in reliance upon a contingent consent or an assumption that, if they put gas company workers in danger, they would assume the risk. The claim that the injured victim assumed the risk by anything approaching consent seems palpably untrue.

Courts applying the traditional rule sometimes say that the plaintiff is barred only if he both voluntarily and *unreasonably* assumed a known risk. *Carrel v. Allied Prods. Corp.*, 677 N.E.2d 795 (Ohio 1997). That formulation can convert the consent idea into a species of contributory fault, as to which the comparative fault reduction in damages would logically follow, as in *Betts*. (Notice that Maryland, the state that decided both *Walker* and *Crews*, cited in this Note, still follows the traditional complete-bar *Butterfield* rule of contributory negligence.)

Note 2 underscores the fact that *Betts* expresses a modern view, and that the traditional approach laid out in Note 1 is not so common any more. The apparent simplicity of this idea, however, gets cloudy in coming materials.

Note 3. Important qualifications of the rule. Our reference in connection with the Restatement's first qualification is to *Stinnett v. Buchele*, Chapter 6. If students remember the point, even vaguely, a Torts Medal to them! If not, it is a reminder that we build on things covered earlier. The difference between plaintiff fault and defendant's non-fault is easy to state in the abstract, but evidently hard to recognize in many situations, so some re-emphasis of the *Stinnett* holding in discussing this qualification may be in order. The other point is that, as we've seen, a contract in which the plaintiff agrees to fully relieve the defendant is usually perfectly acceptable and enforcement. In a way the two points, if not the same, are intimately related, since the defendant's reliance on the plaintiff's knowledge and ability to protect herself works much like a contract.

■*Connection:* The firefighter's assumed risk. The firefighter's rule, Chapter 12, § 3, is sometimes justified on assumed risk grounds. If you want to import the firefighter's rule materials into assumed risk coverage, this is a great place for it. The disadvantage is that the rule arose in premises liability cases and took its early shape from that. The material on invitee-licensee categories may be confusing here in a way that it is not in Chapter 12 where premises material is covered.■

AVILA V. CITRUS COMMUNITY COLLEGE DISTRICT, 131 P.3d 383 (Cal. 2006).

A college baseball player was struck in the head by an intentionally thrown "beanball" thrown in retaliation by the opposing pitcher, and sued the community college district for negligence. The district (on behalf of the host school as well) claimed it owed no duty of reasonable care to the plaintiff. The court said: "When the injury is to a porting participant, the considerations of policy and the question of duty necessary become intertwined with the question of assumption of risk." Then we're off to the races, as it were.

The court reviews California's case law on implied assumption of the risk, starting with *Knight v. Jewett* and its classification of assumption of risk as either "primary" or "secondary," as defined in the case. While *Knight* was a plurality opinion, the majority of the California court has now embraced its rubric, as have many other states. This case deals with primary, not secondary, assumption of the risk. The key in primary assumption, says the court, is the evaluation of "the fundamental nature of the sport and the defendant's role in or relationship to that sport" to determine whether a duty of reasonable care is owed. The court concludes that the core duty is "not to increase the risks inherent in the sport." It then looks at the facts and plaintiff's allegations to assess whether defendant's actions increased those inherent risks. Its conclusion: no.

The court also rejects the plaintiff's argument that not preventing the opposing player from throwing a "beanball" increased the inherent risks of baseball. Rather, looking at testimony and documents, the court concludes that "being intentionally thrown at is a fundamental part and inherent risk of the sport of baseball." Thus a player impliedly assumes the risk of such conduct, in a "primary" way.

Note 1. Inherent risks. In *Bjork*, cited here, the court thought the sports participant assumed not only the risks inherent in the sport but also some risks created by the other participants' active negligence. But the plaintiff did not assume the risk of defective equipment like the frayed ropes. Compare *Hacking v. Town of Belmont*, 736 A.2d 1229 (N.H. 1999): The plaintiff, a child playing school basketball, was injured after coaches and referees allegedly let the game get out of hand. The court said: "While one participating in a sport might 'consent to those commonly appreciated risks which are inherent in and arise out of the nature of the sport generally and flow from such participation,' one does not ordinarily assume an 'unreasonably increased or concealed" risk.'" The plaintiff did not as a matter of law assume the risk. The plaintiffs have alleged in this case that the referees lost control of the game. . . .[W]e cannot say as a matter of law that this was an ordinary risk inherent within the game of basketball that Chelsea or her parents would have known and appreciated."

Note that the California courts have also not limited the "inherent risks" test to co-participants. In *Kahn v. East Side Union High Sch. Dist.*, 75 P.3d 30 (Cal. 2003), a high school athlete sued her swim coach and the school district for negligence after breaking her neck while practicing a racing dive. She alleged that the coach failed to give her any instruction on how to accomplish a shallow-water dive. The defendants argued that the plaintiff assumed the risk of injury, but the court disagreed. It held: "A sports instructor may be found to have breached a duty of care to a student or athlete only if the instructor intentionally injures the student or engages in conduct that is reckless in the sense that it is 'totally outside the range of the ordinary activity' involved in teaching or coaching the sport." Whether the coach's conduct was reckless was a contested fact issue.

Note 2. Duty. In *Sunday*, discussed here, we can see that the "primary" assumption of risk defense must be rejected where the defendant owes the plaintiff a duty of reasonable care that is applicable to the case.

The *Sunday* court recognizes at least two meanings of assumed risk. "In the primary sense," the risk is assumed when there is no breach of duty by the defendant. In a secondary sense, it is merely a form of contributory fault.

In the primary sense, the court says, you assume risks of dangers inherent in the sport. Risks inherent are those that are unavoidable by the defendant's reasonable care. In this sense, then, your assumed risk is only a way of talking about the fact that the defendant is not negligent. That is, if the defendant is negligent, that is not an inherent risk of the sport and not one you assume. If the defendant is negligent, in say, marking the advanced trail as a novice trail, you have not assumed that risk and the defendant is subject to liability.

The court in *Sunday* at one point uses "no duty" language, but later changes this to speak of "no negligence," and "no breach." Some writers have used the term "duty" in a very narrow sense, as you might use it if you said "no duty to stop and get out of your car at the railroad track." In a sentence like that one, "no duty" seems to mean that there is a duty of reasonable care, but that it is not breached merely because you don't get out of your car and look up and down the railroad track before crossing. The casebook does not use "duty" or "no duty" in such a way. It uses the duty term to refer to some standard capable of general statement, such as the usual duty of ordinary care. It uses "negligence" to refer to specific acts which may be regarded as a breach of that duty. *Sunday* apparently used "no duty" in the sense of "no negligence." Unfortunately it confused the issue by saying that there was no breach of duty because there was no duty to begin with; but it later seems to make it clear that the discussion is addressed to the negligence issue. In any event it seems clear that as terminology is used in the casebook, there is a duty of reasonable care.

Skier-students sometimes argue that a hidden bush does not show negligence. The court thought otherwise when the bush was hidden on the novice slope. Be that as it may, however, we need to accept the possibility of negligence here to get to the point about assumed risk. Given negligence on the part of the slope operator, the plaintiff did not assume the risk in the "primary" sense. Nor did he assume the risk in the sense that he consented to the negligent act or to the risks it imposed. He was not guilty of contributory negligence. And it is not a case of non-negligence.

Note 3. Rule violations in sports. *Turcotte*, discussed here, was a primary case in the prior editions of the Casebook. The court expressly recognizes that assumption of the risk, under the comparative negligence statute, "is no longer an absolute defense." At the same time, the "risks assumed by the plaintiff" become important in measuring the defendant's duty (or the standard of care, if that makes more sense to the class). The scope of the defendant's duty to exercise care is only to provide care as to risks not voluntarily assumed. Here risks of contending jockeys weaving in front of the plaintiff were normal risks of the race, even if the defendant actually violated racing rules when he caused the accident. The plaintiff actually if implicitly consented to relieve the defendant of the obligation of care with respect to these risks. That is done by electing to participate in the sport, presumably with knowledge that these were "normal" risks. (Compare "inherent risks of the sport" in *Sunday v. Stratton*). So the defendant escapes liability altogether, even if he is violating a rule of the race.

Notice that the plaintiff's "reasonable expectations" govern, so that interpretation of facts, not interpretation of legal rules, is required. Is the judge persuaded by the facts that the plaintiff consented to relieve the defendant of his ordinary duty of reasonable care? If not, then the issue is simply one of contributory fault to be handled under the comparative negligence regime.

Note 4 tests whether the students get the difference between implied assumption of risk as a rule about contributory negligence (the "secondary" form in states that sill use the name assumption of the risk), and as a rule about no negligence (the "primary" form). The cases say that the "primary" form (or simply the "no duty/no breach" conception, even if it is not called a defense at all), which of course acts as a complete bar to recovery, is not at all inconsistent with comparative negligence. For comparative negligence to apply at all, the defendant must be negligent. And the defendant is not negligent if the defendant does not breach (or owe) a duty of reasonable care.

Note 5. The recklessness approach. *Gauvin*, cited here, is one of a line of cases rejecting a negligence standard for sports participants, and instead adopting a rule that one participant in a sports event may sue another only by proving conduct that is reckless or worse. This approach essentially eliminates the implied assumption of risk issue, focusing the issue on whether the defendant behaved recklessly or worse (such as by committing an intentional tort). *Turcotte* (Note 3) theorized actual if implied consent that eliminates the co-participant's duty of care, so that he is liable only for reckless or intentional harms. *Gauvin* drops the consent language and directly limits the sports participant's duty, as a matter of judicial policy. What policy? To encourage vigorous and active sports participation!

Whether there is good reason to single out sports cases by immunizing negligent behavior seems doubtful, but you might think that ordinary negligence will be hard to adjudicate, given the competitive setting of contact sports. If that is your only concern, you might bear in mind that the negligence standard takes account of circumstances, including the heat of competitive struggle. *Lestina v. West Bend Mutual Ins. Co.,* 501 N.W.2d 28 (Wis. 1993) seems to have had something like this in mind when it adhered to the negligence standard. Likewise you would not immunize negligence in games like golf, but courts in fact have applied the reduced duty in a number of non-contact sports, as noted in **Note 6**. What does your class predict about hunters? Will no hunter ever be held to the standard of reasonable care?

Note 6. Non-contact sports. *Shin,* cited here, discusses the California cases, including *Avila,* at length, and concludes that its assumption of risk approach applies to any activity or sport where "risk is inherent." This is thus not limited to "contact" sports.

Note 7. Expectations of the parties. The *Jagger* court, cited here, focused on reasonable expectations of participants, concluding that skiers owe each other a duty of reasonable care undiminished by any supposed assumed risk.

But some courts seem willing to limit the duty of reasonable care under the circumstances in some rather ordinary activities. In *Pfister v. Shusta,* 657 N.E.2d 1013 (Ill. 1995) the court did so as between participants kicking a crushed can in dormitory lobby. "[S]ome courts have extended the limited duty rule to games like golf and tennis, in which players might expect slightly more civilized behavior, and to playful but noncompetitive activities, in which the enthusiasm of competition does not seem to make negligent or violent behavior the norm."

If it is right to dump the duty of reasonable care in sports cases, including kick-the-can in dormitories, will courts do the same for all activities in which both the plaintiff and defendant participate? A bridge player gets angry and throws his cards at his partner, hitting her in the eye and causing loss of vision. Or one sexual partner negligently fails to adopt appropriate protective measures. Or a hunter is shot by a fellow hunter. Is there no duty of care to fellow hunters because of the well-known propensity of hunters to shoot at anyone wearing a bright orange coat in the woods? Or the plaintiff is injured in a highly active religious exercise. In The Shepard's Fold Church of God it has long been the habit for worshipers to run or "trot" down the aisle "under the Spirit of the Lord." It is also the habit of other worshipers to kneel in the aisle and pray. Would trotters be under the same limited duty to kneelers as hockey players owe to each other? In *Bass v. Aetna Insurance Co.,* 370 So.2d

511 (La. 1979), the defendant tried to argue an "act of God" defense, which of course was absurd. The court did not limit the reasonable-care duty of trotters. In fact, it held that the kneelers did not assume any risk from trotters, since no one had been previously hurt for 25 years. If *Turcotte* and *Gauvin* are right, why wouldn't they be right for all cases in which plaintiff and defendant are co-participants in an activity with known risks?

The sport of wild turkey hunting. Hunting wild turkeys requires the hunter to emulate the female turkey, calling softly to the male, which is then expected to approach with such steady intent that the hunter can shoot him. What risks does such a hunter assume? *Hendricks v. Broderick,* 284 N.W.2d 209 (Iowa 1979). It turns out that the risk of being run down by the aroused male turkey was not in issue. And the court thought the hunter did not assume the risk of negligence by other hunters. Although the court uses the assumed risk terminology, its use is dependent upon a finding that the defendant was negligent.

Note 8. Protective legislation. Distinguish recreational use statutes restricting the duties of landowner who permit but do not charge for use of their lands for recreational use. These are covered in Chapter 12.

After the decision in *Sunday v. Stratton,* supra, the ski industry prevailed upon legislatures to enact somewhat protective statutes in a number of states. This response is reported in *Brett v. Great American Recreation, Inc.,* 677 A.2d 705 (N.J. 1996). Vermont, where *Sunday* was decided, enacted such a statute in VT. STAT. ANN. tit. 12 § 1037. As *Brett* notes, the statutes are somewhat favorable to operators, but for the most part provide results similar to common law result. Some of the ski statutes, however, are much more extreme. A particular statute may impose upon the skier risks that the individual may not have assumed. E.g., UTAH CODE ANN. § 78-27-51 et seq. (forcing an assumed risk of hidden dangers). *Rantapaa v. Black Hills Chair Lift Co.,* 633 N.W.2d 196 (S.D. 2001) held an ordinance like this invalid because it imposed risks not assumed under the law of assumed risk. But *Rayeski v. Gunstock Area/Gunstock Area Com'n,* 776 A.2d 1265 (N.H. 2001), dealing with a similar statute, held that the plaintiff who struck a not-so-visible unpadded light pole in late afternoon skiing was barred because the light pole was an inherent risk of skiing. And ski statues may make specific provisions limiting the duty of operators. See the New Mexico statute quoted in this note and *Philippi v. Sipapu, Inc.,* 961 F.2d 1492 (10th Cir. 1992). Other provisions protect sports entrepreneurs in everything from Little League Baseball to equine activities.

Note 9. Spectators at sporting events. The tendency in spectator cases is to treat assumed risk as meaning a limited duty, but it is a duty to provide reasonable safety, including (for example) screening in the most dangerous

areas, so that the spectator will have a safety choice to make. *See, e.g., Lawson v. Salt Lake Trappers, Inc.,* 901 P.2d 1013 (Utah 1995).
In *Akins v. Glen Falls City Sch. Dist.,* 424 N.E.2d 531 (N.Y. 1981), the plaintiff attended a baseball game and sat outside the area protected by a backstop. He was struck in the eye by a sharp foul ball and the jury returned a verdict for the plaintiff with a reduction for contributory negligence. Holding this was really a case of no negligence, the court decided that the plaintiff could not recover at all.

NOTE: BEYOND THE SPORTS CONTEXT

While many implied assumption of risk cases arise in the sports context, the principles are not limited to that setting. This Note makes this important point for students who might be misled by the preceding sports-oriented coverage.

¶1. *Testing the limits: Assumption of risk by criminals.* Muggers assuming a risk? In *McCummings v. New York City Transit Auth.,* cited here, the plaintiff seems to have committed a violent crime ("mugging") and then fled. A Transit Authority guard, who saw the victim and perhaps some of the mugging, shot the plaintiff twice in the back as he was fleeing, severing his spinal cord and paralyzing him from the chest down. In the robber's suit against the Transit Authority based on a negligence theory, a jury found for the plaintiff. *Held,* affirmed. "To be sure, plaintiff committed a crime but it is the province of the criminal, not the civil, justice system to punish him for his wrong. He has been convicted and will be dealt with as the law requires." Dissenters thought that the officer was privileged to use deadly force to prevent the escape of a felon who had committed a violent crime. But *Tennessee v. Garner,* 471 U. S. 1 (1985), seems more in line with the majority. There a statute was held to be unconstitutional under the Fourth Amendment because it allowed officers to use deadly force to prevent escape of a felon where there was no serious threat of bodily injury or death to others. Be that as it may, shouldn't the *McCummings* majority have explained how to square its ruling with the ruling in *Barker v. Kallash?* And even with *Turcotte v. Fell?*

¶2. *Thinking about alternative locutions. Washington Metro. Area Transit Auth. v. Cross,* cited here, quotes the jury instruction but does not deal with it. We hope students will say the judge could have simply instructed on negligence or could have said that needed stops and starts do not constitute negligence. The hypothesized stops and starts show that the case the judge is instructed on is not that of a negligent defendant who escapes liability because of the plaintiff's assumption of the risk. It is a case of a defendant who is not negligent. Assumed risk as an affirmative defense should arise only when there is a jury case for negligence, but the trial court was jumping ahead to deal with assumed risk by describing conduct that was not negligent in the first place. No wonder students are confused.

The defendant could still argue to the jury that under the definition of negligence, the defendant was not negligent in starting or stopping in the ordinary way.

¶3. *Recategorizing the old "assumed risk" defense.* This can be used to stimulate more discussion, or students can work with it on their own. The plaintiff probably is not chargeable with contributory fault, given the utility of immediate medical attention. Did the plaintiff consent to accept the risks so that this is a kind of contractual shift of responsibility? That makes sense. The plaintiff was not merely voluntarily exposing herself; she was communicating her consent to accept the risks as part of a deal between plaintiff and defendant. The plaintiff would be barred entirely; she would not merely suffer a comparative fault reduction in damages.

You could also say that the defendant was not negligent, but the reasons for such a conclusion do not clearly lie in assumed risk. It would be negligent to turn over a dangerous car without a warning and perhaps negligent to do so even with a warning if there were no good purpose to be served. But the same thing that makes us say the plaintiff was not contributorily negligent in using the car for a good purpose should make us say that the defendant is not negligent in lending it for the same good purpose.

CHAPTER 11

DEFENSES NOT ON THE MERITS

►**Changes in the Sixth Edition.** We've added over a dozen new case citations in Notes. To streamline coverage, we've cut the *Grimes* case abstract and we've turned the *Doe v. Maskell* case into a shorter abstract. Otherwise the order and coverage here remains unchanged from the prior edition.

►The **Concise Edition** dramatically cuts this Chapter to about a quarter of its length in the standard edition. Major omissions are, in order: Notes 1 and 2 after *Crumpton*; *Schiele v. Hobart*, its Notes, and Note: Latent Potential Harm; the Note on Exposure without Symptoms; the Note on Tolling for Disabilities; *Dasha* and its Notes; the Note on Limitations Not Based on Accrual; *Hoery* and its Notes; the Note on Policy and Solutions; and Note 3 after *Miller* (§ 2) on preemption in train-headlight cases. We added Notes on the discovery rule in child-abuse cases and on tolling the statute of limitations for minority, so as not to lose those topics entirely. Coverage of this Chapter in the Concise Edition should be very brisk indeed.■

§ 1. STATUTES OF LIMITATION

Preliminary note: We are concerned with making students aware of the very real problem of the statutes, and specifically with the problems of determining when a claim accrues and thus starts the statutory clock, with tolling, and with estoppel and other extenders of the statutes. Beyond that, we are of course concerned with the underlying policies of the statutes and how they weigh up with the underlying policies of tort law – deterrence, compensation, justice.

You can relate a little of this material to students' courses in civil procedure if you like dispelling the prevalent conception of law school courses as water-tight compartments.

Statute of limitations issues raised when the plaintiff is arguably too late in presenting her claim are varied. In court, however, they fall into two large compartments. First, when did the statute start running (and, relatedly, did it stop running at any point)? Second, when was the plaintiff's action commenced? Aside from raising some policy issues about statutes of limitations, this chapter deals primarily with the first category of issues– when did the statute start running and was it stopped? The second issue is considered only in this manual, in the note FYI note just below.

■**FYI: "Commencement."** Perhaps students have learned in civil procedure courses that commencement of an action for statute of limitation purposes is a different date in different court systems. (1) Some say an action is not commenced until service of process is effected. (2) Others treat the action as commenced with filing of the complaint. (3) More commonly, an action is commenced at the time the complaint is filed, but only provisionally. One version of this kind of rule is that if the plaintiff effects service of process within a specified time such as 120 days, the date of filing the complaint counts as commencement of the action, so if the complaint if filed within the statutory period, all is well for the plaintiff. This is the federal approach under Rules 3 & 4, FED. R. CIV. PROC. However, so far as state claims are being adjudicated in federal court under diversity jurisdiction, a state definition of commencement, if viewed as a part of the state's substantive statute of limitations rules, is controlling. *Walker v. Armco Steel Corp.,* 446 U.S. 740 (1980) (barring the plaintiff's claim under state law rule). A second version of this approach treats the date of filing the complaint as a commencement of the action, provided the plaintiff uses due diligence to effect service of process, otherwise not. *Zacharie v. U.S. Natural Resources, Inc.,* 94 S.W.3d 748 (Tex. App. 2002), is an example. Amendments to the complaint to add claims or defendants after the statute has run sometimes "relate back" to the original, timely filing, and sometimes not, depending on factors usually identified in court rules. ■

CRUMPTON V. HUMANA , 661 P.2d 54 (N.M. 1983)

Lawyers are responsible for many statute of limitations problems. You can take a minute to emphasize the lawyer's responsibility and to suggest malpractice liability if the lawyer fails to pursue this claim.

Pleading a claim with a longer statute of limitations. Maybe students should hear it said somewhere that statutes of limitations conventionally provide for different periods of time for different kinds of claims. Sometimes the plaintiff who is too late to assert an intentional tort claim can still assert a negligence claim, so that some manipulation is possible to avoid a statute's effects.

Note 1 first asks a law-practice management question; the answer is to calendar everything, and make sure you know when the statute of limitations is expiring on every case you are working on. The Note also makes the point that not all statute of limitations problems are created by the lawyer. A client might delay contact the lawyer because she does not know she has a claim at all (anticipating the upcoming materials on the discovery rule), or because she thinks suing is too much trouble, or maybe because she does not know any lawyers and does not know how to contact one.

Note 2. Students in many schools are familiar with estoppel by now from their contracts course and some may come up with the estoppel idea. The court in *Hagen v. Faherty,* cited here, did indeed hold that the state itself was estopped to raise the statute of limitations defense because of the misleading about the doctor's status. Estoppel is mentioned twice later in the chapter.

Negotiation estoppel. Sometimes, but rarely, negotiation between plaintiff and defendant misleads the plaintiff into believing settlement is guaranteed and consequently into delaying suit. But mere negotiation does not mislead anyone into failing to file in a timely way. If the defendant's agent says "Don't file, we'll pay," this might be taken as a representation that the statute of limitations would not be urged as a defense if settlement doesn't work. *See generally* Allan E. Korpela, Annotations, Promises to settle or perform as estopping reliance on statute of limitations, 44 A.L.R.3d 482 (1972); Settlement Negotiations as estopping reliance on statute of limitations, 39 A.L.R.3d 127 (1971).

Other estoppels may be possible, as where the defendant represents that the plaintiff was not unsafely exposed to disease. *See Waage v. Cutter Biological Div. of Miles Labs,* 926 P.2d 1145 (Alaska 1996).

SHEARIN V. LLOYD, 98 S.E.2d 508 (N.C. 1957)

Shearin holds that the negligence action accrues when injury occurs, even if the plaintiff does not know of the injury and therefore could not sue for it. This rule sets the stage for what follows. If you teach these materials in a straight-line, ignoring the complications, the movement from the *Shearin* rule to a discovery rule will be clear.

There is another, more permissive side to the *Shearin* rule. It is that the action does not accrue in a negligence claim until legally cognizable harm is inflicted under the rules seen in Chapter 7, § 1. This is a rule you expect to see where actual harm is required but not otherwise. It applies, for example, to an interference with contract claim, which is based upon intentional interference because actual harm is required to establish that claim. But it does not logically apply in battery case where the cause of action arises when the unpermitted touching occurs, not later when harm results. (Some other torts have their own peculiar rules: libel actions accrue when publication occurs, without regard either to harm or to the plaintiff's knowledge of the publication.)

The permissive side of the rule will assist the plaintiff when the defendant's negligent conduct occurs long before injury, because the action will not accrue and the statute will not begin to run until the injury occurs. For example, the defendant negligently constructs a building, but it does not collapse and cause injury to the plaintiff until ten years later.

Perplexing questions may remain. Suppose a doctor misdiagnoses persistent headaches as sinus when in fact they result from a malformed blood vessel in the brain. If misdiagnosis occurs in January of Year 1 and the patient's blood vessel ruptures in January Year 2, resulting in death, when does injury occur? If the pain and symptoms or even the condition itself could have been relieved immediately by a correct diagnosis, in a sense injury occurred shortly after misdiagnosis. But the Wisconsin court said not. "A misdiagnosis, in and of itself, is not, and cannot, be an actionable injury. The misdiagnosis is the negligent omission, not the injury. The actionable injury arises when the misdiagnosis causes a greater harm than existed at the time of the misdiagnosis." *Paul v. Skemp,* 625 N.W.2d 860 (Wis. 2001).

Common law principles do not prevail over statutory language, but common law principles may move the court in its interpretation of the statute. In *LaBello v. Albany Medical Ctr. Hosp.,* 651 N.E.2d 908 (N.Y. 1995), the statute provided that medical malpractice claims accrued at the time of the doctor's act or omission. The claim in *LaBello* was a claim by a child against the mother's physician allegedly inflicted before the child was born. If the statute were literally applied, the claim would accrue before the child was born and, on the facts, it would be barred. The court avoided this extreme result by saying that the statute silently assumed the existence of a person with "juridical capacity to sue," so that the claim did not accrue until the plaintiff came into being as a person, that is, upon the plaintiff's birth.

Notes 1 & 2. Discovery rule. These notes state the rule and describe its widespread adoption, in anticipation of seeing a more specific application in *Schiele,* below.

Note 3. Continuous treatment. This note involves continuous *treatment* cases. On the distinction between a continuous treatment rule and a continuing negligence rule, see DOBBS ON TORTS § 220 (2000). The note hypothetical raises the question whether "continuous treatment" is a workable concept.

The radiologist case: *Montgomery v. South County Radiologists, Inc.,* cited at the end of this Note, gives oblique support to the plaintiff in the casebook hypothetical, but it was both simpler and more complex than the hypothetical. That may be enough to say here, but here is some detail for those interested.

Three different radiologists read a series of x-rays over time, each missing a tumor. The first reading was outside the statute of limitations so that the claim against first radiologist was barred. All three were employed by SCR. SCR argued that so far as its liability would be based upon the first reading, it, too, was protected by the statute of limitations. The court rejected this argument on the ground that, while the individual radiologist had completed his care with the report on the first x-ray, the company itself had not, as evidenced by subsequent readings done by other employees.

The employer's presence in this case makes it more complex than the hypothetical in the note. However, the note hypothetical is more complex in that the second reading is said not to be negligent. Can you have continuing treatment by non-negligent care? Maybe in *Montgomery* it would be possible for the employer to argue that the later readings were not negligent for some reason. That is an issue not involved in the decision. But if that were not the case, why would the employer fight so hard to avoid liability for the first mis-reading – it would be liable in any event for the mis-readings by others employees. One possibility is that its insurance coverage had changed and that it is really the insurer who is making the statute of limitations argument. But if that is not the case, then perhaps the employer has hopes of avoiding liability for the second and third misreadings and thus sought to exclude the first mis-reading on statute of limitations grounds.

Compare *Casey v. Levine,* 621 N.W.2d 482 (Neb. 2001), where a hospital was allegedly negligent in failing to carry out a doctor's orders for a patient, then discharged the patient, who was still suffering symptoms, because insurance would not pay for another day. The hospital then readmitted the patient a few days later for an extended stay in the intensive care unit, but this time was not negligent. The court held that the care terminated in the date of the (first) discharge and that the statute of limitations running from that date protected the hospital. It rooted this decision in rationales for the doctrine – "allowing a physician an opportunity to correct any malpractice and not disrupting the physician-patient relationship are the primary considerations underlying the continuing treatment doctrine in Nebraska" but these considerations have no application to a hospital who has discharged a patient . . . Patients do not. . . remain under the continued care or observation of the hospital's nursing staff after discharge. There may be a significant gap between hospital stays; different nurses may be on staff when the patient is readmitted; or, as in this case, the patient may be readmitted to a completely different department of the hospital."

Note 4. Concealment. Fraudulent concealment of the fact of negligence or injury will surely estop the defendant or toll the statute. In *Florida Dept. of Health Rehabilitative Services v. S.A.P.,* cited here, the court held that the state would be equitably estopped from asserting the statute of limitations defense if it had fraudulently concealed the facts that generated the plaintiff's cause of action. It is not clear that the plaintiff alleged reliance. She alleged she had no independent memory of the abuse she suffered in a foster home, that the state negligently failed to supervise, and that it concealed its failure by falsifying records. One sentence suggests the absence of reliance: "Had any interested adult examined these records prior to December 21, 1992, they would have been misled into believing that the department had reasonably, appropriately, and lawfully discharged its supervision duties. The negligence of the Department was concealed by these falsified records." The majority and concurring opinions did not comment on the reliance elements. Should the statute be tolled for the state's misconduct even without reliance, which is a normal requirement both for fraud and for estoppel?

Arkansas uses a hard line/bright line rule in medical malpractice claims: "The date of the accrual of the cause of action is the date of the wrongful act complained of and no other time." Even so, its Supreme Court held that fraudulent concealment of the cause of action tolls the statute. But it must be fraudulent – "there must be evidence creating a fact question related to some positive act of fraud, something so furtively planned and secretly executed as to keep the plaintiff's cause of action concealed, or perpetrated in a way that it conceals itself." *Meadors v. Still,* 40 S.W.3d 294 (Ark. 2001). The surgeon in Meadors misrecorded the size of the breast implant. Later, in another state, the plaintiff had another implant, but the second surgeon, relying upon the first surgeon's records, did not have the proper size implant on hand at surgery and completed the surgery with the implant he had. The plaintiff's breasts are now different sizes. The court held that none of this showed fraudulent concealment. Nor was the breast implant a foreign object that would trigger a limited discovery rule.

SCHIELE V. HOBART CORP., 587 P.2d 1010 (Or. 1978).

This case illustrates the discovery rule in a "toxic tort" context – the plaintiff incurs a disease that develops over a period of time. Under the discovery rule, what is it that must be "discovered?" The trial judge gave summary judgment for the defendant on the ground that the two-year statute of limitations had run. The Supreme Court, adopting the discovery rule, reversed and remanded for trial.

The plaintiff here allegedly suffered lung diseases as a result of PVC fumes generated when she used defendant's meat wrapping machines, which involved cutting of plastic or polyvinyl chloride wrapping film. She almost immediately began having problems and almost immediately knew they stemmed from the fumes. Her condition grew steadily worse, but there was no sudden event. Her work with the machines began about June, 1972, and she continued to work until March 12, 1974. In April 1974, her doctors told her that the disease was due to the exposure on the job. The court believes that prior authority stands for the proposition that the statute "does not begin to run until the plaintiff knows, or as a reasonably prudent person should know, that he has the condition for which his action is brought and that defendant has caused it." It then turns to specific issues and holds:

(1) The plaintiff will be chargeable with knowledge of the disease and with knowledge that the defendant caused it if that knowledge could reasonably be gained, even without a positive diagnosis by a physician.

(2) Knowledge of symptoms alone does not necessarily suffice.

(3) The statute begins to run when a reasonable person would (a) associate symptoms with a serious or permanent condition and (b) would perceive the defendant's role in creating that condition.

(4) If knowledge of all this is widespread among similarly situated persons, the plaintiff as a reasonable person should have recognized these facts and should have brought the action sooner. But, by implication, the

defendant has the burden of showing that there is such widespread knowledge, and it has not done so here.

The summary judgment for defendant on statute of limitations grounds was reversed because there was no showing that the plaintiff should have realized the seriousness of the condition.

When *should* the plaintiff have discovered those things that will start the statute running? *Schiele* gives us a little help on that. In *Bibeau v. Pacific Northwest Research Found.*, 188 F.3d 1105 (9th Cir. 1999), the plaintiff, then a prisoner, was asked to take part in an experiment. He consented, perhaps without knowing the nature of the risks. Heller then exposed his testicles to 18.5 rads of radiation to see what the effects would be. He eventually left prison, settled down and got married (but had no children; he had been given a vasectomy). At various times he had testicular pains, but did not consult a doctor and did not associate the pains with the much earlier experiments. When he heard a speech in which the government apologized for experiments on human subjects, however, he began an investigation. He brought suit within two years after that but some thirty years after being irradiated. The court considered whether he should have seen a doctor and if so whether the doctor would have given him information that would have made him aware of the Heller experiments. This could not be decided as a matter of law but had to be resolved on the facts.

Certainty is one of the prized attributes of any law. There is not much of it in negligence law, but until recent years, the statutes of limitation operated to provide a certain terminus of liability. This might be unfair in particular cases, but it cut the high costs of uncertainty. Was the certain terminus too unfair? In judging this question, the student might need a reminder: not everyone who is sued is in fact legally liable or even morally at fault. The statutes of limitation protect the guilty, but also the innocent. Another reminder: *Crumpton* gives us one of the reasons why the plaintiff might delay.

Nevertheless, there are innocent plaintiffs who would be barred by a statute of limitations that is applied efficiently—that is, without any room for judgments. The injection of normative and other judgments into the statute, via the discovery rule, now makes the statute uncertain and in that sense, inefficient. The costs it is intended to save cannot be saved—the "long tail" on the cause of action may mean that the door cannot be shut on that particular dog for twenty or thirty years. *Schiele* adds even further judgments. Did the plaintiff discover not only an injury, but its "nature" as a "serious" injury? Is there any simpler way to deal with this?

The notes should help the student walk through some of the main points. *Schiele* makes no great point of it, but it does adopt the discovery rule and moves on from there to question what discovery ought to count.

Note 2. *Rotella v. Wood,* 528 U.S. 549 (2000), is in accord with *Kubrick,* cited here: the statute starts for a RICO plaintiff upon discovery of injury, not discovery of injury plus a the pattern of racketeering activity required to establish a cause of action. Notice that the first two state-court decisions, *Walk* and *Lagassey,* are more favorable to the plaintiff, but that under either of them the defendant might still prevail on the facts if the plaintiff, knowing causation and injury should have been on notice to investigate further. California also does not start the statute until the plaintiff knows or should know of the factual basis of a claim, but holds in *Fox,* cited here, that the identity of the defendant is not an "element" that must be discovered for the clock to commence. Note that California does allow "Doe" filings even where you don't know the identity of one or more defendants.

Are these cases overly harsh? Or do they only force plaintiffs to be more diligent in discovering the whole truth once they have half of it?

Note 3 points out that the discovery rule's adoption produces fact issues that will often have to be resolved by a jury. The critical question at the end can spark a discussion about trade-offs between certainty (which the traditional rule provided) and achieving individualized justice (which is always less efficient), which is briefly raised in the discussion in Note 1 above as well.

Note 4. Statutes limiting the discovery rule. See also our materials on the "statutes of repose" in the note on limitations not based on accrual.

Note 5. Statutes adopting the discovery rule. The federal statute discussed here, 42 U.S.C.A. § 9658, is an addition to the Superfund (CERCLA) package. The casebook statement of the statute simplifies the structure. The federal statute does not directly add years to the state's statutory period. Instead it lengthens the traditional statute by treating the claim as not commencing until discovery was or should have been made. Within its scope, it will preempt state law to the contrary, although only so far as state law would apply an earlier accrual or commencement date. Not every toxic tort will be within the scope of the statute: the claim must be that the substance was "released into the environment from a facility" which is statutorily defined. The ALI Reporters' Study recommends adoption of the statutory standard in common law cases to which the statute does not apply. *See* II REPORTERS' STUDY, ENTERPRISE RESPONSIBILITY FOR PERSONAL INJURY 364 (ALI 1991).

NOTE: LATENT POTENTIAL HARM

Partial Injury, Latent Potential

Some cases allow the exposed plaintiff who has no present symptoms to recover the costs of medical monitoring aimed at early detection of disease. See *Bourgeois v. A.P. Green Indus., Inc.,* 716 So.2d 355 (La. 1998). Medical monitoring will come up again in the Casebook. A recovery for increased risk, on analogy to recovery for lost chance, might also be possible.

Exposure without Symptoms

Almost everyone is exposed to some airborne chemicals daily, and unfortunately many of us are exposed to worse. The normal rule in negligence claims is that no tort exists unless harm is inflicted. What if the railroad overturns a tank car carrying dangerous chemicals; they escape as a gas and everyone within two miles may have breathed some of the gas, which in turn may cause terrible harm and even death in the years to come. Is there a present cause of action? See *Harper v. Illinois Central Gulf R.R.*, 808 F.2d 1139 (5th Cir. 1987) (toxic spill a mile from plaintiff's home, recovery for lost use of home during precautionary evacuation, but not for mental distress where there was no exposure).

Pathological changes or the presence of bacteria or viruses from the disease might be enough to trigger a cause of action. E.g., *Plummer v. United States*, 580 F.2d 72 (3d Cir. 1978) ("a tubercle bacillus" was enough to establish a tort); but cf. *Simmons v. Pacor, Inc.*, 674 A.2d 232 (Pa. 1996) (exposure led to pleural thickening but no disease or pain, not an injury that would permit claim for emotional distress). In *Bibeau v. Pacific Northwest Research Found.*, 188 F.3d 1105 (9th Cir. 1999), where the plaintiff's testicles had been exposed to substantial radiation as an experiment, the court dealt with the statute of limitations but did not pass on whether there was any actionable tort. Exposure to HIV has provided illustrations of the problem, too. These exposures and others are considered in Chapter 19 on the topic of emotional distress.

MCCOLLUM V. D'ARCY, 638 A.2d 797 (N.H. 1994)
DOE V. MASKELL, 679 A.2d 1087 (Md. 1996)

McCollum allows the plaintiff to postpone the statute of limitations under the discovery rule on the claim that she had repressed memories of childhood sexual abuse by parents. *Doe v. Maskell* refuses to permit use of the discovery rule by alleged victims of childhood sexual abuse at the hands of a priest at their parochial school on the ground that repression has not been proved to exist. The two cases reflect a split complicated by statutes, mentioned in **Note 7**.

In *Doe v. Maskell,* the plaintiffs, women, alleged that in the late 1960s and early 1970s, as students at parochial Seton Keough High School in Baltimore City, they were referred to the school chaplain, Father Maskell, for counseling. Maskell allegedly committed a wide range of sexual acts. The plaintiffs brought suit in 1994. Responding to the statute of limitations argument, they claimed repression and recovery of memories in 1992.

We've cut this case down to its essentials, but you might like to know some more details. The *Maskell* court first recognized two models of repression, serial and collective. In the serial repression model, the court said, repression would occur after each event. In the collective model, repression would occur after all abuse terminated. The court noted that the plaintiffs had not been clear about when repression occurred and that if the repression they claimed was the "collective" kind and occurred only after they reached majority, the statute would have run. The court did not mention insanity or incompetency in this regard. In any event these observations did not control the court's ultimate determination.

The court then observed that the discovery rule would not come to the aid of one who simply forgot. The question thus became: Is there any difference between forgetting and repression? Is there evidence for any repression mechanism, as distinct from a theory or way of looking at things? Expert testimony on summary judgment indicated that no empirical evidence supports the claim of repression, that the psychological community has not reached any consensus that it exists, and that in any event the "recovery" of memories is itself suspect, in part because this may be therapist-induced or influenced.

The court concluded that forgetting and repressing are "indistinguishable scientifically" and hence should be treated the same. Accordingly, the discovery rule would not apply.

Notes 1, 2, 4 & 5. There is no doubt that childhood sexual abuse really occurs, but a debate does go on about whether "repression" is genuine, and whether "recovered memory" is valid. The repression debate is far too elaborate to be fully summarized here. Many talk therapists (as distinct from those who administer drugs) have grounded their livelihood in the idea that there is an unconscious, and that repression is like storing peas in the freezer, that the frozen peas of memory can be recovered more or less intact, and that we should trust therapists to do that. The scientists approach things differently and question or reject each of the propositions asserted by the therapists who believe in repression. The foremost student of memory, Elizabeth Loftus, has convincingly argued that there is no such thing. *See* Elizabeth Loftus, *The Reality of Repressed Memories*, 48 AM. PSYCHOLOGIST 518 (May 1993).

Others might worry more about the "recovery" of repressed memories, and particularly about the potential for abusive practices by therapists who suggest, hypnotize, or browbeat patients to produce false memories. (See the next paragraph.) On this point, we think it unwise to teach about the problem of countersuits against therapists here. That point depends upon entirely different doctrine in spite of the underlying factual connection. And it is a distraction to the statute of limitations coverage. You might want to be personally aware, however, that although some patients have recovered against therapists for implanting memories, *see* Sheila Taub, *Legal Treatment of Recovered Memories of Child Sexual Abuse,* 17 J. LEGAL MED. 183 (1996), the parents who are falsely accused as a result of a therapist's manipulation of patients will almost never be able to recover against the therapist, so there are few if any brakes on the therapist with an agenda or obsession of his own. See Joel Jay Finer, *Therapists' Liability to the Falsely Accused for Inducing Illusory Memories of Childhood Sexual Abuse – Current Remedies and a Proposed Statute,* 11 J. L. & HEALTH 45 (1996-97) (summarizing some horrific practices and proposing a very modest statute). Therapists, of course, argue that there is such a thing as good therapy and that legal liability for misdeeds will diminish its value. Cynthia Grant Bowman and Elizabeth Mertz, *A Dangerous*

Direction: Legal Intervention in Sexual Abuse Survivor Therapy, 109 HARV. L. REV. 549 (1996). On the whole topic of repressed memories, see DAVID L. FAIGMAN, DAVID H. KAYE, MICHAEL J. SAKS, AND JOSEPH SANDERS, MODERN SCIENTIFIC EVIDENCE–THE LAW AND SCIENCE OF EXPERT TESTIMONY Chapter 13 (2 vols. 1997 and Supp.). Elizabeth F. Loftus and Laura A. Rosenwald wrote §§ 13-2.1– 13-2.4 dealing with the scientific status of repressed memory theory.

Note 3. Choosing up your experts. *Doe v. Creighton,* cited here, says it imposes an objective test to determine whether a victim should have recognized the connection between abuse and the harm suffered. This rule, logically applied, would sidestep the repression debate while effectively ruling out claims by victims who claimed to have repressed memories. This might avoid the pitfall of judicial subscription to one set of battling experts. Is it, however, a good rule? Can we determine the answer to that question without knowing whether we believe in repression?

Note 6. Memory intact but other psychological impediments to suit. The New Jersey statute provides: "the cause of action shall accrue at the time of reasonable discovery of the injury and its causal relationship to the act of sexual abuse." *Ross v. Garabedian,* 433 Mass. 360, 742 N.E.2d 1046 (2001) applied a similar statute to reject a summary judgment motion even though the plaintiff was conscious at all times of childhood sexual contact and conscious as well of his own feelings that the contact was shameful. The court thought that he might still have been unaware that the sexual contact was responsible for his later emotional difficulties, and that would be a jury question. Other cases and statutes are cited in DOBBS ON TORTS § 222 (2000).

NOTE: TOLLING FOR DISABILITIES

Distinguish *tolling* from the discovery rule. Under the discovery rule, the clock does not begin to run until the plaintiff discovered or should have discovered certain facts (although some people will call this tolling). With tolling, the clock does not run during the period of the plaintiff's disability, regardless of discovery. A grace period differs from both; it is a time extension but one that is not necessarily coincident with either the plaintiff's ignorance or her disability. *See* DOBBS ON TORTS § 221 (2000).

Courts have not used tolling for unsound mind to assist the plaintiff as often as they have used the discovery rule. Unsound mind can be defined to exclude many adverse psychological states and hence to restrict the use of tolling in many childhood sexual abuse cases and others. In *McCarthy v. Volkswagen of America, Inc.,* 55 N.Y.2d 543, 450 N.Y.S.2d 457, 435 N.E.2d 1072 (1982) the court held that post-traumatic neurosis was insufficient to toll the statute. However, some courts have defined unsound mind to permit tolling whenever the plaintiff's mental state effectively prevents the plaintiff from suing. See *Doe v. Roe*, 191 Ariz. 313, 955 P.2d 951 (1998) (Notes 3 & 4 following *Doe v. Maskell*); *Jones v. Jones*, 242 N.J. Super. 195, 576 A.2d 316 (1990).

The special statutes mentioned in **Note 8** will assist the plaintiff claiming childhood sexual abuse within limits, but notice that they are only addressed to the statute of limitations. They do not address admissibility of evidence. If the testimony of "therapists" on repressed memory is excluded, these statutes won't be of any ultimate assistance to the plaintiff. The statutes, like most, are narrowly conceived in response to a particular incident or particular pressure group. Consequently they do not assist the *Pritzlaff* plaintiff. Is there something wrong with treating the two cases differently?

DASHA V. MAINE MED. CTR., 665 A.2d 993 (Me. 1995)

The Maine Court was unwilling to toll the statute for incapacity that occurred because of, but after the defendant's negligence. The plaintiff's guardian then argued estoppel, but the court rejected this as well. The misdiagnosis was not equivalent to fraud and the plaintiff did not rely upon a misrepresentation. If this is too harsh, what caused the problem?

Note 1 gives the elements of an equitable estoppel claim.

Note 2. Threats and equitable estoppel. In appropriate cases, then, the defendant may be estopped to plead the statute of limitations. In *John R. v. Oakland Unified Sch. Dist.*, cited here, a suit against school district for a teacher's alleged molestation of a male student, the court held that threats against the victim that delayed his filing of suit could count as an estoppel under some circumstances. *Ortega v. Pajaro Valley Unified Sch. Dist.*, also cited here, similarly a suit against a school for a teacher's molestation of a 12-year old female student, found estoppel and analyzed in detail the basis for it in the various forms of oppressive conduct.

Note 3. *Valdez,* cited here, held that fraudulent concealment was not necessary to establish equitable tolling of the statute of limitations. The case arose under the FTCA and involved alleged medical malpractice in obstetrical care. The trial judge dismissed on statute of limitations grounds. On appeal, the court vacated and remanded, holding that the plaintiff should be allowed to prove facts showing that despite her due diligence, she was not aware that the clinics providing the care were federally-funded and thus subject to FTCA rules. The court's application of the rule seems quite similar to a discovery-rule inquiry: whether a reasonable person should have known or discovered necessary facts in order to bring a claim in a timely manner.

NOTE: LIMITATIONS NOT BASED ON ACCRUAL

The discussion of options leads naturally into the possibility of enacting some added limitation. Notice requirements are used in a number of particular situations and the student who is going to practice law must be aware of the trap this can create. The pre-accrual bar, or what is now being called a statute of repose, accepts the discovery rule for some purposes, but then adds an outer limit on recovery, such as ten years from the defendant's act. This is a compromise that gives the plaintiff more than the usual two or three years from the time of the undiscovered injury, but does not leave the claim open indefinitely. This kind of limitation has been especially important in medical malpractice and products liability cases.

1518-1525 Lakeview Boulevard Condominium Ass'n v. Apartment Sales Corporation, 29 P.3d 1249 (Wash. 2001), is much like the introductory example in the text at the head of this section. Condo units were constructed on a hillside, completed in 1990. Buyers received representations about safety. In 1997 landslides damaged the condos severely, but the statute protected builders by a six-year-from-completion rule. So the statute had run a year before the injury occurred.

Another interesting example involved two conflicting statutes of repose, one favoring products manufacturers and the other favoring those who made improvement on land. The court held that when the product was permanently attached to real property, it became real property so the property repose statute applied. *Henningsen v. Eastern Iowa Propane, Ltd,* 652 N.W.2d 462 (Iowa 2002).

The court in *1518-1525 Lakeview Boulevard Condominium Ass'n* upheld the statute against constitutional challenges, but some courts have held these statutes to be unconstitutional under state constitutional provision. A strongly worded decision is *State v. Sheward,* 715 N.E.2d 1062 Ohio 1999).

On this topic see DOBBS ON TORTS § 219 (2000).

HOERY V. UNITED STATES , 64 P.3d 214 (Colo. 2003)

In 1993, the plaintiffs bought a residence with a groundwater well. It turned out that the United States had been dumping toxic chemicals on its nearby Lowry Air Force Base. It quit in 1994, but (a) some toxic substances remain underneath the plaintiffs' property and (b) some others continue to migrate there. The plaintiffs brought suit in 1998. The trial judge dismissed the claim on the ground that the statute of limitations had run. The Tenth Circuit then certified questions to which the Colorado Supreme Court's opinion is addressed. The opinion asserts these propositions:

1. For continuing torts or intrusions, each continuance amounts to another wrong.

2. In the case of a continuing tort, the plaintiff can sue for all the wrongs committed within the limitation period preceding commencement of the action. [I.e., with a two year statute of limitations, for all the harms done in the two years preceding the commencement of the action.]

3. A permanent trespass or nuisance is one that will or should continue indefinitely [i.e., the court cannot or will not require abatement.]

4. In the case of a permanent trespass, there is only one cause of action and the plaintiff must sue within the limitation period for all damages, past and future. [By implication.]

5. The record does not show that the toxic contamination will or should continue indefinitely. It is remediable and in addition should be remedied. Hence it is classed as continuing.

The idea of a continuing tort vs. a permanent one is a difficult idea and we hope the notes together with *Hoery* itself make it reasonably clear, although authorities are not easy to reconcile. A recent case with a quite different take on temporary versus permanent is *Schneider Nat'l Carriers, Inc. v. Bates,* 47 S.W.3d 264 (Tex. 2004). In the past, we've resisted raising the problem because it traditionally occurs with trespass or nuisance suits– not ordinary negligence suits. Yet the trespass and nuisance here are rather formal elements; the plaintiff suffers actual damage to his property (maybe to his person) from acts that look like negligence. So maybe the topic should be included with other statute of limitations problems. Indeed, as *Feltmeier v. Feltmeier,* 798 N.E.2d 75 (Ill. 2003) in **Note 7** shows, similar ideas, though not altogether similar rules, apply in injury cases.

We hope that with the help of the notes, students will be able to see that the *Hoery* court treated the invasion of the plaintiff's land as a continuing one so that the plaintiff could sue for all damages accruing from invasions during the statute of limitations period immediately preceding commencement of the suit.

Note 1. See discussion above.

Notes 2 & 3. Effect on damages and abatement. The problem is not only part of statute of limitations issues, though. It is also critical in measuring damages (to provide appropriate incentives) and in determining whether the plaintiff sues only once or potentially many times.

Two damages statements in Hoery? On the damages issue the court in *Hoery* may have stated two different versions of damages for continuing tort cases. The usual notion is that a new cause of action arises each day of a continuing tort. If the statute is two years and the intrusion started two years and one day before suit was filed, the plaintiff recover damages only for the past two years; he cannot recover for harm done in the period preceding that, because, as to that, the statute has run. The court seems to adopt that view, but also says "the claim does not begin to accrue until the tortious conduct has ceased."

Permanent invasions. If the effects of the tort cannot be abated– if the well is polluted forever– you would have to say that the trespass or nuisance is permanent. That coincides with the fact that the potential for continuing suits would not add to any needed incentive to remove the harm, since the harm is done. If the effects of the tort could be abated but the court would refuse an injunction to make the railway destroy its embankment or the water master remove the irrigation ditch, then the effects of the tort, though in fact capable of abatement, are legally permanent; that is what the refusal of an injunction would mean. That in turn is a policy question. If the railroad has the power of eminent domain, for example, injunction to make it move the railroad, then reinstall it exercising its power of eminent domain would be wasteful without helping the plaintiff.

Note 4. Incentives. If permanent, even the plaintiff who sues in time will get market value of something he did not wish to sell and the defendant is in effect licensed to do nothing to abate the toxic conditions. Continuing tort classification allows the plaintiff to keep suing until the costs of the plaintiffs' suits (and neighbors' maybe) make it more efficient to clean up the toxic condition.

Note 5 sets out factors that may be used in drawing the distinction; we've found it helps facilitate discussion if students have something to hang their hats on.

Note 6. Scope of the problem. Discussion can also turn to possible expansions of the Hoery analysis. We looked earlier at continuing *treatment* by physicians. How about a continuing *tort* analysis where the physician can at any time intervene to stop the harm— by making a correct diagnosis, or by removing a foreign object left in the body. The latter case is especially comparable to *Hoery*.

Note 7 also suggests ways of grouping disparate acts (or omissions, in the case of malpractice) into a single tort.

NOTE: POLICY AND SOLUTIONS

This note provides a further basis for policy discussion. The plaintiff's side of the case is easy to understand and identify with. But as the "medical malpractice crisis" of the early 1970s may have shown us, indefinite liabilities in time will entail heavy costs. The most certain limitation on claims is the one that will be the cheapest. This was the old rule seen in *Shearin v. Lloyd*. But a certain rule, cheaper for society, will be the rule most costly to individual victims. Maybe some compromise would protect more people without sacrificing too much of the certainty.

A second basis for statutes of limitations is that testimony is not very trustworthy in the first place, that triers of fact are not usually very good at discriminating between accurate and inaccurate testimony (Chapter 6, §3), and that testimony becomes less reliable and harder to assess as the claim grows stale. Whether this is true or not, some witnesses simply forget and cannot testify at all. Some move away; some die. But so far as the problem is one of stale testimony, a bright-line, certain bar may not be what is needed.

Could a judge determine from evidence whether the defendant was unduly prejudiced by a claim brought one year late?

A third idea may be too subtle to see in this context, but it will appear again in connection with product liability: we run severe risks of injustice when we use hindsight with too long a telescope. Today's standards and expectations may impinge our vision of another generation's wrongdoing. In the products case, a suit charging that defendant negligently designed a 1938 car runs serious risks of imposing unfair standards.

A final idea in support of statutes of limitation may be that most of us have a strong feeling that at some point even a wrongdoer is entitled to a fresh start. There may be something troubling about the idea that fifty years after a botched medical procedure, the 75-year-old retired doctor can be dragged through the courts, even if her insurance still covers her.

Do these considerations suggest that we might manage to improve the statutes of limitations? For instance, statutes might operate on a sliding scale, scaling down the plaintiff's damages over a period of, say, five years, after the normal statute runs, and barring the claim entirely after a further period of time. Do your students have some ideas of their own or ideas about combining some of the alternatives suggested?

§ 2. COMPLIANCE WITH STATUTE

Preliminary Note: The traditional rule holds that while violation of a statute is negligence per se, compliance with a statute does not show freedom from negligence. The statute is a minimum standard so that violation is negligence; but it says nothing about whether the defendant should exercise more care under given circumstances.

Besides furnishing the information that compliance with statute is seldom a defense, this section has three purposes. First, foreshadows a similar argument in products liability cases; second, introduces without exploring federal preemption; and third, it obliquely recalls two familiar and related rules on violation of statute and compliance with custom.

MILLER V. WARREN , 390 S.E.2d 207 (W.Va. 1990).

This case gives a good statement of the general rule that compliance with statute is not a defense. On that rule, *see* DOBBS ON TORTS § 224 (2000).

Bases for rule. What is the basis for the rule? If we have no evidence of legislative intent to the contrary, we probably should interpret the statute as setting minimum standards. The point is easy to see if you imagine a speed limit statute. A 35 m.p.h. speed limit is certainly demanding; but if you see children playing soccer beside the street you might think that an even lower speed is required by reasonable care. Given The *T.J. Hooper's* view (Chapter 6, § 3) that an industry cannot set its own standard of care, courts cannot allow statutes to set the maximum obligation of the industry.

A third reason is that technology changes, so that statutes that once pre-scribed the perfect amount of care are no longer sufficient to indicate the care a reasonable person would exercise. Arguably, the regulations of a well-staffed, well-managed, up-to-date, and adequately financed regulatory agency would be different. But even here, some of us might worry about whether the agency's "safety" decisions had more to do with a political agenda.

Rejecting the rule: compliance as defense. Occasional cases hold that, on the facts, compliance with a statute or regulation furnishes a defense or at least a presumptive defense. Omitted portions of *Miller* suggest that these cases may turn out to be something else altogether, namely cases in which the plaintiff simply has not proved any unreasonable risk to begin with.

Notes 2-4. Statutes and preemption. Where preemption occurs, com-pliance with the federal statute is effectively a defense to any tort suit based on state law. See *Norfolk Southern Ry. v. Shanklin,* 529 U.S. 344 (2000); *CSX Transp. v. Easterwood,* 507 U.S. 658 (1993) (train speed preempted). As Note 4 points out, even where a federal regulation or statute is violated, the federal provision may preempt inconsistent state law, as a matter of Federal Suprem-acy. Preemption and compliance become major issues in Chapter 24 on products liability. You probably cannot develop this complex topic here in any depth at all, nor should you.

PART 3

LIMITING OR EXPANDING THE DUTY OF CARE ACCORDING TO CONTEXT OR RELATIONSHIP

Preliminary note to Part 3. Taken together, Chapters 12-21 inform students about several important tort doctrines and reflect the use of "duty" as well as immunities to limit access to the jury and, ultimately, to limit liability.

TOPIC A. LIMITING DUTIES ACCORDING TO
CLASS OR STATUS OF THE PARTIES

CHAPTER 12

CARRIERS, HOST-DRIVERS AND LANDOWNERS

►**Changes in the Sixth Edition.** Note material is updated throughout the chapter, with 20 new cases cited or discussed. Some notes have been cut entirely, while some new ones have been added. No primary cases or case abstracts have been changed from the prior edition.

►The **Concise Edition** cuts 20% of the length of this Chapter in the standard edition. In most cases we have achieved this by cutting cases or long notes or text and substituting shorter textual material on the same topic, meaning that the basic coverage is the same in both editions. For the Concise Edition we have cut *Rowland v. Christian* and Notes, substituting a page of text discussing some states' adoption of a reasonable person standard for all entrants; Note 2 after *Scurti*; and most of the materials in § 5 (Recreational Use Statutes) and § 6 (Lessors), explaining both of those topics in text.■

Preliminary Note: This chapter is full of fruitful comparisons and contrasts. It begins with carriers, who are said to owe an especially high duty of care to passengers—one of the very few enhanced duties to be found this side of strict liability. The carrier cases lead naturally into the auto guest cases, where the duty is modified in the opposite direction: under the guest statutes the host owes less than ordinary care.

The guest statute cases in turn push us into the landowner cases, where the common law itself provided a diminished standard of care for landowners in the case of certain entrants on land, including "guests." From this, special rules develop limiting the duties of reasonable care owed to firefighters and other public safety officers. Why special rules for landowners? If the guest statute was unwise and even unconstitutional, as today's consensus implies, why not the landowner rules? Indeed, some courts have begun to abolish the special rules for landowners. But at the end of the chapter we see the first of many occasions in which legislatures have passed special legislation called recreational use statutes to limit liability of special groups, in this case, landowners.

Suggested omissions. If you want to reduce the landowners' coverage to an absolute minimum, try omitting everything but § 2 and lecturing on the other topics in the chapter. That may be easier than it looks for everything except the laundry list of exceptions on the duties of lessors. If the property course in your school covers lessors' tort duties, you might even omit that section with a lecture and a caveat. You could also cover only § 2 and § 4 only, which gives you cases to discuss the theme of common law change, filling in other key points with brief lecture. That being said, if you drop the short § 5 on recreational use, you lose all detail on an important statutory change and another piece of the picture that shows how legislatures have been working in the last generation. Thus if you are particularly interested in statutory revisions of common law rules, you probably want to retain § 5.

NARRATIVE SUMMARY

Section 1. The courts tell us that public carriers owe the highest care or some other extraordinary care for the personal safety of passengers (but not for their goods). In contrast, the guest statutes, a product of the 1920s and 1930s provided that drivers of private automobiles owed no duty of reasonable care to their guests, only a duty to avoid willful, wanton, reckless, or grossly negligent conduct. These have mostly been held unconstitutional or repealed. These points are made in *Doser,* the Alabama Code, and notes.

Section 2. The guest statute limitation on duty has mostly been nullified, but many courts have continued to impose a similar rule about landowners and various entrants upon their lands. To trespasses and licensees, landowners owe no duty of reasonable care, only the duty (as it developed), not to harm by intentional or willful or wanton misconduct. As those terms are traditionally defined, this might require landowners to exercise reasonable care for licensees after discovering both their presence and some immediate danger to them. Social guests are in the licensee category and thus often barred from recovery when the host negligently caused injury. Invitees, meaning business visitors or those invited to enter land open to the public, are entitled to the ordinary due care of the reasonable person under the circumstances. These points are made in *Gladon* and the following notes.

Child trespassers have often been given a little tolerance under the attractive nuisance doctrine, that is, treated as invitees if the landowner maintained a certain dangerous conditions on the land and a child would foreseeably come on the land and be injured by the condition because, given her tender years, she was unable to appreciate its danger. This is fleshed out with the *Bennett* case.

O'Sullivan v. Shaw, a head-first-dive-in-the-pool case, deals with the open and obvious danger idea, so important in landowner and products cases. That case explains that when the danger is blatantly obvious, the problem for the plaintiff is not assumed risk, which has been converted into comparative fault, but rather that the defendant is not negligent at all because he reasonably believes the plaintiff will avoid harm from obvious dangers. As notes indicate, some harm is foreseeable some of the time in spite of the obvious danger.

Section 3. Courts had trouble characterizing firefighters and other public safety officers as trespassers, licensees, or invitees, but eventually came up with a rule that narrowed the landowners' duties to such entrants upon the land in the course of their duties. So long as the safety officer was injured by conditions that prompted his presence in the first place, he has no cause of action based upon the landowner's negligence in creating that condition. These ideas and the exceptions and qualifications to them are advanced in *Minnich v. Med-Waste, Inc.* and the following notes.

Section 4. Beginning in 1968, some courts began to discard the old tripartite classification of entrants as invitees, licensees, and trespassers, and to substitute a rule of ordinary care, or at least a rule of ordinary care for both licensees and invitees. About half the American jurisdictions have now made these or similar reforms. The reasons pro and con and the way the reasonable care rule works are considered in *Rowland v. Christian* and in *Scurti v. City of New York* and the notes that follow each of those cases.

Section 5. Text of this section explains that the reforms seen in § 4 may be undermined by contemporary recreational use statutes, which immunize the landowner from a duty of reasonable care and substitute some standard such as willful or wanton misconduct. These apply where the landowner permits the public to use the land for recreational purposes without a specific fee.

Section 6. Lessors traditionally owed the tenant no duty of care concerning the condition of rented premises in the tenant's control, although the lessor owed a duty of care as to portions of the premises left open for all tenants to use as in the case of stairways. There were a handful of exceptions or qualifications. *Pagelsdorf v. Safeco Ins. Co. of America* explains the traditional rules and rejects them, imposing a duty of ordinary care. Notes summarize the exceptions.

Problems. Four short problems permit review and application of the main rules and ideas in this chapter.

COMMENTS

§ 1. CARRIERS & HOST-DRIVERS

[*a. Common carriers*]

DOSER V. INTERSTATE POWER CO., 173 N.W.2d 556 (Iowa 1970).

A true case of higher duty. A common carrier is said to owe a higher degree of care. Sometimes "higher duty of care" seems only to mean "use care commensurate with the danger," a standard that seems consistent with the ordinary reasonable, prudent person standard. But that does not seem to be the case with common carriers. Driving a bus as a common carrier is not an activity that seems any more risky than driving a private bus, or even a car. The common carrier rule, then, seems to be really a rule of higher duty. This is a good place to terminate discussion if you are rushed or the class is slow. Under more favorable classroom conditions, you can milk this case for more.

Bases for a higher duty? Why should the rule exist? One possibility is that the carrier is understood to undertake a duty of special care. But if that is the understanding or expectation about public carriers, why is there no similar undertaking by or expectation of private carriers? Private persons carrying guests? If there is a difference, is it to be found in considerations of justice or considerations of policy?

Enterprise liability? Perhaps the higher standard for common carriers is a mild version of enterprise liability which has come to be so important in products litigation. To be sure, we have services, not products here. But they are services that have a standard expectation of safety and if that standard is not met, they can be thought defective.

Harms from income-producing activity. Later, in comparing carriers with private drivers and landowners, it will be possible to observe that public carriers would ordinarily have a stream of income from the activity causing harm, and that landowners and private drivers may not. Landowners' income, like income of private drivers, might be erratic and not associated with the activity that produced the injury. The idea before insurance may well have been that the costs of injuries could be amortized in a feasible way by an enterprise, but not by an ordinary homeowner or private car driver.

Reciprocal vs. Non-Reciprocal Risks. We encountered the distinction between reciprocal and non-reciprocal risks with *Bexiga* in the last chapter. Here we can noticed that the *Doser* risk is non-reciprocal–the company-defendant has imposed risks on customers not even remotely like any risks imposed by customers on the company. Is that a distinction without a difference, or do some students think those who derive income from imposing non-reciprocal risks should be under a special duty of care?

Effects of the higher duty. What effect does the higher duty of carriers have in the case? To say the carrier owes the highest care or duty hardly tells the carrier what to do; it merely offers the jury an emphatic suggestion that liability is in order, and of course permits an appellate court to uphold a verdict on scant evidence of fault.

Can jurors or judge really find any basis for concluding that a defendant exercised ordinary care but not great care? Older writings on the subject of degrees of care can sound very peculiar. AMES & SMITH'S CASES ON TORTS of 1900 quoted the 4th edition of SHEARMAN & REDFIELD, NEGLIGENCE (4th ed.) § 47:

> Our conclusion is, therefore, that three degrees of care are and should be recognized and enforced by the law of modern times, to wit: (1) Slight care. . . . (2) Ordinary care. . . . (3) Great care. . . .

Professional (or academic) opinion has run the other way in even more "modern times," toward a universal standard of the prudent person. There is Baron Rolfe's famous statement in *Wilson v. Brett*, 11 M. & W. 113, 152 Eng. Rep. 737 (1843) that there was "no difference between negligence and gross negligence, –that it was the same thing, with the addition of a vituperative epithet. . . ."

Because "highest care", like "slight care", is not a measure of anything, is a standard based on such an abstraction cutting it too fine?

Who is a carrier? Note 2 gives one modern definition, from the Texas high court, which also applies a higher standard of care to such carriers. By its terms, the carrier rule applies to common carriers, not private or contract carriers. You might be surprised to find, however, that besides railroads, bus companies, airlines, and passenger cruise ships, even an elevator may be considered a common carrier. *Cash v. Otis Elevator Co.*, 684 P.2d 1041 (Mont. 1984). On the other hand, in *McKethean v. Washington Metropolitan Area Transit Authority*, 588 A.2d 708 (D.C. App. 1991), the court held that a bus company owed no special duty of care to nine intending passengers who were injured by another person while waiting for a bus. *Gomez* sounds like an extraordinary case, holding that Disneyland is a common carrier when it operates its rides, but the court built its conclusion on earlier cases from a number of jurisdictions that held that roller-coaster operators were common carriers, too.

[*b. Host-drivers: The guest statutes*]

ALA. CODE. § 32-1-2. Walking through statutes with students may be a good idea, if for no other reason than to help ease their fear of statutes. This statute sets up a willful or wanton misconduct standard when a "guest being transported without payment" sues for motor vehicle injuries.

Every student should know of the existence of guest statutes as a matter of professional knowledge. However, the statutes are more important for other reasons.

First, they furnish a close comparison to the landowner's rules. In both cases duties are limited because of status on the defendant's property. This comparison becomes tremendously important when a court considers abolishing the landowners' rules or holding a guest statute unconstitutional. If the guest statute is unconstitutional, surely the landowners' rules, developed by the courts, are at least of doubtful integrity.

Second, the guest statute reminds us that law changes, and furnishes a good opportunity to suggest to the student that how change comes about is important. Is everyone represented in the legislature? In the arguments before the court?

Finally, the guest statutes furnish a good situation for reminding students of some basic purposes of tort law and law in general. Will guest statutes influence conduct? Perhaps they never did. If not, we might then consider whether the guest statute represents some kind of justice, some idea about right and wrong.

Why were guest statutes enacted? There may be no single answer, but one possibility may bear on the landowners' rules as well. It is the possibility of a conceptual failure. It may be that the special rules are not intended to relieve landowners or automobile drivers from the duty of reasonable care. Perhaps the special rules for landowners and guests are fumbling attempts to recognize that reasonable care may vary with some circumstances, including, in some circumstances, the circumstance that the plaintiff is a non-paying guest.

But if that was the idea behind the special rules, the expression of the idea proved to be far off the mark. The courts have lost their sympathy with special protections for the car driver. Mysteriously, however, they have generally retained that sympathy for the landowner.

The process of changing–to the guest statute in the 1930s and back to the common law standard of ordinary care in the 1970s and 1980s–is itself interesting. The casebook has been suggesting that change in tort law is an important theme since the introduction of battery cases based on "offense" rather than on "violence." Was the adoption of guest statutes merely the result of the conceptual failure, and is the repeal and repudiation merely a correction of that failure? Or was the adoption of the guest statute a political act? Should legislatures have intervened in the administration of tort law? Access to legislators differs from access to courts.

§ 2. LANDOWNERS' DUTIES TO TRESPASSERS, LICENSEES, INVITEES, AND CHILDREN

[*a. The classifications of entrants and duties owed to them*]

GLADON V. GREATER CLEVELAND REGIONAL TRANSIT AUTHORITY, 662 N.E.2d 287 (Ohio 1996).

Gladon purchased a ticket for the defendant's rapid transit train. On the platform he was attacked chased by unknown males. He ended up on the tracks. The operator of the next train hit the emergency brake but the train struck Gladon and caused serious injury. Gladon alleged (1) negligent security in the premises and (2) negligent operation of the train. The trial court gave summary judgment for the defendant on the first claim. The second claim went to the jury. The trial judge characterized the plaintiff as an invitee and told the jury that the defendant owed a duty of ordinary care to discover and avoid danger to him. The case establishes the following propositions of law:

(1) An invitee who goes outside the area of his invitation becomes a trespasser or licensee.

(2) Neither Gladon's lack of intent to enter the track area nor any privilege he might have had to do so affect his status as a trespasser or licensee; if he was outside the scope of invitation, he was trespasser or licensee (to whom the duties are the same).

(3) Gladon was outside the scope of his invitation and the trial judge therefore erred in giving the ordinary care instruction. because (a) there was no duty to use care to discover a trespasser and (b) no duty of ordinary care arises as to a trespasser until the landowner is on notice or knows his peril.

(4) However, the evidence is sufficient to permit a properly instructed jury to find for the plaintiff (a) on the ground that the train's speed met the wanton standard and (b) whether the operator was on notice from sight of a tennis shoe that someone was on the track in time to avert the impact by ordinary care.

■**FYI: Trespass to Chattels.** You might want to know that courts sometimes carry over the landowner rules to chattel cases. The court in *Basham v. Hunt*, 773 N.E.2d 1213 (Ill. Ct. App. 2002), applied the rules to a trespasser on a garbage truck. In *Olivier v. Snowden*, 426 S.W.2d 545 (Tex. 1968), and *Payne v. M. Greenberg Const.*, 636 P.2d 116 (Ariz. Ct. App. 1981), workers using another's scaffold were treated as trespasser. *See* DOBBS ON TORTS § 232 n.3 (2000).

The implications of *Harris v. Best Business Products, Inc.*, 651 N.W.2d 875 (S.D. 2002), may be even more interesting. There, the plaintiff may have been a "trespasser" in the defendant's motor vehicle because she had been invited to be there by an agent who had no authority to permit her to ride in the vehicle. The tire blew out and the vehicle rolled, injuring the plaintiff. The court held that even if the plaintiff was a trespasser, the defendant owed her a duty of reasonable care. The exact ground is not fully elaborated, but one idea seemed to be that the defendant owed a duty to the traveling public and that the plaintiff, trespasser or not, was a member of that larger class. Anyone in the vicinity of a dangerous vehicle, whether in a car or not, would be at risk. ■

Note 1 simply underscores the importance of the entrant's classification. It is good to remind classes in those states that have abolished the classifications that half of the states still preserve them.

There are, of course, a lot of close calls on which category an entrant falls into, a rather recurring theme in these materials. You might be a trespasser under these landowner rules even if you were not a trespasser in the sense that you could be held liable to the landowner for trespass. See *Copeland v. Baltimore & O.R.R.*, 416 A.2d 1 (D.C. App. 1980) (one carried unconscious onto the defendant's land has the status of a trespasser to whom no duty of reasonable care is owed). On the other hand, one who intentionally enters the land because the land reasonably appeared to be open to the public, as part of a highway, say, is not a trespasser.

Note 2. Social guests may be "invited over," but they are not invitees in the traditional scheme. You should probably emphasize this counter-intuitive point with the class to remind them that legal terms of art are not always consonant with normal English usage.

In the traditional common law scheme, business visitors and public invitees exhaust the invitee category. So ordinary guests such as friends gather for dinner or a party are not invitees. Instead, they are licensees. Too often, one's status is doubtful. In *Zuther v. Schild*, 581 P.2d 385 (Kan 1978), for example, the plaintiff was at the defendant's home as adult helping with a Girl Scout meeting. The court considered the plaintiff to be a guest. (The cases is no longer technically important in Kansas law, because that state has now abolished the categories). In *Bader v. Lawson*, 898 S.W.2d 40 (Ark. 1995) neighbors watched each other's children from time to time on casual basis, but a child on the neighbor's land was not an invitee.

The question about Indiana's *Burrell v. Meads* approach anticipates later materials in § 4, which get into other state variations (or outright rejections) of the entrant categories. The question here is whether it makes more sense to students to group social guests into a classification that is lumped in with trespassers in terms of the landowner's duty, or whether social guests should be "elevated" to the same status as invitees, and thus owed a duty of reasonable care. You can probably postpone any discussion of this until you get into § 4.Treating social guests as "invitees," as Indiana has done, may achieve much the same thing as treating invitees and licensees alike, a modern variant considered in upcoming materials.

Note 3. Changing categories. As *Gladon* indicates, one who otherwise an invitee or licensee exceeds the scope of the invitation or license, becomes a trespasser, as where, invited into the bar, he enters quarters marked private. *Monsivais v. Winzenried*, 508 N.W.2d 620 (Wis. 1993). The *area* of invitation cases are usually easy enough. You are not an invitee in private portions of the grocery store. If you try to apply similar rules to the entrant's *purpose* you have troubles. In *Woodty* the court held that Mrs. Woodty was an invitee. Although her actions violated motel rules, "the activity in which Mrs. Woodty was engaged did not enhance the risk of causing a fire. . . . . [She was] engaging in the same type of activity (sleeping in a bed) in which a registered guest would normally engage."

Note 4. Duty owed to invitees. Students should realize that the duty owed to invitees is the same reasonable and prudent person under the same or similar circumstances duty they have already studied. Some believe that something must be different about it, but that general duty of care *is* what we are talking about here.

Note 5. Duties to trespassers and licensees. *Discovery of trespasser and his peril.* See DOBBS ON TORTS § 232, at 594. Restatement Second of Torts § 334 imposes liability to trespassers if (a) trespassers constantly intrude in a limited area, and (b) the injury results from the landowner's failure to use reasonable care in carrying on dangerous activities that risk death or serious bodily harm. This is the Restatement's version of the "footpath" exception. Section 335 imposes liability for artificial conditions highly dangerous to "constant" trespassers, and § 336 and § 337 impose liability to known trespassers for activities and artificial conditions. The condition-activity distinction was difficult enough that the drafters covered the case of moving machinery separately in § 338, providing for liability of the landowner to known trespassers who might be injured by "controllable forces."

Scope of the implied license. Courts sometimes explain the footpath or "constant trespassers" exception as an implied license. This may not be an accurate way of looking at the rule, but it does facilitate asking an important question: what is the scope of the license?

The California statute cited here, Civil Code § 847, appears to protect the landowner even if he inflicts injury by active conduct, not merely by reason of a dangerous condition on the land. Does that differ from the common law privilege to defend self and property and to repel trespassers? Seemingly so; its broad language at least arguably protects unreasonable force so long as the landowner is not chargeable with "willful, wanton, or criminal conduct." The statute by its terms applies only to immunize the landowner (not an occupier) when the plaintiff is injured in the course of committing one of the particular felonies listed in the statute; among those felonies are burglary and robbery. Thus the statute would apply, typically, only to a subset of those who would be classified as trespassers in other states. (Remember that California has abolished all of the entrant categories in favor of a reasonable care standard for all entrants. See *Rowland v. Christian*, § 4.)

Licensees. In *Park v. Rogers*, 825 A.2d 1128 (N.J. 2003), a social guest (thus a licensee) fell down a dark stairway with a short railing and sued the homeowner. Reaffirming the "settled principle that a homeowner has a duty to warn the unwary social guest of a condition of the premises that a homeowner knows or has reason to know creates an unreasonable risk of harm," the court reversed a defense summary judgment. Genuine issues of fact remained as to whether the property owners knew or should have known that the handrail posed an unreasonable risk of harm, and whether the plaintiff as a licensee should have observed where the handrail ended through the reasonable use of her faculties. If the licensee would have observed the hazard through the use of reasonable care, the court said, there would be no liability on "open and obvious" grounds. (More on "open and obvious" is coming up, in *O'Sullivan* and Notes.)

Note 6. Conditions versus activities. A good statement of the rule that the status of the plaintiff on the land is irrelevant when it comes to active negligence, as distinct from dangerous conditions, is found in *Lipham v. Federated Department Stores,* Inc., 440 S.E.2d 193 (Ga. 1994). What counts as a condition can be puzzling. If you actively dig a hole in the ground and one minute later the plaintiff falls in it, is it a condition or were you actively negligent? Cf. *Hofer v. Meyer*, 295 N.W.2d 333 (S.D. 1980) (is a horse an artificial condition on the land); *Mercer v. Fritts*, 676 P.2d 150 (Kan. Ct. App. 1984) (licensee injured when the stallion became sexually excited in the presence of a mare and, getting rid of all impediments, threw the guest, held, case not governed by landowner rules but by injury-by-animals law, Restatement Second of Torts § 518).

Perceptive students may recognize that the Ohio court in *Gladon* applies the entrant classifications to the plaintiff there when the alleged negligence of the defendant is in driving a train – an activity if there ever was one. If the court had held that the landowner duty/entrant classification scheme did not apply because the negligence did not concern a "condition on the land," then presumably the plaintiff would have recovered, based on the jury's determination at trial. The case again emphasizes the importance of the classifications to the outcome of cases.

Note 7. Hazards originating on adjacent land. It is doubtful whether the landowner had any right to cut a tree not on his property. If he had no ability to control the hazard, it makes sense not to place him under any duty to do so.

Note 8. Duties to persons outside the land. Lack of control over adjacent land is often a very often important factor in the cases. Compare *Rhudy v. Bottlecaps, Inc.,* 830 A.2d 402 (Del. 2003) (bar owner held not liable for murder of patron in public parking lot promoted as the bar's "free parking" because bar did not increase the risk of crime on the lot, bar owner could not control crime on the lot, and bar did not own lot) with *Mata v. Mata*, 105 Cal.App.4th 1121 (2003) (bar owner owed a duty to take reasonable measures to prevent foreseeable violence in adjacent parking lot because the bar "maintained" the lot, even though it did not own it).

Vegetation obscuring intersection. To some extent, the landowner's duties to those outside the land overlaps the "natural conditions" category. Some courts reject any duty on the part of the landowner to trim vegetation that obscures vision at an intersection for the benefit of drivers on abutting roads.

Others see these as cases raising breach of duty or scope of duty issues. See generally DOBBS ON TORTS § 231 (2000).

[*b. Child trespassers*]

BENNETT V. STANLEY, 748 N.E.2d 41 (Ohio 2001)

A five-year-old child trespassed into his next-door neighbor's (the Stanleys') back yard and fell into their pool, which had been allowed to "go natural," filling with rainwater and full of tadpoles, frogs and snakes. He fell in; his mother tried vainly to save him, and both drowned. The husband/father sued the Stanleys on a negligence theory. The trial court granted the Stanley's motion for summary judgment on the ground that both the boy and his mother were trespassers and thus owed only a duty not to willfully or wantonly injury them, a level of misconduct not alleged by the plaintiff. The court here discusses the child trespasser rules in some detail and announces its adoption of the "attractive nuisance" doctrine for the first time. Thus the summary judgment is reversed.

Note 1. The "attractive nuisance" rule. As the *Bennett* court makes clear, the rule is well-accepted in the vast majority of states. A few states reject it. See *Baisley v. Missisquoi Cemetery Ass'n*, 708 A.2d 924 (Vt. 1998) (but nonetheless holding that a claim based upon a child's falling on a dangerous fence was to be judged under the reasonable care, not the trespasser standard).

Judges sometimes seem to feel that if the "attractive nuisance" doctrine applies, the defendant will then be liable without fault, but of course that is not so. The defendant is liable only for negligence. To invoke the doctrine only allows the child to escape the trespasser category. She must still prove that she was harmed by negligence. Conversely, the child who loses the attractive nuisance issue and is thus classed as a trespasser or licensee may still win if she can show that the defendant the defendant was guilty of willful or wanton misconduct. That happened in *Wiles v. Metzger*, 473 N.W.2d 113 (Neb. 1991), where boys 12 and 18 camped in a cave and were killed when it caved in. The landowner knew of previous cave-ins but had not closed off the cave. The court held that boys would appreciate the risk of cave-ins and thus could not claim the attractive nuisance doctrine. At the same time, however, the landowner, because he knew the danger, might be guilty of wanton misconduct and might still be liable, so summary judgment for the defendant was inappropriate.

History. In addition to those cited in *Bennett*, another leading case is *Keefe v. Milwaukee & St. P. Ry.*, 21 Minn. 207 (1875) (children were "allured into a danger whose nature and extent they, being without judgment or discretion, could neither apprehend nor appreciate, and against which they could not protect themselves. . . .[W]hat an express invitation would be to an adult, the temptation of an attractive plaything is to a child.").

Do we need a child trespasser or "attractive nuisance" rule at all? If you restate the rules, they look very much like ordinary negligence rules with the addition of the requirement that the landowner must know or have reason to know of the danger. If he does, then he may be liable if he should foresee that a child will be on the land and that because of her tender years she would not appreciate the danger and fails to act as a reasonable person to avoid or minimize the danger. The Restatement's § 339 is stated solely in terms of duty, but it seems easier to state the rule as a duty of ordinary care that is triggered when certain circumstances occur—the child's presence is foreseeable, she cannot take care of herself, and the landowner either knows or has reason to know of the danger. The topic of child trespassers is summarized in See DOBBS ON TORTS § 236 (2000).

Suppose the landowner foresees that children of tender years will be on his property and that because of their age and inexperience they will not appreciate the risk of moving machinery on the land. The special rules for child trespassers would apply so that the child would not be classed as a licensee or trespasser and the defendant would owe a duty of care. If he breached that duty, say by failing to fence off the machinery, can he still plead comparative fault on the part of the child?

To invoke the special trespasser rules, the trier must find that because of their age and inexperience, children of age like the plaintiff's would be predictably unable to protect themselves. Does such a finding also necessarily mean that the child was not chargeable with comparative fault under the child standard of care, at least if the child was not herself of unusual ability or experience? Alternatively, might it mean that the landowner owed a *Bexiga* duty to protect the foreseeable child from her own inability and therefore could not plead comparative fault?

Florida has struggled with the problem, taking the view that comparative fault of a child could not be a defense if attractive nuisance is established. *Larnel Builders, Inc. v. Martin*, 110 So.2d 649, 650 (1959). This has led to some strange stratagems in which the defendant seeks to admit a duty of care so the attractive nuisance doctrine is unnecessary and the plaintiff declines the admission. See *Martinello v. B & P USA, Inc.*, 566 So.2d 761 (Fla. 1990).

New Jersey, though, has held that the child's contributory fault is to be considered in attractive nuisance cases In addition, the child's appreciation of the risk would negate the landowner's duty of protection. *Vega v. Piedilato*, 713 A.2d 442 (N.J. 1998).

Note 2. Tender years. From about puberty onwards, the "child" is a trespasser when he enters the land even though some courts claim he cannot be negligent by ordinary standards. In addition, the landowner is not liable unless there is reason to think that the child will be unable to protect himself, so some children are not at risk because the landowner can expect them to avoid the danger. (See *O'Sullivan v. Shaw*, the next case.)

How should the age issue work if the child is 15 but has the mental age of nine? In *Crosby v. Savannah Elec. & Power Co.*, 150 S.E.2d 563 (Ga. Ct. App.

1966) a 15-year-old boy with a mental age of 8 or 9 climbed the defendant's utility pole, trying to retrieve his balloon. He was large enough because of his age to reach the parapet of a nearby building and from there to attain the upper reaches of the pole. But he was mentally limited enough to ignore the risk. He touched an uninsulated wire and fell to the ground. The court said that neither his physical nor mental condition affected the fact that this was a trespass.

Note 3. The leading case requiring that the child be attracted by the instrumentality that harmed her was *United Zinc & Chemical Co. v. Britt*, 258 U.S. 268 (1921) (Holmes, J.). Children eight and eleven, traveling in Kansas in July and camping near the defendants' land, wandered onto the land and discovered a clear pool of water. The pool was probably not visible from outside the land, and in any event it was not what led them to enter the land. They swam in the pool. They were poisoned by the sulfuric acid and zinc smelter and died. Holmes held that since they had not been attracted by this dangerous condition, there was no duty to them. There is some contemporary support for this rule, but the mainstream cases now reject it. That is, if a child is attracted by one hazard but injured by another, the "attractive nuisance" doctrine still applies. *See.e.g., Kessler v. Mortenson*, 16 P.3d 1225 (Utah 2000).

Note 4. Common hazards. *Authorities.* Many courts continue to state the rule that this "attractive nuisance" doctrine does not apply to common hazards, especially waters and fires, but sometime including heights and moving railroad trains. Some courts have explicitly rejected the broad common hazard limitation, while others continue to state it but ignore it in some appealing cases.

Real basis for denying relief? The real basis for the common hazard rule is probably akin to the real basis for the categories—it states the negligence rules in terms of duty so that courts can more readily maintain control over the issue. Thus in Arizona, an arid state where irrigation is of critical importance, an irrigation canal cannot be considered an attractive nuisance, *Dombrowski v. Maricopa County Munc. Water Consev. Dist.*, 496 P.2d 136 (Ariz. 1972), but a swimming pool can, see *Giacona v. Tapley*, 428 P.2d 439 (Ariz. Ct. App. 1967). The difference lies in the social and economic importance of the two activities and the relative cost of making them safe—in other words, in a cost-benefit analysis that seems very much like the kind of negligence analysis so commonly used. But it is not treated as a negligence issue for the jury, rather as a duty issue for the court so that close control over liability can be maintained.

[*c. Open and obvious hazards*]

O'SULLIVAN V. SHAW, 726 N.E.2d 951 (Mass. 2000)

This case gives you a chance to see how well students are retaining their learning of assumed risk. It also gives you a chance to relate the underlying idea back to *Stinnett v. Buchele,* Chapter 6, § 1.

Duty to invitee (and some licensees). The landowner owes an invitee the duty of ordinary care, the care of a reasonable and prudent person under the circumstances. He may owe a similar duty to a licensee whose presence is known if he also knows of the danger. The duty of reasonable care may require affirmative action if a reasonable person would take it, for example, action to inspect the premises. What if the invitee can perceive the danger for herself?

Open and obvious danger. The rule barring recovery against landowners for obvious dangers is often framed as a no-duty rule, both about invitees and licensees. *See, e.g., Armstrong v. Best Buy Co.,* 788 N.E.2d 1088 (Ohio 2003) (no duty owed by store to shopper who crashed into a shopping cart guardrail that was an "open and obvious" hazard). We'll see this no-duty conception arising again in products liability cases. The idea that the landowner owes no duty to protect from an obvious danger has great appeal if you don't give it a lot of thought, but thoughtful analysis shows it needs some adjustment, at least in comparative fault jurisdictions. The notes introduce two sets of closely related problems about the rule. The issues can be discussed in connection with case analysis of *O'Sullivan* or separately.

Notes 2 & 3. Is the supposed rule against liability based upon the conclusion that the defendant has no duty? That he was not negligent on the facts? Or that the plaintiff was chargeable with contributory negligence or assumed risk? All three views can be found in the cases. See, e.g., *Lilya v. Greater Gulf State Fair, Inc.,* 855 So.2d 1049 (Ala. 2003) (reciting factors that appear to go to all views, in case involving man thrown from state fair ride called "Rolling Thunder") On the foreseeability theory advanced in *O'Sullivan,* however, it seems most logical to say that obvious danger is related both to the negligence and to the comparative fault issue. Cf. *Wal-Mart Stores, Inc. v. Miller,* 102 S.W.3d 706 (Tex. 2003) (holding that a plumber had actual knowledge of the condition of stairs before he fell on them and thus could not recover).

"No duty" seems an exaggerated expression, for that implies either that the landowner would escape liability even when harm was foreseeable or that judges rather than jurors would decide foreseeability. If we regard the issue is one of negligence in the first instance, the jury would decide whether, given obvious danger, harm was foreseeable. It would then decide whether the plaintiff's encounter with the obvious danger involved comparative fault. In extreme cases, judges might think that reasonable persons could not differ or that the plaintiff failed to prove that harm was foreseeable to the defendant in spite of the obviousness of the danger. In such cases, judges should direct a verdict or grant summary judgment. That would not be like saying that no duty exists, because a literal no duty rule would eliminate claims on which people might reasonably differ.

Note 4. Harm foreseeable in spite of obvious danger. In some cases, harm is foreseeable in spite of the obviousness of the danger. The underlying principle is one we saw in *Stinnett v. Buchele* in Chapter 6. It is that the defendant is not negligent at all if he reasonably thinks no harm will come to the plaintiff. He might reasonably think that if the plaintiff is in position to protect herself. Obvious danger correlates highly with those conditions; that is why the rule has proved to be such an attractive one to courts.

Yet while obvious danger and foreseeability of harm do correlate, they do not match. In some cases, the defendant can definitely foresee harm to others from obvious dangers. The shopper who is distracted, whose vision is obscured by crowds or partly blocked by packages she is carrying, is certainly foreseeable. Since a shopper would not ever expect to find a large hole in a department store's aisle, she would not necessarily even be negligent if she fell in it under those circumstances.

a. In *Hale*, cited here, the court held that the "open and obvious" nature of the hazard did not bar the plaintiff's claim. A landowner may be liable to an invitee if the landowner has reason to believe that the invitee will proceed to encounter the known or obvious hazard because to a reasonable person in his position the advantages of doing so would outweigh the risks. Equally, a landowner may breach a duty of care for failing to take reasonable steps to protect and invitee from an obvious danger that an invitee might encounter because he is distracted, or has forgotten about the hazard. *Fulmer v. Timber Inn Restaurant Lounge, Inc.,* also raised here, is a variation on these common ideas that will be hard for some to take. The court held that harm was foreseeable if you serve a lot of alcohol to patrons at the top of a long flight of stairs and take no steps to prevent it. At the same time, the court recognized that the intoxicated plaintiff's comparative fault could be considered in reducing damages.

In the third edition we used a shopper case to deal with the open and obvious danger problem. The shopper there was carrying a large mirror sold in the store and did not see an inappropriately-placed pillar. He walked into it on the mirror side and was injured. The Illinois court held that open and obvious danger was relevant to the issues of plaintiff-fault and defendant-negligence, but that a rule forbidding recovery when danger was obvious was inappropriate. This was *Ward v. K Mart Corp.,* 554 N.E.2d 223 (Ill. 1990). We removed the case and substituted *O'Sullivan* because the Illinois legislature prescribed a rule of law that the landowner had no duty to warn or protect from an obvious danger. 740 ILCS 130/2. But it remains a great case to bring up in class as an example of a foreseeable open and obvious hazard, since many students will laughingly admit to having walked into a pillar or two in their lives.

Many falling-down and bumping-into claims are unattractive. We tend to feel that the pedestrian is in charge and should watch where she is going. In addition, many students probably assume that injuries are minor. But the point of the justice system is to determine claims on their individual merits, not on the merits or demerits of the collective claims of other individuals.

b. The example in subparagraph *b.* is one you can develop or ignore as time permits. It may differ from the shopper case. In this example, the plaintiff knows of the danger but is pressed by circumstances to encounter it anyway—no one wants to be without power in the dead of winter. Furthermore, she has a public right to enter a utility office. This example harks back to ideas of plaintiff-no-duty raised in Chapter 9.

Note 5. Children and "open and obvious" hazards. In the *Bragan* case cited here, the court held that the child standard of care did apply when applying the "open and obvious" rule – that is, that a landowner owed a child a "heightened duty" and the issue was whether the hazard was open and obvious to a child of the same age, intelligence and experience as the injured child. In *Grant*, also cited, the court agreed, stressing that the test in determining the foreseeability of injury to a child is whether a typical child "old enough to be at large" would lack the maturity to understand and appreciate the risk involved in the hazard on the land. In other words, the answer to the first question in the note is "yes."

Note 6. Natural conditions: Snow and ice. In *Tarricone v. State*, 571 N.Y.S.2d 845 (App. Div. 1991), the plaintiff had eaten at an overlook or pull-off on a scenic highway maintained by the state along the Delaware River. After lunch she climbed over the low wall to a ledge on its river side. The ledge was small and unfenced. She fell off the 200 foot escarpment, suffering injuries that rendered her paraplegic. The court held that the natural conditions rule precluded recovery. Why is it not the open and obvious danger rule? Put otherwise, isn't this a simple case of no negligence? The difference between a rule about natural conditions and a no-negligence conclusion becomes apparent if you imagine the same case but with a ledge that (quite naturally) creates a misleading appearance of safety. The ledge is still "natural" and the state would avoid liability if the natural condition rule is applied. But the misleading appearance makes it all too likely that someone will be injured who *cannot* take care of herself. To say that the balance of costs and benefits favors the defendant when the plaintiff can care for herself is most definitely not to say that when the defendant knows exactly the contrary. Some people want to go much further because the state does know that SOME people who CAN care for themselves will not in fact do so and will thus be injured. So harm is foreseeable even if the ledge is not misleading in appearance, as the *Tarricone* Court recognized. Even so, the costs of protecting people count heavily indeed when they can protect themselves and when the defendant can reasonably expect them to do so. So maybe the *Tarricone* court could plausibly have refused to impose liability on the ground that, absent a misleading appearance or knowledge that the ledge was used for human sacrifice, the state was simply not negligent.

Note 7. The rescue doctrine and "open and obvious" hazards. *Clinkscales* answers this question "no." The plaintiff in that case, a patron in defendant's bar, rushed to help try to put out a propane gas leak that had started a fire; when he approached the tank, it exploded. The defendant argued that it "owed no duty as a matter of law because the fire and gas leak constituted a known and obvious danger." The court noted that generally in Iowa, "[t]he possessor of land ... is not liable when the injuries sustained by a business invitee were caused by a known or obvious danger." But it concluded that a rescue situation calls for a different analysis and result: "Fire and escaping gas is obviously dangerous. That is not in doubt. This is not your garden-variety premises-liability case, however – it involves an attempted rescue. . . . In a rescue case such as this, it is *axiomatic* that the danger approached is obviously dangerous. *Danger* invites the rescue. To rule the presence of a known and obvious dangerous condition would, as a matter of law, negate any duty to invitee-rescuers would completely eviscerate the rescue doctrine where the rescuer happened to be an invitee of the defendant when the condition first occurred."

§ 3. THE FIREFIGHTER'S RULE

Preliminary note. The firefighters' rule originated as a premises liability rule – or rather, a premises non-liability rule. But it has lost its root in land law and now generally applies to remove tort law protections from public safety officers in many situations outside the land. With this expansion, courts have given new reasons associated with assumed risk or good or bad public policy. Accordingly, you could take up this material with assumed risk or even as a separate unique chapter, as in DOBBS ON TORTS Chapter 17 (2000). The assumed risk approach is unrelated to any contributory fault; it is a no-duty approach grounded in courts' perceptions of policy, so something could be said for considering the topic almost anywhere after you have covered both assumed risk and the licensee category. We've kept it in the landowner materials in default of a good clear place for it. If you are going to cover the next section on abolition of the categories, this section may get in your way. You could consider taking it up at the end of the chapter instead of at this location.

MINNICH V. MED-WASTE, INC., 564 S.E.2d 98 (S.C. 2002)

Minnich soundly rejects the firefighter's rule, holding that South Carolina has not and does not "singl[e] out police officers and firefighters for discriminatory treatment." This is not the majority approach, as **Note 1** points out. But the *Minnich* case helpfully discusses both the rationales for the rule and the various forms of the rule in reaching its decision.

Theories for barring firefighters. The court reviews three rationales for the rule barring firefighters' recovery for injuries sustained in the performance of their duties, and finds them all lacking merit: (1) The firefighter was a licensee on the land to whom no duty of care was owed. (2) The firefighter assumed the risk. (3) Public policy disfavors liability. Policies include (a) that liability for injuries is properly borne by the public, not the individual property owner; (b) that injuries are often unforeseeable because firefighters enter property at strange times and in places off-limits to the public; and (c) because the public already compensates firefighters for confronting dangers, landowners would be paying "multiple penalties" if they had to compensate injured firefighters.

The court also helpfully summarizes various state approaches to the firefighter's rule, and finds them wildly inconsistent. The rule, in sum, is "riddled with exceptions, and criticism of the rule abounds."

You can talk about the *Minnich* court's statements in connection with the final Note in this section, or you can bring the final Note into your discussion of *Minnich*. The big question is whether the firefighter's rule is a good one, and why or why not. Do the policies put forth in support seem sound to the class? A secondary question is one of prediction; the cases seem to pull in opposite directions, with some courts and legislatures cutting back on the rule, or eliminating it, and others expanding it (see **Note 4**). Which trend is going to win out, and why?

Note 2. Assumed risk/no duty. Courts have often adopted an assumed risk analysis. This is not necessarily different from a policy analysis that yields the no- duty conclusion. The *Neighbarger* court quoted here also said, "Under the firefighter's rule, a member of the public who negligently starts a fire owes no duty of care to assure that the firefighter who is summoned to combat the fire is not injured thereby." But the same court said later that "undergirding legal principle of the rule is assumption of the risk." *Calatayud v. State,* 959 P.2d 360 (Cal. 1998). Assumed risk in these cases makes sense as no-duty rule, not as contributory fault. Conceivably, the no duty conclusion might result from the firefighter's contract, but that does not seem to be factually supported. One reason it is not is that the contract is with his employer, while the negligence claim is against someone else altogether.

Note 3. No duty/public policy. The worker's compensation type argument is one we encounter in the *Feres* cases in Chapter 15 on governmental immunity. It does not make much sense, because other workers protected by workers' compensation are permitted to sue third-party tortfeasors. If they recover, part of their recovery in fact goes to repay the employer for his worker's compensation payments. For this reason, the firefighter would not be overcompensated. The firefighter's rule actually prevents the public employer from recovering any part of the compensation payment from the negligent actor.

In *Neighbarger*, cited in Note 2, Justice Mosk argued that the publicly paid firefighter was in the role of the contractor because the firesetter was to be identified with the "public" that paid the firefighter through taxes: "When the firefighter is publicly employed, the public, having secured the services of the firefighter by taxing itself, stands in the shoes of the person who hires a contractor to cure a dangerous condition. In effect, the public has purchased exoneration from the duty of care and should not have to pay twice, through taxation and through individual liability, for that service." But you might wonder whether this conception–and it is a conception, not a fact–is merely another way of expressing the conclusion rather than a reason for it. The "public" (meaning individuals in the public) does not literally stand in someone's shoes. About all you can say is that the judge wants to think of the case that way.

Notes 4-7. Expansions and Persons covered. These notes seem largely self-explanatory. The rule has been applied to volunteer firefighters as well as to paid firefighters, *see* DOBBS ON TORTS § 287 (2000), albeit not by all courts.

Note 8. Wrongdoing not covered. (1) Intentional, wanton misconduct is not immunized by the firefighter's rule, as the *Baldonado* court held. However, *Young v. Sherwin-Williams Co.*, 569 A.2d 1173 (D.C. App.1990) refused to recognize this limitation. A man named Sprouse was driver for Sherwin-Williams. He first overloaded his truck, then consumed large quantities of alcohol before setting off with the rig. He crashed into a bridge rail. The cab of the truck hung over the edge. The door flew open, and Sprouse was dangling over a 50-foot drop to the ground, hanging on to the steering wheel with one hand. Young, a professional firefighter (a pumper driver) arrived on the scene. When Sprouse fell, Young attempted to catch him. He probably saved Sprouse's life, but Young himself was seriously injured. Sprouse and Sherwin-Williams sought to avoid liability under the professional rescuers' doctrine. Young countered with the argument that Sprouse's drunk driving was wilfull and wanton misconduct. The court rejected the argument on the ground the firefighter or professional rescuer doctrine was based on assumed risk, not the degree of culpability of the rescued person.

(2) If the defendant's negligent conduct violates a fire safety ordinance or statute, he may lose the special protection of the firefighter's rule.

(3) The rule does not bar claims resulting from risks not inherent in the job undertaken. This assumed-risk type reasoning permits recovery when the injury occurs from misconduct that did not necessitate the firefighter's presence. That would include all misconduct occurring after the firefighter arrives at the scene. It may also include other tortious conduct of the defendant that is unrelated to fire protection, for instance, the attack by the defendant's dogs in the second example.

When a public safety officer is injured by a defective product that necessitated the officer's presence in the first place–say a burning car– the firefighters' rule may be applied. See DOBBS ON TORTS § 287, p. 778 (2000). However, when the product defect caused harm to the officer but was not the reason for the officer's presence, recovery may be permitted. See *McKernan v. General Motors Corp.*, 3 P.3d 1261 (Kan. 2000). This topic is included in the notes following *Bowling v. Heil*, Chapter 24, § 8.

§ 4. ADOPTING A REASONABLE CARE STANDARD FOR LANDOWNERS

Preliminary Note. This section considers whether the special rules for landowners are desirable. If you just covered the firefighters' rule, you may need to review your class on the trespasser, licensee, and invitee rules.

Do the special privileges that exempt the landowner from an obligation of reasonable care to licensees and trespassers deviate from the fault principle? Professor Robert Rabin, considering these rules and some others, has observed that the fault principle was far from universal and that it was indeed something of a myth. He suggested, in line with many others, that the landowners' rules arose out of a special regard for the "sanctity of land." *See* Robert Rabin, *The Historical Development of the Fault Principle: A Reinterpretation*, 15 GA. L. REV. 925, 934 (1981).

An alternative interpretation is that the landowners' rules are merely inept expressions of a half-formed idea of the negligence standard. In this view, the landowners' rules might represent a conceptual failure–a failure to understand that the negligence concept is sufficiently flexible to take status on the land into account. It would not be the only example of that failure. For instance, you might have a strong suspicion that courts protecting emergency vehicles under a recklessness or wanton misconduct standard, *e.g., Saarinen v. Kerr,* 644 N.E.2d 988 (N.Y. 1994), are really only thinking that the exigencies of the case require conduct that would be too risky in other circumstances, and that on analysis they'd get the same results by applying the reasonable-person-under-the-circumstances standard. One law review article suggests that the equine activity statutes, immunizing various persons involved in providing "equine activities" might be best justified because they "provide immunity for benevolent sponsors who employ reasonable efforts to facilitate safe equine activities." Terence J. Centner, *The New Equine Liability Statutes,* 62 TENN. L. REV. 997, 1004 (1995). But of course if the sponsor met the standards described in this justification, the sponsor would not be negligent at all because the sponsor would have made "reasonable efforts" for "safe equine activities."

To the extent that these statutes are lobbied by interest groups, they don't represent anything but the best deal the group can get the legislature to cut for them. But the thinking of a court or legislator attempting to do the right thing may well be based on nothing more than a failure to appreciate that the reasonable person standard takes circumstances into account.

In *Southcote v. Stanley,* 1 H. & N. 247, 156 Eng. Rep. 1195 (1856), the court explained the rules for licensees by saying that while the licensee is in the landowner's premises "he is in the same position as any other member of the establishment . . . and he must take his chance with the rest." This sounds very much like some form of assumed risk. And as observed in presentation of the assumed risk materials, the assumed risk rules and no-duty rules might be regarded as merely two ways of expressing the same thing. But it might have been an assumed risk based in actual expectations–customs of the parties, who were in a position to provide for their own safety. If that is what the judges meant, it sounds like a case of no negligence. If you choose to spend the weekend with people who drop greasy uncooked bacon on the kitchen floor, you are in the same position as Mr. Stinnett. You had better protect yourself by watching where you step: if you can't take the grease, stay out of the kitchen. The family is disgusting and sloppy but it is not negligent in behaving according to its custom, so long as you become an "insider" pro temp. *Southcote* itself might well be based on the idea that one's status was an important factor in how a reasonable landowner would prepare the conditions on the land.

There is another strand in the desire to use special landowner rules. It is fear of the jury and the desire of judges to have handy rules for keeping control over verdicts in landowner cases. *See* Marsh, *The History and Comparative Law of Invitees, Licensees and Trespassers*, 69 L.Q. REV. 182, 185-86. In the days when these rules were first applied, we might speculate that jurors would seldom have been landowners themselves and landowners would have been viewed a rich who could afford to pay. Correspondingly, there was no homeowner's insurance policy available. In that situation, tight judicial control, at least in England, is not surprising.

Professor James Henderson has suggested a different justification. He is afraid that without such rules courts cannot be protected from "potentially unmanageable openendedness." He sees the ordinary negligence rules as difficult and the categories as relatively manageable, a view that faces 180° away from the *Rowland* decision below. He feels the landowners rules–or some similar rules–are needed not only to make the cases manageable, but also to permit courts to frame issues in a way that permits meaningful adjudication. *See* James Henderson, *Expanding the Negligence Concept: Retreat from the Rule of Law*, 51 IND. L.J. 467 (1976).

Yet the implications of the *Carroll Towing* risk-utility formula seem to be that you must judge risks and utilities by the facts of individual cases, or as Judge Linde said in *Donaca v. Curry County,* 734 P.2d 1339 (Or. 1987), you need empirical data to determine risks and costs; you cannot apply any analysis of risks and costs to all driveways alike. To make a rule that treats all landowners in one category is to reject a risk-utility analysis for everything in that category. That might be justified if the risk-utility balance were almost invariably the same in landowner cases, but that is simply not the case. A huge pit near the road almost certainly has a different set of risks and its repair a different set of costs than a scrap of bacon dropped on the kitchen floor. You might similarly think the categories of entrants are too broad to permit judgment about the real costs and utilities.

A less formal way to consider the justice, policy, and utility of the landowners' rules might be to consider the facts in *Christensen v. Potratz,* 597 P.2d 595 (Idaho 1979). The plaintiff was on a hunting trip with defendant, both sleeping in a camper which fit into the well of defendant's pick-up trick. A propane stove or some part of it exploded, causing injury to the plaintiff. In a guest statute state, would the duty owed vary according to whether the camper was being driven at the time? Under the landowner rules, would it matter whether the camper was parked on the defendant's land or in a public campground? Would the activity-condition distinction be involved if defendant had installed the stove three days earlier? Such questions are essential under the landowner rules, but they take us far from the merits of the case.

ROWLAND V. CHRISTIAN , 443 P.2d 561 (Cal. 1968)

Under the normal licensee rules, the plaintiff could have recovered if defendant knew of the danger and knew plaintiff was about to encounter it. California's rule as to licensees, however, seems to have been more stringent and the court was forced to discard the categories entirely or to otherwise modify its rules if recovery was to be allowed.

The *Rowland* case, and the *Scurti* abstract case that follows, together raise questions of policy and justice. The radical view would presumably hold that the landowners' rules simply intend to protect the landowner, even if he is at fault. A more moderate view would be that the rules are intended to protect the landowner from the vagaries of the jury, but not from responsibility for fault, and that the rules are designed to let judges decide fault rather than juries. Still another view is that the rules are needed to provide a basis for meaningful adjudication. *Rowland* holds a simple view: (1) the rules lead to wrong results and (2) the rules are too complex compared to a simple assessment of negligence. Both rules and adjudication—justice tailored to the individual facts—are required for successful law. Whatever the balance should be in tort cases generally, is there any reason to make it different in landowner cases?

There is at least some reason to doubt that the rules lead to wrong results in a substantial body of cases, though they surely do lead to wrong results in some. If it is true, as Professor Hawkins has suggested (see Note 3 following *Scurti*) that most cases would come out the same way, *Rowland's* first premise is undercut. But even if there is only *some* difference in the landowners rules and the negligence standard, *Rowland* might be sound if that difference reflected injustice. Does it?

Rowland's second premise is that the whole process of classification on the one hand and restating the duty on the other is simply too complex. Can the students see any justification for this view?

Although the case is heavily edited, students can see that the *Rowland* court tries to assess the validity of the categorical rules by assessing a series of factors. These are factors taken from earlier decisions in determining whether to recognize a duty. They are: (1) closeness of connection between injury and defendant's conduct, (2) moral blame, (3) the policy of preventing future harm [deterrence]; (4) prevalence and availability of insurance; (5) foreseeability of harm, (6) certainty of injury, (7) burden to the defendant, (8) consequences to the community of imposing a duty of reasonable care, and (9) cost of insurance. The court thought that the first three factors had almost nothing to justify the categories and that the remainder were not persuasive.

For example, the burden of avoiding injury (number 7) might be same in many cases whether you used categories or reasonable care rules.

Note 2. Status of the traditional rule. About half of the states have modified the traditional classification scheme in some significant way. At this writing, Alaska, California, Hawaii, Louisiana, Nevada, New Hampshire and New York follow the rule in *Rowland,* thus imposing a duty of reasonable care even to trespassers. The District of Columbia, Illinois, Iowa, Kansas, Maine, Massachusetts, Minnesota, Nebraska, North Carolina, North Dakota, Rhode Island, Tennessee, West Virginia, Wisconsin, and Wyoming have in some form abolished the distinction between invitees and licensees while retaining the trespasser category. *See* DOBBS ON TORTS § 237 (2000). *See also* JOSEPH PAGE, THE LAW OF PREMISES LIABILITY § 6.4 (3d ed. 1988 & David Elder supp.). In *Sheets v. Ritt, Ritt & Ritt, Inc.,* 581 N.W.2d 602 (Iowa 1998), Iowa left open the possibility of joining the *Rowland* group, but that has not yet occurred. See *Alexander v. Medical Assocs. Clinic,* 646 N.W.2d 74 (2002) (reaffirming preserving the trespasser category). The Illinois rule is statutory, as reflected in *Ward.* The English statute (discussed below) adopts a similar rule. Rhode Island and the District of Columbia originally followed the *Rowland* rule, but then decided to keep the trespasser category. See *Holland v. Baltimore & Ohio R.R.,* 431 A.2d 597 (D.C. App. 1981); *Tantimonico v. Allendale Mutual Ins. Co.,* 637 A.2d 1056 (R.I. 1994). Other courts have done almost as well by treating social guests as invitees. See, e.g., *Burrell v. Meads,* 561 N.E.2d 637 (Ind. 1991). A similar list can be constructed from the Annotation in 22 A.L.R.4th 294. Some of the cases have slightly overstated the count. See *Nelson v. Freeland,* 507 S.E.2d 882 (N.C. 1998) (including Colorado in the reform group although legislation has put it back in the traditional column; also listing decisions that merely broadened the invitee category to include social guests); *Mallet v. Pickens,* 522 S.E.2d 436 (W.Va. 1999) (listing in the reform cases that did not abolish the categorical way of analyzing premises liability cases). Nevertheless, the reform group is now a large one and at several courts have joined the count in the last dozen or so years, suggesting that the categories are on their way out.

Reluctance to accept complete abolition of categories shows up in at least three ways: (1) Felons may be subject to special disabilities, see *Calvillo-Silva v. Home Grocery,* 968 P.2d 65 (Cal. 1998), mentioned in the notes following *Gladon.* (2) A number of states abolish the special rules for licensees, merging that category with the invitee category, but retain the trespasser category. (3) About half the states at last count still retain all the duty limiting rules for all categories.

Note 3. Retaining the trespasser category. In *Schofield v. Merrill,* 435 N.E.2d 339 (Mass. 1982), the Massachusetts court said: "We can say with confidence that landowners of ordinary prudence customarily exercise care for the safety of trespassers who are known to be in a position of peril, certain foreseeable child trespassers, and all lawful visitors. However, we are not convinced that landowners of ordinary prudence customarily exercise care for the safety of adult trespassers generally." The facts in *Schofield*, however, suggest that a negligence rule would work quite well. The plaintiff there jumped into a water-filled quarry. He struck a hidden ledge, and suffered a spine injury. He had no permission to be on the land and the trial court granted a summary judgment for the defendant. The Supreme Judicial Court affirmed. Wouldn't this be the rule you'd get if we abolished all categories and tried the case under a reasonable understanding of ordinary negligence rules? Surely no trespasser can rightly think the landowner has made a quarry safe for his trespassing use.

The same is true with the more recent decision of the Rhode Island Court in *Tantimonico v. Allendale Mutual Ins. Co.*, 637 A.2d 1056 (R.I. 1994). Two motorcyclists, trepassers on the defendant's land, collided head on. The court's statement of the facts does not suggest any act of negligence of the defendant's part, so under any version of any rule the defendant would not be liable. Indeed, the defendant should escape liability on a motion for summary judgment if not on a motion to dismiss even if all categories are abolished. Yet the court thought that "The case at bar is the incarnation of the worst fears of many opponents to the movement away from common-law status categories."

Privilege to prevent trespass and the landowner's duty. The *Schofield* Court also argued that since the landowner would be privileged to use reasonable force to prevent a trespass, the landowner should be privileged to "forbear from acting with care toward a trespasser." But the landowners' privilege exists to prevent trespass and to eject, and only by reasonable force. There is no privilege to punish for an accomplished trespass and no privilege to inflict serious bodily harm merely to prevent trespass. If the defendant *risks* serious bodily harm, is it thought that this is privileged because it is not actually intended either in the sense of desire or certainty? Is serious risk, in other words, equated with reasonable force because, although deadly when it causes harm, it will not often cause harm? If this is the thought, there is still a problem. The force involved in *Schofield* neither serves to eject the trespasser nor to prevent the trespass. So it is not like the privileged use of force. It can only be punishment, and that is a purpose for which the privilege does not exist. One answer to this argument might be that the threat of unknown risks, including this risk, are like the threat of intended harm, and that one may be privileged to threaten acts one is not privileged to carry out. But there is no threat here, only harm. All this might make one think the privilege argument is under-analyzed in *Schofield*, or at least that it is not wholly persuasive.

Can a trespasser-burglar recover? Still, what about the burglar? If *Schofield* is rejected in favor of *Scurti* (just below), may a burglar recover when she slips on marbles left on the floor of the entrance hall? If no burglar was foreseeable, perhaps there is no negligence at all and the issue ends there. If burglars come regularly, though, must the homeowner pick up the child's toys to protect the burglar against a pratfall? Surely privilege could be utilized as an analytical tool to this extent: one cannot be held liable for negligence for doing the very acts one would be privileged to do intentionally. If marbles constituted a reasonable defense of a dwelling, such a principle would protect the homeowner.

A variation might occur if the homeowner is negligent in leaving the marbles because she expects an invitee. An innocent but befuddled professor bumbles his way into the wrong house, as a bungler, not a burglar. He slips on the marbles. He is not in fact or appearance a burglar. No question of privilege arises. Is the homeowner, liable under the new dispensation? It must be remembered that the homeowner is said to be negligent because an invitee is expected and the invitee might slip on the marbles. Does it follow that there would be liability to anyone who is injured?

As suggested in the casebook a few pages down the road, one answer to this might be found in *Palsgraf.* Classification of persons is required by that distinguished decision. Might the judge say there was negligence to the expected invitee, but not to the unexpected bumbler? This could lead into a long byway, the gist of which is that the classification process may have to begin anew. Just imagine that the landowner expected invitee A, but not invitee B. Invitee B and the bumbling professor show up at the same time and do a duo slip-and-fall routine. If *Palsgraf* furnishes such a nice answer to the professor's claim, does it rightly eliminate invitee B's claim as well? If rejection of categories will force a new classification process along these lines, it might be as easy to keep the categories. But this is a point that can keep if need be.

Note 4. Retaining the categories. About half the states have now liberalized their premises liability rules, but some contemporary cases continue to adhere to the categories. *Pinnell v. Bates,* cited here, said that "Eliminating the distinction [among entrants] curtails the right of unbridled use of private property." See also *Carter v. Kinney,* 896 S.W.2d 926 (Mo. 1995). *Stitt v. Holland Abundant Life Fellowship,* 614 N.W.2d 88 (Mich. 2000), does not address the abolition of the categories, but it resurrected the old business visitor test and rejected the public invitee test. The court may believe that invitees are entitled to something more than reasonable care – that defendants are under a specific to invitees to inspect premises even when reasonable care does not require it. If you the court thinks that, you can see why it might want to retain the old categories.

SCURTI V. CITY OF NEW YORK, 354 N.E.2d 794 (N.Y. 1976)

Schofield (discussed immediately above) said that landowners of ordinary prudence did not vary their conduct according to the licensee category. *Rowland* said about the same. But *Scurti* takes the exact opposite view as a basis for adjudication. For the *Scurti* court, status on the land is a factor affecting the decision-maker's judgment about what constitutes reasonable care. This seems to be an application of the reasonable care under the circumstances rules, with trespass as one of the circumstances. Would juries come up with verdicts pretty much in line with the known and constant trespassers rules, simply by applying the ordinary care standard?

■**FYI: The English rules.** The English have a statute, known as the Occupiers' Liability Act, 1957, 5 & 6 ELIZ. c. 31, as amended (with respect to lessors) in the Defective Premises Act, 1972, c. 35. Section 2, that provides in part that:

> "An occupier of premises owes the same duty, the 'common duty of care,' to all his visitors, except in so far as he is free to and does extend, restrict, modify or exclude his duty to any visitor or visitors by agreement or otherwise."

The common duty of care is in substance the reasonable person standard. The statute in effect retains the trespasser rules, however. See *Videan v. British Transport Comm.*, [1963] 2 All. Eng. Rep. 86 (C.A.) (child trespasser barred but not rescuer.) The effect is that the statute abolishes the invitee-licensee distinction. Professor Rogers explains that the entrant's purpose on the land is relevant but no longer conclusive. W.V.H. ROGERS, WINFIELD & JOLOWICZ ON TORT 233 (14th ed. 1994). This seems to be in accord with *Scurti's* view. Rogers goes on to say a landowner might not be negligent because he could expect the entrant to exercise care for himself. That's an idea we saw in general form back in *Stinnett v. Buchele* and have reviewed with the open and obvious danger cases in this chapter. A burglar would seldom if ever expect that the premises had been made safe for his benefit, for example.■

Note 1. This is to remind students that if the traditional status categories are abolished, the injured entrant wins only upon proof that the defendant was negligent, and that his negligence caused the entrant's harm. Might the reasonable and prudent person standard be flexible enough to take account of the status (non-categorically, perhaps) of the plaintiff? Students might enjoy trying their hand at answering our last question here. **Notes 2 and 3** are related, as is **Note 5.**

Note 4. Categories as facilitating summary judgment or directed verdicts. As already suggested, the categories might implicitly reject the *Carroll Towing*/risk-utility formula. The good and bad side of that is reflected in the fact that they facilitate summary judgment. As we know from Chapter 6, § 3, summary judgment would not be given readily under the ordinary negligence standard. The categories may have at least this effect, then, even if they end up getting the same result that the negligence standard would get: they will save the defendant the cost of the full-scale defense. This is desirable and just if the landowners' rules get exactly the same result as the negligence standard. If the landowners' rules protect 10% too much, however, is the cost saving to the innocent defendants sufficient to justify the rules?

Note 5 allows you to revisit the firefighter's rule, if you wish, and even the assumption of risk "defense." It also relates to the question asked in Note 1.

§ 5. RECREATIONAL USES: RE-CREATION OF THE STATUS CATEGORIES

Virtually all states have now enacted some form of a recreational use statute, sometimes expanding the original immunity to protect landowners against suits for negligence even by invitees, such as those buying produce on a farm. The theory behind the statutes was that they would induce owners of large unused lands to open them for recreational use, much needed as society becomes more and more crowded. Even if that was a good idea, in practice, the statutes often go a good deal beyond that, for example, by protecting negligent public entities whose park lands were already open to the public. The development of these statutes is important in itself and as a part of the growing web of legislative immunities that have set aside many liabilities for unreasonably dangerous activities.

¶3. **Constitutionality.***Guest statutes and recreational use statutes.* Compare the constitutional decisions in guest statute cases. How can a court like the California court, which decided *Rowland* and also held guest statutes to be unconstitutional, appropriately leave room for legislative policy on the recreational statutes? After all, are they not merely new versions of the "unconstitutional" guest statutes? This point brings us almost full circle to the beginning of this section.

¶4. **Scope**. *Attractive nuisance and recreational activity.* Maybe those recreational use statutes that immunize negligent landowners in cases of injuries to young children represent oversights or one of the conceptual failures that occur when we confuse the question of analysis with the question of ultimate liability. While tort liability may impose costs on identifiable interest groups, the withdrawal of tort liability can impose costs on equally identifiable groups. Women, children, ethnic groups, and the poor, are sometimes mentioned as the victims of immunities or restrictive rules of liability, just as tort reformers see doctors, product manufacturers and landowners as victims of tort liability. To the extent that the recreational use statutes exclude liability to children playing on the land, they can be perceived as establishing rules against the welfare of children and certainly as a step backward. *Cf.* Kathryn D. Horning, Comment, *The End of Innocence: The Effect of California's Recreational Use Statute on Children at Play*, 32 SAN DIEGO L. REV. 857 (1995).

What counts as recreational use? The scope of the statute depends in part upon what counts as a recreational use. Some statutes give us long lists, some define such activities abstractly. Suppose a child hunts comic books in a dump and suffers terrible burns when she falls through the crust into smoldering fire. Such a child was allowed recovery in *Dehn v. S. Brand Coal and Oil Co.*,

63 N.W.2d 6 (Minn. 1954) under the attractive nuisance doctrine. Would she be barred today under the recreational use statute? If you are poor enough, hunting for comics in a smoldering dump is a kind of recreational activity, but it might possibly escape a statute that relies on lists of activities if "hunting comic books" or some equivalent phrase is not on the list. Suppose instead that the child was hunting rats in the dump with a BB gun. The Michigan statute specifically covers "hunting" so the 11-year old hunting comic books might not be barred but the 11-year old hunting rats in the same dump might be. The statutes invite litigation, an invitation quickly accepted by defendants who sometimes raise issues that are hard to take seriously. In *Herman v. City of Tucson,* 4 P.3d 973 (Ariz. Ct. App. 2000) the plaintiff was employed by a licensed vendor in a public park when she was injured. The city claimed that she was a recreational user even though it admitted that she was there solely to work. The city's contention was rejected.

Public land, public entities. Coverage of public lands and urban lands is discussed briefly in DOBBS ON TORTS §238, p. 623.

Open for recreational activities or not. In *Verdoljak v. Mosinee Paper Corp.,* 547 N.W.2d 602 (Wis. 1996) the plaintiff, a motorcycle rider on the defendant's land argued that the defendant could not claim the recreational statute's immunity because the defendant had not opened the land for recreational use. The court rejected the argument, saying if the land was used for recreation by the biker, the statute applied. It is not clear why the statute would matter.

Land unsuited to recreational use. In *Ornelas v. Randolph,* 847 P.2d 560 (Cal. 1993), the court rejected any requirement that the land be "suitable" for recreational purposes. Ownership by the defendant plus a recreational purpose by the plaintiff were the only two elements needed to invoke the statute. In *Ornelas,* the plaintiff was an eight-year-old child who (arguably) had tagged alone with other children. The other children were playing on farm machinery and pipes stored on the land, but the plaintiff was sitting to one side, playing with a hand-held toy. The pipes dislodged and fell on the plaintiff. The court thought that whether he tagged along or entered to play on the machinery and whether he was playing on it at the time or not, he was engaged in a recreational purpose. And since suitability of the land for recreation was of no significance, the defendant could properly claim the statutory immunity.

Comments. Larger themes are at the core of these statutes. Should courts or legislatures make the changes made in *Rowland*? How can we make the interaction of courts and legislatures productive? With recreational use statutes you wonder whether the legislatures had access to a complete understanding of the probable scope of liabilities imposed under either the traditional landowners' rules or the *Rowland* regime. Maybe the legislatures had access to only one viewpoint. Relatedly and as we'll see again more than once, the legislative inclination in recent years has been to restrict liability for negligence.

§ 6. LESSORS

PAGELSDORF V. SAFECO INS. CO., 284 N.W.2d 55 (Wis. 1979).

This case summarizes the common law rule and its exceptions, and rejects the whole thing in favor of a common standard based on the prudent person. It is thus comparable to *Rowland's* decision as to landowners other than lessors. You may want to use a hypothetical or so to stress some of the exceptions since most states will analyze cases based upon those rather than upon ordinary negligence.

Note 2. The lessor or landlord was liable in spite of the traditional rule when one of the exceptions applied. The exceptions seem readily understood and are only briefly sketched here.

Note 3 should also be self-explanatory.

Note 4. Implied warranty of habitability. On the limits on warranty liability, *see* DOBBS ON TORTS § 241 (2000). Sometimes courts use the term but in effect apply the rules of negligence. *See Estate of Vazquez v. Hepner,* 564 N.W.2d 426 (Iowa 1997) (seemingly, if reasonable care does not require the landlord to inspect premises, he is not liable on a warranty theory). One case, *Becker v. IRM Corp.,* 698 P.2d 116 (Cal. 1985), did impose strict liability upon for "defective" premises but that case was overruled ten years later in *Peterson v. Superior Court, Peterson v. Superior Court,* 899 P.2d 905 (1995).

Note 5. Statutory duties. A good candidate for concern is the problem of lead-based paint, left on older tenements to poison for life any small children who may peel and lick it, as small children tend to do. Lead paint injuries still arise because some paint antedates 1978 when it was banned. Most courts have not required action by landlords in these cases unless the landlord had actual notice that the paint contained lead. Wisconsin, however, took a notably different view in *Antwaun A. v. Heritage Mutual Ins. Co.,* 596 N.W.2d 456 (Wis. 1999), holding that if the landlord knew of peeling paint in a pre-1978 tenement, the lead danger would be foreseeable as a matter of law and he would be under a duty to test the paint. As the Note points out, statutes often apply here.

––––––––––

PROBLEMS

These mini-problems give the student a chance to apply, and thus capture, one or two main points about the duties in each category. You can discuss them in class as a means of teaching the duties in each category, or you can let students work them out for themselves. We've put the problems at the end of the chapter for review and reinforcement but you can take up each problem with the case materials to which it relates if you prefer.

Paton v. Missouri & Atlantic Ry.

In the Paton problem, if the regulation about headlights is a state regulation that is not preempted by federal law, it might be intended to impose a duty to trespassers where none existed before; but this seems unlikely. Our negligence per se cases usually set a standard or a specific rule of conduct in cases where a duty of care in some degree was already owed. Just as bad from the plaintiff's viewpoint, there is now the possibility that the federal statutes and regulations on train headlights preempt any state law on the subject in any event. (More on preemption in covering products liability, Chapter 22.) The statute probably imposes a duty only to those to whom care is already owed–passengers, cargo shippers, and persons rightfully on the track. If so, the regulation is not a new source of duty and we are forced to fall back on the common law.

In states requiring a lookout, perhaps the trier could infer that the engineer did not keep a lookout, since the train ran over Paton. In such states, perhaps, lawyers would have to reach the issue of contributory negligence/last chance or comparative negligence. (A mini-review here is easy.)

In most states, however, there is no duty to keep a lookout for trespassers, only a duty once the danger is discovered. This seems to be true even with active operations, such as running the train except where the footpath or "constant trespassers" rule applies.

Harper, James & Gray, in § 27.6, state the authority this way for undiscovered trespassers: "a majority of courts impose such a duty where, and only where, the likelihood of trespass at some particular point, or limited locality, on defendant's premises is considerable. Where, for instance, trespassers have beaten a path across railroad tracks near a village, the railroad crews must use reasonable care, e.g., by lookout, warning, and the like, in operating trains at that point."

And Paton is a trespasser. Even if he had been carried unconscious on the land by Talbot, he would be a trespasser for these purposes according to many courts. See *Copeland v. Baltimore & O.R.R.*, 416 A.2d 1 (D.C. App. 1980), though in such a case he would not be affirmatively liable as a trespasser since he committed no "act."

Thus the inquiry is whether any duty is owed under the rules stated. Since Paton was not in fact discovered, there is no duty to warn or otherwise avoid injury under the general rule. Since he is evidently not misled by the premises to enter in the belief that they are part of the public way, he cannot take advantage of that exception. And since he is not shown to be in a limited area frequented by trespassers to the knowledge of the railroad, he has no claim under that rule. Thus there is "no duty" under the usual rules. Were he at a public crossing or even a trespassory crossing known to the railroad, a duty of care would be owed and liability could be imposed for negligence.

A very similar case is *Steffey v. Soo Line R.R.*, 498 N.W.2d 304 (Minn. Ct. App. 1993) where the plaintiff had become intoxicated and lay in a fetal position on the track. A headlight allegedly failed to meet a federal statutory standard of illumination, but this was not for the protection of trespassers, who were left to state law claims. Under Minnesota law, the railroad owed no duty to keep a lookout for trespassers, so summary judgment for defendant was proper.

Christie v. Embry Corp.

Against an adult trespasser, Embry could defend on the ground that it was not shown to have known of the embers and fire. But proof that spontaneous fires had been a problem earlier probably is proof that it *had reason to know* of this danger. Would it then foresee the presence of child trespassers who would not appreciate the danger of fire? Perhaps some courts would feel that although Embry had reason to know of "fire," this proof fails to show that it had reason to know of a hidden danger of burning embers. Something like this was said in *Rush v. Plains Township*, 89 A.2d 200 (Pa. 1952), on similar facts. But other courts may well feel quite differently. Since a foreseeable child trespasser might be injured in a number of ways by fire, perhaps notice of fire in general is sufficient. This seems to be the view in *Dehn v. S. Brand Coal & Oil Co.*, 63 N.W.2d 6 (Minn. 1954), also on very similar facts.

The common hazard rule might preclude application of the attractive nuisance rules in some courts, but not if that rule is interpreted along the lines suggested in our coverage. In that interpretation, the common hazard rule is merely an inappropriate statement of the idea of negligence, a statement that the hazard is socially useful enough to warrant the risk. Thus in *Dehn* and some other cases on such facts, recovery has been allowed.

Christie was not attracted by the fire or embers, but although Holmes once held this would defeat the claim, *United Zinc & Chem. Co. v. Britt, supra*, courts no longer so hold, as we've noted in this chapter. Thus, the main focus of inquiry would probably be whether the defendant could foresee the presence of children too young to care for themselves.

What if Christie's father had taken her to the dump? In *Cullinane v. Interstate Iron & Metal, Inc.*, 343 N.W.2d 725 (Neb. 1984), a ten-year-old boy's recovery was not precluded merely because his father had taken him to the defendant's dangerous property because the father had not taken him to the specific source of danger and because the boy's presence at the specific danger site was foreseeable.

Paget v. Owen.

(1) Owen did not know of the danger on the north road and hence was under no duty to warn as to that. And of course he was under no duty to use care to inspect for the benefit of Paget, even if a reasonable person would have done so. This is the point on which the duty to invitees and licensees differs: to an invitee, a duty to use care in inspection would be required. (We think the duty to inspect is only the duty to make reasonable inspections, that is, to in-

spect when reasonable persons would do so and to the extent they would do so. Recall that some judicial language seems to assume a duty to inspect even when reasonable persons would not do so. Thus, if Paget was injured on the north road, there would no recovery in the absence of proof showing that Owen had reason to know of the danger. An added fact could show the student the "had reason to know" idea: suppose Owen did not know of the washout but did know of heavy creek flooding and of a washout on the south road from the same causes. This might suffice to show he was on notice or "had reason to know" of the danger.

(2) If Paget took the south road: some students will immediately say that since Owen knew of the danger he would be liable. But even under a duty of ordinary care this might not be so. Paget was not expected to be on the south road. There was no foreseeable harm to him there. One could reason even under the ordinary care standard that there is no negligence as a matter of law. Sometimes this seems to be dealt with as a different measure of duty, and the same result is obtained. Thus, it can be said that the landowner only owes a duty when he or she had reason to know both of the danger and the licensee's prospect of encountering it. A third way to get this result is more stringent: outside the scope of the license, the licensee becomes a mere trespasser, and as to those entrants, the landowner owed a duty only if both the danger and the prospect of encounter are actually known.

In re Claims of Picklesimer, et al.

If you don't like problems, omit this one. It permits increased student identification with the lawyer role, some review, and some analysis. The facts of the problem, with some additions, will come up again later in the casebook, and that will permit some continuity. However, the problem is in no sense a major matter.

The problem sounds too important if you write up a complete analysis. You can discuss Picklesimer's claims against Dalzell, by recognizing that Dalzell might be responsible in some way for the misleading appearance, and if so, could be held liable for Picklesimer's original crash. In that case there would be no immunity to a landowner who has mislead someone onto the land. See DOBBS ON TORTS § 231 (2000). If Dalzell is not liable for the original crash, however, Picklesimer will have difficulties, because he appears to be a trespasser as to the excavation. (Dalzell may not even be negligent at all, and thus may not be liable even under a *Rowland* test, but he certainly is not proved to be guilty of willful or wanton misconduct; he did not know of both the excavation and Picklesimer's presence.) As to Pickleseimer's trespasser status, see the note on Classification. Finally, Dalzell, if liable at all, might be liable for the medical negligence that follows. See the rules stated in the scope of duty (proximate cause) chapter, Chapter 8.

You can also spend a little time on the claims by Patrick and Plangent, though there is not a great deal of evidence here. They might conceivably have a claim against Dalzell, too, if he was responsible for the misleading appearance of the road/land.

You can discuss the problem without spending a great deal of time or trying to cover every issue here. The facts are very general and do not lend themselves to definitive construction. One of the values of the problem is that it can be used again later for other issues. You can bring it up in medical malpractice, for example, elaborating on the facts there if you like. The casebook itself brings in new facts further on in connection with suing governmental entities and again in connection with no-fault auto insurance.

CHAPTER 13

DUTIES OF MEDICAL AND OTHER PROFESSIONALS

▶**Changes in the Sixth Edition.** We have added three new cases and deleted three others. An additional case was shortened. Many notes and some other text has also been updated and revised. Specifically, in § 1 on traditional duties, we cut V*alazaquez v. Jiminez* and *Smith v. Knowles*. In § 2 concerning res ipsa loquitur, we have shortened *States v. Lourdes* to a squib case. In § 3 on informed consent we added *Marsingill v. O'Malley* and *Wlosinski v. Cohn*. In § 4—changing medicine, changing law—we added some recent empirical evidence and a section concerning state constitutional challenges to tort reform. Also, on EMTALA, we substituted *Lewellen v. Schneck* for *Arrington v. Wong*. Section 5 on nursing homes, long-term care and elder abuse and § 6 on intentional torts and harassment by professionals remain largely the same.

▶The **Concise Edition** reduces this Chapter's length by almost one-half. Specifically, we've made the following changes, not including small deletions in existing Notes: In § 2 (res ipsa): Note 3 after *States,* necessitating renumbering the remaining Note. In § 3 (informed consent): *Marsingill* and its Notes and *Brown v. Dibbell*. In § 4 (changing medicine, changing law): Much of the text, including most of subsections C, D, E, F, and G. In § 5 (nursing homes), all cases and text, replaced by three paragraphs on elder abuse. In § 6 (intentional torts by professionals), replaced entire section with three paragraphs addressing the same issues.■

Goals. This chapter aims to cover professional negligence that results in physical or emotional harm, with emphasis on medical malpractice. It also aims to introduce non-doctrinal materials such as strategic effects of the medical standard of care, criticisms of liability, and the impact of changes in health care organization. This chapter also briefly introduces regulatory approaches to injury (regulation of nursing homes) and non-tort sources of law. It does not deal with purely financial injury and hence does not cover accountants or lawyers. It covers some issues of professional sexual misconduct with patients, clients, or parishioners in the last section. From a broader perspective, this chapter, like the others in this part, deals in part with special constrictions on the duty of care, especially the limited duties owed in several medical situations.

Scheduling Omissions. Traditional rules are covered in §§ 1-3. Sections 4-6 should help provide a more sophisticated and more up-to-date course – they contain fascinating material reflecting some of the changes in medical practice and the cost containment goals, nursing home negligence, and sexual misbehavior of professionals. If you must limit coverage to core topics, you might omit these sections, especially if advanced courses in your school will take up this material.   If you cover §§ 4-6 on the new medical world of Tort Reform, MCOs, and EMTALA, you might omit discrete portions of that material if you must. Section 5 is pretty much an all-or-nothing section. Section 6 on sexual exploitation and harassment by professionals is important, but the problem of sexual misbehavior arises a good deal in this course, and you may feel you can afford to drop that particular section.

OUTLINE

SUMMARY

§ 1. TRADITIONAL DUTIES OF HEALTH CARE PROVIDERS IN TRADITIONAL PRACTICE

WALSKI V. TIESENGA. This case introduces the medical standard of care and its implication that medical testimony is required in most cases to establish a specific duty. A doctor's testimony that the procedure used by the defendant is not the best, or is "improper in my opinion," or is not very safe will not suffice. Instead, testimony must show that the defendant's procedure did not meet the standard accepted by the relevant medical community.

VERGARA V. DOAN. The medical standard was once set by the defendant's own community of doctors. Courts now often use similar community or even a national community standard.

NOTE: SPECIALISTS. A national standard for medical specialists and the question who can testify against a specialist.

NOTE: NONMEDICAL PRACTITIONERS. Chiropractors and other nonmedical practitioners are held to the standards of the practice they profess to follow, not to medical standards. Notes test this with extreme cases and with religious healers.

HIRPA V. IHC HOSPITALS, INC. Good Samaritan statutes give physicians (and sometimes others) immunity from liability when they act negligently in an emergency. In this case, emergency even includes medical work in a hospital. The rationale is to encourage aid by eliminating the requirement of reasonable care.

NOTE: OTHER PROFESSIONALS. Nurses, architects, engineers, accountants, lawyers and others may be classed as professionals to be judged by proven standards of their professions. Educators may escape any duty at all with respect to teaching, testing and classifying.

§ 2. RES IPSA LOQUITUR

STATES V. LOURDES HOSPITAL. A patient's arm and shoulder are injured during an operation to remove an ovarian cyst. The court allows the use of res ipsa loquitur and follows the approach of most courts in allowing expert medical testimony by the plaintiff's expert on the issue of whether this is the kind of injury that normally does not occur without negligence.

YBARRA V. SPANGARD. The leading case on smoking out defendants. With six or seven people directly involved with the patient, it is not rational to believe they are all negligent. Yet all are held liable, apparently in the belief that this judicial tactic will smoke out the guilty party, or at least smoke out testimony against that party. The practical reason for the result may lie in the possibility that a single malpractice insurer covered all parties. That aside, can one really justify a hostage approach to justice?

§ 3. INFORMED CONSENT

SCHLOENDORF V. SOCIETY OF NEW YORK HOSPITAL. This states the principle behind the informed consent doctrine, autonomy over one's own body.

HARNISH V. CHILDREN'S HOSPITAL MED. CENTER. Massachusetts holds that the doctor must inform the patient of any information "material" to the operation proposed and that liability is not limited to those cases in which the doctor violates the medical standard of disclosure (which often did not exist in any event.) The medical standard controls one issue, however: should the doctor have known the medical facts that were material? The plaintiff must also prove that had she been informed neither she nor reasonable persons would have accepted the medical treatment.

WOOLLEY V. HENDERSON. Maine states the opposite view, holding that there is no liability unless the doctor fails to disclose things that would be disclosed by the relevant medical community.

MARSINGILL V. O'MALLEY. Alaska blurs the line between the reasonable patient standard and the reasonable doctor standard, allowing testimony from doctors about what reasonable patients would want to know.

WLOSINSKI V. COHN. In a case in which a high school student needed a kidney transplant, the doctor was required to warn of risks of the procedure. However, the doctor's own success rate (or lack of success) was not a risk related to the procedure.

ARATO V. AVEDON. Doctors discovered that Miklos Arato had a malignant pancreatic tumor. They removed all the visible tumor, but the 5-year survival rate under the circumstances was only 5%. But medical professionals did not tell Arato this although Arato had asked for the truth. The professionals gave neither the objective facts nor their opinions that he would not live long. Instead Arato was subjected to chemotherapy. Arato died about a year after the discovery of the cancer. Mrs. Arato and the children sue, claiming Arato might have arranged business and personal affairs differently, and especially that they would have handled some tax and commercial matters differently. *Held,* standard practice in the medical community sets the disclosure standard for information that is not about risks of a medical procedure. Since disclosure of statistical life expectancy information was not generally made in the medical community, there was no duty to give it here. A request to be told the truth changes nothing.

TRUMAN V. THOMAS. A doctor is here held liable for failure to advise of the risks of *not* having a medical procedure — in this case a diagnostic test for cancer. The doctor advised to have the test, but did not give the reasons for his advice. This departs from the fact-pattern based on the original battery cases since this is not a touching without consent but a pure obligation to inform. The principle might be acceptable to most people, but isn't the risk of cancer well enough known that the doctor might not think to warn?

BROWN V. DIBBELL. The partial defense of comparative fault is available in informed consent claims, as where the patient is not truthful in giving her own medical history. But a patient is not ordinarily at fault for trusting the doctor's recommendation or failing to ask questions.

§ 4. CHANGING MEDICINE, CHANGING LAW

A. The Medical Malpractice "Crisis"
The text of this segment introduces the medical malpractice "crisis."

B. Statutory Responses
This section outlines statutory "reform" proposals.

C. State Constitutional Challenges to Statutory Reform
At times, state constitutions limit legislative reforms. Those limits are discussed in this section.

D. The Medical Malpractice Reality
The Institute of Medicine recognizes the reality of malpractice (under the gentler name of "preventable medical errors"), but proposes to stop "blaming" people and instead to concentrate on designing systems to work better.

E. Medical Costs, Containment Efforts and Tort Standards

Cost containment through managed care may be shifting some of the malpractice problems from erroneous care to under-care, and from traditional medical malpractice to issues of insurance coverage.

F. Mandatory Emergency Treatment and Screening

42 U.S.C.A. § 1395dd. This federal statute against patient dumping provides that covered hospitals must screen anyone who comes to the emergency room to determine whether or not the patient is in a medical emergency or active labor. If so, the hospital must provide treatment until the patient is stabilized. The alternative of transfer to another facility is expressly limited: a transfer may be made if the patient so requests or if a certification is made that the medical benefits of a transfer outweigh increased risks. The statute creates a federal cause of action for violation.

LEWELLEN V. SCHNECK MEDICAL CENTER. To what extent does EMTALA authorize suit when inadequate medical care is given? In this case the hospital gave quick and shoddy emergency treatment to a man who had been driving drunk. As a result of the inadequate treatment, the man suffers permanent neurological impairment. The court interpreted the EMTALA statute to allow the case for liability to go to trial with respect to whether the emergency room examination had been so cursory as not to amount to an "appropriate medical screening."

G. Strict and Limited Liability Proposals

The text of this segment briefly summarizes some ideas for strict liability coupled with limited recovery. This foreshadows more to come on both issues.

§ 5. NURSING HOMES, LONG-TERM CARE AND ELDER ABUSE

HORIZON/CMS HEALTHCARE CORP. V. AULD. A tort claim for nursing home neglect (abuse?), including failure to prevent or treat bed sores that had rotted the decedent's flesh literally to the bone. Evidence included surveys conducted by a state agency as part of the "regulation" by the federal Centers for Medicare and Medicaid Services (CMS). Given the surveys that gave the nursing home notice of deficiencies, $90 million in punitive damages was justified.

NOTE: REGULATION OR FINANCIAL PARTNERSHIP? A brief summary of the peculiar role of the federal government in both financing health care and then semi-regulating it.

NOTE: THE FALSE CLAIMS ACT AND QUI TAM ACTIONS. Rounding out the main methods of control of health care quality, the government might possibly criminally prosecute low quality health care providers for false claims (Medicaid reimbursement) if the claims are based on substandard care. Even more interesting, private individuals can bring such actions on behalf of the government (qui tam) and share in the proceeds.

§ 6. INTENTIONAL TORTS AND SEXUAL HARASSMENT BY PROFESSIONALS

TEXT. The text distinguishes sexual harassment from sexual exploitation of nominally consenting patients, parishioners or clients. One problem is liability insurance coverage; another is whether sexual misbehavior in either form is "malpractice" and covered by protective legislation or an ordinary tort and not specially protected.

COMMENTS

§1. TRADITIONAL DUTIES OF HEALTH CARE PROVIDERS IN TRADITIONAL PRACTICE

Preliminary Note: Strict liability has gained no foothold in medical cases. See *Finn v. G. D. Searle & Co.*, 677 P. 2d 1147 (Cal. 1984). Even the doctor who uses a defective product that causes harm, though in a position quite analogous to the hairdresser who uses the permanent wave, will not be held strictly liable. See the discussion of the *Magrine* case in *Newmark v. Gimbel's Inc.*, Casebook Chapter 24, §12. On the contrary, to a very large extent, the medical profession sets its own standard of care without much interference from the law. To a degree, but much less importantly, some other professions get some of the same privileges or immunities.

This chapter concentrates on health care providers, but it notes the somewhat similar rules for other professionals such as architects. (Malpractice of accountants and lawyers in civil practice is almost entirely economic malpractice and consequently not a major topic in this book.) This chapter does not cover mental health malpractice as a separate topic. One kind of mental health malpractice is sexual abuse. See § 6 below. Another is breach of confidentiality or invasion of privacy. Still another claim, although perhaps "malpractice" is the wrong name for it, is the claim that a therapist should have recognized that a patient would attack some third person and failed to warn the potential victim. This is the *Tarasoff* claim considered in Chapter 18.

Doctor-patient relationship. The paragraph preceding *Walski* is designed to foreshadow two points considered in later chapters. A doctor-patient relationship is routinely required to establish the doctor's professional duty, but sometimes treatment of a patient requires the doctor to act with reasonable care not to affirmatively injure others. An example of a doctor's liability to a non-patient is *Healthone v. Rodriguez,* 50 P.3d 879 (Colo. 2002), where one doctor left phenol on a cart with nerve block medicines that would be injected intravenously. Phenol would destroy human tissue if so injected. A second doctor mistakenly picked up the phenol and injected it in his patient, the plaintiff, who suffered terrible injuries ending in serious brain damage. The court held that the first doctor owed a common law duty of reasonable care to his non-patient. This outcome is consistent with the point that liability is imposed upon doctors, like anyone else, for affirmative acts creating unreasonable risks. Physicians and surgeons must also take account of the possibility that improper treatment will spread disease or otherwise inflict injuries upon third persons.

WALSKI V. TIESENGA, 381 N.E.2d 279 (Ill. 1978).

During a thyroid operation, the plaintiff's vocal cords are paralyzed. He sues the doctors for medical malpractice. The trial court directed a verdict for the doctors; the intermediate court of appeals affirmed, as does this court.

Walski, which is pretty heavily edited, establishes the following points:

The general rule requires the plaintiff to establish the "medical standard of care" by proof of what the relevant medical community holds to be acceptable practice. A personal opinion of a medical expert is not sufficient. The court recognized the common knowledge or gross negligence exception, in which the medical misconduct is so well understood or so gross that it can be properly appraised by jurors without medical knowledge.

(In a passage we have removed from the book, the court referred to two other exceptions: (1) the hospital rule: medical care of hospitals must meet the standard required by regulations and licensing standards and (2) the drug rule—warnings and instructions accompanying drugs establish the standard for their use and administration. These exceptions are reflected in *Darling v. Charleston Community Memorial Hospital,* 211 N.E.2d 253 (Ill. 1965), and *Ohligschlager v. Proctor Community Hospital,* 55 Ill. 2d 411, 303 N.E.2d 392 (O;;/ 1973), respectively. We've also stricken the court' s discussion on the use of medical treatises, which arises in connection with *Smith v. Knowles* below.)

The court applies these rules to hold that the doctors are not liable for severing the patient's nerves and causing the loss of speech. The plaintiff introduced evidence that Dr. Berger believed their medical procedure improper, and that this was the way he was taught in school. But this form of words did not satisfy the court, since it fell short, in the court's view, of showing any generally accepted practice in the relevant medical community. It is as if the witness had said, "I would have done it differently," and that would not suffice to show the standard or its breach. *Rolon-Alvarado v. Municipality of San Juan,* 1 F.3d 74 (1st Cir. 1993) (Puerto Rico law); *cf. Bowling v. Foster,* 562 S.E.2d 776 (Ga. Ct. App. 2002)(general question "Do you believe the standard of care requires you to try steroid injections on a patient before surgery?" answer "yes," insufficient development of the standard of care).

There is a very good and very brief statement of the basic rule in *Versteeg v. Mowery,* 435 P. 2d 540 (Wash. 1967):

[I]n medical negligence cases doctors are allowed to testify as to the ultimate fact of what constitutes due care, a question generally left to the jury. [The plaintiff] argued that the same jury is able, upon hearing testimony of different doctors, to decide which standard should be applicable. But such a jury is no more capable of choosing between conflicting standards in this highly technical area than it is in creating a standard for itself. For this very reason it has always been the rule that: The testimony of other physicians that they would have followed a different course of treatment than that followed by the defendant, or a disagreement of doctors of equal skill and learning as to what the treatment should have been, does not establish negligence.

The reasonable and prudent person standard. The medical rule differs from the reasonable and prudent person rule normally applied.

(a) Recall that "proof of a standard" is not required or even possible in most non-medical cases. (You can harken back to *District of Columbia v. Shannon,* 696 A.2d 1359 (D.C. Ct. App. 1997) and *Hammons Inc. v. Poletis,* 954 P.2d 1353 (Wyo. 1998) in Chapter 6, § 3.) But proof of a standard of care applied by the relevant medical community is a central requirement in medical malpractice cases.

(b) Medical cases are not the first we've seen that depart from the reasonable, prudent person standard. What we've seen before, however, is that courts (or legislatures) themselves have set a different standard of care, as in the guest statutes or landowner's limited duties. In the medical cases, courts do not set the "standard" or level of care; instead, they defer to the medical profession's customary practice, or at least to the statements of a medical standard by medical experts. Consequently, the plaintiff must prove what the medical custom, practice, or "standard" is. Not even a trespasser has a comparable problem of proof.

(c) To the extent that it relies upon custom to set the standard, this approach differs also from the rules about the effect of custom we saw with The *T.J. Hooper,* 60 F.2d 737 (2d Cir. 1932), also in Chapter 6.

A reason for this special rule for health care practitioners is given in *Walski* – the fear that the jury simply does not know enough to form a judgment. But if this were the real reason, the rule would not require proof of a standard; it would require proof of medical facts or knowable risks, and medical custom would be appropriate but not necessarily required evidence.

On the possibility of expert testimony to establish res ipsa loquitur on *Walski* facts: see *Hightower-Warren v. Silk,* 698 A.2d 52 (Pa. 1997), mentioned below in § 2.

Note 1. Medical "standards." (a) "Standard" in the rule does not refer to an abstract standard like reasonable care that would be capable of application in a variety of cases. Instead, the medical standard refers to the very narrow and particular practice of the profession. In this sense, "standard" looks more like a "rule," as in the sentence "There are virtually thousands of standards of care pertaining to health-care services in the United States today." Eleanor D. Kinney, *The Brave New World of Medical Standards of Care,* 29 J.L. MED. & ETHICS 323 (2001). (b) The standard is not established by testimony of an expert as to what he was taught or believes. *Walski* insists on that point and other courts agree in principle. *District of Columbia v. Wilson,* 721 A.2d 591(D.C.App. 1998) ("The personal opinion of the testifying expert as to what he or she would do in a particular case, without reference to a standard of care, is insufficient to prove the applicable standard of care"). (c) The standard can be established by expert testimony regarding what other physicians would do in the situation. *Palandjian v. Foster,* 842 N.E.2d 916 (Mass. 2006).

Cross-examination from treatises and federal rules of evidence. These two points may be interesting to students in connection with *Walski,* which mentions treatise evidence: (1) (a) treatise and similar evidence was not admissible under common law rules to establish any part of the plaintiff's prima facie case, even though (b) they could be used in cross-examination for impeachment. (2) Treatises are now admissible to establish the plaintiff's case—for instance, the standard of care—under Federal Rule-type systems of evidence. We wouldn't worry if students failed to grasp the distinction between (1) (a) and (1)(b) if they know that treatises are today admissible in many courts. Some witness, of course, must testify that the treatise is authoritative. Even in cross-examination, use of the treatise depends upon the witness' admission that it is authoritative. If the witness says he does not regard the treatise as trustworthy, then it proves nothing to show that he and the treatise disagree and cross-examination from the treatise is not to be allowed. *Stinson v. England,* 633 N.E.2d 532 (Ohio 1994); *Flanagan v. Wesselhoeft,* 765 A.2d 1203 (R.I. 2001) (but in this case not prejudicial to use treatises without first establishing that they state the standard).

Admissibility vs. sufficiency. Admissibility of evidence is a matter entirely different from *sufficiency* of evidence to prove any given point. So the fact that a treatise is admissible does not mean that it is sufficient by itself to get the plaintiff to the jury. Why would treatise evidence be insufficient?

(1) The medical literature or treatise may give medical facts that are relevant but may fail to state a standard of care. That happened in *Landeros v. Flood,* 551 P. 2d 389, 97 A. L. R. 3d 324 (Cal. 1976). The claim was brought by a battered child. The attending physician had failed to recognize the battered-child syndrome and did not order X-rays, which would have revealed a skull fracture. As a result, the child was returned to her mother, who, with a friend, regularly beat the child, and who continued to abuse her. The medical literature on the battered-child syndrome had been available for a long time, so you could believe that diagnosis was possible. But this evidence did not show whether ordinary physicians were conducting medical practice in accord with the literature or not. Hence, the plaintiff might try to prove her case by expert medical testimony, but medical literature would be insufficient.

(2) The standard stated may be too general or imprecise to permit the conclusion that it applied to the particular case before the court or that it was breached. The quotation from Williams on Obstetrics in *Smith v. Knowles* calls for regular and frequent blood pressure checks, but what counts as frequent (every visit to the doctor's office?) is not specified.

(3) Experts may outweigh the written treatise or the plaintiff's lawyer.

Experts denying that treatise is authoritative. Lawyers are often balked by adverse medical experts; at best they can be most difficult to deal with on the witness stand. Consider the testimony quoted in *Jacober v. St. Peter's Medical Center,* 608 A.2d 304 (N.J. 1992). The plaintiff there wanted to show that the defendant doctors used a catheter too large for the premature infant they were treating. The plaintiff's lawyer questioned the defendant's expert on cross examination, intending to establish that a medical treatise was accepted and authoritative. If the defense expert had agreed, the plaintiff's lawyer would then have been able to get the treatise admitted in evidence. The treatise cautioned against using large catheters and advised use of the smallest possible. Even though the defense expert was one of the authors of the treatise, he refused to admit that the treatise was authoritative.

Note 2. Sufficiency of testimony. *Heinrich v. Sweet,* 308 F.3d 48 (1st Cir. 2002), cited here, held that the question and answer failed to establish the standard of care. Aside from the fact that the question was emotionally loaded, "the form of the question was incorrect and did not lead to the required information. While the standard of care question need not be formulaic and some leeway is allowed, we think this question was inadequate to tie Dr. Junck's opinion to the standard of care . . . .To say that Dr. Sweet was in breach of the standard of care, the jury must know what the standard of care was, and neither the question presented to Dr. Junck nor his answer provide this information."

Oakden v. Roland, 988 P.2d 1057 (Wyo. 1999), first rejected the testimony as inadmissible, then held that if admissible it was insufficient. "Oakden attempts to demonstrate the existence of a genuine issue of material fact by presenting evidence that another doctor might have felt Dr. Roland was not sufficiently experienced in the procedure he performed on Oakden. This evidence is not helpful in this particular situation because it does not pertain to the applicable standard of care nor does it demonstrate how Dr. Roland might have deviated from that standard during the procedure."

Note 3. Jury instructions. *McKinnis v. Women and Infants Hosp. of Rhode Island,* 749 A.2d 574 (R.I. 2000), cited here, holds that such instructions emphasizing honest mistake or good faith were error, at least where not cured by a good clean instruction defining the basis of liability. In *Kennelly v. Burgess,* 654 A.2d 1335 (Md. 1995) the court counseled caution in giving a mere happening type instruction, holding it erroneous to have done so in the particular case. You can compare the honest mistake or good faith error type of instruction to the unavoidable accident instruction considered in connection with the emergency doctrine. Some trial judges give a variation, charging the jury that the doctor is not an insurer of good results. Good faith, of course, implies a standard that neither comports with the reasonable prudent person standard nor with the medical standard of care. You might want to emphasize the difference between good faith and reasonable care or even medical care, because it will turn out that good faith, not care, becomes the standard under the Good Samaritan statutes we'll soon see.

Instructions along these lines are egregiously one-sided. In fact, if the normal standards are right, the instructions are flatly and irretrievably wrong. Quite a few courts have now rejected those instructions. *See Riggins v. Mauriello,* 603 A.2d 827 (Del. 1992); *Day v. Morrison,* 657 So.2d 808 (Miss. 1995). But other courts have recently upheld these instructions, a practice that seems logically unaccountable but perhaps explicable in the sense that judges might worry about over-extensive liability or might distrust juries. *Nowatske v. Osterloh,* 543 N.W.2d 265 (Wis. 1996).

Note 4. Expert medical testimony. The medical standard requires testimony. On this, the note merely reinforces *Walski.* Expert medical testimony may also be required to show that the doctor's negligence was a cause in fact of the harm. If the physician negligently delayed in making a diagnosis and the patient died, the plaintiff will need to produce medical evidence that a timely diagnosis would probably have saved the patient. *E.g., Pfiffner v. Correa,* 643 So.2d 1228 (La. 1994). Our point here is merely to forestall error, not investigate causal proof. In the Campbell case cited here, the court said expert testimony was not required on such a claim.

Note 5. Purposes of expert testimony. The fact that mother and child died is not itself evidence of the standard of care, breach of that standard, or that the breach was the actual cause of harm. In Smith v. Knowles (1) Dr. Knowles admitted in testimony that symptoms like those described called for a diagnosis of pre-eclampsia and learned treatises established that immediate attention was required. This minimally establishes the standard of care. (2) However, no testimony showed that Knowles breached the standard. (3) The plaintiff failed to prove cause in fact, *i.e.,* whether earlier diagnosis or different treatment would have saved Diane and the child.

The absence of medical witnesses in this case is a strange thing. Was it the conspiracy of silence or a failure by plaintiff's counsel to put on evidence? Blue Earth County must have been quite small in 1974 when Diane died—it had a population of only 54,000 for the entire county in the 1999 census estimate.

Without the use of treatises, is there enough evidence for lay persons to say the doctor was negligent? If not, what must lawyers do? Minneapolis is only 75 miles from Mankato where Dr. Knowles practiced, but Minneapolis is a major metropolis. Under the traditional locality or similar locality rule, testimony from Minneapolis doctors probably would be inadmissible. [Note on this: The 2000 census (not the census of 1980 which would have been more relevant) shows Mankato with a population of only 32,000 (55,000 for Blue Earth County). In contrast, Minneapolis, along with adjacent St. Paul, sits in Hennepin and Ramsay counties with a combined population of 1.6 million.] Minnesota even now uses the same or similar community standard of care. See *Bauer v. Friedland,* 394 N.W.2d 549 (Minn. Ct. App. 1986). So it is unlikely that a Minneapolis or St. Paul doctor could testify in a suit against a

Mankato doctor. In 2001 an internet yellow pages site showed only five Mankato doctors in family practice (none listed for obstetrics).

Rules of evidence that are not specifically grounded in tort law have an important strategic effect. They tend to narrow the band of cases in which redress can be sought.

Note 6. More than one medical "standard" or practice. *"Two schools of thought." (a) Rule.* When medical authority is divided about whether to use procedure A or procedure B, either one will do. Courts recognize that "where there are distinct and different schools of thought a physician is to be judged only by the practice of his own school of thought. "*Katsetos v. Nolan*, 368 A. 2d 172 (Conn. 1976). The schools of thought in bite case example are reflected in *Reid v. North Caddo Memorial Hospital*, 528 So. 2d 653 (La. Ct. App. 1988).

(b) Qualification. An instruction on the two schools of thought rule is improper unless there is actually evidence that two schools of thought are medically acceptable. *Pesek v. University Neurologists Ass'n, Inc.,* 721 N.E. 2d 1011(Ohio 2000).

(c) Conflict of testimony distinguished. The doctrine has no logical application to a mere conflict of testimony, as where Doctor A testifies to one standard and Doctor B testifies to another. If that were the meaning of the two schools rule, all defendant's would prevail by testifying that the procedure they used met the medical standard. However, it may be difficult in some cases to distinguish between contradictory testimony on the standard of care and testimony showing two schools of thought. *Sinclair v. Block*, 633 A. 2d 1137 (Pa. 1993) may have invoked the two schools rule merely because testimony was in conflict. That court said:

> The Sinclairs presented expert testimony that Dr. Block should not have attempted to use forceps; rather, he should have directly proceeded to perform a Caesarean section. Dr. Block countered with expert testimony that it was reasonable to attempt a vaginal delivery by using forceps prior to performing a Caesarean section.

The court seemed to say that this was enough to invoke the two schools rule.

(d) Hypothetical. What if the plaintiff could show that all the well-regarded contemporary medical studies favor procedure A and that none of the doctors who follow procedure B have read these studies? Under the logic of the rules, that would make no difference. What counts as a division of competent opinion? What if, among 100 doctors in a locality, 90 follow procedure A and 10 follow procedure B? Or 95 and 5?

(e) Defendant as his own school of thought. In *Yates v. University of West Virginia Bd. of Trustees,* 549 S.E.2d 681 (W.Va. 2001), the court was concerned that the defendant might simply testify that his practice represented an accepted school of thought or one of several methods of treatment and thus obtain an instruction on multiple methods or schools of thought even though no other doctors approved. To avoid that, the court insisted that "the 'multiple

methods of treatment' jury instruction (which states that a health care provider is not negligent if he or she selects and utilizes in a non-negligent manner one of two or more generally recognized methods of diagnosis or treatment within the standard of care) is appropriate where the evidence shows that the challenged method of diagnosis or treatment enjoys such substantial support within the medical community that it is, in fact, widely and generally recognized. The necessity of presenting evidence sufficient to support a multiple methods of treatment instruction rests with the defendant."

Note 7. Rejecting *T. J. Hooper*. Learned Hand's opinion in *The T. J. Hooper* held that custom of an industry could never establish the standard of care, although it would certainly be highly relevant. The medical rule rejects the *T. J. Hooper* view and substitutes industry standards for some independently adjudicated standard of care. This might be justified in some abstract kind of way if you thought that the patient was striking a deal with the doctor to follow medical custom, rather than a deal to use the best available procedures. This was the argument raised following the *T. J. Hooper*. It certainly makes sense at least in the case in which the patient is knowledgeable about the practice of medicine and about medical care customs. Does it make sense when the patient is not and the doctor knows it?

Note 8. Rejecting reasonable care. Students need to understand the point of this note before they can make a good evaluation of the rule that uses the medical custom. This note makes the point that a reasonable person would always use the special skill or knowledge that person actually has, so a medical standard of care is not needed to require a physician to use his special skills or knowledge. In *Toth v. Community Hosp. at Glen Cove,* 239 N.E.2d 368 (N.Y. 1968) a pediatrician knew that six liters of oxygen a minute administered to a newborn might cause blindness, so he ordered four instead. The hospital administered six, which was the "standard." If the doctor knew or should have known that the hospital administered the dangerous but standard amount, he was not acting on his own superior knowledge and could be liable. A reasonable care standard–still distinguishing a medical standard– could also require a doctor to use all the skill and knowledge he claims to have by claiming to be a trained doctor. The point? The medical standard is not needed to impose such obligations.

The medical standard can operate, however, to relieve the doctor of using special knowledge or skill to follow the safest practices, for the standard tells us that the safest reasonable procedure is not required, only the customary. Frequently the two will be the same, but when they are not, the customary and unsafe practice sets the standard. If your class doesn't see the difference, this note gives you a kind of mini-hypothetical that poses a risk-utility standard vs. a custom standard.

Policy, justice, or bias: Why use medical custom? One reason might be the one Epstein suggested in connection with the *T. J. Hooper*: if you bargain for services, you might expect services to be delivered according to the custom of the trade. Courts usually emphasize something different. They say or imply that, rare cases aside, juries could not judge negligence of professionals because the matter is too technical and hence the medical standard must be used. That's a non sequitur. Juries (or judges for that matter) would often need to hear expert testimony under any standard, but its purpose would be to identify risks, utilities, and safer procedures, not to identify medical custom. Risk testimony would be the very kind of testimony in fact that *Carroll Towing* would call for. In *Rossell v. Volkswagen of America*, 709 P.2d 517 (Ariz. 1985), the court offered a different explanation. First, it said, the demanding side of the standard holds doctors to a higher standard of care. But as note 6 points out, the "demanding" standard is exactly what a reasonable person standard would require, so it seems doubtful that a medical custom rule is needed for that reason. The court's second reason was not really an affirmative reason at all but basically an assertion that the medical custom rule doesn't do too much harm. This risk that the standard will be too low, he said, is minimized by "professional obligations which tend to prevent the group from setting standards at a low level in order to accommodate other interests."

Is medical custom the same as reasonable care? The studies. Sometimes it is suggested the medical standard will always be a reasonable standard. Medical studies, however, cast doubt on the assumption that physicians will provide the appropriate amount of care. Instead, the evidence is that practices vary "inexplicably" in different geographic areas and even in the same community; hence they are not the result of "scientific understanding" or a careful balance of all the options. *See* Clark Havinghurst, *Practice Guidelines as Legal Standards Governing Physician Liability*, 54 L. & CONTEMP. PROBS. 87 (1991). See also INSTITUTE OF MEDICINE, TO ERR IS HUMAN: BUILDING A SAFER HEALTHY SYSTEM (2000), discussed in Casebook § 4. In turn, this variance gives expert witnesses wide options for presenting their own particular views. Moreover, recent well-regarded studies indicate that much medical malpractice goes undetected and is seldom a basis for suit. Perhaps seven times more patients are injured by medical negligence than actually bring suit. *See* PAUL C. WEILER,, HOWARD H. HIATT, JOSEPH P. NEWHOUSE, WILLIAM G. JOHNSON, TROYEN A. BRENNAN & LUCIAN L. LEAPE, A MEASURE OF MALPRACTICE 69 (1993). The reasons for this may be manifold, but whatever they are, the existence of large amounts of medical malpractice seems to suggest that it might not be best to rely too heavily on the high sense of professional obligation doctors feel.

The conspiracy of silence. At one time, plaintiffs were very much concerned about the "conspiracy of silence" among medical professionals who were reluctant to testify against one another. With the disappearance of the strict locality rule (a point to be seen in *Vegara v. Doan*, next), and the greater availability of expert witnesses, the silence is not so deafening as once it was. You can get a little feel for it from *Mulder v. Parke Davis & Co.*, 181 N. W. 2d 882, 45 A. L. R. 3d 920 (Minn. 1970). *Julien v. Barker*, 272 P.2d 718 (Idaho 1954) reflects the claim that plaintiff's medical witnesses promised to testify, then reneged after trial started because of pressure from the local medical society.

Requiring more than reasonable care. When doctors would generally perform a procedure despite a lack of scientific support, would others truly be required to follow suit? *Palandijan* seems to suggest the answer would be yes. This could make sense. If we think doctors know best, perhaps their practice is ahead of scientific study, which can take many years. On the other hand, we might worry about the cost of requiring the doctor to follow the leader if the leader is simply driving up health care costs in an ineffective way.

Notes 8-10. Where medical testimony is not required. These notes show some instances in which medical testimony is not required to support the plaintiff's case. You can remind the class that there are also some cases of obvious negligence mentioned in Note 4. In addition, a few cases form note 9 accept something like a reasonable care standard rather than a standard of custom. *Ray v. American National Red Cross,* 696 A.2d 399 (D.C. App. 1997); *Advincula v. United Blood Services,* 678 N.E.2d 1009 (Ill. 1996) (the plaintiff could overcome professional standard evidence by any equivalent of expert opinion testimony that showed "the prevailing professional custom or usage itself constitutes negligence"); *Clark v. St. Dominic-Jackson Memorial Hospital,* 660 So.2d 970 (Miss. 1995) (seemingly permitting liability of hospital apart from hospitals' custom or practice); *Nowatske v. Osterloh,* 543 N.W.2d 265 (Wis. 1996).

Medical testimony is of course not required in non-medical negligence cases. It was not necessary in *Self or Powell.*

Sometimes the plaintiff can allege injury from a breach contract or some specific promise distinct from any implied promise to conform to the medical standard of care. In *Zehr v. Haugen,* 871 P. 2d 1006 (Or. 1994), the defendant agreed to perform a tubal ligation upon the plaintiff while she was in the hospital for a different matter. She alleged that the promised procedure was not performed and that no one so advised her. Consequently, she became pregnant. The court held that she could proceed in contract. (Wrongful pregnancy or conception cases are considered along with wrongful life and wrongful birth cases in Chapter 20.)

Note 11. Apology. One of the main issues is about whether it is good for patients to receive an apology. There is certainly some evidence that apologies can be helpful to doctors, not just from a psychological standpoint, but because doctors who apologize for mistakes are less likely to get sued. Should a doctor be able to get the benefits of apologizing but not then have to subsequently take responsibility for making the mistake?

VERGARA V. DOAN , 593 N. E. 2d 185 (1992)

The local medical standard (in its liberalized version) is explained and then ultimately rejected. The court adopts something like a national standard.

The medical community rule may be stated in its three basic forms–"same" community, "same or similar" community, and the general or national standard. Annotation, *Modern Status of 'locality rule'*, 99 A. L. R. 3d 1133 (1980).

The rule requiring conclusory medical testimony is exacerbated by the older rule requiring testimony of doctors from the same locality, since this was the point at which peer pressure was the greatest and most strongly induced the conspiracy of silence. The same or similar community rule helps a little, since courts may be assuming that a community is "similar" if it is of similar size, even where its locale and other characteristics are quite different.

Note 1. *Holmes v. Elliott*, 443 So.2d 825 (Miss. 1983), testimony that the standard of care should be the same in Lumberton and Oklahoma was *not* sufficient grounds for imposing liability. "[E]ven if a national standard exists, it still must be shown that the applicable [state] standard is the same. In order to do this, the expert must have knowledge of the state-wide or local or similar locality standard. In the instant case, expert Dr. Daniel was not shown to have the requisite knowledge of, or familiarity with, the state-wide or Lumberton area or similar locality standard of care . . . ."

In *First Commercial Trust Company v. Rank*, 915 S.W.2d 262 (Ark. 1996), however, the court, applying the similar locality rule, permitted a doctor from Panama City, Florida to testify about the appropriate standard of care in Hots Springs, Arkansas, though Panama City was almost three times larger. The population alone was not the test, the court emphasized, but the medical facilities, practices, and advantages. And conversely, if it is shown that the practices are the same in three cities of disparate size, they are similar localities for the purpose of the similar locality rule.

In *Sheeley v. Mem. Hospital*, 710 A.2d 161 (R.I. 1998), the court said, "we join the growing number of jurisdictions that have repudiated the 'same or similar' communities test in favor of a national standard and hold that a physician is under a duty to use the degree of care and skill that is expected of a reasonably competent practitioner in the same class to which he or she belongs, acting in the same or similar circumstances." The *Sheeley* court listed a number of cases in the growing number liberalizing the locality rule. *See also* DOBBS ON TORTS § 244 (2000).

The national standard pitfall. The national standard has always been regarded as one more favorable to the plaintiff, at least strategically, since it would allow the plaintiff to draw on a witness pool outside the confines of the local community. However, in *Travers v. District of Columbia,* 672 A.2d 566 (D.C. App. 1996) the expert witness testified to a standard of care but did not identify it as a national standard; the court thought that since no "national" standard had been proven, the case had to be dismissed under its national standard approach. You can criticize this ruling. If we assume the witness referred to a national standard, the plaintiff has made her proof. If he refers only to a local standard, it is either the same as, more forgiving, or more demanding than the national standard. If it is the same as or more forgiving, then it is clear that the national standard would have been violated when the local standard is violated. If the local standard is more demanding, you might still think that a national standard sets a floor, a minimum standard, not a ceiling or an immunity. The court appeared to say that the local standard was not only no longer necessary, it was no longer sufficient, either. This in effect presumes that the doctors in the plaintiff's locality are practicing under an aberrant standard of care.

Note 2. Limited resources and the national standard. Mississippi's earlier rule seen in Note 1 may have looked rather bad. If so, *Hall v. Hilbun*, 466 So. 2d 856 (Miss. 1985), cited in this note, makes up for it by establishing a national standard. The national standard could not conceivably require one to use equipment one does not have and cannot get. If the patient needs equipment (or skill) the doctor cannot furnish, the doctor's duty is to refer the patient to a better equipped facility or (in the case of skill) to a specialist. That satisfies the doctor's duty of care, however that duty is formulated. In *Jorgenson v. Vener*, 616 N.W.2d 366 (S.D. 2000) the court, answering an argument that the lost chance rule would somehow "denigrate" rural medical care, said: "Our current medical malpractice regime expects that any physician, rural or urban, who is uncertain about his ability to treat a patient's condition will refer the patient to another who is more skilled or experienced. . . . Whether medical care is administered in a rural or urban setting, among the latest technology or with the most primitive of instruments, a patient still has the right to expect competence in his physician's care."

Hospitals: national standards and equipment. If the defendant is a hospital and holds itself out as one, it might be expected to meet equipment standards of the accrediting committee that are national. On this idea, you might again remind the class of the *T. J. Hooper* and especially of Epstein's ideas about when custom should actually set the standard. Maybe a hospital by its very name implies that it would have customary equipment and perhaps for that reason should be found negligent if it fails to have a working X-ray machine, oxygen, or oxygen monitors. *Birchfield v. Texarkana Memorial Hospital*, 747 S. W. 2d 361 (Tex. 1987), held a hospital liable when a baby was given oxygen and there was no equipment to monitor how much the baby received. Too much oxygen can blind a baby and that happened here. The hospital knew it needed the equipment but did not purchase it. Even so, that was not the only basis for liability. The hospital failed to refer the patient to a better-equipped facility.

Medical guidelines. The medical standard of care is not synonymous with medical practice guidelines. Practice guidelines have recently been proposed as a kind of giant and authoritative list of the most effective procedures for all kinds of medical problems. In fact, the use of any given medical procedure varies enormously among physicians. In other words, *some* physicians are not being guided by "medical science" or by some professional standard. In some instances, medical or surgical or diagnostic procedures were overused, a point related to cost containment issues raised in § 4 below. Perhaps as a result of the ensuing medical and scientific criticisms of the medical profession's practices, many proposals for scientifically acceptable practice guidelines have been put forward. Alternatively, government health agencies may be putting forward *politically* acceptable guidelines for medical procedures. On the topic of practice guidelines, and with suggestions of his own, *see* Michelle M. Mello, *Of Swords and Shields: the Role of Clinical Practice Guidelines in Medical Malpractice Litigation,* 149 U. PA. L. REV. 645 (2001) (arguing against guidelines either to inculpate or exculpate physicians, since guidelines do not represent prevailing medical practice); Clark Havinghurst, *Practice Guidelines as Legal Standards Governing Physician Liability,* 54 L. & CONTEMP. PROBS. 87 (1991). Practice guidelines look more like authoritative regulation than the common law's standard of the medical community. They would be centralized, bureaucratic, and authoritative. They would not necessarily resemble *either* the medical custom standard as we know it *or* the reasonable person standard. Should authoritative guidelines be adopted for most medical, surgical, and diagnostic procedures, their precise legal effect in a malpractice case might still be debated. *See* Havinghurst, *supra.*

NOTE: SPECIALISTS

¶ ¶ **1 & 2.** Specialists are held to the standard of the specialty and that standard is national, not local. E.g., *Bahr v. Harper-Grace Hospitals,* 528 N. W. 2d 170, 172 (Mich. 1995) ("the standard of care for general practitioners is that of the local community or similar communities, and is nationwide for a specialist"). Hence the local medical standard is inappropriate to a claim against a specialist. *Jordan v. Bogner,* 844 P. 2d 664 (Colo. 1993). And "outside" experts in specialties are appropriate. *See* Annotation, 18 A. L. R. 4th 603 (1982).

If the legislature has codified a locality rule (or the court retains it), a non-local specialist might still be permitted to testify. The expert might be able to state that she knows the local standard, for example, if she previously practiced in the locality. She might also be able to state that she knows the local standard because in her specialty the standard is the same in all localities. That is to state that the local standard and the "national" standard are the same. This would comply with a local standard rule and the only question would be whether the court would adopt the expert's self-appraisal as an expert on the "local" standard. See, along these lines, *Piazza v. Behrman Chiropractice Clinic,* Inc., 601 So.2d 1378 (La. 1992).

¶ **3.** In *First Commercial Trust Company v. Rank,* 915 S. W. 2d 262 (Ark. 1996) an emergency room specialist was permitted to testify against a family practitioner on the question of standards for reporting suspected child abuse.

Might even a "lay person" with expertise be permitted to testify? In *Greenberg v. Michael Reese Hosp.,* 415 N. E. 2d 390, 16 A. L. R. 4th 1289 (Ill. 1980), the court permitted a "health physicist," who held a master's degree in "radiological health physics" to testify against a hospital on the ground that he was "highly qualified and familiar with radiation therapy in hospitals." Part of the reasoning was based on the fact that a hospital was a defendant. But in

Reinhardt v. Colton, 337 N. W. 2d 88 (Minn. 1983) the court took a harder line, upholding a trial court's discretion to reject a pathologist's testimony on the inappropriate use of penicillamine because the pathologist was "not a clinician."

Several views on this topic are summarized in DOBBS ON TORTS § 246, at 641 (2000).

NOTE: NON-MEDICAL PRACTITIONERS

¶ **1. The standard.** The term nonmedical of course refers to the nature of the practitioner's credentials–a medical degree or some other degree or none at all. A podiatrist, a chiropractor, and a naturopath may all be delivering health care, but they are not medical doctors and not practicing medicine. We must, then, distinguish "two schools of thought" within the medical profession from "two schools of health care." The standard is the one the practitioner professes to follow, at least so long as he does not mislead the patient and commits no violation of law. You could understand the assumed risk case, *Boyle v. Revici*, 961 F.2d 1060 (2d Cir. 1992), *supra* Chapter 10, as essentially holding the practitioner to the treatment he claimed to give.

Is there a limit? If the doctor's procedure or school of medicine is to wrap the patient in flannels soaked in kerosene, he may be in trouble. Holmes, J. upheld a manslaughter conviction in *Commonwealth v. Pierce*, 138 Mass. 165 (1884). In *Guerrero v. Smith*, 864 S.W.2d 797 (Tex. App. 1993), the defendant was a "licensed medical doctor practicing homeopathic medicine," which included injections of unapproved compounds and directions to the plaintiff to drink her own urine. The plaintiff was most horribly infected and required operations to remove whole parts of her body. The court allowed an M.D. to testify that these practices fell below the standard of care. The standard of care issue seems not to have been raised directly. Instead, the argument was that the plaintiff's witness was not qualified. Is the case really distinguishable from *Boyle v. Revici*, where the doctor provided non-standard cancer treatments that did no good? *Lundman v. McKown*, 530 N. W. 2d 807 (Minn. Ct. App. 1995), the Christian Science case, is another extreme case in which the court seemed to struggle to avoid the excuse that known risks could be excused on the "my school of practice" rule. To make the issue more difficult, *Lundman* adds the religious freedom element. But there is a limit when it comes to children. In that case, the court requires the practitioner to take account of the child's (physical) welfare. How is the practitioner to do this except by what the practitioner believes is the "right" kind of treatment? Is the court implicitly holding that the child's welfare is to be determined by the standard of the medical profession?

¶ **2. Referral.** (1) Chiropractors cannot carry out medical treatment, but (2) in doing whatever is involved in Chiropractic, they are bound only by the standards of Chiropractors, not by the standards of medical doctors. (3) When the patient presents a medical problem, the Chiropractor must not attempt to treat it. *Kerkman v. Hintz*, 418 N.W.2d 795 (Wis. 1988) logically holds that the

Chiropractor need not refer the patient to a medical doctor. *Goldstein v. Janusz Chiropractic Clinics,* 582 N.W.2d 78 (Wis. Ct. App. 1998) goes on to hold that the chiropractor, confronted with an x-ray showing an abnormal mass in the lung need not even recognize it and need not advise the patient that a condition exists beyond the scope of chiropractic.

Some courts go the other way on referral, requiring the chiropractor to refer to a medical doctor. In *Rosenberg v. Cahill,* 492 A.2d 371 (N.J. 1985), the chiropractor took x-rays, as was permitted by the licensing statute for the purpose of determining whether the spine was aligned as chiropractors say it should be. The x-rays clearly showed soft tissue abnormalities that turned out to be a serious disease. Because the chiropractor did not recognize the abnormalities, he did not refer to a medical doctor. The result was that the patient's treatment for his Hodgkin's disease was much delayed. The New Jersey Court held the evidence sufficient to support a finding of negligence in failing to recognize and refer the patient to a medical doctor, although the evidence came from a medical doctor, not from a chiropractor. If you interpret the evidence to mean that the chiropractor's standard itself requires both a recognition of the medical problem and referral, then the chiropractor violated the standard of his own school of practice. If you interpret the evidence to mean only that the chiropractor should have recognized the abnormalities, then it is hard to see why there should be a duty to refer as long as we license Chiropractors.

Must a hospital devoted to religious beliefs that oppose birth control and abortion refer a rape victim to some other hospital if it is unwilling to provide information on pregnancy prevention? *Brownfield v. Daniel Freeman Marina Hospital,* 256 Cal. Rptr. 240 (Ct. App. 1989), supported such a duty to refer in a dictum, but refused to hold for the plaintiff, who failed to allege that she became pregnant as a result of the rape. The plaintiff in that case also sought an injunction but the court seemed to hold that damages would suffice. If the court was saying that the plaintiff who becomes pregnant from a rape is as well off to recover damages as to avoid the pregnancy altogether, the conclusion seems bizarre.

NOTE: OTHER PROFESSIONALS

¶¶ **1 & 2. Nurses, hospitals, and pharmacists.** *Nurses.* Nurse-negligence was once not regarded as malpractice at all, but contemporary thought appears to treat them as professionals who are subject to and beneficiaries of the professional standard and expert testimony rules. *See* DOBBS ON TORTS § 242, at 632, n.11 (2000). In *Sheffield v. Goodwin,* 740 So.2d 854 (Miss. 1999) the court held that the nurse practitioner, because she possessed no specialized knowledge in dentistry or oral surgery, was not qualified to testify as an expert against the doctor.

Hospitals. Some hospital negligence is administrative or non-medical in nature. When that is so, the reasonable care standard applies, not the medical standard. Cf. *Johnson v. Hillcrest Health Care, Inc.,* 70 P.2d 811 (Okla. 2003) (jury could find hospital negligent for failing to post patient's test results on chart where they could be seen by doctors). At least in cases involving ministerial or non-medical negligence, courts sometimes say that the hospital owes care commensurate with the what the hospital knew or should have known was the patient's physical or mental condition. See *Miller v. Trinity Medical Center,* 260 N.W.2d 4 (N.D. 1977). Hospitals are usually accredited by national organizations applying national standards. For this reason if not other, national, not local standards apply to hospitals.

Hospital's duty to supervise physicians and monitor their care. See Dobbs on Torts § 254. The hospital's duty, if any, to supervise doctors who use its facilities, is considered in Chapters 16 & 20. We'll see there that the hospital could be liable for failing to control the quality of care provided by independent physicians. *Darling v. Charleston Com. Mem. Hosp.,* 211 N.E.2d 253 (Ill. 1965).

Hospital's vicarious liability. See Chapter 22.

¶ 3. **Pharmacists.** Some patients have claimed injury from prescription drugs and have sought to recover from pharmacists for failing to provide warnings or necessary information. In a number of cases courts have refused to impose liability, not wishing to set the pharmacist up for a conflict with the physician by second-guessing the prescription. In *Docken v. CIBA-GEIGY,* 790 P. 2d 45 (Or. Ct. App. 1990) the court was willing to impose a duty of care upon the pharmacist to give appropriate warnings, but insisted that the plaintiff would be required to prove the pharmacist's standard of care for warnings and would be denied relief if he did not do so. See Dobbs on Torts § 257 (2000).

¶ 4. **Other callings.** (a) Courts often refer to the reasonable prudent X standard where X refers to the defendant's vocation and is thus a shorthand for "reasonable, prudent person under the circumstances". At least that is the most plausible meaning of many such statements. They do not imply, for instance, that the plaintiff must obtain testimony of dog owners about their customary standards when the plaintiff sues a dog owner.

(b) *Blood banks.* These might be analogized to medical procedures and if so the professional standard might be invoked. That is what the trial judge thought in *Elkerson v. North Jersey Blood Center,* but both the Appellate Division and the New Jersey Supreme Court, cited here, held otherwise, demanding a reasonable care instruction. (We also saw this case back with our discussion of custom following the *T. J. Hooper.*) Whether a blood supplier is a medical professional can also be important on statute of limitations issues. In *Silva v. Southwest Florida Blood Bank, Inc.,* 601 So.2d 1184 (Fla 1992), one of the plaintiff patients allegedly died from AIDS after receiving contaminated blood from the defendant. The issue was whether the malpractice statute of limitations applied to protect the blood bank. The malpractice statute was definitionally limited to cases involving "medical . . . diagnosis, treatment, or care," rendered by a "provider of health care." The court concluded that the blood bank was not a health care provider and had not engaged in diagnosis, treatment or care in this particular case.

¶ **4. Architects, engineers, accountants and lawyers.** All these professionals and an increasing list of others are said to be subject to the professional rather than the reasonable person standard. Some of the rule statements are fuzzy and in some the court may only have in mind reasonable care under the circumstances.

Accountants. Accountants and lawyers usually create economic risks if they are negligent but not risks of personal injury. For this reason, they are outside the scope of our focus on physical injury law. However, the problem of accountants' liability for negligent or fraudulent balance sheets is touched briefly in Chapter 34 in *Ultramares Corp. v. Touche, Niven & Co.*, 255 N.Y. 170, 174 N.E. 441 (1931) and its supporting Notes.

Lawyers. This casebook prints no major cases involving lawyer malpractice. Lawyer malpractice may be considered in courses in professional responsibility and in advanced tort courses dealing with economic and commercial torts. For a brief summary of lawyer malpractice *see* DOBBS ON TORTS, Chapter 36 (2000). The standard treatise is RONALD E. MALLEN & JEFFREY M. SMITH, LEGAL MALPRACTICE (multiple volumes). *See also* PAUL T. HAYDEN, ETHICAL LAWYERING: LEGAL AND PROFESSIONAL RESPONSIBILITIES IN THE PRACTICE OF LAW, Chapter 2 (2d Ed. 2007) (casebook).

¶ **5. Educational malpractice.** (a) *Physical injury, sexual harassment.* Educational malpractice is an unfortunate term because both its factual and legal content is uncertain. For the most part, physical harm on the school ground is a matter of ordinary negligence rules and liability is often appropriate on that basis, as where a student is injured in a chemistry lab fire. *Connett v. Fremont City School Dist.*, 581 P. 2d 1097 (Wyo. 1978). A school might be liable for a sexual assault committed by its principal. See *Galli v. Kirkeby*, 248 N. W. 2d 149 (Mich. 1976).[1] The same is true with other forms of sexual harassment by teachers, which may be actionable under civil rights law or under ordinary tort principles. *See Franklin v. Gwinnett County Public Schools*, 503 U.S. 60 (1992); *Doe v. Taylor Independent School Dist.*, 975 F. 2d 137 (5th Cir. 1992). *Cf. Gagnon v. State*, 570 A. 2d 656 (R. I. 1990) (state subsidized the cost of a child's day care and assigned the child to the Reid's day care center; the state was lax in dealing with complaints about molestation and the child was molested; there was a duty). Nonfeasance rules and duties to protect against harms by third persons can become most significant in some of these cases. For instance, a school may have a duty to protect a student from attacks by others or even from her own suicide. See *Eisel v. Board of Education of Montgomery County*, 597 A. 2d 447 (Md. 1991) and Chapters 16 and 18 below.

---

[1] The allegation was that on more than 100 occasions a school principal had sexually assaulted a pupil, forcing submission to various repulsive acts. The court held that the school board was exercising a discretionary function in screening and hiring principals and that it could not be held liable for negligent hiring, but that the board might be vicariously liable for the definitely non-governmental acts of the principal, if proven.

(b)*Teaching, testing, and social failures.* Failure to teach, if a tort at all, seems mainly an economic or perhaps dignitary tort rather than an injury tort.

Courts have not been receptive to claims that textbooks harmed students by presenting sex education materials or the like; this claim obviously does touch discretionary decisions and in public schools, at least, might well be protected by the discretionary immunity if not by a conventional no-duty rule. See *Aubrey v. Sch. Dist of Philadelphia*, 437 A. 2d 1306 (Pa. Cmwlth. 1981) (claim of emotional harm from reading textbooks denied). Courts have also refused to entertain educational malpractice claims based on misclassification of a student, or on incompetent teaching. Possibly a student deprived of equal educational opportunity would have an action under federal education statutes, but otherwise courts have been opposed to claims against schools for social and educational failure, even when the school committed clear professional error.

Hoffman v. Board of Education of New York, 400 N. E. 2d 317 (N.Y. 1979) involved the classification of a child as subnormal, with the result that he was made to spend 12 years of "school" with seriously defective children where he learned only that he is inadequate as a person. This was a grievous mental and emotional harm with lifetime effects, both economically and personally. The negligence involved can only be gleaned from the Appellate Division's opinion, not from that of the Court of Appeals. The case is instructive in its desire to protect professional judgment. It went much further in that protection than the other malpractice cases go: it did *not* allow for liability when teachers or other school persons violate professional standards.

In *Ross v. Creighton University*, 957 F. 2d 410 (7th Cir. 1992), the plaintiff had been an educationally disadvantaged boy who was a successful high school basketball player. He alleged that Creighton recruited him with promises of special educational help and a chance to play basketball. It turned out, however, that the plaintiff's ACT score was in the bottom one-fifth of all high school seniors, while Creighton's average freshmen admit was in the upper 27 percent. Ross was shunted into courses in Marksmanship. An athletic department employee helped with course papers. Even so, he maintained only a D average and never acquired enough credit hours for graduation. Labeling the claim "educational malpractice," the court held that Illinois law would not recognize any of the variations Ross asserted. Yet the allegations, if true, reveal a cynical manipulation of a disadvantaged human being by a powerful corporation, which ought to be acting as a fiduciary to students, not as a consumer of their talents.

Miller, III v. Loyola University of New Orleans, 829 So.2d 1057 (La. Ct. App. 2002), involved a claim by a law student that the teacher taught a course so badly that he should be entitled at least to reimbursement for the cost of retaking the course with another teacher. The school itself investigated and found a number of deficiencies in the teaching, but the court held that educational malpractice would not be a recognized tort because there were no standards (even though the school itself found standards violated) and because damages could not be calculated (even though this was essentially an economic tort claim with recovery measurable to reimbursement costs) and thus wholly unlike the claim in *Hoffman* (cited in the casebook in this paragraph) for a life ruined by the school's policies.

In *Sain*, cited in this paragraph, the Iowa court recognized that not every claim against educators falls within the "educational malpractice category." If the guidance counselor gave a high school student specific erroneous information upon which the student could be expected to rely, and the result was that the student lost a college scholarship, the student had a good claim. The reasons for the judicially created immunity of educators were said to be "the absence of an adequate standard of care, uncertainty in determining damages, the burden placed on schools by the potential flood of litigation that would probably result, the deference given to the educational system to carry out its internal operations, and the general reluctance of courts to interfere in an area regulated by legislative standards." None of these reasons applied to a case in which the plaintiff assert "a specific act of providing specific information requested by a student under circumstances in which the school knew or should have known the student was relying upon the information to qualify for future educational athletic opportunities. In this context, the resolution of the claim does not require courts to interfere in the daily operation of the school or challenge the policies of education."

Physical risks to student or third persons through bad teaching. If a law school neglected to tell students that civil defendants must file an answer or motion in response to a complaint, or medical schools neglected to mention that sterilization of instruments was necessary, we would certainly be able to measure negligence against a suitable standard. If a graduate, untutored in these essentials, loses a case or a patient as a result, should the victim have a claim against the school? The medical example differs from the other educational malpractice claims in two distinct ways. First, like the law school example, it involves a third party who is injured. Second, unlike the law school example and other educational malpractice cases, it entails a risk of physical harm. Two cases have these characteristics. *Moss Rehab v. White*, 692 A.2d 902 (Del. 1997) and *Moore v. Vanderloo*, 386 N.W.2d 108 (Iowa 1986), involving respectively a driving school graduate whose driving caused a death, and a chiropractic school graduate whose graduate allegedly caused or contributed to a stroke. The courts in each case characterized the claim as one for educational malpractice and thus barred it. Both gave other reasons, however, principally the state's licensing scheme that was viewed as supplying the sole protection for victims.

In *Doe v. Yale University*, 1997 WL 766845 (Conn. Super. 1997) (unpublished), a medical resident was himself allegedly injured, allegedly a result of negligent training. He was directed to change an arterial line in an AIDS patient without either training or supervision. Saying that the claim did not assert an overall failure of the educational program but rather a specific failure to train him in needle safety and failure to supervise the particular task, the court held this was not an "educational malpractice" claim and hence that it could not be dismissed on summary judgment.

It may be a disservice to simply lump all claims in the box labeled educational malpractice. The concern to avoid interference with school administration is justified. But that concern does not prevent courts from redressing outrageous harms that violate clear and well-established norms of the educational culture itself, or from insisting that when a fiduciary promises to protect our interests, he must at least try to honor his promise.

Other professionals not mentioned in this note include mental health practitioners (whose malpractice is touched on in *Tarasoff*, Chapter 18) and members of the clergy (see § 6).

HIRPA V. IHC HOSPITALS, INC., 948 P.2d 785 (Utah 1997)

This case illustrates one type of good Samaritan statute. The rationale given in *Hirpa* is that immunity will encourage humanitarian efforts. Is the premise that (1) It is permissible for humanitarians to take unreasonable risks with the lives of others? *or* (2) The legal system is so bad that it would somehow manage to impose liability upon doctors who act carefully and the immunity is needed to avoid this rather significant failure? *or* (3) Although the legal system is generally sound, doctors wrongly fear liability and will not act as Dr. Daines did unless they are so encouraged by immunity? Why is it that the guest statutes have been repealed or held unconstitutional while the Good Samaritan statutes for physicians are practically universal?

Constitutionality in **Hirpa.** In another part of the *Hirpa* opinion, the court upheld the constitutionality of the Utah statute under the state constitution's provision for "open courts," a clause that imposed limits on the legislature's power to eliminate just claims. It upheld the statute, however, partly because it thought Utah's early history as a sparsely populated state might have protected the volunteer Good Samaritan even without the statute.

For the statutes, *see* 3 LOUISELL & WILLIAMS, MEDICAL MALPRACTICE § 21.01 (1996) and Stewart R. Reuter, *Physicians as Good Samaritans,* 20 J. Legal Med. 157 (1999). *See also* Danny R. Veilleux, Annotation, *Construction and Application of "Good Samaritan" Statutes,* 68 A.L.R.4th 294 (1989).

You may find a jumble of good Samaritan statutes in a single state, directed at various very specific situations or professionals. Some of the California statutes permit liability for wilful misconduct or the like. See, e.g., *Eastburn v. Regional Fire Protection Auth.,* 80 P.3d 656 (Cal. 2003) (applying state statute that immunizes emergency rescue personnel from liability unless their actions were "performed in bad faith" or "grossly negligent"). Others are like the Utah statute in simply immunizing the surgeon who has good intentions. "Thus the goodness of the Samaritan is a description of the quality of his or her intention, not the quality of the aid delivered." *Perkins v. Howard,* 283 Cal.Rptr. 764 (Ct. App. 1991). One student of the topic found 15 statutes like Utah's, providing total immunity. Stewart R. Reuter, *Physicians as Good Samaritans,* 20 J. LEGAL MED. 157 (1999). The remainder recognize liability for gross negligence or wanton misconduct. A few statutes, perhaps explicable as the result of legislative maneuvering, inanely provide that the doctor is protected if he is in good faith *and* not negligent! *E.g.*, ARK. CODE .ANN. § 17-95-101.

Nonpaying-patients version. Sometimes the statute immunizes negligence toward nonpaying patients. In *Washington v. Clark*, 550 S.E.2d 671 (Ga. Ct. App. 2001), an on-call physician was immune because under Georgia statutes "No health care provider 'who voluntarily and without the expectation or receipt of compensation provides professional services ... at the request of a hospital ... shall be liable' for damages or injuries, including death, allegedly sustained by reason of an act or omission in rendering such services, unless such injuries were caused by gross negligence or wilful or wanton misconduct." Can the patient's financial condition really be a good basis for relieving a surgeon from a duty of care? Again, you can compare the now-discredited guest statutes. Even if you thought the patient's poverty justified the physician's negligence, the physician who is on-call is in a real sense paid for his work; his on-call obligation is part of the quid-pro-quo for his staff privileges at the hospital, which in turn provides him services and equipment needed for his income-producing work.

Note 1. Liability for gross negligence. These statutes give the physician more room in which to operate but something short of full immunity.

Note 2. Emergency care. Students should understand that a physician whose duty or job it is to deal with emergencies–the physicians working in the emergency department for example–do not get the statute's immunity; they already owe a duty of care. Statutes may compel the same result by defining emergency. For instance, New York lowers the standard of care for a doctor who "renders first aid or emergency treatment at the scene of an accident or other emergency, outside a hospital, doctor's office or any other place having proper and necessary medical equipment," thus leaving liability for negligence in the course of normal work. N.Y. EDUC. L. § 6527 2. Preexisting duty is not self-defining, however. As the *Hirpa* court suggested, a number of factors might be relevant, including on-call status of the physician.

Which way does it cut that E.R. doctors are more likely to make mistakes? Does that make them better candidates for immunity or better candidates for tort suits on a theory of deterrence?

Note 3. Scope of immunity. Two wispy rationales float around the statutes. One is that a doctor in an emergency (such as a roadside injury) will not have adequate equipment. The second is that regardless of equipment available, the doctor should be encouraged to render aid if he is not already obliged to do so. Which rationale a court adopts greatly effects what it thinks about whether immunity extends to the hospital setting.

Note 4, Need for immunity. The statutes were of course enacted as a result of pressure from the organized medical profession. Quite possibly legislators (and courts, too) failed to understand that the ordinary rules of negligence take account of the emergency setting, both in and out of a hospital. No doctor would be held liable unless his peers could testify that he failed to exercise the care that other doctors would have exercised in the same emergency situation. Some nonmedical statutes may have been enacted or interpreted on the same misunderstanding of tort law and its ability to account for the special pressures that arise in emergencies. A series of strange state statutes resemble the federal model Good Samaritan Food Donation Act, 42 U.S.C.A. § 1791, providing protection for those who donate food to charities.

The medical Good Samaritan statutes have led to litigation that seems to have little or nothing to do with the rights or wrongs involved, with whether the doctor was negligent considering the circumstances. In *Pemberton v. Dharmani,* 525 N.W.2d 497 (Mich. Ct. App. 1994) the court held that a surgeon who was not dealing with an emergency but *thought* he was could enjoy the statutory immunity in a hospital setting.

§ 2. RES IPSA LOQUITUR

STATES V. LOURDES HOSPITAL, 792 N.E.2d 151 (N.Y. 2003).

A caution to teachers: this case has been shortened somewhat in the hope that the central points of the case could be conveyed to students more efficiently. If you have used this case before, please be sure to reread the case as edited in this edition to be sure that you are on the same page as your students.

States applies the "traditional" requirements of res ipsa to a medical malpractice case. Those requirements, which we saw earlier in Chapter 6, are: (1) that the event is of a kind that ordinarily does not occur in the absence of negligence; (2) that the injury was caused by an agent or instrumentality in the defendant's exclusive control; and (3) that no act or negligence on the plaintiff's part contributed to the happening of the event. Recall that the Restatement Second's statement of the requirements of res ipsa, also found in Chapter 6, are somewhat more open-ended on the second and third points.

The case does triple duty here – allowing for a review of res ipsa in general, introducing its use in the medical malpractice area, and showing how, in that area, the admissibility of expert testimony is a relevant issue.

The plaintiff here, whose arm and shoulder were injured during an operation for removal of an ovarian cyst, produced a medical expert who opined that her injuries would not have occurred in the absence of negligence. The trial court held that the jury could rely on this expert testimony in reaching a conclusion that the first requirement of res ipsa was met. The appeals court reversed. This court agrees with the trial court's assessment.

The defendant argued that "res ipsa loquitur cannot apply here because, in order to establish the first prerequisite . . . plaintiff must rely on expert medical opinion, and the doctrinal foundation of res ipsa loquitur can only lie in everyday experience." The court rejects this, holding that expert testimony may properly be admitted to "bridge the gap" between its own knowledge and expert knowledge.

As the court notes, this is both the Restatement Second approach and the majority approach in the states.

Note 1. Common knowledge. The trier of fact can conclude that negligence is more likely than not if it is "common knowledge" that the injury in question would most likely result only from negligence. Typical cases include injury at a remote site and instruments or materials unintentionally left in the abdomen. See *Dalley v. Utah Valley Regional Medical Center,* 791 P.2d 193 (Utah 1990) (caesarean; burn on plaintiff's calf that required skin grafts; common knowledge indicates negligence was probable); *Beaudoin v. Watertown Memorial Hospital,* 145 N.W.2d 166 (Wis. 1966) (operating to remove vaginal polyp, burns on buttocks, res ipsa loquitur applied). Should the courts also recognize a case in which the surgeon operates on the wrong vertebrae, but only because a radiologist assured him he was at the correct site? *Long v. Hacker,* 520 N.W.2d 195 (Neb. 1994) held that res ipsa was established.

The point of the remote site emphasis is not mechanical. It is that the medical procedure normally does not put a remote site at risk. Consequently, res ipsa may be invoked even for an injury at or near the site of the procedure if it is an injury that is not normally risked by the procedure. In *Gold v. Ishak,* 720 N.E.2d 1175 (Ind. App. Ct. 1999) surgeons were performing an operation upon the plaintiff's carotid artery. Her face was covered with an oxygen mask that came in one size only and did not seal well. The surgeons used an electrical cauterizing tool that emitted sparks. The oxygen mask caught fire and the patient was burned on her face and chest. A physician testified about the likelihood of negligence. The court held that res ipsa could apply. Since fire burns were not inherent risks of the operation, this is might be an appropriate result.

Note 2. Expert testimony. As *States* explains, the trier may lack "common knowledge" about a technical field, but this can be remedied by testimony from experts. The expert can testify that although he cannot pinpoint an act of negligence, negligence is nevertheless more likely than not given the facts as developed in the trial. *See Kennelly v. Burgess,* 654 A.2d 1335 (Md. 1995); *Morgan v. Children's Hosp.,* 480 N.E.2d 464, 49 A.L.R.4th 51 (Ohio 1985). On facts similar to *Walski,* a medical witness testified that damage to the nerve does not ordinarily result without negligence. This was enough to invoke res ipsa loquitur and get the plaintiff to the jury. *Hightower-Warren v. Silk,* 698 A.2d 52 (Pa. 1997).

How expert opinion res ipsa differs from other opinion. The expert opinion that furnishes the basis for res ipsa is quite different from that which furnishes the basis for an ordinary negligence claim. In the res ipsa cases all that is required of the expert is a statement that such an injury as the plaintiff received would not ordinarily occur without negligence. This does not require the doctor to state that his colleague, the defendant, has failed to live up to the standard of care and presumably is an easier statement to obtain from many doctors.

Note 3. When is an instruction proper? You can use this note to test students' grasp of res ipsa loquitur. *Kenyon v. Miller,* described here, holds that the res ipsa instruction was improper. How could res ipsa be invoked here? Leaving a part of the mesh in place is a known act. That act was either negligent or not. Testimony was in conflict and that made a jury case of the issue, but res ipsa would have allowed the jury to find for the plaintiff even if the jury believed that leaving the mesh in place was medically right. Perhaps some kinds of untoward medical events strike people more strongly than others. In *Perkins v. Hausladen,* 828 S.W.2d 652 (Ky. 1992), the defendant was drilling a bone in the inner ear to deal with a diseased condition. A prime concern was to avoid tearing the sigmoid sinus, a vein that drains the brain area into the internal jugular vein, but a tearing in fact occurred. The Kentucky Court held that res ipsa applied. That may strike many people as an improbable conclusion without some evidence about the likelihood of non-negligent tearing. Was this a known risk of great magnitude, accepted out of necessity? Was it a low risk but nevertheless one that occurs without negligence? These questions did not trouble the *Perkins* court.

Compare *Walker v. Skiwski,* 529 So.2d 184 (Miss. 1988) where the court held that the fact that an infant's penis was deformed, that he had burning pains when he urinated, that he had to undergo corrective surgery, did *not* warrant a res ipsa loquitur claim against the surgeon who performed the circumcision. Similarly, a mechanical failure, such as the breaking of an endotracheal tube does not show medical negligence. *Rolon-Alvarado v. Municipality of San Juan,* 1 F.3d 74 (1st Cir. 1993) (Puerto Rico law).

Note 4. Abandonment. No claim for abandonment lies unless a duty to act is established in the first place, usually one arising because the doctor or hospital has accepted the patient. This point is closely connected to the Good Samaritan statutes, but one we tried to avoid considering with those statutes. We would also prefer to avoid discussing the affirmative duty to act issue here and save it for Chapters 16-18. What counts as abandonment might turn in part on the doctor-patient contract, which may turn out to be pretty much the same as an informed consent issue. See *Dingle v. Belin* in this note below.

The short answer probably is that in the first hypothetical, breach of duty is obvious or established as a matter of definition, so no standard of care testimony is required. In the second, you expect courts to require evidence about a standard of care, since negligence or abandonment is not obvious. That's about enough for class consumption, but here is a little more detail if you are interested:

Courts sometimes speak of abandonment as if it were some separate kind of tort, but it can easily be perceived as merely one form of malpractice claim. In the first hypothetical put in this note, the doctor simply walks out of the operating room. Maybe he will have an explanation, but on its face that looks like obvious negligence, so if harm results from his absence, the plaintiff probably should get to the jury without expert testimony. Courts sometimes get this result by defining abandonment or simply saying, without any reference to a medical standard, that the conduct was actionable. In *Burnett v. Layman,* 181 S.W. 157 (Tenn. 1915) the doctor "sounded" the patient's urethra and tore the bladder lining in the process. When the sound, evidently a catheter or something like one, was removed, blood and pus flowed. The doctor seemingly panicked, said the plaintiff should find himself a surgeon, and left. This was held an actionable abandonment, apparently as a matter of definition.

The cases do not necessarily use the term abandonment. In *New Biloxi Hosp., Inc. v. Frazier,* 146 So.2d 882 (Miss. 1962) a hospital admitted a bleeding gunshot victim to the emergency room and took his blood pressure, but consciously refused any treatment and in effect let him bleed to death. The victim was an African American. It would be hard to justify requiring expert testimony to show the standard of care. The court affirmed a judgment for the plaintiff.

Many claims are not like the two examples just given. They involve a physician who notifies the patient he will no longer provide treatment, or one who leaves town providing arguably inadequate emergency coverage, or one who fails to refer the patient for appropriate special treatment. Such cases do not often obviously fit the definition of abandonment. When abandonment is not obvious, the plaintiff will need expert testimony to establish the standard for referral or emergency coverage.

In *Tavakoli-Nouri v. Gunther,* 745 A.2d 939 (D.C. App. 2000), the plaintiff claimed that surgery was not scheduled for a long time and visits of the doctor were nine days apart. The court stated that expert testimony was required to show "whether the severance, if any, of that relationship was accomplished in compliance with appropriate standards."

In *McLaughlin v. Hellbusch,* 591 N.W.2d 569 (Neb. 1999), the plaintiff claimed that after surgery, the surgeon should have referred her to specialists who could have monitored her condition, which was likely to and did change. The plaintiff had no clear expert testimony establishing a standard calling for referral on the facts. Nebraska recognizes that "a physician is under the duty to give his patient all necessary and continued attention as long as the case requires it, and that he should not leave his patient at a critical stage without giving reasonable notice or making suitable arrangements for the attendance of another physician." But this rule and its variants did not assist the plaintiff without expert testimony because the plaintiff was not in critical condition at the time. The effect was that for some patients, at least, expert testimony would be required.

Some courts get similar results by concluding as a matter of law that the facts did not show abandonment. *Glenn v. Carlstrom,* 556 N.W.2d 800 (Iowa 1996) (non-referral claim); *Rosen v. Greifenberger,* 513 S.E.2d 861 (Va. 1999) (coverage arrangements). This judicial approach may be adequate in many instances, but if the case were closer and expert testimony showed that coverage arrangements were substandard, the abandonment claim would go to the jury, whether under the rubric of abandonment or the rubric of negligence.

In *Dingle v. Belin,* 749 A.2d 157 (Md. 2000), a surgeon allegedly promised to do "the cutting" himself. He didn't; he delegated this task to another while he performed the delicate task of retracting organs and tissues in the way. A wrong duct was severed with serious complications for the patient. The court saw partial abandonment in any improper delegation. But that was less a claim in itself than potential support for a claim for "traditional professional negligence, lack of informed consent, [or] breach of contract, depending in part on the nature of the consequences that flow from that abandonment." The court thought that the surgeon's alleged contract to operate personally would create a valid claim, but that failure to submit the claim to the jury was not harmful error because it was essentially covered in the informed consent claim, on which the jury found for the defendant.

There is a rather old annotation on abandonment. C. T. Drechsler, Annotation, *Liability of Physician Who Abandons Case,* 57 A.L.R.2d 432 (1958).

YBARRA V. SPANGARD, 154 P.2d 687 (Cal. 1944)

This is the classic case on the potential liability of multiple defendants when the negligence cannot be attributed to any one of them. *Res ipsa loquitur* is said to be the basis for holding all defendants liable.

Was someone negligent? The trier of fact could believe that, more likely than not, someone was negligent. The most notable facts are that a part of the body that was healthy before is now injured, and that it was not a part of the body at risk in the operation.

Could all defendants have been negligent? The basic coverage of *res ipsa loquitur* revealed a long-standing judicial concern to bring the negligence home to the defendant. If the courts believed there was fault, but that it was just as likely that it was the fault of someone other than the defendant, liability was not imposed. Both the old control rule and its contemporary modifications reflect this fundamental point. "The finger of guilt" must be pointed at the defendants who are liable. What has happened to this principle in *Ybarra*? If you believe that *all* those involved in treating the plaintiff–at least seven–were guilty of negligence, it is rational to use *res ipsa loquitur* here. But if you believe that only one or two were probably negligent, how does that justify imposing liability on all of them?

Summers v. Tice. Students with good memories sometimes spontaneously suggest that this is just another version of *Summers v. Tice,* Chapter 7. But *Ybarra* and *Summers* are quite different. In *Summers* we knew both defendants were negligent. We simply did not know which one's act in fact caused the harm. Since both risked the harm, both risked the causal uncertainty. The court appropriately resolved causal doubts against both negligent defendants. We can't resolve causal doubts against negligent defendants in *Ybarra* because we don't know that the defendants are negligent. As likely as not, any given defendant is innocent. *See* Seavey, *Res ipsa loquitur: Tabula in Naufragio*, 63 HARV. L. REV. 643, 648 (1950).

Revealing known facts; duty. The *Ybarra* court seems willing to impose liability as a means of forcing the non-negligent defendants to point the finger at the negligent one. But no evidence shows that any of the defendants, much less all of them, knew any fact about the guilt of others. Any reasonable estimate of likelihoods would be required to accept the probability that some defendants who were held liable did not know any relevant facts. Yet they are subject to liability without evidence of their own fault and without evidence that they were likely to know about the fault of others.

Thode's restatement in terms of duty. The late Professor Thode thought *Ybarra* was best explained by restating the duty of those in the operating room. "I believe the duty of each defendant should be defined to require use of reasonable care to protect the unconscious plaintiff, and a duty to fully inform him about what happened to the healthy part of his body that was unexpectedly injured. In addition, the risk of unexplained injuries to the unconscious plaintiff should be placed on each defendant, with each defendant bearing the burden of proof in establishing that his own conduct meets the above standard." Thode, *The Unconscious Patient: Who Should Bear the Risk of Unexplained Injuries to a Healthy Part of His Body?*, 1969 UTAH L. REV. 1, 10.

A vicarious liability alternative. Thode's proposed rule would put liability upon, say, a nurse who is wholly innocent of any fault herself and who knows nothing about the fault of the doctor. This would make sense if it were first shown that the nurse was negligent, as the hunters were negligent in *Summers v. Tice*. And it would make sense if it were first shown that the nurse in fact had knowledge she would not reveal. It would also make sense, at least to many of us, if it were directed only at the surgeon in charge or the hospital. Liability of the surgeon would be a rule of vicarious liability based on, or substantially identical to, the captain of the ship doctrine and the nondelegable duty rule.[2] But does it persuade us on the facts of *Ybarra,* which imposes liability, not merely upon superiors but also on employees who are not shown to be likely causes?

Smoking out and taking hostages. The court's own theory seems to be, not that one can rationally believe all defendants here were at fault or that justice permits us to impose a duty upon all to guarantee information that may not be known, but that the defendants, faced with liability, will be pres-

---

[2] The captain of the ship doctrine treats the chief surgeon as the "master" of all those in the operating room, a kind of borrowed servant doctrine. Nondelegable duty holds that some duties of care cannot be avoided by delegation to independent contractors. These are vicarious liability doctrines covered in Chapter 22.

sured to reveal what they know. Since this pressure is exerted without proof that any of the defendants knew anything at all about the injury, the moral effect is to take all of the defendants hostage, the innocent and ignorant as well as the guilty and knowing. Can this comport with the idea of justice or individual responsibility? Can one person be held responsible for the acts of another merely because both can be perceived to be in the same "group"?

Insurance behind *Ybarra*. Suppose the X Insurance Company had insured every one of the individual defendants in *Ybarra*. Voluntarily purchased insurance is an approved form of collective responsibility. The premiums of the innocent and ignorant as well as those of the culpable and knowing will be used to pay the judgment, because they have agreed to the scheme. Suppose that although X insured all the defendants, the court exculpated all of them on the ground that although someone was negligent, we did not know which one. Under such a holding, the X Insurance Company, though it ought to pay on behalf of one defendant, will not pay on behalf of anyone. This will strike almost everyone as unjust, and it is an unjustness that would be avoided by the *Ybarra* holding. Could something like this represent the real motive for the *Ybarra* decision?

Caselaw. *(a) Not the Ybarra problem.* A number of cases have cited *Ybarra* favorably, but the opinions on the whole are not very good at reaching the moral issue of collective liability or at formulating an intelligible duty. In fact, however, a number of the cases that purport to follow *Ybarra* are not *Ybarra* cases at all. In *Wick v. Henderson*, 485 N.W.2d 645 (Iowa 1992) there was actually testimony that the anesthetist was responsible for positioning the patient and that the injury probably resulted from improper positioning. The court held this was enough for the anesthetist's liability. This is not collective liability. (The court also recognized a potential for hospital liability as well, but didn't discuss the grounds for that.) *Horner v. Northern Pacific Beneficial Association Hospitals*, 62 Wash.2d 351, 382 P.2d 518 (1963), cited by Prosser as supporting *Ybarra*, is in fact a simple case of vicarious liability on the part of a hospital that employed every single actor in the emergency room.

(b) Cases consistent with vicarious liability rules. Some other *Ybarra*-citing cases are quite consistent with vicarious liability rules based on (1) borrowed servant/captain of the ship and (2) nondelegable duty. Some of the cases actually seem to base liability in part on those doctrines. *Kolakowski v. Voris*, 415 N.E.2d 397 (Ill. 1981); *Swierczek v. Lynch*, 466 N.W.2d 512 (Neb. 1991). Others, including some historical classics, are consistent with those doctrines in the way they are applied to the facts. *See Beaudoin v. Watertown Memorial Hospital*, 145 N.W.2d 166 (Wis. 1966). The difference is that vicarious liability—respondeat superior—works against the persons in charge, not against minor actors like the nurses. (Nothing would prevent liability of a nurse who was probably negligent.)

(c) Cases making individuated judgments of negligence. In some cases roughly similar to *Ybarra*, the facts seem to point to negligence on the part of only some defendants and correspondingly only some are held liable. That was

the case in *Chin v. St. Barnabas Medical Center,* 734 A.2d 778 (N.J. 1999). A physician and three nurses were engaged in performing a hysteroscopy. Some person or persons misconnected the machine, so that instead of circulating water in the womb, it circulated gas that killed the patient. The jury found negligence on the part of the doctor and two of the three nurses. The doctor apparently did not appeal. The trial judge gave NOV for the nurses and the plaintiff appealed that ruling. The appellate and Supreme Courts of New Jersey agreed that the jury verdict should stand. What distinguishes this from *Ybarra* is that judgment about fault is individuated. One of the nurses most probably could not have been responsible for the misconnection; the other two probably were both involved with it.

(d) Other cases mitigating the Ybarra hostage effect. Some other cases not only confine liability to those who, like the plaintiff's own physician or the chief surgeon, might reasonably be understood to have undertaken a special duty to the plaintiff, but even follow more traditional res ipsa thinking in limiting liability to those defendants who are likely to have been at fault, perhaps applying the control rule. In this category is *Darrah v. Bryan Mem. Hospital,* 571 N.W.2d 783 (Neb. 1998) (doctors, nurse, hospital, ulnar nerve injury, no res ipsa loquitur since exclusive control could not be established). *Fieux v. Cardiovascular & Thoracic Clinic, P.C.,* 978 P.2d 429 (Or. Ct. App. 1999) applied res ipsa loquitur to both nurses and an operating surgeon when a clamp was left in the body after open heart surgery, but the court was explicit in demanding that the plaintiff must trace probable negligence to each of the defendants. Others allow the jury to believe the denial of some actors and consequently conclude that other actors must have been negligent. *See Anderson v. Somberg,* 338 A.2d 1 (N.J. 1975).

In *Butler-Tulio v. Scroggins,* 774 A.2d 1209 (Md. Spec. Ct. App. 2001) a small surgical needle tip was left in the plaintiff's wrist at surgery. The plaintiff sued the doctor and the hospital. Testimony indicated that the nurses, hospital employees, not the doctor were responsible for making sure that the needles were all accounted for. There was conflicting testimony about medical standards, the defense doctor testifying that no standard was violated, "it happens all the time." The jury found for the defendants. The plaintiff argued on appeal that a res ipsa loquitur instruction should have been given. The court held that no res ipsa instruction should have been given because (1) no one was in exclusive control even though testimony indicated that needle count was the nurses' responsibility and (2) in any event res ipsa cannot be used "in a case which uses expert testimony to resolve complex issues of fact. . . .[R]es ipsa loquitur* is limited to those instances where, certain criteria having been met, the trier of fact may draw an inference of negligence from the facts alone." [Internal quotation marks omitted.]

A primary caretaker rule. You could impose liability for primary caregivers but not the innocent others by imposing a strict duty rather than by manipulating res ipsa loquitur. Perhaps some students would see the point more clearly in the case of a child left in a nursery. In *Ward v. Forrester Day*

Care, Inc., 547 So.2d 410 (Ala. 1989) an eleven-week-old baby was left at the defendant's day care center. When he was picked up by his parents at the end of the day, he gave an unusual scream. The next day he had a swelling on his wrist after a day at the defendant's day care. His arm had been broken. This case, and cases of elderly patients afflicted with loss of memory or communication skills, represent a problem of a helpless individual in the defendant's care. We can easily imagine that courts could impose a special duty upon the primary caretaker. Indeed, you might think that the caretaker assumed a special duty. We might describe that duty as a strict duty to guarantee reasonable safety. Or we might want to say only that the duty is satisfied if the primary caretaker provides either safety or information fully explaining the injury and exculpating himself. (The cases do not in fact seem to go this far in most instances. In *Persinger v. Step by Step Infant Dev. Ctr.*, 560 S.E.2d 333 (Ga. Ct. App. 2002) the court permitted the infant's claim to go to the jury because (a) he suffered a broken leg while in daycare, (b) the defendant's witnesses claimed he simply ran and fell, (c) but a medical witness testified that the break was inconsistent with a simple fall. This permits rational inferences of negligence on the part of the daycare operator; no liability of others was in issue.)

Against whom would such a duty run? In the nursery care case, surely against the primary caretaker, the owner, and/or the person in charge. But suppose you had twelve teenagers helping out at various times during the day and thirty sets of parents going in and out, sometimes interacting with the babies. The logic of *Ybarra's* massive retaliation would include all of them as well. But the basis of any strict duty upon minor helpers or parents on the scene is most dubious. In contrast, the basis for such a duty on the part of the primary caretaker seems plain: if the caretaker does not actually undertake such a duty, the law reasonably imposes it in almost the identical way it imposes a duty of caretakers to protect the helpless from themselves. (Recall *Bexiga v. Havir Manufacturing Corp.*, 290 A.2d 281 (N.J. 1972), Chapter 9.) None of this looks anything like a rational application of res ipsa loquitur based upon probabilities, but it makes sense. What doesn't make sense is the imposition of liability upon everyone who happened to be around.

Levmore on *Ybarra*. Saul Levmore, *Gomorrah to Ybarra and More: Overextraction and the Puzzle of Immoderate Group Liability*, 81 Va. L. Rev. 1561 (1995) considers *Ybarra* as one kind of model for forcing information, mainly in order to contrast a different model, one he calls overextraction. First he asks us to imagine that you are on an elevator with five other people. You are jostled and you realize that your wallet has been taken, but you cannot identify the culprit. The door opens and a police officer stands there, sympathetic but unable to induce anyone to admit the theft or to permit search. This is obviously in some way comparable to *Ybarra*. Levmore now suggests that all six must pay $150 into the hands of a third person as stakeholder, who would return the funds if the stolen wallet and money were immediately returned. Otherwise he would give it to charity or to a fund for prison construction. If the thief keeps the wallet, with $100, he loses the $150 that is overextracted. This is vintage Levmore, exploring, imagining, distinguishing. Most of the article will interest people who like to see such a mind at work.

Levmore discusses two extreme cases of collective liability. These are *NOPCO Chemical Division v. Blaw-Knox Co.*, 281 A.2d 793 (N.J. 1971) (three unrelated parties handled a machine which was ultimately delivered to the plaintiff with damage; no party could have known if damage had been done by others but liability nonetheless); and *Samson v. Riesing*, 215 N.W.2d 662 (Wis. 1974) (eleven defendants had separately prepared turkeys or turkey salad for a picnic; salmonella poisoning resulted from one but probably not all).

§ 3. INFORMED CONSENT

SCHLOENDORF V. SOC'Y OF NEW YORK HOSPITAL, 105 N.E. 92 (N.Y. 1914)

Cardozo's famous statement is reproduced here as a succinct statement of the principle that actuates informed consent. It can generate discussion here or can be used as background to the discussion of the cases.

The informed consent doctrine may have several good effects, but perhaps most centrally it recognizes and seeks to protect personal autonomy. The principle is not always given its fullest effect, but when it is, it means that, subject to some causal limitations, neither the doctor nor the judge gets to decide what risks are acceptable to the patient. See *Harrison v. United States*, 284 F.3d 293 (1st Cir. 2002) (trial judge erred in weighing risks of accepting and rejecting procedure and determining on that basis that physician owed no duty to reveal risks to patient). Professor Capron pointed out that "autonomy is centrally associated with the notion of individual responsibility" *See* Capron, *Informed Consent in Catastrophic Disease Research and Treatment*, 123 U. PA. L. REV. 340, 364 ff. (1974). Responsibility for decisions, this seems to imply, can only derive from a freedom to make the decisions. In addition, autonomy of individuals is at the root of the political system of any free society and autonomy is a part, after all, of being a human being.

A patient might conceivably exercise autonomy by delegating all decisions to the doctor. No doubt some patients are happy to do this. The patient who expects no information and wants none, who has consciously left the matter to the doctor, would not be entitled to any information. Professor Richard Epstein seems to believe that most or all patients are like this: "The root problem with the informed consent doctrine is that it is forever at war with the mutual expectations of the parties."*Medical Malpractice: The Case for Contract*, [1976] AM. BAR FOUND. J. 87 at 127. If you believe that patients generally do not want or expect information about the medical procedures proposed, the informed consent rules are, at best, needless, and they certainly do not protect autonomy of the patient, who, in this view, has delegated the decision-making to the doctor.

HARNISH V. CHILDREN'S HOSP. MED. CENTER, 439 N.E.2d 240 (Mass. 1982)

WOOLLEY V. HENDERSON , 418 A.2d 1123 (Me. 1980)
MARSINGILL V. O'MALLEY, 128 P.3D 151 (Alaska 2006).

With informed consent seen as a negligence issue, two issues have dominated the topic. First, what is the standard of disclosure, and second, what is the causal test? To reach these points, you must first distinguish and get past the battery cases. *Harnish* and *Woolley* can be discussed together; they raise some key issues for class discussion:

1. What must physician disclose and under what standard? (*Harnish* uses the materiality or "patient" standard, not medical care standard; *Wooley* uses medical standard; pros and cons for discussion)

2. What expert testimony must the plaintiff produce? (Not on standard for disclosure but on whether physician should know of risk.) What expert testimony may the defendant produce? (*Marsingill,* if the standard is what a reasonable patient would want to know, can the defendant doctor put on medical doctors to testify about that issue).

3. Should courts recognize a therapeutic privilege to withhold information and when? (*Harnish*, in dictum, says so, with caution; pros and cons for discussion)

4. What must the plaintiff prove to prove "causation"? (That patient would have rejected the medical procedure and ALSO that the reasonable person would have done so; pros and cons discussable)

Notes 1 & 2. Negligence (informed consent) vs. battery. An operation without consent is a battery under normal battery rules. (Recall that even well-intentioned and helpful touchings are batteries if they are not consented to.) Similarly, your consent to an operation by Dr. A is not a consent to an operation by Dr. B. *Vitale v. Henchey,* 24 S.W.3d 651 (Ky. 2000); *Perna v. Pirozzi,* 457 A.2d 431 (N.J. 1983).The plaintiff who can assert a battery claim may avoid the restrictive rules applied in courts of the *Woolley* persuasion. The plaintiff who proves "no consent" need not adduce expert testimony about whether the doctor should have informed him. See *Gouveia v. Phillips,* 823 So.2d 215 (Fla. Dist. Ct. App. 2002). The no-consent/battery plaintiff may also avoid legislative caps on damages that apply only to negligence claims. See *Perry v. Shaw,* 106 Cal. Rprtr.2d 70 (Ct. App. 2001).

Battery would also be an appropriate theory when consent is induced by intentional (or perhaps negligent) misrepresentation. In *Bloskas v. Murray,* 646 P.2d 907 (Colo. 1982), the court approved a negligent misrepresentation theory, where the physician had allegedly made some affirmative representations but had left some facts undisclosed. Partial disclosure seems to have activated a larger duty of disclosure than otherwise would have existed. Cf. *Rains v. Superior Court,* 198 Cal. Rptr. 249 (Ct. App. 1984). In *Howard v.*

University of Med. & Dentistry of New Jersey, 800 A.2d 73 (N.J. 2002), the court rejected the fraud theory where a surgeon misrepresents his experience in performing the operation. In that case, the plaintiff may have an informed consent claim, but not a fraud claim.

Perhaps some opinions have advanced a battery theory without really intending to adopt the implications of that theory. In *Shadrick v. Coker,* 963 S.W.2d 726 (Tenn. 1998) the court insisted that the informed consent claim was one for battery. A few months later, the same court insisted that the battery theory would work only if the plaintiff did not consent to the operation; if her claim was based on lack of information, it would be an informed consent claim and she would be required to prove the standard of care by expert testimony. *Blanchard v. Kellum,* 975 S.W.2d 522 (Tenn. 1998).

In some states the battery theory may be substantially limited or even barred by the malpractice "reform" statutes.

The no-consent/battery claim is not the informed consent claim. The informed consent claim which asserts that the plaintiff consented to the operation but that the plaintiff is nonetheless aggrieved because she was not given appropriate information about it. The informed consent claim is usually treated under the negligence rules, not the battery rules. This approach and its development are reviewed in *Howard v. University of Med. & Dentistry of New Jersey*, 800 A.2d 73 (N.J. 2002) (summarizing origins and development). *See also Duncan v. Scottsdale Medical Imaging, Ltd.*, 70 P.3d 435 (Ariz. 2003) (distinguishing between a battery claim and an informed consent claim, holding that cases involving the doctor's duty to provide information must be brought as negligence claims for informed consent). But as this Note also reflects, some courts treat both the no-consent and the informed consent claim as a battery. See *Montgomery v. Bazaz-Sehgal,* 798 A.2d 742 (Pa. 2002).

A problem of consent terminology. Judges and lawyers sometimes seem to use the term "informed consent" indiscriminately to mean either "no consent at all" or "consent without appropriate communication of information." As Note 1 shows, the two are not the same. The "informed consent" terminology to mean "no consent" can lead to serious errors. In *Gouveia v. Phillips*, 823 So.2d 215 (Fla. Dist. Ct. App. 2002), the trial judge dismissed the plaintiff's claim that he had not consented to amputation of his fingers (due to incapacity) because the plaintiff's expert witness was excluded from testifying. The trial judge seemed to get this idea from the rule in *informed* consent cases of the *Wooley* persuasion that expert testimony was needed to establish the standard for disclosure. But the no consent/battery claim wasn't about disclosure at all! The appellate court properly reversed on this point, ultimately recognizing that the problem in information and the problem no consent raise different issues. On another issue in the case, however, the court treated a reference to "informed consent" in depositions as including both the problem of conveying adequate information and the problem of the plaintiff who, because of incapacity, does not consent at all.

In *Harnish* and *Woolley* the claim *must* be made for negligence, not battery, because the plaintiff, though lacking important information, consented to the operation that was in fact performed (and of course in *Marsingill,* no procedure was performed).

Although this seems conceptually clear enough, the line between battery and negligence, between no consent and no information, can be difficult to draw. Lacking information, you may be consenting to some operation but not the one performed. In *Blanchard v. Kellum,* 975 S.W.2d 522 (Tenn. 1998), the plaintiff consented to having her teeth extracted, but the doctor did not tell her they would all be extracted at one sitting. The *Blanchard* court held that since the plaintiff claimed she did not consent to "a full extraction," her claim was one for battery! But at the opposite and perhaps shocking extreme, in *Robinson v. Cutchin,* 140 F.Supp.2d 488 (D. Md. 2001), the federal judge held that consent to an emergency cesarean section was consent to a tubal ligation, so the sterilized mother had no battery claim. The judge characterized the sterilization as simply a touching that "was more extensive than agreed," and said it does not amount to a battery.

The problem of distinguishing "no consent" from "consent without adequate information" is one we saw earlier in Chapter 4, with *Doe v. Johnson,* 817 F. Supp. 1382 (W.D. Mich. 1993), where the plaintiff's sexual partner failed to warn her in advance that he was an HIV carrier. In note 4 following that case, we quote from *Desnick v. American Broadcasting Companies, Inc.,* 44 F.3d 1345 (7th Cir. 1994), where Judge Posner advanced his own theory of how to distinguish between no valid consent and a valid consent without adequate information. Those cases did not involve health care defendants, but they raised the same essential question about the legal effect of the plaintiff's "consent" when important information has not been disclosed.

Significance of negligence theory. What does it mean to say that the claim is one for negligence, not battery? (1) In many states, it means that the plaintiff must prove the standard of care for revealing information to patients. (2) In most states it means that the plaintiff cannot have the presumed damages of a battery claim but must prove damages and causation as in any other negligence action. That is the mainstream of informed consent today.

But in some courts, the informed consent claim is *sui generis,* with some characteristics inconsistent with the usual medical negligence claim. In particular, an important number of courts adopt a negligence theory of informed consent claims, yet, as in *Harnish,* dispense with proof of a medical standard of care. And Louisiana has said that the claim is one for negligence, not battery, but that battery-type damages are recoverable nonetheless. Specifically, damages are recoverable for loss of self-determination and other dignitary rights. *Lugenbuhl v. Dowling,* 701 So.2d 447 (La. 1997).

Note 3. Professional standard or the "patient rule"? *(a) Two views.* *Harnish* adopts the view taken in most of the major decisions since the early 1970s, namely, that the doctor owes a duty to disclose material information or what the patient needs to know to make a reasonable decision. Most importantly, this means that the patient need not produce medical experts to describe the "standard" for disclosing information. The fact that doctors in the relevant community would never tell the patient of the risk in question will thus be irrelevant. *Woolley,* of course, adopts the contrary view, holding that the patient must introduce evidence to show the medical standard for revealing information to the patient. If doctors in Maine agree that doctor knows best and that patient is entitled to no information about risk of a proposed operation, then no doctor will be required to enlighten the patient. *Woolley* represents the supposed majority on this issue.

(b) Criticizing Wooley. Does the autonomy principle help us decide between *Harnish* and *Woolley?* What about the reasons given in *Woolley?* (1) The court's idea that a professional standard must be used because this is professional malpractice seems to be an empty tautology, or a kind of play on the word "professional," or simply a non-sequitur. (2) The idea that since the doctor might have withheld information for therapeutic reasons in some cases, the plaintiff would be required to prove violation of medical standards in all cases again does not follow. Therapeutic withholding of information, if it should be recognized at all, could be given as a defense for the doctor to raise. See, e.g., *Bloskas v. Murray,* 646 P.2d 907 (Colo. 1982). (3) The third argument was that since the plaintiff has to find medical testimony in order to prove a negligently performed operation, it is no extra burden to find it to prove lack of informed consent. But at best this misses the point. The issue is not merely whether the plaintiff has to go to some trouble, but whether she should, in justice, lose the case where a reasonable person would have provided her the information but the medical community would not have done so.

In portions of *Woolley* not summarized in the casebook, the court discussed what it considered to be the problem of technical information–that the jury, flooded with technical data might be more likely to do injustice under the more liberal rule. This may contain some assumptions about the form of the proof. What if the proof were that in an operation like that in *Walski* the risk is one in one thousand of cutting a nerve if you use the wide cut technique, and one in ten thousand if you don't? Is this so confusing?

(c) Marsingill. This case suggests that the line between the two standards may collapse in some states. If we have a reasonable patient standard but medical evidence about what reasonable doctors would do, the focus on patient autonomy might be lost.

Statutes on informed consent. Statutes in a number of states regulate informed consent claims. By statute, about 16 states adopt the *Woolley* as opposed to the *Harnish* rule. *See* 1 BARRY R. FURROW, THOMAS L. GREANEY, SANDRA H. JOHNSON, TIMOTHY STOLZFUS JOST AND ROBERT L. SCHWARTZ, HEALTH LAW § 6-10 (1995). For example, the Arkansas Statute provides that in informed consent claims, the plaintiff must prove that "the medical care provider did not supply that type of information regarding the treatment, procedure, or surgery as would customarily have been given to a patient in the position of the injured person . . . by other medical care providers with similar training and experience at the time of the treatment, procedure, or surgery in the locality in which the medical care provider practices or in a similar locality." ARK.. CODE ANN. § 16-114-206. So the plaintiff suing a podiatrist on an informed consent theory must produce an expert who knows the podiatric practice of giving information, or else lose her case, as she did in *Brumley v. Naples,* 320 Ark. 310, 896 S.W.2d 860 (1995). Notice that this statute also returns to the pure locality rule.

The Oregon statute is quite different. It sets patterns of information the physician is required to give to the patient. After the specified information is provided, the physician must ask the patient if she wishes more information and respond accordingly. If the physician fails to ask the prescribed question, the patient has made out the nondisclosure element of the informed consent claim. *Zacher v. Petty,* 826 P.2d 619 (Or. 1992).

Note 4. Causation. *(a) "Objective" causation requirement.* The normal form of causal proof, adjusted to the informed consent claim, would be proof that, but for the failure to give information, the plaintiff would have refused the operation and would thus not have been injured. This has come to be known as the "subjective" test. An "objective" test would require the plaintiff to show that a reasonable person would also have refused the operation had appropriate information been given. Courts seem to impose a dual requirement; the plaintiff must meet both the subjective and the objective test, although a few have more or less dropped the subjective component. *See Backlund v. University of Washington,* 975 P.2d 950, 958 (Wash. 1999) ("The relevant inquiry here is not whether the Backlunds would or would not have consented, but what a reasonably prudent patient/representative under similar circumstances would have done").

(b) Two stated reasons for objective requirements. This requirement might be based on one of several theories: (1) the plaintiff will always testify to a state of mind that would show causation ("I would not have accepted the operation if I had known of the risk") and for this reason the normal rule that the jury is judge of credibility should be put aside for this special case. (2) The legal duty to inform should extend only to the protection of reasonable persons, not to eccentric desires of the plaintiff.

(c) Criticizing the first two reasons. Neither of these theories appeals to the autonomy ideal. On the first point, the plaintiff's credibility, like that of the defendant, is normally for the trier of fact. Both parties often testify in a self-serving manner, one of the things juries consider in determining whether to accept the testimony. We may miss a great deal of truth in trials, but we may not get more truth by refusing to hear what people say. As to the second idea, that only reasonable people deserve protection, sounds like a backdoor way of establishing a paternalistic order or a state of Superpeople, since the result is that people are "allowed" to control their own bodies only if they are reasonable in the estimate of official judges. The trial judge in *Backlund,* supra, took a similar view, saying that no reasonable person would reject the doctor's non-

negligent advice, in effect eliminating the informed consent claim. The Supreme Court of Washington said that went too far, but it seems not so different from the decision to protect only reasonable choices.

(d) A third reason for the objective test. There is, however, another support for the "objective" test of causation that may be more acceptable. (3) In the absence of specific knowledge about the particular patient, doctors should judge what is material to that patient by what reasonable people would act upon. Although the doctor should allow leeway for this judgment, there is no fault on the doctor's part in failing to give information which, in fact, would not be considered by reasonable people. On this ground, something might be said for the objective test of causation, but perhaps if this is really the basis for the test, this principle ought to be expressed, not on the causal issue but on the definition of materiality or in defining negligence.

(e) A middle position or a subjective rule under another name? A little authority strives for a middle position, in some sense adhering to the objective test but at the same time allowing the jury to consider what the individual plaintiff would have reasonably chosen in the light of her individual fears or beliefs. *Fain v. Smith,* 479 So.2d 1150 (Ala. 1985) ("We note, however, that the objective standard requires consideration by the factfinder of what a reasonable person with all of the characteristics of the plaintiff, including his idiosyncrasies and religious beliefs, would have done under the same circumstances); *Bernard v. Char,* 903 P.2d 667 (Haw. 1995); *Ashe v. Radiation Oncology Assocs.,* 9 S.W.3d 119 (Tenn. 1999). *Ashe* cited *Backlund, supra,* for such a rule, but *Backlund* only allowed the jury to consider the risks to which the plaintiff was subjected, not her individual fears or beliefs. The risks to which the plaintiff was subjected would be part of the circumstances in normal application of the reasonable person formula, so *Backlund* does not in fact offer patients the cookie proffered by *Ashe* and *Bernard.*

•*Scope of risk.* [This topic is not included in the casebook. It will be too much for classes moving at a brisk pace, but the teacher can introduce it if is desirable for a particualr class.] What if a surgeon does not inform the plaintiff of Risk A and Risk B, the latter because he is not aware of the risk. The operation goes horribly wrong, but not as a result of Risk A, which does not materialize at all. It goes wrong because of Risk B or because of risks of which the plaintiff was informed. Neither plaintiff nor a reasonable person would have consented to the operation if risks had been properly disclosed. Should the plaintiff have an informed consent claim? See *Canesi v. Wilson,* 730 A.2d 805 (N.J. 1999) (seemingly imposing liability only for injury from risks of which the plaintiff should have been informed); *Schiff v. Friberg,* 771 N.E.2d 517 (Ill. App. Ct. 2002) (seemingly imposing liability for injury, even if it did not result from risks that the defendant should have but did not reveal, so long as the plaintiff shows causation in fact by showing that, upon proper information, she would have rejected the operation and thus avoided injury).

Lugenbuhl v. Dowling, 701 So.2d 447 (La. 1997), *see* Note 5 on damages, seems to imply the same solution.

Some alternative approaches: French law

French law recognizes an informed consent right that seems more extensive than most American courts have been willing to recognize but at the same limits damages recovery on a kind of value-of-the-chance approach:

• First, the physician owes a duty to give a fair, clear, and appropriate information about serious risks, even if those risks are unlikely to eventuate.
• Second, information imparted just before the medical procedure might not constitute a fair warning.
• Third, the burden is on the physician to show that he has fufilled his duty.
• Fourth, the physician's failure to give appropriate information only deprives the plaintiff of the value of the chance to refuse treatment. Recovery is limited to a percentage of the harm suffered. The plaintiff therefore can never recover full damages.
• Fifth, if the physician violates a duty by failing to warn of one risk, say, paralysis, but a different harm eventuates, say, epilepsy, liability may still be imposed. Seemingly this approach imposes liability because the physician has caused harm in fact— the loss of value of the chance— even though epilepsy was not within the risk.

These interesting alternatives to the American approaches are summarized in Suzanne Galand-Carval, *Country Reports– France*, in MICHAEL FAURE & HELMUT KOZIOL (EDS), I TORTS TORT AND INSURANCE LAW: CASES ON MEDICAL MALPRACTICE IN A COMPARATIVE PERSPECTIVE 102, 106-107 (2001). *See also* JULIE A. DAVIES & PAUL T. HAYDEN, GLOBAL ISSUES IN TORT LAW, Chapter 8 (2008).

Note 5. Incompetent patients and life-saving treatment. This is a can of worms you probably won't have time to untangle, but it is a can of which the student should be aware even if its contents cannot be fully explored.

(1) In general, competent patients have the right to refuse treatment, no matter how beneficial it is, even if it is lifesaving treatment. (2) From this, *In re A.C.*, quoted in this note, holds that the dying patient can refuse treatment even if that treatment would save the life of her fetus. (3) As *A.C.* also says, if the patient is incompetent, someone else must make the choice for her, but this must be the choice the incompetent herself would have made had she been competent. *See* DOBBS ON TORTS § 99 (2000). Some of these issues were touched upon in Chapter 4. See the notes following *Kennedy v. Parrott*.

Wrongful prolongation of life. Some recent cases have rejected claims for "wrongful living" or wrongful prolongation of life. In these cases the patient's wishes expressed while competent were to avoid artificial prolongation of life or heroic measures. Family members, one holding a power of attorney, or a guardian objects to artificial life support, but health care providers refuse to discontinue it. Some cases have rejected the subsequent tort claim. See *Estate of Taylor v. Muncie Medical Investors, L.P.,* 727 N.E.2d 466 (Ind. Ct. App. 2000); *Anderson v. St. Francis-St. George Hosp., Inc.,* 671 N.E.2d 255 (Ohio 1996). However, in *Gragg v. Calandra,* 696 N.E.2d 1282 (Ill. App. Ct. 1998) the court sustained a complaint by survivors alleging battery to the now-deceased patient for continuing life support against his wishes expressed in a living will and against their wishes. The court also sustained a claim for infliction of emotional distress upon the survivors. Cases rejecting the claim are criticized in Mark Strasser, *A Jurisprudence in Disarray: On Battery, Wrongful Living, and the Right to Bodily Integrity,* 36 SAN DIEGO L. REV. 997 (1999). Kellen F. Rodriguez, *Suing Health Care Providers for Saving Lives,* 20 J. LEG. MED. 1 (1999) is more detailed; it conveniently summarizes the law and figures on advanced directives, including the federal statutory duty of health care providers to inform patients of their right to refuse life-sustaining treatment and their right to execute advanced directives. This article also reports on studies showing that doctors disregard patient's wishes, sometimes forcing them to die in prolonged pain. It lists the cases pro and con. The footnotes incorporate the Supreme Court of Ohio's decision in *Anderson,* supra, but much of the text in the early portion of the article addresses the intermediate court's decision. When the Ohio Supreme Court's decision is reached in the text, the article is critical.

WLOSINSKI V. COHN, 713 N.W.2d 16 (Mich. Ct. App. 2005)

This case introduces the difficult issue of whether a doctor must not only disclose the risks of the procedure in general, but the doctor's own track record of performance, particularly when asked. A reasonable patient might be quite interested in the fact that five of the doctor's last seven kidney transplants had failed (particularly if other doctors had much better success with the surgeries). If this information would be material to a patient's decision, is the court right to hold that it need not be disclosed? Wouldn't the issue at least raise a fact question for the jury.

ARATO V. AVEDON, 858 P.2d 598 (Cal. 1993)

(1) *Judge and jury.* Whether the defendants should have disclosed the patient's "statistical life expectancy" was a jury question and not to be decided by the court as a matter of law.

(2) *Nonmedical interests.* The core of informed consent doctrine is the protection of patient autonomy over the patient's own body; this "therapeutic focus" indicates that there is not necessarily a duty on the physician's part "to disclose every contingency that might affect the patient's nonmedical 'rights and interests.'" It would thus have been error for the court to instruct the jury,

as the plaintiff proposed, that the physician owed a duty of disclosure of "all facts which materially affect the patient's rights and interests."

(3) *Withholding information for therapeutic reasons or under standard medical practice.* It is not error in this case to admit testimony by other physicians that the standard of medical practice would not require disclosure in this particular instance. Although established California law uses a materiality standard under which the physician must disclose risks material to the patient, there will be times in which the physician must evaluate the "patient's decisional needs against a background of professional understanding that includes a knowledge of what information beyond the significant risks associated with a given treatment would be regarded by the medical community as appropriate for disclosure...." This holding appears to be limited to a second tier of medical information, that is information other than that about "risk of death or serious injury and significant potential complications."

Moore: The Court of Appeal in *Arato* thought *Moore*, which said that maybe a physician who secretly took body cells for commercial development would be liable for failure to secure an informed consent, established the essential point: disclosure is not limited to disclosure of risks about a proposed treatment. The Supreme Court did not directly address this point. First it buried *Moore* in a statement about well-established informed consent rules. Without comment it said that *Moore* recognized a rule that

> a physician must disclose personal interests unrelated to the patient's
> health, whether research or economic, that may affect the physician's
> personal judgment....

But while the Court of Appeal read in this a conclusion that the doctor's duty therefore necessarily went beyond the risks of a proposed treatment, the Supreme Court ignored that point entirely. Its second citation to *Moore* pulled a quotation from that case that said a "physician is not the patient's financial adviser."

The language of *Arato* backs a long distance away from the patient's right to know. It is not the doctor's concern *why* the patient wants medical information. Yet the court may be saying that when the patient wants the medical information for economic reasons, the duty to reveal it is attenuated. But if a human being's rights of autonomy are respected, it must not matter whether he would exercise his autonomy for medical purposes, spiritual purposes, or economic purposes. The court expressly regards "patient sovereignty" as an "extreme" to be avoided.

Possibly the court thinks that the information sought here by the patient and implicitly contracted for as well, is in some sense not purely "medical" information. The court's discussion of "statistical life expectancy" data seems to imply that it regards that information as somehow less than medical information.

Finally, the biggest practical step, and one that will surely require more litigation, is the idea that in some undefined group of cases, the medical "standard" of withholding information is relevant after all. The rule imposed by law that physicians must disclose relevant information was already weak because of the causal requirements attached to it. It is now something less than a rule of law; doctors can testify that they recognized some "medical" standard against disclosure.

This is all the more strange in this case because the plaintiff's implicit contract seems to have been one for disclosure. He checked an express desire to know on the form the physician provided. In *Didato v. Strehler*, 554 S.E.2d 42 (Va. 2001), the court held that a physician might be undertake a duty to provide information that was not required by the prevailing medical standard and could be held liable for a breach of duty so undertaken. The information in that case, however, was genetic information, and the case was a kind of wrongful birth case.

Much of the informed consent problem comes from thinking of it as a substitute for a negligence claim for bodily injury. But the central position of the individual human being in a free society, autonomy, is the gist of the right, and it should not matter whether the patient would use the information to change a medical decision, to decide on an investment program, or to prepare himself for some inevitable loss. The doctor's invasion is not a physical one, but one that strikes at the plaintiff's intangible interests.

Note 1. Physician and procedure success rates. The medical profession is studying the problem of success rates. *Johnson v. Kokemoor*, 545 N.W.2d 495 (Wis. 1996) did hold that the patient was entitled to information from her surgeon that more experienced brain surgeons were available and had a substantially better success rates than inexperienced surgeons. Conceivably, however, that decision applies only in extreme cases like *Kokemoor* itself. Distinguished commentators support the duty to disclose relative success rates and other provider-risk information. Aaron D. Twerski & Neil B. Cohen, *The Second Revolution in Informed Consent: Comparing Physicians to Each Other*, 94 Nw. U. L. Rev. 1 (1999); Lynn M. LoPucki, *Twerski and Cohen's Second Revolution: A Systems/Strategic Perspective*, 94 Nw. U. L. Rev. 55 (1999). LoPucki raises the problem mentioned in the casebook note: providers might fudge records directly or might selectively refuse patients who are high-risk patients in order to improve their standings. He thinks, however, that evaluations based on provider outcomes have been a success already and surgeons with higher mortality rates have had to improve or leave the market. When the procedure is likely to have a bad result no matter which doctor performs it is certainly material information that should be disclosed, as in *Williamson*.

Note 2-6. What must be disclosed under the materiality test? *(a) Types of information generally.* *Harnish* gives us not only the materiality test but also a broad statement of the kind of information it covers—including "the nature of the patient's condition, the nature and probability of risks involved, the benefits to be reasonably expected, the inability of the physician to predict results, if that is the situation, the irreversibility of the procedure, if that be the case, the likely result of no treatment, and the available alternatives, including their risks and benefits." Joan H. Krause, *Reconceptualizing Informed*

Consent in an Era of Health Care Cost Containment, 85 IOWA L. REV. 261 (1999) thinks that while cases, commentators, and statutes speak of alternative treatment disclosure, few cases have actually turned on nondisclosure of treatment alternatives. *Matthies v. Mastromonaco,* 160 N.J. 26, 733 A.2d 456 (1999) is one that does. In *Matthies* since the basis of liability is negligence, not battery, the physician owed the patient a duty to inform of reasonable medical alternatives to his own recommended treatment, even if his treatment was noninvasive and the alternative was. The court said:

> For consent to be informed, the patient must know not only of alternatives that the physician recommends, but of medically reasonable alternatives that the physician does not recommend. Otherwise, the physician, by not discussing these alternatives, effectively makes the choice for the patient. Accordingly, the physician should discuss the medically reasonable courses of treatment, including nontreatment.

So the physician was obliged to discuss surgery. Perhaps more importantly, the patient was entitled to know the effect of the proposed treatment on her independent lifestyle, that is, she should have been told that she would not walk again if treated with bed rest only.

(b) Risks not known to the physician. If the physician does not know of a risk, he is obliged to reveal it only if he should have known the risk and it is material. As *Harnish* says, in that case, the plaintiff must show by medical evidence that the physician should have known the risk, even though the plaintiff is not required to produce medical evidence on the materiality issue. In other words, the duty to disclose is quite different from the duty to find out. *See* Waltz & Scheuneman, *Informed Consent to Therapy,* 64 N.W. L. REV. 628 (1970). As these statements imply, the plaintiff may need expert testimony to show that there is in fact a substantial risk. *See Betterton v. Leichtling,* 124 Cal.Rptr.2d 644 (Ct. App. 2002) ("Whether to disclose a significant risk is not a matter reserved for expert opinion. Whether a particular risk exists, however, may be a matter beyond the knowledge of lay witnesses, and therefore appropriate for determination based on the testimony of experts"). If the risk is a matter of common knowledge, the plaintiff may not need expert testimony, but in that case there may be no need to advise the patient what he presumably already knows.

(c) Materiality. (i) Objective materiality. The patient's need to know or the materiality standard leaves uncertainties that would not exist (for the doctor) under the medical standard. Presumably material information is that information patients in general would want to know about before they make a decision, but not necessarily information they would act on. Presumably the doctor knows they want information that bears strongly on risks, gains, alternative treatments. Information on gains to be expected from a medical procedure comes up in the *Arato* case, next. The physician is not required to provide a medical education or inform the plaintiff of every detail. See

Masquat v. Maguire, 638 P.2d 1105 (Okla. 1981) (surgeon not required to explain different methods for performing a tubal ligation).

(ii) Subjective materiality. If the physician knows that the patient regards a risk as material, the physician presumably must give information about that risk even if it would not be material to most reasonable people. A blood transfusion represents a different order of risks to a Jehovah's Witness than it does to others.

(iii)Risks peculiar to the physician or surgeon but not to the medical procedure itself. What about risks that do accompany a procedure (1) because the particular physician or surgeon has an abnormally low success rate, or, less dramatically, that he was less experienced than he represented; (2) because the physician has a disease like AIDS or uses illegal drugs, or (3) because the physician has an unusual financial stake in performing the operation?

In *Howard v. University of Med. & Dentistry of New Jersey*, 800 A.2d 73 (N.J. 2002), the plaintiff's disputed allegation was that the surgeon informed him of the risk of paralysis but misrepresented the surgeon's credentials ("Board Certified") and experience with the particularly difficult operation. The operation left the plaintiff a quadriplegic. He asserted both fraudulent misrepresentation and lack of informed consent. The New Jersey Court rejected the fraud claim but held that an amended complaint might state an informed consent claim. The court, however, imposed not only the usual materiality and causation requirements but also these: (1) The operation must in fact be riskier than consented to because the harm suffered would be less likely if the representations had been true. (2) Expert tetimony will be required to show that the risk in fact was greater than it would have been had the surgeon's experience been as extensive as he claimed.

(2) Personal dangers. A little authority also suggests that the physician must reveal his AIDS status, though the chance of a patient's contracting AIDS from a properly performed procedure is almost infinitesimally small. In *Albany Urology Clinic, PC v. Cleveland*, 528 S.E.2d 777 (Ga. 2000), the defendant, consulted about a lump on the underside of the plaintiff's penis, advised surgery to remove a possible cancer. After the surgery, the plaintiff "began to experience an acutely painful ninety- degree curvature of his penis upon erection, and a resulting inability to have intercourse." The plaintiff claimed battery and a denial of informed consent on the ground that the surgeon in fact used cocaine and failed to reveal it. The court held that neither claim was valid. Georgia's informed consent law is entirely statutory and the statute does not require the doctor to reveal his use of illegal drugs. The patient has a separate claim for battery for medical touchings, but only if consent is obtained "by an artifice that is directly related to the subject matter of the professional relationship–i.e.: diagnoses, treatments, procedures. . . . However, we decline to extend this rule of law to situations such as the present case, where (1) a physician fails to disclose on their own initiative a negative personal life factor that, although not directly related to the professional relationship, may, depending upon a patient's subjectively held beliefs, impact upon the patient's consent to be touched in the course of treatment, and (2)

there is no direct evidence of record that the physician was impaired or affected by the negative personal life factor at the time consent was obtained and treatment was rendered." As indicated in Dobbs on Torts §251 (2000), a little authority seems contrary.

(3) Financial interests. California has held that a physician must disclose some financial facts to the patient when the physician was using the patient's blood for his own financial gain in a different transaction. This is *Moore,* discussed in this note in the casebook.

In *D.A.B. v. Brown,* 570 N.W.2d 168 (Minn. Ct. App. 1997) the Minnesota Appellate court held that the claim based on the physician's alleged receipt of illegal kickbacks for prescribing a costly drug was "really" one for medical malpractice (not fiduciary breach) and hence that the claim would fail because the plaintiffs alleged no injury, only a conflict of interest. Another financial interest that raises a conflict of interest issue is the doctor's financial interest in delivering less treatment and refusing referrals to specialists. This arises in the HMO setting because the doctor's ultimate income depends upon limiting referrals and costly treatments. Many sources explain this. *E.g.,* Kim Johnston, *Patient Advocates or Patient Adversaries? Using Fiduciary Law to Compel Disclosure of Managed Care Financial Incentives,* 35 SAN DIEGO L. REV. 951 (1998). In *Neade v. Portes,* 710 N.E.2d 418 (Ill. Ct. App. 1999) the court held that the physician was under a fiduciary duty to reveal that conflict, i.e., his financial incentive to withhold specialized tests or treatment. In the comparable suit against the HMO itself for using financial incentives adverse to patient health, ERISA may control. Under ERISA, the suit against a plan fiduciary (the HMO itself, perhaps) for breach of fiduciary duty in failing to reveal its conflicts has been ruled out by the Supreme Court in *Pegram v. Herdrich,* 530 U.S. 211 (2000). *See* § 4 c, below.

(d) Therapeutic privilege. Should the doctor be permitted to withhold material information on the ground the information would be bad for the patient? Courts seem eager to volunteer such a privilege to the doctor. If the patient is competent mentally, is there another solution? How many cases are there of genuine need for therapeutic nondisclosure? In *Cowman v. Hornaday,* 329 N.W.2d 422 (Iowa 1983), the court described the therapeutic privilege as "paternalistic or authoritarian," perhaps hinting some disaffection with the rule and a potential modification of it in later cases. *Barcai v. Betwee,* 50 P.3d 946 (Haw. 2002), gives a substantial discussion of the privilege, insisting on it but holding that it must be grounded in individualized assessment of the patient, not a category wide view that patients in the plaintiff's category would be harmed by information.

(e) Statutory limits. We've already noted that many states have statutes limiting the health care provider's duty to give information. Some attempt to name specific risks that are to be mentioned and provide immunity if the doctor mentions them. *See* IOWA CODE ANN. § 147.137. Others develop a kind of bureaucracy to list risks. Apart from the risk that the list will be incomplete or that the explanation given about the general topic listed will be a poor one, risks do not tell the whole story. Consider the surgeon who recommends mas-

tectomy and fully reveals the risks but does not mention that the mastectomy is not needed or that a biopsy should be done first.

Whose duty to disclose? When several health care providers are involved, information may not be given because each assumes that another provider will give it. Several cases have dealt with the problem. *See Logan v. Greenwich Hosp. Assn.*, 465 A.2d 294 (Conn. 1983) (referring physician had no duty when he told patient that specialist to whom he referred would explain); *Halley v. Birbiglia*, 458 N.E.2d 710 (Mass. 1983) (surgeon who administered procedure, not referring physician had duty to inform where referring physician was not family doctor or admitting physician). A hospital may have a duty to provide information when its activities create the risks. Experimental procedures are governed by FDA rules and require informed consent. *Friter v. Iolab Corp.*, 607 A.2d 1111 (Pa. Super. Ct. 1992) imposes liability upon a hospital for failure to provide information as required by the FDA for experiments.

Note 7. Experiments ("research") performed upon humans. *Grimes v. Kennedy Krieger Institute, Inc.,* cited here, draws a firm distinction between treatment and experimentation. The court alludes to and quotes the detailed federal regulations governing consents required in human experimentation conducted with federal funds. The court also discusses the Nuremberg Code (imposed upon Nazi human experimenters after World War II) as a possible source of duty. But the facts (in their limited summary judgment development) also seem to indicate the ineffectiveness of regulations and the civilized ideals of expressed in the Nuremberg Code to contain the scientific establishment. In *Ancheff v. Hartford Hosp.,* also cited here, the court left to the jury whether the hospital's program was research requiring compliance with federal informed consent and review-board rules, or whether it was treatment. The plaintiff attempted to get into evidence an ethical study produced by the government (the "Belmont Report,") but the trial judge rejected the report as prejudicial because it referred to notorious programs of human experimentation. The Supreme Court's decision is primarily an affirmation of that ruling. That left the conflict expert opinion as the only basis for deciding what counted as research.

Note 8. Damages. Twerski & Cohen, *Informed Decision Making and the Law of Torts: The Myth of Justiciable Causation*, 1988 U. ILL. L. REV. 607, claim to "demonstrate" that the causal issue is not "justiciable" because the law "cannot consider the multitude of factors that influence the way people actually make decisions." (p. 608). Twerski would close the door firmly on personal injury claims resulting from operations performed without informed consent. Cohen would "leave the door slightly ajar" for rare cases. (p. 648). The focus for both would be the value of "the decision rights" destroyed by the defendant's withholding of information. Their discussion on valuing process or participation rights is full of helpful analogies.

On the possibility of damages for dignitary and civil rights invasions that cause no physical or financial harm generally, see *Lugenbuhl v. Dowling*, 701 So.2d 447 (La. 1997) ("While plaintiff failed to prove physical damages or pecuniary loss, he is still entitled to an award of general compensatory damages caused by the doctor's breach of duty. In this type of case, damages for deprivation of self-determination, insult to personal integrity, invasion of privacy, anxiety, worry and mental distress are actual and compensatory); DAN DOBBS, THE LAW OF REMEDIES §§ 7.3 & 7.4 (2d 1992). *Provenzano v. Integrated Genetics,* 22 F.Supp.2d 406 (D.N.J. 1998) was a wrongful birth claim based upon the lab's failure to identify a serious disease in the fetus. The child was born alive suffering from the disease and later died. The parents sued the lab, but admitted that they would not have terminated the pregnancy. Nevertheless, the court held they stated a cause of action; the fact that they would not have terminated only went to the amount of damages to be awarded. More on damages in *Provenzano v. Integrated Genetics,* 66 F.Supp.2d 588 (D.N.J. 1999).

TRUMAN V. THOMAS, 611 P.2d 902 (Cal. 1980)

Truman imposes liability, not for failure to advise of risks of an operation, but for failure to advise of the risks of *refusing* an operation. There is no reason to think this idea is wrong in principle; the risks of refusing an operation would be relevant under the materiality test, which California uses (except where *Arato* controls). *Truman* is a departure, however, from the classic fact pattern, which was based on a touching (the medical procedure) that could be regarded as a battery if consent was ineffective. Although contemporary cases largely prefer a negligence rather than a battery theory, they usually arise in the old touching context. The obligation to provide information suggests that lawyers, too, might be liable for failure to give information necessary for consent to legal actions, which, like *Truman,* involve no touchings. *Truman* provides focus on the fiduciary principle–the duty of the physician to advise and give information, even when not sought. Is the application in *Truman* sound? There was no proof mentioned in the Supreme Court's decision that would suggest that the patient was less than competent. Would not the doctor reasonably believe that patients would know and understand the risk of cancer? Know and understand that pap smears are tests for cancer?

BROWN V. DIBBELL, 595 N.W.2d 358 (Wis. 1999)

The facts are not as detailed as we might like. There seems to be some conflict in the testimony and there are certainly some unknowns. The radiologists found nothing suspicious in the lump that concerns Ms. Brown. She complains that the surgeon did not so advise her, but we don't know whether the radiologists failed to advise her or whether the surgeon knew they had not. The surgeon himself testified he advised Ms. Brown that the lump that worried her was a part of her breast implant. Making of the facts the best we can, the case dovetails with *Truman* on the question whether the patient should ask questions or take some responsibility in selecting the operation or getting information about risks. In *Brown,* that issue is conceived as an issue of contributory fault of the patient. The court thought that inaccurate report of family history might indeed count as contributory negligence, presumably because if family cancer were over-reported the doctor might be led to overrate the risk to the patient. But the court also held that the patient had no duty to question the doctor, to seek independent risk-assessment, or to reject the recommended treatment. We rate autonomy interests highly so this makes sense to us. However, we also think that doctor-patient communication at some point becomes a two-way street. If the doctor has explained enough that he can reasonably believe the patient has the information needed, he should be able to rely upon the patient who appears to be intelligent to say "I don't understand," or to ask questions. So we wonder if the doctor might have been more successful in *Brown v. Dibbel* if he had argued, not contributory fault, but that he had fulfilled his duty by telling a patient who was highly concerned about dying from breast cancer that a mastectomy would be the surest way to reduce the risk. We don't want to put too much weight on this idea, however; people who go to doctors nowadays are quite likely to be rushed through the process before they can formulate all their questions.

FYI: Informed Consent in Other Professions. In departing from the battery pattern, *Truman* suggests that other professions, which do not ordinarily involve themselves in a "touching" of the patient or client, may also have duties to give information. In many professions, the client may need information but it is not necessary as a condition of consent to a touching. For instance, one might argue that an architect should advise the client that there were some optional, cheaper modes of building, but if this is so, it is not because, unless such advice is given, the consent to a touching is invalid. Some independent duty (perhaps arising out of contract) would have to be found.

We mention lawyer informed cases only briefly because lawyer malpractice is usually an economic rather than a personal injury tort. Suppose a lawyer does not tell his client that he can get a light sentence if the client pleads guilty. The lawyer simply defends the case and the client is convicted and sentenced to twenty years.

In *Rogers v. Robson,* 407 N.E.2d 47 (Ill. 1980), a lawyer for a medical malpractice insurer failed to tell the doctor-client-insured that the insurer wanted to settle the case and intended to do so. The lawyer knew that the doctor did not want it settled. Both the doctor and the insurance company were the lawyer's clients. The court, without any discussion of the professional standard or expert testimony, declared that the lawyer was obliged to inform the client and would be liable for any proven damages for failing to do so.

In *Joos v. Auto-Owners Ins. Co.,* 288 N.W.2d 443 (Mich. App. 1979), an insurance attorney did not advise the individual client of an offer to settle within policy limits. Thereafter there was an excess-of-policy judgment for the personal injury claimant and the insured individual sued her lawyer for failing to advise of the within-the-limits offer. The court held that "an attorney has, as a matter of law, a duty to disclose and discuss with his or her client good faith offers to settle," and went on to say it was within "the ordinary knowledge and experience of a layman jury to recognize that . . . the failure of an attorney to disclose" is a breach of the professional standard.

The ABA Model Rules of Professional Conduct, adopted in large part in almost all states (California being one of the last holdouts), place lawyers under a mandatory duty to explain a matter to the extent reasonably necessary to allow the client to make informed decisions about the representation. Model Rule 1.4(b). In a state that has adopted this rule, as most have, this means that a lawyer is subject to discipline by the state bar for a violation; such a violation may be evidence of a breach of a civil duty. *See* Model Rules, *Scope*. *See also* RESTATEMENT OF THE LAW GOVERNING LAWYERS § 20 (Lawyer's Duty to Inform and Consult with a Client); PAUL T. HAYDEN, ETHICAL LAWYERING: LEGAL AND PROFESSIONAL RESPONSIBILITIES IN THE PRACTICE OF LAW (2d Ed. 2007), Chapter 4, § 3 (The Duty to Counsel Effectively).

There is a detailed analysis of the problem of informed consent in lawyer-client relationships in Spiegel, *Lawyering and Client Decisionmaking: Informed Consent and the Legal Profession*, 128 U. PA. L. REV. 41 (1979). The topic is central to the lawyer-client relationship and thus perfect for a course in professional responsibility. As to the professional standard in actions against attorneys in general, *see* Annotation, 17 A.L.R.3d 1442 (1968); also DOBBS ON TORTS § 485 (2000).

Just as the duty to inform may be expanded beyond the medical profession, standing to sue might be expanded as well. In *Hughson v. St. Francis Hosp.*, 459 N.Y.S.2d 814 (App. Div. 1983) the court held that a child injured because of a treatment to the mother before the child's birth could assert a claim based on the mother's lack of informed consent. ■

REFERENCES ON INFORMED CONSENT:
DOBBS ON TORTS §§ 250-251 (2000); 1 BARRY R. FURROW, THOMAS L. GREANEY, SANDRA H. JOHNSON, TIMOTHY STOLZFUS JOST & ROBERT L. SCHWARTZ, HEALTH LAW § 6-10 (1995); 3 DAVID W. LOUISELL & HAROLD WILLIAMS, MEDICAL MALPRACTICE Ch. 22 (various dates); STEVEN E. PEGALIS, & HARVEY F. WACHSMAN, 1 AMERICAN LAW OF MEDICAL MALPRACTICE Ch. 4 (2d Ed. 1992); Peter H. Schuck, *Rethinking Informed Consent,* 103 YALE L. J. 899 (1994); Aaron D. Twerski & Neil B. Cohen, *The Second Revolution in Informed Consent: Comparing Physicians to Each Other,* 94 Nw. U. L. Rev. 1 (1999); Jon R. Waltz & Thomas W. Scheuneman, *Informed Consent to Therapy*, 64 NW. U. L. REV. 628 (1970).

§ 4. CHANGING MEDICINE, CHANGING LAW

A. The Medical Malpractice "Crisis"

Have we had malpractice crises? In part, how many suits are appropriately filed depends on how much malpractice there is. The IOM report starts with some staggering figures on the number of mistakes that are made and the effect that they have. It is an appropriate counterweight to crisis talk to address the magnitude of the problem. However, the IOM report suggests that safety might best be achieved outside tort law, in this case by designing systems to prevent the effects of human error. The Institute definitely doesn't like "blaming" individuals; it sees this as counterproductive, not as a matter of accountability or taking responsibility for your own fault..

The Institute of Medicine is associated with the National Academies and received funding for research from government agencies who seek guidance on health care policy. Those involved in the study are overwhelmingly associated with the health care industry. To get the book, To Err is Human, on the web, try starting use your search engine with a query that includes Institute of Medicine or National Academies.

Whether there is a crisis also depends on whether you look at empirical or anecdotal information about the tort system. Some of the recent empirical work of David Hyman and Charles Silver is particularly compelling on this score. The findings from a study based on pre-tort reform experience also suggests that "there is no crisis." Deborah Jones Merritt & Kathryn Ann Barry, *Is the Tort System in Crisis? New Empirical Evidence,* 60 Ohio St. L.J. 315, 318. (1999). For example, the malpractice win rates for plaintiffs declined significantly during the 12 years preceding the advent of tort reform; correspondingly, verdict size declined. Id. at 380. Professor Patricia Danzon is the author of massive studies on medical malpractice and has produced enormous amounts of data. *See* PATRICIA DANZON, THE FREQUENCY AND SEVERITY OF MEDICAL MALPRACTICE CLAIMS 4-5 (Rand 1982). She summarized the crisis of the 1970s by pointing to data showing that the claims costs per physician in California increased 40% per year in the late 1960s, which eventually precipitated the "crisis" when insurers increased premiums by as much as 300%. See Danzon, *The Effects of Tort Reforms on the Frequency and Severity of Medical Malpractice Claims*, 48 OHIO ST. L.J. 413 (1987).

The strongest claims for massive *abuse* of the tort system, are based on anecdotes rather than systematic studies. They resemble the stories of ungrateful hitchhikers that prompted guest statutes in the '20s and '30s. Some studies indicate that premium costs are not excessive in relation to earnings. Others indicate that most actual victims of untoward medical events don't even assert claims. Since medical organizations are very effective lobbyists but not trained in making balanced social judgments, the statutory results of their displeasure are not necessarily either justified or effective.

If there was a medical malpractice crisis, why so? *Increased litigation?* The reasons for the "crisis" are not entirely clear. Perhaps some malpractice suits are brought that would not have been brought fifty years ago because technology generates new possibilities for error. When there were no kidney dialysis machines, people died of kidney failure but they could not blame the doctor or hospital. Once dialysis machines were invented and in use, any given death from kidney failure might be blamed on the machinery, the system for using it, or human failures in making it work properly. See Mark Grady, *Why Are People Negligent? Technology, Non Durable Precautions, and the Medical Malpractice Explosion*, 82 Nw. U. L. REV. 293 (1988).

Yes, there was increased litigation; yes, there were increased premium costs. Some observers think this will hardly explain any supposed crisis. In any event, students should not too readily accept the idea that increased litigation means increased greed among either lawyers or injured patients. Increased litigation is equally consistent with increased negligence among health care providers or increased awareness of rights. It is also consistent with increased information among victims. One telling statistic is that the proportion of bad claims has not increased. Nearly half of all claims were paid something before and nearly half continue to be paid, even though the total number of claims is higher. PAUL WEILER, MEDICAL MALPRACTICE ON TRIAL 2 (1991). Studies indicating that victims with the best claims do not sue at all add to the puzzle. *See* Localio, Lawthers, Brennan, Laird, Hebert, Peterson, Newhouse, Weiler & Hiatt, *Relation between Malpractice Claims and Adverse Events Due to Negligence*, 325 N. ENG. J. MED. 245 (July 25, 1991); WEILER, *supra*. Professor Michael J. Saks has pointed out that *increase* in litigation does not mean much if you don't have a baseline for measurement: if only 2% of all people with valid claims sue (and that may be close to the mark) you could double the rate of suit but still leave 96% of all reasonable claims without redress. *See* Saks, *Do We Really Know Anything About the Behavior of the Tort Litigation System—And Why Not?*, 140 U. PA. L. REV. 1147 (1992).

Patient satisfaction. Another factor that bore on patient satisfaction and hence on law suits was probably the impersonality of much modern medical practice: the doctor and patient may not know each other, not even remotely. But this speculation, too, has been subjected to scrutiny and it may hold true only in part. One study concluded that, among people who sue, those who evaluate the doctors' competence negatively and those who think doctors fail to show personal concern for them are the most likely to sue. *See* Marlynn May & Daniel Stengel, *Who Sues Their Doctors? How Patients Handle Medical Grievances*, 24 LAW AND SOCIETY REVIEW 105 (1990). The same study shows, on the other hand, efforts by doctors to establish good personal relations with patients, fully informing the patient and the like, do not seem, by themselves, to affect patients' decisions to sue or not.

Insurers' investments. A more important factor may have been the condition of the stock market and the rates of interest payable on the insurers' investments. Insurance companies do not simply put premiums paid into a bank account and pay losses from that account. Instead, they invest the premium funds as long as possible. The return on the investment together with the premium itself must provide a sum of money sufficient to pay the costs of management, claims investigation, lawyer expense, claim payout, and profit. If the investment return is relatively small, it will be obvious that premiums must be raised or that costs or profits must be cut. Again there is little public data about this problem and virtually no regulation.

Actuarial response to cost increases in a given year. One specific source of actuarial concern had to do with the way in which the insurers treated rising costs. If costs (or claims) are rising every year, and not only that but are rising at an increasing rate, some fairly alarming possibilities occur. If costs increased 10% two years ago and 20% last year, should a prudent insurer forecast a 40% rise next year and an 80% rise the year after, going on to 160% and 320% and so on in the ensuing years? The numbers are fictional but they suggest the insurer's dilemma and why the insurer might respond to an increase in claims with great premium increases to protect its ability to make future payouts. Then imagine that after several years of increasing claims, the claims quickly drop again. You can see some actual figures along these lines in PATRICIA DANZON, THE FREQUENCY AND SEVERITY OF MEDICAL MALPRACTICE CLAIMS 4-5 (RAND 1982) (19% overall increase in 1971-75, but the trend did not continue and the 1971-78 period showed an average exponential growth rate of -0.3).

The long tail claims. Along with cost increases that suggested catastrophic projections, there was the problem that liability seemed possible for increasingly long periods. This was due to the recent acceptance in many courts of the rule that the statute of limitations does not start running until the plaintiff has or should have discovered the injury caused by the physician's negligence. This might mean that a physician could be sued and held liable 20 years after he left a sponge in the abdomen. This in turn created actuarial uncertainties, which combined with projections of increased verdicts and other costs naturally led insurers to insist on very large premium charges.

The premiums were and are extremely high. It is not uncommon to talk of premiums of $30,000 a year. Whether these costs were high compared to other costs of doing business, such as rental on a building, and whether they were high in comparison to medical earnings, they nevertheless outraged many physicians.

The statutes. The statutes vary and the provisions are particular in content. One of Danzon's studies suggests that some of the statutory provisions probably have reduced claims or the severity of claims, but that other provisions have had no effect. Danzon, *The Effects of Tort Reforms on the Frequency and Severity of Medical Malpractice Claims*, 48 OHIO ST. L.J. 413 (1987).

A complete discussion of statutory details is probably best left to advanced courses or seminars. The Casebook note is a compromise intended to leave the teacher with a minimal introduction that can be expanded if that proves desirable. If you want to spend a little more time on the topic, one approach is to reproduce or summarize a statute from a single state then parse it with the class, comparing common law rules as you go. Some of the statutes appear to be mere codifications of common law rules.

Exclusion of expert testimony is now a major defense strategy in all kinds of cases. If you want your class to have a picture of professional reality–tort law reality– this is important, even if it is not part of the customary "doctrinal" rules. (More on this in Chapter 24 on products liability.) In *Perdieu v. Blackstone Family Practice Center, Inc.,* 568 S.E.2d 703 (Va. 2002), highly qualified experts were excluded both in a claim against a nursing home for failing to prevent foreseeable falls of a high-risk resident and against doctors for twice failing to diagnose a hip fracture after two (or for failing to supervise the resident who examined the patient). The opinion is one of those that carefully recounts every argument at the trial stage and every trial court response, then dispenses with the appeal in a single paragraph without precisely stating the reasons. It looks as if the Supreme Court of Virginia is relying on the statute's one-year practice rule and also on, with Nurse Corrigan, on the idea that experience in a hospital is not a related field to experience in a nursing home. The exclusions of these witnesses (and one other) left the plaintiff without a case.

Statutes are not the only basis for altering the patient's chances of compensation for medical injury. Arbitration may be based upon contract, as when an HMO contracts require the patient to "assent" to arbitration. *Engalla v. Permanente Medical Group, Inc.,* 938 P.2d 903 (Cal. 1997), contains a detailed description of Kaiser Permanente's statistically terrible performance in arbitrating claims and its seemingly stonewalling conduct in a particular case of a dying patient. Alternative dispute systems have many attractions, but students should think twice before they put the law in the hands of one powerful party, which was the effect of Kaiser's arbitration clause. Students may be enlightened about how defense is conducted in adversary systems–and in Kaiser's arbitration, too–by reading of the various delays. Lawyer McComas, acting for Kaiser, began by refusing to appoint an arbitrator until the patient had first appointed his. At each step in the way, McComas' acts or omissions delayed procedures. We do not know his motives, of course, but the cumulative effect of his actions was delay (while the patient was dying) and this is not an uncommon defense strategy. We think students might see a little more of the "system" in reading this, but of course it is at bottom not a matter of malpractice doctrine.)

The statutes involved in *Hillsborough County Hospital Authority v. Coffaro,* 829 So.2d 862 (Fla. 2002), cited here, required a pre-suit notice of claim followed by a 90-day moratorium on suit, coupled with a statutory tolling of the limitation period. The 90-day moratorium began to run when the different defendants received the notice, not from mailing and it could be ended sooner by a defendant who in return notified the plaintiff that negotiations for settlement were terminated. The plaintiff then had what was left of the original statutory period as tolled or 60 days to sue. The plaintiff could also "purchase" a 90-day extension of time by filing a petition and paying a fee. The case involved a construction of these provisions to determine whether the 90-day purchased extension fit on top of all the other times or not. The theory suggested by the court for all this was that the legislature wanted to encourage negotiations. Maybe so, but parties normally wish to negotiate anyway and there is no impediment to doing so; there is a free market in settlement. Even if there were impediments, it is not clear what new incentive is supplied to an unwilling negotiator by these arrangements. In any event, the negotiation is likely to have preceded filing of suit or notice. So the effect of the statute may be simply added work for plaintiffs' lawyers and added risk of error that will randomly bar some claims because of some error in calculation or giving notice.

As to whether cost-cutting decisions of HMOs are "malpractice" and governed by special medical statutes, see *McEvoy,* below.

B. Statutory Reponses

The purpose of this section is simply to suggest an outline of the types of tort reforms that states have adopted. These are not the only reforms, but they present issues that have been raised in a number of jurisdictions.

C. State Constitutional Challenges to Statutory Reforms

Although legislative action generally overrides common law principles, students should be aware of an important limit. Certain state constitutional provisions require open access to courts, rights of remedy, and equal privileges and immunities.

While these state constitutional guarantees will not necessarily defeat legislative reforms, when legislative reforms are defeated in court, these state constitutional provisions are typically the reason why.

While located in the medical malpractice section, the state constitutional tort provisions may limit many different kinds of tort reforms passed by the legislature. We include them here because this is an area in which so many state legislatures have enacted significant statutory changes.

D. The Medical Practice Reality

Ongoing research in this area continues to illuminate both the problem of malpractice and the feasibility of tort law as an incentive. According to Hyman there is no data suggesting that lawsuits cause the quality of health-care to decline. Does that mean that these suits shouldn't be eliminated or that they won't? The Institute of Medicine favors a regulatory model by analogy to the National Transportation Safety Bureau's investigation into air crashes. These accidents prompt investigations and suggestions for practice reforms. However, there might be differences in air crashes, which are few and public, and acts of medical negligence which are frequent and frequently unknown. Of course, there are also lawsuits in the air crash context.

E. Medical Costs, Containment Efforts and Tort Standards

Barry Furrow, *Enterprise Liability and Health Care Reform: Managing Care and Managing Risk,* 39 ST. LOUIS U. L. J. 77 (1994) argues that malpractice reform, previously engaged in manipulating the interactions of law, medicine and insurance, must now direct attention to managed care organizations. He thinks it now makes sense to introduce some form of enterprise liability. Furrow looks at various proposals and adduces a lot of useful information. He reports, for example, that physicians perceive poor people to pose a special threat of malpractice liability, a perception not based on evidence. If this is the perception, managed care may pose a special threat to health for some groups.

MCO direct liabilities. If cost containment ideals lead an MCO to require physicians to prescribe the least appropriate drug, one with more or more serious side effects, would the MCO itself be liable for harms done? *McKenzie v. Hawai'i Permanente Med. Group, Inc.,* 47 P.3d 1209 (Haw. 2002), cited here, holds that the MCO has no duty to permit its physicians to prescribe the drugs prescribed by others. Seemingly it can make pure cost decisions without regard to medical benefit. The rule may or may not be limited to claims by third persons who are injured as a result of the patient's fainting while driving as a result of the prescription. The court first emphasized complexity of medical/cost decisions and then said that the "stakeholders"– health care professionals, patients and interest groups– should be the decision-makers about cost cutting prescriptions rather than courts. The injured third person and those at risk from cheap but bad prescriptions were not listed among the stakeholders.

Liability for denial of coverage. The managed care organization that denies coverage is not guilty of malpractice; it is not practicing medicine. It might be guilty of contract breach and/or the tort of bad faith contract breach. Conceivably this could be a tortious interference in the relationship between doctor and patient. Several cases cited in the casebook have approved of potential liability. *See also* Kathleen J. McKee, Annotation, *Liability of Third-party Health-care Payor for Injury Arising from Failure to Authorize Required Treatment,* 56 A.L.R.5th 737 (1998). Students should distinguish this liability from malpractice. They do not need to know interference with contract or bad faith contract breach law to do that.

ERISA preemption. One problem with liability of MCOs for coverage delay or denial has been the federal statute known as ERISA, a statute that attempts to guarantee employees their pension and other job benefits such as those associated with health care. ERISA contains a strong preemption clause, which perhaps displaces state law when the claim against an MCO is made under coverage created as an employee benefit. Courts may be gradually coming to the view that the MCO's decisions about coverage –eligibility for treatment– are preempted, so that the plaintiff can assert only whatever rights ERISA gives her (basically to enforce the contract, not to get tort damages). On the other hand, the MCO's medical decisions – a misdiagnosis or conclusion that treatment is not warranted – are state-law medical malpractice decisions that are NOT preempted. Most decisions may be a combination of mixed eligibility and treatment decisions. *Pappas v. Asbel,* 768 A.2d 1089 (Pa. 2001) holds that such mixed decisions fall on the state-law malpractice side and are not preempted. A candle in the darkness with plenty of people who want to blow it out. The Congress has had before it a Patient's Bill of Rights for years, but has been unable to act at all, one way or the other.

In *Pegram v. Herdrich,* 530 U.S. 211 (2000), the plaintiff's HMO physician had delayed providing ultrasound for many days, with the result that the plaintiff's appendix ruptured. The plaintiff sued under ERISA's provision for suit against the plan fiduciaries. She said that the HMO was a fiduciary and breached its duty to her because it structured payment to physicians so that physicians would receive more of the profits if they gave less treatment. The Supreme Court thought the decisions involved here were mixed eligibility and treatment decisions and such decisions did not count as fiduciary decisions. Hence there was no suit under ERISA itself. Note that this did not involve the preemption issue nor was it a case in which the physician's medical decision was overruled by an HMO.

Economic incentives and the medical standard of care. MCOs and health insurers, as purchasers of health care on a wide scale, are in a position to demand safety for patients, but they have not generally done so and have little incentive. *See* INSTITUTE OF MEDICINE, TO ERR IS HUMAN: BUILDING A SAFER HEALTHY SYSTEM, *Executive Summary* 3 (2000). In addition, efforts through utilization review to contain costs may contribute to reduced health care. Many lawyers who specialize in health care issues have worried about how cost containment programs should or will affect legal rights and liability. See, e.g., the extensive and specialized writing in Symposium, *The Legal Implications of Health Care Cost Containment,* 36 CASE WESTERN L. REV. 605 (1986) (with major articles by Wing, Capron, Mehlman, Rosenblatt, Furrow, Grad, Havinghurst and Wadlington).

In *Pegram v. Herdrich, supra,* Justice Souter described the old and new incentives this way:

> In a fee-for-service system, a physician's financial incentive is to provide more care, not less, so long as payment is forthcoming. The check on this incentive is a physician's obligation to exercise reasonable medical skill and judgment in the patient's interest.. . . .
> [I]n an HMO system, a physician's financial interest lies in providing less care, not more. The check on this influence (like that on the converse, fee-for-service incentive) is the professional obligation to provide covered services with a reasonable degree of skill and judgment in the patient's interest.

Jones v. Chicago HMO Ltd. of Illinois, 730 N.E.2d 1119 (Ill. 2000), holds that an HMO can be charged with institutional (corporate) negligence. When its alleged negligence is managerial or administrative, the plaintiff is not necessarily required to prove a "standard of care" by expert medical testimony.

However, she must prove facts that will show negligence. In this case she showed that 3500 was the admitted maximum number of patients that should be assigned to a single physician and created a fact question whether that standard was breached. Her claim was based on the fact that the assigned physician did not actually see her child but prescribed castor oil on the telephone when the symptoms called for a personal examination and/or hospitalization. The child in fact had meningitis and is now permanently disabled, allegedly as a result of this inadequate attention. The court relied on its earlier decision imposing liability upon hospitals for negligence in failing to supervise doctors in the hospital. This was *Darling,* a case we will encounter in Chapters 16 and 20.

Informed consent. Aaron D. Twerski & Neil B. Cohen, *The Second Revolution in Informed Consent: Comparing Physicians to Each Other*, 94 Nw. U. L. Rev. 1 (1999), would require MCOs to disclose provider-risk information and to found liability upon their failure to do so when they actually possess the information in usable form.

One kind of informed consent problem that gets some attention in the world of managed care is the risk arising from the fact that the provider may have financial incentives not to recommend (or even mention) treatment alternatives that require specialists. Likewise, the provider may have no incentive to mention treatment alternatives that are not covered by the health care plan. Susan M. Wolf, *Toward a Systemic Theory of Informed Consent in Managed Care,* 35 HOUS. L. REV. 1631 (1999) argues that with the advent of managed care, information (such as financial incentives of doctors and treatments that are not covered) becomes important at several stages, beginning with a worker's acceptance of a job with a health benefit plan. Thus the managed care world makes "systemic analysis" more important and ultimately requires that information be given by several persons–the employer, for example. She opposes the view that the MCO can simply by contract or by general information included in its plan eliminate the need for informed consent. On the contrary, she thinks it must come at several different stages or parts of the "system."

Joan H. Krause, *Reconceptualizing Informed Consent in an Era of Health Care Cost* 85 IOWA L. REV. 261 (1999), addresses the problem of getting patients information about alternative treatments and in the managed care context, getting them information about non-covered treatment alternatives. She professes little hope for traditional informed consent or even tort law in general, suggesting a combination of statutes and professional discipline of doctors.

F. Mandatory Emergency Treatment and Screening

42 U.S.C.A. § 1395dd.

We decided that the best way to teach EMTALA was to have the students read the actual statute, then read a case applying it. You can parse the statute itself with the class first (using the notes after the statute if you wish), then turn to *Lewellen*, or you can just start with *Lewellen* and refer back to the actual statute as you talk about the case.

To discuss this statute it may be helpful to have a little background about "patient dumping," which was a major problem sought to be addressed by EMTALA. One expert discusses three recent studies analyzing patient dumping. *See* Karen I. Treiger, Note: *Preventing Patient Dumping: Sharpening the COBRA's Fangs,* 61 N.Y.U. L.Rev. at 1190-1191. One study reports that eighty-seven percent of hospitals transferring patients cited the lack of insurance as the sole reason for the transfer. *Id.* at 1190 (citing Schiff, Ansell, Schlosser, Idris, Morrison & Whitman, *Transfers to a Public Hospital--A Prospective Study of 467 Patients,* 314 New Eng. J. Med. 552, 553 (1986)). Another study found that, of the patients transferred, over seventy-two percent required emergency services at the receiving hospital. *See id.* at 1190-1191 (citing Andrulis & Gage, *Patient Transfers to Public Hospitals: A National Assessment* (National Ass'n of Pub. Hosps. Apr. 9, 1986)). A third study found that, of 458 patients transferred to the emergency department of Highland General Hospital in Oakland, sixty-three percent of the transfer patients lacked insurance. There was no evidence patients requested the transfers or that patients were transferred due to lack of beds at the transferring hospital. *See id.* at 1191 (citing Himmelstein, Woolhandler, Harnly, Bader, Silber, Backer & Jones, *Patient Transfers: Medical Practice as Social Triage,* 74 Am. J. Pub. Health 494, 495 (1984)).

Note 2. Private right of action. Are harm and causation required? Yes. The point of this note is to point students to the statute for the answer.

Note 4. Screening and treatment duties. If the language of EMTALA is clear, courts merely read the language (in context) to determine its meaning. If it is ambiguous, courts will invoke interpretative aids unless an agency empowered to construe the statute had done so in a permissible way. In that case, the court will follow the agency's interpretation.

This statute is ambiguous because "come to" could mean the act of going to, that is, approaching. It is unclear "whether Congress required that an emergency patient be present at the emergency room, that the person be on the hospital grounds, or in a hospital-owned ambulance; or whether, as in this case, it is sufficient that the patient be on his way to the hospital in a non-hospital-owned ambulance." Given this ambiguity, the court defers to the agency's interpretation, that is, the regulation promulgated by the Department of Health and Human Services. The regulation treats the patient as coming to the hospital when she reaches any hospital property – sidewalks, outlying facilities, or hospital-owned ambulances. It goes further, providing that if ambulance personnel contact the hospital to inform the hospital that they want to transport the individual to the hospital for examination and treatment, the hospital may deny the individual access only if it lacks the staff or facilities to accept any additional emergency patients. Following this regulation, the court holds that the plaintiff stated a claim.

There are other similar cases: *Smith v. Richmond Mem. Hosp.,* 416 S.E.2d 689 (Va. 1992) and *Lopez-Soto v. Hawayek,* 175 F.3d 170 (1st Cir. 1999), hold that coming to the emergency department is not necessary to invoke the act. The *Lopez-Soto* court emphasized the plain language of the different statutory subsections–"come to the hospital" vs. "comes to the emergency department." However, other cases disagree. *See James v. Sunrise Hospital,* 86 F.3d 885 (9th Cir. 1996).

LEWELLEN V. SCHNECK MEDICAL CENTER, 2007 WL 2363384 (S.D. Ind.).

Lewellen is a factually compelling case. The plaintiff is a drunk driver who caused his own accident so you might expect that this would not be a sympathetic case for the plaintiff. And yet, the story of the poor treatment that he received in the emergency room, his severe pain, the hospital's apparent indifference to it, and the police officer's constant concern, make this a highly sympathetic case for the plaintiff, at least as the facts are relayed by judge Tinder.

The case forces the question of what the statute means when it says that the hospital must provide "an appropriate medical screening." Surely, EMTALA was not crafted as a federal medical malpractice statute, so that plaintiffs have a federal action every time an emergency room doctor was negligent. But is absolutely any examination acceptable, or are there some quality limits?

Note 1. Screening. What is appropriate screening? *(a) Disparate screening.* The statute does not say "discrimination is forbidden," but it does forbid a refusal to screen or a "dumping" for any cause, and the most obvious case for dumping is the patient's inability to pay or to provide payment. Disparate or discriminatory screening might violate the act. That is, unequal treatment is *sufficient* to show a violation of the appropriate screening requirement. But cf. James A. Henderson & John A. Siliciano, *Universal Health Care and the Continued Reliance on Custom in Determining Medical Malpractice,* 79 CORNELL L. REV. 1382 (1994) (arguing against a "unitary, wealth-blinded standard of care" in medical malpractice actions).

(b) Uniform screening. Reverse the case: suppose that the plaintiff gets the same screening procedures as others get, but that the screening was negligent and caused harm. That sounds like screening that is not appropriate, but judges have been extremely anxious not to "federalize malpractice," so they wish to create EMTALA standards that are distinguishable from medical malpractice standards and they interpret the statute in accordance with that desire. The result is that negligent screening is not necessarily inappropriate screening that violates the statute. *E.g., Casey v. Amarillo Hosp. Dist.,* 947 S.W.2d 301 (Tex. App. 1997). Judges may insist that screening is inappropriate and a violation of EMTALA *only* if it violates the hospital's own standards

for screening or differs from screening given to other patients. *Battle v. Memorial Hospital at Gulfport,* 228 F.3d 544 (5th Cir. 2000). In that view, disparate screening is not only *sufficient* to show violation, it is also *necessary.*

In *Battle,* the hospital ran an EEG on a child-patient. It in fact showed gross abnormality which required immediate treatment, but the hospital didn't read the EEG for seven days and consequently treatment of a devastating condition was delayed. The Fifth Circuit held that the delay did not show inappropriate screening because the plaintiff put on no evidence that other EEGs were read more promptly. The effect is that the standard of appropriate screening is based upon equal screening, not upon professional screening.

But what if all emergency department patients are screened by a nurse's aid who simply looks at the patient or reads her palm to determine whether an emergency exists? Can it be that uniformly inane screening is "appropriate" under EMTALA? The command to provide medical screening itself implies some basis for selection, so maybe it would be better to say with *Correa* that a screening must be reasonably calculated to identify medical emergency. If that test were met, screening would be appropriate even if the physician was negligent in some particular way, but the test focuses on professional standards, not merely upon equality.

(c) Subjective standard. Courts have also said that the measure of appropriate screening is subjective in the sense that the screening must be appropriate in light of the hospital's own capabilities and equipment. E.g., *Ingram v. Muskogee Regional Med. Cntr.,* 235 F.3d 550 (10th Cir. 2000) (recognizing this subjective standard both on screening and appropriate transfer). This statement may reflect the court's ambivalence about standards, because the hospital's capabilities could hardly be in question if the only test of duty is to provide equal treatment, bad or good. To emphasize the hospital's limited capabilities is to assume that a medical standard rather than an equality standard applies.

In *Correa v. Hospital San Francisco,* 69 F.3d 1184 (1st Cir. 1995), the court held that the EMTALA law is violated if screening is denied, even if it is denied to all alike. Is this contrary to the equality standard (Note 5 (b), supra) or can we apply the equality standard and still say that *no* screening always violates the statute, even when screening is denied equally to all?

With *Corea* compare *Muse v. Charter Hospital of Winston-Salem, Inc.,* 452 S.E.2d 589 (N.C. Ct. App. 1995). There a hospital had accepted a 16-year-old patient under the care of a doctor for suicidal depression. The hospital had a policy of discharging patients when insurance expired and after a two-day extension (guaranteed by a promissory note from the patient's parents), it acted on this policy. The young man committed suicide shortly thereafter. The court held that the hospital was under a duty to keep the patient if the discharge policy would interfere with the physician's medical judgment.

Note 2. Unpublished opinion. We were torn about whether to use this unpublished case, but it seemed not only to be an interesting teaching case, but also an interesting teaching opportunity. Students will encounter many unpublished opinions in their research. Here is a chance for them to learn how to use (or not use) these cases. We wonder if this case truly is not sufficiently novel to merit publication. In our view, it might well be that the court was instead worried about setting precedent by their ruling.

Note 4. Coordinating with or trumping state law. This is not a vastly interesting subject to many students, but it is professionally important to recognize the problem of meshing different systems of dealing with injury. (We'll see meshing problems with workers' compensation and other non-tort systems, for example). The pre-suit notice of claim requirement imposed in New York on tort claims against municipal corporations (including the hospital involved in *Hardy*) is one of those devices that does not go to the merits but that defendants like because it will trap a certain percentage of meritorious claims. *Hardy* seems to us wrong in using EMTALA's damages measure to import a procedural immunity that does not attempt to measure damages at all. When full scale sovereign immunity was presented to the Eighth Circuit in *Root v. New Liberty Hospital Dist.*, 209 F.3d 1068 (8th Cir. 2000), it refused to treat EMTALA's reference to state damages measures as importing immunity rules. In fact, it concluded that ""Missouri's sovereign immunity statute is in direct conflict with [EMTALA]. The supremacy clause, see U.S. Const. art. VI, cl. 2, therefore dictates that Missouri's sovereign immunity statute must yield." California's damages cap involved in *Barris v. County of Los Angeles,* 972 P.2d 966 (Cal. 1999), is a different animal. It is not a bar to all claims like the sovereign immunity in *Root* or the notice of claim statute in *Hardy*. It is truly a limitation on damages, so if the state's statutory limitation is written broadly enough to cover EMTALA-type claims, EMTALA's direction to import state law damages rules clearly applies, as the *Barris* court held.

FYI: Disability statutes. Some disability statutes may impose liability for failure to provide equal medical accommodation. The Americans with Disabilities Act, which defines disability broadly, provides only for injunctive relief, but state statutes might permit a tort recovery. In *D.B. v. Bloom*, 896 F.Supp. 166 (D.N.J. 1995) a person suffering from AIDS sought dental treatment. When it was denied, along with some unpleasant comments, he claimed emotional trauma and asked for damages under the state discrimination act. This was held to be appropriate. You might think that refusal of treatment in the AIDS case is irrational but that refusal in the case of one who cannot pay is eminently rational from the hospital's point of view. ∎

G. Strict and Limited Liability Proposals

The ALI-Weiler proposal would make hospitals the focus of liability and Weiler would impose a form of limited but strict liability. What about imposing strict liability upon Managed Care Organizations? Clark C. Havinghurst, *Making Health Plans Accountable for the Quality of Care,* 31 GA. L. REV. 587 (1997) proposes that they should bear "exclusive legal responsibility for the negligence of physicians treating their subscribers or enrolees." Reviewing some of the Weiler/Reporter's Study is Sugarman, *"Dr. No,"* (Book Review), 58 U. CHI. L. REV. 1499 (1991).

Material on other legal issues associated with health care–brain death, the human genome project and other broad policy issues–has been dropped from the casebook for want of space and classroom time.

§ 5. NURSING HOMES, LONG-TERM CARE, AND ELDER ABUSE

HORIZON/CMS HEALTHCARE V. AULD, 985 S.W.2d 216 (Tex. App. 1999).

This case does not, standing alone, lend itself so much to traditional rule and policy analysis of the classroom. It rather illustrates one aspect of the nursing home problem and sets the stage for discussing some of the issues raised in notes.

The facts in *Horizon/CMS* are horrifying. Pressure sores are prevented by moving patients periodically. If you don't, the skin and flesh will wear down to the bare bone, eventually with infection and rotting of skin and flesh. The court describes this cleanly and also describes the many, many failures at Horizon/CMS. If you like to take the class through factual analysis, you can take them through not only the harm done but the many stages of Horizon's misconduct, particularly in discussing the propriety of punitive damages.

We are concerned that students may not appreciate the harsh realities of the injuries. We considered publishing a picture of "bedsores" with most of the flesh of one buttock just a bloody mess down to the bone, but we ourselves were so shaken by this and other pictures, we decided they would obstruct learning. There are some pictures on a website. You may wish to view them and then decide whether to refer students to the cite. We don't know whether the pictures will change from time to time but the ones we have viewed are very upsetting, so be warned. The site is:

http://www.geocities.com/Athens/Rhodes/9965/AbusePictures.html

Did the jury go crazy with its 90 Million punitive verdict? Or was it trying to send Horizon a message? Understaffing nursing homes is a serious problem. It leaves residents literally to rot, while saving expenses and maximizing profits for the operators and their administrators. Students may not know that the defendant's wealth is usually admissible in punitive damages cases as one basis for estimating how much its takes to provide deterrence. That is particularly appropriate where the tortious conduct is the very thing that maximizes profits. You might think back to the McDonald's coffee case in Chapter 1, where the jury's award of punitive damages was about the sum of two days' coffee sales by McDonald's.) We don't know what evidence was presented in the trial court, but we do know that Horizon did not argue that the punitive damages were excessive. Its operating revenue in that period was close to $2 billion, as reported in note 3, so the punitive award was about 5%

of its revenue for one year. In 1997, Horizon was acquired by Healthsouth, an aggressive player in the integrated healthcare business.

Students evaluating this case need to understand the risk of underdeterrence and undercompensation so they can see why punitive damages may be needed to offset the first risk if not the second. The idea is that if only one claim is brought out of a hundred valid claims, the nursing home may find it cheaper to neglect patients and pay damages than to provide proper care. Consequently, punitive damages or some other method may be needed to get deterrence to the right level. The reasons why only one claim out of a hundred might be brought are mentioned in note 4.

The role of punitive damages is so important here that you may have some unsuspected options. One is to control and limit the punitive damages discussion and take up the topic more systematically with damages in Chapter 26. Another is to explore the topic rather fully here, importing the rules from Chapter 26 by assigning the relevant pages with this section. Perhaps some middle ground is also possible.

As important as punitive awards may be to bring deterrence up to proper levels, some nursing homes that take in large revenues are nevertheless in financial difficulties. At this writing, a fair number are in bankruptcy and their debts being restructured. With a growing population of elderly, the nursing home industry ideally should represent a reasonably attractive investment if we want the industry to expand and provide appropriate care. But if nursing homes are losing money, the industry will not draw the investment needed to expand and to provide proper services. Big punitive liabilities may therefore make a bad situation worse because profits will go down and services, so obviously missing in *Horizon/CMS*, might be cut even more.

A couple of reasons to doubt that punishment will make bad actors worse. First, the surface appearance that a nursing home is making little or no profit may be misleading to the uninitiated. Notice that even a losing operation may be paying a $1 million every year to its chief executive officer and in fact might not be losing money at all if salaries were more commensurate with success. The surface appearance of loss is also hard to judge because many of the large enterprises operate nursing homes as one component of an integrated health care system that may include home health units, hospitals, and other facilities. Moreover, it may be difficult to trace real income of an operation. Conceivably an operating unit might lose money because it is paying large sums to lease the facility from a corporation that owns the property–but it may turn out that the property owner gaining enormous lease payments is really just another entity owned by the same conglomerate. In that case, the nursing home arm might show little profit while the property owner arm might profit a great deal. If that were the arrangement, the total picture might be one of great profit, not one of loss. Second and perhaps more fundamentally, maybe nursing homes are not the hope of the future; you wouldn't think so from the *Auld* case, would you? If some other system of eldercare becomes feasible, maybe strong punitive measures are highly desirable after all.

In court, the main civil options for dealing with nursing home abuse appear in the notes—awarding attorney fees to prevailing plaintiffs (which should assist the affordability problem) and qui tam actions discussed in the stand-alone note on that topic. More substantial and personal criminal penalties—serious prison time—for individuals who inflict abuse upon the helpless might turn out to be the best solution.

We encounter more conservative students than radicals, but if there are radically minded or thoroughly disgusted students in your class, they might suggest that the government should operate nursing homes to the exclusion of private operators. To that suggestion we might ask, "What if the government itself neglects the helpless patients? Would punitive damages bring the government in line?" (You can then profitably come back to government misbehavior in Chapter 15, where we'll see that punitive damages are not awarded against government and indeed that citizens injured even by intentionally wrong governmental programs may be denied compensation.)

Note 2. The National Elder Abuse Incidence Study was conducted by the National Center on Elder Abuse at the American Public Human Services Association based on funding from The Administration for Children and Families (ACF) and the Administration on Aging (AoA) in the U.S. Department of Health and Human Services. See The National Elder Abuse Incidence Study, Executive Summary. It found that about 450,000 elderly persons suffer abuse or neglect *in domestic settings* in 1996. You can reach this study on the web. http://www.aoa.gov/abuse/report/default.htm. Be warned that the case cited here, *Sieniarecki v. State,* 756 So.2d 68 (Fla. 2000), is strong stuff. It involved conviction of a home caregiver. The victim was fed or allowed to eat her feces. Various parts of her body were rotting. In many such cases, the home caregiver may be simply physically and emotionally overwhelmed as well as untrained and unsupported. In others you suspect that "caregivers" are seriously evil or deranged. (You can read a good many news reports of caregiver rapes and torments.)

Note 3 & 4. We want students to recognize that there are many small nursing homes and other long-term care arrangements, but that many giants now play in this park. That is definitely a part of the evaluation of punitive damages. They also need to know that nursing home care is partly, maybe largely, the creature of federal financing, in particularly through medicaid. Structurally, CMS is part of Health and Human Services, a cabinet Department. Although CMS administers Medicare and Medicaid, the Social Security Administration is a separate entity, not within any cabinet department.

Notes 5 & 6. Under-reporting and affordability. You may need to remind students how lawsuits for the plaintiff are financed—by contingent fees. Lawyers cannot afford to do all their work pro bono. A lawyer who consistently takes small damages cases will predictably not earn enough to pay her office rent, much less support herself and family. Students are not likely to appreciate the effects of chance, either. Even if you took only cases that looked like winners, you would lose some of them because of unexpected testimony, loss of a witness or change of the witness' story, odd biases of judge or jury, and endless other reasons. So your winners must make up for your losers and those that win must bring in enough damages to allow lawyers to make a living. This is the affordability point in Note 6. To this must be added the fact that long-term care neglect and abuse is desperately underreported. Together these notes give students a basis for appreciating the need for something besides "compensatory damages."

Note 8. Standard of care and coverage by med mal statutes. We speak of the health care industry in broad terms, and nursing home negligence certainty can cause health problems. Yet it seems silly to say that providing food and lodging or wheeling a patient down the hallway is a medical matter. Is a cafeteria in the health care business because it provides food? A motel because it provides a bed? The medmal reform statute's terms, of course, will ultimately govern.

Battery. Roberson v. Provident House, 576 So.2d 992 (La. 1991) permitted the plaintiff to claim a battery and hence to sidestep the need for expert testimony when a quadriplegic patient was subjected to an internal catheter over his protest, but as often in Louisiana, the damages award was quite small ($25,000).

False imprisonment, unreasonable restraints. Chemical and physical restraints may present more difficult problems. Professional testimony might be required to show whether the restraint was needed or medically indicated. Another problem with restraint cases is that the nursing home may be liable for failure to restrain or otherwise monitor a patient who is dangerous to herself. Nursing homes can argue that because they can be liable for failure to restrain, they should not be liable for restraint. The key fallacy here is that there is no liability for failure to restrain, only a negligent failure to restrain where restraint is called for. Similarly, liability is appropriate when freedom is called for but the nursing home imposes restraint for its own convenience. See, discussing restraint problems, including the dangers of actual injury from inappropriate restraints, Marshall B. Kapp, *Nursing Home Restraints and Legal Liability,* 13 J. LEGAL MED. 1 (1992). 42 C.F.R. § 483.13 provides: "(a) Restraints. The resident has the right to be free from any physical or chemical restraints imposed for purposes of discipline or convenience, and not required to treat the resident's medical symptoms."

Other claims: contract, civil rights. The contract between resident and the home may set the standard in some cases. *Callens v. Jefferson County Nursing Home,* 769 So.2d 273 (Ala. 2000) (recognizing a breach of contract action). In the special case of a person whom the state has committed to an institution against her will, the institution may be subject to a civil rights action under 42 U.S.C.A. § 1983. *Wadkins v. Gulf Coast Centers, Ltd.,* 77 F.Supp.2d 794 (S.D. Tex. 1999).

Note 10. Regulations as standards of care. You may need to help the class distinguish regulation mentioned in this paragraph from the inspection reports in the next. Many students also appear to be shaky on the state vs. federal distinction, as to which we'll see more in dealing with immunities. The regulation quoted, like others involved in the nursing home problem, applies only to institutions qualified to receive federal funds through medicare or medicaid. The regulation is a good one for students to see. It contains both a statement of lofty goals and some specific language of interest to a lawyer with an *Auld* type case. C.F.R. is of course the Code of Federal Regulations, now mercifully available electronically.

Conservatorship of Gregory, 95 Cal.Rptr.2d 336 (Ct. App. 2000). The points made in the casebook about this case are in the portion certified for publication. The claim was under California's Elder Abuse statute, which requires abuse or neglect. The opinion does not reveal what effect the jury was told to give to the federal regulations. Even if the regulations were not binding, however, the jury must have been allowed to consider them in determining the standards for abuse or neglect. On what ground did the court permit use of federal regulations? It did not attack the problem substantively by saying, for instance, that courts are free to adopt or reject statutory materials as standards. Perhaps it could not well have done that because the state law claim was a statutory claim, not a common law claim. And the court did not assert that the state Elder Abuse statute adopted the federal regulations by reference. The Elder Abuse Statute actually defined abuse and neglect, but even so, it might have implicitly left room to fill gaps or details from standards prevailing in the industry. If so, the federal regulations might be appropriate reflections of those standards. But the court mentioned none of this. Instead it treat the question as a quasi-procedural issue by asking what kind of materials could form the basis for a jury instruction and by answering that all kinds of materials were appropriate. But of course no material would be appropriate unless it reflected governing law, and that was the issue the court slid by. Nevertheless, if the ultimate decision holds up, it will be a major boon to nursing home claimants.

The portion of the case certified for publication does not include the facts. You can get the full opinion, including the portion not certified for publication and citation in California courts, from the Web.

Try http://www.courtinfo.ca.gov/opinions/. There are also private services on the Web.

Note 11. Inspection or survey reports. *See* Jeffrey Spitzer-Resnick & Maya Krajcinovic, *Protecting the Rights of Nursing Home Residents: How Tort Liability Interacts with Statutory Protections,* 19 NOVA L. REV. 629 (1995) recounts a trial court's decision rejecting survey evidence, with the consequent loss of the punitive damages claim. The surveys are a product of federal law and regulation, but the federal government leaves them to the states, which may perform them with varying degrees of commitment. You can check out survey results for nursing homes by state or by zip code location on the web.

Begin with http://www.medicare.gov/nursing/home.asp . You can get your state ombudsman and state survey office telephone numbers from this site as well. The surveys or inspections check a list of standard concerns and reflect violations. The survey distinguishes between isolated cases and patterns and between violations that represent serious risks of harm and those that do not.

Note 12. Elder abuse, residents' rights statutes. Elder rights or nursing home rights statutes usually look pretty weak. In *Beverly Enterprises-Florida, Inc. v. Knowles,* 766 So.2d 335 (Fla. Dist. Ct. App. 2000) the "patient's bill of rights" statute provided that an action under the statute could be brought by the resident or guardian, "or by the personal representative of the estate of a deceased resident *when the cause of death resulted from the deprivation or infringement of the decedent's rights."* (Emphasis added.) It is plausible to say that the list is comprehensive and intended to exclude any plaintiffs not named. The statute may thus have been intended to exclude survival of actions for injuries that did not cause death. In effect, that is what the court said. The court thought that maybe the legislature intended such a result because recovery would not benefit the dead patient. Unfortunately, neither the court nor legislature seems to have considered the need to deter Beverly's misconduct.

As we will see in Chapter 21, some states do not permit pain and suffering claims to survive the death of the plaintiff, so the elder rights statute that permits survival does offer an advantage—but only for that narrow class of actions, which may exclude some claims of "ordinary" medical negligence. See Estate of *McGill v. Albrecht,* 57 P.3d 384 (Ariz. 2002). Some others may resolve a vicarious liability issue by providing that the nursing home is liable for intentional as well as negligent torts, but as we'll see in Chapter 22, that would often be the rule in any event. Perhaps the thing to notice most is that some statutes permit the plaintiff to recover attorney fees and, in California, to sidestep the severe limits, including damages caps, that would be imposed in ordinary malpractice claims. That would give lawyers incentive to take cases that otherwise might seem too unproductive. This is the second of the three ways to deal with the affordability problem, but it may fall short of providing full deterrence.

NOTE: REGULATION OR FINANCIAL PARTNERSHIP?
NOTE ON THE FALSE CLAIMS ACT AND QUI TAM ACTIONS

First, you might note that criminal prosecution could have deterrent effect. While criminal law is no more part of this course than administrative law, it is nonetheless part of the picture and we must assess the success of tort law in the light of other means of social control. Yet, neither criminal law, nor regulation, nor tort law is likely to find and punish individuals in cases like *Horizon/CMS v. Auld.* Unless some individuals are required to take responsibility, you might wonder whether deterrence in the form of financial loss passed on to shareholders, will be as effective as it should be.

Qui tam. Whether claims for reimbursement based on substandard quality of care can be viewed as false claims is not an authoritatively determined issue as of 2000. *United States ex rel. Aranda v. Community Psychiatric Centers of Oklahoma, Inc.,* 945 F.Supp. 1485 (W.D. Okla. 1996) is a moderately well-developed opinion allowing the claim against a motion to dismiss. The complaint was that a psychiatric center, knowing that some of its residents had special needs for security and also knowing that others were sexually or otherwise predatory, failed to provide the first group the security essential to their treatment, yet billed the government. The court seemed to accept an implied certification theory without using the term. Cases settled in favor of the government: *see* John M. Parisi, *A Weapon Against Nursing Home Fraud and Abuse,* 35-DEC Trial 48 (1999).

United States v. NHC Healthcare Corp., 115 F.Supp.2d 1149 (W.D.Mo. 2000) was a government claim under the False Claims Act grounded on the theory that the defendant nursing facility was so woefully understaffed it could not have given the required level of health care to its residents and that the facility's claims for reimbursement were therefore a violation of the false claims act. The court noted that the reimbursement is per diem/per resident, so that the government could not prove failure to deliver a particular service for which a particular payment was made. The court approved *Aranda,* which it thought similar, and held that the government stated a cause of action, although the court noted that proving it might be difficult.

United States ex rel. Mikes v. Straus, 84 F.Supp.2d 427 (S.D.N.Y. 1999) rejected a qui tam action, but it was a weak claim at best. The defendant violated no standard imposed by the government. He was allegedly negligent, but the court observed that "Submitting a claim to the Government for a service that was not provided in accordance with the relevant standard of care, however, without more, does not render that claim false or fraudulent for FCA purposes." It added: "[A] finding of falsity under the FCA is precluded where payment has not been conditioned upon statutory compliance . . . ." The court read several non-health cases to stand for the proposition that "implied false certification is to be found only in those exceptional circumstances where the claimant's adherence to the relevant statutory or regulatory mandates lies at the core of its agreement with the Government, or, in more practical terms, where the Government would have refused to pay had it been aware of the claimant's non-compliance." A similar view was expressed succinctly in *Luckey v. Baxter Healthcare Corp.,* 183 F.3d 730 (7th Cir. 1999).

Some commentators seem to think that the qui tam action has real potential for providing some quality assurance, *see* David C. Hsia, *Application of Qui Tam to the Quality of Health Care,* 14 J. Legal Med. 301 (1993); Carolyn J. Paschke, *The Qui Tam Provision of The Federal False Claims Act: The Statute in Current Form, Its History And Its Unique Position to Influence The Health Care Industry,* 9 J.L. & Health 163 (1994-95). Or conversely, a real danger to health care providers. See a defense lawyer's view in John T. Boese, *When Angry Patients Become Angry Prosecutors: Medical Necessity Determina-*

tions, Quality of Care and the Qui Tam, 43 St. Louis U. L.J. 53 (1999) ("a new and dangerous kind of potential plaintiff").

Qui tam actions may have a very important place, but most especially in financial fraud rather than care quality cases. Large sums have in fact been recovered for wrongful billing of the government, but not in care quality cases. We are doubtful whether qui tam actions will have a profound impact on care quality.

Refocusing. Qui tam claims show us a third method of trying to achieve proper deterrence and of dealing with the affordability problem. Punitive damages, attorney fee awards, and a sharing of the government's recovery—which do students think best?

§ 6. INTENTIONAL TORTS AND SEXUAL HARASSMENT BY PROFESSIONALS

One purpose of this little section is to remind our students that professionals can be guilty of serious mistreatment of their patients/clients/parishioners. That purpose does not require much investment of time; we've seen sexual misconduct before and will see it again.

A broader (and shallower) purpose is to continue this chapter's introduction of practical, non-doctrinal concerns and non-tort approaches to problems. Here we briefly see that insurance coverage as well as medical malpractice crisis statutes may profoundly affect the plaintiff's rights in the practical world. Serious professional misbehavior may go unredressed if insurance does not cover the case. That is for the same reasons we mentioned in the nursing home cases—lawyers who cannot expect to collect cannot afford to take the case.

A professional may mistreat his patient or client either by (a) sexual attack or harassment or (b) sexual exploitation. (We omit any reference to financial torts of professionals). Either kind of claim presents two special problems. First, do the special limits of the malpractice crisis statutes apply to limit the plaintiff in some way, perhaps for example, by barring punitive damages or capping actual damages? Second, is the attack or exploitation covered by the professional's liability insurance? You might expect the answer to be uniformly no to both questions, but that is not the case.

Overt Battery

Does the professional's liability policy cover the claim? In exploitation claims, the *therapist* is often covered by his insurance policy under the theory indicated in the casebook, that he was chargeable with negligent management of "transference." The *physician* can seldom if ever make such an argument and his sexual harassment, attack, or exploitation is perhaps most often seen as a crime and a battery that is by no means the professional activity covered by his liability insurer. *See generally* Christopher Vaeth, Annotation, *Coverage of Professional-liability or-Indemnity Policy For Sexual*

Contact With Patients by Physicians, Surgeons, And Other Healers, 60 A.L.R.5th 239 (1998).

A physician's overt sexual battery (as distinct from a battery based upon manipulation of "consent") will most often fall outside the protection of his liability policy. In *Princeton Ins. Co. v. Chunmuang,* 698 A.2d 9 (N.J. 1997) the court held that a policy's exclusion of coverage for criminal acts defeated coverage when the plaintiff alleged that a physician sexually assaulted her during a gynecological examination. *St. Paul Fire & Marine Ins. Co. v. Engelmann,* 639 N.W.2d 192 (S.D. 2002) involved allegations by gynecological patients that the physician raped them and also had them assume unorthodox positions for the exam. The insurance policy covered professional services, which meant that rape was not covered and the insurer had no obligation to pay for that. "A physician who sexually assaults a patient on the pretense of rendering medical care performs no professional service." It described the minority view as follows: "[A] minority view persists in a few courts. The lead decision in this area is *St. Paul Fire & Marine Ins. Co. v. Asbury,* 720 P.2d 540 (Ariz. Ct. App.1986). There, the court ruled that all tortious acts professionals commit that are intertwined and inseparable from the services provided are covered occurrences." (That included improper sexual manipulation.) Although the *Engelmann* court rejected the minority view and held that rape was not covered by the policy, it thought that improper positions required by the physician could be a bad way of rendering professional services and thus covered. *See also New Mexico Physicians Mutual Liability Co. v. LaMure,* 860 P.2d 734 (N.M. 1993); *but cf. St. Paul Fire & Marine Ins. Co. v. F.H.,* 55 F.3d 1420 (9th Cir. 1995) (no exclusion applied to director of Big Brothers/Big Sisters accused of sexual abuse in the program).

Does a malpractice cap statute cover the claim? The *Hagen* case cited here revisits, in a new context, the issue of what counts as "medical" so as to invoke the special protections offered health care providers. The Virginia Court treats a claimed sexual harassment of a patient as part of the physical examination and hence protected by the special statutory rules for health care professionals. No doubt it was a physical examination. How would the court think rape distinguishable?

The statute of limitations version of malpractice vs. battery arguments. The malpractice-battery distinction becomes important for other reasons besides those mentioned here. In particular, the statute of limitations may treat battery and malpractice to different time limits. In *McCracken v. Walls-Kaufman,* 717 A.2d 346 (D.C. App. 1998) the plaintiff alleged that the defendant chiropractor had indulged in sexual relations with her while she was a patient and that she had been unable to resist because she was on Valium. The battery statute of limitations barred the claim but the negligence statute, if applicable, did not. The court allowed the plaintiff to proceed on a negligence theory if the plaintiff could show that the chiropractor performed psychologist-like functions in their relationship.

Exploitation of the Consenting Patient, Parishioner, or Client

Connections backward: You will probably want to recall the problem, *Payton v. Donner*, in Chapter 4, §2. Discussion of that problem should have put to rest any idea that consent (or by analogy, assumed risk) is a defense where exploitation relies on either duress or abuse of fiduciary or other obligation. *Connections forward*: In many of the cases, the plaintiff complains that the exploitative clergyman's superiors knew or should have known of his conduct and did nothing about it. Those cases raise an added problem for the plaintiff because of the supposed rule that a person need not protect a victim from other persons. *Foreign Mission Board of the Southern Baptist Convention*, 409 S.E.2d 144 (Va. 1991), is such a case.

Clergy sexual exploitation. This nasty little niche is usually under- analyzed and as a result some very broad statements of law have gained currency. Perhaps for the limited coverage here, students need not learn anything about alienation of affections or relational injuries generally. But you might want to draw a clear line between suits by the direct victim of exploitation and, say, suits by the victim's spouse or domestic partner. Most states have abolished claims for alienation of affections or criminal conversation or both. Where that is the case, no spouse of a seduced person has a claim against the seducer, clerical or otherwise because the cause of action has been abolished. But some courts invoke a larger reason in such cases, saying that there is no tort claim for clergy malpractice. On the alienation of affections facts, such statements are correct, but they are unfortunately too general and can be invoked then to deny relief by the direct victim.

The courts rejecting the direct victim's claim against clerical seducers or exploiters have often mentioned the First Amendment's protection of religious freedom. Not everyone will find their explanations intelligible. *F.G. v. MacDonell*, 696 A.2d 697 (N.J. 1997), goes the other way, saying that the claim is for breach of fiduciary duty, not "clergy malpractice." Since "the record supports the inference that MacDonell's alleged misconduct was not an expression of a sincerely held religious belief, but was an egregious violation of the trust and confidence that F.G. reposed in him," the First Amendment did not bar the claim.

The F.G. Court on Consent. "Ordinarily, consenting adults must bear the consequences of their conduct, including sexual conduct. In the sanctuary of the church, however, troubled parishioners should be able to seek pastoral counseling free from the fear that the counselors will sexually abuse them. Our decision does no more than extend to the defenseless the same protection that the dissent would extend to infants and incompetents." Frank battery cases—sexual touching without any pretense that the victim has consented— are easier for the plaintiff since no issue of consent is involved, but even in the sexual battery cases, the church charged with negligent hiring or retention of clergy may try to defend on the ground that liability would violate either the free exercise or the establishment of religion clauses of the First Amendment.

Malicki v. Doe, 814 So.2d 347 (Fla. 2002), rejected that defense in a battery type case.

Lawyers. Students can discuss whether anything like the transference phenomenon can be found in lawyer-client cases. Perhaps the name and theory don't matter; vulnerable clients like those involved in divorce are likely to depend too much on lawyers. Most people, though, probably think that even so, sex between consenting adults is not in and of itself harmful. The therapist and clergy cases might be different on this point. Sex with a lawyer is likely to be just sex (or maybe somewhat less); sex between a member of the clergy and a believer is likely to raise emotional conflicts. Sex between therapist and his patient is dangerous in addition because the patient is by hypothesis already having difficulties. But clients, even vulnerable ones, are not necessarily going to have overwhelming feelings of guilt at having sex with their lawyers, who may be regarded poorly, but not so poorly that sex with a lawyer will cause more anxiety than sex with anyone else.

By anecdote, sexual exploitation by lawyers of their vulnerable clients is a common problem. However, consent of the client is more likely to offer an effective defense in the case of lawyers, whose fiducial obligations tend to be viewed as being more on the financial than the emotional side of the client's interest. See DOBBS ON TORTS § 102, at 239 (2000).

The cases so far are mainly disciplinary cases. California, the state with the most lawyers, has a disciplinary rule, passed in 1992, which makes it a disciplinary offense for a lawyer to (1) require or demand sexual relations with a client; (2) employ coercion, intimidation, or undue influence in entering into sexual relations with a client; or (3) continue representing a client with whom the lawyer has had sexual relations, if that causes the lawyer to perform legal services incompetently. Cal. Rules of Prof. Conduct rule 3-120. A related statute repeats these prohibitions, and reiterates that violations "shall constitute cause for the imposition of discipline of an attorney." CAL. BUS. & PROF. CODE § 6106.9. Section 6106.8(d) of the same title expressly states that disbarment is a potential sanction. The American Bar Association, following the lead of California and some other states, adopted a similar rule in its Model Rules of Professional Conduct, Rule 1.8(j).

CHAPTER 14

FAMILY MEMBERS AND CHARITIES

▶**Changes in the Sixth Edition:** We've updated citations in Notes; otherwise this Chapter is unchanged from the prior edition.

▶**The Concise Edition** makes no revisions in this already-brief Chapter.■

§ 1. FAMILY MEMBERS

Preliminary Note to the Teacher: Family tort issues are important and revealing, but restrained coverage seems advisable, because too much remains to be covered in a basic course and because advanced courses in family law can present a better-rounded picture of the problems, which run far beyond the problems of tort immunity or limited duty and even far beyond tort law. Consequently, the materials in this chapter do not support extended coverage or in-depth discussion.

This section works hard to avoid the contribution issue, but if you covered our simple introduction to contribution in Chapter 6, § 2, it will be feasible to discuss it here. The contribution issue formed a large part of the New York Court's concern in *Holodook* (Note 3 following *Commerce Bank v. Augsburger*, p. 402.). The idea there was that if parents were too readily held liable to their children, then other tortfeasors who jointly caused the child's injury, would seek contribution from the parent. This would, indirectly, retrieve from the family coffers money that had been paid in for the child's injury. To avoid this, the court took a narrow view that parents should seldom be liable to the child so that parents could also avoid liability for contribution to other tortfeasors who injured the child. Connecticut took a similar view in *Crotta v. Home Depot, Inc.*, 732 A.2d 767 (Conn. 1999).

The issue, and *Holodook's* resolution, is a wonderful topic for discussion if you wish to take the time for it. Why, for example, does "negligent supervision" correspond to the cases in which contribution by a joint tortfeasor against the parent is undesirable? Why not abolish all parental liability and prevent contribution in all cases? Or why not call on the family, which is treated as a unit for some purposes, to provide its own insurance for intrafamily injuries? The contribution rule which prevents contribution from one who is not liable to the injured party is developed in Chapter 25.

The broad social issues that can be considered as a part of family living and family law, including issues about effective discrimination against women and children and others are likewise left to the courses in family law in spite of their importance and intrinsic interest.

Some related materials. Some related cases are included in other chapters. In particular the problem of sexual abuse of children in the schools is touched in *Marquay v. Eno,* 662 A.2d 272 (N.H. 1995), in Chapter 18. The duty of police or other public agencies to protect women and children from violent family members and others is touched upon in several places, including Chapters 15, 16, and 18. Among cases of this kind in the casebook are: *Deshaney v. Winnebago County Dept. of Social Services,* 489 U.S. 189 (1989); *Florence v. Goldberg,* 375 N.E.2d 763 (N.Y. 1978); *Kircher v. City of Jamestown,* 543 N.E.2d 443 (N.Y. 1989); and *Navarro v. Block,* 72 F.3d 712 (9th Cir. 1995). As to consortium claims, including cohabitants as family members, see chapter 19. You might also wish to consult Chapter 20 on duties to unborn children, and the much later section on alienation of affections, in Chapter 32. Genetic damage issues occur at several points in the casebook, e.g., in wrongful birth and wrongful pregnancy cases, see Chapter 20, § 2, and in connection with the *Feres* rule against governmental liability to service persons, see Chapter 15.

A. THE TRADITIONAL FAMILY IMMUNITIES

This note attempts to push the student as quickly as possible through the traditional immunities, the basic exceptions, the rationales for the immunities and the current authority rejecting the immunities. After that we can consider how to state the duty imposed. A hypothetical on this note, even on the basic immunity rule, may be in order so you can be sure the class understands that immunity really is immunity. The most important part of the note might be the material on the rationale for the immunities. That is an especially apt topic for class discussion. However, if the class understands the basic rules and exceptions, the best place for discussion of the policy arguments for and against immunity may be later, after the class has considered the problem of imposing liability in particular cases.

Rationale. The rationales can be developed in more detail. The two given in the casebook treat the two immunities more or less alike, but historically they are separate and some of the reasons might also be different. As to the interspousal immunity, Professor Tobias finds that courts have given at least five different reasons, expressing concerns over (1) marital harmony, (2) fraud and collusion, (3) the need to defer to the legislature, (4) excessive and frivolous claims, and (5) the availability of alternative remedies. Carl Tobias, *Interspousal Tort Immunity in America,* 23 GA. L. REV. 359, 441 (1989).

In *Wagner by Griffith v. Smith*, 340 N.W.2d 255 (Iowa 1983) the court listed these reasons against parental liability:

(1) the danger of a parent later inheriting from the child for the parent's own negligence; (2) the drain on family funds; (3) the analogy to interspousal immunity; (4) the immunity of domestic government; (5) the danger of fraud; (6) the disruption of domestic tranquility; and (7) the need for parental discipline and control.

Rejection of spousal immunities. As the casebook note indicates, most states have abolished spousal immunities for motor vehicle cases if nothing else and most states have now done the same for the parent child immunities. Many, however, retain immunity, or some form of limited duty when injury is not caused by a motor vehicle. No casebook cases are provided on spousal immunity. For a few cases, *see* DOBBS ON TORTS § 279 (2000).

Jennifer Wriggins, *Domestic Violence Torts*, 75 S.CAL. L. REV. 121 (2001), cited here, notes that domestic violence is widespread and serious but that there are relatively few suits. One reason, she thinks, is that the abuser has inadequate funds or they would be too difficult to reach. This leaves domestic violence underdeterred. To remedy that, she proposes that mandatory additional insurance against domestic violence be included in automobile insurance policies. The insurer who pays would have a right to recover back from the tortfeasor. Professor Wriggens addresses some of the arguments that might be raised against this proposal and adds that the victim should also be permitted to sue both after and before divorce. For teachers less concerned about logical rationales and more about practical social effects, this is a great topic for discussion. It implicates some of the issues raised below, too.

Sharing insurance funds. Even without Professor Wriggens' new form of insurance, the victimized domestic partner who recovers is likely to recover from an insurance fund. The wrongdoer is likely to share at least indirectly if not directly in this recovery if the relationship continues. In the case of marital partners in community property states, this has represented a formal problem since, initially, each spouse shares in the other's income. It has not in fact proved to be an insuperable difficulty to deal with the formal problem. The personal injury recovery by, say, a wife, can be held to be her own separate property, and certainly the pain and suffering portion can be treated in this way. But this only resolves the purely formal problem. If the wife recovers $100,000 from the husband's insurer is it really possible to imagine that the husband will derive no benefit? What will the wife do with the funds? Will she make no purchases in which the husband will share enjoyment? One problem with this, justice and accountability aside, is that it charges the insurance funds, created by premiums of many persons, with very high costs. Would it be better to say that the marital community should use health and accident insurance and to forego claims based on liability insurance? None of this applies, however, if the victim and abuser have permanently separated or divorced.

Intimate areas of family life. There are "intimate areas" in marriage or other domestic relationships in which courts may be reluctant to intervene. Though these do not involve issues of child-rearing or discipline involved in the "parental discretion" cases, they do involve areas in which the parties should have freedom to develop their own style of living together. Courts in abolishing the spousal immunity have thus spoken of "mutual concessions implied in the marital relationship," *Lewis v. Lewis*, 351 N.E.2d 526 (Mass. 1976), and the "subtle ebb and flow of married life," *Merenoff v. Merenoff*, 388 A.2d 951 (N.J. 1978).

Courts have not hit upon any firm formula, but it seems clear that not all conduct tortious between strangers can be considered tortious between family members if we are to preserve a wide range of freedom for spontaneity and idiosyncrasy in the domestic partnership. This kind of freedom would presumably have its greatest effect in nonphysical claims, such as those for intentional infliction of mental distress, invasion of privacy or slander. But even in an intimate area, one spouse or partner may go too far, as where an estranged husband engages in invasion of privacy by covert electronic eavesdropping. *Burgess v. Burgess*, 447 So. 2d 220 (Fla. 1984).

Divorce or property settlement. Should formerly-married people be permitted to sue one another after a final divorce for torts committed during marriage? Or would the allocation of entitlements at divorce be expected to take marital torts into account? *McCulloh v. Drake*, 24 P.3d 1162 (Wyo. 2001), holds that the wife's claim for emotional distress inflicted during marriage must be pursued as a separate tort suit, not as part of the divorce action. The court said that *res judicata* would not apply, but did not seem to address issue preclusion or collateral estoppel. A different view holds that the tort claim should be presented in the divorce action to avoid the possibility that the defendant's fault would be taken into account twice. *Twyman v. Twyman*, 855 S.W.2d 619 (Tex. 1993). In *Christians v. Christians*, 637 N.W.2d 377 (S.D. 2001), the court permitted the wife to assert a tort claim for emotional distress in the divorce action itself, but only for conduct that was not the basis for divorce and perhaps only for conduct that occurred after a basis for divorce existed). There is a brief discussion in DOBBS ON TORTS § 281 (2000), and Professor Wriggins, echoing some others, takes a strong position against a forced joinder of the divorce petition and the tort claim.

Injury from breach of duty owed to larger class. Schenck is a good illustration of the idea. Another is *Grivas v. Grivas*, 496 N.Y.S.2d 757 (App. Div. 1985), where a mother mowing the lawn with a power mower left her 2 and one-half-year old child near the running mower as she went in to answer the telephone. The child approached the mower and was injured in the revolving blades. Suit against the mother was upheld in spite of New York's rule that negligent supervision of children is not actionable. It was said that although the mother could not be liable for negligent supervision, she could be liable for negligent operation of the lawnmower, since in leaving the mower, she breached a duty to *all* children who might be nearby, not merely to her own child. "With respect to the operator's duty of care, the family relationship between the infant plaintiff and defendant was purely incidental."

GOLLER V. WHITE , 122 N.W.2d 193 (Wis. 1963)
COMMERCE BANK V. AUGSBURGER , 680 N.E.2d 822 (Ill. App. Ct. 1997)

Is the policy purpose behind the *Goller* exceptions clear and defensible? Many acts of "parental discretion" may simply not be negligent at all, but some surely are. Think of the obvious negligence of the person who fails to take a seriously injured child to the hospital. Wouldn't the Wisconsin decision protect perfectly horrifying acts of some parents? *Commerce Bank v. Augsburger* surely answers that question, for Illinois applies the same kind of discretionary immunity to protect alleged acts that would be hard not to characterize as cruel and abusive at best. Are there reasons to permit such treatment of children?

One argument is that parents should have freedom to raise children in their own way and under cultural norms that vary considerably from one group to another. Supporters of this view would not necessarily wish to see parents behave as the defendants are alleged to have behaved in *Augsburger*. They might simply view some abuse as inseparable from freedom and consider that freedom of parents to rear children in their own (often misguided) way may be better in the long run than to have the children reared by juries. Whatever one thinks of the idea, it can at least be understood in a general way from the *Goller* language. Would it be better to recognize that while parents have a privilege to discipline, they are not free to take unreasonable risks with their children?

As with the spousal immunity, courts often began abolishing immunities by abolishing the immunity only for the narrow facts before the court. So a heterogeneous group of exceptions arose: the immunity does not bar claims for intentional tort cases, for motor vehicle cases, for cases involving injury inflicted in the course of a business, for sexual abuse of a child. *See, e.g., Squeglia v. Squeglia,* 661 A.2d 1007 (Conn. 1995) (listing exceptions; immunity retained to reject strict parental liability for injuries inflicted by father's dog); *Henderson v. Woolley,* 644 A.2d 1303 (Conn. 1994) (parental immunity does not bar child's claim for sexual abuse); *Courtney v. Courtney,* 413 S.E.2d 418 (W.Va. 1991) (intentional tort cases); *Shoemake v. Fogel, Ltd.,* 826 S.W.2d 933 (Tex. 1992) (motor vehicle cases); *Newman v. Cole,* 872 So.2d 138 (Ala. 2003) (when clear and convincing evidence shows a parent's willful and intentional injury caused a child's death).

Courts may then go on to reject the immunity under some formula or another for cases generally. *See* DOBBS ON TORTS § 280 (2000).

Its not necessarily a foregone conclusion that the immunity has disappeared. In *Lee v. Mowett Sales Co., Inc.,* 342 S.E.2d 882 (N.C. 1986), the legislature had abolished immunity as to motor vehicles; but the court thought that this limited abolition implied that the immunity was retained in all other cases. Maryland, noting that eight states retained the full parent-child immunity without even permitting an exception for motor vehicle cases, reaffirmed its own complete immunity in *Warren v. Warren*, 650 A.2d 252 (Md. 1994). "Family life and values have not significantly changed since we last addressed this issue in 1990, and we believe that it is still in the best interest of both children and parents to retain parent-child immunity. Abrogating the immunity would result only in further discord within the family and would interfere with the exercise of parental discretion in raising and disciplining children. We are not willing to open the door to rebellious children and frustrated parents and allow the courts to become the arbitrator of parent-child disputes and the overseer of parental decisions." The Maryland Court also refused to open the door to motor vehicle injury claims between parents and children, although by its count 43 American jurisdictions had done so. On the other hand, unlike the *Goller* court, the *Warren* court refused to apply the immunity to a step-parent.

Note 3. Negligent supervision cases. The negligent supervision formula represents an effort to avoid parental liability that would in effect reduce family resources that would otherwise be available for the child. If the child recovers from D but D recovers it all back from the parent, the child's claim will be largely illusory. So the New York courts think anyway, and the idea is closely related to those cases elsewhere that refuse to enforce indemnity agreements against parents when a child is injured. You can refer the class to such cases as *Cooper v. Aspen Skiing Co.*, 48 P.3d 1229 (Colo. 2002) (parental indemnity provisions in releases violate public policy to protect minors and create unacceptable conflicts of interest between parent and child), cited in Chapter 10.

The negligent supervision formula may or may not be coincident with the fear for family resources that sponsors the formula in the first place. It sounds as if it would retain the immunity for failure to supervise or protect, but might impose liability for affirmative negligence such as that involved in operating a motor vehicle. If so, the rule seems to become a variation on and limited application of nonfeasance rules covered in Chapter 16. In a Massachusetts case, *Brown v. Brown*, 409 N.E.2d 717 (Mass. 1980), a wife fell on premises that she and her husband owned together, but alleged that it was the husband's responsibility to provide for sanding and salting the icy areas where she fell. This was held actionable. Would a child have an action in New York if the father had negligently left a marble on the floor and the child was injured? Presumably "supervision" has no part in spousal relations as long as both are competent.

In *Wagner by Griffith v. Smith*, 340 N.W.2d 255 (Iowa 1983), immunity barred recovery where a parent allowed his 4-year-old child near a grain auger, with horrible results. The court had abolished the general immunity but resurrected much of it by installing New York's "supervision" rule. (The court said it adopted *Goller*, but it also said it followed *Holodook*, apparently regarding *Holodook* as an instance of *Goller* rather than as a separate and more demanding test.) But in *Caniglia v. Lary*, 366 N.W.2d 548 (Iowa 1985), a four-year-old child allegedly suffocated as a result of his father's negligent grain-loading operations. The same court that denied recovery in the grain auger case thought this claim would be actionable. One possible difference may be that the court thought the negligence in the first case was inaction, a failure to supervise, but thought that the defendant was actively negligent in the second. Another explanation of the different results in the two cases may be that in the second case there were more detailed allegations. These might have shown that the alleged negligence was outside the parent-child relationship, somewhat along the lines discussed above in connection with *Grivas.*

Could negligent supervision immunity apply to a third party injured by the child? The court in *Buono v. Scalia*, 843 A.2d 1120 (N.J. 2003) said yes. In that case, a minor pedestrian sued a minor bicyclist for negligence, and the bicyclist's parent for negligent supervision. The court held that because the parent's determination that the child could ride a bike without supervision within the confines of a neighborhood block party was a valid exercise of parental authority. Thus, the court reasoned, the parent was immune even from a suit by a third party alleging negligent supervision. Is this really a case of no negligence as a matter of law rather than an immunity case?

HOPPE V. HOPPE, 724 N.Y.S.2d 65 (App. Div. 2001)

A child is injured not in the course of "regular parental supervision," but after having been entrusted with a hammer and a nail gun cartridge. This was not a case of negligent supervision, said the court, but just a case of plain negligence – a duty derived not from one's duties as a parent, but rather from one's duties to the world at large.

Note 1. Applications. *The casebook hypothetical.* The hypothetical and question in this note is meant to emphasize that these brief materials have suggested three different formulations of the retained immunity. *Goller* retains the immunity for exercise of "parental authority," and for discretion in provision of food, shelter and the like. Parental authority sounds like a smaller category than New York's "supervision" category. New York, in contrast, would seem clearly to include this near-drowning case within its concept of supervision, although Hoppe may provide an argument for the contrary position. The facts of this hypo are similar to those in *Shoemake v. Fogel, Ltd.*, 826 S.W.2d 933 (Tex. 1992), where Texas, following a "supervision" rule similar to New York's, held that the immunity protected the parent from a child's suit and hence from a contribution claim by other tortfeasors. (Discretion and supervision are elastic terms and they are meant to be. *Hoffmeyer v. Hoffmeyer*, 869 S.W.2d 667 (Tex. Ct. App. 1994) held that a father who showed his son how to shoot at a target in the father's workshop, then left a gun in plain view, was not liable for the death of his son when the son's friend accidentally shot him, on the ground that this was all discretionary. This case involves none of the concern over contribution actions.) The negligence formulation in *Broadbent, Gibson* and *Anderson* (Note 2 following *Goller* and *Augsburger*) seems the broadest of all, but in application may be a good deal like *Goller*. If the parent is negligent in leaving the child in the pool, immunity would presumably not protect him under this rule.

Note 2. Foster parents, step-parents, and those standing *in loco parentis*. Full-time caretakers who act in the role of parents are usually held to stand in loco parentis and get the parental immunity, whatever it is. Some courts have denied loco parentis status to foster parents who take children under a contract with the state. *See* Annotation, *Foster parent's right to immunity from foster child's negligence claims*, 55 A.L.R.4th 778 (1987). On the other hand, Illinois has extended the loco parentis status and hence the parental immunity to foster parents and even to school teachers. *Palmer v. Mt. Vernon Township High School Dist. 201*, 662 N.E.2d 1260 (Ill. 1996).

§ 2. CHARITIES

This section consists entirely of text, with no cases or case abstracts. It is fair to assign it without spending class time on it, but if you are emphasizing your particular state's law, you might want to bring in some local materials. Most states do have some peculiarity, which is glossed over in a general summary like this text. The topic is covered, along with a state by state analysis in Annot., 25 A.L.R.2d 29 (1952) and supplementing material. The best arguments against the immunity in any form are in Note, *The Quality of Mercy: 'Charitable Torts' and Their Continuing Immunity*, 100 HARV. L. REV. 1382 (1987).

The "next predictable step" after judicial liberalization is legislative reaction. We saw it with the recreational use statutes and the medical malpractice statutes. In both instances, potential defendants with a sufficiently cohesive group to form a lobby were able to get the legislature to take a more conservative line than the courts.

You can consider charitable immunity as a kind of subsidy for charities but one that is not paid by public funds in which we all share as taxpayers; rather, the subsidy is paid by the victims of negligence. In this respect the charitable immunity can be criticized on the same grounds given in some of the cases holding tort reform caps to be unconstitutional. "It is simply unfair and unreasonable," said the New Hampshire Court in a medical malpractice caps case, "to impose the burden of supporting the medical care industry solely upon those persons who are most severely injured. . . ." *Carson v. Maurer*, 424 A.2d 845 (N.H. 1980). To eliminate the tort claim of the charity's putative beneficiary is to compel that beneficiary to subsidize the charity. To cap the liability of the charity, as some states do, is likewise to compel a donation, in the same way the San Francisco citizen was compelled to donate his property in *Surroco v. Geary. See also* Note, 100 HARV. L. REV. at 1388.

When the charitable immunity is limited to "beneficiaries" of the charity and those beneficiaries accept the benefits of the charity's work knowing that they are owed no duty of reasonable care, you can justify the rule on the ground that the beneficiary-victim is free to refuse the benefits if he does not wish to accept the risk of losses. In this situation, the charitable immunity is a kind of platform on which assumed risk is built.

But, first, many "beneficiaries" will have no idea that they are either beneficiaries or that they are legally disfavored, so they could not knowingly assume any risks. In *Rupp v. Brookdale Baptist Church*, 577 A.2d 188 (N.J. Super. 1990), a small child attended a summer day camp operated by the Brookdale Baptist Church, with the usual crafts, games, and swimming. There was no scheduled religious study. The child was held to be a beneficiary of the charity, since that status does not "depend upon a showing that the claimant personally received a benefit from the works of charity;" he is rather a beneficiary if the defendant was engaged in charitable "objectives." The ultimate goal of the church was to promote its religious views, not teach crafts or swimming, hence it was engaged in "charitable" works. And "the fact that plaintiffs did not send William to camp for religious training and that they claim that they were unaware of the camp's religious goals is irrelevant."

Second, in at least some cases, the beneficiary-victim of charity would have little choice; he would be in the position of the plaintiff in *Tunkl*, (Chapter 10), required to waive his ordinary legal rights in order to obtain medical care or some other necessity. If the hospital in *Tunkl* could not legally compel the patient to assume risks of medical negligence as a condition of health care, it is at least strange that courts and legislatures are willing to compel "beneficiaries" of a charity to forgo their ordinary rights.

Individuals engaged in charitable activities. Title 42 U.S.C.A. § 14501 et seq., cited in text in the final paragraph, presents an argumentative set of "findings", then creates an immunity for volunteers to nonprofit and governmental entities for ordinary negligence. Immunities for individuals, as distinct from charitable trusts or corporations, is a new thing, but this federal statute is not the only one; states have enacted others. *E.g.,* COLO. REV. STATS. § 13-21-116; 76 OKLA.STAT. ANN. § 31. (Distinguish statutes that immunize or indemnify directors.)

The federal statute is criticized in Andrew F. Popper, *A One-Term Tort Reform Tale: Victimizing the Vulnerable,* 35 HARV. J. LEGIS. 123 (1998) on the ground that it take the right of reasonable care away from the most vulnerable groups such as disaster victims, school students, day care children, patients in hospice care and others who are served by volunteers. Professor Popper envisions that the statute will protect professionals like doctors and lawyers who volunteer services to the poor.

The federal statute leaves the volunteer liable under state law for criminal, grossly negligent or reckless misconduct. (§ 4(a)(3).) The volunteer also remains potentially liable under state law provisions for harms caused by operation of motor vehicles for which a license or insurance is required. (§

4(a)(4).) As to noneconomic damages, the statute in effect rules out joint and several liability and requires the trier to fix the volunteer's percentage of negligence. (§ 5(b).) The volunteer is then liable only for that percentage of noneconomic harm. Punitive damages are not to be awarded against the volunteer except for wilful or criminal misconduct or the like (§ 4(e)(1)), but that is not much of a restriction since fairly serious misconduct is required to impose liability in the first place. State law is preempted to the extent inconsistent with this act, but the states are permitted to enact even broader immunities. (§ 3 (a).) States are also permitted to elect that the act shall not apply, provided they cite this act specifically and the statute contains no other provisions. (§ 3(b).)

In one case, the individual charity volunteer received a judicially created immunity. *Moore v. Warren,* 463 S.E.2d 459 (Va. 1995) involved a defendant who was a volunteer for the Red Cross. He was driving Mary A. Moore to a medical facility. Allegedly as a result of his negligent driving, a collision occurred, causing injury to the beneficiary-passenger, who later died. The court held that charities were still immune in Virginia and that their immunity should be extended to those who carried out their work, including volunteers like the defendant. Otherwise, it said, the charity's work would be "adversely impacted" in unspecified ways.

Although this seems to be a new immunity, it does not extend to all charitable activities of individuals. On the contrary, it applies only when the individual is an agent or servant of a charity that enjoys immunity and acting for it at the time he causes injury. In *Mooring v. Virginia Wesleyan College,* 514 S.E.2d 619 (Va. 1999), the individual was a professor supervising his recreation and leisure studies students, who in turn were working with children at a Girls' Club. The professor shut the door to keep younger students out, allegedly causing the traumatic amputation of the plaintiff's thumb in the process. But the court thought he was not doing the charity's work and hence could not enjoy the immunity. In *Bhatia v. Mehak, Inc.,* 551 S.E.2d 358 (Va. 2001), the Virginia court went on to say that a donor of services and goods to a religious charity (a catering company, for a religious ceremony involving hot tea) would not share the charitable immunity because the donor shared the immunity only when he was acting "directly" for the charity. In this case, he was not acting directly when he spilled hot tea on children but was acting instead for the donor corporation.

Donors to charities. A Federal model act, the Good Samaritan Food Donation Act, 42 U.S.C.A. § 12672, provides protection for those who donate food to charities. That sounds like a kind of secondary charitable immunity, although a qualified one. A number of states have adopted similar acts. That act, complete with an elaborate set of definitions, provides in essence that

A person . . . shall not be subject to civil or criminal liability arising from the nature, age, packaging, or condition of apparently wholesome food . .

. [donated] in good faith to a nonprofit organization for ultimate distribution to needy individuals. . . .

At least on a charitable reading of the statute, it describes a case of no negligence to begin with. You donate a can of apparently wholesome food or grocery product. You are in good faith. That doesn't sound much like negligence, so at first blush, the statute seems to do nothing. (It prescribes liability for gross negligence and intentional misconduct, but again at first blush, you wonder how anyone donating apparently wholesome food and acting in good faith could be grossly negligent or guilty of intentional misconduct.) Reading at this charitable level, the statute, and its state counterparts appear to do nothing at all, and perhaps were enacted out of a gross misunderstanding about the reasonable prudent person standard of liability for negligence.

At a more cynical level of reading, and one that might be in line with the canons of construction, the statute looks like a dirty trick. First, the statute would accomplish protection for someone if "apparently wholesome" meant something totally bizarre. And it turns out, it does. That phrase is defined so that groceries and food are apparently wholesome if they meet regulatory standards, even if they are unmarketable for some reason. They may even be unmarketable because of "freshness". Freshness is a manipulative word here; only wines, whiskies, and cheeses that should be aged are unmarketable because of "freshness." The statute really means that the goods are unmarketable because they *lack* freshness.

Given this disingenuous definition of "apparently wholesome" you can see how a donor could be negligent: he knows he donates a food that is not fresh and hence that might cause harm to the consumer. Yet, because the food meets regulatory standards for labeling and the like, the donor would be protected. Read this way, the statute does indeed do something, although perhaps not something that consumers or charities should want.

There is one other effect. "Person" is defined to include corporations, so it would seem that a corporation that has manufactured an excess of foods or grocery products that are no longer marketable because of "freshness," might donate the goods to a charity. At a guess, you might expect the corporation to take tax deduction for the donation even though the product is not marketable. Under products liability rules, strict liability might apply to impose liability. This statute at least eliminates any strict liability.

CHAPTER 15

GOVERNMENTAL ENTITIES
AND OFFICERS

▶**Changes in the Sixth Edition.** We have added two new primary cases in § 2 on the FTCA, *Olson* (on the basic scope of the FTCA and its underlying theory) and *Whisnant* (on the discretionary function immunity). To make room for additions and to streamline coverage where possible, we have turned one primary case, *Loge*, into a shorter case abstract, and have cut one primary case, *Maas*. (*Whisnant* and Notes stand in for both.) In § 3 on state-law immunities, we have cut the *Thompson* case and three case abstracts, *Zelig, Barillari*, and *Pletan*, covering all of that material in shorter Notes. Sections 4 and 5 have some revisions in Note materials but are otherwise unchanged. This chapter contains over two dozen new case cites in Notes to keep the material fully updated.

▶The **Concise Edition** cuts about 25 percent of this Chapter's length, primarily by cutting three cases or case abstracts: *Brooks* (§ 2B); *Vaughn v. Ruoff* and its first three Notes (§ 4); and *Navarro v. Block* and its Notes (§ 5). We've also dropped the *Picklesimer* problem, and we've trimmed some still-existing Notes.■

Preliminary Note: The Special Importance of Governmental Liability. If you are deciding whether to cover this section or if you are not familiar with liability-of-government cases, you may wish to glance at this note. The issue of governmental liability in tort is an important one for a number of distinct reasons.

The citizen-government conflict. A moderate legislative view of the conflict presented when citizen sues government for injuries caused by the government is expressed in a Wyoming statute:

The Wyoming legislature recognizes the inherently unfair and inequitable results which occur in the strict application of the doctrine of

452

governmental immunity . . . . It is further recognized that the state and its political subdivisions as trustees of public revenues are constituted to serve the inhabitants of the state of Wyoming and furnish certain services not available through private parties and, in the case of the state, state revenues may only be expended upon legislative appropriation. This act is adopted by the legislature to balance the respective equities between persons injured by governmental actions and the taxpayers of the state of Wyoming whose revenues are utilized by governmental entities on behalf of those taxpayers.

WYO. STATS. § 1-39-102

Understanding tort issues. The issue of governmental liability raises and makes accessible to most students issues about the purposes and accomplishments that can be expected from tort law. Can we deter governmental torts by damages suits? Would regulation be better? How do we assess issues of justice when governmental policy is involved? Do courts consciously or unconsciously treat government as an insurer, liable not for reasons or justice, but only as a very good risk spreader? Or do they treat government as the banker for the public who should not be held liable except for unusually strong reasons? These and other similar issues come up repeatedly in governmental liability cases, and all these issues have importance not only in governmental cases, but in tort law as a whole.

Political structure. Liability of government also raises issues of political concern. On the one hand, courts were not instituted to operate the executive and legislative branches of government, and they should not do so through tort litigation any more than they should do so through injunctions. On the other hand, as one court said, "[t]he more power bureaucrats exercise over our lives, the more we need some sort of ultimate responsibility to lie for their most outrageous conduct." *Grimm v. Arizona Bd. of Pardons and Paroles*, 564 P.2d 1227 (Ariz. 1977). The political balance between citizen and government and among the branches of government is of considerable significance in a free society, and it is very much implicated in governmental tort liability issues.

Practical importance. Finally, on the purely practical side, tort litigation against government has increased considerably. This should be no surprise. Government itself has increased in size. In the 1920s governmental activity accounted, for the first time, for up to 10% of the gross national product; by the 1960s, it accounted for 30%. *See* Clarkson & Muris, Introduction to Symposium, *Civil Liability of Government Officials*, 42 L. & CONTEMP. PROBS. 1 (1978). Governmental power has brought a capacity for harm that once did not exist. And governmental tort liability suits have become big business. And citizens might be injured not only by our own government but also by actions of the United Nations or other governments, which may equally enjoy immunities. See *St. John v. United States*, 240 F.3d 671(8th Cir. 2001) (United States officers acting as part of U.N. Peacekeeping force in Haiti).

Any one of these reasons might call for an extensive treatment of the materials introduced in this section. The regret should be, not that these materials are longer than those in some casebooks, but that they are not long enough. The problem, as always in an introductory course, is to provide a balanced coverage of the system as a whole, and this requires a limit even in the most important segments.

Big Issues: Finding and Achieving Policy Goals. Policy goals in traditional governmental liability cases have been negative: avoid interference with government's ability to govern properly. Should we posit the ordinary goals of tort law in government-defendant cases? Should tort law aim at deterrence in some cases, or getting the right amount of safety? At compensation?

A Word on Torts of Foreign Governments, Agencies, and Individuals in Foreign Countries

With the United Nations, foreign states, and certain officers of foreign states, immunity is the rule, but exceptions are dramatic. Chapter 3 of this manual summarized a kind of civil rights rule in a successful suit against Radovan Karadzic in *Kadic v. Radovan Karadzic,* 70 F.3d 232 (2nd Cir. 1995) (Croats and Muslim plaintiffs claiming that Karadzic was liable under international law for some of the genocide, rape, and other tortures inflicted by the Serbs in Bosnia). Terrorist sponsoring states may also be subject to liability in the United States for terrorist torts abroad, with a potential for enforcement against their frozen bank accounts in the United States. Their agencies may be subject to punitive damages as well. See *Wagner v. Islamic Republic of Iran,* 172 F.Supp.2d 128 (D.D.C. 2001) (American citizen stationed in U.S. embassy in Beirut killed in suicide bombing sponsored by Iran, applying a kind of "federal common law" of damages for wrongful death). In the chapter on nonfeasance we'll see in *A. v. United Kingdom,* 27 E.H.R.R. 611 (1999) that the European Court of Human Rights might hold member states liable for such failure to protect children from abusive parents. There may be some limited liability left in the Alien Tort Statute, 28 U.S.C. § 1350, which gives federal trial courts jurisdiction over "all causes where an alien sues for a tort only in violation of the law of nations or a treaty of the United States. But as we noted in Chapter 3, Casebook 73, the Supreme Court's opinion in *Sosa v. Alvarez-Machain,* 124 S.Ct. 2739 (2004) held that in a case of a Mexican national kidnapped in Mexico on the orders of U.S. officials, then brought to the U.S., no norm of international law was violated and no federal cause of action was stated under the ATS. This reversed a much more liberal reading of the ATS, finding the government liable, by the Ninth Circuit. *Alvarez-Machain v. United States,* 266 F.3d 1045 (9th Cir. 2001). A similar case of the federal Good Neighbor Policy but involving allegedly illegal searches in Canada, is *Nurse v. United States,* 226 F.3d 996 (9th Cir. 2000).

Scheduling omissions: Although government liability is a fundamental topic in today's world, many teachers may feel that time limits dictate the briefest possible coverage. For a bare minimum coverage consider assigning sections 1 and 2A & 2C, and lecturing on the absolute and qualified immunities of officers (which is covered in § 4) without assigning it to be read.

SUMMARY

§ 1. TRADITIONAL IMMUNITIES

This section is text, stating the traditional sovereign immunity. It also briefly refers to the 11th Amendment immunity. Constitutional limits on taking of property is a practical exception. Municipal immunity is distinguished. In most states the immunity is abrogated, but then partly restored.

§ 2. THE FEDERAL TORT CLAIMS ACT (FTCA)

A. The General Structure of the FTCA
UNITED STATES V. OLSON. The Supreme Court explains the basis of the Act's waiver of sovereign immunity. Notes after the case further explain the abolition of immunity, its partial retention in a number of specific exceptions, in particular the assault and battery exception, and the judicially-created exception for strict liability.

B. The *Feres* Rule
BROOKS V. UNITED STATES. The Supreme Court rejects the government's claim of immunity for injuries it inflicts upon furloughed service personnel.

FERES V. UNITED STATES. The Supreme Court invents an immunity to protect government against liability for negligent injuries to on-duty service personnel, including those burned to death in a barracks fire and those injured by army medical negligence.

C. The Discretionary or Basic Policy Immunity
WHISNANT V. UNITED STATES. The discretionary immunity rules out government liability for discretionary decisions of policy. Plaintiff worked for a company that provided seafood to a commissary on a Navy base, and suffered injury from exposure to toxic mold. He sued the U.S. government for negligence in allowing workers and customers to come into contact with the mold, despite its knowledge of the condition and its hazards. The government defended on grounds of discretionary immunity. The court applies a two-part test (from a Supreme Court case) and determines that the suit is not barred by discretionary immunity because the alleged negligence was in the "implementation, rather than the design" of safety regulations.

LOGE V. UNITED STATES. The government approved use of a certain polio vaccine and the plaintiff was stricken with polio from shed virus after her son's inoculation. She claims here that the government was negligent (1) in not requiring the drug manufacturer to comply with existing governmental regulations, and (2) in failing to prescribe additional safety regulations and in licensing use of the vaccine without them. *Held*, the decision to prescribe added regulations is discretionary and not subject to suit; but the government may be liable for failing to follow its own regulations in testing for safety.

§ 3. IMMUNITIES UNDER STATE LAW

RISS V. CITY OF NEW YORK . Linda Riss, terrorized by a rejected suitor, was not given police protection in spite of her many pleas. The suitor threw acid on her face as she was about to be married to a rival. In this suit against the city for alleged negligent failure of the police to protect Riss, *held*, the city is not liable. [Although New York had abolished immunities much earlier,] the city is not liable because, *semble*, liability here would represent too great an interference with limited public resources.

DE LONG V. COUNTY OF ERIE . Mrs. De Long called the 911 emergency number when someone attempted to break into her home; but due to a peculiar routing of the telephone call and a failure to recheck when the officers could not find the address given, no one went to her aid. Mrs. De Long was found dead from stab wounds. A verdict for the plaintiff is *held*, affirmed. The police in this case did not decide, as in *Riss*, to withhold assistance. The municipalities in this case had decided to provide assistance through the 911 emergency system and the police themselves had attempted to provide assistance. This is a sufficient basis for liability for negligence.

HARRY STOLLER AND CO. V. CITY OF LOWELL. Firefighters negligently failed to use the sprinkler system of a building on fire, fighting the fire with hoses instead. *Held*, this is not protected by the state's discretionary immunity, because although there were choices and in that sense discretion, there was no choice among *policy* judgments.

NOTE: THE PUBLIC DUTY DOCTRINE. If a statute imposes a duty upon a public entity or public officers, it may be construed to impose a "public duty" only, not a duty to individuals. In that case, the entity and officer are immune from tort suits based upon their violation of the duty. Once the entity takes affirmative action, however, its duty may be "narrowed" to focus upon the plaintiff, in which case the immunity as to that plaintiff is lost.

PROBLEM: CLAIMS OF PICKLESIMER, ET AL. This problem, introduced first in the landowners' materials, raises the question whether the governmental entity responsible for highway construction and maintenance could be held liable because of the misleading character of the road. Students can consider the discretionary immunity, public duty, and, if the topic has been identified in the discussion of *Riss*, nonfeasance.

§ 4. OFFICERS

STATE V. SECOND JUDICIAL DISTRICT COURT, COUNTY OF WASHOE. Child protective services employees are sued, and claim an absolute quasi-judicial immunity. Held, the quasi-judicial immunity does not apply to state agencies or employees for the day-to-day management and care of their wards, even if it would apply if the employees had been sued for providing information to the court.

VAUGHN V. RUOFF. A state social services worker coerces a woman into having a sterilization procedure based on a promise that she might regain custody of her children. Shortly after this, the social services agency recommended that the parents' parental rights be terminated. The parents sued, claiming violation of their right to procedural due process. The social services worker claimed the executive-branch qualified immunity. Held, the immunity was not available on the facts because a constitutional right was violated, and the right was clearly established at the time of the deprivation.

NOTE: FEDERAL EXECUTIVE BRANCH OFFICERS. Text explains briefly the liability of federal executive branch officers under both federal and state law, including the impact of the Westfall Act.

§ 5. STATE AND MUNICIPAL LIABILITY UNDER § 1983

Notes sketch the rule that states are not generally liable under § 1983 and that municipalities may be liable if, but only if, they have maintained a "policy" that is unconstitutional.

NAVARRO V. BLOCK . Maria Navarro received credible information that her estranged husband, Raymond, was on his way to kill her. She phoned 911, and also revealed that Raymond was under a restraining order. But the dispatcher would not send help. Fifteen minutes later, Raymond entered and killed Maria and four others, incidentally wounding two more. The suit was brought under § 1983. The court first states the rule that municipalities are not liable for random violence, only for constitutionally defective policies. But a policy may be inferred from consistent practice. If the practice was to classify domestic violence calls as non-emergency calls, then that would be gender-neutral on its face. The plaintiff would be required to show discriminatory intent or motive in order to succeed on this ground. No evidence of intent or motive has been presented. However, the Navarros can still succeed on equal protection grounds if the practice does not classify persons in a way that is rationally related to governmental objectives. So if the domestic violence/non-domestic violence classification is irrational, the Navarros might have a claim. In addition, the Navarros claim the county failed to train dispatchers and that this amounts to "deliberate indifference" to the equal protection rights of abused women. But as no evidence was offered on this point, it can furnish no basis for liability.

COMMENTS

§ 1. TRADITIONAL IMMUNITIES AND THEIR PASSING

The initial note gives a compressed statement of the basic rules of immunity. As to contractors carrying out governmental work, the casebook points out a little later that the immunity does not extend to private contractor doing government work such as contractors operating a prison. See *Richardson v. McKnight,* 521 U.S. 399 (1997). However, when federal law is applicable, it does extend to protect contractors who carry out some specific directive in a governmental contract. *See Boyle v. United Technologies Corp.,* 487 U.S. 500 (1988). *Conner v. Quality Coach, Inc.,* 750 A.2d 823 (Pa. 2000), refused to extend the government's immunity to a contractor supplying goods to the state, although it recognized that a contractor who reasonably relies upon a government specification and who does not participate in design, might not be negligent at all.

Some states retain total immunity except as waived by the purchase and coverage of liability insurance. See *Louk v. Isuzu Motors, Inc.,* 479 S.E.2d 211 (W. Va. 1996). In *Fuqua v. Flowers,* 20 S.W.3d 388 (Ark. 2000), the state had notice that a stop sign had been removed at the intersection of two highways. The plaintiff, not faced with the stop sign that should have been there, drove through the intersection and was struck broadside. Both drivers were seriously injured and the plaintiff, six months pregnant, lost her child. But the Arkansas Constitution forbad suits against the state and that was that. Almost all states have passed statutes retaining a large amount of immunity. They may do so either by specifically providing for immunity by statute and then recognizing exceptions or by abolishing immunity and restoring it piecemeal. Either way, substantial immunities remain and it is not possible to say that government is generally responsible to the people it injures by tortious activity. *See generally* DOBBS ON TORTS §§ 260-78 (2000).

Municipalities: *Source of the immunity.* Municipalities are not agencies of a state but are more or less separate entities, chartered by state legislatures and subject to the laws of the state and rules of the charter but otherwise independent. Their immunity was thus not originally associated with the maxim that the King could do no wrong. It is derived instead from an old case, *Russell v. Men of Devon,* 100 Eng. Rep. 359 (K.B. 1788), where the plaintiff was injured on a bridge and sued the men of the county on the theory that they should have repaired it. There was no actual entity such as a corporation or a city, and no one individual had any responsibility. There was obviously no basis for collecting from a treasury that did not exist and recovery was denied. From this strange beginning, municipal immunity became the American norm.

Taking and nuisance. Municipalities are of course liable for a taking of property without just compensation. Since a private nuisance carried on by a local government—a garbage dump in a densely populated area, for instance—

might be a taking or a close analogy to one, many courts recognize a certain amount of municipal liability for nuisance.

Proprietary functions. Many municipalities have carried on both normal governmental functions–operation of police and fire departments, for example–and "proprietary functions," similar to those that might be carried on by private enterprise. For example, many cities operate their own water works or electrical utilities. Municipalities were immune as to governmental operations, but not as to proprietary functions.

Streets. Where a city was obliged by its ownership or by state law to maintain streets, it could often be held liable for negligent maintenance. This applied only to conditions on the way, such as a hole in the street, and not to activities on the streets, such as negligent driving of a police car.

Riots. A few statutes have made cities liable for injuries inflicted in a riot or "mob" action. This statutory liability is limited and leads to peculiar concerns–what constitutes a mob, whether this requires a large number of persons and whether it depends on their motives.

§ 2. THE FEDERAL TORT CLAIMS ACT

A. The General Structure of the FTCA

UNITED STATES V. OLSON, 546 U.S. 43 (2005)

The basic scope of the FTCA, as the Court explains in the first paragraph of this recent opinion, is that the government waives immunity for torts "under circumstances where the U.S., if a private person, would be liable to the claimant in accordance with the law of the place where the act or omission occurred." Reversing a line of Ninth Circuit cases, the Court says that this statutory provision means that courts must focus on whether there is an analogous private-person liability in the particular state involved. It is not correct for a court to ask whether the state law allows liability of the state government. Nor need the court find that state law allows for private-party liability under the same exact circumstances. Rather, the court can look for analogies, and may do so fairly broadly. Thus in this case, where the plaintiffs claimed that the negligence of federal mine inspectors caused injury to mine workers, the focus should be on whether the law of the state (here, Arizona) in which the injury occurred would provide for the liability of a private person in an analogous situation. Because there are "private persons who conduct safety inspections" as the Government itself concedes, the question is what the Arizona state law says about liability of such private inspectors. The parties disagree over that, so there is a remand for a determination of that issue.

Note 1. Some key conditions of the waiver. This brief note states a number of separate rules about suing the federal government under the FTCA. If the class has not yet developed a high degree of self-reliance in preparation, you might walk them through these points.

There is a procedural trap: the plaintiff must assert the claim against the agency involved and give it a chance to make payment. But the agency can sit on the claim up to six months. If the plaintiff has only 119 days before the statute runs and she has not made the claim to the agency, she may be barred. For other problems in the assertion of the administrative claim see *Murrey v. United States,* 73 F.3d 1448 (7th Cir. 1996); David B. Sweet, Annotation, *Failure to Present Prior Administrative Claim to "Appropriate" Federal Agency* . . ., 111 A.L.R. FED. 659 (1993).

Note 2. Governing law. State, not federal law governs duty, breach, causation and proximate cause. (Federal jurisdictional limits and procedures are determined by federal law.) This could mean, for example, that a person might win a claim in one state but lose in another on the same facts, because the state law is different in the two places (choose your own example from many already covered in the casebook, such as perhaps duties owed to entrants onto land). Consequently, also, the federal government is not liable when its only duty is one created by federal law. *Williams v. United States,* 242 F.3d 169 (4th Cir. 2001), holds that EMTALA, which requires hospital emergency departments to screen patients who come to the hospital and then to treat them if an emergency exists, creates only a federal duty. Since state law had not created such a duty by incorporating EMTALA rules or otherwise, the government was not liable for failing to treat a patient who was in severe respiratory distress and who died shortly thereafter as a result. The court also had some back-up reasons.

Notes 3 & 4. Specific statutory exceptions. Students should know one or two of the specific exceptions and where to find the others. The combatant activity exception is interesting because it shows that Congress thought about the armed services, yet did not create a general exception for claims by on-duty service personnel. That will quickly become important in *Feres.* The assault and battery exception has been read by the courts to mean that if the injury arises out of the *facts* of a battery, the claim is barred, even though the plaintiff's legal *theory* or *claim* is not battery but negligence of the government in hiring a batterer.

Other statutes besides the FTCA can and do create immunities. One such statute provides that "No liability of any kind shall attach to or rest upon the United States for any damage from or by floods or flood waters at any place. . ." 33 U.S.C.A. § 702c. On government negligence in connection with flooding see J. D. Perovich, Annot., *Liability of United States under Federal Tort Claims Act for Damage from Flooding,* 4 A.L.R. Fed. 723 (1970).

Note 5. Judicially-established exceptions. The first judicial exception is that government may not be subjected to strict liability. In so deciding, the Court put aside the statute's direction to treat government like a private person in similar circumstances (§ 2674). The Court emphasized instead a mention–in the jurisdictional section–of "wrongful" acts or omissions.

"Wrongful" was thought not to mean tortious, but something much narrower, and hence it was thought to exclude strict liability. *Laird v. Nelms*, 406 U.S. 797 (1972). This is in accord with the view commonly applied by state courts that public entities are not generally liable strictly for punitive damages. The second exception mentioned here is the *Feres* exception dealt with in the next materials. If you are going to skip *Feres* and Notes, you could mention at this point in class what the core of the *Feres* exception is: The government waiver of immunity does not extent to torts committed against active-duty military personnel who are injured "incident to service." It has been broadly construed to bar a number of kinds of claims, sometimes protecting pretty outrageous conduct by the military.

B. The *Feres* Exception

BROOKS V. UNITED STATES, 337 U.S. 49 (1949).

The Brooks brothers, in the army but on furlough, were injured (one of them killed) by a negligently driven army truck. The mere fact that they were in the army did not prevent suit against the United States based on the other driver's negligence. The accident "had nothing to do with the Brooks' army careers." The statute creates exceptions, but this is not one of them. The two quotations are in reverse of the order found in the full case, but their meaning and significance is unaffected by the reversal. This case is a point of departure and a contrast to the vague reading of the statute in *Feres*.

FERES V. UNITED STATES , 340 U.S. 135 (1950).

If you discuss the facts in *Feres* at all, you might pick one to have in mind as the class discusses the rule. The *Jefferson* facts–a medical malpractice case with a 30-inch towel in the abdomen – is least traumatic and serves to emphasize that the rule covers medical malpractice cases as well as others. *Feres* creates a new immunity not recognized in the statute. It applies when the victims is in the service and injuries are "incident to service."

The reasons given in *Feres* seem shabby at best. *See* DOBBS ON TORTS § 263 (2000). Although they are only sketched briefly in the abstract, class discussion is quite feasible. If you ask an open-ended question (e.g., "Do these reasons hold up on analysis?") students are likely to give different responses. Here is one set:

(1) Private persons do not have armies. Partly true, though not quite as true as you might wish. But the claim is not a claim that the government was negligent in having an army. It was negligent in burning its soldier to death, or in leaving 30-inch towels in the soldier's abdomen. And private persons DO cause fires and practice medicine. Since there is always something unique about government operations, if for no other reason than it is government and private persons are not, there would never be any government liability under the Court's idea of a private person analogue because no truly complete

analogue would ever exist. Maybe the Court itself didn't believe what it was saying. Had it believed in this argument it would have simply dismissed on the ground that liability is authorized only "in the same manner and to the same extent as a private individual under like circumstances." But it did not do that.

(2) Uniform soldier law. The Court erected a dual premise not found in the statute, namely, that there should be one law governing the relation of government to soldier and that, somehow, Congress must have implicitly accepted this premise. Accept that and you accept the result in *Feres* and maybe a good deal else as well. Neither aspect of the dual premise is discoverable in the statute. On the contrary, the express words emphasized in *Brooks* say that Congress authorizes "any claim" not excepted. It knew how to create exceptions, including some relating to military activity, but did not create the *Feres* exception. The inference would seem to be that the Congress did NOT accept the Court's premise at all. Where does the Court itself get this premise? Its argument on this point is not summarized in the casebook, but it says that servicemen, having no choice about location, should not be subjected fortuitously to the law of the state where they are posted. This part of the Court's opinion sounds as if it is being protective of service personnel, but in fact the argument is used to deprive them of any benefit of ANY tort law. It cannot offer them a uniform national law as an alternative.

(3) Workers' compensation analogues. It is true that the government provides in-service benefits to military personnel and also pensions and death benefits. Congress could have substituted these benefits for tort liability. After all, civilian employees of the government are usually governed by the Federal Employees Compensation Act, the federal workers' compensation system. See 5 U.S.C.A. § 8101 *et seq.* They recover workers' compensation, perhaps fairly analogous to in-service, death and pension benefits available to members of the armed forces. Under the exclusive remedy provision commonly found in workers' compensation legislation, civilian employees are not permitted to assert tort claims.[1] But it is quite clear that Congress did not enact any such plan. So again the Court is developing a should-be rule that runs across, not with the grain of the statute.

Another difficulty with the exclusive remedy argument is that it has not been applied to bar all claims for injuries for which non-tort government compensation is available. Even prisoners of the United States, who are entitled to a kind of workers' compensation for injury in prison, can also sue the United States in tort. See *United States v. Muniz,* 374 U.S. 150 (1963). Conversely, those who are entitled to no compensation benefits may be denied recovery. See *Stencel Aero Eng'g Corp. v. United States,* 431 U.S. 666, 672-73 (1977).

In short, *Feres* looks like one of those cases in which the Supreme Court was simply determined to get its own way.

---

1. Title 5 U.S.C.A. § 8116(c) "The liability of the United States. . .. with respect to the injury or death of an employee is exclusive and instead of all other liability of the United States. . . ."

Note 1 makes the point that Feres has been used to bar torts claims over some pretty extreme misbehavior.

Note 2. Extending the rationales. "No private armies" has dropped out of the Court's rationales and "military discipline" has appeared in its place. Notice: (a) Cases shifted to a heavy emphasis on the military's freedom from civilian "interference," even when that interference is by courts enforcing laws. (b) The Court invokes this rationale even when the negligence alleged is not that of the military itself. The *Johnson* reasoning suggests that soldiers are expected to be loyal to their country, and hence not sue when the government victimizes them.

In *Taber v. Maine,* 67 F.3d 1029, 1042 (2d Cir. 1995), Judge Calabresi had something to say about the military discipline rationale as well as some other things to be mentioned later. He pointed out that recovery of damages against the government for military negligence does not tell the military how to run its business. The court does not issue an injunction. It merely holds the government liable for the tort. "Injunctions and regulations tell people what they must do and what they must not do, and it is these types of intrusions that would entangle courts in military affairs. Tort judgments do neither of these things." This is a point that common law courts have appreciated in other contexts. We do not wish to discourage appropriate use of dynamite in constructing buildings and highways, for example, but strict liability for dynamite injuries merely requires a business to pay its way, it does not forbid the business. Consequently, strict liability for blasting injuries is generally accepted. See Judge Fuld's comments in *Spano v. Perini Corp.,* 25 N.Y.2d 11, 302 N.Y.S.2d 527, 250 N.E.2d 31 (1969).

Note 3. Spouses and children. *See* LESTER JAYSON, HANDLING FEDERAL TORT CLAIMS § 5-156; DOBBS ON TORTS § 265 (2000). In *Minns v. United States,* cited here, Judge Niemeyer insisted that liability for injury of children through injury to a service person would interfere with military discipline. The fact that the claim is against an individual for an invasion of a constitutional right (and thus not an FTCA claim) has not tempered the courts' approaches. See *Chappel v. Wallace,* 462 U.S. 296 (1983).

Note 4. "Incident to Service." In general, courts view *Feres* as a fairly mechanical rule covering all on-duty military cases. It is not, in other words, a principle that requires analysis of facts on a case-by-case basis to determine whether a military decision is involved. As envisioned by Justice Scalia in *United States v. Stanley,* 483 U.S. 669, 682-83 (1987), the rationale for *Feres* is the protection of military discipline (as expansively understood by the Court), but instead of analyzing facts to determine whether interference with such discipline is a risk, it is better to exclude all cases in which injury is incident to service. (*Stanley* was a civil rights claim under *Bivens,* but the Court applied the *Feres* rule, anyway, and seemingly without any change).

Yet when courts are not sure whether an injury is incident to service, shouldn't they consider whether a suit will disrupt military discipline? Suppose an active duty service member has the afternoon off. She goes to her home off base, changes clothes, and then goes to a recreation area, which happens to be on the base. She spends the afternoon sunbathing and drinking beer. Then she falls into a hidden and dangerous canal and is washed to her death by 60 mile per hour waters. A wrongful death suit claims the army was negligent in not making the premises safer or giving a warning of the hidden danger. In *Dreier v. United States,* 106 F.3d 844 (9th Cir. 1997), the court tried to resolve the incident to service issue on similar facts. It considered (1) the place of the injury, (2) the duty status of the service member, (3) the non-tort benefits that might be payable, and (4) the nature of the plaintiff's activities. It concluded that the case was close but that *Feres* did not bar the claim. Other courts have also weighed factors, although not necessarily factors expressed in the same way. See *Schoemer v. United States,* 59 F.3d 26 (5th Cir. 1995).

Inevitably use of these or similar factors weighs the danger of interfering with military discipline, the very thing that *Stanley* seemed to condemn because *Stanley* assumed that incident to service was a kind of bright line test. On the other hand, Chief Justice Burger had earlier asserted that there was no bright line test for *Feres*, a statement that perhaps invites courts to consider and weigh various factors. See *United States v. Shearer,* 473 U.S. 52, 57 (1985). In any event, how would you determine the incident to service issue if you cannot consider factors such as the place of injury and its connection with military activity by either the plaintiff or defendant?

Judge Calabresi has come up with a solution to the *Feres* problem that is both elegant and sensible. See *Taber v. Maine,* cited in this Note. The solution pares both the compensation benefits rationale and the military discipline rationale.

First, the rationale that service members have compensation benefits analogous to workers' compensation leads to a bar in some cases but not others, like *Brooks,* where the plaintiffs were on furlough but still had compensation. The rationale makes sense, in spite of this seeming inconsistency, because it would bar the tort claim whenever the plaintiff was within the scope of his employment and so that the tort claim would have been barred by the exclusive remedy provision of workers' compensation statutes in analogous civilian situations. On the other hand, when the plaintiff is injured while not in the scope of employment, he still gets compensation from the armed forces, but this should not be treated like workers' compensation; it should be treated as a fringe benefit that does not bar the claim. Thus with a service member who is at liberty,

> coverage is akin to voluntary employee health and injury benefits that accrue independently of the nature of an employee's injury. As such, they are very different from the type of coverage that is required under workers' compensation schemes. Therefore, as in Brooks and Brown,

this type of voluntary coverage will merely serve as a set-off against any FTCA award; it does not bar an FTCA action.

Second, the military discipline rationale is accepted as a sensible general idea, but one that has little scope in the *Feres* case. Discipline can arise in two settings: (1) when the claim implicates the relationship of the plaintiff and the military and (2) when the claim implicates the relationship of the tortfeasor and the military.

The discipline concern in the first instance is more or less automatically taken care of by the scope of employment or incident to service rule; if the victim is injured by activities that are not incident to the victim's service, there is no military discipline problem with respect to him. Conversely, if he is acting incident to service, there might be a military discipline problem but it is not one that calls for attention, because in that case the plaintiff is barred by the *Feres* rule (as interpreted in the preceding paragraph)—the military compensation scheme is exclusive and no more need be said.

In the second instance, the injurer's relationship with the military is important and that does indeed raise the military discipline issue. However, if the plaintiff was not injured incident to service (or in the scope of employment), he is in the position of a civilian. If a civilian sued the army, the army would not be permitted to raise military discipline as a blanket defense. So when the discipline problem arises with respect to the injurer's relationship to the service, we can see that nothing about that problem requires us to dismiss the claim on military discipline grounds. Thus military discipline is not relevant when the problem is generated by the tortfeasor's relationship to the military, except, perhaps, in very extreme or unusual cases.

Calabresi has provided a rational basis for a modified *Feres* rule without resorting to a list of "factors" to be applied indiscriminately. Whether courts are ready for rationality on this point remains to be seen.

Feres does not bar a claim based upon post-discharge negligence. More on that idea in DOBBS ON TORTS § 264, at 708 (2000).

FYI: Contribution and indemnity. The *Feres* doctrine affects the right to contribution against the government as well as the victim's direct suit. A manufacturer held liable to a service person for injuries from a defective product has no contribution claim against the government who negligently used the product to cause injury, because under *Feres*, the service person himself could not have sued the government. *Stencel Aero Engineering Corp. v. United States*, 431 U.S. 666 (1977).■

C. The Discretionary or Basic Policy Immunity

WHISNANT V. UNITED STATES, 400 F.3d 1177 (9th Cir. 2005).

This case introduces the most important condition on the government's waiver of sovereign immunity: the discretionary function exception. (As with Feres, it's an "exception" to the waiver of the immunity, so it's sometimes called, accurately, the discretionary function "immunity."

Plaintiff worked for a company that provided seafood to a commissary on a Navy base, and suffered injury from exposure to toxic mold. He sued the U.S. government for negligence in allowing workers and customers to come into contact with the mold, despite its knowledge of the condition and its hazards. The government defended on grounds of discretionary immunity. The court applies the two-part test from Gaubert and Berkovitz (both from the U.S. Supreme Court) to determine whether the immunity applies: (1) whether the challenged action was discretionary, that is, whether it "was governed by a mandatory statute, policy, or regulation." If the government has no "discretion" at all, because particular actions are mandated, the immunity does not apply. But if the action was discretionary, the next issue is (2) whether the challenged action "involves a decision susceptible to social, economic or political policy analysis. If so, the government retains an immunity, as the statute says, even if that discretion is abused.

The court looks at earlier precedent on the second issue, and finds a focus on whether the challenged government action involved the design of a course of action (in which case it is discretionary, thus immune) or merely the implementation of a course of action (in which it is not).

Here, applying the test, the court holds that the suit is not barred by discretionary immunity because the alleged negligence was in the "implementation, rather than the design" of safety regulations governing the commissary.

Note 1. Purposes. Essentially, this provision of the FTCA has been held to mean that the federal government cannot be held liable in tort under the FTCA for government conduct if (a) it exercises a discretion vested in the government by law, and (b) that discretion is addressed to policy issues. In other words, for this provision to apply to immunize federal government actions, there must be room for discretion and the discretion must be addressed to issues of policy.

The purpose of this immunity, as *Varig Airlines*, cited here, states it, is to prevent judicial "second guessing" of policy decisions made by one of the other two branches. The core concern, then, is preservation of the separation of powers set out in the U.S. Constitution. That's the answer to the question posed at the end of this Note. Students with a good grounding in political science should figure it out, but some others might need help, especially if they have not yet taken the basic structural con law course.

Note 2. Planning-level versus operational-level decisions. Perhaps the simple rules of thumb are not really rules in this area. Picking up on the brief sketch of purposes in Note 1, this Note allows for a little more development. The term "discretionary immunity" is unconsciously used in several different ways.

(1) *Separation of powers.* The discretionary immunity is perhaps foremost a doctrinal expression of the separation of powers principle, as courts have sometimes said. *E.g., Kaisner v. Kolb*, 543 So.2d 732 (Fla. 1989). In *Nusbaum v. Blue Earth County*, 422 N.W.2d 713 (Minn. 1988), the court said: "The major underpinnings for the discretionary function exception to governmental tort liability rest in the notion that the judicial branch of government should not, through the medium of tort actions, second-guess certain policy-making activities that are legislative or executive in nature. '[J]udicial review of major executive policies for "negligence or wrongfulness" could "disrupt the balanced separation of powers of the three branches of government.'"

(2) *A way of talking about "duty" issues.* However, even if there were no immunity at all, there would be questions about the duty owed by government. Is the duty the same as the duty of individuals, that is, the duty of the reasonable and prudent person under the circumstances? If it is the same, do "circumstances" include the fact that the defendant is, after all, the government? Does the government owe any affirmative duty to take action? These questions suggest that a state might abolish immunity and still have some questions that seem very much like immunity questions. And indeed, discretionary immunity cases, including the public duty doctrine cases, often seem to be cases that could be handled better by a conventional duty analysis. Probably many cases of government non-action would be better decided by talking about the scope of the government's affirmative duties rather than by talking about immunity.

(3) *An obscure way of recognizing that the defendant is not negligent or that no standards of care seem workable.* "Discretionary immunity" often seems to mean something like "no negligence," or that there is no standard by which negligence can be judged. If a court decides that the parole board has discretion in making paroles of dangerous criminals because it must balance the policy of rehabilitation and the crowded conditions of jails against the risk to society, it might really be saying that either choice the board makes is justifiable on a reasonable person standard. Or, similarly, it might be saying that no standards can be established for judging a decision that is essentially judicial in nature. In this kind of case, the court's use of immunity analysis rather than negligence analysis leads to blanket rules, to decisions by judges rather than by juries, and to decisions based on generalized contours of the situation rather than on the actual facts, often on the unproven assumption that the government agency exercised judgment when in fact it may not have considered the safety question at all. On the other hand, in this kind of case (but not in cases mentioned in the two preceding paragraphs), the plaintiff can penetrate the immunity if she can convince the court that a knowable standard of conduct has been breached. Thus the city may be liable if its

firefighters fail to use the sprinkler system of a burning building (*Harry Stoller & Co.*).

Note 3. "Maintenance" as discretionary. Another seemingly easy rule of thumb is that if the alleged negligence is simply failure to maintain property or equipment, that cannot be a policy-driven action, and thus can't be immune. But as noted in *Terbush,* cited here, that is perhaps too simplistic because a decision whether or not to maintain could in fact involve discretion.

Note 4. Funding decisions. Yet another rule of thumb. Where the government's action is dependent on a funding decision, you might think that's always protected under the discretionary immunity. But that too turns out to be too simplistic. Indeed, while many cases do find immunity in decisions whether or not to fund some improvement (or maintenance, as in Note 3), if the government could claim an immunity successfully any time an action "involved fiscal concerns," the government would always be immune, and that can't be the intent of the statute. In *Whisnant,* for example, the fact the government may have made a financial decision not to "carry out its responsibility to maintain safe and healthy premises" did not mean that decision was immune from legal attack. Still, however, the government often makes a winning argument that the plaintiff's suit is essentially challenging the policy decision whether to spend scarce government resources on this or that.

Merando, cited here, is such a case. Plaintiffs sued the government for negligence after their family members were killed when a dead oak tree fell on them in the Delaware Water Gap National Recreation Area in New Jersey. Plaintiffs claimed the negligence was in failing "properly to prune, find, and remove the hazardous tree." The government, however, asserted that the plaintiffs were challenging its formulation of the policy on how to manage hazardous trees. The court agreed with the government and noted that it "had to consider how best to use its limited financial and human resources in a manner that balanced visitor safety with visitor enjoyment and conservation of the Park." The government's decisions on how to conduct inspections for dead trees rested on "practical considerations [such] as staffing and funding." At bottom, the government here had to determine "how to distribute its finite resources to locate and remove hazardous trees. . . . [K]nowing it could not inspect every tree in the Park, the Park Service decided to expend the bulk of its resources on high-visitor use areas," as opposed to the area in which the plaintiff's loved ones were killed. This was a decision that "this court should not second-guess."

The court in *Baum v. United States,* 986 F.2d 716 (4th Cir. 1993), held that building defective bridges out of substandard material is a discretionary decision because it requires an allocation of resources. ("The question of what materials to use in such a project is also fundamentally described as a question of how to allocate limited resources among competing needs.

Considered in this light, . . . the Park Service's decision in this regard plainly was one bound up in economic and political policy considerations").

Is there something that does *not* involve an allocation of resources? Maybe. In *O'Toole v. United States,* 295 F.3d 1029 (9th Cir. 2002), the government agency allocated its limited funds to its various needs, but not to maintenance of the irrigation system on land it controlled for the benefit of the Shoshone tribe. The result of no maintenance was that waters backup onto neighboring lands owned by the plaintiffs and allegedly caused harm in excess of $300,000. The court held that the decision to withhold funds from maintenance was not a policy decision. "We hold that an agency's decision to forgo, for fiscal reasons, the routine maintenance of its property– maintenance that would be expected of any other landowner– is not the kind of policy decision that the discretionary function exception protects." The court went on to say that the discretionary function exception could "swallow the FTCA" especially "where the government takes on the role of a private landowner." "Every slip and fall, every failure to warn, every inspection and maintenance decision can be couched in terms of policy choices based on allocation of limited resources. As we have noted before in the discretionary function exception context, "[b]udgetary constraints underlie virtually all governmental activity.'"

Note 5. Where the government makes no conscious decision. In accord with the implication of *Gaubert: Shansky v. United States,* 164 F.3d 688 (1st Cir. 1999) ("The subjective intent of government officials is irrelevant to the discretionary function analysis. It is therefore of no practical consequence that Park Service officials fail to mull particular safety issues when they planned the Trading Post's rehabilitation"). As to conscious choice in state immunity cases, see the notes following *Harry Stoller & Co.,* § 3, below.

LOGE V. UNITED STATES , 662 F.2d 1268 (8th Cir. 1981)

Federal cases on discretionary immunity are sometimes irrational as well as inconsistent. A seminar or class devoted to governmental liability would explore that irrationality. That's not a good project for a first-year class with a great deal of other material to cover. But one simple idea presented in *Loge* is that the judicial branch cannot in effect pass laws or regulations, but it can enforce the standards provided in those regulations.

Failure to comply with regulations. Although the Congress and to some extent the executive may have discretion about what laws to pass or to leave unpassed, there is no discretion to ignore the laws that do exist. The agency is bound by the regulations it itself promulgated, just as any other citizen is bound by their terms if they apply. When the agency failed to follow the Code of Federal Regulations as to testing of the vaccine, it was not exercising discretion because it had no discretion to ignore the law. If the failure to follow the regulation was also negligent (see the next paragraph) then the government could be held liable. In any event, as to this, there was no immunity.

Discretion and negligence issues distinguished. Although the language of "discretionary immunity" may often represent an inappropriate way of saying the government was not negligent, there is a vast theoretical and sometimes a vast practical difference between saying "no discretion" and "no negligence." In *Loge*, the claim is that the agency violated regulations. This shows there was no discretion, but it does not necessarily show that there was negligence. Suppose, for example, that the regulations were not safety regulations, or that if they were, they were intended to protect against some other risk, or to protect some other class of persons. The class should realize that the lawyer will have to go forward from here and prove negligence.

Note 1. Immunity for legislative inaction. You can use *Loge* mainly to reinforce the core idea that the judicial branch should not interfere with the operations of the other branches, and that indeed it would violate our notions of separation of powers to permit judges to control legislation and administration through tort actions. Many courts have made such observations.

Failure to regulate. One claim in *Loge* is that the government was negligent in failing to regulate the drug. (Failing to regulate can include a failure to impose appropriate conditions on a license.) But failure to promulgate appropriate regulations would be a discretionary function and therefore conduct that is immune. Q: Could courts hold that the Congress commits a tort for which the government is liable if it passes a dangerous statute or fails to pass a safety statute? A: Certainly that would do violence to separation of powers; Congress, not the courts, is constitutionally authorized to pass or reject statutes. Q: Would the same reasoning apply to dissuade a court from imposing liability for an administrative agency's passage or failure to pass regulation? A: Yes.

Note 2. Violation of regulations. To be discretionary, a government decision must be one the government is free to make. A regulation that merely states a general objective or expresses a policy that could be carried out in various ways, does not necessarily eliminate the role of discretion. Heinrich v. Sweet, 308 F.3d 48 (1st Cir. 2002). On the other hand, if statutes or regulations mandate a decision one way or the other, the government has no discretion– hence the discretionary immunity cannot protect the government when it violates regulations. E.g., *Miles v. Naval Aviation Museum Found., Inc.,* 289 F.3d 715 (11th Cir. 2002). But this does not establish a cause of action; it only eliminates the immunity. The cause of action is established (or not) by state law. State law can say that violation of either state or federal regulations is negligence per se (or at least evidence of negligence).

As we know, a violation of safety regulations is normally negligence per se. That rule applies under the FTCA when the government actor violates a state statute. *See* Annotation, *Violation of State or Municipal Law or Regulation as*

Affecting Liability under Federal Tort Claims Act, 78 A.L.R.2d 888 (1961). But our case is different: state law governs, but the regulations are those of the federal government. This is a good opportunity to remind the class that the FTCA calls for application of state law, not federal. (Federal tort law, apart from statute, is at best sporadic.) Would states ever hold that it is a violation of *state* law for a citizen to violate a *federal* regulation? It happens. See, e.g., *Coker v. Wal-Mart Stores, Inc.*, 642 So.2d 774 (Fla. Dist. Ct. App. 1994) (violation of federal statute against selling ammunition to minors is negligence per se).

If state law would *not* give such a special effect to a federal regulation, then violation of the regulation in *Loge* would not be negligence per se, since state law is the only governing tort law in an FTCA case. If state law *would* give effect to the federal regulation as negligence per se against a private citizen, can it also give this effect against the federal government? The states could not create a tort rule holding the federal government liable against its wishes, but the effect here is given by the FTCA itself in adopting state law.

Note 3. A case example. In *Navarette*, cited here, the court said that the Army Corps of Engineers' written safety plan comprised an assumption of specific duties that the government could not then violate. Thus the requirements in this plan, albeit one voluntary drafted, became mandatory. "The Safety Plan's instruction that 'dangerous terrain conditions, such as drop-offs, etc, will be properly marked or fenced' is sufficiently specific and mandatory to create clear duties incumbent upon governmental actors." While the government had discretion to decide what conditions were "dangerous," it did not have discretion not to mark off or fence such conditions once that determination was made. Thus the government's acts in failing to mark off or fence the hazard was not immunized by the discretionary function exception.

§ 3. IMMUNITIES UNDER STATE LAW

State law, by judicial decision or by statute, recognizes a discretionary immunity similar to that established by the FTCA. Quite a number of states have enacted language identical or substantially similar to the language of the federal discretionary immunity. E.g., CAL. GOVT. CODE § 8655; GA CODE § 50-21-24; HAWAII REV. STAT. ANN. § 662-15; IOWA CODE ANN. § 669.14; MINN. STATS. ANN. § 3.736, Subd. 3 (a) & (b); 12 VT. STATS. ANN. § 5601. In spite of the general similarity, some states analyze their discretionary immunity under tests that differ from the test we saw in the FTCA cases. Instead of the two-part test of choice and policy judgment, some states accord the immunity only to planning as distinct from operational decisions; some require a substantial policy component or judgment, and some may require a conscious policy decision. *Trujillo v. Utah Dep't of Transp.*, 986 P.2d 752 (Utah Ct. App. 1999), for example, reflects Utah's requirement that a "high degree of discretion" must be involved in planning decisions.

In addition to the general discretionary immunity, state statutes are likely to contain many highly specific provisions protecting particular governmental actions. As one instance among many, KAN. STAT. ANN. § 75-6104 (l) specifically forbids liability for "snow or ice conditions or other temporary or natural conditions on any public way or other public place due to weather conditions". We will see some particular provisions of the California statutes in the *Thompson* case. For the present, the focus is on the general discretionary immunity. Where a statute does not adopt the discretionary immunity terminology, the immunity might go under other names. It might be called, with the Restatement, an immunity for "fundamental governmental policy" or basic policy immunity. See RESTATEMENT SECOND OF TORTS § 895B.

Courts may accomplish the same or added protection for governmental entities by invoking the "public duty" rule, which states that governmental entities are not liable for the breach of duties owed to the public generally, but only for breach of duties owed to an identified class of citizens. That rule is often a form of the nonfeasance rules developed in Chapter 16.

Still another possibility is that the state courts will limit the duty owed by a governmental entity, independent of any public duty rule. For example, if a parole board releases a violent criminal, the court might dispense with talk of immunity or public duty and simply ask whether the parole board owed a duty to citizens to provide warning or supervision. Finally, some courts might analyze what they consider to be relevant policies, and produce a result in the case consistent with their policy beliefs, but fail to establish any rule structure at all. You might think that *Riss* is such a case.

RISS V. CITY OF NEW YORK, 240 N.E.2d 860 (N.Y. 1968).

Riss applies the usually accepted rule that governmental entities are not liable for failure to provide police protection. Although Judge Breitel does not use the discretionary immunity terminology, something like discretionary immunity may be at least a part of the principle behind the police rule. Many courts are likely to invoke the public duty doctrine in police failure cases. Judge Breitel did not use that term, either, although later New York cases have referred the public duty doctrine in police nonaction cases. E.g., *Cuffy v. City of New York,* 505 N.E.2d 937 (N.Y. 1987). If you can manage, it is useful to take up *Riss* and materials that follow it all on one day as a kind of unit to be appreciated in gross before the pieces are examined.

Riss is famous and it has captured the interest of a great many students and lawyers. Linda Riss later married the aggressive Mr. Pugach; you might say their marriage met the acid test (except that lye is an alkali). The natural drama and its talk-show ending in marriage aside, the case is troubling. On the one hand it exemplifies the supposed general rule that governmental entities are not liable for failure to provide police protection, and it is a rule that has its appeals. On the other hand Charles Breitel, who has been called a "judge's judge" and a sophisticated observer, wrote an opinion that leaves many students in doubt both as to its technical and its policy bases. All this makes for good classroom fun and, with luck, some enlightenment. *See* MARSHALL SHAPO, THE DUTY TO ACT 99 (1977) (discussing *Riss* and Judge Breitel's opinion.

The policy basis for the decision seems to be deeply grounded in the belief that the judiciary should not be in the business of allocating resources of the executive department of government. It is a fear that rests, like the discretionary immunity in its most justified sense, on the separation of powers. Judges were not created to appropriate funds, nor to carry on the work of police departments. Yet "ordinary tort law" applied to governments does impose liabilities and does allocate public funds. It is inescapable if there is to be any governmental liability. Recognizing this, Judge Breitel attempts to distinguish good tort cases from bad tort cases. He begins by saying that when government activity has displaced private enterprise, that activity is a good one for tort liability. In the same category, for reasons not given, are "certain activities of government" such as the maintenance of highways and public buildings. If these are negligently maintained, Judge Breitel has no qualms about tort liability because, he says, there is "ground for liability [in] the provision of the services or facilities . . . ." But these two categories are different, for him, from the "provision of a governmental service to protect the public generally." That he is concerned over judicial allocation of public resources through tort suits is clear; why he believes that this is any less involved or any more predictable in the cases of public operation of hospitals is a very murky matter.

One element that looms suggestively in this misty opinion is the duty issue. As we will see in Chapter 16, courts traditionally refuse to impose duties to take affirmative actions; one is free to do nothing without liability, even if reasonable persons would have acted (to rescue, for example.) And, as we will see in Chapter 18, courts have often been reluctant to impose duties to protect the plaintiff from third persons. These two rules about one's duty apply to private citizens and are in no way grounded in immunity theory. They might explain the attitude that Judge Breitel conveys here, although he himself never clearly alludes to them. The next case, *De Long*, might be interpreted as a half step toward an analysis based more or less explicitly on the nonfeasance idea. See the comments to that case.

The facts in *Riss* are amazingly sketchy. We could never be sure on these facts whether the police department was negligent or not. We do not even know whether it made a policy decision or not. One of the difficulties with the habit of going to an immunity theory in these cases is that it seems to give us permission to avoid all the facts and to indulge a quantum leap to a conclusion that we would never reach if the facts were developed.

We might imagine that the police in this case made a decision that their resources were too limited to protect Linda Riss; or that the risk was small; or that there was really very little they could do to guarantee her safety. Such decisions might have been made as a part of a general policy, or they might have been made because of the pressure of some other specific commitment –a demanding murder investigation or illness of officers in the force, for example. In any of these cases we would probably be content with a conclusion that said there was simply no negligence. Cf. *Hamilton v. City of Omaha*, 498 N.W.2d 555 (Neb. 1993) (court concluded that the plaintiff simply had failed to allege negligence when she alleged a failure to protect). Perhaps many would be equally content with a conclusion that said the police decisions were policy or discretionary function decisions and protected for those reasons. But we do not know that any conscious decision was made at all. If the desk sergeant merely lost the information, so that no person responsible for making decisions ever made one, are you willing to say that it is a case of no negligence, or that it was a case of policy judgment? This question raises, in the state-law context, the question posed in Note 5 following *Whisnant* – whether the government can claim discretionary immunity when it made no conscious decision at all.

One trouble with Judge Breitel's opinion is that he never recognizes the alternative non-policy scenarios. Contrast what we'd get if the court started with a negligence analysis. We'd certainly hear a good deal of testimony about why the police department chose not to provide protection, and we'd be able to weigh whether there was policy judgment or not. The *De Long* case, coming up, gives us New York dealing with a full development of the facts, which show, in that case, a mechanical error, not a policy judgment.

DE LONG V. COUNTY OF ERIE , 457 N.E.2d 717 (N.Y. 1983)

This later decision by the New York Court of Appeals obviously connects back to *Riss*. It is not alone in allowing a plaintiff to proceed when the failure to provide police assistance was the result of mechanical error rather than policy judgment. *See Hutcherson v. City of Phoenix*, 961 P.2d 449 (Ariz. 1998) (city's adoption of 911 emergency system was an undertaking that created a duty to use reasonable care); *Ma v. City and County of San Francisco*, 95 Cal.App.4th 488, 115 Cal.Rptr.2d 544 (2002)(911 system); *Bratton v. Welp*, 145 Wash.2d 572, 39 P.3d 959 (2002) (911 call, dispatcher gave assurances that police would come); *Chambers-Castanes v. King County*, 669 P.2d 451(Wash. 1983); *Enright v. Board of Sch. Dir. of City of Milwaukee*, 346 N.W.2d 771 (Wis. 1984) (phone call to school about a suspicious character hanging around was never passed on to the principal, and consequently the man strangled a second grade boy with a wire; state law provides a remedy); cf. *Torres v. State*, 894 P.2d 386 (N.M. 1995) (police investigatory failures).

An allocation of public resources. Part of the language in *DeLong* suggests that the decision to operate an emergency service is the relevant allocation of public resources, and that once the decision had been made, the police were obliged to carry out that decision without negligence. See also *Ma v. City and County of San Francisco*, 95 Cal.App.4th 488, 115 Cal.Rptr.2d 544 (2002) (reasonable care in operation of 911 emergency system required notwithstanding budget concern because public entity already has system in place and is already devoted to good training). *DeLong* offers a very wide ground for liability. It seems wide enough to admit Linda Riss herself into the company of satisfied plaintiffs if in her case the police failure was the result of a clerical mistake rather than a conscious policy decision.

A special relationship established. But the *De Long* court also gives a much narrower reason for liability by saying that a special relationship had been established between the city and the victim, and by saying that her plea for assistance was accepted, not refused. This seems to suggest that the county would not be liable for any negligent management of the 911 system, but only negligent management of a particular call. For example, suppose the county negligently trained those who took the calls, and the result was that a number of 911 calls went unanswered. Or suppose that the county negligently disconnected a whole segment of the county calls by a simple mechanical mistake, so that a dozen victims never reached the police at all. The court's first comment would permit liability, but the second–the one emphasizing relationship with the particular caller–would seem to leave liability excluded under *Riss*. *Riss* could be explained as a public duty doctrine case, and *De Long* as a case where the duty has been "narrowed" by events to focus on the particular plaintiff.

FYI: You may want to know that from the uncertainties of *DeLong* and *Riss*, New York has since developed a quite restrictive doctrine. It has said that the duty to protect is owed when a special relationship exists, but a special relationship exists only when four elements are shown: "(1) an assumption by the municipality, through promises or actions, of an affirmative duty to act on behalf of the party who was injured; (2) knowledge on the part of the municipality's agents that inaction could lead to harm; (3) some form of direct contact between the municipality's agents and the injured party; and (4) that party's justifiable reliance on the municipality's affirmative undertaking." *Cuffy v. City of New York,* 505 N.E.2d 937 (N.Y. 1987). *Cuffy* has been accepted by a number of courts. We'll see the reliance and direct contact requirements in later New York decisions taken up in Chapter 17. You need not develop them here unless you wish to, as they will arise directly in the later materials. ∎

Question for the class. Do you think the important difference between *De Long* and *Riss* lies in the fact that (1) there was a special relationship because the defendants instituted the 911 system? (2) there was a special relationship because the defendants assured the particular caller that help would come and thus induced reliance? (3) the defendants took some affirmative action and did not merely refuse? (4) the defendants made no policy decision about public resources but simply committed an error?

See Jay M. Zitter, Annotation, *Liability for Failure of Police Response to Emergency Call,* 39 A.L.R. 4th 691 (1985); Carol J. Miller, Annotation, *Government Tort Liability for Failure to Provide Police Protection to Specifically Threatened Crime Victim,* 46 A.L.R.4th 948 (1986).

Note 5. See discussion above. To what extent is the deployment of police is always a decision involving "allocation of resources?" Such a conclusion might well immunize all decisions not to deploy. The *Zelig* case cited here is certainly quite protective of government actions (or lack thereof) on that ground, as is *Barillari*, also cited. Does this go too far? If you discussed this allocation idea in the FTCA materials, you can raise it again here.

HARRY STOLLER & CO. V. CITY OF LOWELL, 587 N.E.2d 780 (Mass. 1992)

Plaintiff owned five brick buildings which were destroyed by fire. Firefighters chose not to use a sprinkler system in one of the buildings, in violation of accepted practice, choosing to use hoses instead. The court says the city was not immune since the "negligent conduct that caused the fire to engulf all the plaintiff's building was not founded on planning or policy considerations."

Justice Wilkins' opinion is very different from Judge Breitel's opinion in *Riss*, more detailed in its concerns and in the lines it draws. No doubt it benefitted from the fact that the court below had allowed the plaintiff to develop the facts in a trial, so that the court is working with the realities of negligence and harm and not with the abstraction of discretion. As different as Justice Wilkins' opinion is, it is not contrary to *Riss*. Active negligence is a different case.

Justice Wilkins alludes to a medical case. That gives you a chance to help the class recognize that if professional standards are clear, the professional should have no discretion to act negligently, in violation of the standards. That is what proof showed happened in *Harry Stoller & Co.* Cf. *Gordon v. City of Henderson,* 766 S.W.2d 784 (Tenn. 1989) (in the absence of factual development that might show otherwise, firefighters had no discretion to be absence from their station or intoxicated while on duty). Medical or scientific negligence would be in the same category. In professional service departments of government, professional standards and regulations might coincide. Cf. *Haselhorst v. State*, 240 Neb. 891, 485 N.W.2d 180 (1992) (state placed sexually abusive older child in a foster home where he abused four younger children; the state did not reveal the foster's child's history and did not handle reports of abuse with proper care).

Note 1. Although the basic policy immunity or the discretionary immunity would be most appealing if it protected against liability for conscious decisions of policy, most courts have usually attributed such decision-making to officials without actually requiring any proof on the point. However, some have said that to plead the discretionary or policy immunity, the state must show a conscious exercise of discretion, or a conscious balancing of risks and advantages. See DOBBS ON TORTS § 270, at 721-22 (2000).

Police and fire department failures to act. Chapter 16 is devoted to "nonfeasance." At this point, though, we can notice that many of the discretionary or basic policy immunity problems arise when non-action is a prominent element in the case. See the Note on the public duty doctrine, coming up. Thus if immunity has been abolished, the city is liable for a police officer's negligent driving.

Note 2. *Where the government function is to provide safety.* Arguably this is a separate class of cases and one in which the discretionary immunity should play little or no part. The cases cited do not state any such broad rule, but all are consistent with it and could be read as pointing to a guideline of this sort. However, other cases can be marshaled against the proposed guideline. For instance, in *Jones v. Mississippi Dep't of Transp.*, 744 So.2d 256 (Miss. 1999), the court held that whether to place traffic controls at an intersection was discretionary. (But even so, the government might be under a non-discretionary duty to warn of dangers known to it). Contrast this with *Graber v. City of Ankeny*, 656 N.W.2d 157 (Iowa 2003), which held that the city did not have discretionary immunity in a negligence suit alleging a failure to set the timing of traffic signal properly. The city's judgment in setting the timing was based solely on generic safety concerns, rather than policy-based ones.

The court in *Abdulwali v. Washington Metro. Area Transit Auth.*, 315 F.3d 302 (D.C. Cir. 2003), held that the city transit authority was immune from a suit alleging that bulkhead signs on trains do not adequately warn passengers of the dangers of moving between cars while the train is in motion, because sign specifications are within the scope of the discretionary function.

L.W. v. McComb Separate Mun. Sch. Dist., cited here at the end, concluded that although the school's supervision of students was discretionary to begin with, a statutory obligation to hold pupils to strict account was a ministerial dictate that "trumps the discretionary exceptions," or, we might think, removes the discretion. The duty of schools to protect students is taken up with other duties of protection in Chapter 18.

Note 3 just gives some examples of the state-law immunity variants on the "discretionary immunity" conceptions we saw in the FTCA materials earlier.

Note 4. *Defects in government property.* Many statutes specifically allow a government to be sued when it fails to maintain state property, as the citations here underscore. What about a suit that alleges not a failure to maintain a traffic light, but rather the failure to install one? In *Kohl*, cited here, the City was held immune on discretionary function grounds. The decision not to install a traffic signal was based on a policy decision to utilize a computer program that evaluated criteria and prioritized intersections with respect to their need for signals. The intersection at issue was not prioritized highly by the computer. Thus this was not an "operational" decision, but rather a "fundamental planning" decision.

Note 5. *High-speed chases.* In the high-speed police chase cases, we have affirmative conduct that is alleged to have been negligent. No issue of special relationship, promise, direct contact, or reliance is involved. You might think that the only question would be whether, considering the social usefulness of catching criminals, the speed was unreasonably risky, and hence only an ordinary negligence question to be resolved the ordinary way, and indeed this may be a case of an ordinary negligence analysis taken over by judges and disguised as a question of "official immunity." Some of the cases do in fact simply perform a negligence analysis. In *Sergent v. City of Charleston*, 549 S.E.2d 311 (W.Va. 2001), the court found the police chase could not be negligent or reckless in light of the dangerous felon pursued and the relatively low speeds and risks of the pursuit. In *City of Jackson v. Brister*, 838 So.2d 274 (Miss. 2003), the estate of an innocent bystander killed in a high-speed chase sued the city for the officers' negligence. The court found no immunity because the police acted in reckless disregard of the safety of others, and violated a written departmental policy in pursuing the way they did. What if the fleeing suspect (or his estate or heirs) sues? In City of Winder v. McDonald, 583 S.E.2d 879 (Ga. 2003), the court said that officers could be liable for "reckless disregard of safety," but only to innocent victims. Thus the parents of a suspect killed could not sue the officers involved.

There are a fair number of high-speed chase cases on the books. High speed chases generate a great deal of concern. Some of them are inane and would be deeply funny except for their ending. When a dozen officers join on many roads on a high-noon high speed chase of a traffic violator, a blanket immunity seems cumbersome at best and unjust at worst. Why have courts become more worried about over-deterrence than about deterrence?

Data: Geoffrey P. Alpert, Andrew C. Clarke, & William C. Smith, *The Constitutional Implications of High-Speed Police Pursuits under a Substantive Due Process Analysis: Homeward Through the Haze,* 27 U. MEM. L. REV. 599 (1997), reports some data on police pursuits. They show a high percentage of injuries. They also report efforts to do cost-benefit analysis on the data

California. In California, officers enjoy a blanket, statutory immunity in operating emergency vehicles and in pursuit of an actual or suspected law violator. See *Colvin v. City of Gardena*, 11 Cal. App. 4th 1270, 15 Cal. Rptr. 2d 234 (1992). Another statute specifically confers immunity upon municipalities when they adopt a policy or guidelines governing high speed chases. Although the immunity applies to protect the municipality even when the individual officer does not follow the guidelines, the policy must be specific in detailing what is and is not permitted, according to one California court. If it is not sufficiently detailed, the immunity fails. *Payne v. City of Perris*, 12 Cal. App. 4th 1738, 16 Cal. Rptr. 2d 143 (1993); *Colvin v. City of Gardena, supra.*

Immunity for affirmative misconduct. Although immunity is sometimes applied in negligent police chases, which certainly count as affirmative conduct, in many of the cases the immunity only protects non-action as it did in *Riss*. Even when immunity is invoked to protect police action in negligent pursuit cases, you might sometimes suspect that the immunity is really a surrogate for a negligence analysis or for a kind of deference to executive decision-making when negligence is hard to judge because of the emergency.

Particular statutes may accord immunity to affirmative acts of negligence in specific situations, or at least raise an argument for it. In *Smith v. Burdette,* 566 S.E.2d 614 (W.Va. 2002) an officer responding to a call ran a stop light and in so doing collided with the plaintiff's van. The trial court dismissed without a trial to determine whether he was negligent because the statute immunized from liability for injury resulting from "the method of providing police protection." West Virginia seems to have regarded this as an instance of the planning-operational level discretion, immunizing policy decisions such as the decision about the number of police cruisers and even the policy of permitting police to run red lights; but the statute did not immunize negligence in carrying out that policy. Whether the officer was negligent in light of the circumstances remains an issue on retrial. Students should remember that liability is far from certain even though the immunity is inapplicable.

Connections back: Civil rights claims in high speed chases were rejected in *County of Sacramento v. Lewis,* abstracted in Chapter 3, § 5.

Note 6. *Releasing persons from custody.* Is a public entity immune from liability for its failure to protect a citizen from a prisoner over whom the state has control? This is really part of a different problem – whether an actor is under a duty to protect the plaintiff from another person. This second problem is broader because it is not limited to public entities. The duty to protect from third persons is the subject of Chapter 18. If you are covering that chapter, you'll probably want to just note the immunity points in this Note and move right on.

Grimm v. Arizona Board of Pardons, cited in this note, imposed liability upon a parole board for gross negligence. The effect of using a gross negligence standard is probably to incorporate a wide range for discretion and judgment without automatically barring all recoveries. In that case, the killer was paroled in spite of psychiatric reports showing that he could not control his violent actions and should not be free. Compare *Faile v. South Carolina Dept. of Juvenile Justice,* 350 S.C. 315, 566 S.E.2d 536 (2002), a suit against a probation officer for placing a violent juvenile with his own parents without notifying the court that he had moved the juvenile from a group home. The juvenile then attacked the plaintiff. The court held there would be no discretionary immunity if the officer acted with gross negligence, and that the state had a duty of care because of its special relationship with the juvenile.

The courts have been more disposed to favor the plaintiff when the state has him in custody and fails to take adequate care of him. Ironically, the state owes an unquestioned duty to the violent criminal in prison, but, under many case holdings, none to the innocent citizens he intends to victimize. As with all these cases, non-action is an important element in the courts' decisions. The custody rule will arise again in connection with the *DeShaney* case, Chapter 16.

Should a duty to warn about the impending release of a parolee be limited to those specifically in danger? *Palsgraf,* though it narrowed liability, envisioned liability to the extent that the plaintiff was in the class of persons at risk. This was not an artificial category of persons; it was all who might foreseeably be injured and whose injury might have been avoided by reasonable care. The same is true with the negligence per se cases –the statute violation is negligence per se not merely to named persons but to whole classes of people. Why is *Thompson*, cited at the end of this Note, so limited?

Some courts have rejected the identifiable victim rule and others have spoken of an identifiable class of persons, presumably a standard much less stringent than the *Thompson* rule. A recent Alabama decision rejects the identified victim requirement as a rule of law except for parole board members making discretionary type parole decisions. *Ryan v. Hayes*, 831 So.2d 21 (Ala. 2002). See also DOBBS ON TORTS § 272, at 731-32 (2000).

New Jersey, in *J.S. v. R.T.H.*, 714 A.2d 924 (N.J. 1998), suggested a moderate rule: "In some cases where the nature of the risk or the extent of harm is difficult to ascertain, foreseeability may require that the defendant have a 'special reason to know' that a 'particular plaintiff' or 'identifiable class of plaintiffs' would likely suffer a 'particular type' of injury." In that case, the court held that a wife who knew her husband was a child molester might be subjected to a duty to take reasonable steps to protect an identifiable class of children. In this case, the concerns about imposing any duty at all that would set one spouse against the other might well warrant a "particularized foreseeability" test of this kind.

The Supreme Court in *Martinez v. California*, 444 U.S. 277 (1980), may have lent a little support to the identifiable victim rule. In the course of ruling that negligent parole was too remote to count as a cause of the death of the parolee's victim, the Court observed that "the parole board was not aware that appellants' decedent, as distinguished from the public at large, faced any special danger." Apparently the Court treated this fact as one bearing on remoteness of the injury rather than duty or immunity.

The duty of a therapist who discovers that his patient is dangerous to others is dealt with in *Tarasoff*, covered in Chapter 18. This duty is usually limited to an identifiable victim—or, more flexibly, an identifiable class of victims. E.g., *Fraser v. United States*, 674 A.2d 811 (Conn. 1996). *Tarasoff* statutes may impose the same limitation. See N.H. STAT. ANN. § 329:31 (duty imposed "when the client has communicated to such physician a serious threat of physical violence against a clearly identified or reasonably identifiable victim or victims").

NOTE: THE PUBLIC DUTY DOCTRINE

A few decisions have been skeptical about the public duty doctrine. See DOBBS ON TORTS § 271, at 725-26 n.23 (2000). Louisiana has never adopted the doctrine as distinct from the discretionary immunity. See *Hardy v. Bowie*, 744 So.2d 606 (La. 1999). In *Williams v. City of Tuscumbia*, 426 So. 2d 824 (Ala. 1983), the plaintiff's house burned down when the fire department failed to respond. The engine driver was out with illness and had not been replaced. The court held the plaintiff stated a cause of action. Rejecting the defense that the duty to fight fires is owed only to the public and not to individuals, the court said: "Does this mean that the whole town has to be on fire before the fire department responds to a call?"

Some cases apply the doctrine only to law enforcement activities or even more narrowly to "police" who fail to protect individuals. See *Beaudrie v. Henderson,* 631 N.W.2d 308 (Mich. 2001); *Lovelace v. City of Shelby,* 526 S.E.2d 652 (N.C. 2000). For a few, the doctrine only triggers analysis of several factors, including the state's actual knowledge of danger, reliance by the victim, and whether the statute is aimed at protecting a particular class of persons. See *E.P. v. Riley,* 604 N.W.2d 7 (S.D. 1999).

In the failure-to-arrest-after-a-stop situation, a little authority, contrary to *Ezell,* cited in ¶1, imposes liability for failure to arrest after a stop has been made. See *Irwin v. Town of Ware,* 392 Mass. 745, 467 N.E. 2d 1292 (Mass. 1984).

Defendants increasingly argue a public duty doctrine defense, even when the public entity or officer has affirmatively created dangers or attempted to deal with a danger and managed it negligently.

Some states work on the problem of public entity liability for violation of a statute in slightly different ways. Although California somewhat obliquely applies a public or general duty doctrine, see *Williams v. State,* 664 P.2d 137 (Cal. 1983), a number of California cases approach the problem by asking whether the statute imposed a mandatory duty and to immunize the entity if it does not (and also if the mandatory duty was created to protect against a different risk). See *Haggis v. City of Los Angeles,* 993 P.2d 983 (Cal. 2000). The statute may invite officers to exercise discretion and if so, it is not mandatory.

¶¶ 5-6. Perhaps it is fair to say that to a very large extent the discretionary immunity and the public duty doctrine lead to the same conclusion in most cases, for discretion seems to disappear when a special relationship or affirmative action and reliance are shown. Thus in *Nearing v. Weaver,* 670 P.2d 137 (Or. 1983), where officers knowingly failed to enforce an injunctive order aimed at preventing a husband from attacking a wife, the wife was held to state a claim against the officer. There was no "discretionary immunity." A public duty analysis would presumably say that the court order narrowed the duty so that it protected particular individuals. See also *Sorichetti v. City of New York,* 482 N.E.2d 70 (N.Y. 1985); *Bartunek v. State,* 666 N.W.2d 435 (Neb. 2003) (public duty doctrine bars claim where there was no special relationship between plaintiff and state); *Alabama Dept. of Corrections v. Thompson,* 855 So.2d 1016 (Ala. 2003) (same); *Muthukumarana v. Montgomery County,* 805 A.2d 372 (Md. 2002) (public duty doctrine protects 911 operators, stressing that the operator does not form a special relationship with the victim merely by undertaking to send help).

PROBLEM: CLAIMS OF PICKLESIMER ET AL.

Students can play with at least these ideas: (1) Is this a discretionary immunity situation? That is, would a judicial decision that the highway is negligently designed be an interference with the appropriate political power of a coordinate branch of government? (2) Is there any basis for finding negligence, any standard, custom or community expectation that would permit courts to judge? If there is a professional standard, then perhaps courts could not only assess negligence but also feel that there is no interference in the discretion or policy-making roles of a coordinate branch. (3) Is there room for any public duty type analysis?

Highway systems design as discretionary. Students have no occasion to know what the cases say on the particular subject of highway plans; the problem is presented to permit review and analysis and the kind of learning that comes with an effort to apply knowledge.

For whatever it is worth, however, the cases are somewhat divided. A fair number of cases have said that highway plans involve discretion and that there is an immunity, although not necessarily for everything the state does with a highway. Where the operational planning distinction is drawn, some decisions about highway safety are "operational" and not discretionary. See *Trujillo v. Utah Dep't of Transp.,* 986 P.2d 752 (Utah Ct. App. 1999). In some states, liability for negligence is the norm, not immunity. In *Nusbaum v. Blue Earth County,* 422 N.W.2d 713 (Minn. 1988), the court denied the discretionary immunity protection to highway officials who had ended a slow-down zone just before rather than after a sharp curve. Incidentally, the federal discretionary immunity has been applied to deny liability when federal authorities are responsible for failing to install a guardrail on a narrow highway with a precipitous and deadly drop off. *Bowman v. United States,* 820 F.2d 1393 (4th Cir. 1987) (Blue Ridge Parkway).

Discretionary immunity may attach to other designs or plans as well as highways. In *Garrison v. Deschutes County,* 344 Or. 264, 48 P.3d 807 (2002), the county designed a transfer station—a do it yourself garbage dump—contemplating that users would back up their pickup trucks to a 14.5 foot drop off to a concrete slab below, stand in the back of their trucks, and push garbage over the tailgate and into the drop off. While using the transfer station, the plaintiff fell into the abyss so created. The court assumed that the plaintiff could prove negligence and that a private person in the position of the county would be liable for the negligent design. *Held,* the county is protected by the state's discretionary immunity for negligent design. The designers actually considered safety and costs. "[E]vidence of that thinking process establishes conclusively that this is not a case in which the decision-makers simply disregarded their duty to protect the public. On the contrary, with their decision, even if it was flawed, they exercised their discretion and chose to protect the public in a particular way."

Many states have enacted comprehensive statutes regulating immunities of government, and some of these embody a specific immunity for plans and designs of government property and highways. E.g., N.M. ST. ANN. § 41-4-11;12 VT. STATS. ANN. § 5601. *Cornette v. Department of Transportation,* 26 P.3d 332 (Cal. 2001), where the state failed to install a median divider on a dangerous highway, explains California's law this way:

> A public entity is liable for injury proximately caused by a dangerous condition of its property [including highways] if the dangerous condition created a reasonably foreseeable risk of the kind of injury sustained, and the public entity had actual or constructive notice of the condition a sufficient time before the injury to have taken preventive measures.
>
> However, a public entity may avoid such liability by raising the affirmative defense of *design immunity.* A public entity claiming design immunity must establish three elements: (1) a causal relationship between the plan or design and the accident; (2) discretionary approval of the plan or design prior to construction; and (3) substantial evidence supporting the reasonableness of the plan or design.
>
> Design immunity does not necessarily continue in perpetuity. To demonstrate loss of design immunity a plaintiff must also establish three elements: (1) the plan or design has become dangerous because of a change in physical conditions; (2) the public entity had actual or constructive notice of the dangerous condition thus created; and (3) the public entity had a reasonable time to obtain the funds and carry out the necessary remedial work to bring the property back into conformity with a reasonable design or plan, or the public entity, unable to remedy the condition due to practical impossibility or lack of funds, had not reasonably attempted to provide adequate warnings.
>
> The third element of design immunity, the existence of substantial evidence supporting the reasonableness of the adoption of the plan or design, must be tried by the court, not the jury. . . . A plaintiff [also] has a right to a jury trial as to the issues involved in loss of design immunity.

On cases, *see* Don F. Vaccaro, Annotation, *Liability of Governmental Entity or Public Officer for Personal Injury or Damages Arising out of Vehicular Accident Due to Negligent or Defective Design of a Highway,* 45 A.L.R.3d 875 (1972).

Discussion of the *Picklesimer* problem might bring out several distinctions. Perhaps it is a planning decision to locate the road. It is perhaps less clearly so when it comes to deciding on the grade, curve and banking, but still perhaps within the idea of a large policy decision depending in part on political factors rather than on justice factors —that is, depending on the executive branch decision making rather than on judicial decision making. When it comes to a failure to mark the road or to post signs of warning, this does not look like a political-social decision but a professional one. If there are standards of engineers, or state highway designers or other road builders that would permit us to say that the decision is a professional one by its nature, perhaps for this there should be liability.

§4. OFFICERS

This section briefly addresses the problem of suing individual governmental employees or officers. How should liabilities be imposed to maximize accountability or deterrence effects and at the same time to maximize the possibilities for full compensation to the plaintiff? If the officer but not the public entity is held liable, this may encourage accountability, but it may also limit compensation and drive good employees out of government service. If the public entity is held liable and not the officer, there may be no deterrence effect at all.

The first case here, *Washoe*, deals with the absolute privilege accorded to judicial and quasi-judicial officials (as well as legislative officers). The second, *Vaughn*, explores the qualified immunity – one lost if the defendant acts with malice, or in bad faith – accorded to executive branch officials. Notes fill out the picture.

STATE V. SECOND JUDICIAL DISTRICT COURT, COUNTY OF WASHOE, 55 P.3d 420 (Nev. 2002)

The *Washoe* court and the Notes that follow sketch out the absolute immunity enjoyed by judicial and legislative officers, and persons who at in a quasi-judicial capacity. An absolute immunity is not lost even if the defendant acts with malice or in bad faith. The immunity protects all who participate in the process, such as witnesses in a judicial proceeding. In *Babcock v. State*, 112 Wash.2d 83, 768 P.2d 481 (1989), a juvenile court placed four minor girls in a foster home with Lee Michael. Caseworkers neglected to reveal that Michael had a criminal record. He sexually abused all four girls as well as his own daughter. The court held that the caseworkers shared an absolute immunity because their acts "occurred in the course of judicial proceedings prescribed by statute." On the other hand, even judges and legislators are subject to liability for tortious non-judicial and non-legislative acts. In addition, the judge may be subject to an injunction against illegal conduct, even when she is not liable in damages; and under the civil rights act, liability to an injunction may also entail liability for the plaintiff's attorneys' fees. See *Pulliam v. Allen*, 466 U.S. 522 (1984).

VAUGHN V. RUOFF, 253 F.3d 1124 (8th Cir. 2001)

The defendant, Ruoff, a social service worker assigned to the plaintiffs' case of alleged child neglect, suggests to Mrs. Vaughn that she get sterilized while she is in the hospital giving birth to her second child. The Missouri Department of Family Services ("MDFS") had already taken custody of the Vaughn's first child. Ruoff implies that if she goes forward with a tubal ligation that she and her husband would have a "really great" chance of getting the first child back, and of keeping the second one. Mrs. Vaughn has the sterilization procedure. A couple of months later the MDFS informed the Vaughns that it would recommend termination of their parental rights to both children.

The Vaughns sued, arguing that Ruoff's actions amounted to a procedural due process violation. Ruoff argued that she was entitled to qualified immunity. The court says that qualified immunity analysis asks two questions at the outset: "(1) was there a deprivation of a constitutional right, and if so, (2) was the right clearly established at the time of the deprivation?"

The court holds that the plaintiffs' rights were violated by Ruoff, so that the first question could be answered "yes." The basis for this conclusion is that Ruoff coerced Mrs. Vaughn into being sterilized. She was given no "procedural protections before the sterilization occurred." The court also holds that question two can be answered "yes," explaining that to be "clearly established," the right "must be sufficiently clear that a reasonable official would understand that what [s]he is doing violates that right." Here, while there are no cases on point, any reasonable person, "social worker or not," would have known that compelled sterilization is unconstitutional. Thus *Ruoff* did not enjoy a qualified immunity.

Notes 1-4 walk the students through the rules addressed in the case. You might stress the difference between the qualified immunity granted to executive branch officers and the absolute immunity granted to legislative and judicial officers, if you did not do so already. (You might also make sure that all of your students know what the three branches of government are. Take nothing for granted.)

Note 5. Suing state or local officers under state law. As far as state law goes, officers enjoy a qualified discretionary immunity, one destructible by malice or bad faith. For ministerial, that is, non-discretionary acts, they generally enjoy no immunity. *Fuqua v. Flowers*, 20 S.W.2d 388 (Ark. 2000), states the immunity more broadly: as long as a state employee is acting within the scope of employment, he is immune unless actual malice is shown. Statutes may afford particular immunities.

NOTE: FEDERAL EXECUTIVE BRANCH OFFICERS

Suits under federal law. Although state officers are liable under a federal statute for violation of a citizen's constitutional rights, no federal statute makes any similar provision for federal officers. However, the Court has held that federal officers may be sued individually directly under the constitution. This is usually known as a *Bivens* claim, and it is closely parallel to the § 1983 claim against state officers. The *Bivens* claim, however, is limited to federal officers and does not include any right of action against corporate agents of the government who act under contract with the government, even if they are operating under color of law. See *Correctional Services Corp. v. Malesko*, 534 U.S. 61, 122 S.Ct. 515, 151 L.Ed.2d 456 (2001). There is no general absolute immunity when it comes to official violation of the Constitution. See *Butz v. Economou*, 438 U.S. 478, 98 S. Ct. 2894, 57 L.Ed.2d 895 (1978); *Harlow v. Fitzgerald*, 457 U.S. 800,102 S. Ct. 2727, 73 L.Ed.2d 396 (1982). Notice that this is not to say that the FTCA permits a suit against federal officers or the federal government, only that the officers are not immune. Except for the President of the United States.

Suits under state law. Until very recently, it was possible to sue federal officers under ordinary state tort law. For example, you might sue an FBI agent who negligently drove a car while on duty and who thus ran into your car. However, where there was a discretionary act involved, the Supreme Court gave the officer a complete immunity as to acts within the outer perimeter of the scope of his duties.

FTCA immunity. Suits against federal officers are now virtually impossible under the Westfall Act, discussed in this Note. The Westfall Act as interpreted by the Court protects the federal employee from liability for acts within the scope of employment. The Attorney General certifies to the court that the acts sued upon were within the scope of government employment. The court must then drop the federal employee from the suit and substitute the United States as a defendant. The United States as defendant has all the defenses and immunities the government otherwise has. So, for example, the plaintiff who is injured by a negligent government doctor in Italy has no claim against the doctor because the Westfall Act immunizes him; and she has no claim against the United States because it retains immunity for harms done in foreign countries. *United States v. Smith*, cited here.

The Court, in a 5-4 split, has authorized the plaintiff to contest the attorney general's certificate, in effect to litigate whether the federal employee was actually within the scope of employment at the time of the alleged tort. *Gutierrez de Martinez v. Lamagno,* cited at the end of this Note. *Gutierrez* will provide scant help for most plaintiffs, first because most will find it impossible to show that the employee was outside the scope of employment and second because adding a difficult issue on which the plaintiff may well lose adds a layer to the lawsuit. Added layers mean added risks for plaintiff attorneys under a contingent fee system. That in turn means that lawyers will be unable to afford to take many moderate-sized cases.

What do students think of (a) governmental liability with no officer liability for tort? (b) Officer liability with governmental indemnity? (c) Officer liability without indemnity? (d) Joint and several liability of government and officer and possibly liability of the officer for contribution or indemnity payable to the government? Would any of these approaches tend to deter wrongdoing? Overdeter effective governmental programs and law enforcement? See Jerry Mashaw, *Civil Liability of Government Officers: Property Rights and Official Accountability,* 42 L. & CONTEMP. PROBS. 8, 23 (1978).

If deterrence and accountability of governmental agencies is hard to get, what about holding the individual officer liable? But writers, courts and legislatures have expressed some concerns about the possibility of "overdeterrence" or induced official timidity – driving good government employees out of government employment, or driving them to a timorous posture that prevents effective administration. What about arrests or searches, for example?

A discussion of overdeterrence with a number of references is Ronald A. Cass, *Damage Suits against Public Officers*, 129 U. PA. L. REV. 1110 (1981). Cass believes that the overdeterrence problem in government employee cases differs from that in private enterprise cases because the profit motive of private employers will tend to make them protect the employee with insurance or otherwise whenever the employee would overreact to liability (and thus cut profits). The Westfall Act has now done this in spades, but it differs from Cass' ideas because the government is not always liable where the individual would be, since it has its own special exemptions from liability. Is it good?

§ 5. STATE AND MUNICIPAL LIABILITY UNDER § 1983

State liability. States are not liable under § 1983 because states are not "persons" within the meaning of that statute. State officers or employees may be personally liable, as may local officers. Officer liability is the ordinary grist of the § 1983 mill. Cities and other municipalities are subject to liability, but only for policies or customs that violate federal rights. The significance of that rule is that a spontaneous tort by municipal officer will not be enough. Students should understand that a policy or custom can be found to exist without any explicit declared policy of the city. Consistent practices instituted or approved by officials in charge will suffice.

Municipal liability. The Supreme Court permits municipal liability (as opposed to officer liability) only when constitutional violation occurs through a municipal *policy*. The municipality is not responsible for isolated acts unless those acts represents the municipality's policy. Sometimes a custom or extended practice of the municipality can count as policy; sometimes a single authoritative decision can count as policy. Since municipal negligence will not violate the due process or equal protection clauses, the policy must evince something more, perhaps deliberate indifference. The problems of showing a municipal policy are summarized in DOBBS ON TORTS § 277 (2000).

NAVARRO V. BLOCK, 72 F.3d 712 (9th Cir. 1995)

This is another 9-1-1 failure. This time, however, we know that the 9-1-1 operator made a policy decision and that failure to respond was not one of those mechanical errors or palpable mistakes in judgment about the particular facts. The operator's judgment was, arguably, based on a practice of giving low priority to domestic violence calls. (Consistent practice, the court notes, can show a policy.)

Students must recognize first that not all discrimination is bad and certainly not all is unconstitutional. We discriminate when we make different rules for landowners or doctors, for example. We discriminate between the top score on an exam and the bottom score. The plaintiff claiming a denial of equal protection must show (1) an official policy of discrimination, (2) that the discrimination is intentional (not merely an unintended by-product), and (3) the discrimination must be unjustified.

Justified discrimination is dealt with in constitutional cases by recognizing three (or more) levels of constitutional "scrutiny" or review, but it may be easier to understand these levels of scrutiny in tort terms as types of privilege or justification. (1) Under the strict scrutiny standard, we could say the defendant may not constitutionally discriminate unless there is a *compelling governmental interest*. (2) Under the intermediate standard, the defendant may not discriminate unless there are *important governmental interests* fostered by the discrimination. (3) Under the rational basis test, the defendant may not discriminate unless he has rational (but not necessarily compelling or important) reasons for doing so.

Under constitutional doctrine, the justification in gender discrimination cases is the intermediate one – the defendant is protected if the discrimination serves important governmental objectives, otherwise not. The plaintiff in *Navarro* can perhaps show that the alleged policy discriminates *in fact* against women, because they are the victims of most domestic violence, but she has no evidence of any *intent* to discriminate, so she has no claim of gender discrimination. Her claim of gender discrimination thus fails.

She may still have a claim of some other kind of discrimination –in this case, discrimination against domestic violence victims (regardless whether they are women or not). If there is a policy (derived from the practice of the sheriff), it is on its face discrimination against domestic violence victims because it says in effect "don't give as good protection to those victims." That is the discrimination the court evidently has in mind in saying that the plaintiff still has a potential claim. This claim is harder for the plaintiff than a gender discrimination claim, though, because if discrimination does not touch gender or a suspect category like race, then the level of judicial review or scrutiny is very limited. In tort terms, we might say that the defendant has a very broad privilege to discriminate; he need not have a compelling or even important governmental objective; he need only have some rational basis. So the plaintiff will have to show on remand that (1) the sheriff had an intentional policy to discriminate against domestic violence callers, and (2) the policy was irrational.

Some students will not have had constitutional law when you reach this material, but even if they have, a technical or high-level constitutional approach to class discussion and coverage seems out of place here. The case helps make several practical points that are enough for most tort courses:

(1) The city might be liable under § 1983, regardless of state law, if the city's policy violates the plaintiff's constitutional rights.
(2) A policy can be found in a consistent custom or practice as well as in explicit words.

(3) A policy that has discriminatory impact —as the domestic violence policy undoubtedly does— is not a straight violation of equal protection because of a constitutional rule that says that discriminatory motive or intent is required to show that violation. This means discriminatory impact alone won't do in that particular case. (The class should contain this rule; it does not apply in some other kinds of claims, such as claims based on job discrimination under Title VII; it is an equal protection rule.)

(4) But, according to *Navarro,* the classification of people must still be rationally related to a legitimate governmental purpose. So maybe the plaintiff can prevail if a sufficient argument can be mounted on remand.

All of the police failures are distressing, but a failure based upon a policy not to deal with domestic violence might strike you as doubly damnable, first because it risks severe harm and death as in other cases, and second because it takes aim at a very large group of victims, many of whom simply have no escape unless someone intervenes. For a brief recent recap of some of the figures see Susanne M. Browne, Note, *Due Process and Equal Protection Challenges to the Inadequate Response of the Police in Domestic Violence Situations,* 68 S. CAL. L. REV. 1295 (1995). (If you have students who tend to deny or minimize domestic violence, you might ask them to read a little in the first part of the Browne note, which, among other things, speaks about the personality of the attackers.)

Note 1 provides the holdings of two Supreme Court cases and should be self-explanatory; students don't have much detail here to develop any of this in class.

Note 2 gives the subsequent history of the case.

Note 3. Due process claims in domestic violence cases like *Navarro* are less likely to succeed than equal protection claims, which themselves are hard to pursue because the intent or motive requirement will foreclose many claims. In *Castle Rock,* cited here, the Supreme Court held that a due process claim failed because the plaintiff failed to show a protected property interest in the enforcement of a protective order, when such enforcement was not mandatory under state law.

A closing note:

Student confusion on state and federal law. Some students appear to have only a sketchy notion that we live in a federal system. Talk of state law, which is mostly the common law of torts as applied with differences in each state, confuses some. These short notes are compressed. If you want students to get a handle on the possibility of state-law suits and federal (civil rights) suits and to distinguish those two things from government liability (only under the FTCA), you may need to take more time than the limited amount of material might suggest. For instance, you might pose simple hypotheticals:

A federal employee (don't designate her job yet) fires a gun at the plaintiff, who is an ordinary citizen walking down the street. What options for suit?

One option: sue the federal government under the FTCA if you can prove it was negligent in hiring a gun-happy employee, or in some other way. One difficulty with this: the assault and battery exception. One way around the difficulty: show the employee was a law enforcement officer to whom the battery exception does not apply. A second way around the difficulty: show that the employee was off duty (or perhaps not in the scope of employment), so as to invoke the *Sheridan* exception. *A second option*: sue the employee individually. One difficulty: the exclusive remedy provision of the FTCA, which applies even if the government itself is not liable. One way around this difficulty: show that the employee was violating civil rights so that you sue under the Constitution directly. (*Maybe* this will do the job.)

A second hypothetical will bring in the state employee/municipal liability cases. You can just change the first hypothetical to make the gun-happy employee a municipal employee. The main options then are: First, sue the municipality under § 1983. Difficulty: can you find a municipal policy that caused the event and second can you show it violated a constitutional right? Second, sue the individual officer under § 1983. Possible difficulty: she may enjoy a qualified immunity if she acted in a way that reasonable employees would believe to be constitutional. Finally, you might invoke state law of torts against either the municipality or the officer if the immunities have been waived and no new ones protect these particular acts.

REFERENCES:
Federal Tort Claims generally. LESTER S. JAYSON & ROBERT C. LONGSTRETH, HANDLING FEDERAL TORT CLAIMS (multi-volume, looseleaf); Wests Key Number Digests, *United States*, Key 78, (1-17) (393k78). There are many ALR annotations.

Feres. DOBBS ON TORTS §§ 263-267 (2000).

Discretionary immunity. DOBBS ON TORTS § 262 (2000); Donald N. Zillman, *Protecting Discretion: Judicial Interpretation of the Discretionary Function Exception to the Federal Tort Claims Act*, 47 ME. L. REV. 365 (1995) (short description of the Supreme court cases, followed by a summary of lower court decisions).

States. DOBBS ON TORTS § 268-273 (2000); West's Key Number DIGESTS, *States*, Key 112 (1-2) (360k112). There are a number of annotations, for example, Annotation, Janet Boeth Jones, *Governmental Tort Liability for Injuries Caused by Negligently Released Individual*, 6 A.L.R.4th 1155 (1981).

Municipalities. DOBBS ON TORTS § 269 (2000); West's Key Number DIGESTS, *Municipal Corporations*, Keys 723-857 (268kxxx). A number of annotations are available, some of which overlap state and local liabilities. Both the state and local entities, for example, carry on police activities and construction activities, and annotations may deal with both levels. A sample is Annotation, Dale R. Agthe, *State or Local Governmental Unit's Liability for Injury to Private Highway Construction Worker Based on its Own Negligence*, 28 A.L.R.4th 1188 (1984).

Officers. Dobbs on Torts § 273 (2000); West's Key Number DIGESTS, *Officers*, Keys 114-119 (283k.

In addition to these basic units, you may wish to consult particular topics based on facts—for example, in the West DIGESTS, the topic *Schools* (keys 114-115) (345kxxx)and the topic *Highways* (keys 187-216) (200kxxx) both deal with liabilities of entities or officers in particular situations. Government action (and non-action) is pervasive, so of course there are many other topics that can raise these issues.

TOPIC B. RELATIONSHIPS OR THEIR ABSENCE: NONACTION, CONTRACT AND PROTECTION FROM OTHERS

CHAPTER 16

NONFEASANCE

▶**Changes in the Sixth Edition.** We've added a new primary case, *Podias*, in § 2, along with some new citations in Note material. To make room for the new materials, we've cut the *Newton* case abstract in § 1 (turning it into a shorter Note), and the *Krieg* case abstract in § 2.

▶The **Concise Edition** cuts this Chapter from 20 pages to 12, primarily by deleting *Farwell v. Keaton* and some of its Notes, and *DeShaney* and some of its Notes.■

The Role of This Chapter and Its Relation to Others

This chapter covers the basic nonfeasance rule – the defendant has no duty to act in an affirmative way unless he is in a special relationship with the plaintiff or with others who threaten harm. It also covers the Constitutional analog–the state has no constitutional duty to protect citizens enforceable under § 1983. This chapter stops there. You can think of this chapter as one in a series that involve what the courts think of as the defendant's nonaction. It sets up the basic rules and leaves variations to other chapters where nonfeasance is the background condition and other issues are in the forefront.

In particular, Chapter 15 covered cases of nonfeasance (or putative nonfeasance) in suits against governmental entities. Chapter 17 is based upon nonfeasance rules as they might be modified by the defendant's contract to take action, or, what is much the same, the defendant's conduct that induces reliance by a plaintiff. Chapter 18 involves a series of cases in which the defendant fails to protect the plaintiff from harm, often intentional harm, committed by others but might have a duty to take action for the plaintiff's protection arising out of a special relationship.

This chapter is thus important and basic, but the time commitment for this chapter probably should be commensurate with its length, because we'll have other examples in the next chapters.

OUTLINE

§ 1. **THE NO DUTY TO ACT RULE.** Yania v. Bigan

§ 2. **EXCEPTIONS, QUALIFICATIONS AND QUESTIONS**
[a] Acts causing harm or creating risk as creating a duty of care. Text.
[b] Beginning an act as establishing a duty: action as an undertaking or assumption of duty
    Wakulich v. Mraz
    Farwell v. Keaton
[c] Relationship with victim/implied agreement as establishing a duty of assistance. Farwell v. Keaton; Podias v. Mairs
[d] Civil Rights claims
    [1] Nonprotection. DeShaney v. Winnebago County Dept. of Social Services
    [2] State created danger. Notes

SUMMARY

YANIA V. BIGAN. A defendant taunts a neighbor until he jumps into the water, then fails to rescue him when it appears he is in trouble. There is no liability when the neighbor drowns. Part of the reason may be related to nonfeasance ideas, namely that defendant has "done nothing" because his fault is a failure to rescue. Why is this not like Newton v. Ellis, however? Taking the conduct as a whole, the defendant could be seen to be doing something badly, rather than doing nothing.

WAKULICH V. MRAZ. Allegedly: adult males induce a 16-years-old girl to drink a quart of hard alcohol. She falls unconscious and later dies. They did not call for help. They laid her on a couch and removed her shirt after it was covered with her vomit and also put a pillow beneath her head. The father of these gentlemen order them to get her out of the house, so they took her to a friend's home. She died. The court first holds that neither of the young men nor their father could be liable for providing alcohol as social hosts were simply excluded from liability by Illinois law. The court then holds that they young men undertook to aid her and were under a duty because of that undertaking to exercise reasonable care. Whether they did would be for the jury.

FARWELL V. KEATON. Two teen-aged boys, out for beers, show an interest in some girls, whose male friends proceed to attack the boys. One of them, Farwell, was badly beaten. The other drove him around a while, then left him unconscious in the car. Had he been presented to his family, medical treatment could have been obtained that might have saved his life. The court imposes liability on the teenage friend. Two rules may be the reasons: (1) the defendant took charge of the injured friend, and once having begun this care, he was obliged to exercise reasonable care; (2) the boys had a special relationship for the evening that required reasonable mutual assistance.

PODIAS V. MAIRS. Three 18-year-old college students drove away from a friend's house in the early morning hours after drinking beer. It was raining and the road was wet. Mairs, the driver, lost control of his car on the highway and hit and motorcyclist. All three boys went and looked at the cyclist and decided he was dead. No one else was around. None of them called for assistance. After five or ten minutes they decided to leave the scene. Shortly afterward their car broke down. Mairs hid in the bushes and the other two ran into the woods. Meanwhile a second car ran over the motorcyclist, who was in the middle of the road, killing him. In the estate's suit against the three students, *held*, the defendants owed a duty to assist because of the relationship they had to the accident, including the relationship the two non-drivers had with the driver. Further, they may have breached this duty when they failed to assist; that remains a question of fact.

DESHANEY V. WINNEBAGO COUNTY DEPT. OF SOCIAL SERVICES. The county social services department, in charge of protecting children, received reports that Joshua's father abused him. The agency took charge of Joshua, but then released him to his father on condition that the agency would make regular checks. The agency worker had reason to think Joshua was being abused but the father always made excuses to prevent workers from seeing Joshua. Eventually the father beat Joshua into a profoundly retarded state. Joshua will live the rest of his life in total institutional care. Held, the public entity committed no constitutional tort. The public entity owed no constitutional duties to take affirmative action unless Joshua was in custody. He was not.

COMMENTS

§ 1. THE NO DUTY TO ACT RULE

Introductory Hypothetical

This hypothetical presents a stark form of the setting and the supposed nonfeasance rule. You can use this hypothetical to convey the extreme implications of the rule even if you want to omit everything else.

In a recent notorious criminal case, Strohmeyer sexually molested and then strangled a seven-year-old girl on a toilet seat in a casino. His companion, David Cash, did nothing to avoid it. Yet Cash could not be convicted. That is the essence of the nonfeasance rule. That case, and the nonfeasance rule, is discussed in Marcia M. Ziegler, Comment, *Nonfeasance and the Duty to Assist: The American Seinfeld Syndrome,* 104 DICK. L. REV. 525 (2000).

YANIA V. BIGAN, 155 A.2d 343 (Pa. 1959)

Defendant taunted Yania until he jumped into the water; he then failed to rescue Yania, who drowned. Ordinary rules of responsibility would normally indicate that Yania is responsible for his own decision to jump unless he is known to be peculiarly susceptible to suggestion or otherwise incapacitated. For these reasons, the defendant should not be responsible for Yania's decision to jump.

But why should Yania have no duty of reasonable care to assist the man in the water if it became apparent that, without assistance, he would drown? The court treats this as nonfeasance and refuses to impose any duty to use care for Yania.

Yet the court could have looked at all of the defendant's conduct together and found that taunts coupled with inaction was like excavation coupled with failure to provide a light in *Newton.* This would not necessitate a finding that the taunting itself was actionable –only a taunting, like digging a hole in the ground, is an activity that cannot be meaningfully separated from the failure later on to deal with risks that activity creates.

We begin to see that we deal not so much with cases that are "really" nonfeasance or "really" misfeasance, but with cases in which the judges characterize the conduct in order to achieve a result. It may be a result based in policy, or morals, or intuition, but it is surely not a result based on any "fact" that the conduct is "really" nonfeasance. One pursuing this line of reasoning might even begin to wonder whether the nonfeasance/misfeasance distinction is an accidental or fortuitous feature of cases in which liability is denied on entirely other grounds.

Suppose Bigan had enticed a child to jump into the water, believing with justification that the water was safe. Suppose the child then has difficulty and is obviously in trouble. Would one expect a court to hold that Bigan was under a duty of care to the child? Surely so. The reasoning might be made in two different ways: (1) "Having acted to entice the child into the water — though there was nothing wrong with so doing –the defendant should be obliged to assist his recovery when difficulty is encountered." Much authority, including *South* in the next section, would support this approach. (2) "This was not mere nonfeasance. This was a case of a single course of conduct –of action –which began by encouraging the child to go into the water. It does not become nonfeasance merely because, having got the child into difficulty, the defendant took no further action."

The latter explanation would be along the lines *Newton v. Ellis* advances, and consistent with the brake hypothetical. If we believe the courts would follow either of these lines of reasoning –or any other which would impose liability –then we must see that the decision does not turn on nonfeasance versus misfeasance, but on the court's strong commitment to the autonomy and the personal responsibility for the adult person in full control of his faculties. Nonfeasance, in this view, becomes less the reason for judicial decision than the expression of the judicial conclusion.

Note 1. Nonfeasance versus misfeasance. *Newton*, discussed here, establishes a general view of importance: we can characterize many parts of conduct together in accord with what we perceive to be its general nature, even though some portions of the overall conduct involved doing nothing. We have in a sense known this all along, because we have recognized from the beginning that omissions can constitute negligence.

The point is a significant one, though, in spite of its apparent simplicity. We must recognize that there is no objective basis – certainly none in the judges' statements – for choosing any particular segment of conduct as the basis for characterizing it in terms of nonfeasance or misfeasance. One could describe the failure to light without mentioning the earlier excavating. This is not necessarily the "right" description, if there is a right one. Value judgments have already been built into our case when we describe the conduct to include some (earlier) action.

A simple example. To illustrate the point: Suppose a driver drives very carefully. A child half a block away begins to cross the street. The driver does not move a muscle – does not put on the brake – and thus strikes the child. *Newton* gives us an easy answer and also no doubt a right one: the driver is not merely guilty of nonfeasance, but of active negligence; he was driving a car in a risky way.

On the slippery slope. Suppose, however, that the driver has borrowed a car, driven it safely, brought it to a halt in a safe position and is preparing to get out when the car inexplicably begins to roll. He has set the handbrake and placed the car in gear. Must he now attempt to use the foot brake or otherwise act? What if he has left the car entirely and placed the keys in the owner's house as he promised to do? At some point along this trail, which can be extended easily if one questions a student unwilling to face up to the problem, it will be harder for people to say this was a negligent way of driving. Yet there are no obvious guides to saying where we must stop. (If you like the risk analysis in legal cause cases, you may find this very hard to use as a means of solving nonfeasance issues. If you believe that causal judgments tend to obscure issues of policy or judgment, or that causal analysis is difficult and unpredictable, you might be unwilling to import it to "solve" the issues raised here.)

In one way this may be seen as an all-too-familiar problem of the slippery slope. But it is not merely a slippery slope problem because in this case there are no stated principles to which we can turn as the basis for the judgment that must be made –what segments of conduct do we consider together in order to characterize that conduct as nonfeasance or misfeasance?

Does responsibility follow such legal characterizations –or is a judge's characterization of behavior as action or nonaction a result of judges' notions of responsibility? What concerns does the judge have in mind in making the characterization? If you believe that the judge unavoidably has in mind the ultimate question whether she wishes to impose legal responsibility, and she characterizes the conduct accordingly, then the nonfeasance rule gives us a conclusion without helping us explore a reason for it.

Students find this difficult, and you might choose not to pursue it except in your role as a gadfly, who, having irritated the student-victim, moves on.

Note 2. Characterizing conduct. This Note foreshadows the exceptions to the nonfeasance rule. Even if the general rule makes sense, was it misapplied in *Yania*? First, along the lines suggested in Newton (Note 1 above), why was it a "non-act" when Bigan did not try to save Yania, as opposed to it being an act of misfeasance for Bigan to dare Yania to jump in to a ditch that he, Bigan, had himself dug, *then* not to help him? Consider *Smit v. Anderson,* 72 P.3d 369 (Colo. Ct. App. 2002), where a landowner wanted to construct his own house with the help of untrained friends. To get a building permit and a construction loan, however, he had to have a general contractor. Defendant, to accommodate his friend the landowner, helped the landowner obtain a building permit and construction loan by representing that defendant was the general contractor. Defendant did no supervision. A wall fell on the plaintiff, an untrained friend of the landowner while the plaintiff was helping erect it. Held, the defendant was under a duty of care to supervise untrained workers. If defendant were only chargeable with nonfeasance, he would have no duty absent a special relationship. However, defendant's misrepresentations to facilitate the loan and permit was misfeasance; he created a danger to the landowner's untrained friends that required him to use care in supervision. Would that reasoning apply to *Yania v. Bigan* as well?

Note 3 focuses the students on the power of the distinction, although perhaps Bigan was not negligent here even if he had a duty of care, given Yania's "choice" to jump in. Perhaps the reasoning of *Stinnett v. Buchele* (Chapter 6) might help Bigan – could he assume that Yania was going to act reasonably to help himself? Students might also see this as a case of contributory negligence (which would have barred the claim in most states in 1959) or even implied assumption of the risk of the "primary" variety (See Chapter 10). All of these lines of reasoning, though, go primarily if not completely to Bigan's alleged negligent act of cajoling Yania to jump in. Once in the water, did Bigan have a duty to rescue him? Perhaps an exception to the nonfeasance rule would help (and that's coming up in the next section), but once this conduct is labeled "nonfeasance" it can be outcome-determinative.

Note 4. The *Rocha* case. In *Rocha v. Faltys*, cited here, where one college student/friend encouraged the other to jump into the water, with resulting death, the facts are closely similar to *Yania*, yet arguably quite distinct because the victim was intoxicated. Encouragement is not nonfeasance; it is not actionable in *Yania* because Yania was an adult of sound mind. The *Yania* court recognized that had Yania "been a child of tender years or a person mentally deficient then it is conceivable that taunting and enticement could constitute actionable negligence if it resulted in harm." Wouldn't an intoxicated person be incapacitated like a child of tender years? The *Rocha* court said on this point: "Simply taking George, an adult man, to the location where George could choose to engage in an allegedly dangerous activity does not constitute negligent creation of a dangerous situation. The fact that George was intoxicated does not affect this analysis. It has been long- recognized at common law that an individual who chooses to consume alcohol maintains the ultimate power over his situation and thus the obligation to control his own behavior."

Note 5. Applying the rule. A. *Rockweit v. Senecal,* summarized in this note, holds that Tynan was not liable, but gave a nontraditional line of reasoning. The court held that everyone owes a duty of care[1] and the jury could properly find that Tynan was negligent. But Tynan would not be liable because "Tynan did not participate in the selection of the fire pit site, nor did she start, maintain, or provide any necessary incendiary materials for the fire. The imposition of liability in this case, under the given facts, would place an unreasonable burden upon a guest in Tynan's position." Is this a nonfeasance rule? Except for Wisconsin teachers, the court's reasoning might take you too far afield, but the facts and the result are at least consistent with the nonfeasance rules and the case is much easier on the conscience than *Yania.*

B. After first recounting the landowner-trespasser rules, *Rhodes v. Illinois Cent. Gulf R.R.,* cited here, essentially applied the nonfeasance or no duty to act rule to bar recovery.

Note 6. Rationales. The *Yania* court also stresses "free will." In the *Stockberger* case cited here, a diabetic prison employee became ill at work and was killed in a car accident while driving home. His widow sued the Bureau of Prisons (his employer) for common-law negligence, alleging that it owed him a duty to prevent him from leaving while sick, or to provide transportation to him. The court cast this as a nonfeasance claim, involving "the duty if any to rescue a person in distress." Applying Indiana law, the panel concluded that none of the exceptions to nonfeasance were present. Judge Posner added, "It would not be sensible either to place employers or other invitors on a razor's edge where they face a suit for false imprisonment if they don't let the ill person leave or a suit for negligence if they do."

---

[1] Following Andrews' view in *Palsgraf,* the Wisconsin Court takes the view that a duty of reasonable care is owed to the world, not merely to foreseeable plaintiffs. But instead of saying that the duty is to the world when there is a duty at all, the Court seems to understand its "duty to all" to mean there is always a duty. Once negligence is found, liability is to be avoided not on the usual ground that there is no duty but on the ground that liability is against public policy. Skeptics might wonder how "no duty" differs from "public policy against liability." The court has a hard time avoiding duty or no-duty locutions: "[A]t no time did she assume any responsibility to maintain the fire pit." Different from saying no duty assumed?

§ 2. EXCEPTIONS, QUALIFICATIONS AND QUESTIONS

[a] Acts causing harm, or risking harm, as creating a duty of care

Causing harm. The first "exception" explained in text here is that one who causes harm, even without fault, is then under a duty of reasonable care, requiring assistance or rescue if a reasonable person would give it. Sometimes this is expressed by saying that the duty of care arises if harm is caused by one's instrumentality. The Restatement Second provides that one who has caused harm, or made another helpless, is under a duty of care to prevent further harm. The earlier version of Restatement § 322 did not go this far. It imposed the duty only if the defendant were at fault in the first instance. (Note that Pennsylvania in *Yania* cited the earlier of § 322.)

Comparing Yania *and the Restatement.* Will some bright student suggest that *Yania* might be weak authority under these circumstances? After all, *Yania* does seem contrary to the principle in the current version of § 322 unless one moves into a strong proximate cause rationale –namely, that Bigan was not a cause at all because Yania's volition made the act of jumping into the cut his own act. This line of reasoning –not inconsistent with what the Pennsylvania Court seemed to say and think –suggests that under § 322 "cause" becomes again a critical word.

Perhaps the current § 322 means that a duty of care arises whenever the defendant is an actual cause of harm to the plaintiff. If the same rule is applied to risk that is applied to actual harm, then *Yania* should go the other way under the Restatement Second. This is so because Bigan was an actual cause of the risk, and his failure to attempt rescue is an actual and legal cause of the death that followed.

Innocent cause-of-risk rule. The second "exception" referenced here is that if a person has created an unreasonable risk of harm, a duty of care arises to use reasonable care to prevent the harm from occurring. This is embodied in Restatement Second § 321, and some courts have found a duty to act at a time when the defendant has innocently put the plaintiff in peril, but before harm is actually caused. Defendant runs into a horse on the road and drives on, leaving it dead and in a position on the highway that may cause a collision and injury to another. At this point he has caused no harm to the drivers who follow, but he has created a distinct risk and courts have imposed liability upon the driver who fails to take reasonable steps to minimize this risk. E.g., *Pacht v. Morris*, 489 P.2d 29 (Ariz. 1971).

Duty imposed by statute. A third exception to the common law no duty rule is that a duty will be imposed if a statute says so.

Tor example, most states have enacted statutes that require a driver who is involved in a collision to stop and render aid, independent of any fault on his part. Should this duty be extended by statute or common law to require any drivers on the highway to exercise reasonable care when a highway injury is brought to the drivers' attention? Should it be extended to passengers who are in one of the colliding cars?

[b] Beginning an act as establishing a duty: action as an undertaking or assumption of duty

WAKULICH V. MRAZ, 751 N.E.2d 1 (Ill. App. Ct. 2000).

In different respects, *Wakulich* is factually similar to *Yania* and to *Farwell*. The *Wakulich* court does not regard the taunting and challenge, coupled with peer or social pressure, as significant; instead it regards the case is merely a social host furnishing alcohol. So regarded, the case falls under the Illinois rule that social hosts are not liable for providing alcohol, even, seemingly to underage drinkers subjected to a deadly challenge. (Goldschlager, according to web sources, is 40 or 43% alcohol). We see the rules for furnishing alcohol in Chapter 18; the social host ruling is mainly background for the main point to be made here and a passing forecast of things to come. The real point comes with the second holding, that the men somehow undertook to do something that would have saved Elizabeth Wakulich when they removed her shirt and propped her head up. Really? Did they undertake to get her to the hospital by these acts? Evidently not, because they didn't even begin to go to the hospital. Did they, then, prop her head up negligently? No suggestion of that. The court is determinedly vague about what duty was undertaken and equally about how it was breached. Maybe you could think that this is not a duty undertaken case but one in which the court is merely circumventing the harsh rule (or supposed rule) immunizing social hosts under all circumstances. There is a third point that is easy: if you do something that is in itself harmful, preventing aid from others, for example, you have acted affirmatively and you are liable if that is negligent.

Farwell (the next case) also implicates the "takes charge" exception, briefly, and the first two Notes after that case discuss that exception. So as you get into that case you can start with that ground of decision before developing the "special relationship" exception, which is perhaps the more interesting point in that case.

Notes 1 & 2 set out the Restatement (Third) rules on undertaking to render service and suggest how the rule might be applied by courts. In *Roos*, cited in Note 2, the application is pretty clear: you may not have a duty to be a back-seat driver (in fact, you may have a duty not to), but if you start to tell the driver that all is clear when it is not, you may have breached a duty you created yourself by speaking up. In *Rice v. White*, cited at the end of Note 2, the party hosts did not have to start checking guests for weapons. But once they did, they assumed what the court called a "voluntary duty." But the court held that even though a duty was owed, it was not breached: The duty assumed was only one of reasonable care under the circumstances, and none of them was particularly expert at conducting "pat downs" for weapons.

[c] Relationship with victim/implied agreement as establishing a duty of assistance

FARWELL V. KEATON, 240 N.W.2d 217 (Mich. 1976).

Farwall is a famous case in tort-law circles, primarily for its "special relationship" conception. The case stands on either of two grounds, though – that the defendant by taking charge assumed a duty of reasonable care (see above), as well as the idea that a relationship between plaintiff and defendant can create a duty of reasonable care. The relationship here somewhat resembles that in *Wakulich* in that young people out together for the evening. For the Michigan Court, this is enough to imply an obligation of mutual care. The idea of an implied agreement or tacit understanding about expectations will take us into contracts and promises in the next chapter. Would the relationship/implied agreement idea work in *Wakulich?* Probably not, because a relationship basis for a duty would undermine the court's insistence that social hosts (a relationship to guests) is not itself enough for liability.

Defendant "Takes Charge"

Note 1. Marking matters worse. *Worse off by detrimental reliance.* One kind of "worse off" is detrimental reliance. Detrimental reliance suggests the kind of problem dealt with in the next Chapter, that is, duties based on promises that are either expressed in words or in conduct.

Worse off by imagined alternatives. Another kind of "worse" is the kind the Restatement Second seems to have in mind. In § 324, cmt. *g,* the Restatement supposes a case in which the defendant takes the plaintiff from a trench filled with poison gas. Defendant cannot "throw" the plaintiff back into the trench or even leave him in the street where he might be run over. The example is loaded by the verb "throw," but the Restatement would presumably also say that the rescuer could not gently return the plaintiff to the trench, either. If that is so, how can the Restatement say that the defendant has made the plaintiff worse off by lifting him partly out of the trench and then letting him slip back in? If no other facts appear, he is not worse off than he was before the defendant intervened at all. If the defendant raises the victim in the gas filled trench all the way out, it is possible to say that he is then worse off to be put back in the trench if you use the term "worse off" to mean "worse off than the best position he achieved, thanks to the defendant." In this situation "worse off" does not mean "worse off than he was before the defendant intervened."

In *Krieg v. Massey*, cited here, a landlady took a gun away from a man, but put it on a high shelf in a closet is his apartment. Shortly thereafter he shot himself. The court held that even if she "took charge" by beginning to assist him, she did not leave him in a worse position than he would have been in had she not acted at all. But can we say that he was in a better position at one point, when she had in the gun in her position, and that she left him "worse off" than that?

The Restatement's vision of what counts as "worse off" seems different from the vision of the Montana Court in *Krieg,* because in *Krieg,* the defendant took the gun away from the decedent, then put it back within his reach. That would be like removing the soldier from the gas-filled trench, then putting him back.

If the Restatement's line of demarcation seems morally right, though, what about the defendant who never gets the plaintiff to any higher plane of safety? Suppose the defendant lifts the victim a few inches up, but not out of the range of the poison gas, then decides to hell with it. To declare that the soldier is worse off seems no better than intellectual chicanery. To declare that there is no liability seems morally and humanly wrong. The "worse off" test seems to lead us further into the swamp.

The perception that the swamp gets gloomier is perhaps what leads people to veer off and grasp here for the idea that liability is to be imposed, not for making the plaintiff worse off, but for acting negligently once you have taken charge. See the Restatement's formulation in § 324(a). But this is mysterious, too. If it applies to cases like those in Note 1, it is entirely understandable. If it applies to the drowning man hauled half-way to shore, then the worse off test in § 324(b) is superfluous and confusing.

Note 2. Duty to take charge reasonably. Perhaps a third ground for liability would be better: by taking charge you create a special relationship so that there is a duty to act with reasonable care and to continue aid, regardless of any "worse off" test.Almost everyone would say there is affirmative action here and it was carried out badly. But what counts as affirmative action can be quite uncertain. See *Welsh v. City of Philadelphia,* 627 A.2d 248 (Pa. Cmwlth. Ct. 1993) (police arrival to assist heart attack victim not affirmative action and they were free to refuse assistance for fear that victim had AIDS); *Freeman v. Busch,* 349 F.3d 582 (8th Cir. 2003) (resident assistant in college dorm saw that the plaintiff was drunk, told another student to monitor her condition, and to report back to him, all before she was raped; court held he "took no specific action to exercise control or custody" over her and therefore owed her no duty of reasonable care).

Special Relationships as a Basis for a Duty

Some of the special relationships sketched here will arise again in Chapter 18. In that chapter, the focus is upon the responsibility of actors to protect plaintiffs from third persons, not on nonfeasance as such. Some of the cases will involve nonfeasance, but others will not.

Note 3 lists seven special relationships recognized by the Restatement Third. We will see some of these special relationships implicated in later chapters.

Note 5. Other determinate relationships. It seems plain that there are other determinate relationships, relationships we'd give a name to, like the relationship of parent and child. Could one in the role of a parent, a schoolteacher, for example, stand by and do nothing to save one of her class from serious harm if the child could be helped without a risk to the teacher? If the answer is no, as we think, then it is plain that the Restatement has not listed all the important determinate relationships. We'll revisit relationships in Chapter 18 where protection of the plaintiff from herself or from third persons is the main point, but you can see from the question posed in this note that other relationships are definitely important. In *Brandon v. County of Richardson*, 624 N.W.2d 604 (Neb. 2001), the defendant took no steps to protect a rape victim, who had reported the criminal act by men already know to be dangerous. They later murdered the victim. The sheriff was under a duty of care, not to guarantee safety but to take reasonable steps. But *Dwyer v. Bartlett*, 472 A.2d 431 (Me. 1984), held that the town's officer had no duty to the citizen to report a fire. What if the officer had seen a fire at city hall and failed to report that?

Note 6. Indeterminate or ad hoc relationships. Students already know from *Farwell* that ad hoc or indeterminate relationships may suffice to impose a duty of action. But they may not know that they know. Once students know the Restatement's five categories, they may discard knowledge they have that other relationships may also suffice. When they think about it, however, they can say from *Farwell* that a specific, determinate relationship like custodian-ward is not required and hence that the Restatement may give a misleading picture.

The *Farwell* court says: "Farwell and Siegrist were companions on a social venture. Implicit in such a common undertaking is the understanding that one will render assistance to the other when he is in peril if he can do so without endangering himself." That may be far too broad a statement, but surely it is true that your acts may imply undertakings of care. But compare the Rocha case, cited here (and discussed more fully in Note 4 after *Yania*). Those two guys were also out on a social venture together. Maybe the *Farwell* court would have accepted a duty in the *Rocha* case, but the *Rocha* court itself did not. Later in the *Rocha* opinion, the court says that, after all, Michael did not "actively" encourage or pressure George to jump.

In *Depue v. Flatau*, 111 N.W. 1 (Minn. 1907), the claim was that a dinner guest became ill. The hosts refused to let him spend the night and instead propped him in his wagon, threw the reins over his shoulder and started him toward home. The Supreme Court of Minnesota said that the hosts could be liable for injury to the guest if the jury found negligence. It seems clear that the hosts never undertook anything beyond a dinner, nor did they start a rescue and then stop, leaving the guest in a worse position. Is the host-guest relationship enough? Perhaps the case is not that different from the "implied contract" in *Farwell*. Compare *Tiedman v. Morgan*, 435 N.W.2d 86 (Minn. Ct. App. 1989) (family's duty of care to daughter's boyfriend, who was known to have heart problems).

In *Soldano v. O'Daniels*, 190 Cal. Rptr. 310 (App. Ct. 1983) the plaintiff alleged that a patron of Happy Jack's Saloon went across the street to the Circle Inn and asked the bartender there to call the police or to permit the patron to do so because a man had been threatened in Happy Jack's. The bartender refused to call or to permit the patron to do so. The plaintiff's father was shot and killed in Happy Jack's Saloon, presumably after the effort to call the police. The trial court dismissed the claim against the Circle Inn. *Held*, reversed. There is no special relationship here between the bar owner and a threat to a patron in another bar. But the rule of non-liability for nonfeasance should be re-examined. Legislative policy recognizes the importance of citizen intervention in crime, for example by providing for reimbursement for damages incurred in crime suppression. In addition, legislation in providing for 911 phone calls, recognized the importance of the telephone in dealing with crime. In determining whether a duty exists, a number of factors should be considered, including foreseeability of harm and closeness of connection between conduct and injury, moral blame, the policy of deterrence and the availability and cost of insurance. Here "[t]he employee's conduct displayed a disregard for human life that can be characterized as morally wrong; he was callously indifferent to the possibility that Darrell Soldano would die as the result of his refusal to allow a person to use the telephone.... [T]he bartender's burden was minimal and exposed him to no risk.... It would have cost him or his employer nothing. It could have saved a life.... Finding a duty in these circumstances would promote a policy of preventing future harm.... [W]e note that the liability which is sought to be imposed here is that of employee negligence, which is covered by many insurance policies .... No rule should be adopted which would require a citizen to open up his or her house to a stranger .... It does not follow, however, that use of a telephone in a public portion of a business should be refused for a legitimate emergency call.... The courts have a special responsibility to reshape, refine and guide legal doctrine they have created."

PODIAS V. MAIRS, 926 A.2d 859 (N.J. Super. App. Div. 2007).

Three 18-year-old college students drove away from a friend's house in the early morning hours after drinking beer. It was raining and the road was wet. Mairs, the driver, lost control of his car on the highway and hit and motorcyclist. All three boys went and looked at the cyclist and decided he was dead. No one else was around. None of them called for assistance, but they made a lot of other calls and decided essentially to run away and pretend nothing happened. After five or ten minutes they decided to drive off. Shortly afterward their car broke down. Mairs hid in the bushes waiting for his girlfriend to pick him up and the other two ran into the woods. Meanwhile a second car ran over the motorcyclist, who was in the middle of the road, killing him. In the estate's suit against the three students, *held*, the defendants owed a duty to assist, and breached that duty.

You might begin, after going through the facts, by asking what the basis of the driver's duty would be. The answer is that he caused the harm, one of the first "exceptions" mentioned in the text at the beginning of this chapter. But it's the passengers' duty of care that should command our attention here. If they did not cause the injury initially (indeed, one passenger was asleep when the original wreck occurred), what's the trigger of their duty?

The court is less than crystal clear, doctrinally, although morally it seems certain: "given the circumstances, the imposition of a duty upon defendants does not offend notions of fairness and common decency and is in accord with public policy, [which] encourages gratuitous assistance by those who have no legal obligation to render it."

So what "circumstances" seem most important? The court says the defendants "were far more than innocent bystanders or strangers to the event," thus taking the case out of the kind of example we give at the beginning of this chapter. Specifically, the court says that the "instrumentality of injury" (the car) was "operated for a common purpose and the mutual benefit of defendants." Further, the passengers knew the driver was intoxicated. And the defendants, all of them, "acquiesced in the conditions that may have helped create [the initial risk] and subsequently those conditions that further endangered the victim's safety." Finally, the court points out that the defendants had a kind of "special relationship" to the "incident itself."

Note 1 suggests that perhaps the court was consciously avoiding any attempt to fit the case into narrow categories of duty-triggering situations. But can students fit these reasons into the existing categories we've seen? The court was apparently driving in part at the point that the passengers helped create the original risk (that the intoxicated driver would cause an accident), which would trigger a duty of reasonable care if that risk came to fruition. Might this court have thought that the defendant in *Farwell* also helped create the original risk by drinking with his friend? What of the idea that the car was operated for their "mutual benefit?" How far might this rationale go? Would the court really find a duty of reasonable care on the part of every passive passenger when the care in which they are riding causes harm to someone? Unlikely.

Might the court have concluded that the passengers "took charge" when they began to talk about what to do next about the injured person? Or even that they actively helped convince each other not to help, thus making matters worse than if they had not done anything at all? The court does seem to stress this at at least two points in its opinion (the paragraph beginning "So, too, even though the defendant . . ." and in its next-to-last paragraph). Would that not provide an easy ground for the decision, without going into other matters? Why would the court bring in so many factors if one would clearly suffice? Does the *Wakulich* opinion seem "cleaner" in this respect?

Note 2. Is the court really condemning the basic nonfeasance rule? We saw it defended on moral grounds in *Yania*, where the court said that the situation "imposed upon [Bigan] no legal, although a moral, obligation or duty to go to [Yania's] rescue." We saw attacked on the same grounds in *Farwell* – pointing in the opposite direction – where the court stressed "humanitarian considerations" in finding a duty. In *Podias*, the court stresses "the moral obligation of common humanity" that the law refuses to impose as a general matter. What of the *Podias* court's citation of Prosser for the proposition that a duty might be found where the defendant has "mere knowledge of serious peril, threatening death or great bodily harm to another, which an identified defendant might avoid with little inconvenience"? Would such a formulation not result in a wholesale rejection of the no-duty-to-assist rule? If students think so, remind them that liability would follow only where the defendant then breached such a duty, which would presumably not occur where the rescue would be dangerous to the defendant, or where the defendant's "knowledge" was sketchy. This is essentially the way the rule is structured in countries that follow a German model, although it is a criminal, not a tort, provision. *See* JULIE A. DAVIES & PAUL T. HAYDEN, GLOBAL ISSUES IN TORT LAW 120-21 (2008).

[d] Civil Rights Claims

DESHANEY V. WINNEBAGO COUNTY DEP'T OF SOC. SERVS., 489 U.S. 189 (1989)

Joshua, born in 1979, is profoundly retarded as a result of a severe beating by his father in 1984 when he was four years old. The first complaints went to Winnebago County authorities in January 1982; in January, 1983 an investigation was launched when he had multiple injuries and the child protection (Department of Social Services) team exacted a contract from his father. A third report came in a month later. Social workers regularly visited the living quarters, always observing more injuries to Joshua or being turned away without seeing him. After the final beating and brain surgery, it was too late.

This suit asserts that the county deprived Joshua of "due process" right to life or liberty and is liable under § 1983. The argument that the child protection statutes gave Joshua an entitlement that could not be denied by the state is not before the court. Neither is the argument that the state selectively denied services so as to violate equal protection.

•CHIEF JUSTICE REHNQUIST, for the majority, makes a number of points:

1. **Due process: no affirmative duty**. The Due Process clause does not require the state to protect affirmatively against acts by private citizens.

2. **Special relationships**. The state may be liable to provide protection on the basis of special relationships in a limited class of cases: • *Estelle v. Gamble*. The 8th Amendment (cruel and unusual punishment) requires states not show deliberate indifference to the medical needs of prisoners. • *Youngberg v. Romeo*. Substantive due process extends this obligation to involuntarily committed mental patients. These cases only establish a special relationship where the state takes a person "into custody and holds him there against his will." (p. 484). This is because the state has restrained the individual so that he cannot care for himself. The fact that the state once took Joshua into custody has no bearing on this.

3. **State tort law**. States are free to impose tort liability, although the Court expresses appreciation of a dilemma: if the social worker moves too aggressively, the state will be interfering with the parent-child relationship.

●JUSTICE BRENNAN, dissenting, joined by Justices MARSHALL and BLACKMUN:

1. **Relevance of affirmative actions**. Affirmative actions are not relevant only because they deprive people of the ability to care for themselves; in *Youngberg v. Romeo* Romeo never had sufficient mental capacity so the state deprived him of nothing. If the state cuts off private aid and refuses aid itself, it cannot "wash its hands of the harm" that results.

2. **The state channeled and otherwise took affirmative actions**. The state channeled concerns over child safety to the DSS; it invited and directed dependence on the DSS. A private citizen would feel her job was done when she reported abuse. Joshua should be permitted to prove if he can that failure to help did not arise from professional judgment but from arbitrariness.

3. **Basis of liability**. Negligence is not the basis of liability; a mistake in judgment is not enough. But inaction can be abusive.

●JUSTICE BLACKMUN, dissenting:

The state actively intervened in the life of Joshua. A formal and rigid line between action and inaction has no place in interpreting the broad clauses of the 14th Amendment.

You can't teach constitutional law in the torts course, but *DeShaney* is a tort as well as a constitutional law case. We can skip the subtle points or even major points of constitutional doctrine, but we cannot ignore constitutional torts. And, whether we like those notions or not, we need to compare them to ordinary common law ideas of nonfeasance and to recognize the practical effect of denying civil rights liability.

Background qualifications. *DeShaney* decided ONLY substantive due process points. *DeShaney* did NOT decide any of the following things:

(a) liability of a public entity for discriminatory non-enforcement of law. Battered women who are victims of their partner's violence and of police refusal to protect them, may still be able to claim a civil rights violation if police refusal is discriminatory and denies equal protection of law.

(b) liability of a public entity for failure to train law enforcers properly. This might be regarded as a bad way of operating law enforcement rather than mere nonfeasance. If so, the formal, rigid limits of special relationships to "custody" cases has no application.

(c) liability based on a state-law entitlement to protection. If Joshua did have an entitlement, the state could not deprive him of that entitlement except by due process. As indicated in the Court's footnote 2, that issue was not raised in time.

Although the Court might conceivably answer the questions above in a way to impose liability in some cases, the first interest for us is the Court's concept of constitutional nonfeasance.

Background qualifications out of the way, you can begin by focusing on the issues raised in **Note 1**. If you were asserting a claim or defense under state law, what are the arguments for finding a duty here? There seems to be no neutral ground for asserting that the public entity took no action, that it undertook nothing, or that it lacked any relationship to Joshua. If you say it did "nothing" you must surely be defining "nothing" for the purpose of eliminating liability. If no legal rights turned on the description of the entity's activity, you would surely never think to say the state did nothing at all. The Court's emphasis, however, is on special relationship, conceived as the relationship of custodian to one in custody.

Note 2. Bases for constitutional duties. The court seems to identify a number of grounds, any one of which would be a sufficient trigger of a duty: (1) the plaintiff was in custody and officials intentionally failed to protect her; (2) the plaintiff was a victim of selectively unfavorable treatment of disfavored groups (see also the FYI Note below on discrimination); (3) the plaintiff had an entitlement created by state law and the officials deprived her of that entitlement without due process; or (4) officials actively created the danger that resulted in harm to the plaintiff. In each instance, the plaintiff would have to establish the defendant's culpability – an intentional deprivation of constitutional rights or deliberate indifference, or the like.

Note 3. What about other special relationships? The Court's formal conception of control or custody as the basis for a duty creates a problem. Whatever may be right constitutionally speaking, the common law outlook is much broader, for obligations may arise not only from control or custody but, as we've just seen, from special relationships.

In *Stevens v. Umsted,* 131 F.3d 697 (7th Cir. 1997), the court held that the school had no custody of the disabled child who was free to enroll in a different school. The principal's failure to act was therefore not actionable.

In *Weatherford v. State,* 54 P.3d 342 (Ariz. Ct. App. 2002), the court held that the constitutional right to reasonable safety while in foster care had been established for years (thus defeating a qualified immunity). The court seems to be implicitly hold that foster care is custody analogous to the *Estelle* and *Youngberg* custody cases cited in *DeShaney.*

Flexible custody, irrelevant custody. In the hands of some judges, the custody concept is quite flexible, but sometimes it is irrelevant, too. In a state-law case, *Deppe v. Poweshiek County,* 542 N.W.2d 6 (Iowa Ct. App. 1995), sheriff's officers followed the plaintiff, who was on a motorcycle, then pulled him over. One officer asked the plaintiff to walk around in front of the police car and get into the back passenger seat. The plaintiff had to walk through high weeds in the dark and in doing so fell into a culvert and sustained injuries. Citing *DeShaney,* the court concluded that the state had taken custody of the plaintiff, although he was not under arrest and was only being given a speeding citation. "[P]laintiff's normal opportunity for self-protection was curtailed. The command was specific and directed plaintiff to an area of danger. . . ." So much for formal custody.

The fact that the plaintiff is in custody will not win her lawsuit for her. In *Ladd v. County of San Mateo,* 911 P.2d 496 (Cal. 1996), custody became wholly irrelevant. The plaintiff was a minor, a 15-year-old ward of the juvenile court placed in the custody of her aunt. She ran away from her aunt and officers took her into custody and were driving her, handcuffed, to the juvenile hall. When the vehicle stopped at a traffic signal near railroad tracks, the plaintiff somehow managed to get out. She ran toward a freight train, and though handcuffed, tried to climb aboard. She slipped, fell beneath the wheels and lost both legs. She brought this suit against the county.

You might expect the arguments to be mainly about whether the officers were negligent: should they have foreseen a possible dangerous escape attempt and forestalled it in some way or not? But the California Court, now long accustomed to moving issues about negligence to the duty category where judges decide them, concluded that public entities owed no duty to prisoners to prevent the prisoner's own escape. If you shift the abstraction level a little, you might ask instead whether the custodian owes the ward a duty of reasonable care, including a duty to protect her from herself. In that form, the question does not so clearly invite a negative answer. If guards foresaw a suicide attempt, usual tort law principles would require them to take reasonable steps to prevent it.

Compare *White v. Whiddon,* 670 So.2d 131 (Fla. Dist. Ct. App. 1996). A 15-year-old became violent and irrational and his family took him to the sheriff's office for conveyance to a mental health facility where he had been treated before. The deputy put the boy in the locked cage of the officer's car, then left him alone there for a short while. The boy was handcuffed, but managed to get his arms through the cage, get the deputy's shotgun, and kill himself. The court held that the installer of the cage owed a duty of care, not only to others, but to the person incarcerated in it. Wouldn't it follow that the custodian owed a duty of care?

Comparative fault of person in custody. Del Tufo v. Township of Old Bridge, 685 A.2d 1267 (N.J. 1996), holds that comparative fault principles can be applied to affect recovery when an arrestee, to whom the police owe an affirmative duty of care, ingested an overdose of cocaine shortly before arrest. Both his ingestion (seemingly unknown to the police) and his failure to tell them he needed medical attention could count as contributory fault in a suit for his death. Although police owed a duty of care, the arrestee's comparative fault, consisting of conduct before injury occurred, would not merely count on minimizing damages but as comparative fault.

Note 4. State-created danger. As this note explains briefly, when the state creates a danger, then *DeShaney* is no longer a barrier. A constitutional duty is owed when the state creates a danger. The question then is whether the duty was breached. Some federal courts have hidden the structural simplicity of this idea in talking about state-created danger, sometimes generating multi-part tests. *See* Joseph M. Pellicciotti, Annotation, *"State-created Danger," or Similar Theory, as Basis For Civil Rights Action Under 42 U.S.C.A. § 1983*, 159 A.L.R. Fed. 37 (2000). However, there was never any idea that public entities could actively and intentionally deprive citizens of their rights. Once the officer takes affirmative actions that create a danger, the *DeShaney* problem should be behind you. Still, federal courts may be developing the state-created danger concept as one that differs from the common law concept of affirmative action carried out wrongfully.

A second and quite different question remains, but it is not the nonfeasance question. It is the question of constitutional culpability. Negligence is not a basis for finding a violation of due process or equal protection; the officer is not liable unless he intentionally violates the plaintiff's right or his behavior shocks the conscience by his deliberate indifference. (With professionals undertaking protection of one in custody, the standard may be one of professional judgment, however. As to that, see the "Foster homes" paragraph below.) This second or culpability issue is not the point of this chapter, which is instead about the difference between action and non-action. However, students should remember that even if the officer acts affirmatively, creating a danger that would not otherwise exist, he may not be guilty of wilful indifference –or indeed, even of negligence. You may wish to remind the class of materials in Chapter 3, § 5.

In recognizing the state-created danger "exception," the federal courts do not seem to recognize affirmative action as an undertaking that in itself suffices. Instead, they seem to require that the defendant's conduct make matters worse than if the state had not intervened at all.

In *Estate of Amos v. City of Page*, 257 F.3d 1086 (9th Cir. 2001), the complaint alleged that police investigating car collision, learned that a driver had wandered into the desert, apparently bleeding. Track marks indicated he was disoriented. But officers quickly gave up the search, perhaps in the belief that the driver was a Navajo who would make his way to the nearby reservation. The police not only gave up; they prevented civilian rescue efforts. The driver's remains were found in a canyon a year later. The court held that, although the state did undertake a search, it did not create the danger and did not leave the driver in a worse position. The state also prevented civilian rescue attempts, but this was not enough to show that the driver was worse off, since the civilians were not shown to have special training and they might not have found him, either. For these reasons, the stated-created danger avenue was closed to the plaintiff. The court left room, however, for a claim that the driver had been denied equal protection if the search was called off because the police believed the driver to be a Native American.

In *S.S. v. McMullen,* cited here, the state removed the plaintiff from her father's custody, but then unaccountably returned her to his custody in spite of the known risk that she would be sodomized by her father's associate, a known pedophile. The risk in fact eventuated. The panel held that this was state-created danger and that the plaintiff could recover. *S.S., ex rel. Jervis v. McMullen,* 186 F.3d 1066 (8th Cir. 1999). The Eighth Circuit en banc held that this was not state-created danger because "in returning S.S. to her father, the state did not increase the danger of significant harm to S.S.: It merely placed her back into the situation from which it had originally retrieved her."

This approach seems in line with Chief Justice Rehnquist's comments in *DeShaney*:

> That the State once took temporary custody of Joshua does not alter the analysis, for when it returned him to his father's custody, it placed him in no worse position than that in which he would have been had it not acted at all; the State does not become the permanent guarantor of an individual's safety by having once offered him shelter.

In *K.H. v. Morgan*, also cited here, Judge Posner said "the absence of a duty to rescue does not entitle a rescuer to harm the person whom he has rescued. . . . If, as the complaint alleges, the defendants must have known they were placing K.H. in a sequence of foster homes that would be destructive of her mental health, the ingredients of a valid constitutional claim are present." Is that statement at odds with *DeShaney*?

In *Currier v. Doran*, 242 F.3d 905 (10th Cir. 2001), the mother had custody of small children. The state took custody of the children. In spite of the fact that there were reasons to think the children's father would abuse them, the state officers at least acquiesced in transfer of custody to him. In his custody, they were abused terribly; the father actually poured boiling water of the male child, who later died as a result. The responsible officers were held subject to § 1983 liability. The court distinguished the case in which the state "merely" returned the child to the parent who had custody before, saying this was a state-created danger case.

Foster homes and wilful indifference vs. professional judgment standard. In *Eugene D. v. Karman*, 889 F.2d 701 (6th Cir. 1989), a case in which the state failed to remove a child from foster care when evidence mounted that the child was being mistreated, the court thought it unclear whether the officials would be under a constitutional duty.

However, other courts have held that state placement of a child is equivalent to custody so that a duty is imposed upon the state to at least avoid wilful indifference and perhaps to exercise care of a professional social worker. *Nicini v. Morra,* 212 F.3d 798 (3d Cir. 2000). The underlying due process standard is "shocks the conscience," which in the case of some omissions, seems to be met by the deliberate indifference standard imposed in some 8th Amendment cruel and unusual punishment cases. But *Youngberg* used a professional care standard for those involuntarily committed to a mental institution. *Kara B. v. Dane County*, 555 N.W.2d 630 (Wis. 1996), adapted that professional standard to the state's supervision of a foster home, but some other cases have assumed that intent or the wilful indifference standard would apply. *White v. Chambliss,* 112 F.3d 731 (4th Cir. 1997). *Weatherford v. State,* 54 P.3d 342 (Ariz. Ct. App. 2002), a § 1983 case, said that if professional judgment standard differed from wilful indifference, the former would apply. The court in *Lewis v. Anderson,* 308 F.3d 768 (7th Cir. 2002), looking at none of this but relying on the formulation in *K.H.*, quoted above, concludes that liability can be imposed only if the social workers *know or suspect* the prospective foster parents are dangerous to the child.

In *Kara B. v. Dane County*, 555 N.W.2d 630 (Wis. 1996), however, the court thought that after *DeShaney's* reasoning was considered, a constitutional right of the child to state protection was clearly established, so that state officers who placed the child in a dangerous foster home would not enjoy a qualified immunity. Furthermore, a constitutional violation would be shown not only by wilful indifference to her safety, but by a deviation from professional judgment. The plaintiff in that case was allowed to proceed with a claim that she was sexually abused in the foster home where county officials had placed her.

In *Little v. Utah State Div. of Family Servs.*, 667 P.2d 49 (Utah 1983), the state removed a two-and-one-half-year old child, Jennifer, from the parental home after a juvenile court found that the child was manifesting autistic behavior and that the parents could not provide for her emotionally. The child was placed in a foster home, but the state failed to give any special training to the foster parents for the care of autistic children and also failed to provide protective headgear. Jennifer repeatedly banged her head and bruised herself and died from this repeated self-harm. A jury returned a verdict against the state for $20,000 and funeral expenses. *Held,* affirmed. There was no discretionary immunity. But even if the decision to place the child in a foster home was discretionary, "once that decision was made and the placement occurred, the question was no longer whether the child was to receive foster care but whether due care was exercised under a duty assumed. . . . Negligence under the Federal Tort Claims Act has been consistently held actionable where the conduct involved a non-discretionary duty to perform a professional function unrelated to policy decisions." Id. At 51-52. Some other cases have also found liability in foster-home situations. *E.g., Vonner v. State*, 273 So.2d 252, (La. 1973); *Koepf v. York County*, 251 N.W.2d 866 (Neb. 1977).

Note that where the state court itself has direct involvement in placing a child in a foster home, plaintiffs will have a rough time. Federal courts cannot review the correctness of state decisions, so court-approved placement is not actionable even under federal civil rights statutes. *Lewis v. Anderson*, 308 F.3d 768 (7th Cir. 2003). And state court involvement may raise the possibility that social workers enjoy absolute judicial immunity. *See Miller v. Gammie*, 292 F.3d 982 (9th Cir. 2002). *But see State v. Second Judicial District Court, County of Washoe*, 55 P.3d 420 (Nev. 2002) (social worker implementation of child-placement decisions not absolutely immune, even if social worker input into the decisions may be).

Note 5. A foreign perspective (The European Human Rights Convention). *(a) Alerting students to texts.* As usual, a contrary outcome can throw more light on the subject. First, those who dislike *DeShaney's* outcome might still think that *A. v. United Kingdom*, 27 E.H.R.R. 611 (1999,) went too far in the other direction. More on that in the next paragraph. Second, you can emphasize that there are two distinct reasons why this decision would not be binding in American courts–(a) jurisdictionally, the European Court has no power over American governments and hence its decisions are not binding; (b) more importantly, the court is working under a text that is quite different in language, context, and legal history from the text of the United States Constitution. (And of course quite different from our common law, too, since common law wholly lacks an authoritative initial text). Although the decision in *A.* might still be persuasive-but-not-binding in American courts, the fact that it is rooted in a specific text not applicable in the United States suggests it would lack persuasive value as well as precedential value. In addition, the arguably extreme outcome might persuade many judges NOT to adopt a duty.

(b) A. v. United Kingdom *as an extreme case?* In *A.*, England actually prosecuted the child-beater but the defense in that criminal action persuaded the jury that the defendant's beatings were moderate under all the circumstances, including the circumstance that the boy was "difficult." There was no suggestion that the prosecution was inept. The European Court did seem to think that the absence of guidelines about what counted as moderate or non-degrading punishment plus a burden of proof upon the prosecution helped make England responsible under a clause requiring the signatory states to secure the rights and freedoms recognized in the Convention. The Court, though it proffers very long opinions, does not engage in extensive reasoning.

As the casebook reflects, the court gave at least some weight to the fact that the jury was allowed to decide what counted as moderate punishment without specific guidance. You might wonder whether this concern reflects the biases of the civil law approach based upon codes and a dislike of common law method that allows decision makers to import current and even local standards in deciding questions like reasonableness or moderation.

Note 6. Although it would be hard for us to say that the state took no action in *DeShaney*, there are reasons to exercise caution about imposing liability upon social workers in similar situations. Perhaps if a social worker is too readily held liable, social workers might become more intrusive into family life to avoid liability. If she has probable cause to believe the child is in danger, she would be protected against liability for intervening, even if intervention proved in the end to be unnecessary. Given that protection from suit by the family, liability for failure to act would give her incentive to intrude in doubtful cases. One proposal is to relieve the individual social worker of liability, just as federal employees are relieved. *See* Laura Oren, *The State's Failure to Protect Children and Substantive Due Process: DeShaney in Context*, 68 N.C.L. REV. 659 (1990).

■**FYI: Discriminatory police action or inaction.** There is another constitutional ground for protection, adjacent to the one the *DeShaney* Court impassively barred: Equal protection based on police discrimination. *See Sinthasimphone v. City of Milwaukee*, 785 F.Supp. 1343 (E.D. Wis. 1992) (police released a young Laotian man found naked on the street, severely hurt and drugged, into the custody of mass murderer Jeffrey Dahmer, who killed him soon after; court said the complaint should not be dismissed where it alleged intentional discrimination based on "race, color, national origin, or sexual orientation"). Equal protection ideas might be used in cases where police policy refuses protection in domestic violence cases, even though due process analysis could not. *See* James T.R. Jones, *Battered Spouses' Section 1983 Damage Actions against the Unresponsive Police after DeShaney*, 93 W. VA. L. REV. 251 (1991). (Failure to train, as suggested earlier, may be another option.)

CHAPTER 17

CONTRACT AND DUTY

▶**Changes in the Sixth Edition.** The basic coverage and organization have not been changed from the prior edition, although here as elsewhere we've tried to tighten the material. In § 1, we've cut the *Mobil v. Thorn* case and the *Southwestern Bell v. DeLanney* case abstract. We've added a new primary case in the same section, *Spengler*. In § 3, we've cut the *Folsom* case abstract. Notes have been reorganized in places and updated throughout.

▶The **Concise Edition** trims just a few pages from this Chapter, by substituting a short case abstract of Paz v. State of California for the main case, cutting Notes 2 and 3 after Paz, and cutting subsections B and C of the Note: Content and Duty Derived from "Undertakings" at the very end of the Chapter.■

Preliminary Note. In many instances, tort duties can be created, modified, or limited by contract, informal undertaking, or even by mutual and reasonable expectations between the parties. Saying that a contract, undertaking, or relationships creates tort duties means that liability will be determined under the rules of tort law (the statute of limitations, for example) and that tort damages will be appropriate if the plaintiff prevails. The precise expression of this principle and its exact scope may be uncertain, but not the principle itself.

Authorities tell us that the contract cannot dictate tort duties unless the defendant has actually begun performance. That would make nonfeasance an important factor in determining tort duties arising from contract. You can be skeptical about that. The variables that seem more important when the contract is offered to create or enlarge a duty of care are those exposed by these questions: (1) Was the contract (or undertaking) an economic matter only, or did it attempt to provide for physical safety? (2) Did the plaintiff reasonably and foreseeably rely upon the contract or undertaking, with concomitant loss when the defendant breached? Maybe the reliance demand is overdone at times, and perhaps it ought to be re-worked to require only foreseeable harm, but re-worked or not, the safety promise must be clearly distinguished from the economic promise.

When the contract is offered, not to create a tort duty but to limit a duty or liability, matters are simpler. We've already seen contractual assumed risk. Contracts limiting liability or shifting responsibility do not fundamentally differ in principle from the idea that the plaintiff can assume the risk or shoulder full responsibility for safety. Accordingly, a valid contract limiting the defendant's liability would be enforced according to its terms unless it is against public policy or secured by fraud.

Three other types of question arise. (1) Is the defendant who undertakes a duty to one person bound to perform it for the benefit of another? (2) What is the duty the defendant has undertaken – reasonable care, or something more? (3) What is the scope of the duty undertaken – against what kinds of risks or harms is the defendant obliged to protect?

OUTLINE

§ 1. NONPERFORMANCE OF PROMISES
A. Unenforceable Promises. *Thorne v. Deas*
B. Enforceable Promises. *Spengler v. ADT*; *Grimes v. Kennedy Krieger Institute, Inc.*

§ 2. PROMISES TO THIRD PERSONS
Winterbottom v. Wright; H.R. Moch Co. v.   Rensselaer Water Co.; Palka v. Servicemaster; Paz v. State of California

§ 3. ACTION AS A PROMISE OR UNDERTAKING
Florence v. Goldberg; Kircher v. City of Jamestown;
Note: Content and Scope of Duty Derived from "Undertakings"

COMMENTS

§ 1. NONPERFORMANCE OF PROMISES

A. Unenforceable Promises

THORNE V. DEAS, 4 Johns. (N.Y.) 84 (1809).

This is the classic case, with an opinion by a judge who influenced much early American law. He thought there was no consideration, hence no contract, no misfeasance, hence no tort. A promise not enforceable because contract law opposed enforcement cannot furnish the basis for a tort duty that would undermine the contract law rule.

Cases like *Thorne* have led to the idea that gratuitous promises create no tort duty unless some action is taken toward performance. The Restatement, §

323, takes no position on the point either way. But this restrictive notion is based mostly on economic harm cases like *Thorne*. When a promise is made to minimize the risk of physical harm, and nonperformance negligently creates a risk of that harm, the few modern cases seem inclined to require that the defendant exercise reasonable care to perform his promise, even when he has utterly failed to act on it. See DOBBS ON TORTS § 320 (2000). Cases supporting liability:

• In *Morgan v. County of Yuba,* 41 Cal.Rptr. 508 (Ct. App. 1964), peace officers, before and after arresting a man who had threatened a woman's life, promised to warn her when he was released on bail; they didn't and the man killed her when he was released. The court held that these allegations stated a cause of action based on nonfeasance if the plaintiff could amend to show reliance on the promise.

• *Marsalis v. LaSalle,* 94 So.2d 120 (La. App. 1957) is the famous cat case. Without the defendant's fault, his cat scratched the plaintiff, a customer; defendant promised to keep the cat up for fourteen days to determine whether it had rabies, but took no steps whatever to do so and the cat escaped and could not be found, as a result of which the plaintiff had to undergo the painful Pasteur treatment and some painful reactions to it. The cat reappeared a month later, entirely healthy, showing that the treatments would have been unneeded if the cat had been kept in the house as promised. The court held that the promise created a duty of care to keep the cat up. The case is only slightly marred by the fact that a narrower ground for the duty could have been found under the rule that if the defendant causes harm, however innocently, he must then exercise care to minimize it. See Chapter 16.

Notes 1 & 2. The Restatement of Contracts § 90, which permits a promissory estoppel to substitute for consideration, might change results on facts somewhat like those in *Thorne*. However, one might be very cautious about permitting contract liability that turns the defendant into an insurer. As Kent suggests, the rule might be different for those in the insurance business, and indeed an agent who does not promptly process an application or the home office which does not do so may be liable in tort. A good number of decisions support this liability, and some find liability in contract. *See* Annotation, 32 A.L.R.2d 487 (1953). The casebook does not develop this material, because the focus here is on physical, not economic torts.

Reliance. In *Cunningham v. Braum's Ice Cream & Dairy Stores*, 80 P.3d 35 (Kan. 2003), employees of an ice cream store told customers to leave, despite the fact (unknown to the customers) that a tornado warning was in effect. The customers were injured by a tornado as they drove away. They sued the store in a tort action, claiming that there was a duty either to warn them of the coming tornado or to provide them with shelter. They rested their duty argument on the store's written emergency plan, claiming this was an affirmative undertaking of a duty to customers to protect them in accordance with it. That plan said that if a tornado was sighted, customers who wish to remain in the store should be taken into the milk room. Held, the defendant owed plaintiffs no duty. The emergency plan, which simply said that if a tornado is sighted, customers who wish to remain in the store should be taken to the milk room, "does not compel any particular action by Braum's employees in such a situation," and creates no duties at all. There was no evidence, the court concluded, that Braum's conduct increased the risk to the plaintiffs, or that the plaintiffs relied on the emergency action plan to their detriment. It seems that the plaintiffs could not have relied on the plan if they did not know about it, which would defeat their claim even under the new Restatement quoted in Note 1 after *Spengler*, just below.

Note 3. *Belhumeur*, cited here, focuses on the "increasing the risk of harm" idea touched on above, as well as on the idea that an bald promise, without reliance, should not create a legal duty. The former point may provide a criticism of the Spengler case, coming up.

B. Enforceable Promises

SPENGLER V. ADT SECURITY SERVICES, INC., 505 F.3d 456 (6th Cir. 2007)

Note 1. Critiquing *Spengler*. Doesn't the *Spengler* case fit the Restatement (Third) rule like a glove? Indeed, it seems that both of the conditions in the second part of the rule are met, when only one would suffice: the failure to exercise care increased the risk of harm (unlike the case involving bees mentioned in Note 3 after Thorne, above), and the plaintiff was relying on the undertaking to provide security.

Note 2. Distinguishing contract from tort. Dobbs on Torts § 320, cited here, says that "The general rule is that the defendant is under a duty to perform undertakings made for safety purposes and is liable for physical harm he causes the plaintiff by negligently performing or quitting performance once it has begun." Isn't that *Spengler*?

In *Southwestern Bell Tel. Co. v. DeLanney*, discussed here, Bell's contract to publish a Yellow Pages listing also limited its liability for failure to publish. If the plaintiff could avoid this limitation by saying "I sue in tort, not contract" the agreement of the parties would be dishonored and subverted. If an exception to enforceability does not apply, tort law must bow to a valid agreement of the parties that limits tort liability. (We saw this, in part, in Chapter 10 on contractual or express assumption of the risk.)

The principle of honoring valid contracts and even informal understandings of the parties really resolves *DeLanney*. The court, however, takes the occasion to approach the issue in terms of nonfeasance – if there is no performance of the contract at all, there can be no tort liability. The nonfeasance analysis doesn't seem satisfactory. Suppose the telephone company had actually set the listing in type and proofed it, then had negligently lost the printing plate and gone ahead without it to meet a deadline. That is a case in which performance has begun, but the limitation on liability should still prevail because the parties agreed to it, unless one of the three exceptions listed above applies.

Equally, the nonfeasance analysis doesn't seem desirable when the defendant's promise (or conduct amounting to a promise) is a safety promise that induces reliance, as discussed above with respect to *Spengler*. Even complete nonperformance of a promise that electrical current will be turned off while the plaintiff is working on the electrical circuits should surely be actionable if the plaintiff reasonably relied upon it.

The *DeLanney* case involved purely economic harm, not physical harm as in *Spengler*. As suggested in several places, that is an important distinction with judging whether a contract should create a tort duty as opposed to leaving matters to contract law. The quote from *DeLanney*, though, seems to further undermine the reasoning and result in *Spengler*. When someone has undertaken to provide services that involve minimizing the risks of physical harm to someone, that should create a duty independent of contract, and give rise to a tort duty. That was not the case in *DeLanney*, of course, but it certainly seems like the case in *Spengler*.

GRIMES V. KENNEDY KRIEGER INSTITUTE, INC., 782 A.2d 807 (Md. 2001).

The factual details are not developed, but the children were subjected one way or another to the risk of lead poisoning and the researchers were misleading the families about this. The researcher's affirmative acts, and even the relationship between researcher and human subject itself, might be enough to create a duty, and the court seemed to think so. However, the court was at pains to stress that the consent form created a contract between the parties and in so doing, it created a special relationship from which a tort duty of care could spring. (Confusingly enough, part of the opinion seems to say that the jury will determine whether a special relationship existed, but we can fairly skip that to make the point that contracts can after all create tort duties.)

Note 1. Tort duty from contract. Continuing the theme. As a policy matter, if a tort duty exists separate from the contract, why limit the duty to the contract? That is the *Grimes* view. But this is a complicated issue, covered in several places coming up. See, especially, the NOTE: CONTENT AND SCOPE OF DUTY DERIVED FROM "UNDERTAKINGS," Casebook p. 475.

Note 2. Leases. *Leavitt*, discussed here, is a well-known case. The landlord's promise in that case is no doubt supported by consideration, so it is enforceable as a contract, but only for contract damages. Contract damages reflect the value of the thing promised in the contract, not collateral losses that result from nonperformance. See 3 DAN DOBBS, THE LAW OF REMEDIES § 12.4(4) (2d ed. 1993). That excludes recovery for injury as distinct from the cost of repairing the premises. *Leavitt's* rule eliminating tort damages was logical and might even be reasonable as applied to bargainers on equal footing. It might even be reasonable as to repairs the tenant could be expected to handle for herself. Noncapital repairs – for example a new light switch when the old one appears to have a short – could well be allocated to the tenant in any event, and even if allocated to the lessor, it might be reasonable to let the tenant repair and deduct the cost. This was the effect of the *Leavitt* rule.

But the rule worked rather differently in the case of poor tenants, or where capital repairs were required. (Why should a month-to-month tenant have to purchase a new furnace or water heater and take the chance that the lessor will not pay for it?) These and similar considerations – usually muffled under the general cloak of vague arguments based on "modern conditions" or "unfair bargaining power" or the like – led courts to give a tort effect to the landlord's contract duty in residential cases. So *Leavitt* represents the old guard, now unlikely to be followed.*Mobil Oil Corp. v. Thorn*, cited here, involves a physical risk and physical harm resulting from the conduct that was also a breach of contract. The court was not only comfortable with tort damages, but applied the rule in the case of a commercial as well as a residential lease. You can describe the effect of liability in cases like *Mobil Oil v. Thorn* in at least two different ways. You could say that the plaintiff recovers "in contract" but is permitted to recover an unusual measure of damages. Or you could say that the plaintiff recovers "in tort" and recovers the usual tort measure of damages. Perhaps it does not often matter how whether we conceptualize this kind of recovery as tort or as contract with tort-type damages permitted.

Note 3. Reassessing *Spengler*. As if we had not already invited students to reject the Spengler case more than once, here's another opportunity. From a pedagogical perspective, the Note here invites students (led by the teacher, if you wish) to take a legal standard applicable to Situation A (landlords and leases) and apply it to Situation B (*Spengler*) by analogy. Again, *Spengler* seems to come up short. Perhaps in defense of the opinion, it was a federal court applying, rather than making, state law. Its hands were tied. But the law being applied hardly seems sound.

Note 4. Expired contracts. In *Folsom v. Burger King*, cited here, the issue was whether the defendant's conduct in leaving the alarm system on the premises and in working order amount to an undertaking to provide alarm services, even though in fact the contract for service had been terminated. In the case, we do not know whether the murdered employees knew that the contract had been terminated. The court thought that the security company was not undertaking a "rescue" by leaving the equipment in place. The case so presented looks like a standard nonfeasance decision – the defendant's contract having been terminated, it had no duty unless it began a rescue, but it did not. If the defendant created a misleading appearance that an alarm system was in place, would that be enough to justify liability? Or would the estates of the murdered employee be required to show that the employees relied on a working system? How could they do that? Perhaps by showing that (a) the employees believed the system was working and (b) would not have remained in the employment if they had known the truth. There was evidence in the case that officers were across the street and could have immediately responded had the alarm service provided the call to police.

§ 2. PROMISES TO THIRD PERSONS

WINTERBOTTOM V. WRIGHT, 152 Eng. Rep. 402 (Exch. Pl. 1842).

Winterbottom was a leading case for many years and is still a famous one. The judge is Lord Abinger of *Priestly v. Fowler*, 3 M. & W. 1 (Exch. 1837), the also-famous origin of the fellow-servant rule. The accepted work doctrine, derived in part from *Winterbottom,* had it that once a building contractor had completed a job and the landowner had accepted it, the building contractor had no liability to someone injured by his dangerous and negligent work. That doctrine is now largely obsolete and usually overruled when defendant's argue in contemporary cases. E.g., *Suneson v. Holloway Construction Co.,* 992 S.W.2d 79 (Ark. 1999). And *Winterbottom* itself is obsolete when it comes to active negligence; otherwise the law of products liability would have remained stunted. But if the repair shop did nothing, the case looks like nonfeasance. Cardozo's language in *Moch* would suggest that *Winterbottom* remains sound law on its facts, although we think it is not.

This law is easy to translate into modern life for your class. "Suppose, Ms. Jones, you take your car to your auto repair person and leave it, obtaining an agreement that the brakes will be checked, as you are about to take a long trip. When you return, the station is closed for the night and your keys are under the seat where the attendants have left them before. You drive off, happy in the assumption that the brakes have been checked and are safe. In fact, they were never checked and are not safe. You then have a wreck as a result of the brake defects, and a man named Patridge is injured. Can he sue your repair person?

Both the hypothetical and *Winterbottom* itself differ from *Delanney*. All involve nonfeasance, but *Winterbottom* and the hypothetical are cases in which the defendant has created risks of physical harm. *Winterbottom* and the hypothetical also differ from *Delanney* in that third persons are injured. That is, the injury is not to the person the defendant contracted with.

We have thought that *Winterbottom* was a dead letter, but an Indiana Appellate Court opinion is somewhat similar. In *Holt v. Quality Motor Sales, Inc.,* 776 N.E.2d 361(Ind. Ct. App. 2002), the repairer was not liable to a third party not in privity even though he was guilty of active negligence rather than mere nonfeasance. The court thought Indiana had abolished any distinction between nonfeasance and misfeasance, not with the result that the plaintiff could recover for nonfeasance but with the result that the plaintiff might be denied recovery for misfeasance! In the absence of a special relationship, something we take to be similar to privity, it would all hinge on policy considerations. The policy considerations here were only gestured at. The injured driver of the car who was a relation of the owner, had no driver's license. The court thought that this was somehow a policy consideration:

> We do not mean to suggest that William's lack of a valid license was a proximate cause of his fatal accident, but we do believe that sound public policy weighs against holding Quality accountable for William's illegal operation of Harrison's vehicle. Our policy analysis is further buttressed by the fact that Quality repaired the Pontiac's brakes to Harrison's satisfaction in January 1998 and that Harrison and William experienced no problems with the braking system while driving more than 13,000 miles in three months.

Although we find this case troubling, it is not a rule of law requiring privity because it turns on facts of particular cases so far as they impress the judges as bearing on "public policy."

H.R. MOCH CO. V. RENSSELAER WATER CO., 159 N.E. 896 (N.Y. 1928).

You may want to read the textual NOTE: CONTENT AND SCOPE OF DUTY DERIVED FROM "UNDERTAKINGS" (after the Notes to *Paz*), before you conduct a class on *Moch*.

Moch, of course, is the leading case. Note that the contract between the city and the water company is valid. If the city, finding the water pressure inadequate, had to buy its water elsewhere at a higher price, it would surely have had an action on the contract.

Why not a contract action? Persons within the scope of the contract. Parties to a contract control the scope of their contract. If it is not intended to be enforceable by a non-party, then it is not. This is a kind of autonomy or freedom. If no preexisting rule compels either party to bargain for the benefit of a non-party, it is difficult to see how the rule could be otherwise.

Why not an action in tort? The nonfeasance rule. Why does the citizen not have an action in tort? Cardozo tells us that there is no tort duty because the defendant did nothing; it is a case of nonfeasance.[1] The defendant

---

[1] Cardozo speaks disparagingly of the incompleteness and misleading character of the nonfeasance formula, so students sometimes think he is rejecting a nonfeasance analysis. He is not. He is saying that there are cases in which even nonfeasance will be tortious and actionable if there is a relationship between the parties that requires action. Affirmative action becomes important for Cardozo because it establishes a relationship between the parties; and nonaction is important because in some (but not all) cases it will show the absence of a relationship that engenders a duty. But none of this turns out to be of any importance in the decision. In the end, he goes back to basic nonfeasance reasoning– did action go forward sufficiently? Most students can be led to see that this is just a restatement of the problem, not a revealing test that will facilitate decision-making.

is free – apart from contract or promise – to do nothing. In this respect, the promise of the water utility creates no duty because the plaintiff is not within the class of persons it protects. As to the plaintiff, it is as if there is not contract at all. Since there is no contract duty to the plaintiff and since there is no affirmative action, the case for Cardozo resolves itself into a simple case of no duty to the plaintiff.

Cardozo's answers raise two questions. (1) Is nonfeasance really determinative in these cases if (a) the defendant promises actions to enhance physical safety, and (b) the plaintiff relies? (2) Was the defendant's misconduct really nonfeasance?

The limited relevance of nonfeasance. When the promise is one meant to enhance safety or reduce risk and the plaintiff relies upon it, nonaction would seem not to matter at all. The electric company promises a contractor that it will disconnect electrical current at a job site until workers have finished working on electrical connections. It does nothing toward performance. If a subcontractor suffers electrical burns because of her reasonable reliance upon the promise, liability seems almost beyond serious question. If the plaintiff is defeated, it should be because she did not rely at all, or he relied unreasonably, or was an unforeseeable victim, not because the defendant did nothing. In the case of a purely economic promise, on the other hand, the promisor is almost certainly not liable in tort even if he take action in performance; he is liable instead according to the tenor of his contract.

Was this nonfeasance? On the second question, was Cardozo correct in treating this as a case of nonfeasance by the defendant? All we really know is that the water pressure was not kept up. This could have happened as the result of a specific, affirmative action of negligence – misreading instruments or opening the wrong valve. The plaintiff's complaint in *Moch* does not take us very far in understanding the facts, and the New York courts did not seem any more curious about them than they were in *Riss*. If the water company opened the wrong valve, this might or might not have violated the contract, but it would surely be negligent affirmative action.

A bad way of actively supplying water? More fundamentally, you might go back to *Newton v. Ellis* in Chapter 16 (Nonfeasance), where the contractor failed to light the excavation in the street. Failure to light the excavation was not to be considered as nonfeasance because it was not to be considered standing alone. Failure to light was a bad way of excavating the street. Why is failure to supply pressure not regarded as a bad way of running a water company? If we said that, the case would not be a case of nonfeasance at all, but one of active conduct—the conduct of running the water company and running it in a way that is dangerous if fire occurs.

Characterizing the activity. Some people will say that "running a water company" is too big an action category and that if you use categories of activities like that, almost anything will be counted as misfeasance. Such an argument may be right, or partly right, but nothing has been handed down from above to tell us how to categorize activities. If putting on the brakes is a part of the category of activity called "driving a car," why is not putting the pressure up not part of the activity called "operating a water works?"

A different explanation: avoiding strict liability. The answer may lie in a different direction. It takes a minute to grasp, but once you see it, it does seem to reveal some ideas that are lost in the dark shadows of the nonfeasance talk. The answer may be that lawyers and judges in *Moch* discussed a tort but unconsciously assumed that liability, if any, would be like that in contract –strict liability. And the judges were not willing to impose strict liability. This is one reason the plaintiff's failure to claim any specific act of negligence is significant. The claim was only that the water company failed to live up to the contract promise to provide the water pressure. For a contract claim, non-performance would be enough to establish liability, since, by and large, contract liability is strict liability. Liability in tort for mere breach of contract without proof of some sort of fault would seem extreme. Without articulating any such feelings, the judges may have felt very uncomfortable with the idea that a contract promise would impose strict liability in tort to third persons. Maybe the case would have been very different, then, if the plaintiff had alleged a specific act of negligence, even if it had been an "omission," such as a failure to read the pressure instructions.

Another explanation. Cardozo was worried about indefinite expansion of liability –in "an indeterminate amount for an indeterminate time to an indeterminate class" as he expressed it in *Ultramares*, reprinted in Chapter 34. This is a good thing to worry about when you are talking about pure economic harm. A contractor accepting one liability should not be forced to accept others. But Cardozo failed to recognize that all of the cases he cited and the reasons he gave had to do with economic contracts, not safety arrangements. When we come to strict products liability, we'll see that exactly such a distinction is drawn (as it is also in many other kinds of cases.)

Scope of risk undertaken. If we are to hold the water company either in tort or contract because of its contract promise, we will presumably limit its liability to those harms or risks its promise was intended to avoid. This point is considered in the NOTE: CONTENT AND SCOPE OF DUTY DERIVED FROM "UNDERTAKINGS" but you may want to initiate discussion with *Moch. Libbey v. Hampton Water Works Co.*, 389 A.2d 434 (N.H. 1978) (**Note 6**), sees the uniform pricing of water as a good indication that the water supplier's promise was a guarantee against price increases, not a guarantee against fire. Why so? Because if you were guaranteeing fire protection, you'd charge higher water costs in neighborhoods with higher valued property and those where fires were particularly likely or particularly likely to spread. Uniform costs per hydrant indicate you are only making an economic guarantee. If that is correct, you shouldn't be held liable for fire damages, because that is a guarantee you did not make.

Fire Insurance and scope of risk. This may be a good place to consider the role of fire insurance. The *Libbey* case, Note 6, suggests that given the way water was priced, the water supplier probably had not expected to be charged as an insurer, and was thus contracting only as a price guarantor. The availability and common usage of fire insurance suggests something of the same thing. Given a choice, we would probably prefer insurance companies to base their premium charges on sound actuarial understandings of the risk, which an insurance company can do, but not a water company. Fire insurance is relatively efficient; it pays without necessitating any expensive public investigation into fault that goes on in tort cases. Not only is fire insurance a good solution to cases like *Moch* from a public or judicial viewpoint, but it probably matches the kinds of expectations the parties had –which did not include holding the water company as an insurer.

Added costs of pursuing tort rather than insurance recovery. If we allowed tort recovery against the water company in this kind of case, it would probably add new costs that would not be involved in collecting from a fire insurer. If *Moch* imposed liability, a likely situation is as follows: the water company has liability insurance; the homeowner has a fire insurance policy. When the fire occurs, the homeowner collects from his fire insurer. The insurer, subrogated to the homeowner's rights, now sues the water company in tort. The water company notifies its insurer, who comes in and investigates, defends, negotiates and pays. Can the class see that there are large new costs involved in this set of procedures? If *Moch* cases deny recovery, the fire insurer pays with its more efficient premium dollars and that's the end of it.

Class of person limits on liability premised on undertaking. The contract or promise might also create a duty subject to the *Palsgraf* class of person analysis. A promise to A is not a promise to B or even to all persons who might foreseeably benefit from performance given to A. This is the basis for the limited protection given to third parties. The privity language of the cases and discussions may obscure this fairly simple point. The promisor should be held liable on contract only if he agrees to liability; that is what contract is all about. If he agrees to be liable to A for failure to supply water, the law should not compel him to accept liability to B and C as well as a condition of entering into the contract with A. *Cf. Blake v. Public Service Co.*, 82 P.3d 960 (N.M. Ct. App. 2003) (no duty owed by electrical utility to individual residents; court stressed that no contract existed between utility and residents and that imposing a duty would impose financial burden on all residents).

PALKA V. SERVICEMASTER MANAGEMENT SERVICES CORP., 634 N.E.2d 189 (N.Y. 1994).

In *Palka,* the hospital contracted with Servicemaster to manage maintenance operations that, previously, the hospital had managed for itself. The hospital, in its management of maintenance, undoubtedly owed a duty of care to persons who might be injured by negligent maintenance, including its nurses (unless workers' compensation laws barred them from tort actions). Servicemaster was negligent and its work at the hospital and as a result a wall-mounted fan fell upon the nurse-plaintiff. Servicemaster, like the water company in *Moch,* would have no duty to the plaintiff apart from its contract with the hospital. Yet it is held liable. Part of the reason seems to be that it took affirmative steps in the performance of its contract (but not, evidently, in making the fan safe). The court perhaps senses that this kind of statement standing alone makes the case too much like *Moch* to justify liability. The court adds, then, that Servicemaster's conduct made risks greater than if it had done nothing. The court then goes on to suggest an array of factors justifying liability, including the "displacement and substitution of a particular safety function".

Note 1 is another example of tort-contract cross-fertilization, holding that a contract between Party A and Party B created a tort duty towards Party C, a third-party beneficiary of the contract. Notice that this was a contract intended to protect the beneficiary from physical injury. You might again analogize this to *Spengler* if you haven't thoroughly killed it already. That is, even if the mother in *Spengler* was not the contracting party but only the third party beneficiary, a tort duty should still attach under the reasoning of the *Doe v. Wright* case discussed in this Note.

Notes 2-4. These cases are consistent with a recognition that (1) contracts made in part for physical safety are different from economic contracts, and (2) a contract accepting another's duty to provide safety will suffice to make the defendant liable for negligent failure to perform that duty.

Gazo v. City of Stamford, 765 A.2d 505 (Conn. 2001), is a good example of shifting a duty. Pierni, hired to clean the ice and snow that the bank was duty bound to clean, was contractually assuming the bank's duty. Here the court is explicit: Pierni is "accountable for the plaintiff's injuries if they were caused by Pierni's negligent performance of his contract with Chase Bank." Reliance need not be shown when one person assumes another's duty.

Phinney v. Boston Elevated Ry. Co., 187 N.E. 490 (Mass. 1909), made the same point. In that case, the city dug a ditch that crossed a railroad track. The ditch required barricades for safety, and these had to be removed with the arrival of each train. To avoid the barricade problem, the railroad agreed to post a watchman if the city would withdraw its barricades. The city did so, but the watchman failed to guard the trench and the plaintiff was injured. The railroad was held liable, much as Servicemaster was in the *Palka* case. Notice that here again the contract a contract to achieve a degree of safety and that it is also a contract taking over the duty of care of another person.

Caulfield v. Kitsap County, 29 P.3d 738 (Wash. Ct. App. 2001), is a compelling illustration of the point. There the state department of social services undertook to provide in-home care for the plaintiff, who suffered multiple sclerosis and could not feed or otherwise care for himself but who could nevertheless live at home. This department contracted with Sellers to provide the care, but, within six weeks, the plaintiff had been reduced to a serious condition, whereupon the state contracted with the county to provide the services. The county accepted the obligation but did nothing. By the time help arrived, the plaintiff "had urosepsis, pneumonia, saline depletion, contractures, was malnourished, suffered severe weight loss, and had severe bed sores that had cut through his flesh to his bone" and had lost all capacity for independent living at home. He required hospitalization and was in critical condition. The county had taken no affirmative action at all, but it had accepted the state's duty, and that was enough to subject it to liability (along with the state and the putative "caregiver").

Why does it matter that the defendant is taking over another person's duty of reasonable care rather than contracting such a duty in the first place? First, in such a case the defendant clearly knows the scope of its obligation is to the same persons who would have been protected without the contract. In *Palka, Phinney*, and *Caulfield* the defendants knew that they are assuming the duties of others (the hospital, the city, and the state). Since their contract is made with the understanding that they accept the duty owed by the hospital and the city respectively, the promise extends to all persons who would have been protected by the hospital's or the city's reasonable care. Second, if you held otherwise, the endangered victim might be deprived of the care owed him by the contract promisee (the hospital, the city) without getting the protection that was substituted for it.[2]

A third reason is suggested by a third party beneficiary contract claim. In *L.A.C. v. Ward Parkway Shopping Ctr. Co.*, 75 S.W.3d 247 (Mo. 2002), the plaintiff alleged that she had been raped in a shopping mall. She sued the owners-operators and the company that had contracted to provide security. The court found that the mall owner owed a duty to its invitees to provide reasonable care protection, and that a security company, also a defendant, had contracted to fulfill or help fulfill that duty. The plaintiff asserted that the security company was liable for breach of contract as well as in tort. The court said: "A person is a creditor beneficiary if the performance of the promise will satisfy an actual or supposed or asserted duty of the promisee to the beneficiary." Because the security company contracted with the mall owner "to assist it in its duty to take reasonable measures to protect mall customers from criminal activity. . . . [The] plaintiff is a creditor beneficiary of the contract and has a right to bring suit and recover if she can also establish breach that caused damages." (The plaintiff's negligence claim was also upheld against summary judgment motion.)

Goar; cases in which A's duty can successfully be transferred to B. In *Goar v. Village of Stephen*, 196 N.W. 171 (Minn. 1923), the Village contracted with a company to install an electrical distributing system, including transformers

---

[2] This might not hold up in these examples, because the hospital, the city, and the state might each be deemed to owe a nondelegable duty of care. That would mean that those promisees would still be liable to the plaintiff even if they had contracted quite reasonably for others to provide the necessary care. See Chapter 20. But safety in fact and not a money substitute for it is the aim. If B, taking over A's duty, is not bound to perform it, A may nevertheless rely on him to do so, as seems to be the case in *Caulfield*. That means horrible injury may result in fact. The objective in imposing liability upon B is to encourage safety, not merely to find a solvent person who can pay after the plaintiff's body is ruined. In addition, not every duty of care is nondelegable, so for some class of cases the second reason seems especially sound.

and wires. The company installed it negligently, so that two wires rubbed when blown in the wind, with the result that the insulation wore through and 2300 volts were transmitted into the plaintiff's house, causing injury. The Village had been negligent in not inspecting, and by the clear implication of its contract, the duty of the company had been shifted to the Village. The court held the company not liable.

Transfer of duties is important in practice. We have two forms of the transfer before – by contractual assumed risk and by way of the terminated risk idea in the scope of duty (proximate cause) chapter. Indemnity agreements are another form and they are often important in arranging transactions that involved risks.

Note 5. In *Alder v. Bayer Corp., Agfa Div.,*61 P.3d 1068 (Utah 2002), the reported facts of the transaction between defendant, who was installing the system, and the hospital, do not make it clear in our reading whether the parties expected the hospital to deal with ventilation or the defendant to do so. The dissent asserts the conclusion that the hospital undertook to provide ventilation, but does not relate the facts upon which it relies for that conclusion. If the dissent's conclusion is correct, that would seem prima facie to relieve the defendant of any duty (or to show that its duty of care was not breached). However, if the defendant knew the hospital was not going to check the ventilation or make it adequate, Restatement Second § 389 would warrant holding that the defendant's duty of care, arising from installation of the system dangerous to users, could not be shifted to prevent a recovery by the injured persons. In that case, though, the defendant might well have a good indemnity claim against the hospital. The majority held that summary judgment for the defendant was error. This would be sound if responsibility for the danger created by the defendant's installation-without-good-ventilation had not been shifted by contract or tacit understanding and also if responsibility had been shifted but the defendant knew that the hospital was not making effort to secure safety.

Invoking § 324A in cases of affirmative negligence. Restatement Second § 324A recognizes a duty to take affirmative steps for another's safety. It is a limit on the usual nonfeasance rule and that is all that it is. If the defendant affirmatively creates a risk, § 324A is not involved. (Look at the structure of Restatement Second Chapter 12, Topic 7, which contains § 324A and you will see this at a glance.) Nevertheless, courts have invoked § 324A even when the defendant is not charged merely with failure to act but with affirmatively creating a risk. That seems to be the case in *Alder v. Bayer Corp.* The defendant's act of installing a machine that gave off dangerous fumes without checking ventilation certainly looks like an affirmative creation of risk. (Remember the contractor who dug a hole and didn't put a light or barrier at night?) Yet the court relied heavily on § 324A to justify imposing a duty. The negative implication that there might not be a duty when you affirmatively create risks unless you can find a specific authority for duty may cause difficulties.

PAZ V. STATE OF CALIFORNIA, 994 P.2d 975 (Cal. 2000)

In 1989, the defendant allegedly contracted with public entities to construct traffic signals at a dangerous intersection, but in 1991 the signals still had not been installed and the plaintiff was injured in an accident at the intersection, one that signals might have prevented. Did the defendant owe a duty of care by reason of its contract with a third person? The courts says not. (1) Failure to alleviate a risk is not increasing a risk, so increased risk is not basis for a duty here. (2) This was not a case of taking over a duty owed by the public entity to the plaintiff, so taking over another's duty is no basis either. (3) Neither the plaintiff nor the city relied upon the existence of a traffic signal, so reliance is no basis.

Paz is highly edited and we summarized the facts for brevity. The "contract" took the form of a condition for getting city permits for a development, so it was a kind of conditional undertaking. However, that should not much matter; the contractor had gone forward with the development and was also going forward (albeit slowly) with installation of the traffic signal. There was no deadline for performance. That is definitely a problem, but we've tried to avoid dealing with it so that the more substantial tort issues can be emphasized. The court's theory seems to be that when there is no time for performance specified, the time is a reasonable time.

This case walks through the three clauses of Restatement § 324A, recognizing that a contract (or any undertaking) can create a duty if the promisor's failure to perform as promised (a) increases the risk, (b) the promisor is undertaking to perform a duty already owed by the promisee, or (c) either the promisee or the victim has relied upon the undertaking.

Clauses (a) and (b) harken back to ideas we have already encountered.

Note 1. Increased risk – increase over what? Clause (a) speaks of increased risk. One interpretation of that clause might be that the risk must be greater than it would have been if the contractor had properly performed his contract. That might be more or less equivalent to saying that once he begins performance, he must use reasonable care. However, that does not seem to be what the court has in mind. Perhaps it thinks of increased risk as creating a risk greater than would exist if there were no contract at all. This seems in line with the analysis in the case of the bees-in-the-trees in *Belheumeur v. Zilm*, discussed in Note 3 after *Thorne v. Deas* above.

Note 2. A model for increased risk cases? If *Thirion v. Frederickson & Watson Construction Co.*, cited here, is the only model for increased risk, it does indeed seem as if the court is thinking of affirmative acts creating risks that exist independent of the contract – that is, risks greater than would occur if there were no contract at all. Although a jury might be permitted to find that KOA's conduct was affirmative conduct and that it was negligent, KOA did not make matters worse in the way the contractor did in *Thirion*. KOA did not, for example, install a traffic signal that worked improperly, or, in a closer analogy to *Thirion,* negligently cause some other traffic signal to operate incorrectly. The court seems to be saying, then, that it is not enough that the risk is greater than it would have been had the contract been properly performed.

The *Fung* court's analysis, referenced in this Note, is similar. There, a Port Authority employee slipped on a patch of ice in a parking lot and sued the snow removal contractor hired to remove ice and snow from the lot. The court said the contractor's plowing of snow did not create or exacerbate a dangerous condition so as to trigger a duty to salt or sand the area it had plowed. *See also Alexander v. Mitchell,* 930 A.2d 1016 (Me. 2007), where the court held that a snow-plowing contractor who was contractually obligated to the town to plow its roads did not owe a duty of care to a motorist who was killed in an accident on a snow-covered road. The contract was with the town, said the court; there was no duty flowing to individual motorists. And the "precipitating cause" of the road's condition was the weather.

Note 3. Increased risk and reliance. Clause (c) in § 324 helps propel us forward to the reliance materials that follow. In particular, the *Paz* majority and dissent introduce us to what are perhaps not very well developed ideas about what counts as reliance. Chief Justice George's dissent seems to say that because the city did not need to expend its funds for the light if the contractor was going to install it, it was relying. Can that be enough? Would you have to believe that the city *would* have expended its funds if the contractor had not undertaken to install the light?

With respect to § 324A, clause (b), we see a formalization and reinforcement of the operative idea in *Palka* – the defendant had agreed to perform a preexisting duty the promisee owed the victim.

The *Clay Electric* case cited at the end of this note involved both the reliance and increased risk grounds for finding a duty of care. Based on materials we've seen already, this is perhaps not surprising. Might your students think, however, that placing the burden of paying such damages on a company that had merely agreed to maintain the lights is too severe? Should the court limit liability consonant with the contractual undertaking in some way?

§ 3. ACTION AS A PROMISE OR UNDERTAKING

FLORENCE V. GOLDBERG, 375 N.E.2d 763 (N.Y. 1978).
KIRCHER V. CITY OF JAMESTOWN, 543 N.E.2d 443 (N.Y. 1989).

Two cases decided by the New York Court of Appeals, nine years apart. The results are different. Why? In short, in *Florence* the infant plaintiff's mother relied on the defendant's continued performance of its undertaking, whereas in *Kircher* the plaintiff did not rely; in *Kircher* the plaintiff also failed to meet New York's "direct contact" requirement (see numbered paragraphs 2 and 3 in *Kircher*). Notes explore these requirements; the comments below go to many of the points raised in notes..

Misfeasance or reliance as the basis? The problem of affirmative duties of public entities is pervasive, difficult, and perhaps incapable of solution. In *Florence* the plaintiff is able to recover, perhaps partly because of reliance. Judge Jasen at times appears to speak as though this was a case of affirmative action done badly, and quotes Cardozo's remarks in *Moch* about this. If there is misfeasance, or the action has gone forward so far that it amounts to causing harm rather than withholding a benefit, reliance would presumably not be required. It is difficult to see how furnishing a crossing guard is any more misfeasance than delivering water every day, so perhaps reliance is a necessary ingredient here.

Riss rising. Judge Jasen had a difficult problem in explicating the *Florence* case because of *Riss*, Chapter 15 above, and analogous New York cases. A part of the language emphasizing undertaking is really addressed to the *Riss* problem, not to the nonfeasance problem. In *Riss,* the court refused to permit any liability for failure to provide police protection, ostensibly not on nonfeasance grounds but on grounds like those involved in the discretionary immunity. The undertaking in *Florence*, then, is first mentioned to show that the police had taken on a specific duty, not merely a general duty to the public.

Requiring BOTH reliance AND active negligence? From this Judge Jasen seems to shade off into dealing with the problem of nonfeasance, and it is perhaps never clear that reliance is required. If it is required, where there is an affirmative undertaking, the implication is extremely conservative– that reliance would be required even where there is active negligence. Perhaps it is best to view the undertaking language as addressed mainly to the *Riss* problem. That leaves reliance as the main ground for relief so far as nonfeasance is concerned.

The Restatement. The Restatement Second §§ 323 and 324 (1965) sets up a system for dealing with "nonfeasance" cases that is perhaps not wholly satisfactory. Section 323 provides for liability for "undertakings," e.g., promises. This arises only when the defendant, having undertaken protection, is negligent in increasing the risk to the plaintiff or when the harm suffered results from the plaintiff's reliance on the undertaking.

In § 324, the duty is derived from "taking charge" of another who is helpless to protect himself adequately, and liability results if the defendant acts negligently in taking charge or in discontinuing aid.

Does *Florence* come within either section? Habitual conduct resembles a promise; it is an "undertaking" in that it induces expectations, and one might therefore consider § 323. Under that section, liability might be invoked if the defendant somehow increased the risk –presumably by failing to exercise care in the performance of the crossing guard duties.

Relations back: *Kircher* relates back to material covered in Chapter 15 on public entity liability.

Note 1. Many cases hold that the undertaking to repair is not itself an undertaking to warn, even of discovered defects in the product. However, notice that a repairer might undertake regular servicing, which would call for advice and warnings. This is really a scope of undertaking problem, so you could consider it with the Note on that topic if you like.

Notes 2 & 3 explore some more ramifications of the reliance requirement. If you read *Florence* as recognizing a duty of care based on undertaking without any reliance requirement, then *Kircher* disappoints. Reliance must mean choice or at least awareness by the plaintiff or someone acting for the plaintiff. You could rely on having a guard at the crossing only if you knew of the guard's presence and could choose to use other means of protection. If that is what reliance requires, a duty is owed in *Florence* only because the parents of the boy knew of the practice of having a guard and could have provided their own escort if the guard were withdrawn.

Here's the trouble with the reliance requirement, as opposed to, say, a foreseeable harm requirement. Suppose that two children were struck at the crossing. The *Florence* plaintiff recovers because his parents knew of the guard, could have escorted him themselves, and relied on the guard's presence. The other child is seriously injured, but her parents had to be at work before school started and never learned about the guard and could have done nothing to protect their child even if they had known that no guard was present. Since no one in the second child's family relied upon the guard, that child's injury goes unredressed. How is it possible to support a rule that holds the public entity to a duty to one child in the crosswalk and not to the other? Only if you think reliance is more important than the affirmative conduct.

Kircher on reliance as action in making a choice. Kircher fortifies this idea of reliance as choice. You can't rely if you are helpless; if you never had a choice, you did not rely on police action. *Kircher* – and the implications of *Florence* – protect the public fisc at the expense of the public safety. Do students like this one? If tort law has any tendency to deter dangerous behavior of private corporations, why should we not wish to deter of government agencies who, after all, are supposed to act for our benefit? One thing you can say for sure: reliance upon the courts for devotion to your safety will not be justified under these decisions.

Note 4. In *State Auto Ins. Co. v. B.N.C.*, cited here, the facts get pretty complicated. State Auto insured a car owned by one William Close. Close's daughter, Audry Ault, was taking care of Close's house while Close was on vacation; she was watering plants, letting the cat in, and so on. Unbeknownst to either Close or Ault, Ault's teenaged daughter B.D. (14 years old) and a friend went over to Close's house to go swimming. B.D. also went into the house through a back door that Ault had mistakenly left unlocked. B.D. got the idea to go pick up another friend to go swimming and took Close's car. On this drive, B.D. totaled the car. State Auto paid Close's claim for the car and brought at subrogation action against Ault and B.D. The trial court granted summary judgment for Ault on the theory that Ault did not owe Close a duty of care. The South Dakota Supreme Court held that she did owe him a duty to keep his house secured as part of a "gratuitous undertaking." The court quoted Restatement (Second) § 323 and said that her undertaking increased the risk of harm, which created a special relationship giving rise to a duty. It also said that while there is generally no duty of affirmative action to protect a person from a third party (B.D., in this case), this was a case of misfeasance, not nonfeasance. The court also stressed the high foreseeability of harm that would occur from leaving the back door unlocked.

NOTE: CONTENT AND SCOPE OF DUTY DERIVED FROM UNDERTAKINGS

¶ 1. *Scope of duty imposed by undertaking.* The cases in subparagraphs put this idea together with the problem of conduct that may convey ambiguous messages. The basic rule on the scope of duty is handled by the quote from *Delgado*. In that case, plaintiff was attacked by another patron of the defendant's bar in the defendant's parking lot. The defendant had contracted with a company to provide two security guards. They were both present on the night of the attack but failed to prevent it. The court held that the defendant did owe a duty to provide "minimal measures" to protect its patrons, but rejected the idea that merely hiring a guard created a general duty to use reasonable care to protect patrons. "First, the scope of any duty assumed depends on the nature of the undertaking. Merely because a supermarket or other similar enterprise chooses to have a security program that includes provision of a roving security guard does not signify that the proprietor has assumed a duty to protect invitees from third party violence. . . . Second, . . . a defendant's undertaking with support the finding of a duty to another only if (a) the defendant's action increased the risk of harm to another, or (b) the other person reasonably relied upon the undertaking to his or her detriment."

¶ 1 A. *Jefferson County School District R-1 v. Gilbert*, cited here, thought that if you provide afternoon guards only, you are undertaking afternoon guards only, no matter how it might look to someone who saw afternoon guards at the crossing. But cf. *Jefferson County School District R-1 v. Justus*, 725 P.2d 767 (Colo. 1986). Compare *Jackson v. Post Properties*, 513 S.E.2d 259 (Ga. Ct. App. 1999). There a landlord undertook security at an apartment building by posting a "courtesy officer," but the officer was not present on the night a tenant was raped. The court did not suggest that the landlord only undertook to have a guard some of the time, but rather said that the question was whether failing to have one present on that particular night was negligent.

¶ 1 B. The court in *Bourgonzje v. Machev*, cited here, quoted extensively from Dobbs on Torts. It noted that the plaintiff did not demonstrate that the door buzzer and intercom system were designed for security purposes as opposed to "convenience." Thus the defendant did not undertake to provide security at all, let alone to persons not inside the building.

¶ 1 C. In *Rein v. Benchmark Construction*, cited here, the court held that (1) the construction company could not have reasonably foreseen that the resident would be attacked and killed by the fire ants; the court stressed that the construction had been completed two years before the attack; (2) the first landscaping company did not owe any duty to provide fire ant protection of any kind; but (3) the second company, by virtue of its contract, might well owe a duty of care to inspect and treat ant beds. As to the second company, the court concluded that issues of fact remained as to scope of the duty and the foreseeability of the resident's injuries.

¶ 2. *Scope and breach.* In *Hill v. James Walker Memorial Hospital*, cited here, the point seems not to have been recognized. The contract to provide rodent sanitation services may have been breached, but was the contract intended to protect against falls or only against disease?

Hill *as a transferred duty case.* You can see *Hill* as a case like *Palka* in which the defendant contracts to assume the duty already owed to the plaintiff by the promisee. If the transferred duty idea is carried as far as it was in *Hill*, we might find very little left of the nonfeasance rule.[3] In *Winterbottom*, for example, some duty was owed by the employer, and the promise to care for the coach, which was the employee's place of work, might be seen as a promise to take over a portion of the employer's duty to provide a safe place in which to work. Should cases like *Palka* and *Phinney* be read broadly so that there is nothing left of *Winterbottom*?

¶ 3. *Content of duty.* When a duty is undertaken by conduct, is it a duty of reasonable care? Or a duty to carry out some specific conduct like maintaining guards at school crossings? Or could it be a strict duty, breach of which would impose liability without fault of any kind? We are in largely unexplored territory here, but the afternoon guards and drooping eyelid warning cases are markers of sorts.

In *Sall v. T's*, the later Kansas case cited here, the court held that the golf course did owe a duty of reasonable care to protect golfers from lightning strikes. It voluntarily assumed that duty, the court said, by employing a policy

---

[3] The transfer of duties by contract, subject to the nondelegable duty rule seen Chapter 22, is perfectly sound. But *Hill* may have opened the door too wide. Another court might interpret *Hill* to indicate that the contract with the hospital was in fact breached. Could that be right? Is a contract to kill rats a contract to kill *all* rats? Another court might also interpret *Hill* to mean that the risks against which Orkin guaranteed included all risks of bodily harm and not merely sanitation risks. Finally, another court might read *Hill* to support strict liability, because it seems to assume that breach of the contract without fault would not only support an action by the contract promisee, but also by third persons who are not third party beneficiaries. All three of those interpretations might be very bad law.

or procedures for monitoring the weather and sounding an air horn to warn golfers when inclement weather was approaching. Golfers relied on that system, too, the court said. Whether that duty was breached was a contested issue of fact.

In *South v. McCarter*, decided by the same court a year earlier, the court held that a landlord did not owe a duty to protect a person injured in a fight in the landlord's mobile home park. Nothing in the lease agreement obligated the landlord to provide security, and there was no evidence that the landlord undertook to provide such security. Specifically, on the lease, the court found that a provision that required the landlord to abate noise did not impose any contractual (or tort) duty to provide security or to monitor "the security risk of guests of tenants."

In *Sanderson v. Eckerd Corp.*, 780 So.2d 930 (Fla. Dist. Ct. App. 2001), a pharmacist allegedly undertook by advertising to provide computer generated advice warning of drug interactions. The decedent became drowsy while driving, ran into a tree, and died as a result. In a suit against the pharmacist, the court thought undertaking by the pharmacist was a viable theory but that the plaintiff could not proceed on the complaint because she had not alleged some essential ingredients, including reliance and negligence. The court appeared to think that the tort claims (as distinct from any contract claim) would not lie unless the pharmacist not only failed to provide appropriate advice but was negligent in failing to do so, as by operating the computer incorrectly.

In *Davis v. Westwood Group*, 652 N.E.2d 567 (Mass. 1995), a racetrack's parking lot was on one side of a major, divided highway, while its track was on the other. The track arranged for police officers to control traffic at the crossing, but the plaintiff was struck by a drinking driver in spite of the officer's efforts to bring traffic to a halt. The plaintiff argued that reasonable care required the track to provide a safer crossing, as by constructing a pedestrian bridge. When that argument (predictably) was rejected, the plaintiff argued that the track had undertaken to effectuate a safe crossing when it arranged for the officers to take control. But the court thought that the defendant had only undertaken "the discrete task of hiring municipal police officers to direct traffic during race times," not a general duty of safety.

If courts are as worried about imposing duties as they seem to be, they might reflect that to impose a duty of care is not to impose ultimate liability. The scope of the duty imposed by contract or by action-and-reliance seems to be open for considerable analysis. If the scope of risk and measures-of-duty questions are brought out into the open and identified clearly, much of the conceptual difficulty disappears. Content-of-duty issues supplement the principle that the contractor should be under the duty he contracted for, but only as to person and as to risk.

Conceivably a contractor could assume a strict duty, that is, become a guarantor of a given result. Cf. *St. Joseph Light & Power Co. v. Kaw Valley Tunneling*, 589 S.W.2d 260 (Mo. 1979) (contractor's indemnity agreement in effect guaranteed no damage to third persons from construction work, was obliged to pay damages caused by promisee's negligence). But if he does not undertake a guarantee or strict liability duty, is there any reason to think that courts would consciously impose strict liability based upon an undertaking?

Contracts and non-personal injury torts. Contract, promise, and conduct inducing reliance may have many effects on tort law not covered in this chapter, which, in line with the book as a whole, addresses personal injury and property damage, not economic torts. Some of the most expansive and litigated areas of tort law in the last decade have involve intersections of tort and contract. These include a variety of job rights claims, the putative tort of bad faith in dealing with contracts, professional and especially lawyer malpractice, and interference with contract or with economic opportunities. Misrepresentation claims often also involve contractual or semi-contractual relationships.

We deleted a problem that appeared in the Fifth Edition at the end of this chapter. If you used it before, or if you like to work with problems, we reprint it below with our commentary.

PROBLEM: SALMON V. UNGAR

Salmon was taken by ambulance to the R.C. Henderson Memorial Hospital in a medical emergency. Ungar was the cardiologist on call. The emergency team quickly determined that a cardiologist was required and called Ungar, but he was out of town. It was an hour before Emelia Jones, a cardiologist from a nearby town, could be located. Salmon died shortly after Jones arrived. Salmon could have been saved by prompt attention of a specialist such as Ungar or any qualified substitute. Ungar and all other staff members of the hospital are subject to its on-call assignments as a condition of staff privileges. Ungar claims he arranged for Dr. Prager, another cardiologist, to take his calls, but Prager denies this and the hospital operators had no record showing that Prager should be called instead of Ungar. You represent Salmon's son. Do you advise bringing suit against Ungar?

COMMENTARY:

You can use this problem to review the undertaking and third person/privity materials. You can also introduce a new idea about physician's duties, as explained below.

Back in *Hirpa v. IHC Hospitals, Inc.,* 948 P.2d 785 (Utah 1997) (abstracted regarding good Samaritan statutes in Chapter 13) the court, dealing with the Good Samaritan statute in a hospital emergency, noted that the physician could not have the protection of the statutory immunity if he already owed a preexisting duty. The existence of such a duty might depend on his on-call obligations, hospital rules, contractual obligation, or even practice and custom of doctors to respond. This view grounds the tort duty in tort considerations, which may include but are not limited to contractual relationships. You might expect that if, under hospital rules or his contract with the hospital, a physician is on-call, he would have a duty to respond to emergencies. Some authority so holds. *Hiser v. Randolph,* 617 P.2d 774 (Ariz. Ct. App. 1980), *partially overruled on other grounds; Thompson v. Sun City Community Hospital, Inc.,* 688 P.2d 605 (Ariz. 1984). See also *Lownsbury v. VanBuren,* 762 N.E.2d 354 (Ohio 2002) (physician who had contracted with hospital to supervise resident doctors thereby undertook duty to those treated by residents).

In *Hand v. Tavera,* 864 S.W.2d 678 (Tex. Ct. App. 1993) the plaintiff, exhibited certain symptoms in a hospital's emergency department. The plaintiff had Humana health care coverage and Dr. Tavera, who was not present, was in charge of admissions to the hospital and also a doctor contracting with Humana. Tavera's Humana contract required him to treat Humana patients without discrimination. Tavera refused admission to the hospital, although the emergency department doctor who examined the plaintiff recommended it. The plaintiff accordingly went home and suffered a stroke. The court relied in part upon the Tavera-Humana contract to establish Tavera's duty of care to the plaintiff. Although the plaintiff is not a party to the contract between Tavera and Humana, he is not suing on that contract. The contract, read with the health care plan, served to create a physician patient relationship.

However, some courts have become entangled in the idea that a duty of care arises only when a physician-patient relationship exists, and that such a relationship depends upon a contract or consent by the physician. They then reason that the plaintiff is not a third party beneficiary of the physician's contract to provide on-call services to the hospital. A good example is *Anderson v. Houser,* 523 S.E.2d 342 (Ga. Ct. App. 1999). The net result is that such courts ground tort duty solely in contract, not in public considerations, custom, hospital rules, or expectations of the parties.

In *Anderson,* the court could have decided, and quite rightly, on much narrower grounds, because the physician on call was never physically in town but had left substitutes who were not claimed to be unqualified to perform his on-call duties. But the court reached out to state a much broader proposition, that contractual relationship with the patient was required. This view, shared by some other courts whose decisions are discussed in *Anderson,* seems totally out of touch with reasonable expectations of the patient, but is it in line with *Moch* and other cases?

In *Diggs v. Arizona Cardiologists, Ltd.,* 8 P.3d 386 (Ariz. Ct. App. 2000), Dr. Johnson, seeing an emergency room patient, tentatively concluded from tests that she was not suffering a myocardial infarction ("heart attack") and proposed to discharge her, but sought advice of a heart specialist who happened to be passing through. The specialist wrongly concurred in Johnson's diagnosis and agreed that the patient should be discharged. She was and she died within hours. The specialist admitted that, had she been his own patient, he would have ordered another test, which would have led to treatment rather than discharge, but said he owed no duty. The court recognized that authorities agreed with the no-contract, no-duty analysis but said the specialist had undertaken to give an opinion and would be liable under § 342A for his negligence in doing so, grounding duty in tort policy, not contract.

CHAPTER 18

THE DUTY TO PROTECT FROM THIRD PERSONS

▶**Changes in the Sixth Edition.** We've dramatically reduced the length of this chapter to encourage teachers to cover more of it, given its real-world importance. Specifically, we've cut seven of the case abstracts that appeared in the prior edition: *Parish* and *Mirand* in § 1, and *Rosales, DiMarco, Witthoeft, Vince v. Wilson,* and *West American v. Turner* in § 2. The issues raised by those abstracts are now covered in shorter Notes. We have added one new primary case, *Iseberg* (right up front), which presents the basic question of the existence of a duty to protect from a third person on dramatic facts. Reflective of the amount of current litigation in this area, we've added in Notes three dozen citations to new cases. Notes have been reorganized and revised to reflect these newer case-law developments.

▶The Concise Edition cuts five pages (about 15 %) from this Chapter, by making a few cuts at the end of § 1. Specifically, we substituted a short case abstract of *Marquay v. Eno* for the main case; cut *Young v. Salt Lake City School District* and its Notes; and cut *Funchess* and its Notes 1-3. These cuts should not affect the flow of the Chapter or distract from its main points.■

Preliminary Note: This chapter deals primarily with a group of torts in which one tortfeasor creates or enhances a risk that another tortfeasor will harm the plaintiff. You can speak of tortfeasors who facilitate another's tort, or, as Professor Rabin has it, tortfeasors who enable the torts of others. Robert L. Rabin, *Enabling Torts,* 49 DEPAUL L. REV. 435 (1999). The pattern is that A negligently creates a risk that B will negligently or intentionally cause harm to someone like the plaintiff. We've seen the patterns before with proximate cause cases, but we now seek to determine the conditions under which A has a duty to protect the plaintiff from B.

When the question is whether the tortfeasor owes a duty to protect the plaintiff from the plaintiff's own conduct rather than from a third person, we often expect to see courts resolving the case in terms of assumption of the risk or some close no-duty type of analysis. Sometimes that issue will be dealt with in terms of causation and sometimes in terms of contributory fault. *Cf. Stehlik v. Kimberly Clark Corp.,* 645 N.W.2d 889 (Wis. 2002) (host entrusted new ATV to drinking guests but did not require them to wear a helmet when operating; the guest-operator's failure to use a helmet was self-inflicted harm and the host could not be held responsible for failing to insist that he wear one).

In the third person cases that comprise most of this chapter, the question of apportionment of responsibility between the first and second tortfeasor looms very large indeed. That topic is covered in Chapter 25, especially in connection with the abolition of joint and several liability in many states. Some of the cases in the present chapter could have been considered in Chapter 16 as nonfeasance cases. Some cases may also turn in part on consensual arrangements between the parties (landlord-tenant cases, e.g.); these could have been considered in Chapter 12.

Many courts, perhaps most, continue to see the problem of this chapter as a "duty to control" rather than a duty to protect. *Johnson v. State,* 553 N.W.2d 40 (Minn. 1996) involved release of a sex offender to a halfway house. The halfway house did not report the fact that the offender never showed up. (In fact he went on a crime spree, raping a woman and stabbing her to death several days after he should have been at the halfway house.) The court saw the question in terms of a duty to control the released convict rather than a duty to use care to protect the victim. Viewed as a problem in "control," the plaintiff's claim against the halfway house was doomed, since it could not have controlled the non-arriving offender. If the question were merely one of reasonable care to protect potential victims, however, the halfway house would quickly be condemned for its lax treatment of a known violent offender. The initial characterization of the problem as one of control thus deflects analysis of negligence and tends to determine the outcome.

Courts do specify limited exceptions to the rule that there is no duty to control. The exceptions are based upon very particular relationships, upon custody, or upon control. This chapter is mainly about such cases.

Courts believe the relationship-custody-control exceptions cover the defendant's duty. Yet, there are many cases in which the gist of the defendant's negligence is that he has subjected the plaintiff to a risk from others and in which liability is imposed without mentioning any special rule at all. For example, if you negligently design an access road so that anyone leaving a shopping center may be struck by hard-to-see vehicles, you may be liable to the victim, see *Louk v. Isuzu Motors, Inc.,* 479 S.E.2d 911 (W.Va. 1996), as indeed you may be in most cases in which one driver creates risks of injuries in part caused by others. Perhaps the intentional wrong of third persons more than the nonfeasance of the defendant influences courts in many cases.

Scheduling omissions and imports from other chapters. *Imports*. If you are not going to teach the material in Chapter 25, you might wish import some of its apportionment materials. Alternatively, you can deal with the apportionment problem by merely discussing Note 8 at the very end of § 1, after *Funchess*. If you *are* covering Chapter 25, you can raise the question in the note so the issue can come into play as you discuss further duty cases.

Omissions. If you must omit as much as possible, try covering *Iseberg* and *Posecai* in § 1 and *Tarasoff* and *Brigance* in § 2, with as much of the accompanying Note material as you can manage.

OUTLINE

§ 1. DEFENDANT'S RELATIONSHIP WITH THE PLAINTIFF

§ 2. DEFENDANT'S RELATIONSHIP WITH DANGEROUS PERSONS

SUMMARY

§ 1. DEFENDANT'S RELATIONSHIP WITH THE PLAINTIFF

[a. Special relationships and foreseeability]

ISEBERG V. GROSS. Iseberg was shot four times by a former business associate when he answered his front door. He lived, and sued two other former (mutual) business associates, Gross and Frank, alleging they were negligent in failing to warn him about threats the shooter had made against him. The trial court dismissed, and the Illinois Supreme Court affirmed on the ground that the two defendants owed him no duty because they did not have a recognized "special relationship" with him.

POSECAI V. WAL-MART STORES, INC. The plaintiff shopped at the defendant's store. She was attacked and robbed by a man hiding under her car in the defendant's parking lot. She claimed that the store should have provided security patrols. There had been three robberies over a five or six year period and 83 predatory offenses in nearby businesses. Was the defendant under any duty to protect the plaintiff? This is a question of law, to be answered by the court in the light of moral, social, and economic factors. Courts have taken various approaches to facts like these saying foreseeability is established and the landowner owes a duty of care (1) when and only when he knows that specific imminent harm is about to befall the invitee; (2) when prior similar instances have put him on notice of the danger; (3) when the totality of circumstances make such danger foreseeable; (4) when, balancing foreseeability, gravity of potential harm, and burden of forestalling it, the burden is not too great in light of the threatened harm. The balancing test is adopted as the best one. Applied here, the store did not "possess the requisite degree of foreseeability" to warrant a duty to provide security patrols.

[*b. Defendant as employer, teacher or otherwise*]

NOTE: AN EMPLOYER'S DUTY TO ITS EMPLOYEES. This short notes recites the Restatement rule that an employer owes its employees a duty of reasonable care to protect them from third parties, but only where the employee is in "imminent danger," and this is known to the employer.

MARQUAY V. ENO. *Held,* supervisory school employees, standing in as proxies for parents where school attendance is compulsory, owe a duty to report sexual abuse of students carried out by other school personnel, even though the sexual abuse reporting statute creates no private right of action and its violation does not show negligence per se. The common law duty arises from a supervisory employee's relationship with the student and, in the case of those who can hire or fire, the relationship with the abuser.

YOUNG V. SALT LAKE CITY SCHOOL DISTRICT. An elementary-school student was struck by a car while riding in a crosswalk, as he was going to school to attend a mandatory after-school Parent-Teacher-Student meeting. In his suit against the school for negligence (for failure to supply a crossing guard or warning lights, or to warn the city of dangerous parking conditions around the school), *held,* the school owed him no duty. His injuries did not occur during school or on school property. Nor was he participating in a school-sponsored event; he was merely coming to the school to attend such an event.

[*c. Duties of Colleges*]

NOTE: DUTIES OF COLLEGES. Colleges generally no duty of care to protect students from themselves with respect to sex, drugs, alcohol, overstudy or the like. A series of hypotheticals, with case citations, explore whether colleges might owe a duty to students to protect them from third parties.

[*d. Lessors' duty to tenants*]

FUNCHESS V. CECIL NEWMAN CORP. The outside security door and the intercom system in a tenant's apartment building was not working properly. When someone buzzed the tenant, he had to open his apartment door to see who it was. Unfortunately it was intruders, who killed him. Held, the landlord owed no duty of care with respect to this attack. The court reasoned that the landlord-tenant relationship was not by itself sufficient to create a duty to protect from third persons. Nor was the provision of security measures in the form of an intercom system and a security door a sufficient undertaking of a duty. And since a breach of contract claim was not pleaded, the court could not consider it. Notes explore the merits (or lack thereof) of the court's opinion.

§ 2. DEFENDANT'S RELATIONSHIP WITH DANGEROUS PERSONS

[a. Generally]

DUDLEY V. OFFENDER AID & RESTORATION OF RICHMOND, INC. A halfway house had "custody" of a dangerous criminal and was under a duty of care to protect his foreseeable potential victims, including a woman in the general area whom he raped and murdered.

[b. Parents and their children]

NOTE: A DUTY TO CONTROL CHILDREN? If a child harms the plaintiff, can the plaintiff sue the parents? We saw in Chapter 3 that parents are not vicariously liable, but statutes may make the liable under particular conditions. The question here is whether parents owe a common-law duty to the plaintiff, allowing a suit for negligence against the parents. Courts hold that parents are liable only for failing to control some specific dangerous habit of a child of which the parents know or should know in the exercise of reasonable care. Case examples indicate just how hard it is for a plaintiff to succeed on such a claim.

[c. The physician's or therapist's relation to a dangerous patient]

TARASOFF V. REGENTS OF UNIVERSITY OF CALIFORNIA. The psychiatrist who has reason to believe his patient will attack someone, must warn or otherwise act with reasonable care for the protection of the potential victim in spite of the therapist's confidential relationship with the patient.

[d. Supplying dangerous substances or instrumentalities to source of harm]

BRIGANCE V. VELVET DOVE RESTAURANT, INC. The defendant served intoxicating drinks to a group of minors, even though it knew that they had arrived by car and would probably leave in the same way. One of the minors did leave the restaurant intoxicated and drove in such a way as to cause an accident in which the plaintiff was injured. Held, the traditional common law rule that only the drinker's negligence is a proximate cause is rejected. One who sells intoxicating beverages for on-premises consumption is under a duty of care to third persons not to sell to noticeably intoxicated persons. Notes analogize the situation to negligent entrustment.

[*e. Problems for review and development*]

(1) An employer works an employee for 24 hours and the employee falls asleep driving home, with injury to another person. (2) A physician allegedly mis-prescribes a drug, which causes the patient to become hostile and aggressive and to shoot a third person. (3) A homeowner leaves a pistol in his bedroom, although he has a safe. His child or her friend steal the gun and use it in a robbery-killing. *Is the first actor under a duty to protect against the second in any of these cases?*

COMMENTS

Introductory statement. Courts often state the rule, not by addressing reasonable care, but by saying that the defendant has no duty to "control" a third person's conduct to prevent harm to the plaintiff. In practice, the no-duty-to-control statement means that the defendant is ordinarily not liable for failure to protect the plaintiff even when the defendant could reasonably provide protection without actually controlling third persons. See, e.g., *Johnson v. State,* 553 N.W.2d 40 (Minn. 1996).

§ 1. DEFENDANT'S RELATIONSHIP WITH THE PLAINTIFF

ISEBERG V. GROSS, 879 N.E.2d 278 (Ill. 2007).

Iseberg was shot four times by a former business associate, Slavin, when he answered his front door. He lived, and sued two other former (mutual) business associates, Gross and Frank, alleging they were negligent in failing to warn him about threats Slavin had made against him. The trial court dismissed, and the Illinois Supreme Court affirmed on the ground that the two defendants owed him no duty because they did not have a recognized "special relationship" with him.

The court here recites the "universally accepted rule," one "long adhered to by this court," that "a private person has no duty to act affirmatively to protect another from criminal attack by a third person absent a 'special relationship' between the parties." The plaintiff first argues that he was in a special relationship with the two defendants because they were all former business associates. His fallback position is that the court should abandon the "special relationship" requirement altogether in favor of a general negligence-duty test, which would focus in part at least on the foreseeability of harm. The court here rejects both arguments and reaffirms the "universally accepted rule" it started with.

You can use the Notes to discuss this case and begin to draw comparisons to the *Posecai* approach, which finds the mere existence of a clear "special relationship" (invitor-invitee) insufficient in the absence of the foreseeability of an unreasonable risk of harm. *Iseberg* is the essential opposite problem – foreseeability without a special relationship. In neither case does the court find a duty of care.

Note 1. Special relationships. The Illinois court in Iseberg recites the four "special relationships" that courts have traditionally recognized: common carrier-passenger, innkeeper-guest, business invitor-invitee; and "voluntary custodian-protectee." Isberg could not and did not claim to fall within one of these categories; instead his first argument was that the categories should not be applied inflexibly. He claimed that he was an "agent" of the defendants (he was acting as a lawyer, he said, in addition to being a business associate). The court rejected his invitation to enlarge the list. The *Hills* case cited here is from the same court, to the same effect. Likewise in the *Parish* case (which appeared as an abstract in prior editions), a court read the list literally to find that no duty existed on the part of a homeowner to protect a social guest from a third party attack.

The second paragraph of this Note suggests expansions, first in the list itself (in the Third Restatement), and then in conception. The plaintiff in *Iseberg* wanted the court to enlarge its own four-category list at least to include "agents," but then was hoisted on his own petard when the court determined that he was not an "agent" at all. He would have fared no better, it seems, in arguing that "business associates" are in a special relationship.

You might ask students if there is some case-law support for Iseberg's argument that the special relationships should be viewed broadly. We saw in Chapter 16 the *Farwell* case, where the court said that friends on a social venture (drinking together) were in a special relationship. In the same chapter we saw the *Podias* case, in which the court seemingly identified a special relationship along the same lines, if anything more flexibly. Would that approach be better, or is there something to sticking to a fixed list?

Note 2. Why such a requirement? Iseberg's alternative (and more radical) position was that the "special relationship" requirement should just be abandoned. Might that be the logical next step from *Farwell* and *Podias* anyway? How might the rule look without any requirement of a "special relationship?" Presumably we are in review territory now, looking back to the kinds of factors courts look for in finding a duty of care in the first place, and to the kinds of tests used to determine breach of duty and scope of risk as well. You could just say that and force students to do the review work on their own, or you could walk them through some of the major building blocks of the negligence case once again to reinforce some key concepts.

Note 3. Necessary, but not sufficient? The *Iseberg* court clearly believes that two things must be present in order to find a duty to protect a plaintiff from an attack by a third person: a recognized "special relationship" and a reasonably foreseeable risk posed by a third person. (Its rule statement on this, in the first paragraph on page 478 is: "When one of these special relationships exists between the parties and an unreasonable risk of physical harm arises within the scope of that relationship, an obligation may be imposed on the one to protect the other from such risk, if the risk is reasonably foreseeable, or to render first aid when it is known that such aid is needed." Many other courts have said the same, as these other case citations indicate. Does that make sense? That is, would it make sense to say that a special relationship *alone* creates a duty of reasonable care, then leave the foreseeability of the harm to the breach element, or to the scope of risk element? Perhaps the problem with that is that it would leave too many cases to the jury, thus raising settlement costs to defendants. Or would the flip side make sense, to say that foreseeability of an unreasonable risk of harm by third persons *alone* creates the duty of reasonable care, leaving the relationship between the parties to the breach or scope of risk elements? Perhaps it is again the same problem, from a policy perspective. So those courts inclined to allow defendants to escape liability on motion are much more likely to build in requirements for the "duty" element, whereas those who are less concerned about that dynamic might be more willing to say, for example, that an invitee is always owed a general duty of care by the inviter/landowner, but that liability will follow only where there was some foreseeable and unreasonable risk of harm to the invitee that the inviter failed to take reasonable measures to prevent (breach of duty).

Note 4. Employers and employees. The rules on employers' duties to employees is right in line with the discussion sketched above: the rule in most places, reflected in the Restatement Second, is that the employer owes a duty of reasonable care to employees to protect them from harm, but only if there is also a known, imminent threat (a kind of super-foreseeability) that arises within the scope of the relationship. Once again, the existence of a special relationship alone is not sufficient; neither is the foreseeability of harm.

Note 5. Duty to protect plaintiffs against negligent acts by third parties. We added this Note to remind students and teachers that while third party criminal attacks are the focus of this whole chapter, the rules work in much the same way with third party negligence. We have actually seen many such cases elsewhere in the book, often dealt with in terms of scope of risk (intervening cause, especially) rather than duty.

Note 6. Nonfeasance. Do we need any special rules on "special relationships" where the defendant has acted affirmatively to create a risk of harm? The analogous situations of "duty to rescue" in Chapter 16 all dealt with situations in which the defendant did not himself create a risk, or do the harming. In those situations, a duty arose. Is that the same situation where the alleged negligence is in failing to protect the plaintiff from a third party attack? You might think so, and you can probably mount principled arguments for such a position. But the case law does not uniformly support that position and much of it runs counter. Even where a defendant has created a risk of harm, then, the absence of a "special relationship" will doom the case in many courtrooms. *Iseberg* itself may be an example; a clearer one is perhaps the *Posecai* case, if you see allegedly inadequate security as an instance of an "act done badly" as opposed to nonfeasance. An even clearer example is in the *Parish* case cited in Note 1, in which the defendant threw open the front door without checking to see who it was. It was the criminals who then shot the plaintiff. The court did not differentiate between a "non-act" and an "act" for purposes of applying its "special relationship" requirement to bar the claim.

Anaya v. Turk, 199 Cal. Rptr. 187 (Ct. App. 1984), was similar to *Parish* and got a similar result. And these decisions are not alone in dismissing claims even when the defendant is actively negligent. See *Deppe v. Poweshiek County*, 542 N.W.2d 6 (Iowa Ct. App. 1995); *Lauritzen v. Lauritzen*, 874 P.2d 861 (Wash. Ct. App. 1994) (passenger injured by attack when driver, eschewing directions for a safe route to his Miami hotel, drove into a "very ugly part of town," no liability to passenger).   Although a nonfeasance-no-duty answer seems wrong in cases like these, you might reach a no-duty conclusion on other grounds. You could take the view that one is free even to be actively negligent if the risk created is only the risk of conscious action by third persons. Indeed, this was the idea pursued in some of the intervening causes cases. It is also one of the ideas behind the traditional view that a bartender is not liable for injuries caused by selling alcohol to a drunk.

This sticky issue develops further as the chapter progresses: Is there some special reason behind a particular rule that insulates a defendant from liability for an injury that results from the intervention of a third party? Your best students should see that we've discussed this issue before in connection with scope of risk and intervening causes – asking the same question, and getting the same mixed answers when we look at cases.

POSECAI V. WAL-MART STORES, INC., 752 So.2d 762 (La. 1999)

When does a business or invitor owe a duty to protect customers/invitees from attacks by others on its property? Students should understand that the approaches summarized in this case deal specifically with the invitor-invitee relationship and the duties that grow out of that.

Notice, apropos of points made above in connection with *Iseberg*, that this court is faced with the situation where a "special relationship" clearly exists, yet still holds that there is no duty on grounds of lack of foreseeability of harm. Remember that *Iseberg* found no duty for the mirror-image problem: foreseeability, but no "special relationship."

The *Posecai* court reviews four positions that can be found in (or attributed to) cases in various states on the "reasonable foreseeability" issue. You might not be entirely sympathetic with someone who wears $19,000 worth of jewelry to shop in a discount store, but bear in mind that these attacks on customers can just as well result in rape and death and that more cases are like that than like the once be-jeweled Mrs. Posecai.

Foreseeability. The approaches listed by the *Posecai* court purport to be setting up particular rules for determining foreseeability, so you get courts referring to the "degree of foreseeability" as if foreseeability were about ocular clarity rather to the existence of a risk. What courts evidently mean by such strange phrases is not foreseeability but probability. And indeed you can reasonably refer to degrees of probability. See DOBBS ON TORTS § 143, at 336 (2000).

The risk-utility or balancing approach embedded in all other approaches. In evaluating all the approaches to this problem, students should be conscious of the fact that the risk-utility("balancing") approach adopted in *Posecai* is actually embedded in all the other approaches. The difference in other approaches is that juries, not judges, might determine risks and utilities. For example, the narrowest rule would hold that the defendant has no duty at all except in cases like *Greco,* **Note 3**, a specific threat is taking place and the owner knows it. But even in this strong case for a duty, we do not drop the requirement of negligence with its risk-utility elements. To hold the landowner liable, we'd have to believe that a reasonable person in his position would have taken effective steps to forestall the attack, and that in turn would take account of risks and utilities, including the costs of making the patrons safe.

Relative merits of the approaches. *Rules of law.* We ask about duty versus negligence in **Note 7**. Given that risk-utility assessments will be made in all cases, either by juries or by judges, which approach is best? As we've said, courts have often dealt with the problem as if they were dealing with problems of foreseeability. They might then make rules of law that harm to the customer is not foreseeable unless harm is known and imminent, or that specific similar incidents have occurred that put the landowner on notice that such harm is likely. These two approaches have something in common with the *Posecai* balancing approach–they make rules of law rather than leaving the matter to the trier of fact to determine foreseeability on the facts of the case.

A case from the same court that decided *Posecai* reconfirms its basic approach, insofar as division of labor between judge and jury goes. In *Pinsonneault v. Merchants & Farmers Bank & Trust Co.*, 816 So.2d 270 (La. 2002), decedent was murdered by robbers as decedent attempted to make a night deposit of $64 at the defendant's bank. The trial court held that the bank was not liable. The Supreme Court first seemed to say that the bank had "no duty" to provide security guards because foreseeability (probability?) was low compared to the cost of providing guards. However, it would still be possible that even low probability of injury (low "foreseeability") would require some lesser precautions, such as trimmed shrubbery, lighting, and surveillance cameras. The trial judge as trier of fact, however, found the bank's actions in all these respects to be reasonable. The Supreme Court held that such findings on the breach or negligence issue were permissible even if the trier could also have gone the other way.

Similar instances. Under the similar instance rule, discussed in **Note 4**, courts may in effect protect the defendant who foresees serious crime against its invitees but does not foresee the very specific form the crime took. This looks like a rejection of the usual rule we saw in proximate cause cases, that the defendant is responsible if he should foresee the general type of risk or harm. Or possibly it is just a case of judges losing sight of the point as they entangle themselves in analysis of what counts as similar. In *Wood v. Centermark Properties, Inc.,* 984 S.W.2d 517 (Mo. Ct. App. 1998), for example, the plaintiff adduced evidence of 80 crimes at a mall, but the court excluded evidence of indecent acts because they were not similar to carjacking, and it excluded violence committed by escaping shoplifters, and finally concluded that even the crimes of strong-arm robberies and holdups with weapons were not sufficiently similar. The mall already had security guards; the question was whether they were qualified and acted negligently. Even though the same security patrols that would protect against armed robbery would have also protected against car-jacking and abduction, the robberies and other crimes were not enough to show a duty to protect against carjacking.

Totality of circumstances. The third rule, the totality of circumstances rule (**Note 5**) is really the absence of special rules; it permits the trier of fact to consider any relevant evidence that tends to show "foreseeability" (or probability of harm). As in all negligence cases, judges would still be able to hold that the evidence was insufficient to show foreseeable harm in particular cases.

In *Stanton v. University of Maine System,* 773 A.2d 1045 (Me. 2001), the court treated a college student as an invitee of the college. She was sexually assaulted in her dorm room. Although the college had had no reports of sexual attacks for years and had a good deal of security, the court thought attacks might be foreseeable without prior similar instances and that was a question for the jury. The defendant's own security precautions provided some evidence that an attack was foreseeable. The jury could find that the plaintiff was at least entitled to a warning and an explanation how the security worked.

Clohesy v. Food Circus Supermarkets, Inc., 149 N.J. 496, 694 A.2d 1017 (N.J. 1997) and *Delta Tau Delta, Beta Alpha Chapter v. Johnson,* 712 N.E.2d 968 (Ind. 1999) both cited in **Note 5**, give good reviews of cases and good analyses of the problem.

A duty to warn? If a store or mall-owner knows of crimes in the parking lot, should it at least have a duty to warn patrons? In *Erichsen v. No-Frills Supermarkets of Omaha, Inc.,* 518 N.W.2d 116 (Neb. 1994), a store patron was attacked in the defendant's parking lot and suffered injuries. She became entangled in the safety belt of her assailant's vehicle and she was dragged for over a mile and a half. The owner knew of other such incidents. The plaintiff argued her case on a failure to warn theory. The court responded with a general duty to use reasonable care, holding that past incidents were sufficient impose that obligation. Recall the new argument in informed consent cases that physicians must inform patients of their track record on proposed medical procedures.

Note 1. Applying *Posecai*. This note is intended to require students to understand the most obvious workings of the balancing test by applying it. Under the balancing test, costs to the defendant are a significant consideration. Security guards are costly, so the balancing test requires a relatively high probability of harm before the landowner will be required to have guards. But surveillance cameras and better lighting are both more commonly used and cheaper and both those things might reduce crime. Unless causal issues (next note) get in the way, a balancing test court might say that security guards are not required but better lighting, surveillance cameras, or the like might be.

But in *Sharon P. v. Arman, Ltd.,* cited here, the California court concluded that no such measures would be required because no personal assaults had previously taken place in the garage, almost a return to the similar incidents rule —every dog gets one bite, every parking garage can be part of the urban blight until someone is raped. *Sharon P.* differs from the customer cases like *Posecai*; it could be taken up with the discussion of lessors later in the chapter, but it seems most relevant on the cluster of issues raised here. Should the duty be different because the parties are in a contractual relationship?

Note 2. In *Nixon v. Mr. Property Management Co., Inc.,* 690 S.W.2d 546 (Tex. 1985) the plaintiff was not on the premises when abducted. She was a stranger to the property. Affirmative duties of the property owner in *Nixon* could not be explained by the relationship between the plaintiff and the property owner, but the court found a duty in a rather bland ordinance requiring doors and windows on vacant property. (There was also evidence that crime was foreseeable, an issue the court regarded as relating to proximate cause.) See also *Scialabba v. Brandise Construction Co.,* Inc., 112 Nev. 965, 921 P.2d 928 (1996) (contractor left door in new apartment building unlocked, permitting attacker to hide in the empty apartment and attack a woman who moved in across the hall).

In contrast, *Waters v. New York City Housing Authority*, 69 N.Y.2d 225, 513 N.Y.S.2d 356, 505 N.E.2d 922 (1987), on quite similar facts, holds that the property owner has no duty to a "stranger" who stands in no particular relationship to the vacant property.

Salazar v. Crown Enterprises, Inc., 328 Ill.App.3d 735, 767 N.E.2d 366, 262 Ill.Dec. 906 (2002), held that the estate of a homeless person who had sought shelter in the defendant's abandoned building had no claim, even though the owner's neglect of the building and violation of code requirements encouraged a sub-culture's dangerous use of the building. The homeless person was a trespasser, so he could not claim the duty owed to invitees and tenants. (In addition, the court thought murderous attacks as distinct from other harms was not foreseeable on the basis of prior experience.) Having denied the claim, the court recommended an authoritative revisitation of the law:

> [W]e urge the legislature (or the supreme court) to consider such a duty. What we have in this case are nonresident landowners who have allowed their property to fall into a complete state of disrepair, with various citations being issued to them over quite a few years concerning the condition of the premises. Defendants did nothing to rectify the situation. Rather than repair and/or secure the structure or surrounding perimeter, defendants, like many other landowners in this city, await the government or municipality's response by condemning the property and tearing down any structures at its cost. This is precisely what occurred in the instant case. Approximately three months after decedent's death, defendants' property was condemned and torn down. Based on the law as it exists today, no amount of notice or knowledge by a landowner that, because its property is in such a state of disrepair, vagrants live on it and commit criminal acts, would impose any duty upon the owner to protect individuals entering thereupon, irrespective of their entry status.

Note 3. *Grimes*, discussed briefly in this Note, involved American researchers who allegedly subjected children to uninformed and dangerous exposures to lead. The researchers got a federal grant for a study in which children would be exposed to different levels of lead dust in low-cost rental housing. Families were asked to sign a "consent" form to allow periodic testing of the houses, and their children's blood, for lead. The children selected had no pre-existing health problems, but it was foreseeable that some of them would suffer from elevated lead levels in their blood as a result of living in the homes. No medical treatment was part of the deal. Two children who suffered elevated lead levels sued the researchers, who argued they owed no duty of care. The case is interesting on a number of points other than the one made here, most notably on its construction and application of informed consent. *See* Chapter 13 (medical malpractice).

In *Wilkins v. Siplin*, 13 Cal.Rptr. 2d 634 (1992) a woman named Siplin, who was separated from her husband, invited Wilkins, a man, to spend the night at her remote cabin. She called her husband twice, checking, she said, on the welfare of their child who was with him. Several hours later he showed up at the cabin, where both Siplin's and Wilkins' vehicle were parked. He entered and stabbed Wilkins 17 times. The best laid plans, and so forth. The defendant explicitly made the argument that defendant owed no duty to prevent harm because the she was not in any special relationship with Wilkins. Be that as it may, the court was quick to say that no special relationship was required to impose a duty of care upon a defendant who acts affirmatively.

Resisting robbers. In *Kentucky Fried Chicken of California, Inc. v. Superior Court*, 927 P.2d 1260 (Cal. 1997) the plaintiff was a customer at defendant's place of business when she was seized and held at gun point by a robber, who demanded that the defendant open the cash drawer. The clerk used a delaying ploy, and the robber became agitated and as a result may have injured the plaintiff further. The court held that there was no duty to comply with the robber's demand, but purported not to pass on the question whether a duty might exist to avoid physical resistance that would endanger the customer.

In *Boyd v. Racine Currency Exchange, Inc.*, 306 N.E.2d 39 (Ill. 1973) a robber demanded that a teller in the currency exchange give him money, else he would shoot a customer. The teller didn't and the robber did. Boyd, the victim, was killed by the shot. The court said any duty would only benefit criminals, who would then be encouraged to take hostages, and that by denying the duty it could stiffen the resolve of business to stand up to the criminals. But the rejection of a duty is fact-specific here, not a rejection of a landowner's general duty of care.

Outside the premises. *Simpson v. Big Bear Stores, Co.*, 652 N.E.2d 702 (Ohio 1995) takes the view that even if a grocery store knows of dangers on a parking lot adjacent to the grocery's property, the store owes no duty to its patrons. The property line is the bright line that marks off duty from no-duty. As to dangers outside the premises besides attacks, *see Davis v. Westwood Group,* 420 Mass. 739, 652 N.E.2d 567 (Mass. 1995); *Ferreira v. Strack,* 636 A.2d 682 (R.I. 1994).

Banks v. Hyatt Corp., 722 F.2d 214 (5th Cir. 1984), imposed a duty upon a hotel to use care for protection of a guest against assaults, even on adjacent property, so long as the hotel "has sufficient control of property adjacent to his premises so that he is capable of taking reasonable actions to reduce the risk of injury to guests present on the adjacent property. . . ." Since Hyatt had perimeter patrols, it had sufficient control over a sidewalk to require reasonable care to reduce the risks to guests on the sidewalk.

Notes 4-6. See discussion in *Posecai*, above.

Note 7. Duty vs. breach analysis. See above discussion. The *Posecai* court adopts the balancing test, which overtly moves the court into risk-utility analysis that seems to be very much like the risk-utility analysis we performed in negligence cases. But here the court is performing that analysis on the duty issue. As the court notes, that is an issue for the judge to decide, not the jury. In contrast, negligence is an issue for the jury to decide, not the judge.

If the judge deciding duty is determining issues that we previously said were for the jury deciding negligence, isn't something badly wrong? The more traditional approach would be to leave negligence issues to the jury except where reasonable people could not differ. That would also require proof about matters like costs and burdens to the landowner, not speculation that costs would be great in comparison to risks. Yet Judge Marcus is able to reach a conclusion about the costs and the safety gains without alluding to any evidence about costs or the value of potential safety gains, either from the record or from data generally available. You might think this looks like a decision about negligence performed by judges (and to be performed in each case in the future, since it turns on factual details). *See* DOBBS ON TORTS §§ 226-229 (2000).

Note 8. Negligence and causation. Students must remember that negligence (breach of duty) must be shown. This is a difficult point to make under the balancing test, because, as we emphasized above, it looks very much like an analysis of the negligence or breach issue being performed by judges instead of juries. In *Shadday*, cited here, Judge Posner wrote the opinion that found for the defendant on the ground that the hotel was not negligent in failing to protect the plaintiff from guest-on-guest crime, as a matter of law. That kind of crime, as opposed to some attack by an outsider, was completely unheard of (thus not reasonably foreseeable), the court said. Thus the hotel did not breach any duty of care by failing to have security measures in place to minimize guest-on-guest crime.

Causation is also required. Good lighting and maintenance do tend to minimize criminal activity in an area, as evidence showed in *Nallan v. Helmsley-Spear, Inc.,* cited in **Note 4**. That proposition does not show that the particular crime would not have been committed and some courts have dismissed such claims on the ground that cause in fact had not been demonstrated.

In *Shaner v. Tucson Airport Authority Inc.*, 573 P.2d 518 (Ariz. Ct. App. 1978), a woman parked her car in a dimly lit airport parking lot, intending to meet her husband who was returning from an overseas tour of duty. Her body was found several months later, partially buried many miles away. The court held that the parking lot's bad lighting could not be shown to be a cause in fact of her abduction and it upheld a directed verdict.

One antidote to *Shaner* might be the rule that if the defendant negligently creates the specific risk that befell the plaintiff, the defendant won't be heard to say that causation cannot be established. See *Zuchowicz v. United States,* 140 F.3d 381 (2d Cir. 1998) (Chapter 7) and *Liriano v. Hobart Corp.,* 170 F.3d 264 (2d Cir. 1999) (Chapter 24, § 6). Other possibilities are a liberal inference of causation approach. See *First Commercial Trust Company v. Rank,* 915 S.W.2d 262 (Ark. 1996) (defendant should have reported suspected child abuse because that might have caused an investigation that might in turn have forestalled further abuse). Or at least a value of the chance approach; increased risk is enough according to *Nebel v. Avichal Enterprises, Inc.,* 704 F.Supp. 570 (D.N.J. 1989).

MARQUAY V. ENO, 662 A.2d 272 (N.H. 1995)

Back in Chapter 16, we saw the Restatement's limited list of special relationships that might create a duty of care. We questioned the adequacy of that list then. We questioned it in connection with *Iseberg*. And we question it again here by including these cases on school-student duty.

These next two cases discuss the duty of the school, or its personnel, to protect students. In the first a duty is found: In *Marquay* the students are protected from teachers and other authorities. In *Young,* by contrast, the court rejects a duty where the student is injured by a neutral third person (not a student, not a teacher), off the school ground, and before he had arrived at a mandatory school meeting. The *Young* case should by now be easy for students to distinguish.

In *Marquay,* three female public school students or former students complained that they had been sexually abused by authorities –teachers and a coach– and that non-abusing personnel knew or should have known about the abuse and should have done something about it but did not. The main discussion is directed at the liability of the non-abusers who allegedly averted their gaze.

The court first discards the child abuse reporting statute as a source of duty, distinguishing statutes that create a private right of action from those that might be adopted by courts as a standard of care and given negligence per se effect. This statute, though, had no effect at all. It created no private right of action. Why not use it as a standard of care? Because the court appears to think that the care owed is supervision of the student, while reporting is something else. You might wonder about that, but in the end it makes no difference because the court erects its own common law standards with both rigor and flexibility.

The court perceives various actors in the school system as having different roles and duties. School authorities with supervisory duties over students owe students a duty because of their relationship with the student. Considering a number of factors, including compulsory school attendance, the expectation of parents, and reliance upon the school, the court thought that the supervisory authorities had a duty to stand-in as proxy for parents, but only during times when they served as proxies. That did not entirely exclude liability for after-hours and off-premises abuse if the non-abusing supervisory authorities should have prevented the abuse by actions taken while they served as proxies.

A very different basis for liability of non-abusers applies to those who are not directly supervising students but who hire and fire teachers or coaches who are abusers. *Those* authorities owe a duty to students because of their relationship with the abuser. If they know or should know of his abuse, the authorities must take reasonable steps to protect the student, as by not hiring the abuser or not retaining him.

Marquay's duty is more favorable to the victim than the statutory reporting duty in some ways. *Marquay* imposes a duty of reasonable care. What it would take to fulfill that duty might vary with circumstances; perhaps reporting would be one way to fulfill that duty but not the only one and perhaps in some cases reporting alone might not be enough. What if a teacher learns that the coach is having sexual relations with a 15-year old student, but instead of reporting to anyone, goes to the student and counsels her? *Doe v. Rains County*

Independent School District, 66 F.3d 1402 (5th Cir. 1995) (no § 1983 liability because non-reporting was not under color of law).

Notes 1 & 2 remind students that there are other defendants to sue in these cases. Remember, though, that the actual attacker may not have sufficient assets to pay a judgment, and cannot cover any intentional tort judgment with insurance, as point we see again later in these materials.

Note 3. Primary liability of schools. Schools may also be held liable where the school knows of abuse or harassment and do nothing about it, a point we emphasize here that was strongly implied in *Marquay*.

Note 4. Child-abuse reporting statutes. We've just summarized the case law here. As we say, all states have some kind of statute. There are at least three distinct statutory directives that can arise in tort cases. (1) The statute directs a child protective agency to investigate suspected child abuse and to act for the protection of the child. This was the kind of problem seen in *DeShaney, supra* Ch. 16. (2) The statute directs a public agency to investigate child-care facilities and to refuse or cancel a license if these facilities present dangers to children. (3) The statute directs anyone who reasonably suspects child abuse to report it to the protective agency.

Note 5. Student-on-student violence. *Mirand*, cited here, holds that schools owe a duty to protect students from other students. The duty could be founded on either "special relationship," as this chapter indicates.

YOUNG V. SALT LAKE CITY SCH. DIST., 52 P.3d 1230 (Utah 2002).

An elementary-school student was struck by a car while in a crosswalk, as he was going to school to attend a mandatory after-school Parent-Teacher-Student meeting. In his suit against the school for negligence (for failure to supply a crossing guard or warning lights, or to warn the city of dangerous parking conditions around the school), *held*, the school owed him no duty. His injuries did not occur during school or on school property. Nor was he participating in a school-sponsored event; he was merely coming to the school to attend such an event.

Note 1. In *Young* we are one further step removed from the situation in the immediately-preceding materials. The student is struck in the crosswalk leading to the school, after the school day had ended, while on his way to a mandatory meeting. You can draw some interesting contrasts to the *Fazzaroli* case, discussed in this Note. While the school day had not started in *Fazzolari* and the attack came from outside the school system, the student-victim was on school property for the purpose of attending school. From one perspective, *Young* is just a line-drawing problem and the student fell outside the line because he was not on school property.

Note 2. Perhaps one who is in "custody" is by definition dependent upon the "custodian," and thus must rely on that custodian to protect him.

Small children must rely on parents, often. And as in *Mirand,* courts say that schools stand in place of parents – in loco parentis. Thus school duties to younger children seem uncontroversial. By the time of high school, however, ideas about the student's personhood and citizenship are inconsistent with detailed supervision. Are notions of "custody" similarly misplaced as students get older?

Note 3. In *Edson,* cited here, the court affirmed a summary judgment for the school, on the ground that the evidence failed to show that the school had the requisite degree of knowledge or notice of the risk that the student would be murdered off campus. The court said (apropos of the discussion in Note 2, above) that the school did stand in loco parentis, and owed the student a duty of reasonable supervision pursuant to a state statute. But that duty – which the statute itself set at "reasonable care" -- did not mean that there was a "duty of immediate supervision at all times and under all circumstances." The court thought there might be circumstances where a school could be held liable for negligent supervision even when the student left school grounds without permission and was injured, but that here the student's death was "a result of the premeditated criminal act of a third party," and therefore generally unforeseeable. In this case, there was no showing that the school had any "special knowledge or notice" that would bring it within an exception to the general rule.

NOTE: DUTIES OF COLLEGES

¶ **1. *College temptations and stress.*** Colleges have no "school day." Although many students are ill-prepared for college, emotionally, socially, and intellectually, courts have been reluctant to impose general supervisory duties upon colleges or to impose a protectionist Big Brother upon adult students. Suppose a college student, unaccustomed to the freedom of college life, becomes intoxicated at a social hour on a college field trip. She is seriously and permanent paralyzed when she falls into a crevice. Or suppose a college student succumbs to the temptations of drugs and sex and suffers the consequences. Finally, suppose the student suffers an emotional breakdown as a result of the pressures of college life. The cited cases represent something of these patterns. You might find room for a little doubt about whether colleges do their job. What if data showed that for every 100 students entering college as a freshman at Big State University, 25 became alcoholics or drug addicts? Given that personal supervision of individuals would be inappropriate to our social and political values in a free society, does that mean the college should offer no educational programs, no counseling, or no fair warnings of any kind?

¶ **2. *Risks of attacks.***

A. In *Coghlan v. Beta Theta Pi Fraternity*, discussed here, the court held that the university did not owe a duty of care to protect its students. However, the allegations in the complaint stated a claim for breach of a voluntarily-assumed duty since the college provided employees to supervise the parties that the plaintiff attended. *Tanja H. v. Regents of the University of California*, also discussed here, refused to recognize a duty on the part of the university to use care to protect the plaintiff or even a vicarious liability for non-enforcement of its own regulations. That's a much tougher decision than one that merely refuses to take a parental attitude toward college students generally. If you accept a formulation that says the university does indeed owe a duty of reasonable care (no more, no less), then *Tanja H.* would simply raise the question whether the university was negligent and contributed causally to the injury. But the court treated the case like a stress and temptation case, saying courts should not require colleges to institute curfews and install hall monitors.

B. *Eiseman v. State*, raised in this paragraph, goes yet one step further because the college knows of a specific risk in the person of a specific student. (Football player risks seen in *Tanja H.* are presumably only generic if there are indeed any risks at all.) *Eiseman* held that the college was under no duty to use care to shield its students, or to "brand" the former prisoner. Any liability, the Court suggested, would be "at odds with the laws and public policy regarding the release of prisoners" because it would be premised on the notion that they represent a continuing threat. Would the students in your class feel that the law school mistreated them if the person sitting next to them had a long history of sadistic murders and the law school knew it but never provided any warning? On the other hand, would a law school dean be expected to publicly warn all students when a former prisoner is admitted after having served his or her sentence?

C. *Nova Southeastern University, Inc. v. Gross*, discussed here, is the only case among those in this Note that holds for the plaintiff. The court rejects the argument that since the plaintiff was an adult, the college owed her no duty. (That would have been an appropriate argument if the plaintiff had succumbed to college temptations, but when the college creates a risk from others, the argument seems outrageously misplaced. Relationships among adults have been a basis for duties since deep medieval times. We have only to think of doctor-patient relationships, for example, not to mention the business-invitee relationships with which we started this chapter.) What about the defendant's claim that the plaintiff already knew of the danger? So far as the plaintiff's suit was based upon assignment to a dangerous place (rather than a failure to warn), the court thought her knowledge did not negate the duty; it went to issues of negligence, proximate cause, and comparative fault. "Issues of Gross's knowledge should be considered when determining the issues of breach of duty and proximate cause of her injury and in attributing proportional fault. However, it does not eliminate the university's duty to use reasonable care in assigning students to practicum locations."

For more cases on this subject, see Joel E. Smith, Annotation, *Liability of University. . . etc. for failure to protect student from crime*, 1 A.L.R.4th 1099 (1980).

FUNCHESS V. CECIL NEWMAN CORP., 632 N.W.2d 666 (Minn. 2001).

A tenant is killed by intruders. They got in, allegedly, because the security door in the apartment building and the buzzer-intercom system were not functional. In a suit against the landlord for negligence, held, the landlord owed no duty of care to protect the tenant from third-party attacks. The landlord-tenant relationship is insufficient to create a duty, in part because the landlord is not in a position to offer such protection. The landlord's provision of security measures (the security door and intercom) is insufficient to constitute an undertaking of a duty. The court feared a contrary holding on that issue would incentivize landlords not to institute security measures in the first place, or to upgrade them. And finally, the plaintiff failed to allege a breach of contract as a separate legal theory, so it could not be considered. (The landlord had agreed in the lease to provide security and to make prompt repairs.)

Note 1 should remind students that a no-duty approach allows the court to make a decision as a matter of law. If the issue is seen as one of causation, it's a matter for the jury if reasonable people could differ.

Notes 2-4. In an opinion pretty squarely opposed to the position taken in *Funchess*, the Maryland high court held in *Hemmings v. Pelham Wood Ltd. Liability Partnership*, 826 A.2d 443 (Md. 2003), that a "landlord has a duty to maintain and regularly inspect devices implemented to deter criminal activity. That is, if the security devices that the landlord provides require regular maintenance or inspection for them to properly function, the landlord must do what is reasonable to maintain or inspect the devices." Do you think Maryland apartment buildings will, in the coming years, be less safe than apartment buildings in Minnesota?

Among the cases imposing a duty of care to protect tenants from third persons, *Kline* (**Note 4**) is the leading case, but not a very demanding one. It is fundamentally contractual in its orientation, requiring the lessor to retain the level of protection that existed when the tenant leased the premises. Where the lease provisions create a duty of protection, or, as in *Kline*, the circumstances of leasing create reasonable expectations on the part of the tenant, some other cases have imposed a duty of care. See *Holley v. Mt. Zion Terrace Apartments, Inc.*, 382 So. 2d 98 (Fla. Dist. Ct. App. 1980) (a charge for guards may have been included in the rental, but no guards were furnished); *Jackson v. Post Properties*, 513 S.E.2d 259 (Ga. Ct. App. 1999) (landlord, confronted with rape and burglary, posted a guard, but guard was absent on the night plaintiff was raped by intruder in her apartment). Misrepresentation by the lessor would predictably have the same effect, and perhaps a failure to warn of highly specific and known dangers would also result in liability. See *O'Hara* *v. Western Seven Trees Corp.*, 142 Cal. Rptr. 487 (App. Ct. 1977). When the alleged undertaking is less than explicit or based in part on the landlord's conduct, the same ambiguity we saw in Chapter 17 arises. In *Hall v. Rental Management, Inc.*, 913 S.W.2d 293 (Ark. 1996), the landlord's policy statements repeatedly reflected a concern about security and expressed an attitude of concern for it; in addition, it instituted regular property patrols by on-site managers. But it did not provide security guards. The court thought it had not undertaken to do so merely because it had instituted patrols by managers.

Some courts have extended the principle to commercial leases, others have not. *Doe v. Grosvenor Properties (Hawaii) Ltd.*, also cited in **Note 4**, is a rape-in-an-office-building case, where security was poor and the elevator stopped between floors. Hawaii rejected a duty of reasonable care to protect against third persons. Although it laid this down as a rule, its view was largely influenced by its perception that the attack was unforeseeable on the facts. The court was at pains to insist that an office worker in the building was to be considered as a tenant, not as an invitee. That created a discontinuity between the duties owed by the landlord as to areas of retained control and those owed by invitors. Why could the worker not be an invitee?

Note 5. *Landlord introduces the risk.* If the landlord introduces the risk, as in *Samson v. Saginaw Professional Building, Inc.*, cited here, liability should follow easily enough if the landlord is also negligent. In *Samson,* the owner leased the fourth floor of an office building to a mental health clinic, which was in the business of seeing mentally disturbed persons, including violent criminals on parole or "convalescent leave." The clinic was presented to any who might see its name as "Saginaw Valley Consultation Center," and it took up to 25 patients a day. The inevitable eventually occurred when one of these patients, a man named Butzin, caught a legal secretary in the elevator, knifed and robbed her. The court held the lessor liable. Although there was a dissent, the lessor itself introduced the danger into the building and knew of it.

Note 6. *Reasonable care.* Some courts simply require reasonable care on the part of landlords with respect to common areas, as the citations here indicate. Some would even go beyond this. In *Sharp v. W.H. Moore, Inc.*, 796 P.2d 506 (Idaho 1990), the court, quoting an earlier decision, said: "[W]e adopt the rule that a landlord is under a duty to exercise reasonable care in light of all the circumstances. We stress that adoption of this rule is not tantamount to making the landlord an insurer for all injury occurring on the premises, but merely constitutes our removal of the landlord's common-law cloak of immunity. . . ." This was another in the long line of rape cases. The plaintiff was raped at her office. There was a faulty lock on the door.

See Tracy A. Bateman & Susan Thomas, Annotation, *Landlord's Liability for Failure to Protect Tenant from Criminal Acts of Third Person,* 43 A.L.R.5th 207 (1996); DOBBS ON TORTS § 325 (2000).

Note 7. *Guest of tenant.* In *Martinez*, cited here, the court applied the Restatement rule that any person on the land with the consent of a lessee is owed the same duty of care as the lessee. In the case, the court held that a condo owner was to be treated like a landlord, and the condo owner like a tenant, for these purposes. The guest in the case was shot (not fatally) in the condo parking lot; the court held the duty of care extended not only to conditions on the land, but also to dangerous activities such as criminal intrusions. There were issues of fact remaining on whether that duty was breached, however.

Note 8. *Thinking about damages allocation.* This is an issue that pops up more than once in the casebook; most pointedly it appeared in Chapter 9 (in connection with *Wassell v. Adams* and the comparative fault between the plaintiff and the defendant) and will appear in Chapter 25 on apportionment. For now, you can simply point out that in a several liability situation, where the intentional tort of the defendant/third party attacker may be compared to the negligence of the defendant landlord, the attacker will certainly be assigned the lion's share of the responsibility. Where this occurs the plaintiff is the real loser, since the attacker's share will likely go unpaid. Should courts not allow the joinder of the attacker, or not allow the landlord's share to be reduced in such a situation? We don't provide answers here and you should probably not be looking to do so, either; the point is to make students think like lawyers about the fact that the person who seems most at fault may not be the person from whom money can be obtained.

•*Further questions on the relationships that can give rise to a duty.*

At times, a defendant may fall into more than one "special relationship" with a given plaintiff. Which one a court chooses to identify may be determinative. Some additional thoughts on this are set forth below for possible class discussion purposes.

Innkeepers, lodging houses, and invitors. The *Parish* court recited the rote formula – the duty to protect is limited to carriers, innkeepers, invitors and custodians. The lessor was not in the same category as the innkeeper. The lessor conveyed premises while the innkeeper provided a service and retained control. This distinction led to what the law came to perceive as special duties of the innkeeper (although you could say just as well that the innkeeper's duties were normal and the lessor enjoyed special immunities). Since guests are invitees, the invitor-invitee category seems broad enough to cover all the innkeeper cases.

But in *Donaldson v. Young Women's Christian Association of Duluth,* 539 N.W.2d 789 (Minn. 1995) the court insisted that the operator of a 97-room residence for low-income persons, many of whom had mental health problems, was not in the innkeeper category and that it was under no duty to protect a resident from her own suicide. When it formulated the duty to protect rule, it did not list invitees as such, only carriers, innkeepers, possessors of land who hold it open to the public, and persons who have custody. Any duty to protect a person from her own suicide is analogous to a duty to protect her from another person. Why should it matter that the YWCA is not an innkeeper but a "lodging house"? Whatever it is, isn't the resident an invitee to whom a duty of care is owed? Since the YWCA was not acting as custodian, what counts as reasonable care might be very little care indeed. Reasonable care would not require it to lock the resident in or stand guard at all hours. But it seems strange to say that *if* the YWCA failed to act as a reasonable person would have acted, given its role as a lodging house, if its personnel simply watched a resident take out the razor blades and slit her wrist and did nothing, that no duty of care existed.

Lessor or employer. Where courts have not expanded the lessor's duty, the defendant's status as lessor gives him the benefit of a no-duty rule. We saw in *Hosein* that the taxi company escaped responsibility for failing to use safe cabs for its drivers on the ground that the drivers were (in form) lessees, not employees. The same idea arose in a different context in *Exxon Corporation v. Tidwell*, 867 S.W.2d 19 (Tex. 1993), where an oil company leased a gas station selling its products to Morgan. An employee was shot during a robbery. The oil company's obligation to maintain a safe workplace depended upon whether it was only a lessor or whether, because it controlled day to day details of the work, it was an employer. If it was a lessor only, it had no obligation.

College as invitor or landlord. The earlier notes suggested that a college might escape general responsibility for the moral or emotional well being of its students, but to the extent that a college is an invitor or a landlord —leasing to dorm students, for example— it may be under a duty to students created by the invitor or landlord relationship.

College as invitor. In *Sharkey v. Board of Regents, University of Nebraska*, 615 N.W.2d 889 (Neb. 2000), one student attacked another. The university had long known that the attacker had stalked and harassed women but had not pursued an investigation. The attacker stabbed the plaintiff when the plaintiff told him to stop harassing the plaintiff's wife. The court recognized a duty of care based upon the invitor-invitee relationship and the foreseeability that the attacker would commit some such crimes. Whether the university was negligent was a matter for the trier.

In *Peterson v. San Francisco Comm. College Dist.*, 685 P.2d 1193 (Cal. 1984), the plaintiff was a college student who was assaulted while ascending a stair in the school's parking lot. An unidentified male attacked her from behind untrimmed foliage. The untrimmed foliage was regarded as a dangerous condition in the college's control and it was held under a duty to use care with respect to this condition. The court held that California's immunity statutes protected the college from any liability grounded on a theory of inadequate police protection, but that this furnished no protection as to claims of inadequate warning or failure to trim foliage behind which an attacker could hide.

College as landlord. In *Nero v. Kansas State University*, 861 P.2d 768 (Kan. 1993), the plaintiff was a female student at a university and a resident in a co-ed university housing unit. A student named Ramon Davenport was also a resident. Davenport had been accused of raping another woman in another co-ed hall (he later pleaded guilty). The university carefully removed him from that hall while charges were pending, but when summer session came, he was allowed to move into the co-ed hall where the plaintiff lived. The plaintiff alleged that he sexually assaulted her in the laundry-recreation room. The court reversed a summary judgment for the university, concluding that on the basis of the landlord-tenant relationship, the university owed the plaintiff a duty of reasonable care that might have been breached. The court insisted that the care was like the care owed by a private landowner to its tenants. The court did not rely on the university's relationship to Davenport.

In *Mullins v. Pine Manor College*, 449 N.E.2d 331 (Mass. 1983), where an intruder entered a dorm late at night in spite of some rather careful security precautions. He raped the plaintiff in her room. The Massachusetts Court imposed a duty of care. It thought that "colleges of ordinary prudence customarily exercise care to protect the well-being of their resident students, including seeking to protect them against the criminal acts of third parties." The court added: "The fact that a college need not police the morals of its resident students, however, does not entitle it to abandon any effort to ensure their physical safety."

See also Stanton v. University of Maine System, 773 A.2d 1045 (Me. 2001)(specifically characterizing a student as an invitee rather than as a tenant).

In *Miller v. State*, 467 N.E.2d 493 (N.Y. 1984), a college student was in the laundry room of her dormitory early one morning when a large man with a butcher knife captured her, blindfolded her, and led her to another room in the dormitory, where he raped her. The trial court found he was an outsider who found entry easy because there were ten doors to the dorm, all of which were left unlocked at all times. This was found negligent and a small judgment in favor of the college student was rendered. The Appellate Division reversed because –*Riss* rises again– this was regarded as a claim of inadequate police protection as to which there would be no liability, relationship or not relationship. The Court of Appeals, however, reversed, holding that the claim against the state in its capacity as landlord was on the same footing as a claim against a private landlord.

Contract obligations. Colleges may undertake protection of the student by contract or by promises or representations inducing reliance. Cf. *Delaney v. University of Houston*, 835 S.W.2d 56 (Tex. 1992) (university gave assurances of security, then refused to repair broken lock in dormitory). In *Savannah College*, supra, the plaintiff argued that the college was in breach of contract to protect the student, who was raped by a dormitory intruder. This claim was dismissed, on the ground that any contract would have to be "expressed plainly and explicitly." But other courts might find the contract terms between student and college in a series of documents such as the faculty-student handbook or customs and usages. *George v. University of Idaho*, 822 P.2d 549

(Idaho Ct. App. 1991). (a university's failure to prevent repeated sexual harassment by a law teacher).

§ 2. DEFENDANT'S RELATIONSHIP WITH DANGEROUS PERSONS

DUDLEY V. OFFENDER AID & RESTORATION OF RICHMOND, INC., 401 S.E.2d 878 (Va. 1991).

Dudley should be an easy case: The defendant was under some specific duties (rules) aimed at controlling a very dangerous person. The defendant did not perform those duties and one result seems to have been the injury and death of a citizen. The court is careful to find "custody," or at least a custodial relationship. Perhaps the Virginia Court would not have imposed liability if this had been a suit against the state or one of its agencies, but it was not. Notice that the court imposes the duty of care not only to victims that might be identified in advance or against whom specific threats are made, but to all who might foreseeably be injured. If that rule is right for private organizations who have custody of state prisoners, why is it not right for the state itself, a major duty of which is protection of citizens?

The same year Virginia decided *Dudley* it also decided *Foreign Mission Board of the Southern Baptist Convention v. Wade*, 409 S.E.2d 144 (Va. 1991). Beginning in 1976 George Thomas Wade worked as a career missionary in Africa under an appointment by the defendant, the Foreign Mission Board of the Southern Baptist Convention. In 1982 Wade's daughter Renee told Fray, the associate director of the defendant board, that her father had sexually molested her. The response of that gentleman was to tell her not to repeat her statements to her mother or anyone else. Fray did confront Wade, however, and Wade admitted the molestation. Fray did not advise the child's mother. After the family returned to the United States Renee told her mother and molestation of other children then came to light. This is a suit by Renee, now an adult, and by her mother on behalf of the other children on the ground that the Board, knowing of the injury to Renee, failed to secure medical care for Renee and failed to protect the other children. The trial court dismissed the negligence claim but permitted a breach of contract claim to go to the jury, which awarded $1.5 million in damages. *Held*, reversed for a judgment in favor of the defendant. (1) Although the Board did guarantee the safety of the family, this obligation did not relate to dangers from the father. No contract obligation existed to require the Board to protect the children. (2) The trial court held that the Board had no common law duty of care to the Wades and there was no appeal on that ruling. Should the lawyers have appealed from dismissal of the negligence claim?

Note 1. "Custody." *Parole officers, child protective services, employers.* (a) *Schmidt v. HTG, Inc.,* cited here, was a suit for the wrongful death of a young woman who, like the parolee, worked in the HTG restaurant. The parole officer had provided no information to HTG as the new employer of a man who had been in prison ten years for aggravated rape and sodomy of a young woman and who was rated as high risk. The parolee's fellow employee, ignorant of the risk, accepted a ride home from him and was never again seen alive. The court concluded that the that the parole officer, though in control of the relevant information, was not sufficiently in control or in charge of the parolee. As usual, the court used the control test to defeat liability even though the plaintiff did not claim a failure of control but only that the parole officer should have provided appropriate warning or information that would have permitted her protection. (The court also relied on the idea that no specific threat was directed at an identifiable person, the point raised in *Thompson v. County of Alameda,* 614 P.2d 728 (Cal. 1980), discussed in Note 2 after *Tarasoff* in this chapter.

(b) *E.P. v. Riley,* cited here, held that the DSS "had both legal custody and supervisory control" of JH even after he had been placed with foster parents. They owed a duty of care to "control him," apparently by giving information to foster parents or by providing psychiatric help. The foster parents were not subject to liability because, deprived of information by the DSS, they could not reasonably foresee that JH would harm others. Incidentally, the court disposed of the public duty argument by saying it applied only to law enforcement failures, not cases like this.

(c) *Employers:* Under the Restatement, employers have a duty to control when danger is at hand. But the duty is not absolute. In *K.M. v. Publix Super Markets,* cited here, the court held that the employer had no duty to warn on these facts. The key fact to the court was that the warning pertained to the employees' "personal relationship outside of work." An employer does not owe a duty, said the court, to protect anyone from his employees while those employees are off duty, not acting for the employer's benefit, not on the employer's premises and not using the employer's equipment.

Note 2. A duty to control spouses or family members? Conflicts might be promoted between spouses if each spouse becomes liable to "control" or manipulate the other. The extreme case posed in this note is based upon the allegations in *Pamela L. v. Farmer,* the first case cited here. The court held that a cause of action was stated. The allegation was that the husband had a propensity for sexual molestation of young girls and that the wife had represented to the parents of the girls that it would be safe for them to swim at her home while she was away because her husband would be there to take care of them. The husband allegedly molested the children while the wife was away. The court emphasized that in this case the wife was not guilty merely of nonfeasance because she had actively assured the parents of the girls that they would be safe.

J.S. v. R.T.H., the second cited case in this Note, suggested that a duty might be focused on the plaintiffs with whom the defendant had a long neighborly relationship and would not necessary require a warning; the knowledgeable wife might simply arrange to be present when the children were there. *D.W. v. Bliss,* by comparison, the more recent Kansas case cited next, held that there was no special relationship between a sex offender's wife and his minor victim, on the ground that the wife had no ability to control the husband. The plaintiff's attempt to ground a duty in the wife's landowner status was equally unavailing.

Eric J. v. Betty M., next cited here, put great weight on the parole system's assumption that repentance was possible and seemed to say that the relatives of a parolee were entitled to share the same heroic assumption. The logic of that line of reasoning suggests that, given liability in *Pamela L.,* maybe the victim would be able to maintain the claim against the do-nothing relatives if the molester had never been convicted, but that after his conviction his knowledgeable relatives would be free to do nothing in the happy belief in his repentance (and self control). This is the more puzzling because they would, as the court suggests, be liable for harm done by a pit bull on their property–unless, perhaps, the pit bull was on parole.

In *Bebry v. Zanauskas,* the final citation in this Note, the court held that there was no duty, since neither the parents nor the brother had "taken control" over him.

Additional cases. Control (or the right to, at least) was key to the court in *Volpe v. Gallagher,* 821 A.2d 699 (R.I. 2003), which held that liability could be imposed upon a homeowner for death of a neighbor at the hands of the homeowner's adult son. The son stored weapons and ammunition in the house in obvious places and the mother knew generally that something was wrong with the son, although she was not aware of anything leading to the incident and was inside the house when her son erupted from his basement lair and shot and killed a neighbor a few feet away. The court relied on Restatement Second § 318, would impose a duty of care upon a landowner who (1) is present, (2) knows or "has reason to know" he can control the third person, and (3) knows of the need to do so, and (4) knows of the opportunity to do so.

Some of the spousal control cases can come up in a negligent entrustment type situation. Compare *Andrade v. Baptiste,* 583 N.E.2d 837 (Mass. 1992) (wife allowed husband to keep assault rifle in her house and to have access to it, she had no duty to control it) with *Williams v. Bumpass,* 568 So.2d 979 (Fla. 1990) (friend liable for handing enraged fighter a gun when he was losing fight).

Parent's duty to protect child. Distinguish the case in which the parent fails to protect her child from an abuser. In that case, the parent has a relationship with, and an obligation to, the child, regardless of her relationship with the abuser. See *Hite v. Brown,* 654 N.E.2d 452 (Ohio 1995) where the court said a mother was under a duty to protect her child from her husband's abuse. "[W]e conclude a parent or guardian of a child has a special relationship with the child, and the duty to be exercised in that relationship can be defined with reference to the duties of care, protection and support set forth in R.C. 2919.22(A)." The statute did not seem to add anything, as it merely recognized the duty by providing that no parent " shall create a substantial risk to the health or safety of the child, by violating a duty of care, protection, or support."

Note 3. A duty to control tenants? In *Rosales v. Stewart*, cited here, the court required the landlord to use his economic and legal power over the tenant to control the tenant.

Does this create some problems? What about the situation where the landlord suspects the prospective tenant is a gang member? Does he owe a duty not to rent to that person for fear of liability if he does, and the person injures someone else? In *Castaneda*, cited here, the California Supreme Court held that there is no such duty unless the circumstances indicate to the landlord that gang violence is "extraordinarily foreseeable," which it was not on the facts. The court said, "we are not persuaded that imposing a duty on landlords to withhold rental units from those they believe to be gang members is a fair and workable solution to this problem [of gang violence], or one consistent with our state's public policy as a whole." Because gang members "do not announce their gang affiliations on housing applications," placing landlords under a duty not to rent would result in "arbitrary discrimination on the basis of race, ethnicity, family composition, dress and appearance, or reputation. All of these are, in at least some circumstances, illegal and against public policy and could themselves subject the landlord to liability."

In *Strunk v. Zoltanski*, also cited here, the court held that if the landlord knows before the lease is entered into that the tenant may be expected to carry on activities dangerous to others, the landlord has a duty to use care. Since there was evidence that the lessor knew of the dog's vicious nature and that it would be kept on the premises, the courts below correctly denied a summary judgment for the landlord. Judge Jones envisioned that the landlord might exercise the reasonable care required by inserting lease provisions for the confinement or control of the dog. The dissent by Judge Kaye calls this a "new duty" and says it effectively subjects the landlord to absolute liability. What is absolute about a duty to exercise reasonable care?

Accord, that the landlord owes a duty of care to those in a common area once he knows or should know of the tenant's dangerous animal: *Fouts v. Mason*, 592 N.W.2d 33 (Iowa 1999); *Shields v. Wagman*, 350 Md. 666, 714 A.2d 881 (Md. 1998). See also *Alaskan Village, Inc. v. Smalley*, 720 P.2d 945 (Alaska 1986) (pit bulls, landlord should have enforced its own rules.) *Contra*, at least where the dog owner tenant was not in violation of the lease and the landlord merely had the option not to renew at the end of the month, *Stewart v. Aldrich*, 788 A.2d 603 (Me. 2002) (landlord's right of control " does not include the incidental control that comes from being able to threaten tenants with nonrenewal of a lease or with eviction"); *Smaxwell*, cited here (no liability for tenant's dogs unless the landlord himself is also an owner or keeper of the dogs).

In *Klitzka*, also cited here, the court said even where the landlords new the tenants' dog was dangerous, they owed no duty to the tenant's guest from the dog because they had no control over the leased premises where the dog attack occurred. the court further noted that imposing liability on landlords in these cases by requiring them to evict tenants with dangerous dogs "leads to the relocation, not elimination, of the danger the animal presents."

Drug trafficking. In *Muniz by Gonzales v. Flohern, Inc.*, also cited in this Note, the court held that the landlord owed no duty to the plaintiff. The plaintiff alleged that the defendant leased a building to a tenant known to be illegally trafficking in drugs. A would-be robber fired a gun, pellets from which struck and blinded the plaintiff, who was merely a passerby. "There was no relationship between defendants and the gunman who robbed the streetfront store of their building. Nor was there any relationship between the attempted robbery and the illicit drug activity such as to require defendants to attempt to control the conduct of either the tenant or the gunman. Moreover, there was no relationship between defendants and the infant plaintiff requiring defendants to afford protection from potential dangers springing from the tenant's illicit drug trafficking in the streetfront store."

—*Tiger, tiger burning bright. Frobig v. Gordon*, 881 P.2d 226 (Wash. 1994), holds that landlords who lease land to a tenant for purposes of harboring wild animals, are not liable to a third person injured by the tenant's tiger. Liability "flows from ownership or direct control." The court disagreed with *Strunk v. Zoltani*, but thought that even under *Strunk* the landlords would not be liable here because they would only be held to take precautions within their control; the landlords had specifically required some safety precautions in the lease and in addition had notified the tenant to vacate the premises when complaints were made.

See Annotation, Landlord's liability to third person for injury resulting from attack off leased premises by dangerous vicious animal kept by tenant, 89 A.L.R.4th 374 (1991).

Note 4. A duty to control employees? Yes, an employer can be liable for negligently hiring or supervising a dangerous person. All of the cases here so hold. In *Keller*, cited here, the court held that the employer did not owe a duty to the victim, since harm to her was not a foreseeable risk. The establishment was closed for business that entire day (it was Sunday); the employer did not know the employee was bringing the victim to the business; and knowledge that the employee had acted inappropriately towards adult females did not make a sexual assault on a child foreseeable. This result may remind us of the "special relationship plus foreseeability" requirements we saw at the beginning of this chapter.

Negligent recommendations of a dangerous person. Could a person be held liable for negligently recommending a dangerous person for a job with someone else, which results in hiring, which further results in the dangerous person harming someone? In *Randi W. v. Muroc Joint Unified School District*, 929 P.2d 582 (Cal. 1997), the plaintiff, claiming molestation by a school administrator, sued the administrator's former employers who had given him a positive recommendation for the job that put him in position to molest the plaintiff. *Held,* if the plaintiff's injury resulted from action taken by the current employer in reliance on the recommendation, the plaintiff has a claim. In

Richland Sch. Dist. v. Mabton Sch. Dist., 45 P.3d 580 (Wash. Ct. App. 2002), the first school district wrote laudatory recommendations for an employee who in fact was forced to resign after he had been charged with sexual molestation of students. The second school district hired the employee, then terminated him after it learned of the dropped charges. The termination cost the second school district "front pay" of $100,000, for which it sued the first district. The court rejected liability, partly because it regarded the claim as one of negligence or negligent misrepresentation rather than a knowing misrepresentation and partly because, unlike *Randi W.*, it asserted only an economic interest, not an interest in freedom from personal injury.

Negligent hiring or supervision of dangerous clergy. *Connection:* See the discussion of First Amendment barriers to claims for intentional infliction of emotional distress in Chapter 19, § 1.

NOTE: A DUTY TO CONTROL CHILDREN?

¶ **1. Basic limits.** You probably need to remind students of the first basic rule here: No vicarious liability (but possible liability based on statute, as we saw in Chapter 3). Beyond that, we see that the liability of parents for negligent supervision is extremely limited by most courts.

Parent of a dangerous person. Even if parents owed a full duty of reasonable care to control their children, they would not be subject to liability unless they were negligent. If they cannot foresee that their child would have engaged in deadly gay bashing, they are not liable for it. *Rodriguez v. Spencer*, 902 S.W.2d 37 (Tex. App. 1995). But in fact courts appear to exculpate parents even when their children's torts are foreseeable. *Bebry*, cited in Note 2 after *Dudley*, may be such a case, since the court rested its "no duty" holding on the family members' lack of virtual custody (or lack of sufficient control) over him.

¶ **2. Normal children.** In *McNamee v. A.J.W.*, cited here, the court thought parents had no duty based upon their son's sex with the 15-year-old plaintiff while they were away. *But cf. Huston v. Konieczny*, 556 N.E.2d 505 (Ohio 1990) (parents who permit children under drinking age to use their house for a New Year's Eve party, with the expectation that some would drink beer, might be liable for injuries resulting from intoxication of one of the minors, emphasis on negligent entrustment rather than duty to control).

¶ **3. Children known to be violent.** In some cases, the specific danger requirement seems silly. The *Parsons* court apparently would hold parents responsible for the attacks on the women there only if they knew of their son's propensity to attack with hammers and saws. Yet they knew of his propensity for violence and at least some of it was directed at women.

In other cases, however, the requirement coincides with ordinary care. Parents should balance control with increased freedom as the child grows. Choices between demonstrating trust and demonstrating distrust and control can be difficult. The parent and step-parent in the gun cases (*Dinsmore-Poff v.*

Alvord, and *Williamson v. Daniels*, had plenty of notice that the teenagers were dangerous, but may have made choices in upbringing that were within the range of the reasonable.

In *Gritzner v. Michael R.*, 611 N.W.2d 906 (Wis. 2000), cited at the end of this Note, Michael, a ten-year-old, had a propensity for sexually abusing young girls—or least had engaged in such abuse before. A four-year old girl was visiting at Michael's house and he allegedly abused her. The court held that one Bubner might be held liable for Michael's abuse if he was negligent in failing to control Michael or in failing to give appropriate warning of Michael's alleged propensity. The basis for this liability was that Bubner lived with Michael's mother in a "romantic" relationship; he stood in a loco parentis relationship and also had undertaken a duty of parental supervision.

At the end of the chapter, with the problems presented there, we'll have a chance to distinguish between failure of parents to control a child and negligent entrustment, as where the parent allows a child to have a pistol. By then we will have covered negligent entrustment and we can ask whether the parent would be liable for that.

¶ 4. *Is ability to control important?* This question foreshadows the *Tarasoff* case coming up; while we have seen some courts stress the ability to control as a major justification for imposing a duty of care, *Tarasoff* focuses on something else entirely.

TARASOFF V. REGENTS OF UNIVERSITY OF CALIFORNIA , 551 P.2d 334 (Cal. 1976).

First, notice that though the relationship between the defendant and the source of harm is the basis for the duty in this case, there is no legal power to control the source of harm except through commitment. In this respect the case differs from *Rosales,* where the court suggested termination of the tenancy and from parental control cases where there is a legal power to control one's child. There might indeed be a legal power to commit in a case like *Tarasoff* but in fact the court refuses to permit liability on that ground because of the California immunity statutes. The basis of the duty here, then, is not power of *control* the killer but merely an ability to *protect* the victim, by warning, for example.

The therapeutic role of the doctor in *Tarasoff* leads to the confidentiality problem, the problem most discussed in this connection. If patients do not believe what they say is held in confidence they will be reluctant to talk and treatment will be accordingly even less effective than it already is. One solution to this would be to keep patients in ignorance of law as much as possible. This however would presumably violate the notions behind the informed consent rules. What should a psychiatrist do in California under the *Tarasoff* decision? Should there be a sign on the door "Under the law of California no statements may be held in confidence"? As troubling as this might be to those who think talk is therapy, it is might be at least tolerable with ongoing therapy. In the case of crisis counseling the difficulties may become more intense.

Distinguish failure to control. *Tarasoff* required reasonable care, whatever that might be, but the context suggested that a warning to the potential victim would be in order. If the victim already knows the danger –the ever-present abused wife, for example– then the claim must be that the duty of reasonable care required some kind of control over the patient, by treatment, commitment, or otherwise. In *Estates of Morgan v. Fairfield Family Counseling Center,* 673 N.E.2d 1311 (Ohio 1997), where the doctor withdrew the patient's anti-schizophrenia medication, the court recognized potential liability when the patient then killed his parents. However, in *Weitz v. Lovelace Health System, Inc.,* 214 F.3d 1175 (10th Cir. 2000), the federal court concluded that New Mexico would not impose a "duty to control" an outpatient even though New Mexico accepted the *Tarasoff* warning duty. Instead of asking whether control was reasonable and possible in the particular case, the court departed from the principle of reasonable care. It suggested that in general outpatient status would give the doctor less opportunity for control so that, regardless of the facts and justice of a particular case, there would be no duty in outpatient cases.

Note 1. Scope. This note is intended to remind the student that the negligence and causation issues remain; to impose the duty of care is not to determine liability. Suppose the patient's threat is a threat to "key" the plaintiff's new car–scratch it with a key. Students can argue that under *Carroll Towing,* both the likelihood of injury and the kind of injury that would occur are small, so that the balance of utility might weigh in favor of confidentiality. This is consistent with *Tarasoff's* view that confidentiality is not an absolute; it does not prevent the imposition of a duty of care, but that does not say it plays no part in the determination of *negligence.* However, as we know, the standards set by custom are at least potentially opposed to standards set by the *Carroll Towing* principle. In professional malpractice cases the habit of courts is to consider expert testimony, and experts are so guided by their own professional ideas, which may not include any notions similar to *Carroll Towing's* balance.

The California Court was in its giving mode when *Tarasoff* was decided and it found negligence in spite of the fact that the therapist in fact DID warn the police. Why was he not reasonable in relying upon them? The California statute now provides expressly that a warning to law enforcement authorities will suffice to fulfill the therapist's duty of care.

Note 2. *Tarasoff* and *Thompson*. Strangely enough, in the *Thompson* case all the signs would point to liability but there it was denied. The public entity in *Thompson* was in actual control and had legal authority to control the violent actor. It took affirmative action by releasing him and was not merely guilty of nonfeasance. Yet the same court found no liability and suggested that the difference between that case and *Tarasoff* lay in the fact that the violent actor in *Thompson* had not threatened a specific victim. It was also true that in *Thompson* one supposes that the therapeutic role of the public entity is minor or non-existent, while in *Tarasoff* the therapeutic role is the major one.

Most states have followed the *Thompson* limitation, as the citations to *Cowles* and *Osborn* indicate, and as we reiterate in **Note 3** below. Some other states, represented here by the *Schuster* case from Wisconsin, go the other way.

We have just seen the *Dudley* court rejecting that limitation in facts closer to the *Thompson* case. In *Estates of Morgan v. Fairfield Family Counseling Center,* 673 N.E.2d 1311 (Ohio 1997), the court held that the *Thompson* limitation to identified victims could apply only if the act of negligence was a failure to warn (as it was in *Thompson*). In *Morgan,* the allegations and testimony had it that the defendants failed to protect the patient's victims by failing in their duty to the patient himself. One doctor withdrew the patient's schizophrenia-controlling medicine, apparently believing the patient to be a malingerer seeking Social Security money; unqualified people made all kinds of medical/psychiatric judgments and failed to commit the patient who needed care. The patient got worse and worse after medication was withdrawn, but nothing was done and he eventually killed his parents. The case seems much easier than *Tarasoff* because all the defendants had to do to avoid potential liability was to properly treat their own patient; they did not need to breach confidence or identify who might be a victim. In this respect, compare *Reisner* and *Amos,* below.

In evaluating *Thompson's* limitation, students must remember that even without the limitation, the plaintiff must still prove negligence and causation. If there is no identifiable victim, the therapist may have no reasonable options and in that case could not be found negligent, even if he were under a duty to exercise reasonable care. For instance, if the therapist judges the balance of danger as barely justifying a warning, but there is no one to whom the warning can go, the therapist might well conclude that the same balance of danger would not justify any more extreme protective actions such as commitment.

Note 3. Accepting the *Tarasoff* duty. For a sample statute, see CAL. CIV. CODE. § 43.92. *Tarasoff* is discussed in a broader context in DOBBS ON TORTS § 331 (2000). All of the cases cited here accept *Tarasoff* with the *Thompson* limitation, as described in the parentheticals.

Note 4. Rejecting or modifying *Tarasoff*. Most courts have fully accepted *Tarasoff;* we provide a few examples here of courts that have either rejected it or have limited it to particular facts, or have found *Tarasoff*-like duties but on a different theory from the *Tarasoff* case. For example, in the *Gregory* case cited here, the court held that while there is a duty to control a dangerous patient, there is no duty to warn those endangered by the patient.

Texas rejected the *Tarasoff* duty of reasonable care so far as it required a diagnosis or treatment of a patient, in *Van Horn v. Chambers,* 970 S.W.2d 542

(Tex. 1998). The same court rejected a *Tarasoff* duty to warn because it implicated confidentiality and because of its view of legislative policy. *Thapar v. Zezulka,* cited here. Yet it has now recognized that a defendant might have a duty to *control* a dangerous person. In *Texas Home Management, Inc. v. Peavy,* also cited here, the state contracted with an "intermediate"care facility for mentally limited persons, to take care of a teenager, Dixon. Dixon exhibited increasing violence in attacks on others, and he was less controlled when allowed to leave the facility's structured living on extended home visits. On such visits, he committed a number of crimes over time, ending (we hope) with the murder of the plaintiffs' daughter and the theft of her car. The majority held that given the contractual obligation and the concomitant right of control, the defendant facility had a relationship with Dixon, and the relationship in turn established a duty to control. Perhaps the court would not want to stick with this exact and seemingly circular formulation. Indeed, it might have minimized conflict with concurring judges if all the judges had seen the issue in terms of a duty to use care, a duty that might be breached by unreasonably failing to exercise control. However that may be, the jurisprudence of these cases seems complicated. Texas seems to say no duty at all to diagnose, to treat, or to warn, at least if the defendant is in a doctor-patient relationship, yet a duty to "control" the patient by confinement where he is already confined. A duty to warn of a discovered danger is easy to carry out, and a duty of reasonable care to diagnose would not add burdens to the duty already owed to the patient himself. So, at least in the abstract, it looks as if some defendants may be absolved of a relatively undemanding duty, while others may be required to exercise full "control." On the facts of *Texas Home Management*, however, there might be good reason to impose duty to control where the care facility has an incentive (payment for care) to retain persons whose violence make a more restrictive environment desirable.

Note 5. Extending *Tarasoff*. *Note:* Emotional harm resulting from injury to another is considered as a separate topic in Chapter 19.

Eisel v. Board of Education of Montgomery County, cited here: The training and education of school counselors might be quite different from the training and education of many licensed psychotherapists, but, again, notice that reasonable care is all that is required. The Maryland Court does NOT require the school counselor who hears a suicide threat to make a diagnosis that only a psychiatrist could make. She is only required to act reasonably on a danger she should have perceived. Presumably she is to be judged by the standards of care of her profession; in any event the court does not suggest that she is judged by the standards of care of better psychiatrists unless she is so trained herself. *Eisel* rejected any requirement of custody or control. In rejecting that requirement, the court pointed out that "The negligence relied on is a failure to communicate to the parent the information allegedly possessed by the defendants concerning the child's contemplated suicide, not a failure by the school authorities physically to prevent the suicide by exercising custody or control."

In *Bellah v. Greenson*, also cited, the court held that the *Tarasoff* duty did not extend to the protection of a suicidal patient. The psychiatrist there noted that his patient, Tammy, was disposed to suicide, but he did not warn Tammy's parents. Tammy did commit suicide. In a suit against the psychiatrist for her wrongful death, the court said: "We conclude that Tarasoff . . . required only that a therapist disclose the contents of a confidential communication where the risk to be prevented thereby is the danger of violent assault, and not where the risk of harm is self-inflicted harm or mere property damage. We decline to further extend the holding of *Tarasoff*."

Lawlor v. Orlando, 795 So.2d 147 (Fla. Dist. Ct. App. 2001), also held that a therapist had no duty to prevent an outpatient's suicide because suicide was not foreseeable, even though expert opinion said it was. Since the court considered the question to be one of duty, it made its own decision on foreseeability without deference to what a jury might have found. Once the question is framed as a duty to prevent an outpatient's suicide the answer seems foredoomed. If the court had asked whether the therapist had a duty of reasonable care and whether evidence would permit a finding that the duty was breached because no protection was instituted to avoid foreseeable suicide, the answer would presumably have been that the issue of foreseeability was for the jury.

Note 6. Doctors' warnings to patients. This is but a variant on *Tarasoff*, albeit an easier one for reasons described below. The penultimate questions, followed by the citation to *Witthoeft*, are actually answered by the first case cited: The idea is that a doctor does not owe a duty to warn the patient of something that should be obvious to the patient, such as the patient's poor eyesight. This is entirely different from the kind of situation in *DiMarco* (from the same court that decided *Witthoeft*) where the patient has a communicable disease that is not an obvious condition from the patient's perspective.

Reisner v. Regents of University of California, 37 Cal.Rptr.2d 518 (Ct. App. 1995) is similar to *DiMarco*. A young woman named Jennifer was given a blood transfusion in the course of surgery at UCLA Medical Center. Her physician discovered the next day that she had HIV antibodies in her blood, but did not tell her or her parents. Jennifer was treated for five years before anyone told her she had AIDS. By that time, she had been intimate with Daniel. After Jennifer discovered the infection and told Daniel, Daniel tested positive for HIV. Daniel sued the doctor and the University of California. The defendant made a *Thompson*-type argument: Daniel was not a known or readily identifiable person, so he was not protected by a *Tarasoff* duty to warn. The court rejected this argument in part because the defendant could have protected Daniel by warning its own patient.

Amos v. Vanderbilt University, 62 S.W.3d 133 (Tenn. 2001), is a little like *Reisner*. The defendant allegedly should have warned its former patient that she had been given blood that might have been AIDs contaminated. Unwarned, he later married and had a child. The child contracted AIDs in utero and died of it. The court held that the hospital owed a duty to warn the patient for the benefit of others, including her husband. The court had previously limited the duty to warn to "identifiable victims," but here it seemed to say that an identifiable victim was anyone foreseeably endangered. "The zone of danger in this case, therefore, is much larger than the zone of danger in *Bradshaw*. As a result, the identifiable third parties may be extended beyond the patient's immediate family members."

These cases are much easier for the plaintiff than *Tarasoff* because on their facts the patient *wants* to follow the safe practice and avoid risks to others. All the doctor need do is fully inform the patient. The cases raise no concern over whether the doctor should warn third persons. Neither the confidentiality problem of *Tarasoff* nor the identifiable victim rule in *Thompson* presents any basis for defensive arguments.

Note 7. Doctors' warnings to non-patients. This setting is obviously closer to the *Tarasoff* case than the **Note 6** cases are. When the plaintiff cannot be protected solely by a warning to the patient herself, some courts support a duty to warn others.

In disease cases, privacy issues are the counterpart to confidentiality issues in the *Tarasoff*-therapeutic cases. In *Santa Rosa Health Care Corp. v. Garcia,* cited in this note, B was perhaps exposed to HIV through administration of a blood factor provided by the defendant for hemophiliacs. The defendant did not warn him directly and did not warn Garcia, his friend who later became his wife. But the statute prohibited divulging any information about AIDS, positive or negative or about any risk and its exception did not apply. So Garcia had no claim. For a privacy-type claim under a statute by an AIDS victim whose status was revealed to protect others, see *Doe v. Marselle,* 675 A.2d 835 (Conn. 1996) (claim valid).

Bradshaw v. Daniel, 854 S.W.2d 865 (Tenn. 1993), holds that a physician treating a man for Rocky Mountain Spotted Fever is under a duty to warn the wife. The wife was at risk even though the disease was not contagious because tick activity that infected the husband may have infected her as well. In *McIntosh v. Milano,* 403 A.2d 500 (N.J. Super. 1979), a case imposing a *Tarasoff* duty, the court said: "[A] physician has the duty to warn third persons against possible exposure to contagious or infectious diseases, e. g., tuberculosis, venereal diseases, and so forth. That duty extends to instances where the physician should have known of the infectious disease." Until recent years, the duty of physicians to warn others of contagious disease did not seem very controversial. "It would . . . be their duty to exercise reasonable care to advise members of the family and others, who are liable to be exposed thereto, of the nature of the disease and the danger of exposure." *Davis v. Rodman,* 227 S.W. 612, 13 A.L.R. 1459 (Ark. 1921) (but denying liability on causal grounds).

See Tracy A. Bateman, Annotation, *Liability of Doctor or Other Health Practitioner to Third Party contracting Contagious Disease from Doctor's Patient,* 3 A.L.R.5th 370 (1992).

Prescription cases. Although *McKenzie v. Hawai'i Permanente Med. Group, Inc.,* 47 P.3d 1209 (Haw. 2002), and some other cases do hold the doctor liable for a negligent failure to warn that prescribed medication can make driving dangerous, a number of others reject liability to third persons. Sometimes the claim is discussed dismissively on the ground that there is no "privity," as if that were a reason. See *Webb v. Jarvis,* 575 N.E.2d 992 (Ind. 1991). *Lester v. Hall,* 970 P.2d 590 (N.M. 1998), is more policy oriented, but hard to interpret because it invokes policies that do not seem to apply when the issue is whether a doctor must warn his own patient. If the warning must be given to the patient anyway, the fact that the warning protects others does not add to any burden and certainly such a warning is no intrusion upon the doctor-patient relationship. We note incidentally that *McKenzie* rejected any duty to use reasonable care in choose medication or in prescribing the dosage.

BRIGANCE V. VELVET DOVE RESTAURANT, INC., 725 P. 2d 300 (Okla. 1986).

Most courts now seem willing to impose *Brigance* type liability even in the absence of a true dram shop statute. It is enough that the defendant negligently sells alcohol in violation of a regulatory statute. The violation is ordinarily sale to a minor or sale to an intoxicated person. *See generally* DOBBS ON TORTS § 332 (2000).

Part of the omission in the quotation about changing needs and the modern trend is: "If this were not so, we must succumb to a rule that a judge should let others 'long dead and unaware of the problems of the age in which he lives do his thinking for him.'"

Ordinary negligence rules applied. The *Brigance* Court seems to think that if you decide alcohol provider cases under ordinary negligence rules, with no special rules to help the defense, the provider would be liable. The student can try it out for herself. Would it ever be negligence to serve a person who is getting drunk and who is likely to drive away in a car? What kinds of harm would you think foreseeable? Doubters can be supplied with added facts: the bartender knows the drinker is getting intoxicated and will get much worse if permitted to do so; the bartender knows he drove to the bar and will drive away; it is 3:00 p.m. and throngs of school children are in the streets, along with singing nuns, tail-wagging dogs, and honest laborers, all at risk from a drunken driver. If the bartender is negligent at all, isn't it that he can recognize a risk of intoxication, negligent driving, and consequent injury?

So it looks as if negligence and ordinary foreseeability would be established at least in some cases. Could the bartender escape liability on the ground that in selling whiskey he was guilty only of nonfeasance? That cannot be so, either. He does not merely stand by and watch while another plies the drinker. He actively sells a product. Even *DeShaney,* with its seeming insistence on something close to custody, might not insist on custody if the social worker had handed Joshua's vicious father a baseball bat or a bottle of Jack Daniel's.

One judge, justifying the traditional rule, argued that "Problems arising out of intoxication are perhaps as old as mankind. . . . It is basically a social problem and not a legal problem." His colleague on the bench argued: "Of course, drinking is a social problem but the function of law is to help solve social problems." *Garcia v. Hargrove*, 176 N.W.2d 566 (Wis. 1970).

The negligence requirement. How would the rule of liability work? One argument advanced in older decisions was essentially that the bartender should not be held liable because in some cases she could not determine whether a customer was intoxicated. One example was the case of a hotel serving a large private party in which servers might not even identify different guests as individuals. The argument seems inherently incredible, because it simply says that because in some cases the bartender is not negligent she should not be liable even in those cases where she is. If in fact the bartender cannot reasonably recognize that a customer is intoxicated, then he is not liable either under the traditional rule or the rule in *Brigance*.

As a mater of evidence, the plaintiffs may show the number of drinks served, the boisterous, loud behavior of the drinker, slurred speech and the like. In *Cusenbary v. Mortensen,* 296 Mont. 25, 987 P.2d 351 (1999) the plaintiff put on expert testimony that blood alcohol content was very high and that with high blood alcohol content, symptoms of intoxication become visible to observers. "[B]ased upon Dr. Finkle's estimate of bloo alcohol concentration, it was probable that Wells was displaying observable signs of intoxication while served alcohol by Mortensen."

Notes 1 & 2. The negligent entrustment analogy. Broadly put, one is under a duty not to create unreasonable risks to third persons by entrusting chattels that are dangerous themselves or that are dangerous in the hands of the person to whom they are entrusted. *See generally* RESTATEMENT SECOND OF TORTS §§ 308 & 390 (1965), quoted in *Brigance.* As you can see from the quotations in that case, § 308 addresses risks created to persons *other than* the entrustee, while § 390 permits recovery by anyone, including the entrustee herself, but only risks from the driver's known incompetence "because of his youth, inexperience, or otherwise"

The court in *Brigance* then, is appealing to negligent entrustment ideas in its citation to the these Restatement sections. Section 308's Illustration 2 has the defendant lending his car to a friend whom he knows to be intoxicated. The friend drives negligently and injures the plaintiff. The lender is liable under the rule stated in § 308. Or as the illustration puts it, the defendant "is negligent toward" the plaintiff. Section 390 is similar, but focuses on the characteristics of the injurer. The defendant lends a car to a person whose characteristics make this dangerous: the person is too young to drive, or is known to be a habitual drunk although not intoxicated at the time. The Restatement regards this as a special case of the rule stated in § 308.

The implicit argument of *Brigance* on this point seems to be something like this: (a) you are liable if you entrust a car to a person whom you know or should know has already had drinks and thus create the risk that drinking and driving will be combined; (b) there is no material difference if you entrust a drink to a person who already has a car, since you create the same risk of combining drinking and driving. (c) Therefore, the rules of negligent entrustment apply.

As pointed out here, most cases of negligent entrustment involve giving a dangerous thing to a person whom the entruster knows or should know would be apt to use it in a dangerous way – things like guns, or knives, or cars, or cigarette lighters. In negligent entrustment cases the owner provides a car to an already intoxicated person, with the resulting dangerous combination of driving and alcohol. In the alcohol dispenser cases, the order is reversed: the owner of the alcohol sells it to someone who already has a car, but the resulting dangerous combination is the same. So does the analogy hold, as *Brigance* insists?

As discussed briefly in **Note 2**, some courts have pressed negligent entrustment pretty far. If you can agree with *Vince* or *West*, then you should have no trouble with the extension, or analogy, in *Brigance*.

Perhaps it is most helpful to think of negligent entrustment, not as a separate doctrine, but merely as a factual category of negligence cases – a set of facts in which courts agree that duty and negligence are sufficiently demonstrated. To speak of negligent entrustment as a technical doctrine or as something different from "ordinary negligence" may be to invite mis-analysis. The Restatement Second itself saw § 390 as merely an instance of § 308, and the Restatement Third § 19 seems to see both as merely instances of negligence.

Scope of risk in negligent entrustment cases. Suppose the defendant negligently entrusts a vehicle to a driver known for his spectacularly-bad alcoholic driving. Suppose, however, that on this occasion the driver in fact does not drink at all while driving the car. Instead, while driving quite carefully, he unfortunately strikes a pedestrian. The driver would not be liable and the lender of the car should not be liable either. The risks the lender created were risks associated with intoxicated driving, not careful driving. His fault is not a legal cause of the harm.

Duty to the entrustee. In *Casebolt v. Cowan*, 829 P.2d 352 (Colo. 1992), the court extended the doctrine of negligent entrustment so that the entruster was under a duty to the entrustee and potentially liable for the entrustee's own injury. The parallel questions of an alcohol dispenser's liability to the drinker himself is raised in **Note 6** below.

Note 3. The traditional approach to alcohol-sales cases. In Chapter 8 on scope of risk (proximate cause) we saw the older idea that treated conscious choices of intervening actors as invariably a superseding cause and we saw that this idea has been supplanted by the view that the second actor (like the drinker) is NOT a superseding cause if his conduct was foreseeable. Doctrinal support for the argument that the drinker not the provider is "the" proximate cause has thus evaporated. However, as reflected in *Wegleitner*, cited here, a legislature may declare its own traditional proximate cause rule and defeat the claim. In addition, some courts still adhere to the old view of "proximate cause."

Note 4. Rulings as a matter of law. This is an especially good situation for letting the students see that courts can often reach the no-liability result either by advancing proximate cause reasoning or by advancing no-duty reasoning. The no-duty rule makes sense as a prescription that is repeatable for a describable, general class of cases while proximate cause rules make sense, not as prescriptive rules that decide whole classes of cases, but as steps in the analysis of cases one by one.

Proximate cause: case by case decision making on the scope of risk issue. The normal result of a proximate cause decision is not a rule of law (except in the sense that any adjudication is precedent); it is application of a rule to particular facts, just as application of negligence rules are. Take *Derdiarian* (Chapter 8). To say that the jury gets to decide the proximate cause issue there is to say that similar cases will *not* be decided by a rule of law. Even if the court had concluded that there was NO proximate cause in *Derdiarian*, other cases that did not present precisely the same facts would still require case-by-case adjudication. You could not state a rule from a decision of no-proximate-cause in *Ventricelli* for example, that would exclude any particular describable class of cases except trunk-lid, parallel-parked car cases. The difference is not only rule vs. adjudication but judge vs. jury.

Duty cases: classes of cases decided in advance on policy or class-wide grounds. In contrast, no-duty rules exclude liability in classes of cases that can be described in advance. In no-duty decisions, courts feel comfortable in determining that, no matter what the factual peculiarities might be in particular cases, the liability ought always to be denied in the described class of cases. Since foreseeability varies with the facts of each case, no-duty rules cannot be truly about foreseeability; they are rules of policy or prejudice. They decide whole groups of cases in advance.

Which cases are which? As the last paragraph implies, the appropriate scope of the proximate cause issue is about scope of risk, and it must be decided case by case, usually by the jury. When courts have tried to make general rules about scope of risk, it doesn't work well. The one-time rule that the last intentional wrongdoer would be the only one liable simply does not describe scope of foreseeable risk for all cases. Similarly, the claim that the intoxicated drinker's negligence was not foreseeable to the bartender defies all sense. If alcohol providers as a class are not liable, the reasons are reasons of policy that have nothing to do with foreseeability or scope of risk.

True scope of risk issues. There are true scope-of-the-risk or proximate cause issues in alcohol provider cases, of course. If you discuss this note, you might pull into the discussion Note 8.D, which gives you a true scope of risk issue that contrasts with the broad duty question.

Scope of duty vs. scope of risk. If a duty of care is imposed upon alcohol providers, that duty might still be limited in some ways not related to foreseeability or the scope of the risk. Not every "scope" question is about foreseeability. Quick examples: (1) the duty might be limited to cases in which alcohol is served to minors, or to people already intoxicated, even though similar harm might be foreseeable when alcohol is served to sober adults who are likely to become intoxicated later; (2) the duty might be limited to the direct provider, so that those who encourage the provider or the drinker are not liable, even if they do so commercially, see *Triplex Communications, Inc. v. Riley*, 900 S.W.2d 716 (Tex. 1995) (radio station encouraging drinking not liable for terrible results that followed); (3) the duty might be imposed only upon commercial providers of alcohol, not upon social hosts.

In *Dettmann v. Kruckenberg*, 613 N.W.2d 238 (Iowa 2000) boys stole a good deal of beer from a beer delivery truck parked unlocked in front of a convenience store. They apparently drank this and other alcohol and one drunkenly drove a car into the decedent's car, killing her. The court concluded that the delivery truck driver had no duty to secure the beer. This view, however, was apparently based upon the belief that theft was unforeseeable on the facts of the particular case, so some might regard it as equivalent to saying that, as a matter of law, the driver was not negligent on the facts. What if he had reason to believe (as he does now) that thefts might take place with horrible results? *Petolicchio v. Santa Cruz County Fair and Rodeo Ass'n*, Inc., 866 P.2d 1342 (Ariz. 1994), held that where theft of alcohol was foreseeable, a liquor licensee who controlled it was subject to liability for negligently failing to secure it properly. That was case of a minor who stole alcohol, gave some to another minor, who ultimately caused a driving death. If such things are a foreseeable result from theft of alcohol, are they not equally foreseeable from providing it directly to a minor or intoxicated person?

Note 5. Fixing responsibility. What policies can the class come up with for exculpating the alcohol provider, given that he knows or should know the drinker is intoxicated or a minor and may harm others as a result of his condition? The policy in favor of liability is obvious enough. The drinker is either a minor or an intoxicated person, in either event, a person whose incentives to stay sober are likely to be low, and whose ability to drive is impaired. Giving the bartender incentives to cut service to drunks sounds like an obvious safety measure. Some students may want to be sure that the drinker is held responsible and may feel that bartender liability diminishes responsibility of the drinker. That is an understandable first reaction, but it doesn't hold up. If the drinker has no funds and no insurance, there is no meaningful civil responsibility in any event. If he is in funds or covered by insurance, then he can be held liable for contribution (maybe even indemnity) when the bartender is forced to pay. See *Red Flame, Inc. v. Martinez*, 996 P.2d 540 (Utah 2000). Further, he is subject to criminal liability. So we need not protect the bartender to impose responsibility upon the drinker.

Note 6. Suits by the drinker. The cases are divided, as noted here.. *See* DOBBS ON TORTS § 332, pp. 900-961 (2000). Some courts hold that, at least in the case of a minor drinker who is also the injury victim, the bartender cannot invoke the comparative fault defense. *Loeb v. Rasmussen*, 822 P.2d 914 (Alaska 1991), argued a position similar to the idea in *Bexiga* and to the idea that statutes may intend to protect the plaintiff against her own fault or incompetence. Other courts have insisted that the plaintiff's recovery is to be reduced by her own fault in drinking. *E.g., Schooley v. Pinch's Deli Market, Inc.*, 951 P.2d 749 (Wash. 1998).

Note 7. Liability of social hosts. You might want to distinguish large corporate social events and organized fraternity parties from ordinary home gatherings. Although both are social, it might make sense to impose special responsibility in the case of the former. *See* DOBBS ON TORTS § 332, pp. 901-902 (2000) for citations to both kinds of case.

When courts impose social host liability, or even render a decision that suggests social host liability might follow, legislatures may react firmly against it. Some of the cases and the legislative reactions are reviewed in PAUL LEBEL, JOHN BARLEYCORN MUST PAY: COMPENSATING THE VICTIMS OF DRINKING DRIVERS 135-148 (1992).

In *Panagakos v. Walsh,* 434 Mass. 353, 749 N.E.2d 670 (2001), the defendants allegedly obtained alcohol for Paquet by forging documents to represent that they were of legal age; they provided alcohol to Paquet who was an adult by Massachusetts law but nevertheless underage for drinking. They then dropped Paquet somewhere–the facts are sketchy–and he was killed while walking on the road, presumably struck by a car, although the court does not say how. The Massachusetts court treated the defendants like social hosts. Following a rule it had earlier established, it held that social hosts owed no duty of care to their adult guests for the guests' own injuries. The court thought its social host rule precluded application of the Restatement rules imposing a duty of care when the defendant innocently creates a risk or harm. It did not cite by name the famous case of *Farwell v. Keaton,* 396 Mich. 281, 240 N.W.2d 217 (1976), but said that the plaintiffs had cited no authority for treating companions on a social venture as having a 'special relationship that would impose any added duty and it refused to recognize one. What if the "hosts" had seen their intoxicated guest about to step in front of a car? Can it be right to say that once they have served alcohol they are absolved of any responsibility arising from their joint activities?

Luoni v. Berube, 431 Mass. 729, 729 N.E.2d 1108 (2000), cited at the end of this Note, held that the social host had no duty to intervene for the safety of his guests when some guests began setting off illegal fireworks, even though the host knew of the fireworks. You can do some fact discrimination exercises with this one if you wish. Alcohol is not itself illegal, but fireworks are. Yet the host did not provide the fireworks and the Massachusetts Court thought that made a big difference.

Note 8. Scope of risk, redux. Alcohol provider claims are likely to involve a number of more or less impossible cause in fact issues before we get the proximate cause problem. Causal problems abound if the dispenser is held liable. In *Munford, Inc. v. Peterson,* 368 So.2d 213 (Miss. 1979), some teenaged boys found some vodka and drank it, then bought beer from defendant's store in violation of the liquor control laws. A spectacular wreck followed. If the vodka was consumed at 3:00 and the beer at 3:30, with intoxicated driving and injury following, would it matter whether the injury occurred at 3:35, 4:00 or 6:00?

What risks are created by serving alcohol to an intoxicated or minor drinker who is also likely to drive? Surely the main risks are road risks, although if the drinker is known to be a hostile and quarrelsome one, there might be risks of direct attacks as well. But we might doubt whether risks that the intoxicated person would start a fire are big enough risks to be part of the decision that the defendant provider was negligent. If not, perhaps the court will say "no proximate cause" if the drinker falls asleep with a burning cigarette and sets the house afire. If this is a problem, it is a true scope-of-risk problem and not a duty problem in disguise. Cf. *Griesenbeck v. Walker*, 488 A.2d 1038 (N.J. Super. 1985) (alcohol provider not liable for fire caused by intoxicated smoker). An intervening cause analysis might come up with the same answer in many cases. In *Kunza v. Pantze*, 531 N.W.2d 839 (Minn. 1995), the defendant served drinks to an intoxicated H who allegedly attacked W while they were driving home. W, trying to escape the attack, either jumped or fell out of the car and was injured. Not even a jury question on proximate cause, according to the Minnesota Court.

Passing along alcohol seems to us eminently foreseeable, maybe even more likely among minors. In *Schooley v. Pinch's Deli Market, Inc.*, 951 P.2d 749 (Wash. 1998), one minor purchased alcohol illegally–he was not even challenged for ID–and then shared it with other minors. Some in the group were going to throw the plaintiff into the pool. She dove in, perhaps to circumvent this. The water was two feet deep and she is now quadriplegic. The court rejected the defendant's argument that the injury was "remote" because sale was not to the injured person.

In *Cusenbary v. Mortensen*, 987 P.2d 351 (Mont. 1999), the defendant served alcohol repeatedly to a man in a wheel chair, who by all accounts was quite intoxicated, in a foul mood, and being quite obnoxious. His companions eventually took him to their car and put him in the passenger seat, but he managed to get behind the wheel and drive the car through the wall of the tavern, injuring the plaintiff. The defendant argued that provision of alcohol was not a proximate cause of the plaintiff's harm. The emphasis of the argument seems to have been that it was unforeseeable that a disabled patron who needed help of family to move would be able to somehow get into the driver's seat and run through the wall. This argument is not that serving alcohol is never a proximate cause, only that these particular events were unforeseeable. The court rejected the argument, saying that drunken conduct of an intoxicated person, including drunken driving, was foreseeable. In effect, the court moved up the abstraction ladder in conceptualizing the foreseeable conduct; it was not "a disabled person driving through a wall" but "drunken driving." This is in line with the rule that foreseeability of details is not the test in scope of risk decisions.

There is another kind of scope of risk or proximate cause problem. Lest there be any doubt, it may pay to make sure the class understands it. Suppose the defendant negligently provides alcohol to a drinker-driver, who then does in fact drive into a pedestrian, who is injured. Will this prove the plaintiff's case? No. The injury must result from the intoxication and this will have to be proved. What if the driver is not negligent at all? Then the defendant alcohol-provider is not liable, because he has created a risk, but only a risk of negligent driving, not a risk of safe driving. See the discussion of the similar idea in connection with negligent entrustment.

NOTE: DRAM SHOP STATUTES

Dram shop statutes are different from ordinary regulatory statutes dealing with alcohol. Dram shop statutes create private causes of action; regulatory statutes do not. Most states do not have dram shop statutes and did not traditionally treat violation of regulatory statutes as negligence per se. That is why cases like *Brigance* are important. Some students don't notice the difference between dram shop and regulatory statutes and you may need to emphasize the point.

Some statutes (Wisconsin's is an example) immunize providers and procurers of alcohol for adults but not minors. In *Stephenson v. Universal Metrics, Inc.*, 641 N.W.2d 158 (Wis. 2002), the court held that since defendant secured alcohol for the intoxicated drinker, he "procured" it and was therefore immune. The court also engaged in one of those many-factored public policy discussions, with factors so numerous and general that any outcome can be achieved. The majority found liability would be against public policy; the dissenter (Chief Justice Shirley S. Abrahamson) observed in this respect: "The majority opinion appears to conclude that of the six public policy factors to be considered, three factors point to imposing liability on Kreuser. In contrast, I apply the same six public policy considerations to the facts of the present case and conclude that none of them points to relieving Kreuser of liability in this case."

Note that there is limited authority for the proposition that a state dram shop act is not the exclusive remedy. In *Craig v. Driscoll*, 813 A.2d 1003 (Conn. 2003), the dram shop act was held not to bar a common-law negligence action against purveyors of alcohol who served an intoxicated adult who drove drunk and killed a pedestrian. Overruling an earlier case, the court held that a tort action supplements rather than conflicts with the dram shop act. The court also held that harm from drunk driving is a foreseeable risk caused by negligently serving alcohol to an intoxicated person, rejecting the tavern's argument on scope of risk.

PROBLEMS

1. The overworked employee. In *Robertson v. LeMaster*, 301 S.E.2d 563 (W. Va. 1983), the court recognized a claim against the railroad and rejected the "no duty" argument of the defendant. Liability was not based upon failure to control the employee on the highway but upon the employer's earlier acts creating a risk of foreseeable harm when the employee drove.

2. The physician's prescription. *Webb v. Jarvis*, 575 N.E.2d 992 (Ind. 1991), ruled against liability, chiefly on the ground that the doctor was not in privity with the injured third person. The court relied upon some economic harm cases.

3. Insecure guns. Cases go both ways. Some cases lend support to liability for failing to secure guns with reasonable care. In *Adames v. Sheahan*, 880 N.E.2d 559 (Ill. Ct. App. 2007), the court held that a policeman who stored his handgun at home in a box owed a duty of reasonable care to secure it in such a manner that a child could not find and use it (which is what happened), and suggested that this duty was breached; fact questions remained as to whether the negligent act of improper storage was a proximate cause of the death of the shooter's friend. In any event, the court noted that it was entirely foreseeable for an unauthorized person to find a gun that has been stored improperly, then use it to harm others. *Estate of Strever v. Cline*, 924 P.2d 666 (Mont. 1996), held that a defendant owes a duty to all to secure his firearms with reasonable care, but rejected liability on proximate cause reasoning when the injury occurred in an unusual way. *Pavlides v. Niles Gun Show, Inc.*, 637 N.E.2d 404 (Ohio 1994) held that a gun show operator who took no steps to require independent vendors sited in the "show" to secure their guns, could be held liable when teenagers stole guns that were unsecured, then stole a car, and shot the plaintiff.

Other cases have gone the other way. In *McGrane v. Cline*, 973 P.2d 1092 (Wash. Ct. App. 1999), the defendant left his pistol in his bedroom. His 16-year-old daughter invited guests while he was away and one of them stole the gun and used it in a robbery, killing McGrane. The court rejected the wrongful death claim against the defendant, on the ground that courts should not "recognize a duty on the part of a firearm owner to prevent the theft of that firearm from his or her residence." Since negligence was alleged, the court presumably means "no duty" to exercise reasonable care to prevent theft.

Valentine v. On Target, Inc., 727 A.2d 947 (Md. 1999), held that a "gun store owner does not owe a duty to a third person and thus can not be held liable in negligence" when its guns are stolen and used in a murder. "[A]lthough the inherent nature of guns suggests that their use may likely result in serious personal injury or death to another this does not create a duty of gun dealers to all persons who may be subject of the harm." The court appeared to feel that the store's burden of protecting its own property from theft would be very heavy while the benefit to the public would be "hypothetical" at best. How can it be a heavy burden to use reasonable means to protect your own property?

In *Heck v. Stoffer,* 786 N.E.2d 265 (Ind. 2003), Timothy, an adult fugitive felon with a history of crime, including theft from his family, stole a gun from his parents' bedroom and shot and killed officer Heck when Heck attempted to apprehend Timothy. The parents knew he was fleeing and likely confront police attempting to apprehend him. In fact, the parents had given him keys to their house, permitted him to hide at their lake cottage to avoid arrest, and had warned him of a police tracking device. The Heck estate sued the parents, who prevailed on no-duty rulings in the lower courts. *Held,* reversed. The defendants had no relationship with officer Heck, and that counts against a duty. However, it was foreseeable that Timothy might steal the gun, both because of his past stealing from his parents, and the exigency of an expected police action against him. The gun was in the cushions of a chair, not otherwise hidden and not locked away. Timothy still had the keys to the house. The foreseeability evidence weighs in favor of a duty. The public policy factors also weigh in favor of a duty. A quarter of a million guns are stolen yearly and in Indiana alone, 4,000 people were killed in gun violence in the more recent five-years period for which data is available, plus 8,000 more injured. (The court also noted the slight burden of reducing risk by locking guns away in connection with this factor.)

The *Heck* court also said that the right to bear arms, emphasized by the intermediate court as a policy factor against recognizing a duty, is not an absolute right. "A constitutional guarantee does not shield parties from negligence claims tangentially related to the exercise thereof. Several constitutional provisions guarantee the free exercise of religion, but nothing precludes a person from suing for slip-and-fall injuries that occur on a church's premises. In the same vein, the press has the right to free exchange of thought and opinion, but newspaper distributors are not shielded from negligence suits for injuries caused by their delivery drivers. Similarly, Indiana gun owners are guaranteed the right to bear arms, but this right does not entitle owners to impose on their fellow citizens all the external human and economic costs associated with their ownership." Finally, the defendant's intervening cause argument is rejected. See the proximate cause chapter.

Topic C. LIMITING DUTIES TO PROTECT AGAINST
SPECIAL TYPES OF HARM

CHAPTER 19

EMOTIONAL HARM

►**Changes in the Sixth Edition.** You'll find some dramatic revisions here. We have reduced this chapter by five pages (over 15%) by revising and reorganizing Notes substantially and cutting some cases and case abstracts. The division of sections within the chapter remains the same. We have also added some new materials, including over two dozen recent case citations in Notes. Specifically, in § 1 we have added the text of the Restatement (Third) on intentional infliction of emotional distress, plus one of its Comments. We've reduced the *GTE v. Bruce* case to a shorter abstract, and we've cut three case abstracts: *Taylor, Winkler,* and *Bettis.* In § 2, we've cut two case abstracts, Miley and Bird, but we've added *Dillon v. Legg* (formerly discussed in a Note) as a longer case abstract to accompany *Thing v. LaChusa* on bystander negligent infliction. In § 3 we've cut the *Sacco* case. All in all, these changes should make the chapter a bit simpler to teach without oversimplifying this difficult doctrinal area.

►The **Concise Edition** trims three more pages of this Chapter by cutting *Boucher,* the main case on loss of consortium, plus its Notes 1 and 5; that topic is now covered in even briefer fashion.■

Preliminary Note. This chapter groups the main emotional harm issues together, including intentional and negligent infliction cases and loss of consortium. (Intentional infliction is in § 1; negligent infliction of emotional distress is covered in §§ 2-4; consortium appears in § 2.) Notes also point to, but do not develop, a few torts that often redress emotional harm under their own rules. Intentional torts, including trespass, can readily support mental distress and kindred elements of damage, at least as parasitic damages. The negligent infliction materials are presented not only in terms of the conflicting and often silly rules that may be applied, but more importantly in terms of three distinct fact patterns as indicated by the section titles.

Scope of coverage. Although an entire chapter is devoted to this important topic, it cannot cover all the issues. It does not attempt to deal with defenses, even though conceivably they apply rather differently in the case of emotional harm. Nor does it attempt to integrate emotional harm cases into special settings. For instance, it does not raise the question of recovery for emotional harm under the Federal Tort Claims Act. Obvious problems here would be the discretionary function exception, and the assault and battery exception, but there are other problems as well. *See* Gregory G. Sarno, Annotation, *Recovery of Damages for Infliction of Emotional Distress under Federal Tort Claims Act,* 107 A.L.R. FED. 309 (1992).

Scheduling omissions and rearrangements. (1) If you prefer to deal with intentional infliction in the early part of the course, along with assault for example, you can simply assign all of § 1 to be read there. However, if you teach this chapter as is, you may find that students will have a different and quite possibly better understanding of the topic as a whole. (2) If omissions are necessary, you might consider omissions in § 4, which deals with the specific case of fear for future harm due to toxic exposure. The section is factually and socially important because it reveals some of the courts' continuing concerns about their own fears – unlimited litigation. However, outside of California you might consider omitting *Potter v. Firestone.* (3) If you want maximum omissions, the very least coverage possible, you'll lose a lot, but you might consider omitting the NOTE ON FIRST AMENDMENT CONSIDERATIONS and *Homer v. Long* and its Notes (in § 1)(perhaps covering in a quick lecture the Restatement's rules on recovery when the outrageous conduct is directed at a third person); *Boucher* (§ 2, consortium and how it compares to the emotional harm claim) (covering the note material by lecture, perhaps); and *Potter* (§ 4, fear of future harm from toxic exposure.) With each omission, you'd probably want to explain the problem and some of the rules in lecture.

OUTLINE

Subchapter A. Intentional and Reckless Harms

§ 1. INTENTIONAL INFLICTION OF EMOTIONAL DISTRESS
[a] General rules of liability for intentional infliction of severe distress by outrageous conduct. *Restatement (Third) §45; GTE Southwest v. Bruce.*
[b] Conduct directed at one person causing distress to another person or to one not present. *Homer v. Long*

Subchapter B. Negligent Infliction of Distress or Emotional Harm

§ 2. FRIGHT OR SHOCK FROM RISKS OF PHYSICAL HARM

A. Emotional Harm Directly Inflicted on the Plaintiff. *Mitchell v. Rochester Ry. Co.; Note: Development of a Stand-Alone Claim*

B. Emotional Harm Resulting from Injury to Another

    1. The Emotional Distress Claim

        [a] Plaintiff in the zone of danger. *Grube v. Union Pacific R.R.*

        [b] Plaintiff as bystander. Dillon v. Legg; *Thing v. LaChusa*

        [c] The independent duty undertaken in special relationships. *Burgess v. Superior Court.*

    2. The Loss of Consortium Claim

        [a] Consortium identified. *Text.*

        [b] Consortium rights of spouses, parents, children, and domestic partners. *Boucher v. Dixie Medical Center*

§ 3. DUTIES OF CARE TO PROTECT EMOTIONAL WELL-BEING INDEPENDENT OF PHYSICAL RISKS

[a] The no-risk model and dead-body cases. *Washington v. John T. Rhines Co.*

[b] Misinformation *to* the plaintiff: negligent diagnosis of AIDS. *Heiner v. Moretuzzo.*

[c] Truthful information *about* the plaintiff: sex, truth, and videotape. *Boyles v. Kerr.*

[d] Discarding constraining rules. *Camper v. Minor*

§ 4. TOXIC EXPOSURE: FEAR OF FUTURE HARM: LIMITS ON RECOVERY?

[a] Fear of future harm after environmental exposure; causation. *Potter v. Firestone Tire and Rubber Co.; Norfolk & Western Ry. v. Ayers.*

[b] Fear of AIDS and the exposure rules. *Note: Recovery in "No Exposure" Cases.*

SUMMARY

Subchapter A. Intentional and Reckless Harms

§ 1. INTENTIONAL INFLICTION OF EMOTIONAL DISTRESS

RESTATEMENT (THIRD) § 45 & COMMENT *g* (2005). The new Restatement sets out the elements of the tort: (1) an intentional or reckless act that is (2) extreme and outrageous (3) causing severe emotional distress. The Comment explains what "recklessly" means here, and explains why that state of mind (and not just intent) supports the claim.

GTE SOUTHWEST, INC. V. BRUCE. An immediate supervisor carried on systematic abuse and humiliation of several employees. Probably so one incident would have been sufficient to count as outrageous conduct but the repetition of anger, threats, and humiliating tactics (e.g., making employees clean their own offices in spite of janitorial services devoted to that job) was sufficient to show outrage. The fact that it occurs in employment makes the Texas Court want to be especially cautious to protect employers' rights to criticize and discipline, but even with that attitude, this was too much for the Court.

NOTE: FIRST AMENDMENT CONSIDERATIONS. Sometimes this tort is accomplished through words, and if the setting is right (or wrong), that can implicate First Amendment free speech concerns. At other times the tort is set within religious orders and the allegation is that the religiously-motivated conduct is "extreme and outrageous," raising First Amendment religion clauses issues. This note briefly touches on both of these cautions.

HOMER V. LONG. The plaintiff sued a therapist who had treated his former wife. He alleged that defendant, in the course of therapy, took advantage of the wife's needy and vulnerable condition to seduce her, that her personality changed, and that he and his wife were later divorced. On the intentional infliction of distress claim, *held,* outrageous conduct directed at A does not necessarily give B a cause of action. Conduct outrageous as to A is also outrageous to B in some cases where B is present, but the court thinks the presence requirement must be maintained as a pragmatic way of drawing a line against otherwise extensive liability.

Subchapter B. Negligent Infliction of Distress or Emotional Harm

§ 2. FRIGHT OR SHOCK FROM NEGLIGENTLY INFLICTED RISKS OF PHYSICAL HARM

A. Emotional Harm Directly Inflicted on the Plaintiff

MITCHELL V. ROCHESTER RY. CO. A team of horses almost ran the plaintiff down, but they did not in fact touch her. She suffered "shock" and a miscarriage as a result. *Held,* (1) there is no recovery for fright alone and (2) there can be no recovery for the consequences of fright, including the physical consequences like a miscarriage.

NOTE: DEVELOPMENT OF A STAND-ALONE CLAIM. The history of this tort in the courts is not linear, but we can trace a gradual if incomplete evolution from *Mitchell* (which essentially rejected the claim) through the Restatement (Third)'s latest iteration. The possibly final "evolutionary stage" actually appears via the Camper v. Minor case at the end of § 3, where all constraining rules are discarded. But few courts have reached that stage at this point, and undoubtedly some will never get there.

B. Emotional Harm Resulting from Injury to Another

1. The Emotional Distress Claim

GRUBE V. UNION PACIFIC R.R. The plaintiff was a railroad engineer whose train collided with a car trapped on the railroad track, allegedly by reason of the negligence of the railroad. He perceived that a crash was impending and after it occurred he touched the deceased driver, attempting to find a pulse. He became ill immediately. He admitted that he was not afraid for himself. The minor impact inside his cab caused neither physical harm nor his emotional harm. In an FELA suit against the railroad as his employer, the court *held:* A plaintiff who suffers emotional harm when another is threatened with or suffers physical harm must show that he himself was in the zone of danger and feared for his own safety. The rule does not change merely because the plaintiff himself suffered an impact, where that impact causes none of the emotional harm claimed.

DILLON V. LEGG. The original "bystander" claim. Two family members saw another (a child) struck by a negligently-driven car. The trial court applied the then-current rule, zone of danger, and held against one of the plaintiffs (the mother) on the ground that she did not fear for her own safety. The court reversed, discarding the zone of danger test, and replacing it with a multi-factor approach in which the court considers (1) whether plaintiff was near the scene; (2) contemporaneously observed the accident; and (3) whether the plaintiff and the victim were "closely related."

THING V. LA CHUSA. Restricting the court's earlier *Dillon* decision, *held,* the plaintiff must prove as elements (1) that she is a close relation to the victim (which the court narrowly defined); (2) that she was present at the scene of the injury-producing event and aware of it at the time and (3) as a result suffered severe emotional distress. Under this rule, a mother could not recover for emotional distress resulting when she rushed to the scene of her son's injury and saw him unconscious in the road. She was not there and did not see or even hear the impact.

BURGESS V. SUPERIOR COURT. A mother giving birth to a child sued her doctor for alleged negligence in delivering the child that caused brain damage to the child. The limiting rules in *Thing* do not apply to bar her claim, even if she were not aware of the brain damage when it occurred. This is a "direct victim" case, in which the doctor, because of his relationship to the mother, owes her a duty of care with respect to emotional harm. She is not a mere bystander.

2. The Loss of Consortium Claim

Text. Loss of consortium claims are historically derived from the master's right to recover when his servant was tortiously injured, but they now reflect intangible interests akin to emotional distress – the loss of society and companionship of one spouse when another is injured, for example.

BOUCHER V. DIXIE MEDICAL CENTER. Consortium rights, originally vested in the husband (or master of servants) included the right to receive the wife's (or servant's) services or the money they earned. Nowadays wives have correlative rights in the services of their husbands (except where the consortium rights have been abolished for both sexes) and we see "services" in a broad light as including not only gainful economic activity or sexual relationships but also society, love, affection, and companionship. Utah has achieved a non-sexist rule by abolishing the consortium claim for either spouse and that leads Utah here to say that it will also refuse to recognize the claim of parents for loss of consortium or society of a permanently brain-damaged child. The parents were not in the zone of danger so they lost the general mental distress claim. And the court rejects loss of filial consortium altogether, so the parents whose son lapsed into a coma after surgery had no claim of their own at all against the allegedly negligent health care providers.

§ 3. DUTIES OF CARE TO PROTECT EMOTIONAL WELL-BEING INDEPENDENT OF PHYSICAL RISKS

[a. Transitional cases: bodies]

WASHINGTON V. JOHN T. RHINES CO. A surviving wife contracted with the defendant for undertaking services and for shipment from the District of Columbia to El Paso for the funeral. When the body arrived for the funeral, it was discolored and rapidly decomposing; the casket was filled with the odor of embalming fluid, and a catheter was still in the body. *Held*, the plaintiff cannot recover for emotional distress as she was not in the zone of danger.

[b. *Misinformation to the plaintiff—including negligent diagnosis*]

HEINER V. MORETUZZO. The defendant's mistakenly concluded that the plaintiff was suffering from AIDS and then mistakenly confirmed that misdiagnosis. *Held*, the plaintiff cannot recover for emotional distress since she was never actually in peril.

[c. *Correct but private information about the plaintiff*]

BOYLES V. KERR . The plaintiff and defendant had sexual intercourse. The defendant secretly video-taped their encounter, then added comments of his friends to the tape and showed it on various occasions to others. *Held*, the plaintiff has no emotional distress claim. There is no general duty to use care to avoid inflicting emotional distress in Texas. A limitation to severe distress cases would not be workable.

[d. *The abolition of constraining rules*]

CAMPER V. MINOR. The decedent negligently caused a vehicular collision with the plaintiff. The decedent was killed and the plaintiff saw her body at close range. In the plaintiff's suit against her estate, held, physical manifestation of injury will no longer be required and general negligence rules apply instead, except that the plaintiff can only recover for severe distress as supported by medical or scientific proof.

§4. TOXIC EXPOSURES: FEAR OF FUTURE HARM: LIMITS ON RECOVERY?

POTTER V. FIRESTONE TIRE & RUBBER CO. Defendant, knowingly and illegally, dumped toxic materials into a landfill not equipped to handle them. The toxins leached into the ground water and contaminated the plaintiffs' water wells. The toxins include known and suspected carcinogens, so the plaintiffs reasonably feared that they would in the future develop cancers as a result. They claim damages for that fear. *Held,* (1) To recover in negligence for the fear of future cancers, the plaintiffs must show that such cancers are more likely than not to occur. This is necessary to avoid (a) overwhelming liability that could compromise the affordability of insurance; (b) adverse affects on the pharmaceutical industry, which fears that today's useful drugs might some-day prove to carry harmful side effects, which in turn would lead to many fear claims; (c) exhausting available insurance coverages in paying fear claims and leaving nothing with which to pay actual physical injury claims that may oc-cur later; (d) an unpredictable rule of recovery that cannot be consistently applied. (2) The more likely than not standard need not be met when the de-fendant is guilty of intentional infliction of mental distress or acts with oppression, malice, or fraud, or in the willful disregard of others' rights. That is the case here.

NORFOLK & WESTERN RY. V. AYERS. In a FELA suit, plaintiffs claim that their railroad employer negligently exposed them to asbestos. They claimed not only that they contracted asbestosis (a non-cancerous lung dis-ease), but also that they suffer from a fear of developing cancer. The Court affirms a jury verdict for the plaintiffs. Once a person has suffered physical harms, as have these plaintiffs, emotional distress damages are recoverable upon proof that the emotional distress if both genuine and serious.

NOTE: RECOVERY IN "NO EXPOSURE" CASES. When a plaintiff claims emotional distress based on a fear of getting a disease in the future, most courts hold that he must prove "actual exposure" to the disease-causing toxin or virus. Some courts have allowed recovery without such a showing. Because the jurisdictions vary in their approach, this note provides ample opportunity for compare and contrast discussion.

COMMENTS

Subchapter A. Intentional and Reckless Harms

§ 1. INTENTIONAL INFLICTION OF EMOTIONAL DISTRESS

RESTATEMENT (THIRD) § 45 & COMMENT *g* (2005). You can walk the students through the elements here: (1) an intentional or reckless act – defined in the accompanying comment, that is (2) extreme and outrageous; (3) causing se-vere emotional distress. Once you do that you can begin to see how they apply in the cases that follow.

The Comment provides a nice review of what "intent" means in all inten-tional torts: purposefulness, or knowledge that the particular bad result (depending on the tort) is substantially certain to occur – material that we covered back in Chapter 3. It also explains what "reckless" means, in more de-tail than we have seen before or will see again. You probably don't need to delve into the Comment's statements of why recklessness is sufficient to state a claim here; you can wait to do that when you reach the end of this section, after you've seen more about how the tort is applied in the cases.

GTE SOUTHWEST, INC. V. BRUCE, 998 S.W.2d 605 (Tex. 1999).

This case states and applies the generally recognized rules that were laid out more completely in the Restatement provision quoted above. The suit is actually against Mr. Shield's employer, GTE Southwest, and the court actually held that GTE was vicariously liable. But as our point is to focus on what counts as outrage.

[In some early printings (spell-check alert) the summary says that at times the defendant "simply started" at employees in his office. That should read "simply stared," which is less active, but much weirder. Later printings have corrected this error.]

What we see in Shield's behavior is continued, repeated abusive conduct. It would almost certainly not count as outrage if he had only lost his temper once or twice, or had merely once required office workers to clean their own offices. It is the totality of his behavior carried out over a substantial period of time that makes this sufficiently outrageous. The other element is one the Texas Court seeks to discount but does at least implicitly recognize. It is the power Shields holds over these employees. He is their supervisor and evidently was given a good deal of control. Abusive behavior toward a stranger might be different.

Note 1. History of the tort. This should be self-explanatory; the only thing to highlight, if you mention it at all, is that this tort is relatively new. It is not a tort like those we saw in Chapter 3 (battery, assault, false imprisonment, trespass, and so on) that have century upon century of development. Any common law rule that is new will have some judicial fits and starts, and we see that in this tort – even more so in the negligent infliction version coming up in the next sections of this chapter.

Employment disputes (such as that involved in *Bruce*) are often the source of emotional harm claims, but we wanted to quickly dispel the idea that intentional infliction of emotional distress claims are grounded solely in such a setting. Older dead body cases and some current ones as well ascribe liability to a property interest in the body. With the recognition of a claim for emotional distress, this property reasoning seems superfluous if not ridiculous. Rudeness and insensitivity are not enough for the tort in the dead body setting any more than elsewhere. See *Crockett v. Essex*, 19 S.W.3d 585 (Ark. 2000) (hurried funeral service). *Travelers Ins. Co. v. Smith*, cited here, may be a case of reckless rather than intentional interference. As we saw in the Restatement excerpt, recklessness as well as intent suffices as a basis for liability. In § 3 we'll see *Washington v. John T. Rhines Co.*, a dead body case based upon negligence; there the plaintiff loses.

Note 2. Markers of outrage. While a determination of "outrageous" conduct is fact-sensitive, as *Almy* says, one of three features appears in many cases: (1) repeated conduct, (2) abuse of power, or (3) particular vulnerability of the plaintiff, known to the defendant. In many settings all markers are present; those are the easiest cases for plaintiffs, although even then the results in cases are highly variable. *GTE v. Bruce* certainly fits both (1) and (2), and probably (3) as well, at least with respect to some of the plaintiffs as the horrible misconduct continued. **Notes 3-5** explore briefly each of these three "markers of outrage" in turn.

Note 3. Repeated conduct. The idea here is that a single isolated bit of conduct may not be "extreme and outrageous" but may become so when repeated. (Note, however, that this is not an "element," so that a single instance may be actionable if other factors are present, as discussed below.) *Jones v. Clinton*, cited here, is Paula Jones v. Bill Clinton, which some of your students will remember. Jones sued Clinton for allegedly propositioning her once in his hotel room when he was the Governor of Arkansas and she was a state employee who had never met him before. According to her allegations, he made only one request for a sexual act, and when she refused he did not repeat it and she left the room. The court held as a matter of law that a single act such as this was not "outrageous" under Arkansas law.

With S*amms v. Eccles* cited here, compare *Morgan v. Anthony,* 27 S.W.3d 928 (Tex. 2000).

Note 4. Abuse of power. We first cite here *Brandon v. County of Richardson,* which inspired a movie, *Boys Don't Cry.* As a teen-ager Brandon, born a female, underwent a gender identity crisis and began to dress and present as a man. Brandon dated a young woman. Two men with criminal records discovered the truth, then raped Brandon. They warned Brandon of harm or death if Brandon went to the police. Brandon reported the rapes anyway. Sheriff Laux interviewed Brandon on the same day as the rapes. His interview was crude and perhaps hostile and he referred to Brandon as an "it." Some questions, the court later said, were irrelevant; they merely showed prurient interest in the details. The sheriff did not then arrest the rapists and did not institute any protection plan for Brandon. The rapists then murdered Brandon. Brandon's mother brought suit against the sheriff for (a) wrongful death and (b) intentional infliction of emotional distress. On the wrongful death claim, the court thought the sheriff owed a duty of reasonable protection because a "special relationship was created when the victim went to law enforcement officials and offered to testify and aid in the prosecution of Lotter and Nissen." On the emotional distress claim, the trial judge rejected the claim because the sheriff's conduct was not sufficiently outrageous and because there was no evidence that Brandon suffered severe distress as a result of the sheriff's prurient, crude, and hostile questioning. On appeal, the Nebraska Supreme Court held that the sheriff's conduct was outrageous as a matter of law and that the nature of his conduct furnished some evidence that serious distress probably resulted. On the wrongful death claim, the court went on to hold that the sheriff or county could not reduce liability because of the "comparative fault" of the rapist-murderers; comparative fault does not apply to intentional torts. The trial judge's conclusion that Brandon was chargeable with contributory fault for unspecified reasons was also reversed. The court could not find any basis for holding Brandon at fault and in any event any such supposed fault was not a cause in fact of Brandon's death. Obviously the case would fit the "knowledge of plaintiff's vulnerability" pattern described in **Note 5** below, as well.

The *Washington v. Mother Works* case, cited next, reminds us that "mere insult" is not enough to establish this tort, even where the defendant is abusing power over an employee. In that case, a supervisor ridiculed an employee with racial slurs when she missed work; this was held not to be outrageous because the conduct lasted "only" a few weeks and did not go beyond mere insult.

Some other courts have taken a decidedly different view of racial slurs in the workplace. For example, in *Taylor v. Metzger*, 706 A.2d 685 (N.J. 1998), the sheriff referred to an African-American deputy as a "jungle bunny" in front of another supervisor. The court said that "mere insults" were not actionable, but that "a racial slur uttered by a sheriff directed against a subordinate officer is not, as a matter of law, a mere insult or triviality. . . . [W]hen defendant called plaintiff a 'jungle bunny,' he may have stepped beyond our civilized community's bounds of decency." The *Taylor* court recognized that some other courts (*Washington* is an example for us) have held as a matter of law that isolated uses of racial epithets by supervisors in the work place cannot constitute "extreme and outrageous behavior" but disagreed with those cases, instead holding that such conduct created an issue of fact for the jury, considering all the circumstances. This kind of case, too, may overlap with the "vulnerable plaintiff" pattern described in **Note 5**; a white person would not have the same visceral emotional reaction to being called a "jungle bunny" by another white person, nor would the plaintiff be as vulnerable if the plaintiff and defendants were equal.

In *Langeslag v. KYMN Inc.*, also cited here, the court found that outrageous conduct was not shown, resting that view primarily on the fact that the plaintiff was the defendant's superior. Thus there could be no abuse of power (although there were repeated harassing acts).

With *Langeslag*, compare *Nims v. Harrison*, 768 So.2d 1198 (Fla. Dist. Ct. App. 2000). This was a suit by a high school teacher against students who allegedly published, apparently as the ubiquitous "award," comments that were racist, obscene, and threatening. "Mrs. Nims for being a stupid bitch ass bitch who has black skin and is a fucking gigaboo so fuck you, you stupid ass bitch I will kill you you fucking whore ass faget maggot burger I will rape you and all of your children and cousins you stupid mother fucking bitch die nigger." The court, without assessing the seriousness of the threat or any issue of free speech, thought that "Justice, reason and common sense compel a remedy for the revilement inflicted upon the teacher in the instant case," partly because the language allegedly used was "offensive" and partly because children were threatened.

In *Kroger Co. v. Willgruber,* 920 S.W.2d 61 (Ky. 1996), the jury found that the plaintiff, an employee of 32 years with a record of successful management, was wrongfully discharged after he refused to violate company ethical rules at the instance of a new manager. The plant manager wrote fictitious evaluations of the plaintiff who was then –at a Christmas luncheon– presented with a demand that he resign and also exonerate the company from all potential liability. He was promised a job at a Bakery in South Carolina and went to interview there, but found the promised job was entirely fictitious. He suffered a severe breakdown. The court approved a recovery first for wrongful discharge and then separately for infliction of mental distress.

Note 5. Knowledge of plaintiff's vulnerability. As we suggest here, known vulnerability of the plaintiff may accurately be seen as the counterpart of power abuse by the defendant. And that power is not merely a position of formal authority as in the employment cases. It includes any practical power, as in the creditor cases. Not all such cases succeed. If the defendant's acts would be outrageous *only* because the plaintiff is especially vulnerable the defendant would not be liable unless he was on notice of the plaintiff's vulnerability. See *Hollomon v. Keadle,* 931 S.W.2d 413 (Ark. 1996).

Sometimes, though, the plaintiff's vulnerability is obviously known to the defendant, and is even exploited. That may well support a claim, of course. In *Drejza v. Vaccaro,* 650 A.2d 1308 (D.C. App. 1994), a police officer, now the defendant, interviewed the plaintiff an hour after a rape by her former boyfriend. According to the plaintiff's version, the officer snickered and laughed at her, tossed her undergarments at her with the comment, "take your little panties and go home," joked about her "marital hymen," and was otherwise contemptuous and degrading. The trial judge gave summary judgment for the defendant, apparently under the impression that the recent trauma inflicted upon the plaintiff was irrelevant unless it was worse than that of other rape victims! On appeal, the summary judgment was reversed. "An hour or so before the first interview, as Vaccaro well knew, Ms. Drejza had endured a violent rape – one of the most harrowing ordeals that can befall a woman. '[A]cts which are not generally considered outrageous may become so when the actor knows that the other person is peculiarly susceptible to emotional distress.'" One judge dissented, believing that the conduct was not extreme or outrageous.

In *Robel v. Roundup Corp.,* 59 P.3d 611 (Wash. 2002), the plaintiff was injured on the job and filed a workers' compensation claim. Co-workers taunted the plaintiff mercilessly and repeatedly, sometimes in front of customers. They acted out a slip and fall, as "one of them yelled Oh, I hurt my back, L & I, L & I! They audibly called [Robel] a bitch and cunt. They also told customers she had lied about her back and was being punished by Fred Meyer by demoing pizzas." [All internal quotation marks omitted.] This conduct was actionable. Apparently the court felt that the plaintiff was vulnerable and that the conduct took on added significance because it occurred in the workplace. "Robel was called *in her workplace* names so vulgar that they have acquired nicknames, such as 'the C word,' for example." and that this was more than name calling, although that is exactly what it was on the plaintiff's defamation count.

Tenants vs. landlords. If a tenant is forced repeatedly to do without heat in the winter, or electric service is cut off, or the toilet is left unrepaired for weeks, would this be a good claim? Does it fit the "outrage marker" patterns described thus far? Clearly yes. See *Birkenhead v. Coombs,* 465 A.2d 244 (Vt. 1983); *Simon v. Solomon,* 431 N.E.2d 556 (Mass. 1982). These landlord cases in may fit both patterns – repeated harassment and the vulnerability-power pattern. A more recent case is *Harris v. Soley,* 756 A.2d 499 (Me. 2000), where the landlord (in violation of his promise) provided a woeful apartment, infested, with smells of urine, a dead cat under the floorboards, snow falling into the living room in winter, no heat, and so on. He also broke in and took the tenants' belongings. The emotional harm verdict was quite modest, $15,000 for each tenant's emotional distress, but we are happy to report that the jury also awarded, and the court approved, an award of $1 million in punitive damages. We only hope that the judgment does not drive the landlord in our direction.

Some of the results in cases are rather mysterious to us. In *Costello v. Mitchell Pub. Sch. Dist. 79,* 266 F.3d 916 (8th Cir. 2001), Sadonya was a new seventh grade student in the school. Her band teacher "daily called her 'retarded,' 'stupid,' and 'dumb,' in front of her classmates. He once threw a notebook at her in class. There were other similar incidents. Sadonya took an emotional nose dive, was diagnosed with severe depression and ultimately was home-schooled. In her suit for intentional infliction of emotional distress, the court held that the teacher's conduct "did not rise to the level that would satisfy" the outrage requirement. There was no mention at all of the teacher's abuse of power or the repeated nature of the behavior, or the public humiliation.

Note 6. Exercising legal rights. Some exercises of legal rights, as mentioned here, are known to cause emotional distress. But that does not make them actionable, since such acts are not considered "extreme and outrageous," defined by many courts as "conduct intolerable in civilized society." But where legal rights are exercised in a way that brings them within the patterns described above, the fact that the defendant was also exercising a legal right does not provide any immunity. This is a theme of the debtor-creditor cases. For example, In *Cadle Company v. Hobbs,* 673 So.2d 1363 (La. Ct. App. 1996) a debtor had actually paid her installment debt until the creditor failed and she was unable to discover its proper successor. The debt collector pursued her by repeated phone calls, threatening garnishment and other forms of enforcement, even threatening to take her dog and her parents' furniture. (That was just before Christmas.) The debtor testified:

He said you remember what color you are. He said you are a nigger and I am a white boy. He said and anything I send those stupid Southerners down South, they will believe when a Northern white man tell [sic] them down there.

Maybe this did not go down well with the Louisiana Court; the debtor got a judgment for $5,000.

Note 7. Intent to do what? You may well have already answered this question with your class if you have parsed the Restatement provision and the comment. The intent of the defendant must be to inflict severe emotional distress, or knows of the risk of severe emotional harm and is indifferent to it. We placed this Note here to invite students to see the forest again after being lost in the trees, perhaps, in the preceding Notes. The patterns of outrageous behavior are instances in which the defendant is shown to have either intended to inflict emotional distress or has caused such distress recklessly.

Note 8. Causation. The outrageous conduct must cause the severe emotional distress or the claim will fail. Comment *j* to the Restatement, cited here, says that the intentional infliction tort is established "only when the actor's extreme and outrageous conduct is a factual cause of the plaintiff's severe emotional distress."

The sketchy hypothetical in this note is based upon *State Rubbish Collectors Assn. v. Siliznoff,* 240 P.2d 282 (Cal. 1952), which required no proof of physical symptoms. *Miller v. Willbanks*, cited here, adds that no expert testimony is required, either, although Tennessee requires such testimony when the tort is based upon negligence rather than intent. Predictably, a few courts have required special evidence. *Vallinoto v. DiSandro,* 688 A.2d 830 (R.I. 1997), a claim based upon assertions that the plaintiff's attorney had sexually exploited her, required both objective symptoms of harm and medical evidence to show that the symptoms were caused by the outrageous conduct. *Powell v. Grant Medical Ctr.,* cited in this Note, was a negligent infliction case. The court acknowledged that expert testimony was not generally required, but held that it was required in that particular case because the plaintiffs were claiming emotional harm resulting from accidental injury to their mother's body shortly after her death and this was inextricably intertwined with their grieving at her death itself, for which the defendant was not responsible. Expert testimony, then, was needed in part on the causal link between the outrageous conduct and the emotional distress.

Note 9. Severity of emotional distress. The Ohio court in *Fisher v. American Red Cross Blood Services*, cited here, held that the plaintiff had not shown serious mental distress, although the notification caused marital strife and necessitated counseling. In *Morgan v. Anthony,* 27 S.W.3d 928 (Tex. 2000) the defendant, a male, stopped his truck by the disabled vehicle of the plaintiff, a female. He held her car door open, refusing to let her close it, and proceeded to harass her with sexual innuendo and/or demands long after she rejected his advances. The Texas Court noted that the plaintiff's distress and fear at the time as well as her distress later, were to be considered in determining severity and thought that the distress was severe enough.

Note 10. Overlap with other tort claims. Should courts permit a claim for emotional distress if it is based solely on a touching and if the battery claim is outlawed by the statute of limitations? Is that not like permitting an intentional infliction claim based on a touching that itself is privileged? The court in *GTE v. Bruce* said, in portion of the opinion not reprinted in the casebook, that the intentional infliction tort would lie only if some other tort is not involved. In *Dickens v. Puryear*, cited here, the court allowed a claim for intentional infliction of emotional distress when the outrageous acts complained of could not form the basis of any other tort claim. Thus in *Dickens* when defendants beat the plaintiff and held a knife to him, those claims were for battery and assault (and in the case, barred by the statute of limitations), but where defendants made threats of killing plaintiff in the future, those acts could support an intentional infliction claim since they were neither assaults nor batteries.

Similarly, in *K.G. v. R.T.R.*, 918 S.W.2d 795 (Mo. 1996), the court disallowed an intentional infliction claim where the facts established the elements of another tort. The facts showed sexual touchings, so the court characterized the case as a battery case. So characterized, the case was late and the statute barred recovery. The plaintiff attempted to say that it was also an intentional or reckless infliction of distress, as to which the statute had not run. The Missouri Court rejected this argument as an attempt to do an end run around the statute. If the facts showed a battery, it said, then a claim for intentional infliction would not lie. *See also Veilleux v. Nat'l Broadcasting Co.*, 206 F.3d 92 (1st Cir. 2000)(distress caused by misrepresentation barred if tort action for misrepresentation was barred); *Banks v. Fritsch,* 39 S.W.3d 474 (Ky. Ct. App. 2001) (intentional infliction of emotional distress is a gap-filler and lies only when no other tort redresses the emotional injury; in this case, the claim for false imprisonment, battery, and assault potentially allow recovery for emotional distress and the outrage claim was properly dismissed).

But not all courts agree with this conception. In *Winkler v. Rocky Mountain Conference of the United Methodist Church*, cited here, the plaintiff was a member of a church in which defendant Chambers was the senior pastor. The plaintiff also did volunteer work at the church on the recommendation of her therapist to work in a safe environment as a means of overcoming her fears of the workplace. The defendant on several occasions put his arm around the plaintiff, stroked her thigh, or rubbed his body against hers, expressing love for her. The plaintiff sued for intentional infliction of emotional distress and breach of fiduciary duty. The jury awarded $28,675 on each of these two claims. The appeals court cited here affirmed, holding that although Chambers' conduct would be a battery, the same conduct can amount to intentional infliction of distress. That is an independent tort and the plaintiff is not required to sue on a battery theory merely because the facts would have sufficed to show a battery. Where the plaintiff can assert an intentional infliction claim, the fact that the battery claim is barred by the statute of limitations is irrelevant.

To take another example, in *McQuay v. Guntharp,* 963 S.W.2d 583 (Ark. 1998), the court held that a doctor's improper fondling of patients was not merely a battery, which was barred by the statute of limitations, but an intentional infliction of distress or outrage. The outrage "flows not merely from the physical touching of the women's breasts, which would make out a claim for battery, but from the violation of a trusted relationship." Without discussing the problem, *Smith v. Welch,* 967 P.2d 727 (Kan. 1998), also a doctor-fondling claim, also said an intentional infliction claim would lie.

If you allow intentional infliction claims when other torts are more to the point, the distress claim could potentially take over many torts, perhaps eliminating special requirements they impose. It might be used in lieu of torts like libel or slander, malicious prosecution, or privacy invasion. That probably is not an overall good.

On the other hand, on facts like those in *Winkler,* cited here and discussed more fully just above, there was a battery but also more than a battery. The facts showed a composite breach of professional duties and human treatment. This is a good point to affirm in class. So reckless or intentional infliction claims in *Winkler* might be sound even if the facts also showed a battery. But that surely should not mean that all batteries are also intentional infliction cases and if it does not mean that, then there will be difficult problems in drawing the line.

Note 11. Statutes. This Note is informational and is designed simply to make students aware (if they are not already) that the common law claim for intentional infliction of emotional distress is not the only legal avenue open to plaintiffs in many of these cases. Disability discrimination may be covered by the Americans with Disability Act, 42 U.S.C.A. § 12101 and The Rehabilitation Act, 29 U.S.C.A. § 701 and a variety of others as well as state statutes.

Students should know that there is a large body of law on Title VII addressed to sexual discrimination in the work place, including sexual harassment. Workers' compensation is the usual exclusive remedy for workplace injuries, so this is another wrinkle when the victim sues the employer. See Chapter 28.

NOTE: FIRST AMENDMENT CONSIDERATIONS

1. *First Amendment and public figures.* Free speech is guaranteed by the First Amendment of the United States Constitution. "Speech" includes all forms of communication. The First Amendment's narrow terms may mislead some students, because it only prohibits interference with speech by Congress. For reasons we need not consider, however, the First Amendment legally protects against any state interference with speech, including interference by

judicial decision. Besides the First Amendment's text, free speech is central to a democratic society, which depends upon information and discussion. To foster good information exchange and discussion, you may have to tolerate some error and excess.

It is enough here for students to recognize that when intentional infliction of mental distress is based on publication to third persons (like a magazine, newspaper or television publication), free speech interests will have to be considered. Private speech, speech between the defendant and the plaintiff alone, might not raise the free speech issue, or at least not so cogently.

2. *The First Amendment and religion.* At least in the absence of fraud or coercion, a minority religious group must be permitted to hold its beliefs and to persuade others to join them, even if those beliefs are antisocial and degrading. A religious doctrine that "the female form is the form of evil" is as intolerable as the teachings of the Nazi party. But the remedy, as always in the realm of free speech, is more speech, not less. If you believe that a religious group holds evil beliefs, you are as free as the religious group itself to persuade others to your position. The First Amendment's free speech provisions are provisions of hope and optimism; they work on the belief that we can still talk to each other enough to work and live together in our communities.

Courts work with this backdrop. *Tilton v. Marshall,* discussed here, holds that no emotional distress claim can proceed if it must question the sincerity of the defendant's belief. Tilton, the defendant in the trial court, allegedly make insincere religious representations in his television "ministry," inducing plaintiff contributors to send him money. This might lead to a fraud claim, but the court could not adjudicate the intentional infliction of distress claim without judging the sincerity of the defendant's belief and necessarily the truth or falsity of his religious doctrine. That is the very thing forbidden by the First Amendment so the insincerity claim could not stand. The plaintiffs were also distressed by Tilton's promises, elaborate promises to pray in certain ways, suggestive of a direct line of God. But the answer was the same; in judging this claim, courts would all too likely get involved in judging the validity of religious ideas. *See also Dushkin v. Desai,* 18 F.Supp.2d 117 (D. Mass. 1998) (defendant set himself up as a guru having no interest in sexual or financial matters and urges his follows to adopt the same attitude; followers discover various sexual behaviors and that he has taken a very substantial income from their donations to his organization; fraud adequately pleaded but emotional distress claim disallowed).

In *Sands v. Living Word Fellowship,* also cited here, the Alaska court held that the church-ordered shunning was protected free exercise of religion. *See also Lybrand v. Trask,* 31 P.3d 801 (Alaska 2001) (sign on the defendant's roof, clearly visible from the plaintiff's house and offering Biblical quotations directed at plaintiff, is not outrageous).

In *Checkley v. Boyd,* also cited here, the court refused to dismiss the emotional distress claim without a trial, saying that although some communications might be religious in all cases, others might be religious only if asserted for religious purposes. The Satan assertions might prove to be religious upon trial, but perhaps the other assertions would prove to be unconnected with religion.

On well known case in this area is *Murphy v. I.S.K.Con. of New England, Inc.*, 571 N.E.2d 340 (Mass. 1991). A 13-year-old, Susan Murphy, became interested in Krishna consciousness and stayed a while at a Krishna temple. Eventually, however, she returned home and later brought a claim against the religious group for intentional infliction of emotional distress. Part of this claim was that Susan Murphy suffered emotional distress as a result of the defendant's teachings, including, specifically that (1) "women are inferior to men," and (2) "the female form is the form of evil." The court held that, even though Susan was a minor, she could not predicate an intentional infliction claim upon the teaching of religious beliefs. "Inherent in the claim that exposure to ISKCON N.E.'s religious beliefs causes tortious emotional damage is the notion that the disputed beliefs are fundamentally flawed and inconsistent with a proper notion of human development. While this issue may be the subject of a theological or academic debate, it has no place in the courts of this Commonwealth." The court said that at least in the absence of fraud or coercion, a minority religious group must be permitted to hold its beliefs and to persuade others to join them, even if those beliefs are antisocial and degrading. The doctrine that "the female form is the form of evil" is as intolerable as the teachings of the Nazi party. But the remedy, as always in the realm of free speech, is more speech, not less. If you believe that a religious group holds evil beliefs, you are as free as the religious group itself to persuade others to your position. The First Amendment's free speech provisions are provisions of hope and optimism; they work on the belief that we can still talk to each other enough to work and live together in our communities.

Before *Winkler,* cited in Note 10 after *GTE v. Bruce* and discussed above in this Manual, the Colorado Supreme Court held that a clergy person who seduces a married parishioner while acting as a marriage counselor to both the parishioner and spouse would be liable to the spouse for an intentional infliction of mental distress claim. *Destefano v. Grabrian*, 763 P.2d 275 (Colo. 1988). Since the defendant did not profess to be acting under the dictates of religious doctrine but *did* seem to be acting in violation of his fiduciary or special relationship to the non-participating spouse, liability does not seem to infringe the First Amendment's freedom of religion protections. What if the clergy induces a spouse to leave the other spouse for religious reasons? Cf. *O'Neil v. Schuckardt*, 733 P.2d 693, 67 A.L.R.4th 1065 (Idaho 1986) (clergyman enticed family from husband-father).

For a deeper analysis of the religion cases, *see* Paul T. Hayden, *Religiously Motivated "Outrageous Conduct: Intentional Infliction of Emotional Distress as a Weapon against "Other People's Faiths,"* 34 WM. & MARY L. REV. 579 (1993).

HOMER V. LONG, 599 A.2d 1193 (Md. Ct. Spec. App. 1992)

This case presents the problem of a plaintiff suing for intentional infliction of emotional distress when the allegedly outrageous conduct was directed at some third person. Often, of course, this third person is someone about whom the plaintiff has close feelings, but that is not always true in the cases. The Restatement Second, in § 46, requires that the plaintiff be (1) present and (2) either (a) a family member of the victim, or (b) suffer bodily harm from the emotional distress. Many courts continue to use that standard. As the court says in Homer, "Outrageous conduct directed at A does not necessarily give B a cause of action." The court concludes that the plaintiff cannot recover here.

In accord with *Homer v. Long* where the defendant initiated sexual relationships with the plaintiff's former wife, his wife, and his former fiancé, *Padwa v. Hadley*, 981 P.2d 1234 (N.M. Ct. App. 1999).

Policy behind denial of relief in Homer. Homer sounds like a traditional alienation of affections or criminal conversation case. Those torts respectively allowed the plaintiff to sue anyone who alienated the spouse's affections or engaged in sexual relations with the spouse. Such claims represented an intangible harm that seems to be a species of emotional distress −"lost honor," hurt feelings, and so on. So infliction of distress was recognized under the special rules for those separate torts. Symbolically at least, they seemed to recognize a kind of ownership of one spouse by the other. The participating spouse's knowing and valid consent was no defense! For these and other reasons, many states have abolished alienation of affections or criminal conversation or both. The reasons for abolishing those claims might counsel against recovery in *Homer*; if so, we can say the court used the presence rule when it should have obtained the same result on a policy analysis or on the ground that this claim is merely a disguise for one of the claims that have been abolished.

(b) Duty arising from special relationship of therapist to patient. Even in jurisdictions that have abolished alienation of affections and criminal conversation, however, the therapist's violation of his duty of care to the patient might be a special case. The therapist ought to be liable even if the alienation/criminal conversations actions are abolished if he violates a duty as therapist to the person who is suing. But he did not. His fiduciary duty is to the patient, not to the spouse of the patient. This point has a neat ending: if *both* spouses are the therapist's patients, say in joint counseling, the therapist might indeed be liable to the husband and even if the alienation/criminal conversation actions were abolished. *Horak v. Biris*, 474 N.E.2d 13 (Ill. App. Ct. 1985). In *Rowe v. Bennett*, 514 A.2d 802 (Me. 1986), a non-married couple, J and K, consulted a marriage counselor, who seduced J and thereby further imperiled the non-marital but real relationship. K sued the marriage counselor. The counselor's conduct was not actionable as an alienation of affections or criminal conversation. But the court held it actionable as an intentional or

reckless infliction of distress. Cf. *Odenthal v. Minnesota Conference of Seventh-Day Adventists*, 649 N.W.2d 426 (Minn. 2002) (a minister providing marriage counseling to both partners secretly established relationship with one of them; neutral standards applied to all mental health practitioners in negligence claim would not violate First Amendment prohibition against religious interference).

Note 1. *Transferred intent.* How does the third-person presence requirement fit with transferred intent? The rule is essentially a rejection of transferred intent, although substantial certainty intent is still recognized. A little review of the concepts is possible here. "Outrageous to A" is a good concept to contrast with transferred intent. "Outrageous to A" reminds us of *Palsgraf's* idea that you might be negligent toward A but not toward B.

Recklessness, intent, and negligence. The intent required is intent to produce severe emotional distress, though the intent is usually inferred from the outrageous conduct. The Restatement also recognizes that recklessness will be sufficient –that is, the defendant may be held for a "deliberate disregard of a high degree of probability that emotional distress will follow." Maybe you can find "outrageous to A, reckless to B" when you cannot find "outrageous to B." Consider on this point the fact that the therapist in *Homer*, if guilty as alleged, would presumably not have wanted the husband to discover his misdeeds. He would therefore have had no purpose to inflict distress upon the husband. But perhaps he could be considered to have been reckless to the husband. Sometimes courts seem not so demanding about proof of recklessness and even use focus on "natural and probable" distress rather than on "deliberate disregard" or "high probability." See the peculiar case of *Chuy v. Philadelphia Eagles Football Club*, 595 F.2d 1265 (3d Cir. 1979).

Note 2. What "presence" means. There are at least two ways for a court to bend a seemingly rigid rule: changing the definition of the operative term (as in the example here), or create exceptions (as discussed in the next Note). Presence at its core means physical presence, period. But some courts have said it could mean something else, too, as mentioned here. In *Bevan v. Fix,* cited here, the court held that children who perceived verbal and physical attacks upon their mother at the time they took place were "present" under the Restatement rule even if they did not visually witness the attacks, provided they could show "sensory and contemporaneous" awareness through other senses.

Note 3. Exceptions to the presence requirement. The presence rule could be viewed as an arbitrary rule, one that excludes liability for harms actually and demonstrably caused. Its justification is pragmatic, not moral. The *Homer* court fears an unlimited liability unless the presence rule is used. This is the first of a series of more or less arbitrary rules that constrain emotional harm recoveries. If you want to test it, you can consider the unpleasant case of child abuse, of which parents learn much later.

In *Reid v. Pierce County*, cited here, the court said because the plaintiffs were not present, they did not have a claim. This is not a dead body case, but surely it is equally offensive to think that your close relative's dissected body might be used by someone who simply likes to look at bodies. You may want to foreshadow *Christensen v. Superior Court*, 54 Cal. 3d 868, 2 Cal. Rptr. 2d 79, 820 P.2d 181 (1991), cited in the notes following *Washington v. John T. Rhines Co.* in § 3, by raising the facts of that case hypothetically. The point is that recovery was allowed to third persons in *Christensen* where the defendant undertakers had a relationship with the plaintiffs and denied in *Reid* where the court treats the parties as strangers.

But *Homer* also suggests there are some exceptions to this requirement, and we give a couple of examples here.

In *Bettis v. Islamic Republic of Iran*, cited here, Jenco was kidnaped and tortured by persons acting under the auspices of Iran. The trial court recognized claims of siblings (not nephews and nieces) even though they were not present. The case in the trial court was styled *Jenco v. Islamic Republic of Iran*, 154 F.Supp.2d 27 (D.D.C. 2001). Even if the presence rule is a good idea, does this present a good case for an exception?

On the appeal, the emotional-distress claims of the Jenco's siblings and his estate were not involved, only the claims brought by the nieces and nephews. The court gave a very long discussion of the law to be applied, under the federal statutory exception to foreign immunity; ultimately it relied primarily on the Restatement's § 46. There was no doubt that the emotional distress of the whole family, all of whom worked for Jenco's release constantly for 19 months, was severe. But the nieces and nephews were not "direct" victims and they were not immediate family as required by the Restatement. The *Bettis* court distinguished a case in which owners of an animal were permitted to recover for their distress at its intentional killing. "Although appellants are correct that the defendant in *Gill* targeted the plaintiffs by striking at something dear to them, the donkey was property and not another person with an independent legal right to be free from outrageous conduct. Thus, killing the donkey directly targeted the plaintiffs. *Gill* is therefore consistent with the general rule that courts do not consider a plaintiff to be a direct victim of the defendant's conduct where that conduct more directly targeted another victim."

Even if "presence" was not required, the *Bettis* court said, no recovery could be had because the nieces and nephews did not qualify as immediate family. *Is the "family members" rule fair?* A discussion here can foreshadow a discussion of the "bystander" negligent infliction of emotional distress cases later in this chapter. Who should count as family? Why family and not just someone who can demonstrate a strong emotional connection to the victim? In other words, why allow an estranged brother to recover when a favorite nephew could not?

The *Hatch* opinion cited at the end of this Note is decidedly odd, we think, in saying that a plaintiff seeking to come within a presence exception must show, in addition to the factors mentioned, that the defendant intended to inflict injury on the "absent plaintiff." That would seem to mean that the presence requirement would be irrelevant anyway, as our rhetorical question says.

Subchapter B. Negligent Infliction of Distress or Emotional Harm

§ 2. FRIGHT OR SHOCK FROM RISKS OF PHYSICAL HARM

In this section, we shift from intent and recklessness to negligence. The cases originally confronted the claim of negligently inflicted emotional harm resulting from a risk of physical harm. That factual pattern has dominated or limited the courts' thinking about the subject of negligently inflicted emotional harm. Hereafter, we refer to the claim for negligent infliction of emotional distress by its acronym, NIED.

A. Emotional Harm Directly Inflicted on the Plaintiff

MITCHELL V. ROCHESTER RY. CO., 45 N.E. 354 (N.Y. 1896)

This case and *Victorian Railways Commissioners v. Coultas*, [1888] A.C. 222 (Privy Council), are the classic cases. *Spade v. Lynn & B.R.R.*, 47 N.E. 88 (Mass. 1897), also requiring initial injury, appeared shortly thereafter. In *Coultas*, members of the Coultas family were in a horse drawn buggy one evening in 1886. The buggy approached the defendant's railroad tracks in Australia. The gatekeeper negligently opened the gate to let them on the track, then closed it and left them trapped with gates down both before and behind them. A train approached and only narrowly missed the trapped buggy. Mary Coultas suffered a severe shock and the jury awarded damages for it. But the Privy Council held that recovery was improper because the shock was not a consequence which, in the ordinary course of things, would flow from the negligence of the gate-keeper.

The *Mitchell* rationale is a little firmer or hard-edged. *Mitchell* sets up (1) the fright-for-self pattern of cases and (2) the rejection of a stand-alone NIED-claim entirely. In our coverage, *Mitchell* is the beginning of a trip, not merely through time, but also through various rules and fact patterns to be seen even today. The most important thing for the class to observe is the character of the case. It is a claim that seems to be based on negligence in risking physical harm to the plaintiff. As it happens, the court refused to impose liability even in that case, and one fork of the analysis will show us that this holding has now been set aside. The other fork of the analysis lays the groundwork for much else in this chapter. Negligence creating physical risks is the important scenery on this road.

Note 1. Parasitic damages. You should point out to your class that in *Mitchell*, if harm had eventuated – if the horses had run over her – she would have been permitted to recover for that physical harm and also for any pain and suffering and emotional distress. That is the parasitic damages rule. Thus a stand-alone claim for NIED is not being allowed by Mitchell; rather, the plaintiff must show a physical injury (as in virtually all of the negligence cases we've seen in the course up until now) caused by defendant's negligence. Where that is shown, one category of damages, in addition to the damages for the physical harm, is "pain and suffering," which is in part compensation for the kind of emotional distress that is our subject here.

Note 2. The fright or shock pattern. This should be self-explanatory. It simply sets the stage for what is to come.

NOTE: DEVELOPMENT OF A STAND-ALONE CLAIM

1. ***Impact.*** Early courts like *Mitchell* required an impact because they required a physical injury in order to justify the emotional harm damages. The impact rule, then, was originally a rule that emotional harm damages could be recovered as parasitic damages but not otherwise. But courts took one step away from that restrictive view, and began to allow a stand-alone negligent infliction (NIED) claim, when they dropped the "physical injury" linkage and began only to require an impact – something physically striking the plaintiff – but not that the impact caused any actionable injury. *See, e.g., Helsel v. Hoosier Ins. Co.*, 827 N.E.2d 155 (Ind. 2005). A handful of states continue to require impact, as noted here, but it is a small number.

It may be fair to say that Florida continues to use the impact rule, but that it does so selectively. The *Abril* case, cited here, is one example (no impact needed where the defendant has violated a duty of confidentiality in causing the emotional distress). In an earlier case, *Hagan v. Coca-Cola Bottling Co.*, 804 So.2d 1234 (Fla. 2001), the court held that an emotional distress recovery might be permitted to consumers who drank Coca-Cola from a bottle, then discovered what appeared to be a used condom in it. The court seemed to say this was an exception to the impact rule, although it also said that ingestion of the food or drink was itself an impact.(On remand, however, the plaintiffs lost under the special dual rules for AIDS fear, see NOTE: RECOVERY IN "NO EXPOSURE CASES," § 4 of this chapter.) Note that the *Abril* case may stand on another ground – that no "impact" is logically required to support emotional distress damages where there is a completed underlying tort that itself does not require any physical touching. An actionable invasion of privacy, for example, permits recovery of emotional harm damages that result. This was the holding of *Fairfax Hosp. v. Curtis,* 492 S.E.2d 642 (Va. 1997) (medical providers release of plaintiff's confidential records was actionable for emotional harm without physical harm). But this truly is a form of parasitic damages, not a stand-alone NIED claim.

The slightest touching rule. Some cases in "impact" states have treated the slightest touching as sufficient to meet the impact requirement. *See Plummer v. United States,* 580 F.2d 72 (3d Cir. 1978) (under the "however slight" rule, the "'impact' of the tubercle bacilli which infected the bodies of the plaintiffs constitutes a sufficient physical nexus to allow compensation for the mental affliction of the plaintiffs"); *Zelinsky v. Chimics,* 175 A.2d 351 (Pa. Super. Ct. 1961) (jostling of the plaintiff without cutting or bruising him in a minor fender-bender collision sufficient for emotional distress claim).

A famous Georgia case allowed emotional distress recovery when a circus horse evacuated his bowels in a spectator's lap in *Christy Bros. Circus v. Turnage,* 144 S.E. 680 (Ga. Ct. App. 1928) ("Any unlawful touching of a person's body, although no actual physical hurt may ensue therefrom, yet, since it violates a personal right, constitutes a physical injury to that person."). In 1989, the Georgia Court overruled *Christy Bros. Circus,* requiring not merely impact but also injury. *OB-GYN Associates of Albany v. Littleton,* 386 S.E.2d 146 (Ga. 1989), *overruled on other grounds, Lee v. State Farm Mut. Ins. Co.,* 533 S.E.2d 82 (Ga. 2000). Indeed, some of the few impact states have now clearly stated that the impact must cause physical injury that then causes emotional distress. Others have not been so clear on the point.

In any event, the "impact" rule is dying if not entirely dead, perhaps a vestige of the time when a negligent infliction claim was not allowed at all, dependent on the plaintiff having suffered a physical injury first, then claiming emotional distress in the form of parasitic damages for pain and suffering.

Next we take up the "physical manifestations" rule, followed by the "zone of danger" rule, both of which have more adherents today. Query whether those tests are any better at filtering out invalid claims, or limiting claims (even if meritorious) than the "impact" requirement appears to be.

2. ***Physical manifestation of objective symptoms***. Although the impact rule has been largely abandoned, a greater number of states continue to bar NIED claims unless the plaintiff can demonstrate some physical manifestation of emotional injury. *Reilly v. United States*, 547 A.2d 894 (R.I. 1988). In some settings, courts have even strengthened the rule. See *Simmons v. Pacor, Inc.*, 674 A.2d 232 (Pa. 1996) (asbestos caused pleural thickening, an objectively determined condition characterized by calcified tissue of the membranes surrounding the lungs and testable by x-rays, nevertheless not "injury" that supports an emotional distress claim, citing cases from other jurisdictions as well). The difference between the impact rule and the physical manifestation rule can be seen in the sequence. Classes may appreciate a diagram, although the idea is simple enough. The sample diagram below depicts one way to show the distinction. The third row in the diagram also shows the abolition of the physical injury rule (taken up following the diagram). The diagram elements themselves can be placed on the board sequentially, one at a time, with discussion of each as you go. You can use different shapes such as squares, triangles, or circles, different chalk colors, or different shadings, to clearly distinguish among the ideas in the sequence. If you provide materials to your students on computer, you can use this or a more sophisticated diagram.

The sequence reflects the theory or rule. In the first line a tort is committed that causes "actual harm," meaning some degree of physical injury that would be actionable. Emotional harm damages are recoverable as parasitic damages. Line two reversed the sequences–the tort causes emotional harm, which in turn produces physical injury or at least a physical manifestation of the distress. The parasitic damages rule won't work there, so there was originally no recovery. The physical harm (or manifestation) rule recognized in most courts today will permit recovery in the sequence shown in line two. Line three shows a tort causing stand-alone emotional harm, without physical injury or physical manifestation. The physical manifestation rule by its terms does not permit recovery in that scenario.

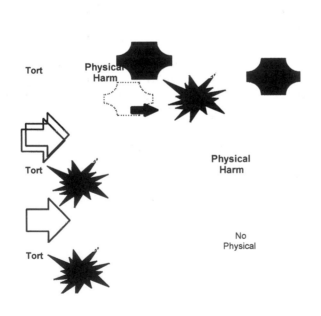

Courts are in the process chipping away at the physical manifestation rule and a good number, as we'll see, have discarded it entirely. For instance, a number of courts have allowed recovery for pre-impact fright in survival actions. In *Beynon v. Montgomery Cablevision Limited Partnership,* 718 A.2d 1161 (Md. 1998). the court did so by liberalizing its objective manifestation rule. It said that there was actual injury (the death that followed the fright) and that there was also an objective basis for determining fright because the decedent laid down 71 feet of skid marks before the impact in which he died.

In addition to *Sullivan,* cited here, see *Armstrong v. Paoli Memorial Hospital,* 633 A.2d 605 (Pa. Super. Ct. 1993). It factually belongs in the next section because there was no physical risk to anyone, but it illustrates the dilution of the physical injury requirement. The plaintiff, called to the hospital because her husband was seriously injured, eventually discovered the man was not her husband, at which point, "I just lost it. I urinated, defecated, and I just lost it completely". This "loss of continence" coupled with nightmares and insomnia was considered "physical injury."

Quite a few courts now seem to be requiring "severe" injury, a rule that is standard in the intentional infliction area and now gaining currency in the negligent infliction case as well. Some have required that the injury be "diagnosable." See, e.g., *Paz, Hegel, and Johnson,* cited here. Some require both severity and a medically-diagnosable mental disorder, as illustrated in *Hamilton v. Nestor,* cited here, which required both that the distress be "so severe that no reasonable person could be expected to endure it" and that it be "medically diagnosable and must be of sufficient severity that it is medically significant." These sorts of requirements may be well on their way to replacing the physical manifestation rule. "Diagnosable" may prove to be too narrow and too focused on the categories of psychotherapeutic culture.

3. ***Zone of danger.*** We deal more fully with the zone of danger test in the next section, but it logically belongs here as well. Many courts have placed a limit on NIED cases not based on whether or not there was an impact (1), or whether there were physical manifestations of the emotional distress (2), but instead on whether the plaintiff was in the "zone of danger," which usually means that the plaintiff's distress flows from a fear for the plaintiff's own physical safety. Seen in this way, the zone of danger test is not a "bystander" rule at all, it's rather a rule that does not allow true "bystander" recovery, where the theory is that the plaintiff suffered emotional harm flowing from seeing someone else injured. (This is the clear implication of the *Dillon v. Legg* opinion from California, coming up in the next section.)

4. ***Combinations.*** As described here, the specific combination of restrictive rules in stand-alone NIED claims varies from state to state. Some use restrictive tests in the alternative (for example, allowing plaintiff to succeed upon proof of either an impact or a physical manifestation, or either of those or zone of danger). Others require some combination of additional elements

(such as impact, plus, if the impact is slight, some additional proof of genuineness of the distress; or zone of danger and physical symptoms.

This Note is not an attempt to survey all fifty states, obviously, but rather to give students the idea that there is tremendous variation at this point from state to state. It should perhaps go without saying, then, that it is not a fruitful exercise for the Torts class to go into an exhaustive listing of all of the various approaches, literally; it's enough to examine the basic building blocks and then recognize that different states combine different blocks – all to the point of saying that the NIED claim is not treated in most states as the usual physical injury cases we have been exploring the course up until this point.

5. *The Restatement Third approach.* You can parse this now with your class if you wish, or come back to it when you have seen some more cases. The Restatement combines a number of approaches, and does so in the alternative. If the defendant's negligence places plaintiff in immediate danger of bodily harm, and causes serious emotional distress, that is sufficient to state a claim. This is much like the *Grube* approach to the zone of danger, it seems, as we will see just below. The alternative rule, allowing recovery for serious distress if the defendant negligently performs some duty owed as part of any of "specified categories of activities, undertakings, or relationships in which negligent conduct is especially likely to cause serious emotional disturbance," would allow recovery in such cases as where the defendant negligently handles the dead body of one of the plaintiff's loved ones (a case we see coming up later (*Washington v. John P. Rhines*), in which the court denied recovery because the plaintiffs were not in the "zone of danger").

Comment *d* to the Restatement says that there have been traditionally two kinds of "categories" of cases where recovery has been allowed: (1) delivering a telegram or other communication falsely announcing death or illness; and (2) the mishandling of dead bodies cases. It adds that more modern courts appear to have recognized NIED in cases involving consumption of food containing some "repulsive foreign objects," cases involving doctors who negligently caused the death of a fetus (as in *Burgess*, coming up), or who negligently misdiagnosed an illness or disease (another set of cases coming up), and cases in which employers abuse employees or one spouse mentally abuses another. The comment notes that "courts have not provided clear guidelines to identify precisely which activities, undertakings or relationships will support liability," which underscores the fluidity of the doctrine in this early stage of this tort's development.

6. *Questions.* The three hypotheticals give students a chance to drill themselves, with or without your help. (a) Parasitic damages rule allows recovery. Physical manifestation or symptoms would not be important if the plaintiff is physically injured, which seems to be the case. (b) This is the fright-shock pattern seen in *Mitchell*. The logic of *Mitchell* would deny recovery. Once the impact rule is eliminated, the plaintiff can recover or not, depending upon whether physical manifestation or injury is required. The

question asks what result where physical manifestation is still required, so the answer is that the plaintiff cannot recover. (c) This set of facts demonstrates physical manifestation (rashes, possibly the fainting as well). So recovery would be permitted.

B. Emotional Harm Resulting from Injury to Another

(1) The General Mental Distress Claim

GRUBE V. UNION PACIFIC R.R., 886 P.2d 845 (Kan. 1994)

These cases are often called "bystander" cases. They resemble *Mitchell's* basic pattern in that the defendant has negligently created a risk of physical harm to someone. The element of shock from sudden, traumatic events is in the forefront. These cases differ from *Mitchell* only in that (in some instances) the risk the defendant created is a risk of physical harm to another person, not to the plaintiff. This segment deals with the main approaches and some of the subsidiary rules.

In *Grube*, the plaintiff was an engineer on a Union Pacific Railroad and was emotionally distressed when his train struck a car on the track and he saw the occupants before and after the crash. The claim is actually not against the driver of the car, but is rather a claim under the Federal Employers Liability Act (FELA), which allows employees of "common carriers" such as trains to collect for negligently-caused harms. This, then, was an action based on a different area of law than what we've seen in this Chapter, but that is of little moment. Our focus is on the NIED analysis, which translates well to a non-FELA setting as well.

The courts interpreting the federal statute here have held that a plaintiff must be in the "zone of danger" in order to recover for emotional distress caused by a defendant's negligence. The rule says in effect that the defendant must have created a risk to the plaintiff as well as to another person; the plaintiff must at least theoretically fear for herself and not merely for another. Zone of danger cases are not so much an "exception" as a special instance of the physical risk rules. (Under one name or another, as noted earlier, a number of courts continue to use the zone of danger rule for NIED cases.)

The court here holds that Grube was not in the zone of danger and therefore cannot recover – meaning that he did not fear for his own safety in the accident. This conclusion was based in part on his own (presumably truthful) testimony, recited in the case, that he "expressed no fear at the time of the collision." The court says that such fear need not be "contemporaneously" expressed at the time of the accident, but does say that it "must be expressed at or near the time of the danger in order for plaintiff to prevail."

Note 1. The classic "bystander" case is one in which a person watches in fear as another person is injured by the defendant's negligence. The difference between the "direct victim" case and the "bystander" case, then, is usually in who is actually in peril. If the plaintiff is in peril for his own safety, that's a "direct victim" case, at least where the emotional distress flows from the fear of that very peril. If the plaintiff is in fear for the other's safety, and the emotional distress flows from that, it's a "bystander" case. Not all courts draw this line so cleanly, but that is a decent thumbnail description of the difference. Notice that *Grube* is a case in which the plaintiff seeks to recover for the emotional distress of seeing another person injured, so it's a bystander case by definition. But the court denies recovery on the ground that he did not fear for his own safety – usually a test (zone of danger) that is not really a "bystander" test at all. This "mismatch" of using a test that does not fit the allegations at all is similar to what happens in the *Washington v. John T. Rhines* case at the beginning of section 3, in which the court denies recovery in a "dead body" case on grounds that the plaintiffs were not in the zone of danger.

Note 2. One twist in the *Grube* case is mentioned here, which demonstrates that the court knew that the plaintiff was seeking "bystander" recovery after all. The court suggests that once a plaintiff does fear for his own safety, he can then recover for the emotional distress resulting from witnessing an injury to another person in the same accident. This certainly makes *Grube* a true bystander case, albeit one that rejects such a claim on the facts. Most other FELA cases do not allow bystander recovery at all, meaning that the damages recoverable must all be attributable to the fear for one's own safety. *See Lukowski*, cited here.

DILLON V. LEGG, 441 P.2d 912 (Cal. 1968)
THING V. LACHUSA, 771 P.2d 814 (Cal. 1989)

The next two cases establish special rules for bystanders, rules that have no application to any other facts. In each case the plaintiff is suing for the emotional distress of seeing someone else injured. In each case there is no fear for the plaintiff's own safety (at least not as it relates to the court's discussion). As we note after these abstracts, some states have continued to use *Dillon* for bystander NIED cases, even though California no longer does. *E.g., Masaki v. General Motors Corp.*, 780 P.2d 566 (Haw. 1989); *James v. Lieb*, 375 N.W.2d 109 (Neb. 1985); *Johnson v. Ruark Obstetrics and Gynecology Associates, P.A.*, 395 S.E.2d 85 (N.C. 1990); *Graves v. Estabrook*, 818 A.2d 1255 (N.H. 2003) (liberalizing "close relationship" to include a fiancee). And another group of states has followed California's lead by adopting *Thing* or something similar. *E.g., Clohessy v. Bachelor*, 675 A.2d 852 (Conn. 1996); *Cameron v. Pepin*, 610 A.2d 279 (Me. 1992).

Dillon guidelines approach. The *Dillon* approach aims at a foreseeability test constrained by some specific factors or guidelines. The court wants to know whether the plaintiff was nearby, whether she had a direct sensory and contemporary perception of the accident and whether she was closely related. But these are merely factors to be weighed in judging foreseeability of emotional harm. To see how it contrasts with *Grube's* rule, you can ask whether Mr. Grube could perhaps get to the jury under *Dillon*. The answer is presumably yes under its basic rules, but notice that the emotional distress claim is derivative– it can only be pursued if the "direct victim" would have a tort claim. If the victim would be barred by contributory fault, for example, the bystander's emotional harm claim would be lost along with it.

Thing bright-line rules approach. The third approach is that taken in *Thing v. La Chusa*. The factors or guidelines in *Dillon* become bright-line or hard-and-fast rules. Thus the plaintiffs in *Bird v. Saenz,* cited in **Note 2**, cannot recover because the second *Thing* element – present at the scene of the injury-producing event at the time it occurs and are then aware that it is causing injury to the victim – is not satisfied. Would Mr. Grube be permitted to get to the jury under the *Thing* elements? Definitely not. He is not closely related to the primary victim. On the other hand, the plaintiff need not be in the zone of danger. So a parent who witnesses injury to a child from vantage point of personal safety may recover though she would be barred under the *Grube* rule.

Thing's limitation on "thin skin" recovery. Notice that the *Thing* court restricts the recoverable emotional damages to compensation for distress that is not an "abnormal response to the circumstances." Students might recognize that this is disallowing "thin skull" recovery, which in this context is sometimes called "thin skin" recovery. Under the thin skin rule, a plaintiff should recover all damages – even if they represent an "abnormally" severe emotional reaction – if a "normal" person would have been emotionally affected, albeit to a lesser extent.

Jurisdictions that have adopted *Thing* in toto, then, don't apply the thin skin rule to bystander NIED cases. But other courts have allowed thin skin recovery in NIED cases. *See, e.g., Miley v. Landry*, 582 So.2d 833 (La. 1991) (a "direct victim" case).

In *Brackett v. Peters,* 11 F.3d 78 (7th Cir. 1993), Judge Posner said: "It has long been the rule in tort law (the 'thin-skull' or 'eggshell-skull' rule) not only that the tortfeasor takes his victim as he finds him, but also that psychological vulnerability is on the same footing with physical. If for example the victim is predisposed to schizophrenia, and the tortfeasor inflicts a minor injury which precipitates the schizophrenia, he is liable for the entire consequences even though they were both highly unlikely and unforeseen."

In *Poole v. Copland,* 498 S.E.2d 602 (N.C. 1998) the plaintiff, a female who had been sexually abused as a child and abused later as well, was sexually harassed at work by a co-worker's sexual bravado. She may have suffered more damages than some persons might because of her previous experience and the jury was allowed to consider that. The Supreme Court of North Carolina held that the instruction on the thin skin rule (allowing full recovery) was correctly given.

Is there a meaningful distinction between "bystanders" and "direct victims" in terms of restricting "thin skin" recovery? Or is there a meaningful distinction between "thin skin" (emotional) recovery and "thin skull" (physical) recovery, despite what Judge Posner said in *Brackett*, quoted above?

Note 1. The Restatement Third, cited here, lists all of the states as of 2007, although it does not clearly distinguish between *Dillon* and *Thing* in its list. The black-letter is closer to *Thing*, allowing recovery for "serious emotional disturbance" caused by a defendant's negligently causing "serious bodily injury to a third person" if the plaintiff "(a) perceives the event contemporaneously, and (b) is a close family member of the person suffering the bodily injury." The Restatement also makes the bystander claim derivative of the physical-injury victim's claim, meaning that the NIED plaintiff "must prove that the physically injured person could recover from the tortfeasor."

Note 2. See discussion above. The classic sudden-event pattern has a strong hold on the courts' thinking. You might suffer more watching a child's long suffering than watching a sudden injury to the child, but the *Fernandez* court nonetheless requires a "sudden, traumatic injury-producing event." *Finnegan* is in line with this. Is such a result justified by a need to limit the number of people who can sue for emotional distress? What if the number is already limited by a requirement of severe (and perhaps diagnosable) emotional harm? Does it make sense to deny recovery to the plaintiffs in *Bird v. Saenz* on this basis?

The Restatement (Third) § 47, in Comment *d*, requires "contemporaneous perception" as opposed to "contemporaneous observation," specifically noting that "the perception required . . . is not limited to sight." However, "it is not enough that the person later learned about the events, later viewed a recording of them, or later observed the resulting bodily injuries."

Note 3. Delayed perception. Recall that *Thing* itself is a case of a mother who arrived shortly after the accident and that recovery was denied there. All of the courts cited at the beginning of this Note follow the Thing rule, and so deny recovery (as would the Restatement Third) in "delayed perception" cases. For courts that accept a more flexible approach, there is still a limit somewhere. Most, as suggested or stated in the *Eskin, Smith* and *Colbert* cases cited here, say that for a delayed-perception case to win, the plaintiff must arrive before changes take place. To take another example, the court in *Bowen v. Lumbermens Mutual Casualty Co.*, 517 N.W.2d 432 (Wis. 1994), said the plaintiff need not see or hear the accident but must arrive within a few minutes and must witness some of its effects. New Mexico has said it requires contemporaneous sensory perception by the plaintiff and that this is a bright-line rule, but at the same time allows recovery if the plaintiff observed death or serious injury "before the arrival of emergency medical professionals at the scene." *Gabaldon v. Jay-Bi Property Management, Inc.*, 925 P.2d 510 (N.M. 1996). As noted at the end here, a *Dillon* jurisdiction – using contemporaneous perception or observance as a factor rather than an element – is more likely to be flexible.

Note 4. Close relationship. *Thing* sets up a requirement of a close family relationship. Thus states that follow Thing will deny claims of financees, best friends, long-time lovers, and so forth. Does this kind of bright-line test make sense, or should some notion of "foreseeable plaintiffs" be used instead? What about same-sex partners in states that don't allow gay people to marry? Should they be denied NIED recovery on the basis of another state law that does not allow them to enter into a "family relationship" that would give them this protection? New Hampshire cases, as noted here, engage in a case-by-case examination of whether the plaintiff and victim have a "close emotional relationship" regardless of the familial connection. Is that workable, especially in a larger state with more litigation? Is such an inquiry too intrusive? Or is it focused on the true issues: whether emotional distress to the plaintiff is foreseeable and genuine?

In the *Smith v. Toney* case cited at the end of this Note, the Indiana court answered a certified question from the federal district court: can a fiancée make a bystander NIED claim under Indiana law. An earlier Indiana opinion said that a plaintiff could satisfy the "closely related" element if the plaintiff was in a "relationship that is analogous to a spouse" with the victim. *Groves v. Taylor*, 729 N.E.2d 569 (Ind. 2000). The *Smith* court looked at other jurisdictions for guidance, finding that a few had allowed fiancées to recover (citing, among other cases, *Graves v. Estabrook*), but concluding that most had not. The court said, "Cases have cited three major policy reasons in rejecting claims for bystander recovery of negligent infliction of emotional distress by unmarried cohabitants or engaged persons: (1) promoting the strong state interest in the marriage relationship; (2) preventing an unreasonable burden on the courts; and (3) limiting the number of persons to whom a negligent defendant owes a duty of care." The court found all of these persuasive. On the second, the court essentially took issue with New Hampshire's approach, saying that even the fact of "engagement" is not clear in many cases and determining whether two people were "engaged" would force courts "to evaluate and rank a variety of personal relationships even though the quality of those relationship[s] would turn on factors not readily knowable. Moreover, defendants would be at a serious disadvantage because the only person in a position to know the true intimate details of the relationship will be the surviving claimant asserting the 'bystander' claim."

Note 5. Beyond the family? Courts have shown little disposition to extend protection beyond the immediate family, as suggested in the previous Note. But you could say that *participants* in the event are in the same position as the primary victim, not "bystanders" at all. That would be consistent with the analogous idea seen in *Bennett v. Stanley*, 748 N.E.2d 41 (Ohio 2001), that the rescuer of a child on the defendant's land is not a trespasser because he takes the status of the child he's rescuing. But as the casebook indicates, the *Michaud* and *Hislop* cases refuse to hold a negligent defendant for emotional harm to rescuers who attempt to aid a co-worker suffering a horrible death.

Slaton v. Vansickle, 872 P.2d 929 (Okla. 1994), declared in a conclusory way that there was no legal distinction between a bystander and a participant.

Most courts seem concerned with preventing an expansion of liability to participants, either rescuers or innocent causes of harm. In *Kallstrom v. United States,* cited here, where the defendant left a pitcher of caustic lye on a kitchen counter at a dance that was consumed by a child by accident, although the defendant was negligent as a matter of law because this was clearly foreseeable, the court held her not liable since she did not meet the *Dillon*-type bystander rules and the court was unwilling to treat the plaintiff's unwilling participation in causing harm as a substitute for close family relationship.

Note 6. Combining the rules. Special bystander rules such as those applied in *Thing* and *Dillon v. Legg* are obviously inapplicable to non-bystander claims. But in those states that have special bystander rules, what is the rule for non-bystanders? Just as we saw with the basic (or non-bystander) NIED claim, there is a good deal of state to state variation in rule-combination here. When you combine all the possible variations, the list is almost too long to recount, let alone to try to teach to a class. Furthermore, we write on shifting sands. For example, Pennsylvania abolished the physical manifestation requirement in *Sinn v. Burd,* 404 A.2d 672 (Pa. 1979), then held that its abolition was only for bystander cases in *Simmons v. Pacor, Inc.,* 674 A.2d 232 (Pa. 1995). Alaska and Illinois did the opposite – they eliminated the physical manifestation requirement in "direct victim" cases but left it standing in bystander cases. See *Chizmar v. Mackie,* 896 P.2d 196 (Alaska 1995) and *Corgan v.Muehling,* 574 N.E.2d 602 (Ill. 1991).

The Note gives a couple of more recent examples; Indiana retains the impact rule for non-bystanders but has dropped it for bystanders. In *Helsel,* cited here, the court held that an NIED claim requires the plaintiff to prove either (1) a "direct impact," or (2) that the plaintiff witnesses or comes upon an accident caused by another's negligence and sustains emotional distress upon learning the accident involves "a loved one with a relationship to the plaintiff analogous to a spouse, parent, child, grandparent, grandchild or sibling." The court referred to the second type of case as a "direct involvement" case, distinguished from the "direct impact" case. The *Helsel* case further suggests that if one suffers a "direct impact," recovery could include damages for the emotional distress of seeing another person injured – rather like the *Grube* court's formulation of the "zone of danger" test.

There are of course many more particular rules that we have not included the casebook. For example – and we are not attempting a complete list here, either -- some courts have adopted one or more of these bystander rules: The plaintiff must suffer serious (or diagnosable) emotional harm, *Clohessy v. Bachelor,* 675 A.2d 852 (Conn. 1996); the primary victim must have suffered serious injury or death or the bystander reasonably so believed, *Pekin Ins. Co. v. Hugh,* 501 N.W.2d 508 (Iowa 1993); and a normally constituted person would have suffered serious emotional harm. This last is an old idea expressed in slightly different language in English courts. It goes back some years in

American courts, too, see *Caputzal v. Lindsay Co.,* 222 A.2d 513 (N.J. 1966), but has gained more currency in recent years. *See Holland v. Sebunya,* 759 A.2d 205 (Me. 2000).

BURGESS V. SUPERIOR COURT, 831 P.2d 1197 (Cal. 1992)

In some ways this case offers the most important idea. The classic fright and shock cases and the bystander version of those cases usually involved strangers who had no special relationship to each other. *Burgess* involves a doctor-patient relationship and it seems easy to say that the doctor owes the patient a duty of reasonable care not to cause her *either* physical *or* emotional harm. That independent duty – independent, that is, from the duty he owes the child– seems to be ample ground for saying that no special constraining rules will bar the mother-patient's claim.

The *Burgess* rule is not about mothers and children, but rather about the relationship between the plaintiff and defendant that might generate a duty of care. In *Burgess,* it was a doctor-patient relationship. In the next section, we'll see that other relationships might generate the same duty, even when the defendant imposes no risks of physical harm upon any person. Because *Burgess* is about duties stemming from contracts or relationships rather than about parents and children, the non-patient father might be denied recovery on similar facts. We should also recognize that the mother, too, would be denied recovery under the *Burgess* logic if she is not a patient. She was a patient in *Burgess* because the *Burgess* facts involved delivery of her child; she and the child were both patients. But it seems probable that the mother whose role is merely to bring an older child to the doctor is not a patient. Such a mother would presumably be required to meet the jurisdiction's rules for bystander recovery. *See Williams v. Baker,* 572 A.2d 1062 (D.C. App. 1990) (applying zone of danger rules to bar the mother's claim). And in *Clark v. Estate of Rice,* 653 N.W.2d 166 (Iowa 2002), where a mother negligently caused her own death in the presence of her daughter, the mother's estate was not liable to the daughter. In spite of emotional ties, the mother had not undertaken or contracted to protect her daughter from emotional harm, of this kind; the act of driving an automobile was too far removed from emotional concerns.

The *Burgess* implicit undertaking might conceivably create duties of care that would override other restrictive rules, not only the bystander or fear-for-another rules. See *Curtis v. MRI Imaging Services II,* 327 Or. 9, 956 P.2d 960 (Or. 1998), and our discussion below.

Notes 1 & 2. *Burgess* yields a rule that can expand liability, as it did in *Burgess* itself. But it also states limits on that expanded liability. As noted above, if the father who is not a patient claims emotional harm for the child's injury, he is merely a bystander and he must meet whichever rule the jurisdiction adopts for bystander claims. He must be aware of the injury at the time it occurred in a *Dillon-Thing* jurisdiction, or be within the zone of danger in a *Grube* type jurisdiction. Thus in *Carey v. Lovett,* cited in **Note 2**, the court denied recovery to the father under the *Thing* rules. Although it may sound strange to speak of the zone of danger rule on facts similar to those in *Burgess,* the District of Columbia applied that rule to bar *both* parents in *Cauman v. George Washington University,* 630 A.2d 1104 (D.C. App. 1993).

"Direct victim" locution. Burgess is derived from but modifies the language in *Molien v. Kaiser Foundation Hospitals,* 616 P.2d 813, 16 A.L.R.4th 518 (Cal. 1980). Where *Burgess* speaks of undertakings and independent duties, *Molien* spoke of a direct duty or a "direct victim" of the defendant's tort. If direct in that case meant anything besides an independent duty or undertaking, it was certainly vague. We have used the term "direct victim" at times to distinguish the bystander or fear-for-another situation and perhaps at times that term is a reference to the independent duty idea. However, the term is ambiguous. Some courts use "direct victim" to mean one who is physically placed in danger and exclude liability unless danger to the plaintiff is demonstrated. See *Straub v. Fisher and Paykel Health Care,* 990 P.2d 384 (Utah 1999). The *Burgess* idea of undertaking and independent duty is assuredly a better-developed concept and one capable of use in rational adjudication.

Drawing the bystander/ "direct victim" distinction. As we've discussed already in the Casebook and in this Manual, a large number of states apply different rules to "bystanders" as to others – call them "non-bystanders," or "participants," or "direct victims," or what have you (and different states use different terms). You need, then, to be able to distinguish the two classes of plaintiffs. But this is frustratingly difficult, as the cases have indicated, especially if you are trying to state generally-applicable concepts as opposed to focusing narrowly on a single state's definitions, which is a lot easier.

The *Burgess* idea, as we've said above, would recognize that where a plaintiff is owed a preexisting duty, either from a relationship (as doctor and patient in the case itself) or from an undertaking, the plaintiff is not a "bystander." It may be seen, then, as a way to enlarge the "direct victim" or "non-bystander" category, to include persons who are actually suing for the distress of seeing another person injured, but who do not have to meet the special "bystander" rules.

In *Page v. Smith,* [1995] 2 All E.R. 736 (H.L.), Lord Lloyd of Berwick also drew a distinction between primary or direct victims on the one hand and secondary or indirect victims on the other. Although the distinction may not exactly parallel the distinction drawn in *Burgess,* there are some similarities. In Lord Lloyd of Berwick's judgment, if either physical or emotional injury is foreseeable to a primary victim, then the negligent defendant is responsible. He thought that in cases of primary victims, none of the special limiting rules is needed. "Since liability depends on foreseeability of physical injury, there could be no question of the defendant finding himself liable to all the world."

Some courts have dropped all limiting rules for NIED claims in cases that fit the assumed duty pattern but have not mentioned the assumed duty rationale. In *McAllister v. Ha,* 496 S.E.2d 577 (N.C. 1998) the court (quoting earlier authority) stated that the elements of the claim were negligence, foreseeability of severe emotional harm, and resulting severe emotional harm.

That case was in fact a doctor-patient case. In *Tanner v. Hartog,* 696 So.2d 705 (Fla. 1997), both a husband and wife claimed damages for emotional distress against doctors who were allegedly negligent in causing the stillbirth of their child. Florida had two conservative rules that seemed to forbid recovery. (1) Florida's rule allowed no claim for wrongful death of the child, who was not considered a person under the wrongful death statute and (2) Florida still retained the full impact rule. As Florida stated the rule, it "requires that before a plaintiff can recover damages for emotional distress caused by the negligence of another, the emotional stress suffered must flow from physical injuries the plaintiff sustained in an impact." But in this case the court thought it should make an exception. The scope of the exception was not clear and seemed grounded in no particular principle.

(2) The Loss of Consortium Claim

NOTE ON CONSORTIUM .

Between spouses, loss of consortium includes loss of sexual relationships, but of course that is only one element of the loss covered: consortium rights include "the mutual right of the husband and wife to that affection, solace, comfort, companionship, society, assistance, and sexual relations necessary to a successful marriage." *Wal-Mart Stores, Inc. v. Alexander,* 868 S.W.2d 322 (Tex. 1994).

Since loss of society, affection, and companionship surely leaves a sense of loss of important elements of emotional life, why do some courts think it is so different from the general mental distress claim? Partly because of its history and its use in the law courts before any separate emotional harm claim was recognized, partly because it focuses on rather particular elements of emotional harm, partly because it has a different name. We have worked in mental compartments so long that they seem real.

Perhaps the distinction is breaking down. In *Archer v. Roadrunner Trucking, Inc.,* 930 P.2d 1155, 1157 (N.M. 1996), repeated New Mexico's version of consortium: "In other words, '[l]oss of consortium is simply the emotional distress suffered by one spouse who loses the normal company of his or her mate when the mate is physically injured due to the tortious conduct of another.'"

BOUCHER V. DIXIE MEDICAL CENTER, 850 P.2d 1179 (Utah. 1992).

Traditionally, damages for loss of consortium were allowed only to husbands for injury to the wife, but are now allowed to wives for injury to husbands as well. In awarding loss of consortium damages courts have imposed none of the restrictive rules applied in other kinds of claim emotional distress. Zone of danger, *Dillon/Thing* rules, physical manifestation–none of these appear to restrict the consortium claim. The relationship, the fact of injury and the fact of loss suffice.

Boucher and the note preceding it attempt to present the loss of consortium claim as a part of the web of rules that – erratically – permit compensation for emotional harm or loss. In fact, the Bouchers asserted both the general mental distress claim and the loss of consortium claim as theories for recovery on one set of facts. On the consortium issue, Utah takes a very conservative position, denying it equally to all comers. But the *Boucher* case nevertheless presents the alternatives clearly.

Consortium claims potentially raise several problems. First, should tort law recognize *both* a general mental distress *and* a consortium claim? What if the Boucher son had been injured in a more liberal state, say one governed by the *Dillon v. Legg* rule and a state that also recognized filial consortium rights? Would that mean the parents would recover damages twice, once for mental distress and once for loss of society, affection, companionship and so on? Some other problems are discussed in the notes.

Note 1. Spousal consortium claims. Loss of sexual relationships, or diminished enjoyment of sexual relations is what people think of first, but the consortium claim includes all the quality of life lost by reason of the other spouse's injury. That seems to lead inexorably to the conclusion that the claim could lie when the injured spouse suffers emotional harm without physical injury. The logical question is how the injury, whatever it is, has diminished the life of the non-injured spouse. *Barnes v. Outlaw,* 964 P.2d 484 (Ariz. 1998) recognizes that courts are divided and that the rule is not settled, but favors allowing the claim for loss of consortium based upon emotional injury to the other spouse.

Note 2. Derivative nature of spousal consortium claims. Is the consortium claim an independent claim or a derivative one? The traditional view is that it is derivative, at least in the sense that the primary victim's comparative fault or contributory negligence reduces or bar the consortium claim. Some courts reject this view and allow the spouse to recover fully from the tortfeasor. A middle position is possible: the consortium claim is derivative in the sense that the primary victim's fault will reduce or bar recovery, but independent in the sense that the primary victim has no right to release the spousal consortium claim. On this, compare *Kibble v. Weeks Dredging & Constr. Co.,* 735 A.2d 1142 (N.J. 1999) (primary victim's release no bar) with *Tichenor v. Santillo,* 527 A.2d 78 (N.J. Super. 1987) (comparative fault applies to consortium claim; cited with seeming approval in *Kibble*). Still another possibility is that where joint and several liability has been abolished, the tortfeasor will be liable only for a percentage of the spouse's consortium loss, not because the claim is derivative but under a principle that each tortfeasor is liable only for his own comparative fault share. *See* Chapter 25.

In *Ferriter v. Daniel O'Connell's Sons, Inc.,* 413 N.E.2d 690, 11 A.L.R.4th 518 (Mass. 1980), cited in **Note 3** on the child's claim, the court also held that the child and wife could recover for loss of consortium even though the husband's claim was barred by the exclusive remedy provision of the workers' compensation system. That rule was legislatively changed to bar the consortium claim when the husband was barred under workers' compensation law. M.G.L.A. 152 § 24.

Notes 3-5. Parents and children. Many courts have not permitted children or parents to recover on a consortium theory for the loss of the other's society, affection, companionship or guidance, which is the traditional approach as indicated in these Notes. But a substantial number have gone the other way in both kinds of cases. *Rolf v. Tri State Motor Transit Co.*, cited in **Note 3**, goes further in permitting adult children to recover, even when they were living apart from the injured parent. The parent's physical injury in *Rolf* was quite substantial and he would require convalescent care and medical treatment for the rest of his life. Another case supporting recovery is *Giuliani v. Guiler,* 951 S.W.2d 318 (Ky. 1997).

Thompson v. Love, 661 So.2d 1131 (Miss. 1995) gave a long list of policy objections to the child's claim: (1) possible increased litigation and multiple claims; (2) inclusion of this claim would hinder settlement; (3) increased liability means high premiums; (4) difficulty in assessing damages to the child; (5) emotional distress upon the child resulting from additional scrutiny of child's relationship with the parent; (6) difficulty for the trier in distinguishing losses of parent and child and potential "double" recovery. Additional logistical problems: (1) longer statute of limitation problems & (2) compulsory joinder problems.

Note 6. Unmarried cohabitants. Courts have often said that the consortium claim is a claim restricted to nuclear families. The usual rule is that couples who cohabit, who regard themselves as committed domestic partners, and who are utterly devoted to one another cannot recover for loss of consortium. On the other hand, marriage partners who are temporarily separated are said to have consortium rights so that if one is injured during the separation, the other can still recover for loss of consortium, presumably to be determined on the basis of losses likely to occur upon being reunited. *Planned Parenthood of Northwest Indiana, Inc. v. Vines,* 543 N.E.2d 654 (1989).

New Jersey's decision in *Dunphy v. Gregor,* New Mexico's in *Lozoya v.Sanchez,* Vermont's Civil Union statute, 15 VT. STAT. §§ 1204(a) & 1204(e) (2) and California's provision for emotional harm damages in CAL. CIV. CODE § 1714.01, all cited in this Note, reflect a more liberal view and others may be encouraged to accept it. (Another California statute gives domestic partners standing to sue for wrongful death.) The reluctance of courts to permit a claim may have several sources. For one thing it is undoubtedly true that such claims would generate the need for a lot of evidence that need not be provided in routine consortium claims, evidence about the depth and commitment of the relationship, for example. For another, until same-sex marriage or civil union become possible, many courts may be reluctant to face the issue whether same-sex couples, gays and lesbians, could assert the consortium claim.

In *Trombley v. Starr-Wood Cardiac Group, PC,* cited at the end of this Note, the plaintiff claimed injury by medical malpractice occurring in 1991. At the date of the surgery, she was married to Bradrick. Two years later, when suit was filed, she was married to Trombley. When surgery occurred, Bradrick, an Alzheimer's patient, was in a critical care facility. Presumably he could have suffered little or no loss of consortium, and certainly none after the divorce in 1992. Trombley claimed that he was a de facto spouse at the time of the surgery. (We've discovered that Australians use de facto as a noun to mean domestic but unmarried partner, as in "This is Bob, my de facto." But the Alaska court continued traditional use as an adjective.) The Alaska court thought there were reasonable arguments for allowing an unmarried cohabitant to recover for loss of consortium in some cases, but not here. Since the injured victim was already married to Bradrick, to allow Trombley's consortium claim might open the door to allowance to consortium claims by at least two persons, the legal and the de facto spouses.

In *Owens-Illinois v. Cook,* also cited at the end of this Note, a worker developed mesothelioma after being exposed to asbestos on the job. The court held that the wife was entitled to bring a loss of consortium claim based on her husband's illness, even though his exposure to the asbestos occurred prior to the marriage, where the diagnosis of the disease occurred after the marriage.

Some other cases have permitted a consortium recovery for a premarital tort when the plaintiff was unaware of the tort at the time of marriage. *Stager v. Schneider,* 494 A.2d 1307 (D.C. Ct. App. 1985) (arguably a continuing tort in that the claim was based upon a physician's non-disclosure of cancer and that non-disclosure "continued" even after the marriage); *Green v. A.P.C.,* 960 P.2d 912 (Wash. 1998)(primary victim a DES daughter, whose injury occurred before she was born and in Washington consortium claim is separate, not derivative).

A number of other courts have denied the spouse's loss of consortium claim when the injury suffered by the other spouse occurred before marriage, even though the injury continues to cause harm after the marriage. E.g., *Sawyer v. Bailey,* 413 A.2d 165 (Me. 1980) (operation followed by long and painful convalescence); *Hite v. Brown,* 654 N.E.2d 452 (Ohio Ct. App. 1995) (sexual abuse of W as a child, leaving emotional scars causing loss of consortium to H after H and W married). The fact that the spouse knew nothing of a premarital injury until after marriage seems logically irrelevant; delayed discovery may postpone the bar of the statute of limitations, but it could hardly create a cause of action that never existed. *Zwicker v. Altamont Emergency Room Physicians Med. Group.,* 118 Cal. Rptr.2d 912 (2002), takes that view.

Note 7. Consortium and the *Dillon-Thing* rules. *See* discussion above preceding Note 1. *See also* DOBBS ON TORTS § 310 (2000). Notice that the two claims (loss of consortium and NIED) are not identical and do not protect identical interests. Recovery, then, for both, would not appear duplicative as a general matter.

Note 8. Animals. Animals are considered property, and courts generally deny emotional distress damages for loss of property. Of course, the owner of the race horse definitely has actual harm – the loss of the horse and the financial loss that goes with that. Courts in these and similar cases simply reject all claims for emotional harm based upon negligently inflicting (actual) damage to property and likewise upon loss of property value due to contract breach.

By locating this material with consortium claims we implicitly suggest an analogy between loss of quality in an animal's companionship and loss of quality in human companionship (although it also serves as a basis for thinking about the dead body cases coming up next). We wouldn't carry any analogy between companion animals and companion persons very far. Yet it is true that companion animals bring enormous benefits to many people and that the animal is not necessarily a fungible that can be readily replaced. In *Rabideau v. City of Racine,* cited at the end of this Note, the defendant shot and killed the plaintiff's dog, perhaps in defense of his own property or family, perhaps not, depending upon whose testimony you accept. The Wisconsin court rejected the intentional infliction claim, as mentioned earlier. It also rejected the negligent infliction claim, partly on the ground that the claim cannot be asserted for negligent harm to property and partly on the ground that the rules of bystander recovery foreclosed an emotional distress action unless the plaintiff was in a close family relation to the injured person. The dog was not a family relation. More policy-oriented grounds were that there was no just stopping place for liability. The class of animals covered is potentially unlimited– people can form bonds of affection even with a parakeet. The class of plaintiffs who could regard an animal as a companion was similarly unlimited– even the next door neighbor or the kid in the downstairs apartment might regard the animal as his special companion. Accord in this policy reasoning is *Harabes v. Barkery, Inc.*, 791 A.2d 1142 (N.J. Super. 2001).

To some extent, loss of your dream home may be for you what loss of a companion animal is for others, but as *Erlich v. Menezes,* cited here, indicates, that is not ground for emotional distress, either. In that case, the contractor had agreed to build the plaintiff's dream house; it was a miserable piece of work. After it leaked everywhere, the plaintiffs discovered that it was structurally unsound as well. The details are striking. But emotional distress was not allowed under the rules mentioned. Interestingly, intentional interference with a contract might deprive the plaintiffs of their dream house but this will be actionable and justify an emotional distress award. See *Maloney v. Home and Investment Cntr., Inc.*, 994 P.2d 1124 (Mont. 2000) (also recognizing emotional distress damages are recoverable in nuisance cases, that is, those arising out of actionable interference with use and enjoyment of land).

A qualifier or two. First, the rule against emotional harm/loss of consortium damages for harms to property is a negligence-law rule; it does not forbid recovery for intentionally inflicted harm. Second, some real property cases involving trespass or nuisance may generate emotional harm claims. In *Hawkins v. Scituate Oil Co.*, Inc., 723 A.2d 771 (R.I. 1999), defendant poured oil down wrong pipe, flooding basement and dispossessing owners. They sued on a negligence, not a nuisance or trespass theory, and were allowed to recover for inconvenience, discomfort, and annoyance–the standard language in nuisance claims.

§ 3. DUTIES OF CARE TO PROTECT EMOTIONAL WELL-BEING INDEPENDENT OF PHYSICAL RISKS

Introduction. Cases in the fright or shock pattern did not seem to create all of the risks of extensive liability that courts sometimes imagined. Those cases involved definite occasions in which someone, the plaintiff herself or someone nearby, was negligently put at risk of physical harm. More particularly, the fright cases did not suggest that the defendant's negligent use of words could warrant any recovery. The impact rule would exclude such cases, as would the zone of danger rule if either requirement were applied to harm done through words or non-threatening conduct. The *Dillon-Thing* rules or guidelines would also seem to exclude recovery unless some particular threatening event or actual harm occurred.

Some courts did recognize two very limited cases in which the plaintiff could be permitted a recovery for distress even though neither the plaintiff nor any other person was put in physical danger. Emotional distress damages could once sometimes be recovered (1) for negligently transmitted or delivered telegraphic death messages and (2) for negligent mishandling of a close relative's dead body. These exceptions gained little currency. Most dead body cases appear to require some fault greater than negligence. *See Gonzalez v. Metropolitan Dade County Public Health Trust,* 651 So.2d 673 (Fla. 1995). And the liability of telegraph companies was soon superseded as to all interstate messages by a federal rule rejecting emotional distress claims. Most of the nominate torts that permit a recovery of emotional distress damages require wrongful intent or impose some other limits on recovery.

Section 3 in effect asks: Will today's courts go beyond the fright pattern of cases and permit some kind of mental distress claim based on negligent words or deeds that do not threaten the plaintiff or any one else? If so, will the limits be more stringent than those imposed under (a) the physical manifestation rules, (b) the *Dillon-Thing* rules or guidelines or (c) the zone of danger rules?

[A. *Transitional cases: bodies*]

WASHINGTON V. JOHN T. RHINES CO., 646 A.2d 345 (D.C. App. 1994)

Plaintiff contracted with the defendant, a funeral home, to embalm and prepare her deceased husband's body. Due to negligence, the body arrived in Texas in a rather hideous state of decomposition. The court rejects her emotional distress claim on the ground that she was not within the zone of danger.

Notes 1 & 3. Even if a body is property, we've just seen that damage to property is usually no basis for emotional harm damages. And without a theory that the body is someone's property, you cannot say that the defendant created a risk of physical harm to *either* person *or* property.

The most plausible approach to the facts in *Washington* would be to drop property theories and to reason from *Burgess*. The undertaker's undertaking is surely to use professional care to guard against emotional harm to survivors. He is to preserve and dress the body to provide a small solace to survivors, not to make the body presentable for sale. *Burgess* would presumably hold that no limiting rules apply to undermine the undertaker's undertaking. Indeed, the zone of danger rule sounds positively absurd on the facts. What danger threatened the family members? Bad embalming?

Christensen v. Superior Court, discussed in **Note 3**, sets up a model for such cases. Notice that we seem to have left the pattern of sudden threats, fright, and shock. If you insist that, after all, survivors will be shocked if not frightened when they see the body in *Washington* or learn that pop's kidneys were sold to someone, there is still a great divorce between the time of the defendant's act and the plaintiff's perception.

Wrongful autopsy is often regarded as a mutilation of the body and an intentional tort actionable by survivors. *See* James O. Pearson, Jr., *Annotation, Liability for Wrongful Autopsy*, 18 A.L.R.4th 858 (1982).

Note 2. In *Perry-Rogers*, cited at the end of this Note, the court held that a claim for emotional distress was stated. The court said, "Damages for emotional harm can be recovered even in the absence of physical injury when there is a duty owed by defendant to plaintiff, [and a] breach of that duty result[s] directly in emotional harm. There is no requirement that the plaintiff must be in fear of his or her own physical safety."

[B. *Misinformation to the plaintiff—including negligent diagnosis*]

HEINER V. MORETUZZO, 652 N.E.2d 664 (Ohio 1995), and **Notes**.

Heiner is one kind of misinformation case, not a case of physical risk, not even to a dead body. It is therefore a definite break in the pattern of fright and shock from physical risk to one's self or to others. (Misdiagnosis in the other direction, a false negative, would be risky, but the false positive is not unless it leads to harmful treatment.) You could look at *Heiner* as simply a manifestation of the physical injury rule, but it is more than that (or a good deal less) because it ignores the defendant's undertaking of care and the concomitant expectations of the plaintiff and because physical injury will seldom result from bad information standing alone.

Many case of negligent gathering or dissemination of information create non-physical risks dealt with through nominate torts like libel, deceit, privacy invasion, or trademark infringement. We might doubt whether liability should be readily imposed for negligent communication (as distinct from negligent testing or other information gathering); the negligence standard hardly seems workable when it comes to choice among limitless locutions and inept expressions. But that problem does not impact *Heiner*. The negligence claimed is not that the defendants tested carefully and communicated carelessly. It is that the testing or the record-keeping in testing was done badly, leading to the misinformation.

One famous case, *Molien v. Kaiser Foundation Hospitals*, 616 P.2d 813, 16 A.L.R.4th 518 (Cal. 1980), held that emotional distress resulting to a husband would be actionable if the defendant had negligently given a diagnosis that the wife had syphilis when she did not. The court concluded that the husband was not a bystander subject to the bystander rules, but a "direct victim." *Burgess* shifted from the direct victim locution to the language of undertaking and relationship, but *Molien* remains at odds with the *Heiner* rule.

As in *Washington*, the classic model of physical danger and fright emotional distress seems greatly to influence the *Heiner* court's ideas. *Burgess'* idea that a doctor undertakes duties to patients he does not owe to strangers was not considered. Students should understand that although relationships have long been significant in creating tort duties, the idea in this context is a new one to the profession. Indeed, that is one of the lessons of *Washington* and *Heiner* –that the courts are still influenced by a whole conception of mental distress claims that assumes (a) they proceed from a platform of physical risks to person and (b) that you must have a single general rule covering all cases. *Burgess'* strength is its recognition that there is a principled basis for protecting emotional interests in some cases even if not in all.

Information about injury or health of plaintiff's spouse, partner or family. It is not so easy to apply the *Burgess* principle when the defendant's primary relationship is with a patient but it is a family member who is emotionally harmed by misinformation. In *Molien*, supra, the husband's claim was no doubt buttressed by the fact that the defendant instructed the wife to inform the husband of her supposed syphilis and to have him tested. But suppose that a hospital mis-identifies a patient and advises the plaintiff that her husband or daughter has been grievously injured or is dead.

In *Johnson v. State*, 334 N.E.2d 590 (N.Y. 1975), a hospital advised the plaintiff that her mother had died. This was false and the hospital conceded its negligence in identification of the patient who died. Judge Breitel held that the plaintiff stated a good claim. "Key to liability, of course, is the hospital's duty, borne or assumed, to advise the proper next of kin of the death of a patient." The plaintiff was not a bystander; a duty was owed "directly" to her. The New York Court later interpreted this to mean that "Liability was based entirely on a duty the defendant had undertaken to inform the plaintiff of her mother's status." *Bovsun v. Sanperi*, 461 N.E.2d 843 (N.Y. 1984).

Some cases have rejected liability on similar facts. The plaintiff is not in fact a family member of the person reputedly injured or deceased, so if this is a bystander case, the plaintiff might be ruled out for that reason. Courts in these cases may also require physical injury in the plaintiff. See *Hoard v. Shawnee Mission Med. Cntr.*, 233 Kan. 267, 662 P.2d 1214 (1983); *Armstrong v. Paoli Memorial Hospital,* 430 Pa.Super. 36, 633 A.2d 605 (1993). Would the *Burgess* court hold otherwise? The hospital in these cases had no preexisting duty to plaintiff, who was not even related to the hospital's patient. But perhaps it undertook a duty when it misinformed the plaintiff.

Information between sexual partners. In some cases, the defendant as a prospective sexual partner misrepresents either his disease status or his reproductive status. The plaintiff in reliance engages in sexual intercourse. Either disease is communicated or pregnancy results. Battery and misrepresentation are potential theories of liability in such cases, though not always accepted. In *Hogan v. Tavzel,* 660 So.2d 350 (Fla. Dist. Ct. App. 1995), H and W had intercourse at a time when H knew he had contagious genital warts but W did not. H took no precautions against spread of the disease, nor did he warn W. W contracted the warts. Thereafter, W and H were divorced. Later still, W brought this action. *Held,* such allegations state a valid claim for battery on the ground that consent was fraudulent procured. If the battery claim is valid, emotional distress damages would normally be recoverable as parasitic damages. *See* Gregory G. Sarno, Annotation, *Tort Liability for Infliction of Venereal Disease,* 40 A.L.R.4th 1089 (1985).

[C. *Correct but private information about the plaintiff*]

BOYLES v. KERR , 855 S.W.2d 593 (Tex. 1993)

This abstract serves at least three purposes. (1) It models an accurate-information-to-others setting; (2) along with the notes, it introduces (but does not develop) the idea that some kinds of emotional harm might be redressed under the rules for privacy invasions; (3) it allows us to discuss whether a "severe injury" limitation would be useful; and finally (4) it provides a little insight into the strategic importance of the negligence theory as opposed to an intentional tort or other theory of the claim.

This case would ordinarily be conceived as either a reckless infliction case or an invasion of privacy/breach of duty of confidentiality. All three of those theories might leave the defendant without liability insurance coverage and hence leave the plaintiff with an uncollectible judgment. That is probably why the plaintiff's lawyers tried hard to make a case for negligent infliction – so the defendant's liability insurance for negligence would apply, as suggested in **Note 2**.

Privacy. Although the *Boyles* court adamantly insists that no emotional harm claim can be asserted, it does not rule out a privacy invasion claim or an intentional infliction claim. A claim for breach of privacy or breach of a duty of confidentiality based on the relationship and expectations of the parties would probably be recognized in most courts, as **Note 3** suggests. This topic is covered briefly in Chapter 32. Absent a confidential relationship or something like it, revelation of private facts presents some serious First Amendment issues, but that does not seem so on facts like those in *Boyles*. Privacy is mentioned here to indicate that while a negligence claim may fail, a claim based upon some other theory might succeed and to suggest that courts are not really all that worried about the reality or foreseeability of emotional injury, since they allow it when privacy rights can be asserted –and, we'd add, in libel, malicious prosecution, and other torts, too.

The *Boyles* quotation from Professor Richard Pearson attacks what may be the real problem for emotional distress claims. Could you either limit damages in some reasonable way or limit the kinds and numbers of cases? The question is doubly important if you go beyond the classic fright cases seen in § 2, because none of us lives a life without some degree of emotional distress, often the result of someone else's words or deeds.

Does the class share Pearson's certainty that severe or serious distress furnishes no useful limitation? It has been the limiting feature in the Restatement's intentional infliction rules from the beginning. As to the argument that severity is a matter of degree and therefore not manageable, much about this argument turns on your view of law, juries, and the legal process. It doesn't seem so persuasive if you think that trials are held in part to determine matters that have not been fully determined in advance and if you recognize that there are many gatekeepers that dissuade prospective claimants. Some of those include lawyers, who do not generally wish to take unproductive cases. Much also depends upon your view of the American culture. Many anecdotes (some in the form of cases) demonstrate that some people are willing to sue quite readily. But many more are not. Cultural norms, inertia, and self-interest keep many potential claimants out of court. If you think these things, you might not be persuaded by Professor Pearson's argument. Students might also recall that many issues in torts, including the issue of negligence itself, is a matter of degree and one that usually must be estimated rather than measured precisely.

Note 1. You might connect this case to the "special relationship" cases from Chapter 16, especially those that recognize an "ad hoc" relationship creating a duty to assist someone. Does it seem inconsistent that one court would say that two friends out drinking together are in a "special relationship" (*Farwell v. Keaton*) whereas this court says that two people having sex are not?

Note 2. *Insurance coverage.* Professor Roger Henderson, an expert both in torts and insurance, points out that liability insurance might still cover recklessness or gross negligence, even though it does not cover intentional torts. He goes on to say, however, that insurance is likely to cover only bodily injury, and hence that coverage for stand-alone emotional harm may be avoided on that ground.

Note 3. See discussion above.

[D. *The abolition of constraining rules*]

CAMPER V. MINOR, 915 S.W.2d 437 (Tenn. 1996)

This case eliminates any requirement of impact, sudden event or shock, physical risk, and physical manifestation of emotional harm. As the Tennessee court said more recently, "Tennessee is one of an exceedingly small minority of jurisdictions which currently follow a general foreseeability approach for negligent infliction of emotional distress," (citing Dobbs on Torts § 312). *Doe v. Roman Catholic Diocese of Nashville*, 154 S.W.3d 22, 40 (Tenn. 2005).

The case is a foil for *Boyles*. Where *Boyles* rejects any general duty and even any duty arising out of the special relationship of Boyles and Kerr, *Camper* posits a duty to protect against emotional distress that, as formulated, seems indiscriminate in its breadth.

You could be skeptical about the ultimate meaning of both – skeptical about *Camper* because the decision may be far broader than necessary of the facts, and because the court's new rules seem to cover bystanders and strangers as well as those to whom the defendant has undertaken a duty of special care.

In *Camper*, the defendant was negligent in creating a physical risk to the plaintiff, although it turned out that the risk to herself and her ultimate death is what triggered the plaintiff's emotional harm, not risk to the plaintiff. That is a little peculiar, but otherwise the *Camper* case is in the traditional physical risk pattern. That might make you wonder whether the Tennessee Court really means to apply its generous rule to, say, overrule its cautious approach to fear of AIDS cases discussed later.

About the same time that *Camper* was decided, the House of Lords was deciding *Page v. Smith*, [1995] 2 All E.R. 736 (H.L.). In this case, the defendant negligently caused a collision. No one suffered any observable injury. The plaintiff seems to have been like the engineer in *Grube*, that is, physically touched but not physically harmed by the touching. But the collision caused the plaintiff's long-standing condition to become worse or chronic. The condition was called "myalgic encephalomyelitis" (ME) or chronic fatigue syndrome (CFS). The plaintiff had been recovering and hoped to return to work. His theory was that the accident has made the condition permanent so he would never work again. The plaintiff testified to no fright or the like, but did say that three hours after the accident "he began to suffer symptoms indicative of a recrudescence of CFS."

Note 1. Taken together, these cases may raise the possibility that, in spite of the impulse to push back the lines of tort liability in an age of tort reform, some courts may have had their fill of the special and rather arbitrary rules. They also raise the possibility that courts might oversimplify the rules too much.

Note 2 points out that *Camper* and many of these other "progressive" courts require a plaintiff to prove the mental distress using expert medical testimony. If the concern that gave rise to the earlier-adopted restrictions on NIED recovery was primarily one of genuineness of the claim, does this fix it?

Note 3. Bystanders. This makes the same point made earlier in Notes in the prior section, but asks a new question: Is there a reason to retain special bystander rules, or not? Perhaps the strongest reasons to say yes are the same reasons courts have given for restricting bystander recovery to family members. On this, see our discussion in this Manual above. But if you disagreed with those policy reasons, you will likely answer no to the question.

§ 4. TOXIC EXPOSURE: FEAR OF FUTURE HARM

Introductory comments. This section is about toxic exposures that cause the victims to fear future disease such as cancer or AIDS, but that, so far have not actually caused such disease. Other fears about future harms are possible, but we focus on toxins and disease and on damages rather than injunctions. These cases take us back to the classic cases because the defendant has acted tortiously toward the plaintiff by subjecting the plaintiff to a definite physical risk, as surely as the horses in *Mitchell* created a risk to the plaintiff when they almost ran her down. In some cases, we even have an impact because the toxic horses have actually touched and affected the plaintiff's body. In other cases, because viruses are not so easy to trace as horses, we cannot be sure whether the toxic horses actually invaded the plaintiff's body or not and the very uncertainty is the basis for the plaintiff's fear of future harm.

Courts that require a physical injury resulting from the tort as a basis for the emotional harm recovery can simply dismiss some of these cases on the ground that no physical injury objective symptom has been shown. Courts that have abolished the physical injury requirement, however, may find themselves inventing some new limitations on recovery for this particular kind of case.

If science becomes precise enough, there remains the possibility, mentioned in *Potter*, that the plaintiffs exposed to carcinogens will be able to show some actual physical changes at the cellular level, even though those changes are not presently causing any symptoms. In that case, a court could conceivably treat the fear of future harm as parasitic to a claim for physical harm.

POTTER V. FIRESTONE TIRE AND RUBBER CO., 863 P.2d 795 (Cal. 1993)

Before going to the merits of the court's reasoning and decision, you might want to deal with two side-issues that bear on the students' evaluation. (1) Whatever the court does in the present case, it might still permit a suit later for physical harm damages if cancer actually occurs, a point made in Chapter 11, § 1, *Hagerty v. L. & L. Marine Serv. Inc.*, 788 F.2d 315 (5th Cir. 1986). (2) If a court were to use the value of the chance approach to future harm on facts like those in *Potter,* the plaintiff would recover now for the cancer, discounted by the probability that cancer would occur, but would not have a later claim when the cancer actually eventuated. Loss of chance was covered in Chapter 7. Whether courts will extend value of the chance analysis beyond special relationships (like doctor and patient relationships) remains to be seen. Both increased risk and fear cases are discussed in David Carl Minneman, Annotation, *Future Disease or Condition, or Anxiety Relating Thereto, as Element of Recovery*, 50 A.L.R.4th 13 (1986). Students may need to get these two issues set to one side so they can consider the fear claim on its own two feet.

Potter presents the classic fact pattern: defendant has created a physical risk to the plaintiff, which so far has brought about no physical harm, but has caused emotional harm in the form of fear. You can compare *Mitchell's* horses. The cases are more favorable to the plaintiff in one respect: the carcinogens were actually ingested here in *Potter*. So in courts that no longer require manifestation of physical harm or symptoms, you'd expect the plaintiffs to recover, at least if their fears were reasonable. But that is not the *Potter* court's rule.

The *Potter* court holds that when the defendant is merely negligent in subjecting the plaintiff to toxic exposures, the plaintiff cannot recover for fear of a future resulting disease unless that disease is more likely than not to occur. This is the court's rule even though the plaintiff's fear is entirely reasonable. (Who would not fear cancer if the chance of getting it was 40%?)

This case is heavily edited, but as edited is rather straightforward in listing four policy grounds why the court is unwilling to impose liability for negligently inflicted toxic exposure that does not make physical harm more likely than not. You can discuss whether the reasons themselves are persuasive. Somewhat separately, you can discuss whether they are the kind of reasons that ought to be considered by courts and whether they should be supported by factual studies before they are given any weight in a judicial proceeding.

1. *Affordability and availability of insurance.* The court asserts that if liability were imposed here based only upon negligence of the defendant claims for fear of cancer would proliferate wildly and that this "might" result in unaffordable insurance costs, or might even affect the availability of insurance. Affordability and availability are terms taken from the medical malpractice "crisis." Malpractice insurance costs did rise at one time and some practitioners did at one time have difficulty getting insurance. The court needs two factual premises to support this policy argument. First, it must say that there will be many, many claims for emotional distress based upon fear; and second it must assert that claims will not merely affect insurance costs (all claims do that) but that they will do so dramatically, so that insurance may become unaffordable. The court presented no factual basis for these assertions, so one question is whether they merely represent the court's own fears of the future or whether there is a factual basis for the concerns.

Another question about this reason is evaluative rather than factual. Consider *Carroll Towing*. If you think that claims for fear or other adverse emotional states are genuine and worth compensating, a rule that excludes compensation for a substantial number of reasonable fears is going to distort the desired incentive effects in favor of more toxic dumping. Toxic dumpers as a class do not seem to warrant treatment more favorable than that given to others.

2. *Detriment to the health care field.* A second guess about the future is based on the argument of the medical association as amicus curiae. (Students should understand that an amicus is a kind of judicial lobbyist.) The medical association's fear of the future is almost certainly not based on a provably more likely than not scenario it wants to impose on the claimants. That fear is that "thousands" of drugs in current use might someday prove to have harmful side effects. If that happens, then "one can expect numerous lawsuits" by people who currently are using the drugs and who have no illness from them, but who assert fear. This could lead drug manufacturers to "diminish the availability" of new beneficial drugs or increase the price of such drugs.

This argument is exactly the same argument as the first one and in fact is merely an example of the first argument or a more specific fear of liability. It is an assertion that an overwhelming number of claims would be filed and that those claims would drive up costs (of insurance, of products). So this argument stands or falls with the first, but its speculative nature, because it is related to a specific factual situation, is maybe clearer. Later we will see that for many years courts supported the idea that the price of the product should reflect the costs of injuries the products causes, but that in recent years courts have withdrawn from that position most especially in drug cases. If you want to foreshadow the products liability policy discussion you can focus on the question whether it would be bad if some particular products had to be priced higher because they tended to cause harms.

3. *Saving the limited resources.* The third policy argument is an echo of the idea dear to the hearts of the older tort reformers who favored no-fault or some other alternative and those who counseled limitations on emotional harm damages generally. Their idea was "first things first," secure compensation for economic losses first, and only if something is left over pay other less pressing claims. The argument is predicated on a belief that as a practical matter, only a limited amount of money is available for payment of injuries, so that we must use it wisely.

The value-judgments in this argument might be sound if the physical harms that will be compensated from the fund result in financial losses and the emotional harms do not. (In this respect, you might note that in a portion of the opinion not included in the casebook, the California Court approved a recovery now for medical monitoring costs designed to provide early detection of cancer. These costs are recoverable although (1) the claim is only one for negligence, (2) no present physical harm is proven, and (3) the feared harm is NOT more likely than not to occur, provided medical monitoring is reasonably needed.)

When this kind of first-things-first argument was made in favor of alternative systems to displace tort law, it was made on the basis of substantial evidence that much of the torts compensation dollar did not actually go to pay for financial losses but to pay for pain and suffering or for financial losses that had been compensated from other sources. But the argument in *Potter* is not based on such studies; it is based instead on the court's belief that if the fear claim is allowed, it will overwhelm the system. So this argument, like the first two, is based on a factual premise for which no substantiation was offered.

4. *Definite rules needed.* The fourth policy reason offered is that the more likely than not limitation is needed to establish a definite and predictable threshold for recovery. It is not so clear why questions of reasonable fear are different from the many other reasonableness questions in tort cases, including the most basic ones turning on the reasonableness at the heart of the negligence determination. The only specific reason given by the court (not included in the casebook version) was that juries might give inconsistent answers, some concluding a 5% chance is enough for a reasonable fear, others concluding it was not. If that is the only problem, the extreme more likely than not standard is certainly not required to enforce some consistency; the court could set any threshold it chose. Or, more in line with traditional adjudication, it could recognize some fears might be reasonable when the risk is only 5% while others might be unreasonable unless the risk is extremely likely.

Are these policy reasons adequate to the result? Or does the class think that maybe they represent complex ways of talking about the underlying feeling that emotional harm is not real or not worthy of compensation?

The physical injury possibility.. The *Potter* court suggested that it might not require more likely than not evidence if the plaintiff had suffered actual physical injury, even if that injury was some kind of damage to the immune system that had produced no symptoms. Presumably the idea is that such a scenario would trigger the parasitic damages rule–actual physical harm being done, the plaintiff recovers for emotional harm as well.

Other legal theories for constraining recovery.. *Potter* is not the only rule that could exclude recovery. On facts like *Potter's*, the plaintiff could lose in an impact jurisdiction and even in one merely requiring some physical or objective manifestation of emotional harm.

Other courts. Outside California, Potter's more-likely-than-not rule has so far received no support, although a number of courts have cited *Potter* for its approval of medical monitoring recovery.

On facts similar to *Potter's*, some courts have rejected fear claims for different reasons – under the limiting rules they apply to emotional distress generally. E.g., *Dodge v. Cotter Corp.*, 203 F.3d 1190 (10th Cir. 2000) (plaintiffs had not proved a "chronic objective condition caused by their increased risk of developing cancer" necessary to support an emotional distress claim under Colorado law as the court interpreted it); *Temple-Inland Forest Prods. Corp. v. Carter*, 993 S.W.2d 88 (Tex. 1999) (rejecting claim based on asbestos exposure on the basis of *Boyles v. Kerr's* holding that Texas does not recognize negligent infliction of emotional distress and because although the plaintiff's inhaled asbestos fibers, they did not presently show serious bodily injury). James A. Henderson, Jr. & Aaron D. Twerski, *Asbestos Litigation Gone Mad:*

Exposure-based Recovery for Increased Risk, Mental Distress, and Medical Monitoring, 53 S.C. L. REV. 815 (2002), addressing asbestos exposure cases, opposes emotional distress claims based on "pre-injury" fears of future disease. The same article also opposes medical monitoring costs. The authors say that the emotional distress action was not "designed" to redress "general malaise" but to permit recovery for serious emotional distress arising from violent or traumatic conduct.

Some courts have expressly rejected *Potter. John and Jane Roes, 1-100 v. FHP, Inc.,* 985 P.2d 661 (Haw. 1999); *Madrid v. Lincoln County Med. Ctr.,* 923 P.2d 1154 (N.M. 1996); cf. *Boryla v. Pash,* 960 P.2d 123 (Colo. 1998) (doctor's failure to diagnose existing cancer). See also **Note 3**.

The federal Price-Anderson Act imports state substantive law of torts to govern private companies' liabilities for nuclear incidents; but (as we've seen with the FTCA), there are some preliminary limits, more or less jurisdictional. The claim must be one for "bodily injury," else there is no claim at all. Where many people were exposed to radiation from a nuclear development installation, those who claimed emotional harm and prospective but not existing physical injury had no claim because they had no "bodily injury." In re *Berg Litigation,* 293 F.3d 1127 (9th Cir. 2002). The court also excluded medical monitoring claims on the same basis. The Warsaw Convention (covering airline injuries on international flights) makes the same requirement of bodily injury, with similar results.

NORFOLK & WESTERN RY. V. AYERS, 538 U.S. 135 (2003)

Held, Railroad workers, who were exposed to asbestos and suffered noncancerous asbestosis as a result, could recover under the FELA for "genuine and serious" fear of contracting cancer. Given the bodily harm (asbestosis), the plaintiffs are not required to prove physical manifestations of emotional distress. It is true that the plaintiffs' bodily harm– asbestosis– cannot cause cancer. However, exposure to asbestos *does* cause cancer and that suffices to justify the claim. Hence a verdict for the plaintiff was affirmed.

The Supreme Court is recognizing here what is often called parasitic damages. Given a tort resulting in bodily harm, all proximately caused damages, including pain, suffering, and emotional distress, are fully recoverable. In such cases, the rules imposed in many states that require physical manifestation have no application whatever.

The unusual feature here is that while the plaintiffs' bodily harms – asbestosis– are the basis for permitting emotional distress recovery for fear of cancer, the fear of cancer itself cannot arise from that bodily harm, because asbestosis does not cause cancer. Instead, the fear arises from the tortious exposure to asbestos. The Restatement specifically dealt with this problem by saying the defendant would be liable for emotional distress "resulting from the bodily harm *or from the conduct which causes it*" – that conduct being the exposure to asbestos. Does this strike students as strange? The plaintiffs are allowed to recover for emotional distress only because of bodily harm, but it is emotional distress that does not flow from that bodily harm! And had the plaintiffs suffered no bodily harm, they could not have recovered under the FELA in the absence of impact or physical symptoms. *Metro-North Commuter R.R. Co. v. Buckley,* 521 U.S. 424 (1997).

Justice Kennedy, dissenting in *Ayers,* argued first that awards of this type will bankrupt companies involved in asbestos litigation, leaving nothing for those who actually get cancer. This is a broad argument that actually seems to apply to any claim for pain, suffering, or emotional distress if we cannot be sure that enough money remains available to pay for the more fundamental needs such as medical expenses and lost of wages. Justice Kennedy's dissent foreshadows the argument we address in Chapter 27– that tort law misuses limited resources. You can come back to Justice Kennedy's point there.

Justice Kennedy's second argument might be viewed as a kind of play on words– the fear resulted from what the plaintiffs read about cancer danger rather than from the asbestosis. As a matter of causation, though, isn't all of that part of the foreseeable causation of emotional distress?

We did not include Justice Breyer's dissenting argument in our case abstract because it could further distract from the parasitic damages issue. You might want to know, though, that Justice Breyer would "rule out recovery for fear of disease when the following conditions are met: (1) actual development of the disease can neither be expected nor ruled out for many years; (2) fear of the disease is separately compensable if the disease occurs; *and* (3) fear of the disease is based upon risks not significantly different in kind from the background risks that all individuals face." If you discuss this line of argument with your class, you might want to remind students of the *Hagerty* case discussed in text in Chapter 11 § 1.

NOTE: RECOVERY IN "NO EXPOSURE" CASES

¶ 1. In *Hartwig,* discussed here and in subsequent paragraphs of this Note, the defendant negligently disposed of medical waste (sharps in this case) in ordinary trash. The risk is that someone may be hurt by a puncture and also that infection will spread. Given the injury, quite traditional rules of parasitic damages would allow recovery not only for the injury itself but for pain and suffering, including emotional distress that results. The court took that very approach, and in so doing rejected, for needle sticks and other physical impacts, the dual exposure rules requiring both a channel of exposure and proof that a virus existed in it (¶ 5). That does not necessarily cover cases like those in which the patient consents to a touching by a doctor but does not know the risks attached to it.

Justice. On the justice of the *Hartwig* claim, (as distinct from its deterrent effect), the Nebraska Court strikes us as commonsensical. Of *course* people worry, and worry reasonably, about AIDS when they've been stuck with a discarded needle or scalpel. The channel of exposure is shown; the plaintiff is seeking to recover because she doesn't know whether she's been exposed or not and can't find out. Perhaps if the plaintiff had obtained counsel the same day, the needle would have been tested, but you can hardly expect every lay person to recognize the importance of doing that when the health care professionals themselves not only violate the rules for medical waste but then don't test the needle.

Defendants captured rhetorical advantage very early conflict over AIDS claims by getting courts to think of these cases as claims for AIDS phobia, as if to say a person who is afraid of AIDS is a little nutty and maybe also socially insensitive, a theme that runs loosely through the cases. In line with this, a number of courts have constructed the dual-exposure rule of law that eliminates any consideration of the plaintiff's reasonableness in fearing AIDs. Even so, at least six cases from courts of last resort now support recovery where the plaintiff shows a plausible channel of infection and where infection cannot be ruled out, or where the defendant misdiagnoses AIDS. *See also De Milio v. Schranger*, 666 A.2d 627 (N.J. Super. 1995) presumed exposure when the defendant was guilty of a reckless "mindset" (another medical waste case in which sharps were disposed up in ordinary trash).

¶ 2.What counts as physical injury? *Cell or immune system damage without pain or symptoms* . In toxic tort cases, the parasitic damages possibility elevates the importance of two issues: (1) As a matter of fact, can some small cellular change in the plaintiff's body be shown to exist as a result of the exposure? and (2) If it does exist without symptoms, can that legally count as physical injury?

The California Court in *Potter* suggested the possibility that cellular change, even though non-symptomatic, might be enough, though it did not pass on that issue. But recall that in *Grube*, the engineer's bumps in the cabin of the train were not enough to induce the court to permit recovery. *Simmons v. Pacor, Inc.*, 674 A.2d 232 (Pa. 1996), appears to reject any possibility that physical changes in the body that are not themselves painful and that do not limit the plaintiff's functioning could trigger the parasitic damages rule. In that case, the plaintiff suffered actual changes in the body in the form of thickened or calcified tissues surrounding the lung, but that was not enough to support a fear claim. Even a needle stick was not a sufficient injury to support a parasitic approach to a fear claim in *Herbert v. Regents of University of California*, 31 Cal.Rptr.2d 709 (Ct. App. 1994). The court thought that the *Potter* standard applied even though the injury was not from a general environmental exposure.

But in *Howard v. Alexandria Hospital*, 429 S.E.2d 22 (Va. 1993), the defendant hospital failed to sterilize instruments used in surgery upon the plaintiff. The danger was quickly recognized. The plaintiff was immediately given intravenous antibiotics and kept in the hospital several additional days. When she was discharged, she was told that she would need another test for AIDS in six months. In the meantime, she suffered the physical invasions of hospital treatments, a physical reaction to the antibiotics, and fear and anxiety. The defendant somehow persuaded the trial judge that there was no injury to support an emotional distress claim. The Supreme Court of Virginia reversed. "[T]he plaintiff sustained positive, physical and mental hurt." The court seemed to view the mental anguish claim as one which directly resulted from the physical invasions.

In *Duarte v. Zachariah,* 28 Cal.Rptr.2d 88 (Ct. App. 1994), the court emphasized the question whether any actionable injury at all occurred when the plaintiff's bone marrow was destroyed by a negligently administered overdose of cytoxin as a part of chemotherapy. The plaintiff was unable to prove that the overdose caused recurrence of the cancer but the court thought that the destruction of bone marrow cells was itself an injury that would be actionable. "The Restatement Second of Torts applies the term "injury" to any invasion of a legally protected interest, such as the interest in bodily security. (§ 7.) Such an invasion may occasion "harm": "Physical changes or alterations may be either beneficial, detrimental, or of no consequence to a person. In so far as physical changes have a detrimental effect on a person, that person suffers harm." (§ 7, com. b.) . . . .the change in Duarte's bone marrow was an appreciable functional impairment of the immune system. As a result of the overdose of cytoxin her bone marrow is no longer able to function in a manner that allows her to engage in a beneficial medical treatment, chemotherapy. This adverse change can only be fairly characterized as a detriment, "a loss or harm suffered in person" (Civ.Code, § 3282) and is a sufficient predicate for a cause of action for personal injury."

¶ 3. Have courts been overtaken by undue concerns in the AIDS and asbestos cases? If the plaintiff is tortiously blinded in one eye, he can surely recover for the pain and distress he suffers from the fear that the other eye may be lost, too. See *Danaher v. Patridge Creek Country Club*, 323 N.W.2d 376 (Mich. Ct. App. 1982). If he is bitten by a dog supposed to be rabid, he can surely have damages based on his terror at the prospect of rabies. *Ayers v. Macoughtry*, 117 P. 1088 (Okla. 1911). Some courts have applied the same idea in toxic tort cases, as where the plaintiff was splashed with a dangerous chemical. *Sterling v. Velsicol Chem. Corp.*, 855 F.2d 1188 (6th Cir. 1988). Why do the supposed majority resist parasitic damages in the AIDS-fear cases?

¶ 4. What is the alternative to the exposure rule? Instead of positing a rule that governs all cases, regardless of the facts, the courts could use simply require that the fear be "reasonable." If that were the approach, the judge would be required to analyze the facts of each particular case and tailor justice to the facts. Under the "rule" approach, the facts can be ignored, so that cases in which the plaintiff showed no reason to fear AIDS at all are lumped with cases in which the plaintiff's body has been punctured with a bloody needle that could not be tested for HIV.

The "majority" dual exposure rules (channel plus actual infection of the instrument) includes some of the needle-stick cases, but also cases that look more like informed consent claims. It also includes a number of intermediate and trial court decisions. These are of course valid and important cases, but they are not necessarily the final word. This is a good place to discuss the "majority rule" syndrome that afflicts some students. Law in the courts is not a matter of counting the decisions of other courts. And if it were, how meaningful would it be to say that the "majority" holds thus and such when only 13 cases have been decided?

One of the "majority" cases, *Carroll v. Sisters of Saint Francis Health Services,* cited here, is a needle stick case. Because the plaintiff could not show that the needle itself was contaminated the actual exposure rule excluded recovery for distress even during the period of uncertainty. The Tennessee Court reasoned that it had always required some kind of objective component in emotional distress claims. Traditionally, that objective component was physical injury, but actual exposure would suffice as an equally objective matter. The court did not explain why a puncture by a used needle would not also be objective. In *Camper v. Minor*, see above, Tennessee said it was moving to a more generous rule about emotional distress claims, under which emotional distress claims are to be decided under general negligence rules of unreasonable risk and foreseeable harm. If we take that statement literally, it looks as if *Carroll's* restrictive requirement is overruled. Should we believe that?

On the arguments, sometimes explicit, that ignorant people will flood the courts with AIDS fear suits if all that is required is some kind of incident plus a reasonable fear, there is a specific reason to think this is not likely. Lawyers for plaintiffs, being paid only if they win, will not take cases unless they have a chance to win. If the lawyer thinks, "I cannot persuade judge and jury to accept my client's fear as reasonable," that lawyer will not bring the case. The lawyer cannot afford to.

Finally, deterrence might be especially important idea here to raise with the class if you haven't discussed it lately. The plaintiff's claim supports public health interests, for there are many people at risk when the defendant mishandles medical waste. The Mississippi and New Mexico cases cited here allow recovery and emphasize the importance of deterrence. Mississippi noted both the need to encourage hospitals to use care and the need to require them to conduct tests on instruments that have caused harm.

CHAPTER 20

PRENATAL HARMS

▶**Changes in the Sixth Edition.** Except for updating and cutting some Note materials, this Chapter is unchanged from the previous edition.

▶The Concise Edition makes no changes in this brief Chapter.■

Preliminary note to the chapter. This chapter is short and interesting to most students, but almost all of the material raises controversial issues on which most of us have strong feelings. In class discussion, you may want to be especially careful of those feelings on all sides. One set of feelings has to do with the genetic damage cases. Some of the class members may have siblings or children who suffer from serious disabilities similar to those in the cases. To talk about the mother's lost opportunity for abortion in those cases is very difficult for some people. Second, all of these cases touch a nerve on the abortion issue generally and the way different groups in society look at "life." You can spend a minute before covering this material outlining the emotional difficulties and asking for professional (but not pallid) discussion.

Scheduling omissions. The material in this chapter is fairly basic and is already quite trim. We would not recommend any omissions if you decide to cover this topic at all.

§ 1. PRENATAL AND PRECONCEPTION INJURY

REMY V. MACDONALD, 801 N.E.2d 260 (Mass. 2004)

The facts of this case are summarized in the first paragraph, and the issue posed: can a child, born alive, sue her mother for personal injuries caused by the mother's negligently causing a car crash that harmed the child in utero?

The court sees this as a duty issue, and holds there is no duty. Thus a summary judgment for the defendant is affirmed.

The court found that everything had to do with the fact that this was a child suing its own mother. The court here said it agreed in principle with the trial court's observation that the "'unique symbiotic relationship' between a mother and her unborn child" made the creation of a tort duty between them "problematic." One problem, thought the court, would be to invade potentially the woman's right to choose (see **Note 6**).

The court raises the "floodgates" spectre, reasoning that imposing a duty might well lead to litigation in "an almost unlimited number of circumstances." Notice too the court's focus on "existing social values and customs" – and its conclusion that no "settled social policy" exists that would justify imposing a duty on the mother here.

How does the court distinguish the three appellate cases from other jurisdictions that go the other way? Essentially by criticizing their failure to distinguish injuries caused by the mother's negligence from injuries caused by some other person's negligence, and on the ground that such a failure proves they had undertaken "no serious analysis" of the issue. The court's distinction between moral duties and legal ones might remind the class of *Yania v. Bigan* in Chapter 16, where the court said that the defendant was under a moral, but not a legal, duty to rescue the decedent who jumped into a trench filled with water.

Is this really a family immunity ruling? Not really, although obviously the court's concerns about the relationship between mother and unborn child might remind you of some of the issues that gave rise to familial immunities (Chapter 14). The court recognizes that had the child been born at the time of the accident, "even if only one hour of age," she would have been able to sue her mother for negligently-caused injuries. But a "bright line" must be drawn "around the zone of potential tort liability of one who is still biologically joined to an injured plaintiff."

You might engage the class in a discussion, invited by the court's broad reasoning, about whether certain kinds of injurious wrongs are simply not addressable by courts. Do they agree that the line-drawing in which courts would have to engage in these fetus/mother tort cases would cause havoc? Several of the notes raise this broad question more specifically.

Note 1. Traditional rule. As referenced here, traditionally there was no cause of action at all for harm done to a fetus before the child was born.

Note 2. Contemporary rules: Child born alive. When a child is born alive, most courts now allow recovery for prenatal injury (at least against persons other than the mother), even if that injury was inflicted before the child was viable. The problem case is the wrongful death claim for a stillborn fetus or a fetus that, though born alive, never attained viability in the sense that it could be expected to sustain life for an appreciable time independent of the mother. The Oklahoma statement of the rule in *Nealis* is a useful one: the court said: "[A] wrongful death action can generally be said to lie where the child's death is caused by prenatal injury inflicted any time during gestation if either (1) the child is subsequently born alive after reaching the point of viability or (2) the child is stillborn but survived the injury in utero to reach the point of viability." If you did not require either viability or live birth at some point, you might find yourself entertaining a wrongful death action when a test tube breaks during an attempt at in vitro fertilization. But if you impose those requirements, the problem disappears.

Note 3. Contemporary rules: Child not born alive but viable at injury. Most courts that have addressed such cases have held that a wrongful death action is available if the fetus was viable at the time of the injury but born dead. You may wish to emphasize that in the wrongful death action for a stillborn fetus, the claim, like virtually all death claims, is entirely statutory. Wrongful death statutes speak of death of a "person," so one technical problem to anticipate with stillborn wrongful death claims is whether the fetus was a "person" within the meaning of the statute. Each state, obviously, can arrive at its own interpretation, and wrongful death statutes do vary (see Chapter 21).

Note 4. Contemporary rules: Child not born alive and not viable at injury. Most courts reject liability here, although some decisions have allowed recovery, as noted.. The same point about wrongful death statutes applies here: where the claim is for wrongful death, the claim is entirely statutory and success will depend on whether the fetus was a person entitled to recover under the statute. See *Humes v. Clinton*, 792 P.2d 1032 (Kan 1990) (injury to fetus that is not viable and not born alive was not injury to a "person" under the wrongful death statute); *Bolin v. Wingert*, 764 N.E.2d 201 (Ind. 2002)(same). Thus both *Farley* and *Weirsma*, cited in this Note, hold that a nonviable fetus is a "person" within the meaning of the death statutes.

In *Nealis v. Baird,* briefly discussed in this Note, the fetus was arguably born alive but died almost immediately. On the supposition that the child, though born alive, had never become capable of sustaining existence independent of the mother, the Oklahoma Court held that once the child is born alive, "the debate over whether the fetus is or is not a person ends and the live born child attains" personhood that permits a wrongful death action.

––––––––––

Summary. It can be easy to get drawn into drawing confusing distinctions. A table or matrix on the board might help. In this one, boxes marked with P represent settings in which the plaintiff is more likely to prevail; in the setting represented by the box marked D, the defendant will probably prevail.

	Viable at injury	Not viable at injury
Born alive	**P**. Stated in Note 2.	**P**. Note 2.
Not born alive	**P** Stated in Note 3. Recovery still rejected in cases such as Shaw, cited in Note 3..	**D**. Stated in Note 4. (*Santana* & *Crosby*) Recovery has been allowed in some states. (*Wiersma* & *Farley*)

Note 5. Recovery of emotional distress damages. *Smith v. Borello,* cited here, seems to be an attempt to apportion damages between wrongful death and emotional distress claims in cases of fetal death, both viable and nonviable. Roughly, the court said emotional distress or psychic injury claims of the mother could be recovered in her action, whether or not a wrongful death suit could actually be maintained, while loss of consortium could be recovered in the wrongful death suit,. (It could not be in Maryland for loss of a nonviable fetus.) This allocation does not seem to prevent duplicated damages if you take the Maryland death statute literally, since it specifically allows damages both for the survivor's emotional distress and loss of consortium. What does the class think should be done to prevent duplication?

Note 6. Parental liability: Some hard questions. The mother's right to control her own body is a critical issue here. When she does something that she is generally free to do—refusing blood transfusions, for example—her rights may be paramount even if her conduct is harmful to a viable fetus. *In re Fetus Brown*, 689 N.E.2d 397 (Ill. App. Ct. 1997). This is in line with the right to refuse medical treatment. See *Shine v. Vega,* 709 N.E.2d 58 (Mass. 1999) and Chapter 13.

When the mother's conduct is illegal or tortious irrespective of harm to the fetus, the case for the mother's freedom of action is harder to establish. *Stallman v. Youngquist*, cited here, refused to impose liability upon a mother for pre-natal injury in an automobile accident, saying it was unwilling to subordinate the mother's control over her own life to the interests of the fetus by imposing tort liability. But as the mother had no legal right to drive negligently in the first place, the argument that her rights outweigh those of the fetus is misdirected. Perhaps the real point is the slippery slope argument that liability for wrongs might lead to liability in the quite different cases in which the mother is exercising her rights. *Chennault v. Huie,* also cited here, approved *Stallman* in the case of a cocaine mother. The court argued that liability could interfere "with a woman's legal rights," a point that is even less convincing here than in *Stallman,* since the mother had no rights to ingest illegal drugs. The court made some other arguments that seem insupportable.

On the technical and policy problems in criminal cases, see *State v. Deborah J.Z*, 596 N.W.2d 490 (Wis. 1999). On toxic injury to the fetus caused by parents and employers, see DOBBS ON TORTS § 289 (2000).

Someone might think that *Roe v. Wade*, 410 U.S. 113 (1973), treats a fetus in the first trimester as not a "person." But *Roe v. Wade* does not say that. *Roe* protects the mother's choice to have or not have an abortion. The *mother's* right to choose, however, is not the same as a *tortfeasor's* right to choose. The mother's right to choose is not only protected by *Roe*, but also by the tort law which allows a claim against the tortfeasor who disrupts her choice. In terms of function and operation, tort liability is not in logically in conflict with *Roe v. Wade*.

RENSLOW V. MENNONITE HOSPITAL, 367 N.E.2d 1250 (Ill. 1977)
ALBALA V. CITY OF NEW YORK, 429 N.E.2d 786 (N.Y. 1981)

Skipping over the question of viability, *Renslow* raises the question whether injury to a mother even before conception can form the basis of a claim by the child who later suffers. The court, much divided, answered "yes."

Albala appears in principle to go the other way from *Renslow*. Why is it that a negligent motorist should be protected from liability in the case supposed? Is this merely a way of assuming the answer to the present case, or is it so clear that no argument is needed? The Court of Appeals appears to think that its obligation in deciding this case is to decide in a way that would leave no obvious unresolved problems for the future, such as the problem of the chromosome damage which would lead to claims for generations to come. Is this right, or is Illinois correct in saying it would deal with those issues when they arose?

Note 1. The hypothetical put is similar to *Albala* in that the defendant's conduct occurs before the plaintiff's building, which is the "victim" here, is in existence. Yet it does not quite capture all of the problem the *Albala* Court worried about because it does not suggest the potential for an infinite string of injury. The preconception injury could cause medical problems not only to the later-conceived child, but to that child's child, and so on to the nth generation. The DES cases help us see the reality of that possibility.

But two points about New York's holding in *Albala*: (1) The problem of infinite replication of injury through the generations is not a problem for preconception torts; it is a problem for *genetic* torts. A preconception tort might *not* cause injury that will be replicated in the next generation. And vice versa: a genetic tort might occur *after* conception but could present the infinite injury problem. So New York has put an ill-fitting suit of rules on the *Albala* problem; the suit is too big for some cases and too small for others. (2) The DES grandchild cases (note 2) show ironically that New York knows how to limit the liability to one generation without denying a remedy to the first generation. Whether it should limit that liability is a different question. The point is that you don't have to deny all damage for the spread of fire merely because you could imagine that Mrs. O'Leary's fire burned all the way from Chicago to Los Angeles.

What about the supposed conflict between duties to the mother and those to the child? First, such cases have not appeared yet, so it is unnecessary to bar this plaintiff because some other, hypothetical plaintiff might be barred. Second, if a conflict arises, the mother will normally have the right to determine the medical treatment to be accorded; she can consent for herself and also as agent for the child. See See Julie A. Greenberg, *Reconceptualizing Preconception Torts*, 64 TENN. L. REV. 315 (1997); DOBBS ON TORTS § 290.

Note 2. *Enright v. Eli Lilly & Co.*, cited here, applied *Albala* to deny the claim. A claim was made by a male grandchild in *Grover v. Eli Lilly and Co.*, 591 N.E.2d 696 (Ohio 1992). The Ohio Court seemed to criticize the flat rule of law in *Albala*.

Note 3. *Taylor v. Cutler,* cited here, rejected liability on the ground that injury to a child seven years later was unforeseeable. The decision is couched in the language of duty but since it analyzes the facts of the particular case for foreseeability, it looks like a traditional "proximate cause" decision. The Appellate Division appeared to support liability for preconception injury in cases like *Renslow* and in products liability cases on the ground that injury to an un-conceived child would be foreseeable there. However, the Supreme Court in affirming specifically avoided passing on this point.

§ 2. WRONGFUL LIFE, BIRTH, OR CONCEPTION

Preliminary note. You have some options here. You can either discuss *Chaffee* in whatever way you usually introduce cases, and use the Notes (roughly in order) to fill out the discussion, or you can use *Chaffee* and its notes to engage in a full-blown discussion of whether these claims should be allowed (and the extent courts and legislatures now allow or disallow them) and the kinds of damages that should be awarded. If you are inclined to do the latter, we provide a template for such a discussion at the end of this section, following the comments on all the Notes.

CHAFFEE V. SESLAR, 751 N.E.2d 773 (Ind. Ct. App. 2001)

A woman sues her doctor for the costs of rearing a healthy child whose birth would have been avoided had the defendant properly performed the sterilization procedure he had attempted earlier. The court here sees this not as a case of "wrongful pregnancy" or "wrongful birth," but simply as a medical malpractice claim subject to all of the rules of negligence. Negligence rules permit the recovery of all proximately caused harms. Harms are allowable, generally, when they are foreseeable. Applying those rules here, the plaintiff is allowed to recover damages. In short, "the healthcare provider's negligence has resulted in the imposition of financial burdens which the parent desired to avoid." What about the argument that the mother seeks to recover damages for conduct that resulted in the birth of a healthy child, and that that is against public policy? The court says "a parent's injury [in such a case] is not the birth of her child, but rather is the invasion of her interest in the financial security of her family and the attendant desire to limit her family size, and the deprivation of her right to limit procreation." Indeed, the court says, "[T]he sanctity of life is more undermined by a parent being financially unable to provide the basic necessities of life than allowing the recovery of child-rearing expenses."

Are damages too speculative? The court says no. Juries have to make even more difficult determinations, and we allow the recovery of pain and suffering and future damages.

Must damages be mitigated? Yes, but the argument is limited. The defendant can "present evidence to limit the amount of the recovery of child-rearing damages by the benefits resulting from the child's birth," although the court does not specify what kinds of benefits to which it refers. But the defendant cannot argue that the plaintiff's failure to obtain an abortion or have her child adopted was a failure to mitigate. This, said the court, would be an affront to Supreme Court precedent guaranteeing a woman's right to control procreation decisions.

Note 1. Was the Indiana court right here to avoid the "wrongful conception" label? Was the court right to allow the damages it did? You can run through the court's recitation of the three views it found it in the case law from various jurisdictions: (1) full recovery rule, allowing all child-rearing costs; (2) benefit rule, allowing child-rearing costs but offsetting benefits the parent will receive by having the child; and (3) the no-recovery rule. By the court's own count, over three-fifths of the states are in category three.

Wrongful conception and genetic defects. If the risk of the physician's negligence is that a normal but unwanted child will be born, there seems to be no basis for making the physician liable for the "unforeseeable" genetic harm. That surely seems to be the answer under scope of risk ("proximate cause") rules. A recent case to the same effect is *Simmerer v. Dabbas,* 733 N.E.2d 1169 (Ohio 2000) (citing a number of cases).

For a good discussion of the "wrongful conception" or "wrongful pregnancy" cases, *see* Mark Strasser, *Misconceptions and Wrongful Births: A Call for a Principled Jurisprudence,* 31 ARIZ. ST. L.J. 161 (1999).

Notes 2 & 4. *The shorthand terms.* When health care providers negligently fail to diagnose a serious genetic defect in a fetus so that the mother loses the opportunity to lawfully terminate pregnancy, two types of claim have been presented to the courts. These too are claims for a species of medical malpractice, that is, negligence, but as a matter of convenient shorthand these claims are often designated as claims for (1) Wrongful life (an action by the child who suffers horrible defects, essentially a claim that "I should not have been born"). (2) Wrongful birth (a claim by the mother that she would have terminated the pregnancy had she been properly advised and that because she was not advised, she must care for a seriously damaged child). *See Greco v. United States*, 893 P.2d 345 (Nev. 1995) (distinguishing the two claims and recognizing one for wrongful birth but not one for wrongful life).

Note 4. Wrongful life. For representative cases, see DOBBS ON TORTS § 291 (2000). A recent rejection of the wrongful life claim is *Hester v. Dwivedi*, 733 N.E.2d 1161 (Ohio 2000). California, which does accept wrongful life claims, limits recovery to the cost of care. That excludes lost earnings and emotional harm. In *Johnson v. Superior Court*, 101 Cal.App.4th 869 (2002), the defendants allegedly supplied defective sperm for artificial insemination knowing that the donor's family had a history of polycystic kidney disease likely to be inherited. Brittany, the child born of this arrangement, suffered the disease as a result. In her suit against these suppliers, the court held that she could not recover for emotional distress because this was essentially a wrongful life claim. Although California recognizes wrongful life claims, it does not permit damages award in those claims for emotional distress. The plaintiffs argued that defendant's *caused* the harm by supplying defective sperm; but the parents' only choice would be that the sperm would not be used, in which case Brittany would not have been born; that makes this a wrongful life claim, subject to the damages limit.

In *Grubbs v. Barbourville Family Health Center*, 120 S.W.3d 682 (Ky. 2003), the court held that parents and children do not have claims for wrongful life or wrongful birth against doctors who failed to diagnose a medical condition in the fetus in time for the mother to have an abortion. The court said, however, that the parents could sue for breach of contract if doctors failed to report the results of prenatal tests when they were under a contractual duty to do so.

Note 5. Emotional distress damages. See DOBBS ON TORTS § 292 (2000) for a summary of how the special emotional harm rules differ from ordinary negligent malpractice rules and for cases going both ways.

Notes 6 & 7. Damages. Damages issues in these cases are difficult, and we only scratch the surface in these Notes. The question of child-rearing costs is especially dicey. Does the Chaffee court's formulation, full child-rearing costs minus "benefits" of the child's birth, seem workable? Is a rule allowing for only "extraordinary" costs better? Or is it better still to not allow any damages on a theory that someone who has a healthy child is not, in fact, damaged at all (remember Chaffee addressed that position directly, and rejected it). See generally Michael A. Mogill, *Misconceptions of the Law: Providing Full Recovery for the Birth of an Unplanned Child*, 1996 UTAH L. REV. 827.

●Possible discussion agenda for § 2:

You could begin by getting the students to outline the types of claims that can be made in this setting – Wrongful Life (the child's claim), Wrongful Birth (the parents' claim), and Wrongful Conception (birth of an unwanted healthy child).

1. Invite discussion of each kind of claim. You can limit discussion by asking students to assume the constitutional given, namely that the mother has a right to terminate the pregnancy. This is probably not a good occasion for generating a whole abortion debate. Discussion might distinguish the three types of cases, then invite students to say whether all should be treated alike.

    a. *Wrongful birth vs. wrongful conception or pregnancy.* Some students who accept birth control but deplore abortion might be willing to accept the wrongful conception claim, which does not entail a claimed right of abortion.

    b. *The merits of the wrongful birth and wrongful conception claims.* In tort terms the question on the merits seems to be "why would you NOT impose liability" upon a negligent health care provider for harms caused by his negligence? The courts' answers in wrongful life cases have usually been satisfying enough. A court that denies relief in wrongful birth or wrongful conception cases must give some unusual answers. We see in *Chaffee* the court rejecting the notion that the harm in such cases is the birth of a healthy child – i.e, an argument that the birth of a healthy child is not a legally-cognizable injury. In fact, as the *Chaffee* court says, it is a terrible economic injury to a family that cannot afford to feed another person. Denial of relief in wrongful birth cases must be explained by even more extreme reasons or by confused assertions. The class can consider *Wilson v. Kuenzi* (**Note 3**) on this point.

    c. *Wrongful life.* Wrongful life claims have little support except that a few states have allowed the claim for all economic damages such as cost of support. Those states that allow wrongful life claims are mainly allocating the recovery for expenses from the parents' cause of action to the child's. Instead of the parents recovering the cost of support, the child recovers it. That automatically fixes the time period for computing damages at the child's lifetime. To allocate the claim to the child may also give the child some protection against parental dissipation of the recovery, since the recovery would be handled by a guardian or some other person with a degree of formal control.

2. Outline the main elements of damages and possible adjustments, without going into too much detail. Courts sometimes say explicitly that these are

medical malpractice claims to be decided under accepted principles of negligence law, e.g., *Hester v. Dwivedi,* 733 N.E.2d 1161 (Ohio 2000), but that is precisely what most courts do not do in limiting damages.

a. Should the mother recover for all costs of caring for the seriously damaged child, including medical and custodial costs? Or should the recovery be limited to costs that would exceed those of a normal child? This question embodies the question whether an "offset" should be allowed for the normal child-rearing costs. You might ask whether the student speaker would distinguish a wrongful birth claim from a wrongful conception claim.

b. Should the mother (and father?) recover for emotional suffering resulting from the birth of a seriously damaged child?

c. If emotional harm damages are recoverable, should the defendant get an offset equal to the emotional benefits of having the child? Might the answer be different for some students depending upon whether the claim was for wrongful birth or wrongful conception?

Note that even a general discussion of damages may require you to state the general rules about avoidable consequences ("mitigation of damages") and the direct benefits rule. On all these issues, *see* DOBBS ON TORTS § 293 (2000); 2 DAN DOBBS, REMEDIES § 8.2, p. 419-420 (1993).

CHAPTER 21

DEATH

▶**Changes in the Sixth Edition.** A new main case, *Weigel v. Lee* (N.D. 2008), substitutes for *Smith v. Whitaker* right up front. Notes have been streamlined in some instances, and updated with some new citations.

▶The **Concise Edition** makes no changes in this short Chapter.■

Preliminary Note. The common law no-duty or immunity rule in death cases has now been supplanted by two types of statutory actions. The basis of liability is now the usually same as in other cases – intent, negligence, or occasionally strict liability. Particular provisions in particular statutes may provide special protections or require more than negligence in special cases. See, e.g., *Monnin v. Fifth Third Bank of Miami Valley,* 658 N.E.2d 1140 (Ohio Ct. App. 1995) (reflecting a statute that limits liability of premises owner for wrongful death caused by third person). The point is not that there may be more oddball statutes in death cases, but that death cases are still subject to special remedial and procedural limitations and even to an arguably shameful allocation of damages among those who recover.

Scheduling omissions. The special place of death actions and the accompanying procedures are important in personal injury practice, but if you want to minimize coverage, you can lecture on this topic. Students probably should know the distinction between wrongful death and survival actions.

Governing law: State statutes, FELA, Jones Act, and maritime law. Wrongful death actions are governed almost exclusively by statutes, mostly statutes of the states. However, the Federal Employers Liability Act (FELA) and the Jones Act are among the few important federal statutes that create wrongful death liability in matters within the federal sphere. There is also a judge-made right to recover for wrongful death under general maritime law (the judge-made law under federal Admiralty jurisdiction). Statutes differ in their terms and provisions. This chapter does not pursue the differences, but it does show differences among statutes on three topics: (1) the treatment of survival vs. wrongful death claims; (2) wrongful death damages; and (3) allocation of wrongful death damages to survivors.

States usually have both a general wrongful death statute and a survival statute. In addition, states may enact special statutes creating death actions in special circumstances, as in the case of some Dram Shop statutes, for example. So lawyers must search for alternatives, but they are not discussed in this chapter.

INTRODUCTORY TEXT

If students can get the main point of the text that precedes the first case, everything else falls quickly into place. The point is to distinguish wrongful death actions from survival actions. The wrongful death statute creates a wholly new claim in favor of designated survivors, such as children, spouse, or parents, for their losses resulting from the decedent's death. The survival action merely continues whatever claim the decedent had at the moment of his death, such as his claim for pain and suffering and the damages are payable to the decedent's estate. The survival claim is not limited to harms that result in death but includes any tort claim that the decedent could have pursued during the decedent's lifetime. These points, and some specific examples of damages differences, can be made in parsing *Smith v. Whitaker* with your class.

WEIGEL V. LEE, 752 N.W.2d 618 (N.D. 2008)

Darlyne Rogers died just after being admitted to a regular hospital room despite being critically ill. Her adult children sued for loss of consortium and for their own emotional distress, claiming negligence (in not putting her in intensive care).

The trial court, in a series of rulings, held that the children's claims failed as a matter of law, and that they could bring only claims for Darlyne Rogers' own emotional distress she suffered before she died. *Held*, reversed.

In reversing, the court here distinguishes among three "distinct claims": (1) loss of consortium; (2) survival actions; and (3) wrongful death actions.

The latter two claims (our focus here) are statutory. The court quotes the North Dakota survival statute first, and points out that the plaintiffs did not seek recovery under that statute.

Next the court discusses the wrongful death statute, and quotes the main part of it in its entirety, distinguishing it from the survival action. The court's discussion is straightforward and you can walk the students through it by asking what the difference is between the two claims. **Note 1** draws out the distinction, when compared to **Note 9**.

Ultimately the court concludes here that plaintiffs do state a claim under the wrongful death statute, since they are entitled to sue, and persons entitled to recover.

Notes 2-8 deal with damages that may be recovered in a wrongful death case; *Weigel* only touches briefly on this issue. Under most statutes, wrongful death damages are measured by pecuniary contributions the decedent would have made to the survivors.

These notes summarize the two main measures of pecuniary loss – the only loss that counts under traditional statutes – and reflect the difficulties with both measures, especially in the case of non-earning decedents (**Note 6**). Students may need concrete examples to see why each measure might yield zero damages for negligently killing someone or alternatively might overcompensate for financial loss. Apart from specially provided-for items like funeral expenses, the loss of survivors measure will yield a zero award in the case of any decedent who has no dependents. The loss to the estate award will yield a zero award for any non-earner such as a retired person. It might also yield a zero award for any earner who spends all his earnings in playing the horses unless the courts literally mean that the estate recovers all his earnings with a subtraction only for his *own* support rather than for his own normal expenditures. In that case, however, his estate would be overcompensated.

The two basic measures are different but not complementary; even taken together they may leave inadequate compensation in the case of non-earning decedents.

For a case rejecting a claim for loss of inheritance to be added to loss of support, see *Pfau v. Comair Holdings, Inc.*, 15 P.3d 1160 (Idaho 2000). On the combination of the two measures *see* James T. Tucker, Annotation, *Wrongful Death Damages For Loss of Expectancy of Inheritance From Decedent*, 42 A.L.R.5th 465 (1996); DAN B. DOBBS, THE LAW OF REMEDIES § 8.3 (4) (1993); DOBBS ON TORTS § 296 (2000).

Derogation of Common Law

Courts have developed a series of seemingly contradictory maxims of statutory construction. One pair is that statutes in derogation of common law must be construed narrowly or strictly, but that statutes that are remedial must be construed liberally. Remedial here is not a technical distinction between right and remedy, only a reference to a perceived correction of a common law defect. Many courts have said that death statutes are in derogation of common law and to be strictly construed, but some have taken the opposite maxim and said they are remedial, deserving of liberal construction. Perhaps the choice seldom matters directly. These maxims are usually used in argument as part of the softening up process, intended to create an attitude rather than to insert a logical or policy proposition. Strict construction: *see, e.g., Estate of Kronemeyer v. Meinig,* 948 P.2d 119 (Colo. Ct. App. 1997); liberal construction: e.g., *Beck v. Groe,* 70 N.W.2d 886 (Minn. 1955). Outside the constraints of dueling maxims, a few cases take the view that common law in America (not England) once allowed a wrongful death action. This proposition then becomes the basis for flexible, liberal, or equitable interpretation of the death statute. See *LaFage v. Jani,* 766 A.2d 1066 (N.J. 2001).

Note 7. Non-pecuniary claims generally. Given the inadequacies of both measures of pecuniary loss, emotional harm damages for survivors would be a seemingly appropriate addition. Some statutes do permit that item of recovery, but that is not the case with traditional death statutes. However, statutes now often permit loss of consortium or guidance recoveries, although courts stress that this does not include emotional distress.

Note 8. Future losses. All death action losses necessarily require an estimate about what the decedent would have earned, contributed, or saved in the future—sometimes 40 years after the death. (This is also true with permanent injury cases.) You might pause long enough to notice this point, for it may trouble students much later when we get to damages in Chapter 26. However, there is no need to consider technical problems of calculating taxes, inflation, and discount to present value –those are merely problems that show how much we must rely upon estimates.

Notes 9-13 focus on survival cases, as opposed to wrongful death cases. A survivor claim is one that belongs to the decedent's estate, as explained in **Note 9.** Survival statutes may provide for the continuation of a plaintiff's claim after the plaintiff's death (**Note 10**), or may provide for the survival of a claim against a defendant's estate after the death of the defendant (**Note 11**).

Note 12. Survival damages. Under survival statutes, the claim is merely for the losses suffered by the decedent himself between injury and death. Statutes control. The action survives only when the statute so provides. Under some statutes, the claim for pain and suffering does not survive. Under others, particular actions such as a claim for loss of consortium or alienation of affections may not survive while a claim for emotional distress might. Note that the claim here is definitely for the pain or anguish suffered by the decedent himself, not the anguish of survivors. If death is instantaneous, there can be no recovery for pain even if the state otherwise allows pain as an element of damages. *Long v. Broadlawns Medical Ctr.*, 656 N.W.2d 71 (Iowa 2002).

CHAVEZ V. CARPENTER, 111 Cal.Rptr.2d 534 (Ct. App. 2001).

The full facts are complicated, which is why the case got litigated in the first place. Altie Chavez was killed by a drunk driver. Altie was not married. Altie had a two-year old daughter who died the following month. Altie lived with his parents, and contributed to their support. Altie's parents sued the defendant for Altie's death, and the daughter's mother (Maria Garcia) also sued. The California statute allows a suit by "heirs." The parents cannot sue here as heirs because Altie's daughter was an heir who survived him. But the statute also authorizes suit by "dependents," and fact questions remain about whether they were their son's "dependents." The daughter had a cause of action under the statute, and that cause of action survives her death and may be pursued by her estate. The operative California statute, Civ. Proc. Code § 377.60, reads as follows:

> A cause of action for the death of a person caused by the wrongful act or neglect of another may be asserted by any of the following persons or by the decedent's personal representative on their behalf:
>
> (a) The decedent's surviving spouse, children, and issue of deceased children, or, if there is no surviving issue of the decedent, the persons, including the surviving spouse, who would be entitled to the property of the decedent by intestate succession.
>
> (b) Whether or not qualified under subdivision (a), if they were dependent on the decedent, the putative spouse, children of the putative spouse, stepchildren, or parents. As used in this subdivision, "putative spouse" means the surviving spouse of a void or voidable marriage who is found by the court to have believed in good faith that the marriage to the decedent was valid.
>
> (c) A minor, whether or not qualified under subdivision (a) or (b), if, at the time of the decedent's death, the minor resided for the previous 180 days in the decedent's household and was dependent on the decedent for one-half or more of the minor's support.

Distribution of recovery. *Chavez* and its notes introduce a few of the problems in distribution of the death act recovery. Most statutes designate classes of beneficiaries, such as children, parents, heirs or the like; sometimes there is a preferred class, then a second class that can share if there are no members of the first class. Although damages are usually calculated by determining the support lost, the statutory beneficiaries may not be the persons who lost the support.

For example, suppose that the statute designates "child or children, if any" as the sole beneficiaries, then parents if there are no children. Decedent, aged 50, has two grown, self-sufficient children, but she supports her 75-year-old mother. It is plain that the financial loss resulting from decedent's death will be borne by the mother, not the children, but it is also plain that the statute gives the award to the children.

To complicate a set of laws already thoroughly botched, the person who is authorized to bring the death action may not be either the person who was dependent upon the decedent or the person who will take the award. In *Goodleft v. Gullickson,* 556 N.W.2d 303 (N.D. 1996) the decedent was a five-year-old child. His grandmother sued for his death, but both parents were living and the statute authorized suit only by parents. The court rejected the grandmother's argument "that she was entitled to bring this wrongful death claim because she was Dustin's 'psychological' or 'de facto' mother. It is generally held, notwithstanding the care and support of a child, a person standing in loco parentis is not a child's father or mother for purposes of a wrongful death action."

Most of the statutes' failures to distribute the proceeds rationally seem to result from conceptual failures, some from drafting failures, and some from outright fear that allowing recovery by those who are actually dependent upon the decedent might bring on suits by lovers and other disfavored persons. For whatever reason, the legislatures' general failure to provide a rational scheme of distribution creates both injustice and misery. Sometimes courts find a way out themselves. For example, in *Shelton v. DeWitte*, 2 P.3d 650 (Kan. 2001), both mother and fetus were killed. The father, normally the sole heir, was unknown. Rather than giving no one at all the right to sue for recovery, the majority of the court held that the grandparents could sue since there was no means of identifying the "heir."

Note 3. Claims by non-custodial parents for a child's death. Divorce of the parents of a decedent is not the only divorce. The statutes often divorce the measure and purpose of damages from their distribution. If you measure damages by loss of support or consortium, why would you not distributed damages where the loss falls? Neither the half-and-half approach in *Sindelar* nor the award entirely to one parent in *Carter* will always approximate the losses.

Note 4. Stepchildren. Statutes that fail to include "stepchildren" in the definition of "children" seem mistaken to us. It is true that the decedent's step child, unless adopted, has no legal right to inheritance. But she might be receiving support as a member of the reconstituted family. In a jurisdiction that measures damages by lost support, why write a statute like the *Klossner* statute that excludes her because she does not fit any of the categories, even the category of "child"? This seems to be either a conceptual or a drafting failure. But maldistribution along these lines is not at all uncommon. Accord, *Brown v. Brown,* 309 S.E.2d 586 (Va. 1983).

Steed v. Imperial Airlines, cited here, reached a similar result. The statute applied in *Chavez,* supra, and quoted in this manual in the discussion of the case, was then adopted to address some specific instances of perceived maldistribution.

The problem in these cases sometimes is only that someone's loss won't be counted and that someone will not recover. But in many of them the problem is worse. It is that *A* will suffer the loss but that *B* will recover it.

Claims by illegitimate children. Some states once denied illegitimate children any recovery for death of a parent. The Supreme Court, however, held this practice to be a violation of the Equal Protection Clause of the 14th Amendment in *Levy v. Louisiana,* 391 U.S. 68 (1968). Why is it that the illegitimate child may recover but the stepchild cannot?

Claims by parents of illegitimate children. In *Glona v. American Guarantee & Liability Insurance Co.,* 391 U.S. 73 (1968), the Supreme Court held similarly that it was a denial of equal protection for a state to exclude parents of an illegitimate child from a death action recovery. However, states may limit the recovery to the mother and exclude the father. *Parham v. Hughes,* 441 U.S. 347 (1979).

Note 5. Unmarried cohabitants. The Vermont Civil Union statute (and Vermont may go further on this issue in the future) seems to permit recovery by the survivor of a civil union analogous to a marriage. This parallels the issue of consortium and bystander emotional distress we covered in Chapter 19. CAL. CIV. CODE § 1714.01 permits emotional distress claims brought by domestic partners, but says nothing of wrongful death or loss of consortium. In *Surette v. Islamic Republic of Iran,* 231 F.Supp.2d 260 (D.D.C. 2002), one of the Iran-sponsored hostage torture and death cases, the court held, as a matter of federal common law, that a long-time companion of the torture victim could recover "solatium," said to be "for mental anguish resulting from the loss of a decedent's society and companionship" upon his death by torture.

Damages for death under workers' compensation and dram shop statutes may sometimes be distributed differently. In *Soto v. Montanez,* 578 N.Y.S.2d 758 (App. Div. 1991), a former wife was entitled to nothing from the decedent in his lifetime, but he was making contributions to her anyway. That was the first miracle. In an action for the husband' death, the court held that upon proper evidence, the former wife could recover in a wrongful death action under a dram shop statute. That was the second miracle.

Note 7. Jury awards. Should we try to fix the maldistribution problems? Perhaps by allowing recovery by any person who loses reasonably probable support from the decedent? What should we do about the maldistribution reflected in discriminatory awards? Notice how the discrimination reported in this note works: women survivors of male decedents get more in damages. Nice if you can get it, but maybe the implication is that males are worth more. Is it possible that these discriminatory awards merely reflect the jury's awareness that women survivors will often have a cruelly hard time in the work place and will often not command a wage that male survivors would get? If the class thinks these awards are discriminatory in fact, what should be done?

NOTE: DEFENSES

1. *Decedent's contributory negligence or assumed risk.* Wrongful death statutes give at least two contradictory signals. First, they are and purport to be new causes of action for the survivors. But second, they give no claim to survivors unless the decedent himself could have sued had he lived. This rule sounds as if the wrongful death action is somehow derivative, so that the plaintiff would fail if for any reason the decedent himself would have failed had he sued. That is the rule usually applied, so the decedent's negligence reduces the beneficiaries' damages or, even the decedent's negligence is great enough in a modified comparative fault jurisdiction, it bars the claim. *See* DOBBS ON TORTS § 299.

Some people argue that the decedent's contributory negligence should be irrelevant because the wrongful death action is "new and independent." If you like this idea, you might have a hard time implementing it under the statutes abolishing joint and several liability, because under those statutes each defendant is liable only for his fault-share. In any event, comparative fault may make the whole thing easier, since the decedent's fault would not always bar the survivor's recovery. And whatever exceptions still allow a complete recovery without regard to the plaintiff's contributory fault would also allow such a recovery in the death action. The *Bexiga* duty to protect the decedent from his own fault would be an example.

2. *Beneficiary's contributory negligence or assumed risk.* In a survival action, the fault of some party who will share in the estate does not appear relevant as contributory fault; the question is what claim the decedent had at the moment of death and if the decedent was not at fault, his claim is good. However, the fault of some party who might share in the estate might be relevant in two other ways. First he might be liable as a joint tortfeasor, and hence liable for contribution if the defendant pays more than his equitable share of liability. Second, under statutes abolishing joint and several liability, the fault of the person sharing in the estate might be considered in determining the appropriate fault-share of the defendant.

However, the beneficiary might still avoid losing her comparative fault share of the survival action proceeds if she was immune from liability to the decedent. In *Shoemake v. Fogel,* 826 S.W.2d 933 (Tex. 1992), a small child drowned due to the negligence of both the defendant and the child's mother. The jury charged the defendant with 55% of the fault, the plaintiff-mother 45% of the fault. In the wrongful death action, the mother's fault reduced her recovery. The defendant claimed the same result should be obtained in the survival action because it was entitled to contribution from the mother. That argument did not work because the mother had parental immunity as to supervision of the child. The child could not have recovered from the mother and hence the defendant could not get contribution under the rule requiring joint liability to support contribution.

3, 4 & 5. *Statutes of limitations.* Wrongful death statutes may be more precise than others by specifying that the statute runs from the time of death. This may be construed to give the court none of the usual options. For example, in *Moreno v. Sterling Drug, Inc.*, 787 S.W.2d 348 (Tex. 1990) the court concluded that the legislature, in saying that the cause of action accrued at death, meant just what it said and therefore that the discovery doctrine could not apply. (The plaintiff's there knew of the fact of death when it occurred, but not until later did they learn that the defendant's product might have had causal significance in that death.) Later, in *Russell v. Ingersoll-Rand Company*, 841 S.W.2d 343 (Tex. 1992), cited in the casebook, the Texas court held that the wrongful death claim was "derivative" and barred if the personal injury claim from which it was derived would have been barred by the statute of limitations (or any other defense). The death action was brought in a matter of weeks after death, but it will still too late because had the deceased himself been alive and sued on the same date, he would have been barred by the statute. In accord, *Weinberg v. Johns-Manville Sales Corp.*, 473 A.2d 22 (Md. 1984) (New York law).

Some courts are convinced that there was a common law wrongful death action. If that is true, the time limitation prescribed in the statute for bringing a death action is not a "condition precedent" or "substantive" limitation but a true statute of limitations. As such, it can be construed with provisions of the statutes of limitation for personal injury, which in turn means courts could import tolling and other provisions into the death statute. That is what happened in *LaFage v. Jani*, 766 A.2d 1066 (N.J. 2001) (tolling for minority). But even if there was a common law death action, decisions like *LaFage* do not resurrect it; as the casebook text says, the actions today are entirely statutory apart from the small Admiralty exception.

If a court takes the view that expiration of the statute of limitations during the decedent's lifetime is not bar to a death suit, would it be required, as a matter of logic, to hold that the decedent's contributory negligence is no bar to the death claim? And that settlement of the claim by the decedent during his lifetime is not bar? The common premise is that the wrongful death suit is independent of the decedent's rights.

6. *Damages caps.* In *Jenkins v. Patel*, cited here, the court held that the medical malpractice damages cap applied in a wrongful death case where the

underlying claim was one for medical malpractice. Two judges dissented, arguing that the majority's opinion is at odds with the plain language of the wrongful death statute, which is the "exclusive remedy" in wrongful death cases and mentions nothing at all about caps being imported from any other statutes. *Bartholomew*, also cited, goes the other way (that is, with the dissenters in *Jenkins*), based on the Wisconsin statute.

PART 4

THE EBB AND FLOW OF COMMON LAW STRICT LIABILITY FOR PHYSICAL HARMS

CHAPTER 22

VICARIOUS LIABILITY

▶**Changes in the Sixth Edition.** We have added one new main case, *Puckrein*, in § 2, on selecting an incompetent independent contractor; new and reorganized Notes on that subject (and the primary liability of an employer generally) appear after the case. We have also added a number of new case discussions or cites, including many citations to the newest Restatement (Third) of Agency, in Notes to fully update the Chapter. To make room for these new materials, and to cut the length by about 10 percent, we've cut two main cases (*Kastner* and *Otero*) and two case abstracts (*Jackson* and *Fletcher*) in § 2. The issues addressed by the omitted cases are described and discussed in text and Notes. We have reorganized the materials in § 2 to flow logically given the changes.

▶This Concise Edition Chapter is six pages (just over 15%) shorter than the standard edition. Cuts are modest; most notably *Faul v. Jelco* and *Ahlstrom v. Salt Lake City Corp.*, both case abstracts in § 1, and the substitution of short textual material for all of § 3 (other forms of vicarious liability). We have also edited *Edgewater Hotels v. Gatzke*, although nothing substantive is lost, and we've cut some Note materials after the *Rodebush* and *Fahrendorff* cases.■

Scheduling omissions. This chapter gives a compact coverage of major issues in vicarious liability and also introduces some ideas associated with enterprise (strict) liability. Consequently, it is difficult to find substantial omissions. (1) You might omit *Lisa M.* and perhaps some of the accompanying notes if you are pressed for time or just can't stand any more trashy sex cases. But be aware that *Lisa M.* is a decision of a major court on a major problem for women and also an a doorway to good discussions about fundamental reasons for vicarious liability; (2) You can omit *O'Banner* on apparent authority/estoppel and give a brief lecture instead; (3) You can omit *Puckrein* if you discuss the possibility that the employer should be liable for hiring incompetent or insolvent contractors, leaving out the technical, nondelegable duty and collateral negligence issue. (4) You might omit discussion of § 3 or selective portions of that section on other forms of vicarious liability. But be aware that the concept of concerted action will arise again and the little introduction to the point in ¶¶ 3 & 4 of the text is useful groundwork.

Preliminary Note:

In Chapter 18, defendants were sometimes held liable for harms done to the plaintiff by other people. The liability of defendants there was not vicarious, however. It was instead based upon the defendant's own fault in failing to protect the plaintiff when there was some special duty to do so. In the present chapter, we resume exploration of liability for the acts of others, but responsibility here is not based on the defendant's fault, except in the narrow instance of hiring incompetent independent contractors (raised by *Puckrein* and its Notes).

This Chapter, then, is an introduction to strict liability – because the liability of the employer is strict, with the single exception noted above. The Chapter also connects forward to the strict liability concerns of Chapters 23 and 24. The three chapters together present the great bulk of common law strict liability in tort, although products liability is not *entirely* strict. These chapters present an opportunity to delineate and discuss the somewhat different rationales of strict liability as well. For this reason, they are well considered as a unit, in spite of the diverse nature of some of the materials. Strict liability is of course common in alternative compensation systems, as well (Chapters 28-30) but that is arguably a different story.

OUTLINE

§ 1. RESPONDEAT SUPERIOR AND SCOPE OF EMPLOYMENT
[a] Introduction and Rationales for Vicarious Liability. Riviello v. Waldron; Fruit v. Schreiner; Note: Enterprise Liability

[b] What is a "master," and what is a "servant?" Note: Serving Two Masters; Note: Serving Gratuitously;

[c] Scope of employment: the going and coming rule. Hinman v. Westinghouse Electric Co.; Faul v. Jelco, Inc.; Ahlstrom v. Salt Lake City Corp.

[d] Scope of employment: "arising out of employment." Edgewater Motels, Inc. v. Gatzke

[e] Scope of employment: intentional acts by those in positions of trust or authority. Lisa M. v. Henry Mayo Newhall Memorial Hospital; Rodebush v. Oklahoma Nursing Homes, Ltd.; Fahrendorff v. North Homes, Inc.

§ 2. EMPLOYERS WHO ARE NOT MASTERS
[a] Basic independent contractor rule. District of Columbia v. Hampton
[b] Nondelegable duties. Pusey v. Bator
[c] Apparent agency. O'Banner v. McDonald's Corp.
[d] Primary negligence; hiring incompetent contractors. Puckrin v. ATI Transport, Inc.

§ 3. OTHER FORMS OF VICARIOUS RESPONSIBILITY

SUMMARY

§ 1. RESPONDEAT SUPERIOR AND SCOPE OF EMPLOYMENT

[a] Introduction and Rationales for Vicarious Liability

RIVIELLO V. WALDRON; FRUIT V. SCHREINER; NOTE: ENTERPRISE LIABILITY. Why is the employer liable for the torts of the employee? Cases and text suggest these possible reasons: (1) employers might reduce accidents if liable. (2) it is desirable to spread the costs of injury to the community and this can be done by holding the employer liable, who in turn will pass it to the community in the form of higher prices). (3) The employer has "control" of the employee and so should be liable for his torts. (4) If the employer's work is being done it is fair, *semble*, that the employer be liable for the torts. (5) The employee may not have assets and the employer is more likely able to pay. (6) Inevitable losses caused by a business are properly considered expenses of the business and should be charged to it; in turn, it can increase the price of its product.

[b] What is a "master" and what is a "servant?"

NOTE: SERVING TWO MASTERS. At times, it is not clear which "master" is responsible for the "servant's" torts. This Note deals with three such cases, briefly: (1) Borrowed servants (a servant who is loaned from one master to another, a common practice in the building trade); (2) the "captain of the ship" doctrine (common in medical practice); and (3) the "police officer" problem (as when a police officer moonlights as a security guard).

NOTE: SERVING GRATUITOUSLY. Is a person a "servant" if working without pay, or having volunteered to perform a task outside normal job functions? Yes is the answer, as long as the "servant" submits himself or herself to the employer's control.

[c] Scope of employment; the going and coming rule

HINMAN V. WESTINGHOUSE ELEC. CO. A construction worker, Herman, was returning home from a job site when he struck the plaintiff. The plaintiff sued Herman's employer, Westinghouse. Westinghouse had paid Herman for travel time and provided some expenses as well. The trial court refused to charge the jury that Herman was within the scope of his employment, but instead told the jury that whether he was depended upon a number of factors. The jury found Herman to be negligent, but nevertheless returned a verdict for Westinghouse. *Held*, it was error to refuse the charge that Herman was within the scope of his employment as a matter of law. Under the going and coming rule, the employee was not acting within the scope of his employment in going to work or coming home. But here there was a substantial benefit to the employer to reach out into other labor markets, a fact reflected by the extra pay. This increases the risk incident to travel. Where the employer has made travel time part of the working day by paying for it, he is liable for the employee's torts during that travel.

FAUL V. JELCO, INC. A construction worker caused an injury while traveling home from the construction site on a weekend. There was no separate compensation for travel, but he was paid "zone pay, an increased hourly wage" because he was working away from home. Held, summary judgment for the defendant affirmed. Although there is an exception to the going and coming rule where there are special hazards, distance alone is not such a hazard. There is also an exception where the employee is performing an employment service while commuting, but this had no application here. The ability of the employer to reach out into other labor markets is not an employment service.

AHLSTROM V. SALT LAKE CITY CORP. Ross, a police officer, driving a marked police vehicle, was in a collision on her way home. She had a right to use the car because she had paid a small fee and agreed to be on call while she had the car. *Held,* the plaintiff is not entitled to a partial summary judgment against the employer. The going and coming rule applies because the city derive insufficient benefit and exercised insufficient control. There was no dual purpose because there was no evidence that the city would have sent anyone else had Ross not gone.

[d] Scope of employment: "arising out of employment"

EDGEWATER MOTELS, INC. V. GATZKE. An employee of Walgreen's living away from home while supervising the opening of a new restaurant, worked late, drank, went to his room and worked on an expense account part of the time. He smoked, fell asleep and set fire to the motel. The motel sues the employer. Held, the trier could find he was within the scope of his employment so that the employer would be liable. Although part of his purposes were personal, there was some employer benefit and there was enough employment relation to justify a finding that he was within the scope of employment.

[e] Scope of employment: intentional acts by those in positions of trust or authority

LISA M. V. HENRY MAYO NEWHALL MEMORIAL HOSPITAL. The pregnant plaintiff fell. She sought treatment in the defendant's emergency room. Tripoli, the technician, purporting to administer ultrasound tests, used the occasion to sexually fondle her, actually inserting the ultrasound wand and his finger into her vagina. She sued the hospital. (1) Vicarious responsibility is no longer limited to cases in which the employee is motivated to serve the employer. (2) But vicarious liability is not acceptable where the act is based on personal malice not engendered by the employment itself. Liability is limited to injuries that are "sure" or likely to occur in the employment. (3) Although sex crimes can be within the scope of employment, they are not so unless something in the employment triggers them. Specifically, nothing in the employment put Tripoli in a position of special power or special trust. Here, there was only "propinquity and lust," so the employee was not within the scope of his employment and the employer hospital not vicariously liable. (4) Policy goals support this analysis. Prevention of future harm, compensation, and risk spreading do not suggest liability. Spreading the loss to the beneficiaries of the enterprise is justified only if the act is closely related to the enterprise itself.

RODEBUSH V. OKLAHOMA NURSING HOMES, LTD. A drunken nurse's aide (with a criminal record) slapped an Alzheimer's patient who lived at defendant's long-term facility. Vicarious liability was imposed because the act was incident to the business, done while the aide was engaged in that business, and arose from "some impulse of emotion which naturally grew out of or was incident to the attempt to perform" that business.

FAHRENDORFF V. NORTH HOMES, INC. A counselor in a group home made sexual advances towards the plaintiff. Vicarious liability was a jury question because this kind of activity is a "well-known hazard" of this kind of enterprise.

§ 2. EMPLOYERS WHO ARE NOT MASTERS

[a] Basic independent contractor rule

DISTRICT OF COLUMBIA V. HAMPTON. The District of Columbia's Department of Human Services (DHS) removed two-year old Mykeeda Hampton from her mother and placed her in foster care. The foster mother left Mykeeda with her two sons for over ten hours, during which time Mykeeda was beaten to death by the 12-year-old son. Mykeeda's mother sued DHS, alleging among other things that the foster mother was its agent or employee. The trial court allowed the respondeat superior claim to go to the jury, which found for the plaintiff. *Held*, reversed for entry of judgment N.O.V. No reasonable juror could have concluded that the foster mother was the DHS's agent. Of the many factors to be considered in making such a judgment, the most important is "the right to control an employee in the performance of a task and in its result." Here, there was no evidence suggesting that DHS had a right to control the foster mother's daily performance of her duties. That DHS has the authority to dictate many aspects of a child's life while in foster care does not establish that the foster parent is under the DHS's actual control to a degree sufficient to impose vicarious liability.

[b] Nondelegable duties

PUSEY V. BATOR. Bator was employed by Youngstown Security Patrol (YSP). YSP contracted to provide guards at the Greif Brothers property. Bator was the guard provided. In an incident on the Greif property, Bator shot and killed a trespasser, Pusey. The plaintiff here filed a wrongful death and survival action against Bator, YSP and Greif Brothers. The trial judge directed a verdict for Greit and the Court of Appeals affirmed. *Held*, reversed. Employers of independent contractors, normally not liable for the torts of those contractors, are nevertheless liable if they have a nondelegable duty of care. Such a duty exists when the work is inherently dangerous because it creates a peculiar risk to others. "The work must create a risk that is not a normal, routine matter of customary human activity, such as driving an automobile, but is rather a special danger to those in the vicinity arising out of the particular situation created, and calling for special precautions. . . ." That is the case here.

[c] Apparent agency

O'BANNER V. MCDONALD'S CORP. O'Banner slipped and fell in the bathroom of a McDonald's restaurant. He sued McDonald's Corp., the franchisor, which defended on the ground that the restaurant was actually owned by its franchisor and that it did not operate, maintain or control the restaurant. The court affirmed summary judgment for McDonald's, holding that the appeals court erred in reversing on the ground that fact questions remained on the issue of apparent agency. Apparent agency or apparent authority is based on principles of estoppel. If a principal creates the appearance that someone is his agent, and a third party reasonably relies on that apparent agency and is injured as a result, the principal cannot deny the agency relationship. Here, there was no evidence suggesting that O'Banner relied on the apparent agency in going to the restaurant. It might have been irrelevant to him that this was a McDonald's restaurant.

[d] Hiring incompetent independent contractors; the employer's primary negligence

PUCKREIN V. ATI TRANSPORT, INC. Another exception to the usual rule that an employer is not liable for the torts of an independent contractor is when the employer hires an incompetent contractor. Here, the defendant hired a contractor knowing that the contractor lacked the necessary license and insurance to perform the job legally. Note that this is not an instance of vicarious liability at all, but rather of the employer's primary negligence. Where the negligent hiring is an actual and proximate cause of the plaintiff's injury, the defendant will be liable, just as in any other negligence case.

§ 3. OTHER FORMS OF VICARIOUS RESPONSIBILITY

This note summarizes a number of other instances in which one person is held liable for the acts of another, including some cases in which the defendant is himself partly at fault. The situations summarized include partnership, joint enterprise, negligent hiring, negligent entrustment, owner-in-the-car, owner-consent statutes, family purpose doctrine, imputed negligence and imputed contributory negligence.

COMMENTS

§ 1. RESPONDEAT SUPERIOR AND SCOPE OF EMPLOYMENT

RIVIELLO V. WALDRON, 391 N.E. 2d 1278 (N.Y. 1979)
FRUIT V. SCHREINER, 502 P.2d 133 (Alaska 1972)
NOTE: ENTERPRISE LIABILITY

The employer is generally liable for the torts of the "servant" committed in the scope of the servant's employment. This liability is based on fault of the servant, not on the fault of the employer. Thus the liability is strict liability at least in some important sense.

Why is strict liability visited upon the employer? The question would not be difficult or interesting if the employer's liability were limited to cases in which the servant follows exact instructions. If the employer tells the employee to drive fast, it is easy to feel the employer is negligent for simply doing through another what he might do himself. *See South Carolina Ins. Co. v. Greene*, 348 S.E.2d 617 (S.C. 1986) ("Although the tortious act was that of the servant, liability was imposed on the master on the principle 'qui facit per alium facit per se' [he who acts through another acts himself]. This maxim applied only where the tortious act had been commanded by the master; it did not apply to the case of negligence, since the master does not ordinarily direct his servant to be negligent"). But why is the employer liable when he is not negligent, when the employee, though instructed to be careful, drives negligently, or even engages in an intentional tort?

The answers are important because they effect how we will deal with other issues of strict liability and how we evaluate this kind of liability. They are also important because they will have an impact on courts in deciding how far to take this vicarious liability.

On the other hand, the answers don't have to be perfectly developed at this point or even in this chapter; the ideas behind strict liability will haunt us in the two succeeding chapters, and there will be much opportunity to develop them further. The class can consider:

(1) **Control.** As *Riviello* indicates, vicarious liability was early justified on the ground that the employer is in "control" of the employee. Control correlates closely with the *qui facit* idea that the employer is acting through another much as a puppet master controls the puppets. But this obviously explains only a few cases in spite of the fact that courts commonly repeat "control" formulas. *See, e.g., Anderson v. Eichner,* 890 P.2d 1329 (Okla. 1994) ("Qui facit per alium facit per se" . . . . This rule rests on the premise that, when exercising delegated authority, the employee stands under the complete control of the employer.").

(2) **Assuring compensation.** The *Lisa M* paraphrase in the introductory note offers assurance of compensation as one goal of vicarious liability. Certainly that is a *goal,* but it is hardly a *justification,* is it?

(3) **Prevention of future injuries.** This justification for vicarious liability (also stated in *Lisa M*) needs some elaboration if it is not to be subject to the same problems as the "assuring compensation" reasoning. The prevention justification is a deterrence argument. But we don't want to deter all activities that produce injuries. (If we did, we'd prohibit the use of automobiles, drugs, and even swimming pools.) This is the point of *Carroll Towing* or the risk-utility weighing. Calabresi argues (**Note: Enterprise Liability**) that holding an enterprise strictly liable for the harms it causes reduces the costs of accidents and the costs of accident avoidance. Because consumers favor cheaper products, if products reflect true accident costs, the safer products will be favored over the more dangerous. This gives companies an incentive to make their products safer in order to more effectively compete. The same is true for services offered to the public for a price. If the price a business charges for its products or services truly reflects the costs of accidents caused by the employees of the business, then consumers will use this information to choose to patronize the safer businesses. Strict liability accomplishes this result more effectively than fault-based schemes. Would this reasoning support strict liability regardless of *employee* fault?

(4) **Distributing losses.** The last ground suggested in *Lisa M* is distribution of losses. One practical good of this is that no one pays an overwhelming loss. But is it morally justified to force those who buy the business' products to pay higher prices for products in order to "distribute" the losses?

What does *Fruit* mean in suggesting that the compensation costs will be absorbed by those benefitted by the enterprise"? If costs are indeed absorbed by those benefitted, the idea might be transmuted from a practical notion that no one will have to pay too much into a claim that in justice risks of the enterprise should be absorbed by those who benefit. On this ground, *Fruit's* arguments become a kind of statistical version of the arguments we began in *Vincent*. If you get the benefits of imposing a risk, in justice you should also pay the costs; you take the sour with the sweet; you have to internalize your costs, not thrust them upon others. What costs are "yours," though, and what costs "belong" to others? In *Richard v. Hall*, 874 So.2d 131, 137-138 (La. 2004), the court said: "In determining whether a particular accident may be associated with the employer's business enterprise, the court must essentially decide whether the particular accident is a part of the more or less inevitable toll of a lawful enterprise."

Note 1. That the employer is vicariously liable does not mean that the employee somehow escapes legal liability. As noted here, the employer rarely enforces the right to collect from the employee. The usual "sanction" against the employee is probably being fired.

FYI, corporate officers as employees of the corporation are generally subject to the rule that employees are liable for their own tortious behavior and that which they authorize or in which they participate with others. Although victims seldom attempt to collect from the employee-tortfeasor, there may be some small potential for actually enforcing judgments against the employee who, as a corporate officer, authorizes or participates in the "corporate" tort. See *State ex rel. The Doe Run Resources Corp. v. Neill*, 128 S.W.3d 502 (Mo. 2004) ("An individual is not protected from liability simply because the acts constituting the tort 'were done in the scope and course, and pertained to, the duties of his employment'"); *Saltiel v. GSI Consultants, Inc.*, 788 A.2d 268 (N.J. 2002) (recognizing that a corporate officer who "takes part in the commission of a tort by the corporation" will be held liable, although he is not liable (i) for the torts of other officers or employees nor for (ii) the corporation's breach of contract). Since negligent infliction of pure economic loss without physical or emotional harms is seldom actionable in tort, the plaintiff will often have only a contract claim for pure economic injury. The rule that the officer is not liable for his participation in the corporation's breach of contract will also mean that he may often escape liability for infliction of pure economic loss. *See Greg Allen Construction Co. v. Estelle*, 798 N.E.2d 171 (Ind. 2003). On the other hand, if a corporate officer authorizes illegal dumping of toxic wastes that cause harm, it looks as if she should be personally liable along with the corporation itself.

NOTE: SERVING TWO MASTERS

¶ 1. *Borrowed servants.* In *Kastner v. Toombs*, cited here, defendants leased a backhoe to Clearwater for digging a pipe ditch. The lease called for defendants to furnish both the backhoe and its operator, who in turn worked under direction of Clearwater. Following Clearwater's directions, the defendant's backhoe operator dug a dangerously deep ditch, which caved in and injured Kastner, who was employed by Clearwater. The trial court gave summary judgment for the defendants on the ground that they were not liable for any negligence of the backhoe operator while he was working under Clearwater's directions. The Alaska court reversed and remanded, rejecting the traditional rule. Traditionally courts decide which of two "masters" is vicariously liable by emphasizing the right of control, but the court found this an ambiguous test since general control is in the general employer, while on the spot control is in the special employer. Since the servant is acting within the scope of employment of both masters, both should be liable; principles of contribution and indemnity can adjust the loss between the two masters.

Although the *Kastner* case makes good sense on its facts, it is not the usual way of resolving this problem, as the Note makes clear. It is usually said that the servant remains in the general employment even after he is loaned out, subject to the possibility that evidence will somehow lead to a different conclusion. This sounds more like a rule than it is. It has led to interminable discussions of the right of control, which of course often rests with both the general and the special employer. For example, in *Jones v. James Reeves Contractors, Inc.*, also cited here, a plumbing and heating contractor (McCaskill) arranged to have another company (Contractors) supply a backhoe and an operator (Reeves) to excavate a large hole. During this dig, the walls caved in, killing three of McCaskill's employees. The court held that Reeves remained an employee of Contractors, since no implied or express contract existed between Reeves and McCaskill (the borrowing employer) which would "transform the relationship into a master servant relationship," and because the instructions that McCaskill gave Reeves "were in the nature of cooperation and not subordination," thus "not evidencing the kind of control needed" to make McCaskill vicariously liable.

¶2. *Captain of the ship.* The captain of the ship doctrine is a special case of the borrowed servant problem. A nurse or other person employed by the hospital assists in some way in the operating room. The nurse is negligent and the patient is injured. Since the doctor in charge of the operation can give specific orders to the nurse during the operation and is thus in "control" in the sense used in agency law, it is possible to think of the nurse as a hospital employee who has been loaned to the doctor. The doctor is then the special employer, and given this high degree of "control," could be held liable. A few courts have imposed vicarious liability on the doctor in situations like this. See DOBBS ON TORTS § 339, at 931-32 (2000 & Supp.). The trouble with the captain of the ship doctrine is that it automatically held the surgeon liable, even if the plaintiff failed to show that he was in control of or supervised the hospital nurses. For this reason, a number of courts reject the captain of the ship doctrine, and rely upon the borrowed servant approach, which would inquire in each case whether the doctor actually had control and became a special employer upon vicarious liability should be visited. See *Lewis v. Physicians Ins. Co. of Wisconsin,* 627 N.W.2d 484 (Wis. 2001) (the concurring opinion of Abrahamson, J., noting that although the captain doctrine was rejected, borrowed servant theory was not).

Captain of the ship and Ybarra. Is *Ybarra v. Spangard,* 25 Cal. 2d 486, 154 P.2d 687 (1944), considered as a res ipsa case in Chapter 11, § 2, really a borrowed servant/vicarious liability case? No. Some of the hospital-multiple defendant cases might well be understood as merely vicarious liability cases because they impose liability only upon principals. But *Ybarra* imposed liability upon everyone, from top to bottom. Still, the question promotes some insight. Most of the legal result and perhaps all of the practical result in *Ybarra* could be justified under a vicarious liability rule if you think the captain of the ship doctrine or even anything close to it would be good law.

¶3. *Moonlighting police officers.* Many businesses employ off-duty police officers a security guards. The officer may sometimes wear a police uniform and carry official sidearms. The business gets the advantage not only of a security guard but also the appearance of official authority. Courts have not generally been disturbed at this private capture of official power. Some have even said it should be encouraged. In addition, they have often reasoned that the officer has a duty in his public job to enforce the law, even when he is in some sense "off duty." If his acts are acts that would be within the scope of his public employment while on duty, then they are regarded as acts for his public employer. These courts then conclude that the officer, though on duty for the private employer at the time of his tort, is not within the scope of his private employment. In other words, it is an either/or thing –he is a public employee or a private employee. *See Mansfield v. C.F. Bent Tree Apartment Limited Partnership,* 37 S.W.3d 145 (Tex. Ct. App. 2001) where a security guard for an apartment complex encountered a male trespasser at 4:30 a.m., pointed his gun, showed his badge, and placed the trespasser on the ground. The officer-guard then kicked the trespasser, fracturing his ribs and rupturing his spleen. We don't know why, but in fact the trespasser was wearing only a bra and panties, with his penis "hanging out." The court reasoned that even if the officer-guard was not acting as a police officer when he first spotted the trespasser, he was doing so when he showed he badge and sought assistance. This meant no vicarious liability for his employer. Although any citizen could have arrested the trespasser, the officer-guard, as a police officer, had a duty to do so.

Since either/or reasoning, as applied to most of an officer's acts against violence or criminality, would place the officer in his public employment, the effect is that the private employer not only gets the advantage of official powers but has none of the responsibilities. This can be the end of the case for the plaintiff, because the public employer may be immune.

In *White v. Revco Discount Drug Centers, Inc.,* 33 S.W.3d 713 (Tenn. 2001), the court rejected that kind of reasoning, saying that ordinary agency principles should apply. The court denied that an off-duty officer was always "on duty" for the police department. It held that both employers might be vicariously liable in some situations. The private employer was not to be immunized if the officer was acting within the scope of his private employment, even if he was also acting within the scope of his public employment. Maryland's highest court quickly decided the same, holding that the evidence was sufficient to show that an off-duty police officer shooting at a robber was within the scope of employment with his hotel-employer even if he were also within his employment with the police department. *Lovelace v. Anderson,* 785 A.2d 726 (Md. 2001).

NOTE: SERVING GRATUITOUSLY.

Some cases turn more on whether someone is an employee (or "servant") at all, rather than on whether an act was performed within the scope of employment. We focus most of our attention on the latter issue, but pause here on the former.

A person is a "servant" only if he submits himself to the employer's control. One need not be paid, or doing paid work, however, to have submitted himself to such control. Thus a church member who volunteers to deliver cookies to shut-ins, agreeing to submit to the church's directions, subjects the church to vicarious liability for his negligent driving (*Trinity Lutheran Church*); but the dutiful son who feeds his parents' cats while they are away does not become their agent when he has not so submitted (*Austin*).

HINMAN V. WESTINGHOUSE ELECTRIC CO., 471 P. 2d 988 (Cal. 1970)

Hinman begins with another look at some of the reasons for imposing vicarious liability, then narrows to focus on the going and coming rule, to which it creates an exception on the facts. The employer benefits from reaching out into a distant labor market; the employer pays for the travel time; and the travel increases risk on the highways. These facts convince the court that the going and coming rule should not be applied.

Are these facts relevant to any reason for liability? If I hire a consulting engineer from Japan, who must fly to the United States to examine my project, I may benefit from his travel, but why does that mean his travel torts are my responsibility? And true, travel increases risks, but not necessarily unreasonably. In *Hinman*, travel by a skilled worker might be safer overall than using local, unskilled labors to construct elevators. Payment for travel time might be more convincing: that suggests that the employer and employee themselves regard the travel time as work time. In omitted material, *Hinman* in fact relied on a theory that the master and servant implicitly agreed to continue employment during travel.

Hinman is unusual but has some support. When you work out of town, you may be on the job portal-to-portal. See *Carroll Air Systems, Inc. v. Greenbaum,* 629 So.2d 914 (Fla. Dist. Ct. App. 1993); also *Gatzke,* the next main case.

FAUL V. JELCO, INC., 595 P.2d 1035 (Ariz. Ct. App. 1979)

A case similar to *Hinman* on its facts, but with one important difference— the worker was not given pay based on time spent traveling but he was paid extra because he worked away from home. What difference does it make whether the employer pays a higher hourly rate for commuting to work or a mileage allowance or nothing extra at all? If there is an oversupply of labor, the employer might pay no extra sum at all to those who commute. Should the injured plaintiff's rights turn on this?

The *Faul* court points out that vicarious responsibility is often said to rest upon "control" by the employer, a mechanical ground set up for us in *Riviello*. But, according to *Faul*, *Hinman* departed from a control test and used a risk justification— the employer's use of distant labor increased highway risks. This observation in *Faul* gives you a chance to emphasize the traditional formal statement that control or right to control forms the basis of and limits the scope of vicarious liability. Control is an extremely vague word, of course. That very vagueness may explain why it was popular with the courts: it permitted wide latitude in the decisions while absolving the courts from responsibility for giving any really clear reasons for any given holding.

Faul also recognizes two exceptions to the going and coming rule: (1) the special hazard exception, in which the travel itself is a hazard for which (presumably) the worker is being paid; (2) the dual purpose doctrine, under which the worker is considered on the job if, in addition simply to "going home," she is performing some work-related task taking tools to the repair shop on the way home, for example.

AHLSTROM V. SALT LAKE CITY CORP., 73 P.3d 315 (Utah 2003)

This abstract adds a slight emphasis to the dual purpose exception raised so briefly in *Faul*. Here the court demands some rather definite kind of benefit— so much so that the plaintiff must prove some other employee would have been sent on the trip if the employee in question had not undertaken to go. The special errand exception, though given a different name, is an essentially a subset of the dual purpose exception— the employee engages in a special activity or errand during the coming and going trip. The *Ahlstrom* court held that this exception applied only in workers' compensation cases but that in any event the plaintiff could not show such an errand. Finally, *Ahlstrom* held that while another exception to the going and coming rule could be found when the employer provided the transport, at least when the employee was required to use that transport, that exception did not apply here where the employee, not the employer, was seeking the benefit of using the employer's car.

On the dual purpose exception, maybe the amount of "purpose" or benefit requires a judgment call and maybe the court's judgment call here was entirely reasonable. However, the implication that dual purpose could not be demonstrated unless some other employee would have been sent on the trip if the employee in question had not gone could be too demanding. Suppose an employee is about to leave work and the boss says, "Hey, you want to go a block out of your way to pick up that repaired gizmo at the other shop? If not, I can get it when I'm out tomorrow." Wouldn't it be fair to hold the employer liable for an injury inflicted in the one-block drive to get the gizmo? If so, would the class treat this like a kind of reverse frolic and detour and say that once the employee is back on his regular route home the going and coming rule applies?

Note 1. *Carter v. Reynolds,* cited here, imposed vicarious liability, even though the employee was headed home from the client's offices. Had the employee first gone back to her place of employment and *then* headed home, the answer would be different. The rationale is that both benefit to the employer and control could be found. The employer benefits from requiring the employee to use her own car in that the employer need to purchase or rent one; the employer has control—this is a little tricky—in its ability to require use of the employee's car.

Note 2. Factual variations. *Obst v. United States Postal Service,* 427 F.Supp. 696 (N.D. Cal. 1977): The employee took a postal vehicle beyond the authorized area in order to eat lunch with an unauthorized passenger and to enjoy a scenic view. The court invoked the dual purpose doctrine because he was also guarding the mail.

District of Columbia v. Davis, 386 A.2d 1195 (D.C. Ct. App. 1978): An off duty officer was required to carry a service revolver, even at social gatherings. The officer accidentally shot the plaintiff. "By wearing it at all times, he was furthering his employer's function of maintaining public order . . . . The act of unholstering it was surely conduct incidental to that authorized . . . ."

National Convenience Stores, Inc. v. Fantauzzi, 584 P.2d 6879 (Nev. 1978): The employee, on his day off, intended to stop in at a convenience market owned by his employer to get some shelf measurements, a duty that was part of his on-the-job responsibility. On the way to the store he got into a drag race, crossed the center line and collided with another vehicle, killing two persons and injuring another. The court found the employee within the scope of his employment on the special errand exception to the going and coming rule that is, he abandoned his personal objective in order to perform a job-related task.

Note 3. Frolic and detour. This presents infinite possibilities for variation and a good many basic patterns. If you have time to teach a course devoted to fact-discrimination and patterning, this is a wonderful subject to use. In an ordinary torts course, the subject warrants enough attention to induce recognition of the general pattern.

Re-entry problems are especially fact-sensitive. In *McNair v. Lend Lease Trucks, Inc.,* 95 F.3d 325 (4th Cir. 1996), a trucker took a break and drank for four hours at a roadside bar. As he was walking back to his truck, he suddenly darted into the path of a motorcyclist, and both the trucker and the cyclist were killed. The court held the drinking was a "frolic" as a matter of law, but concluded that there was a jury question as to whether the trucker had reentered the scope of employment when he started towards his truck.

EDGEWATER MOTELS, INC. V. GATZKE, 277 N.W. 2d 11 (Minn. 1979)

Hinman parallels the problem which, in workers' compensation, is called the "course of employment" issue. *Gatzke* parallels the problem which, in workers' compensation, is called the "arising out of employment" problem. The two are usually regarded as largely distinct problems. The "course of" problem relates to time, place and circumstance; has the job started and not ended? The "arising out of employment" problem has a more qualitative component; in fact, it resembles strongly the issues associated with scope of the risk.

Specifically, one might be in the course of employment, but pursuing some entirely personal end at the same time so that the activity does not seem significantly related to employment. The frolic and detour materials, immediately preceding, are a bridge into this idea, since they involve both time-place limits and personal purposes of the employee.

The idea that one may be on the job but still outside the scope of employment in carrying out a particular act is easiest to see in cases of intentional torts. If the bartender gets in a fight as the result of trying to manage an unruly drunk, he is still pursuing employment objectives and the employer is responsible for his acts. But if he gets in a fight because a customer makes fun of the bartender's domestic partner, his purposes and his acts may be "unrelated" to the job.

Gatzke is a subtler version of this kind of argument. Should the argument have won there? *Gatzke* was assuredly carrying out some very personal purposes. Does the somewhat incidental benefit the company might derive from having expense accounts filled out really justify characterizing all this as being in the scope of employment? You might enjoy asking the class to apply the rationales seen earlier to this case. Why is a burning motel room "really" a business risk of Walgreen's, for example, rather than a routine business risk of the motel itself?

Some personal acts do not further the business of the employer at all. Suppose an employee of a restaurant sits down at a table with a customer and has a drink, not to encourage the customer's consumption of the restaurant's food or drink, but to make a date. The employee negligently breaks a wine glass and cuts the customer with it.

Other personal acts might be carried on more or less concurrently with employment, as in the case of ordinary smoking and to a lesser extent ordinary drinking. Still others might further the employer's business in the attenuated sense that they relieve employee discomfort and promote better morale and production. An employee who negligently injures another while on the way to the bathroom might thus be in the scope of employment. As to smoking, see Annotation, 20 A.L.R.3d 893 (1968).

The opinion in *Gatzke* seems concerned with at least two distinct issues. (1) Smoking as a "personal" versus enterprise activity. This is to us the less important; many personal activities can be carried on with the work; it doesn't take the employee outside employment merely because, concurrently, he smokes. You might compare the knife-flipping cook in *Riviello*. (2) Was Gatzke outside the scope of employment back in his room? This issue is raised in a somewhat narrow way, by the defendant's assertion that Gatzke left employment when he went to the bar. The court gives three responses to this. In reverse order: (a) The last one says he was an executive or 24-hour man and hence within employment in the room. This response may be addressed as much to the "course of" problem as to the "arising out of" problem. (b) The second response is that even if Gatzke left employment in the bar, he had resumed it back in his room by filling out expenses reports. (c) The first response is aimed only at the narrow issue framed by the defendant, that Gatzke was outside employment (i.e., carrying on his personal life) while in the bar. The answer to this narrow version of the issue was that he was also doing company business, learning about bars.

The opinion is complex enough to warrant class analysis. At the same time it can hide the central point– purely personal acts, even when carried out during employment hours are not acts arising out of employment, but purely personal acts that are incidental and concurrent with employment duties (such as smoking) do not take the employee outside employment.

Notes 1 & 2. The idea that an employee remains within the scope of employment while "temporarily deviating" from the job is conceptually related to the "frolic and detour" concept addressed in Notes 3 and 4 after *Ahlstrom*. Were this not the rule, employers would often escape vicarious liability, it seems – by arguing that whatever the employee was doing was a deviation from work. An example might be the knife-flipper in *Riviello*.

LISA M. V. HENRY MAYO NEWHALL MEM. HOSP. , 907 P.2d 358 (Cal. 1995)
RODEBUSH V. OKLAHOMA NURSING HOMES, 867 P.2d 1241 (Okla. 1993)
FAHRENDORFF V. NORTH HOMES, INC., 597 N.W.2d 905 (Minn. 1999)

If you wish to take the time, the *Lisa M.* case (coupled with *Rodebush* and *Fahrendorff*) allows room for a very good discussion. Since *Lisa M.* is essentially a case of rape, albeit one not accomplished by force, you might want to encourage the class to discuss the issues professionally and with great respect not only for what others say but for feelings of class members who may say nothing.

California rejects the Restatement's rule that the conduct must be motivated in part by a desire to serve the employer, but it reintroduces that rule in a flexible form as a factor to consider in determining whether an act is "personal" on the one hand or one "generated by the employment." You can interpret the court to mean that the employment must cause the employee's act as both an actual and a legal cause, that is, that employment must have created the risk of the employee's act.

But even that is not enough, as it turns out. The act that counts as an intentional tort will form no basis for vicarious liability unless the resulting injury is "sure to occur in the conduct of the enterprise." Maybe the court won't insist on "sure," because it then talks of "foreseeable," but its idea seems to be in either event that the injury is a risk correlated with the business and not merely a casual or occasional occurrence, perhaps a risk that occurs more with the defendant's business than with businesses in general.

In applying its principle that employment must generate the risk as a more or less sure thing, the court concludes that the employment was merely a cause in fact, not a typical risk or one broadly associated with the enterprise.

The court then injects a very narrow rule. It says that the employment must not only risk the employee's act, but his "motivating emotions." That is big change from the idea that vicarious liability could be imposed if employment regularly generated the risk of such conduct. Employment might generate risks by generating opportunities. Those opportunities might even be distinctive to the employment. That would not be enough under the rule the court adopts. The technician here simply "took advantage of solitude with a naive patient" to commit a sexual assault; his sexual "emotions" were not generated by the job.

In a second part of the opinion in *Lisa M*, the court purports to shift analysis to foreseeability and to reach the same conclusion. A focus on foreseeability is perhaps not so odd; other courts have utilized it. For example, in *Porter v. Harshfield*, 948 S.W.2d 83 (Ark. 1997), the court held as a matter of law that an because an employee's sexual assault was "purely personal" and "not expectable in view of his duties as a radiology technician," there could be no employer vicarious liability. But there is a strange line in the *Lisa M* opinion during this discussion, or so some might think. "[T]here is no evidence of emotional involvement. . . arising from the medical relationship." Indeed not; this is essentially a species of rape, not an act of love. That the medical procedure would not normally arouse emotions seems supremely irrelevant to the question whether abuse of power is foreseeable, either out of a rapist's rage or out of lust.

Does the employee's position of authority and trust matter? Not really. It is different, the court thinks, from the police officer's position of "unique authority."

The *Lisa M* court's test for vicarious liability on its facts— that the employment must not only risk the employee's act, but his "motivating emotions" – is a great topic for lively classroom discussion. First off, contrast the California court's statement of this "rule" with the statement in *Penn Central Transportation Co. v. Reddick*, 398 A.2d 27 (D.C. Ct. App. 1979): "The present trend is to extend liability for intentional torts to situations where the employment provides a 'peculiar opportunity and . . . incentive for such loss of temper,' . . . as where an argument is likely by virtue of the servant's duties, and the conduct is wholly or partially in furtherance of the master's business." But, as the same court recognized, there is no liability "for those 'willful acts, intended by the agent only to further his own interest. . . .' "

The case excerpts of *Fahrendorff* and *Rodebush*, and the notes following them, allow for fuller development of this point. The Oklahoma court's opinion in *Rodebush* seems to echo the view expressed in *Lisa M*: vicarious liability can be imposed for an employee's intentional tort only where it is not only incident to the business, but also arises from some "impulse of emotion which naturally grew out of or was incident to the attempt to perform the master's business." By contrast, in *Fahrendorff*, the fact that inappropriate sexual contact was a "well-known" (that is, foreseeable) hazard in the group-home business created a fact question as to a group home's vicarious liability for a counselor's improper advances — advances that were surely aimed solely at furthering the "interests" of the counselor. This does not sound at all like the "test" applied in *Lisa M*.

Note that the Restatement's intent-to-serve-the-employer rule points in the opposite direction from *Fahrendorff*, *Lourim*, and *Lyon*. What about an auto accident or macho road encounter in the course of employment that leads to an actual fight? In *Kuehn v. White*, 24 Wash. App. 274, 600 P.2d 679 (1979), White was driving a tractor-trailer for Inter-City Auto Freight. White drove in a way that forced dangerous maneuvers by Kuehn, then braked suddenly and pulled off the road. Kuehn pulled off behind him. White got out of his truck with a 2-foot length of pipe and announced: "There is no son of a bitch going to give me the finger." He proceeded to hit Kuehn on the head three times. The court held that when White hit Kuehn it was "because of his personal anger towards Kuehn and not because of any intent to serve the employer." This was thought to warrant summary judgment for White's employer. What about the fact that this all arose out of White's driving? Similarly, in *Nichols v. Land Transport Corp.*, 223 F.3d 21 (1st Cir. 2000), the employer's summary judgment was affirmed in a case in which a truck driver stabbed a motorist in a "road rage" attack. Applying Maine law and citing *Kuehn*, the court reasoned that a servant's tort is within the scope of employment only if actuated, at least in part, by a purpose to serve the master, and that the trucker's attack was not so actuated.

Three tests? A good starting point for discussion is to ask students to recognize the different tests used in *(a) Lisa M* and *Rodebush*, *(b) Fahrendorf* and *Lourim* (**Note 2**) and (c) the Restatement Second's intent-to-serve-the-master approach. The next step is to explore with the students which of the various approaches seems to better support the goals of vicarious liability which were presumably teased out earlier. The cases raised in **Note 3** can be used to prompt discussion of different fact patterns. The question in each case is whether vicarious liability should be imposed; students can be asked whether it would be imposed under the various tests that have been identified earlier.

Negligence of the hospital. We don't want to distract from the main issues of vicarious liability, but at some point it is appropriate to raise the lawyering possibility here. Could the plaintiff argue that, if the hospital was not vicariously liable, it was nevertheless negligent in failing to supervise Tripoli? Or, if this is different, that it was negligent in failing to have another person in the room when the examination was taking place?

In *Regions Bank & Trust v. Stone County Skilled Nursing Facility, Inc.,* 49 S.W.3d 107 (Ark. 2001), testimony was that a male nursing home attendant named Bill McConnaughey –formerly a housekeeper for the nursing home but recently promoted to "certified nursing assistant" – sexually assaulted a female patient who was quadriplegic, unable to move and also unable to speak. The court rejected a claim based upon failure to supervise because the facility had no reason to think McConnaughey was dangerous. It also rejected respondeat superior liability because McConnaughey's act was "personal" and outside the scope of employment. But the court, noting that the patient "was a helpless, semi-comatose quadriplegic," held that the nursing facility "assumed responsibility for her care and required payment therefor. They were therefore under a duty of ordinary care to provide such attention as her condition reasonably required. Given Elder's total inability to take care of herself, Stone County Skilled Nursing Facility was responsible for every aspect of her well being." Although this might sound as if the court were flirting (perhaps unintentionally) with strict liability, the court probably had negligence in mind based upon the nursing home's "policy which permitted unaccompanied access to helpless female patients . . . by male aides with little or no previous health care experience. This policy was not in keeping with accepted nursing practice. Further, and also contrary to accepted nursing practice, the facility failed to supervise its aides, particularly those such as Mr. McConnaughey, who had not been on the job long enough to establish a record of patient care and dependability."

If a student represented the plaintiff, what problem would the student anticipate in claiming that the hospital was negligent in failing to have another person in the examination room? Would the plaintiff have to prove a medical standard of care?

Note 2. Two cases: Scout leaders and priests. In *Lourim,* the court allows the imposition of vicarious liability on the Boy Scout organization when a Boy Scout leader's position was a "necessary precursor" to his sexual abuse of a scout. The court stressed that the Scouts "sponsored and encouraged" the development of a relationship between the Scout leader and the plaintiff; that the Scout leader used this relationship for his own perverse purposes was not determinative. *Fearing* is somewhat similar. In both cases, the point seems to be that while the abuse of the plaintiff was personal to the employee and not within the scope of employment, it nevertheless had roots in something that definitely was within the scope of employment. Maybe even the *Lisa M.* court would agree that the "motivating emotions" in these cases could have grown out of employment? Would the class agree that these are stronger cases for vicarious liability, or would some argue that they are weaker?

Note 3. Trust, authority, and incentive. When the employee is placed by his employment in a position of trust, so that normal social forces may not constrain misbehavior, maybe there is special reason to support vicarious liability. The *Lisa M.* dissenters might support some such idea as a specific instance in which employees are placed by their work in a position to victimize the plaintiff. On that reasoning, though, would a primary negligence claim against the employer be more appropriate as in *Regions Bank,* supra? Cf. *Juarez v. Boy Scouts of America, Inc.*, 97 Cal. Rptr. 2d 12 (Ct. App. 2000) (rejecting respondeat superior theory in sexual molestation case on the authority of *Lisa M.*, but holding that Boy Scouts had a duty of care to take reasonable measures to protect plaintiff scout from sexual abuse by adult scout leaders).

In the five cases set out in this note, what would most justify vicarious liability– trust, or authority? Certainly use of authority or power created by the job is a strong ground for respondeat superior liability and maybe a trust relationship is, too. But is there any coherent pattern in these cases?

• *John R. v. Oakland Unified School District*, 769 P.2d 948 (Cal. 1989): The school teacher threatens a failing grade unless the student engages in sexual acts. The school district is not liable. The court rejected the lower court's position that vicarious liability was justified because the official, job-created hierarchical relationship gave the teacher authority and the power to abuse it. See the reasoning in *Godar v. Edwards*, 588 N.W.2d 701 (Iowa 1999) (school district employee repeatedly molested student; held to be outside scope of employment because the torts were not "of the same general nature" as the duties authorized by the employer, were not committed in furtherance of his duties, and represented a "substantial deviation" from those duties).

• *Mary M. v. City of Los Angeles*, 814 P.2d 1341 (Cal. 1991): A police officer, having arrested a woman, takes her home and rapes her. The city is liable. *John R.* is distinguishable because liability of the school there would encourage the school to over-react by discouraging extra-curricular contacts altogether, while liability of the city for police rape would not lead cities to deprive their officers of weapons. The court emphasized that the "authority" of a police officer is reflected in tangible symbols "his uniform, badge and firearm, and only slightly less so by the prospect of criminal sanctions. . . ." The reasoning, as so often the case when a court lists a group of factors, is mechanical at best.

Cockrell v. Pearl River Valley Water Supply Dist., 865 So.2d 357 (Miss. 2004), cited with *Mary M.* in the casebook, held that the alleged kissing officer was outside the scope of his employment. "Mississippi law provides that an activity must be in furtherance of the employer's business to be within the scope and course of employment. , , , An employee's personal unsanctioned recreational endeavors are beyond the course and scope of his employment." There was no discussion of the risks associated with the job.

In *Primeaux v. U.S.*, 181 F.3d 876 (8th Cir. 1999), which applied South Dakota law, a tribal police officer driving a government vehicle offered a ride to a stranded motorist, then raped her. The court held that the government was not vicariously liable, reasoning that the connection between government employment and the rape was "too tenuous to have been foreseen" by the employer, given that the employee was off duty, unarmed and out of uniform. No uniform, no badge, no liability?

• *Destefano v. Grabrian*, 763 P.2d 275 (Colo. 1988): A priest, encouraged in marriage counseling by his church, engaged in sexual activity with one of the partners he counseled. The court held that a church which encouraged its priests to engage in marriage counseling was not vicariously liable for the priest's tortious sexual intercourse with one of the marital partners he was counseling. *Byrd v. Faber*, 565 N.E.2d 584, 5 A.L.R.5th 1115 (Ohio 1991) is in accord, stating a most restrictive test: was the act "calculated to facilitate or promote the business for which the servant was employed." The church "did not hire Faber to rape, seduce, or otherwise physically assault members of his congregation," and could not have foreseen that he would behave in this manner, hence the church is not liable. See also *N.H. v. Presbyterian Church (U.S.A.)*, 998 P.2d 592 (Okla. 1999), a case in which twelve minors sued the defendant national church, claiming it was vicariously liable for sexual molestation committed by a Presbyterian minister. Holding that the minister's actions were outside the scope of employment as a matter of law, the court stressed that the minister's acts were motivated entirely by his personal gratification and that it is "inconceivable" that his acts were in the nature of those he was hired to perform.

• *Baker v. Saint Francis Hosp.*, 126 P.3d 602 (Okla. 2005), reversed a summary judgment for the hospital. Citing *Rodebush*, the court held that an employer could be held vicariously liable where the act of the employee "is incidental to and done in furtherance of the business of the employer even though the servant or agent acted in excess of the authority or willfully or maliciously committed the wrongs." Contested fact issues remained, however: The court said that "the answer to the respondeat superior issue primarily lies in determining whether [the employee] had stepped aside from her employment at the time of the offending tortious act(s) on some mission or conduct to serve her own personal needs, motivations or purposes. . . . [T]he purpose or motivation behind Davis's act(s) is an important, and potentially an overriding, consideration. . . ."

• *Buck v. Blum*, 130 S.W.3d 285 (Tex. App. 2004): the doctor was not within the scope of employment in using his penis to test the strength of the patient's hands. "Nor can it be said the assault was so connected with and immediately arising out of Yen's employment tasks as to merge the activities into one indivisible tort. A club bouncer has an inherently confrontational job that may well require physical force; whereas, neurology is not an inherently sexual profession and never requires the action allegedly perpetrated by Yen. As a matter of law, Yen's alleged conduct did not arise out of the course and scope of his employment, and, thus, his employers cannot be held liable under respondeat superior."

We are not suggesting that trust and authority are the only sound bases for liability. If courts can be persuaded that the employee's act really is one strongly associated with the employer's business activity, courts will impose vicarious liability even for acts like rape. In *Lyon v. Carey*, 533 F.2d 649 (D.C. Cir. 1976), a 19-old-driver for Pep Line was delivering a mattress to the plaintiff. An argument about delivery of the mattress, and payment for it, culminated in the driver's raping the plaintiff at knifepoint in her bedroom. The court held that a jury could find Pep Line vicariously liable for the attack, if the assault was "triggered off or motivated or occasioned by a dispute over the conduct . . . of the employer's business."

Nevertheless the series of five bulleted cases show us that courts differ quite a bit in their willingness to find a strong association between the employee's highly personal acts and the employment.

§ 2. EMPLOYERS WHO ARE NOT MASTERS

DISTRICT OF COLUMBIA V. HAMPTON, 666 A.2d 30 (D.C. 1995)

Hampton is a particularly tragic case that presents the independent contractor rule in a somewhat unusual context. Is a foster parent considered an agent or employee of the state family services agency, thus making the agency vicariously liable for the foster parent's torts (often against foster children)? The court, in accord with most, says no. It gets there by invoking a multi-factor test for determining whether a master-servant relationship exists: (1) the selection and engagement of the servant; (2) the payment of wages; (3) the power to discharge; (4) the power to control the servant's conduct; and (5) whether the work is part of the employer's "regular business." Along with most courts, this one says that the determinative factor is number four, the right of control. (The Restatement (Second) of Agency § 220 lists ten factors to be considered.)

Commerce Bank v. Youth Services of Mid-Illinois, Inc., 775 N.E.2d 297 (Ill. Ct. App. 2002) is in accord where the defendant was a private corporation hired by the state agency to carry out the functions of the state agency. The defendant exercised or had the right to exercise enormous day-to-day control, but the court said this was merely monitoring regulations of the state agency. The case is a sequel to *Commerce Bank v. Augsburger*, 680 N.E.2d 822 (Ill. Ct. App. 1997), a case abstract printed in Chapter 14. In that case, the court held that if the foster parents had confined the child to a shelf a closet with the door closed and where she died of asphyxia and hypothermia, the foster parents were merely exercising parental discretion and were immune.

Courts most often look to the *right* to control the details of the purported servant's work, as opposed to the actual exercise of that control. On the facts of *Hampton*, did the agency have the right to control the details of the foster parent's conduct? Perhaps to ask the question that way (that is, focusing on details) provides its own answer. Obviously an agency is not going to control the "daily details" of parenting, foster or otherwise. Even where the agency had assigned a particular social worker to the foster parent, that social worker did not direct the foster parent in decisions about what the child would eat and wear, when the child would bathe, and how the child would be disciplined. If the right to control the larger things were considered, would the analysis and result differ? Certainly the agency here had the right to remove the child from the foster parent entirely. But this court looks at the trees, not the forest.

Hampton also allows for a discussion of how right of control can be proved. In the independent contractor context, the "actual relationship" between the parties is the focus. Where a written agreement exists (as it often will), then that will provide key evidence about the nature of that relationship. Where there is no such writing, the task of proving what the relationship is will be more difficult. Notice that in *Hampton*, there was "very little testimony" about the relationship between the foster mother and the agency's social workers, which suggests in part a failure of *proof,* even if the reality were somehow different. Teachers can use this opportunity to stress a legal ethics point: lawyers have an ethical duty to investigate claims competently, to know the applicable legal standards, and to raise relevant points in litigation effectively. The court will not do the research or make the arguments for the party who has the burden of proof. That is, if an employer does in fact have the right to control the details of a contractor's work, but the contractor's lawyer fails to prove that, the result will likely be the same as if the employer did *not* have such a right of control.

Foster parents as state actors in a civil rights action– NOT. Would the foster parent be subject to a federal civil rights action on the ground that the foster parent is a state actor? This is not the same issue as the *Hampton* independent contractor issue and it is not tested by the same tests. Still, the issues are parallel and you might be surprised if the foster parent was treated as an independent contractor and also a state actor. *Rayburn v. Hogue,* 241 F.3d 1341(11th Cir. 2001), holds that such parents are *not* state actors. The court applied a tripartite test, which asks whether the state has coerced or encouraged the unconstitutional action of the foster parents, whether the foster parents performed a traditional state function, or whether the foster parents and the state were essentially in a joint enterprise. The answer to all these questions was no, so the foster parents were not state actors.

Note 1. Employer's liability for torts of independent contractor. Stressing this note might be important to make it clear to the class that the issue of whether an employer is liable for the torts of an independent contractor most commonly arises in a business setting, rather than in anything resembling *Hampton.*

Note 2. Tests for the status of independent contractor. Right to control is usually the test except when courts don't use it! The medical group's right to control the details of a physician's medical treatment is zero; control would interfere with the doctor-patient relationship. Yet the doctor doesn't become an independent contractor for that reason. *Dias v. Brigham Med. Assocs., Inc.,* cited here, said:

> The *Bing* case [Bing v. Thunig, 2 N.Y.2d 656, 163 N.Y.S.2d 3, 143 N.E.2d 3 (1957)], and other cases across jurisdictions that have followed it, stand for the proposition that although a corporate entity may not control the precise treatment decisions of physicians, the entity should not be able to escape liability for physician malpractice.

Note 3. Structuring relationships by contract. *Zirkle v. Winkler,* cited here, refused to accept the parties' contractual label, "independent contractor" as governing the newspaper's relationship with its delivery personnel, although courts often do treat the parties' agreement as one factor to be considered. In *Zirkle* the court held that the independent contractor status was for the jury. What would the student do as a lawyer for a taxi company that owns its own fleet of cabs but wants to say its drivers are independent contractors? One ploy is to "lease" the cab to the driver and structure all the finances to fit the independent contractor mold. Such legal structuring may work. Factual details in the cab cases are quite varied. *See* R. L. Martyn, Annotation, *Owning, Leasing, or Otherwise Engaging in Business of Furnishing Services for Taxicabs as Basis of Tort Liability for Acts of Taxi Driver under Respondeat Superior Doctrine,* 8 A.L.R.3d 818 (1966). The independent contractor status may be irrelevant where the cab company is liable (to passengers) under estoppel doctrines. *See Mitchell v. DCX,* Inc., 274 F.Supp.2d 33 (D.D.C. 2003). The estoppel or apparent agency idea is developed later in this section in *O'Banner.*

Note 4. Retained control. Retained control gets complicated quickly. We've tried to resist piling up note material on this narrow topic. We simply say (1) retained control might also tend to show that the "independent contractor" is really NOT an independent contractor at all but is instead a servant –at least when he acts within the scope of control retained by the defendant-employer, but (2) that in many cases, retained control might be understood as warranting a finding of direct negligence by the employer in failing to exercise the control he has.

PUSEY V. BATOR, 762 N.E.2d 968 (Ohio 2002)

The independent contractor's employee, Bator, guarding the defendant's plant, caused a death by using a handgun.

One who uses an independent contractor to do inherently dangerous work creating a peculiar risk is liable for that contractor's negligence. Inherent danger, according to the court is not routine or the general possibility of danger. Rather, it must involve a danger that is not normal, routine, or customary and one that calls for special precautions. We'll see vaguely similar ideas behind strict liability for activities that are abnormally or significantly dangerous when we get to the next chapter. But in this chapter, the inherent danger conception is a little milder in nature and also in effect – it only holds the employer liable vicariously as if the contractor were a traditional employee.

The court's application of the vague inherent danger principle the court seems looser than the principle itself. On the danger, the court seems to say the principle is satisfied if it is foreseeable that some one might be injured by inappropriate use of the weapon. The court then adds that the risk is not a normal one like driving an automobile. That's it. Hiring armed guards is an inherently dangerous activity, so vicarious liability for any negligence is appropriate.

Maybe "armed guards" is only an inherently dangerous activity for injuries that result from the weapon. Suppose Bator kept his weapon holstered but killed Pusey with a blow to the neck. The fact that he had a weapon (other than his fists) seems irrelevant in that instance, doesn't it?

Note 1. "Nondelegable" terminology. Students sometimes get confused about what this means, believing that the negligent contractor is not liable. No need to emphasize this if your class is in the habit of reading the notes.

Note 2. Inherent danger and peculiar risk. The Restatement Second of Torts is particularly detailed on the subject of nondelegable duties, but may add more to the confusion by failing to sift out the chaff and get to the principles. Maybe there aren't any if the diverse cases of negligence in this note are fair examples. This is a place where even law students who still just want to memorize black letter rules will see that the rules themselves won't be good predictors or very useful platforms for arguing cases.

Note 3. Duties imposed by statutory instruments. Is a statutory duty nondelegable? The two cases in this note relied on that idea. Would every single statute impose a nondelegable duty? *Maloney* suggests the idea is broad indeed.

Another recent example of a statute imposing a nondelegable duty is *Park v. Burlington Northern Santa Fe Ry.,* 133 Cal. Rptr. 2d 757 (Ct. App. 2003). Burlington generated hazardous wastes and hired a competent contractor to make proper disposal. The contractor did not handle the wastes properly and they caused serious injuries to the plaintiff. The court thought "the hazardous waste disposal statutes and regulations impose nondelegable duties on the generator of hazardous waste to see that the waste is properly disposed of." A good rule, we think. And it is hardly believable that Burlington would not have had an indemnity clause in the contract or required insurance by the contractor.

Note 4. Duties to maintain safety of land open to the public or chattels supplied for business use. Another specific case of nondelegable duty. The plumber example is especially clear. At the end of this note, we offer the first glimpse of the indemnity possibility, one of the reasons we need not be concerned if courts freely find nondelegable duties.

Note 5. Landowners and construction contractors. In *Otero v. Jordon Restaurant Enterprises*, cited here, a bar owner hired an independent contractor to do work on the premises that included installation of bleachers so customers could watch TV. As a result of the contractor's negligence, the bleachers collapsed about four months after the work was done. The plaintiff was injured and seeks to hold that the bar owner is vicariously liable. *Held,* the owner is vicariously liable. Once a contractor's work is done and the landowner resumes possession, the landowner is liable for injuries as if the landowner had personally done the work. This case is not a collateral negligence case in which the harm done is not normal to the work, such as a temporarily unsafe condition while the work is in progress.

Note 6. Nondelegable duty as open-ended policy. Although the Restatement provides "rules" covering some situations, the decision to declare that a duty is nondelegable is essentially a decision of policy and justice, leaving open the possibility that any given duty can be placed in that category. We give two case examples you can consider in class.

A. In *Stropes v. Heritage House Childrens Center of Shelbyville, Inc.*, cited here, the children's center cared for a severely retarded and disabled child of 14, who had the mental capacity of a five-month-old. One of its attendants engaged in oral and anal sex with the child. The trial court granted summary judgment for the center on the ground that the employee who committed the crimes was not within the scope of his employment. The Indiana Supreme Court held first that the jury could find the acts to be sufficiently employment related to warrant vicarious liability.

The *Stropes* result is consistent with an opportunity and incentive approach, *cf. Fahrendorff v. North Homes, supra,* and maybe a risk-of-the-business approach, but probably not with the California Court's approach in *Lisa M.* The court then went on to hold that the trial judge should also have considered the nondelegable duty theory as a basis for the employer's liability. It analogized the case to the case of a common carrier. The carrier, it is said, has a nondelegable duty to provide safety for the passenger and is liable to protect the passenger from assaults even if they are assaults by the carrier's servants acting outside the scope of their employment. In the case of the children's center, the victim is even more strikingly vulnerable. The "contract of passage" is not for transportation but for the comfort, safety, and maintenance that the child's dependence requires. The basis for the nondelegable duty seems to be found in the expectations of the parties, which in turn is derived from the helplessness of the child.

But there may be other layers to the problem.

(1) The usual application of nondelegable duty theory makes the employer liable for the work of an independent contractor. Should the theory be applied as well in cases of employees who are acting outside the scope of their employment? Notice that when the employer is liable for acts of the independent contractor, the contractor is still within the scope of his employment.

(2) Do grounds for nondelegable duty exist? The child was utterly dependent upon the employer for protection. As a result, all the parties expected some kind of enhanced obligation. The nondelegable duty the court erects is rooted in the general expectations of the parties and their understanding that if safety is not provided by the employer it won't be provided at all. See the further comments on *Ybarra* below.

On facts similar to *Stropes*, the Washington Supreme Court held that a group home for the developmentally disabled could *not* be held vicariously liable for an employee's rape of a resident, because his act was for purely personal gratification. *Niece v. Elmview Group Home*, 929 P.2d 420 (Wash. 1997). That court also held that the imposition of a nondelegable duty should be left to the state legislature.

Ybarra and nondelegable duty. Recall that *Ybarra,* considered in Chapter 13, got a result that went beyond the nondelegable duty or Captain of the Ship doctrines because it held the employees as well as the employer liable. However, many of the cases that are cited in support of *Ybarra* only hold the "Captain" or employer liable and could be explained as nondelegable duty cases or as Captain of the Ship cases. That result might be especially supportable when the defendant undertakes to care for the helpless, as in *Stropes*.

B. In *Breeden v. Anesthesia West, P.C.*, cited here, the court held that the anesthesiologist owed a nondelegable duty to his patient "to be aware of reasonably available medical information significant to the health of his or her patient prior to administering anesthesia," which is to say he could not escape liability by relying on the nurse to come forward with the information, even though such reliance fulfilled the medical standard of care.

The court does not theorize that the defendant was negligent as a matter of law in failing to check a readily available chart, but its reasoning for creating a nondelegable duty might also support such a judicial intervention in the medical standard. It said the nondelegable duties should be imposed when "the responsibility is so important to the community that the employer should not be permitted to transfer it to another." Here it was important because of the danger of not gathering the information– "because a patient can sustain severe injuries and even death if anesthesia is not administered properly." These reasons sound closely similar to reasons you would give for finding negligence as a matter of law. There is even an implicit weighing of costs: the *Breedon* court noted that the nurse's notes on the patient's chart could be accessed by computer and that there were at least three computers in the pre-op holding area where the anesthesia was administered.

The court also reasoned that "Under established principles, the client's reasonable expectations and beliefs about who will render a particular service are a significant factor in identifying duties that should be deemed to be nondelegable." This, too, sounds like a reason that might be given for saying that the defendant owed the plaintiff a duty to obtain the information himself and that he was negligent if he failed to do so.

Arguably, then, *Breedon*, with its nondelegable terminology, is pretty much identical to a ruling that an anesthesiologist owes a duty to personally check charts and that he is negligent if he doesn't do so.

O'BANNER V. MCDONALD'S CORP., 670 N.E.2d 632 (Ill. 1996)

We do not develop all the details of "apparent authority" and "agency by estoppel," some of which are difficult. For these, *see* RESTATEMENT THIRD OF AGENCY §§ 2.03 & 2.05.

O'Banner and its notes consider the possibilities that the employer of an independent contractor can be held liable because the employer created the appearance of agency. Courts speak of ostensible agency, apparent authority, and agency by estoppel.

Franchising takes many forms, but students probably understand the gist of the idea. The franchisor, such as McDonald's, has a valuable trademark or trade name. It licenses, that is permits use of, the name and often provides ancillary services and advice, such as an accounting system. Along with this goes a certain amount of franchisor control over quality in order to protect the value of the name or mark. Franchising in some form or degree is extremely common in motels, fast food enterprises, service stations, and many other business. If the owner of a trademark merely licenses the mark to another without any control at all, he is not a franchisor but a licensor and incurs no serious risk of liability for operations. When a franchisor exercises quality controls that invade day to day operations, there is a risk that the court will regard the franchisee, not as an independent contractor, but as an actual agent. And, as *O'Banner* suggests but does not hold, a franchisor might also be held on an apparent authority or estoppel theory.

Would the result be any different if the court was to say that some duties are "nondelegable?" Courts can always choose as a matter of policy to impose a nondelegable duty – meaning that one who uses an independent contractor cannot avoid the duty to provide due care and is thus liable for the independent contractor's negligence. Courts seem more willing to accept the apparent agency approach in the emergency department situations than the nondelegable duty approach. In *Baptist Mem. Hospital System v. Sampson*, 969 S.W.2d 945 (Tex. 1998), the court refused to impose a nondelegable duty on hospitals for the malpractice of emergency room doctors and instead reaffirmed its traditional ostensible agency requirements.

Note that the imposition of a nondelegable duty does not impose unlimited liability. In *Ward v. Lutheran Hospitals & Homes Soc'y of America, Inc.*, 963

P.2d 1031 (Alaska 1998), the court found that such a duty did not encompass the particular facts. The plaintiff alleged that three doctors negligently failed to obtain her informed consent to a blood transfusion in the hospital. The doctors were not employees of the hospital; indeed, the lead doctor was the plaintiff's personal obstetrician and the other two were his associates. They were treating the plaintiff in the hospital solely for the convenience of the main doctor. On these facts, neither the nondelegable duty nor ostensible agency theory could support hospital liability.

Annotations: Phoebe Carter, *Franchisor's Tort Liability for Injuries Allegedly Caused by Assault Etc.*, 2 A.L.R.5th 369 (1992); Ronald J. Sinesio, *Primary Liability of Private Chain Franchisor for Injury or Death Caused by Franchise Premises of Equipment*, 59 A.L.R.4th 1142 (1988).

Note 1. The meaning of reliance. *(a) Mere belief or action in reliance?* The *O'Banner* court seems to think that but-for reliance would be required to establish a claim for apparent or ostensible agency. The plaintiff in that case would evidence be required to show that but-for the appearance that McDonald's was the national franchisor, he would *not* have gone into the bathroom. Surely not a persuasive claim. The quotation from *Burless* seems on its face to require much less– a reasonable belief by the plaintiff that the actor was the agent of the putative employer. If only belief is required, the plaintiff would not be required to make the argument that the plaintiff would have followed some different course of conduct had the plaintiff known the truth.

(b) The Restatement Third of Agency. The RESTATEMENT THIRD OF AGENCY §§ 2.03, 3.03 & 2.05 deal with apparent authority and estoppel to deny agency. The first two (apparent authority) require only that the plaintiff *reasonably believe* the actor has authority but the last requires the plaintiff to make a "detrimental change in position" because of his reasonable belief that a person is the agent of the defendant. It looks as reasonable belief, as opposed to detrimental, but-for reliance, is enough in many cases, certainly those in which the defendant has created the misleading appearance. Other examples are spelled out in DOBBS ON TORTS § 338. Perhaps that was not enough in *O'Banner* but it seems to have been enough in *Petrovich*, **Note 2**, below– and *Petrovich* is also an Illinois case.

Note 2. Managed health care or HMOs. The court in *Petrovich v. Share Health Plan of Illinois, Inc.*, cited here, noted a "national trend of courts to hold HMOs accountable for medical malpractice under a variety of theories."

PUCKREIN V. ATI TRANSPORT, INC., 897 A.2d 1034 (N.J. 2006)

Browning-Ferris (BFI-NY) hired ATI Transport to haul glass residue as part of its business. On an ill-fated journey an ATI truck with defective brakes crashed into the Puckreins, killing them. In the Puckrein estate's suit against BFI, ATI, and a related company (World Carting), the trial judge held that

BFI could not be held liable because ATI/World Carting was an independent contractor, granting summary judgment for BFI. Here the court reverses, holding that BFI cannot use the "independent contractor" shield where those contractors were incompetent.

The case and **Note 1** state the general rule: "An employer may be charged with negligence in hiring an independent contractor where it is demonstrated that he should have known, or might by the exercise of reasonable care have ascertained, that the contractor was not competent." Incompetence takes many forms. In *Puckrein* it was the lack of registration, insurance and other licenses. These were all legally required to haul goods, which is what BFI hired ATI to do.

Notice that this is a negligence theory, pure and simple. BFI could be held liable for its own negligence in hiring an independent contractor, as long as that negligence was an actual and proximate cause of the plaintiff's harm.

Note 2. The employer's primary negligence. An employer may be negligent in hiring an employee who is dangerous to those with whom he may deal. The same is true as to training and retaining the employee. In *Foradori*, cited here, a customer of defendant's fast-food restaurant was attacked on its premises by an off-duty employee. The court affirmed a jury's findings that the restaurant operator's negligence in failing to train, supervise and control its off-duty employees on the premises was a proximate cause of the customer's serious injuries. (The plaintiff was rendered a paraplegic by the attack, and won a judgment of over $20 million. To take another couple of examples, in *Welsh Manufacturing Division of Textron, Inc. v. Pinkerton's, Inc., Inc.*, 474 A.2d 436 (R.I. 1984), the employer of a security guard was held liable when the guard used his position to assist in a theft from the business he was supposed to guard. In *Ponticas v. K.M.S. Investments*, 331 N.W.2d 907 (Minn. 1983), the landlord was held liable for the manager's sexual assault upon a tenant. In *Scott Fetzer Co. v. Read*, 945 S.W.2d 854 (Tex. App. 1997), *aff'd*, 990 S.W.2d 732 (Tex. 1998), a vacuum cleaner manufacturer and distributor were held liable for a salesman's sexual assault on a customer. In these cases there had been negligence in failing adequately to investigate the character of the employee. Again, this is a ground of liability that is wholly unrelated to respondeat superior. Thus liability does not depend on whether the employee was within the scope of his employment.

Note 3. "Corporate negligence." You may not need to mention this in class; it is yet another particular form of primary negligence, applied most often to hospitals and HMO's.

§ 3. OTHER FORMS OF VICARIOUS RESPONSIBILITY

This section is designed to be largely self-explanatory; teachers can probably just have students read it and ask if there are any questions. The issues raised are more fully discussed in DOBBS ON TORTS §§ 340-41 (2000).

Law firm partnerships do not necessarily fit the partnership principles described in paragraph 1, because, with law firms, the limited liability partnership ("LLP") form of business is in widespread use.

¶ ¶ **3 & 4. Concert of action, conspiring, aiding and abetting.** This note might be worth a moment's attention because we are going to talk about concert of action or conspiracy twice more, first in connection with *Lewis* in the products liability chapter, Casebook 739, and second in connection with market share liability following *Hymowitz*, Casebook 825. In addition, even where joint and several liability is abolished (Chapter 25), it may be retained for concert of action or conspiracy cases.

¶ **5 (a). Negligent entrustment.** Negligent entrustment is not vicarious liability; the owner who entrusts his vehicle to a known drunken driver is himself negligent. If he were vicariously liable, he would be liable to the plaintiff for all the plaintiff's recoverable damages, although he might then have an action over against the driver for indemnity. Most courts do not treat negligent entrustment as a case for vicarious liability of the entrustor. Instead, they apportion liability between the entrustor and the negligent driver, as in *Ali v. Fisher*, cited here. It might not matter much if joint and the several liability system were in force, since in that case the entrustor would be potentially liable for 100% of the plaintiff's damages even without vicarious liability. But Tennessee had judicially abolished joint and several liability, so fault apportionment limited the entrustor's liability to his percentage of fault as assessed by the jury.

The *Ali* plaintiff argued that once the entrustor was found to be negligent in making the entrustment to a dangerous driver, the entrustor would be vicariously liable. Respondeat superior would not lead to such a result, but you can see why there is a problem in apportionment between the entrustor and the entrustee. It is the same problem we face with how to apportion liability of other facilitators. The drunken entrustee is somewhat like a force of nature, not a rational human being capable of responsible conduct. To unleash such a force is a serious wrong, without which the injury would not have occurred. That is a strong case for retaining joint and several liability. Even where joint and several liability has been abolished, though, there is room for argument that a major portion of the responsibility should fall on the rational person who is in control, so that an apportionment of 80% of the fault to the entrustor would not necessarily be wrong-headed. The *Ali* plaintiff did not argue that, but sought to get 100% of the damages from the entrustor under a vicarious liability theory and lost that argument.

¶ **5 (d). Owner consent statutes.** If you teach local law in an owner-consent state, you might want to call the class' attention to the expansive liabilities possible. In *Murdza v. Zimmerman*, 786 N.E.2d 440 (N.Y. 2003), the court succinctly explained the rationale for the owner liability statutes, saying that the owner liability statute simultaneously increases the likelihood of compensation for those injured in motor vehicle accidents and decreases the probability of such accidents by encouraging an owner's prudent selection of drivers.

In that case, A was a leasing company, leasing vehicles to B, Brown & Williamson Tobacco Corporation. Brown and Williamson made the leased vehicle available to its employee, C, subject to a rule in its employee manual that the vehicle was only available to employees and spouses, not others. C nevertheless permitted her boyfriend to drive. The boyfriend, driving the car, struck the plaintiff. The court held that the presumption of consent was negated as to Brown & Williamson because of their restriction in the employee manual. But A, the leasing company, in the business of putting large numbers of vehicles on the road, had to anticipate that others besides the lessee would drive and accordingly was liable in spite of the restriction on consent imposed by the lessee.

In Florida, a judge-made doctrine imposes strict vicarious liability upon the owner who provides a motor vehicle to another. But Florida recognizes an exception if the bailee goes so far beyond the owner's consent that the bailee in effect becomes a thief or converter. *Hertz Corporation v. Jackson,* 617 So.2d 1051 (Fla. 1993).

Fojtik v. Hunter, 828 A.2d 589 (Conn. 2003): Under a lessor-liability statute, lessor would not be liable for negligence of unauthorized driver, but would remain liable for negligence of driver who breached lease agreement by not having valid driver's license.

CHAPTER 23

THE DEVELOPMENT OF
COMMON LAW STRICT LIABILITY

▶**Changes in the Sixth Edition.** We have updated text and notes, trimming some material when possible. Otherwise this chapter is unchanged from the prior edition.

▶The **Concise Edition** reduces the length of this Chapter by almost one-third, by cutting the introductory materials (including the Weaver v. Ward and Brown v. Kendall cases) and substituting textual discussion of the development of common-law negligence; shortening the text on trespassing animals; and making various cuts to the text describing "The Subjects of Strict Liability."◾

Preliminary Note:

This chapter treats traditional strict liability subjects and bridges directly into the next chapter, which deals with products liability. It has one major side purpose, to provide a little sense of how changes can come about in tort law.

The chapter is organized chronologically, beginning with the medieval strict liability in those actions in which the writ of Trespass could be used. The shift to a fault standard, and the shifts back toward some degree of strict liability are then presented. Each main case is decided at a later date than the case preceding it. (Notes following the cases bring in some non-chronological materials.) Chronology is not history, of course, but it does tend to help make a developmental approach possible in this chapter. History and legal development mean change, and this chapter furnishes an opportunity to consider how the changes are occurring and why.

The main doctrinal function of the chapter is to provide a survey of the forms, subjects, and rationales for traditional strict liability. This begins with the formal rules of the writ of trespass, and moves to the rejection of strict liability based on such formalities (*Brown v. Kendall*). As soon, however, as the strict liability is rejected, it rises again, this time with new rationales, surprisingly and wonderfully expressed in Baron Bramwell's judgment in *Bamford*. This judgment opens up the discussion both to economic analysis of strict liability and a humanistic or even a moral analysis. *Rylands v. Fletcher* branches to the idea of a non-natural user as grounds for strict liability. The American cases, rejecting this, are then shown gradually to accept a branch of the branch — liability for abnormally dangerous activities, as formulated by the Restatement Second of Torts in sections 519 and 520. But this, too, gives away to a narrower formulation in the Restatement Third based on Jones' ideas that strict liability only applies when the defendant's activity is the most significant cause and others are not involved.

The remainder of the chapter is less interesting but some of it may be a relief to students. It runs through a number of activities held to be, or not to be, strict liability activities, then considers scope of risk issues and the defenses of contributory fault and assumed risk.

OUTLINE

§ 1. STRICT LIABILITY FOR TRESPASSORY TORTS AND THE ADVENT OF FAULT THEORY

§ 2. STRICT LIABILITY AFTER *BROWN V. KENDALL*

§ 3. STRICT LIABILITY TODAY

C. Affirmative Defenses to Strict Liability Claims. Text (Contributory negligence, assumed risk, comparative negligence, and plaintiff's abnormal sensitivity.)

SUMMARY

§ 1. STRICT LIABILITY FOR TRESPASSORY TORTS AND THE ADVENT OF FAULT THEORY

TEXT. c. 1200-1400. This states the rule of strict liability followed in the medieval period whenever the appropriate writ was *Trespass*. This was, at least in theory, in any situation in which the injury was "direct" and forcible. Where the injury was "indirect," the writ of *Case* was used and some kind of fault was required.

WEAVER V. WARD. 1616. Weaver alleged that Ward "trespassed" against him by assault and battery. Ward pleaded that the two were skirmishing as part of a military exercise and that his piece accidentally and against his will discharged and caused the wound of which the plaintiff complains. The plaintiff demurred to this defensive plea, and the court sustained the demurrer and gave judgment for the plaintiff. This holding illustrates the strict liability as applied in trespass (direct and forcible injury) cases. But the court goes on in dicta to suggest that if it is "utterly without his fault," as where the plaintiff crossed the weapon when it was discharging, then there would be no liability. Notes take up the development of fault as an important element in these cases.

BROWN V. KENDALL. 1850. Defendant, beating two fighting dogs with a stick, raised it over his head and in so doing struck the plaintiff in the eye. There seems to have been no intent to hit the plaintiff, but the injury was direct and thus within the writ of trespass. But the court holds that negligence must be proved. The old regime of strict liability based on direct harms is at an end. Notes raise questions as to the forces that may have led to this shift from strict liability.

§ 2. STRICT LIABILITY AFTER *BROWN V. KENDALL*

A. Trespassing Animals

TEXT. Although cattle trespasses were not the direct result of an owner's acts in most cases, there was strict liability at common law. The happenstantial aspects of this rule are emphasized in the note. Strict liability for wild animals seems to have a different source and that topic is treated after *Rylands v. Fletcher*.

B. Nuisance

[1] Strict Liability for Nuisance and Non-Natural Activities

BAMFORD V. TURNLEY. 1862. Defendant constructed brick kilns on his land and made brick, using the clay on his own land, intending to provide bricks for the building of his own house. The kilns were as far from the plaintiff's property as possible, but they gave off offensive "vapours, smokes, fumes, stinks and stenches." The trial judge ruled that if the spot chosen for the kilns was a reasonable use of the defendant's own land under the circumstances, the defendant would be entitled to a verdict. Held: reversed. In separate judgments, the judges held that if the acts amount to a nuisance, it is no defense to say that the defendant was using his land in a reasonable manner. The Bramwell judgment provides a basis for both moral and economic analysis of strict liability claims.

NOTE: A SHORT SIDE-TRIP – NUISANCES TODAY. This note summarizes the main current doctrines– the invasion must be "substantial" to be a nuisance at all, and it must be unreasonable in the sense that it interferes unduly with the plaintiff's rights (but not necessarily in the sense that the defendant behaves unreasonably). It also considers sensitive plaintiffs, coming to the nuisance and the nature of intent that can be found in nuisance cases. This note is in the nature of an extended footnote, intended to explain the main points of nuisance law without developing them in any depth.

RYLANDS V. FLETCHER. 1865-1868. We think *Rylands* is a special case of "nuisance," but if you don't want to think of it that way, you can insert a new subsection marker here. The defendant hired an independent contractor to construct a pond. Though the area was one devoted to mining, no one knew or had reason to know that the pond was situated over old vertical mine shafts which had been loosely filled. When water was collected the weight caused the material in the old shafts to give way and the water flooded these shafts. They were connected to horizontal shafts, which in turn connected to the plaintiff's nearby mine. His mine was flooded as a result and he sued the defendant landowner. When the case reaches the House of Lords, the result is that there is liability, which is said to be because the land was used in a "non-natural" way, or because some non-natural thing (water) was introduced "into the close." Notes begin to suggest the economic problem of inconsistent land uses.

C. Slouching Toward the Abnormal Danger Conception

SULLIVAN V. DUNHAM. 1900. Annie E. Harten, 19, was struck by a stump as she walked on the public highway. The stump had been blasted by the defendant, who was not shown to be negligent. The court reasoned that because the blaster would have been liable for a trespass to land even if he was not at fault, he should be held liable here. However, this is only to the extent that there is direct forcible injury; if the injury results from shock waves, there would be no liability without fault.

EXNER V. SHERMAN POWER CONST. CO. A blasting caused concussion damages (by shaking the earth) but did not involve any actual physical trespass by debris (or stumps). The court here rejects any universal rule that liability is based solely on fault and suggests that when one has engaged in "perilous activity" such as using large quantities of explosives, that one rather than a third person should bear the loss that results. Perilous activity rather than enterprise liability becomes the basis for the new synthesis.

NOTE: THE RESTATEMENTS' RULES OF STRICT LIABILITY. The Restatement Third requires a foreseeable risk of physical harm that is so significant that it remains even when reasonable care is used. The risk must result from an activity that is not a common usage. The harm must result predominantly from the defendant's activity alone, not from, say, a train and car collision where others must be involved. The Restatement Second used some of these ideas, but considered also the appropriateness of the activity to the place where it was carried on. And it did not insist that the plaintiff and others be uninvolved.

§ 3. STRICT LIABILITY TODAY

A. The Subjects of Strict Liability

In text, we summarize a number of the contemporary fact-patterns or issues in strict liability – impoundment cases, hazardous wastes, lateral support, blasting, nuclear energy, fire, other high-energy activities, poisons, and ground damage from aircraft. There is a brief mention of environmental statutes and the superfund.

B. Scope of Risk Limitations in Strict Liability Cases

The risk rule works in strict liability cases if you adjust the statement of its rationale. If liability is strict, then the scope of liability should be limited to harms that result from the reasons for making liability strict in the first place. The note provides the familiar illustration of the blasting which causes mother mink, bred for commercial purposes, to eat their young and also some "intervening cause" type cases, in which a third person deliberately causes an explosion.

C. Affirmative Defenses to Strict Liability Claims

Under the Restatement view, contributory negligence is no bar, but that something like assumed risk is.

COMMENTS

§ 1. STRICT LIABILITY FOR TRESPASSORY TORTS AND THE ADVENT OF FAULT THEORY

[a] Strict liability under Trespass at early common law

Textual Note

A historical development in a torts casebook must necessarily be so limited that, to a professional historian, it would seem to be a caricature of history rather than a map of it. But as stylized as this historical development may be, it can still add a great deal to an understanding of both the process of tort law and the current doctrine.

If the class got a rough idea of the enterprise liability theories of strict liability in Chapter 20, the old form of strict liability for direct and forcible harms will come as a jolt. It is strict liability, but it does not turn on deep pocket, risk spreading, or any idea that the risk involved is incident to an enterprise and ought to be borne by the enterprise. It seems to turn on what may strike us now as a rather arbitrary or accidental feature – was the injury "direct?"

For some thinkers, directness seems a suitable touchstone, a word that brings intuitive responses that seem adequate to mark off grounds for liability. Directness is the test, the class might remember, that many people have used in "proximate cause" or scope-of-risk cases. But it perhaps is not so appealing a method of deciding between fault and strict liability. Why should the plaintiff who is hit by a thrown log recover without proof of the defendant's fault, when a plaintiff who stumbles over it two seconds later must prove fault or be denied relief? To ask this question seems to suggest that the Trespass-Case distinction was a formal one, not related to considerations of substance, either moral or economic. Discussion of *Weaver v. Ward* is likely to accentuate this feeling that the strict liability rule there is an arbitrary one.

Yet it may be that only the formulation of the rule is wrong, not the underlying idea of strict liability. The idea that there should be strict liability for direct and physical harms may be a crude expression of the ideas advanced in connection with *Vincent v. Lake Erie Transp. Co.*– namely that if you choose to act, you'll get the benefits of the act and you ought to bear the losses as well. See also *Bamford*.

[b] Application of strict liability and signs of change to come

WEAVER V. WARD, 80 Eng.Rep. 284 (K.B. 1616)

This case applies a rule of strict liability in Trespass. It also recognizes that a defendant might in some cases carry the burden of justifying his action (self-defense would be an example). The justification offered here is that he was not at fault, but this was not an acceptable justification. The court seems to be willing to impose liability upon others who might act without fault, as well, though they may sometimes escape criminal punishment– the prize fighter who without fault kills his opponent, or the "lunatick" who causes harm without fault. No moral justification is suggested; instead the court suggests that tort law is mainly compensatory– it "tends only to give damages according to hurt or loss" and not fault.

Discussion of this first part of the case bears on the idea that the early courts had fed the pie of strict liability to the wrong plaintiffs. It may pay to ask the class directly if this means that courts should discard strict liability in all cases. If the answer is yes, they should, then you might ask if this means abolishing vicarious responsibility. This may help the class to see that the direct-indirect test of strict liability may be unsatisfactory but to see that this does not by itself condemn strict liability in all cases.

Having declared that the defendant is liable though he never intended to hit the plaintiff and only discharged his piece by accident, the *Weaver* court then advances the suggestion that there might be cases, after all, in which the absence of fault would excuse the defendant. On this point, you could think that it is a forecast of changes to come. There is a certain merit in making this point and moving on, dealing with the theme of change in the notes.

However, the court gives examples of non-liability cases that suggest not only the absence of fault but also the absence of act or cause. If someone takes my hand and strikes you with it, there is plenty of reason to say there is no liability: there is no act by me at all. In the illustration of the plaintiff who runs across the defendant's piece as it is discharging, liability might be denied because of the defendant's innocence, but that would not seem to be very consistent with *Weaver v. Ward* itself. However, liability in such a case could be denied on some kind of proximate cause reasoning.

The court's notion of fault or negligence as expressed in these examples, then, may not be quite the same as ours. The last words of the reporter who summarized this decision have the court telling us that a more specific pleading by the defendant might have sufficed to exculpate him if it had shown that injury was "inevitable, and that the defendant had committed no negligence . . . ." Given the court's understanding about what would constitute a case of "no negligence" this sentence might be read with a grain of salt. Nevertheless, it will, like any case, have its readers who see in it the prospect of a shift to a fault standard.

Note 2. Eighteenth century development. The directness test was supplemented, seemingly, by an unlawfulness test, glimmerings of which you can see in the trial court's charge in *Brown v. Kendall*.

Vosberg v. Putney, 50 N.W. 403 (Wis. 1891) is familiar to many torts teachers. Some regard it as an essential case for a torts casebook and even as THE case that ought to come first in a casebook.[1] There, a 12-year-old boy

---

1. James Henderson, *Why Vosburg Comes First*, 1992 WIS. L. REV. 853. *Vosburg* was celebrated at great length in a series of articles in 1992. Zigurds Zile, *Vosburg v. Putney: A Centennial Story*, 1992 WIS. L. REV. 877. Shorter articles, besides Henderson's, are Robert

kicked a 14-year-old boy while they were both in class at school. The kick caused some unexpected harm and the 14-year-old sued. The jury found that the defendant had no intent to harm, but the court held he could be liable even though he lacked the intent, if the act was "unlawful." The court thought that, in the classroom, the act was indeed "unlawful," though it might have been otherwise on the playground. As others have noted, there are plenty of issues in *Vosburg*, including a thin skull or thin shin issue. In connection with Note 2, however, *Vosburg* makes a kind of historical sense because it uses unlawfulness to condemn a touching that might have been perfectly acceptable elsewhere. The unlawfulness test might add to the number of cases in which liability could be found. Yet, with the perverseness that seems almost characteristic of legal change, the addition of the unlawfulness test provided an indirect emphasis on something very similar to fault, which, as we now know, came to dominate the thinking about tort liability.

Note 3. Nineteenth century development. By this time the courts would allow the plaintiff to "waive the trespass" and prove fault if he could. This meant he could use Case, with whatever procedural advantages that writ might carry. It is better to prove fault, if you can do so, since this will mean you can use Case and you will not be thrown out of court for using the wrong writ. Lawyers, proving fault for strategy reasons like this, are becoming accustomed to proving fault. What is customarily done is very likely to become the standard, even though there was not one iota of policy or moral thinking behind it. What we have as the fault system is the result of odd accidents, not conscious choice. So, at least, the material summarized here seems to suggest.

Note 4. Recognizing change. Lawyers of the time probably had only the vaguest inkling that change was taking place. They continued to cite old precedents as they always had. Can we as lawyers today sensitize ourselves so that we will recognize change before our clients are struck down by it?

[c] Change arrives: the fault theory is adopted

BROWN V. KENDALL, 60 Mass. 292 (1850)

Brown v. Kendall was a direct physical ("forcible") harm. It was the kind of case that fits under the writ of Trespass. Unless the law is to be changed in this case, then, the defendant should be held liable. But the law *is* changed and the defendant is *not* held liable.

If the orthodox understanding of the history is correct— and it may not be— Chief Justice Shaw's decision in *Brown v. Kendall* was a major shift in the

---

Rabin, *Vosburg v. Putney in Three-Part Disharmony*, 1992 WIS. L. REV. 863 (a delightful series of comments by three fictional professors); and James Willard Hurst, *The Use of Case Histories*, 1992 WIS. L. REV. 875. These articles are not primarily or at all concerned with the fact that unlawfulness became a kind of optional substitute for the older directness test.

law, and perhaps a somewhat conscious one. The trial judge evidently had some ideas about "unlawfulness," and also about the use of privilege as a defense. His ideas sound strange to us today, but they show some awareness of the strict liability rules in cases of direct and forcible harm. So do the cases cited by Shaw. Yet Shaw is able to distinguish those cases.

His distinction is one students have trouble in finding and interpreting. His distinction turns on a separation of the formal problem of choosing the right writ from the problem of substance – does any cause of action at all exist on a given state of facts? All of the cases which have imposed strict liability for direct torts are interpreted to mean, not that there is liability, but that Trespass is the correct writ. Could that really have been the idea in the judge's mind in *Weaver v. Ward*? It does not seem credible.

Whether Shaw was consciously undermining the precedent or not, *Brown v. Kendall* either created important shifts in thinking or expressed shifts that were already taking place. Three changes loomed: (1) Fault, not strict liability, would govern legal responsibility. (2) The content of fault judges would be (a) intent, (b) negligence, based on the ordinary person standard, or (c) unlawfulness. (3) This principle of liability would be, as far as we could tell from the text, rather general. It was not a rule about duties between particular classes of people.

How did this change come about? Was it merely the result of an accretion of small changes, none of which was directed toward this end? Or was it by design? Some of the notes suggest possibilities for discussion.

Note 2. Procedural change. By the middle of the 19th century, procedural reform was well underway, as the Field Code shows. It became possible to separate the procedure or the writ from the substantial right. It may be that Shaw's thinking was influenced by this. We can separate the procedural side of the case from the justice of the case, so that mere choice of a writ no longer controls your rights. We have eliminated the writs, one might say, and we thus no longer are required to accept the strict liability that went with them.

If this was the thinking, it is interesting to notice that it was not carried out to the limits of its logic. It starts with a sense of freedom – we are not limited by the procedural system. But that freedom comes to a quick end because there is no sign that Shaw thought about the possibility of developing some other form of strict liability or applying it to other cases. To abolish the procedural writ was to abolish the whole case for strict liability, not merely to abolish the directness rule.

Note 3. Subsidizing industry. You could easily think that Shaw's decision prepared the way for industrial development. Most industrial accidents would involve moving machinery, such as trains, winches, cranes and booms, or possibly explosives and boilers. These would cause harm directly and forcibly. If industry were made to pay without fault, under the old directness test for Trespass, then industry might not long survive in a world without large capital aggregations and risk-sharing devices such as insurance. Did Shaw make it possible for industrial development to be paid for with the blood of the working man, as the saying goes? Gary Schwartz concluded that courts were sympathetic with injured workers. As a practical lawyer, is there anything like this you should take into account today in assessing the probable direction of law that affects your clients?

Note 4. Universalizing principles. G. Edward White's wonderful book, cited here, sees Shaw's decision as a part of a larger tendency to conceptualize or generalize. The common law originated and carried on for many years as a series of more or less discrete decisions. To be sure, the courts were bound by precedent, but the precedential decisions were not often generalized to the broadest possible principle. Their force was therefore limited. White sees in *Brown v. Kendall* a part of the tendency of the time to generalize.

Reading *Brown v. Kendall* in 1850, a lawyer might have concluded that strict liability was dead. If so, it was a case of strict liability is dead, long live strict liability, as the next section seems to show.

§ 2. STRICT LIABILITY AFTER *BROWN V. KENDALL*

A. Trespassing Animals

Some teachers like to spend some time on trespassing animals, partly because this little topic in itself can demonstrate change in the law and also its adaptation to social conditions. This is so because the English strict liability rule, which was presumptively carried over to this country by way of statutes providing for the "reception" of common law, was in fact changed in the American courts to reflect local conditions. In the West, for example, open range was sometimes the preferred solution to cattle raising, and naturally strict liability was not a desirable rule in such cases.

The casebook does not develop the trespassing animals topic extensively, or even animals-on-the-highway cases. For more on this history, and several ways of viewing the rule-choices, *see* DOBBS ON TORTS § 343 (2000).

Some books present cases of wild animals and those with vicious propensities in the same segment with the cattle trespass cases. But the wild animal cases stand on a different footing. They fit more neatly into the category of abnormal or at least nonreciprocal danger. They are thus dealt with (though rather briskly) after we take up *Rylands*.

B. Nuisance

Most of the casebook is devoted to development of tort law as applied to physical harms. Some of these are harms to persons, some harms to property, but all are physical. Nuisance cases do sometimes involve physical invasions, as in *Rylands v. Fletcher*, but most often the invasion is by smells, smoke, odors, or even offensive sights. There is, of course, a physical basis for this kind of invasion— smoke has particles, and even sight nuisances are carried by light waves. But the courts have almost always treated such cases differently from the kind of physical invasion that may do immediate physical harm or may dispossess the landowner.

You can see one difference in the way courts treated idiosyncratic preferences of the landowner. These preferences were fully protected by the law of trespass in the case of gross physical entry, but were not protected at all under the law of nuisance: the man who hates church bells on Sunday morning may be obliged to put up with them if his preference is abnormal. This is reflected in the fact that damages are often based on diminished value of the property. Indeed in some states, the primary guide to finding that a nuisance exists at all lay in the reduction of the property's value. *See Arnoldt v. Ashland Oil, Inc.*, 412 S.E.2d 795 (W. Va. 1991) (applying Kentucky law). There will be no reduction in property value if only the landowner cares about the church bells; market value is an objective way of finding out that the annoyance is not purely personal. Predominantly, then, nuisance is an economic tort with overtones of emotional distress, not a physical injury tort; the damage we are most often concerned with is that the quality of life of those on the property is less and the value of the property is driven down in the market. Occasionally, a landowner will complain that he has been made ill by smells, but such claims are almost never the substantial basis of the case. On the distinction between nuisance and trespass, with reference to cases that attempt to break down the distinction, *see* DOBBS ON TORTS § 463. Recent decisions discussing the issue are *Public Service Co. of Colorado v. Van Wyk,* 27 P.3d 377 (Colo. 2001) and *Adams v. Cleveland-Cliffs Iron Co.,* 602 N.W.2d 215 (Mich. Ct. App. 1999).

Thus if the casebook were to develop nuisance materials fully, the place for that development would probably be in Part VII with the economic torts. In fact, the casebook provides very little material on nuisance, and most of it is here. The reason for providing such limited material is that much of nuisance law relates to the problem of land use control, while another part is relates to environmental law, so that it is likely to be covered with the aid of related materials in advanced courses.

The reason for putting the nuisance materials at this particular place is perhaps more obvious. No torts course can ignore *Rylands v. Fletcher*, and whether you regard that as a nuisance case or not, it certainly calls for some comparison to nuisance. More importantly, it is perfect material for development of certain aspects of strict liability. Bramwell's judgment in *Bamford* is a wonderful expression of a viewpoint that promotes a great deal of both moral and economic discussion on strict liability. And because students should know something about what a nuisance is, there is a little added material on nuisances today.

BAMFORD V. TURNLEY , 122 Eng. Rep. 27 (1862).

Strict liability and intent in *Bamford*. Several things make *Bamford* special. One is the possibility that it imposes strict liability. If the defendant is reasonable in his conduct there is at least some sense in which liability is strict here. This may, however, be an intentional tort. Defendant knows his smoke invades the plaintiff's property and knows as well that the invasion is substantial and annoying. (You can be sure he's heard about the annoyance.) Once he's heard of the annoyance to the plaintiff, he continues to make brick with substantial certainty that harm is being caused. This could lead you to the view that he is an intentional tortfeasor under the ordinary intent rules. But if so, it is still meaningful to say that he is being held strictly liable. He is acting reasonably to exploit his property, even if he is causing harm. When a defendant acts reasonably to protect himself in self-defense cases he is definitely not held liable and if he were so held, we'd probably feel that there was something "strict" in the liability thus imposed.

Bramwell's judgment. This is not to say the rule of strict liability in *Bamford* —if that is what it is— is a bad one. Bramwell's opinion, believe it or not, actually does excite interest in some students. His judgment is a significant part of legal lore and has seemingly had its impact on thinkers like Richard Epstein and George Fletcher. (See references to Fletcher, *Fairness and Utility in Tort Theory*, Casebook, Chapter 22 § 2; Epstein, *Nuisance Law: Corrective Justice and Its Utilitarian Constraints*, 8 J. LEG STUD. 49 (1979).) Bramwell creates a two-part structure for analysis of nuisance law that picks up two important threads, both of which are at odds with any effort to elevate *Carroll Towing* to the rank of overarching principle in tort law. The first thread leads us back to the community standard rather than the reasonableness standard. The second thread uses a cost-benefit analysis as in *Carroll Towing*, but rejects the *Carroll Towing* conclusion that the defendant's acts are justified if they produce or conserve enough benefit to the defendant.

— *Reciprocal nuisances*. First, there are nuisances such as burning weeds, emptying cesspools and the like which he thinks are not actionable. They are "common and ordinary," and they fall under the rule of live and let live. That is, it is desirable to hold such activities not to be actionable because all neighbors will want to carry on those or very similar activities. They are "reciprocal nuisances."

— *Productive nuisances*. Second, there are nuisances that are productive. They create benefits for society and for those who carry on the nuisances. But as to these, Bramwell does not apply the rule of *Carroll Towing*. That case told us that if the benefits to be derived from a risk-taking activity outweighed the cost of the harm discounted by its likelihood, there would be no liability. Here Bramwell tells us that, on the contrary, if you want to carry on an activity that is costly to others, it should be valuable enough to pay for the harm it causes. If he had stopped there, his view might be consistent with *Carroll Towing*. But where *Carroll Towing* concludes that the defendant is not to be liable when its activities produce a net benefit, Bramwell draws the opposite conclusion. "[U]nless the defendant's profits are enough to compensate [plaintiff's loss], I deny that it is for the public benefit. . ." But if the profits *are* enough to compensate the plaintiff, that is produce benefits that exceed the costs, then the defendant "ought to compensate." "[T]he loss to the individuals of the public who lose will bear compensation out of the gains of those who gain." There is a public benefit in running trains; but this does not mean they may take property without paying for it. Similarly, Bramwell thinks, for nuisances: if there is benefit in making brick, then take the benefit and pay the freight.

Bramwell's judgment and *Surroco, Vincent* and *Carroll Towing*. Bramwell's judgment brings us back with a jolt to issues specifically introduced in connection with such cases as *Surroco v. Geary, Vincent v. Lake Erie Transp. Co.* and *Carroll Towing*. Bramwell's judgment gives a reason for *Vincent* —take what you want and pay for it. But it is not technically contrary to *Carroll Towing*. This is so partly because Bramwell seems to envision *intentional* choices to inflict certain harm on neighbors, not a choice to inflict only a risk upon them. If you choose to inflict a risk, but not a certain harm, should you be liable? Perhaps if you like enterprise liability theories of respondeat superior, your answer will be "yes," with an exception, perhaps, for reciprocal risks. This view could wipe out the entire field of negligence law. Is Bramwell's idea so potent as this?

The narrow view of causation in Bramwell's judgment; a reference forward. There is very much that is appealing in Bramwell's judgment and in the thought of jurists that have been influenced by it. But it does turn on a narrow vision of causation. It takes both a brickyard and a residence to create the problem. What makes it a "choice" on the part of the defendant to burn bricks but not a "choice" on the part of the plaintiff to live next door? This is a problem that can best be dealt with perhaps after looking at *Rylands v. Fletcher*, but it definitely will be important to deal with it. It is a form of a problem we will have many times in strict liability cases. Other forms of the problem can be seen in the enterprise liability cases in Chapter 22 (whose enterprise is it, who should bear the cost of an activity as "his" activity?), and in products cases in Chapter 24 (is the allergy to a product the problem of the manufacturer or the consumer?).

Note 4. This note is a tip-off to students to compare or contrast *Bamford* with *Carroll Towing*, so discussion of the points raised above can proceed without undue delays. The reference to *T.J. Hooper* in this question is intended to contrast another Hand opinion, one which rejects customs as a controlling force. Bramwell, of course, makes custom the standard of conduct, protecting all conduct that is matched by like conduct in the community.

NOTE: A SHORT SIDE-TRIP – NUISANCES TODAY

If you feel nuisance must be covered with some care, you'll have to spend a little time on this. Otherwise, you might simply invite questions from the class about it (there usually are some). The points made here are basic ones in nuisance law. *See* DOBBS ON TORTS §§ 462-68 (2000).

Although *Bamford* and some of the cases sketched in this note are claims by residential homeowners, many of the nuisance situations sketched in this note are — typically — economic harm cases that can also be considered as cases of interference with contract or interference with prospective business dealings. Sometimes when one claim won't work, the other will. *See Page County Appliance Center v. Honeywell*, 347 N.W.2d 171 (Iowa 1984) ("radiation" from travel agency's computer affecting TV reception in nearby appliance store). Many of the public nuisance cases are also like this.

¶ 6. **Injunctions.** We inserted this paragraph to inform students of the fact that the remedy often sought in nuisance cases is not the one the students have been seeing almost exclusively up until now – damages. Rather, plaintiffs in nuisance cases often seek to have the nuisance abated, in other words to have the court grant injunctive relief ordering the defendant to stop doing something (or start, like cleaning up the mess). Your students may or may not have encountered this remedy in other classes; in any event you probably need do no more than mention it in class and tell them that it's typically a major focus of a remedies class.

¶ 7. **Public nuisances.** *(a) Public claims.* Many statutes declare some activity to be a nuisance, then authorize its abatement. These do not concern us. Apart from statute, public nuisance involves a substantial interference with a public right, usually access to or use of public ways or waters. The public entity may seek abatement (by injunction) or may seek damages.

(b) Private persons harmed by a public nuisance. The private nuisance claim we have considered up to this point is enforceable only by land occupiers and their families. Public nuisances that cause harm to private persons, though, are actionable by the private plaintiff independent of any land ownership, provided the private plaintiff suffers harm different from the kind of harm suffered by people generally. The commercial fisher who cannot fish because public waters are polluted is probably a good example. As this example shows, public nuisance with private harm is definitely not tied to landownership the way private nuisance is.

(c) Public nuisance causing private physical injury. Sometimes a personal injury claim is pursued as a public nuisance claim with damages different in kind. If the ultimate basis of liability is negligence, even though it is encased in a nuisance theory, perhaps all the negligence rules should apply – which seems to make it just a negligence case. In *Physicians Plus Ins. Corp. v. Medwest Mut. Ins. Co.*, 646 N.W.2d 777 (Wis.. 2002), a city, county, and private landowner did nothing about the landowner's tree branches that had obstructed a view of a stop sign for at least two months. Diane Smith, who had had four or five beers in the preceding two hours and had one open in the car, said she didn't see the sign; she ran into the plaintiff who, on his motorcycle, was crossing the intersection on the dominant road. The court held that the plaintiff could proceed past summary judgment on a public nuisance theory. The court concluded that the defendants would be liable only if they knew or

should have known of the dangerous condition, and that liability would be apportioned under comparative fault rules. Justice Ann Walsh Bradley concurred, arguing that it would be more straightforward to say that when negligence was the basis of liability, the "nuisance" case is simply a negligence case and all the negligence rules apply.

There are plenty of debates about nuisance law. Should you recognize a nuisance at all in cases that involve no invasion of the land, not even by particles? For example, suppose defendant sets up a "half-way house" in a residential neighborhood, a place designed to house paroled convicts who are to be "re-integrated" into the community. Or creates a truly ugly sign within view of the plaintiff's living room window. Or opens a funeral parlor across the street. In these cases there is not invasion of the plaintiff's land at all unless you count the light waves that allow perception of the funeral parlor. See, e.g., *Heston v. Ousler*, 398 A.2d 536 (N.H. 1979) (view obstructed); *Arkansas Release Guidance Foundation v. Needler*, 477 S.W.2d 821 (Ark. 1972) (halfway house); *Mitchell v. Bearden*, 503 S.W.2d 904 (Ark. 1974) (mortuary).

Another interesting version of this kind of nuisance is one that occurs from storage of dangerous materials, such as dynamite. (Perhaps a good comparison, from the neighbor's viewpoint, to the halfway house). Professor Barry Furrow describes this as a "dread" nuisance, and he argues that if this can be enjoined, then so can dangerous laboratory experiments, such as those involving research in recombinant DNA. See Furrow, *Governing Science: Public Risks and Private Remedies*, 131 U. PA. L. REV. 1403 (1983).

The end of the textual note, not separately titled, is intended to bring back the focus on the state of strict liability after *Brown v. Kendall*. It also suggests, as these comments do, that even if you find intent in *Bamford*, there is still strict liability in some important sense.

RYLANDS V. FLETCHER , L.R. 3 H.L. 330 (1868).

A First Analysis

The Exchequer. Baron Bramwell's opinion in the Exchequer Court is no surprise, is it? Could Baron Martin have distinguished *Bamford* if he were minded to do so? Certainly. In *Bamford,* the defendant intended to do the act that was causing harm and must have known eventually that it was in fact causing harm. In *Rylands,* the defendant not only has no intent to inflict the harm, he did not even *risk* it. Liability in *Rylands,* then, would require the law to go much further than liability in *Bamford.*

The Exchequer Chamber. The Exchequer Chamber reversed, holding that the defendant is liable because he brought something on the land that will do mischief if it escapes. Blackburn's argument is interesting and useful for students to see, because Blackburn uses cases on quite different facts to suggest a generalization that will cover this case. It is a fundamental part of legal method, inductive, but far from scientific.

— *Blackburn's three case-situations.* Blackburn takes three kinds of cases. The first is the case of cattle trespass. The owner is to keep them at his peril, that is, the owner is strictly liable for the trespass of cattle. The second is the case of the landowner whose privy leaks to the detriment of his neighbor. In this and like cases, the landowner is again held strictly liable. The third case is the case of the alkali works in Liverpool, from which escaped chlorine gas. The parties in that case all assumed that there would be strict liability if the defendant's gas in fact escaped.

— *Blackburn's generalization.* The generalization or rule that Blackburn thinks these cases support was that "the person who, for his own purposes, bring on his land, and collects and keeps there anything likely to do mischief if it escapes, must keep it in at his peril . . . ." He is strictly liable, subject only to excuse such as the act of God defense.

— *Induction and generalization.* Blackburn's argument is subject to criticism, but it is a good example of the inductive or synthetic argument. It may be worth the effort to be sure students see how they, too, can construct arguments by seeing case decisions as example of some broader, though unexpressed, principle. Such an argument may be risky, though, unless judges are ready to accept the outcome. Risky because, after all, for many lawyers and judges, a cow case is not much like a mill-pond case.

— *Criticisms of Blackburn's generalization; the cattle cases.* It is true you can think of cattle trespass cases as cases in which the defendant has brought cattle on his land and kept them there, and it is true that they are likely to do mischief if they escape. But you can also think of cattle cases in many other ways. (i) In a given society or locality, it may be easier/cheaper for the cattle owner to fence them in than for the gardener to fence them out, especially if the number of cattle are few and the number of gardens are great. So you can think of the cattle cases as decisions that favor economic efficiency. (ii) Or perhaps as cases that favor the little guy with the garden over the rich guy with the cows. (iii) Certainly, you can also think of the cattle cases as cases of known danger– not cases of unknown danger like *Rylands*. You can even also think of the cattle cases as merely primitive holdovers from a time in which the owner is identified with his beasts in much the way we identify the employer with his servant today. (iv) Finally, you might think that strict liability for trespassing cattle was a historical accident based on the absence of the writ of *Case* at the time the early cases were decided. Characterized as accidents of the 14th Century, those cases would support no rational or policy-based generalization at all. So Blackburn's generalization was not required by the cases and some other generalizations might be more pertinent.

— *Other generalizations; the privy cases.* The privy case furnishes even more doubtful a support for Blackburn's generalization. What was it Blackburn thought the landowner brought on the land? The wall? Himself? That point aside, might you not use the privy case to support an entirely different generalization– one about public health, for example? There is also the question whether the privy case can hold up under Bramwell's analysis in *Bamford*. If all neighbors at the time used privies, the use of a privy would be a reciprocal risk and there would be no action except for fault!

— *Other generalizations; the chlorine gas.* This case is also susceptible to other generalizations. Maybe chlorine gas is a case of special (and public) danger, not just a case of bringing "anything" on the land. Abnormal danger is definitely not a part of the express reasoning the Rylands judges advanced. If the chlorine gas case is seen as supporting an abnormal danger rationale, perhaps the defendant in *Rylands* would have won.

The House of Lords. (a) Lord Cairns formulates the principle somewhat differently. The defendant is free to make "natural use" of his land and cannot be held liable for that (in the absence of negligence, anyway). Non-natural use, however, subjects him to strict liability for harm resulting from that non-natural use.

(b) Lord Cranworth appeared to accept the formulation by Blackburn, J. in the Exchequer Chamber. He does not emphasize "user" of the land but "bringing or accumulating" anything likely to harm if it escapes. In fact, he goes back to the general proposition that strict liability is the rule: "the question in general is, not whether the defendant has acted with due care and caution, but whether his acts have occasioned the damage." (Cf. *Weaver v. Ward.*)

The rule; non-natural user vs. not naturally there. What rule comes out of this? The House of Lords, at least if you take Lord Cairns' judgment, at first seems to confine the strict liability to cases of non-natural use– perhaps a much narrower view than that taken by Blackburn in the Exchequer Chamber. But to take this view, you have to eliminate one of the three legs on which Blackburn constructed his grounds– the cattle cases. Cattle are not naturally on the land, but to bring them and raise them there is not a non-natural use in most localities. This leaves Blackburn's inductive generalization very weak indeed, and the House of Lords provides nothing better. Perhaps Lord Cairns' judgment suggests a "bringing to the land" rationale like Blackburn's, since he speaks of "introducing" something on the land. If you give weight to that, the cattle cases can still exemplify the rule. Did Cairns' deliberately propose two different rules of different scope? Isn't it more likely that his formula emphasizing "user" is what he intended?

— *Locality, custom.* The Cairns' non-natural user version of the rule turns on some conception of what is a "natural use" of land. This might refer merely to custom in the relevant locality, a kind of strict liability for departing from custom. That would be a close parallel to Bramwell's contention in *Bamford*. A conservative, class oriented society might well take such a view. But the economic explanation is more likely. To bring an unusual enterprise to the area runs the risk of conflicts with the existing investment. See the comments to those notes below.

Economic Analysis

Rylands and *Bamford* present wonderful opportunities for a little economic analysis if you want to pursue it here. You don't have to have economic training to play productively with these ideas.

Thomas Galligan has pointed out that one kind of analysis is NOT done in *Rylands*-type cases. They do no risk-utility balancing at "the case-specific level." Galligan, *Strict Liability in Action: The Truncated Learned Hand Formula*, 52 LA. L. REV. 323, 336 (1991). In this respect, *Rylands* cases differ both from negligence cases using the ideas behind *Carroll Towing* and from products liability design defect cases covered in Chapter 22. If there is any risk-utility balancing in *Rylands* cases, it takes place at a more abstract level, one in which we compare the abnormal activity in general to the normal activities around it, without worrying whether the abnormal activity really is more productive than the harm it causes in the particular case. Galligan's observation may be helpful later in considering products forms of strict liability.

Note 1. Trespass or nuisance alternatives? The analysis in *Rylands* is required only if there is no other theory already in existence that will explain its results. Sometimes students need to get these other theories out of the way to appreciate that *Rylands* may be a new departure. If trespass requires an "act," with reference to the land, it is easy to see why this is not a trespass. Similarly, if trespass requires an intent to enter the land, this is not a trespass. That was perhaps not the understanding at the time of *Rylands,* and Bohlen's explanation that the entry was "indirect," which reverts to the formal distinction between *Trespass* and *Case,* may explain what the courts had in mind. The implication of this reasoning is that the English courts still adhered to a general pattern of strict liability based on direct harm (Trespass.) Even if they had moved to a fault principle, however, it is hard to see how this would be a trespass in the absence of any intent to enter or any negligence in doing so.

Bohlen's explanation why this is not a nuisance is also formal —the seepage is not "continuous," but on the contrary, the flood was wreaked at once. Although most nuisance cases do involve continuous conditions and continuous injury, this is not an invariable necessity, certainly not if you take Bramwell's rationale in *Bamford*. In this view, *Rylands* is a nuisance-type case, but that does not mean there was nothing new for the courts to decide there. Whereas in *Bamford* liability was held proper where the defendant imposed a certainty of harm (though he may have been uncertain as to the legal effect of the harm), *Rylands* involves a defendant who seems to have had no inkling that even a risk existed, much less that there was any certainty of harm. In any view, then, *Rylands* does seem to be deciding something new.

Notes 2 & 3. Note 2 poses a general issue — what is the scope of *Rylands*? This is intended to ask the student to focus on stating the rule or principle. Note 3 tries to help out by asking the student to recognize that this rule is not based on hazard (as the chlorine gas case might have been) but on non-natural use, or, if you take the formulation in the Exchequer Chamber, on bringing something on the land likely to do mischief if it escapes. Does the class think that either of these formulations is equivalent to negligence? If so, you have only to point to the cattle cases as an example of something likely to do mischief if it escapes; but no one will contend it is negligent to bring cattle to your farm or ranch. Does the class think that the two formulas, that in the Exchequer Chamber and the House of Lords, are the same? If so, the cattle example is again helpful. Cattle are not "naturally" on the land, and they are likely to do mischief if they escape. But to raise cattle in an area where cattle are usually raised is not a non-natural use. The Cairns' judgment in the House of Lords thus came up with a narrower formulation of the rule, but in so doing may have lost one of the main supports for that rule, the cattle cases. You could explore cattle escaping and causing highway accidents here if you wish. Open range states usually but not always dislike imposing even a duty of reasonable care on cattle owners to prevent escape. *See Andersen v. Two Dot Ranch,* Inc., 49 P.3d 1011(Wyo. 2002); *contra, Carrow Co. v. Lusby,* 167 Ariz. 18, 804 P.2d 747 (1990).

Notes 4-7. Economic and moral interpretations. These notes suggest some possible economic interpretations. If you want to pursue economic discussion in more depth, see the references above.

Note 4. Hypothetical. Two new enterprises move into the Valley of the Murg (a fictitious grain). One enterprise is beekeeping. It is inconsistent with the Murg growing, because growing Murg requires spraying and this is deleterious to the pollen and the honey. The other enterprise is an industry which pollutes the delicate grain fields and, presumably, lowers production. The point of presenting two enterprises in this hypothetical is that one is harmed by and the other harms the Murg interests. Both are newcomers, making a use of the land that is "non-natural" for that locality– at least if non-natural includes non-customary. Although no one is at fault in either case, the situation provides a good illustration of the economic and moral claims that can be asserted on both sides. You can ask the student to assume for now that the judges want a rule that will get the most desirable economic outcomes. The assumption can be discarded or tested in debate later.

Note 5. Does Rylands fit the inconsistent land uses pattern? The note then asks what happens where bringing the factory to the Murg field presents danger to the existing investment. This can be expressed by saying that the factory is a "non-natural" use. (Blackburn's "bringing anything" formulation would work here, too.) This applies in spades to the mining interests in *Rylands*, since if you want exploitation of natural resources, as people in the 19th century undoubtedly did, then you are likely to favor the coal owner. One cannot move the coal mine, but in a wet country like England, one can set up a mill pond almost anywhere.

Note 6. A test case (*Turner v. Big Lake Oil*). This is a famous case in the development of strict liability. Texas rejected "strict liability," but on the facts of the case any court with a similar locality might have rejected liability, even if the court otherwise followed *Rylands*. The point is that in Texas, oil exploitation required collection of salt water. If the economic implications of the discussion above are correct, then you would expect Texas (or the House of Lords) to favor exploitation of natural resources. In *Rylands* this was done by allowing the exploiter to recover for harm done to its enterprise. In *Turner* this was done by protecting the exploiter from liability to others. This is the beekeeper case.

Note 7. Coming to the nuisance. This doctrine means many things. One is that there is no nuisance at all, as where a homeowner moves his residence to an established factory district and then complains because it is like a factory district. Another is that the plaintiff has already been compensated for the "nuisance," as where he buys a home next to an airport– the purchase price of the land will reflect public assessment of the harm done by the nuisance. The beekeeper who moves operations into the Murg fields is perhaps like the homeowner who moves to the factory district. Just as the homeowner in such a case must accept ordinary factory noise, the beekeeper must accept ordinary operations of the Murg growers — that is, risks that were reciprocal before he arrived.

How does the class evaluate all this? Does it impose a stasis on development, maybe bad economics instead of good? Or should we be considering economics at all? If a student takes that view, consider the possibility that the feelings involved are as much moral as they are economic– in some sense, maybe it is "wrong" to move your different and demanding land use into the community and demand that it conform to your needs.

Note 8. Animals. If you are doing local law, you might want to check for leash laws and other statutes or ordinances regulating liability for dogs. The common law strict liability for dogs, horses and the like, was only for cases in which the animal was known to have a "vicious propensity," such as a propensity to bite. One still sees this formulation today, as in the *Bard* case cited here. In such a case, even the most careful owner could be held liable if the animal was able to exercise its vicious propensity upon the plaintiff. But if the animal did some other harm, not related to the vicious propensity, there was no strict liability. This is a scope of the risk rule, as to which see § 3 below. What about a dog with a vicious propensity to lunge at guests, one of whom is frightened but not physically hurt?

Liability for negligence might still be possible even if the owner knows of no vicious propensity. In *Williams v. Tysinger*, 399 S.E.2d 108 (N.C. 1991) the owner of a horse allowed a boy who had no experience with animals to enter a horse lot, where a horse kicked him. Although the horse had no known vicious propensities, the owner knew that horses might kick without warning or step on a child. Because of their age and inexperience, the boys might not realize the danger. The court held that a jury could properly find the owner to be negligent in permitting the boys to go into the lot unsupervised.

In *Henkel v. Jordan*, 644 P.2d 1348 (Kan. Ct. App. 1982) a dog frightened a boy on a bike, who lost control and fell as a result. The court affirmed a judgment for the plaintiff, but expressed the view that "[l]iability in animal cases, as in all negligence cases, is based on the 'fault' of the animal owner." Comparative negligence was applied. As to dog fright cases, see Annotation, 30 A.L.R.4th 986 (1984).

Students can usually recognize that wild animal cases bear a resemblance to *Rylands*. To bring a wild animal such as a bear onto the land is at least as good a case for strict liability as *Rylands'*, and either the Blackburn or the Cairns judgment would provide a formula that would call for strict liability. In terms of reciprocal risks there is again a good ground for imposing strict liability.

THOMALEN V. MARRIOTT CORP. , 845 F.Supp. 33 (D. Mass. 1994).

When lighter fluid used in a stage act ignited, causing burns to the plaintiff, strict liability under *Rylands* was not appropriate since there was no "escape." As we'll see, escape does not figure in the Restatement's emphasis on abnormal danger.

C. SLOUCHING TOWARD THE ABNORMAL DANGER CONCEPTION

SULLIVAN V. DUNHAM, 55 N.E. 923 (N.Y. 1900).

Dramatically enough, Annie E. Harten was killed by a flying stump while she was walking on the public highway. The stump was propelled through the air by the defendant's blasting. The New York Court had already rejected *Rylands,* a fact the student can glean by implication from the *Sullivan* excerpt itself and which is iterated in Note 3 following. It retained, for land cases, the old pre-*Brown v. Kendall* law, however. This meant it could impose liability upon the blaster who caused a direct and forcible (physical) injury to another's land. If the explosives had propelled the stump so that it fell on a neighbor's land, there would be "trespass." As the court in *Sullivan* says, the same legal result would not follow if the blasting only caused concussion damage, since this would not comport with the idea of direct and physical harm required by the old Trespass writ. Analogizing from the trespass-to-land cases, the court imposes liability without fault. This is a trespass to person.

Sullivan is very much like *Brown v. Kendall*, but with an opposite result. There was a direct application of force in both cases. It is odd how very close both are to the classic illustration of Trespass – the log thrown by the defendant and striking the plaintiff. In *Brown* it was a stick wielded and in *Sullivan* it was a stump thrown by explosive force. In neither case was there any intent to harm. Unless you think it is unreasonably risky to use explosives under the circumstances, you have to say that there is no ground for liability under *Brown v. Kendall. Sullivan*, clearly implies a rejection of the fault requirement in *Brown v. Kendall*. But for our purposes the interesting thing to notice is that it does so in circumstances that suggest some new possibilities for liability. As courts come more and more to believe that fault is the ordinary standard of liability and that the formalistic strict liability under the writ of Trespass is undesirable, they will grope for some theory of strict liability that will explain the cases without going back to the broad liability for direct harm. *Sullivan* provided the setting which suggested the new and more restrictive form of strict liability – use of unusually hazardous materials. This leads directly to *Exner*.

EXNER V. SHERMAN POWER CONST. CO. , 54 F.2d 510, 80 A.L.R. 686 (2d Cir. 1931).

The abstract case provided in the casebook does not reflect the panel of judges, but you might be interested in knowing that the panel was distinguished by Learned Hand, Thomas Swan (who came to the Second Circuit from the Deanship of Yale Law School) and Augustus Hand (Learned's "Cousin Gus"), the last signing the opinion.

The defendant's blast causes harm, but not by the application of direct tangible force, as in *Sullivan*. The blast causes concussion type damages only (the shock shook the house and threw Mrs. Exner out of bed.) This is the situation the New York Court in *Sullivan*, though not trespassory and therefore not within the strict liability rules. The *Exner* court rejects any distinction between harm caused by physical intrusion and harm caused by concussion. In this respect it is aligned with *Brown v. Kendall*. "In every practical sense there can be no difference" between the "direct" injury caused by rocks blasted onto the land and concussion damage or shock.

But the court disagrees with the solution in *Brown v. Kendall. Brown* will eliminate strict liability; *Exner* will preserve it, but in a different class of cases. *Exner's* approach is the one that the court in *Brown v. Kendall* seems not to have considered.

In what cases is strict liability to be retained under *Exner*? About this the court is not so clear. The court thinks there is no universal rule. Interestingly, it sees the problem, not as one of logic or even history, but as one of practicality– of the "adjustment of conflicting interests." In a portion of the opinion not reproduced here, the court acknowledged that in cases of personal injury, fault is usually required. In the casebook version, the court then states a rather substantial universal of its own, apparently about property cases:

> If damage is inflicted, there ordinarily is liability in the absence of excuse.

What cases it has in mind cannot be discerned from this statement, but the court does go on to narrow the rule to the facts:

> When, as here, the defendant though without fault, has engaged in the perilous activity of storing large quantities of a dangerous explosive for use in his business, we think there is no justification for relieving it of liability. . . .

The defendant's liability under this decision might be broad, a kind of nuisance liability, somewhat like that in *Bamford*. But this would seem to be very close to the acceptance of *Rylands v. Fletcher*. And we know from the *Exner* opinion that the rule in *Rylands* had been rejected in major decisions in New York, New Jersey and New Hampshire. Even though *Exner* was decided before *Erie*, it would be a difficult thing for the federal court here to adopt *Rylands* in the face of these major decisions.

You could reject *Rylands* and still follow *Exner* by noticing that in *Bamford* the defendant knew he was imposing actual harm, while in *Rylands* the defendant did not know that he was imposing harm and did not even know that he was imposing even a risk of harm. *Exner* is the in-between-case. The defendant, though acting with care, must have known it was imposing some risks (risks of harm as distinct from harm itself in *Bamford*), though it rightly deemed them to be reasonable.

This was not the line of distinction adopted. The distinction adopted in the Restatement First of Torts instead emphasized the extreme peril of the defendant's activity with the claim that an ultrahazardous activity rule was different from *Rylands*.

NOTE: THE RESTATEMENTS' RULES OF STRICT LIABILITY

The new Restatement, almost completed as the Sixth Edition is published, substantially revises the Restatement Second's strict liability rule and presents a substantially different set of attitudes as well.

¶ 1. The formulation of strict liability rules. *(a) Blackletter requirements*. The Second Restatement's factors turned strict liability into something uncomfortably close to negligence. The Third Restatement evidently aims to avoid that mistake. So its blackletter is formally simple: the defendant is strictly liable if it creates a reasonably foreseeable risk of physical harm, the risk is highly significant and remains even when everyone exercises reasonable care, and the activity is not one of common usage.

(b) "Significant" risks. The risk of harm may be highly significant either because the probability is great or because the magnitude of harm if it occurs will be great. Although this sounds like part of the negligence formula under *Carroll Towing*, liability is not imposed because of a risk-utility balance. No matter how great the utility of the defendant's activity, liability may be imposed for a significant risk, provided the other elements of the claim are met.

(c) Significant risk and commensurate care. But there is a more subtle point. If the risk must be significant, then ordinary negligence law would require commensurate care. The greater the risk, the greater the care required. So the more the plaintiff proves the great risk need for strict liability, the more likely it is that the care required could have avoided injury– which would take us back to negligence!

¶ 2. **When plaintiff or others contribute.** Paragraphs 2 and 3 of the casebook Note point to the Third Restatement's limiting ideas. The Restatement comments seem to eliminate the defendant's strict liability if the plaintiff's own conduct is involved. The core illustration of this idea is the car-train crash at a crossing. It results from the defendant's activity, but also from the plaintiff's activity in using a car; and as the Restatement notes, in the background there is the city's activity in building a grade level crossing. Most injuries will result from the activities of two or more persons and thus exclude strict liability even when the activity of one is quite dangerous. The idea is reminiscent of the reciprocity idea we've raised periodically, most recently in *Bamford.* But it seems to go further because a railroad engine might be thought to impose risks upon car passengers that are not reciprocal simply because the risks imposed by the car are usually insignificant. If reciprocity were the sole test of strict liability, then, the railroad might be liable in train-car crashes at crossings.

¶ 3. **Risks or harms avoidable by reasonable care.** Paragraph 3 raises a distinct but related idea– that if any one could have avoided injury by the exercise of reasonable care, the case is not appropriate for strict liability. That means that if the plaintiff, defendant, or others could have avoided injury by reasonable care, the defendant will not be strictly liable. The logic of this point eliminates the issue of comparative responsibility taken up in § 3 c, below. If the plaintiff is causally at fault, both the reasons in Comment e and Comment h would exclude strict liability; the plaintiff will have to make his case on proof of fault, not on strict liability.

¶ 4. **The Second Restatement's factors.** The factors approach, so common in the Restatement Second, was not irrational, but it did create the appearance that strict liability might really be negligence under a different name. If abnormal danger is judged in part by the appropriateness of the location of the defendant's activity, that might seem like risk-utility balancing or negligence analysis. The Third Restatement eliminates such factors as appropriateness of the defendant's activity at the location. Location is often important in nuisance cases, but the Third Restatement seems to recognize that nuisance liability is a separate matter, so it is not required to write a rule that covers both nuisance and "significant danger" cases.

¶ 5. *Rylands* **and abnormal danger.** Whether you interpret *Rylands* as a nuisance case or not, it seems clear that significant danger is not required in *Rylands*. Non-natural user might possibly be surrogate test for non-common usage, but otherwise the American effort to find a basis for strict liability went in different directions entirely, not tied to landowners, not tied to escape of substances, and definitely tied to significant (or abnormal) danger of an activity not in common usage. Where the idea of special danger come from? The *Sullivan* case, maybe, though abnormal danger was an adventitious feature, because it relied on the formal strict liability of a direct trespass. The *Exner* case is a more direct ancestor in emphasizing peril albeit without a real rationale for strict liability. *(Exner,* you might notice, is like a mule— without pride of ancestry or hope of posterity; it was decided under the federal common law that we now know to be illicit.) Yet it was one of the straws Bohlen grabbed at to construct the First Restatement's materials on strict liability for "ultrahazardous activity" in a country that had largely rejected *Rylands*. Are we still grabbing at straws?

¶ 6. **Justifications for strict liability.** This paragraph mentions only two elements— the defendant's choice to carry out a dangerous activity and the possibility that there is negligence we cannot see. Many people will be unconvinced by either ground standing alone.

(a) Defendant's chosen activity. If the defendant chooses to cause harm, as he did in *Vincent v. Lake Erie Transportation Co.* (Chapter 4), certainly he should take the bitter with the sweet, the costs as well as the potential benefits. But choosing a dangerous activity is not choosing to cause a harm, only choosing to impose a risk. And, given that the risk-utility balance necessarily favor the defendant (else this would be a negligence case), it is a risk we as a society want the defendant to take. We need blasting activities, for example. So standing alone, a decision to carry out an activity that is good for society seems a poor reason for strict liability, even if that same activity is potentially good for the defendant as well.

(b) If you can't find it, it must be there? It is true that in many instances the defendant may be unprovably negligent. Should we infer negligence or impose strict liability merely because we cannot find the negligence? We *think* the Restatement justifies strict liability partly on this ground, although only where the defendant's significantly dangerous activity is the "unitary" cause of injury. Yet this is not a res ipsa loquitur argument that negligence is more likely than not. If we think negligence is probable, then strict liability is ruled out and the plaintiff will win on negligence grounds. What exactly is the argument? In all too recent times, some therapists argued that if a patient thinks her parents did NOT abuse here, then they certainly did. Could you similarly argue that since we *cannot* reasonably infer that every single office holder is corrupt, we should hold them all liable for corruption? The Reporters certainly made no such extreme arguments, but the extreme arguments might warrant a doubt or at least an abundantly clear explanation why the absence of provable negligence should assist the plaintiff's recovery.

(c) Cause of harm is enough? A very different reason given in the Restatement Third's § 20 and *not* presented in the casebook Note, is that "the

person in the street" believes you should bear responsibility of paying for the harm you caused. The implication, insinuated by imputing views to the person in the street, is that strict liability, is always appropriate or at least attractive unless this cause-harm connection is blurred. The connection is in fact blurred in most cases, the Restatement suggests, because in most cases the plaintiff's activity will also be connected to the injury– the train-car crash again. The suggestions that "unitary" causation alone is or should be enough to impose liability, maybe begs the question. One of two citizens must bear the loss. Neither had done wrong. Is this really ground enough for strict liability?

¶ 7. **Common usage.** If common usage is really a proxy for other reasons, it might be better to address those other reasons than to muffle them under the common usage blanket. And the reasons may not convince everyone. (1) If we are concerned about the acceptability of the activity, should we not identify that concern and tell actors in advance what concerns us? (2) Why should care whether benefits are concentrated in the defendant unless we are adopting a deep pocket approach? You might believe that one who chooses an activity should pay the costs his activity imposes, but do you really have to believe he will be the only one to benefit? That he will be the only one to benefit is actually unlikely. After all, we already think there is probably social utility to his activity; if there were none, the defendant would not be negligent in choosing to carry out the activity. You might suspect common usage is a pragmatic rather than a principled limitation. But if you think that, maybe you've undermined the rationales for strict liability.

Many people like the idea of strict liability instinctively and seek grounds to justify it. The many formulations and rationales, though might leave you wondering whether, aside from nuisance with its incompatible land uses, there is much room for significant danger types of strict liability.

The meandering path from strict liability for direct and forcible harms to strict liability for abnormally dangerous activities shows little sign of rational development, or even of conscious choice. Chief Justice Shaw in *Brown* did not seem to consider the possibility that he could eliminate the seemingly irrational distinction between direct and indirect harms and keep some degree of strict liability. *Bamford* gave some good reasons for strict liability if you see the defendant as the sole cause of harm, but *Rylands* expanded this without showing much awareness that there could be an important distinction between choosing to impose a certain harm, as in *Bamford*, and choosing conduct that seems to offer no prospects at all for harm (as in *Rylands*.) The Third Restatement, though quite possibly imperfect, seems by far the best balanced analysis by imposing strict liability only when the defendant's activity is uncommon, when it imposes a foreseeable and significant risk of harm, and when other causes of harm are not closely connected. Perhaps it is no coincidence that the Restatement's current view is also one that applies strict liability rules in a narrow set of cases.

§ 3. STRICT LIABILITY TODAY

The focus of this section shifts. It uses textual notes and illustrations to describe the general picture of strict liability today (so far as it arises from the *Bamford-Rylands*-abnormal danger rules). The focus here is not on historical development so much as it is on the state of the law on several specific points. The focus of class discussion naturally also shifts. On the other hand, you can use these specific illustrations of strict liability to develop some of the ideas raised above, for example, the difference, if any, between *Rylands* strict liability and the Restatement's strict liability. If you've covered the preceding materials well, however, you may wish to assign § 3 a. as readings, not for class discussion.

A. The Subjects of Strict Liability

¶1. **Impoundments**. The escape of known toxic wastes in *State Dept. of Environmental Protetion v. Ventron*, cited here, seems an easy case. It meets the *Rylands* test and also the Restatement's abnormal danger test. The various corporate entities involved were responsible for contaminating a land site with a total of 268 tons of toxic waste, mostly mercury, as a result of mercury processing. This has now contaminated creeks and tidal areas. "Even if they did not intend to pollute or adhered to the standards of the time, all of these parties remain liable. Those who poison the land must pay for its cure." (463 A.2d at 903). If it was substantially certain that the mercury would penetrate to waters or lands outside the defendants', then the *Bamford* rationale would also support liability, since in that case there would be a non-reciprocal harm substantially certain to occur and not merely a risk of such harm.

Some cases have gone the other way and required some kind of fault. In the current state of affairs does the class think that most courts would continue to protect toxic waste leaks?

¶ 2. **Hazardous wastes**. T & E Industries, cited here, held that the seller would be strictly be liable to the buyer of property contaminated by radium. *Spendorio v. Bilbray Demolition Co.*, 682 A.2d 461 (R.I. 1996), recognized that strict liability should be imposed for abnormally dangerous activities involving toxic substances like asbestos, overruling *en passant* a once-well-known case, *Rose v. Socony-Vacuum Corp.*, 173 A. 627 (R.I. 1934). The court insisted, though, that strict liability was appropriate only for abnormally dangerous *activities*, not for socially-useful activities merely involving abnormally dangerous *materials*. Thus an inspector looking for asbestos (and finding it) was not strictly liable for a plaintiff's injuries caused by his activities.

¶ 3. **Environmental statutes; the Superfund**. The environmental statutes, both state and federal, may help a plaintiff in some instances. The superfund allows the government to clean up pollution (using the fund) and then obtain reimbursement from the responsible industry. The government may also order clean up by an owner. Four classes of persons are potentially responsible to the government for the costs of clean up. These are (1) the present owner, (2) the operator of the facility at the time substances were disposed of there, (3) any person who arranged for disposal and (4) any person who accepted hazardous substances for disposal or transportation. 42 U.S.C.A. § 9701(a)(1)–(4). Liability is strict, so the owner may be liable even if someone else dumped hazardous wastes on her land. The innocent plaintiff who cleans up the site can under some circumstances recover from a person in one of those categories. This leads to economic harm claims and fascinating problems in determining who counts as a disposer, an arranger for disposal, owner, or operator of the facility. The statute also permits recovery for damage to natural resources.

¶ 4. **Lateral Support**. Lateral support strict liability has been around a long time. The Restatement recognizes this form of strict liability, but under a separate rule, not under the principle of abnormal danger. The existence of strict liability on these facts does not prove much, but it certainly suggests that the abnormal danger theory is (a) an inaccurate formulation, or, at best, one that is (b) not comprehensive. Is there any theory that would encompass both the blasting and the adjacent support cases?

¶ 5. **Blasting and explosives**. This states the rule, now accepted generally, that concussion damage is within the scope of strict liability for blasting. Note that unintended detonation of stored explosives is treated like blasting in many cases. Some states limit abnormal-danger strict liability to blasting. *See, e.g., Saiz v. Belen School Dist.,* 827 P.2d 102 (N.M. 1992); see also LA. CIV. CODE ANN. art 667 (1999)(blasting and pile driving the only grounds for such liability).

¶ 6. **Nuclear energy**. There is no general acceptance of governmental liability for abnormal danger. 42 U.S.C.A. § 2211 appears to contemplate a limited strict liability for nuclear accidents resulting from nuclear warships. *Silkwood v. Kerr-McGee,* 104 S. Ct. 615 (1984) involved plutonium contamination of a worker in the Kerr-McGee plant. (The worker was played by Meryl Streep in the movie, *Silkwood.*) The Supreme court held that state law governed liability, including the award of punitive damages. The *Silkwood* decision seemed to leave states free to impose strict liability. Since 1988, the act covers "nuclear incidents" and not merely the "extraordinary nuclear occurrences" formerly covered. The nuclear plant that obtains the benefits of limited liability must waive defenses relating to contributory fault, certain immunities, and certain statutes of limitation.

¶ 7 & 8. **Other high-energy activities; Utilities**. Abnormal danger has been found and strict liability imposed in some other high energy activities. But not with the ordinary transmission of natural gas or of electricity before it enters the home. See, e.g., *Foster v. City of Keyser*, 501 S.E.2d 165 (W.Va. 1997) (no strict liability for transmitters of natural gas that caused an explosion). Why not? You might want to recall that courts have often said that suppliers of gas and electricity must use the "highest degree of care." The *Foster* court said that the high degree of care and the availability of res ipsa loquitur sufficiently address "the concerns that argue for strict liability." Is that convincing?

¶ 9. **Fireworks**. Fireworks cases should give the students a good chance to apply the Third Restatement's test. Is a celebratory display an activity that foreseeably risks significant harm even when reasonable care is exercised by everyone? And is it not a "matter of common usage?" Under the new Restatement, the activity is abnormally dangerous only if we can answer "yes" to BOTH questions. If every town in the U.S. has fireworks displays on Independence Day, could such an activity possibly be "not a matter of common usage?" But does the nature of the display matter? Who is in charge of it? When it occurs? Where it occurs? How about a Millennium display? Surely the focus should be on the commonness of fireworks displays generally, rather than on the commonness of the specific event being celebrated. Under the Restatement Third, would location still matter in determining whether the activity was common, even though that Restatement drops location as well as the other factors of the Restatement Second? *Cadena v. Chicago Fireworks Mfg. Co.*, cited here, rejected strict liability on the grounds that Fourth of July fireworks displays are a matter of common usage, can be made safer by the exercise of reasonable care, and have "some social utility." *Klein v. Pyrodyne Corp.*, on the other hand, concluded that fireworks displays were not in common usage, and imposed strict liability primarily on that ground, stressing that while many people watch such displays, very few people actually conduct them.

¶ 10. **Poisons**. The note asks whether liability for crop dusting with poison might be justified on *Rylands* grounds even if it is not "abnormally dangerous." Actually, it is a better case for liability than *Rylands* in one respect, since the crop duster knows he is subjecting others to a risk of harm, as the defendant in *Rylands* did not. On the other hand, crop dusting may not be a nonnatural use of land in some agricultural areas. You might want to suggest that strict liability should correlate with those nondelegable duties based upon special danger.

B. Scope of Risk Limitations in Strict Liability Cases

This short text states the basic rule, which adapts the risk rule of negligence law to the strict liability setting. It furnishes a chance for the class to get reacquainted with basic doctrine, and also, because it is basic doctrine, to feel a little relief from the pressure of new materials.

In *Herman v. Welland Chem. Ltd.*, 580 F. Supp. 823 (D. Pa. 1984), a carrier of chemicals was in an road accident and complicated accident-injury sequence resulted. A strict liability claim was dismissed in the trial court on the ground that even if the shipment of chemicals qualified as abnormally dangerous activity, strict liability would be limited to "the kind of harm, the possibility of which makes the activity abnormally dangerous," quoting Restatement of Torts Second § 519, cmt. *e*.

Cambridge Water Co. Ltd. v. Eastern Counties Leather, cited here, uses the language of foreseeability to express what essentially seems to be the *Medcalf/Wagon Mound* risk rule. The reasonably foreseeable harm from the non-natural user (if that is what it was) was that someone might be overcome by fumes, not that ground-water might be polluted. Although we now know that there were other risks, not much was known at the time. Later, in considering products liability, we'll have a very similar question: whether the manufacturer is strictly liable for a design or warning defect the risk of which could not have been known at the time the product was sold. The answer in those cases is usually the same as in *Cambridge Water* – although liability is strict, it is only for known or reasonably knowable risks. Students should understand that a defendant is not negligent merely because he takes a foreseeable risk. To be negligent, he would also have to handle that risk in an unreasonable way. If strict liability is imposed, the plaintiff will have to show foreseeability of the risk, but won't have to show that the defendant handled that risk in an unreasonable way.

It is easy to understand the scope of risk idea with some kinds of strict liability. Students usually understand that even some foreseeable risks are outside the scope of abnormal danger. That would be the case with the mother minks who, frightened by blasting, eat their young. It is also easy in the animal cases: you might be strictly liable if your dog bites your guest, but not if the dog merely licks her ankles and lights up a latent sore. It is harder to translate the idea from an abnormal danger system to a *Rylands* system. Under the abnormal danger rule, we can ask what are the risks that made the activity abnormally dangerous? How should we ask the question under a *Rylands* rule? What are the risks that made the activity non-natural? That seems almost a contradiction in terms, because non-natural describes customary usage (or possibly a condition of the land), not risks.

A related problem on the facts of *Cambridge Water Co.* is whether you can use a non-natural user test at all when the escaping substance travels completely out of the neighborhood (173 miles in this case). The idea of natural user seems to involve some idea of local custom or usage, so it is puzzling how the test can be used to benefit someone who is no part of the neighborhood custom and who is not even in the neighborhood when injury occurred. Maybe if you consider *Cambridge Water Co.* to be a *Rylands* case at all, you are thinking more of escape of something not naturally on the land and less of non-natural user.

C. Affirmative Defenses to Strict Liability Claims

¶¶ 1 & 2. **Traditional rule; Comparative responsibility.** *(a) Applicability in principle.* The traditional rule ignored the plaintiff's contributory fault when the defendant was strictly liable, so the plaintiff could make a full recovery of all damages in spite of her own fault. This viewpoint will arise again with products strict liability. The Apportionment Restatement recognizes that comparative fault rules should now apply in strict liability cases and the Physical Harms Restatement reinforces that view in § 25.

(b) Limits of strict liability to a contributorily negligent plaintiff under Restatement Third of Torts § 20. We have already noted that under the Third Restatement's § 20, strict liability is ruled out when the plaintiff is involved in some causal way, irrespective of the plaintiff's fault. It is also ruled out if the plaintiff, defendant, or anyone else under a duty of care could have made the activity reasonably safe by the exercise of ordinary care. *See* Note: The Restatements' Rules of Strict Liability, *supra.* Under those rules, strict liability would almost certainly be ruled out if the plaintiff is chargeable with causal contributory fault, because such a plaintiff would be involved and not merely a passive victim. In addition, the plaintiff's ability to act with care would normally mean that care of all involved could have made the activity reasonably safe. ("Reasonable care" would have little meaning if reasonable care could not reduce the risk.) With strict liability ruled out in such cases, the issue raised in ¶ 2 seems to disappear. We won't have to determine whether contributory/comparative fault is a defense to strict liability because there will be not strict liability. Even so, the Restatement Third of Torts, Liability for Physical Harms § 25 (Proposed Final Draft No. 1, 2005), provides for use of comparative fault rules in strict liability cases, just in case plaintiff-fault-involvement issues do not rule out strict liability altogether.

¶ 3. **Non-negligent activity by the plaintiff.** What if the plaintiff, through no fault of his own, is abnormally sensitive, and that is one of the necessary causes of for his injury? You could exclude the plaintiff from recovery here by saying he is an abnormally sensitive person; the Restatement Second adopts this as a principle in § 524A. The principle is essentially one of legal cause. The plaintiff's injury is not one of the risks that made us mark off the defendant's activity for strict liability in the first place. The result may be right, but the reason might lie in our inadequate formulation of the rule of strict liability in the first place. The Third (Physical Harms) Restatement § 20, discussed in ¶ 2 above, recognizes just that. It is not a case for strict liability if it involves two activities, plaintiff's and defendant's, each of which contribute to the injury. One advantage of the newer Restatement on this point is that you are not required to make scope of risk judgments to resolve cases like this.

CHAPTER 24

TORT LIABILITY
FOR DEFECTIVE PRODUCTS

▶**Changes in the Sixth Edition.** Although we have cut over ten percent of the length of this Chapter, it remains the longest in the book. Section divisions and the order of basic presentation remain the same. Notes have been updated throughout, with the addition of over 30 citations and/or discussions of new cases; Notes have also been reordered in some places. The most significant changes are these: in § 7, we have cut the *Turpin* case and substituted a shorter case, *Merck v. Garza*, which discusses evidence of general and specific causation; in § 10, we have cut *Ramirez*, turned *Boyle* into a shorter case abstract, and have added *Doyle,* a Georgia case from 1997, on statutory compliance; in § 12, we have cut the *Quintana* case at the very end.

▶The **Concise Edition** slashes this Chapter by over 50% while retaining the real core of this topic. The major changes are, in their order of appearance: In §3 (stand-alone economic harm), cut *Moorman Mfg. Co.* and Notes, substituting text on the topic. In §4 (manufacturing defects), cut *Mexicali Rose* and some Note material, substituting shorter notes on defects in food. In §5 (design defects), cut *McCarthy v. Olin* and Notes 1 & 2. In §6 (warning defects), cut several Notes after *Liriano;* the *Carruth* case abstract and its Notes; and the *Lewis* case and its Note; cut material from the Note on Learned Intermediaries; cut the *Comstock* and *Gregory* case abstracts and Notes. In §7 (special issues of proof), substituted two paragraphs of text for the entire section. In §9 (proximate cause and misuse), substituted just over one page of text for the entire section. In §10 (compliance with overriding standards), substituted a page of text for the entire section. In §11 (statutes of limitation), substituted three paragraphs for the entire section. In §12 (beyond the manufacturer of new goods), substituted three paragraphs of text for the entire section. Throughout the chapter we've trimmed some text and Note materials.■

Scheduling omissions: If you have only one day in Rome.... If modest omissions will suit you, some suggestions appear in the Quick Summary below. If you must cover products in only one, two, or three days, we offer suggestions for packages below and encourage you to think it can be done. Products law has been so significant that we want to make it possible for all teachers to cover some basics, even if only a few hours are allocated to the torts course.

If you have only one day:

Cover basic contours of manufacturing, design and warning defects; introduction of consumer expectation and risk-utility balancing tests, including some coverage of RAD. You won't have time for more than passing mention of defenses.

• Begin with a brief lecture on the development of legal theories and mention rationales thought to support strict liability (§ 1 and 2) (5-10 minutes). • On manufacturing defects, § 4, cover *Lee* and its notes; Omit from *Mexicali Rose* to end of section. • On design defects, § 5, cover *Leichtamer* and *Knitz, & Barker v. Lull*, and notes to all. • Cover Notes 2-9 following *Honda* (but not *Honda* itself). • Lecture on warning defects, § 6, without details, without assigning any reading on it (10 min. max). This is only 20 pages of reading for students, but very demanding for the teacher and could easily take up two days if you have discussion or class confusion or if your lectures are detailed.

If you have two days:

Add depth to RAD coverage and warnings.

• Expand discussion of sections 1 and 2 to be sure students understand warranty vs. strict tort liability and economic harm vs. physical injury and that they grasp some rationales for strict liability. • Design defects, cover *Honda* and note 1. • Warning defects: Cover *Liriano* and notes, and *Carruth* and notes.

If you have three days:

• On design defects, § 5, explore the limits of consumer expectation if you have not already done so; cover *McCarthy v. Olin* and notes, omitting the lecture on the topic listed for one day's coverage. • Defenses: cover *Bowling*, § 8 and as many of its notes as you can; cover *Hughes* § 9 *or* lecture on "misuse."

The Challenge and Significance of the Products Chapter

Products liability is a difficult subject. Although we have already spoken of strict liability in two chapters, we have not yet seen a detailed development of a strict liability *system*. In Chapter 24 we have an opportunity to see the difficulties in a strict liability system, especially when it must mesh with a tort law that is more often based on fault. We see this tension reflected in the modern trend (goaded on by the Restatement (Third) of Torts: Products Liability) that retains true strict liability only for manufacturing defects, and bases liability for design and information/warning defects on negligence, even if the N word is not used. The law remains in a state of flux at the moment as states decide what the basis of liability should be for various kinds of product defect. This situation provides both a challenge and an opportunity for the class to think again about the proper role of fault (and change) in tort law.

Conceptually, the chapter is difficult on a number of points. It raises these questions among others: What is a defective product? Can we honestly distinguish "defect" in a product from negligence of the producer? Is the issue of defect distinguishable from the issue of proximate cause? Or assumed risk or contributory negligence? Indeed, an even more fundamental question is whether we are (or should be) dealing with strict liability at all in some cases.

The focus of this chapter is on today's products-liability tort law. Beyond highlighting the issues recited above, this chapter (1) helps furnish a detailed working picture of a strict liability system, with all attendant growing and aging pains; (2) provokes a more thorough examination of the grounds offered in support of strict liability; (3) as a whole provides a datum in the students' understanding of legal change, and especially in the debate whether courts or legislatures should be the primary instigator of change; (4) initiates some important issues about new forms of apportioning responsibility (can you compare fault with strict liability in a comparative fault regime?); and (5) reflects the most ambitious of judicial restructuring of tort law and the contemporary backlash of the defendants and the professional community.

A Quick Summary with Notes on Omissions

Section 1. The privity requirement applied in negligence actions is qualified piecemeal, then abolished (*MacPherson*). The warranty form of strict liability is recognized, but privity bars the way. Ultimately, the privity requirement for warranty is sidestepped by holding that the warranty cases are "really" strict tort liability cases and that privity is not required in tort. (*Greenman*). This becomes the basis for the Restatement Second's § 402A. If you are really pressed for time, you could consider omitting this section, in which case you would probably need to lecture briefly on the privity rule and on warranty.

Section 2. This section provides a brief discussion of the various rationales most often invoked in favor of strict products liability. Students should be able to see connections between this section and the beginning material in

Chapter 22, as well as some of the ideas trotted out in Chapter 23. Teachers can return to these rationales virtually at will as the class goes through the chapter to question whether particular rule-formulations make good sense from the perspective of justice or policy. The end of this section reports the Third Restatement's retreat from strict liability for all but manufacturing defects.

Section 3. The strict tort liability idea applies only to cases of physical harm to persons or to property; it does not apply to stand-alone economic harm, as where the product simply doesn't work well. For economic harm cases, the consumer is left to claims based on the contract, that is, to warranty claims. (*Moorman.*) You can readily omit this section, if you state the gist of the preceding two sentences to the class. You could also retain it but shift it so that it is covered with § 12 (or move some of that section's information forward to this point), which considers the scope of strict tort liability.

Section 4. Manufacturing defects. Strict liability is applied to manufacturing flaws, even under the new Restatement. You must prove that harm was caused by a flaw or defect, but if you do, you've proved your case without proving negligence. A limit or exception is noted. The consumer expectation test is introduced. The ideas in this section are indispensable to any coverage of products liability, but some of the material can readily be presented by lecture.

Section 5. Design defects. This has been a major battleground in the products area in the last several years, and we see a number of different experiments in the law. The risk-utility balance and consumer expectations tests are compared. Is it really strict liability if a risk-utility balance is used? What is to be done about a danger that the manufacturer simply could not have known about? The Restatement of Products Liability shuns the strict liability terminology but essentially treats these cases as negligence cases. This section introduces the issues that have caused much of the problem and the new Restatement's requirement that, to prove design defect, the plaintiff must also prove a reasonable alternative design. An end note on adjudication of design defects focus on some broad policy issues that are central to the debate about tort doctrine in this volatile and timely area. This section, too, seems key to adequate coverage, but again, some of the ideas can be presented by lecture.

Section 6. Warning or information defects. Beyond manufacturing and design defects, a product can be defective because its dangers, reasonable in themselves, are excessive without adequate warnings or instructions on use. This kind of defect, like design defects, has produced a great deal of litigation in the last few years. Most of this section also seems indispensable, but if you need to omit something, the material running from the note on Learned Intermediaries through the end of this section (covering post-sale warnings) is probably the best choice. If you do that, you might want to lecture briefly on both topics.

Section 7. Special issues of proof. This section is included mainly for the chance to let students see some special proof issues that can arise in products cases. You can easily omit this section and certainly can omit *Garza*.

Section 8. Defenses. Given the adoption of comparative fault, should the plaintiff's contributory negligence or "assumed risk" reduce her recovery or should the strictly liable defendant be liable for full damages? If comparative fault reduces damages, is there still room for *Bexiga* in some particular cases? Comparative fault/assumed risk arguments are standard stuff in products cases. You can omit this section and lecture on the division of opinion if you wish, but omission will make it especially difficult to cover the already-difficult materials that come next.

Section 9. This section could be called "Three faces of misuse." Proximate cause, assumed risk, and misuse: are these separate ways to defeat liability or merely labels for the conclusion that the product was not defective? This is difficult, but even teachers providing minimal coverage should hesitate to omit it. Indeed, if you teach only one thing on defenses, *Hughes* provides the most bang for the buck.

Section 10. The compliance with statute defense, then federal preemption (which is a case of compliance with federal law) is introduced. This material is difficult. For minimal coverage, or with a class having trouble, this is a good section to omit. If you omit it, you might raise the simple compliance with statute by a hypothetical or in lecture; you can connect it to the same basic points students saw in the negligence defenses chapter.

Section 11. Statutes of limitation work much as they do in other cases. This is important for professional-level coverage and it reinforces earlier learning, but you can easily omit this section if your approach is to cover or emphasize only the large ideas.

Section 12. If strict liability is indeed strict, what kinds of defects are covered? Is a sale required? Does strict liability apply to real property, or to "defective" services? Cover this section if you can; you can even move it up earlier when discussing the basic scope of strict products liability.

COMMENTS

Subchapter A. Developing Core Concepts

§ 1. EVOLUTION OF LIABILITY THEORIES

This section presents some of the basics on the development of the various theories of liability for injuries caused by defective products, permitting the class to move quickly to the current issues.

The chief aims of the section are to acquaint the students with the following new ideas: (1) the privity rule (and its gradual confinement); (2) the idea that a product might be defective even though the defendant is not negligent and that the defendant might be liable in such a case; and (3) the basic distinctions among (a) negligence, (b) warranty and (c) strict tort liability claims. Rationales for strict products liability are presented in the next section.

We try here to summarize succinctly the main stopping points along the route from *Winterbottom v. Wright* to the promulgation of § 402A. *Winterbottom* (Casebook 507) barred claims where there was no privity. The privity requirement in negligence cases was abolished in *McPherson v. Buick Motor Co.*, a case in which Cardozo thought privity was merely a poor expression of the basic idea of liability for foreseeable harm. Plaintiffs who could not prove fault, though, were left to warranty claims, conceived as a species of claim on the contract. Courts retained the privity requirement in these warranty claims. But ultimately, *Henningsen* allowed plaintiffs to recover for breach of warranty without privity. This was an uncomfortable anomaly; why should a plaintiff be permitted to recover on someone else's contract?

At that point *Greenman* enters to inaugurate strict liability in tort for product defects. The main ground for the *Greenman* court's decision to uphold a plaintiff's verdict was that the court could impose strict liability on the manufacturer apart from any warranty liability and that in consumer injury actions it should do so. This was strict liability in tort, not a warranty claim. Hence it was not subject to whatever limits are imposed in warranty claims and the plaintiff need not have given any notice of breach. Suddenly it all made some kind of sense in a way that the warranty claim did not.

The American Law Institute's adoption of § 402A seemed to follow naturally. We provide a summary of the essential provisions of § 402A in the final paragraph of the section. Much products law was built on these core notions; the new Restatement departs from them (or limits them) in several respects, as we see in the next section. The key provisions are:

(a) Persons injured by a defective product can sue the "seller" without proving fault. It turns out that the term "seller" is outmoded as a limiting term; as we see in § 12, lessors and others may be strictly liable. You can use seller as shorthand, however, for one who supplies chattels in the course of business. Casual suppliers of chattels are *not* covered by § 402A. That is, this form of liability applies only to those in the business of supplying the product, not to those who might occasionally do so.

(b) Privity requirements are abolished as to physical harms to person or property.

(c) The "seller" is strictly liable if the product is defective, meaning unreasonably dangerous, and causes physical harm to person or property.

(d) The test of defectiveness is the consumer's reasonable expectations.

FYI: Warranty. Clearly, warranty is not as important in products cases as it once was. But it is not irrelevant, and some states continue to deal in warranty terms (usually in addition to using tort theories). *See, e.g., Denny v. Ford Motor Co.*, 662 N.E.2d 730 (N.Y. 1995), in which the court rejected the invitation to hold that warranty theories were no longer viable in personal injury cases involving defective products. Express warranties, especially, might create a consumer expectation that the consumer would not otherwise have, or might provide a specific guarantee more favorable to the plaintiff than offered by § 402A. In addition, the statute of limitations may be calculated in a different way under warranty claims and this conceivably might prove more favorable to the plaintiff in some cases. (See § 11.) We give warranty short treatment primarily because it is not central to physical-injury products cases in most states, and because it is not tort law. Students usually get some coverage of warranty in the basic contracts class or in advanced courses in commercial law or products liability. If you nonetheless want to say a few things (or answer a few questions) about warranty at this point, here are some essentials.

Types of warranties. The most important warranties in products cases are the *express warranty*, arising from the seller's representation about the product's characteristics or uses; the *implied warranty of merchantability*, which is implied in every contract for the sale of goods and which says that an item is fit for the ordinary purposes for which such goods are used; and the *implied warranty of fitness for a particular purpose.*

Privity in warranty claims. The UCC has eliminated the total privity requirement in some cases. But many states adopt only the "Alternative A" version of § 2-318, which limits liability of a seller to a "natural person" in the buyer's household and to certain guests. ("Natural person" excludes corporations and other artificial entities.) This is a very restrictive provision. If your neighbor were injured by an exploding bottle manufactured by the defendant, your neighbor would not meet this standard. She'd have to recover under tort law, or not at all.

Disclaimers. Disclaimers are permitted under the UCC, but are limited. Most importantly, a limitation on damages for personal injury is unconscionable and not enforceable. However, a seller might exclude the warranty altogether in some cases. If this does not work, the seller might get the same effect by describing what he sells in such a way that the warranty would not be breached. Suppose a car dealer has an old, unsafe car for sale. If he sells it as a car, there is an implied warranty of reasonable safety. But if he sells it as junk to a scrap dealer there is not. Strict liability in tort is different; it is imposed, not because the parties agreed to it but because the law regarded it as good policy. Accordingly, the parties' disclaimers in tort liability cases will work only if they comport with the legal policy – which would usually be not at all. ■

§ 2. RATIONALES FOR STRICT PRODUCTS LIABILITY

You can use this section to establish some of the basic rationales for imposing strict products liability at the outset. You can then discuss the materials that follow in the light of the reasons given in support of strict liability. It may pay to take a few minutes with the reasons listed and to tie them back into the reasons given in Chapter 22 for strict vicarious liability and Chapter 23 for abnormally dangerous strict liability. Are the reasons given sufficient to justify strict products liability? Since the class has not yet covered the issues and rules, any final judgment here is premature, so skepticism coupled with suspended judgment seems to be the appropriate attitude.

It has been argued at times that many of the reasons given for strict products liability would also support strict liability in other settings. For example, enterprise liability or risk spreading (see Note 2) would justify liability in many kinds of cases to which strict liability is not applied. *See* William C. Powers, *Distinguishing Between Products and Services in Strict Liability*, 62 N.C. L. REV. 415 (1984). This seems to suggest that strict liability ought to be expanded or else that it is fundamentally illegitimate. (Powers favors expansion to cover some services.)

If the problem with a particular class is not to induce a skeptical attitude but to induce an open mind, you might have to suggest that distinctions are possible. As we get further in thinking about strict products liability (and its cutback), some in-between positions might be discovered; we might adopt a risk-spreading rationale, but subject it to some moral or efficiency limits. It might make sense to use risk-spreading in the case of non-reciprocal risks, which is the normal products case, but it might make no sense at all to use strict liability in tort to spread risks in the case of two auto drivers. Why not? First, perhaps because in the case where the plaintiff is causally involved in a significant (not necessarily faulty) way, the plaintiff's "enterprise" or activity deserves no better treatment than the defendant's. This is a rough version of the ideas advanced in Chapter 23 on the Restatements' Rules for strict liability in significant danger cases. Second, each driver could spread his or her own risks through accident insurance. This is perhaps morally fair enough since the risks are reciprocal (drivers generally share similar risks). It is also perhaps an efficient solution, since liability insurance is extremely inefficient in the return of premium dollars. (See Chapter 27, Casebook 907-908.) Thus we could reasonably adopt a risk-spreading rationale to justify the adoption of strict liability in products cases without impose strict liability in all cases.

¶4. *Fairness.* The fairness rationale should not be difficult for students to grasp, at least in broad brush, and they should recognize one basic argument from Chapter 22; there we saw that one rationale for vicarious liability is that it is fair for the employer to bear the costs of injuries inflicted by its employees because it gets the benefits of the employees' work. The argument in this context is quite similar.

The nonreciprocal risks idea may be more somewhat more difficult, but it is worth taking a little time on. George Fletcher, discussed here, wants corrective justice. He thinks strict liability would achieve justice if it is imposed whenever the plaintiff is harmed by way of a risk created by the defendant that is not reciprocal. If the risks imposed by the defendant upon the plaintiff are different in nature (or maybe extreme degree) from the risks imposed by the plaintiff upon the defendant, then those risks are nonreciprocal. Ultimately the moral content of this approach is derived from what people actually do in some relevant community. The utilitarian *Carroll Towing* approach is specifically rejected.

Fletcher is especially discussible. The summary is so brief that you cannot always determine what Fletcher would say or do about a given situation, but you can still discuss the possibilities. Here are some discussion ideas, any one of which might suffice.

Would Fletcher always impose strict liability? No. He'd impose liability when the defendant causes harm through a nonreciprocal risk, but otherwise no liability at all. Negligence cases like ordinary automobile cases are cases of nonreciprocal risks; to prove negligence is to prove that the driver created a risk that was not a general risk of motoring, and hence to prove grounds for liability.

How can you understand products liability in terms of Fletcher's theory? This note gives some clue. A manufacturer imposes risks on the consumer that are quite different, and much more significant than, any risks the consumer imposes on the manufacturer.

If you have time, you can ask the students to harken back to Chapter 23 to think more deeply about Fletcher's nonreciprocal risks idea. Would Fletcher agree with Judge Bramwell in *Bamford*? It seems likely; indeed Fletcher must have been influenced by Bramwell or someone like him. You can refer the class back to Bramwell's arguments to see the underlying similarity.

STEPHEN SUGARMAN, DOING AWAY WITH PERSONAL INJURY LAW 57-62 (1989) gives a good summary of Fletcher (as well as Epstein, Coleman, Weinrib and Glanville Williams). Some of Sugarman's ideas appear in the Casebook, Chapters 27 and 29, and in this manual in Chapter 31. He thinks that if victims can obtain compensation from some other source, a system that denies victims access to the defendant's funds or insurance does no substantial disservice to any corrective justice norms we could agree upon. Ultimately, Sugarman believes that corrective justice is an extravagance, and one that primarily benefits lawyers and insurance companies. See SUGARMAN at 62.

¶ **5. *Deterrence*.** Guido Calabresi's economic ideas are deep and important. They are highly simplified here, and even if you never read one iota of economics, you can lead a discussion through them. Students in your class who have had economics courses may find all this too simple, but they are glad for a chance to apply something they really know and you can enlist their aid in discussion quite readily.

Carroll Towing and its risk-utility analysis came up a great deal in discussions of negligence. According to economic thinkers, *Carroll Towing* follows utilitarian, economic ideals, judging legal liability by efficiency. Although we could judge efficiency in some ways not measured in money, money measures of efficiency lend themselves to communication and analysis.

Calabresi proposes a system of strict liability, grounded in notions of deterrence and accident reduction. Liability for some category of injuries is placed on some category of "activity," such as manufacturing cars. This is not because the manufacturer is at fault, or even necessarily because cars cause the injury. The idea is rather, that the manufacturer will then seek the cheapest way of avoiding liability –by making cars safer or paying someone else to accept the liability –someone who can achieve safety more cheaply.

If all this fails, then liability will drive the price of the cars up, and even that, in this best of all possible worlds, will help achieve safety, because the price of the car will reflect its connection with injury. Buyers, faced with this higher price, may catch the subway, thus achieving increased safety from cars, though perhaps not from muggers. The end result (muggers aside) is increased safety achieved through voluntary choice of the consumer.

There is a kind of second stage. Since there are many ways to avoid injuries, the ideal of efficiency would be to get the cheapest way. If liability is placed on A, but B can avoid the injury more cheaply, A may be able to pay B to take the necessary steps to avoid the injury and still come out ahead. If we could assign the liability in the first place to the cheapest injury avoider, we could save even more, since there would be no transaction costs (the cost of bargaining between A and B). If we cannot assign the liability to the best avoider, then we might place liability initially on someone who is likely to find and bargain with the best avoider. The one person who should not bear the initial liability is anyone who will find bargaining so expensive that liability cannot be shifted to the cheapest cost avoider.

(In a kind of third stage, Calabresi deals with the question how to categorize the activity against which the liability is to be levied. Is it, for example, "driving," or "driving at night," or "driving by teenagers?" We don't raise this level of his theory here; if you want to raise it with the class, Calabresi's own works are the place to go.)

A good way to get into Calabresi's ideas is through the Athens and Sparta examples discussed briefly in this note. What point is he trying to make? When the Sparta-Athens example is understood, the rest seems to move fairly well, often in a series of student comments that begin "But what about . . .?"

Would specific deterrence be better than Calabresi's general deterrence? Perhaps the economic approach– Calabresi's general deterrence– has the merit of giving people more decision-making power over their own lives with less regulation. Regulation is also itself costly and often ineffective.

Could Calabresi's ideas ever actually be implemented? Do they in fact explain strict products liability? Strict liability in any other area of law? Would you think they would work for judicial decision making, or only for large legislative determinations? Note that taxes on dangerous activities could have some effects similar to Calabresi's "general deterrence" system. Would direct taxation of product manufacturers, or the manufacturers of particularly dangerous products, be a better solution than strict tort liability?

Maybe the ideal outlook for students after discussing the rationales in Paragraphs 1-5 would be "I can see both pros and cons, but I'm not sure; show me more."

The (Partial) Decline of Strict Products Liability. These two paragraphs discuss the most recent development in products liability law: the retreat from strict liability in cases other than manufacturing defects. For design defects and warning/information defects, we appear to be moving rather inexorably towards (or back to) negligence as the legal theory. In some ways, as we will see in the materials that follow, this "development" is nothing more than a recognition that strict liability was an in-name-only affair in design and warning cases in many states, anyway. Strict liability was not distinct from negligence if it utilized a risk-utility balancing test, took account only of reasonably foreseeable risks, and placed the burden of proof on the plaintiff. However, not all states presently limit strict liability to manufacturing flaw cases. The new Restatement has the effect of declaring that, apart from manufacturing flaw cases, strict liability is out of step with the times. It thus has an impact both in the debate and in the process of legal change.

The Products Restatement almost never uses the terms "negligence" or "strict liability," even in comments. Its structure is not at all around legal theories, but rather around the various categories of product defect. Our Subchapter B on establishing a prima facie case is also organized by type of defect rather than by underlying legal theory. This does not mean that the question of what the best underlying theory is very far away, however.

§ 3. EXCLUDING STAND-ALONE ECONOMIC HARM

This short section is placed here to delimit the discussion: we are not talking about economic tort claims, only about physical harms to persons or property.

MOORMAN MFG. CO. V. NATIONAL TANK CO. 435 N.E.2d 443 (Ill. 1982)

The plaintiff purchased a steel storage tank, which developed a crack ten years later. The plaintiff sued the manufacturer on claims of negligence and strict tort liability. But the Supreme Court of Illinois held the claims properly dismissed because they were claims of economic loss only, not claims for physical injury to person or property. As to economic claims, the claim must be on warranty and meet warranty law requirements.

The *Moorman* opinion briefly restates *MacPherson* and *Greenman,* a helpful reinforcement for some students. It then reviews two leading and important cases on the question of economic loss. New Jersey, in *Santor,* held that strict liability applied to stand-alone economic loss in the absence of privity. But *Seely v. White Motor* held that strict liability does NOT apply to stand-alone economic loss. (New Jersey got rid of the last vestiges of *Santor* in *Alloway v. General Marines Industries, L.P.,* 695 A.2d 264 (N.J. 1997).)

Reasons. Reasons for denial of strict liability for stand-alone loss: (1) Sales law rules (UCC/warranty), such as those governing disclaimers and parol evidence are appropriate to govern economic relations and should not be eviscerated by strict tort liability. For example, the normal contract rules should not be overridden by the tort rule that disclaimers are ineffective. (2) Strict tort liability might [unfairly] impose liability for economic needs of a business even though not communicated to the manufacturer. (3) The rule against recovery of stand-alone economic loss in the absence of warranty permits maximum freedom: Purchasers can bargain for a warranty if they want one; but equally, they can do without a warranty and pay less. If courts imposed a automatic recovery of economic loss, this second option would be lost.

Property damage. Property damage is not the excluded economic loss; property damage is recoverable on analogy to personal injury. However, damage to the *product itself* is not covered property damage that is recoverable for "qualitative defects" defeating the purchaser's expectations, unless it results from a sudden dangerous occurrence.

Negligence liability. Contract liability for pure economic harm is more appropriate than tort, so negligence liability is excluded as well as strict tort liability.

Innocent representation. In economic loss cases, there is to be no recovery for innocent misrepresentations. The statute has run on warranty claims.

Effects. The effects of *Moorman* can be stated by saying that (1) the plaintiff who claims as buyer of goods and who asserts only an economic harm to the product itself has no claim at all unless he has a warranty (contract) claim; and (2) if he has a warranty claim, remedies are limited to remedies applied under contract law, and tort remedies are excluded. The first effect can be illustrated by a claim in which the statute of limitations has run on the warranty claim. In such a case the plaintiff has no claim at all. A conscionable disclaimer by the seller would have the same effect. The second effect can be illustrated by cases in which the plaintiff suffers a loss of $30,000 in attempting to repair the faulty product but the contract or warranty limits his remedy to a return of the goods or to repair by the manufacturer. Likewise, courts usually deny punitive damages in contract actions and so would deny punitive damages against the manufacturer of a defective product which causes only economic harm. *E.g., Waggoner v. Town & Country Mobile Homes, Inc.*, 808 P.2d 649 (Okla. 1990).

Distinguishing Economic and Physical Harms. What is economic loss? Sometimes students have difficulty with the term, which is conventional here. They point out that if you injure someone who is confined to the hospital or loses work, she has economic loss, yet that kind of economic loss is evidently recoverable. This is quite correct. The term economic loss is a shorthand convention meaning stand-alone economic loss– "economic loss without physical harm or damage to person or property." And in this case, "property" means property other than the product itself.

— *Examples: the vacuum cleaner.* Suppose you buy a vacuum cleaner. But when you get it home, the motor quits. The cleaner has not damaged your rug or you or even itself. It is just a pile of junk that is not worth what you paid. Your obvious remedy is to get your money back– your loss is wholly economic. Thus if the seller had sold the machine to you with the disclaimer, "I'm not sure how long this will last, it is very old and not in good shape, but you can have the machine for $5," the disclaimer is valid and you could not recover on strict tort liability or in negligence. But if the motor in the cleaner somehow blew up and shattered the bone in your leg, you'd have a physical injury and a potential claim based on strict tort liability or negligence. If instead of injuring your leg, the explosion burned down your house, you would also have a "physical injury" to "other property," also giving rise to a potential tort claim.

Note 1. The economic loss rule. The *Moorman* court's holdings track Traynor's decision in *Seely v. White Motor Co.* and rejects the New Jersey rule in *Santor v. A & M Karagheusian, Inc.*, which would allow economic recoveries. These were the two leading cases at the time *Moorman* was decided and both are discussed in the opinion.

It may be difficult at times to distinguish the two categories of "economic harm" and "physical harm." What does the class think the court did with the plaintiff's claim in *Moorman*? In fact the court held it was an economic claim and not one for physical harm. Is it apparent to the class that this is so? What is the test? Courts have struggled some with this little problem of drawing the line. If the crack here had developed suddenly, say within minutes, and if it had caused the tank to burst suddenly and collapse on a worker, would it not be clear that the claim was one for physical harm? What if the tank burst suddenly and damaged other property of the plaintiff? The court is quick to recognize such property damage as a ground for strict liability; the test is physical harm, not personal injury. But what if the product merely damaged itself? Some courts might make the issue turn on whether it damages itself or something else.

In any event, most courts accept the rule that stand-alone economic loss is not subject to strict tort liability. *See East River Steamship Corp. v. Transamerica Delaval, Inc.*, 476 U.S. 858 (1986); *Oceanside at Pine Point Condominium Owners Assn v. Peachtree Doors, Inc.*, 659 A.2d 267 (Me. 1995); Jay M. Zitter, *Annotation, Strict Products Liability: Recovery for Damage to Product Alone*, 72 A.L.R.4TH 12 (1989); DOBBS ON TORTS § 352. The same rule applies to cases of innocent misrepresentation about the product: strict liability or negligence liability may attach if physical harm is done, but there is no liability for pure economic loss resulting from innocent misrepresentation. *See Ritter v. Custom Chemicides, Inc.*, 912 S.W.2d 128 (Tenn. 1995). *See also* DOBBS ON TORTS § 482.

Notes 2 & 3. What constitutes "separate property?" If the defective product causes harm to some property other than the product itself, ordinary product liability and negligence rules can apply to permit recovery. E.g., *A. J. Decoster Co. v. Westinghouse Electric Corp.*, 634 A.2d 1330 (Md. 1994) (electrical back-up ventilation system failed, resulting in death of chickens, liability).

Saying that added equipment is not part of the product itself does restrict the sweep of the economic damages rule. But it may sometimes be difficult to decide what constitutes "added equipment." After the Supreme Court's *Saratoga Fishing* opinion, the Third Circuit decided to allow a strict liability theory to proceed in a case where a prefab warehouse collapsed, damaging the merchandise inside. *2-J Corp. v. Tice*, 126 F.3d 539 (3d Cir. 1997). But the Fourth Circuit held that where a $50,000 coin collection was stolen from a safe manufactured by defendants, the economic loss rule barred a strict liability design-defect claim. *Redman v. John D. Brush & Co.*, 111 F3d 1174 (4th Cir. 1997). Are the two cases distinguishable, or do the differences reflect some disagreement over the merits of the economic harm rule itself? The Florida Supreme Court, in *Comptech Int'l Inc. v. Milam Commerce Park, Ltd.*, 753 So.2d 1219 (Fla. 1999), held that a tort action for negligence in renovating a warehouse could be maintained despite a contract governing that renovation, on the ground that the computers damaged in the renovation were "other property." The court said the economic loss rule has "some genuine, albeit limited, value in tort and contract law."

(1) The main point is that the hypothetical facts in **Note 3** do *not* seem to be governed by the *Moorman* restrictions. Although cleanup costs are financial costs, they are costs of dealing with actual *damage to property* which is *not* the property sold by the defendant.

(2) *Abnormal danger.* Conceivably a non-product principle of strict liability could be invoked against TankCo. TankCo is furnishing containers for the express purpose of providing safe controls of materials that may well be classified as abnormally dangerous. So perhaps TankCo should be strictly liable on the ground that it imposed a significant risk, rather than on the grounds that it sold a product. The common usage rule might defeat that claim, however. See Chapter 23. And if there is significant danger, that fact may not help if you think the interest protected by those rules excludes pure economic interests. (Recall that the Restatement Third of Torts: Liability for Physical Harm addresses only physical, not stand-alone economic harms.)

(3) *Strangers.* In the hypothetical in **Note 3,** we can see that the plaintiff is not in the chain of contract. The plaintiff is merely a person injured by way of the defendant's defective product. When the plaintiff is not a buyer at all, he has no ability to contract for greater or lesser safety. The warranty option is not his as it is when he is a buyer of the goods, either from the manufacturer or from a dealer. When he is a complete stranger to the transaction, it looks as if the reasons for the *Moorman* rules disappear. It is, after all, the ability to contract about the scope of protection and to trade price saving for more risk or extra cost for more safety, that makes sense. So you can argue that when damage is done outside the scope of the contract the products rules do not create the basis for recovery and do not limit it. See *Paramount Aviation Corp. v. Agusta,* 288 F.3d 67 (3d Cir. 2002).

Nevertheless, the economic loss rule is broader than products liability. If you negligently pollute the river wholly apart from the sale of any product, you may be liable to a governmental entity to clean it up, but, statutes aside, you are not usually liable to the owner of the bar who loses business because people do not patronize the bar during the clean up period. Cf. *State of Louisiana ex rel. Guste v. M/V Testbank,* 752 F.2d 1019 (5th Cir. 1985) (pollution of the Mississippi River, polluter not liable for purely economic harm to some of the businesses dependent upon the river or its traffic).

Note 4. Present economic harm resulting from product's risk of physical harm. This is a challenging note with good potential payoff for students who work through it. *First,* it challenges student to recognize that

Moorman does NOT preclude liability for breach of warranty.

Second: It challenges students to consider, then reject, a comparison to the increased risk of harm cases first seen with loss of the chance/increased risk cases in Chapter 7. This IS a risk of future harm case, to be sure, but it differs from the risk of future cancer or other medical impairment because the allegation here is that the risk of future harm causes a *present loss* in economic value. We quite commonly measure economic injury by diminished market value. Most assuredly we do NOT require physical harm in claims for contract or warranty breach. Nor do we require any actual sale in order to invoke the loss of market value as a measure of damages. *See generally* on market measures of damages, DAN B. DOBBS, THE LAW OF REMEDIES § 3.3(1) (1993). In *In re Bridgestone/Firestone, Inc.*, 288 F.3d 1012 (7th Cir. 2002), Judge Easterbrook asserted that most states would deny recovery on facts like those in *Frank*, but in support he cited two cases involving only increased risk of personal harm or fear of future injury, *Willett v. Baxter International, Inc.*, 929 F.2d 1094 (5th Cir. 1991) and *Capital Holding Corp. v. Bailey*, 873 S.W.2d 187 (Ky. 1994).

Third, if you are so minded, you can discuss the *Carroll Towing* "efficiency" argument Judge Easterbrook made in *Bridgestone*, supra, but this will require you to check the case because we have not printed it.

The cases cited here take the view that there is no defect at all because the product is still functioning properly. A few cases have gone the other way. It may be that cases like *Briehl* and *Frank* are justified in holding for the defendants, but maybe not on the ground they assert. If you buy a house and the defendant either fraudulently represents that it has a new roof or guarantees the roof in a deed warranty, you have a claim when it turns out that the roof is twenty years old and will start leaking any day. You don't have to wait for the leak to occur. One reason this makes sense is that the objective market will tell you that the value of the house is less than it should have been under the representation or warranty. On this topic see DOBBS ON TORTS § 483A (Supp.).

Comparative law. Products are likely to be in international trade, so products liability law may require much broad perspectives of lawyers, or at least familiarity with foreign products laws. That, of course, is beyond the scope of this book, although you might consider adopting a supplemental text if the topic really interests you. *See* JULIE A. DAVIES & PAUL T. HAYDEN, GLOBAL ISSUES IN TORT LAW (2008) (containing a chapter on products liability).

The European Union (European Communities) Council of European Communities (now known as the European Economic Community, or EEC) issued a directive governing products liability in 1985. That directive, theoretically authoritative, provides in language much simpler than the Restatement's, "The producer shall be liable for damage caused by a defect in his product." When France passed legislation implementing the directive in 1998, all of the EEC nations had finally passed products laws in compliance with the directive. For analysis of European products law and the directive, see Howells & Mildred, *Is European Products Liability More Protective than the Restatement (3d) of Torts: Products Liability?*, 65 TENN. L. REV. 985 (1998) and Alfred E. Mottur, *The European Product Liability Directive: a Comparison with U.S. Law, an Analysis of its Impact on Trade, and a Recommendation for Reform So as to Accomplish Harmonization and Consumer Protection*, 25 LAW & POLICY IN INT'L BUS. 983 (1994). Local cultures may or may not be receptive to the whole idea of strict liability. See Anita Bernstein & Paul Fanning, *Heirs of Leonardo: Cultural Obstacles to Strict Products Liability in Italy*, 27 VAND. J. TRANSNAT'L L. 1 (1994). See also BRUCE FELDTHUSEN, ECONOMIC NEGLIGENCE 167-198 (2d ed. 1988), discussing American, Canadian and English (British Commonwealth) decisions. For a comparison to German law, which shares the same problems reflected in *Moorman*-related cases, and some of the same results on different technical grounds, see Bungert, *Compensating Harm to the Defective Product Itself—A Comparative Analysis of American and German Products Liability Law*, 66 TUL. L. REV. 1179 (1992). There is a good brief overview of EEC products law in 1 MADDEN & OWEN ON PRODUCTS LIABILITY § 1:9 (3d Ed. 2000).

Subchapter B. Establishing a Prima Facie Case

§ 4. MANUFACTURING DEFECTS

This short section introduces the first and easiest kind of strict products case, the manufacturing flaw. It also introduces (or re-introduces) the consumer expectation test, now rejected by the Restatement of Products Liability except in food cases.

LEE V. CROOKSTON COCA-COLA BOTTLING CO., 188 N.W.2d. 426 (Minn. 1971)

The plaintiff was injured when a bottle exploded in her hand. She sued the bottler. The trial judge submitted only her claims based on negligence and warranty theories. The jury found for the bottler. On appeal, the plaintiff argues that her strict tort liability theory should have been submitted to the jury. *Held*, for the plaintiff, new trial. The mere fact of injury is not sufficient to show a defect any more than it is to show negligence. But circumstantial evidence that is sufficient to submit the case on res ipsa loquitur grounds also justifies submission on strict liability grounds. There was such evidence here. The jury's finding of no negligence does not dispense with the strict tort claim, since a bottle may be defective even if the defendant used due care. Likewise, the jury's finding for the defendant on the warranty claim does not exclude the possibility that the defendant would be strictly liable in tort.

Distinguishing Strict Liability, Negligence and Warranty

This case allows the student an opportunity to begin distinguishing negligence and warranty claims from strict tort liability claims. It is then necessary to define what we mean by "defective" products.

Warranty. Warranty is a form of strict liability. The jury might find it hard to accept the idea that the defendant "warranted" a safe bottle, yet might believe that the bottle was "defective" when it left the defendant's hands. Thus the jury's finding against the plaintiff on the warranty claim would not necessarily establish that the bottle was not defective, although a different wording of the warranty instruction might produce a different result on this issue.

Negligence. In one respect this resembles a negligence case, as the court recognizes when it says that evidence that justifies res ipsa loquitur also justifies a finding of a defect. Has the jury already rejected the idea that the bottle was defective, since it found no negligence? The court is correct in saying "not necessarily." You might believe a bottle is defective even though the defendant has done everything in its power to avoid the defects. This point pushes us directly into a discussion of what we mean by "defective."

What is "Defective?"

Note 1. Manufacturing defects. This note gives a clear definition of a manufacturing defect, including the definition contained in the Restatement (Third) of Torts: Products Liability (which we call the Restatement of Products Liability). That Restatement maintains strict liability for manufacturing flaws by the way it defines a defect. You might pause on this note to emphasize the that the students need to keep the old Restatement Second and new Restatements separate in their minds. Section 402A is the old Restatement. The new Restatement has sections numbered from § 1 up. Old 402A was expansive in approach, looking forward to an interesting new development of liabilities. The new Restatement of Products Liability is constrictive and categorical, attempting to state general concepts partly opposed to strict liability and particular rules that define the scope of liability carefully.

Notes 2 & 3. The consumer expectation test. The Restatement (Third) of Torts: Products Liability did not render the consumer expectation test a complete nullity, although it reduces it to a factor to be considered in determining "defectiveness" and eliminates it as an independent test for judging design and information defects. See § 2, cmt. *g*. With respect to manufacturing defects, however, the consumer expectation test would appear to retain its essential vitality. Comment *c* to § 2 provides, "More distinctly than any other type of defect, manufacturing defects disappoint consumer expectations." That is, consumer expectations are clearly not met when a product "departs from its intended design." So it looks as if the Restatement of Products Liability is recognizing the consumer expectations test for product flaw cases by defining defect to be a departure from intended design.

Note 4. An informational note – the courts use consumer expectations and it is widely used in other countries.

Proving a Case of Manufacturing Defect

Note 5. Elements of a strict liability claim. This note reflects the essential elements of strict products liability behind the somewhat varied formulations you can find in some cases. Note that the causation of actual harm is still required for a prima facie case. Just as negligence in the air, so to speak, will not do, neither will defectiveness in the air. The requirement that the product be "defective" when it leaves the defendant's hands is most fundamentally a requirement that the defect be fairly attributable to the defendant before liability can be imposed. The requirement of a defect in the product when it left the defendant's hands also relates to notions of proximate cause, misuse, assumed risk and contributory negligence, issues developed more fully in §§ 8 and 9.

Note 6. Inferences of cause and defect. Students may need a reminder that drawing inferences is as necessary in proving a strict liability case as it is in a negligence case. The new Restatement's § 3, quoted here, of course parallels the rule of res ipsa loquitur. The section is titled "Circumstantial Evidence Supporting Inference of Product Defect," and both the comments and the Reporters' Note make explicit references to res ipsa. However, the rule seems even more like an instance the rule of inferred causation we've seen in cases like *Zuchowicz v. United States,* 140 F. 3d 381, 390-391 (2d Cir. 1998) (Chapter 7, Casebook 206). We see that again in *Liriano,* and its Note 10 following that case, below. We are here drawing a distinction between an inference of defect on the one hand and an inference of causation on the other. One, the other, or both may be involved.

Note 7. Applications. Do differences in the results in these cases turn on fact-distinctions or changed attitudes? If a bottle explodes, what are we to think except that (a) someone was negligent or (b) the bottle was defective? Courts have struggled with proof problems and their attitudes have perhaps become more liberal as they have become accustomed to strict liability. Perhaps Minnesota and New Jersey can distinguish their later from their earlier cases, but the developing liberal attitude of the later period may be a more likely explanation for the difference.

In *Cooper Tire v. Mendez,* the Texas case cited here, the court held for the defendant, on the ground that an expert's opinion about what caused the blowout was legally insufficient given the other evidence. There was, thought the court, no scientific basis for the expert's conclusion that something other than the nail caused the blowout.

The remaining case here, *Mixon v. Chrysler Corp.,* also held for the defendant. The plaintiff must prove a defect in the product that existed when the product left the defendant's hands (see Note 5 above) and the court thought that burden had not been met. (Some quite different proof issues appear in § 7 below.)

Other examples of the issue include *Crawford v. Sears Roebuck & Co.,* 295 F.3d 884 (8th Cir. 2002). There, a ladder manufactured at least 20 years earlier buckled laterally, throwing plaintiff to the ground. This was not enough to show either negligence or defect. Because the plaintiff offered no evidence to exclude other forces that might have affected ladder during its long pre-injury history, there could be no inference of defect at the time ladder left the seller's hands). In *Parsons v. Ford Motor Co.,* 85 S.W.3d 323 (Tex. App. 2002), the plaintiff claimed a design rather than manufacturing defect, but the problem of inferring defect or negligence was the same. The plaintiff's car, engine switched off, burst into flames, justifying inference of negligence or defect. But since the probable source of flames was ignition that had been worked on by a dealer after the car left the manufacturer's hands, the dealer's work rather than the design defect may have been the only cognizable cause. We are not so sure that this one comes out right. The dealer's work had been necessitated by the original design defect. Even if the dealer did a bad job and enhanced the risk, wouldn't the design defect still be a cause in the same way that a negligent driver is a cause of the initial injury and also its aggravation by a negligent doctor?

Note 8. Proof of specific defect. This note ties in directly to Note 6 above. Specifically, an inference of defect may be drawn in a case even without proof of the specific defect. Comment *c* to § 3 explains that "quite apart from the question of what type of defect was involved, the plaintiff need not explain specifically what constituent part of the product failed." The comment goes on to give the example of the catastrophic failure of an airplane. In such a situation, the plaintiff does not have to prove whether the failure was caused by a fuel-tank explosion or an engine malfunction in order to prove the plane's defect caused the harm.

Note 9. Defect and negligence. *Lee*'s res ipsa analogies and the note materials above do indeed suggest that negligence and strict liability are not so many miles apart in many respects. Indeed, it may turn out in the end that you won't be able to distinguish negligence from strict liability; or at least that you won't be able to distinguish it in all cases. Be that as it may, students are entitled to see the constant iteration of the courts and most writers that the two are indeed different and to see why they say so. The manufacturing defect cases generally, and *Lee* specifically, is a good vehicle for this. The manufacturer has produced a "defective" bottle that explodes in the purchaser's hand. The manufacturer has used the highest possible care. In such a case, if there is liability at all, it is strict. A determined student may insist that such a case is really one of negligence because res ipsa loquitur. Indeed, *Escola v. Coca Cola Bottling Co. of Fresno,* 150 P.2d 436 (Cal. 1944), decided exactly that, so maybe, you'll let the student bask in some credit for a moment before trying out a case that definitely is not a *res ipsa* case: suppose a can of food produced in the most modern factory and under the best methods possible contains a virus hitherto unknown and entirely undetectable except by its devastating effects on the human digestive system. The logic of the Restatement is that liability will be imposed, but this is hardly a case explicable on res ipsa grounds.

It is true, however, that although the plaintiff may not prove negligence, negligence might actually exist in many of these products cases. If you believe this, you might believe that the defendant's liability is not strict liability, but really liability for probable negligence. Yet, even if you think this way, you have to admit that the rule of strict liability makes a profound difference – it allows the plaintiff to recover without *proof* of negligence. Under the negligence rule he would have to suffer a directed verdict unless he offered some substantial evidence of that negligence..

MEXICALI ROSE V. SUPERIOR COURT, 822 P.2d 1292 (Cal. 1992)

The plaintiff was injured on a chicken bone in a chicken enchilada served at the defendant's restaurant. The court thought a demurrer to both strict tort liability and to warranty claims should be sustained.

The old natural-foreign distinction was a rule of law that the plaintiff could not recover either on a negligence or warranty theory for injuries due to materials natural to the food, so long as the food was unspoiled. The same rule might be carried over to strict liability in tort as it was in *Mexicali Rose*. The court modifies the rule to permit proof that the restaurant was negligent in preparing the enchilada and to permit a recovery if it was. However, as to strict liability either in warranty or tort the answer is that the plaintiff simply cannot recover as long as the item causing harm was "natural" rather than foreign to the food. You can make this rule commensurate with the consumer expectation test only by ignoring actual consumer expectations and stating that, as a matter of law in all cases consumers do not expect their restaurant food to eliminate natural dangers. The case may be a sport, reflecting more about the 1992 California Court than about the law generally: even the Products Restatement does not accept it.

JACKSON V. NESTLE-BEICH, INC., 589 N.E. 2d 547 (Ill. 1992)

The plaintiff broke a tooth on a pecan shell embedded in a pecan-candy. The Illinois Court rejects the rule adopted in California, adhering to a consumer expectation test and hence eliminating any rule of law that "natural" items are always within the consumer's expectation.

Note. Food products and consumer expectations. The Restatement resolves the split between *Mexicali Rose* and *Jackson* by siding with *Jackson* and the consumer expectation test in food cases. The consumer expectation test does raise some sticky problems, some of which relate closely to defenses such as assumed risk, open and obvious danger, or contributory fault. For this reason, you might prefer to delay talking about its ambiguities or limits until other materials are covered. (See the discussion of consumer expectations in § 5 below.)

These two cases can, however, nicely illustrate some of the test's ambiguities: (1) What if the consumer in *Jackson* knew from bad experience that pecan shells turned up in the candy, but consumers generally did not? (2) Vice versa: what if reasonable consumers generally knew of the pecan-shell risk but the plaintiff did not? (3) What if the consumer was a child who knew nothing about danger, but reasonably informed adult consumers would know that danger? (4) What if the particular consumer and also consumers generally would never have thought of pecan-shell dangers and had no expectations about danger from that particular source, but did expect candy to be safe except for the excessive sugar content?

The doubts these questions might create about the consumer expectation test become much more serious when the consumer has no expectation of safety because she can see the product's "obvious danger." That means that if you use a consumer expectation test as the sole test of defect, the consumer's contributory negligence or assumed risk with respect to an obviously dangerous product will not simply reduce damages but will bar recovery because the product would not be defective at all if the consumer could see its danger and thus expected no safety.

§ 5. DESIGN DEFECTS

LEICHTAMER V. AMERICAN MOTORS CO., 424 N.E. 2d 568 (Ohio 1981)

The plaintiff was injured when a Jeep did a back-to-front flip. The rollbar displaced toward the passengers and the plaintiff was paralyzed. There was no production flaw, but the vehicle's design was defective because the rollbar was designed only to protect against sideway turnovers. This is a defect because it is not as safe as an ordinary consumer would expect. Strict liability applies to crashworthiness or "second collision" cases.

This simple case introduces the design defect in contrast to the manufacturing flaw. It also states the consumer expectation test in the design defect context. That test works well for the plaintiff in *Leichtamer* because the design's defectiveness was probably actually misleading about safety. With the help of notes, *Leichtamer* also provides two important pieces of information, namely the rule that a product may be defective in some instances if it is not crashworthy, and the rule that bystanders as well as purchasers, users and repairers may recover.

Note 1. Design defects. One significance of the design defect category is mentioned in the casebook– if the design of a product is defective, the entire product line is defective and represents potential for liability. Another significance is that for the most part it will be very difficult to know whether a design is defective if there is no norm in custom on which to rely– a norm readily supplied by other similar products in the case of production flaws. Most soft drink bottles do not explode in our hands and if a bottle is an exploding one, other, safer, bottles give us a standard of expectation. But we cannot make a similar statement about a car without a roll bar or a side-impact airbag. The car was designed that way; how are we to say it was defective, especially under the consumer expectation test? In *Leichtamer* it is not difficult because the roll bar gave the appearance of safety to the ordinary consumer when it was not in fact safe. Design defect cases will quickly become more difficult to judge, however.

Notes 2 & 3. Consumer expectations. The Restatement Second rather casually tossed off the consumer expectation test in the comments to 402A: a product defect, says comment *g*, is one which "leaves the seller's hands, in a condition not contemplated by the ultimate consumer, which will be unreasonably dangerous to him." And comment *i* defines an "unreasonably dangerous"product as one that is "dangerous to an extent beyond that which would be contemplated by the ordinary consumer who purchases it, with the ordinary knowledge common to the community as to its characteristics." As we have learned, that test has now been rejected by the Restatement Third as an independent ground for liability, except in food-manufacturing defect cases. If you wish to discuss the test further, Notes 2 & 3 and the *Knitz* case will furnish a springboard. The notes are meant to raise a question for thought or discussion: Does the test work if you try to apply it? If a consumer doesn't know anything about whether cars have roll bars or other reinforcements in the roof, can she nevertheless expect that the roof will not collapse and crush her in case of a rollover? This is one of the fundamental difficulties presented by the consumer expectation test. At least it is a difficulty if you want the answer to be that the manufacturer should not be liable in such a case. If you use a general expectation of safety, irrespective of knowledge about roll bars, you have extensive liability and a constantly changing standard. If you require a specific expectation of safety based on the common knowledge that roll bars are usually built into cars, then you foreclose liability in a very large number of cases because such a specific expectation is not justified.

Soule v. General Motors Corporation, cited in **Note 2**, more or less stands for the view that the consumer expectation test works for the plaintiff only when consumers have a *specific* expectation about a design based on their common experience or knowledge; it is not enough that they expect general safety in the product, or that they would not expect a car roof to collapse. The facts in *Soule* are almost exactly like a roof collapse case except that it was a floorboard displaced upward instead of a roof displaced downward. "[T]he consumer expectations test is reserved for cases in which the everyday experience of the product's users permits a conclusion that the product's design violated minimum safety assumptions, and is thus defective regardless of expert opinion about the merits of the design." The consumer has no reasonable expectation that the floorboard would not be displaced into the car upon a collision. The case has also been read as limiting the consumer expectation test in California to "simple" products. If too many experts are called to testify as to the design, then it looks like the product is "complex," and, on the ground stated above, the consumer expectation test becomes unusable.

In *Jackson v. General Motors Corp.*, 60 S.W.3d 800 (Tenn. 2001), the plaintiff broke his jaw when, while wearing a seatbelt, his face struck the steering wheel in a crash. The court rejected the manufacturer's argument that the consumer expectation test (recognized in Tennessee statutes) could not apply to complex products. (Both sides had cited *Soule*). However, the plaintiff would still be required to prove that consumers with ordinary knowledge of the product would have reasonable expectations that were not met.

Morson v. Superior Court, 109 Cal. Rptr. 2d 343 (Ct. App. 2001), said the consumer expectation test could be used even if the product could be complex—but its *failure* must be simple. The court there refused to apply the consumer expectation to claims that the defendants' latex rubber gloves used in health care industry resulting in serious allergenic injuries. The mechanism of the alleged product failure was complex, involving the interactions of proteins naturally in rubber and personal allergies. Knowing nothing of such matters, consumers would have no expectation about them. The court suggested that if the product had failed to provide a safety barrier, so that the user was infected by a disease because the gloves were permeable, the answer might be different. *Contra*, applying the consumer expectation test to alleged allergies resulting from use of to latex rubber gloves, *Green v. Smith & Nephew AHP, Inc.,* 629 N.W.2d 727 (Wis. 2001).

Hansen v. Baxter Healthcare Corp., 764 N.E.2d 35 (Ill. 2002) approved use of a consumer expectation test as a basis for liability of a medical device supplier. The device was a connector that united two pieces of tubing, one feeding into the plaintiff's veins. One connector was a pressure connection—you pushed a smaller tube into a larger one. The trouble was that such connections sometimes came apart and one did so in this case. That allowed air bubbles to enter the vein and cause an embolism in the brain, which in turn caused the patient brain damage and ultimately death. The same manufacturer also offered hospitals—who were the purchasers of this equipment—a locking collar that prevented separation. The manufacturer did not withdraw the unsafe connector from the market or even warn the healthcare providers that the safer product was available at a few cents advance in price. On these facts the court thought a consumer expectation test was an appropriate basis of liability. Who did the court think was the consumer? The patient. "Andrina, who was conscious after surgery, could have reasonably expected that her IV catheter connection, if properly designed and manufactured, would be safe to use for its intended purpose. She was the person who would be harmed if the device failed." This seems to be an anti-*Soule* approach, requiring only some general expectation of safety, not even knowledge that a particular connection was used, much less knowledge that it might disconnect. Why not use the expectation of the healthcare professionals who purchased or used the product and who had a rather more specific assumption about safety? These were the persons to whom a warning was owed, so why is it not their expectations? The answer to that question might matter greatly if you were in a *Soule* jurisdiction where general expectation of safety would be irrelevant. The question itself also helps reveal one of the difficulties in applying consumer expectations tests.

Defending the consumer expectation test. Does the consumer expectation test really have all the problems attributed to it? Some think not. When you can identify the level of safety the reasonable consumer would expect in using the product as the manufacturer expects, the test tells you exactly the right amount of liability, at least when the plaintiff is the purchaser or a voluntary user. In a broad sense, you can compare consumer expectations to custom in the community. If consumers really would expect a safe rollbar, that speaks of a community-wide understanding about particular products and it would be shared and understood by manufacturers, too. The consumer expectation test is closely related to the idea of custom. As with custom in negligence cases, the consumer expectation-community standard is at odds with the risk-utility test. But, as suggested in **Note 3**, although the consumer expectation test might defeat an old § 402A strict liability claim when the danger was obvious – since the consumer, aware of the danger, would not expect greater safety – the plaintiff in such a case would still have an ordinary negligence claim if the product was unreasonably risky. What's so bad about that?

Note 4. Bystanders or strangers. The passengers in *Leichtamer* might be "consumers" of the product in the sense that they are users of it. Bystanders, however, are not in any sense consumers of the very product that causes harm. Nevertheless, courts decided early on after the promulgation of § 402A that, with privity abolished, anyone who foreseeably might be injured by a product's defect, could assert a claim against the manufacturer or other appropriate defendant. Even if a bystander is injured partly because of a product defect and partly because a another person misused the product, the manufacturer can be subjected to liability; the old saw there is no duty to control others has no application. *See Smith v. Bryco Arms,* 33 P.3d 638 (N.M. Ct. App. 2001).

Can the consumer expectation test explain such liability to strangers who have not purchased or used or even serviced the product? Suppose that a parsimonious professor still has his first car, purchased in 1951. He drives it to work but one day the steering fails and he loses control. The car runs up on the sidewalk and into a pedestrian there. The pedestrian could have little or no expectation about the car's specific engineering devices or even about its probable safety performance. So does the bystander's right to recover suggest that the consumer expectation test is itself defectively designed?

Should products liability extend to cases of emotional distress of bystanders who see a horrible accident caused by the product? *Walker v. Clark Equipment Co.,* 320 N.W.2d 561 (Iowa 1982), allowed such a recovery. Illinois, which finally abolished its impact requirement in favor of a zone of danger rule in negligence cases, adhered to that requirement for strict liability cases. *Pasquale v. Speed Products Engineering,* 654 N.E.2d 1365 (Ill. 1995). In fact, the court insisted that even though the plaintiff was struck by his wife's body when the product exploded and struck her, that would not count as sufficient physical harm required under Restatement § 402A. The ruling rested entirely on the distinction between negligence and strict liability theories of the case. *See* Dale Joseph Gilsinger, Annotation, *Bystander Recovery under State Law for Emotional Distress from Witnessing Another's Injury in Products Liability Context*, 90 A.L.R.5th 179 (2001). If, because of your use of your defective product, a friend or client is injured or killed, but the victim is not a family member, should the restrictions imposed in the emotional distress cases like *Thing v. La Chusa* be lifted to permit recovery? See *Kately v. Wilkinson*, 148 Cal. App. 3d 576, 195 Cal. Rptr. 902 (1983) (permitting recovery before *Thing v. La Chusa* was decided); *Kennedy v. McKesson Co.*, 58 N.Y.2d 500, 462 N.Y.S.2d 421, 448 N.E.2d 1332 (1983) (negligent product repair to dental gas machine, dentist using it without fault killed patient, repairer liable for dentist's emotional harm). Cf. *Washington State Physicians Ins. Exchange & Ass'n v. Fisons Corp.*, 122 Wash.2d 299, 858 P.2d 1054 (1993); *Oskenholt v. Lederle Labs.*, 294 Or. 213, 656 P.2d 293 (1982) (doctors prescribing injury causing drugs could recover for damages resulting from lost reputation). However, *Straub v. Fisher and Paykel Health Care*, 990 P.2d 384 (Utah 1999) denied recovery to a nurse who allegedly suffered serious emotional consequences when her use of a defectively designed product led to the horrible death of her patient. The court there insisted that the plaintiff claiming emotional harm would have to be physically endangered, whether her claim was in negligence or strict liability.

Note 5. Crashworthiness. The manufacturers have pretty well lost this issue so far as it is based on the "unintended use" argument. They are required at their peril to produce a product that is safe for foreseeable uses, including, in the case of motor vehicles, crashes. This seems incongruous with the consumer expectation test. The foreseeable use test allows a finding of defectiveness even if the danger was obvious to the consumer. Thus, lurking beneath the surface, the foreseeable use test, which is the support for the manufacturer's duty to provide a reasonably crashworthy vehicle, is in potential conflict with the consumer expectation test. Both were adopted in *Leichtamer*. The range of liability under the foreseeable use test, however, is rather narrow, because if the danger is obvious to people in general, through warnings supplied by the manufacturer or otherwise, the use will not be will often be characterized as an unforeseeable one. This may be described as misuse, but that will often be a shorthand expression for the proposition that the product was not defective for foreseeable uses.
The misuse idea is considered in § 9.

KNITZ V. MINSTER MACHINE CO., 432 N.E.2d 814 (Ohio 1982)

Although it does not affect analysis of the problem, you may wish to know that the Ohio legislature first codified the *Knitz* court's alternative test for design defects, then eliminated the consumer expectation test entirely. *See Perkins v. Wilkinson Sword, Inc.*, 700 N.E.2d 1247 (Ohio 1998)(discussing statutory history).

Knitz begins to describe a problem and takes us to the top of a slippery slope. It represents the second step in appreciating design defect cases, but not a solution to those cases. That step is to recognize that consumer expectation tests will not allow the plaintiff to recover in many design cases.

Although that test worked well in *Leichtamer* because the consumer probably did have an expectation of safety induced by the appearance of the vehicle if not by the advertisements for it, the consumer in *Knitz* knew exactly what the physical structure of the machine was —it was operated by a foot pedal— and they probably also understood the risks this presented. A straight application of the consumer-expectation-of-safety test would almost certainly defeat recovery in a case like this one, unless you created a special rule for those who are compelled by practical exigencies of employment to confront the risk.

Feeling that this is a good kind of case for strict liability, courts have substituted the risk-utility balance for the consumer expectation test. This sounds like negligence. How can we say we are imposing strict liability if we are adopting the same test used in *Carroll Towing* negligence cases? This point is thrust upon students in Note 5 below.

Note 2. The fundamental distinction. Other countries ignore the design-manufacturing flaw distinction. Possibly we have drawn too many distinctions; or possibly European law is generally simply not as (usefully) analytical as American law. Discussion of this point will be easier later; right now, it serves to alert students to the possibility that there may be other ways to handle products, so perhaps they can read these materials with a mind open to different approaches.

Note 3. Risks and utilities balanced. The risk-utility balancing contemplated by the court allows a finding of defect in the product even if it meets consumer expectations of safety, so long as the risk of the design outweighs the benefits of the design. Doesn't adoption of a risk-utility test mean that we have reverted to negligence law? Most courts and commentators think so, although some courts continue to insist that they are applying "strict" liability even when using risk-utility balancing.

We emphasize this problem in Note 6 below and test it out in some of the materials that follow.

Note 5. Restatement of Products Liability. Alert classes will not need emphasis to see that the Products Restatement junks the consumer expectation test in design defect cases; sleepy students may need a teacher to highlight this point. The Restatement accepts consumer expectation as relevant to an assessment of risks and utilities, in particular, as relevant to foreseeability and frequency of the risk.

Note 6. Negligence disguised in strict liability? This Note sets a question to be pursued in following materials and hence discussion of it may be a good use of class time. The adoption of a risk-utility test raises the question whether strict liability has simply been eliminated for design defect cases. This note tries to get us ready to look seriously at the question by first disposing of a hackneyed distinction we think meaningless and with what looks like a court's simply refusal to cope with the issue. (a) The saw that strict liability is about the quality of the product, if meaningful when defect is tested by consumer expectations, is no ground for distinction if the liability is tested by the same risk-utility weighing we use in negligence law. (b) The *Connelly* court seems to perform a risk-utility balance to conclude that the airbag system was not defective, yet to say that the jury could find negligence on the same facts. Unless the court has in mind some *other* negligence, this seems to imply that the court is not testing negligence by a risk-utility approach. That would be possible, as suggested when we covered *Carroll Towing*, but that would mean that we must rewrite a good deal of negligence analysis to maintain the distinction.

The materials that follow try to test whether some distinction remains between strict liability and negligence once a risk-utility test has become the sole test of liability. Maybe you could say that a strict liability approach is still distinguishable from a negligence approach if: (1) The risk-utility balancing in products cases is somehow more exacting, say because we tolerate less risk or require more utility. If that is what courts are doing, they are not doing it openly. (2) The courts weigh unknowable and unforeseen risks against known utilities. This idea, once very much on the table, was used by manufacturers to push statutory limits on liability and it now has little support. The Restatement of Products Liability has rejected it. (3) The risk-utility balance might be the same, but the defendant might be required to should the burden of proving a favorable balance. (*Barker*, below). (4) the risk-utility balance is the same but defenses available in negligence suits are less favorable to product liability defendants; for example, the faulty plaintiff might be permitted to make a full recovery in strict liability (*Bowling*, Casebook 756), or the statute of limitations might be more generous to the plaintiff. The immediately following materials give you a chance to show that none of these assertions hold up in most states. So, to the extent that risk-utility balance is the sole test of "strict liability" in design cases, there is no real strict liability in those cases. Where the consumer expectations test is still available, however, strict liability may indeed remain distinct from negligence liability.

BARKER V. LULL ENGINEERING CO., 573 P.2d 443 (Cal. 1978).

In some cases, the plaintiff would lose under a risk-utility test. In other cases, the plaintiff would lose under the consumer expectation test. *Barker* might be such a case because the consumer had no expectation of safety from a canopy or the like. *See also, e.g., Horton v. American Tobacco Co.*, 667 So.2d 1289 (Miss. 1995) (in suit against a tobacco company for wrongful death of a smoker, the estate sought a risk utility-instruction since the smoker may have had no expectation of safety).

Barker allows the plaintiff, at her option, to use either the consumer expectation or the risk-utility test, giving the plaintiff the best of both worlds. That in itself is not so surprising, because in a court using the consumer expectation test, the plaintiff could always assert negligence with its emphasis on risks and utilities when the consumer expectation test would fail. *See Green v. Smith & Nephew AHP, Inc.,* 629 N.W.2d 727 (Wis. 2001).

But *Barker* does not stop there; it is quite distinguishable from a negligence case, because the court shifts the burden of proof to the defendant in a way wholly inconsistent with negligence law. *Barker* draws a very real distinction between risk-utility in negligence and risk-utility in strict liability; the risk-utility balance is the same as in negligence cases, but the burden of proof is not.

In short, *Barker* contains two distinct and pro-plaintiff rules: (1) The plaintiff has an option to use either the consumer expectation test or the risk-utility test, whichever is more favorable, and (2) the burden shifts to the defendant to show the design was nondefective once the plaintiff shows the design caused harm.

Soule, cited below in **Note 3**, cuts back on the first *Barker* rule, by limiting the use of the consumer expectation test to cases in which consumers have a *specific* expectation about a design based on their common experience or knowledge. This effectively means that *Barker* in its full glory is applied in California only to rather simple products.

Note 1. The first *Barker* rule (plaintiff choice of test) has some limited support outside California. The Products Restatement, rejecting the independent consumer expectation test altogether, is to the contrary. Burden-shifting has even less support outside California.

Note 2. *Campbell* is primarily an illustration of the burden shifting. The plaintiff has made her case against the bus manufacturer by showing that she sat in the one seat on the bus without a nearby handle, that the bus turned, and that she fell off her seat. Does anyone think this proof would suffice in an ordinary negligence case?

HONDA OF AMERICA MFG. V. NORMAN , 104 S.W.3d 600 (Tex. App. 2003)

The decedent, seemingly intoxicated, backed into Galveston Bay. Her companion escaped, but, as the jury must have found, the decedent's seatbelt jammed and she drowned. The plaintiffs suing for her death claimed the seat-belt-harness was defective because it could strap the driver in tightly with no good chance of release. No good chance of release because the release button was over the driver's left shoulder, possibly unreachable if she were strapped in tightly. Alternative designs could have positioned the release at the driver's hip, used a timer to retract and loosen the belt when it jammed, or could have used two release buttons. The jury found for the plaintiff, although it also found the decedent to be chargeable with 25% of the negligence, a finding that presumably reduced damages proportionately, although the court does not say that.

The case, in contrast to *Barker v. Lull*, establishes (a) a burden of proof on the plaintiff to prove a defect, and (b) the requirement that the plaintiff prove a reasonable alternative design existed. The RAD requirement breaks down into more demands for proof, namely, that

(1) there was a safer alternative;

(2) the safer alternative would have

(i) prevented or significantly reduced the risk of injury,

(ii) without substantially impairing the product's utility ("that is, that the alternative design not only would have reduced the risk of harm in the instant case, but also would not, 'under other circumstances, impose an equal or greater risk of harm'"); and

(3) the safer alternative was both

(i) technologically and

(ii) economically feasible

when the product left the control of the manufacturer.

On the timer alternative, an expert testified that "it would have been 'simple within the electronics' to have created such a system." This was inadequate testimony. The court seems to have in mind that the testimony was too general: "Horton did not identify any such available design, nor did he discuss the economic or technological feasibility of such a hypothetical alternative design." But then it veers to a different idea altogether in stating its conclusion: "[T]he Normans failed to prove that a timer-controlled mouse was a safer alternative design to the seatbelt system in Karen's Honda."

On the location of the release button, testimony indicated that a more easily reachable release was actually in use; Toyota used a hip-side release on its cars. The court held that this testimony might establish technical feasibility, but that it did not establish economic feasibility. "While the use of an alternative design by another manufacturer may establish technological feasibility, we have held that, as a matter of law, it does not establish economic feasibility."

Finally, as the court goes on, it again veers from the path it had followed: "[E]ven if the Normans presented more than a scintilla of evidence from which the jury could reasonably have inferred that the Toyota passive-restraint system was technologically and economically feasible, they did not establish that the right hip release would have prevented or significantly reduced the risk of Karen's death without 'under other circumstances, impos[ing] an equal or greater risk of harm.'"

Clearing non-issue debris. (1) The decedent was intoxicated, but that should at most only reduce her damages under comparative fault rules. Arguably, the decedent's fault is totally irrelevant because a safe seatbelt should protect drivers no matter how they got in a predicament. We've seen a similar rule with physicians– they should treat patients with reasonable care, even if when treating the patient for an injury resulting from the patient's own negligence. Whatever your take is on this, the comparative fault of the plaintiff should in no way be relevant to the issue of defectiveness, only at most to the amount of damages recoverable. (2) Similarly, there was no issue raised in the case whether the plaintiff had enough evidence to show that the mouse jammed in the way the plaintiff postulated. Perhaps there was evidence not mentioned in the opinion that supported a finding that the belt locked up on the decedent. Again, this problem is a distraction, not at issue in the case, although students would be right to say that in real life, at the trial, that might be a big issue, depending on the evidence. (3) Finally, there was a products liability statute, but the court apparently acts on the common law rules as well, and that is our interest here.

Rejecting the burden shift. The *Honda-Norman* case is using the risk-utility test and under that test, it implicitly rejects the *Barker v. Lull* burden shifting by requiring that the plaintiff to produce some evidence beyond mere proof that the design "caused" injury. That is one of the large points students should take from this case. If you discuss this case in tandem with *Barker v. Lull*, the contract in proof burden– and the effects–will be strikingly clear.

Requiring proof of a reasonable alternative design. The second big point is that the plaintiff not only has the burden of proving a defect, but that she must prove a defect by including evidence that there is a reasonable alternative design (RAD). This also contrasts with *Barker v. Lull*. The plaintiff cannot get to the jury under the *Honda-Norman* rule by proving that the design caused harm. The plaintiff must prove instead a basis for finding that the manufacturer could have used a reasonable alternative design that would have (probably) avoided harm– in shorthand, that it was technically and economically feasible, would have probably avoided injury to the plaintiff (decedent here), and would have been overall safer. Evaluation of this RAD requirement can come right along with development of the specific application of it in this case.

Application in the Honda-Norman case. You might accept the requirement of RAD evidence, in some if not all products cases, but still think the requirement was applied too stringently here.

(1) General testimony that the design was feasible was insufficient. Apparently the court is requiring discussion of a detailed actual design, not merely a verbal statement of the expert that the mouse could have been on a timer and that was feasible.

(2) (a) The cost effectiveness of another of the proposed alternative designs– an emergency button at the hip rather than over the shoulder– requires explicit evidence of dollar costs. At least that is what we think the court means when it says that "the plaintiff must introduce proof of the 'cost of incorporating this technology'" when that language is coupled with the court's rejection of the plaintiff's evidence. If the court is requiring dollar cost figures, that seems both extreme and unwarranted. (b) You can also criticize the court's more specific statement that a competing manufacturer's use of an alternative design is insufficient to show that the alternative design can be used at reasonable cost. You might well think that actual use of the alternative design in the industry is sufficient for a prima facie showing that it is cost effective. Competitors won't use it if it is economically wasteful. To be sure, Toyota might have chosen a too-expensive release because it could fit better with other design elements. The defendant could certainly adduce evidence to that effect if in the unlikely event that it is so. But prima facie, actual use in the market place is highly valuable and objective evidence of cost effectiveness and it is hard to see why it would be rejected. Certainly the court gave no reasons for rejecting it.

Finally, the court's use of precedent. The casebook does not give the students a basis for judging the court's use of precedent, but some teachers may be interested.

The *Honda-Norman* court cites two other Texas cases, like *Honda-Norman* itself, from Houston, for the proposition that "use of an alternative design by another manufacturer . . . as a matter of law . . . does not establish economic feasibility." We don't read them as supporting that proposition.

The first was *Smith v. Aqua-Flo, Inc.,* 23 S.W.3d 473 (Tex. App. 2000). It did cite with approval a case in which the plaintiff had actually proved the cost per unit of the proposed alternative design. You might speculate that the court thought that was required, but what it actually said was that "the Smiths offered no evidence of economic feasibility." It did *not* say, "the Smiths offered no dollar cost evidence." On the contrary, the *Smith* court seemed to think that actual adoption of a design in the industry would be significant and seemed to say the plaintiff failed in part because there was no such evidence. That's a separate and difficult issue, to be sure– whether the defendant's compliance with industry custom is some kind of defense. Nevertheless, the court seems to think that industry usage would be important element of proof for the plaintiff: "Without any evidence of the economic feasibility of pressure sensitive shut- off switches in 1980, any research in the spa industry, or any evidence that anyone in 1980 was of the opinion that pressure sensitive shut-off switches should be applied to spa pumps, there was not even a scintilla of evidence that a reasonably safer alternative design existed for a shut-off switch when the pump was manufactured in 1980." It does not look as if *Smith* can be made to stand for the proposition that economic feasibility of an alternative design can only be shown by proof of dollar costs. The *Honda-Norman* court's firm rule that as a matter of law evidence of usage of the design in the industry is totally useless to the plaintiff, that it is not even a "scintilla" of evidence about reasonableness of cost of the design, seems as un-justified in precedent as in policy.

The other Texas cited by the *Honda-Norman* court for the "matter of law" proposition was *Jaimes v. Fiesta Mart, Inc.,* 21 S.W.3d 301(Tex. App. 1999). In *Jaimes* a small child choked to death on a latex balloon. The plaintiff argued that the seller should have coated the balloons with an unpalatable substance or used something besides latex. The something available besides latex was mylar, but mylar balloons cost up to 20 times as much wholesale. As to the unpalatable coating on latex, the plaintiff seems not to have present any evi-dence at all about costs. It was definitely not a case in which other manufacturers used an unpalatable coating. So this case stood for the proposi-tion that the plaintiff must provide some evidence about costs of the proposed alternative but it does not seem to say that an alternative design's use in the industry must be rejected as evidence of economic feasibility.

Notes 1 & 2. These two notes emphasize that *Honda-Norman* differs from *Barker v. Lull* on two more or less distinct points– in placing the burden on the plaintiff to make proof that the design was defective and in requiring the plaintiff to prove that some reasonable alternative design was available.

– *Reasonable alternative design.* The Restatement Third of Torts (Products Liability) rejects *Barker's* burden shifting, requiring the plaintiff to prove not only that the product was defective but that there was a reasonable alterna-tive design ("RAD"). Before going too far in exploring RAD, you might want to be sure students understand that RAD by itself does not show grounds for re-covery. *Slisze v. Stanley-Bostich,* 979 P.2d 317 (Utah 1999), points out that a defendant does not have a duty to discontinue manufacture of the more dan-gerous model merely because there is a safer one. After all, some danger is tolerable. In the other case cited in this note, *Grzanka v. Pfeifer,* 694 A.2d 295 (N.J. Super. App. Div. 1997), the plaintiff was injured in an intersection colli-sion. The collision resulted in part from the fact that vandals had tampered with the traffic signal. Plaintiff, suing the manufacturer of the signal, offered evidence of a feasible design that would have foiled the vandals. But the court affirmed a summary judgment for the defendants on the ground that the plaintiff failed to prove that tampering with the controls (which were locked) was foreseeable.

Back to the main point: The RAD proof requirement. A number of states, in accord with the *Honda-Norman* rule, now require such evidence in design defect cases. See, e.g., *Lewis v. American Cyanamid Co.,* 715 A.2d 967 (N.J. 1998) (also holding that whether plaintiff has met this burden is a jury ques-tion, unless the evidence presented cannot reasonably support the proposed design as a feasible alternative).

At least initially you might regard the RAD requirement as simply an-other reflection of the negligence orientation that risk-utility analysis brings to "strict" products liability. In routine negligence cases, the plaintiff must or-dinarily demonstrate, or the jury must be able to say from common knowledge, that the defendant should have engaged in some safer alternative *conduct*. You can recall the *Mathew* case in Chapter 6, the burning mower case, as a simple example. The RAD is similar, though it applies to the product rather than to conduct. But in spite of this similarity, practical differences, some seen in *Honda-Norman,* give the RAD requirement in products cases a sinister appearance to plaintiffs. It is one thing to argue to a jury that a reasonable person would have pushed a mower out of the garage before starting it. It is quite another to retain an expert who can testify that a complicated product would have been safer if designed differently, and that the alternative design was feasible because it would not raise production costs too severely, and because it would not negatively affect the product's longevity, maintenance, repair or esthetics. See RESTATEMENT OF PRODUCTS LIABILITY § 2, cmt. *f* (listing factors to be considered in determining reasonableness of a proposed alternative design). This is likely to be very expensive proof. In fact we are going to see suggestions that many people injured by defective products will not find relief because lawyers cannot afford to take their cases.

Note 3. Contours of the reasonable alternative design. In *Rose*, cited here, the court held that in a smoker's product design suit against cigarette manufacturers, she had to prove that alternative "light" cigarettes would be acceptable to consumers. The court reasoned that the "inherent usefulness" of cigarettes was intimately and necessarily tied to "subjective feelings and sensations" of users.

Note 4. The R.A.D. requirement: a middle ground?. In *Vautour v. Body Masters Sports Industries, Inc.,* cited here, the New Hampshire court said that while the availability of a reasonable alternative design was a factor, it should not become an essential element of the plaintiff's claim. It gave several reasons: a requirement of reasonable alternative design might eliminate just claims because of the expense, especially claims that were relatively small; it would be difficult for courts to apply; and "the rigid prerequisite of a reasonable alternative design places too much emphasis on one of many possible factors that could potentially affect the risk-utility analysis."

The Restatement gave some assurances, perhaps not always fulfilled in the caselaw, that the RAD requirement would not be used to for extreme demands upon the plaintiff. The plaintiff is not required to show that the design was actually available at that time, only that it could reasonably have been. Nor need the expert actually construct a prototype of the proposed alternative design, if the expert's "qualified" testimony "reasonably supports the conclusion that a reasonable alternative design could have been practically adopted at the time of sale." RESTATEMENT OF PRODUCTS LIABILITY § 2, cmt. *f.*

Note 5. Manifestly unreasonable designs. A partial answer to the question in Note 4 is that a design might be manifestly dangerous and unreasonable designs, so clear that no proof is required. You can think of two different reasons why a design might be manifestly unreasonable (on analogy to res ipsa loquitur). (1) In the most extreme case, low utility coupled with great danger might be so obvious so that no alternatives need be presented– because even there were no better design possible, the danger would be unjustified. The Restatement of Products Liability § 2, cmt. *e* gives the example of a dangerous toy gun that shoots hard pellets. The danger is part of the allure to consumers and thus a characteristic that could not be avoided by substituting soft gelatin missiles. Yet, a court might well think that the product is unreasonably dangerous even if there are no suitable alternatives. (2) In a way, the case of ornamental but sharp revolving blades on a hub cab presents about the same considerations. The blade could slice human flesh (for example if the wheel were turning after a collision put the vehicle on its side). Maybe there is no substitute for idiosyncratic ornament and if so, a decision that the blades were unreasonably dangerous is like the same decision about dangerous toy guns. Alternatively, you might think that the essential quality of the hub cab is not necessarily a vicious ornament but something milder. In that case, even without expert testimony, the jury might apply its common knowledge to say that, yes, there are reasonable alternative designs for hubcaps.

Note 6. Unidentified defect. We don't have much doubt that there is a defect in a Ford Aerostar if it sometimes accelerates to full throttle when you start it. Maybe you think (again a close analogy to res ipsa loquitur) that there *must* be a better design even though we don't know what it is. In *Jarvis*, cited here, the court allowed the plaintiff to get to the jury. We observe that the expert did postulate a theory that suggested a defect, but that no evidence of the supposed defect was ever found apart from the fact that the vehicle throttled up and couldn't be stopped. The case was approached as a design defect case and the court held that the plaintiff was not required to prove a specific defect. It is not so easy to say there is a manifestly unreasonable design in *Jarvis unless we know what counts as the defect*– if the design's problem is manifest, we must know what it is, and maybe we don't. Yet it is clear that given the facts found by the jury, the Aerostar was defective.

Note 7. Consumer expectation test eliminating the reasonable alternative design requirement. This is simply a reminder to students that the problems and rules we are addressing result from the risk-utility test. They do not arise under the consumer expectation test.

Note 8. Plaintiff strategy. If RAD evidence can only be adduced via an expert, plaintiffs in modest cases might omit such evidence out of financial necessity (especially if the expert must build a model, a topic considered following *Turpin,* below.) But such evidence would be useful to the plaintiff in providing a favorable risk-utility balance even when it is not absolutely required by law. Maybe it would also help prove consumer expectations. If the RAD actually existed in the market at the time the challenged design was sold (if, for example, competitors' product designs were safer), evidence of that fact might satisfy both the RAD requirement and the consumer expectation test.

Note 9. What is an "alternative" design? What is the chance that courts will bog down in secondary inquiries about what counts as a reasonable alternative design and overlook the real question of negligence? If you think a pellet gun is "a toy" then in a sense balls, rubber horseshoes, or video games are reasonable alternatives. But surely that is meaningless. Will it be productive, however, for courts to consider what counts as a reasonable alternative to a pellet gun? And relatedly, is it true that you can only judge the negligence in selling children guns by judging whether ping-pong guns would be better?

Note 10. Another middle ground? The *Honda-Norman* court's demands for specific costing of alternative designs is a serious problem for plaintiffs in any but very large cases. And it is not necessary to accept this demand merely because you demand some kind of evidence about reasonable alternative designs. A middle ground would certainly recognize that with some simple products consumers-jurors know enough to make cost evidence unnecessary. Don't we know that hubcaps without slicing blades are probably cheaper than hubcaps with spinning blades attached? And a sensible middle ground would also permit evidence of reasonable cost of the alternative design that is not reduced to dollars and cents, such as evidence that the alternative design was used by others in the industry.

MCCARTHY V. OLIN CORP., 119 F.3d 148 (2d Cir. 1997)

This is a lawsuit by people who were shot aboard a Long Island Railroad commuter train and by survivors of people who were killed. The suit is not against the shooter but rather against the manufacturer of the bullets (Black Talons) used in the attack. Legal theories against the manufacturer, Olin Corp., ran the gamut from negligent advertising and marketing to various design-defect claims (both negligence and strict liability) to a claim that the bullets were "unreasonable and ultrahazardous." The court rejected all theories.

Design defect. (a) The first claim raised and rejected was that the Black Talons were defectively designed "because the expansion mechanism of the bullets, which causes ripping and tearing in its victims, results in enhanced injuries beyond ordinary bullets." Under an approach like that of the old § 402A, plaintiffs must allege that the bullet was "unreasonably dangerous for its intended use." But here, its intended use is to kill and maim. The analogy is to the sharp knife that can cut or the bottle of whiskey that can cause alcoholism. The bullets here performed precisely as intended. Thus there was "nothing wrong" with them. (b) Under a risk-utility analysis like that adopted by the Restatement of Products Liability, the court rejected plaintiff's attempt to use risk-utility balancing on the ground that such a balance could never occur without a showing, first, that there was "something wrong" with the product. The risks identified here "arise from the function of the product, not any defect in the product."

Unreasonably dangerous per se. The court rejected this theory, saying that New York courts did not recognize it. (Under the *Erie* doctrine, the federal court was applying New York law.) The court noted that plaintiffs' assertion of this theory was simply another attempt to get the court to apply risk-utility balancing, which it had already decided was inappropriate given the nature of this product.

Negligent distribution and marketing. Finally, the court rejected a negligent marketing claim, again on the ground that New York courts have not recognized it. Further, the court thought that to impose such a duty would result in driving ammunition off the market, suggesting that only a legislature should take such a step.

Notes 1 & 2. These notes question the court's reasoning on risk-utility balancing and ask students to consider the possible use of the consumer expectations test here. Is the court right in saying that risk-utility balancing should never occur unless the product is first shown to be defective –that there is "something wrong" with it? Consider the case of the butane cigarette lighter. Lighters are designed to start fires, albeit controlled ones, and fire can burn. If a child uses a properly-functioning butane lighter and gets burned, can a risk-utility balancing test be utilized to judge whether the design was defective for not being child-proof? The court in *Perkins v. Wilkinson Sword, Inc.*, 700 N.E.2d 1247 (Ohio 1998), said yes, rejecting the trial court's holding that the risk-benefit test applied only to improperly-functioning products. See also *Hernandez v. Tokai Corp.*, 2 S.W.3d 251 (Tex. 1999) (allowing risk-utility balancing on similar facts, with properly-working lighter).

Perhaps the real reason that risk-utility balancing does not work in *McCarthy* is that there is no reasonable alternative design. In the lighter cases discussed above, the plaintiffs could argue that a safer, child-proof design was feasible. Gary Schwartz wrote over 30 years ago that "one simply cannot talk meaningfully about a risk-benefit defect until and unless one has identified some design alternative (including any design omission) that can serve as the basis for a risk-benefit analysis." Gary T. Schwartz, *Foreward: Understanding Products Liability*, 67 CAL.L.REV. 435, 468 (1979). If this is true, then is it ever possible to condemn the design of products that are by their nature extremely dangerous, and have no reasonable alternative given their essential purposes? Does this reasoning (which seems to be that of the court in *McCarthy*) effectively immunize certain dangerous but "established" classes of products from design defect lawsuits? Does it leave the legislature and administrative agencies as the key actors in dealing with such dangerous products? Is this a socially desirable result?

Note 3. Firearms: Design defect theories. Guns are treated by courts much as knives are: such products are by their very nature dangerous, and their dangerousness is what gives them their utility. A dull knife would be safer but it would not have the very characteristic that make knives both useful and dangerous. There is not, then, a reasonable alternative design, when viewed at this broad product level. Said another way, there is simply no way to "design away" such products' inherent risks. The Products Restatement explicitly states that firearms can be held to be defective in design only upon proof of a reasonable alternative design. You might play devil's advocate with a class that is prone to challenge this approach, by asking what would happen if handguns, alcohol or tobacco were subjected to a true risk-utility balancing in lawsuit after lawsuit. Could these products would be driven from the market? (The *McCarthy* court suggests this result if a negligent marketing theory were imposed on ammunition manufacturers.) And should that big a step occur through litigation, or is it better left to regulatory bodies and legislatures?

Note 4 alerts students to a federal immunity for firearms manufacturers passed during the George W. Bush administration. As noted here, thus far it has withstood constitutional attack.

Note 5. Firearms: Other theories of liability. Negligent distribution and marketing, rejected as a viable theory in *McCarthy*, has become a fairly common theory in gun litigation, as design defect theories fail. Such a theory attacks the defendant's conduct in selling its products, for example selling in certain markets or to certain people. A slingshot might be reasonably marketed to adults in a sporting goods store, but negligently marketed to children in a toy store. A Black Talon bullet might be reasonably marketed to law enforcement personnel, but negligently marketed to the general public. The *McCarthy* court rejected this theory less on the basis of analysis or policy than on the absence of favorable New York precedent for such a theory of liability. What does the class think of imposing such a duty of care in marketing? Suppose Olin had advertised Black Talon bullets in a magazine intended to appeal to violent and disturbed persons? The cases on this topic are divided. Many of these cases invoke theories of public nuisance and/or interference with economic prospects. *See* DOBBS ON TORTS §§ 452, 467. A few cases have upheld such claims in principle. See *Gary ex rel. King v. Smith & Wesson Corp.*, 801 N.E.2d 1222 (Ind. 2003); *James v. Arms Technology Inc.*, 820 A.2d 27 (N.J. Super. 2003). Some, however, have not allowed them under the PLCAA discussed in **Note 4** above.

Note that it is still possible to sue a gun manufacturer on a design defect theory if the gun at issue has some design that makes it function improperly. For example, in *Endresen v. Scheels Hardware & Sports Shop, Inc.*, 560 N.W.2d 225 (N.D. 1997), a handgun manufacturer was held liable on the basis of risk-utility balancing in a case alleging that the defendant's gun was improperly designed to handle defective ammunition. What's the distinction between *Endresen* and *McCarthy*? In the former there was "something wrong" with the product.

Note 6. Tobacco. The tobacco-liability picture is ever-changing, as is the situation with firearms. This note just gives some recent examples. One can predict that if one set of theories will not work, others will be tried. For example, in *American Tobacco Co. v. Grinnell*, 951 S.W.2d 420 (Tex. 1997), the Texas high court rejected a design defect theory on the ground that the plaintiff failed to prove a reasonable alternative design as required by Texas statute. But it allowed both a manufacturing defect claim (based on the presence of pesticides in the cigarettes) and a "strict liability" marketing claim to proceed. Still, a Texas statute applicable to cases filed after *Grinnell*, however, probably guts almost all tobacco claims except those based upon a manufacturing defects. See TEX. CIV. PRAC. & REMEDIES CODE § 82.004. The tobacco settlement mentioned here did not, as some might believe, bar lawsuits by injured individuals, so we can expect these lawsuits to continue.

Note 7. Drugs. Drugs get special treatment in design defect law. Drugs are incapable of being made safe for their intended use, but to label them "defective" would have a grossly antisocial result. The Restatement Second, in comment k to 402A, says that drugs (using the Pasteur rabies vaccine as an example) is neither defective nor unreasonably dangerous, a clear application of risk-utility balancing in which both sides of the scales are weighty but utility is far weightier. Comment k addresses the problem which it calls the problem of "unavoidably unsafe products." Its rule is essentially that strict liability does not apply in such cases, which means that the plaintiff must prove negligence; courts may analyze such cases by invoking Comment k or by saying that negligence is required or by doing both. E.g., *Hahn v. Richter*, 673 A.2d 888 (Pa. 1996).

In rejecting strict liability for the products covered, Comment k also of course rejects any test that would produce strict liability. So, within its scope, it rejects the consumer expectation test. You can see the way the consumer expectation test might work in *Allison v. Merck and Co., Inc.*, 878 P.2d 948 (Nev. 1994). In that case, a children's vaccine caused serious permanent harms, including blindness and brain damage, to a child. A majority, for various reasons, permitted the claim to go to the jury. The test of strict liability in one opinion was to ask whether products are "dangerous because they fail to perform in the manner reasonably to be expected in the light of their nature and intended function. . . . The nature and intended function of this vaccine, of course, is to create an immunity to measles, mumps, and rubella without attendant blindness, deafness, mental retardation and permanent brain damage." And "a vaccine that causes blindness and deafness is a defective product." (*Allison* was, however, a 2-1-2 decision in which only the first 2 joined in the consumer expectation type language quoted; one favored the plaintiff on another ground and another two argued for Comment *k*.) Note that the National Childhood Vaccine Act would have applied to *Allison* if the injury had occurred a little later. *Cochran v. Brooke*, cited here, relied on comment *k* to affirm a directed verdict for a drug manufacturer. In that case, the arthritis drug's design or formula (or, if you prefer, its inherent qualities) was such that blindness would result in a very small number of people. It was known that the drug sometimes caused visual blurring.

Query whether comment *k* is properly extended to all prescription drugs, or just certain ones whose benefits clearly outweigh their risks. Certainly, the single illustration given in comment k differs materially from the facts in *Cochran*. It would be very hard to argue that the plaintiff who suffered a side reaction from the Pasteur treatment should make the manufacturer bear his loss, even though he knew the risk in advance and chose to accept it. But it is a very different thing to argue that a plaintiff who knows no more of the risk than the manufacturer should bear the loss alone. In terms of risk-spreading, internalization of costs, safety and other ideas behind products liability, how does it work to deny liability here? Would there be anything wrong with imposing liability, the costs of which would then be passed on to drug users as a class in the form of higher drug prices? (Maybe it would be even better if costs were passed on to users of this particular drug.) Do your students feel that drug users, many of whom are poor and old, should have to pay extra or do without because of some other individual's problems? Or conversely, that those lucky enough to escape blindness should avoid paying "their share" of the true cost of the drug? Maybe neither of those things adequately describes the likelihoods. Instead, some of the high drug costs would be paid by Medicaid, which necessitate public, tax dollar support.

Note 8. The Products Restatement. The Products Restatement's § 6 virtually immunizes prescription drug producers for design defects. It does NOT utilize the risk-utility test by asking whether the manufacturer could have made a drug that was safer overall at reasonable cost. Instead it asks, in effect, whether the drug that was produced had benefits exceeding risks. That is by no means the same thing. A drug's benefits might outweigh its risks, yet it would be possible that the same benefits could be retained by using a different drug with fewer risks. This is the basic basis for criticism by the court in *Bryant* and by George W. Conk, both cited here. Many of the other articles that criticize the Restatement are cited in the Henderson & Twerski Yale Law Journal article cited at the end of the Note. The dispute is perhaps a narrow one, because when safer drugs are actually marketed, the Restatement test is so phrased as to permit a risk-utility test that compares the safety of the defendant's drug with other drugs on the market.

Note 9. Manufacturing flaws in drugs. This reminds students that just because a design defect theory won't work, that does not mean a manufacturing defect theory will necessarily suffer the same fate.

Note 10. Unknowable risks. What if a manufacturer is treated as if it had full knowledge of risks, even if it could not in fact have had such knowledge? If you took that approach under a risk-utility balancing test, you would then ask whether the manufacturer would have been considered negligent if it had known of the risks, even though it could not have known them. This form of "superstrict liability" has little support in the case law, and is rejected in the Products Restatement, both generally (§ 2(b)) and specifically for prescription drugs (§ 6). It was accepted, however, in *Sternhagen*, a 1997 Montana case cited here. Is such superstrict liability a good idea in general? Certainly, holding a manufacturer to knowledge of unknowable risks would retain a very real kind of strict liability even if risk-utility balancing were used.

Note 11. State of the art. We've resisted introducing this term, but the defendant's argument in *Falada,* cited here, makes us think this could be a productive Note. The court rejected the defendant's argument. We are tempted to say, of course. A design defect is not the same as a product or manufacturing flaw claimed here – bad workmanship in executing the design. The Iowa's court's decision is also of course in line with its earlier holding that state of the art meant feasibility, not custom. Could custom to produce defectively welded products ever count as a defense? State of the art statutes require individual construction in practice and some of them might be applied to flaws, but it is hard to see how Iowa's could be, given the Iowa Court's construction of the term to mean feasibility.

AN END NOTE: ADJUDICATION OF DESIGN DEFECTS

The limits of adjudication. Is it true that courts and juries are "designing products" in making these risk-utility decisions? Notice that if a reasonable alternative design must be proven, juries are not asked to design the *best* product, but merely to say whether the one designed was one of several acceptable models. To continue the football example used here, the jury is not asked to say whether Dubbs should play guard, but whether it was unreasonable to put Dubbs at guard in the light of all the other decisions made by the coach. Thus the product need not be the safest possible, only reasonably safe. *Cover v. Cohen,* 461 N.E.2d 864 (N.Y. 1984). And the product is judged as a whole, so that an imperfect door lock may be offset by excellent seat belts. See *Daly v. General Motors Corp.,* 575 P.2d 1162 (Cal. 1978). Do these rules support or detract from Professor Henderson's thesis? Does the polycentric task argument prove too much, so that, if you accept it you have to discard the entire *Carroll Towing* negligence system? Or is a design defect case somehow different from other negligence cases?

Jury role. This paragraph should give you enough to lead a brief discussion of the merits of judges deciding cases, rather than juries. There is little empirical evidence that juries run amok, but many people clearly believe they do. Do judges as a class have, or lack, certain biases that lay people do not? Are judges better able to deal with complex issues of design than are juries? *Liriano,* in the next section, talks about the proper function of juries in judging the reasonableness of conduct and the foreseeability of harm; the court notes the modern trend to enlarge the sphere of the jury.

Social or economic factors. Cases like *McCarthy v. Olin* may give one pause about the ability of courts to make the world safer from dangerous products. Tobacco is used as an example here, with Professor Vandall's absolute liability argument summarized. Would an "absolute liability" system best come from the legislature rather than from a court? Why or why not?

Is there a products liability "crisis?" The Merritt & Barry article is worth reading in its entirety. This note allows a renewal of the topic first raised in Chapter 1 about anecdotal evidence versus empirical evidence. Newspapers have recently picked up on similar data with specific relevance to products liability. According to a front-page article in the New York Times in January, 2001, the number of products cases filed in federal court dropped from 32,856 in 1997 to 14,428 in 2000. (The source of this data is the Administrative Office of the U.S. Courts.) The story goes on to say, however, that the median award in products cases tripled from 1993 to 1999, to $1.8 million. The author's analysis is that lawyers are taking only the "big" cases now because products liability cases are so expensive to bring, especially given the rising costs of expert witnesses. Greg Winter, *Jury Awards Soar as Lawsuits Decline on Defective Goods*, N.Y. TIMES, Jan. 30, 2001, at A1. A front-page story in the Los Angeles Times two days later reported that tort lawsuits generally have dropped in recent years, dramatically so in California. Among the reasons for California's dramatic decline in tort suits – with such suits only half as frequent as they were a decade ago– were the spread of ADR processes (most notably private judging) and improvements in products safety. Ted Rohrlich, *We Aren't Seeing You in Court*, L.A. TIMES, Feb. 1, 2001, at A1. All of these studies and statistics raise questions about the need for restrictions on lawsuits, but people on each side of the debate can of course quote the statistics that best support their position. Opponents of restrictions and damages caps point to the decline in lawsuits, and the low percentage of disputes that ever reach the lawsuit stage; proponents point to large and unpredictable jury awards, especially against businesses. You may have to be careful in raising this material with certain classes, but it does present an excellent opportunity for a civil debate that goes beyond anecdote.

§ 6. WARNING OR INFORMATION DEFECTS

A. Focusing on Point-of-Sale and On-Product Warnings

In the 1960s, courts and thinkers began to construct the notion that a failure to provide proper warnings or other information necessary for safe use of a product would subject the manufacturer to "strict liability." But you judged the warning by a risk-utility standard, so it always appeared that the warning "defect" was merely negligence unless some special rules were applied. It is pretty well-established now that warning cases in most states proceed on a negligence theory, regardless of whether they are labeled negligence, breach of warranty, or strict liability claims. The new Restatement takes that position in § 2(c), placing manufacturers under a duty to provide a reasonable warning when it would reduce foreseeable risks of harm. For a fuller discussion of the various legal theories, see 1 MADDEN & OWEN ON PRODUCTS LIABILITY § 9:1, at 514-17 (3d Ed. 2000).

LIRIANO V. HOBART CORP., 170 F.3d 264 (2d Cir. 1999)

Liriano, a 17-year old who had recently immigrated to the United States, had been on the job a week when he caught his hand in a Hobart meat grinder. His employer had purchased the grinder with a safety guard that would have prevented the accident, but that guard had been removed. The grinder bore no warning that it should be operated only with the guard attached. Liriano won a jury verdict on his failure-to-warn claim against Hobart and the employer; this appeal followed. The court, per Calabresi, affirmed.

This case raises three important points to discuss with the class: (1) the different functions of warnings; (2) the role of the "open and obvious hazard" in warning defect cases; and (3) the causation requirement in warning cases. Notes discuss each of these in some detail.

Duty to Provide Information

Note 2. This is a good place to start discussion. A duty to warn arises when a reasonable person in defendant's circumstances would foresee a risk of harm by the product in the absence of warnings. A warning defect may be found even if the product is not defective in design. Although Hobart provided a guard that would have protected the user, a reasonable manufacturer might still foresee that the guard would be removed, thus exposing the user to a danger that required a warning. This was the essential holding of the state court in answering one of the questions certified to it in this case. *Liriano v. Hobart Corp.*, 700 N.E.2d 303 (N.Y. 1998).

Note 3. Functions of product information. Warnings and information serve different purposes. This is the key to *Liriano* and it explains why an information-type warning could be required even when danger is obvious. The court recognizes that everyone knows that meat grinders are dangerous. No one could reasonably believe that a suggested warning saying "Meat grinders are dangerous," or "Keep hands out of meat grinder," would serve any useful purpose at all. But, Calabresi reasons (quoting Henderson & Twerski), warnings serve more complex functions. Not only can they exhort people to be careful; they can assist people in making choices, for example, by "making known the existence of [safer] alternatives." His example of the driver on the steep road illustrates this distinction well. Thus a jury could find that a reasonable manufacturer would provide a warning that would let users know guards are both available and needed, because that information is not obvious even if the danger is.

Similarly, information about the degree or frequency of a known danger might make a product safer. In *Chronister v. Bryco Arms,* 125 F.3d 624 (8th Cir. 1997), the plaintiff suffered hearing damage resulting from a misfire of defendant's handgun. The defendant provided warnings that ear protection should be worn, but the plaintiff argued that a more specific warning that misfeeds were common would have changed his conduct. The court agreed.

Note 4. Duty to provide a risk-utility balanced warning. The question at the end of this note can get students talking about an important idea: that too many warnings about obvious things tend to dilute warnings about more important (and non-obvious) risks. That is, the rule that a manufacturer does not have to warn of open and obvious risks (as qualified by *Liriano* itself; see Note 3 above) not only requires plaintiffs to exercise reasonable care for themselves but also recognizes that unneeded warnings would be static that interfered with the effectiveness of needed warnings. Are you more likely to pay attention to a single warning that appears at the top of an instruction manual on a power drill, or to a list of 50 warnings that includes such things as "do not stick fingers into light socket" and "do not operate drill while standing in a bathtub full of water"? You might analogize this to informed consent in medical malpractice cases. Are the risks of a common procedure being reasonably conveyed if the doctor lists 100 possible side-effects, including minor headaches with a one-in-100,000 chance, or does reasonableness require a more limited recitation of risks?

Cases cited here give some examples of unnecessary warnings, given the obviousness of the risk. Sometimes when courts say the manufacturer need not warn of known or obvious dangers, it looks like less a rule and more a matter of assessing evidence in each case. For example, in *Maneely v. General Motors Corp.*, 108 F.3d 1176 (9th Cir. 1997), the court concluded as a matter of law that the dangers of riding in the cargo compartment of a pickup truck were obvious so that no warning was needed. "If the public recognizes that traveling in the passenger compartment of an automobile without a seatbelt is dangerous, it only follows as night the day that the public also recognizes that riding in the cargo bed of a pickup, where seatbelts and other occupant packaging are conspicuously absent, presents even greater risks. . . . At some point, manufacturers must be relieved of the paternalistic responsibility of warning users of every possible risk that could arise from foreseeable use of their product." Those who smile at Polonius' speech to his son may enjoy this quotation.

Note 5. Unknowable risks. If a defendant is held to knowledge of unknowable risks in this context, then the duty to warn would be a matter of strict liability. There is some case support for such a standard, but not much, and the Restatement rejects it. (The same issue arose with design defects in the preceding section, with the same bottom line.)

Obvious Danger

Obvious dangers are often said to be obvious not because of the product's structure, but because the product's risks are generally well-known. This might be true with alcohol, for example, although we have plenty of evidence that the dangers of alcohol are generally ignored. If the defendant argues that the risks of a product are obvious because they are a matter of common knowledge, it may become important to focus on what particular risks are actually "well-known" by the public. This was an important issue in the closely-watched smoker's case of *American Tobacco Co. v. Grinnell*, 951 S.W.2d 420

(Tex. 1997). The smoker claimed that the defendant was liable for failure to warn of the risks of smoking, including the risks of nicotine addiction. The court held that the "general health risks of smoking" were a matter of common knowledge when plaintiff began smoking in 1952, thus freeing cigarette companies from any duty to warn of those general risks. But it was not common knowledge at that time that cigarettes are addictive. Thus a defense summary judgment on the failure-to-warn-of-addiction-risks claim was reversed.

Note 6. Obvious dangers and the no duty rule. This topic is not new. We began seeing it with *Stinnett v. Buchele* in Chapter 6 and continued analysis with *O'Sullivan v. Shaw*, 726 N.E.2d 951 (Mass. 2000) in Chapter 12. The Texas case cited here, *Caterpillar, Inc. v. Shears*, recognizes that obvious dangers give their own warnings. The question is whether the danger is within the ordinary knowledge common to the community. That is judged by an objective standard, because it speaks to the defendant's duty (or, you might say, its negligence). If all dangers are obvious, then users can protect themselves so that harm is not likely. Alternatively, if users choose to confront the danger, they must rate the utility highly. Thus the product seems non-defective on a risk-utility analysis, and even more clearly on a consumer expectation analysis. In spite of this, the *Shears* court held that a product may be defective even in the case of apparent dangers, because risks must be balanced against utilities. In the end, it came down to feasible safer alternatives. Perhaps that means the court recognizes that workers may not have the choice implied in the obvious danger analysis.

Note 7. Obvious dangers and comparative fault. If the danger is obvious and no further information is needed (as it was in *Liriano*), then the defendant is under no duty or the product is not defective at all. If the harm is foreseeable in spite of obvious danger, then the product may be defective, in which case the issue of comparative fault may arise. This note alerts students to the possibility. We cover comparative fault and other proposed defenses in §§ 8 & 9.

Note 8. Obvious danger and design defect. If danger is obvious, the product is usually not defective for lack of a warning about that danger – although the nature of the proposed warning may be critical to the analysis, as we see in *Liriano*. A product that is not defective for lack of a warning, however, may still be unreasonably dangerous in design. For example, it might be unreasonable to produce an unguarded drill press for industrial use when a simple switch could protect the workers' hands, even though the danger of an unguarded press is obvious and even though there is a warning on the press. In such a case a warning to "keep hands away" does nothing to make the product safer because the worker already knows the danger and because, usually, the worker can do nothing about it but is at the mercy of the job. *See, e.g, Uniroyal Goodrich Tire Co. v. Martinez*, 977 S.W.2d 328 (Tex. 1998) (holding that a plaintiff who ignored a very specific warning on a tire could recover from the manufacturer on the ground that the tire was defective in design despite the warning). So in such cases the viable claim is bad design, not failure to warn. *See* James A. Henderson & Aaron D. Twerski, *Doctrinal Collapse in Products Liability: The Empty Shall of Failure to Warn*, 65 N.Y.U. L. REV. 265, 280-282 (1990).

In other words, if the manufacturer foresees that the product will be used and will be dangerous in spite of the obvious danger, then the manufacturer may be required to design around the danger if that is feasible, even where a warning itself may add nothing. Employees who are required to use dangerous products are foreseeable victims of the product's danger, for example, as are bystanders and sometimes children. This may explain why the California Court once said the manufacturer is "callous" if its product was dangerous, even if the danger was thought to be obvious. *Luque v. McLean*, 8 Cal. 3d 136, 501 P.2d 1163, 1169, 104 Cal. Rptr. 443 (1972).

Note 9. Obvious danger and consumer expectations. Notice that if the consumer had no reasonable expectation of safety, he could not prevail on the consumer expectation test, but might still prevail either on an ordinary negligence claim or a "strict liability" risk-utility claim by asserting that the manufacturer could have made the product significantly safer at little cost.

Causation

Note 10. Causation in warning failure cases. (a) The heeding presumption. Courts commonly recognize a rebuttable heeding presumption. They presume that if a proper warning had been given, the plaintiff would have heeded it and avoided harm. But this is a rebuttable presumption, and evidence adduced by the defendant may disestablish it. For example, in *Bloxom v. Bloxom*, 512 So.2d 839 (La. 1987), GM sold a car prophetically called a Firebird, providing a warning in the owner's manual that said "Do not drive through, idle, or park your car over combustible materials, such as grass or leaves. They could touch the hot exhaust system and ignite." Lonnie Bloxom parked the car on door-high hay in a barn after driving it at 60 mph for 20 minutes. The barn, the hay and the car all burned. Even though the court said the warning was not sufficiently obvious, Bloxom lost his case on causation grounds based on his admission that he had not read the owner's manual and would not have read the warning even if it was in a prominent place in the manual. This rebutted the heeding presumption by showing that even an adequate warning would have not changed his behavior. *See* DOBBS ON TORTS § 367 (2000).

(b) Plaintiff's persons knowledge distinct from obvious danger. The opinion in *Burke v. Spartanics Ltd.*, 252 F.3d 131 (2d Cir. 2001), cited with a question in Note 10, was also written by Judge Calabresi, but this time he upheld a jury verdict for the defendant. The trial judge gave an instruction that the defendant owed no duty to warn of obvious danger, sound under New York law if the danger was in fact obvious. But the trial judge also told the jury that the defendant owed no duty to warn if the plaintiff himself knew of the danger. That was error, as the duty to warn arises when safety for some, not necessarily all, foreseeable users will be improved. Nevertheless, Judge Calabresi thought the error harmless because, given its other findings, the jury would have found that the plaintiff's knowledge of the danger negated cause in fact.

Comment on the "heeding presumption" language. It might be better to drop the language of presumptions and simply say that the jury is permitted to draw the inference that a proper warning would have been heeded. We doubt that any more need be said to first year students, but you may want to see why we say so. *Golonka v. General Motors Corp.,* 65 P.3d 956 (Ariz. Ct. App. 2003), took the language of presumption quite seriously and then applied the bursting bubble theory, so that once rebuttal evidence of any caliber is introduced, the presumption disappeared. This led to what some jurists might think is a technical labyrinth that does not seem to further any insight into the central substantive issue. "[E]ven if the fact-finder might disbelieve the rebuttal evidence, the 'bubble is burst,' and the existence or non-existence of the presumed fact must be determined as if the presumption had never operated in the case." This is view was outcome-determinative and may have undercut the requirement of a proper warning. The plaintiff was killed when, after placing her truck in the parking gear, she began loading the truck at the rear. It popped into reverse, backed into and killed her. The gear was so designed that the user might believe she had shifted into Park when in fact she had placed the gear on a hump between Park and Reverse. An adequate warning of this danger would presumably have warned that the vehicle might begin motion when the driver believed it was in the Park gear. No such warning was given. However, the manufacturer gave routine instructions that the handbrakes should be set and the ignition turned off when leaving the car. These instructions gave no hint that the driver might lose her life if she did not follow them, so they would not have been adequate warnings of the danger. Yet they indirectly defeated the claim, because, the court reasoned, the fact that those routine instructions were not heeded was *some* evidence, however, weak, that an adequate warning would not have been heeded either. Given the bursting bubble approach, that mean that heeding presumptions disappeared, even if the trier would have rejected the proposition that a failure to use the handbrake as instructed also meant the decedent would have ignored a proper warning. It is possible that this approach will not defeat the plaintiff in cases when a new trial is ordered, because as the *Golonka* court recognized, "the jury may still draw reasonable inferences from the facts originally giving rise to the presumption." The general view that it is human nature to avoid serious injury supports the "presumption." Whether that view of human nature constitutes a fact "originally giving rise to the presumption" may be uncertain, but if it is, the plaintiff would still get to the jury on new trial.

Note 11. Shifting burden of proof on causation. To prevail on a warning defect claim, the plaintiff must prove that the lack of a warning was a cause-in-fact (and proximate cause) of the harm. That is, the plaintiff must prove that he would have avoided the risk if adequately warned. *See, e.g., Phillips v. A-Best Products Co.*, 665 A.2d 1167 (Pa. 1995). Yet Judge Calabresi in *Liriano* said that the defendant had the burden of proving the absence of causation. Why so? Calabresi begins addressing this problem by referring to an idea we encountered in Chapter 7 on cause in fact: if the plaintiff suffers an injury within the risk (maybe within the core risk) created by the defendant's negligence, the reason you say the defendant was negligent is that you think harm of this sort is all too likely to befall someone. When the harm risked does in fact occur, it may be reasonable to think it would not have happened except for the negligence that risked it. See *Zuchowicz*, Chapter 7. The same point is mentioned above in Notes after *Lee*. Judge Calabresi seems to be saying that prima facie, causation is established in such a case.

The idea is attractive, but we suggest some cautions. When we address the *negligence* issue as distinct from the causation issue, to say that harm is all too likely to occur is to consider probability of harm in the light of cost to the defendant (low in the case of a warning) and in the light of potential harm. On the negligence issue we might find harm "all too likely" if it is cheap and easy to avoid the risk, even if the probability is very low that injury would be avoided by safer conduct. On the issue of causation, the question is whether probability of harm exceeds .50, not whether a low probability is sufficient to indicate that simple safety measures are worth taking. So to find negligence is not to find causation by the more-probable-than-not standard. Even so, a finding of negligence in many cases strongly suggests causation and permits an inference. Calabresi seems to be saying there is an inference sufficient to make out a prima facie case, but the defendant may rebut it if he can.

CARRUTH V. PITTWAY CORP., 643 So.2d 1340 (Ala. 1994)

The appalling loss of an entire family in this case highlights the issue of the adequacy of a warning. Once a warning is given, it is still subject to attack as being unreasonable in content, form, or location. The adequacy of a warning is a jury question, unless reasonable people can't differ. The confusing and contradictory elements in the defendant's instructions here were enough to make a jury question on the adequacy of warning. You might ask the class to come up with an adequate warning (in content, form and location) for this smoke-detector.

Note 1. Content or expression. This should be easy for students to grasp. Note that where the potential harm is severe, a warning that offers only a vague statement of a danger may be worse than no warning at all. If something might kill you if you inhale it, a warning that says, "May cause illness" may in fact mislead you into believing that it will NOT kill you. This ties in to **Note 3** below.

Note 2. Form and location. Even a warning with unassailably reasonable content is inadequate if the form or location is not reasonable. For example, a warning in *Liriano* that said "A guard was provided with this grinder. Do not operate without it," might have been adequate in content, but would still be unreasonable if placed on the bottom of the machine where it would not be seen.

Why was the father's admission that he never read the manual not sufficient to support the defendant's summary judgment? The answer in this case is that the diagram on the box and the format of the manual left a reasonable impression that the manual did not contain any essential information about installation. That is to say that his failure to read the manual was itself foreseeable, given the apparently complete information about installation provided elsewhere on the packaging. If a plaintiff is induced NOT to read warnings because of other statements made by the manufacturer in packaging materials, then the failure to read the warnings will not defeat the plaintiff's claim.

Note 3. Nature and seriousness of harm. *Pavlik v. Lane Ltd./Tobacco Exporters International*, cited here: How about "CAN BE FATAL IF INHALED"?

Benjamin v. Wal-Mart Stores, Inc., cited here, held the jury could find the warning was inadequate (1) because it did not identify the hazard—death— (2) and, in spite of directions never to use in a tent, was too vague when coupled with the "outdoor use only" direction; and (3) that the warning was not displayed in type, location, or color to call adequate attention to itself. The latter point meant that even if the deceased did not read the warning, the estate could recover.

Note 4. Language of the warning. This hypo is taken from a California Supreme Court case from 1993. U.S. Census data from the 1990 census showed that in California the numbers who reported speaking Spanish and not speaking English at all or not very well were 248,586 in the 5-17 age group; 1,434,927 in the 18-64 age group, and 98,654 in the over 65 age group. (While Spanish was the main non-English language, the census listed 24 other substantial language groups as representing the language spoken at home.) Do these numbers mean that a manufacturer who markets its product in California should provide warnings in Spanish? In *Ramirez v. Plough, Inc.*, 863 P.2d 167 (Cal. 1993), an aspirin manufacturer advertised in Spanish, but warnings that aspirin could cause serious side-effects in children were not given in Spanish. The court held that no non-English warnings were needed. It reasoned that the legislature, by requiring English language warnings, implied that no others were required. In *Stanley Indus., Inc. v. W.M. Barr & Co., Inc.*, 784 F.Supp. 1570 (S.D. Fla. 1992), the court thought it was for the jury to determine whether an English-only warning was adequate where the sellers advertised in Spanish to Hispanics and where the users could not understand the English-only warning. What if the manufacturer expects illiterate persons to use its poison products? *See* DOBBS ON TORTS § 364, p. 1010 (2000).

LEWIS v. LEAD INDUSTRIES ASS'N, 793 N.E.2d 869 (Ill App. Ct. 2003)

The plaintiffs sue for children who have been exposed to lead and may develop serious medical conditions, seeking damages for the costs of medical monitoring. Defendants include both the producers of lead pigment for paint and their trade association that promoted the use of such pigments. The plaintiffs did not identify which manufacturer produced the pigments to which the children were exposed. The only theory of liability the court recognizes is the claim labeled "civil conspiracy." The allegation is multifarious but seems to include the assertion that defendants conspired to market dangerous lead-based paint and not only to fail to warn but to actively suppress or conceal information about its dangers.

The court points out that conspiracy itself is not the wrong; there must be an underlying tort that the defendants conspire to commit. What tort here? The court doesn't say. Perhaps the court believes that the tort is the marketing of lead pigments that foreseeably would expose children to the terrible effects of lead. We do not know which defendant actually produced the pigment that led to the potential lead poisoning, but if any one of them did so, all would be liable if they conspired. Yet it is hard to imagine that the defendants conspired to produce and market in competition with each other. Maybe what they conspired to do was, as alleged, to uniformly suppress warnings and information. That would make some kind of sense even though the defendants were competing with each other, for if any one of them let the cat out of the bag, all would be likely to suffer loss of sales.

The conspiracy theory, difficult as it probably will be to prove, has some advantages. We've seen a glimpse of conspiracy type vicarious liability before, back in Chapter 22. In this case, the conspiracy theory, if it works, is going to keep the plaintiffs in court even though they cannot show which one of the conspirators actually delivered the lead that exposed the particular plaintiffs. If students have difficulty, you can imagine a case of two conspirators who agree to beat the plaintiff. Both approach him in the dark but only one of them actually delivers the blows. Both are liable as conspirators, though we cannot say which one struck the plaintiff.

You can hope that some good students will realize that this situation is a close parallel to the situation in *Summers v. Tice.* In the broad rationale we might be willing to give to *Summers,* both actors did something tortious that either caused the harm directly or operated to conceal the cause. Either way, both should be liable. Can the same be said here? If so, should we have doubts about how the scope of sophisticated user rule, our next topic?

Connections: (1) *Lewis* foreshadows the problem we will see in market-share case, *Hymowitz,* covered in Chapter 25 on apportionment (p. 747). (2) Medical monitoring costs as elements of damages for exposure cases are discussed in Chapter 26 on damages. We have actually seen medical monitoring claims before, in *Hagerty* (p. 299) and in *Potter v. Firestone Tire & Rubber* (p.

538). (3) You can keep discussing *Lewis* as you cover the note on Learned Intermediaries and Sophisticated Users, coming up next, because it is not so clear under the sophisticated user rules that the pigment producers should have warned the paint manufacturers – and if not them, then who? Active supersession or concealment or misrepresentation would presumably be another matter, but a conspiracy to suppress may be much harder to prove than a conspiracy to give no warning, especially since the warning may not have been due anyway under the sophisticated user rules.

Note. Product combinations. Lead pigment produced by defendants in *Lewis* was combined by paint manufacturers with other substances to make paint. When two products are to be combined for use, you might think that the manufacturers of both would owe a warning of the dangers that arise upon combination. But *Rastelli v. Goodyear Tire & Rubber Co.,* cited here, holds that Goodyear had no duty to warn of the danger created when its tires, which were safe in themselves, were used for their only purpose, namely, with inherently dangerous multi-piece rims. The reasoning is that component manufacturers are sometimes in a position similar to sellers to sophisticated users. If the component itself is dangerous, a warning might be required, but not merely because the total integrated product is dangerous. *See Zaza v. Marquess and Nell, Inc.,* 675 A.2d 620 (N.J. 1996). Compare *Firestone Steel Products Co. v. Barajas,* 927 S.W.2d 608 (Tex. 1996). In that case, Firestone designed and patented a wheel rim to permit trucks to use tubeless tires. It permitted anyone to manufacturer the rim without payment of royalties. Kelsey-Hayes did manufacture a modified version of the wheel. The decedent was killed in attempting to change a tire on the Kelsey-Hayes wheel. "A manufacturer generally does not have a duty to warn or instruct about another manufacturer's products, even though a third party might use those products in connection with the manufacturer's own product." If it makes any difference, how about an ordinary negligence claim? As a matter of ordinary negligence law, if a defendant instructs someone how to make a dangerous item and foresees that it will be made with the dangerous characteristics he has specified, should he not be liable for the foreseeable harms? The Texas Court said Firestone did not manufacture, design or sell the wheel that caused harm and hence that it "owed no duty" to the decedent. Yet if Firestone's design features were the ones that caused the harm, why should it matter that the wheel was modified in some other respect?

NOTE: LEARNED INTERMEDIARIES AND SOPHISTICATED USERS.

¶1. *Prescription drugs.* A warning to your doctor about a prescription drug usually suffices, as does the warning to a bulk buyer or sophisticated user (¶ 2). The idea is to shift responsibility: the adequately warned physician or bulk buyer will pass along the warning to the end user, as required. The majority appear to follow the learned intermediary rule, even in the case of birth control devices.

¶2. *Direct marketing.* Since the advent of direct marketing of drugs in 1997, does the learned intermediary rule still make sense? As you can see, authorities are divided. Asking students what they think might be an interesting exercise, with the added benefit of clarifying their understanding of what the learned intermediary rule is designed to accomplish in the first place.

¶3. *The Products Restatement.* When it is foreseeable that the intermediary will *not* pass on the warning, a few courts require reasonable efforts to communicate directly with the persons affected. The Restatement Third takes a hard line on unreliable intermediaries; only if "no" health care provider would pass on a warning would the manufacturer of prescription drugs be required to warn the consumer directly. In the mass inoculation case, however, the manufacturer would be required to give the best direct warning it could reasonably provide.

¶4. **Sophisticated users**. You can plug in *Lewis* here. If the plaintiffs there can prove only that the defendants failed to warn, would the defendant's be relieved of a duty to warn? Would warning to the paint manufacturers be enough? Would even that be needed?

Some courts seem to have in mind a rule of law that relieves the defendant, but maybe others want to know what the facts are, whether a warning was foreseeably needed and cost-effective. Maybe the facts will show that lead pigment manufacturers had far more information about danger than paint manufacturers and that they knew it. If so, should the sophisticated user rule bar the plaintiff's claim that a warning was owed? It may be, as the Mohr court suggested, that this rule is essentially kin to the "open and obvious" rule – that no warning is needed where the hazard is obvious.

¶5. *Suppliers of bulk goods.* In *Ritchie v. Glidden Co.,* cited here, the plaintiff was operating a high-pressure paint sprayer for her employer. She hadn't been trained; much less had she been given safety instruction. According to her testimony and that of others, there were no warnings on the pump or sprayer itself. When a leak occurred, she felt the hose. She found the hole – her finger was injected with paint. It did not hurt immediately so the employer decided it best to "forget it." The finger was swollen to three times its normal size a few hours later, however, and when operations were performed, it was found to be full of paint. Doctors attempted to remove it without success and the finger was ultimately amputated. The plaintiff claimed against the supplier and manufacturer on the ground that no warnings had been given. One argument for the defense seems without any basis: that no warning is owed unless the product is defective. That was quickly dismissed. Another argument was the sophisticated user argument, that the manufacturer and supplier fulfilled their duty by providing safety manuals to the employer. The court held that this argument furnished no ground for summary judgment. Whether the defense would apply was basically a question that in other contexts we call the negligence question. The court must consider the "likelihood or unlikelihood that harm will occur if the intermediary does not pass on the warning to the ultimate user, the trivial nature of the probable harm, the probability or improbability that the particular intermediary will not pass on the warning and the ease or burden of the giving of the warning by the manufacturer to the ultimate user." Whether, considering these factors, the manufacturer adequately discharged its duty to warn is a question of fact for the jury.

FYI: Complicating reasonable care warnings. Warnings to bulk buyers, sophisticated users, and learned intermediaries all present the same essential problem–should the manufacturer be permitted to avoid liability by warning its immediate buyer? Yet some courts have been at pains to say that these three "doctrines" differ from one another. The Connecticut Court has drawn a distinction between learned intermediaries and sophisticated users. That court says that the sophisticated user "defense" raises a question of fact for the trier– whether the manufacturer was reasonable in relying upon the user to pass along warnings. But the learned intermediary doctrine, in contrast, is a rule of law applicable only in the medical setting, that the drug manufacturer need only warn the prescribing doctor, with no reasonableness question for the jury at all. *Vitanza v. Upjohn Co.*, 778 A.2d 829 (Conn. 2001). Massachusetts drew a different distinction, one between the "bulk supplier doctrine" and the "sophisticated user defense," but the distinction is difficult to follow: "[T]he bulk supplier doctrine allows a fact finder to find that the duty to warn has been satisfied; the sophisticated user doctrine allows the fact finder to determine that no such duty was owed." *Hoffman v. Houghton Chemical Corp.*, 751 N.E.2d 848 (Mass. 2001). Why isn't all of this a matter of reasonableness under the circumstances, not a matter of a doctrine or rule of law, and why isn't it an element of the plaintiff's case rather than a "defense?"■

Note 6. *Government as "learned intermediary?"* *Macias*, discussed here, is an odd case in the eyes of many. The court held that the manufacturers had no duty to prove an honest warning, even when they knew the state was misleading citizens about the risks of its product and thereby risking serious harm to them. Why? Because such warnings might interfere with the state's handling of a Medfly emergency, and thus represent an intrusion upon the state's sovereignty. Was it reasonable for the manufacturer to "rely on the state" to give an adequate warning when the manufacturer knew the state was NOT giving an adequate warning? Would it have been a significant interference with state sovereignty to place a burden on the manufacturer to make a good faith *attempt* to get the state to give such a warning? Do the mass inoculation cases provide any support for a manufacturer's duty to warn directly?

B. Focusing on Post-Sale Warnings

COMSTOCK V. GENERAL MOTORS CORP., 99 N.W.2d 627 (Mich. 1959)
GREGORY V. CINCINNATI, INC., 538 N.W.2d 325 (Mich. 1995)

In *Comstock,* the manufacturer, GM, discovered brake problems on a certain model soon after it was introduced, but failed to notify owners. When Friend's car lost its brakes, he took it to the dealer for repairs. A dealer employee, moving the car, forgot that it was brakeless and ran into Comstock. Comstock sued GM. *Held,* GM had a duty to convey an effective warning when it discovered the defect. In *Gregory,* the same court said that before there is a continuing duty to warn, recall, or repair, there must have been a defect that was itself actionable at the time of manufacture and in any event that there was no duty to recall or repair.

Notes 1 & 2. Under Michigan's view in *Gregory,* is there any function for a claim that the manufacturer failed to give a post-sale warning? Since the warning is due only if there was a defect to begin with, the plaintiff could sue on the original defect and the failure to warn claim would not be needed. Even under that view, failure to warn might conceivably still be important on two issues: punitive damages and the statute of limitations. What result under *Gregory* if the product was not defective to begin with because the danger was unknowable when the product was manufactured but the manufacturer later discovers the defect and says nothing about it? Suppose Burro Company makes a butter substitute that actually tastes like butter and that no harmful side effects were knowable under the present state of technology. If Burro discovers that its product kills heavy users and it changes the formula to avoid that, has it done everything it must? Or should it warn those who might still be harmed by the original product? The Products Restatement (**Note 5** below) rejects the *Gregory* approach and adopts a reasonableness standard on the post-sale duty to warn.

§ 7. SPECIAL ISSUES OF PROOF

BITTNER V. AMERICAN HONDA MOTOR CO. , 533 N.W.2d 476 (Wis. 1995)

The plaintiff was injured when the defendant's ATV turned over. On the first and less important point: The court permitted the defendant to introduce evidence that "similar products" like snowmobiles had an injury rate less than the ATVs. It wanted to draw the unlikely inference that the higher ATV rate must have been due to operator error. The court permits use of the evidence and presumably would permit the defendant to make the accompanying argument to the jury. The defendant's reasoning, accepted by the court, went this way: (a) Snowmobiles and like vehicles are like ATVs. (b) But the accident rate for snowmobiles and like vehicles is much lower than for ATVs. (c) Therefore, the high ATV accident rate must be due to operator error. The court seems to have gone off on the word "similar." Snowmobiles had a similar purpose, so the defendant's syllogism worked for the court. But similar purpose is not similar design. Nor do we know that snowmobiles face the same number and kind of hazards. *Designs* of snowmobiles and ATVs do not rely on common elements related to the risk in question. So if snowmobiles had a poor safety record, for example, that would hardly justify admitting evidence of that safety record to prove that ATVs were defective. Likewise, their good safety record compared to ATVs seems to prove nothing at all about ATVs. Not only is the major premise of the syllogism doubtful at best, the court also seemed to suggest that its result was merely an extension of the safety history rules stated in note 1. That also seems wrong and for the same reason: similar purposes do not bespeak similar risks or designs. It is as if the court had said that fish and chicken are similar because both are non-red-meat foods. If more people get sick eating fish than chicken, it would hardly prove that it was error in preparation. *Kava v. American Honda Motor Co.,* Inc., 48 P.3d 1170 (Alaska 2002), also permitted comparative risk testimony but only to contextualize and impeach similar statistical evidence introduced by the plaintiff. (*Bittner* also relied on a similar idea as to one, but only one, segment of the comparative risk testimony.)

On safety history, note that if the defendant offers evidence that the product has a good safety history, it is probably really offering evidence of a negative, that is, evidence that few or no injuries had resulted from the product's use. This is permissible, but only if the witness is in a position to know of injuries if they had occurred. The defendant probably cannot simply testify, "we never heard of any injuries," but probably would have to prove evidence of an effective investigation or study. This point is made at length in *Jones v. Pak-Mor Mfg. Co.,* 700 P.2d 819 (Ariz. 1985).

The second set of evidence in *Bittner* raises a more substantive issue of torts. Risk-utility weighing under *Carroll Towing* does not attempt to measure customarily accepted risks. That is really what the evidence offered by the defendant as to "dissimilar" activities proposed to do. It would have allowed the jury to say that since people accept much higher risks in scuba-diving and football, the risks of ATVs must be acceptable. So the court seems clearly right in rejecting comparative risks figures if they are offered to permit a *Carroll Towing* assessment of reasonable risk.

NOTE: SUBSEQUENT REMEDIAL MEASURES.

This topic deserves little attention in a busy torts course. It is included partly because the notes following *Bittner* seemed too much like a half-truth without some reference to this issue. But there are two affirmative reasons for including the topic now that the Restatement of Products Liability has eliminated "strict liability" for design defects.

First, the rule in some cases that subsequent remedial measures are admissible in strict liability cases but not in negligence cases shows that a shift away from strict liability theory in the Restatement Third might have logical and ideological consequences. That is, if we accept that there is essentially no such thing as strict liability in design defect cases, subsequent remedial measures might not be admissible even in the liberal view. (Or do those cases deal with products rather than with strict liability?) *Ault* and *Caparara*, both cited here, might seem weak cases. Both were decided when the bloom was on the strict liability rose, while in this day, strict liability is not so much blooming as blushing.

Second, if you try to sensitize students to the trial process and to the tight connection between evidentiary facts and legal argument, you can recall the discussion of custom in Chapter 6. The notes there indicated that even when evidence of custom might be excluded as bearing on the appropriate level or standard of care, it might be admitted as bearing on other issues like foreseeability and feasibility. The same is true here. If the defendant argues that a safer practice was not feasible, or would carry too many dis-utilities, the court would be well justified in admitting evidence that the defendant itself adopted the safer practice after the injury occurred.

MERCK & CO. V. GARZA, 277 S.W.3d 430 (Tex. App. 2008)

Seventy-one year old Leonel Garza died of a heart attack after taking Vioxx, manufactured by the defendant Merck. His heirs sued. Merck on design defect and marketing defect theories. In the portion of the opinion reprinted here, the court analyzes the sufficiency of the plaintiffs' proof of causation. The court explains the concepts of general and specific causation, and holds that the plaintiffs met their burden on both. However, as noted at the end of the excerpt, the trial court's judgment for plaintiffs was reversed on other grounds.

The case is here to make students aware of the requirements of general and specific causation used in these design defect cases, particularly those involving drugs, and to introduce some Notes that raise other evidentiary issues.

Because students will not have had evidence when they study this, you cannot expect much depth – and few will have the luxury of time to provide it. But as a general awareness matter, these materials are justified.

Note 1 reiterates the basic definitions and invites you to ask your class what these causation requirements mean, and perhaps why they are there. It is, of course, an "actual cause" matter, also connected to duty and breach.

If a product is incapable of causing harm, then it is not defective. Put in terms of duty-breach, the defendant has breached no duty to provide a non-defective product. Although this seems plain, jurists have begun using different terminology, speaking of general causation and specific causation. The general causation question is whether the product harms anyone or has capacity to harm; the specific causation question asks whether the product harmed the plaintiff as claimed. See Joseph Sanders & Julie Machal-Fulks, *The Admissibility of Differential Diagnosis Testimony to Prove Causation in Toxic Tort Cases: The Interplay of Adjective and Substantive Law*, 64-AUT LAW & CONTEMP. PROBS. 107, 110 (2001). "General causation" is a fairly sensible description of the idea. We would probably prefer not to create new terminology when it seems clear that the issue is one already described in terms of the traditional tort law elements by reference to duty or breach. Still, courts seem to have quickly accustomed themselves to the general or "generic" causation language.

The disadvantage of the "general causation" language is that it may tend to obscure an important point. If, using the language of duty or defect, you conclude that the product is defective because it can too often cause harm, then you might be willing to permit an inference of causation in the particular case. We also think if a product is defective because it has a propensity to cause harm, this fact can at times, in conjunction with other evidence, warrant a causal inference. To speak in terms of general causation instead of defect is perhaps to lose this point.

To put a clear example, suppose that some massive study is done and eventually a drug is found to be defective and unreasonably dangerous because 120 birth defects result among users' children for every 100 birth defects suffered in the general population. Suppose the plaintiff's mother took the drug at relevant times and the plaintiff suffers from birth defects of the kind generally associated with the drug. Notice that it is still five times as likely that the plaintiff suffered a "normal" birth defect than that the plaintiff suffered the "drug" birth defect. Unless the product is like the old Pasteur rabies treatment – the only treatment, without which most series consequences are likely– the product seems to be defective. If you concede that a 20% increase in serious risk makes the product defective, then this case really DOES present a causal issue, not a defect issue.

Note 2. Proof of dosage or exposure levels. The reasoning in *Alder v. Bayer Corp., Agfa Div.*, cited here, seems subject to criticism if the issue is causation (or "specific causation.") The thin or eggshell skull argument–that you take the plaintiff as you find her–supports the plaintiff's recovery without further proof if you already know that the plaintiff suffered a level of exposure that, more likely than not, would have caused *some* harm to foreseeable victims. But if you don't know that, the thin skull argument doesn't seem to help the plaintiff. First, the fact that *some* level of exposure would cause foreseeable harm doesn't prove that *every* level of exposure would have done so. Second, that some level of exposure would cause foreseeable harm doesn't prove that there was enough exposure to permit a finding of negligence. Only if you know that the exposure caused by the defendant was sufficient to cause foreseeable harm can you find both negligence and causation. So the court seems in error here unless the thin skull doctrine permits strict liability and without causal proof for the benefit of unusually vulnerable people while enforcing the usual rules of negligence and causation for others.

Note 3. Admissibility of expert testimony. Under traditional practice, once the witness is shown to be qualified, the question was "relevancy" of the witnesses' opinion, not its validity. In 1923, a federal court in *Frye v. United*

States, 293 F. 1013 (D.C. Cir. 1923), laid down a restrictive rule for admission of "scientific" evidence alongside the laissez-faire attitude toward "opinion" evidence. Under the *Frye* rule, scientific propositions had to garner "general acceptance" in the particular field to be admissible.The potential conflict between these two rules was not initially recognized. It is now, and much of the discussion has turned on admissibility of expert or scientific evidence under the federal rules. *See* John Strong, *Language and Logic in Expert Testimony: Limiting Expert Testimony by Restrictions of Function, Reliability and Form*, 71 OR. L. REV. 349 (1992). Students should see the difference between *admissibility* of expert testimony and its *sufficiency*. If expert testimony is excluded because it is inadmissible, then the issue is cut off at the pass. If it is admitted, however, the important issue remains: Is the evidence *sufficient* to warrant a jury finding based on that testimony?

The *Daubert* case is of course the big topic here, although full development should and must await the evidence course's coverage. Hundreds of articles and thousands of cases have cited *Daubert*. It, and its interpretation, raise interesting issues about the nature of science and the nature of law, and how law can, should, or might put its faith in science. Those issues transcend tort law and are much too large for extensive development in a tort course. Yet tort law outcomes depend in part on these issues, and the issue also fits the larger picture of tort reform, so you may feel justified in providing your class with a little discussion.

If you discuss *Daubert* with your class, perhaps you will want to emphasize that it can cut both ways. As a matter of form, *Daubert* initially purports to liberalize the old *Frye* rule, under which expert presentation of scientific propositions was excluded unless those propositions had gained general acceptance. *Daubert* made general acceptance a sometime-factor, not a bright-line test for exclusion. In criminal cases, the *Frye* rule of general acceptance often favored the defendant by excluding "scientific" tests that might establish guilt. In those cases, you find the state as prosecutor arguing for *Daubert* as a *liberalizing* test that would admit evidence. *E.g., State v. Jones*, 922 P.2d 806 (Wash. 1996).

However, the liberalizing side of *Daubert* Court may not be so significant in many civil cases. The *Daubert* court, having rejected *Frye*, went on to elaborate the role of federal judges as gatekeepers excluding unreliable evidence and listed a number of factors to consider in determining reliability. The overall effect was not to enhance admissibility but to provide many grounds besides relevance for excluding the evidence, and the *Daubert* line of cases is most often asserted in tort cases to exclude, not to admit, testimony. Thus in a number of products cases, the defendant is arguing on the basis of *Daubert* for exclusion of expert testimony. In these cases, the court that rejects *Daubert* or finds it inapplicable to the facts is often holding for the plaintiff, while the court that applies *Daubert* is holding for the defendant by excluding the plaintiff's evidence. We cite several such cases below. This effect is not universal; a strict application of *Daubert* might sometimes exclude evidence offered by the defendant to rebut the plaintiff's claim. See *Baker v. Dalkon Shield Claimants*

Trust, 156 F.3d 248 (1st Cir. 1998) (reversing the trial court's exclusion of the defendant's evidence).

The trial judge's gatekeeping function —the power to exclude evidence – is largely a matter of discretion, reviewable only for abuse. *Kumho Tire Co., Ltd. v. Carmichael,* 526 U.S. 137 (1999). *Kumho* also recognized the trial judge's discretion to determine the kind of proceedings needed to make the reliability determination. The Court contemplated that the trial judge would "avoid unnecessary 'reliability' proceedings in ordinary cases where the reliability of an expert's methods is properly taken for granted. . . ." But the main message seems to have been "take pains to exclude doubtful expert testimony." In line with this, some decisions expressly or impliedly put the burden upon the plaintiff to show affirmatively, not only that her expert is qualified as an expert but also to show that the testimony is "reliable" in the light of the factors or considerations spelled out in *Daubert.* See *E.I. du Pont de Nemours & Co., Inc. v. Robinson,* 923 S.W.2d 549, 557 (Tex. 1996).

Unreviewable discretion can be a serious problem to the party with the burden of proof, and so can a rule that puts the burden of proof on the plaintiff to convince the judge that testimony is not only relevant, but that it is also "reliable." *Daubert* and *Kumho,* then may reduce the number of viable tort lawsuits. They are likely to make production of expert testimony much more expensive. In addition, they are determining the outcome for the defendant by preventing the jury from hearing expert testimony. This is quite different from the traditional way of seeking truth in trials— production of testimony and counter-testimony, vigorous cross-examination of witnesses to expose the shakiness of their conclusions, and, if after full development of the evidence it falls short, then directed verdict.

You might think there is little or no harm in broad exclusion of expert testimony. After all, the trial judge's assessment of admissibility is theoretically about the credentials of witnesses and the reliability and relevance of their testimony. *Daubert* sought to eliminate unreliable testimony and said that the test reliability was methodology, not the expert's conclusions. But determination of reliability (and hence admissibility) easily shades into a judge's decision that the witness is not credible or that his testimony is not entitled to much weight, displacing the jury's traditional function.

For instance, on remand of the Supreme Court's decision in *Daubert,* the Ninth Circuit insisted that a factor to be considered in excluding expert testimony was "whether the experts are proposing to testify about matters growing naturally and directly out of research they have conducted independent of the litigation, or whether they have developed their opinions expressly for purposes of testifying." *Daubert v. Merrell Dow Pharmaceuticals, Inc.,* 43 F.3d 1311, 1317 (9th Cir. 1995). A trier of fact should certainly consider the expert's interest in assessing his credibility and in determining the weight of his testimony, so the fact that he is paid and the further fact that his opinion was developed for the purpose of consulting in the case are highly relevant. But if the Ninth Circuit's view applies, a trial judge might refuse to admit testimony of an expert who developed his opinion for purpose of providing testimony.

That would mean that the judge would be in effect determining credibility, not credentials.

You can see a concrete example in *Bogosian v. Mercedes-Benz of North America, Inc.,* 104 F.3d 472 (1st Cir. 1997), where a Mercedes distributed by the defendant rolled over the plaintiff after she left the car, even though she had placed it in parking gear. She offered testimony of a master mechanic who was not a degreed engineer but who had 15 years of transmission experience and training in engineering that the design was defective in permitting a false sense that the gear was lodged in "park" when it was not. His testimony was rejected and the plaintiff lost the case. "While not dispositive, the lack of a mechanical engineering degree or other engineering expertise certainly calls into question Davidson's ability to criticize the design of a transmission parking mechanism and its operation under various circumstances." Is this a decision about weight or credibility of testimony, or does the court mean that it would be irrational to give weight to 15 years of hands-on experience? Would a rancher be incapable of assessing the health of a new calf because he had never designed one or taken a course in bio-engineering?

Another example of exclusion of expert testimony that might once have been admitted is *Moore v. Ashland Chemical Inc.,* 151 F.3d 269 (5th Cir. 1998) (en banc), where a doctor's opinion on the causation of plaintiff's respiratory illness inadmissible since the doctor had never conducted any research on the specific subject and had never treated a patient who had been exposed to the substance at issue.

On the other side of the equation, however, courts have long recognized that expert testimony on matters that jurors could decide from their own knowledge and evaluation the established facts would invade the province of the jury. Exclusion of unsupported expert testimony on matters that jurors might decide for themselves, while done in the name of reliability, may actually revert to the habits of the pre-expert era, shielding jurors of the impression that experts know it all. In *Calhoun v. Yamaha Motor Corp.,* 350 F.3d 316 (3d Cir. 2003), experts wanted to opine that jet skies should not be operated by young people under sixteen, but they had no studies to support that view nor any demonstrated expertise in judging age-capacity. Their testimony on this point was excluded in a measured opinion. The effect of cases like this may be to leave to the jury to its own good sense about what can be expected of young people, who, after all operate bicycles, snowmobiles, motorcycles, cars, trucks, and tractors, and sometimes fly airplanes.

Perhaps judges should recognize that reliability of an expert's testimony must be considered in the light of other evidence in the case and when it involves issues of causation, in the light of other possible causes. Suppose the mechanic's testimony in *Bogosian* was about the possibility that the gear shift could give user a tactile sensation that the gear was firmly lodged in Park when it was not. Should his testimony be considered in isolation or in connection with all the facts that tend to show that possibility, including, if the jury believes the plaintiff's testimony, the absence of other explanations?

Taking all the facts into account in assessing possible causes is somewhat like the differential diagnosis issue in medical causation cases. The physician who concludes that PCBs are the cause of cancer without considering whether the plaintiff was also exposed to heavy cigarette smoke may not be sufficiently reliable. See *Re Paoli R.R. Yard PCB Litigation*, 35 F.3d 717 (3d Cir. 1994). Conversely, however, if the witness concludes that force A caused harm B by ruling out other causes, that testimony seems eminently reliable and admissible. See *Baker v. Dalkon Shield Claimants Trust*, 156 F.3d 248 (1st Cir. 1998) (findings more consistent with the conclusion that plaintiff's PID was caused by chlamydia, hence expert concluded defendant's IUD did not cause the harm); *Courtaulds Fibers, Inc. v. Long*, 779 So.2d 198 (Ala. 2000) (vet ruled out causes for harm to the plaintiff's horses except releases from defendant's plant; testimony was admissible). But the plaintiff still must prove a basis for "ruling in" the defendant's product. Mere case reports that some other persons who have ingested the defendant's prescription drug have suffered harms similar to the plaintiff's are insufficient. *Glastetter v. Novartis Pharmaceuticals Corp.*, 252 F.3d 986 (8th Cir. 2001).

Rule 702. If you want to investigate this further, law reviews and practice materials abound, but you might take a look a Rule 702 of the Federal Rules of Evidence. That rule was the basis for *Daubert's* rejection of *Frye*. Rule 702 has since been amended to spell out greater restriction. The amended (post-*Daubert*) Rule 702 went into effect December 1, 2000. It provides:

> If scientific, technical, or other specialized knowledge will assist the trier of fact to understand the evidence or to determine a fact in issue, a witness qualified as an expert by knowledge, skill, experience, training, or education, may testify thereto in the form of an opinion or otherwise, if (1) the testimony is based upon sufficient facts or data, (2) the testimony is the product of reliable principles and methods, and (3) the witness has applied the principles and methods reliably to the facts of the case.

The Advisory Committee Notes contain an excellent brief summary of *Daubert* and related cases up to 2000.

Note 4. State law differences. States are free to accept either *Frye* or *Daubert-Kumho* or to reject either or both and to construct their own rules of evidence. *Logerquist v. McVey*, 1 P.3d 113 (Ariz. 2000), dealing with testimony about repression of memory, rejects *Daubert* and points out that even testimony from Einstein might have been rejected under the *Frye* "general acceptance" standard. Iowa does not follow the *Daubert* analysis, but seemingly doesn't follow *Frye's* general acceptance standard, either; instead, it permits trial judges to consider particular factors listed in *Daubert* if they find it helpful in complex cases. See *Mercer v. Pittway Corp.*, 616 N.W.2d 602 (Iowa 2000) (applying this rule to uphold admission of testimony). The Nevada Court, regarding *Daubert* as a work in progress, saw no need to adopt it to exclude evidence of causation in a breast implant case. The court held that the plaintiff "did not need to wait until the scientific community developed a consensus that breast implants caused her diseases," observing that a wait might preclude recovery under statutes of limitation. Moreover, the plaintiffs' claim "was not tried in the court of scientific opinion, but before a jury of her peers who considered the evidence and concluded that Dow Corning silicone gel breast implants caused her injuries. . . . Science may properly require a higher standard of proof before declaring the truth, but that standard did not guide the jury, nor do we use that standard to evaluate the judgment on appeal." *Dow Chemical Co. v. Mahlum,* 970 P.2d 98 (Nev. 1998).

Note 5 is a bone for the civ pro mavens.

Note 6. Epidemiological and animal studies. Epidemiology is the study of disease occurrence in humans, usually based on statistical methodology intended to show correlations or lack of correlations between disease and some other conditions. This is little more than an "awareness" Note. The Kaye and Green articles cited here are readable, understandable, and helpful, if you want more information for yourself or your students. Epidemiological evidence is generally considered to be not only an acceptable type of evidence, but a very desirable type. See Green, *supra* (of the five types of scientific evidence, epidemiology, animal toxicology, in vitro testing, chemical structural analysis, and case reports, epidemiologic evidence is the most desirable).

Some epidemiological evidence is poor or even unacceptable because it is based on poorly designed studies. A political poll that questioned only men or only persons who lived in a single-family dwelling is an understandable example of bias in selection of the group studied. Another defect may occur in measurement itself.

There are obvious problems with animal studies, first because dosage comparisons are difficult and second because extrapolation of animal toxicity to predict human toxicity is at best tricky. The technique of the defendants in these cases is to divide and conquer. Animal studies are tossed out *entirely* because of such difficulties; they are never revisited as part of the larger picture. Yet, even if you think the animal study proves nothing by itself, you might also think that when animal studies show toxicity to embryos, that fact changes the probabilities that the relative risk statistics are right, even when their initial confidence interval is very broad. Epidemiologists are the elite of this corner of science and some of the courts have converted the pecking order of their chicken-yard to a kind of jurisprudential principle.

Note 7. Legal vs. scientific purposes. The *Daubert* Court recognized that science is not committed to final answers but to a method of continuous inquiry. Heidi Li Feldman, *Science and Uncertainty in Mass Exposure Litigation*, 74 TEX. L. REV. 1, 16 (1995), summarizes by saying that "Science is dynamic." New data or new ways of looking at data lead scientists to revise their conclusions or hypotheses. This view of science means that "science does not produce fixed, unassailable conclusions" but a range of opinions, some shared more widely than others (and some that change over time). So a rule limiting access of the legal system to the current majority view of scientists would be too restrictive; it would give the factfinder an "edited version of science." More than that, the less editing you do the more you find uncertainty in scientific ideas. In contrast, legal resolution of disputes must take place now, not some indefinite time in the future. Science can accept uncertainty while it works towards perfect ruth, but law must accept imperfections in order to get disputes decided. Jurists should not demand certainty or perfection, only human efforts to be rational and reasonable.

Note 8. Experts and reasonable alternative design. Maybe the *Dhillon* court, cited here, did not really mean that the plaintiff injured by an industrial machine must always build a competing and safer version; perhaps the model could be a conceptual model or a blueprint. Whatever *Dhillon* meant, though, it seems to suggest that the plaintiff must invest a sizeable sum in engineering a better product just to be admitted to the courtroom. The RAD rule and the gatekeeper approach combine to reduce the number of claims by putting them beyond the financial reach of many plaintiffs. Do we really need a model to determine whether a rear door is needed and feasible? Would it reduce law courts to witchcraft if instead we listened to people knowledgeable in the use and dangers of forklifts and took general estimates of costs? After all, judges estimate costs themselves–without expert help – when they do risk-utility analyses, and those estimates are seldom based on precise figures. *Carroll Towing* itself was like that.

And testing – is testing really necessary, especially where the expert's testimony is based on practical experience? Consider the testimony in *Persinger v. Step by Step Infant Dev. Ctr.*, 560 S.E.2d 333 (Ga. Ct. App. 2002), where an 18-month-old child broke his leg at a day-care center. The defendant center witnesses said he just fell. An orthopedic surgeon testified that a simple fall could not have broken his leg; he would have to have twisted it with the foot locked into position, as might be the case if his foot had been caught between crib slats. This testimony was the only thing that allowed the plaintiff to get to the jury; it permitted an inference that the center was covering up the real cause of injury and that the real cause must have been the center's fault. No objection to the doctor's testimony is mentioned in the case. If a federal court under *Daubert-Kumho*-Rule 702 were deciding the case, would the doctor have to break thousands of infant legs and tabulate results before he could testify that a simple fall would be insufficient to cause the break?

What evidence is sufficient or necessary perhaps depends in part on what evidence is reasonably available. In *Norris v. Baxter Healthcare Corp.*, 397 F.3d 878 (10th Cir. 2005), the defendant offered epidemiological evidence that breast implants did not cause autoimmune disease and the court appeared to have independent knowledge of a substantial body of epidemiological evidence to like effect. In those circumstances, the court thought that the plaintiff who produced no contrary epidemiology should lose on summary judgment.

But look at the cases in Note 4 where there is no body of epidemiological evidence. To be sure, these are state cases, not federal, but they quite reasonably take the view that in the absence of epidemiological studies, the trier could rely on the cruder bases for causal judgments. If we don't expect plaintiffs to conduct a national epidemiological study and are willing to rule on reasonably available evidence, why would we insist in cases like *Dhillon* that the plaintiff must build a new forklift to demonstrate the defect in the old one?

Alternatives. Causal issues in mass toxic tort cases have led many thinkers to a considerable disenchantment with the tort system as it works in such cases. The suggestion of some writers, therefore, has been that such cases should be removed from the torts system altogether, in favor of some kind of social insurance model. Professor Rabin, a distinguished scholar of torts has even said "that continuing resort to the tort system in these mass toxics cases seems indefensible." Robert Rabin, Book Review, 98 YALE L. J. 813 (1989) (reviewing PETER.SCHUCK, TORT SYSTEM ON TRIAL: THE BURDEN OF MASS TOXICS LITIGATION (1987)). Some alternate institutions might include reliance on the market or on contracting, on government regulation of specific risks, and on various social insurance programs, usually with limited but more assured compensation. Among the trenchant discussions of the general idea of allocating mass torts to alternate institutions, *see* Kip Viscusi, *Toward a Diminished Role for Tort Liability: Social Insurance, Government Regulation, and Contemporary Risks to Health and Safety*, 6 YALE J. ON REG. 65 (1989).

The American Law Institute's *Reporters' Study, Enterprise Responsibility for Personal Injury* deals with toxic and "environmental" torts as an entirely separate category and treats the causal problem in such tort cases differently. The Study mainly recommends use of court appointed experts, or a blue ribbon expert panel, developing these ideas into a permanent federal science board to help courts decide toxic causation issues. (Vol. II, pp. 339 ff.). However, the *Study* also draws two sets of distinctions. First, it distinguishes four types of scientific uncertainty in toxic causation cases (one of which is the confidence interval uncertainty discussed above). Second, it distinguishes mass tort cases from individual injury cases. One importance in this second distinction lies in the idea that the more sophisticated proof might well be required in mass tort cases where many people are exposed; but such proof might not necessarily be required in other cases. (II-329). Mass torts would be likely to generate more epidemiological data and it might be more cost effective to use it when costs could be spread among a class. The Study also favors proportionate compensation when liability is established. This shares a core with value-of-the-chance or probabilistic causation rules.

Subchapter C. Defenses and Defeats

§ 8. COMPARATIVE FAULT AND ASSUMPTION OF RISK

BOWLING V. HEIL, 511 N.E.2d 373 (Ohio 1987)

The decedent was killed when he put his head under an upraised bed of a dump truck and manipulated the lever in an attempt to make the bed go down. He succeeded. The Ohio Court held that his conduct was not to be considered at all, either as a bar or as grounds for reducing damages, because liability of the defendant is "enterprise liability" with a focus on the product, not on conduct, and because, it seems, the defective product could injure the careful and careless alike.

Bowling applies the traditional rule, that contributory negligence is no defense to a "strict liability" claim. (This is the same as the traditional approach in the abnormally dangerous activity cases we saw in Chapter 23). Could the court's reasoning survive in any way the tide of negligence law that is flooding strict products liability in design defect cases? Perhaps. The court reasons that strict liability can now be perceived as enterprise liability for products. In this view, the products or "enterprise liability" rules are not necessarily strict liability rules, and they are not very different from negligence rules, but they are different in a few particulars. One of those particulars is the rule of contributory or comparative fault; another (already mentioned) is the rule in some courts admitting evidence of subsequent remedial measures (§ 7).

Bowling's rule is a minority; most courts do allow a defendant in a products case (even one brought on a strict liability theory) to defend on grounds that the plaintiff was contributorily negligent, with the result that damages are reduced if the defense succeeds. Interestingly, of the four states that retain contributory negligence as a complete bar to recovery in ordinary negligence cases, two hold or provide that contributory negligence is a defense (and a complete defense) in a products action. See *Uniroyal Goodrich Tire Co. v. Hall*, 681 So.2d 126 (Ala. 1996); N.C. Gen. Stat. § 99B-4. The other two disregard contributory negligence. *Ellsworth v. Sherne Lingerie, Inc.*, 495 A.2d 348, 52 A.L.R.4th 247 (Md. 1984); *Wood v. Bass Pro Shops, Inc.*, 462 S.E.2d 101 (Va. 1995) (warranty theory; also disregarded assumed risk, but recognizing product misuse as a complete defense).

Comparing negligence to strict liability. How can a jury ever compare the negligence of a plaintiff to the strict liability of a defendant? One thing is for sure: "comparative negligence" cannot be the proper term for it. The Restatement of Apportionment now uses the term "comparative responsibility." (The California Court has switched to the term "equitable apportionment," which still does not describe what it is you are asking the jury to do, not even in theory.) We printed the Restatement of Apportionment § 8 in Chapter 9. You may wish to look back at its list of factors to consider and the criticisms in this manual. The best place for discussing this point in detail, if you wish to, is with *Safeway Stores*, Chapter 25, where the topic of apportionment generally is considered and where supporting notes suggest some ways to compare causation. The only reason to mention the topic here at all is to acknowledge the problem so the substantive comparative fault rule choices can be discussed.

The options. How should you deal with the plaintiff's fault when the defendant's liability is "strict"? The most obvious options are:

(1) You can follow the Second Restatement's rule and hold that where the defendant is strictly liable, the plaintiff's ordinary contributory negligence has no effect at all either to bar the claim or reduce the damages.

(2) You can apply comparative negligence rules as a partial defense and reduce recovery accordingly.

Less obvious options are considered in the next section. They include:

(3) You can bar the plaintiff completely on the ground that the plaintiff's fault is the sole proximate cause of the harm. This will probably be called "misuse."

(4) You can bar the plaintiff completely on the ground that the defendant breached no duty to the plaintiff, or in strict liability terms, that the product was not defective at all because the plaintiff's dangerous conduct was not foreseeable. That, too, is considered in the next section.

A fifth option is to distinguish between types of contributory negligence/comparative fault, ignoring the plaintiff's failure to discover a defect but reducing damages if the plaintiff does not exercise care in the face of a discovered defect. See **Note 5** below.

If you teach this short section quickly, you can concentrate on the first two options and add the third and fourth options in the next section, after which the class can put together an complete view.

Note 1. Comparative fault reductions. In *Daly v. General Motors Corp.*, cited here, the decedent's car collided with a metal fence. Allegedly as a result of a defective latch design, a car door flew open. The driver, intoxicated and using neither the door lock nor the seat-belt devices, was ejected from the car and suffered fatal injuries. The court permitted evidence of the decedent's fault on the ground that his contributory negligence will reduce the damages recovered under California's comparative negligence rules.

The Products Restatement § 17 essentially adopts the *Daly* view that contributory negligence is a defense to a products suit, as it is in any other kind of suit. As noted above, most courts confronting the issue agree with *Daly* and the new Restatement. *See* DOBBS ON TORTS § 369 (2000); *Annotation, Applicability of Comparative Negligence Doctrine to Actions Based on Strict Liability in Tort*, 9 A.L.R.4th 633 (1981). Statutes may answer the question specifically, and in some instances statutory answers have superseded those given by the courts.

Note 3. Causal apportionment. This Note reminds us that causal apportionment is entirely different from fault apportionment. Even if you hold with *Bowling v. Heil* that the plaintiff's contributory fault is wholly irrelevant, the defendant is still liable only for harms caused by the defective product. If it only caused a broken arm, it is liable for that, not the broken leg that resulted from other causes.

This concept is easy to confuse and abuse, though. It is very easy to slide from analysis of cause in fact to a kind of vague "proximate cause" or scope of risk reasoning. Suppose the plaintiff was contributorily negligent in skydiving with a broken leg in a cast. Where the defendant's parachute partially fails, the plaintiff lands hard and injures his leg even more and also breaks his arm. This kind of case probably should NOT be handled as a causal apportionment case. Although the plaintiff is chargeable with fault (or even assumed risk), both he AND the defendant are causes of the broken leg. The confusion issue can be discussed with the avoidable consequences or minimizing damages rules, which we raise in Chapters 25 & 26 (*see* Casebook Index).

Note 4. Misuse. The question in this note forecasts the problems in the next section or can be used to transport your discussion into that section.

Note 5. Discovered vs. undiscovered defect. The Texas Supreme Court in *Sanchez*, discussed at the end of this Note, said that to reduce a plaintiff's recovery based on his own negligence in failing to discover a defect would be to "defeat the purposes of strict liability." *Jay v. Moog Automotive, Inc.*, 652 N.W.2d 872 (Neb. 2002) is a more recent case stating the idea that contributory negligence "in the sense of a failure to discover a defect or to guard against it, is not a defense to a suit in strict tort, [but] misuse of the product is." Maybe it would make for a more coherent approach to say that the plaintiff who trusts the product simply is not chargeable with contributory negligence at all unless he has reason to think it is dangerous. Such a recognition would obviate the necessary for multiple kinds of contributory fault and re-focus on the merits of the defense. *See* DOBBS ON TORTS § 369, p. 1023 (2000).

Note 7. Assumed risk. The distinction in effect between contributory negligence and assumed risk is also part of the traditional abnormal danger type of strict liability. However, we saw in Chapter 10 that the distinction has proved difficult to maintain in the era of comparative responsibility. When the phrase assumed risk is only an obscure way of saying that the defendant was not at fault or that the product was not defective, then of course the defendant is not liable at all because there is no case against it to begin with. But if the product is defective or the defendant negligent, why treat the plaintiff's fault as having no effect when it is called contributory negligence and as barring the plaintiff completely when it is called assumed risk?

In *Onderko v. Richmond Mfg. Co.*, 511 N.E.2d 388 (Ohio 1987), decided the same day as *Bowling*, the plaintiff lost his arm when the auger of an earth-boring machine lurched forward and entangled his clothing. The trial court reduced his damages on a finding that he had assumed the risk, which was treated as comparative negligence. This was reversed on appeal on the ground that "Voluntary and unreasonable assumption of a known risk posed by a product constitutes an absolute bar to recovery in a products liability action based upon strict liability in tort." There were two special peculiarities about this decision. First, it made assumed risk an absolute bar only when the assumed risk was unreasonable —a fair warning that assumed risk as the court viewed it was merely another species of contributory fault. Second, the court held that the same assumed risk would not be an absolute bar to the plaintiff's *negligence* claim based on the same facts; as to the negligence claim, the assumed risk would be treated as comparative fault, the effect of which would be only to reduce damages. Ohio has now gone on to hold that an encounter with known danger as required by employment does not count as assumed risk. *Carrel v. Allied Products Corp.*, 677 N.E.2d 795 (Ohio 1997) (cited in this Note).

Note 8. Recalling *Bexiga*. This note reminds the students of *Bexiga* (Chapter 9), which, after all, was a products liability case. If the principle there is that in some cases the manufacturer must protect the plaintiff against his own fault, does that principle extend to every case in which the manufacturer can foresee harm to the careless user of the product? Could you support the principle and the result in *Bexiga*, for example, and still think that *Bowling* was wrong? Or that *Bowling* should be limited to cases in which the manufacturer should recognize in advance that the worker is in no position to protect himself?

Cotita v. Pharma-Plast, U.S.A., Inc., cited here, applied Louisiana law on comparative negligence in products cases. As the *Cotita* court explained it:

[A] two-pronged test has been distilled to ascertain whether comparative fault should be used to reduce a plaintiff's award in a products liability action: (1) Would the reduction of the award realistically provide incentive for user care? If this query is affirmatively answered, a court must then ask (2) would the application of comparative fault drastically undermine the manufacturer's incentive to make a safe product? If this latter question is answered affirmatively, "Louisiana law prohibits the application of comparative fault."

In *Cotita*, the nurse had been working with an AIDS patient. The nurse properly wore gloves. Some of the patient's blood was on the gloves when he opened a syringe manufactured by the defendant. The needle lacked its usual protective cover and the nurse was stuck. The glove was pierced so the nurse feared that he had been exposed to AIDS. His claim is for the emotional harm resulting. (*See* Chapter 19, § 4 for more on fear of future harm.) The court thought comparative fault could apply under the Louisiana standard because the "district court here was entitled to determine that the application of comparative fault will ultimately encourage workers in the health care field to follow the established procedures for handling syringes" and because "no reasonably prudent manufacturer will 'rely on future careless use of its products to offset its full liability with any predictability that would alter the manufacturer's duty to produce the safest product possible.'" Should contributory fault rules apply if the plaintiff is able to formulate a claim for breach of express or implied warranty rather than in tort?

Note 9. Seatbelts. If you view failure to wear a seatbelt as contributory fault *and* you adopt the Ohio rule in *Bowling*, then you must say that the plaintiff's failure to wear a seatbelt has NO effect on the recovery. This was the view in *Dillinger v. Caterpillar, Inc.*, 959 F.2d 430 (3d Cir. 1992). What if you regard failure to wear a seatbelt as a kind of avoidable consequences issue with causal apportionment of damages? In that case the defendant might make a little headway even in a jurisdiction like Ohio.

The "seatbelt defense" is often barred by statute. See, classifying statutes, DOBBS ON TORTS § 205 (2000). The statutes can sometimes bar a plaintiff's products claim for injuries resulting from defective seatbelts, too. See *Carlson v. Hyundai Motor Co.*, 164 F.3d 1160 (8th Cir. 1999) (Minnesota statute forbidding evidence of use or failure to use seatbelts in an auto crash case barred plaintiff's design defect claim in which she claimed the car's door frame had deformed in an accident, allowing her ejection from a car; alleged defects in the seat belt system and the door frame were intertwined). Sometimes these seatbelt statutes are held not to apply at all to products liability cases. See *Klinke v. Mitsubishi Motors Corp.*, 581 N.W.2d 272 (Mich. 1998) (construing Michigan statute forbidding evidence of plaintiff's use or non-use of seatbelts).

Note 10. The firefighter's rule. More remembrance of things past. When the firefighter's rule is presented in the products context instead of the landowner's context, do we feel that the rule has a sound underlying basis and can be generalized to all situations? Or do we come to doubt it even in the landowner cases?

Note 11. Effect on deterrence. These questions may be used for class discussion, or simply to make students think. You might conclude that taking account of a plaintiff's contributory negligence is a less dramatic development in a pure comparative jurisdiction, in which the recovery will only be reduced, not barred. But what about the majority of states, that follow modified comparative schemes? There is a very real possibility of a negligent plaintiff being barred from recovery because he is deemed "more responsible" than the defendant manufacturer. Should manufacturers have a general duty to protect product users from their own negligence in using the products, a la *Bexiga*?

§ 9. DISTINGUISHING DEFENSES FROM FAILURE TO PROVE DEFECT: PROXIMATE CAUSE AND MISUSE

A. Misuse, Defectiveness, and Comparative Fault/Assumed Risk

HUGHES V. MAGIC CHEF, INC., 288 N.W.2d 542 (Iowa 1980)

The plaintiff was burned by the explosion of a home propane stove. One version of the facts was that the propane had run dry and when it was reconnected not all the pilots lights were lit. The gas built up in the stove and exploded. *Held:* (1) misuse by the plaintiff is not an affirmative defense like assumed risk but instead related to the question whether the product was defective in the first place. The plaintiff must prove that the product was unreasonably dangerous for reasonably foreseeable uses. [If its danger is a result of any unforeseen use (whether *mis*use or not) and not from a properly used product, then the product simply isn't defective with respect to the risk that caused harm. At least the plaintiff has not proved the defect.] (2) At the same time, the plaintiff is not held to a reasonableness standard – that would be contributory negligence, which is no defense to a strict liability claim. So it was error for the trial judge to instruct the jury on misuse as a complete defense and then to define misuse.

"The misuse defense" and equivalent locutions are common, but they are very unfortunate sources of confusion. "Misuse" –because of the prefix, "mis"– suggests fault, so you might confuse the term with contributory negligence or assumed risk. "Defense" in the same phrase seems to confirm that idea, implying that the burden is upon the defendant. But neither of these implications is correct, as *Hughes* shows us. Further, it is not merely misuse that defeats the claim in the ordinary case, but "unforeseeable misuse."

Why does unforeseeable misuse defeat the claim? Because unforeseeable misuse means the product is not defective or at least has not be proved to be so. To be defective, the product must be put to an intended or foreseeable use. A golf cart may not be safe for highway use, but is danger for highway use does not make it defective unless highway use is intended or foreseeable.

The *Hughes* Court also helps us distinguish assumed risk from contributory fault. If those defenses apply in a product case at all, they turn on whether the plaintiff took unreasonable risks under the circumstances or knowingly assumed the risk. Misuse, in contrast, turns on whether the plaintiff's conduct was foreseeable to the defendant. Note 1 tries to give you a handle for helping students to draw the distinction. The distinction is not found in any difference in the character of the plaintiff's conduct, but in the question of foreseeability. If the plaintiff's use of the product is not foreseeable, and that use creates the danger, then the product is not defective; the unforeseeable use is not a danger against which the product should have protected. If the use is foreseeable, on the other hand, the product may be defective, and in that case, the issue may be about comparative fault.

Note 4. This note ends by trying to reinforce the idea that unforeseeable misuse, if the only relevant cause of the plaintiff's harm, might merely mean that the product is not defective at all, but that foreseeable misuse, while permitting a conclusion that the product is defective, could still represent comparative fault and operate to reduce damages accordingly. That is the point of the last question.

B. Misuse, Defectiveness, and Proximate Cause

REID V. SPADONE MACHINE CO., 404 A.2d 1094 (N.H. 1979)

The defendant manufactured a cutting machine for cutting blocks of molded plastic. The machine was sold to manufacturers, whose employees operated it in production. The original safety device was in the form of a two-button trigger: both hands had to be out of the way to trigger the cutter. Workers circumvented this by using a wooden bar to push both at once, so the defendant put the buttons on one side of the machine instead of the front. The plaintiff, a worker using the machine for an employer, circumvented this safety design by working the machine with a co-worker who would push the buttons while the worker inserted and turned the material to be cut. The two workers inevitably got out of synch and the plaintiff lost some fingers. This is his action against the manufacturer. The manufacturer argued the *employer's* negligence in permitting or encouraging misuse was a superseding cause. *Held*, the manufacturer is liable for a foreseeable misuse; since the machine's defect was its failure to prevent this very kind of misuse, the misuse was foreseeable. The proximate cause defense is therefore unacceptable.

Proximate cause. Reid gives us more of the misuse formula. If misuse IS foreseeable, then the product is defective when it fails to provide reasonable protection against that misuse. Could misuse still raise an issue of proximate cause? The court seems to think so, but only if the misuse is unforeseeable. But something is funny here. If the misuse is unforeseeable, then according to *Hughes,* the products would not be defective at all, so discussion of proximate cause would be superfluous or confusing. Perhaps use of proximate (superseding) cause here is an alternate expression of a no-liability rule. Courts often seem to invoke proximate cause when the real problem is that the defendant is not negligent, so maybe in products cases it should not surprise us if they do so when the real problem is that the product is not defective.

Forseeability. Misuse of almost anything is foreseeable. Must the manufacturer always provide protection against foreseeable misuse?

Note 1. Defectiveness or superseding cause? Statutes, constitutional provisions, and local legal culture sometimes lead courts to reject both these approaches. In *Jimenez v. Sears, Roebuck and Company,* 904 P.2d 861 (Ariz. 1995), the court concluded that misuse under a statutory provision governing products liability was not the same as contributory fault but that comparative negligence principles nevertheless applied in misuse cases.

Note 2. Plaintiff's misuse as superseding cause. As we saw in Chapter 9, § 4, labeling a plaintiff's negligent conduct a superseding cause of harm, thus barring his recovery altogether, is a controversial use of a doctrine, especially insofar as it may undercut the workings of comparative fault approaches. *See* Michael D. Green, *The Unanticipated Ripples of Comparative Negligence: Superseding Cause In Products Liability and Beyond*, 53 S.C. L. REV. 1103 (2002). But courts do use it, disproportionately those in states that follow a pure form of comparative responsibility. For an argument that this use of superseding cause serves as a "safety valve" in pure states to soften the arguably harsh effects of pure comparison on defendants, *see* Paul T. Hayden, *Butterfield Rides Again: Plaintiff's Negligence as Superseding or Sole Proximate Cause in Systems of Pure Comparative Responsibility,* 33 LOYOLA L.A. L.REV. 887 (2000).

Jeld-Wen, Inc. v. Gamble, 501 S.E.2d 393 (Va. 1998): *Held,* the child's misuse of the screen (by "using it to provide balance and restraining support") was unforeseeable, precluding liability since the manufacturer owed no duty to guard against such misuse.

Note 3. Intended users. *Phillips v. Cricket Lighters,* 841 A.2d 1000 (Pa. 2003): the lead opinion argued that foreseeable use test would inject a negligence concept into strict liability, which it thought should remain unsullied by negligence concepts. Three other justices rejected strict liability on a different ground—that the risk-utility balance of negligence law was a better way to deal with such products. (This could have been done under the rubric of strict liability in courts that regard the risk-utility analysis as a mode of establishing strict liability for design defects.) All but one of the Justices in Phillips agreed that although strict liability was inappropriate, the plaintiff might still get to the jury on a negligence theory in which foreseeability of use was the foundation.

Notes 4 & 5. Foreseeability of misuse. In *Slone v. General Motors Corp.,* 457 S.E.2d 51 (Va. 1995), a dump truck, loaded with gravel, was backed toward the edge of a high dump site. The ground gave way under the back wheels and the truck flipped over backwards and slid down the side of the dump site. The driver was partially crushed and suffered brain damage. The court insisted that it was rejecting the crashworthiness doctrine but at the same time held that a manufacturer could be liable for foreseeable misuse and that the use here could be found to be foreseeable. Hence early summary judgment for the defendant was not proper.

Note 5 is just a reminder about the shifting meanings of "foreseeability."

Note 6. Shifting responsibility. The *Robinson* case evinces an attitude about products liability rather more cautious than that shown in *Reid. Robinson* is obviously distinguishable, but notice that the manufacturer knew other machines had been modified and foresaw that this one would be. The court seemed to be willing in *Robinson* to shift the responsibility entirely to the employer, who, of course, had little incentive to exercise responsibility under the workers' compensation laws, which generally limit the employer's liability to workers' compensation payments.

The "proximate cause" argument in *Reid* seems to be a kind of shifting responsibility argument. If the buyer actually discovers the product's defect, should all responsibility shift to the buyer so that the manufacturer is relieved? If your answer is yes, then the same should happen if the manufacturer adequately warns the buyer, even though the buyer does not pass on the warning. On the other hand, if the manufacturer should foresee that its warning will not be heeded, the warning should not shift responsibility. See Restatement Second § 389. Likewise if it should foresee that its post-sale warning would not be heeded by an employer and that employees might suffer as a result, perhaps the warning should not shift responsibility. In *Gracyalny v. Westinghouse Elec. Corp.*, 723 F.2d 1311 (7th Cir. 1983), the court held that even though the manufacturer gave a post-sale warning to buyers, the buyer's failure to make the simple correction needed did not as a matter of law shift all responsibility to the buyer under superseding cause theories. This is in accord with the view that actual discovery by the buyer would not do so either.

As the note indicates, New York has said that *Robinson* does not apply to relieve the manufacturer who purposefully designs goods to permit removal of their safety devices. *See Colon v. BIC USA,* Inc.199 F.Supp.2d 53 (S.D.N.Y. 2001). The same court thought that New York could not apply *Robinson* at all to consumer users of household products. That seems a surprising discrimination against workers who may have no economically viable choice about facing product dangers. The court thought the distinction would be justified because "the users in the typical *Robinson* setting are trained adults. Their employers share responsibility for their employees' workplace injuries through statutorily-prescribed vehicles of recovery such as Workers' Compensation. Many widely-used consumer household products have a failsafe feature, for example food processors which do not mince, cut or dice when the top is unlatched."

Notes 6 & 7 should be straightforward, bringing students back to earth with respect to "obvious" or well-known dangers.

VAUGHN V. NISSAN MOTOR CORP., 77 F.3d 736 (4th Cir. 1996)

Not all "proximate cause," scope of risk, or scope of duty problems arise from misuse, and we've included two such non-misuse cases here for completeness.

Vaughn raises the question much like the thin skull question we looked at in the proximate cause chapter. The plaintiff may have suffered harms that most people would not suffer, but if there was a defect in the product so that some people would suffer harm, then the plaintiff can recover damages even if she is especially sensitive.

On the technical side, the trial judge's instruction could be viewed as addressing the issue of defect, telling the jury that there was no defect and hence no liability unless the plaintiff was herself an ordinary consumer. But the court holds that although governing South Carolina law applies the ordinary consumer test of the old Restatement Second's § 402A, that test goes only to the issue of defect. Once a defect is established, then other questions arise, including proximate cause, but on the proximate cause issue the thin skull rule governs. So if there is a defect, the fact that the plaintiff suffered more than ordinary consumers would suffer is of no consequence. Presumably, a defect could be found quite readily, since ordinary consumers would suffer *some* harm from inhaling the fumes, even if they would not suffer such extreme harm. Once again, in other words, it may be important to know whether we are addressing the issue of defectiveness or some other issue.

Allergic reactions and "defectiveness." Query whether a product would be defective if it created a risk of serious skin rash for one user out of 100,000 and the manufacturer knew of this risk. The manufacturer in such a case knows of the risk but does not know which customers will suffer the reaction. If the manufacturer provides some appropriate warning that a small number of people may be allergic, is the productive defective?

Some cases have said that the product is not defective when only a small group of people would suffer adverse reactions to it. This made – and makes– some kind of sense under the law of warranty and its reliance on the ordinary consumer as a standard. When the question arises under the contemporary risk-utility assessment, however, rules exculpating the manufacturer unless the allergy is common are unnecessary. Courts can simply weigh the likelihood and potential seriousness and extent harm (many people? few people?). If few people would be harmed and those not seriously, perhaps no product redesign is called for, but maybe a warning is. But if the harm is serious, the answer might be different. Small groups are entitled to reasonable care. *See* DOBBS ON TORTS § 363, p. 1008 (2000). On allergies and against strict liability, *see* Henderson, *Process Norms in Products Litigation: Liability for Allergic Reactions*, 51 U. PITT. L. REV. 761 (1990).

STAHLECKER V. FORD MOTOR CO., 667 N.W.2d 244 (Neb. 2003)

Like *Vaughn,* this case presents a scope of risk/scope of duty issue unrelated to misuse. This one emphasizes, not the type of harm suffered so much as the intervening criminal act. On the negligence claim the court concludes that there was no duty under the general rule that there is no duty to control third persons in the absence of a relationship to such a person or control over the premises. On the strict liability claim the court seems to have the same idea in mind, but says there was no causal relationship between defect and harm, suggesting that it is thinking more in terms of efficient intervening cause expressions than scope-of-risk, scope-of-duty ideas. That's no surprise, even though the court insists that foreseeability on the duty issue and foreseeability on the proximate cause issue are somehow different.

C. Misuse, Defectiveness, Warnings, and Disclaimers

Warnings and misuse. To some extent, perhaps an enormous extent under *Halliday,* manufacturers can define the field of misuse by appropriate warnings, since use against a warning can be regarded as misuse. How far can this go? Could Ford avoid all liability for roll-overs by warning people not to drive fast?

Given the effect of warnings in cases like *Halliday*, cited here, would total disclaimers of all liability be effective to bar products liability claims? For tort law personal injury claims, no. For warranty claims under the UCC, though, a warranty can be disclaimed. Likewise under the UCC remedies for breach can be limited except that limitations of remedies for personal injuries are prima facie unconscionable.

The last paragraph of this text segment is a mini-problem. The car would be defective if sold as an operating vehicle. If sold as scrap, or for parts, perhaps it is not defective at all. Is the product's description – scrap, for parts– a warning? Or a disclaimer? Descriptions can operate like warnings and hence the question of foreseeable misuse should be judged in the light of the description/warning. But in some cases the supplier will foresee misuse in spite of the description or warning and the misuse will be unreasonably risky. Suppose the car is sold by a scrap dealer to a teen-ager for $50. The dealer would surely expect that the teenager is not in the scrap business and would be likely to drive. That's very different from the not-very-likely case of a new car manufacturer who discovers its new product has so many defects that it decides to sell the whole thing for scrap or parts to a scrap dealer.

§ 10. COMPLIANCE WITH OVERRIDING STANDARDS — STATUTE, SPECIFICATIONS AND FEDERAL PREEMPTION

A. Compliance with Statute

DOYLE V. VOLKSWAGENWERK AKTIENGESELLSCHAFT, 481 S.E.2d 518 (Ga. 1997)

The general rule, well illustrated by *Doyle*, is that compliance with statute is no defense. But evidence of compliance with government regulations or statutes may be admitted for the trier's consideration, as mentioned in **Note 1**. Statutes may make similar provisions, as recited in **Note 2**.

Note that the rule that compliance, though some evidence of a defect, does not necessarily by itself furnish a defense, does not preclude a defense based upon a statutory immunity. A statute that says Good Samaritans are not liable for ordinary negligence in donating unwholesome food to a charity sets up a kind of immunity or a standard of care on which the defendant can rely. The model Good Samaritan Food Donation Act is 42 U.S.C.A. § 12672.

Advocates of limiting tort liability have repeatedly suggested that evidence of the defendant's compliance with a statute regulating product safety should be a complete defense, not merely an item of factor in judging defectiveness. What problems would you anticipate about this? *See* Teresa Moran Schwartz, *The Role of Federal Safety Regulations in Products Liability Actions*, 41 VAND. L. REV. 1121 (1988), arguing that regulatory standards should not be either conclusively or presumptively adequate safety measures, partly because they are too general and often ambiguous and partly because regulations cannot keep standards sufficiently up to date. What other matters should be considered and how do you evaluate the following statute in the light of those considerations?

Some possibilities are: (1) a statutory standard is fair if it is as safe as possible when it is passed, but subsequent technology in the industry makes it feasible to have a much safer product at little cost; (2) the statutory standard is inadequately drafted, without enough knowledge about industrial feasibility or consumer safety needs; (3) the industry whose product is regulated by the statute is the chief lobbyist and the legislature never hears about different possible standards; (4) the statute provides for many safety features but says nothing about others; it provides for brakes, headlights, and windshield wipers on cars but says nothing about whether the gas tank should be protected from crashes; (5) the statute was never intended to do more than set *minimum* standards.

Many first year students seem to be naive about how statutes and regulations are passed and about the length of time involved in the process. The "agency capture" theory sometimes seems right and sometimes not, but it is at least a risk that the industry being regulated is also effectively drafting the regulations. See, discussing the theory and some of the literature, *Wood v. General Motors Corp.*, 865 F.2d 395 (1st Cir. 1988).

A concrete example may suggest some of the difficulties in making compliance with statute or regulation a conclusive defense. In *Garcia v. Rivera,* 541 N.Y.S.2d 880 (App. Div. 1989) where the plaintiff, a passenger in a car, was quite seriously injured when the vehicle in which he was riding struck the rear of a large tractor-trailer unit, the bumper of which was so high that the trailer could "override" the car. In an extreme case, the effect would be that the portion of the car above the hood level would be sheared off. In *Garcia* the trailer merely "invaded" the passenger compartment, leaving the plaintiff blinded in one eye, with fractures of his skull and other bones, and with disfigurement. The claim was that the trailer should have been designed with a lower bumper to prevent such "override" by the trailer.

The defense was that the bumper design complied with federal standards expressed in 49 CFR § 393.86. That standard was promulgated in 1953, some thirty years before the accident. Since that time much dissatisfaction had been expressed with the standard, and the National Highway Traffic Safety Administration itself proposed to strengthen the requirements in 1967. It announced a proposed new standard two years later, but then in two more years, 1971, it seems to have bowed to the industry objections that changing bumper designs would be too costly. It terminated consideration of the proposed changes at that time, even though it had also concluded that the changes could save 50-100 lives. Congress held hearings after that and new proposals were made in the 1980s, partly in the light of further studies and partly in the light of developing bumper technology in Europe. But for whatever reasons, the new proposals were never enacted. Perhaps this is explicable by the ideology of the administration; perhaps it is explicable because the new proposals were themselves inadequate or cost too much. Either way, however, the history of a concrete regulatory statute suggests that few statutes should be given too much deference.

(In *Garcia* itself, the trial court's denial of the defendant's summary judgment motion was reversed on appeal. The appellate court held that the plaintiff failed to establish that a defect in the bumper caused his enhanced injuries.

Note 2.   Some particular statutes on special causes of action may provide for a complete compliance defense. *See* 42 U.S.C.A. § 300aa-22 (national vaccine injury statute, compliance with FDA regulations leads to presumption of adequate warning, etc.). Michigan's statute provides an absolute defense — not a "presumption"– in suits against drug companies if the drug at issue had been approved by the FDA without fraud or bribery on the part of the defendant. This was held constitutional as against an improper delegation of power argument in *Taylor v. SmithKline Beecham Corp.*, 658 N.W.2d 127 (Mich. 2003). A statute might also of course establish some particular affirmative defense by reference to a statutory rule, in effect providing that a defendant who does X shall not be liable.

Note 3. In *Ramirez*, cited here, the defendant targeted Spanish-speaking groups by using ads in Spanish. The court held, however, that the defendant was under no duty to provide necessary warnings in any language besides English. The result was defended on the ground that the federal statute provided only for English-language warnings. Can this be right, on the basis of the statute or otherwise?

B. "Preemption" of Liability Rules by Compliance with Overriding Law

Preemption is important as constitutional doctrine, but for our purposes, preemption is primarily an *effect* and that effect is to say that compliance with federal statute is a complete defense to any state-law claim. The course in torts is not the place to study the reasoning of courts or the constitutional dimensions of preemption, but it is professionally important to recognize that the compliance with statute defense may be effectuated under the completely different doctrine of preemption.

Federal preemption. This paragraph is only background to help first-year students get the hang of the idea. *Medtronic, Inc. v. Lohr*, cited here, held that the Medical Device Amendments of 1976 did not preempt the plaintiff's claim that the defendant's pacemaker was defective. The technical statutory construction is interesting, but too complex to warrant treatment in the casebook.

Effect in products cases. The main point of the casebook's presentation of preemption is in these paragraphs. When a federal statutory standard preempts the state standard, the federal standard becomes the *only* standard, so compliance with that standard is in effect a defense to the state tort law claim. The second paragraph under this heading discusses two big Supreme Court cases (*Geier and Riegel v. Medtronic*) that raised preemption issues.

The third paragraph here focuses on a series of more recent cases, the impact of which has not yet made itself clear. After the casebook went to press, the Supreme Court in *Wyeth v. Levine*, 129 S.Ct. 1187 (2009), affirmed the Vermont Court's ruling cited here. By a 6-3 vote (Alito, Roberts and Scalia dissenting), the Court held that state law failure-to-warn claims were not preempted by federal law, either on a theory that the manufacturer could not have modified its warning after it had been approved by the FDA, or that the manufacturer could not comply with state law duties to provide a stronger warning without obstructing the purposes and objectives of federal drug-labeling regulations.

Two effects of preemption. It may also be important to recognize that from the tort practitioner's viewpoint, there are really two kinds of preemption. One kind sets up a cause of action for the plaintiff that was *not* available under state law. The Federal Employer's Liability Act is like this. The effect there is to "preempt" the no-liability rules or the defenses created by state law. The other kind preemption sets limits to liabilities. In effect, this second kind of preemptive statute says that the defendant can NOT be held liable if it complies with some minimal standard set by federal law. This is the kind of preemption under consideration here because this kind of preemption is in effect a compliance-with-statute defense.

Distinguish: state law rejection of claims that meet federal standards. If a claim is not preempted by federal law the plaintiff can present her claim, but of course she may lose on any number of grounds not associated with preemption. One interesting possibility is that the state's product liability law might itself choose the federal regulatory standard as the measure of defectiveness. So if the plaintiff complied with a federal regulation –producing a car with a federally acceptable seatbelt, for example– the state might deny the claim by incorporating the federal standard into state products liability law. This is what the court did in *Doyle*, supra.

What is and is not regulated and therefore preempted? Characterizing "aspects of performance." A federal regulation governs standards for automobile seatbelts. The defendant complies with the seatbelt requirement. The plaintiff is rendered quadriplegic when a car manufactured by the defendant overturns and the plaintiff's head strikes the roof of the car. She asserts that the seatbelt is defective because it should have restrained such a bodily movement. The statute seems to provide for preemption to exclude state law that regulates the "the same aspect of performance" as covered by the federal regulation. Since the federal regulation covered "seatbelt standards" you might think that no state law rule could regulate "seatbelt standards."

But notice the statutory language: it is the "same aspect of *performance*" that the state must not regulate. Perhaps the seatbelt performance regulated by the statute is performance of seatbelts to protect against ejection or harm done in front-end collisions, not performance in rollover cases. In *Hernandez-Gomez v. Leonardo*, 917 P.2d 238 (Ariz. 1996), the court on such facts concluded that the federal statute did not expressly preempt the claim. Part of the reasoning was that the seatbelt standard "does not address the performance aspect at issue:... rollover protection. ..."

FYI: Bases for finding preemption. In the case of many federal statutes, Congress has not said in so many words that it intended to preempt state law. However, it would usually be entirely clear that state law is preempted so far as it actually conflicts with rules laid down in federal statutes. Beyond this, Congress may regulate so completely that it is fair to interpret the federal statute as "occupying the field," leaving no room for state law. Another kind of preemption occurs when a statute does not speak in so many words to the issue but might be understood to imply that states could not impose duties or rights different from those specified in federal law.

Federal statutes speak with forked tongue. The federal statutes sometimes seem to send two different messages about preemption. The statute on motor vehicle standards[5] provides that the states can not use any safety standard "applicable to the same aspect of performance" except one identical to that provided by federal law. This sounds like preemption. On the other hand, the same statute provided that compliance with the safety standards issued pursuant to the statute "does not exempt any person from any liability under common law." This sounds like a rejection of preemption. The interaction between the preemptive-sounding language and the "savings clause" language makes the question of preemption and its scope quite difficult. See, dealing with this kind of conflict in the statutory language, *Wood v. General Motors Corp.*, 865 F.2d 395 (1st Cir. 1988); *Hernandez-Gomez v. Leonardo*, 917 P.2d 238 (Ariz. 1996). Perhaps you could explain the two statements on the ground that Congress was thinking of legislation or regulation in the preemptive language but of tort suits in the savings clause, even though the two might end up having much the same effects. *See* Ralph Nader and Joseph A. Page, *Automobile Design Liability and Compliance with Federal Standards*, 64 GEO. WASH. L. REV. 415 (1996). But some parts of *Cipollone* seem to throw cold water on that reasonable explanation. The Supreme Court not surprisingly splits badly when grappling with such cases, as in *Geier v. American Honda Motor Co.*, 529 U.S. 861 (2000), discussed in this section, in which a 5-justice majority held that a state claim of negligence in failing to equip a 1987 Honda Accord with an air bag was preempted by this very statute.

If the statute (like the one in the preceding paragraph) is construed not to expressly preempt state law, can it still impliedly do so? *Geier* so held. Case-

---

5. National Traffic and Motor Vehicle Safety Act of 1966, originally as in 15 U.S.C. § 1397(k) and now recodified in slightly different language. The preemption section is now 49 U.S.C.A. § 30103 (b); the savings clause is 49 U.S.C.A. § 30103 (e). That subsection provides: "Compliance with a motor vehicle safety standard prescribed under this chapter does not exempt a person from liability at common law."

by-case analysis is often required. This is so partly because the arguments for preemption may differ from statute to statute. It is also partly so because a single statute may preempt some claims but not others, so detailed factual analysis is sometimes required. ■

Does Preemption "Nationalize" Products Liability Law?

Federal preemption is a partial nationalization of whatever issue is involved, products or something else. For a number of years, members of Congress have proposed various federal rules for products (and sometimes other tort law issues.) This can be viewed as one piece of "tort reform", aspects of which are considered in Chapters 23 and 24. It can also be considered as an aspect of federalism. Is it a good idea to nationalize tort law? In the products field, one advantage for manufacturers would be uniformity. But uniformity is also a disadvantage; one function of federalism is to encourage development of a variety of solutions. Even worse disadvantages might ensue. Gary T. Schwartz, *Considering the Proper Federal Role in American Tort Law*, 38 ARIZ. L. REV. 917 (1996) reviews a number. One you might not have thought of is a national standard makes the Supreme Court the final arbiter, so that products liability cases would compete for the Court's limited time with Equal Protection, Due Process, First Amendment claims and many others. (Id. at 945.) Schwartz emphasizes alternative routes to greater uniformity –the Restatement process and the use of Uniform State Laws. On the constitutional bases for nationalization, including the limits of the commerce clause, see Robert M. Ackerman, *Tort Law and Federalism: Whatever Happened to Devolution?*, 14 YALE L. & POL'Y REV. 429 (1996).

FYI: Other preemption cases. Preemption issues can arise almost any time a federal statute speaks on a subject. Here are some examples.

(1) Various federal statutes deal with labeling and warnings on products. Preemption issues are likely to arise. (a) The Federal Insecticide, Fungicide, and Rodenticide Act (FIFRA), 7 U.S.C. § 136 et seq. (1988) covers labeling on various hazardous materials like insecticides and provides that states may not require a different labeling or packaging. So some courts have held that no common law tort claims can be asserted on the basis of misleading or inadequate label or package warnings. *Grenier v. Vermont Log Buildings*, Inc., 96 F.3d 559 (1st Cir. 1996). See Beverly L. Jacklin, *Annotation, Federal Preemption of State Common-law Products Liability Claims Pertaining to Pesticides*, 101 A.L.R. FED. 887 (1991). (b) The Federal Hazardous Substances Act (FHSA), 15 U.S.C. § 1261 et seq. has been treated in much the same way. *Comeaux v. National Tea Co.*, 81 F.3d 42 (5th Cir. 1996) (boy ignited by Ronsonol lighter fluid he poured into a pumpkin, FHSA preempted any duty based on warning).

(2) Federal standards for various aspects of railroad operations may be preemptive. *CSX Transportation, Inc. v. Easterwood*, 507 U.S. 658 (1993), so held with respect to railroad crossing safety provisions.

(3) On the preemptive force of federal motor vehicle standards, see Beverly

L. Jacklin, *Annotation, Federal Pre-emption of State Common-law Products Liability Claims Pertaining to Motor Vehicles,* 97 A.L.R. FED. 853 (1990).

(4) The Medical Device Amendments Act of 1976 was considered by the Supreme Court in *Medtronic, Inc. v. Lohr,* 518 U.S. 470 (1996). The Court held the statute did not preempt the plaintiff's claim that the defendant's pacemaker was defective. ■

C. Compliance with Specification: Government Contractors and Others

BOYLE V. UNITED TECHNOLOGIES CORP., 487 U.S. 500 (1988)

A marine helicopter pilot drowned when his plane went down and he could not escape. He could not escape because the hatch was designed to open outward, impossible under the pressure of water. This is a wrongful death suit against the manufacturer of the plane. It claims that the defendant (1) defectively repaired the plane and (2) defectively designed it with respect to the hatch opening and access to the mechanisms. The jury found for the plaintiff, but the appeals court reversed, ordering a judgment for the defendant under the military contractor defense. *Held,* affirmed as to the defense but remanded for reassessment of the evidence.

The key question is whether the manufacturer is immune because it made the plane to government-approved specifications. The Court upholds the defense in principle: federal common law must preempt or displace state tort law when federal interests are involved and when they are in significant conflict with the state tort demands. That conflict can be found whenever the government itself would be immune under the discretionary function immunity, as it would be in choosing at least some specifications for military equipment. The contractor is immune whenever "(1) the United States approved reasonably precise specifications; (2) the equipment conformed to those specifications; and (3) the supplier warned the United States about the dangers in the use of the equipment that were known to the supplier but not to the United States."

The first two conditions – government specification and conformity to it – show that discretionary immunity is involved by showing that the design feature was considered by the government itself.

The third condition – that the contractor must warn of known dangers – is imposed to avoid the incentive the contractor would otherwise have to withhold knowledge of risks. This would not protect the discretionary functions; it would "perversely impede them" by cutting off information.

Note 1. Manufacturing defects. The *Boyle* decision has no apparent effect on manufacturing defect cases; the government's discretionary immunity goes to "specifications" –that is, to design– not to manufacturing. The note simply calls this to the student's attention. See, recognizing this point, *Harduvel v. General Dynamics Corp.,* 878 F.2d 1311 (11th Cir. 1989); *Torrington Co. v. Stutzman,* 46 S.W.3d 829 (Tex. 2001) ("manufacturing defects are deviations from intended designs and therefore cannot be considered the product of an exercise of discretion;" but federal law determines whether a defect is classified as a manufacturing or as a design defect).

Warning defects. *Boyle* deals with design defects, but its logic or policy may require a similar but separate rule for warnings. Some federal courts have said in substance that the government contractor is to be protected under a *Boyle*-type rule when the government made a discretionary decision against furnishing warnings to users, but is to be denied that protection when the government's discretionary decisions did not foreclose use of a warning. *See Oliver v. Oshkosh Truck Corp.,* 96 F.3d 992 (7th Cir. 1996); *Tate v. Boeing Helicopters,* 55 F.3d 1150 (6th Cir. 1995); *but cf. Perez v. Lockheed Corp.,* 88 F.3d 340 (5th Cir. 1996) (*semble,* if warning claim is a claim of product "defect," then rules of *Boyle* govern). Put in negative form, the *Boyle* defense is inapplicable unless the contractor's decision not to warn was prompted by government specifications. *Butler v. Ingalls Shipbuilding, Inc.,* 89 F.3d 582 (9th Cir. 1996). Other courts pursue a similar analysis. *E.g., Miller v. United Technologies Corp.,* 660 A.2d 810 (Conn. 1995).

Even if *Boyle* does not defeat the plaintiff's failure-to-warn claim, the claim may be in for trouble under ordinary state-law rules. If the plaintiff contends that the warning should have been given directly to the plaintiff, she may find herself barred by ordinary tort law under the bulk-seller, sophisticated user rule. That is, a warning to the government would fulfill the manufacturer's duty to the plaintiff.

If the plaintiff contends that the warning should have been given to the *government* rather than to users, *Boyle* probably would not apply in any event, because *Boyle* itself requires the manufacturer to warn the government of dangers known to the manufacturer and unknown to the government. In *Densberger v. United Technologies Corp.,* 297 F.3d 66 (2d Cir. 2002), a Blackhawk helicopter manufactured by the defendant went down, causing deaths and injuries. The plaintiff claimed that the manufacturer should have given a post-sale warning to the government when the manufacturer discovered the problem that caused the crash. The defendant urged the *Boyle* government contractor defense. Judge Calabresi, affirming a judgment of almost $23 million for the several plaintiffs, held that the defense was inapplicable: "[T]he government contractor defense applies only when the government, for reasons of federal interest, chooses to limit the warnings provided by the seller *to end-users.* It does not apply to limit the warnings that a reasonable seller would provide to the government itself."

If warning to the government would fulfill the defendant's duty, the plaintiff may also be defeated when no warning at all was given but the government actually knew of the danger or even if the manufacturer reasonably thought the government actually knew it. That seems to be what the court in *Oliver v. Oshkosh Truck Corp., supra,* had in mind. In that case, the manufacturer's dangerous placement of spare gasoline carriers on a military vehicle would have been obvious to the government.

Suppose the manufacturer meets government specifications for a helicopter supplied to the army. The copter is later treated as surplus and sold to the plaintiff. Although *Boyle* precludes liability based on design specified by the government, *held*, it does not preclude liability based upon a failure to give an appropriate post-sale warning about newly discovered dangers. *Timberline Air Service, Inc. v. Bell Helicopter-Textron, Inc.*, 884 P.2d 920 (Wash. 1994).

Note 2. *Boyle* **as a compliance case.** This note makes two quick points. First, it is the contractor's *compliance* with federal specifications that furnishes a defense. The contractor's violation of specifications, as far as we know, might have no effect at all on liability. At best, noncompliance with federal specifications might be evidence of state-law negligence. Second, we began with displacement of state law by a federal statute, the highest law of the land apart from the Constitution and treaties. When we read *Boyle*, we realize that state law is displaced by the specifications written in the executive (not the legislative) branch and in the service of a "federal" policy as conceived by judges. That is in a sense extreme.

Notes 3 & 4. Is Boyle limited to military contractors or product manufacturers? The Court's discretionary function rationale of the *Boyle* case is both broad and narrow. It is broad in that is covers much more than a military contractor. It is narrow in that it would seem to apply only when the government, if it were sued, could claim the discretionary function immunity. The Court's *formula*, however, if read literally and without implicit reformation to conform to the rationale, seems to offer contractors protection that would be most doubtful under the discretionary function rationale.

For example, suppose the United States, presented with specifications drawn up by the contractor merely rubber stamps them. Should the contractor then escape liability under the *Boyle* defense because the government "approved" the specifications and the contractor complied with them?

The formula does not seem to provide a category for considering this possibility. Indeed, it seems the Court intended the formula to be taken as a formula, independent of the discretionary function rationale on which it was erected.

The Ninth Circuit seems committed to the view that *Boyle* applies only to military contractors. Although it recognizes that *Boyle* shifts the "intellectual mooring" of the defense, it has insisted that the policy remains the same as the *Feres* policy and "rooted in considerations peculiar to the military." *Nielsen v. George Diamond Vogel Paint Co.*, 892 F.2d 1450 (9th Cir. 1990) (holding that a manufacturer supplying paint to government specifications for a civilian job did not enjoy the immunity). When the government has made no specifications for the product, you'd expect that to disqualify the case for the government contractor defense. The Ninth Circuit has disqualified the case all right but partly on the ground that the product was not *military* equipment! *In re Hawaii Federal Asbestos Cases*, 960 F.2d 806 (9th Cir. 1992). In *Butler v. Ingalls Shipbuilding, Inc.*, 89 F.3d 582 (9th Cir. 1996) that attitude forced the Ninth Circuit to characterize a ladder on a ship as military equipment in order to invoke the *Boyle* rule.

These cases are puzzling. The *Boyle* reasoning on its face covers much broader ground that military contractors. In addition, the Court favorably cited a non-military case, *Yearsley v. W.A. Ross Construction Co.*, 309 U.S. 18 (1940). The statement that the *Feres* rationale was underinclusive points in the same direction. *Carley v. Wheeled Coach*, 991 F.2d 1117 (3d Cir. 1993) holds that *Boyle* is not limited to military contractors at all. That case noted the split in authority in which the Ninth Circuit seems to be the only Circuit limiting *Boyle* to military contractors. However, a number of decisions have casually referred to the "military contractor defense" since the *Boyle* decision. *E.g., Miller v. Diamond Shamrock Co.*, 275 F.3d 414 (5th Cir. 2001).

If a student likes strict liability for consumer products, does she or he feel differently when it comes to military products? Suppose it is true that liability imposed upon contractors would drive up the price of military equipment, so that in the end it would be government which pays the costs of tort liability. That no doubt implicates a federal interest, as Justice Scalia says in *Boyle*. But is there any essential reason why the government should not pay for the harm it does by ordering products? One effect of *Boyle* is that individual citizen's safety (and lives) are sacrificed at random. No one has suggested that the government cannot legally choose such a sacrifice in the interest of military development, but just why is it that government's payment for harm done is so delicate a matter? Perhaps we should know the true costs of the product, including the costs incurred in accidents caused through its negligent design. Maybe the judges feel that the problem is not so much the payment but the evidence. The evidence might invade national security. But even this reason, if it has any factual basis at all, does not seem to require a rule as broad as the general defense; individual plaintiffs might be denied recovery because proof they need involves secrets, without denying all claims.

Note 5. *Feres* and *Boyle*. The court of appeals in *Boyle* reasoned that *Feres* barred recovery because the government is not liable to service personnel [for improper designs] and hence should not be liable indirectly by way of increased contracting costs arising out of injury to those persons. The Supreme Court, however, found that this *Feres* reasoning goes too far because it could relieve government of liability even in the case of the helicopter purchased from stock. The Court also said that *Feres* is too narrow a base. *Feres* only covers service personnel and hence if the government contractor defense is based on *Feres,* it would not protect the contractor against civilian suits for injuries. Yet the government interest and the conflict would still exist.

Note 6. State (not federal) contractors. If the rationale for the government contractor defense is that the contractor is immune so far as it executes the sovereign will of the government, which is itself immune, then you would expect that contractors with state governments would enjoy similar protection when they execute projects falling within the state's basic policy immunity. As the Pennsylvania Supreme Court said almost a half-century ago, "if the contractor . . . performs the contract work which the State is privileged to have done, the privilege operates to relieve the contractor from liability to third persons except for negligence or wilful tort in performance of the work." *Valley Forge Gardens, Inc. v. James D. Morrissey, Inc.*, 123 A.2d 888 (Pa. 1956). But the same court in 2000 distinguished *Boyle* in *Conner v. Quality Coach, Inc.*, as described in this note. The court stressed that the contractor in *Conner* participated in the design decision itself, removing it from the usual protections given to contractors who reasonably rely on government specifications. The court also noted that Pennsylvania has abolished common law immunity, and that the legislature had established no state-contractor immunity. In *Engelhardt v. Rogers Group, Inc.*, 132 F.Supp.2d 757 (E.D. Ark. 2001), the federal district court applying Arkansas law seemed to say that the contractor who knows of a dangerous specification owes a duty to warn or else "to decline to enter the contract. . . ." The state's specifications there called for an inappropriate grade of asphalt for a major road, making hydroplaning and injury all too likely. The contractor knew it and should have warned the state. State statutes may control.

Note 7. Private contractors providing products to private customers. In *Michalko v. Cooke Color & Chemical Corp.*, 451 A.2d 179 (N.J. 1982), a repairer-rebuilder of a machine followed dangerous specs, delivering a machine that was defective for lack of a safety device. It was held liable even though it followed the private owner's specifications. But in *Zaza v. Marquess and Nell, Inc.*, 675 A.2d 620 (N.J. 1996), a fabricator of a part to be used in a large complex machine was treated differently: "In contrast, the fabricator of a component part that is not inherently dangerous has no control over whether the purchaser properly installs the component part into the final system. . . . Where a finished product is the result of work by more than one party, a court must examine at what stage installation of safety devices is feasible and practicable." The court noted that the Products Restatement (then in draft) provides that a component part manufacturer generally is not liable unless the component itself is defective or the component provider substantially participated in the design of the final product. It concluded that in *Michalko*, "the defendant knew that safety devices were not included in the design plans and that the owner was unlikely to install safety devices on his own. In contrast, plaintiff [here in *Zaza*] has provided no evidence that the quench tank was in a defective condition when it was delivered to Maxwell House or that International knew or should have known that Maxwell House was unlikely to install safety devices."

§ 11. STATUTES OF LIMITATION

This brief section only manages to renew acquaintance with the statute of limitations encountered in Chapter 11 and to introduce the special problems that products liability suits may be characterized as negligence claims or "products" claims, or as suits in contract (warranty) or tort, so that the court may be forced to choose between two rather different statutes of limitations. It recalls the time-of-accrual problem we have already seen and the special "statutes of repose" problem. The hypothetical in ¶ 1 is based on *Alder v. Bayer Corp., Agfa Div.*, 61 P.3d 1068 (Utah 2002), where the court held that the claim was "really" one for negligence, not "products," since no defect in the product was claimed, only defective installation.

¶ 2. ***Accrual of the claim. (b) Injury or later date***. In *Schiele v. Hobart Corp.*, Chapter 11, an insidious disease case involving the effects of repeated exposures to toxic substances over a long period, the court held that the statute of limitations did not begin to run until the plaintiff, or a reasonable person in the plaintiff's position, would associate the symptoms with a "serious or permanent condition," and perceive "the role which the defendant has played. . . ." This rule obviously makes it possible to postpone the start of the statute for a long time after the symptoms themselves are discovered, if the plaintiff reasonably failed to recognize them as "serious and permanent" or failed to recognize defendant's connection with them.

Does this rule undercut the purposes of the statute of limitations, perhaps especially in the products liability setting? In *Olsen v. Bell Telephone Laboratories, Inc.*, 445 N.E.2d 609 (Mass. 1983), the plaintiff was exposed to an allegedly toxic substance beginning in 1964. He experienced symptoms as early as 1968 and they became severe by 1970. The condition was diagnosed in 1973. The court observed:

> "A cause of action to recover for an insidious disease could be deemed to accrue on one of several dates: the date of the defendant's negligent act; the date of the plaintiff's first exposure to the product; the date of the plaintiff's last exposure to the product; the date of the first physiological effect on the plaintiff, whether recognized by the plaintiff or not; the date of the discovery of injury; and the date on which the plaintiff discovered, or reasonably should have discovered, that he has been harmed as a result of the defendant's conduct . . . [or] the date that the plaintiff knows, or should know, that the injury is permanent."

The court thought that in the case of "inherently unknowable" wrongs, the claim cannot accrue and the statute cannot begin to run before the claimant knew or should have known of harm resulting from the defendant's conduct. But the court rejected the *Schiele* rule under which the statute began to run with discovery that the harm was permanent. The purpose of the statute of limitations, the court thought, was to provide a "fixed time period, " a purpose that would be subverted by the permanency rule.

Which of these two rules is better? Does the "fixed time period" policy suggest that the discovery rule is also vulnerable to attack? Courts have taken a wide variety of positions on the possible dates listed in the *Olsen* opinion.

Even under the discovery rule there are still problems. Compare *Schiele* with *Klempka v. G.D. Searle and Company*, 963 F.2d 168 (8th Cir. 1992). In the latter case the plaintiff was fitted with a Cu-7 intrauterine device manufactured by the defendant. From the beginning, in October, 1976, she suffered problems. In January 1977 the device was removed and she was informed that she suffered Pelvic Inflammatory Disease (PID) caused by the Cu-7. The plaintiff married in September 1978. She wanted children but did not conceive. In 1982, for the first time, she learned that the Cu-7 may have been ultimately responsible for her infertility. She commenced suit in 1986. Suit would be timely if the action accrued in 1982, but would be barred if it accrued in 1977. The court held it accrued in 1977 when she learned of the PID. The court saw it this way: "Although she did not know the full extent of her injuries, she clearly knew in February 1977 that she was injured and that the injuries were, in her physician's opinion, caused by the Cu-7. A plaintiff who is aware of both her injury and the likely cause of her injury is not permitted to circumvent the statute of limitations by waiting for a more serious injury to develop from the same cause."

Apgar v. Lederle Laboratories, 588 A.2d 380 (N.J. 1991) involved a plaintiff who had ingested an antibiotic as a small child and who suffered tooth discoloration, allegedly as a result. By the time she was 21 years old (August, 1982) if not sooner, she knew of the discoloration and had reason to think it was due to some kind of medicine she had taken as a child. She did not bring suit until March 1988. The statutory period was two years. The court rejected her argument that the discovery rule gave her two years from the time she discovered the identity of the manufacturers of the drug. Accordingly the court forcclosed her claim.

¶ **3. *Statutes of Repose.* (a) *The problem.*** You might cover future potential liabilities by insurance, but that solves no problems, since it merely shifts the need to plan to the insurance company. Insurance companies handle this by charging premiums based on this long tail of potential claims –and this means premiums must be very large, since no one can guess the potential. The premiums in turn are reflected in the manufacturer's cost of doing business, and if possible it will pass these increased costs on to consumers to insure themselves by purchasing accident or hospital insurance of injuries rooted so deeply in the remote past.

(b) *Statutory response.* This was the proposal of the Uniform Products Liability Act § 110(B). Another proposal provides a 25 year period of ultimate repose, but only for "capital goods," and only when the claim is based on defective design or defective warning. (§ 12(a).)

(c) *Constitutionality.* There are cases on both sides. *Perkins v. Northeastern Log Homes*, 808 S.W.2d 809 (Ky. 1991) sides with *Heath* on the basis of special provisions of Kentucky's constitution. The court made this comment: "Recognizing that a majority of the states have upheld the construction industry's statute of repose against attack on constitutional grounds, our obligation is to comply with the letter and spirit of the Kentucky Constitution. If that places us in a statistical minority, we can only commiserate with the citizens of other states who do not enjoy similar protection." Alabama described such statutes as "arbitrary." *Lankford v. Sullivan, Long & Haggerty*, 416 So.2d 996 (Ala. 1982). *Sealey v. Hicks*, 788 P.2d 435 (Or. 1990) upholds the statute under Oregon's constitution and under federal constitutional attacks. .

The quotation from Judge Frank is from *Dincher v. Marlin Firearms Co.*, 198 F.2d 821, 823 (2d Cir. 1952). In a portion of that opinion not quoted by the *Heath* court, Judge Frank added that the policy behind the statute of limitations is to penalize one who sleeps on his rights, but "no student of such legal somnolence has ever explained how a man can sleep on a right he does not have." This is great stuff, but "legal somnolence" probably is no longer the explanation we would hear. The concern here is instead the "long tail" on the products action, together with the supposed insurance consequences of that long tail.

Is the problem of products liability special enough to warrant these repose statutes? In manufacturing flaw cases, strict liability is imposed without any corresponding limits on damages such as we find in workers' compensation. The trigger of liability is often unclear (do we have a design defect or don't we?). At least for a period in the development of this liability, some courts put little or no emphasis on the consumer's self-accountability. All of these things combined to make some cases of products liability somewhat harsher than perhaps would have been initially predicted. But worst of all in the eyes of some is the "long tail" on the claim.

An example is *Daugaard v. Baltic Co-Op. Bldg. Supply Ass'n*, 349 N.W.2d 419 (S.D. 1984), where the court held both the products statute and the building-construction statute unconstitutional under the "open courts" provision of the South Dakota constitution. The statutes were characterized as "a locked deadbolt and a shackle on our courtroom doors." The dissent complained that it was difficult to address an "opinion that relies upon rhetoric rather than reason. . . . Talk of locks and shackles on our courtroom doors . . . makes good newspaper copy, but it is hardly the currency of serious analysis."

The statutes of repose have been enacted in several distinct areas – products, building and construction, and medical malpractice. To some extent judicial reactions in one area may tend to carry over to others, as all the statutes operate on a similar principle. Thus in *Kenyon v. Hammer*, 688 P.2d 961 (Ariz. 1984) the court held a medical malpractice statute of repose unconstitutional under a local equal protection analysis. Among the many cases cited by the court here was the *Daugaard* case, supra, which did not involve the medical malpractice statute, but the products and construction statutes.

Back in Chapter 11's discussion of the statute of limitations, some alternative solutions were suggested for discussion. Instead of the all-or-nothing rule we now use, these proposals suggested various compromises that might reduce damages after the statute has run. One limited liability to actual medical expenses and lost wages; another reduced the ordinary damages by a percentage for each year after the statutory bar.

Would these proposals be unconstitutional means of dealing with the long tail? These proposals might remind us that there has been a long slow movement toward a statistical reduction in claims – you can go back to the idea introduced with *Lord v. Lovett* (Chapter 7) and to comparative negligence (Chapter 9) to find similarities. If you would be willing to let the plaintiff recover a percentage of his damages when causation is uncertain, why not a percentage when suit is brought long after the defendant's sale of the product?

But even if you like this idea, what about the last of the proposals – let everyone purchase insurance against the possibility of a barred action? Wouldn't that just pin the "long tail" on another donkey?

(d) Continuing duty to warn. In *Watkins v. Ford Motor Co.,* 190 F.3d 1213 (11th Cir. 1999), Georgia's 10-year statute of repose for design defect claims was held inapplicable to a failure-to-warn claim. The court reasoned that a manufacturer's duty under Georgia law to warn of dangers is a continuing one, which may arise decades after the first sale of the product.

Subchapter D. Scope of Products Liability

§ 12. BEYOND THE MANUFACTURER OF NEW GOODS

In the first part of this section, materials are compacted, but they contain some concrete legal information and rules. Even where rules cannot be stated, it is easy to spot the central issues and to understand the range of answers. In the latter part of the section, though, we move back toward some problems of determining what is a defect. If services are to be covered, how will we judge which services are defective?

A. Tangible Goods and Property

¶ 1. ***Distributors and only distributors.*** This should be self-explanatory, but you may wish to make sure students understand this point. If there are any special products liability rules to be applied, they apply only to people who are considered "distributors." So-called "casual sellers" are not covered. This means that even a business may not be covered by the products rules if the defective product it sold was not something it usually sells, as the *Griffin Industries* case cited here makes clear.

¶ 2. ***Retailers, wholesalers, component manufacturers.*** *Retailers.* Recall that in earlier days, a buyer would be in privity with his retailer and so might get the benefits of strict liability based on an express or implied warranty. That is still so, of course. In addition, retailers have been subjected to strict tort liability. 2 MADDEN & OWEN ON PRODUCTS LIABILITY, § 19:1 (3d ed) contains a good brief summary. As Madden and Owen point out in the same section, statutes in a number of states protect retailers to some extent. But the statutory protection is usually withdrawn if the retailer is himself had some control over the product's design or condition and if the manufacturer is insolvent or beyond the reach of local process. See, e.g., *Claypotch v. Heller, Inc.,* 823 A.2d 844 (N.J. Super. 2003).

Components. The defective component of course invites liability; an altimeter that doesn't work foreseeably leads to an airplane's crash. But a component that is not defective in itself does not become defective merely because it is to be part of a larger machine that requires safety devices. The component manufacturer in such a case is neither required to provide the safety device nor to warn the builder of the integrated machinery. *Zaza v. Marquess and Nell,* Inc., 675 A.2d 620 (N.J. 1996). A component part manufacturer may, however, be liable to the ultimate user if it has participated in the integration of the component into the completed product's ultimate design. *Buonanno v. Colmar Belting Co.,* 733 A.2d 712 (R.I. 1999). The Products Restatement § 5 is in accord.

Components, raw materials in medical devices. Congress has now restricted the liability of suppliers of raw materials and component parts for use in medical devices that are to be implanted in the human body. Such defendants are liable only if they are considered "manufacturers" or "sellers" of the implant, or if the raw materials or component parts fail to meet applicable contractual requirements or specifications. 21 U.S.C. §§ 1601 *et seq.* (1998).

Endorsers, testers, franchisors, etc. Except for the passing reference to *Torres v. Goodyear Tire & Rubber Co., Inc.,* 786 P.2d 939 (Ariz. 1990), the problem of endorsers, franchisors and others similarly situated was simply omitted as more suited to a specialized course.

¶ 3. ***The former requirement of a sale.*** *Gunning v. Small Feast Caterers,* Inc., 777 N.Y.S.2d 268 (Sup. Ct. 2004) held that a restaurant which provided patron a glass of water that exploded in patron's hand, would be liable for breach of warranty or strict tort liability, even though no charge was made for the water.

¶ 4. ***Used goods. (a) Negligence.*** A dealer in used goods could obviously be held for negligence in creating a dangerous condition. In addition, there may be a duty to use care to inspect the goods and to discover and correct or warn of dangers. However, sellers of used products are not part of the original chain of distribution and in no sense are they responsible for the original design, so the dealer in used goods is likely to be mainly responsible for negligent failure to warn of defects he did or should discover.

(b) Warranty. A dealer in used goods may be held for an express warranty. In the absence of an express warranty, would one be implied with used goods? And could the dealer exclude the warranty by an "as is" clause?

(c) Strict liability. *(1) Cases.* As the casebook indicates, the cases are divided. See Tracy A. Bateman, *Annotation, Products Liability: Application of Strict Liability Doctrine to Seller of Used Product,* 9 A.L.R.5TH 1 (1993).

(2) Products Restatement. Under the Restatement of Products Liability, design and warning defects are treated much like negligence claims with the risk-utility weighing. In those cases, on essential issues of liability (as distinct from, say, the statute of limitations), the distinction between new and used products seems not much to matter. But strict liability remains in manufac-

turing defect cases. In manufacturing flaw cases, then, the new-used distinction may matter in jurisdictions that reject strict liability for used products. Consumers ordinarily expect used products to suffer the defects of aging, so some conditions of a used product that would count as flaws if the product were new do not represent defects at all when the product is used. See PRODUCTS RESTATEMENT § 8, cmt. *b*. These products rules apply pursuant to § 8 only to those "engaged in the business of selling or otherwise distributing used products," so strict liability would not be applied to you for reselling your car to a neighbor.

(d) Rental of used products. A commercial lessor of goods necessarily deals in used goods for all leases after the first one. Lessors are held to the usual rules of products liability, at least when the products are "like new" and generate consumer expectations of "like new" quality, as in the case of most car rentals. See PRODUCTS RESTATEMENT § 8, cmt. *j*.

In *Nelson v. Nelson Hardware, Inc.*, 467 N.W.2d 518, 9 A.L.R.5th 983 (Wis. 1991) the court held that strict liability would be imposed upon the seller of used goods who was in the business of selling goods of the same kind, where the defective condition arose from the original manufacture or design. In that case, there was good evidence of an original defect not arising from mere use or wear and tear. The product was a used shotgun that would go off if dropped on its butt 10 inches or more, even though it was uncocked and set on safety. The original manufacture had filed for bankruptcy, so the plaintiff sued the retailer who sold the used gun. Hence summary judgment for the defendant was error. In *Nelson,* the dealer who sold the gun was not a dealer in new guns of the same brand. Nevertheless, the dealer did deal in guns and that was enough.

Sales for limited purpose. A warranty can be excluded under the UCC by selling an item "as is." Is there any comparable way of excluding strict tort liability? The traditional view is that strict liability could not be excluded by a disclaimer, though a warranty could be, and that this in fact was one advantage of strict liability in tort. Suppose, however, a used car is sold for a limited purpose —as scrap metal. Can it then be defective when it is used for transportation? Suppose the purchaser is a 16-year-old, and the car, while unsafe, can actually be made to move.

¶ 5. *Builders and sellers of real property.* For a long time, the old *Winterbottom v. Wright* rule of privity continued to dominate thought about the work of a builder or contractor who negligently constructed something on land. The rule was that once the contract work had been accepted as completed by the landowner, the contractor's liability, even for negligence, was at an end except for concealed dangers or the like. This rule has gradually given way to a rule of foreseeability. *See, e.g., Louk v. Isuzu Motors,* Inc., 479 S.E.2d 911 (W.Va. 1996).

When it comes to strict liability, some courts have refused to extend strict liability to real property sellers in any form. *See* CCH Products Liability Reporter ¶ 4180; 2 MADDEN & OWEN ON PRODUCTS LIABILITY § 20:8 (3d ed.).

Distinguish sales of products to be incorporated in buildings. The seller of asbestos that is later incorporated into a building, for example, may be liable because asbestos is dangerous. E.g., *U.S. Gypsum Co. v. Mayor and City Council of Baltimore,* 647 A.2d 405 (Md. 1994). Some discussions do not draw this distinction clearly and some courts have not passed on the question. *See,* collecting cases, *Annotation, Recovery, Under Strict Liability in Tort, for Injury or Damage Caused by Defects in Building or Land,* 25 A.L.R.4TH 351 (1983).

¶ **6. *Lessors of real property.*** *Becker* never gained support on its facts, but managed to last in California for ten years. Massachusetts interprets its statute to impose strict liability upon landlords who fail to remove lead-based paint from premises occupied in part by small children. *Bencosme v. Kokoras,* 507 N.E.2d 748 (Mass. 1987). But other courts have been holding to the negligence standard. *Gore v. People's Savings Bank,* 665 A.2d 1341 (Conn. 1995); *Redwind Joint Venture v. Bruson,* 645 A.2d 1147 (Md. 1994). *See* Sonja Larsen, *Annotation, Landlord's Liability for Injury or Death of Tenant's Child From Lead Paint Poisoning,* 19 A.L.R.5TH 405 (1994). A federal statute forbids further use of lead-based paint, so maybe the problem will eventually be resolved.

¶ **7. *Animals and animal products.*** Would the fact that animals are "natural" and not the work of an artificer or manufacturer mean that they are not products? In *Kaplan v. C Lazy U. Ranch,* 615 F.Supp. 234 (D. Colo. 1985), the judge asserted that living things do not constitute products, since their condition is not fixed when it leaves the manufacturer's control. Really? What about a breeding bull's semen containing defective genes? Restatement § 19 suggests it depends on mutability of the danger in question. Some animal defects may risk personal injury, as where the animal has rabies. Other defects may risk only economic harm, as with the case of defective semen from a breeding bull.

B. Intangibles – Services and Endorsements

NEWMARK V. GIMBEL'S INC., 258 A.2d 697 (N.J. 1969)

A now-classic case struggling with the hybrid sales-service transaction. The difficulty becomes apparent if discussion is focused on the *Magrine* case, which the *Newmark* court attempts to distinguish. But both involved delivery of a service using a defective product. The distinctions may be one of social class.

There are two major kinds of issues about services raised in this short subsection.

(1) Assuming that some "product" of a tangible sort is required to show grounds for strict liability, what is to be done with transactions having tangible products and services? This includes a great many cases potentially

involving examples such as restaurant food service, blood transfusions, hair treatments, massages, medical treatments, repair-replacement of tangible items in cars and houses and so on. This is the *Newmark* problem.

(2) Should there be strict liability for pure services? This problem is explored by questions and examples in the notes. On services generally, see E.C. Cowley, *Annotation, Application of Rule of Strict Liability in Tort to Person Rendering Services*, 29 A.L.R.3D 1425 (1970).

Note 1. Pure services. Only tangible goods can be products according to the ruling orthodoxy. So pure services do not fall under the products rules. Even if strict liability would apply to products, it does not apply to pure services.

Note 2. Hybrid transactions. The first question in this note is phrased generally to avoid suggesting particular criticisms and to invite the class to consider whether *Newmark's* discussion is adequate. There may be a distinction between "beauty operators" and dentists, but is it really one that should count, or is it, as many students think, merely a social distinction? The *Newmark* court observes the role of judgment in the case of professionals like dentists, doctors, and lawyers. This role leads to the proposition that the professional is not guaranteeing the outcome. That's fine, but the issue is liability for defects in a product used by the service provider, not the overall outcome.

The test of predominance: In *Hill v. Rieth-Riley Construction Co., Inc.,* 670 N.E.2d 940 (Ind. Ct. App. 1996), Rieth-Riley and its subcontractor, the Hoosier Company, resurfaced a state road and removed and reset guardrails respectively. The plaintiff was injured when her car ran into the reset guardrail and flipped onto its side, amputating her arm. *Held,* under Indiana's product liability statute, strict liability attaches only to products, not to services. In the case of mixed sales and service, the sale must be predominant. There was no evidence that goods supplied, such as concrete plugs or nails formed the predominant part of the jobs, so there was not factual issue on this point and a summary judgment for the defendant was justified. But in *Hyman v. Gordon,* 111 Cal. Rptr. 262 (Ct. App. 1973), the court recognized that a builder-vendor who defectively designs a house may be liable for design defects. What would make the transaction "predominantly" a sale or "predominantly" a service?

UCC: restaurant sales/services. When you suffer harm from deleterious food served in a restaurant, do you have a products liability action because it is a sale of the food, or only a negligence claim because it is a service? Or must we try to figure out in each case whether it is a sale or a service (as the "predominance" test would presumably require)? UCC § 2-314 simply declares that "the serving for value of food or drink to be consumed either on the premises or elsewhere is a sale." The UCC is addressing warranties and most of the cases seem to be based on a warranty theory, but courts have entertained claims against restaurants on a strict liability theory as well. E.g., *Livingston v. Marie Callender's Inc.,* 85 Cal. Rptr. 2d 528 (Ct. App. 1999) (strict liability failure-to-warn of allergen).

Note 3. Hybrid medical transactions.   (a) Most cases hold that medical providers are not "sellers" of these products, but rather are providers of "services." See, e.g., *Royer v. Catholic Medical Center*, 741 A.2d 74 (N.H. 1999) (prosthetic devices).

(b) What if X brand breast implants were defectively designed and likely to cause harm. The surgeon who uses them on patients does not know of the defect, but he has been given financial incentives or kickbacks to use them. That may deprive the patient of the surgeon's objective judgment, but does it warrant strict liability?

(c) The surgeon is not strictly liable for the product he uses, yet a contractor who builds a house and sells it with a defective water heater may be strictly liable. *State Stove Manufacturing Co. v. Hodges,* 189 So. 2d 113 (Miss. 1966). So is a contractor who remodels a house and provides defective parts in the process. Why the difference?

Note 4. Separate billing. *Bell v. Precision Airmotive Corp.,* cited here, involved repair and service of an airplane, but is broad outlines is like the hypothetical. The court accepted the Restatement of Products Liability, § 20, cmt. *d*, to the effect that separate billing for tangible products makes the supplier of those products a seller (and thus subject to whatever rules, including strict liability rules, the jurisdiction applies to sellers.) Is this matter of formality, how the charge is listed in the books, a surrogate for something else or merely an expedient, imposed because you must draw the line somewhere?

Note 5. Products must be tangible; dangerous media communications. The Restatement of Products § 19 defines products to include tangible goods but to exclude intangibles. Some judges have succumbed to the temptation to resolve some difficult cases by simply deciding that the instrument of harm was not, definitionally, a product, thus avoiding serious issues of policy.

Most cases deny relief to those injured from copy-cat behavior depicted in the media. In *Wilson v. Midway Games, Inc.,* 198 F.Supp. 2d 167 (D. Conn. 2002), a 13-year-old was stabbed to death by his friend, Yancey, who was allegedly addicted to a video game called Mortal Kombat. In a suit against the game maker, the mother of the dead boy alleged that the virtual reality game attempted to "make players physically feel as if they are killing the characters in the game, and rewards players when they tap their 'killer responses.'" Yancey was addicted to the game and evidently much influenced by it. The plaintiff alleged that Yancey identified with a game character Cyrax. In the game, Cyrax "kills his opponents by grabbing them around the neck in a 'headlock' and stabbing them in the chest. Wilson claims that Yancy used this same maneuver to stab her son, and that Yancy was addicted to Mortal Kombat when he killed Noah. She further alleges that Midway designed Mortal Kombat to addict players to the exhilaration of violence, and specifically targeted a young audience, intending to addict them to the game." None of this aided the plaintiff, however. One of the interesting arguments the class can get without backgrounding the First Amendment was that a game like chess or pinball would not be protected by speech and that an interactive video game is not different. The court rejected the argument, saying: "While video games that are merely digitized pinball machines are not protected speech, those that are analytically indistinguishable from other protected media, such as motion pictures or books, which convey information or evoke emotions by imagery, are protected under the First Amendment. . . . In short, the label "video game" is not talismanic. . . ."

James v. Meow Media, Inc., cited here, involved suits against manufacturers of violent computer games, brought for the for death of several students murdered by classmate Michael Carneal in Paducah, Kentucky. The games allegedly inspired the killings. The court found the games were not products for strict liability purposes. On the separate negligence claim, the court held that foreseeability is required to establish duty, that on the duty issue, foreseeability is determined by judges, not by the trier of fact, that the shooting was so idiosyncratic that it was unforeseeable, and hence that the manufacturers owed no duty to the victims. Thus according to the court, the trial judge properly sustained a motion to dismiss without investigating foreseeability (which the court agreed was a matter of probability). In so concluding, the court argued that one generally need not anticipate violations of law by others, thus treating mass marketers who create many potentials for unlawful behavior as if they were like motorists who have no reason to assume that others approaching an intersection will fail to obey stop signals on a particular occasion. The court also suggested that, had there been a duty, it would probably have found no proximate cause, the idiosyncratic response of Carneal being a superseding cause. (But duty requires foreseeability in the first place, that would mean that Carneal's acts would be foreseeable and hence not a superseding cause.) The court also thought it would like to resolve the case without getting into the First Amendment/free speech problem and that approach reinforced its no duty idea.

In *Walt Disney Prods., Inc. v. Shannon,* cited here, the court held that the suit was barred by First Amendment considerations. *See also DeFilippo v. National Broadcasting Co.,* 446 A.2d 1036 (R.I. 1982) (13-year old attempted to emulate "hanging" stunt on TV show, but succeeded only in killing himself; First Amendment barred recovery); *Olivia N. v. National Broadcasting Co., Inc.,* 178 Cal. Rptr. 888 (Ct. App. 1982) (movie showing "artificial rape" with a "plumber's helper" allegedly stimulated some viewers to imitate such an attack; this was protected speech unless actual incitement was proved). *See also Bill v. Superior Court,* 187 Cal. Rptr. 625 (Ct. App. 1983).

In *Byers v. Edmonson,* 712 So.2d 681 (La. Ct. App. 1998), the court held that, taking the allegations of the complaint as true, the plaintiff stated a cause of action that would hold the media liable for an alleged copy-cat crime spree. The critical allegation both in recognizing a duty of care and dodging the First Amendment was that the defendants intended to incite such behavior. The court noted that foreseeability alone would not suffice. Cf. *Rice v.*

Paladin Enterprises, Inc., 128 F.3d 233 (4th Cir. 1997) (instructional manual on how to commit murder for fun and profit used by a reader in preparing to kill and then killing two people; First Amendment does not bar claim in light of intend to aid and abet crime). Is this so different from teaching teenagers that murder solves problems and rewarding them for learning how to commit murder in the game?

Information suppliers. The Restatement Second, § 324A, provides that one who undertakes to render services which he should recognize as necessary for the protection of a third persons can be liable to the third person if his failure to exercise reasonable care increases the risk of harm, or if he has undertaken the duty of another person, or if the harm is suffered because of reliance. On this basis, the court in *Silicone Gel Breast Implants Products Liability Litigation,* 887 F.Supp. 1455 (N.D. Ala. 1995), held that Dow Chemical might be held liable for misinformation derived for its silicone tests, because it knew that Dow-Corning would use the information in making and marketing breast implants. This situation is closely parallel to the problem of information providers in the economic arena, as where accountants provide incorrect information to a company, which then uses the information to secure a loan from the bank, which loses its money because the accountant's numbers are unsound..

In *Winter v. G.P. Putnam's Sons,* 938 F.2d 1033 (9th Cir. 1991), a book about mushrooms was published in Britain. The defendant bought copies of the book and distributed them in the United States. Defendant did not edit the book or, apparently, even buy the right to print it. The plaintiffs relied on its information which was allegedly faulty. As a result they ate a poisonous growth and required liver transplants to survive. Judge Sneed went off on the idea that although the paper and binding might be a product, the information or ideas contained in a book are not. Claims against publishers must be brought under the law of copyright, libel, misrepresentation, and negligence, not the law of product liability. This is because the named laws are "aimed at the delicate issues that arise with respect to intangibles such as ideas and expressions," while products liability law "is geared to the tangible world."

Henderson, *Extending the Boundaries of Strict Products Liability: Implications of the Theory of The Second Best,* 128 U. Pa. L. Rev. 1036 (1980) used economic arguments to suggest caution in extending strict liability to services and similar cases. One example: If repairers of houses were held strictly liable, do-it-yourself repairs would become more attractive – "attract consumers at the margin," (p. 1079). This might be so because if repairers were strictly liable, their charges for work would reflect the increased costs of strict liability. Some homeowners would find this too expensive and would substitute some other "activity" –their own labor in this instance. But their own labor might be riskier overall than that of experienced contractors. Their labor would not bear strict liability costs, and it would be deceptively cheaper, perhaps not actually cheaper when we add in the cost of injury. Thus the extension of strict liability to repairers might lead homeowners into riskier substitutes, with greater harm to themselves and greater distortion of the economics involved. You might add that it is very likely that the people who would bear the brunt of this extra cost would be poorer rather than richer people. Daddy Warbucks probably will not paint his own house, but a lot of older and poorer people will. The increased injury would be borne by those people rather than by those whose time is too valuable to permit such activities.

Note 6. Should some providers be strictly liable for pure service defects? The hybrid sales-service cases mainly raise line-drawing problems. This note asks students to consider the more fundamental question whether even pure services, with no sales and goods involved at all, should be exempt from a strict liability regime?

The slippery slope argument suggests that no distinction between services and services-with-product is justifiable.

Professor Furrow argued that psychiatry exposes the patient to a significant risk of harm. He describes the "Deterioration Effect" occurring in some patients and argues for strict liability. Would there be problems in determining what services are defective and whether the "defect" caused the harm? Professor Furrow believes that courts could develop workable and fair rules to deal with these questions. Furrow, *Defective Mental Treatment: A Proposal for the Application of Strict Liability to Psychiatric Services,* 58 B.U. L. REV. 391(1978). In Greenfield, *Consumer Protection in Service Transactions – Implied Warranties and Strict Liability in Torts,* 1974 UTAH L. REV. 661, the proposal is to extend strict liability to services generally.

Dean Powers argued that services or hybrid transactions can be brought within strict liability rules or not, depending on the rationale behind strict liability. He rejects some of the rationales for products strict liability on the ground that they fail to distinguish products from other cases. The risk-spreading rationale is like this in his view, since it would also call for strict liability in some cases involving neither products nor services. On the other hand, two rationales are important. The first is consumer expectation. If consumer expectations are emphasized, even pure service transactions might be brought within the rules of strict liability. If this is rejected, the remaining rationale is that strict liability is justified in products cases because once a defect is shown, negligence is fairly likely and because the plaintiff will typically have a difficult time in proving the negligence of a distant manufacturer. This rationale works equally for some hybrid sales-service transactions. It could, in Professor Powers' view, then form the basis for courts decision to apply strict liability rules or to reject them in favor of negligence. William C. Powers, *Distinguishing between Products and Services in Strict Liability,* 62 N.C. L. REV. 415 (1984).

Against strict liability in many services cases is the difficulty of proving a defect. This is surely a problem whenever services are known to have uncertain outcomes, like legal services and medical services.

Electricity. Courts have not regarded electricity to be in the category of "ultrahazardous activities." The Products Restatement, § 19(a), provides that electricity is a product when "the context of [its] distribution and use is sufficiently analogous to the distribution and use of tangible personal property that it is appropriate to apply the rules stated in this Restatement." *Monroe v. Savannah Electric and Power Co.*, 471 S.E.2d 854 (Ga. 1996) held that electricity was a product but that since it had not been sold – it was in power lines touched by metal– no strict liability would attach. But to say it is a product is not necessarily to impose strict liability. Courts usually do not do so when someone touches a power line, for example. *See Houston Lighting & Power Co. v. Reynolds*, 765 S.W.2d 784 (Tex. 1988). And some courts have denied that electricity is a product at all. *Otte v. Dayton Power & Light Co.*, 523 N.E.2d 835 (Ohio 1988).

Would it make sense to hold the electric company strictly liable for substantial and damaging power surges? In *Ransome v. Wisconsin Elec. Power Co.*, 275 N.W.2d 641 (Wis. 1979), there was an electrical overload which caused a house fire. Strict tort liability was held to apply to "defective" electricity. Wisconsin imposed liability for "defective" electricity and in *Beacon Bowl, Inc. v. Wisconsin Elec. Power Co.*, 501 N.W.2d 788 (Wis. 1993) (spikes in electricity caused fire; consumer expectation test). Similarly, in *Stein v. Southern California Edison Co.*, 8 Cal. Rptr. 2d 907 (Ct. App. 1992), an electrical overload hit the plaintiff's electrical meter, causing a fire. The debate there was over the supposed rule that electricity becomes a product subject to strict liability only when it passes through the customer's meter. Since it did not pass through the meter and hence was not sold, the defendant argued that the electricity was merely a "service" or at least not subject to strict liability. The court held, however, that strict liability could be imposed for damage it does after it leaves the "control" of the utility.

The Council of European Communities (the European Union) adopted a products liability directive that includes electricity within its definition of product. *See* Alfred E. Mottur, *The European Product Liability Directive: a Comparison with U.S. Law, an Analysis of its Impact on Trade, and a Recommendation for Reform So as to Accomplish Harmonization and Consumer Protection*, 25 LAW & POLICY IN INT'L BUS. 983 (1994) (discussing the directive generally). Products liability statutes, generally aimed at restricting liability, exclude electricity.

Aircraft crashes. The passenger on a plane has not bought, or even leased, a product. She has no interest in the chattel or any right to use it. She has bought transportation only. This is a service. But it is a service which, on the facts, can be judged defective against the normal standard (delivery of passengers to their destination, or at least to some destination). Cf. *Saks v. Air France*, 724 F.2d 1383 (9th Cir. 1984) (normal pressure changes caused hearing loss, liability imposed under Warsaw Convention, which requires only "accident" on aircraft.)

Note 7. Blood and other body products. Statutes routinely eliminate strict liability for the supplier of blood and the Products Restatement § 19(c) is in accord.

PART 5

PRACTICALITIES AND VALUES

————————

CHAPTER 25

═══════════════

SETTLEMENT AND APPORTIONMENT

▶**Changes in the Sixth Edition.** Although this Chapter remains substantial, we've reduced its length by seven pages by cutting one main case in § 3 on contribution (*Ascheman*), by cutting two case abstracts, *Bernstein* (§ 2) and *Dunn v. Praiss* (§ 3), and by turning the *Turner* case into a shorter case abstract. We have also trimmed some Note material, even while updating Notes with new citations.

▶The **Concise Edition** cuts this Chapter by one-third as compared to the standard edition. We reduced § 1 (insurance) and § 2 (settlements) to "awareness" sections of very brief text. In §4 (new forms of apportionment), we substituted a shorter case abstract of *Safeway Stores v. Nest-Kart* for the main case version, and cut and Notes 3-8 after that case.■

Scheduling omissions. This chapter contains wonderful material. The practical professional business of settling law suits and arranging to get or avoid contribution is well worthwhile; the effects of abolishing joint and several liability are socially enormous. There is nothing we really want to omit.

If you do need to make omissions, you'll have some difficulties. These materials are not intellectually modular; all the materials lean on all the other materials to a large extent. And some of the chapter is difficult for many students. These two points suggest that if you are pressed for time or your students move at a slow pace, you might want to omit this chapter altogether. We say that with some pain, because it really is good material, closer to the engine room than to the bridge of the ship.

If you want to try to omit some of the material but not all, consider covering the basic insurance information; review materials; market-share apportionment; and the tort reform materials on abolition of joint and several liability. That would omit the most of the difficult problems of how settlement with one tortfeasor affects liability and/or contribution rights of the other. Coverage might be as follows:

(1) Insurance (pages 726-29)

(2) Reviewing basics: Notes: Reviewing Joint and Several Liability; Reviewing Causal Apportionment; Traditional Forms of Settlement with one of Several Tortfeasors; Contribution and Indemnity (738-42);

(3) Market share: *Hymowitz*, 747-52 (with such notes as you feel are useful given the limited time);

(4) Contribution after settlement: Cal. Code Civ. Proc. § 877 & *Cardio Systems*, 757-58, coupled with a simplified version of the a comparative fault credit of the kind you can see in *Cartel Capital*, 758;

(5) Abolishing joint and several liability. Cal. Civ. Code § 1431.2 (761); *Price*, (763-64), and *Turner* (771-72).

This is a total of about 21 pages or so, but it is probably too much for many students to master quickly, so it would probably require two full days and some teaching effort to fill in gaps.

COMMENTS

Subchapter A. Insurance and Settlement

§ 1. AN INTRODUCTION TO THE INSTITUTION OF INSURANCE

This short textual section summarizes some main points about insurance. Both subrogation and liability insurance have been briefly explained before. Classes seem to understand this material. You can assign it without devoting class time to it except to answer questions.

§ 2. SETTLEMENT AND NEGOTIATION

Preliminary Note:

Many potential tort claims are not even asserted; those asserted are almost all settled; those that go as far as a suit are almost all settled, too. So settlement is an important institution of the tort system. At a minimum, lawyers must be prepared on the law and on the facts in order to make appropriate judgments about settlement. Until the plaintiff is paid, she is often under economic pressure to settle, a fact that may induce systematic underpayment of certain kinds of claims. Under pressure or not, undercompensation is quite possible if injury turns out to be worse than the plaintiff suspected when she settled. But only in a few cases can the plaintiff set aside the settlement and claim full compensation. This in turn leads to problems of administration—which settlements should be set aside and how can that be done fairly. Finally, the claimant's own lawyer may fail to provide appropriate information for settlement, as in the aggregate settlement situation or simply by failing to provide full information in the informed consent sense.

There is a philosophic side to settlement. In fact, debate about the legitimacy of settlement– as distinguished from adjudication– once aroused intense academic interest. See, discussing some of the literature, Carrie Menkel-Meadow, *Whose Dispute Is It Anyway?: A Philosophical and Democratic Defense of Settlement (In Some Cases)*, 83 GEO. L. J. 2663 (1995) .

Fascinating (and sometimes troubling) as this debate may be, this section's purpose is limited. It considers briefly one or two practical problems in making the tort rules work. It is not that broader issues are irrelevant to our understanding of how tort law works in fact. To the extent that you think settlement of tort cases is likely to work against the disempowered, or that adjusters with their power and experience systematically take advantage of inexperienced, one-time victims, tort law could be seen as a very large failure, because most cases are in fact settled. But this leads inevitably to an ever larger problem, because many just claims are never identified by the victims at all and never asserted. *See* PAUL C. WEILER, HOWARD H. HIATT, JOSEPH P. NEWHOUSE, WILLIAM G. JOHNSON, TROYEN A. BRENNAN, & LUCIAN L. LEAPE, A MEASURE OF MALPRACTICE (1993) (reflecting, in one study, 27,179 negligent medical injuries with only 3,682 claims).

Neither courtroom skills nor briefing skills necessarily assist negotiation. Lawyers as negotiators need to be facilitators more than adversaries. They may need the ability to identify points on which seemingly competing interests share common ground. Cooperative negotiation may be more successful than competitive negotiation. Perhaps students should hear that negotiation practice may require personal development beyond any technical learning. Some other skills of negotiation have intense intellectual content. Courses in negotiation are taught in law schools and you can find books dealing with both attitude and intellectual content of negotiation. *E.g.,* H.T. EDWARDS AND J.J. WHITE, THE LAWYER AS NEGOTIATOR (1977); G.R. WILLIAMS, LEGAL NEGOTIATION AND SETTLEMENT (1983).

Negotiation requires intense preparation. You must have a vision of how your claim or defense can be presented, where the decision points are, and how the decisions of judge and jury are likely to come out. A plaintiff's lawyer may present a settlement brochure to the defendant, sometimes quite candidly stating the proof and the damages figures. Sometimes they include photographs. Possibly a lawyer who intends to use a film showing a day in the life of his injured client will make this available to the defense counsel as a part of the settlement negotiations.

A. Settlement

The text here is mainly informational. It may require no classroom attention. However, it may be good to emphasize that lawyers can only settle when they (a) know all the potential testimony (the "facts") and (b) all the legal rules and theories that may bear on the case. The text also leads logically through a series of small points to the improvident settlement seen in *Gleason*.

The lawyer's judgment about what would happen if the case were tried also involves, quite heavily, a legal component. Lawyers on both sides must ask themselves at the outset whether the plaintiff's case can get to the jury. There will be little negotiation and small settlement if both lawyers come to the conclusion that the defendant will win on motion to dismiss or summary judgment.

B. Improvident Settlement

The plaintiff, having made a final settlement, finds her injuries to be worse than anticipated or otherwise concludes that she settled too cheaply. (1) Does the plaintiff have grounds for making a second claim in spite of the fact that she has given a release and accepted a "final" settlement? (2) What procedure can be invented to permit trial of this issue without prejudicing the defendant?

Two prejudicial effects may hit the defendant if the plaintiff sues after she has given a release. First, the plaintiff may not be required to restore the consideration given for the release; this means the defendant, intending to buy its peace in a final settlement, is in effect financing the lawsuit against himself. Suppose, for example, that the defendant wins this second suit because the jury finds that although the defendant has paid $10,000 for a release, the defendant was not at fault. If the defendant does not get its $10,000 back, it will be out $10,000 it did not owe and will not have got the peace it paid for when it gave the plaintiff the money.

Second, if the defendant wants to defend by presenting the release, won't it seem to the jury that the release is an admission of liability? The introductory text suggests outlines of this problem.

GLEASON V. GUZMAN, 623 P.2d 378 (Colo. 1981)

The plaintiff, then a minor, suffered a head injury when a vending machine fell from the defendant's truck. She was given medical attention and everyone appeared to think that her injury was minor and that she had fully recovered. The parties settled for about $6,000. Almost four years later, the plaintiff began to have epileptic seizures. Tracing these to the injury, the plaintiff then filed this action in tort against the defendant, suing for the original injury. The trial judge granted a summary judgment in favor of the defendant. On appeal, this was reversed and the plaintiff was allowed to proceed with her second claim. (1) The plaintiff's mistake about the nature of her injury was grounds for avoiding the release. (2) Release language purporting to release claims for unknown injuries was not given effect to bar the plaintiff.

We see a new manifestation of the nature-versus- extent distinction that was central in scope of risk judgments on the topic of proximate cause. The

Gleason court embraced the mainstream rule: if there was a mistake about the *nature* or existence of the injury, so that the parties thought they were releasing a claim for X when it was in reality a claim for Y, the release can be avoided. A mere mistake as to *extent* of injury (including the duration, or consequences that might flow from it), would not suffice. On the other hand, the court recognizes that the "nature of the injury" involves at least some element of forecast about extent of the injury. If you settle for a bruise, part of your idea about what a bruise is may include the idea that it will heal. If it develops a deadly clot, or cancer, or gangrene, a court might plausibly take the view that you mistook the nature of your injury, not merely some future consequences. This is the idea the *Gleason* court seems to embrace, quoting Learned Hand.

Lawyers might easily fail to recognize a serious injury, but it does not follow that the defendant should bear this risk any more than the plaintiff. Has the plaintiff not contractually assumed the risk as to future developments? Put differently, is the plaintiff mistaken at all when she knows that she does not know the future course of her injury? Cf. Dobbs, *Conclusiveness of Personal Injury Settlements: Basic Problems*, 41 N.C. L. REV. 665 (1963).

But perhaps the policy should be to encourage settlement even if, occasionally, some settlements must be set aside. Perhaps we do not really want plaintiffs to wait to receive needed funds until they are absolutely out of pain and fully restored. That might take years, during which time the plaintiff might be out of work, suffering pain and incurring heavy bills. These factors in mind, we might want to follow the mainstream approach– or at least one that permits full recovery to tort-injured plaintiffs who settle reasonably and in good faith.

The second holding in *Gleason* was that the release could be avoided even though its own provisions specified that it was intended to cover unknown and later-developing injuries. The court suggests that this is because the parties did not really "intend" this result, in spite of the language, and that the subjective or "real" intention of the parties will be investigated at trial. But this may be too narrow a rule. If the plaintiff was led into execution of the release on the basis of mistake in the first place, does that mistake not vitiate the whole release, including the "unknown injury" provisions? You might be reminded of the problem:

> Every statement in this box is false.

If the statement is false, it is true. If it is true, it is false. The plaintiff is caught in a similar box with these releases, and perhaps the courts are wise not to be too technical.

Note 1. *Nevue v. Close*, discussed here, holds that the plaintiff may avoid the release based on neck sprain and sue for the back injury. The court's rule is like that in *Gleason,* but stated in bottom line form rather than as an application of the mistake rules.

   Hypothetical. What if a plaintiff in Colorado is mistaken about the nature of her injury when she signs a release: she has a broken foot, which, as she understands, will never be usable again. She will always have to walk on crutches. She does not know that at the time she signs a release for $100,000, the crushed foot is harboring gangrene. The gangrene eventually leads to removal of one toe months after the release is signed. She brings a suit, as in *Gleason.* Projected additional damages would be $50,000. Should the court entertain her suit? Or does someone in the class think the rules for relief from releases ought to take into account the (1) total payment (large) and (2) the difference between payment and likely additional recovery? Would it make economic sense to entertain the second suit if its prospects were for only an added $10,000?

   Comparing the statute of limitations bar. Darlene's injury occurred in 1970. Seizures began in 1974, almost four years later. Suppose the statute of limitations was two years. Should the mistake rule and the discovery rule be congruent, so that if Darlene's mistake would allow her to ignore the release and sue, the discovery rule would also postpone accrual of the claim until the mistake was recognized? That sounds reasonable enough, but if we can set aside settlements and ignore statutes of limitations, why not actual judgments? That question takes us to the *Alfone* problem.

   Note 2. Another problem for setting aside releases: how can you find a mutual mistake? The quotation from the Vermont Court in *Maglin* pointedly raises this problem. You can only be mistaken if you have a state of mind not in accord with the facts. Even if the plaintiff is mistaken, the defendant seemingly is not. We say that, not because the defendant knows the injury is worse, but because the defendant knows he doesn't know. He has not state of mind that is not in accord with the facts. Furthermore, he doesn't care; he wants to be out of danger from a suit, so to the defendant, the issue is not even material. If the class follows this line of thought, then it might want to consider whether all rescission of releases is wrong or whether rescission is only nominally for "mistake" and really based on something else, say policy or prejudice.

   Note 3. In *Bernstein,* cited here, as in *Gleason,* the plaintiff developed epileptic symptoms. But the Maryland Court refused to give the plaintiff any relief. This court emphasized the idea that if you wish to encourage compromise, you must encourage defendants as well as plaintiffs. If an insurer cannot get a high degree of assurance that it has bought peace, it will not settle. The Maryland Court saw the question as an "intent of the parties" issue.

   Note 4. According to *Williams v. Glash,* cited here, the plaintiff who settles all her injury claims by accepting a check for her property damage, in the belief that she had no personal injury at all, may be allowed to avoid the settlement unless evidence indicates she intended to assume the risk of unknown injury, and the fact that the release specifically released claims for unknown injury is not controlling. "The law of mutual mistake does not, of course, preclude a person from intentionally assuming the risk of unknown injuries in a valid release. However, whether the parties to a release intended to cover an unknown injury cannot always be determined exclusively by reference to the language of the release itself. It may require consideration of the conduct of the parties and the information available to them at the time of signing. . . . The question of mutual mistake is determined not by self-serving subjective statements of the parties' intent, which would necessitate trial to a jury in all such cases, but rather solely by objective circumstances surrounding execution of the release, such as the knowledge of the parties at the time of signing concerning the injury, the amount of consideration paid, the extent of negotiations and discussions as to personal injuries, and the haste or lack thereof in obtaining the release."

Smothers v. Richland Mem. Hospital, also cited here, on the other hand, takes a view much like that of *Bernstein v. Kapneck* court (**Note 3**). The *Smothers* court gave effect to a release provision barring further claims, even those for unknown injuries, saying "if the parties did in fact intentionally agree upon a settlement for unknown injuries, the release will be binding." The plaintiff there had sued for medical malpractice because a pad had been left in his body after surgery. He accepted a settlement and signed an "unknown injuries" release, then discovered that a surgical clip had also been left in his body. The court held his claim barred by the release.

We saw long ago that assumed risk might simply turn out to be no duty or no negligence. In the release cases, assumed risk may turn out to be the same as no mistake— you are not mistaken about future injuries or even about the present injury if you know you don't know its nature. If the plaintiff has not subjectively assumed the risk (and thus is mistaken about the nature of her injuries), is there any reason to say that a contractual assumed risk is against public policy as it was back in *Tunkl,* Chapter 10 § 1?

Note 5. Counsel, counsel, counsel. (Ever wonder why lawyers are called "counselor?") That involves communication, a core ethical duty of all lawyers. *See* PAUL T. HAYDEN, ETHICAL LAWYERING, Chapter 4 §§ 2 & 3 (2d Ed. 2007).

Note 6. In the release cases, the plaintiff can simply sue on the tort claim and leave the defendant to plead the release as a defense. Can the defendant insist that, in order to sue at all, the plaintiff must restore what she received in settlement? In *Doe v. Golnick,* 556 N.W.2d 20 (Neb. 1996), the court held that the plaintiff would not be required to tender a restoration of the consideration paid for the release if she sued in equity to rescind, but that since she had simply sued "at law" on the tort and had made no tender, she was barred. The consideration for the release in that case was $75,000. The plaintiff claimed that the release was void because it had been induced by undue influence, duress, and fraud. What if the plaintiff had spent the money in payment of medical bills and legal fees?

Note 7. Fraud, coercion, incapacity. Coercion has been pleaded in many forms. Suppose a jailer beats a prisoner, puts him in solitary confinement for 19 days, then takes him to meet an insurance adjuster, who pays him $500 for a release? On allegation of similar facts in a civil rights claim, *Jones v. Taber*, 648 F.2d 1201 (9th Cir. 1981) held that whether the release could be avoided presented triable issues of fact.

A statutory rule. Vermont statutes permit the plaintiff to rescind a release that was given within 15 days after the injury or death and gives the plaintiff three years in which to make that decision. 12 VT. STAT. ANN. § 1076. But the plaintiff must tender a return of the consideration she received. Id. § 1077. Won't that effectively limit relief to cases in which small sums are paid? – because plaintiffs will seldom be able to return payments of, say, $100,000 even if it turns out that the ultimate loss is a million dollars. Apart from the tender of consideration requirement, is the statute a good idea? Maybe insurers in Vermont will simply not settle cases within the first 15 days. That will make the statute a dead letter that can form no basis for setting aside the release that is ultimately given later. At the same time, small claims that are important to low-income people living on the edge would not be paid when most needed–$500 to get the pick-up truck running again so the plaintiff can get to work. But maybe this dire forecast is purely academic. In *Maglin v. Tschannerl,* 800 A.2d 486 (Vt. 2002) (quoted on another point in **Note 2**, supra), the insurer settled on the 10th day and the plaintiff, when she sought to avoid the release, didn't try to take advantage of the statute in the trial court, raising the issue for the first time only on appeal. This suggests that neither plaintiffs nor defendants in Vermont have treated the statute as central to their settlements.

ALFONE V. SARNO, 432 A.2d 857 (N.J. 1981)

An injured plaintiff recovered for malpractice during her lifetime. She then died and her administrator brought a second action against the doctor for the same alleged malpractice. The court held that the inter vivos action of the decedent-victim did not bar recovery by the administrator for death. The death action is treated as if it were an independent action for some issues in the case, so that the administrator is not barred. For other issues, however, it is not an independent action, and the administrator is bound by findings on contributory negligence of the decedent. Likewise, prior recovery must be, in effect, credited.

Costs and benefits. The gain from permitting this kind of suit may be small compared to the costs. The initial trial would seek to show all the damages, present and future. Unless we move to a periodic payment system like that used in workers' compensation, it would seem that reopening the case is not desirable where a fair trial has guaranteed careful evidence and estimates of loss. If cases should be opened again for a second shot after a trial, there is really no special reason to limit those cases to death actions: dependents will suffer equally from a too-low award, whether the victim dies or lives.

Inter vivos settlements with relatives? If you represented the insurer in a settlement, would you try to pay some small sum to a host of relatives, taking a release from all of them as well as from the injured person? This would add to settlement costs, both in money and in negotiating and administrative time; but from the insurer's point of view, that might be preferable to a second suit based on the same injury. Whatever relatives are around might get an extra $100 or so for nothing, and premium payers would have to pay the costs. A couple of courts once played with the idea that even this costly protection would not be available because such releases would be against public policy. This view now seems to be at least implicitly rejected. See *Brown v. Drillers, Inc.,* 630 So.2d 741 (La. 1994); *Kibble v. Weeks Dredging & Construction Co.,* 735 A.2d 1142 (N.J. 1999) (lump sum settlement of workers' compensation benefits, spouse with right to death benefits may be barred if she knowingly joins waiver of death benefits). Annotations: Wayne D. Foster, *Validity of Release of Prospective Right to Wrongful Death Action,* 92 A.L.R.3d 1232 (1979); Vitauts M. Gulbis, *Judgment in Favor Of, or Adverse To, Person Injured as Barring Action for His Death,* 26 A.L.R.4th 1264 (1983). That leaves defendants in *Alfone* jurisdictions with the cost of locating potential survivors and obtaining releases for their contingent interests. What can the defendant do if relatives will not sign an *Alfone* release and the case goes to trial? Could the defendant make the relatives parties so that they would be bound by the judgment?

Note 3. *Gershon v. Regency Diving Ctr., Inc.,* cited here, differs from *Alfone* because the "release" there is a species of express assumed risk, not settlement of a tort claim after it arises. An express or contractual assumed risk looks much like assumed risk in the "primary sense," which is to say the defendant has no duty or at least that he breached none. New Jersey led the way in that interpretation of assumed risk in the primary sense. *Meistrich v. Casino Arena Attractions, Inc.,* 155 A.2d 90 (N.J. 1959). Although *Meistrich* was not discussing contractual assumed risk, if the contract is valid, that contractual form of assumed risk would operate in the same way. How can a defendant who has no duty or who has breached none be liable to anyone, heirs or not?

NOTE: CLIENTS' RIGHTS AGAINST THEIR OWN LAWYERS

This Note is narrowly focused on limited issues in the settlement process, not on the general law of lawyer malpractice. The emphasis is on workability of the tort system. The exact form of settlement– whether proceeds are paid into a trust, or whether a release is in the right form to preserve claims against non-settling tortfeasors, for example– is not important here, although it may be a good idea if students know that there are highly technical details that must be learned elsewhere. (The issue of release versus covenant is treated in §3 below. Plaintiffs who have or may get public assistance benefits, through social security or Medicaid or otherwise, may need special trust documents. Taxation of tort awards is another specialized area. Some injury lawyers will now use tax and trust experts to deal with such issues.)

Aggregating claims for settlement. The plaintiff has run the obstacle course— she has survived injury and managed to stay financially alive even though she may be out of a job and incurring medical bills; she has not given an improvident release; she has retained an attorney and settlement negotiations are proceeding. She still confronts one obstacle, though she probably does not know it.

A lawyer representing the plaintiff Perales tells adjuster for the defendant's insurance company, he would settle for $100,000. The adjuster responds by saying, "that's way too much for Perales' case, but we are the insurer on ten of your clients and we'll settle the whole batch for $500,000. You can cut the dough up any way your clients will agree to." The lawyer may be tempted to come to this arrangement, especially if the lawyer's estimate of all ten cases comes to a similar total figure. But the lawyer who begins to think like this will soon be trying to get some of the ten clients to accept less than they should so the lawyer can make the whole (secret) deal go through. Further, the lawyer's interest may be in conflict with the client's. The lawyer's interest may be to make the whole group settlement go through to maximize the lawyer's contingent fee even if this sacrifices the interest of an individual client. This might require the lawyer to minimize the claim of Client A so that there will be enough settlement money to satisfy Client B. A lawyer who succumbs to this kind of temptation is not likely to advise the client that the cases are settled as a batch.

What can the client do to for protection? Does the professional rule, of which the client knows nothing, help? Is it self-enforcing?

Legal informed consent. A related problem is informed consent as it might be applied to lawyers. The client may find himself bound by a settlement made through his attorney, even if his attorney did not get the client's informed consent, at least where the case is pending in court and the attorney of record dismisses it pursuant to settlement. *See Arnold v. Yarborough*, 316 S.E.2d 416 (S.C. Ct. App. 1984). Any major action taken by the lawyer today without informing the client may be ground for a client's claim against the attorney. *Rogers v. Robson, Masters, Ryan, Brumund and Belom*, 407 N.E.2d 47 (Ill. 1980); cf. *Rodriguez v. Horton*, 622 P.2d 261 (N.M. Ct. App. 1980).

Subchapter B. Settlement and Trial with Multiple Defendants

§ 3. THE TRADITIONAL ALLOCATION OF RESPONSIBILITY AMONG MULTIPLE DEFENDANTS

The four textual notes deal with basic rules of(1) joint and several liability; (2) the possibility of causal rather than fault apportionment (a topic we've seen before but one that also arises repeatedly later on); (3) traditional settlement options (release, covenant); and (4) contribution and indemnity.

Although much is familiar, you may find that a question or two reveals some lingering doubts or uncertainties. This is bedrock material, so students should master it before going on.

NOTE: REVIEWING JOINT AND SEVERAL LIABILITY
NOTE: REVIEWING CAUSAL APPORTIONMENT

While students may need the review in these two notes, we doubt that comments from us will prove especially helpful. We first looked at joint and several liability in Chapter 6. We first investigated causal apportionment in Chapter 7, as well as several times thereafter.

NOTE: TRADITIONAL FORMS OF SETTLEMENT WITH ONE OF SEVERAL TORTFEASORS

¶ ¶ 1 & 2. The distinction between satisfaction and release seems well established, and we've never thought it needed great emphasis, but two recent cases show a potential disaster awaiting any lawyer who doesn't have the distinction in mind. See *Bridgestone/Firestone North America Tire, L.L.C. v. Naranjo,* 79 P.3d 1206 (Ariz. 2003); *Saichek v. Lupa,* 787 N.E.2d 827 (Ill. 2003). In both, the plaintiff suffered a single indivisible injury, then recovered damages from tortfeasor A. The recovery in both cases appears to have been a recovery of the full damages assessed in the trial. In both cases, the plaintiff seems to have intended all along to pursue the claim against tortfeasor B. In fact, in *Saichek,* when the plaintiff satisfied the judgment against A, she stipulated that releasing that judgment did not release her claim against B. However, in both cases, the court held that full satisfaction is a bar and that the amount of the judgment in the first case determines the amount of damages once and for all, so that the plaintiff cannot argue that damages were really more than the courts found in the trial against A. The principles of release had no bearing, and the plaintiff's intent to leave open the claim against B is irrelevant; she is barred, not by a consensual arrangement, but because she has been fully compensated. *Distinguish* the case in which A and B are liable for different injuries and also the case in which A paid only a fraction of the total damages.

NOTE: CONTRIBUTION AND INDEMNITY

Some courts have made the term indemnity ambiguous by using it to mean a species of judicially created contribution. See notes following *American Motorcycle,* below. Consequently, you might want to stress the traditional usage and the difference between the two terms.

¶1. *Contribution.* The common liability requirement means that one claiming contribution must show that both tortfeasors were liable to the plaintiff. As that implies, A, as the tortfeasor seeking contribution would thus have to prove that he himself, as well as B, was negligent (or maybe strictly liable). What else? The settlement must have discharged B as well as A; if B is not protected by the settlement, he owes no contribution. And the settlement amount must have been reasonable, or, if it is not, contribution should be figured on such smaller sum as would have constituted a reasonable settlement. *M. Pierre Equipment Co., Inc. v.* Griffith Consumers Co., 831 A.2d 1036 (D.C. App. 2003) so holds. These points should assist students in recognizing the problem to be considered in the Problem, Perkins v. Alter and Bain below.

¶2. *Indemnity.* The indemnity idea made perfect sense when one tortfeasor was held strictly liable for the fault of another, as in the employer-employee cases, but before comparative fault was adopted, indemnity was sometimes also permitted in favor of a tortfeasor whose negligent conduct facilitated or enabled torts, sometimes intentional torts, committed more directly by others. Courts would sometimes say that the enabler's tort was only "secondary," or "passive." The cases were peculiar at best and with the adoption of comparative fault systems little logical or policy basis remains for the active-passive type of indemnity as distinct from the employer's and retailer's indemnity. See *Miller v. American President Lines, Ltd.*, 989 F.2d 1450 (6th Cir. 1993); VICTOR SCHWARTZ, COMPARATIVE NEGLIGENCE § 16.9 (2d ed. 1985 & Supp.). However, in the puzzle created by apportioning fault among negligent and intentional tortfeasors, indemnity in this sense may be resurrected. *See Degener v. Hall Contracting Corp.*, 27 S.W.3d 775(Ky. 2000).

§ 4. NEW FORMS OF APPORTIONMENT AMONG TORTFEASORS

[A. Comparative fault– contribution and effect on joint and several liability]

AMERICAN MOTORCYCLE ASS'N V. SUPERIOR COURT, 578 P.2d 899 (Cal. 1978)

Students often get confused about the two points made in this case. Although we'll see that some courts and legislatures have abolished joint and several liability (see California's statute, Casebook p. 761), comparative fault statutes on their face did not initially do any such thing. They provided for reduction of the plaintiff's damages to reflect the plaintiff's fault, but, at least as far as their words went, they did not alter joint and several liability. That is the California court's first holding here. (Students may need to remember that even after comparative fault, one defendant may be immune or insolvent, so that retaining the joint and several liability system after comparative fault has a major purpose –the blameworthy tortfeasors, not the innocent plaintiff, should bear the risk of each other's insolvency. Maybe a different answer is called for when the plaintiff herself is negligent.)

On the court's second holding, you may need to remind students that the original idea of contribution was a rough-hewn equal-shares apportionment system. The plaintiff in the earlier cases was never negligent (if she had been negligent, she would have recovered nothing). If one defendant paid the entire judgment, he would be entitled to contribution for the other defendant for one-half, regardless of fault shares. With the adoption of comparative fault, it becomes possible to say that contribution should effect an apportionment according to fault, not equal shares. That is the California Court's second holding. Although a few courts initially held on to the old equal shares apportionment, most followed this comparative fault apportionment systems. *See* Annotation, *Contribution or indemnity between joint tortfeasors on basis of relative fault*, 53 A.L.R.3d 184 (1973).

Note 3. "Indemnity." New York and California have both used the term "indemnity" to describe comparative fault contribution. They are obviously not talking about indemnity in the traditional sense, in which one tortfeasor must fully repay the other. Perhaps they chose to inflict this confusion on the law and its students out of an embarrassment. Statutes called for contribution on a pro rata or equal shares basis. There was obviously some problem in ignoring the statute or in arbitrarily re-writing it to say that contribution would be on a comparative fault basis. It must have seemed easier to those courts to say they were not dealing with "contribution," a topic covered by the statute, but "equitable indemnity," as to which they could invent their own rules. Odd limitations on contribution rights may also prompt courts to deny contribution but grant "equitable indemnity" proportioned to the rights of the settling tortfeasor.

[B. New Forms of Causal Apportionment: Comparative Causation [?]]

SAFEWAY STORES, INC. V. NEST-KART, 579 P.2d 441 (Cal. 1978)

The court extends comparative fault contribution principle of *American Motorcycle* to cases in which one tortfeasor is not at fault at all but is instead only strictly liable. It is an extension of *Daly v. General Motors Corp.*, 575 P.2d 1162 (Cal. 1978), which applied a comparative fault rule as between a contributorily negligent plaintiff and strictly liable defendant. The result is that a tortfeasor who is at fault will be able to make a tortfeasor who is not at fault pay a share of contribution. The extension seems predictable as a formal matter if you look at this table showing how the two variables had been decided before *Safeway*.

	Negligence/ Negligence	Negli-gence	Negligence/Strict Liability
Comparing Plaintiff-Defendant:	Li v. Yellow Cab (1975)		Daly v. Gen. Motors (1978)
Comparing Defendant-Defendant:	American Motorcycle (1978)		[Safeway v. Nest Kart] (1978)

Two questions: Can a rule be just or politic that requires a non-faulty defendant to bear a portion of responsibility with the faulty defendant? How can it work, what can you apportion?

Beginning an argument. The reasons supporting *Daly* (plaintiff-defendant comparison) may not also support *Safeway-Nest-Kart*. The use of comparative fault in *Daly* worked to allow a negligent plaintiff to recover from a strictly liable (and presumably non-negligent) defendant, but to reduce damages. In *Daly* the adoption of this rule put more responsibility upon the negligent party than had existed under the Restatement rule, which ignored the plaintiff's fault in strict liability cases. Furthermore, a plaintiff taking advantage of the *Daly* rule to recover in spite of her own fault would often be imposing no risks at all upon other persons; whereas defendants in a *Safeway*-type situation are necessarily imposing risks upon others. These differences suggest that you could cheerfully and honestly adopt *Daly* but at the same time reject *Safeway* so far as it would permit any right of contribution in favor of a negligent defendant against a non-negligent defendant.

Notes 4-7. What to apportion. Be that as it may, what is to be done with the second question – if one party is not at fault, what are we apportioning? One possible explanation was stated by the Texas Court, that we are somehow comparing causation. Two possible ways of thinking about comparative causation as distinct from comparative fault are suggested in notes 4-7, mainly to show that it might be a meaningful approach, or at least as meaningful as we usually expect tort law to be. Some classes, perhaps surprisingly, have been more than willing to discuss these ideas.

Notes 8 & 9. Strassfeld, and the Restatement. For practical administration of tort law, Strassfeld's point seems strong. Although causal apportionment makes sense when one defendant is not a cause in fact of some identified and measurable harm, comparative causation is an idea not likely to be efficient or workable in ordinary jury trials. The Restatement of Apportionment deals with the whole problem by saying that we compare "responsibility" not negligence, intent, or strict liability. (This section of the Restatement of Apportionment is reprinted at Casebook pp. 261-62.) Not only does the Restatement insert into tort law the subjectivism we rejected in setting the standard of care (each person's abilities, for example), it seems to reject any measured assessment of risk in favor of vague abstractions– the extent to which the conduct failed to meet applicable legal standards, for example. Try applying that one to the manufacturer's responsibility in *Safeway*. We have no doubt that juries can reach verdicts, but in the absence of a method and rationale the jurors may simply inflict their worst biases.

Other approaches to the problem? It is easy to criticize both the comparative causation and the Restatement's approach to the problem generated when you compare responsibility for negligence with responsibility for strict liability. It is much harder to come up with a good solution. Does your class have any ideas?

–Rejecting strict liability? What about rejecting the comparison altogether, either in *Safeway* as distinct from *Daly* type cases or in both kinds of case? With the new focus on risk-utility assessment in the Restatement of Products Liability, perhaps we will hear less of strict liability in products cases; perhaps plaintiffs will assert and prove fault and juries will be able to assess comparative responsibility on that basis.

–Apportionment by business role of the risk? Would anyone in the class want to allocate responsibility in *Safeway* according to the share that these dangerous carts play in the business of each defendant? Safeway's use of carts is important in its business, but figured by its expenditure on carts or the time spent in management of carts, you have to believe that carts form a very small part of its operation. For Nest-Kart, however, carts seem to be very important indeed. If the policy of strict liability is invoked on the ground that manufacturers should bear the inevitable losses caused by their products and should pass along the loss to their consumers, should liability be apportioned more or less in accord with the relative importance of the product in each defendant's business, at least if each defendant is held strictly liable? Or, in a case like *Safeway*, perhaps not apportioned at all, and left entirely to Nest-Kart, whose prices will then reflect the costs back to Safeway and other cart purchasers? Or does it really matter, in a case like *Safeway*, where Safeway and Nest-Kart could bargain with each other for an allocation of responsibility before any injury occurred?

–Arbitrary apportionment. Still another approach would be to allocate responsibility among strictly liable defendants by conventional, easily applied rules, such as the pro rata rule. We should recognize that we often use conventional rules rather than accurate measurements. *See* DAN B. DOBBS, THE LAW OF REMEDIES § 1.7 (2d ed. 1993). So a 50-50 division might be more justified than an extended investigation of the comparative causal significance of two acts.

[C. Market Share Apportionment and Similar Theories]

HYMOWITZ V. ELI LILLY & CO., 539 N.E.2d 1069 (N.Y. 1989)

Facts: DES daughters' suits against manufacturers. During the many relevant years, some 300 manufacturers made the drug, which is a generic chemical compound. Druggists filled prescriptions with whatever brand was at hand since all were identical. Manufacturers of particular pills ingested by the plaintiffs' mothers cannot be identified. *Held:* National market-share standard is adopted. Even if manufacturer may not have sold in New York, liability is to be imposed according to national market-share. Plaintiffs will not be fully compensated because no manufacturer is liable beyond its own share (and some have gone out of business).

1. *Alternative liability. Summers v. Tice* represents alternative liability. Defendant should have better access to information than plaintiff to justify this joint and several liability rule. (Also the likelihood is high that one of the two "did it.")

2. *Inapplicable to DES cases.* Great number of possible wrongdoers in DES cases and they are not in better position than plaintiff to identify who did it.

3. *Concerted action.* The companies were engaged in extensive parallel conduct in marketing, but nothing shows they had any agreement, tacit or otherwise, to market DES without proper steps to ensure safety.

4. Sindell *and* Brown *reviewed. Sindell* modified *Summers* to impose market-share liability upon manufacturers. This will result over the course of many cases in liability roughly equal to injuries the defendant actually caused. There is no joint and several liability, only several.

5. *Relevant market.* Although some cases support the idea that the relevant market can be a particular pharmacy, city, county, or state, we adopt a national market concept as the best solution. Reliable determination of less than national market is not practicable. Nor is the risk each defendant caused (Wisconsin) a good solution. Given hundreds of cases, such an open-ended inquiry is not feasible. The national market formula will create disproportions in liability between the manufacturer's national and local market share, so it would not approximate local share liability. But the national market corresponds to the over all culpability of each defendant

. . . because liability here is based on the over-all risk produced, and not causation in a single case, there should be no exculpation of a defendant who, although a member of the market producing DES for pregnancy use, appears not to have caused a particular plaintiff's injury.

6. *Several liability for market share only.* Liability is several and limited to market share. Some plaintiffs will not recover all their damages.

When the facts and the options have been outlined in class discussion, a good line of questions might begin with reference to the court's statement that the manufacturer can exculpate itself by showing it was not in the market, but *cannot* exculpate itself by showing it did not cause the plaintiff any harm. The court said:

because liability here is based on the over-all risk produced, and not causation in a single case, there should be no exculpation of a defendant who, although a member of the market producing DES for pregnancy use, appears not to have caused a particular plaintiff's injury. It is merely a wind-fall for a producer to escape liability solely because it manufactured a more identifiable pill, or sold only to certain drugstores.

What does the class make of this? Is it merely a concomitant of using the national market? It seems addressed to the questions that arise when a manu-facturer can show that the plaintiff's mother purchased the drug only in New York and that it never sold the drug there; or when the mother purchased only in a particular drug store, which was never supplied by the particular de-fendant. At first glance this may seem wrong to many. The court suggests its national market scheme is right for purely pragmatic reasons, but maybe it understates the justifications. If all courts were to adopt something like a na-tional market standard, the rule in the quoted language would tend to work toward the right allocation of liability. Particular exclusions would tend, quite the contrary, to lead to fortuitous windfalls.

Most of the controversy stems from the perception that market-share pro-duces too much liability, or at least that it does not require enough proof from the plaintiff.

But maybe market-share liability is not enough to get the right deterrence or caretaking. Unless firms producing DES could have agreed to jointly pur-sue research or other caretaking activities, no one firm wants to do it because that firm will spend the money to develop the technology but all firms will benefit. The caretaking firm would never recoup its expenses. Joint efforts might avoid this, but might run into antitrust considerations. *See* Rose-Ackerman, *Market-Share Allocations in Tort Law: Strengths and Weaknesses*, XIX J. LEGAL STUDIES 739, 745 (1990).

Conley v. Boyle Drug Co., 570 So.2d 275 (Fla. 1991) specifically adopts the Washington view that the relevant market should be "as narrowly defined as the evidence in a given case allows. . . . where it can be determined that the DES ingested by the mother was purchased from a particular pharmacy, that pharmacy should be considered the relevant market." (570 So.2d at 284). The market share theory is a theory of "last resort" according to the *Conley* court. So the plaintiff can use that theory only upon a showing that she has made a genuine attempt to locate and to identify the manufacturer responsible. The court also specifically limited the use of the theory to negligence cases; it can-not be used if the claim is strict liability in tort or warranty.

Note 6. Concert of action, enterprise liability. This is the place to connect back to *Lewis v. Lead Indus. Ass'n*, Chapter 24, Casebook p. 676. Re-call that *Lewis* upheld a rather vague allegation of concerned action among producers of lead pigment for paint, which in turn was likely to expose young children. The plaintiffs there, suing for young children who were in fact ex-posed, were unable to show which manufacturer produced the pigments to which the plaintiff was exposed. Market-share liability in cases like *Hy-mowitz* will not only limit each defendant's liability but will also almost certainly prevent plaintiffs from recovering their full damages, since they will never collect from the marketers who are out of business or cannot be identified. You can find out a student's understanding by asking whether the plaintiff prefer market-share liability or concerted action/enterprise liability of *Lewis*? Undoubtedly the latter, providing a basis can be proved. Although enterprise liability and market-share liability resolve the same practical problem– inability to identify particular defendants as causes of the plaintiffs' harm– enterprise or concerted action liability is full joint and several liability. If any one of the pigment manufacturers is liable at all, it is liable for all the damages.

Note 7. Cases for excluding market-share liability? Market share theories seem inappropriate to, or at least less justifiable in the first two instances given here and perhaps even in the third.

(a) If the defect is only a manufacturing defect, there is no reason to think that all other products share this defect. *But see Smith v. Cutter Biological, Inc.,* discussed in **Note 8** below.

(b) If the product is not uniform, or does not uniformly expose people to risks, the foundation for market share liability disappears. The fair share for all manufacturers cannot be determined, at least without a whole different range of proof. The worker exposed to asbestos in massive quantities on the job probably should have no market share claim against the manufacturer of asbestos-lined hair dryers. Arguably, such a worker should have a market share claim against the several manufacturers who provided insulation asbestos, but if so, we seem to depart from the pure market share theory by eliminating some producers (those manufacturing hair dryers and other products using asbestos). A number of courts have thus concluded that market-share theories should not apply to asbestos products. *E.g., Blackston v. Shook & Fletcher Insul. Co.,* 764 F.2d 1480 (11th Cir. 1985). But what if the plaintiff is exposed to asbestos from a single type of product that is nearly uniform in asbestos content but made by a variety of manufacturers? *Wheeler v. Raybestos-Manhattan,* 11 Cal.Rptr.2d 109 (Ct. App. 1992) (brake pads of different manufacturers, all with similar levels of asbestos, market-share liability not to be excluded); but cf. *Black v. Abex Corp.,* 603 N.W.2d 182 (N.D. 1999) (defendants' "friction products" including brake pads not sufficiently uniform where asbestos content varied from 7 to 70%).

(c) If a product exposes only a small number of people to risk of injury, does that exclude market share liability? Maybe under the national market test in *Hymowitz* you would feel that if only a hundred people around the country were exposed, the chance that each manufacturer would ultimately share appropriately in liability would be reduced. This might be especially so if there were numerous manufacturers. If market-share is an estimate of probable overall causation, the case of the small group of victims might be a bad case for market share liability. If you think that causation is simply dropped out and the causal potential or proportionate risk is enough, they perhaps it does not matter.

Bly v. Tri-Continental Industries, Inc., 663 A.2d 1232 (D.C. App. 1995) rejected market share where the plaintiffs had been exposed to benzene in petroleum products of different companies over many years.

In *Skipworth v. Lead Industries Ass'n, Inc.*, 690 A.2d 169 (Pa. 1997), the plaintiff child suffered from effects of lead paint poisoning resulting from such paint in her home. The plaintiff could not identify makers but allegedly joined as defendants all lead pigment manufacturers or their successors from 1870 to the time manufacture of this poison was discontinued in 1977. The court rejected market share liability on the ground that proximate cause (seemingly in the sense of cause in fact) was required and that market share would grotesquely distort liability. That was so because manufacturers would have entered and left the market over such an extended time as one hundred years as compared to nine months for DES. Second, the lead pigments had different formulations with different levels of lead and bioavailability. Alternative liability a la *Summers v. Tice* was also rejected because the defendants did not act simultaneously and because not all were joined. Finally the court rejected conspiracy and concert of action theories.

Note 8. Blood products. *Smith v. Cutter Biological, Inc.*, cited here, held: (a) Hawaii would adopt the market share approach; (b) it would use the national market standard of *Hymowitz*; (c) the blood shield statute did not intend to bar market share approach to blood products by using the "its own negligence" language; and (d) the fact that the Factor VIII products were not uniform, did not prevent using the market share theory. The court leaned heavily in favor of the enterprise liability theory, but did not actually adopt it.

In *King v. Cutter Laboratories*, 714 So.2d 351(Fla. 1998), another Factor VIII case, the Florida Court held that an evidentiary hearing was required to determine whether "all of these products were uniformly infectious with the HIV virus." Later in the opinion the court said the question was whether the products were "sufficiently uniformly infectious to justify the application of the market share alternate theory." The latter formulation suggests that the court might tolerate some deviation in uniformity. This appears to recognize that the problem is not like the DES problem where injury resulted from an inherent characteristic of the product itself rather than from a contaminant.

The uniform product requirement in other cases would seem to bar the *Smith* claim. So would the useful drug idea seen in Note 9. But the court seems to have a point in *Smith*, and one that shows its affinity with the enterprise liability, quasi-conspiracy theory, or negligent marketing idea. It seems to say that because the claim is that the manufacturers were negligent in failing to screen out dangerous blood donations, and because in that respect they were more or less alike, they were more or less equally culpable in marketing the product.

Actually, if all the manufacturers were negligent in distributing unscreened blood, the case is *exactly* like *Summers v. Tice* except that we deal with four manufacturers instead of two. *Exactly* because the relevant comparison is that the defendants in both cases were negligent, and that the defendants in both cases by their acts of negligence deprived the plaintiff of causal proof. That there are more than two does not make it harder to apply *Summers* if you think the loss of proof is within the scope of the risk created by the defendants (a difficult point even in *Summers* itself). In fact, that there are more numerous defendants seems to make it easier to apply *Summers* because the effect is to spread the costs so that the ultimate liability of each is smaller than if there were only two actors.

In *Wysocki v. Reed*, 583 N.E.2d 1139 (Ill. App. Ct. 1991), the plaintiff sued for the death of her husband resulting from use of heparin, which was manufactured either by Upjohn or Wyeth. The claim that was neither provided adequate warning. If their failure to warn was negligent and was causal, then you can say that a warning by either would have prevented the harm or else would have revealed that the other defendant was the negligent cause of the harm. This brings the case within the pattern of *Summers* and the court so held, even though the Supreme Court of Illinois had rejected market-share liability and had made some very strong statements about the importance of causation and the plaintiff's burden.

Our comments about alternative liability may be true to the ideas in *Summers v. Tice*, regardless how many defendants there are; but our comments are definitely at odds with Judge Wachtler's version of *Summers*, which he sees as primarily a holding intended to smoke out the testimony of a defendant who knows the truth but won't disclose it.

Note 10. Questions for evaluation. Some courts speak as if market-share were harmful to defendants, but it may be plaintiffs who suffer most. Defendants held liable for market share will never be liable for more than the "correct" amount of their liability if their market-share is properly figured. Imagine that only ten women were injured by drugs produced entirely by three manufacturers. The manufacturers sold 10%, 30% and 60% of all the drug sold. If each woman could identify each manufacturer, it would turn out that 1 was injured by the 10% manufacturer, 3 by the 30% manufacturer and so on.

The only reasons why this might not be so are (1) the number of victims is so small that the distribution of injury might not follow the odds, and (2) the market share is not properly calculated. As to the first objection, the distribution will be very likely correct when large numbers are involved. As to the second objection, calculation of market share is a fact to be proved like any other fact in the case, and of course errors may occur, but not more so than with other facts.

The plaintiff, on the other hand, does not get the advantage of *Summers v. Tice* and that means that she will never fully recover unless all manufacturers are found and all are capable of paying the judgment. In the simplified example just given, suppose the manufacturer with 30% of the market was no longer in business. The plaintiff could only recover 70% of her damages under market share. In the DES cases this will always be so because all manufacturers cannot be identified and some no longer exist.

§ 5. MULTIPLE DEFENDANTS: SETTLEMENT AND SUIT IN A JOINT AND SEVERAL LIABILITY SYSTEM

COMMENTS

[A. Settling to Preserve the Settling of Tortfeasor's Right of Contribution]

Both the *Perkins* and the *Parrott* problems are set in joint and several liability situations. (In several liability jurisdictions, there is no occasion for contribution.) We have seen the idea of contribution from time to time, beginning in Chapter 1. Now we see some of the problems.

PROBLEM: PERKINS V. ALTER AND BAIN

The *Perkins* problem is here very largely because it furnishes a basis for comparing and contrasting the situation in the next problem, but it is no less important for that reason.

One tortfeasor, fearing a large verdict, wishes to settle, but the other will not join in the settlement and the plaintiff will not accept a partial settlement. What can be done? (In some jurisdictions one tortfeasor can settle by obtaining a release in which the plaintiff releases both tortfeasors; the paying tortfeasor can then pursue a contribution claim against the non-settling tortfeasor.)

The student represents Bain (B), a tortfeasor who would be happy to settle for his share of the loss, but who cannot do so because A, the other tortfeasor, refuses to engage in any settlement. The lawyer believes B runs a risk of being hit for a verdict in excess of his share of the loss. The ideal solution for B is to settle for his share only. But in this instance the plaintiff is unwilling to do that. B's options are:

(1) Go to trial and run the risk of a verdict up to $200,000 or so; or
(2) Settle with the plaintiff for the entire claim for $100,000 and seek contribution against A.

If B wishes to pursue this second option, the lawyer will have to arrange a settlement in a way to permit B to seek contribution from A. Examples of cases in this pattern are *Dunn v. Praiss*, 656 A.2d 413 (N.J. 1995), and *Bervoets v. Harde Ralls Pontiac-Olds*, Inc., 891 S.W.2d 905 (Tenn. 1994). Three major points emerge in the discussion of this rather simple problem.

(1) Contribution without judgment. In some states such a settlement might not be possible because the contribution statute permits contribution only when B has paid a judgment. See, reflecting Mississippi law to that effect, *Estate of Hunter v. General Motors Corp.*, 729 So.2d 1264 (Miss. 1999) ("contribution among joint tortfeasors is unavailable absent a joint judgment against the tortfeasors"). In other words, there would have to be a trial before contribution would be permitted.

(2) **Releasing both tortfeasors.** B will have to use a settlement document that will release A. **Q:** "Do you use a release or covenant not to sue?" (See § 3.) If A is still liable to the plaintiff, A will not be liable to B for contribution. Only if their common liability is released will A owe contribution. This means, specifically, that the release must state in so many words that both B and A are released.

(3) **Proving B's own liability as a predicate for a contribution suit.** B will then have to prove the contribution claim against A by proving that the two actors were jointly and severally liable. Proving one's own negligence as part of a claim is as unappealing as a jury tactic as it is necessary under the common liability rule. This is one of the reasons that B is unlikely to pursue this course in the absence of very strong reasons to do so.

Limited reasons for settlement in hope of a separate contribution success. What reasons of tactics or strategy would lead a lawyer to recommend a settlement with the plaintiff on the hope of contribution from A? One reason is that the lawyer has a strong opinion that the risk of going to trial is very high. If she thinks the verdict really is likely to be $200,000, the settlement at $100,000 may be a good buy even if no contribution is forthcoming. If she thinks that the judgment is likely to be only $100,000, the settlement may not be such a good deal.

Another reason to recommend such a settlement is a fear that the other defendant has very little insurance coverage and no assets. In that case, going to trial would entail the risk of a judgment which would be collected entirely against B without any effective contribution. If this is the forecast, a settlement at or near the projected bottom jury range would be desirable, since it would save the cost to the defendant of trying the case. Further it would avoid the danger of increased verdict size that sometimes occurs when there are multiple defendants.

Reality is much more complicated if only because you don't know the true value of the case and you don't know whether or not any negotiating partners are stating their true willingness to settle or their genuine estimates of the case value. It is also more complicated because the insurer in this example is faced with an interesting question. Its own lawyer ("you," the student) says the risks are high. But two other lawyers, whose interests are to be as accurate as possible, are saying that the risks are low. B's lawyer is saying so directly; the plaintiff's lawyer is saying so by his willingness to accept a total of $100,000. So you, the lawyer for Bain will have another pressure: your client may doubt your estimates. Very personal matters will influence issues like these. For instance, if your opinion is that Alter's lawyer is always rigid and makes poor estimates of liability, you'll be somewhat reinforced in your own estimate.

[B. Settling to Preserve the Plaintiff's Right Against the Non-Settling Tortfeasor and to Protect the Settling Tortfeasor From Contribution]

PROBLEM: PARROTT V. AMLYN AND BUMGARTNER

This is the reverse of the previous problem. It is parallel with, but in contrast to, the Perkins situation in that the present client-defendant wants to settle his share only and to be protected against any possible contribution claim. Many students do not have a very good grasp of the forces and pressures at work in these situations and it is an enlightenment to them to work through the problems and the strategies for resolution. Illustrations use pro rata or equal shares contribution to simplify the figures.

One tortfeasor wishes to settle for his estimated share and the plaintiff is willing. Can he safely settle in the light of the possibility that the non-settling tortfeasor might be held liable for a large judgment and might then claim contribution? In such a case, the settlement must protect him from contribution or he will not settle.

The student here represents A. The insurer wants to settle at or near the policy limit, since it believes its insured may be subjected to much higher liability. (There are legal obligations that pressure the insurer to settle at policy limits when damages are high.) But settlement would be acceptable only if A could be assured he would not be sued for contribution. The potential scenario that most students don't seem instinctively to grasp is suggested in Note 1: Plaintiff recovers a large judgment against B, who, in paying it off, will have paid more than his share of the total liability. B will then seek contribution from A. The object of the negotiating partners here is to assure A that he will not be liable for contribution. If he cannot be so assured, he will not settle in most instances.

Since settlement is desirable and even essential to the tort system, we want to set up a system that permits and encourages settlement. On the other hand, it often strikes people that there is something unfair about letting A settle for $300,000 and holding B liable for $900,000. Many students may take the view initially that contribution in favor of B would be desirable. But if it is permitted by law, A will not settle. That means that the plaintiff, who may badly need funds, will not get a settlement now and may indeed lose at trial.

The supposed rule —maybe it doesn't exist very often in practice because of the *Pierringer* possibility, see **Note 5**– that even if A settles, B can get contribution. This is a rule the class might see as a logical result of the common liability rule advanced in *Ascheman*. At the time of the injury, both A and B were liable, hence subsequent defenses are not significant, the Minnesota Court might say under *Ascheman*.

But *Pierringer v. Hoger*, **Note 5**, suggests a way out. Notes 5 and 6 try to spell this out for the student because experience indicated that working it out in class without the support of a note took too much time. You may still need to work through it with most classes.

On the illustration in **Note 6,** the *Pierringer* release would work the same as the pro rata (equal shares) rule sometimes imposed by courts. That is, the credit is based on an equal share liability rather than on the amount of money actually paid or on comparative fault shares. The traditional term, pro rata, meant equal shares, but it could literally be applied to comparative fault shares, too, so maybe it is a good time to drop the old pro rata language and use "equal shares." You can use the term "equal shares" to describe the credit authorized by *Pierringer* as applied to this illustration, but *Pierringer* itself happens to have been a comparative fault case more like *Cartel Capital.* The equal shares term is useful because it will be helpful for use in identifying three systems of credit– equal shares (pro rata), pro tanto, and comparative fault or "percent" credit.

Settlement documents. Applying these ideas to the problem, we can see that the settlement document to be used must *not* be one that releases B. Plaintiff will thus have to insist on a covenant not to sue or some form of release that permits the plaintiff to proceed with his claim against B. In addition, if you are in a state following the rule stated in **Note 2**, you will have to use a *Pierringer* type release to get the protection A needs against contribution.

This is a good opportunity to set the distinction between covenants not to sue and release at common law. The modern provision of many statutes is that a release of one tortfeasor no longer releases the other unless the release terms so provide –more or less the reverse of the common law rule. Thus the plaintiff could use either a covenant not to sue here or a release under one of the modern statutes and still preserve the right to sue B.

As with the first problem, this one has many reality wrinkles. One question here is whether the plaintiff would, on balance, want to accept the $300,000 settlement. The motive to do so is clear enough. Amlyn has limited insurance and is willing to pay it all; the insurance gives the plaintiff up-front funds, which may be needed by the plaintiff or by the lawyers. But notice that if a *Pierringer*-type solution is accepted here, the plaintiff may end up reducing his ultimate claim against B. On the $300,000 settlement followed by a $900,000 verdict against B, plaintiff would only recover $750,000 total (in a pro rata jurisdiction and also in a comparative fault regime if A and B were equally negligent). Compare that to the recovery the plaintiff would make if she accepts no settlement and there is joint and several liability –a full $900,000.

Here are our numbers:

Parrott's total damages as found by the jury	900,000
Credit to Bumgartner for partial satisfaction (paid by Amlyn in settlement)	300,000
Gross liability of Bumgartner before contribution credits	600,000
Bumgartner's pro rata (equal) share of liability (900,000/2)	450,000

Plaintiff reduces claim v. B under Pierringer to	450,000
Parrott's total recovery– $300,000 + 450,000	<u>750,000</u>

Instead of this rigamarole, a rule of law that credits the non-settling defendant might get the same outcome more simply. That's what we look at next.

[C. Credits to the Non-Settling Tortfeasor]

[1.] Pro Tanto Rule or Dollar Credit Rule

WEST'S ANN. CAL. CODE CIV. PROC. § 877

Section 877 is affected by Cal. Civ. Code § 1431.2, reprinted in the very next section, Casebook p. 761, which limits joint and several liability as to nonpecuniary losses such as pain and suffering. To the extent that joint and several liability remains, § 877 represents another solution to the problems of settlement by one of the tortfeasors.

A release can protect the settling defendant from contribution claims. To make up to other defendants for their loss of contribution rights against A, the plaintiff who takes a settlement with A must reduce her claim against B at least by the amount she received from A.

Clause (b) states the main objective –to encourage settlement by protecting the settling tortfeasor from contribution suits brought against him by the nonsettling tortfeasor. That seems straightforward enough. But what about Clause (a) of the California statute? *Cardio* will show us how it could operate and the new problem it creates.

The statutory solution, like the Uniform Act, is to bar the nonsettling tortfeasor's contribution claim against the settling tortfeasor (clause (b)), but in exchange give the settling tortfeasor a credit that reduces his liability. The credit is pro tanto– to the extent that the settling tortfeasor paid the plaintiff. Thus in the Parrott problem, if A paid $300,000 and there was a judgment for $900,000 against B, B would have to pay $600,000 ($900,000 minus the statutory credit of $300,000). Under the *Pierringer* release, however, we've already seen that B would pay only $450,000, an equal share. This example sets up some of the basic conflict that follows.

CARDIO SYSTEMS V. SUPERIOR COURT, 176 Cal. Rptr. 254 (Ct. App. 1981)

Summary: Plaintiff sued A and B. A settled for court costs and B later settled for $1 million. *Held*, B cannot seek contribution from A, even if A did not pay his share, so long as the settlement by A was "in good faith." *Cardio* reflects the problem; *Tech-Bilt*, in **Note 1**, reflects a change in this rule.

Please note that Cardio has been overruled. See **Note 1**. *It is retained here because it illustrates the underlying problem.* Plaintiff settles as to one defendant for a nominal sum, then with the other, Hospital, for $1 million. Hospital, like Bain in the Perkins problem, wanted contribution from the first tortfeasor, who had settled for a few dollars. But under the California statute set out above and under the Uniform Act, Hospital is not entitled to contribution. The purpose is the same purpose as the *Pierringer* release— to create a situation in which plaintiff and one tortfeasor can settle if they wish. But a *Pierringer* settlement would have reduced the Hospital's share substantially. Under the pro rata or equal shares contribution system we used to illustrate the Perkins problem and the *Pierringer* release, the Hospital's liability would have been reduced to half a million. Under the California statutory provision, the liability is not reduced in any material way at all.

The statute provides that reduction is to be by the amount paid by the settling tortfeasor, so long as the settlement is in good faith. What kind of settlement would be a bad faith settlement? One intended solely to help out a friend or to harm the non-settling defendant? It is not clear.

In any case in which the plaintiff's settlement with the first tortfeasor is likely to be less than the judgment against or settlement with the second tortfeasor, the plaintiff would prefer the system used in the California statute to the *Pierringer* release. Plaintiffs are very much encouraged to settle by this system. The tortfeasor who wishes to settle is indifferent between the two, as he will escape liability for contribution in either system. Does it matter which system is used, either from the point of view of justice or from the point of view of policy?

One of the problems the student should consider on this issue is that the plaintiff may be confronted with one tortfeasor who has very little insurance protection. When that tortfeasor wishes to settle for the amount of his policy limits, there is really every reason for the plaintiff to accept this settlement and plenty of public policy to encourage him to do so, since early receipt of funds may provide much needed support for him and his family at a critical time. The *Pierringer* solution requires the plaintiff to give up a part of his claim in order to take advantage of the settlement offer.

You can see the plaintiff's loss under a *Pierringer* release by comparing the Parrott hypotheticals with what would happen at trial. Remember that Parrott would get the $300,000 from A on settlement, plus a $900,000 judgment against B. But B would end up paying only $450,000 (in a pro rata contribution system) under the *Pierringer* release. To take advantage of A's settlement offer, Parrott in effect had to give up the advantage of joint and several liability. If he had sued both tortfeasors, refusing to accept a settlement from either, his recovery would have been $900,000, not $750,000 he would get under the *Pierringer* release. That is so because B would be jointly and severally liable. B, if solvent or insured, would have to pay the entire $900,000 and as a practical matter could not get contribution from A for more than A had.

Thus the Uniform Act and the California statute are more in line with the idea of joint and several liability and they represent a solution that will seem more fair to plaintiffs, since under the statutory credit, the plaintiff is still able to collect full damages without any reduction.

From the defendant's point of view, however, this is grossly unfair. The defendant in a *Pierringer* release bears his share of liability, no more and no less, but in a *Cardio* type system, one defendant might bear virtually the entire liability, even though the settling defendant was equally or more at fault.

Tech-Bilt deals with the *Cardio* problem by adding another layer or two of adjudication, not by providing a rule. A California statute, CAL. CIV. PRO. CODE § 877.6, spells out the right of the any party to get a pre-trial or pre-verdict hearing on good faith and in addition a potential right to review in a higher court. "The issue of the good faith of a settlement may be determined by the court on the basis of affidavits served with the notice of hearing, and any counter-affidavits filed in response thereto, or the court may, in its discretion, receive other evidence at the hearing."

The State of Washington provides for notice of intent to settle to all other parties and the court, followed by a reasonableness hearing as to the amount to be paid. The pro tanto reduction in liability of the non-settling tortfeasor is retained, as under the California procedure, but if the settlement amount is unreasonable, then the liability is reduced by the amount that would have been "reasonable" in settlement. *See* REV. CODE WASH. § 4.22.060.

Illinois also holds good faith hearings on proposed settlements affecting nonsettling tortfeasors. In *Johnson v. United Airlines*, 784 N.E.2d 812 (Ill. 2003), two planes collided as one attempted to take off and another attempted to land at an airport without a tower. That airport was operated by the City of Quincy. All aboard both flights were killed. and death suits for eight of them were brought against operators of the planes and also against Raytheon Aircraft Co. as manufacturer of one plane. Raytheon impleaded Quincy, seeking contribution in the event Raytheon was held liable. Raytheon alleged negligence in Quincy's failure to regulate dangerous approaches by landing planes. Quincy moved to dismiss on grounds of venue and immunity, but before that motion was decided, Quincy settled with all eight plaintiffs for $1,000 each, conditioned on a release that passed muster at a good faith hearing. The Supreme Court of Illinois upheld the release after determining that the proponent of the release must first establish some preliminary baseline of good faith. Once that is done, the opponent of the release – Raytheon, here – could still attack the release by proving bad faith by a preponderance of the evidence.

The court acknowledged that the statute did not define good faith. The court did not formally define good faith, either. Instead it relied heavily on " totality of the circumstances," and the trial court's discretion (as opposed to an articulate standard or definition).

Some gleanings: (1) The trial judge's hearing on good faith should not be a trial on the merits, but the possibility that the settling tortfeasor would be immune is a factor to consider. (2) The ratio of settlement amount to probable damages is a factor, but again not conclusive and one committed to discretion. (3) If plaintiffs' settlement with Quincy was motivated by a desire to impede a legitimate claim for contribution" that would be at least evidence of bad faith. (4) But the plaintiff's strategic purpose to get the settling tortfeasor out of the case to prevent a venue transfer is not bad faith.

Should courts be concerned with the *plaintiffs'* bad faith or the settling defendant's?

Can this kind of collateral litigation, only indirectly concerned with the merits, be avoided by a different rule? Yes, as we'll see in *Cartel Capital*.

Overpayment by settling tortfeasor. The California statute does not focus on the legal responsibility of the settling tortfeasor at all, only on the amount of the payment. In fact, it has been held that the non-settling tortfeasor is entitled to the credit even if the jury later determines that the person making the settlement is not a tortfeasor at all. *Poire v. C.L. Peck/Jones Bros. Constr. Corp.,* 46 Cal.Rptr.2d 631 (Ct. App. 1995).

Note 2. *Baker v. ACandS,* cited here, held that the fifth defendant, as a joint tortfeasor, would be liable for the entire judgment, less credits. It was entitled to a full pro rata credit for the first three defendants because their releases so provided and because the statute permitted the parties to specify the amount of the credit. However, the fifth defendant could not claim a pro rata credit for the Manville settlement because the release there provided for pro tanto only. Consequently, the fifth defendant was liable for its own proportionate share, $440,000, plus Manville's share, $440,000, with a credit pro tanto for what Manville actually paid, $30,000. That worked out to be $880,000 minus $30,000 or $850,000. There were complications and arguments not reflected in this summary.

What could ACandS have done to avoid this burden? It could have correctly forecast that it would be held liable, in which case it could seemingly have settled for its share like the first three defendants. ACandS wanted the opportunity to avoid all liability, apparently, so it litigated and lost. The cost of the opportunity was the risk of the added cost of Manville's unpaid share. This is not different from other missed opportunities to settle except that the costs of a misestimation may be higher. For example, suppose a single tortfeasor who estimates that he can escape liability by trial, or that if liability is imposed, it will not exceed $100,000. He therefore gives up an opportunity to settle for $200,000. It turns out that he has misestimated: the court holds him liable for $400,000. A high price to pay but one that is not at all related to joint and several liability. It is related instead to uncertainties inherent in disputes.

Note 3. Secret settlements. Some kinds of settlements raise ethical issues for lawyers. As noted here, where courts know of a Mary Carter agreement they often disapprove of it on the ground that it changes the "adversarial nature" of the proceedings; at a minimum, most courts say that such agreements must be disclosed to the court, to other co-defendants, and sometimes to the jury. With the "high low" agreement, courts seem less uniformly disapproving, but the court in *Monti,* cited here, held that a high-low agreement had to be disclosed both to the court and to the non-settling defendant promptly upon its execution. The court said that settlement generally is a good thing, and these agreements promote settlement, so a prohibition is not called for; but because they can pose "a threat to the fairness of the trial for nonsettling defendants," safeguards (such as full prompt disclosure) are necessary.

[2.] Percent or Comparative Fault Credit

CARTEL CAPITAL CORP. V. FIRECO, 410 A.2d 674 (N.J. 1980)

Held, when one tortfeasor settles, the plaintiff's claim against the other is reduced by the percentage of fault attributable to the settling tortfeasor. (No matter what A pays in settlement, if his fault is 10%, B's liability to the plaintiff is for 90% of the damages.)

Although the figures may be a little difficult, the principle seems easy enough −we use a variation of the pro rata rule, crediting the non-settling defendant with the pro rata share of the settling defendant, but judging pro rata by comparative fault rather than by equal shares standards. In other words, the plaintiff's judgment against the non-settling defendant is to be reduced by a percentage equal to the percentage of fault attributable the settling defendant. This makes the nonsettling defendant liable only for his appropriate comparative fault share. However, this is not an abolition of joint and several liability. If the first tortfeasor had not settled, the second could still be jointly and severally liable for the plaintiff's entire damages.

Suppose the plaintiff's total damages, established in the trial with the non-settling defendant, are $100,000. On the blackboard a simple hypothetical looks like this:

Party	Per Cent Fault	Settlement or Judgment	P's Recovery
P	-0-	—	
A	10%	100,000	100,000
B	90%	100,000	90,000

Spelling it out: A settles for $100,000. Plaintiff proceeds to judgment against *B*. The jury awards $100,000. *B* is entitled to a credit of $10,000. That is, he is liable for 90% of the judgment, the proper share under comparative fault. So *P* gets $100,000 from his settlement with a defendant who was not much at fault, and $90,000 from the judgment against the defendant who was mainly at fault, a total of $190,000. The jury supposedly fixed the total of the plaintiff's damages at $100,000, but the plaintiff has recovered almost twice that much.

On these facts some students may say *B* gets off lightly. But he pays his comparative fault share, no more and no less. **A** does get hurt, but he is hurt by his own settlement, which, in retrospect looks foolish, but must have seemed like a good deal at the time. Plaintiff is overpaid, but only because he made a bargain for it. **A** is held to his bargain and **B** is held to his comparative fault share. This is the problem discussed by the *Duncan* case in **Note 3**.

The reverse can also happen: the settling tortfeasor may underpay his liability, in which case the plaintiff is hurt. Suppose:

Party	% Fault	Settlement or Judgment	P's Recovery
P	-0-		—
A	50%	10,000	10,000
B	50%	100,000	50,000

On these facts the plaintiff will be underpaid. He will suffer harm of $100,000, but he will collect only $60,000 –$10,000 in the settlement with *A*, and $50,000 from the judgment against *B*. The principle, again, is to hold *B* liable for his ratable share, judging that share by comparative fault standards. And again, what any party bargains for by contract is what he gets or pays.

You can see from this second example that the problem for the plaintiff is the same here as it was with the pro rata equal shares or *Pierringer* release rule. Under either the equal shares or comparative fault shares versions of a pro rata rule, the plaintiff who settles will be forced to lose the advantage of joint and several liability. Thus if *A* has only a $10,000 insurance coverage, the plaintiff may have to forego getting all he can at an early stage in order to proceed on to trial against both defendants if he wants to hold *B*, who has complete insurance coverage, fully liable.

In short, *Cartel Capital* does not do any better with one of the major problems of unfairness than other forms of the pro rata rule. Arguably the rule is not unfair as long as the plaintiff has a choice of proceeding to trial. And, after all, the plaintiff is able to decide whether advance payment now is worth the risk or not. But that still has the effect of forcing a trial between two parties who want to settle in a system that must regard settlement as being of prime importance.

Notes 3 & 4. Potential windfalls. This note and the next taken together compare the "windfall" effect of the *Cartel Capital* or pro rata rules with the pro tanto rule. On the windfall issue, *Cartel Capital* seems superior. Each defendant is held either to (a) his contract obligation or (b) his tort obligation. The plaintiff in turn is free to contract if she can reach an agreement and if she does, she gets the benefits and burdens of her contract. If no contract controls, she recovers the defendant's legal obligation. From this perspective, no one gets a windfall.

But the pro tanto rule creates the opposite situation. That is because the settlement of A under the pro tanto rule can operate to fully relieve a non-settling tortfeasor of all liability. In *Dobson v. Camden*, sketched in **Note 4**, the court thought that the pro tanto rule, as applied to § 1983 actions, would violate federal policies. The § 1983 plaintiff "deserves, in some moral sense, to be made whole," and in addition, § 1983 is intended to deter constitutional violations. To enhance deterrence, the court thought that it would not be appropriate to relieve a non-settling defendant of his share of responsibility because of payments made by other tortfeasors.

Note 5. The problem of settlement with underinsured tortfeasor. As a solution to most problems, the *Cartel Capital* rule seems to come out better than the pro tanto rule. But that rule does nothing to solve the plaintiff's problem when he has a chance to settle with an underinsured tortfeasor for substantially all the tortfeasors assets. Notice that the non-settling defendant is not prejudiced by this settlement,since he could get no more in contribution than the plaintiff gets in settlement. In this situation, the pro tanto rule of the Uniform Act (*Cardio*, the California statute) looks pretty good.

Note 6. Trial: What should the jury know about settlements? This issue is crucial in many cases. Before you dismiss this as a piddling matter of trial practice, consider whether the difficulties on this point suggest that the tort system, at least in complex cases, is simply too unlikely to deliver fair results. If it cannot do so, no amount of theory will sustain its claim to do justice. (This issue is also touched upon in the earlier Note on secret settlements.)

What does the jury think when the evidence shows negligence on the part of both the hospital who is not a party, and the doctor who is? That the hospital has settled, indicating that the hospital alone was responsible? That the hospital has settled, indicating that both were responsible? That the hospital's payment reflects half the damages? Might it imagine a settlement bigger than was in fact made? Or that the absent party has no money and will never be held liable? Would these possibilities affect the jury's decision about the existence and extent of liability for the defendant who is before it?

This problem is minimized or even eliminated where joint and several liability is abolished and the jury is instructed merely to determine percentage fault of each party and allocated liability accordingly. In that case, prior settlements make sense to the jury and their absence is irrelevant. In the regime of joint and several liability, however, the issue is of considerable concern.

A lot of courts support the view that the jury should be told nothing. See e.g., *Holger v. Irish,* 851 P.2d 1122 (Or. 1993). For difficulties in maintaining the don't-tell rule, see the discussion of *Belton v. Fibreboard Corp.,* 724 F.2d 500 (5th Cir. 1984). In *Quirion v.Forcier,* 632 A.2d 365 (Vt. 1993), the court left a measure of discretion to the trial judge to admit evidence of settlement, at least where the settlement might affect credibility of a witness.

§ 6. MULTIPLE DEFENDANTS: SETTLEMENT AND SUIT (MOSTLY) IN A PROPORTIONATE SHARE SYSTEM

COMMENTS

A. Abolishing or Limiting Joint and Several Liability

CAL. CIV. CODE § 1431.2.

In injury, death, and property damage claims, the liability of joint tortfeasors is hereafter made to be several, not joint, as to the recovery for *noneconomic* damages such as pain and suffering damages. For such damages, each tortfeasor is liable for his or her percentage share only.

This statute, then, abolishes joint and several liability of defendants where comparative negligence is involved, but only as to non-economic damages such as pain and suffering.

Note 3. Causal apportionment. The situation in this note is perhaps distinguishable from *D'Amario,* but it provides a simple hypothetical that forecasts the *D'Amario* problem and makes it easier to deal with. You can also ignore this note here and come back to it if you wish after you cover *D'Amario.*

Under traditional rules, A might be jointly and severally liable for the entire damage if A was not only negligent in breaking the arm but also in foreseeably causing a second injury. But this note present only a pure causal apportionment issue because P does not ask A to share in the damages for the broken pelvis, only for the broken arm. Likewise, P asks B only for damages attributable to the broken pelvis. Thus P has made a reasonable causal apportionment and each would be liable for the damages claimed. That was would have been the result under traditional law, given P's limited claim, and nothing about statutes abolishing joint and several liability should affect causal apportionment.

In the Fourth Edition that we made it more complicated. We posed two problems. The first problem imagined that A negligently caused injury to the plaintiff. B, a health care practitioner, then negligently aggravated that injury. Under traditional proximate cause rules, A is jointly and severally liable with B for the aggravation as well as severally liable for the initial harm. *Haff v. Hettich,* 593 N.W.2d 383 (N.D. 1999) held that A is no longer liable for aggravation, only for the initial injury. This seems to impose a causal apportionments, not a fault apportionment required by the abolition statutes. Abolishing joint and several liability would logically mean only that each defendant is liable for his comparative fault share; it would not address causal apportionments. A's fault extends to all foreseeable harm, including harm caused by B's fault if that is foreseeable. A look at the California statute makes it clear that you proportion A's liability to his *fault,* not to some causal principle. A's percentage of fault does not necessarily. Further, the causal apportionment is not a cause-in-fact apportionment; the initial tortfeasor is a cause in fact of the aggravation as well as the initial injury. The apportionment is then necessarily some kind of "proximate cause" apportionment based on some conception of scope of risk. Yet scope of risk issues have not changed under statutes abolishing joint and several liability, so the basis for this holding is subject to debate. It will also be relevant to *D'Amario,* where the "causal" apportionment worked in favor of the plaintiff rather than the defendant.

The second issue in the Fourth Edition note involved B's liability as the second tortfeasor. Suppose Dentist A negligently treats the patient so that all her teeth must be removed. Dentist B then negligently injures her in attempted transplant surgery. Dentist A's negligence is 20%, B's 80%, The patient sues B only for the damages he caused. The jury finds that B caused $500,000 in damages and A $10,000 in damages. Should we ignore A's negligence and hold B liable for the entire $500,000 because a statute abolishing joint and several liability does not affect causal apportionment? *Kitzig v. Nordquist,* 97 Cal. Rptr.2d 762 (Ct. App. 2000), on somewhat similar facts with different numbers (the first dentist was allocated only 1% of the negligence), held that B is liable for all damages he caused. That accords with the view that you take the plaintiff as you find her and seems to be based on an understanding that if you make a causal apportionment, seeking only damages caused by B, you are not involved with joint and several liability or its abolition. Whether a causal apportionment is in fact justified on the facts is an entirely different question.

Notes 6-9. Three types of statutes. These notes reflect three of the major kinds of statutes. If the plaintiff's damages are mainly "out of pocket" losses such as medical expense, the economic loss statute will not deeply affect the plaintiff's claim. In a jurisdiction like New York, the relatively innocent plaintiff may still have the advantages of joint and several liability recoveries. In harsh jurisdictions like Arizona, the plaintiff may be ruined if the insured defendant was guilty of only a small percent of the fault. Students should recognize that both the statutes and the factual configurations are important in determining the defendants' liabilities and the plaintiff's recoveries under this new dispensation.

Some Problems in Interpretation. Although statutory terms differ from state to state, it is instructive to consider some of the construction problems presented by the California statute.

—*Market-share cases.* Does the California statute eliminate market-share apportionment? Remember that market-share liability is several, not joint. So market-share liability seems consistent with the most obvious of the statutory goals. The anti-joint-liability statute applies only in actions "based upon principles of comparative fault." Since market-share is NOT based on comparative fault but upon strict liability with a market share apportionment, the statute does not on its face seem to apply.

—*Non-faulty plaintiffs.* Does the California statute apply at all if the plaintiff is guilty of no fault? Again, the statute seems to apply only to cases "based upon principles of comparative fault." If the plaintiff is not at fault at all, is her claim "based upon principles of comparative fault?" If not, the joint and several liability limits would not apply. Some statutes answer this specific question directly. *E.g.,* MICH. STAT. ANN. § 27A.6304 (3) (joint and several liability if plaintiff not at fault); WASH. REV. CODE ANN. § 4.22.070 (1)(b) (same).

—*Grouping defendants.* An employer is normally liable for the negligence of employees acting within the scope of employment. This liability is joint and several. If an employee is guilty of 60% of the negligence and the employer none, what is to be done under the California statute? Some statutes expressly retain joint and several liability for employer liability cases. *E.g.,* ARIZ. REV. STATS. §12-2506.

Are there other cases in which it is appropriate to group several defendants together for a single assessment of fault? Suppose two college coaches working for a city's summer recreation program plan a gymnastics course for children. They design the plan negligently, failing to take into account either the children's limits or the limits of untrained persons who will teach the course. As a direct result of their negligence a child is seriously injured. The negligently designed plan is found to represent 90% of the negligence in the case. Does this mean that each coach is liable for only 45% of the damage? And if there were four coaches planning the course, each would be liable for 22 1/2 %? What if nine coaches were responsible? What if 200 manufacturers of drugs jointly agree on a formula and negligently agree on manufacturing standards that are unsafe. This looks like a good concert of action claim; is the plaintiff injured by the drug limited to 1/200 from each manufacturer? In a slightly different context, this possibility seemed to strike the court as inherently preposterous in *Lyon v. Ranger III*, 858 F.2d 22 (1st Cir. 1988). But, under the statute, can it be avoided?

—*Construing in pro tanto settlement cases.* Section 1431.2 does not rule out all joint and several liability. Hence you suppose that Cal. Code Civ. Proc. § 877 (§ 5), prescribing a pro tanto solution to the problem of credits for the nonsettling defendant, will still apply to the extent that joint and several liability remains, that is, as to pecuniary losses. So if A settles and at trial the plaintiff proves both "economic" and "noneconomic" damages, B's liability for the noneconomic damages must be determined by his comparative fault share, but B's liability for the economic damages must be determined by the pro tanto setoff rule under § 877. See *Poire v. C.L. Peck/Jones Bros. Constr. Corp.,* 46 Cal. Rptr. 2d 631 (CT. App. 1995); *Roslan v. Permea, Inc.,* 21 Cal. Rptr. 2d 66 (Ct. App. 1993). This raises new problems–how much of the settlement was for economic damages, how much for non-economic? One solution is to assume that the settlement with A reflected the same proportion of economic to noneconomic damages as awarded by the jury against B. *Ehret v. Congoleum Corp.,* 87 Cal. Rptr. 2d 363 (Ct. App. 1999).

B. Comparative Fault Effects and Adjustments

PRICE V. KITSAP TRANSIT, 886 P.2d 556 (Wash. 1994)

A tort reform statute required apportionment of liability according to fault. A four-year-old boy hit the emergency stop switch on a bus, bring the vehicle to a sudden stop and causing serious injury to the plaintiff, a passenger. The jury attributed 80% of the fault to the boy, 10% each to the bus company and the boy's father. *Held,* no fault can be apportioned to the boy. Children under six are incapable of negligence. Notes consider who should be eliminated from the comparative calculus and the effects of eliminating an actor.

Some of the class may not get it. If the boy's "fault" is dropped out of the calculation, that leaves two tortfeasors whose fault has been found to be equal. As in *Cartel Capital*, you can recalculate readily: it comes to 50-50. Does the plaintiff, who is not at fault at all, care? If the four-year-old-boy had no insurance coverage and no trust fund (do beneficiaries of substantial trusts ride buses?), then under a several liability system, the most the plaintiff could recover would be 20% of his damages. If the boy's "fault" is dropped out of the picture, then he can recover all of his damages if both the company and the father are insured, or at least half if only the bus company is.

All of this flows from the several liability system that is the subject of this section. Under a joint and several liability system, any one of the three actors would have been liable for the plaintiff's entire injury and, so far as the plaintiff was concerned, the boy's fault would not matter.

In *S.H. v. Bistryski*, 923 P.2d 1376 (Utah 1996) a three-year-old child was bitten by the defendant's dog. Under a statute, the defendant was strictly liable but the court concluded that comparative fault apportionment was nonetheless proper. Although the court concluded that, as a matter of law, a child under seven could not be guilty of contributory negligence, the mother's negligence was relevant, not on a theory that the mother's negligence was attributed to the child, but on the theory that to determine the defendant's comparative fault share, the mother's negligence had to be calculated and compared.

Note 3. Phantom and non-party tortfeasors. What about tortfeasors who are not joined and those who cannot even be identified? Can we drop them out as the court dropped out the boy in *Price*? Because if we can, the plaintiff will be far better off, perhaps able to collect an entire judgment from the named defendant. Courts usually reject this view and require the jury to consider the negligence of, say, a hit and run driver as well as the negligence of the named defendant. The result, in a several liability system, is to push down the defendant's "share" of liability and to guarantee that the plaintiff will not be compensated. The RESTATEMENT OF APPORTIONMENT § 29B, cmt. *d,* supports this result (for several liability systems) where the nonparty is "identified" and evidence suffices for attributing a share of the responsibility.

The Uniform Apportionment of Tort Responsibility Act gets a different result– in part. It ignores non-parties in calculating the percentages of fault, except that it considers the negligence or fault of released persons. Connecticut makes similar provisions in its statute, as the court explained in *Donner v. Kearse,* 662 A.2d 1269 (Conn. 1995), the statute originally provided for comparative fault and abolished joint and several liability. "[T]o avoid the possibility that a jury would find that the negligence of a nonparty was a proximate cause of his or her injuries, a plaintiff was required to name as defendants all persons whose actions suggested even the slightest hint of negligence. The unwanted practical effect, therefore, was that plaintiffs were 'required to pursue claims of weak liability against third parties, thereby fostering marginal and costly litigation in our courts.'" Accordingly, the legislature amended the statute to require a comparison of fault as among those who were "parties" plus all person who had settled. The plaintiff exercised substantial control over both categories, but the defendant could implead a person who might be liable if the plaintiff did not initially sue.

Notice that the California statute specifies *defendants*, not tortfeasors, actors or negligent persons. Does that suggest that non-party negligence is to be ignored? Cf. *Plante v. Johnson,* 565 A.2d 1346 (Vt. 1989) ("the statute provides for apportionment among defendants, suggesting that only those joined in the same action should be considered in apportioning damages;" plaintiff brought separate suits against two defendants and the two suits were tried together).

Note 4. Immune tortfeasors. The casebook simplifies the problem in *Unzicker v. Kraft Food Ingredients Corp.,* 783 N.E.2d 1024 (Ill. 2002). The point is to see how the immunity works to exclude one defendant's liability and also the plaintiff's compensation with joint and several liability out of the picture. More detail if you are interested: As the casebook says, the plaintiff was not at fault at all. The plaintiff had damages of almost $900,000. As reported earlier in the casebook, Illinois modifies joint and several liability by providing several liability only as to nonmedical damages for tortfeasors whose fault is less than 25%. Given attribution of 99% of the fault to the employer, the other tortfeasor would be liable only for 1% and that is what the court held. The non-constitutional arguments hinged on whether to count the fault of an immune tortfeasor at all. The statutory answer was to count the fault of any tortfeasor as a party to the action if the plaintiff *could* have sued that tortfeasor. The employer was an actual party because the defendant joined the employer, claiming contribution. But whether that counted depended on whether the plaintiff could have have sued his employer. The answer was yes. The employer's immunity under workers' compensation laws is an affirmative defense. If the employer had not raised the immunity the plaintiff could not only literally sue the employer but could also collect. That meant that the immune employer fit the statutory concept of persons whose fault was to be considered under the 25% rule. In turn, that meant that the third person was liable only for its several share, 1%. The plaintiff had $788,000 nonmedical damages. Of this, the third person was liable only for $7,880.

Note 5. Settlement effects. *Wells v. Tallahassee Memorial Regional Medical Center.*, Inc., 659 So.2d 249 (Fla. 1995) would say "yes," each defendant is liable for its respective share. Accord, the UNIFORM APPORTIONMENT ACT, §§ 8 & 9 (2002). In *Donner v. Kearse*, supra, the plaintiff settled with R for $100,000 and dropped R from the suit, leaving only Kearse as the defendant. The jury found plaintiff's damages to be $554,000 and attributed all fault to Kearse, none to R . The driver of the plaintiff's vehicle, the plaintiff's husband, had originally sued, but he dismissed his complaint and Kearse never impleaded him. The statute limited comparative fault apportionment to parties, and since Kearse had not impleaded him, his fault, if any, was not to be considered. The jury was within its province in finding that R was chargeable with no fault, in spite of her settlement. Consequently, Kerse was properly held liable for all the plaintiff's damages.

Recall the single satisfaction rule, NOTE: TRADITIONAL FORMS OF SETTLEMENT WITH ONE OF SEVERAL TORTFEASORS, § 3, supra this manual. Consider whether that rule rather than the fault apportionment rules, should the non-settling tortfeasor in extreme cases like *Shantigar Foundation v. Bear Mountain Builders*, 804 N.E.2d 324 (Mass. 2004) still get credit for what the settling person paid?

D'AMARIO V. FORD MOTOR CO., 806 So.2d 424 (Fla. 2001)

D'Amario involves two cases, but we have excluded the facts of the second case to save space. The cases arise in a jurisdiction that has abolished joint and several liability and that considers negligence of non-parties as well as parties in apportioning liability to any given defendant.

A minor, Clifford Harris, was severely burned and lost three limbs when the car in which he was a passenger, collided with a tree burst into flames, and, some minutes later, exploded. Harris and his mother, D'Amario, sued Ford, alleging that the vehicle had a defective relay switch, which caused injuries from fire and explosion. The plaintiffs sought no damages for injuries from the initial collision with the tree.

Ford offered evidence that the driver of the car was intoxicated and speeding so that the injuries were caused by the fault of the driver. With this evidence before the jury, it returned a verdict in favor of Ford. the trial court set this aside because it became convinced that the evidence should not have been submitted to the jury. The District Court of Appeal reversed that decision, in effect reinstating the jury verdict.

Held, the District Court of Appeal decision is quashed. It was erroneous to permit the jury to consider the fault of the driver.

The opinion appears to advance two separate and perhaps inconsistent arguments. First, relying on *Jimenez,* the court says that excluding consideration of the driver's fault while limiting liability of Ford to the enhanced injuries "effectively apportions fault and damages on a comparative basis; defendant is liable only for the increased injury caused by its own conduct, not for the injury resulting from the crash itself." Second, the court makes it clear that its apportionment is a proximate cause apportionment, not a comparative fault apportionment. It specifically relies on the analogy to the case of a plaintiff who is injured through his own or another's negligence and is then injured further by a physician's negligence, asserting various proximate cause terminology, such as "condition not cause."

The class will need to understand several things to assess the significance of this case.

(1) The class should recognize that Florida is a several or comparative fault jurisdiction, not a joint and several liability jurisdiction. (See the penultimate paragraph, Casebook 845).

(2) The practical effect of the court's separation of the injuries into two components, is that Ford can be held liable for 100% of the second and greater injury, that resulting from the fire and explosion as distinct from that resulting from the crash itself.

(3) The separation of the injuries and avoidance of a fault apportionment would clearly be right if the tortfeasors each cause separate injuries and neither is a but-for cause of the injury caused by the other, conceivably the case in Note 3, Casebook 840. But that is not the case here. The allegedly drunken driver is one of the but-for causes of every injury here. But for his drunken driving, but for his drunken driving, there would have been no impact, no fire, and no explosion. So the ordinary causal apportionment rule does not seem to work in *D'Amario.*

(4) The court is making neither fault nor cause-in-fact apportionment but a kind of "proximate cause" apportionment. The drunken driver is not a proximate cause of the fire-explosion injuries even if he is a cause in fact of those injuries. This is illustrated by the court's use of a medical aggravation case (Casebook 846). The court concludes that if a tortfeasor causes an injury later aggravated by a physician's negligence, the initial tortfeasor is not liable, and by analogy gets the same result here.

The fourth point produces several questions worth discussion:

• Even if you don't like the statutory several liability system, you might think that analysis really undermines it, leaving a potentially large bundle of cases that may fall outside the system of several liability because of the courts' reasoning on proximate cause.

• Florida's view on proximate cause is at odds with what we've seen in *Anaya*, Casebook p. 246, where we learned that the initial tortfeasor *is* traditionally regarded as one of the proximate causes (as well as one of the but-for causes) of medical aggravation of the injury.

•. Moreover, the court bases its general conclusion that an initial tortfeasor is not liable for subsequent medical aggravation of the injury he caused on *Whitehead v. Linkous*, 404 So.2d 377 (Fla. Dist. Ct. App. 1981). But in *Whitehead* it was not a tortfeasor who was at fault causing an initial injury, it was the plaintiff himself. The question in a case like that is whether to reduce damages for a plaintiff who negligently injures himself when the doctor's liability is only for the separate injury the doctor himself caused. And that kind of case, we've seen, is *not* treated like the *Anaya* situation. (The plaintiff fault case is covered in *Mercer*, Casebook p. 268).

• What if the shoe is on the other foot and the initial tortfeasor is the one with insurance and also the one who is most at fault. He will escape liability for the greater portion of the injury because he is liable only for the initial injury, not for the fire-caused injury.

Taken together, these points might make you think that several liability has its serious downsides and that efforts to cope with them by "proximate cause" apportionment will only get good solutions by happenstance.

Note 1. A chance for students to check their understanding of *D'Amario*. The *Jackson* court did mention proximate cause and the potential for confusion and prejudice emphasized in *D'Amario*, but it seemed to take the view that the essential thing was distinct injury. *D'Amario* did mention distinct injury, but it did not seem to rule out the possibility that any enhancement would be considered distinct. On a scope of risk/proximate cause rationale, it would seem that all of the enhancement, distinct or not distinct, would be attributable to the second

tortfeasor. On the potential for confusing the jury to the prejudice of the plaintiff's claim, you could conceivably distinguish *Jackson,* but that would require you to say that there would be more confusion/prejudice when the first tortfeasor is a drunk driver than when the first tortfeasor is a professional caregiver who woefully failed in basic duties of care. The *Jackson* court did not assert that and if it had we'd have to wonder whether that is really enough of a difference to call for an entirely different result.

C. Comparing Negligence with Intentional and Strict Liability Wrongs

BOARD OF COUNTY COMN'RS OF TETON COUNTY V. BASSETT, 8 P.3d 1079 (Wyo. 2000)

The Wyoming Highway Patrol, Sheriff's deputies, and Park Police acting together pursued the dangerous Ortega at high speeds, set up a road block, and failed to warn the plaintiffs, approaching the scene in another car. Negligence of the three sets of police officers led to a high speech crash in which Ortega struck the plaintiffs' vehicle. The jury found the plaintiffs to be free of fault and attributed 100% of the fault to the various police officers. *Held,* the jury should have been required to attribute some fault to Ortega [even though he was guilty of wanton or intentional misconduct]. The statute requires apportionment of "fault," not merely negligence. In addition, its purpose in abolishing joint and several liability is to limit each tortfeasor's liability to his own proportionate share, a policy that would be defeated by ignoring Ortega's fault.

TURNER V. JORDAN, 957 S.W.2d 815 (Tenn. 1997)

The defendant, a psychiatrist, knew one of his patients was dangerous to nurses and others but took no steps to protect them. The patient beat the plaintiff, a nurse, inflicting serious head injuries. The jury apportioned all fault to the defendant and awarded $1.8 million. The trial judge thought all fault could not be allocated to the defendant and ordered a new trial. *Held,* remanded for entry of judgment on the jury's verdict. A negligent defendant is not entitled to have his percentage of fault reduced by the fault of an intentional tortfeasor whose intentional misconduct is within the foreseeable risk created by the negligent tortfeasor.

Both of these cases are decided under several liability regimes. *Teton County v. Bassett,* on the basis of statutory construction, holds that a negligent defendant's liability must be reduced by the fault attributed to an intentional or wanton tortfeasor, even though the defendant negligently created a risk of the wanton or intentional tort. *Turner* takes the opposite view.

These cases raise three distinct questions: (1) Is the comparison sound as a matter of philosophy or jurisprudence? (2) Is it based upon sound statutory construction? (3) What is its practical effect?

Although you might try to resolve the problem in *Bassett* and *Turner* by refusing to compare intentional torts to reduce the liability of the negligent tortfeasor who created a risk of those very torts, the larger underlying problem arises from the enforcement of a several liability system. Some of the notes reflect efforts that seem, like *D'Amario,* aimed at ameliorating the several liability system. If it needs ameliorating, maybe it is not such a good system to adopt. What does the class think, now that we've had a close look?

CHAPTER 26

DAMAGES

▶**Changes in the Sixth Edition.** While this Chapter is fully updated with over 20 new cases cited or discussed in text and Notes and a new case abstract (*Philip Morris v. Williams* in § 3), we have cut over ten percent of the pages here by deleting one main case and three case abstracts and by trimming some Note material. Specifically, we've cut the *Mercado* case from § 1, and the case abstracts of *Clark*, *Doe v. Isaacs*, and *Bardonardo* from § 3. The chapter is thus leaner and should be easier to teach, while maintaining sufficient depth to remain quite challenging.

▶The **Concise Edition** cuts 25% from this Chapter by converting some main cases into shorter case abstracts and by trimming some Notes. Specifically, we've replaced *McDougald v. Garber* (at the end of §1.A) with a case abstract version; cut Notes 4 to 11 following the two state statutes on capping and limiting damages (at the beginning of §1.B); eliminated the Note on Abolishing or Limiting Pain and Suffering Damages; replaced *Keans v. Bottiarelli* (at the beginning of §2) with a shorter case abstract; cut the long abstract from Dobbs, The Law of Remedies (at the beginning of §3) and replaced it with shorter text; and cut a Note on the litigation-finance function of punitive damages.■

Scheduling omissions. For reasons sketched in the preliminary note to § 1, below, we think some coverage of damages material is desirable, if for no other reason than to round out the picture of torts today. Caps on compensatory and punitive damages call for special attention. At a minimum we'd cover (1) *Martin*, with notes 4, 5, and 9 (Casebook pp. 776-81); (2) Subsection 1.B. on Capping and Limiting Damages, pp. 786-90; (3) Notes and textual material on punitive damages, pp. 796-800. This runs about 13 pages. With effort this can might be covered in one class meeting, though a little more time would be desirable.

If you can do more, we'd cover (1) all of the short § 2 on Adjustments in Damages, which includes the avoidable consequences rule and the collateral source rule, pp. 791-96; and/or (2) the Supreme Court's punitive damages cases, *State Farm v. Campbell* and *Philip Morris v. Williams,* pp. 803-14 (with the problem that follows if you can manage it). If all of that material is added, you will probably need close to three class hours.

§ 1. COMPENSATORY DAMAGES GENERALLY

Preliminary Note to the Teacher:

This section is assuredly not a complete coverage of tort damages or even of personal injury damages. For example, although lost earning capacity and medical monitoring damages are of course mentioned, we do not develop those interesting topics in the casebook. The section instead focuses on trying to provide a well-rounded, if limited coverage and on exhibiting issues that are central to the ongoing debates about the proper scope of tort damages.

You might think that damages are best taught in the remedies course and that teaching damages in torts serves mainly to explain something about the costs, the time-consumption and elaborate effort that goes into tort cases. Tort reform statutes and the expansion of immunities compel a different vision of damages in the torts course. Cutting damages to the bone through comparative fault, several-only liability rules, and damages caps – not to mention barring meritorious claims through the proliferation of immunities – eliminates large numbers of tort claims. In *form,* the rules limiting damages are not about the existence of rights or liabilities; but in *fact* a reduction of damages can rule out many suits altogether, just as surely as an immunity. This, then, is about substance.

We began the course with some damages materials. If you did not cover those in Chapter 1, you may wish to consider using them here. If you did cover them, you may wish to review them.

COMMENTS

A. Proving and Computing Basic Damages

Constitutional torts. Given the casebook's emphasis on person or property injury – the physical torts – the text does not develop this rule in detail and you may wish to leave coverage to assigned reading.

Where the constitutional tort causes personal injury, the ordinary personal injury damages are recoverable. Where the constitutional tort is of the kind we saw in Chapter 3, much like the common law trespassory tort, again common law damages for, say, unconstitutional detention, are recoverable. However, where the constitutional right in issue is not a protection of the integrity of personal or property, the Supreme Court has limited damages severely. In *Carey v. Piphus,* 435 U.S. 247 (1978), a student was suspended without a due process hearing for allegedly smoking marijuana; he had no money or physical losses and could recover only actual or nominal damages. *Memphis Community School Dist. v. Stachura*, 477 U.S. 299 (1986), was much the same– except that the plaintiff was denied free speech rights instead of due process. Maybe the intangible right represented in the right to vote will prove a tougher case. *See generally* DOBBS ON REMEDIES § 7.4(2) (2d ed. 1993). Certain discrimination cases that may or may not involve constitutional rights can be brought under statutes that authorize damages, notably employment discrimination.

Property torts. The Casebook summary, though quite short, is probably sufficient for a torts courts.

Personal injury torts. The note lists the main elements of a personal injury recovery. On these elements, *see* DOBBS ON TORTS § 377 (2000). Pain and suffering, lost enjoyment of life, proof issues, and medical monitoring damages are considered in greater detail in this Chapter.

MARTIN V. UNITED STATES, 471 F.Supp. 6 (D. Ariz. 1979).

Each of the main elements of damage is involved here– lost wage or earning capacity, medical expense, and pain, together with the future losses in each category. This case is frankly illustrative and requires little analysis. If you are using this case without the remainder of the materials, discussion can be generated to consider the problems of future loss, pain and other issues. If the remaining materials are also to be used, discussion here may focus on the uncertainty, and on the difficulty for the lawyers – on both sides – in dealing with the projections of probable earnings of these boys. Such a discussion can tie directly to the materials that follow. The basic elements of damages can be summarized by student or teacher.

If you reach a discussion on the desirability of pain and suffering awards later in this chapter, or in discussing no-fault or workers' compensation, this case is a good one to have in mind. There are many cases in which the suffering is depicted more graphically, but this one seems to suffice as a model for judging whether you are really willing to give up entirely on pain awards.

Note 1. Proving causation. When a plaintiff offers medical evidence to corroborate her claim that she suffers pain, defendants have often object to the admission of that evidence on the ground that only the plaintiff can know her subjective pain. *See* J. Evans, Annotation, *Admissibility, in Civil Case, of Expert Evidence as to Existence or Nonexistence, or Severity, of Pain*, 11 A.L.R.3d 1249 (1967) (reflecting the argument and the courts' contemporary rejection of it). When the plaintiff does not offer medical evidence of pain, the defendant may argue just the contrary, that the plaintiff's subjective knowledge of pain is not to be trusted and that medical testimony is required. The Nebraska court has said that the plaintiff claiming "subjective" injuries must establish both injury and causation by medical testimony. *See Eiting v. Godding*, 214 N.W.2d 241 (Neb. 1974) ("When symptoms from which personal injury may be inferred are subjective only, medical testimony is required");

Eno v. Watkins, 429 N.W.2d 371 (Neb. 1988) ("Before a plaintiff can recover damages for such injuries, there must be expert medical testimony to establish causation and the extent and nature of the injuries"). *Choi v. Anvil,* 32 P.3d 1 (Alaska 2001), rejects Nebraska's extreme rule of law.

Defendants have succeeded in persuading some courts that the soft-tissue injury is suspect or worse. But you can see how aggressive stance against soft-tissue injuries played out against the insurer who was held subject to tort liability in *Crackel v. Allstate Ins. Co.,* 92 P.3d 882 (Ariz. Ct. App. 2004) on the basis of evidence that its policy was to make soft-tissue injury claims so expensive to litigate that lawyers and injured persons would not pursue them but would accept small settlements instead. Requiring medical experts to testify for plaintiffs' soft-tissue, "subjective" claims certainly has the effect of making small-claim litigation financially difficult to impossible.

In spite of the criticisms implicit in the paragraphs above, some claims will indeed be justifiable only if expert testimony is presented in support. There are *some* subjective complaints that the victim cannot truly know resulted from, say an automobile accident. In much the same way, jurors simply have no experience or common knowledge from which to conclude that the plaintiff's condition was caused by the defendant's negligence. That would likely be the case if the plaintiff proposes to testify about the future course of injury, for example, that she will always have headaches resulting from the accident.

We may be guilty of offering too many lessons in **Note 1**; you may wish to choose only one for emphasis. First, there really are substantial impediments to getting just compensation, especially for people who have relatively small injuries but who may need compensation far more than some people with larger injuries. Second, lawyers must takes rules of law as guides to the evidence they need; even logic can guide them some of the time. If the plaintiff's lawyer waltzes into court with the bare assertion that she has muscle injury, she may fail to convince the jury (or the judge before that). And your research in advance is the only way to save your client's claim (or present a good defense) if it has not occurred to you that your court may demand medical proof for subjective injuries.

Note 2. Inflation and reduction to present value. This is a technical problem. Students should understand the gist, not necessarily the details. For more, but still non-technical details, *see* 1 & 2 DAN DOBBS, THE LAW OF REMEDIES §§ 3.7 & 8.5(3) − 8.5(4) (2d ed. 1993). A related practical problem is to establish the loss period. How long would the plaintiff have lived and worked but for the tort? *See* 2 ID., § 8.5(2).

Note 3. Periodic payments. Some periodic payment statutes have been held unconstitutional under state constitutional provisions. See *Smith v. Myers, (Bellina),* 887 P.2d 541 (Ariz. 1994) (under provision that "[n]o law shall be enacted in this State limiting the amount of damages to be recovered for causing the death or injury of any person"); *Galayda v. Lake Hospital Systems, Inc.,* , 644 N.E.2d 298 (Ohio 1994).

Students might be interested to know that other countries use periodic payment plans extensively. France and the Netherlands allow judges the discretion to award damages as periodic payments in any torts case. *See* JULIE A. DAVIES & PAUL T. HAYDEN, GLOBAL ISSUES IN TORT LAW 11 (2008).

Note 5. Dollarizing pain. When the defendant argues that an award should be reduced because it exceeds any possible justification, reviewing courts do sometimes say that awards made in comparable cases can be considered and may be instructive, as stated in **Note 6.** You could approach the problem differently by standardizing pain awards in various ways. *Surette v. Islamic Republic of Iran,* cited here, is a simple way of doing so, and one that still leaves a good deal of flexibility. (If you covered governmental immunity and death damages, you'll want to note that claim was brought under statutory exceptions to the usual immunity of foreign states and that the damages are essentially the kind recognized in survival actions. The law applied was the federal common law.) In American law, however, standardized damages (so much per day, or so much per violation, for example) are almost invariably the result of legislation, not judicial action like that in *Surette. See* DOBBS ON REMEDIES § 3.3(2) (2d ed. 1993).

Note 6. Considering comparable awards. Prior awards might be used in at least two distinct ways, one reflecting something like a use of precedent and one not.

(1) Suppose a prior court decision held that an award of $100,000 for a broken arm with no complications was excessive. Today's court may hold that on similar facts an award of $100,000 or more is still excessive. Such a holding focuses not on the award itself but on the prior court decision as precedent. The same thing could be said if the prior decision held that the earlier award was not excessive, or that it was inadequate.

(2) Instead of looking to the appellate court's precedent, courts could look at the triers' awards themselves as guidelines, emphasizing averages or ranges. This approach would give weight to what other triers in other cases found acceptable, not to precedential value of an appellate decision that approved or disapproved the award. It is the second kind of use of prior awards that is controversial here.

Some courts have adopted a formula called the maximum recovery rule that suggests a degree of precision that is perhaps illusory. It is stated as a rule favorable to the plaintiff: "we will decline to reduce damages where the amount awarded is not disproportionate to at least *one factually similar* case from the relevant jurisdiction" and it is not disproportionate unless it exceeds 133% of the highest previous recovery in the relevant jurisdiction. *Lebron v. United States,* 279 F.3d 321 (5th Cir. 2002) (quoting earlier authority).

Note 7. Argumentation. The per diem or unit-of-time argument is often effective. Some courts once held that plaintiffs' attorney would not be permitted to make such an argument to the jury. That view seems largely passed. *See* 2 DAN B. DOBBS, THE LAW OF REMEDIES § 8.1(4), at 394 (2d ed. 1993). But it is still possible to go too far in arguing pain and suffering, as for example by repeated references to the sale price of a Picasso, the earnings of ballplayers or high awards in other suits. Likewise, the "golden rule" argument to the effect that jurors should give what they would like to receive, or what the plaintiff would have to pay to get someone else to bear the pain, is impermissible because it asks the jury to use the wrong standard.

Note 8. Reinforcing pain. Pain and suffering awards are supposed to compensate for suffering, and if there is a future component, you would hope that the recovery would make the plaintiff feel better. Some research suggests that is not so. If pain and suffering awards don't make the plaintiff feel better, should we just forget about giving them? Not so fast; see Note 9 below.

Note 9. Pain and suffering pays attorney fees. Another bit of legal realism here. Most plaintiffs' lawyers are working on a contingent fee basis — they are paid only if the plaintiff wins a recovery, and then that fee is a percentage of that recovery. Legal fees are not recoverable in general as a line-item of damages. This means that if the lawyer is to receive her 25% or 33% or whatever, the money must come from the plaintiff's recovery of compensatory damages. This would leave the plaintiff that percentage short of adequate compensation for lost future wages or future medical expenses, for example, except for the rather "sloshy" amount of money recoverable for pain and suffering. Tort "reformers" are fully aware of this litigation-finance function of pain and suffering damages, of course — caps on pain and suffering may amount to caps on fees, which in turn may discourage lawyers from bringing certain cases at all.

McDOUGALD v. GARBER, 536 N.E.2d 372 (N.Y. 1989)

The plaintiff Emma was deprived of oxygen during surgery. She is brain damaged and permanently comatose. The trial judge charged that Emma could not recover for pain unless she was aware of it, but could recover, aware or not, for the loss of pleasures and pursuits of life. The jury awarded Emma almost $10 million, which included $3.5 million for loss of pleasures. The trial judge reduced the awards substantially, combining the pain and the lost pleasure award in a single award of $2 million.

Held, reversed. The instruction is error. The goal is compensation. That includes compensation for nonpecuniary loss but compensation is fictional because money cannot ease the pain. The money award for lost enjoyment has no utility and we cannot extend the fiction of compensation that far. "Some" level of awareness is required. Likewise, the award is not different from a pain award. Pain and suffering includes lost enjoyment. Treating the two forms of suffering separately would merely be likely to distort the award.

Judge Titone dissented. He argued loss of enjoyment is a separate item of damages from pain, that the loss is real without regard to the plaintiff's awareness of it, and that it should be compensated.

If you hold that loss of enjoyment of life is merely a form of pain and suffering damages, you probably dictate the majority's outcome because you cannot very well say that a person is in pain if she is unaware of it.

Some courts like to conceptualize loss of enjoyment as something different from pain and suffering. A court may say, for example, that although suffering is a psychological state, it does not encompass loss of ability to engage in life's pleasurable activities. "These types of experiences are all positive sensations of pleasure" which differ from suffering, which the court may see in terms of "nervousness, grief, shock, anxiety, and so forth." *Fantozzi v. Sandusky Cement Products Co.*, 597 N.E.2d 474 (Ohio 1992). Somewhat similarly, South Carolina has now held that loss of enjoyment is a separate item of recovery when such loss is proven and it is to be distinguished from pain and suffering in instructing the jury. *Boan v. Blackwell*, 541 S.E.2d 242 (S.C. 2001). It seems clear that (unless pain and suffering awards are to be abolished), recovery ought to be permitted for one's inability to play golf as she could before injury, but whether this is called "suffering" or not doesn't seem to matter at an intellectual level.

Note 2. Plaintiff aware of loss. Several cases have approved instructions on separate awards for pain and loss of enjoyment. *Ogden v. J.M. Steel Erecting*, Inc., 31 P.3d 806 (Ariz. Ct. App. 2001); *Boan v. Blackwell*, 541 S.E.2d 242 (S.C. 2001); *Kirk v. Washington State University*, 746 P.2d 285 (Wash. 1987). Recovery for conscious loss of enjoyment seems as sound as recovery for other forms of suffering, as long as the instruction does not encourage the jury to cumulate damages. Would an instruction that the plaintiff is entitled to recover for all forms of pain and suffering be adequate? *See Anderson v. Nebraska Dept. of Social Services*, 538 N.W.2d 732 (Neb. 1995). There is an Annotation, *Loss of enjoyment of life as a distinct element or factor in awarding damages for bodily injury*, 34 A.L.R.4th 293 (1984). As to expert testimony on pain, *see* Annotation, 11 A.L.R.3d 1249 (1967).

Note 3. Plaintiff unaware of loss. When the plaintiff is aware of nothing, and can become aware of nothing, she can have no pain or sense of loss. That is *McDougald's* core. The plaintiff has a loss in the sense that she will fail to reap happiness that otherwise she would have reaped in life, but as happiness is an idea wholly dependent upon consciousness, you must wonder a little about what it might mean to say that she who knows nothing can "recover" for a loss that can only be defined by a consciousness that she lacks. *Flannery v. United States*, cited here, goes very far indeed by holding that there can be a recovery for loss of life's enjoyments on behalf of a comatose patient who was not aware of any loss.

Note 4. Proof. In *Mercado*, cited here, the plaintiff sought to introduce the "loss of enjoyment of life" testimony of an economist based on "willingness-to-pay" studies. Since people pay more or less determinable amounts to protect their lives by smoke detectors and the like, the testimony assumed that life can be valued by aggregating the sums so paid. The court rejected this testimony on the ground that it does not in fact adequately represent how people value life, partly because some purchases may be dictated by government regulations (airbags). The court also thought safety purchases are not necessarily good indicators of value because some people buy because they are led like cattle by advertising and because some are extremely cautious. Similarly, the court rejected the testimony based on increased wages paid to those in risky jobs. On this, however, the court's reasons were a little different. It thought that the pay for risky jobs like police work is dictated by government, which in turn is influenced by budget and political considerations. It also thought that some people will accept risky work because they are moved by civic duty.

In the end, however, the court backed off these comments and relied on an entirely different notion: The expert can give testimony only if he can assist the jury; maybe his methodology was all right after all, but "Smith [the economist] was no more expert in valuing life than the average person" because, (evidently as a matter of faith) no person can achieve "unique knowledge of the value of life."

Most courts have rejected such testimony. *See, e.g., Loth v. Truck-A-Way Corp.*, 70 Cal.Rptr.2d 571 (Ct. App. 1998) (commenting that the very same expert's "impersonal method of valuing life assumes that for the most part, all lives have the same basic value." Such testimony has been rejected even in West Virginia, a state that approves recovery for the loss of pleasure even when the plaintiff is unaware of that "loss". *Wilt v. Buracker*, 443 S.E.2d 196 (W.Va. 1994).

There are a couple of cases in which such testimony has been admitted. *See Couch v. Astec Indus., Inc.*, 53 P.3d 398 (N.M. Ct. App. 2002); *Dorn v. Burlington Northern Santa Fe R.R.*, 397 F.3d 1183 (9th Cir. 2005) (noting in dictum that value of life testimony might be useful as giving "some finitude to a question that can sound like a probe into the infinite").

NOTE: THE SPECIAL CASE OF MEDICAL MONITORING DAMAGES

Is it madness to permit recovery of medical monitoring damages when the plaintiff has suffered no compensable physical or mental harm? Theoretically, the plaintiffs could pay their own medical costs of periodic monitoring, suing only if some disease for which the defendants were responsible actually appeared at some future time. But the defendant's tort has caused at least one thing, hasn't it? – the plaintiffs' economic costs of obtaining medical oversight. Such economic losses, even if regarded as stand-alone economic harms, are not within the rule excluding economic losses where the parties have contracted with reference to the safety issues. You might recall *Moorman Mfg. Co. v. Na-*

tional Tank Co. on that point, Casebook pp. 638. You might also recall that the defendant is a tortfeasor. Another thing to think about: If the plaintiffs fail to have medical monitoring then suffer cancer that is advanced before it is detected, you can be sure defendants will argue that the plaintiff should have minimized damages by having medical monitoring. To that point, we can add that plaintiffs are usually entitled to recover the costs they incurred in reasonably minimizing damages.

Maybe some students will balk at the suggestion that the defendant "caused" the need for economic expenditure. The plaintiffs themselves choose to have medical monitoring, they might say. Yet it definitely is the defendant's tortious activity that causes the need for the monitoring.

As the last sentence implies, the plaintiff would in any event be required to establish a reasonable medical need for the monitoring, such as exposure that is significant and has real possibility of causing future harm that could be minimized by early detection. And if nothing more is required for good medical surveillance than is required for the public at large, there is no basis for an award for medical monitoring. Some authority has said that the plaintiff must also prove that useful or accurate tests can be made as part of the monitoring and that the tests are themselves reasonably safe in comparison to the risks they aimed to detect. See In re *Paoli Railroad Yard Master File PCB Litigation,* 2000 WL 274262 (E.D. Pa. 2000); and *Bourgeois v. A.P. Green Indus.,* Inc., 716 So.2d 355 (La. 1998). Beyond that, medical expert testimony to establish the need, risks, and safety, must meet admissibility standards (Casebook pp. 688-69) and will be excluded if it does not.

With all these restrictions, you might like the idea of awarding medical monitoring damages for people who have suffered no injury beyond significant exposure. Still, there are problems of administration. Apart from family litigation (divorce, child custody) and a few "equity" cases, the American judicial system is not bureaucratic. It is not geared to periodic supervision and repeated litigation that undoubtedly would erupt over particular expenses. If the defendants are liable for medical monitoring expense, just how is that to work? A trust fund, administered by a trustee, maybe? Sounds like extra costs, doesn't it?

B. Capping and Limiting Damages

CAL. CIV. CODE § 3333.2
MD. ANN. CODE, CT. & JUD. PROC. § 11-108

Two statutes capping damages in personal injury cases. California's statute applies only in suits against a "health care provider," and then only to claims based upon "professional negligence." This latter phrase limits the apparent scope of the statute. In the malpractice chapter, we drew a distinction between informed consent claims based upon negligence and battery claims. That distinction can be asserted when the surgeon performs some unconsented-to operation, for which the plaintiff may well recover uncapped damages for a medical battery. *Perry v. Shaw*, 106 Cal. Rptr. 2d 70 (Ct. App. 2001) (the surgeon performed breast augmentation not consented to).

Maryland's statute applies in "any action for . . . personal injury." California caps "noneconomic losses" such as pain and suffering at $250,000. Maryland caps all damages at $350,000. Notes to these statutes work through some interpretations and applications.

Caps and joint and several liability limits. In *McCarty v. City of Minneapolis*, 654 N.W.2d 353 (Minn. Ct. App. 2002), a police car went out of control and ran into a crowd of people as a result of both driver negligence and a defect in electronics installed in the car and manufactured by Federal Signal. Many people were injured and two killed. Only two (with their father) are before the court here, both of whom were children at the time, neither at fault. One, Erin, lost her right arm. Her damages as found by the jury came to $3.815 million. Her brother's and father's came to about $200,000. The problem for the plaintiffs was two-fold. Municipal liability in Minnesota is capped by a maximum of $300,000 for any one victim, but a total of $750,000 for any one event. That had the effect of capping the brother/father's claim against the city at about $21,500, apparently because the court allocated some of the $750,000 cap to other victims not part of this case. Erin's claim was capped at $300,000. In a pure joint and several liability system, Federal Signal would be liable for any damage not collectible from the municipality, but Minnesota had an unusual provision, to the effect that for tortfeasors whose fault was less than 15%, their joint and several liability would be limited to four times the percentage allocated by the trier. The trier allocated negligence 87.5% to the municipality and 12.5% to Federal Signal. If both statutes applied, then, the plaintiffs' recovery against the city would be a relatively small percentage of their actual damages and Federal Signal's liability would be limited to 50% (4 x 12.5%) of their actual damages. The plaintiff argued in effect that with the liability of municipalities capped, that meant they were not joint tortfeasors at all for any amount above the capped amount. So Federal Signal could not take advantage of the special limit on joint and several liability, since, for amounts over the capped sum, Federal Signal was not a joint tortfeasor at all. The court rejected this argument and limited the plaintiffs to capped sums against the city and 50% of the plaintiffs' damages against Federal Signal.

Note 6. Capping plaintiffs vs. capping defendants. Whether the cap applies per defendant or per plaintiff is at least theoretically a question of statutory construction. Authority cited in Note 6 construes the statutes in favor of the plaintiff, allowing the capped amount against each severally liable defendant. But some statutes may be construed to limit the total amount the plaintiff can recover, so that given a $250,000 cap and five defendants who are severally liable, no one of them could be held for more than $50,000. *Garhart v. Tinsman*, 95 P.3d 571(Colo. 2004) (medical cap statute provided "total amount recoverable for a course of care for all defendants;" held, non-party tortfeasors are "defendants" within the meaning of the statute, so that the cap should be first applied to the award, then the judge should apportion the capped award "according to the percentages the jury found to exist for each tortfeasor").This problem will be much exacerbated where joint and several liability is abolished.

Note 7. Caps and comparative fault. This note raises a specific problem that is more detailed than students really need to have here, but it illustrates the fact that caps introduce many new problems and suggests something of the kind of thought lawyers must devote to new legal systems. Cap first, then make comparative negligence reduction is the effect of *McAdory*. Some other California authority supports that rule, some does not. Some similar problems in capping can be seen in *Salgado v. County of Los Angeles*, 967 P.2d 585 (Cal. 1998, as modified 1999) (integrating caps with periodic payment rules); *General Electric Co. v. Niemet*, 866 P.2d 1361 (Colo. 1994) (apportion liability among defendants, then cap).

Note 11. Attorney fees. A reiteration of an important point made earlier. Students may tend to think that caps merely reduce what the plaintiff recovers. The most drastic effect of caps, however, may be to make many complicated, expensive claims too unrewarding for lawyers to pursue at all. To see this, students must recall the relationship between pain and suffering awards and lawyer's fees. In a sense, pain and suffering awards are often mostly attorney fee awards, without which the case could not be pursued properly

NOTE: ABOLISHING OR LIMITING PAIN AND SUFFERING DAMAGES

This short Note can support a class discussion on the topic of pain and suffering awards. You can start provocatively by suggesting abolition (or suggesting that pain awards should be expanded). Moderately inclined students may suggest a middle ground. Some of the note material furnishes arguments. One is a freedom argument. You want to buy cars more cheaply, but you must necessarily pay a price that will reflect the manufacturer's cost of paying pain and suffering damages in some cases. You really cannot effectively renounce those damages to get a lower price.

If pain and suffering awards are "really" countenanced mainly because they fund an attorney fee, then if you abolish pain and suffering damages, you'll need to allow a fee recovery by the winning attorney against the defendant. Would that be cheaper, or would it add a new layer of secondary litigation in the fee assessment hearing? There is already such a litigation layer where fees are charged to defendants under the federal civil rights act and other statutes. *See* DOBBS ON REMEDIES, §§ 3.10(8) – 3.10 (11).

§ 2. ADJUSTMENTS IN DAMAGES

KEANS V. BOTTIARELLI, 645 A.2d 1029 (Conn. App. Ct. 1994).

Plaintiff had a blood disorder that could interfere with blood clotting. She informed her dentist, the defendant here, but, without checking with the plaintiff's hematologist, he performed a tooth extraction. This was found to be malpractice. The site of the extraction began to bleed after the plaintiff went home; she called the dentist who gave some advice. The next day she saw her hematologist, who confined her to the hospital for several days. The plaintiff did not follow the dentist's instructions for post-op care; in particularly, she did not fill the penicillin prescription. The trial court thought that damages should be "mitigated" to the extent of hospital expenses, which could have been avoided otherwise. *Held*, the reduction was not clearly erroneous.

The biggest teaching concerns here are about causal apportionment (again) and whether the separate avoidable consequences rule should be dropped entirely.

Keans approaches the problem as one of avoidable consequences or "mitigation of damages," not as a comparative fault problem. This is review if you covered the fault vs. causal apportionment distinction in Chapter 9, § 4, and in *D'Amario*, Chapter 25, Casebook p. 765, but the topic may be more meaningful here. Notice that the problem is structured exactly like the seatbelt cases: the plaintiff could not have avoided the initial injury and her "fault" occurs after the injury. Perhaps most important, though, a non-fault-based apportionment is practical here; we can see that some specific parts of her recovery were caused by her own failure to minimize damages.

Yet if the plaintiff's is a but-for cause of her own hospitalization, so is the defendant. But for the defendant's negligence, the plaintiff would not have required hospitalization. But for the plaintiff's negligence, the plaintiff would not have required hospitalization. And both parties create the risk of hospitalization as well. Thus both are but-for causes of hospitalization, which was within the risk each created. In an important way, then, we can say that there is really no basis for causal apportionment here and that we should use comparative fault instead.

When the plaintiff suffers a single indivisible injury– that is, one that cannot be apportioned to causes– the comparative fault system will work when causal apportionment is impossible. Cf. *Owens Corning Fiberglas Corp. v. Parrish*, 58 S.W.3d 467 (Ky. 2001) (plaintiff's smoking contributed to lung disease resulting in shortness of breath; defendant's asbestos caused asbestosis, a distinct lung disease that also results in shortness of breath; in the absence of evidence that would permit causal apportionment, the trial judge rightly instructed the jury to apportion by comparative fault). When causal apportionment is possible, is it a superior or inferior method for dealing with apportionment between a plaintiff and a defendant? If the moral character of the parties' acts lie in the fault element rather than the cause element, wouldn't comparative fault apportionment be preferred?

Del Tufo v. Township of Old Bridge, 685 A.2d 1267 (N.J. 1996) holds that comparative fault principles can be applied to affect recovery when an arrestee, to whom the police owe an affirmative duty of care, ingested an overdose of cocaine shortly before arrest. Both his ingestion (seemingly unknown to the police) and his failure to tell them he needed medical attention could count as contributory fault in a suit for his death. Although police owed a duty of care, the arrestee's comparative fault, consisting of conduct before injury occurred, would not merely count on minimizing damages but as comparative fault.

NOTE: OTHER DAMAGES ADJUSTMENTS: THE COLLATERAL SOURCE RULE AND ITS COUSINS

An example of the collateral source rule is *Montgomery Ward & Co., Inc. v. G.W. Anderson,* 976 S.W.2d 382 (Ark. 1998). The plaintiff, injured by the defendant's negligence, incurred almost $25,000 in medical bills at a hospital. But the hospital agreed with her lawyer to discount its bills by 50%. The court held that this discount was subject to the collateral source rule and hence that the plaintiff could make a full recovery against the defendant. It rejected several cases that gratuitous medical services do not fall under the rule.

Maybe teachers should be satisfied with a superficial coverage of the collateral source rule. Students can master it well, but usually only with a heavy time investment and with a focus that may be rapidly diminishing by the time you reach these materials. If the material is too long, too hard, or too detailed, you might stick with the core rule and the distinction between collateral and direct sources, then notice that some states have abolished the rule, at least for particular kinds of cases.

¶ 4. *The direct source or direct benefits rule.* The direct benefits rule must be contrasted with the collateral benefit or collateral source rule. The defendant gets a credit against his liability when he confers a benefit upon the plaintiff directly, either by commission of the tort itself or by conferring a benefit upon the plaintiff solely because of the tort-caused injury.

When the defendant makes a cash payment to the plaintiff (or when the payment is made on the defendant's behalf by his insurer, but as part of his med pay insurance that has nothing to do with liability), the defendant (or his insurer) will be entitled to credit for the payment made in any tort suit by a plaintiff.

A slightly different form of the direct benefits idea occurs when the tort itself creates a benefit as well as a loss. Suppose the defendant trespasses on the plaintiff's land, and cuts a drainage ditch that destroys a valuable wild orchid worth $1,000. But the ditch will drain both the defendant's land and the plaintiff's. This improves the plaintiff's property so that it is now worth $500 more than before. The plaintiff keeps the ditch and enjoys its benefits. He has his action for trespass but damages must be reduced to reflect the benefit resulting from the trespass, at least if he accepts the benefit. This is the benefits rule defendants sometimes argue in wrongful birth and wrongful conception cases– that the mother gets the benefit of the child and must credit intangible benefit against both the intangible damages (pain, suffering) and the tangible, money loss. *Chaffee v. Seslar,* Chapter 20, Casebook p. 550, went against some other authority to reject that kind of set off. What kinds of benefits can be traded against what kinds of loss represents a difficult problem, but for many reasons unwanted benefits that do not increase the plaintiff's net worth probably should never be credited to the tortfeasor. *See* DOBBS ON TORTS § 293 (2001). There is a parallel problem with collateral source matching. See ¶ 8 below.

¶ **5. *Criticizing the collateral source rule.*** If time permits you to walk through ¶ 5, that may be desirable because it shows some of the reasons why you might think the collateral source rule to be inefficient. If you want more explanation of these steps, *see* Conard, *The Economic Treatment of Automobile Injuries,* 63 MICH. L. REV. 279, 311 (1964), or 2 DAN B. DOBBS, THE LAW OF REMEDIES 8.6(3), pp. 495-f. (2d ed. 1993).

One counter argument you might inject in the discussion is that the defendant would get a windfall if he got credit for the plaintiff's insurance, and that implies that the defendant would be inadequately deterred. That argument, however, may be circular: if we want the plaintiff to bear the loss through her own insurance, then it overdeters the defendant if we require him to pay for the loss that is already paid for.

¶¶ **6 & 7. *Abolishing the collateral source rule; credits.*** This topic probably should be covered as a part of understanding tort reform packages. About half the states appear to have adopted statutes substantially altering the collateral source rule. Some subsidiary points:

• Some statutes are addressed to civil or tort actions generally. Others apply only to discrete categories of cases like medical malpractice actions.

• Some statutes retain the collateral source rule to the extent that it is needed to protect a subrogation right, such as the right of the workers' compensation carrier to reimbursement from the tortfeasor.

• *Public benefits.* Suppose the plaintiff is severely injured and the state provides major benefits, say life care for a plaintiff in a vegetative state. Should the defendant be permitted to avoid liability for a lifetime of care because the state has picked up the tab? In *Schuff v. A.T. Klemens & Son,* 16 P.3d 1002 (Mont. 2000), the statute abolished the collateral source rule, but the court construed it not to apply to social security death benefits, with the result that the plaintiff could collect both damages and social security benefits. In accord as to social security disability payments, *Schroeder v. Triangulum Assocs.,* 789 A.2d 459 (Conn. 2002). But, as reflected in ¶ 7, *Woodger v. Christ Hospital,* 834 A.2d 1047 (N.J. Super. 2003), allowed the defendant a deduction for the sums the plaintiff received in social security less the sums the plaintiff had paid in contributions to the social security system. The same question whether to credit the defendant for public benefits received by the plaintiff arises when the plaintiff receives workers' compensation benefits instead of a tort judgment. If the workers' compensation statute is construed *not* to require a reduction of workers' compensation to account for social security benefits received, then the social security statute and regulation may require a reduction in social security payments to account for worker's compensation benefits received. *See* 20 C.F.R. § 404.408.

When the defendant gets credit for collateral source payments to the plaintiff, the statute abolishing the collateral source rule may allow a deduction from this credit for the plaintiff's costs in obtaining those benefits—premiums in the case of insurance, or, as in *Woodger,* tax contributions in the case of social security. More issues arise in computation— premiums for how long? How long will benefits continue? Are we bogged down, creating issues collateral to the merits, or just being careful?

Taxes. Personal injury and other litigators must now recognize that tax liabilities can raise important issues in settling cases. The plaintiff's lawyer must consider creating a trust when the plaintiff is disabled and entitled to public assistance, and to that end might retain a specialist who deals in such trusts. Something similar applies with taxes. First-year students certainly do not need professional-level information on this subject. They should be aware, however, that the compensatory damage award for some personal injuries is not subject to federal tax, but that many state courts continue to hide this fact from the jury, a rule that may doubly hurt the defendant, first by imposing liability upon the defendant for losses the plaintiff will not have (because of the tax savings), and second by hiding the saving from the jury, which may covertly increase the award in the erroneous belief that it will be subject to a giant tax bill. The rule seems to be a leftover from the days when courts were sympathetic to plaintiffs. It was arguably unjustified to begin with and its survival in the era of tort reform seems surprising. In *Norfolk & W. Ry. v. Liepelt,* 444 U.S. 490 (1980), the Court held, (1) that, ordinarily, evidence on the tax savings must be admitted; (2) the jury must be told about the tax effects. The *Liepelt* rules apply in any FELA claim, whether it is brought in federal court or state court.∎

§ 3. PUNITIVE DAMAGES

The topic of punitive damages is almost entirely a tort topic, because such damages are almost never available in ordinary contract cases. Chapter 1 contains a brief mention; we are now in a position to review the topic and add some important detail. Punitive damages is a subject you *cannot* cover fully in a torts course. The excerpt included in the casebook counts for less than two pages out of 90 in the treatise from which it was taken. There are whole books on the subject. *See, e.g.,* JAMES D. GHIARDI & JOHN J. KIRCHER, & CHRISTINE M. WISEMAN, PUNITIVE DAMAGES LAW AND PRACTICE (1998). Three topics can be considered here:

(1) What good does the punitive award do? (Why do we ever make such awards?) If you covered Chapter 1 and perhaps some other material, this will be review.

(2) How can we fairly and effectively measure a punitive award?

(3) Are the rules for limiting punitive damages, including the supposed constitutional rules, good or bad?

A fourth topic might be: Can you fit punitive damages with *Carroll Towing*? The *Carroll Towing* formula wants defendants to take risks, provided only that they are economically sound –that they will cost less in harms than they produce in economic value. Taxing activities with punitive damages means that some activities that would be risky but useful may be "taxed" out of existence by the punitive award, especially since punitive awards are often based in part on state of mind rather than on objective conduct. But punitive damages might still be justified, even if you are a root-and-branch supporter of *Carroll Towing*, since punitive damages would allow courts to charge against a defendant "real" costs of the defendant's activity that otherwise could be externalized.

Students can raise quite a few questions not covered here. If your students are taking criminal procedure, they might ask about double jeopardy. Can the defendant be held criminally liable and also punitively liable? You can simply say, "Courts have usually said there is no double jeopardy, and also that punitive damages does not violate the Constitution's excessive fines clause." The courts' answer on double jeopardy is surely right if you measure punitive damages only to the extent that further deterrence is required or if you measure them to pay the plaintiff's attorney fee.

A. General Rules

DAN B. DOBBS, THE LAW OF REMEDIES § 3.11(1)

This excerpt summarizes some of the main common law rules about punitive damages. The notes that follow emphasize several particular points.

¶ ¶ 1 & 2. **State of mind**. You might want to emphasize that some kind of bad state of mind is required, not merely high risk. You cannot describe the bad state of mind with precision. Courts speak of malice, "evil mind", wilfulness or wantonness. Lots of adjectives, but none that can be verified by looking or listening. The adjective in the sentence "He has brown eyes" can be verified; the adjective in the sentence "He has an evil mind" cannot, although we might all have opinions. Maybe for now it's enough to say that some kind of mental state the court will condemn is required in addition to seriously wrong conduct.

Gross negligence, a classification used to state a standard of care in some circumstances, usually means merely extreme negligence, nothing more. That is not enough to warrant punitive damages. Wilful, wanton, or reckless misconduct might include conscious indifference. A court can, of course, define gross negligence to mean what we usually mean by wanton or reckless misconduct. In *Mobil Oil Corp. v. Ellender,* 968 S.W.2d 917, 921 (Tex. 1998), following earlier authority, the Texas Court used the term gross negligence as a basis for punitive damages, but said that it was defined to require "actual, subjective awareness of the risk involved" and that the defendant must have proceeded "in conscious indifference to the rights, safety, or welfare or others." That makes gross negligence for the Texas Court pretty much the same as wanton misconduct or recklessness is for others– it entails a punishment-worthy state of mind.

OWENS-CORNING FIBERGLAS CORP. V. BALLARD, 749 So.2d 483 (Fla. 1999)

Facts like these suggest the reason why punitive damages may be needed for deterrence. If selling Kaylo is profitable and the business has no human concerns, you will need to be sure that it is unprofitable to carry on such humanly destructive activities. Whether we have any way to measure the right amount of punitive damages is another question.

Note 1. Deterrence function. Courts often speak of punishment as well as deterrence, presumably meaning that, independent of deterrence, added damages are a matter of "just deserts." These notes concentrate on deterrence and litigation finance functions.

You might recall that in the McDonald's coffee case, Chapter 1, Casebook p. 18, evidence indicated that McDonalds knew of many customer burns but nevertheless continued to heat its coffee to an unusually high temperature. *Gonzales v. Surgidev Corp.,* 899 P.2d 576 (N.M. 1995), was a suit against a manufacturer of intraocular lens implants who had known for a long time that Style 10 lens implants caused serious problems in vision when implanted by certain procedures and that some patients developed secondary glaucoma. Nevertheless, it continued to promote Style 10 for use with this procedure and gave no warning. This was quite sufficient to show utter indifference to the consequences and thus to justify punitive damages. The court also permitted introduction of evidence that the defendant has similarly turned its back on patients' safety concern with other models that were not substantially the same. This evidence was relevant because it showed a reckless disregard for the safety of others even though not with the same product. For details on a number of corporate concealment cases leading to harm from products, *see* Cynthia R. Mabry, *Warning! The Manufacturer of this Product May Have Engaged in Cover-Ups, Lies, and Concealment: Making the Case for Limitless Punitive Awards in Product Liability Lawsuits,* 73 IND. L.J. 187, 216-234 (1997) (detailing Dalkon Shield, asbestos, tobacco and other cases).

Death of a tortfeasor. Could you deter a tortfeasor who has died? Most courts hold that punitive damages are not to be levied against the estate of a deceased. A few, however, have held that the award is permissible, at least in some cases. In *G.J.D. v. Johnson,* 713 A.2d 1127 (Pa. 1998), the plaintiff had lived with one Darwin Thebes (a real name?) for several years. Thebes made

sexually explicit photographs of the plaintiff. When she terminated their relationship, Thebes circulated copies of the photographs widely in the
community, identifying the plaintiff by name, giving her phone number, and
suggesting she was a prostitute. He made sure that copies would be seen by
the plaintiff's mother, her children, and her employer. He then committee suicide. The court held that punitive damages against the estate would be
permitted and that the jury in determining the amount could take into account the estate's assets. What about deterring a corporation that produced or
used asbestos to the everlasting harm of its employees and others but no
longer deals in that substance? A judge who abuses his power from the bench
but has lost the election and is no longer a judge? Is it ever just to punish one
person solely because that will provide an example to others?

Note 4. Litigation finance function. The reality of the "American rule"
of attorney fees, in which each side bears its own fees and the loser does not
pay, coupled with the lack of universal health care or the kind of social-
security safety net you see in most other industrialized nations, is a central
part of any sensible assessment of tort law damages. Punitive damages, like
pain and suffering awards, may help finance litigation. If you oppose litigation, that's bad. If you take a more measured view, then the assessment about
what to do about punitive damages is, well, more complex than that.

B. Measurement of Punitive Damages

Note : Traditional Factors in Measuring Punitive Damages

Profiteers and Terrorists. You can think of punitive damages cases in
two large categories – (1) the tort-for-profit case in which a manufacturer deliberately chooses a dangerous design because it can make more money than it
expects to lose in damages awards; (2) the tort-for-pleasure-or-rage case,
which encompasses the bully on the street corner, Dickens' socio-pathic aristo-
crats in *Tale of Two Cities*, racist hate crimes, and the terrorist tortfeasors
who blow people up with bombs. Contemporary American law has been more
concerned with the first category. Deterrence and deterrence measures are
surely important in the first category, and some of the factors named below
might well be important. But the second category exists. Can we intelligently
measure punitive damages against a state agency that sponsors terrorism? In
Wagner v. Islamic Republic of Iran, 172 F. Supp.2d 128 (D. D.C. 2001) the
court, following some similar cases, held that MOIS, an agency of Iran that
sponsored a terrorist bombing of the American Embassy in Beirut, killing the
decedent, would be liable for $300 million in punitive damages, a figure repre-
senting three times the amount of MOIS's estimated annual budget for
terrorist activities.

In the tort-for-profit kind of case, you might think deterrence would be the
primary function of punitive damages, so that the trier should consider the
tort's profitability rather than capital wealth in determining the right amount
of punitive damages. The ratio of actual harm or the amount of compensatory

damages to punitive damages might strike some of us as an arbitrary consideration in a single-injury case. If the damages are small, the profit already made or the profit to be made by continued repetition of the tort may still be high. In *Parrott v. Carr Chevrolet, Inc.,* 17 P.3d 473 (Or. 2001), the punitive award was 87 times the actual damages suffered by the plaintiff, but the court avoided the ratio guideline by considering also the damages inflicted on others in the past and potential future damages– which is to say that the actual ratio is not necessarily of any consequence at all.

In mass tort cases, a ratio rule or factor might have some merit. If the defendant is liable for many punitive awards to different claimants arising from the same or conduct, the ratio rule would tend to prevent excessive punishment/deterrence. Wealth and ratio issues usually prompt discussion.

NOTE: LIMITING PUNITIVE AWARDS

Part of tort reform is aimed at punitive damages in particular. This note summarizes some of the kinds of limitations reformers have imposed. One or two statutes virtually abolish punitive awards against health care practitioners, *e.g.,* OR. REV. STATS. § 18.550. Most attempt to cut the awards by less drastic means.

Students exposed to discussion can usually see that redirection of awards could affect the attorney and hence the attorney's financial ability to take the case if compensatory damages are small and proof is complex. Although *Kirk v. Denver Pub. Co.,* cited in ¶ **6**, held the statute to be unconstitutional, *Gordon v. State,* 608 So.2d 800 (Fla. 1992), upheld such a statute, including its specific provision that the attorney's contingent fee could not be calculated on the portion of the award that was redirected. *Evans v. Kutch,* 56 P.3d 1046 (Alaska 2002), is a split decision on the issue. The judges who thought the statute unconstitutional argued that the "forfeiture" of half the punitive damages added nothing to deterrence, so the legislature had to have some other purpose and that no legitimate other purpose existed. They believed that in those circumstances, the statute violated due process and also constituted a taking without just compensation. As to the idea of discouraging frivolous claims advanced in support of the redirection of half the punitive award, these judges said: "Because the state receives its fifty-percent share of punitive damages . . . only if the jury's award of punitive damages withstands scrutiny by the trial judge and is upheld on appeal, the actual source of forfeiture under the statute will *always* consist of punitive damages that have been conclusively established to be factually and legally justified. While purporting to target frivolous and excessive claims, then, the forfeiture statute paradoxically does just the opposite: it attacks only meritorious judgments . . . . As a deterrent to frivolous claims, then, this regime is worse than irrational; it is perverse." For other cases, *see* Sonja Larsen, Annotation, *Validity, Construction, and Application of Statutes Requiring That Percentage of Punitive Damages Awards Be Paid Directly to State or Court-Administered Fund,* 16 A.L.R.5th 129 (1993).

Some statutes protect the attorney fee by computing it on the total award, then redirect the punitive award or some portion. Such a statute does not seem to discourage any suits at all unless you believe there are a good many monster plaintiffs out there manufacturing claims, but some defendants, in line with the tort reform picture of Americans as greedy and dishonest, do believe that. None of the redirection statutes seem likely to discourage false as opposed legitimate suits.

¶ 8. When caps are fixed by a ratio rule, they merely make the ratio rule, which is already arbitrary and potentially inconsistent with deterrence and punishment, more arbitrary. It becomes a rule, not a guideline. If you didn't discuss the ratio rule earlier, it can come in for discussion here.

Constitutionality of tort reform statutes. Tort reform statutes limiting punitive damages may sometimes run into constitutional difficulties, mostly on the basis of narrow and particular state constitutional provisions. The whole Illinois statute, which among other things, limited punitive damages to three times the economic harm inflicted, was held unconstitutional in *Best v. Taylor Machine Works*, 689 N.E.2d 1057 (Ill. 1997). The Ohio statute, including its punitive damages limitations, was held unconstitutional in *State v. Sheward*, 715 N.E.2d 1062 (Ohio 1999). *Williams v. Wilson*, 972 S.W.2d 260 (Ky. 1998), following the Kentucky view that some common law rights were "impervious" to legislative modification, held some punitive damages limitations unconstitutional. Most constitutional discussions now, however, are directed toward limiting punitive damages, not toward the tort reform statutes. Montana's statutory requirement of a unanimous jury for punitive damages awards ran afoul of that state's constitutional provision permitting a verdict on two-thirds' vote. *Finstad v. W.R. Grace & Co.*, 8 P.3d 778 (Mont. 2000).

[*Constitutional Limits on Punitive Damages*]

Due process limits before *Campbell*

Not per se unconstitutional. The Supreme Court entered the punitive damages battle gingerly, holding, as stated in ¶ 4, Casebook p. 796, that punitive damages are not per se unconstitutional under the double jeopardy, excessive fines, or due process provisions of the United States Constitution.

Procedural safeguards required. In *Pacific Mutual Ins. Co. v. Haslip*, 499 U.S. 1 (1991), though, the Court signaled that punitive damages might run afoul of a kind of procedural due process unless the jury was told to consider relevant factors, notably reprehensibility of the defendant's conduct, and maybe also told that an award of punitive damages was not required. Also in the procedural realm, the state had to conduct a post-trial review to assure that the issue was fairly presented. *See Honda Motor Co. Ltd. v. Oberg*, 512 U.S. 415 (1994).

And maybe punitive damages could be constitutionally excessive; factors. Then the Court began to say that punitive damages might be constitutionally excessive even if the procedural safeguards were in place. Whether damages were excessive would be judged largely by the same factors the jury was told to consider in the first place. Of these, reprehensibility of the defendant's misconduct was a major factor. In addition, the ratio between the damage potential and the punitive award was highly significant. Notice that this is not the actual damage/punitive ratio but the potential damage/punitive ratio. The Court discussed this moderate version of the ratio factor in See *Haslip, supra,* and *TXO Production Corp. v. Alliance Resources Corp.,* 509 U.S. 443 (1993) ("Taking account of the potential harm that might result from the defendant's conduct in calculating punitive damages . . ."). In the latter case, the Court upheld an award of $10 million in punitive damages, partly because of evidence of the defendant's net worth and potential for profit from its misconduct.

Yes, by golly, punitive damages are excessive in this case. Then in in *BMW of North America v. Gore,* 517 U.S. 559 (1996), the Court struck down a punitive award for the first time.

BMW v. Gore. (a) *The* Gore *facts.* When BMW cars were damaged while still in its control, BMW would repair or repaint as required. If the damage was quite small, it would simply sell these cars as new cars; if it was larger, BMW would use them in-house. The car Gore bought had been repainted by BMW as a result of damage, probably from acid rain. The painting cost was only $600 and Gore was not told of the repainting. This might have cost him $4,000 in resale value and $4,000 was the jury's award of compensatory damages. The jury then awarded $4 million in punitive damages, reduced to $2 million by the Alabama Court.

(b) *The* Gore *factors, theory and a distinction.* In striking the award, the Supreme Court emphasized the three factors from a longer list it had previously recognized— (a) the degree of reprehensibility of the nondisclosure; (b) the disparity between the harm or potential harm suffered by Dr. Gore and his punitive damages award; and (c) the difference between this remedy and the civil penalties authorized or imposed in comparable cases. It tied these factors to the larger idea that the punitive award could not be justified unless the defendant had received fair notice of the "magnitude of the sanction that" the state might impose for the conduct. The Court thought that of the factors it selected from the longer list, reprehensibility of the defendant's conduct was perhaps the "most important indicium of the reasonableness of a punitive damage award". In assessing this, the Court emphasized that the harm was economic only, creating no risks personal harm, and that there were no deliberate false statements or the like.

(c) *Gore's comparison of punitive awards to criminal penalties.* One of the factors had received little attention in earlier punitive damages jurisprudence. This factor compares the punitive award to the criminal penalty that might be imposed for the same conduct, the idea being that the punitive award should not exceed the criminal penalty by an enormous sum. Although that comparison might bear on the question whether the defendant had fair notice that a severe penalty might be exacted for serious misconduct, the use of criminal penalties as a serious guideline to punitive damages runs heavy risks that the goal of deterrence will be routinely defeated, since the criminal penalty is seldom if ever geared to the defendant's profit from his illicit activity.

(d) *Gore's alternation of the ratio rule formula.* The *BMW* Court also altered the formulation of the ratio rule, so that it became "ratio to the actual harm inflicted on the plaintiff." As we've already pointed out, in *TXO* and *Haslip,* both cited by the Court for this formulation, the Court had specifically recognized that the important ratio was not necessarily a comparison between punitive award and *actual* damages but between the punitive award and *potential harm.*

(e) *Gore on out of state conduct.* Finally, although the Court had recognized deterrence as a goal of punitive damages, the Court in *BMW* put great emphasis on the idea that a state must not attempt to deter by punishing out-of-state conduct, which might, after all, be entirely legal in other states, or might be subject to the most limited kind of penalty. This turned out to be a prelude to *Campbell*

STATE FARM MUT. AUTO. INS. CO. V. CAMPBELL, 538 U.S. 406 (2003)

Campbell sets out the Supreme Court's current ideas about due process limits on punitive damages. In the belief that most teachers will need to minimize the time spent on this case, we'll first give a brief summary-comment, then more detailed background for those who want more. You may wish to know up front that on remand to the Utah Court, that court reassessed punitive damages in accordance with the Supreme Court's direction and came up with punitive damages in accord with the single-digit demand, exactly nine times the compensatory damages, $9,018,780.75. *Campbell v. State Farm Mutual Auto. Ins. Co.,* 98 P.3d 409 (Utah 2004).

Facts. The evidence indicated that State Farm insured Campbell, that Campbell was negligent in causing a serious collision between two other cars by trying to pass six cars on a two-lane road. Campbell wasn't hurt, but Ospital, driver of one other car, was killed, and Slusher, driver of the third vehicle, was permanently disabled. Campbell is a thoroughly bad guy on this evidence, so some students won't feel even an iota of sympathy for him. Yet, though the claim begins as Campbell's claim against his insurer, it will be the victims who benefit from any judgment against State Farm.

Ospital estate's suit against Campbell. Ospital's estate sued Campbell. State Farm refused to settle with the estate for its policy limit of $25,000, so the case went to trial. The ultimate judgment against Campbell came to just over $185,000, about $135,000 more than State Farm's policy limit. State Farm told Campbell that he might as well put his house up for sale because State Farm refused to pay the excess over the policy limit, even though it could have protected Campbell by paying the policy limit in the first place.

The insured's claim and assignment. Students need to understand the insured's bad faith claim outlined in **Note 1.** If State Farm as Campbell's liability insurer, fails to take advantage of an opportunity to settle a clear case of liability for a reasonable sum within its policy limits, that leaves the insured unprotected for a potentially very large verdict. In the absence of a duty to behave in good faith, State Farm would have nothing to lose but the costs of defense; its policy limit of $25,000 per claimant, would protect it, even though that might leave its insured exposed for hundreds of thousands of dollars. The duty courts impose on State Farm and other insurers with settlement opportunities is to consider whether, if it had something to lose, it would accept the settlement offer that is in fact within its policy limits. If it does not accept the offer and is in bad faith (or maybe even just unreasonable), then it will be liable to the insured for any part of the ultimate judgment against the insured that runs over the policy limits. That will give the insured the protection against liability he tried to get by buying insurance. In this case, State Farm initially refused to pay the excess over policy limits (about $125,000). To protect his assets from the judgment that was in excess of State Farm's policy, Campbell sold his claim against State Farm to Ospital's estate in exchange for the estate's covenant not to sue him. Thus, if Campbell had a right to recover against State Farm, that right has now passed to the victim. Eventually, in suit by Ospital's estate against Campbell, the judgment against Campbell was affirmed. At that point State Farm finally agreed to pay the excess.

Campbell's bad faith claim against State Farm. Campbell then filed his bad faith claim (the proceeds of which now belong to Ospital's estate). After reduction by the trial court, the judgment in this suit came to $1 million in actual damages and $25 million in punitive damages. The latter was based on evidence that State Farm had a systematic policy, effectuated in many states, to cap payouts on legitimate claims. This is the punitive award up for review in the Supreme Court.

The Supreme Court's ratio approach. The Court's majority heavily emphasized a concern with the ratio between harm or potential harm and the punitive damages. However, the Court did not attempt to estimate potential harmful effects of the defendant's conduct– much less the effects on other State Farm insureds and injured persons. Instead, the Court shifted slipped from the potential harm-punitive ratio into a totally different emphasis– the actual harm-punitive ratio. Having slipped into this entirely different test, the Court went on to divorce it as much as possible from the merits of the punitive award by making it largely a mechanical test. While the Court said there were no automatic benchmark ratios, it strongly suggested that 4 to 1 would often be the constitutional limit and that in any event a punitive award exceeding a single-digit ratio would seldom if ever be constitutional. See Casebook 895.

Comment: The risk of harm– meaning both the likelihood of harm and its potential magnitude– bears strongly on the reprehensibility issue, but the actual award to a particular plaintiff does not except by happenstance. The emphasis on the actual compensatory award seems hard to square with the reprehensibility guidepost, which the Court recognizes. It is also hard to square with the deterrence function of punitive awards. **Note 5** alerts students to take a careful look at the ratio approach.

Activities of State Farm in other states. The *Campbell* Court also emphasized the plaintiff's use of evidence about State Farm's egregious misconduct in other states. The evidence was offered, not to measure punitive damages but for other purposes, such as to rebut State Farm's claim of inadvertence. The Court recognized that even though the state could not punish lawful out-of-state conduct, the court could admit evidence of such conduct when "it demonstrates the deliberateness and culpability of the defendant's action in the State where it is tortious." **Note 2** alerts students to this point. Still, the evidence could not simply show evil doing; it would have to show conduct with "a nexus to the specific harm suffered by the plaintiff." "A defendant's dissimilar acts, independent from the acts upon which liability was premised, may not serve as the basis for punitive damages." The Court believed that had happened in the Utah Courts.

Note 3 poses a hypothetical about this issue. Could an insurance commissioner exclude State Farm from doing business in the state because of its activities elsewhere? Could the United States have excluded immigration to this country of Nazi Party members, even though the Nazi activities were legal where carried out? One distinction is that both those examples involve administrative or legislation action, not judicial action. Is the Court perhaps feeling that judicial action must be more limited than action in the political arena? The feeling that criminal legislation furnishes some kind of guide that limits judicial imposition of punitive damages is also in line with this suggestion.

Note 4 continues to explore this issue by raising the characterization problem. The Court insists that "dissimilar acts" cannot be the basis for punitive awards. What acts count as similar, though, depend on how you describe State Farm's acts and how you generalize your description. Justice Ginsburg's dissent raises this issue, too; she sees an overarching underpayment scheme, thus generalizing State Farm's conduct broadly enough to

Criminal punishment as a measure of punitive damages. The existence of a criminal penalty bears on the seriousness of the defendant's misconduct, the Court says, but isn't so useful in measuring the punitive damages. What the Court seems to mean by that comment is that the punitive damages should not necessarily be a great as the criminal penalties. The Court seems to think, however, that the criminal penalties should not be "dwarfed" by the punitive award and that an award that far outstrips the criminal penalties may well violate the Constitutional due process right of the defendant.

Note 5. Ratio rule limitations. The Court in *Campbell* did not specify exactly what kind of ratio would violate due process, so lower courts and state courts have been working that out themselves, as noted here. The Court rendered a more recent decision on the ratio rules, however, in *Exxon v. Baker*, cited here, holding that in admiralty cases, a 1:1 ratio was the constitutional limit. The Court made clear that such a limit was only for admiralty cases, however, so the experimentation continues.

Model Act. The Commissioners on Uniform State Laws promulgated a Model Act on punitive damages in the summer of 1996. It emphasizes the egregiousness of the defendant's bad conduct and the ratio of punitive to compensatory damages. The ratio rule remains a problem, though, because seriously bad and wonderfully profitable misconduct might cause a particular plaintiff to suffer only small actual harm.

Note 6. Profits, attorney fees as limits. As we know, courts consider wealth, sometimes in the form of profits, in evaluating the amount of a punitive award. We can add that they also consider the plaintiff's attorney fees. *Kunewa v. Joshua,* 924 P.2d 559 (Haw. Ct. App. 1996). The note, however, discusses these elements as possible limits on the award, not merely as relevant factors.

PHILIP MORRIS USA V. WILLIAMS, 549 U.S. 346 (2007)

Williams deals primarily with the "harm to non-parties" idea. By a 5-4 majority, the Court holds that a punitive damages award based in part upon a jury's desire to punish a defendant for harming non-parties (i.e., persons or entities not before the court) violates due process. Even if you disagree with this basic holding, it makes sense. But the dissenters (**Note 3**) thought that the second part of the Court's holding does not make sense: That evidence of harm to non-parties may be admitted, but only to show "reprehensibility," not to influence the amount of punitive damages. Is this analogous to the *Campbell* Court's attempt to cabin evidence of out-of-state conduct? You might ask students what they think of Justice Stevens's "bomb-thrower" example in **Note 3**. Isn't he right?

Note 2 raises the practical problem with the Court's distinction. Does you class think a jury can hear non-party harm evidence, consider it on the reprehensibility issue, but then disregard it when it comes time to fix the damages? Are they not supposed to fix the amount of damages based in part upon reprehensibility?

PROBLEM : O'BRIEN V. SPRING DEPARTMENT STORE

Most importantly, this problem gives students a chance to look at and apply some of the factors that are said to guide the punitive award. They may feel that when the factors are fully considered, they still have almost no basis for determining a given sum of punitive damages.

A secondary possibility in teaching this problem is to use it in an engaging experiment. In *Assessing Punitive Damages (With Notes on Cognition and Valuation in Law)*, 107 YALE L.J. 2071 (1998), authors Cass R. Sunstein, Daniel Kahneman and David Schkade reported an experimental study on punitive damages in which they asked mock jurors to rate conduct for punishment on a scale of one to six, not in dollars. They reported high agreement in the result. A classroom won't replicate all the controls, but it might still be useful to ask the class to rate the conduct on such a scale. You might want to have prepared ballots for this. If most students come up with similar numbers, you might then discuss the possibility of a legally prescribed range to go with each number of the scale. (Notice you might lose all deterrent effect or equally you might over-deter.) If you can spend the class time, you might also try taking the class votes both before discussion and afterward.

The problem is based upon *Bowden v. Caldor, Inc.*, 710 A.2d 267 (Md. 1998), which is substantially similar both in the main facts and in the quoted words. The trial judge in the second trial concluded that the punitive award in the first trial was a cap on the punitive award that could be made in the second trial, for otherwise the defendant would be robbed of its victory on appeal. The Maryland Court reversed this, holding that the first trial's award was not a limitation punitive damages.

However, although acknowledging that the jury could have "reasonably concluded that the Caldor officials involved in this matter were motivated by racial hatred," the court went on to hold that the award of $9 million was excessive as a matter of law. In so holding, it considered factors of the kind discussed in the casebook. It then remanded the case to permit the trial judge to review the award and reduce it for excessiveness. With compensatory damages, at least, a trial judge implements a finding of excessiveness by ordering a new trial unless the plaintiff consents to a reduction in a specified amount. In this case the Maryland Court held that reduction of punitive damages was in the power of the judge without ordering a new trial. The trial judge will therefore pick a number between 1 and 9 million and that will be the end of the matter.

The Maryland Court listed a several factors that influenced its judgment that the award was excessive. We've added numbers in these quotations:

[1] Caldor's malicious and wrongful conduct was not life threatening or the type of conduct which would likely lead to permanent physical injuries. [2] There was no evidence in the record that the plaintiff has suffered any serious lasting effects from the events. [3] There was also no evidence that Caldor personnel had previously or have subsequently engaged in similar wrongful conduct. [4] The $9,000,000 punitive damages award is nine times higher than the greatest criminal fine authorized by the Maryland Legislature. [5] It is about thirteen times higher than the largest punitive damages award ever

upheld by this Court. [6] It is one hundred and fifty times higher than the compensatory damages awarded in the case

Are all these factors really relevant to appropriate levels of deterrence?

CHAPTER 27

EVALUATING TORT LAW

▶**Changes in the Sixth Edition.** We have updated the data on injuries and economic effects. The chapter otherwise remains much the same as in the Fifth Edition. However, if you teach this chapter but not all the chapters on alternatives to the tort system, you might want to bring in materials on the alternatives. The 9-11 compensation system (from public funds) is an alternative not very popular with scholars and a good one to import for contrast with the tort system if you are not covering Chapter 29.

▶The **Concise Edition** trims a couple of pages from this Chapter by omitting some paragraphs in various places; the main ideas remain.■

This chapter not only permits a backward glance at the materials covered in the course, it allows students to begin evaluating the tort system as a whole. At the same time, this chapter projects forward and gives a basis for taking seriously the non-tort systems that follow.

The introductory sketch indicates something about the incidence and costs of injury. The data come from the National Safety Council, Report on Injuries in America (2008), available online at http://www.nsc.org/lrs/injuriesinamerica08.aspx. The National Safety Council website at www.nsc.org has a number of other interesting safety-related statistics and reports that might interest torts teachers as well.

The National Center for State Courts (NCSC) has a web site with a lot of statistics, but some are stated too broadly to permit you to pull out tort suits. The total number of cases filed approaches 100 million, but only 16 million civil cases. Of the civil cases, tort case filings have actually declined in most states, while contract claims have increased. When you consider that tort claims may include economic tort claims, usually involving entrepreneurial disputes, and that for some years economic tort claims have increased, this figure is fairly striking. You can reach the NCSC home page http://www.ncsconline.org/. Click on Court Statistics to reach statistical summaries.

Other statistical information on tort cases can be found at the Bureau of Justice Statistics: website http://www.ojp.usdoj.gov/bjs/welcome.html. The median total award in a tort case was only $24,000, hardly the image portrayed by the media. This is lower than the median contract award and less than half of what the National Safety Council estimates is the average economic cost of an automobile injury. It may be worth looking at a number of statistics about what is really happening in the tort system. Links to the BJS site and many other helpful sites can also be found at http://www.nsc.org/lrs/statinfo/statlink.htm.

Death from injury has actually declined over the years. Some of the decline in driving deaths year surely stemmed from the very high price of gasoline and the resulting decrease in number of miles driven. Given that alcohol is associated with a high percentage of vehicle injuries and deaths, it is possible that Mothers Against Drunk Driving's campaign for more stringent DUI enforcement has been responsible for some of the reduction in death in previous years. Other possibilities include better-designed highways and safer cars. The remaining deaths and injuries, however, are very numerous and very costly in both economic and human terms.

§ 1. RULES, PRACTICES AND THEORIES OF TORT LAW

These short paragraphs ask the student to begin looking at torts from a public point of view, but with the knowledge of a professional. You don't have to discuss them directly, but, treating them as introductory, you can begin with § 2.

§ 2. TORT WARS

The "new" tort reform seeks to limit liability without providing any alternatives for injured people. In this respect tort reform is essentially negative (and often based on shamefully inaccurate or undocumented statements). We come again to some of the ideas introduced in Chapter 1, but this chapter presents more basis for evaluation of tort reformers' claims. Still, you may want to review the McDonald's coffee case and like material from Chapter 1.

Evaluating Criticisms

One way to discuss ideas in this chapter is to take up each of the bulleted items one by one (or select ones you'd prefer to discuss).

In the first item, recent study confirms that the gross number of claims seems to have remained fairly stable in spite of the critics' claims. One reason for widely divergent views about what is happening in tort claims may arise from critics' reliance upon anecdotes, but another is that there are many kinds of tort cases and the data about one kind may reveal an increase in suits while data about another may reveal a different story. See Deborah R. Hensler, *Trends in Tort Litigation: Findings from the Institute for Civil Justice's Research,* 48 OHIO ST. L.J. 479, 480 (1987). Scholarly study indicates that asserting tort claims for injury is "a statistically *unusual* behavior." DEBORAH HENSLER, SUSAN MARQUIS, ALLAN ABRAHAMSE, SANDRA BERRY, PATRICIA EBENER, ELIZABETH LEWIS, ALLAN LIND, ROBERT MACCOUN, WILLARD MANNING, JEANNETTE ROGOWSKI & MARY VAIANA, COMPENSATION FOR ACCIDENTAL INJURIES IN THE UNITED STATES 142 (Rand Corporation 1991).

We have removed from the casebook an interesting paragraph summarizing a piece in the summer 1995 issue of *Civil Justice Digest,* published by the Roscoe Pound Foundation. It reported a study concluding that corporate members of the American Tort Reform Association and Product Liability Alliance themselves brought 38,000 lawsuits from 1991 through 1994 in five populous states alone. This was a rate of one new suit every 12.5 minutes the courthouses were open. The authors considered many of these cases to be as frivolous as any of the absurd personal injury cases publicized by tort reformers. The study also asserted that contract suits were ten times more numerous than tort suits. The figures in the Merritt & Barry study, presented in a chart in Chapter 1, this manual, are not so extreme. Still, their figures showed that contract litigation exceeded even the common automobile case. As these comments suggest, there are many kinds of cases, even many kinds of tort cases, and data about one kind may not reflect what is going on with others.

The text following the bullets asserts that tort reform critics got their rhetoric from anecdotes, not studies of the system as a whole. And some of the anecdotes were misleadingly presented. But if the tort reformers used misleading anecdotes, did they nevertheless get the conclusion right? By calling on the students' own experience with the wide assortment of cases we have read and discussed, you give students a chance to put opinions together and to review at the same time.

Similarly you can ask a student what she makes of the fact stated in the fourth item, that half of all medical malpractice payouts are paying on behalf of doctors against whom others have collected before. Do we conclude: (a) some doctors are natural victims; (b) this is just a coincidence; (c) there must be some real malpractice going on and maybe most of it is by the same group of doctors over and over; (d) maybe the tort system is not deterring very well and some system for medical review would better serve to stop repeat offenders.

There is an enormous amount of politicized comment on the topic of increased litigation. The Saks article is especially helpful on analysis. The Sanders and Joyce article gives you, in addition, some arresting political or factual detail about the "reform" process.

§ 3. THE IMPACT OF TORT LAW ON THE INJURY PROBLEM

It may be helpful if students are led to visualize some of the kinds of social problems that could be created by uncompensated injury, or even injury for which compensation is delayed. The barest questioning can usually prompt a recognition that the uncompensated injured may absorb tax funds from welfare, public or private. It may not be obvious to all students that employers, too, may suffer losses when an employee is injured. There will be in many instances production losses—goods or services that bring in income are not produced at all, or the employer must pay overtime to get replacement work.

It is really important for students to try to see what it is like on the edge. Our dramatic powers may not suffice to overcome the limited imagination of a well-fed life. A single young worker has purchased a truck on which he makes payments. He needs the truck to get to work. He is injured and the truck is damaged in a minor collision. He misses two weeks of work as a result and his employer, needing a replacement, discharges him. Now he cannot make payments on the truck and it is repossessed. He has no savings, no medical plan, and no transportation. Now he has no job, either. His landlord evicts him. What began as a minor cost that could easily have been limited to truck repair costs and a little medical expense has spiraled into a serious matter. The young man's life is substantially disrupted. Without support from family or friends, he may never get it on track again. Unless, of course, a lawyer can blow up this once-minor case into a claim large enough to get the plaintiff going again.

If we imagine injury within a family unit some things are easier and some are harder. The radiating effects of pain and worry are likely first to destroy personal relationships within the family, by destruction of both authority and affection. Children or young persons may be led to drop out of school or to forego college. Some will certainly be led into increasingly anti-social activities—abuse of substances, crime. Quite aside from the sad effects on individuals, all these things can cost the rest of us, and this is what we mean by social loss. If a student in your class—perhaps a former counselor or social worker— can be led to describe some of these effects, it will be possible to get a grip on the idea that there is a societal interest involved.

Problems with the Tort System?

Discussion of each of these items, if time permits, is a useful way to break up this material. Most torts students are not accustomed to dealing with figures, but this works well if one takes one question at a time.

1. Undercompensation. Reasons for undercompensation. Are all the reasons bad? After all, the fault system attempts to reduce recovery for fault of the plaintiff on the ground that liability for fault should be in proportion to fault. Won't that explain some of the cases of apparent undercompensation— the plaintiff is guilty of negligence? One can, at this point or later, question whether this principle itself is sound, after all, in the light of the social impact of injury. But even if the principle is still sound, it seems clear that undercompensation exceeds anything that would ordinarily be explained by contributory negligence. This is so for reasons given in paragraph 3—that is, the compensation is distributed in a most peculiar way, with overcompensation to some claimants and undercompensation to others. The distribution of compensation is obviously also related to the undercompensation addressed in paragraph 1. Hence even if we are complete adherents of the fault principles, we have to say that tort law is not achieving its goals here. Much more serious is the prevalence of the uninsured driver. The estimate that one in five or six vehicles is uninsured is based upon Gary Schwartz' estimate, in turn based upon an unpublished study. That estimate is an average of 17%, with some areas of uninsurance as high at 80%. Gary T. Schwartz, *Auto No-fault and First-party Insurance: Advantages and Problems,* 73 S. CAL. L. REV. 611 (2000).

Social impact of undercompensation. It is easy for most law students to underestimate this. What do they think might be some of the impact? Answers are usually vague and unenthusiastic. But the impact is enormous. As the introductory figures indicate, direct losses from auto accidents are at least 5 to 10 billion annually. But direct costs are not the only real costs impacting society. Accidents cause economic loss to people who are not injured at all. The employer may lose production or may incur added costs (overtime) paid to other workers to keep production up, for example. Work accidents alone cost almost $15 billion in wage losses and medical expenses way back in 1982. The astonishing figure, though, is that indirect costs doubled this figure. In other words, the money value of the time lost by workers not injured, the time taken to investigate accidents and so on, came to another $15 billion. This does not include such costs as court time in law suits.

A system of injury law that is either inefficient or fails to rehabilitate as quickly as possible will increase costs of this kind. Assured compensation systems might be superior to the tort system on both counts—providing speedy, immediate medical attention and thus improving rehabilitation, and by minimizing the costs of investigating and proving fault. It is easy to imagine a fracture that is not properly attended as an example: it may not heal so quickly, or it may require extensive medical attention later if not attended to immediately, in either case with resulting production losses.

More important impacts may occur in the home. Even if injury does not cause loss of work time, any economic harm at all can be disastrous for economically marginal families. Medical expense, car damage or a day's loss of work may mean severe economic dislocation to many families. What is the social impact of this? The impacts may be hard to trace, but they are easy to imagine if the student will try. A breadwinner's injury or even damage to a family car may trigger new work patterns in the family; the home parent may begin work, a marginal child who most needs education may drop out of high school to work. Delinquency may rise. Compensation may tend to avoid or minimize any of these impacts even if it does not involve rehabilitation.

2. Overcompensation. Overcompensation represents, in the words of Morris and Paul, "large areas of economic waste." Morris & Paul, *The Financial Impact of Automobile Accidents,* 110 U. PA. L. REV. 913 (1962). Economic waste is not, as some students may wish to believe, merely a matter of taking from those who can afford it and giving to those who cannot. On the contrary, it represents money that flows randomly sometimes to those who do not need it and certainly to those who do not deserve it; and likewise, it is derived most often from insurance, to which we all do or should contribute. It inevitably adds to the cost of insurance, and any increase in the cost of insurance will eventually drive some insurance buyers out of the market unless insurance is compulsory. If liability insurance is made compulsory, it will cost even more, and even then it will drive down the amounts of insurance people will purchase. If it is not made compulsory, many drivers will "go bare," and be unable to pay the damages they cause. Overcompensation is a positive evil from many points of view and the students can be led to take an unsentimental, clear sighted view of this.

Some students may have difficulty accepting that there is both over-and undercompensation especially in the light of the claim made in Morris & Paul that the poor may be hardest hit. It must be remembered, though, that while the average $330 claim was paid $829, only 70% of those having injuries under $500 received anything at all. The table shows payouts are relatively high for low-loss claims, relatively low for high-loss claims, but a smaller percentage of low-loss claims are paid. Thus in the range of $1-499, the average loss is $330 and the reparation is $829, but only 70% receive any reparations at all. When the loss ranges from $1,500 to $2,499, the average loss is $1,947 and the average payout is $2,234, but by this time some 88% of the claimants are being paid. Between $10,000 and $24,999, the loss is $16,482, the payout only $9,681, but 91 percent are paid.

3. Misuse of limited resources. The insurance pie simply is not big enough to go around—not even for actual economic losses. It is still less adequate to cover pain and suffering losses as well.[1] The figures given here from the DOT study are not the only ones, but they sufficiently illustrate the point. The main options on which class discussion can center might be:

(a) Leave things alone.

(b) Collect added insurance premiums so that there will be a sufficient fund to pay out all losses. One problem is that, as the next note says, the liability insurance dollar is inefficient. Another problem is that if premiums are raised, we will have a new dilemma—either we will have to make insurance

---

1. A somewhat similar point was made in *Norfolk & Western Ry. v. Ayers*, 538 U.S. 135 (2003) (Kennedy J., dissenting) — that defendants who must pay emotional harm damages to the first plaintiff in mass tort cases may have no funds left for payment of even more serious claims for pain or actual financial costs suffered by later plaintiffs. The comment on that point in Dobbs on Torts § 302 (Supp.) is: "This problem, however, is not really about emotional harm claims but about equitable distribution to multiple victims when the wrongdoer's funds are inadequate to cover the harms he has inflicted. The problem occurs not only with emotional harm claims but also with punitive damages awarded to an early claimant and even with ordinary economic loss claims paid to the first plaintiff and leaving nothing for claims of the second. It may be that the legal solution should aim at the whole problem and not merely at the isolated instance of it when emotional harm is claimed."

compulsory or we will have an increased number of uninsured motorists and therefore an increased number of victims who cannot collect. The mandatory insurance feature may not trouble some people—after all, it is a feature of no-fault as well—but it would almost certainly drive people to purchase the minimum required insurance. If the liability dollar is inefficient as compared to some other insurance dollars, this mandatory waste would be counterproductive at best. Since it would necessarily be a higher cost than a more efficient insurance scheme, it might even be viewed as particularly hard on poorer drivers.

(c) Limit pain and suffering. This will not solve the problem, given the figures reported here. That is because the pain and suffering figures are not included here and the insurance fund is insufficient even without any pain and suffering recovery. It would, however, tend to bring a better balance—some of the money now going for pain and suffering could go to pay economic losses instead, or alternatively, premiums could be reduced. People get very excited about proposals like this and class discussion is not hard to generate. One way to consider the idea is to ask the student whether it would be preferable, given the lack of insurance funds, simply to let individuals insure themselves for their own losses. The most important losses might be left for the tort-insurance system, and those generally of lesser importance might be insured for by individuals interested. If this approach were taken, which losses would remain in the tort system—economic losses or pain and suffering? Would individuals ever insure themselves for pain and suffering? Since pain is highly individualized, might it be best to let people insure themselves for pain in the same way they can buy their own accident insurance? Notice that we are compelled now to insure for pain if we want liability insurance, since pain represents half or more of many recoveries. Even if we as individuals would rather pay a lower premium and not get a pain award if injured, we have no choice because we must purchase insurance to protect against what the law says the other fellow can recover.

4. Inefficiency of the tort-liability insurance system. "Inefficiency" implies a cheaper way of accomplishing our goals. Some students may have trouble grasping the comparative costs of liability insurance as compared to other kinds. Maybe you can pry open the idea of costs of the tort system by noticing the great volume of litigation. Students of the problem now estimate that there are hundreds of thousands of mass tort claims involving asbestos and Dalkon Shield. These are pursued mainly in class actions and in bankruptcy litigation, which may lead to bulk treatment. On the other hand, if class actions cannot be used, many individuals will be unable to pursue claims and the judicial system would be overwhelmed if they could. The literature of mass torts is itself now massive.

The argument that inefficiency results from the costs of paying injury losses through liability insurance and a tort trial system is more persuasive. Costs may have varied over time and data are always incomplete, but contemporary estimates indicate that administrative costs of the tort system run about 50%, with some variation depending upon the type of tort case involved. In terms of premium dollar, this would mean that when a driver pays $1,000 for liability insurance, only about $500 of that sum is actually paid out for injury. In some toxic litigation the costs are much higher and the returns in payouts are much lower. *See* Deborah R. Hensler, *Trends in Tort Litigation: Findings from the Institute for Civil Justice's Research,* 48 OHIO ST. L.J. 479, 492 (1987).

The data is old but it indicates that workers' compensation and first party insurance is more efficient, that is returns a higher proportion of the premium dollar in payouts. Conard group's study provided some gross figures, although they denied the figures represented relative efficiency. These figures showed that, for 1960, the tort system provided net benefits of $1,413 million, but at a total cost of $3,202 million. CONARD, MORGAN, PRATT, VOLZ & BOMBAUGH, AUTOMOBILE ACCIDENT COSTS AND PAYMENTS (1964). (The figures are not the same as those given in the DOT study, but it must be understood that, definitional and procedural differences aside, we are dealing with estimates at best.)

Another approach to the inefficiency argument can be posed on the board, and will have some payoffs in later discussion of subrogation costs as well. Professor Alfred Conard gave an illustration in which Policyholder of a Blue Cross policy is injured in an accident with Driver. Policyholder incurs $1,000 in medical costs paid by Blue Cross at a total cost to Blue Cross of $1,080. (Professor Conard had his reasons for estimating $80 as the cost of handling the claim.) If Blue Cross then attempts subrogation against Driver and recovers $1,000, its net recovery will only be $750 after expenses and legal fees. Driver's liability insurer, on the other hand, will spend not only the $1,000 necessary to pay the judgment, but also an added $600 in expenses. Thus the liability insurer will pay $1,600 to net the Blue Cross $750. See Conard, *The Economic Treatment of Automobile Injuries,* 63 MICH. L. REV. 279, 311 (1964). This example does not give a full comparison of premium return of the two system, but it furnishes a dramatic illustration of the costs in the two different systems, nonetheless. If this illustration is used in class, with a blackboard and the figures, it can also serve as a foundation for discussions of subrogation later on when we come to it in workers' compensation. There is no need to alert the class to this prospective use and it is sufficiently striking that it will be easy to recapture the idea later.

5. Delay in payment under the tort system. Delay is a serious problem to the injured plaintiff. Although many plaintiffs, supported by their own private insurance and other resources, will not suffer greatly from the delay in payment, many others would have to endure considerable hardship. The delay is independent of the problem of undercompensation, but it also feeds into that problem, since it may be a tool for inducing a settlement that is undercompensatory.

The casebook suggests three separate problems of delay. Conceivably two of those problems could be dealt with without altering the torts system. Delay due to the problems of identifying and proving future injury might be dealt with by using a periodic payments system rather than a lump sum system. There is in fact a MODEL PERIODIC PAYMENT OF JUDGMENTS ACT, 14 U.L.A. (Supp.). The best analysis of periodic payment problems is Roger Henderson, *Designing a Responsible Periodic Payment System for Tort Awards*, 32 ARIZ. L. REV. 21 (1990). You'll recall from Chapter 23 that some courts have already held some periodic payment statutes unconstitutional.

The other less-than-radical effort to cut delay would be to charge interest and/or penalties. The traditional rule is that defendants are not liable for interest on amounts owed unless the amount is liquidated or readily ascertainable. This did not traditionally include tort claims. Thus defendants may actually profit by delay, not only strategically, but also by retaining the money owed and investing it. Some states now have adopted some major interest statutes or court rules. These may not be sufficiently strong to discourage delay, but they do reflect ways in which intended, strategic delay could be reduced.

But none of this, even if carried out vigorously, could attack the fundamental problem of delay resulting from the detailed analysis of fault, cause, and damage. Law's commitment to due process and to analysis and full argument is a proud achievement, but it may be that not every issue in the world should be treated to these benefits. You might be reminded of the comments with which the late Professor Grant Gilmore ended his lectures on the Ages of American Law. Hell will be filled with law, he said, and "due process will be meticulously observed." G. GILMORE, THE AGES OF AMERICAN LAW 111 (1977). Those who want to see the tort system replaced in accident cases would no doubt take the position that the elaborate trial and investigation into fault we now know might be appropriate for some things, but not for the massive problem represented by millions of injured. But the question is open to debate, nonetheless: if fault is important in the justice of the matter, then careful investigation may be worth the costs. What does the class think about this?

6. The failure to deter or compensate. Maximum deterrence will occur on an individual level when there is a direct and perceived relationship between tort liability and fault, and when the defendant is personally made to suffer as a result of the fault. Insurance tends to prevent this, however. What about increases in insurance rates? Actually, the threat of insurance rate increases may be more real to some drivers than tort liability. Insurance rates are monthly, quarterly or annual, and they come up again and again. They are not risks, but certainties to those who buy insurance. While a driver might ignore mere risks of tort liability—quite unrealistically, perhaps—it may not be so likely that the driver will ignore insurance premiums, which may be raised after an accident, as the driver well knows. Since there are many factors involved in fixing premiums besides fault as such—the potential for high damages being one—it is doubtful whether there is a sufficient direct relationship to accomplish deterrence goals on a substantial basis. It is, perhaps, possible to alter this somewhat if one is determined to save the tort system. A deductible liability policy is not impossible; a tax against the tortfeasor to fund an unsatisfied judgment fund would not be an entirely bad idea, either.

7. Participation in the insurance fund—lack of reciprocity. X buys no insurance but is injured in an accident. X may recover thousands or even millions from funds provided by Y, the driver of the other car, even though X will provide nothing to those he may injure. Some students may be tempted to say that you can't expect X to buy insurance if X is poor, and it matters not that he drew on funds provided by others, since, after all, the other in this case was at fault (otherwise he would not be liable). The fact that X has not bought insurance to cover some other accident is just as irrelevant as the fact that X once abused a spouse. This argument, however, assumes what is in issue—the fault system. Why should X be protected by the good conscience of others when he refuses to provide equivalent protection for harm he wrongfully causes?

Students may here resort to the idea that this situation is just a small redistribution of wealth in favor of the poor. If X cannot afford insurance, fine, then let the wealthy who may be his victims buy their own. The merits of this form of wealth redistribution might be arguable if it could work that way. But in fact there are two problems that prevent its working at all. First, X may not be poor, or "too poor" to provide insurance. (For an X who is too poor, some other arrangement might be made.) Second, wealth is not redistributed this way unless we imagine that X will selectively carry out his negligent driving toward wealthy, and only wealthy, victims. That is of course impossible, and a moment's reflection will indicate that X may cause more harms to poor person or persons of quite limited means. His failure to carry insurance may increase any inequalities in wealth distribution, not the other way around.

Evincing similar concerns, but proceeding from a different kind of non-reciprocity, is it possible to argue that poor people as a class will not get their share of the insurance pie? This argument is based on grouping of contributors to the funds, and implicitly asserts that the group should recover in at least rough proportion to its input. The first argument on reciprocity was not necessarily based on a rejection of the fault system; it might be answered, for example, by compulsory insurance. This second argument seems, however, to assume that the fault system is wrong, for if it is right, the fact that one group pays in more than it withdraws cannot itself be important. (It is important if it reflects undercompensation, but only as an argument about adequate compensation, not as an argument about reciprocity.)

8. Is the tort system a lottery? (a) Is there really a problem here? We could adopt a single system of reparations—one based on fault, for example—and eliminate the disparity of treatment among those who are injured in car accidents, in products accidents, and in work accidents. And as to the "luck" of striking someone whose damages are limited by contributory negligence or by a thick skull, that is simply a reflection of the compensatory purpose of tort law or of the notion that there is liability only to the extent of fault. If this is too lucky for words, we could certainly add criminal charges if we thought it worth it. If the student likes the casebook suggestions, these comments should furnish room for further questioning.

(b) There is luck in getting an attractive party or witness, and maybe jurors are misled by stage management of lawyers. But this is not limited to tort cases, is it? Is this "luck" argument merely a counsel of despair?

(c) The lottery might encourage the bringing of claims that should not win. The small chance of the big recovery is what keeps the gambler betting on the 20-1 horse or buying lottery tickets. It also keeps lawyers and clients going to court. If one wants to consider the "dishonesty" argument this can be added here, but the lottery element does not depend on dishonesty; cupidity or self-delusion is quite sufficient.

9. The lump-sum award and pain and suffering. The lump-sum award is all too likely to be mismanaged. Unfortunately there are few data, but plenty of anecdotes. If the plaintiff recovers a large sum but loses it to unscrupulous friends, advisors or salespeople, or simply cannot manage it, the funds from insurance accomplish, to that extent, no useful purpose. If the pain and suffering award accomplishes no clear good, it, too, is wasted and would be better spent on economic losses that now go uncompensated. This will provoke a considerable debate in most classes.

New Directions

This segment begins to suggest that some or all of the injury problem could be dealt with by other means than a tort-liability-insurance system. Some of the traditional alternative institutions for dealing with injury are considered in the next three chapters.

PART 6

ALTERNATIVES TO TORT LAW

The next four Chapters deal with alternatives to tort law. Chapter 28 covers workers' compensation. Chapter 29 covers public compensation systems, focusing mainly on Social Security disability. Chapter 30 addresses private insurance solutions, mainly no-fault automobile insurance. Finally, Chapter 31 presents a brief discussion agenda for evaluating the various systems we have seen for injury compensation.

▶The **Concise Edition** combines these four Chapters into a single brief Chapter 28, titled Being Aware of Compensation Options. That Chapter offers a most succinct summary of these tort law alternatives without going into any detail. The point is to make students aware that these alternatives exist, and perhaps to interest them in further study.■

CHAPTER 28

WORKERS' COMPENSATION

▶**Changes in the Sixth Edition.** We have cut over 10 percent of the length of this Chapter, in part to encourage more professors to teach it (or part of it). Most of the cuts are in § 2, where we have cut the *Jaeger Baking* and *Leff* cases, and the case abstracts of *McCann, Kolson,* and *Kerr McGee v. Hutto.* We have added a new main case in that section, *Wait.* In § 3 we've reduced the *Kerans* case to a case abstract. Notes and text have been fully updated and include 18 new cases cited and/or discussed.

Scheduling omissions: *One day:* If you only have time to make students aware of the general idea, assign § 1, with or without class discussion. If you have a day or less, that will convey the general idea and you can lecture briefly on the most serious connection with tort law, the exclusive remedy rules. You can read over §§ 3 & 4 in preparation for such a lecture.

More than one day: If you can cover more than one day, add *Wait* and its Notes in § 2.A, and the first part of § 2.B, to the end of the Notes to *Harris.* That will give students the basics of the "arising out of and in the course of employment" core requirement, plus enough application for it to make sense. You should probably also emphasize, if you have no time for anything else, the main point made in § 1.C (¶8) and at the beginning of § 4 – that workers' compensation does not provide the exclusive remedy when the injury is caused by a third party. If you can cover more on exclusive remedy (§ 3), that topic is the major tort law connection and will help complete the picture of tort law itself.

§ 1. INTRODUCTION

The class can probably read this subsection on its own, but you might want to emphasize the drastically different working conditions that prevailed in many places in the 19th century coupled with the complete lack of social support in the form of health care, job security, unemployment benefits and so on.

A. The Employer's Tort Liability at Common Law

You might highlight the "fellow servant" rule here, given its connection to assumption of the risk.

B. The Adoption of Workers' Compensation

Ives v. South Buffalo Ry. Co., discussed here, is a horrendously long piece of work. The court has a very clear picture in its mind: "The right of property rests, not upon philosophical or scientific speculations, nor upon the commendable impulses of benevolence or charity, nor yet upon the dictates of natural justice. The right has its foundation in the fundamental law. That can be changed by the people, but not by the Legislature."

Two federal workers' compensation statutes are the Longshore and Harbor Workers' Compensation Act is 33 U.S.C.A. § 901 *et seq.*, and the Federal Emplolyees Compensation Act (FECA), 5 U.S.C.A. § 8102 *et seq.* Given world enough and time, a good deal could be done with these, especially the latter, because they present additional dimensions to the problem of making compensation systems mesh with tort systems. That is not only because they are federal systems, but because of the problems encountered in determining whether the general maritimc law, the Jones Act, or conceivably the Death on the High Seas Act applies in various situations. All of this must be left to those who pursue the study of admiralty, however.

C. Characteristics of the Statutes

You might consider highlighting several of the main characteristics of workers' compensation with a snapshot of the process: In routine cases, the employee fills out a form supplied by the compensation tribunal and may also submit a doctor's report. This may be the end of the matter. Payments will be made until the recovery period is over. The doctor's periodic reports will establish this. The casebook deals with none of this but instead presents litigated issues, but the student should remember that there are many, many cases without litigation.

The text describes the informal administrative hearing that occurs when there is a dispute. On issues of law, and where there is no evidence to support the tribunal's award, there may be review in the courts. This is what we see in the present chapter. In the main, the litigated issues are similar regardless whether the insurance scheme behind workers' compensation is public or private. Those who favor public control, however, might note that public finance leads to cost cutting not unlike that lobbied for under private schemes. *See* Karen O'Kasey and Carolos Martinez, *Recent Developments in Workers'*

Compensation Law, 31 TORT & INS. L.J. 559 (1996) (reviewing cost-cutting "reforms" in Oregon and New Mexico).

D. Coverage

You might try a simple hypothetical here that can establish the lawyer's need to consult the statute and test whether the students have absorbed the fellow servant rule: A farm worker is injured when another worker runs a tractor over her. What rights of the injured worker?\

E. Benefits

We get only a peek at the big topic of benefits. Medical costs aside, benefits were initially meant only to replace actual wage losses. That approach still governs many cases.

In *Metropolitan Stevedore Co. v. Rambo,* The 1995 Supreme Court case cited here, the compensation claim was brought under the Longshore and Harbor Workers' Compensation Act, 33 U.S.C.A. § 901 *et seq.* The statute specifically provided for modification of the disability award in the case of changed conditions, part of the flexibility implied in the periodic payment regime of compensation statutes. The claimant had injured his back and leg as a longshoreman and had received a compensation award of $80.16 per week representing the statutory two-thirds of his imputed lost wages. ("Imputed" because the computation was based on the idea that he sustained a 22 ½ % disability rather than on any actual lost wages.) After the award was made, the claimant attended crane school. He acquired the skill to work as a crane operator and received average weekly wages of between $1300 and almost $1700, much more than he made before. His physical injury remained, but his actual capacity to earn money was greater. Since disability was defined to mean incapacity because of injury to earn the wages received before injury, no disability remained, even though the physical injury itself had not been ameliorated. Moreover, the fundamental purpose of the act was to compensate for wage loss. Hence the award was subject to downward modification. As it turned out, however, Rambo was entitled to recover nominal compensation even though he lost nothing. This was permitted so that he would not be foreclosed under the LHWCA from claiming in the future when his incapacity might actually result in loss.

Benefits have been widely criticized as inadequate. Partly this may be based on an assumption that tort damages reflect "real" compensation, when in fact many tort damages recoveries appear to be excessive as compensation, especially at the lower end. However, the level of benefits fixed could affect safety. If benefits are low, employers will have little incentive to make a plant safer. This does not tell us what the proper amount of benefits should be, but it should quite probably come to a high percentage of the employee's actual wage loss, at least if safety is a concern. *See* Note, *Exceptions to the Exclusive Remedy Requirements of Workers' Compensation Statutes,* 96 HARV. L. REV.

1641 (1983), giving a good brief statement of this view of workers' compensation as a potential source of internalization of the costs of injury. This led the notewriter, and has led others more recently, to suggest expanded possibilities for tort claims against the employer, but if injury is properly attributable to the work (rather than, for example, a product defect), it might be more desirable simply to raise the benefits.

Low benefits were intentionally adopted and they continued to be defended in certain respects. Professor Richard Epstein has pointed out that benefits were made to represent less than 100% of wage loss as a part of the initial bargain by which workers recovered without proof of negligence, and that low compensation reduces overall costs of the plan. Low benefits also help prevent fraud, and, in his view, they also leave some incentive on the worker to provide for self-protection. This provides an "implicit substitute" for the trinity of defenses embodied in the contributory negligence, assumption of risk, and fellow servant rules. Epstein, *The Historical Origins and Economic Structure of Workers' Compensation Law*, 16 GA. L. REV. 775, 800-01 (1982). Part of the basis for this last statement is that the fellow servant rule was justified by some writers as putting the burden of safety on the worker, who was seen as having the greatest ability to achieve safety.

Epstein also advances the idea that low benefits represent limited damages that go with strict liability in the same way *Hadley v. Baxendale* provides for limited damages for breach of contract. The success of the system is thus seen as a reflection of the fact that it matches what the bargaining parties would agree to in a contract. Epstein, *supra* at 805-06.

Justifications of low benefits, however, do not extend to the problem created when low benefits are lowered further by inflation, or to the problem of benefits subjected to a maximum recovery at the end of some arbitrary period of time. Benefits given an arbitrary top amount mean that high-pay workers may recover less than the 66% of their wages, but high paid workers are in a position to buy added protection if they wish, so this problem of low benefits may not be so great. But inflation and arbitrary termination of benefits after a certain time period, and low death benefits may not be so readily justified.

§ 2. JOB-RELATED INJURY

SUMMARY

A. Arising Out of and in the Course of Employment

WAIT V. TRAVELERS INDEMNITY CO. OF ILLINOIS. A telecommuter working in her home is attacked by a neighbor for no apparent reason. She was preparing lunch in her kitchen at the time. Plaintiff sought workers' compensation benefits from her employer's insurer. The reviewing court held that the injuries did not arise out of or occur in the course of her employment. On appeal, the Tennessee Supreme Court holds that the injuries (1) occurred during the course of her employment, but (2) did not arise out of her employment. Thus the injury was not compensable under workers' compensation.

CARVALHO V. DECORATIVE FABRICS CO. Horseplay: The claimant was injured when a fellow employee placed an air hose used in the employment "in the vicinity of" the claimant's rectum and claimant's stomach was expanded with air and his rectum perforated. *Held,* where horseplay has become customary, the horseplay injury is arising out of employment. Where horseplay is not customary, the question is whether it is a substantial deviation from employment. Compensation would be denied only if it is. Here, since use of the hose is a daily part of the work, play with the hose is a risk of employment and thus is compensable. The court also notes that even participants in horseplay may recover since only specified faults (intoxication, for example) constitute a bar.

UNION COLLIERY CO. V. INDUSTRIAL COM'N. A coal miner is killed when he rides up in the "cage" with a load of coal, in violation of state statutes on mining safety. Clearly the employee was injured during working hours and was physically present, but the employer argued that the injury did not arise out of employment because the employee was carrying out his work in violation of a statute. The court holds the injury is compensable; when the employee is "in the course of" employment, his violation of statute or rule does not take him out of employment. To hold otherwise would be to introduce contributory negligence in a strict liability system.

B. Accident, Injury and Disease

NOTE: "ACCIDENT" AND "ACCIDENTAL INJURY." This Note parses some of the possible meanings of the terms– not intended, a definite occasion, something external (not a spontaneous heart attack, for example). The note also considers suicide and self inflicted injury.

HARRIS V. BD. OF EDUC. OF HOWARD COUNTY . A 58-year-old worker suffered debilitating back pain while doing her regular work, which, however, did involve lifting and moving heavy objects. Judicial review of an award of compensation took the form of a jury trial and the jury found that the back problem arose in the course of the claimant's usual work – a finding that eliminated workers' compensation under the supposed rule that such a claim would count as a compensable accident only if the claimant's was doing something "unusual." But *held,* in Maryland's highest court, the "unusual activity" requirement is discarded as unwarranted under the statutory language. The court recognizes, however, that a causal link between employment and injury must be shown and perhaps also that a "sudden" injury might be required in some cases.

SHEALY V. AIKEN COUNTY . This court holds that for emotional disability, there must be some unusual condition of employment. An undercover police officer's disabling stress met this test because in addition to the stress of his work, he was subjected to death threats, gun incidents, violent drug dealers and the like. But here the claimant still cannot recover because, his personal stresses–finances, divorce, and other issues– caused his emotional disability, not the job.

C. Multiple Exposure or Injury

UNION CARBIDE CORP. V. INDUSTRIAL COMM'N. An employer hired claimant "on condition" that he was shown to be healthy. He was allowed to begin working before the exam results were in. A few days later, the results came in and showed he had lung cancer. He was dismissed because the condition of employment was not met, but during his brief tenure, he had been exposed to radiation. *Held*, the employer is liable for death benefits, since there was an injurious exposure, even though he already had the disease.

BRACKE V. BAZA'R, INC. Claimant was exposed in employments first with A and then with B. Employment A sensitized the claimant to "meat wrapper's asthma." There was further exposure while working for employer B, but this exposure did not aggravate the underlying disease. *Held,* employer A is liable, not employer B. The rationale for the last injurious exposure rule is that it will spread liability fairly among employers by the "law of averages," but this rationale has no application where the second exposure did not aggravate the disease.

COMMENTS

A. Arising Out of and in the Course of Employment

WAIT V. TRAVELERS INDEMNITY CO. OF ILLINOIS, 240 S.W.3d 220 (Tenn. 2007).

A telecommuter working in her home is attacked by a neighbor for no apparent reason. She was preparing lunch in her kitchen at the time. Plaintiff sought workers' compensation benefits from her employer's insurer. The reviewing court held that the injuries did not arise out of or occur in the course of her employment. On appeal, the Tennessee Supreme Court holds that the injuries (1) occurred during the course of her employment, but (2) did not arise out of her employment. Thus the injury was not compensable under workers' compensation.

The case is a good one for many reasons – it focuses on the dual requirement of "during the course of" and "arising out of" employment, and clearly shows that both requirements must be met, and are not identical. Further, the case arises in a modern context (telecommuting). Finally, the case also presents the issue of whether a worker on an allegedly "personal break" from work can still be acting "in the course of employment" – an issue analogous to those we saw in Chapter 22 in the *Edgewater v. Gatzke* case and its Notes.

At a minimum, you should make sure the class understands the dual "arising out of" and "in the course of" requirements. The first requirement, "arising out of," refers to "cause or origin" of the injury. We look for a "causal connection . . . between the employment conditions and the resulting injuries." Generally, as the court explains, the injury must "emanate from a peculiar danger or risk inherent to the nature of the employment." The second, "in the course of," denotes the "time, place and circumstances" of the injury. Factually, we look for whether the injury "takes place within the period of the employment, at a place where the employee reasonably may be, and while the employee is fulfilling work duties or engaged in doing something incidental thereto."

Note 1. Increased risk. In *Jivan*, cited here, the Arkansas court reasoned that the employee was placed in a greater risk of injury by hotel fire because she had to live at the hotel for a long time, unlike usual hotel guests. The "street risk" doctrine as described at the end of *Wait* applies when the employee's job requires her to be "indiscriminately exposed to the general public." The *Wait* court found that doctrine inapplicable because the attack here was not causally connected to the job in any way. The "street risk" doctrine may look more like the "positional risk" rule than the "increased risk" approach described in Note 2 below.

Note 2. Positional risks. This is a much broader test than the "increased risk" test described in Note 1, but also one is that far easier to apply consistently and efficiently. As explained here, courts using this test basically require a "but for" connection between the employment and the injury, period. *Kerr-McGee Corp. v. Hutto*, cited here, is a noteworthy example. A husband, perhaps out of jealousy, shot his wife's employee while the employee was at work. The court held that since the wife-employer had told the employee to speak to her husband, the employee's death is not disassociated from employment and is compensable. *See also, e.g., Wilson v. State Farm Ins. Co.*, 952 P.2d 528 (Or. 1998) (the plaintiff "skip stepped" while at work and tore her tendon; held compensable even if she was carrying out her tasks in an unusual way); *Mulready v. University Research Corp.*, 756 A.2d 575 (Md. 2000)(employee fell in the bathtub of her hotel during a business conference; held compensable). Note that courts do not find the "positional risk" test met where the employee was engaged in a purely personal activity.

A number of cases involve spouses of employees who, convinced that the working spouse is having an on-the-job affair, come to the premises and kill the suspected spouse or the suspected paramour or both. In *Bell v. Kelso Oil Co.*, 597 S.W.2d 731 (Tenn. 1980), the claimant, a man, was stabbed by a "boy friend" of a co-employee who, apparently without much reason, had decided the claimant was "messing" with his "girl friend." The stabbing took place at the end of a night meeting that involved dinner and drinks at a motel. The boy friend stated, "Well, I'm tired of you all trying to mess with my girl friend in there" and at that point stabbed the claimant. The court held the injury compensable.

> First, it was the employment which subjected the employee to the hazard of assault and, secondly, the motive of the assailant to make the assault on the plaintiff arose out of the nature of the "work," i.e., the wining and dining of his girl friend . . . in the late hours of the night at a motel.

In *Robbins v. Nicholson*, 188 S.E.2d 350 (N.C. 1972), however, a wife worked in a grocery store where she came into routine contact with male co-workers. In a fit of jealously, her husband came into the grocery store, where he shot and killed his wife and co-employee Robbins. The Commission held that dependents of both the wife and co-worker Robbins could recover compensation. The Supreme Court held this in error. Employment was not the chief source of the matrimonial difficulties which led to the assault. "The origin was his alcoholism, and it was the fact that she finally left him which motivated the assaults." Even if the wife's employment was a major source of friction between her and her husband, "that friction was not a risk arising out of the nature of her employment."

No class should be denied an opportunity to know about *Brookhaven Steam Laundry v. Watts*, 59 So. 2d 294 (Miss. 1952). Watts was employed at a laundry, engaged in the delivery and pick-up of laundry. He was having an affair with one Mrs. Garrett, a married woman, who would signal her husband's absence by leaving laundry on her porch. When this happened, Watts would sojourn a while inside with Mrs. Garrett, then take the laundry with him as part of his job. Mr. Garrett became suspicious and laid in wait; when Watts appeared in response to the laundry signal and held an incriminating conversation with Mrs. Garrett, the aggrieved husband burst from his hiding place and shot Watts. The court originally awarded compensation but on rehearing denied it on the ground that Watts was killed for personal reasons.

Note 3. "In the course of" employment and the going and coming rule. The going and coming rule holds there will be no compensation for injuries sustained while going to work or coming from it. This parallels the rule seen in agency cases (Chapter 22), though workers' compensation cases are almost always more liberal. In statutory terms, too, the issue is formed, not as "going and coming" but as "course of employment." In *Jaeger Baking Co. v. Kretschmann*, cited here, the worker was injured by an attacker just outside his place of employment as he was going to work at 2:00 a.m. He was in a place where he might have been had he parked in the company parking lot and headed for the door; but in fact he arrived by bus and was never in the company parking lot. Under an explicit statute in Wisconsin, one injured on public property while on the way from the company parking lot to the place of work is covered by workers' compensation. But *held*, since he was *not* on his way from the parking lot, he is subject to the ordinary going and coming rule and is thus not within the course of employment.

The exceptions, too, parallel those we saw in Chapter 22, as the Nevada and Utah case cites indicate. *See also McLin v. Indus. Specialty Contractors, Inc.*, 851 So.2d 1135 (La. 2003) (when an employee was required to attend a safety meeting away from his work location, that is a special mission for the employer, essentially having a "dual purpose"; he was within the course of employment until he arrived home, so long as he was returning from the special mission rather than from his regular work place). In *Snowbarger*, cited at the end of this Note, the court held that the employee's death was compensable. His employer had required him to work "extraordinary overtime" doing manual labor during an ice storm; he worked 86 hours out of 100 in the stretch before he died when he fell asleep behind the wheel of his car driving home. The Missouri court cited cases from many other jurisdictions which held similar injuries compensable.

Note 4. Traveling employees. *McCann v. Hatchett,* cited here, treats all injuries of traveling employees away from home as within the course of employment and asks only whether the particular activity has become so personal that it does not arise out of employment. The effect of applying this rule to telecommuters would be that all such employees would be within the course of employment continually, except for "purely personal" activities. Note that as described in Note 5 below, a mere incidental departure from working, such as making a sandwich in your kitchen, would not take you out of the course of employment.

Note 5. Incidental departures from working. The main point should be clear here – mere incidental departures from work do not remove the employee from "the course of employment." This is very similar to the rule for vicarious liability that we saw in *Edgewater Hotels v. Gatzke*, the "smoking case," in Chapter 22.

CARVALHO V. DECORATIVE FABRICS CO., 366 A.2d 157 (R.I. 1976)

Although horseplay is not usually considered as a personal risk, horseplay and assaults, as well as more interesting personal activities, may create risks that come to fruition on the job. The horseplay cases are pretty well settled, though there are problems in its application. *Carvalho* is a good example of the horseplay problem. No serious harm is intended, but serious harm results. This is not a battery, presumably, because neither harmful nor offensive touching was intended; put otherwise, the touching intended would have been within the scope of apparent consent.

The classic case on horseplay is *Leonbruno v. Champlain Silk Mills*, 229 N.Y. 470, 128 N.E. 711 (1920). In addition to the comments quoted in *Carvalho*, Cardozo said, "The claimant's presence in a factory in association with other workmen involved exposure to the risk of injury from the careless acts of those about him . . . . Whatever men and boys will do, when gathered together in such surroundings, at all events if it is something reasonably to be expected, was one of the perils of his service."

Note 1. In *Hilton*, cited at the end of this Note, the victim's estate sued the co-employee for assault and battery, and the employer for negligent hiring and retention. The defendants claimed that workers' comp was the exclusive remedy. The court held that the fatal injuries did not "arise out of" the victim's employment, thus siding with the plaintiff. The court concluded that the co-worker's sudden attack had nothing to do with the employee's status as an employee, and was "purely personal." The employer's workplace requirements (which forbade unauthorized use of defibrillators) had no causal connection to the risk of injury by battery, and the co-worker's decision was entirely his own, unconnected with the conditions of his employment.

Note 2 should be self-explanatory.

Note 3. Intended battery. The issue here is whether the attack is based on personal rather than job-related animosity.

Note 4. Company-sponsored recreation. Recreation in the form of horseplay "co-mingled" with work is readily classed as arising out of employment. Recreation organized by the company may be similarly classified, but in many instances it reflects mere personal pleasure or activity of the employee, though it has the imprimatur of the company. Suppose, for example, the company gives an annual award to its top salesperson, in the form of a vacation for the employee and spouse. This clearly has a business purpose to encourage sales but that business purpose is accomplished by providing a non-job benefit.

Resolution of the recreational cases turns on extensive factual analysis. Larson states as rules that recreational and social activities are within the "course of employment" when they occur on the premises. Company sponsorship is not required in such cases, provided this is customary or expectable. LARSON §§ 22.00 and those following. The company picnic and similar activities are ambiguously related to employment. If the employee dies of excess drink, or drowns swimming, or chokes on his salami at the company picnic, can it be said that it was an employment activity rather than a personal one? Courts consider a number of factors, and as usual, rely heavily on Larson's analysis in many instances.

In some cases, injury occurs after a Christmas party, while the claimant is on the way home. In *Oklahoma Natural Gas Co. v. Williams*, 639 P.2d 1222 (Okla. 1981), the company placed considerable emphasis on attendance of company functions for those who wanted "to get ahead in the company." Claimant was reminded of the party's importance to his success in the company when he showed signs of evading the party. Afterwards, on the way to pick up a baby-sitter, there was a vehicular collision. The court thought compensation would be justified.

UNION COLLIERY CO. V. INDUSTRIAL COMM'N, 132 N.E. 200 (Ill. 1921)

This case involves no issue about course of employment; the employee was clearly within the working hours and physically present at the job site. The employer's argument is that injury did not arise out of employment because the employee was carrying out his work in violation of a statute. The analogy is to the scope of employment issue in vicarious liability cases. The court holds in favor of workers' compensation. When the employee is in the course of employment, her violation of statute or rule does not take her out of employment in the metaphysical sense that arising out of tests.

B. Accident, Injury and Disease

NOTE: "ACCIDENT" AND "ACCIDENTAL INJURY"

We would go over with the class some potential meanings of "accident" or "accidental" – that injury must not be intentional in the sense of self-inflicted, that it must occur on a definite occasion, and that injury must proceed from external causes as distinct from a degenerative breakdown. The latter two are especially relevant in the heart attack, stroke, hernia, and mental disability cases. You may need to tease out the rest of the note material in questions or discussion.

Intended injury. Accident excludes the idea of intended injury. Where statutes make specific provision against compensation for self-inflicted wounds, such provisions may be used instead to reach suicide. The suicide cases could easily have been a centerpiece here as well as in the proximate cause chapter. They certainly do reach into the core of problems of accountability with ideas like free will and duress, meaningful choice. The worker who is in pain and commits suicide as an escape may today be condemned by the Church, but not by the courts. What really seems required is not insanity of the worker but understanding by the court. If suicide is understandable, whether because of insanity or pain or depression, compensation will be recoverable in many instances. This seems also the general direction of the common law tort cases, so that if the tortfeasor injures a person, who then commits suicide, a very similar analysis is followed.

In *Zach,* cited in ¶ 4, the court held the injury non-compensable, on the ground that the suicide was caused by "mental stimulus," thus was not an "accident," which requires that there be some "violence to the physical structure of the body."

In *Glodo v. Indus. Comm'n of Arizona,* 955 P.2d 15 (Ariz. Ct. App. 1997), and *McKay Dee Hospital v. Indus. Comm'n of Utah,* 598 P.2d 375 (Utah 1979), the worker slammed his fist into a metal door when angered as a result of on the job friction. *McKay* said this was a "foreseeable and expected injury" to his hand and he could not recover. *Glodo* agreed, saying it because injury was to be expected, the injury was not an "accident." Does this import contributory negligence reasoning? The *Glodo* court suggested that the employee's misconduct was the basis of its "accident" reasoning when it said "It would be patently unwise to reward individuals who engage in this type of self-injurious conduct."

Definite occasion. A series of events would often be sufficient today. But was there an event? The problem today is sometimes called repetitive stress injury or "cumulative trauma disorder." Carpal tunnel syndrome, familiar to those who use computers extensively, is a modern version of the *Young* case. In *Noble v. Lamoni Products*, 512 N.W.2d 290 (Iowa 1994), the court held that carpal tunnel syndrome was an injury rather than an occupational disease and thus compensable under the rules for injury rather than those for occupational disease. In part this holding resulted from the fact that Iowa's statutory requirement of injury does not also contain a requirement of "accident."

Where "accident" is required, the implication may be that a definite occasion for the injury must be identified. That point takes us directly to the next subsection on occupational disease. In *Roseburg Forest Products v. Rowe*, 865 P.2d 1329 (Or. Ct. App. 1993), the court affirmed an award for carpal tunnel syndrome as an occupational disease.

External events. See comments following *Harris*, below.

HARRIS V. BD. OF EDUC. OF HOWARD COUNTY, 825 A.2d 365 (Md. 2003)

Harris raises the problems associated with various "internal" injuries not easily connected with a particular "external" event–heart attacks, strokes, hernias, general backache. Heart attack and stroke cases may be the most dramatic forms of the problem. Heart attacks may occur in connection with work, and even in connection with stress or effort, but even so, we might have doubts that work caused the underlying condition or even triggered the injury. In addition, we might think that if work did indeed trigger the injury, the preexisting condition – aging, genetic predisposition to heart attack and so on– is the more significant cause. Tort law might deal with this by discounting the recovery (see Note 4), but there seems to be no system for any such approach in workers' compensation. So the claimant, if compensated at all, gets full compensation, even though it is likely that he would suffer a similar heart attack even if he did not work at all. Maybe this is why courts have often tried to exclude compensation in heart attack and similar cases by insisting on evidence that the claimant show unusual exertion or a sudden event precipitating the injury. *E.g., Virginia Elec. & Power Co. v. Cogbill*, 288 S.E.2d 485 (Va. 1982).

On reflection, however, the unusual exertion test is both over-and under-inclusive. It will compensate claims on the basis of exertion that may not prove causation. And it will exclude claims even when causation can be proved. So you may think that *Harris* is right in rejecting the test. Still, students should not read too much into *Harris*. While it rejects the unusual exertion test, it retains the requirement of causation and causation must be proved somehow. In *Bush v. Industrial Com'n,* 667 P.2d 222 (Ariz. 1983), for example, the court thought that heart attack induced by job stress would be compensable if

> the exertion, whether usual or unusual, is of such a character that the injury can be traced to it with reasonable assurance that the work caused or contributed to the injury. . . . Put another way, the claimant must show that the work and exertions of the job precipitated the heart attack.

Unusual exertion might conceivably be relevant to proof of causation and in some cases even necessary. What the *Harris* court did most clearly was to eliminate the test as a rule of law to be applied in all cases. Instead, the court wants to look for evidence of causation. One passage seems to make it clear that on the causal issue, exertion would remain relevant and might even be required, depending on other factors. What other factors? The *Farrington* case, **Note 2**, suggested that "age, weight, diet, previous cardiac ailments or injuries, genetic predispositions, and the claimant's consumption of alcohol and use of tobacco or other drugs" would be relevant as and might tend to show that the work was not a significant cause." In that case, the plaintiff's only hope might lie in showing unusual exertion.

Statutes may control. The Michigan requirement that the work be not only a cause but a significant cause is perhaps a reasonable approach if the tort discount under *Dillon* cannot be invoked.

Notes 1-2. Scope and alternatives. Because students may read too much into *Harris,* this note implicitly suggests that the back problem is like the heart attack problem, then asks students to question whether every heart attack, stroke, or hernia that occurs during working hours would be compensable under *Harris.* The information given – that many courts do in fact require either extraordinary exertion or a sudden event preceding the heart attack – should help suggest that *Harris* has some limits. **Note 2** suggests alternatives that are consistent with *Harris* –namely that job relatededness must be established even if no unusual exertion is required. The quotation is especially helpful; it permits us to see that personal rather than job factors may appear more significant in judging causation. The preexisting injury cases should logically require the same as a preexisting heart condition and the question is asked only to lead students to see that for themselves if they can. In *Rakestraw,* cited at the end of **Note 2**, much of the argument was about the distinction between injury and symptoms of injury, but the essential point seems to be that the plaintiff must prove job-relatedly or causation no matter what. "[W]here the symptoms complained of are *equally* attributable to the progression of a preexisting condition or a work-related injury, a plaintiff will fail to meet his burden of proving by a preponderance of the evidence that the injury arose "out of and in the course of employment"; stated otherwise, plaintiff will have failed to establish causation."

Note 3. Statutes. Some states by statute or otherwise impose very particular requirements. The Michigan example in Note 2 might suggest that ANY evidence that shows job related causation should suffice, not merely evidence of unusual exertion. But this note tells us that in many states the overall goal of requiring job relatedness is subordinated to very particular tests that may be over- or under-inclusive.

Note 4. Pre-existing conditions and amount of award. Part of the problem may be that workers' compensation statutes do not allow for discounted damages based on a finding that the same harm would occur anyway within a predictable period. The idea of discounted damages takes us back to *Dillon v. Twin States Electric Co.*, mentioned briefly in the casebook earlier in Chapter 7. If a job contributes to a worker's heart attack, maybe the question should be: how soon would he have had the same heart attack were it not for the job stress? But, as we say, that is not an approach adopted by the statutes, so we get roundabout approaches to limit the recovery.

SHEALY V. AIKEN COUNTY , 535 S.E.2d 438 (S.C. 2000)

Shealy deals with emotional distress as a potentially compensable injury. A good deal of emotional distress will be uncompensated because the claimant, however distressed, will not suffer impairment or a disabling injury from the distress. Even the worker who is unable to work because of distress may find that she has no compensation. If the distress results from "personal" rather than job events, it won't qualify because it does not arise out of employment. If it arises out of employment, it still may not qualify unless there is an "accident." (An accident is not required under all statutes, however; nor is it required if the distress counts as an occupational disease.) *Shealy* acknowledges a potential claim even in a case of cumulative job stress (as opposed to a sudden event), but then rejects the claim because the claimant's emotional troubles were not proved to result from the job but were rather personal in nature. In this latter respect, the case fortifies the point we made with *Harris*, that ultimately the issue should be less about "accident" and more about job connection.

Shealy is the hard case – a "mental-mental" injury rather than a physical-mental injury, meaning that both the stimuli and the injury were "mental" or emotional in nature. And harder still because it involves no sudden event or unusual stress. The court's liberal approach to unusual stress is countered, however, by its actual holding that causation was not shown in the light of the claimant's existing emotional problems.

Note 1. Mental or emotional disorders: Sudden event in the fright-shock pattern. The easiest legal claim for disability or impairment resulting from emotional distress is parallel to the easiest case for distress recovery under common law tort doctrines – where distress results from physical injury. In workers' compensation cases, the physical injury itself must be sustained in the course of and arising out of employment. If it is, then distress that is further disabling may be compensable.

When the employee's emotional condition does not arise from a physical injury, it may still be compensable, but the case is harder to establish. A number of statutes expressly recognize emotional distress as a compensable injury or occupational disease, but these may impose their own specific limitations. California's statute is long and detailed, see CAL. LABOR CODE § 3208.3, but most statutes impose limitations somewhat analogous to the accident requirement: the emotional harm must result from unusual or extraordinary stress or events, or must be extraordinary in comparison to stress experienced by other employees in similar jobs. *E.g.*, ARIZ. REV. STATS. § 23-1043.0; 39-A ME. REV. STATS. ANN. § 201 par 3. See, denying compensation for stress based disability, *Spencer v. Time Warner Cable,* 717 N.Y.S.2d 711 (App. Div. 2000) (office worker taking large number of customer calls); *Davis v. W.C.A.B.,* 751 A.2d 168 (Pa. 2000) (police officer dealing with stressful situations, but not unlike situations other officers had to deal with). By the same token, if emotional injury results from a sudden traumatic event, as distinct from the stress of job demands, may be compensable without physical injury, the *Ivey* case, cited here, holds.

Guess v. Sharp Mfg. Co. Of America, cited at the end of this Note, involved a sudden event– a touching of blood of a co-worker which might have exposed the claimant to HIV. Not surprisingly, the court added a particular requirement that the plaintiff must prove, as in tort claims, "actual exposure," no matter how real or how reasonable the fear of HIV/AIDS might be. One point to be made here is that the overall generalization is only a pointer; particular facts may turn out to be more important. Another example of the same thing is that when the emotional stress results from discrimination, the courts may apply the job discrimination statutes rather than workers' compensation statute.

One effect students might not expect: if the emotional harm is not an injury within the meaning of the compensation act, then it may be actionable as a tort in spite of the exclusive remedy provision. See *Kerans v. Porter Paint Co.,* § 3 below.

Note 2. Mental or emotional disorders: Cumulative stress. Cumulative job stress involves no sudden event, and, as with tort claims for negligent infliction of emotional distress, courts seem overall less inclined to permit recovery. But this is merely an overall generalization, not a rule that will always control. Many illustrative cases, classified in multiple layers, are found in a series annotations. *See* Emmanuel S. Tipon, Annotation, *Right to Workers' Compensation for Emotional Distress or like Injury Suffered by Claimant as Result of Sudden Stimuli Involving Nonpersonnel Action–Right to Compensation under Particular Statutory Provisions and Requisites of, and*

Factors Affecting, Compensability, 83 A.L.R.5th 103 (2000); Emmanuel S. Tipon, Annotation, *Right to Workers' Compensation for Emotional Distress or Like Injury Suffered by Claimant as Result of Sudden Stimuli Involving Nonpersonnel Action–Compensability under Particular Circumstances*, 84 A.L.R.5th 249 (2000); Emmanuel S. Tipon, Annotation, *Right to Workers' Compensation for Emotional Distress or like Injury Suffered by Claimant as Result of Nonsudden Stimuli–Right to Compensation under Particular Statutory Provisions*, 97 A.L.R.5th 1 (2002); Emmanuel S. Tipon, Anno., *Right to Workers' Compensation for Physical Injury or Illness Suffered by Claimant as Result of Sudden Mental Stimuli– Compensability under Particular Circumstances*, 107 A.L.R.5th 441 (2003); Emmanuel S. Tipon, Anno., *Right to Workers' Compensation for Emotional Distress or like Injury Suffered by Claimant as Result of Nonsudden Stimuli--Compensability under Particular Circumstances*, 108 A.L.R.5th 1 (2003).

Note 3. Occupational disease. On addiction: A job may expose the employee to greater risk of taking drugs and becoming addicted, so it would be possible for addiction to arise out of employment if, on the facts, it is not a "personal" rather than a job matter. But if recreational drug usage is intentional, it looks less like an accident. In any event, courts are careful to exclude cases of personal choice. See *Petersen v. O'Malley*, 272 Minn. 17, 136 N.W.2d 586 (1965) (employee was user before employment, dependency does not arise from employment even though she appropriated employer's drugs in quantity); *DiGloria v. Chief of Police of Methuen*, 8 Mass. App. Ct. 506, 395 N.E.2d 1297 (1979) (undercover narcotics officer at fault in becoming addicted, no compensation); cf. *Pierce v. General Motors Corp.*, 443 Mich. 137, 504 N.W.2d 648 (1993) (alcoholism is not compensable "injury," though a separate analysis would be required to determine whether it would be compensable as an occupational disease).

Virginia's refusal to recognize repetitive stress injury in *Stenrich Group v. Jemmott*, cited here, might still leave a door open for a few cases. *Ogden Aviation Services v. Saghy*, 526 S.E.2d 756 (Va. Ct. App. 2000), held that carpal tunnel syndrome may be compensable as injury by accident if it qualifies as injury because of sudden onset on a particular occasion.

Brunell v. Wildwood Crest Police Dept., cited at the end of this Note, recognizes that the initial stress may count as an accident in some cases but that in others the officer suffering from PTSD might have an occupational disease claim. This is a fence that must be walked carefully; occupational disease must be typical or at least expected in the particular occupation, while "accident" must be the opposite, unexpected.

C. Multiple Exposure or Injury

UNION CARBIDE CORP. V. INDUSTRIAL COM'N , 581 P.2d 734 (Colo. 1978)
BRACKE V. BAZA'R, INC., 646 P.2d 1330 (Or. 1982)

Two different job-relatedness problems appear in these cases. The first is whether the disease is job related rather than personal or a risk of life in general. The second is, if it is job-related, then "which job?" The tests for the two problems are different.

Where there is on-the-job injury by accident, the employer takes the employee as it finds her, with whatever predisposition the employee may have for accident and for greater injury. Indeed, this rule is the reason why second injury funds are needed, since without such funds, employers, caught with excessive dangers of susceptible employees, might simply refuse to hire those who are handicapped. See **Note 3.** However, when disease rather than injury is the source of disability, the court may impose a requirement of "significant contribution" by the job, a rule that seems at least potentially in conflict with the thin-skull rule as applied in compensation cases to "injury." See *Rutledge v. Tultex Corp./Kings Yarn*, 301 S.E.2d 359 (N.C. 1983). Why not rely on the familiar "arising out of employment" test without additional requirements?

Last employer's liability. Union Carbide and Bracke concentrate on the second of the two problems. Both are extreme cases. In *Union Carbide*, the employee worked only 8 days for the last employer, yet that employer was held liable for death benefits from lung disease the employee had undoubtedly had much earlier. *Bracke* involves similar facts. The employee worked only a very brief time for the last employer, but the earlier, not later employer is held liable. This serves as a warning that injurious exposure is the test, and if the last employer's exposure was not injurious, there is no liability. No doubt we might argue about the court's rather narrow notion of what is injurious in *Bracke*, but the principle does not seem debatable. One might in fact think that it should have been recognized in *Union Carbide*.

These two cases differ in their rationale for the last injurious exposure rule. *Union Carbide* seems to say the rule is merely a practical adaptation to what otherwise would be an overwhelming burden of proof upon the employee. *Summers v. Tice* shows this is not essential because employers could be held liable, subject to proof they might be able to make that they were responsible for less than all the harm. However, apportionment among employers would be time-consuming and costly. If any reasonably fair system could be devised short of getting into this individualized proof, it would be preferred. The Oregon court in *Bracke* suggests that the last injurious exposure rule is reasonably fair because it works on the law of averages. Carriers (who will pay the compensation) are relatively few in number and a carrier stuck with an 8-day worker like Benally will no doubt on some other occasion avoid liability when its insured exposed the employee most of his life. This kind of approach may remind us how expensive the common law methods really are and, if one thinks this is reasonably suitable, how easy it is to find a cheaper substitute. The substitute found in the last employer rule works almost exactly like the market-share rule in cases like *Hymowitz*.

Note 4. Compensable injury causing further injury. *See* LARSON § 13.21. Prevention of treatment of existing ailment: LARSON § 13.11. Injury causing second injury: LARSON § 13.12. What if a worker, injured on the job, suffers a second injury on the way to the doctor's office? On this see LARSON § 13.13. Larson says these are generally held compensable where the work-connected injury is the reason for the visit to the doctor.

§ 3. WORKERS' COMPENSATION AS THE EXCLUSIVE REMEDY

SUMMARY

SNYDER V. MICHAEL'S STORES, INC. A child exposed to a gas in utero at her mother's workplace is not barred by the exclusive remedy provision that would bar the mother's tort claim.

HESSE V. ASHLAND OIL . Held, parents who witnessed their son's on-the-job death had no claim against the son's employer; the statute barred the claim of any person whose claim arises by reason of the employee's death. There is a dissent.

MARTIN V. LANCASTER BATTERY CO. After on-the-job blood testing revealed that employee Martin was suffering from lead-related medical problems, the manager withheld that information and altered the blood test results. Because Martin did not know the correct test results, his condition became worse. When he discovered the truth, he sued the employer and Manix, the manager who altered the test results. *Held*, the exclusive remedy provision of the compensation statute does not bar the claim. It is not a risk of employment that employers will deprive workers of statutory rights to medical treatment and compensation; fraud is not one of the risks covered in the compensation "bargain." The plaintiff may assert a fraudulent misrepresentation action. The court distinguished an earlier case (*Poyser*) on the ground that it involved (a) a representation to a third person, not the employee and (b) the misrepresentation there did not lead to aggravation of a work-related injury.

BERCAW V. DOMINO'S PIZZA, INC. The defendant dispatched its employee to deliver pizza under suspicious circumstances; the employee was attacked and killed in making the delivery. *Held*, the workers' compensation remedy is exclusive and bars a death action. The substantial certainty standard is inappropriate for distinguishing between accidental and non-accidental injuries because it is too hard to distinguish risk from certainty, and semble, the test is not met here in any event.

KERANS V. PORTER PAINT CO. The plaintiff, a woman, was sexually molested on the job by a store manager, Levine. The incidents included some touching of her person and some visual displays. She sued him and the employer. She settled with Levine. The claim on appeal in this case is against the employer. She claims that the employer had a policy of encouraging or permitting sexual harassment by Levine and that it negligently or intentionally inflicted emotional distress. The plaintiff suffered no physical injury. *Held*, (1) the exclusive remedy provision does not bar this claim because the claim is not for an "injury" within the meaning of the statute.

Although a physical injury resulting from emotional stress is compensable, a purely emotional or "psychological" injury is not. The plaintiff's claim is purely for psychological injury. The exclusive remedy provision only covers "injury" covered by the statute. (2) The employer may be liable in tort if the facts developed at trial show: (a) grounds for respondeat superior liability; this may be based on Levine's power as a supervisor if he used that power to make plaintiff feel she must endure his advances; or (b) the employer failed to use reasonable care to control the dangerous employee.

COMMENTS

We don't explore the rules that retain the tort claims of seamen and railroad employees, but a little later we do re-emphasize that job discrimination victims do not lose their tort claims under federal law by reason of the exclusive remedy provision of either state or federal compensation acts. See Note 8 following *Kerans*.

Workers' compensation is often thought of as a kind of "bargain" between employer and employee in which the employer accepts the costs of strict liability for all on-the-job injuries but in turn gets the benefit of limited liability. That limited liability trade can only be effected by immunizing the employer from tort suits, as the statutes have done. This can create a number of problems, where the employer is guilty of intentional harms, or wrongfully inflicts injuries for which workers' compensation, with its medical and wage loss benefit scheme, simply does not compensate at all.

Viewed in a broader perspective, workers' compensation provisions must mesh —more or less— with a number of other laws, not merely tort law. In this section we see the problem of meshing with ordinary tort law and with statutes on discrimination or sexual harassment. But these are not the only potential conflicts. Workers' compensation potentially conflicts with disability and other anti-discrimination statutes as well, as where the employer terminates an injured employee after her healing period is completed. *See City of Moorpark,* 959 P.2d 752 (Cal. 1998) (holding that workers' compensation is not the exclusive remedy and that the employee so terminated may pursue both common law wrongful discharge and statutory disability discrimination claims).

SNYDER V. MICHAEL'S STORES, INC., 945 P.2d 781 (Cal. 1997)

Accord, citing a number of cases, *Meyer v. Burger King Corp.,* 2 P.3d 1015 (Wash. Ct. App. 2000) (injury to fetus from abruption of the placenta in work-injury of mother was not "derived" from mother's injury but was independent injury to child, who is therefore not barred); *Raney v. Walter O. Moss Regional Hosp.,* 629 So.2d 485 (La. Ct. App. 1993) (independent injury since it was not based on worker's loss of wage).

Distinguish a consortium claim by the worker's spouse; that claim would depend upon the validity of a tort claim by the worker herself and would be barred because under the exclusive remedy clause, she has no remedy. In *Pizza Hut of America, Inc. v. Keefe,* 900 P.2d 97 (Colo. 1995), an injury to a pregnant employee caused injury to her fetus. The child was born alive but later died. The court first recognized that even non-employees would be barred by the exclusive remedy provision if their claim derived from the employee's injury. According to the court, the derivative injury doctrine bars claims for wrongful death of the employee herself, claims by a family member for loss of consortium, and contribution and indemnity claims by third persons who are liable to the employee. However, the court regarded the prenatal injury to the child as independent, although occurring at the same time as injury to the mother. Consequently, the child could have recovered for her own injury had she lived. That means that the child's survivors –the mother-employee– can recover for the child's wrongful death.

HESSE V. ASHLAND OIL, INC., 642 N.W.2d 330 (Mich. 2002)

The parents either witnessed the death or came to the scene immediately afterward, either of which would suffice to give them standing as bystander emotional distress plaintiffs in many jurisdictions. That is not in issue in *Hesse,* only the exclusive remedy clause. The Michigan statute was worded to exclude the remedy that "any person" might otherwise have arising from the employee's death. Perhaps what you think of immediately on reading this statute is the consortium claim, often held to be derivative and barred when the primary victim's own claim is barred. But the parents' claim here was not for loss of consortium; it was their own claim for their own distress at witnessing the death of their son. The Federal Tort Claims Act which bars claims "arising" out of battery. The Michigan statute similarly provides that a claim is barred if it "accrues" by reason of the employee's death. Arising and accruing are ambiguous expressions; they might refer to the idea that the claim is rooted in the legal concept of battery or the legal right of the employee. Or they might mean something much broader– that the claim is rooted in some of the same facts that would count as a battery or some of the same facts that would support an employee's claim. In both instances, we've seen courts choosing the broader meaning to exclude liability. Judge Kelly, dissenting in *Hesse,* evidently chooses the narrower meaning of "accrues," emphasizing that regardless of the factual conditions for the parents' claim, they are not asserting a claim rooted in the son's legal right and therefore not barred.

MARTIN V. LANCASTER BATTERY CO., 606 A.2d 444 (Pa. 1992)

The employer's concealment of an employee's injury or disease is not only a wrongdoing but is one that defeats the whole scheme of workers' compensation. *Johns-Manville Products Corp. v. Superior Court,* 612 P.2d 948, 9 A.L.R.4th 758 (Cal. 1980), is in accord with *Martin* in imposing liability upon the employer who aggravates employment injury by concealing industrial injury or disease.

These cases may be at the top of a slippery slope. What distinguishes them from any kind of intentional tort to the employee? What if the "fraud" or duress is merely the termination of monthly benefits, or bad faith breach of a settlement agreement? In such a case, the claimant's remedy may be to apply to the industrial commission for compensation rather than to seek tort damages. *Cruz v. Liberty Mut. Ins. Co.*, 889 P.2d 1223 (N.M. 1995).

Note 2. Negligence of employer. *Burns v. Smith*, cited here, held that the supervisor's act of applying a weld to a water pressure tank was outside of his duty to provide a reasonably safe place to work, and thus took the injury outside the exclusivity of workers' comp. The court said that where a supervising co-employee commits an affirmative act that creates a danger "beyond that normally faced in the job-specific work environment," workers' compensation is not the exclusive remedy.

Weaver v. Kimberly-Clark Corp., also cited here, holds, with most other cases on point, that the former employer gets no immunity. Larson put its in terms of time: the employment relationship must exist at the time of injury (not the time of negligence) if the exclusive remedy provision is to apply. The Alabama court took Larson to heart, but also read the statute's definition of employer. That would, of course, be a good place for the lawyer to start research. The statutory definition spoke of employment in the present tense, and from this the court concluded that the statute's immunity applied only to employers who remain employers at the time of injury. Some other cases proceeded with the same reasoning. It seems strained or at least inadequate to reach the conclusion. We'd stop class discussion with the observation that reading the statute and particularly the definitions of employer and employee, might be a good place to start research– a way of emphasizing the statutory nature of workers' comp claims.

Notes 3-5. Intentional torts. As these three notes indicate, where the employer, coworker or even insurance carrier commits an intentional tort, most states would not limit the employee to workers' compensation recovery.

BERCAW V. DOMINO'S PIZZA, INC., 630 N.E.2d 166 (Ill. App. Ct. 1994)

You may need to review substantial certainty rules here. Did the *Bercaw* court need to reject substantial certainty as a rule, or could it merely have said that there was no such certainty on the facts? Maybe that is in fact what it meant. Would the class favor a rule that imposed liability short of substantial certainty, say for wilful or wanton or reckless risks?

Note 1. For the court in *Padney,* cited here, substantial certainty is a legal doctrine, a term of art, not really a determination about certainty. You could hardly find certainty in everyday usage when a risk is in the neighborhood of

35%. And you can't be certain of harm merely because the harm, if it occurs, would be serious. (See also paragraph (c) below.) So students should recognize that an old label (substantial certainty) has been used, but the doctrinal content is entirely new and quite unrelated to anything that would ordinarily be called substantial certainty. You might want to impose tort liability upon reckless employers who take advantage of the workers' compensation immunity to behave atrociously, yet wonder whether a distorted version of substantial certainty is the best way to achieve that result.

Laidlow v. Hariton Mach. Co., Inc., 790 A.2d 884 (N.J. 2002), like some of the Ohio authorities, is willing to use substantial certainty to mean a very high statistical probability *over time.* That is, given continued operation of a dangerous process, sooner or later injury will occur. This does not seem to be the idea behind traditional concepts of substantial certainty, which focuses on the here and now. As this manual explains in that connection, probability over time is merely the same as risk, not certainty.

Laidlow is also like *Padney* in treating seriousness of potential injury as a factor indicating certainty of injury. Again, that can hardly be so in any literal sense. If your machine has a one-in-a-billion chance of causing injury, injury is no more certain (probable) because it turns out that the injury is death rather than loss of a finger. Seriousness of potential injury might indeed show that the employer is acting atrociously in subjecting employees to a risk, but atrocity and certainty are not equivalent concepts.

However, New Jersey inserts an added requirement besides substantial certainty, and it is one to which seriousness of potential injury might be relevant. Its added requirement is that "the resulting injury and the circumstances of its infliction on the worker must be (a) more than a fact of life of industrial employment and (b) plainly beyond anything the Legislature intended the Workers' Compensation Act to immunize."

Several similar cases in which an employer knows of a danger but fails to warn or instruct are listed in Wanda Ellen Wakefield, Annotation, Concealed Hazard– Employer's Tort Liability, 9 A.L.R.4th 778 (1981), denying liability.

Note 2. Given that the ordinary meaning of substantial certainty is distorted in cases like *Padney,* it is no wonder that some courts are uncomfortable with the whole idea and reject it. Cases rejecting the use of substantial certainty intent altogether as a means of avoiding the exclusive remedy provision are *Birklid v. Boeing Co.,* 904 P.2d 278 (Wash. 1995), and *Baker v. Westinghouse Elec. Corp.,* 637 N.E.2d 1271 (Ind. 1994). Yet, if the state recognizes tort liability of employer's for intentional torts, shouldn't that include intentional torts based upon "real" substantial certainty as opposed to the doctrine in *Padney*? Or is it that the exclusive remedy clause itself is the wrong way to go?

KERANS V. PORTER PAINT CO., 575 N.E.2d 428 (Ohio 1991)

Rationale and its effect in physical harm cases. Kerans' rationale for putting the claim in the realm of tort, not workers' compensation, is that purely emotional harms are not covered by the statute and hence not by the exclusive remedy clause. *Ford v. Revlon*, infra, offers a slight variation on this idea– that emotional harm is not a covered "accident" unless it occurs suddenly or traumatically. This line of reasoning risks the result in *Driscoll*, namely that emotional harm resulting from physical injury was covered and hence the tort action was barred. See "Catch 22" below.

Other Rationales. The *Kerans'* rationale is not the only one available. As shown in **Note 2**, *Horodyskyj v. Karanian* asks, not whether the injury is the type covered, but whether the sexual assault or harassment arose out of employment, using the three familiar categories for analysis. Since sexual assault or harassment here (and generally, the court thinks) was personal, that meant it did not arise out of employment and hence that the exclusive remedy provision was no bar.

Catch-22. (a) Personal attacks. In some cases, workers' compensation might be denied because the rape or harassment does not "arise out of employment." Why not? Because if it is "personal" to the attacker, not job-related. *Anderson v. Save-A-Lot, Ltd.,* 989 S.W.2d 277 (Tenn. 1999) (so holding). Some statutes codify this idea.

(b) Recovery in tort? If compensation is denied, could the victim then recover in tort? Maybe not. If the attacker's motives were "personal," the exclusive remedy provision would not apply, but the employer might escape tort liability on the ground that the attacker was not acting within the scope of employment and that the employer was not independently negligent in making the attack possible.

(c) Work related attacks. Finally, suppose the employer is at fault, say in letting security lapse. In that case the employer may assert that the attack was work related after all, so that he is immune to tort liability and pays workers' compensation only. See *Holland v. Commonwealth*, 584 A.2d 1056 (Pa. Cmwlth. 1990) (rapist's lack of personal animosity toward the plaintiff showed the attack was work-related, so plaintiff was limited to compensation claim); cf. *Melo v. Jewish Bd. of Family and Children's Services, Inc.*, 706 N.Y.S.2d 569 (App. Div. 1999) (employee attacked on employer's premises by unidentified assailant; work environment increased risk of attack, so it was work related and exclusive remedy provision limited employer's liability to workers' compensation).

Do you think that the *Kerans* court would allow a recovery in tort against the employer if an employee was raped by another employee or by a supervisor?

FYI: Employer's vicarious liability for sexual harassment. Federal sexual harassment law distinguishes between quid pro quo and hostile work environment sexual discrimination or harassment. In the quid pro quo sexual harassment, tangible job benefits are at stake because a supervisor demands something in exchange for retaining or gaining benefits. Hostile work environment harassment does not implicate tangible job benefits but reflects pervasive discrimination or harassment. Under Title VII, the employer is vicariously liable in both cases, but in the hostile work environment case, the employer can defend itself by showing that it exercised reasonable care to prevent and promptly correct sexually harassing behavior and that the plaintiff unreasonably failed to take advantage of the preventive or corrective opportunities provided. *Burlington Indus., Inc. v. Ellerth,* 524 U.S. 742 (1998); *Faragher v. City of Boca Raton,* 524 U.S. 775. ■

Dignitary torts. Sexual harassment on the job is a real problem. If sexual harassment produced a single kind of injury, it might be possible to address the problem more readily. Judge Resnick described the injury in *Kerans* as psychological, meaning, presumably, non-physical.

Sexual harassment cases may be sui generis. Certainly they are in that they invoke a specific set of policies and statutes. Even so, it is useful to recognize that sexual harassment cases like *Kerans,* where there is no physical harm, can be compared in some ways to torts like assault, false imprisonment, infliction of mental distress and privacy invasion. Those torts have in common not only a recognition that dignitary interests, interests in the self, are important and recognized by law, but also that they quite often do not entail any economic loss or direct physical harm. The gist of many such claims is neither wage loss nor medical expense, but a kind of emotional suffering from the outrage. The significance of this point is that workers' compensation statutes were never structured to deal with non-physical, dignitary torts.

So there is sense in what Judge Resnick says: the injury claim displaced by workers' compensation is physical injury, or at least emotional injury that is physically debilitating. If you took that view, you'd allow *Kerans*-type sexual harassment tort claims, but also probably a wide variety of other tort claims against the employer because they are outside the "bargain" made with workers' compensation. That is the import of the notes preceding *Kerans.*

Note 2. *Where injury is not compensable under workers' compensation. Kerans'* exclusion of emotional injuries from workers' copmpensation is based on a rather narrow ground. *Horodyskyj v. Karanian,* cited here, and some other cases seem broader in allowing the tort claim whenever the injury does not "arise out of employment." Other cases allowing the tort recovery for sexual harassment or assault include: *Onstad v. Payless Shoesource,* 9 P.3d 98 (Mont. 2000) (stranger attack, employer negligence); *Coates v. Wal-Mart Stores, Inc.,* 976 P.2d 999 (N.M. 1999) (tort action may proceed if injuries are not compensable, or if they do not arise out of employment, or if the employer intended injury); *GTE Southwest, Inc. v. Bruce,* 998 S.W.2d 605 (Tex. 1999) (supervisor's harassment did not give rise to compensation claim because it was not rooted in particular event, tort claim is actionable).

When the employer knows of the harassment and does nothing to stop it, the employer itself is at fault at least for negligently failing to provide a reasonably safe place of employment. It is not implausible to say that, given the employer's duty to provide a reasonably safe place of work, the employer who deliberately looks the other way in sexual harassment cases is guilty of an intentional tort for which punitive damages are appropriate. In *Ford v. Revlon*, 734 P.2d 580 (Ariz. 1987), the plaintiff recovered $10,000 in compensatory and $100,000 in punitive damages from her employer, who knew of continuous physical and verbal sexual harassment but refused to interfere. The court held that the exclusive remedy provision did not apply because the tort was not inflicted by "accident" and because the statute specifically provided that a "mental injury" was not an accident "unless ... unexpected, unusual or extraordinary stress ... or some physical injury ... was a substantial contributing cause." This second ground, like the reasoning in *Kerans*, seems to leave open the possibility that an employer might escape tort liability for a worker's actual physical assault. That is confirmed by *Driscoll v. General Nutrition Corp.*, which is cited in **Note 1**.

Note 7. *Workers' compensation interaction with federal statutes.* The exclusive remedy clause of the federal government employees' workers' compensation statute (FECA) does not bar Title VII claims, either, although this obviously is not based upon the Supremacy Clause. *Nichols v. Frank*, 42 F.3d 503 (9th Cir. 1994) (sexual harassment was not an "injury by accident" under the compensation statute and hence is not covered; and even if it were, the exclusive remedy clause does not preclude the "equitable" relief authorized under Title VII).

§ 4. TORT CLAIMS AGAINST THIRD PARTIES

COMMENTS

A. Who Is a "Third Party?"

Notes give two examples. Co-workers are usually not "third parties" who can be sued, but when they deviate from employment to engage in an attack that results from their personal lives, they are liable. The other example is the workers' compensation insurance carrier. These are typically identified with the work in the same way that co-employees are, and hence get the same immunity from tort suit. However, in some cases the carrier's activities at the work site are tortious and in a few cases the carrier has been held liable in tort.

B. The Statutory Employer and Borrowed Servants

1. *The statutory employer's compensation obligation.* If the employer hires an independent contractor to carry out the employer's regular work, the

employer is treated by the statutes as if he employed the contractor's workers and he is liable for compensation to them. As we saw in covering vicarious liability, the employer can always protect himself by requiring the independent contractor to maintain full insurance, including, in this case, workers' compensation insurance.

2. *Immunity of the statutory employer.* If the employer is a statutory employer of the independent contractor's employees, they presumably could not sue him in tort; their remedy would be a workers' compensation claim only.

3. *Borrowed servants.* If you treat both the lender and the borrower as employers, both owe compensation but neither is liable in tort for his negligence.

C. Adjustments Among the Parties

This may be hard for some students to follow. If you are good with the chalk board or its modern electronic equivalents, diagrams may help you explicate it.

1. *The employer's lien.* The employer who pays workers' compensation gets to share in the employee's tort recovery. That is the bottom line about what it means to say that the employer has a lien on that recovery. As we pointed out in discussing matching of direct and collateral benefits, *supra* Chapter 26, this manual, the employer (almost always the employer's insurance carrier in reality) may pay only for wage loss or medical benefits, but may get to enforce its lien against the employee's recovery for entirely different elements, such as emotional distress or pain and suffering.

If you want an illustration you can take this one or simplify it for presentation to the class. Suppose the plaintiff is injured on the job by a product. The manufacturer is negligent and so is the employer. The plaintiff suffers intense and lasting pain, and has medical bills, but does not miss work. She recovers workers' compensation benefits of $2,000, none of which include pain and suffering. She then sues the product manufacturer. The manufacturer persuades the jury that it was chargeable only with 10% of the negligence, and that the employer was chargeable with 90%. Total damages were $2,000 in medical expenses and $20,000 in pain and suffering, but the plaintiff had personal insurance policies that paid her the medical expenses and the jurisdiction has eliminated the collateral source rule. With joint and several liability also abolished, the product manufacturer will be liable for only 10% of the total damages (as reduced by the anti-collateral source rule), a net of only $2,000. The employer, of course, is immune from tort liability. To add insult to injury, the employer's lien against the tort recovery will be for $2,000, the amount it paid in benefits. That will leave the employee with no tort recovery against the product manufacturer. The employer/carrier, though guilty of most of the fault, recovers everything it paid or will pay in workers' compensation benefits. Since the ultimate judgment for the employee only covered pain and suffering, not the medical costs, this means the employer's lien claim arose out of medical payments but is recouped against pain and suffering payments.

2. *The employer's subrogation rights.* If the employee does not sue the third party tortfeasor, the employer/carrier may do so, by way of their subrogation right. In amounts and application, it works like the lien claim except that the employer/carrier brings the suit when the employee fails to do so.

3. *The third-person tortfeasor's claim against the negligent employer.* Both the third person and the employer are negligent in this scenario. In a joint and several liability system, the third person tortfeasor is liable for all the plaintiff's damages (except as reduced by the plaintiff's comparative fault). Only a few cases have allowed some kind of incomplete and limited contribution by the third person against the employer, say, up to the amount of the workers' compensation payments. To reject all contribution is exactly in line with the common liability rule.

4. *In a several liability jurisdiction.* The plaintiff here would recover against the third person tortfeasor only that tortfeasor's percentage share. If the employer is the person guilty of most fault, the plaintiff's recovery would be limited and even part of that might be taken by the employer/carrier via the lien or subrogation rights. Is the employer immunity really such a good idea?

CHAPTER 29

PUBLIC COMPENSATION SYSTEMS, INCLUDING SOCIAL SECURITY

▶**Changes in the Sixth Edition.** We have cut the length of this chapter slightly, updating and trimming text and cutting the *Cleveland* case abstract. The federal statute reprinted in § 2 (42 U.S.C.A. § 423) has been updated to reflect 2004 amendments that occurred after the Fifth Edition had gone to press. We also cut one of the two Grids we had reprinted in the prior edition (in the NOTE: THE MEDICAL-VOCATIONAL GUIDELINES) on a theory that one Grid provides enough of an example.

Scheduling omissions. The materials in this chapter do not call for more than one day's coverage, although you can spend more time on them.

§ 1. PROTECTING INDUSTRIES THROUGH COMPENSATION SCHEMES THAT REPLACE TORT LIABILITY

A. Taxing Industry and Eliminating Its Tort Liability

The quotation from *Schafer v. American Cyanamid Co.,* 20 F.3d 1 (1st Cir. 1994), summarizes the National Childhood Vaccine Injury Act. This section does not support extended analysis, only the kernel of an idea about a tort alternative.

The facts of the *Schafer* case are not given here because the point is not case analysis or critique, but introduction to the system created by the Act. As a matter of fact, however, you may wish to know that in the *Schafer* case a *parent* contracted polio after a child's was vaccinated for that disease. That parent recovered an award under the Vaccine Act, some $750,000. The *other* parent and the *child* then withdrew their Vaccine Act petitions and brought tort claims. The *Schafer* court held that the act did not bar the tort claim of the uninjured parent for loss of the child's consortium or the child's own claim for injury merely because a family member had accepted compensation under the Act.

Strategically, what's in this Vaccine Act for the manufacturers? According to Judge Breyer, the plaintiff could reject the Vaccine Court's award and go into the tort system. This sounds like the best of both worlds for the plaintiff, and quite different from the workers' compensation system with its exclusive remedy provision. Part of the answer is that in tort, the rights are reduced, damages limited, and procedural disadvantages imposed.

One group of cases has involved childhood injuries resulting from preservatives added to the vaccine, notably mercury. The Act requires forbids tort actions unless the plaintiff has first presented her claim through the Vaccine Court, but it permits the plaintiff to proceed in tort for injuries caused by an adulterant or contaminant in the vaccine. Is mercury, intentionally added as a preservative, an adulterant or contaminant? The cases have almost all held not. Consequently the plaintiff who attempt to present a tort claim must lose. A good review of the issues and cases can be found in *Troxclair v. Aventis Pasteur,* Inc., 864 A.2d 1147 (N.J. Super. 2005).

The Vaccine Act approach is not much like the more thorough-going public system we see in social security disability benefits. You might call it a quasi-public system rather than a public system. In one respect, however, the Vaccine Act uses a procedure that can remind you of the grids in social security cases. The act provides that the plaintiff can either prove that the vaccine caused injury or can rely on a table showing vaccines, symptoms, and time-intervals for the symptoms to create a prima facie case of causation. The table specifies injuries covered and the number of days within which symptoms must appear to obtain the presumption of the table. It is this table that somewhat resembles the grids approach.

Construction of the statute and its table: See *Shalala v. Whitecotton,* 514 U.S. 268 (1995); Russell G. Donaldson, Annotation, Construction and Application of National Childhood Vaccine Injury Act (42 U.S.C.A. §§ 300aa et seq.), 129 A.L.R. Fed. 1 (1996).

This tiny section ends with three discussion questions, one of which uses the term "plaintiffs as a whole." The phrase is important. Tort law has traditionally tailored its relief to individual victims, not to groups of victims "as a whole." An individual plaintiff is not ordinarily denied relief merely because most other victims in similar circumstances would have no claim.

Figures. Better chance among some masters: Among the six masters, success rates varied from 32.8 percent to 65.8 in the period studied, even though negligence was not an issue. Derry Ridgway, *No-fault Vaccine Insurance: Lessons From The National Vaccine Injury Compensation Program,* 24 J. HEALTH POL. POL'Y & L. 59 (1999). Once you eliminate issues like those associated with negligence, duty, and scope of risk, you expect that even-handed administration of the law would produce similar results. Why is it not doing so here?

B. Taxing the Public to Protect Industries and Provide Compensation to Victims – The 9-11 Compensation System

The workers' compensation system gives the plaintiff no choice at all to sue in tort. The Vaccine Act gives the plaintiff such a choice, but only after she has pursued the Vaccine Court claim and rejects its judgment. In the September 11 compensation system, the plaintiff the plaintiff can sue either in tort or under the administrative system provided, and need not jump through the administrative hoops first. Why the differences? In workers' compensation we commonly hear of an implicit "bargain" by which the worker gets strict liability but limits his claim to the benefits provided. If there were a bargain between workers and employers, then we might think that there was a bargain between parents and drug makers and a bargain between the direct victims of terrorism on September 11 and the airlines. In that case, we could explain the differences as simply the outcomes of different bargain. But of course there were no bargains. All these systems were imposed by legislators, mainly for the benefit of the employers, the drug manufacturers, and airlines (who also got a bail-out in cash). Did the three kinds of legislation treat tort rights differently because legislators had a reason? If the September 11 option to sue in tort works there, would it equally work with workers' compensation?

The last question forces us to recognize that the September 11 system directly uses tax money to pay victims. It is unique in that respect. Even the Vaccine Act, which taxes the industry to provide the funds, is not using general tax funds. The September 11 system has raised big doubts about the appropriate scope of public aid to victims. Can we distinguish the victims of September 11 terrorism from the victim's of Tim McVeigh's terrorism? Can we even distinguish them from the victims of terrorism on our streets every night with random rapes, shootings, and tortures?

To the extent that tax money is used to pay tort-like awards, say for pain and suffering and in somewhat individuated amounts, may public compensation should be for all victims of everything or for none. *See* **Note 3.** But look at the summary of the Special Master's regulations. Consider flattening, the effort, apparently, to say, all the victims, whatever their losses, are in the same boat and that there should not be too much individuation except on a need basis. Is more like compensation systems, more like welfare, or more like tort? Whatever the answer, isn't there some uneasy feeling victims of other torts are no less victims and that the government should be even-handed in disbursing the public treasury? One big difference between McVeigh's victims and those of September 11– there were no airlines crying for help in Oklahoma City. Another is that we are not giving up the hope of deterring unsafe activities in administering the September 11 system. We are giving that up in the workers' compensation system with its exclusive remedy clause and to a large extent with the Vaccine Act.

With some discussion of such issues, perhaps your class will have opinions which of the systems we've just mentioned, including tort law, is most desirable– or at least which of them is the *least* desirable.

§ 2. SOCIAL SECURITY DISABILITY BENEFITS

Cash benefits, sometimes called quasi-insurance benefits, are provided by the social security program for retired individuals and their dependents. Certain *disabled* persons may also qualify for benefits independent of retirement.

OASDI and SSI versions. Title II of the Social Security Act provides disability benefits for eligible workers who have paid into the Social Security Trust Fund. Title XVI provides benefits to disabled adults and children based on financial need. The latter is essentially a welfare program, not based on contributions by the claimant. The two programs, one based in part on contributions, the other not, have different statutory and financial bases and are referred to separately. The contribution-based program is the Old Age and Survivors Insurance or Old Age and Survivors and Disability Insurance program (OASDI). The other is the Supplemental Security Income or SSI program. The distinction is important because the terms are used constantly in almost all discussions; and it is important in pursuing claims and in reading the statistics. However, the sketch of disability claims in this chapter does not make anything turn on the difference between OASDI and SSI claims.

Benefits generally. Benefits are paid as if the worker had retired at the age of 62. See 20 C.F.R. § 404.317. At lower wage levels, these benefits reach to 90% of average wages, with a much smaller percentage payable for wages in the higher brackets. In addition, there are family benefits.

Disability generally. A claimant may qualify for disability benefits even though the disability did not arise from injury and was unconnected with any job. Personal illnesses, disease, or breakdown will be sufficient. Personal limitations in education, experience and ability will be considered in determining whether one is disabled. The disability, however, must be one that prevents work and it must be long lasting, a year or more. The system, then, roughly aims at wage replacement for disabilities that are more or less total and permanent.

Reasons for our coverage. (1) These materials represent one way law can respond adjudicatively to injury and disability. The tort way of dealing can be judged in part only by comparing it to other ways, of which this government benefits program is one. As an adjudicative system, this program uses both individual adjudication of rights (like the tort system) and statistical methods (the grids) that may not reflect disability in the particular case.

(2) Social security represents different ways in which injury compensation can be financed, through a combination of contributions and tax dollars. To some extent, the scheme is an insurance scheme, so that the worker gets what he or she has paid for. However, the scheme is also a welfare or subsidy scheme in the sense that the worker does not often get benefits in proportion to premiums (payroll taxes). The lower-paid worker may get 90% of his wages in benefits, the higher-paid worker much less. In addition, family benefits and SSI benefits are not related to premiums or taxes paid. Thus this scheme has

elements of financing that we can compare and contrast with torts and workers' compensation as to safety incentives and general deterrence.

(3) Professional lawyers must be aware of this scheme for practical reasons. The plaintiff may best hold out for a good settlement, for example, if she has the security of a monthly disability check. Tort lawyers must also engage other legal experts in some cases to make sure that settlement of the tort suit is consummated with appropriate trust documents when the client is disabled and entitled to public assistance through SSI or Medicaid, because public assistance is withdrawn when the client has countable assets or income over a certain level. *See* Jersey M. Green & Marilyn W. McWilliams, *Preserving the Disabled Plaintiff's Access to Public Benefits with Special Needs Trust,* 25 MAY COLO. LAW. 49 (1996); Joel A. Mendler, *Using Trusts for Disabled Clients: Preserving Governmental Benefits,* 44 LA. B. J. 26 (1996). This is a technical point not developed in these materials, but it is a good indication that tort lawyers today had best be aware of a wide range of non-tort personal injury law.

(4) The least important reason is that this chapter gives a minuscule introduction to a complex statute and to the idea of extensive administrative regulations. As the torts student approaches the end of the first year, this seems especially appropriate.

COMMENTS

INTRODUCTORY NOTE

For current figures, see the Social Security Bulletin (Annual Statistical Supplement) for the latest year, or access Westlaw or Internet materials listed in references below.

A 1995 law removed the Social Security Administration from the Department of Health and Human Services and set it up as an independent federal agency, headed by the Commissioner of Social Security. Formerly, the nominal defendant in suits to claim disability benefits was the Secretary of HHS; it is now the Commissioner of Social Security. Hence cases before the change refer occasionally to decisions of the Secretary, while later cases and the notes in the casebook refer to the decisions of the Commissioner.

42 U.S.C.A. § 423

Some teachers may want to parse this statute with the students. As the course moves toward a close, the introduction of more complicated statutory material seems appropriate.

It may be easy to teach students here how to read a statute. Some students will be helped a lot by a warning that statutes are like mathematical equations, graphs, and poetry in that a great deal may be compressed into a very few words or symbols. The reading speed for statutes is much, much slower than for cases, and the student should expect that.

Subsection (a) is not really hard, but it may confuse some students on first reading. After reading it through, you can see that it is attempting to state the four elements necessary to establish a claim. A reader who learns to reorganize the statute, at least provisionally, can grasp its meanings very quickly. In addition, some readers will be helped if they learn to use the system of "temporary dropouts" — in (a)(1)(A) the parenthetical clause is merely like a footnote cross reference, to tell you that you can find out more about the definition of "insured" in Subsection (c). As soon as a reader gets to this, it is possible to drop it out (temporarily, mentally), because it is an interruption in the list.

The definition of disability in Subsection (d) is more difficult. Here some temporary translations may help. In (d)(1)(A), a student reader might summarize for him or herself by saying, "To have a disability, you have to have a medical impairment that prevents work for at least a year." This is obviously not a complete statement. You might have to wonder whether "substantial gainful activity" differs from "work," and what "medically determinable" might mean. You would also have to include a statement about death as "disability." Still, the temporary translation may help the student get the gist of the idea and some students will be helped if this is pointed out. Another kind of translation occurs with the "or" at the end of (d)(1)(A). This translates: "You can also have a disability if . . . ."

Another helpful approach in parsing complex statutes is to try to imagine the cases they cover (or don't). Why, for example, did the Congress add (B) here? Rough translation: "if you go blind after 55, we don't expect you to acquire wholly new skills, and if you can't do your former work, or something like it, we'll say you are disabled."

Parsing the statute like this is sometimes helpful to introduce students to statute, but if you don't have the time or inclination to do so, you can point out to the student some key rules: Disability must be more or less permanent –it must last a year or more– and it must be more or less total– it must prevent any substantial gainful activity. Furthermore, proof of this requires: (a) medically determinable impairment resulting from anatomical, physiological or psychological abnormalities demonstrable by clinical or laboratory diagnostic techniques; and (b) inability to work in a job that exists in the national economy, whether or not there is actually a vacancy he could fill. However, this ability to work is judged by a subjective standard, based on the claimant's own education, background, and ability.

Note 1. Procedures for claim. There is no jury at any stage. In the first stage, the decision is based on the paperwork only. When the ALJ is called in, usually in or near the claimant's locality, there is a "hearing" at which the claimant and a representative may appear and present evidence. A transcript is made and this becomes the basis for appeals. It is usually attached to a motion for summary judgment if the appeals get as far as a new suit in District Court to review the decision. The district judge usually decides these cases on cross motions for summary judgment. The proceeding is not "judicial" but administrative. In that respect, it is like the workers' compensation proceeding in most states. When the United States District Judge gets into the picture, she is not trying the case but is giving judicial review to an administrative proceeding. The administrators are sometimes in conflict with the judges. Something of the tug-of-war over administrative versus judicial standards can be seen in *Hyatt v. Sullivan*, 899 F.2d 329 (4th Cir. 1990), where the courts actually had to use injunctive powers to force the recalcitrant Secretary to comply with the law (on standards for pain). *See* Erin Margaret Masson, *Social Security Administration Nonacquiescence on the Standard for Evaluating Pain*, 36 WM. & MARY L. REV. 1819 (1995).

Note 2. Insured status. Social security "premiums" are actually taxes and the system is compulsory. It is important to realize that the premiums (taxes) are allocated to separate funds. They do not go into general revenues of the government. As pointed out above, the premiums or taxes paid to the fund by Jane Doe in working from 1947 to 1982 are *not* in any sense returned to her. Her social security benefits do not equal contributions plus interest or investment proceeds. Her contributions were long ago paid out to others. Her benefits will come from contributions being made today by younger people. This is the source of agony, controversy and (some argue) the near-bankruptcy of the system. Whether it is right or wrong need not concern us very greatly in this course. What may be more important for us is whether, in spite of this "current cost financing," the program resembles insurance in the sense that benefits have some relationship to contributions. In some degree at least, the basic social security payments are insurance payments. There is no need to introduce the current cost financing discussion unless it becomes relevant to a particular line of discussion. The SSI materials track the disability definition under general social security provisions, but they appear in different sections.

Note 3. Benefits. As indicated in the preliminary note, the average monthly disability benefit under OASDI is around $600 in 1992, but total benefits to the family may be more.

The casebook note on benefits is grossly simplified and that seems proper. The benefits computation is extremely complex and time consuming. However, the regulations are now written in English and are addressed to the claimant ("We calculate your indexing year under this paragraph if you, the insured worker, die before reaching age 62..."). CFR §§ 404.211 and 404.212 spell out the basic processes generalized here. They give considerably more detail and are quite easy to follow if you have already mastered basic statute reading under the Internal Revenue Code. They also give examples.

There are also some provisions not mentioned in the note. For instance, claimants may drop out some years from the averaging process to get rid of years with low production. (See § 404.211(e)).

When the Average Indexed Monthly Earnings (AIME) is computed, the benefit formula is applied along the lines indicated in the note. See § 404.212. A table of the formulas for 1979-82 is given in Appendix III to Subpart C.

Note 4. Disability. This note shifts the student's attention to the concept of disability under the statute. And disability IS a concept, not merely a discoverable fact. To have disability you must (a) have an impairment, (b) be unable to work in substantial gainful employment and (c) fulfill a process or evidentiary requirement by showing that the impairment is medically determinable. This little note is mainly intended to shift directions toward the *McLain* case.

MCLAIN V. SCHWEIKER, 715 F.2d 866 (4th Cir. 1983)

McLain, 49, has a high school education with two years college, and has been employed as a salesman and security guard but claims he can no longer work because he cannot tolerate noise, etc. A psychiatrist reports a paranoid-like trend in his thought and concludes he cannot interrelate or withstand job pressures. The ALJ found impairment but concluded that he would be able to perform his previous work in non-stressful environments, e.g., as a sedentary security guard. The ALJ denied benefits.

Held: remanded.

(1) Once the claimant shows inability to perform former work because of impairment, burden shifts to commissioner to show that the claimant has sufficient "residual functional capacity" to engage in some other job existing in the national economy. Plaintiff's proof made the prima facie case.

(2) The commissioner came forward with no evidence to show an alternative real job for one of the claimant's age, experience and impairment. A vocational expert is needed to show job availability that matches the impairment. Administrative notice of job positions does not establish correlation with the plaintiff's residual abilities.

"Administrative notice" may puzzle some students. It is a phrase parallel to "judicial notice," that is, the power of a judge to accept as proven (or take notice of) some facts of general knowledge. The ALJ then was taking as proven that there are sales positions and sedentary security guard positions which would not involve stress and crowds. (An unlikely proposition one might think.)

Notes 1. Applying the statute. Both paragraphs of this note end with the question, readily answerable, "what does the statute say?" The point is to throw the student on the statute as the authoritative source of law. The answer to both questions must be located in (d)(2)(A). The statute imposes a national job market standard: the claimant must be unable to obtain substantial gainful work "which exists in the national economy, regardless of whether such work exists in the immediate area in which he lives, or whether a specific job vacancy exists for him, or whether he would be hired if he applied for work." Reading this language alone, you must say that if the claimant can work sorting potatoes, he is not disabled, even if potato sorting jobs are all

1,000 miles away. Similarly, you have to say that if he can sort potatoes, the fact that there are few jobs and many applicants makes no difference.

However, the next sentence in (d)(2)(A) may qualify that conclusion. "For purposes of the preceding sentence (with respect to any individual), 'work which exists in the national economy' means work which exists in significant numbers either in the region where such individual lives or in several regions of the country." If the potato sorting job is really *only* located in a region 1,000 miles away, it is not located in the claimant's region or in "several regions." Under those circumstances, if the claimant could *only* work at potato sorting, he would be disabled after all. Similarly, if there is only one potato sorting job in the whole country, the "significant numbers" test used in this section would allow an award for disability if that is the only job the claimant could perform. In real life, a person who could sort potatoes could probably sort beets and perform other similar tasks, so you would have to consider the regions and significant numbers tests about all the jobs the claimant could perform.

The preceding materials and some of those that follow reflect the fact that disability under the statute is a product of both the claimant's condition and the job market. Bodily impairment has meaning under the express terms of the statute only as it affects an ability to work in some real job somewhere. On the other hand, the statute is not to be used as an unemployment compensation statute, so making these two factors work for the statutory purposes is difficult. Although we did not explore disability in the workers' compensation materials, there is in fact a comparable problem there. E.g., *Guyton v. Irving Jensen Company,* 373 N.W.2d 101 (1985) (describing the problem in terms of the "odd-lot" doctrine).

Note 4. The Listings. In *Sullivan v. Zebley*, 493 U.S. 521 (1990), a child was excluded by the listings. The Court held that the child should be permitted to show that he was nonetheless disabled under the statute's standard for children, namely that his impairment was of comparable severity. So the Court is unwilling to give up tailored adjudication based on the individual merits of the individual case. (The statutory standard for child coverage has since been change to restrict coverage, but that is irrelevant to the larger point in *Zebley,* that some individuation remains possible in determining whether the statutory standard is met.) Individuation may sometimes be illusory, however. In reality, any presumptive barrier like the listings, as applied to a mass of potential claimants, will have the effect of excluding a large percentage of claimants who could prove comparably severe impairments if they pursued their rights to the nth degree. Is this, however, any different from a burden of proof rule in tort law?

NOTE: THE MEDICAL-VOCATIONAL GUIDELINES – THE GRIDS

The grids, or medical vocational guidelines, combine various relevant factors for determining disability, mainly the degree of impairment, age, education, and work experience. Once the administrative law judge fills in the blanks, it is a matter of reading across the table. For instance, an older person with a given impairment may be disabled when a younger person is not. But an older person with a J.D. degree may not be disabled merely because she must limit herself to sedentary work. Sometimes the grids mandate a finding of disability, sometimes the other way around. Like the five-step analysis above, the grids reflect a bureaucratic channel for analysis. Is any of this different from the judicial process of analysis in tort cases? Mainly perhaps in the fact that judges working with a series of factors usually allow themselves enormous discretion. They do not tell us how much weight they will give each factor. (Think of the Restatement's factors for determining conversion, for example.) In the case of the grids, a rather precise decision has already been made for the ALJ.

HECKLER V. CAMPBELL, 461 U.S. 458 (1983)

The Court upholds the Grids as permissible regulations. First year students in some law schools may be unfamiliar with regulations and indeed some may be unsure about the traditional three divisions of government unless you clarified that in teaching the nursing home materials or the EMTALA regulations (both in Chapter 13 on medical malpractice). With social security, as with workers' compensation, we have moved out of traditional tort law into administration; and administration here is combining both judicial decision making (a determination what the impairment is, for example) and "legislative" activity (the promulgation of binding regulations). All rules are likely to encompass too much or too little; an effective rule will not merely tell the judge (or ALJ) to decide the case. It will very likely classify or define and prescribe results to be obtained whenever the classification or definition is met. ("Guest" under guest statutes, for example.)

Some courts have thought the grids to be unconstitutional as overbroad and others have differed. Here the Court thought the regulations did not decide any matter that should be left for adjudication and that the claimant still got individually tailored justice on all the individual matters involved –what her impairment actually was, how old she was, what her experience was and what her education was. Yet, as suggested in the notes, this may effectively undo the burden shifting we see in the other cases. The claimant shows she cannot do her former work; the burden shifts to the Commissioner; he meets it by prescribing a regulation. Implicit in the regulation is the assertion that there are jobs in the economy this claimant, with her impairments, can handle. What are they? The secretary's (Commissioner's) position is that he won't tell. Even if the regulations are valid, as far as they go, why should the secretary not be required to give at least some examples?

Notice that the claimant escapes the grid if her disability is nonexertional, e.g., a result of mental limitations.

Another means of putting flexibility into the grid system is shown in *Tejada v. Apfel,* 167 F.3d 770 (2d Cir. 1999), an opinion expressing some disquiet about the hearings before the ALJ:

It is the rule in our circuit that the ALJ, unlike a judge in a trial, must ... affirmatively develop the record in light of the essentially non-adversarial nature of a benefits proceeding, even if the claimant is represented by counsel. In this case, we question the decision of the ALJ not to develop the record further concerning Tejada's arthritis or her depression, particularly since the ALJ himself referred to the fact that Tejada was under treatment for both conditions. . . .

Legal rules often tell the lawyer what evidence to look for and what arguments to make. The grids do that, too. After *Campbell,* the claimant will push proof that tends to show greater impairment, or less education or work experience. By showing such items, the plaintiff will be able to claim a more favorable position on the grid. One way impairments may be enhanced is by testimony as to pain. Does this conflict with the "medically determinable" rule, which seems to require objective evidence? Courts have readily permitted pain testimony by the claimant, if it is based on some other impairment that is medically determinable.

Professor Ellen Pryor's article reveals a wealth of material on pain. She makes a significant distinction between acute and chronic pain. The latter seems to be more related to psycho-social factors and is also harder to rate. She proposes different attitudes about pain, especially in social security cases, but also in workers' compensation cases.

On a broader level, this chapter is one of the units necessary for a picture of injury law. It helps give a picture of what is actually there. It also helps give a picture of what is possible and what might be perceived by some as normatively desirable. Sugarman's proposal may strike many students as a strange one to encounter in an era when welfare is a political no-no. It may also seem strange in light of the problems that seem to be present in determining social security disability claims; although fault and causation issues have disappeared, we seem to be caught in the need to adjudicate particular cases in spite of listings and grids. However, you can recall that the alternatives we are now considering must always be compared to the tort system and that system does not look so good. You might also consult the always-thoughtful Conard, who brings some skepticism, or at least caution, to Sugarman's ideas, but thinks that reformers should at least have *some* comprehensive program in mind and justify proposed reforms as part of such a program. Conard, *Coup de Grace for Personal Injury Torts?*, 88 MICH. L. REV. 1557 (1990) (reviewing STEPHEN SUGARMAN, DOING AWAY WITH PERSONAL INJURY LAW (1989)).

Evaluating and Looking Ahead

You can pause at the end of this coverage to ask for some evaluation. Would some kind of approach like social security, expanded to cover all injury, be better than tort law? Better than workers' compensation? When we reach the end of the present chapter, then, we will have seen a number of distinct systems by which injury or disability is dealt with in our society–the torts-fault system, the torts strict liability system, workers' compensation, industry tax coupled with tort immunities and benefits to the injury, public benefits, and social security, with both welfare and insurance components. We next examine private insurance as an alternative.

REFERENCES:

When we last looked, two books are on Westlaw: CHARLES T. HALL, SOCIAL SECURITY DISABILITY PRACTICE and HARVEY MCCORMICK, SOCIAL SECURITY AND CLAIMS PROCEDURE. Use the data bases SSDISP and SSCLP respectively. WEST'S DIGESTS: *Social Security and Public Welfare.* Use the Federal Practice Digest for this topic. There are other materials on Westlaw, which of course include the cases.

The Social Security Administration is accessible on the Net. Try starting with http://www.ssa.gov/policy/. From here you can link to statistics and other information. You can get it in bulk, but there is a Fast Facts short summary you can easily download for such information as the average amount of benefit. Downloading is possible in PDF format.

CHAPTER 30

PRIVATE INSURANCE SOLUTIONS

▶**Changes in the Sixth Edition.** There are no changes in this chapter.

NOTE: INSURANCE INSIDE AND OUTSIDE THE TORT SYSTEM

Within the tort system. *Financial responsibility laws. See* A. WIDISS, A GUIDE TO UNINSURED MOTORIST COVERAGE §§ 1.2-1.4 (1969 & Supp.); R. KEETON & J. O'CONNELL, BASIC PROTECTION FOR THE TRAFFIC VICTIM 102-109 (1965). *Unsatisfied judgment funds.* This is another experiment that seemed to go nowhere. On the topic, *see* G.V. HALLMAN, UNSATISFIED JUDGMENT FUNDS (1968).

Uninsured motorist coverage. This attempts to provide for the same problem by letting victim-drivers protect themselves by purchasing insurance that would pay what the faulty but uninsured driver should pay under the tort system. The victim pays an additional premium and still faces the need to prove fault of the other driver. *See* WIDISS, *supra*; M. WOODROFF, J. FONESCA & A. SQUILLANTE, AUTOMOBILE INSURANCE AND NO-FAULT LAWS, Chapter 7 (1974).

Outside the tort system. *Accident insurance.* The advantage of a fixed payment is efficiency, since it is not necessary to determine actual losses and the only uncertainty for the insurer is how many persons will suffer a disability. There is another potential advantage in flat payment policies: anyone who wants to insure against pain and suffering can use such a policy for this purpose, by building it on top of basic medical coverages. Issues remain, of course, as to whether there was an "accident" (recall workers' compensation problems with this) and whether the plaintiff suffered a disability. E.g., *Kasper v. Provident Life Insurance Co.*, 285 N.W.2d 548, 1 A.L.R.4th 1305 (N.D. 1979) (heart attack while fighting a fire).

Medical payments insurance. This kind of insurance is one component of the no-fault auto schemes, though it is not so broad in coverage, and, as with other existing coverages, it will duplicate tort recoveries, and hence duplicate premium charges. It is a good background to understanding no-fault.

Disability and medical insurance. Although this insurance is "efficient" in many instances as compared with liability insurance because it returns a higher percent of the premium dollar in benefits it may be inefficient in promoting higher medical costs. The current problems with Managed Care arises from the impetus to reduce care once payments for it are fixed by the insurance available.

NOTE: NO-FAULT AUTO INSURANCE

Five of the major features of no-fault, as conceived by Robert Keeton and Jeffrey O'Connell, are listed here. In a fast class, you won't need to discuss each one in order as they will come up in discussion of other matters. For example, if you have some really good students, they will propose plans of their own which will raise most of these issues. If the class is a little slower, (or tired or bored), a one-by-one discussion or comment on each of these characteristics is desirable.

To a large extent, no-fault comes down to saying that the legal system will not accept minor cases, as to which drivers must accept personal responsibility for themselves under a compulsory insurance provision.

Although people might differ about what is minor, this is the kind of idea we accept in many situations. It is a kind of "deductible" provision like one in your collision policy. It may be aggravating when you have to pay the first $100 of your collision damage, but the provision probably saves your premium money in the long run.

But compulsion to use self-insurance is different. We don't accept compulsion readily, nor should we. Any compulsion is bad if it can be avoided, though no complex society runs without a great deal of it. We have building restrictions, taxes, tort law rules and thousands of regulations affecting our lives. Social security is compulsory and so is workers' compensation. So perhaps one should not automatically discard a compulsory no-fault system if there are good reasons for compulsion.

What reasons could there be? One argument is that without compulsion many injuries would go uncompensated. Some of these injuries would be to children who had no say in the decision to reject insurance coverage. Uncompensated injury would have many effects on others in society, many of them the source of current criticisms of the tort system. Some of the possible effects of undercompensation have already been mentioned —increases in crime, family disintegration, and increasing reliance on welfare solutions. Later we will see that some compulsion may be required to create an efficient system.

NEW YORK INSURANCE LAW § 5103

This section spells out the conditions for payment of "first party" benefits to everyone except those in another motor vehicle or motorcycle. In addition, the named insured and members of the insured household are covered even if they are in another automobile. Death benefits are specified in (d), and in the second paragraph, the insurer is allowed to exclude certain risk, such as intentional self-injury.

You can see much of the basic scheme in this kernel. You buy your own insurance. It covers you wherever you go. In addition, it covers your household. What about pedestrians? It covers them, too, since they are not occupants of another vehicle. What if the driver of another vehicle is injured? His own insurance covers him, and as the next statute excerpt shows, his tort action is abolished to the extent that he has no-fault coverage.

Some details about benefits are set out in the Note following this segment of the statute. The benefits are chiefly medical and wage loss, subject to limits in amount.

New York Insurance Law § 5104

This is the other side of the self-insurance coin –what is covered by one's own insurance is *not* covered by the tort/liability insurance system. If the driver of the other car is injured, he recovers economic losses from his own insurance, up to the limits. He may not sue you in tort for those covered losses.

The tort action is retained, however, for economic losses in excess of those covered by the no-fault basic benefits. Thus, to the extent that the economic injury has been covered by the first party benefits –to the extent the economic injury is under $50,000 -- there is no tort claim for that. Once the injury is more than this sum, the tort system can be brought into play to deal with the excess.

The tort action is also retained under the New York statute for "serious" noneconomic losses such as pain and suffering.

Problem: In re Claims of Picklesimer, et al.

The basIC facts for this problem were given at the end of Chapter 12. The problem can be used to make sure the students get the general ideas. Aside from issues pointed to in the notes, discussed separately below, students can recognize:

(1) Picklesimer recovers even if he is at fault.

(2) He recovers even if no one else is at fault.

(3) His benefits do not include anything for pain or inconvenience, but, in this case, would be mainly medical bills.

(4) He would have to subtract his personal medical coverage from no-fault coverage. Students may need to be reminded again that the point of this is to eliminate duplicative premiums: if no subtraction is made, he will be compelled to pay duplicative premiums even if he wants only one recovery. This is the compulsory element in the present system.

(5) Picklesimer's no-fault policy also includes a liability policy. This may be important, for it may be Picklesimer who is at fault here, and both Plangent and Patrick may sue him. Of course, Picklesimer has a tort exemption up to the $5,000/$10,000 level (under Keeton-O'Connell), but if their damages exceed one of these sums for pain or economic loss, Picklesimer might be liable. At this point, the liability insurance feature of the no-fault coverage is invoked.

(6) Comparisons to tort might be worthwhile. It may be hard here to determine fault, and if it goes to court we'll invest a lot of resources in trying to do so, especially if there are multiple defendants. Quite possibly no one is at fault, and in that case, Picklesimer would recover nothing under the tort system. Under no-fault, he simply recovers on his own, personally paid-for, no-fault policy, just as he recovers on his own medical disability insurance.

The partner's questions. The first question asked by the partner at the end of the problem is in effect taken up in Note 1. See the comments to that.

The second question is a misconception of no-fault and gives the student a chance to catch the partner's misunderstanding. Since under no-fault, each auto owner insures himself and his occupants, claims by Patrick and Plangent would be covered by the Patrick insurance and would be no threat to Picklesimer's own recovery from his own no-fault policy. This is what is meant by first party insurance. You can take the students through the New York statute on this point if you like. Section 5103(a) excludes occupants of other vehicles from no-fault coverage.

If a pedestrian had been injured, it is conceivable that the pedestrian's claim would compete with Picklesimer's claims for the limited insurance funds under Picklesimer's policy. The Keeton-O'Connell Plan proposed to deal with this by requiring the insurer to pay benefits proportioned to losses or to make an "equitable allocation." These authors rejected the first-come, first serve approach applicable to common law judgments. See § 2.71 and p. 314 of KEETON-O'CONNELL. There seems no reason to go into this detail here.

Note 1. From this, students should see a little about the scope of coverage and the meshing with torts. The no-fault system is intended to cover auto injuries only —those arising from the use, occupation, or maintenance of automobiles. As always, borderline cases arise. If you are a no-fault insured and suffer injury in a carjacking, you might or might not be covered. *See* Diane L. Schmauder, Annotation, *No-fault Insurance Coverage For Injury or Death of Insured Occurring During Carjacking or Attempted Carjacking*, 42 A.L.R.5th 727 (1996) (reflecting cases going both ways). But when autos are not involved at all, the tort exemption, essential to the system if duplicative premiums are to be avoided, has no application when autos are not involved.

Examples:

(a) D throws a Tootsie Pop at P and puts out P's eye. There is no no-fault coverage and no tort exemption.

(b) Dr. Noh negligently leaves a forceps in Pat's thoracic cavity at the close of an operation. Noh has no no-fault coverage and no exemption.

The *Grof* case is used not only because it involves a suit against the state, as our case might, but also because it shows the relation between the deduction and the exemption. If the state had been a no-fault insured with respect to this injury —if it had caused the wreck by its own automobile, for example— then it would be entitled to the exemption. And, equally, if the plaintiff had met the threshold and sued the state, the state would be entitled to have the plaintiff's no-fault benefits deducted. The court holds here that there is no deduction, because the state is not a no-fault insured.

This same principle answers the question whether there is an exemption in the first place. A number of decisions are in accord. In *Citizens Ins. Co. of America v. Tuttle*, 309 N.W.2d 174 (Mich. 1981), the plaintiff ran into a cow, negligently left running loose on the highway. The cow owner was held to have no tort exemptions.

Note 2. The answer to this question turns in part on the principle just covered in Note 1. Dalzell's interests as a landowner are no part of the no-fault system. As to them, Picklesimer probably has no tort exemption. Dalzell's claim against Picklesimer, if legally sound on the substantive of tort law, is still good. Picklesimer's policy includes both a no-fault and a liability component and he is thus covered against any claims by Dalzell.

Note 3. *Ownership and use of an automobile.* In terms of the New York statute, this kind of question might be resolved by recognizing that the no-fault law applies only to injuries arising out of use or operation. (Keeton-O'Connell used "ownership, maintenance or use," and Massachusetts speaks of "ownership, operation, maintenance or use.") The phrase "arising out of" is also suggestive. Courts have sometimes said specifically that this statutory requirement is a "proximate cause" issue, as in *McConnell v. Fireman's Fund American Ins. Co.*, 370 N.Y.S.2d 730 (App. Div. 1975) and *Reliance Ins. Co. v. O'Neill*, 430 N.Y.S.2d 239 (Sup. Ct. 1980).

In *Picklesimer*, we might be reminded of the "proximate cause" problem in *Marshall v. Nugent*, Chapter 8. We might roughly parallel Judge Magruder's ideas by asking whether the risks of operation of an automobile were still in operation as Picklesimer was walking on Dalzell's land.

Though a problem like this can be fun, it does not reflect the concerns of the drafters and the critics of tort law. They were concerned with the great mass of cases, not these border incidents. It really does not much matter, in the larger picture, whether decisions in such atypical cases go one way or another. No-fault is to tort law as compulsory vaccinations are to heart transplants. We might spend less on vaccinations than on heart transplants, but the vaccinations will save many thousands of lives while heart transplants will save a handful. Although the Picklesimer problem serves its teaching function and permits application of the law to a concrete and interesting set of facts, no one should be led to judge no-fault laws by their capacity to deal with outlandish cases of this sort.

Note 4. Section 5104 (b) of the New York statute specifically authorizes a lien in favor of the no-fault insurer on the damages recoverable by the no-fault insured. This covers claims only against non-covered persons. What should be done about the no-fault insured's claim against a covered person? Suppose the insurer pays its policy limits to the no-fault insured, whose injuries are serious enough to support a tort claim for further economic loss and also for pain and suffering against another covered person? Is it clear that there should be no subrogation or lien in favor of the no-fault insurer?

LICARI V. ELLIOTT, 441 N.E.2d 1088 (N.Y. 1982)

This case is useful because it is not dramatic or bizarre. It is an ordinary small injury case that most will agree ought to be compensated summarily rather than through elaborate proceedings of tort law. Are there students in the class who oppose no-fault and adhere to tort rules? If so, would they agree with the statement above? The claim in *Licari* is the kind of claim that is easily overblown. The leverage for overcompensation is that the insurer can pay more than the relatively minor loss at an early stage of the claim and that this will be cheaper than going to trial and successfully defending the claim. So the case is a good example of the kind of case that we might want to exclude from full scale tort trial. If there are supporters of the tort system in the class, however, discussion might take another and productive tact: even if we are to keep the tort rules, might this be the kind of case that ought to be limited to summary disposition, for example, by a minor judicial official, without a jury?

This last question would lead in turn back to the specific issue here: how well do thresholds work? Presumably the New York Court of Appeals is issuing in *Licari* a general message to the trial courts not to retain such dubious tort claims. But whatever the general policy, will we continue to suffer endless litigation over where to draw the line between PIP and tort, just as we have suffered teeming litigation over where to draw the line between no-liability and tort?

NOTE: ADOPTING OR EXTENDING NO-FAULT

This short text summarizes the basic kinds of no-fault plans and their adoption in the states and District. If you are teaching local law, you can fit your state into this list or indicate that no form of no-fault has been adopted.

Add-on statutes. A minute with pencil and paper or chalk and blackboard should make it clear that these will be costly and will not result in the savings potentially available under pure no-fault. It is much as if the law were to permit you to buy added accident insurance; you could do it, but it would not relieve you of tort liability and hence could not reduce the amount of funds spent on the tort system.

NOTE: EVALUATING NO FAULT

Is no-fault a good idea? If no-fault is good for automobile cases, why not for everything? This might be a place to resurrect the distinction between reciprocal and non-reciprocal risks. The auto accident is the chief example of a reciprocal risk. Even in pedestrian cases, many pedestrians will use automobiles or other vehicular transportation on other, similar occasions. Does this reciprocity justify a rule for autos that is entirely different from the rule in say, a products case? Maybe practicality and need are more important than a principle here. Auto accidents account for a very high percentage of claims and small injuries.

REFERENCES: Gary T. Schwartz, *Auto No-fault and First-party Insurance: Advantages and Problems,* 73 S. CAL. L. REV. 611 (2000), cited in the casebook, might be the best place to start if you are unfamiliar with no-fault. Books include ROBERT KEETON & JEFFREY O'CONNELL, BASIC PROTECTION FOR THE TRAFFIC VICTIM (1965); JEFFREY O'CONNELL & ROGER C. HENDERSON, TORT LAW, NO-FAULT AND BEYOND (1975). Jeffrey O'Connell has written many articles on variant proposals for no fault in various settings. Older articles include Roger C. Henderson, *No-Fault Insurance for Automobile Accidents,* 56 OR. L. REV. 287 (1977); Roger C. Henderson, *Crisis in Accident Loss Reparations Systems: Where We Are and How We Got There,* 1976 ARIZ. ST. L.J. 401.

CHAPTER 31

EVALUATING INJURY SYSTEMS:
A DISCUSSION AGENDA

▶**Changes in the Sixth Edition.** This chapter has not been changed, other than some tightening in the text to cut length.

This short text is the opportunity to wrap up the course if you are not covering the economic-dignitary tort material that follows. Where the last chapter ended in raising some policy issues about no-fault, this chapter quickly broadens the focus again. How well do the injury systems stack up? This is the time the class can think aloud with you about the different systems we've seen for dealing with various injuries. The text first asks students to consider the judicial process itself and its ideals. Perhaps most teachers have had students who think they know from reading an appellate opinion which witnesses are telling the truth and whether some of them are fraudulent. Yet the students have never seen these witnesses or even read the actual detailed transcript of testimony. You might want to remind students of the ideal of adjudication with its focus on human individuals in their individual circumstances. Some characteristics of the bureaucratic alternatives – the social security grids, perhaps – can be directly contrasted. So can rules-of-law created by legislatures that immunize large categories of defendants.

The text then launches into themes we've seen from the beginning – personal accountability, social responsibility, safety, and deterrence. It then asks students to compare tort law with alternatives in connection with some specific problems like costs and delay. Students have ample room to sum up and try to articulate their concerns and appreciations, with a little review in the process.

Some of Stephen Sugarman's work could furnish a basis for working through these ideas. Stephen Sugarman, *A Restatement of Torts*, 44 STAN. L. REV. 1163 (1992). Professor Sugarman reviews the American Law Institute's REPORTER'S STUDY. He reminds us that he has "devalued" the corrective justice goal of tort law in favor or some alternative system. The Study's policy approach, he thinks, is an improvement over the Restatement's doctrinal approach; he commends the *Study's* effort to consider alternative institutions for resolution of injury problems. Although the *Study* proposes to reform rather than to replace tort law, Sugarman thinks he and the *Study* agree at times in departing from efforts to deter (behavioral channeling"). Instead, compensation is the goal.

Sugarman then considers what he calls five models of tort law and its alternatives. These range from the "libertarian" model based largely on markets and self-protection and the "liberal" model represented by workers' compensation, through a collective model and a socialist model, based largely on "social insurance." Sugarman then reviews these possibilities, more or less in line with his book, STEPHEN SUGARMAN, DOING AWAY WITH PERSONAL INJURY LAW (1989).

As to the specific recommendations of the *Study* (better assessment of real damages by changing the collateral source rule, limiting pain and suffering recoveries), Sugarman believes they move us closer to a system that meets "actual need" and away from one focused on punishing wrongdoing. He likes that. He then considers the options and, in line with his book, favors social insurance systems.

Sugarman's book review would be a manageable assignment in lieu of this chapter and would allow you to focus on the competing claims. But maybe the short text of this chapter will be adequate to permit you to pull the strings that work the now-familiar shadow puppets – justice, deterrence, accountability, compensation, social responsibility, costs and so on.

On a very high plane you might consider the nature of the process of torts adjudication. Kenneth Abraham (*What Is a Tort claim? An Interpretation of Contemporary Tort Reform*, 51 MD. L. REV. 172 (1992)) thinks tort law always individuates the decision and that this is true in applying liability standards, causal rules, and damages. (Perhaps this is true of most judicial approaches, not merely to tort law approaches, but that changes nothing about the point here.) He thinks that recent developments move tort law away from this each-case-is-unique approach.

One obvious de-individualization occurs with value of the chance or proportional cause cases and with market share. In those cases we quit worrying about whether *this* plaintiff was harmed by *this* defendant. Damages changes furnish another basic shift. If you cap damages you do NOT treat everyone equally (since seriously injured persons recover less than all their damages), and you assuredly stop treating everyone according to his own deserts and injury. Scheduling would make more sense he thinks but either way these standardized rather than individuated decisions about recovery are hallmarks of the compensation system. As Abraham notices, the individuation of decisions for each case is not necessarily all to the good. It is this individuation that injects the lottery elements and even worse the elements of discrimination.

REFERENCES: We cut some citations from the previous edition that also might be helpful to you before discussing this with your class. On the issue of safety and deterrence, *see* Daniel Shuman, *The Psychology of Deterrence in Tort Law*, 42 U. KAN. L. REV. 115 (1993) and Daniel Shuman, *The Psychology of Compensation in Tort Law*, 43 U. KAN. L. REV. 39 (1994). On no-fault insurance, see two articles cited in Chapter 30: Gary T. Schwartz, *Auto No-Fault and First-Party Insurance: Advantages and Problems*, 73 S. CAL. L. REV. 611 (2000) and Roger C. Henderson, *No-Fault Insurance for Automobile Accidents: Status and Effect in the United States*, 56 OR. L. REV. 287 (1977).

PART 7

ECONOMIC AND DIGNITARY TORTS

The final three Chapters of the book cover economic and dignitary torts, although in-depth coverage must be left to advanced courses. Chapter 32 deals with the communication of personally harmful impressions to others, and most notably includes defamation, malicious prosecution, and some types of privacy invasions. Chapter 33 turns to the communication of commercially harmful impressions to others, covering such torts as injurious falsehood, intentional interference with contract, unfair competition, and misappropriation of commercial value. Chapter 34, on misrepresentation and other misdealings, focuses on fraud and negligent misrepresentation.

▶The **Concise Edition** combines these three Chapters into a single brief Chapter 29, titled Being Aware of Dignitary and Economic Torts. That Chapter, as the name implies, is simply designed to make students aware that these other torts exist, not to teach them anything substantive. ■

Given the compression of the materials in this part, and the expectation that many teachers would prefer to cover them by lecture, we present here a rather different set of teacher's notes. The notes will sketch the cases and try to indicate, as briefly as possible, the general direction the cases mark out. They will also attempt to explain a couple of unusual organizational decisions. Beyond that, there will be no comments or analysis.

First Amendment. To the extent that any tort depends on communications to a third person, there is a potential for a free speech argument. Thus in Chapters 32 and 33, which are devoted exclusively to communicative torts, the free speech issue runs thematically through the materials.

Privacy. The organization in Part 7 permits you to divide privacy in an unorthodox but helpful way. Instead of presenting privacy as a monolithic tort, and then carefully explaining that it is "really" four separate torts, these materials present privacy issues where they fall naturally. The communicative privacy issues involving personal harms fall in Chapter 32; they resemble defamation and they raise the same kinds of constitutional problems. But commercial appropriation versions of privacy fall naturally with the "right of publicity" cases in Chapter 33. Finally, the non-communicative or intrusive privacy cases naturally fall with other dignitary invasions, which we placed in the now-dropped materials on civil rights. Intrusive privacy invasion thus requires a brief acknowledgment or lecture from the teacher.

You might consider offering a lecture on the materials covered in this part, or on some of them, in which case you can get through this very quickly. If you cover them fully, you will probably need four to six hours of class time.

———

CHAPTER 32

COMMUNICATION OF PERSONALLY HARMFUL IMPRESSIONS TO OTHERS

▶**Changes in the Sixth Edition.** We have cut over ten percent of the length from this already-slim Chapter, primarily by cutting some Note material. We have fully updated the Chapter nonetheless, with over a dozen new case citations in Notes. We have reorganized Part I.A somewhat to emphasize the continuing importance of the common law rules of defamation, lest our leading with an 80-year-old case left the wrong impression. To that same end, we have added in that section a new case abstract, *Stanton*, a 2006 case with a factual similarity to the *Cassidy* case it now follows.

§ 1. DEFAMATION — LIBEL AND SLANDER

A. The Common Law Defamation Rules

CASSIDY V. DAILY MIRROR NEWSPAPERS, LTD., [1929] 2 K.B. 331, 69 A.L.R. 720

The newspaper published an accurate quotation from Mr. "Corrigan," who said he was going to marry Miss X. This was not in fact true and Mr. "Corrigan's" wife sued on the ground that the newspaper's quotation made it appear that she was not married to Corrigan and hence that she was an immoral woman. The newspaper had no reason to know of Mrs. Corrigan's existence, but it is held liable.

Conceivably you could support this case and not impose any general form of strict liability, but it furnishes a quick, piquant example of strict liability for publishing libelous statements at common law. The newspaper had one intent– the intent to publish. The law required only that the publisher have intent to publish or that it be negligent in doing so. That established, no fault was required as to the content of the publication.

The Note after the case emphasizes the strict nature of common law defamation in its pristine form. As we will see in upcoming materials, most courts have voluntarily departed from strict liability for this tort, at least requiring some form of negligence, even where not required by the Constitution.

STANTON V. METRO CORP., 438 F.3d 119 (1st Cir. 2006)

A high-school girl in New Hampshire is mortified to find her photograph in *Boston* magazine accompanying a story about teenage sex in the Boston suburbs. The story describes the promiscuity and alcohol use of the teenagers, and quotes many in the story by first name. Apparently the New Hampshire girl has no connection whatsoever to the activities being described; a small notation in text at the bottom of the first page issues the explanation that the photographs were taken as part of a "five-year project on teen sexuality," and the disclaimer that "the individuals pictured are unrelated to people or events described in this story." The teenager sued the magazine's publisher for defamation, and here the appeals court (sitting in diversity) reverses the district court's order dismissing the complaint. The court applies the common law rules of defamation – there is no constitutional dimension involved – and holds that a jury could find the publication defamatory, and that the publication was about the plaintiff, even with the disclaimer.

Note 1. Common law evolution. The only change from the rules applied in *Cassidy*, it seems, is that the court used a negligence standard rather than strict liability – a clear modern trend. The Note gives the common-law elements of defamation as they exist today in most states. The Constitutional rules we see in the next section are an overlay or qualification of these basic rules; Stanton makes the point that not all cases implicate these Constitutional restrictions.

Note 2. Publication. More on the basics. "Publication" is required in all defamation cases, and it has a particular meaning in this context. The end of the Note underscores that many (most) courts require negligence in making a false or defamatory statement, which represents a change in the common law strict liability applied in *Cassidy*.

Note 3. Repeaters. Notice that *Cassidy* itself is an instance of the repeater's liability.

Note 4. Reference to plaintiff. Proving a defamation claim requires proof that the defamatory statement can reasonably be taken by readers as being about the plaintiff. This was found to be so in *Cassidy*, and possibly so in *Stanton*, even though the plaintiff was only pictured, not named, and a disclaimer said the story was not about the people in the pictures.

Defamation can be found, then, even where the publication refers to some particular individual without naming her. This can even occur with fiction. The facts in *Muzikowski v. Paramount Pictures Corp.,* as summarized here illustrate the idea. The *Muzikowski* court upheld the plaintiff's complaint.

Note 5. Defamatory meaning. The issue on whether something is defamatory is whether the publication tends to lower the plaintiff in the esteem of some substantial segment of the community. As mentioned here, this is a common issue in defamation cases today, even when the Constitution is implicated. Complexities are of course left to more advanced courses, but the point can be made here that mere name-calling is not defamatory.

Note 6. Judge and jury. Whether a statement is defamatory is a jury question, but that does not mean that a judge will not take the question away from the jury if she believes that reasonable people cannot differ on it. In the Evel Knievel case cited here, the judge looked at the statements in the context of the publication (a "light-hearted" website) to conclude that no reasonable person could take it seriously – thus no reasonable person could believe that the publication would lower Knievel's esteem among a substantial segment of the community.

Note 7. Damages. This Note is an important foundation for what follows in the Constitutional cases discussed in the next section, because the Constitutional rules impact on the damages recoverable. At common law, damages were presumed in many defamation cases (as they still are in the intentional torts we saw in Chapter 3). As with the modification of the strict liability rule (see **Notes 1 & 2** above), many courts have now modified this common law rule as well, even when the Constitution does not require it.

Notes 8 & 9. Libel and Slander; Slander per se. The common law rules contain[ed] somewhat complicated distinctions based on whether the defamatory publication was oral (slander) or written (libel), and on what the statement was about (certain subjects were considered defamatory *per se*). These rules have not lost all currency today, but are of lesser importance than they used to be.

Note 10. Truth defeating the claim. The common law puts the burden on the defendant to prove truth if he can. Constitutional law has changed that for at least some cases, but the casebook doesn't get to the burden of proof shift yet. One way of another, truth defeats the defamation claim. Truth is judged by the sting, not by details. That cuts two ways. First, the defendant must show truth of the sting, not merely the literal words. Defamation committed by publishing "the newspaper reported. . . [or, in my opinion. . . or is it true that. . .] the plaintiff doctored the evidence" is still defamation; it cannot be defended on the ground that the newspaper really did report it, or that it really was your opinion, or that your statement was in the form of a question. The sting is in the suggested that the plaintiff doctored the evidence and that is enough. This is easily explained as a result of the repeaters' rule in the first instance, but the other examples seem to reflect only the gist/sting idea.

NOTE: COMMON-LAW PRIVILEGES

This Note is a brief survey of the common-law privileges that a defendant may use to defeat a defamation claim. There is probably not enough depth here to develop much of this in class discussion, but we thought a class studying defamation at all needed to see the defense side before launching off into the Constitutional cases. The large point is that these sometimes complicated privileges are not irrelevant today, even after the Constitutional cases; the modern case citations more than demonstrate that.

Indeed, Constitutional protections have disappointed the some people's expectations. With the now-certainty that Constitutional protections are much less than complete, state law privileges are quite significant in any state that retains the common law presumptions of fault and damages to the full extent permitted by Constitutional rules.

Courts continue to develop and apply these privileges. The absolute privilege (or immunity) granted to the judicial process itself may be expanded, for example, to include statements made in the course of investigation for trial. See *Hawkins v. Harris,* 661 A.2d 284 (N.J. 1995). California has held that its statutory absolute privilege protects even defamatory reports to police or administrative agencies. *Hagberg v. California Fed. Bank FSB*, 81 P.3d 244 (Cal. 2004). Further elaboration must be left to more advanced courses.

B. The Constitutional Constraints of Free Speech

NEW YORK TIMES CO. v. SULLIVAN , 376 U.S. 254 (1964)

At one time libel was thought to be excluded from the first amendment's protection, but in *Times-Sullivan* the Court recognized that when a public official sues for defamation, his suit may tend to silence criticism. Yet criticism of government and its officials is not merely permissible, it is desirable in a free society. With this in mind, the Court held that in public official suits, the official cannot recover unless he proves knowing falsehood or reckless disregard of the truth. It called this "actual malice," but that term engendered a lot of confusion and it may be best to explain it to the class as "knowing or reckless falsehood," which, in fact, is the specific test.

The test is a trade-off. It sanctions some degree of unintended falsehood in order not to shut off criticisms. It has an enormous side-effect, too: it requires the plaintiff to prove the un-truth of the statement, as we underscore in **Note 4**. In contrast, as we saw in the preceding section, the common law put the burden on the defendant to show the statement was true. All this focuses the inquiry on the content of the statement — a matter often of little importance at common law.

Times-Sullivan was quickly extended to cover not only public officials, but also public figures, as noted in **Note 1**. But did it cover private plaintiffs who might be in the public eye?

Note 2. Actual malice. Experience indicates that many students need to pause on the terminology to understand that "actual malice" is a technical term (and maybe one best avoided). It means knowing or reckless falsehood, not spite or ill-will. Spite or ill-will might conceivably tend to support an inference of knowing falsehood if other evidence already points in that direction. See *Celle v. Filipino Reporter Enterprises,* Inc., 209 F.3d 163 (2d Cir. 2000). And proof of knowing or even reckless falsehood might tend to show spite or ill will or "malice" in the non-technical sense. But what the plaintiff in a *Times-Sullivan* type case must prove is definitely not spite or ill-will but knowing or reckless falsehood.

GERTZ V. ROBERT WELCH, INC., 418 U.S. 323 (1974)

Gertz, a lawyer who was active in a controversial case, was attacked in the defendant's publication, which associated him with leftist movements and a Communist campaign to discredit the police. Gertz sued. Although the statements were not true, the defendant argued that the *Times-Sullivan* rule ought to protect it. Discussion of matters of public concern ought to be protected, it argued, as much as matters that are technically official. The Court rejected this argument. It held:

1. Private persons– as distinct from public officials and public figures– can recover without proving the defendant published a reckless or intentional falsehood. However, the private plaintiff will be required to prove these elements not required at common law:
   (a) Some degree of fault, to be defined by law of the states. (Most states have used a negligence standard.), and
   (b) Actual damages.

2. To invoke the more stringent public figures rules, the plaintiff must have been either an all purpose or special purpose public figure. It may be possible for one to be an involuntary public figure, but this will be rare. Ordinarily, people can become public figures only if they have thrust themselves to the forefront of a particular controversy.

Many commentators have noticed the increase in libel suits in the post *Times-Sullivan* era, and some have suggested that difficulties now being encountered in the cases results from the Court's decision in *Gertz* to use "multiple standards where unified ones could be applied." *See* Rodney Smolla,

Let the Author Beware: The Rejuvenation of the American Law of Libel, 132 U. PA. L. REV. 1, 93 (1983); *cf.* George Christie, *Injury to Reputation and the Constitution: Confusion Amid Conflicting Approaches*, 75 MICH. L. REV. 43 (1976).

Although *Gertz* substantially re-wrote the state law of libel, it did not go as far as *Times-Sullivan*. It provided a middle ground between the strict rules of common law and the free-speech orientation of *Times-Sullivan*. In doing so, it provided a place for compromise and a focal point for argument. The notes take the class through the main issues associated with *Gertz*. You can use discuss most of them if time permits, but because discussion of these notes could easily take an hour or more, you may have to pick a couple for emphasis in your comments and a couple of others for discussion.

Note 3. Types of fault. The states must require the plaintiff to prove "some fault," whatever level of fault the states wish to require. What counts as "some fault" and how can it be judged? Most states talk in terms of negligence, but what real meaning can be given to the concept of negligence as applied to a published statement? Negligent investigation of facts is probably the prime claim. But what about negligent drawing of inferences? Negligent phrasing of a report so that some readers will see in it defamatory material? And how can either *Gertz* or *Times-Sullivan* be related to fiction? Or to private publications, such as letters? (On the last, see **Note 8.**)

Note 4. Actual damages. The *Gertz* requirement of actual damages does not exclude recovery for emotional harm, even though there are no "special damages" in the form of cash costs. Notice that the actual damages proof is a demand of *Gertz*, not a demand of *Times-Sullivan*. If you make *Times-Sullivan* proof of knowing or reckless falsehood, you apparently do not have to prove actual damages.

Notes 5-7. Public figures and public officials. Under *Gertz*, you have to argue about whether the plaintiff is a public figure or not. The Court has actually held that a public employee who receives substantial grant monies from the United States is not a "public figure," *Hutchinson v. Proxmire*, 443 U.S. 111 (1979). And that one who has been charged with crime and found guilty is not, for that reason alone, a public figure. *Wolston v. Reader's Digest Assn., Inc.*, 443 U.S. 157 (1979). And that one who invokes the divorce courts and is involved in a divorce from an heir to a famous fortune is not a public figure. *Time, Inc. v. Firestone*, 424 U.S. 448 (1976). Many commentators believe the Court has backed away from the speech protection it afforded in *Times-Sullivan*. If so, it may be because *Gertz* provided a compromise fall-back position.

8. Publishers and broadcasters. Is there any point is giving more protection to media publishers than to individual human beings who want to criticize government, society, or even publishers and broadcasters? Could you argue just the opposite, that publishers who are in the business of producing publications as a product should be strictly liable? (Recall that the First Amendment seems to say something about that.) Maybe the most dramatic or extreme case refusing *Gertz* protection to non-media defendants is *Denny v. Mertz*, 318 N.W.2d 141 (Wis. 1982). *Casso v. Brand*, 776 S.W.2d 551 (Tex. 1989), held that a public figure suing a private person (not a media publisher) was required to meet the standards of *Times-Sullivan* or lose.

Note 9. Truth (redux). The plaintiff must prove falsehood in cases that fit in the *Times-Sullivan* box or the *Gertz* box. *Hepps*, discussed briefly here, does not address the case of a private plaintiff suing a defendant over a publication that lacks any public concern issue, that is, does not address facts like those in *Dun & Bradstreet* case, coming up next. So we don't know whether Constitutional rules put the burden on the plaintiff to prove fault in that kind of case or not.

Note 10. Constitutional protection for "opinion" statements. The Supreme Court has protected what many people would call "opinion" or publications that are not intended to be taken as factual and are not so taken. Metaphor and hyperbole, satire and the like are properly understood to assert *something*, but not the literal fact stated. Many thinkers understood this kind of rule as one that immunized "opinion" statements. In *Milkovich v. Lorain Journal*, cited here, the Court said there was no special constitutional protection for "opinion." Yet at the same time it said the author of a statement could not be held liable unless the statement asserted or implied a fact, something "provably false." The statement at issue in that case was to the effect that if the reader had been in the courtroom, the reader would know that the plaintiff was lying. Clearly enough, you cannot escape liability by saying "in my opinion she stole money from her employer throughout the year she worked there." *See, e.g., Flamm v. American Ass'n of University Women*, 201 F.3d 144 (2d Cir. 2000) (statement in directory of lawyers that "At least one [client] has described [plaintiff] as an 'ambulance chaser' with interest only in 'slam dunk' cases" held actionable, since it implies the fact that plaintiff engages in unethical solicitation).

DUN & BRADSTREET V. GREENMOSS BUILDERS, 472 U.S. 749 (1985)

Dun and Bradstreet published a negligently prepared credit report to several of its subscribers, the effect of which was to suggest that the plaintiff, upon whom the report was made, was in bankruptcy. This was false and the plaintiff sued without establishing any actual damages. The state court held he could recover traditional "presumed" damages because *Gertz* would have no application except to media publishers. The Supreme Court passed up the opportunity to limit *Gertz* to media publishers, presumably because the judges did not think it was so limited. Instead, the Supreme court upheld the unproved damages award on the ground that the publication was not about any matter of public concern.

The result of *Dun & Bradstreet*, when read with *Times-Sullivan* and *Gertz* is to create three levels of rules and to suggest a possible fourth. (1) If the plaintiff is a public official or figure, he must prove fault at the level of knowing or reckless falsehood; (2) If the plaintiff is a private person but the topic of the publication is a matter of public concern, the plaintiff must prove only some degree of fault plus actual damages; (3) If the plaintiff is a private person and the topic of the publication is a matter of private concern, the plaintiff may recover without proof of actual damages.

In the third or *Dun & Bradstreet* category, will the Court also relieve the plaintiff of any burden to prove fault? Notice that is NOT what the Court held. It has not authoritatively decided that issue.

In the first *Times-Sullivan* category, is there any private concern publication comparable to the private concern publication in *Dun & Bradstreet*? The Court has not held so. Publication of private matters about a public figure, if the information was obtained in breach of confidence, might be actionable as a privacy invasion and perhaps on those facts, no First Amendment right would protect the defendant.

Notes bring us back around to the point that the Constitution does not displace all of the common law rules for defamation, not by a long shot.

§ 2. MALICIOUS PROSECUTION AND OTHER ABUSES OF THE LEGAL SYSTEM

Malicious prosecution also involves communication—in particular, a communication which, regarded purely as a libel or slander, would be privileged. Malicious prosecution, therefore, at least potentially involves the same free speech issues as defamation. But, as it turns out, the common law courts applied to this species of defamation not only a new name, but also protective rules very similar to those applied under the *Times-Sullivan* rule.

A. Malicious Prosecution

Teaching illustrative cases. These illustrative cases are used as an economical presentation of some common fact patterns and to give the student some paradigms against which to apply the rules stated later. The teacher can discuss these cases, but it may be easiest to go straight to the rules, using the cases to question or illustrate. Thus one could ask: "what is the 'malice' in Illustration 1?" See the notes to the rules.

Illustration 1. The facts are suggested by the facts in *Lambert v. Sears, Roebuck & Co.*, 570 P.2d 357 (Or. 1977). The court affirmed an award of $1,350 specials, $10,000 generals and $10,000 punitives. This set of facts is typical of many store-customer cases. Notice there may also be a false arrest claim based on detention before the prosecution is initiated. The court found there was no probable cause because the detective failed to obtain the plaintiff's version before deciding to prosecute, then permitted an inference of malice on the ground that the want of probable cause showed a lack of genuine belief in the guilt, which in turn permitted a finding of malice. In addition, the fact that the detective did not listen to the plaintiff's version permitted that inference. As in some of the libel cases involving a privilege to convey information by a former employer to a prospective one, there is sometimes a hint that the courts wish to insist on some kind of private due process. Thus here the detective is guilty of malicious prosecution because he did not hear the plaintiff's side.

Illustration 2. The facts are suggested by *Martin v. City of Albany*, 364 N.E.2d 1304 (N.Y. 1977). An officer (or the city, his employer) may be held for malicious prosecution. Recall that the judge and prosecuting attorney will normally enjoy an absolute immunity. The want of probable cause in this case seems obvious. Malice may be harder. There was no evidence that the officer ever heard of the plaintiffs before, so personal spite is not possible here. Yet in fact a number of cases, this one and Illustration 1, seem to involve an abuse of position or authority.

False imprisonment and malicious prosecution. The distinction is sketched in the first paragraph after Illustration 2. A series of New York cases have dealt with the burden of proof difference and also with damages. *See Broughton v. State of New York*, 335 N.E.2d 310 (N.Y. 1975); *Hollender v. Trump Village Cooperative, Inc.*, 448 N.E.2d 432 (N.Y. 1983).

Defamation and malicious prosecution. As briefly noted here, there is also an overlap between these two torts; in both the courts must balance important competing interests. The paragraph here leads into the next, which sketches the elements of a malicious prosecution claim in light of this necessary balance.

The common law rule. (1) *Prosecution.* The rules are usually stated as four, here those numbered (2) through (5). The rule is stated here in five parts to emphasize that a report alone would not suffice to permit a cause of action. Defamation law would protect it if it was made in good faith, and malicious prosecution creates a limited exception — there must not only be a report of crime to authorities, a prosecution must follow. Although the rule is not usually stated in this five-part form, this statement is accurate — a prosecution is required to have malicious prosecution.

(2) *Instigation.* This is under-analyzed in most cases. In the great majority of cases the accuser who gives information to the authorities should probably

not be regarded as the instigator; he relies upon the authorities to make the decision. Only if he acts in such a way that their independent judgment is precluded should a private citizen be regarded as instigating the prosecution. Thus he may be an instigator where he lies about the facts, or omits critical facts; or where he pressures the authorities to prosecute. *See Dellums v. Powell*, 566 F.2d 167 (D.C. Cir. 1977). Instigation is not quite an adequate word; some courts have allowed the malicious prosecution action for continuing a prosecution after facts exonerating the accused come to light.

(3) *Malice*. The trickiest word in torts. The statements in the casebook on this seem correct to us. Courts have not often stated the rule as involving abuse of power or authority, but the cases, including those on which Illustrations 1 and 2 are based, seem to be consistent with this statement. The same is true with the award of punitive damages in many kinds of cases — abuse of power or authority seems at times the key to the "malice" found in those cases. See 1 DAN DOBBS, THE LAW OF REMEDIES § 3.11(2) (2d ed. 1993). This also comports with practice in intentional infliction of mental anguish cases, where "outrage" often turns on the special vulnerability of the plaintiff or special authority or position of the defendant.

(4) *Probable cause*. In many cases there is the possibility of inferring a lack of probable cause from the magistrate's discharge at the probable cause hearing, or the grand jury's refusal to indict. All this gets much more complicated than is pleasant to contemplate or possible to cover. *See* DOBBS ON TORTS § 432 (2000). The probable cause issue is the most litigated one in the cases. One might wish to refer back to the Illustrations and ask the class to find the want of probable cause that would justify imposing liability. In **Illustration 1**, the refusal to examine information available (the plaintiff's side of the story), is one basis for saying the detective lacked probable cause. Another is the detective's own version of the facts that he watched the plaintiff the whole time. If one believes this and also believes the plaintiff when he said he brought the wrench into the store, the detective must have seen him remove it from his pocket and must have had reason to think it was his own. Thus the court in *Lambert* reasoned.

(5) *Termination*. A compromise of the criminal case in which the case is dismissed does not usually adjudicate guilt. In many such cases the accused is in fact guilty, though in others this is not so. Courts have often said that compromised dismissals under the various names of procedures used for this, are not such terminations as will permit the accused to later sue. *See Hollender v. Trump Village Co-op., Inc.*, 448 N.E.2d 432 (N.Y. 1983).

Dismissal conditioned upon a release. Should the prosecuting attorney, in agreeing to dismiss, demand, as a condition of dismissal, that the accused release any potential malicious prosecution claim against the instigators? In *Hoines v. Barney's Club, Inc.*, 620 P.2d 628 (Cal. 1980), plaintiff was arrested on a charge of disturbing the peace. The district attorney agreed to dismiss the complaint if plaintiff would sign a release of any malicious prosecution charge. The plaintiff testified he was concerned about admission to the California bar and the effect of an arrest and conviction record, so he accepted this dismissal. He then sued in spite of the release, contending it was coerced by these circumstances. The California court held that the exchange of dismissal for release did not violate public policy and upheld dismissal of the plaintiff's claim. The Supreme Court has likewise held that the release is a good one, even in civil rights litigation, at least in the absence of special facts that show it was exacted for no purpose or without voluntary assent of the accused. *Town of Newton v. Rumery*, 480 U.S. 386 (1987). On the other hand, *Cowles v. Brownell*, 538 N.E.2d 973 (N.Y. 1989), held that the integrity of the criminal justice system was not served by such releases; if the plaintiff was guilty, he was not prosecuted; if he was not, the prosecutor was under an ethical duty to dismiss the prosecution. Accordingly, the release was no bar.

Malicious prosecution after Times-Sullivan. There is a little discussion in Dan B. Dobbs, *Belief and Doubt in Malicious Prosecution and Libel*, 21 ARIZ. L. REV. 608, 613-615 (1970).

On malicious prosecution generally, *see* DOBBS ON TORTS §§ 429-35 (2000).

B. Improper Civil Litigation

FRIEDMAN V. DOZORC, 312 N.W.2d 585 (Mich. 1981)

The court holds (1) that negligence is not a ground of liability, since the attorney for A owes no duty to A's adversary, and (2) that malicious prosecution cannot be maintained against the attorney for an adversary in the absence of "special injury." Special injury requires physician detention of person or property, or at least repeated re-litigation of the same case.

The case is included to permit discussion and development of these two basic holdings. In addition the remark of the court that litigation is not always the solution to problems may be an interesting source of discussion to some teachers.

Omitted portions of the opinion deal with abuse of process and with the case in which an attorney might properly be held liable. The court made these points among others:

(1) "[W]hether an attorney acted without probable cause in initiating, defending or continuing proceedings on behalf of a client should not normally depend upon the extent of the investigation conducted." (312 N.W.2d at 605).

(2) "A lawyer is entitled to accept his client's version of the facts and to proceed on the assumption that they are true absent compelling evidence to the contrary." Id.

(3) [The Restatement's standard in § 675] would allow lack of probable cause to be found where the lawyer proceeded with knowledge that the claim had no factual or legal basis, but would impose no obligation to investigate if the lawyer could reasonably believe the facts to be as his client alleged." Id. at 606.

Note 1. Special injury rule. *Ackerman v. Kaufman*, 15 P.2d 966 (Ariz. 1932) rejected the rule, but it was a case in which Ackerman had brought at least six claims against Kaufman, many repeating already-litigated claims. So the case would probably have been no different if the special injury rule had been approved. Is the rejection meaningful under those circumstances? *See also Greenberg v. Wolfberg*, 890 P.2d 895 (Okla. 1994) (rejecting special injury rule with similar facts).

Note 2. Physician countersuits. Success is very low in these cases. The CPR was rejected as a ground for relief in parts of *Friedman* that have been omitted. After *O'Toole*, cited here, the Oregon Court, also held it furnished no ground for relief. *Bob Godfrey Pontiac, Inc. v. Roloff*, 630 P.2d 840 (Or. 1981).

The principle of *Friedman* and other similar cases is of course not limited to physicians; physicians have merely been prominent as plaintiffs and their sense of grievance at malpractice suits pretty frequently aired. Thus a lawyer, having escaped malpractice liability, sued the lawyer who had sued him in *Madda v. Reliance Ins. Co.*, 368 N.E.2d 580 (Ill. Ct. App. 1977), but lost on the same principle — which is primarily concerned to protect lawyers in their traditional adversary role and to avoid chilling access to courts. In *Beecy v. Pucciarelli*, 441 N.E.2d 1035 (Mass. 1982), a lawyer for Filene's erroneously commenced a collection action for Filene's against Beecy. The Beecys sued him, but the Massachusetts Court denied that any claim was stated. The Court said, among other things, that there was no "malice." "To succeed on a claim of malice in a malicious prosecution action, the Beecys must demonstrate that (1) Mr. Pucciarelli knew that there was no probable cause for the prosecution and (2) Mr. Pucciarelli either personally acted with an improper motive or he knew that Filene's was motivated by malice. The Beecys do not allege any improper motive on Mr. Pucciarelli's part." Mere negligence is not sufficient, the Court said, to impose liability upon an attorney to his adversary.

Cases that go the other way might conceivably be justified even if you accept most of the court's reasoning in *Friedman*. Conceivably the duty to investigate basic facts is non-adversary — a duty owed the client in any event. It is also possible to hold, and Friedman may have recognized this, that the attorney is liable for a knowing advancement of an unwarranted claim, where the attorney knows the client has an ulterior purpose and that the client does not believe the facts alleged. This is cutting it much too fine for most first year discussions of this problem.

On tortious civil litigation generally, *see* DOBBS ON TORTS §§ 436 & 437 (2000).

Note 3. Rules of ethics and procedure. While you probably need not develop the point in class, students should know that whenever a lawyer's conduct is at issue in a case, the legal ethics rules (and often procedural rules) might provide an additional sanction. The answer to the last question is no, because these other sanctions do not aim to compensate the plaintiff – rather, the typical remedy in a disciplinary proceeding is some discipline against an attorney (and as noted here, discipline may be severe for this kind of misconduct), and with Rule 11 and analogous violations the sanction is often a reimbursement of attorney fees paid by the other side, the plaintiff in this instance, traceable to the attorney's rule violation.

C. Abuse of Process

Illustration 1. Perhaps some courts would reject the conclusion that Dominic is guilty of an abuse of process, since no process has issued after the threat or to enforce it. In *Union National Bank of Little Rock v. Kutait,* 846 S.W.2d 652 (Ark. 1993), the court insisted, in line with many others, that "The key is improper use of process after issuance, even when issuance has been properly obtained."

Illustration 2. Notes below the illustration explain why Dalmar is not liable for abuse of process on these facts.

———————

Elements. This paragraph attempts to set out the elements of this tort succinctly, allowing for quick coverage by running through the illustrations above.

Settlement. A typical setting for abuse of process is when the defendant commences a suit and then offers to drop it in exchange for some "collateral advantage" unrelated to the suit itself, or that a court would be unable to order. *See* DOBBS ON TORTS § 438 (2000). Thus there could be an abuse of process suit against A on this hypothetical, based on the demand for B to settle claims "that have no bearing on the attached car."

SLAPP suits. Anti-SLAPP statutes arose in the past decade or so. They present somewhat stereotyped figures: the Bad Developer and the Good Citizen. The Bad Developer sues the Good Citizen because the Good Citizen's earlier suit or political activity has held up and maybe destroyed a commercial opportunity. But the Bad Developer does not expect to win: he merely wishes silence or punish the Good Citizen. This is an idea closely related to the immunity developed by the Supreme Court for the right to petition government, even if the petitioning activity would otherwise violate the antitrust laws. *See Professional Real Estate Investors, Inc. v.Columbia Pictures Industries, Inc.,* 508 U.S. 49 (1993). The requirements of California's SLAPP statute are found in *Briggs v. Eden Council for Hope and Opportunity,* 969 P.2d 564 (Cal. 1999).

Taus v. Loftus, cited here, shows that the SLAPP world extends beyond developers. *Taus* is a very long opinion, involving a suit by a person who was a subject in a case study (unnamed there) reported in a scholarly article. Noted scholar Elizabeth Loftus — an expert on, among other things, repressed memory – wrote two subsequent articles questioning the case study's basic premise, in which she recounted details of plaintiff's life, without revealing plaintiff's identity. Loftus also discussed her articles at scholarly conferences, again without ever mentioning the plaintiff's name or revealing her identity. The plaintiff sued for invasion of privacy, among other torts. Loftus and her publisher moved to strike pursuant to the anti-SLAPP statute. The Supreme Court of California held that defendants' course of conduct was in furtherance of free speech, as required by the statute, and most (but not all) of plaintiff's claims should be stricken under the anti-SLAPP statute, largely because of various privileges.

§ 3. PRIVACY

The casebook sketches the four separate torts or patterns in privacy cases. However, intrusive invasion cases do not entail communications to their persons (or even to the plaintiff); consequently, they do not belong in this chapter on communicative torts. We deal with commercial appropriation only in connection with the "right of publicity" in the next chapter. And we deal with intrusive invasions of privacy only in the brief Paragraph 1, which you can use as a springboard for a hypothetical, for discussion, or for comment. What remains for this chapter is false light and private fact invasions, both of which involved communication and hence potential constitutional/free speech issues.

¶1. *Intrusive invasions.* In *Irvine v. Akron Beacon Journal,* 770 N.E.2d 1105 (Ohio Ct. App.), *appeal denied,* 774 N.E.2d 765 (Ohio 2002), the court upheld a privacy invasion and a statutory violation claim against a newspaper that programmed autodial calling in such a way as to result in predictably repeated calls to the same numbers. There is a federal statute, the Telephone Consumer Protection Act or TCPA, 47 USCA § 227. It gains what strength it has from FCC rules based on it. See 47 C.F.R. § 64.1200. State statutes may do better in some instances. Most of us remain victims of these aggressive oral spammers. The remaining privacy cases are communicative versions of privacy invasion. These, naturally, raise free speech issues similar to those considered with *Times-Sullivan* and *Gertz.*

SOLANO V. PLAYGIRL, INC., 292 F.3d 1078 (9th Cir. 2002)

A highly edited version here, but enough to raise central issues. Solano claimed false light privacy invasion and the court accepts that characterization, but the court' s list of elements makes it sound like libel. And it may well be. Is there really any difference? Constitutionally, false light privacy claims will have to meet the *Times-Sullivan* standards of proof when they are brought by public figures or public officials and, we guess, the *Gertz* standards when private figures sue on issues of public concern. How do you meet those standards? The *Solano* court seems to assume that the defendant must know not only of the falsehood but the offensiveness. Given free speech interests, should we just drop this tort? *Godbehere,* cited in **Note 3**, insists there is something worth keeping. Maybe the best case is the systematically false presentation of personal facts that glorify the plaintiff. That is a pretty small category, we'd guess.

THE FLORIDA STAR V. B.J.F., 491 U.S. 524 (1989)

This brief summary leaves out some of the tight and useful reasoning, but it presents the issue starkly. The Court's formula emphasizes that the defendant's protection is limited to truthful facts lawfully obtained. But that way trouble lies. Do we really want to invite governments to restrict information any further? What could be restricted? What about information illegally gained by an individual, then passed on to the publisher? In *Bartnicki v. Vopper,* 531 U.S. 990 (2001), not a private facts case, the defendant published some illegally taped conversations on matters of public concern. The court assumed that the defendant knew that the information had been obtained in violation of federal statutes, though the defendant did not prompt the violation and was not responsible for it. Since the matter was one of public concern, and since the defendant did not himself have any role in the law violation, he could not constitutionally be held liable for the publication.

Allegations in *Burgess v. Busby,* 544 S.E.2d 4 (N.C. Ct. App. 2001), asserted that the plaintiffs had all been jurors in a medical practice case in which Dr. Busby had been a defendant. The jurors found one doctor negligent, but not Dr. Busby. Busby then sent out a letter listing the jurors with their addresses as jurors who had found a doctor guilty of negligence. The letter went to medical practitioners in the county. The plaintiffs alleged that Busby had done so in retaliation and for the purpose of encouraging doctors to refuse or limit medical care to the plaintiffs. The court permitted the plaintiff to proceed on an emotional distress theory and obstruction of justice theory. *Florida Star* was not cited. Would its protection for lawfully obtained and truthful information forbid the emotional distress claim?

§ 4. INTERFERENCE WITH FAMILY RELATIONSHIPS

This short section may require no class time at all. But: Are there free speech issues here, too? A number of rationales for free speech are possible. The political interpretation of free speech is behind *Times-Sullivan.* Yet it is possible to see free speech is a personal right, a part of every one's humanness, an instrument of self-fulfillment rather than of political debate. If defendant, by speech that is not (a) defamatory, (b) privacy-invading, or (c) fraudulent, induces one spouse to leave another, on what grounds can this speech-activity be punished? If there is a ground for imposing liability here, can these cases really be distinguished on neutral grounds from the libel cases?

CHAPTER 33

COMMUNICATION OF COMMERCIALLY HARMFUL IMPRESSIONS TO OTHERS

▶**Changes in the Sixth Edition.** We have shortened this chapter by cutting two cases, *Jeffrey* (§1) and *Caruso* (§2). Their essential points are now made in text or Notes. We've added a half-dozen recent case cites to Notes to assure that our materials remain fully up-to-date, even if the chapter is quite brief.

§ 1. INJURIOUS FALSEHOOD

BRUNSON COMMUNICATIONS, INC. V. ARBITRON, INC., 266 F.Supp.2d 377 (E.D.Pa. 2003)

The plaintiff in this case asserts a commercial disparagement version of injurious falsehood. He claims that the defendant's measurement of television viewers in effect falsely communicated to advertisers that few viewers actually watched the plaintiff's television channel. This would allegedly lead marketers to avoid advertising on the plaintiff's channel. The plaintiff alleged pecuniary loss, although it is not spelled out in terms of any actual loss of advertisers. Although the defendant did not mention the plaintiff's television station, the total effect of its published assessments in effect disparaged the plaintiff's business. However, the court requires the plaintiff to alleged specific loss of sales, perhaps by alleging sales before the statement and after.

Note 1. In *Jeffrey v. Cathers* , cited here, the defendant, using a forged document, placed a mechanic's lien on the plaintiff's property. The plaintiff alleged that the existence of the lien prevent disbursement of monies to him from other persons and the loss of use of those monies [presumably until the lien could be cleared.] The plaintiff claimed the form of injurious falsehood usually known as slander of title, the elements of which we set out here.

Note 2. Unlike a libel or slander per se case, the plaintiff who claims injurious falsehood must prove "malice," probably meaning intentionally false or unjustified claim that demeans the plaintiff's property rights. Also unlike common law libel or slander per se, the plaintiff must prove actual pecuniary loss. This may be taken to mean that he has no action merely because his property would be worth less because of the defendant's words or actions; he would have to show an actual lost sale or some other realized loss, such as the delay in getting access to his money alleged here.

The special or pecuniary damage requirement as applied in *Brunson* is very demanding, isn't it? Even if the plaintiff's pre-publication advertising sales were not great, they might have gone up but for the publication.

You might guess that what courts really are concerned about in requiring special or pecuniary damages is to avoid allowing a recovery for a paper loss in value that would be made good as a soon as the false impression left by the defendant's words was corrected. For instance, if defendant stated that the demand for chips was down this quarter, the plaintiff's stock in a chip manufacturer might drop in value. But tomorrow when the statement is shown to be false, the stock might recover its earlier value. To permit a recovery for the transient diminution of the stock's value might be a bad idea. This is explained in DOBBS ON REMEDIES § 6.8 (2) (2d ed. 1993). But that doesn't necessary mean you have to require proof of special damages by proving specific lost sales. If it is reasonably probable that some advertisers would have lodged advertising with the plaintiff but for the defendant's allegedly false publication, and some reasonable estimate can be made of the lost advertising revenue, why isn't that good enough? Later, when we look at interference with business opportunity, we can wonder why anyone would bother with injurious falsehood claims when a tort with few traditional inhibitions might be available to circumvent demands for proof of pre-publication sales compared to post-publication sales.

Note that commercial speech enjoys at least some of the first amendment protections, but it is not settled whether the protections afforded by *Times-Sullivan* or *Gertz* in libel cases will apply in some injurious falsehood cases. Sometimes courts struggle to protect disparaging speech of public importance even when the constitutional doctrine does not plainly require protection. See *Auvil v. CBS 60 Minutes*, 67 F.3d 816 (9th Cir. 1995) (CBS' feature of Alar sprayed on apples). Perhaps the free speech problem will not often be important. Under the Restatement version of injurious falsehood, the plaintiff will already be required to prove knowing or reckless falsehood *and* special damages– requirements more demanding that the *Times-Sullivan* requirement, first because *Times-Sullivan* imposed to damages rule at all and second because it applies only to cases in which the plaintiff is a public official or public figure.

Note 3 mentions but does not develop the idea that the Lanham Act may provide a better remedy in some of these cases. Students would typically see that Act in advanced courses in intellectual property.

§ 2. INTENTIONAL INTERFERENCE WITH CONTRACT AND OTHER ECONOMIC VALUES

A. Prima Facie Liability for Interference

LUMLEY V. GYE , 2 El. & Bl. 216, 118 Eng.Rep. 749 (1853)

Defendant hired a singer to perform in his theater, knowing she was under exclusive contract to sing for his competitor, the plaintiff. The plaintiff sued, not the contract-breaching singer, but the defendant who induced her to breach. This is the classic case of inducing breach of contract. The court sees it in stark terms. Procuring violation of the plaintiff's contract right IS a cause of action. If you know of the contract and induce a party to breach it, you are liable in tort, which may include punitive damages. The defendant might in some cases be able to justify his action, but that would come as an affirmative defense, and few justifications were recognized.

Notice that the court does not require any bad state of mind or any action that is wrongful, unless you consider the honest persuasion to be wrongful. If it is, that is the only wrong required. No misstatements of fact, no bad motive, no knowing or reckless falsehoods, no physical harm, no damage to property or to property rights.

Why can't you seek to persuade another by perfectly honest statements? Suppose the defendant said: "I'll pay you more; you can decide for yourself whether it is enough for you to pay damages for breaching your contract."

Note 2. Inducing and other forms of interference. On the facts here, Empson's new employer did not know she was under exclusive contract with the plaintiff. The new employer had already hired her when it found it. It continued to employer and that was enough to make it liable for interference of the older employer's contract with Empson.

Note 3. Negligent interference. Negligent interference is usually not enough for liability, but there are a few cases that favor such liability and a few situations when perhaps a number of courts would do so.

Note 5. Interference by disparagement. Some dissonance here. Why do lawyers pursue claims of injurious falsehood when interference with contract is so easy to prove? The other side of the question is why do we have an interference with contract tort based on perfectly honest statements, or on opinions, or market promises? And what happened to free speech that involves no falsity whatever?

ALYESKA PIPELINE SERVICE V. AURORA AIR SERVICE, 604 P.2d 1090 (Alaska 1979)

RCA had a contract with Alyeska to supply certain air services. RCA's contract with Alyeska was terminable by Alyeska at any time. RCA provided air services by subcontracting to Aurora, with the provision in its contract with Aurora that it could terminate the contract at any time. After Alyeska had a dispute with Aurora, it decided to run its own air services, and accordingly terminated this portion of RCA's contract, knowing that RCA would then terminate Aurora. The Alaska Court held that this could be viewed as an interference with Aurora's expectancy and that Aurora could recover from Alyeska.

Notice that Aurora's had no enforceable contract to sell its services. It was an "at will" contract, or terminable, which is to say it was no contract at all as to future performances. Where does free speech fit into this tort? Does the Alaska Court mean that you lose your free speech rights if you have ill will (or a disputed claim)? Or is there simply no free speech in commercial speech cases?

B. Traditional Privileges and Changing Rules

¶ 1. *Two identifiable privileges.* The privilege to compete applies only to interference with economic prospects, not to interference with contract. *Lumley* itself illustrates liability of a competitor who interferes with an actual contract. In contrast, one grocery store can compete with another for customers, since grocery stores don't have customers under contract.

¶ 2. *Good motive and other uncertain privileges.* The Restatement thinks there may be privileges to interfere even with contract, but only advances a series of factors to consider. Taken together, do those factors merely suggest that the court gets to follow its biases and relieve good guys from liability but not guys the court thinks are "bad?"

¶ 3. *Mixed motive.* Good motives (including competition) are especially likely to help a defendant avoid liability when the interference is with economic prospects, not actual contracts. What about both good and bad motives? Assuming we have the right to judge motives arising out of ill-will, what is to be done if the defendant also has good and socially useful motives? That is *Aleyska*. The court decided it could know which motive was dominant (the bad one, of course) and imposed liability. But why a dominant motive test? Can we really know which motives are both bad and dominant? What if the good motive alone would have caused the interference? In that case, should the defendant avoid liability? The *Mt. Healthy* approach is something like that.

¶ 4. *Putting the burden on the plaintiff.* Prima facie torts are rare. Usually we require the plaintiff to prove something and don't require the defendant to justify his conduct until the plaintiff has a proved it wrongful. This note leads us to *Wal-Mart v. Sturges*, next.

WAL-MART STORES V. STURGES , 52 S.W.3d 711 (Tex. 2001)

Note first that this is an interference with prospects case, not an interference with an existing contract. In that context, the Texas Court requires the plaintiff to shoulder the burden of proving, not mere ill-will as in *Alyeska*, but conduct that is independently tortious, illustratively, fraud or defamation that interferes. Courts may be working toward some such requirement, but this case is perhaps the most stringent, because it requires actual tortious behavior before imposing liability. Notice that this does not extend to interference with contract claims.

Notes 2-5. Boycotts. We have cut this material down dramatically in this Edition. While the boycott represents a form of interference with contract, development of this fact pattern must await advanced courses in labor law, anti-discrimination law, or antitrust law.

§ 3. INTELLECTUAL PROPERTY AND UNFAIR COMPETITION–TRADEMARK INFRINGEMENT

NOTE: INTELLECTUAL PROPERTY AND UNFAIR COMPETITION

This note surveys several types of intellectual property rights: patents, copyrights, and trade secrets. Notice that patents and copyrights are monopolies for a limited time. The time limit is significant (see Note 2). That's a point we'll want to remember when we get to rights of publicity (§ 4 below).

¶ **2. *Patents.*** The free competition theme that was missing interference with contract cases, comes on strong in *Bonito Boats*. In the world of functioning goods, you are free to copy your competitor's work in detail, so long as it is not patented (or conceivably, copyrighted as a work of art). We'll see, however, that you can't present your product as your competitor's – the law of trademark or unfair competition will prevent that. On the other hand, we will also see that unfair competition law won't give you trademark type protection for functional designs– that has to be left to patents.

¶ **3. *Copyrights.*** There are some highly specialized parts of copyright law (music, for example). If we take ordinary printed materials, art, and the like as our example, there is a lot that mysterious, but plenty that is also straightforward. If you create ("author") an original work, you hold copyright under federal law. Maybe it will be a good idea to register the copyright, otherwise your remedies may be limited. How original does it have to be? Not very. It can't be merely alphabetizing a list, but it could be very bad (or even pornographic) story. What is copyrighted is the specific tangible form, not the ideas. If the theme is about obsession with a white whale or a cache or gold at the bottom of the river or a secret cache of weapons hidden in desert, it won't matter that someone else has already used those ideas because it is not the idea that is copyrighted. It is the specific presentation of it, organization, words, and so on.

With this wide notion of copyright on the table, the problem is: won't copyright law hamper free speech? Maybe not, since ideas are not copyrighted; anybody can discuss insane obsessions or hidden gold. In addition, the statute specifically recognizes fair use – determined by considering the four factors listed in this paragraph. In *Hustler Magazine, Inc. v. Moral Majority*, 796 F.2d 1148 (9th Cir. 1986), Hustler magazine published a nasty satire about Jerry Falwell. Falwell lost his claim against Hustler on free speech grounds, but then turned the tables by sending out copies of the Hustler satire to potential donors, asking for money. Hustler claimed a violation of its copyright. But Falwell's Moral Majority won on fair use grounds. Can the class see elements in the list that might apply to relieve the Moral Majority from liability for using copyrighted material?

¶ 4. *Trade secrets.* Just about any information that is economically useful can be a trade secret -- the formula for a popular soft drink, for example. Trade secret protection might last forever if the owner can keep the secret. No law is required for that. What does the law of trade secrets do? It holds liable those who obtain the secret by improper means, such as breach of confidence, breach of contract, out right theft or the like. If you buy the popular soft drink, analyze it, and come up with its formula without breach of confidence or contract, fine, you can use it and make it public.

QUALITEX CO. V. JACOBSON PRODUCTS CO., 514 U.S. 159 (1995)

Qualitex has sold green-gold pads to dry cleaning establishments for use on presses since the 1950s. In 1989, Jacobson began selling competing pads with the same color. Qualitex brought an unfair competition suit, then registered the color as a trademark and added an infringement count. The trial court found for Qualitext, but the Ninth Circuit reversed, holding that color alone could not count as a trademark. *Held*: reversed. Color alone *can* count as a trademark.

Qualitex introduces some important trademark ideas– identification of the mark owner as the source of goods, the likelihood of confusion, the use of trade dress or product configuration (like a non-functional color) as a "mark," and the functionality rule.

A mark must be distinctive, capable of distinguishing the plaintiff's goods from others. It might be inherently distinctive because it is a totally arbitrary word or symbol. If not, it might acquire distinctiveness by use and association with the plaintiff's product. The Court thought a color could be in that category. The type of distinctiveness is often called secondary meaning. Some words or symbols cannot be distinctive; they describe the whole class of goods. So "Lumber" for a lumber company cannot very well count as a trademark.

On the other hand, trade dress, the way a product is packaged or displayed, may well count as a trademark, provided it is not functional. Functional features cannot be trademarks; that would undermine *Bonito Boats*, Casebook 1029.

Note 1. Infringement. Infringement of a trademark, either under the Lanham Act or under the common law, is a tort. Infringement will occur with outright copying of a valid mark, of course, but also when the defendant uses a mark (including trade dress) that creates confusion. Even the likelihood of confusion will be enough if the mark owner seeks an injunction rather than damages.

Note 2. Dilution. This shades into a kind of statutory disparagement claim. Conventionally, dilution might be tarnishment, association of the protected mark with something unsavory; or it might be merely blurring, making the plaintiff's mark non-unique. These are not infringement cases. No one really thinks Tiffany's Cat Chow is made in the back rooms at the jewelers, but the jeweler's mark– its name– is perhaps diluted. Dilution claims cannot be made to protect weak marks, that is, marks are not very distinctive or that are distinctive only in a narrow context, like "Blue Ribbon." Dilution claims were created by statute, first in some states, but now under the federal statute, 15 U.S.C. § 1125(c).

Note 3. Free speech: trademark cases. Where the plaintiff's mark is not used to describe or identify the *defendant's* product but only the plaintiff's, there is probably no trademark infringement. At any rate the Ninth Circuit has so held and other cases get similar result. *New Kids on the Block v. News American Publishing, Inc.,* 971 F.2d 302 (9th Cir. 1992) (imposing, however, some limitations); see also *Ty Inc. v. Perryman,* 306 F.3d 509 (7th Cir. 2002). Does this bear on free speech? Surely. Suppose a public interest group runs an ad attacking Philip Morris for selling a cancer causing product. Philip Morris is a trademark. But even without the First Amendment's help, the attack seems not to be a violation of trademark.

§ 4. MISAPPROPRIATION OF COMMERCIAL VALUE

A. Appropriation of Personality or "Identity"

CARSON V. HERE'S JOHNNY PORTABLE TOILETS, INC., 698 F.2d 831 (6th Cir. 1983)

"Here's Johnny," a phrase of the English language peculiarly associated with the plaintiff, who is a famous person, was used as the trademark for a maker of toilets. (Sadly, you may have to tell some of your students how famous Johnny Carson once was, and how distinctive Ed McMahon's utterance was.) Since the mark was weak — that is, not arbitrary like "ALZAK" cookies– it could be used in a variety of goods not competing with the owner's goods or services. The idea here is that there would be little risk of confusion if the mark is weak and the goods or services are not competing (hence a "Gold Medal Beer" probably does not infringe a "Gold Medal Computer.") But even though there is no good trademark claim here, the plaintiff has a claim for invasion of his right of publicity, analogous to, if not identical to, the kind of privacy invasion known as commercial appropriation. The idea is that he owns a valuable commercial identity – his image, personality, features, etc. – and should be able to have exclusive rights to sell it. If anyone can use his name in this way, he will not be able to sell it because users could take it without charge.

Is there a free speech issue here? How did Carson acquire a right to preempt those particular words of the English language? If Carson's claim is less commercial and more personal, if it is a claim that he is diminished as a person because of the unseemly association with toilet, is the free speech argument for the defense stronger or weaker?

B. Misappropriation of Commercial Values

INTERNATIONAL NEWS SERVICE V. ASSOCIATED PRESS , 248 U.S. 215 (1918)

The plaintiff generated news materials, which it disseminated to its customers, newspapers. The defendant copied these news materials from the newspapers and their bulletin boards, then distributed the material to its own customers, other newspapers, who published it in some form. The material was not copyrighted. The plaintiff was entitled to no protection under the copyright laws, but the Court held it was entitled to protection under a federal common law which would recognize quasi property in the work. It explained this narrowly as a case of unfair competition, limited to the situation in which one competitor takes the work of another; but it also used broad language, condemning the defendant's effort to "reap where it has not sown . . . ."

INS preceded the heyday of free speech. It was also a pre-*Erie* decision, so presumably would not be duplicated today by a Federal court. If a state court attempted to impose such a liability today, would the Supreme Court accept it?

SEARS, ROEBUCK & CO. V. STIFFEL CO., 376 U.S. 225 (1964)

Here a state court did impose liability somewhat analogous to that imposed in *INS*, but the Supreme Court will have none of it! Stiffel invested its work effort in creating a pole lamp which sold very well. Noticing this, Sears copied the lamp and sold identical copies more cheaply. Just as the news stories in *INS* enjoyed no copyright, the lamp in *Sears-Stiffel* enjoyed no patent. Thus Sears could claim it had every right to do as it did– just as INS could claim the same when it copied AP news stories. But in *Sears-Stiffel* the Court held that copying could be carried out freely. Any other rule would give the lamp maker a perpetual monopoly on the lamp's design– even though it failed to qualify for the monopoly of limited duration under the patent laws!

Note 1. *Bonito Boats* is reprised here. Its stance is like *Sears,'* but it recognizes the possibility of appropriate trademark protection if a product design is not functional but is distinctive of the plaintiff's product.

Note 2. *INS* raised a problem in free speech and free competition. *Sears-Stiffel* raised a problem in free competition only. Yet the *Stiffel* solution provides a wider protection for competition than *INS* provides for both competition and free speech. Is *INS* impliedly left to rot in the limbo of federal common law? See the comments on and following *Zacchini,* the next case.

ZACCHINI V. SCRIPPS HOWARD BROADCASTING CO., 433 U.S. 562 (1977).

You are free to copy an unpatented pole lamp, but not an uncopyrighted cannonball act?

Mr. Zacchini can prohibit copying of his act where Stiffel could not permit the copying of its lamp. *Zacchini* would not be so shocking except for the fact that no restrictions were placed by contract on the plaintiff's rights; its ticket seems not to have contained the usual restrictions on cameras. You might think that this puts the defendant in the same position it would be in if it made pictures of Zacchini performing in a public park. What happened to the free speech concerns of *Times-Sullivan?* Did Zacchini not "thrust himself" into the public eye?

After *Zacchini,* the Court in *Bonito Boats,* Note 1 following *Sears,* reaffirmed the *Sears* principle. The rule then is that your product's design, or its trade dress, can serve as a trademark-like identifier and can be protected as such if it is distinctive and identified the product/source in the public mind. Is Zacchini's "identity" expressed in his complete performance to be treated like trade dress?

Note. We saw the uncertain pull of the First Amendment throughout this Chapter, and we close with that issue here. We give a pretty fair amount of factual detail on the *C.B.C.* case, perhaps enough (with its holding) to kick the issue around with your class, if you are so inclined.

CHAPTER 34

MISREPRESENTATION AND OTHER MISDEALINGS

▶ **Changes in the Sixth Edition.** We have cut this Chapter slightly by turning the *Pinnacle Peak* case into a shorter case abstract. Some Notes have been revised, and we've added eight new case citations or discussions in Notes.

§ 1. THEORIES OF LIABILITY AND THEIR CONSEQUENCES

This section is organized to permit highly compressed presentation of basic material. Though it is compressed, it seems to work. Here is the sequence:

First, the context of simple fraud cases is set up by **Illustration 1**: there is a misrepresentation of fact, with economic loss following. Then in quick sequence we get the two most common bases for liability: scienter fraud, presented in *Derry v. Peek*; and negligence, presented in the Restatement § 552.

Note 3 after *Derry v. Peek* asks first whether the employer in *Randi W. v. Muroc* would be liable for physical harms resulting from a false-positive letter of recommendation. The court answered yes. Second, we ask whether the publisher of the Yellow Pages ad in *Knepper* could be liable for physical harms resulting from an ad that intentionally misrepresented a doctor's qualifications. The court there held that the plaintiff proved a case of fraud against the publisher, and that the physical damages were a reasonably foreseeable consequence of the fraud, thus recoverable. A jury verdict for $1.5 million was affirmed.

Before looking at the possibility of strict liability, we look at some of the consequences of proceeding on a negligence theory rather than a scienter

973

fraud theory. One major consequence is that if the defendant is merely negligent, he may have no liability to third persons who have relied on his (negligent) misstatements. This is *Ultramares v. Touche, Niven & Co.* Some important cases rejected this rule, but recent decisions accept some version of it. The second major consequence of proceeding on a negligence theory is that damages may be limited. The damages rules for the two types of misrepresentation claims are presented in **Illustrations 2, 3 and 4**.

Note 4 following Illustration 4 cites *BDO Seidman, LLP v. Mindis Acquisition Corp.*, for the rule that with negligent misrepresentation, the plaintiff gets only out of pocket damages. It may be that the court meant this rule to apply only in cases of negligent misrepresentation by a defendant who was not in privity. The court said: "A benefit-of-the-bargain standard gives the wronged party the benefit of the contract he made, but it also ensures that the fraudfeasor does not enjoy any fruits of his misdeeds. The dual purposes of this standard have no application in a negligent misrepresentation case where there was no privity because the defendant was not a party to the transaction and thus, has not been unjustly enriched."

Gauerke v. Rozga then takes us to the end of the section. It introduces the possibility of strict liability for innocent misstatements, and at the same time presents the student opportunities to consolidate the learning of the previous materials. One of those opportunities is to analyze whether, after all, some statements made of one's own knowledge might not fit the definition of scienter fraud. If you don't know the facts and you are conscious of your own ignorance, a positive assertion is reckless, "careless whether it be true or false," under the test in *Derry v. Peek*. The second opportunity is to extrapolate the principles about damages and third party liability just covered in the materials that distinguish between scienter fraud and negligent misrepresentation.

§ 2. RELIANCE AND RELATED DOCTRINES

The topic of reliance is mostly covered in the introductory text. *Pinnacle Peak Developers v. TRW Investment Corp.* presents a problem that is only partly one of reasonable reliance. The fraud rule is that the plaintiff must prove misrepresentation of fact. A promise will be a token of contract, not fraud, and the plaintiff's claim for breach of promise must stand or fall on the law of contract. And there is no such thing as a misrepresentation of fact about the future— it cannot be a "fact" until it exists.

These statements can be interpreted to express in a formal way the underlying policies. First, you honor the contract rules when you deal with promises. If the parol evidence rule excludes evidence of a deal made before the written contract and that is ruled out by the written contract, then you should not make an end run around that rule by calling a promise fraud. Second, the fraud rules themselves reject the claim unless the plaintiff has relied in fact on the misrepresentation and relied reasonably. It is generally not reasonable to rely on a statement about the future. Hence if the defendant's communication about the future is a promise, the plaintiff has no tort claim. If it is not, he still has no claim because he cannot reasonably rely on such "non-factual" statements.

Pinnacle Peak deals with an exception. If you state now your present intention to do something in the future, you can misstate one fact – the fact of your present intention, as repeated in **Note 1**. Thus if you say you intend to install tennis courts and swimming pools for the owners of the condominium, but you have no such intention, you have misstated your state of mind – and that is a present fact. This line of reasoning gets you off one horn of the dilemma, since it shows that there was a factual misstatement.

Pinnacle Peak then goes on to consider the other horn of the dilemma. Although the statement of present intent can be thought of as a misstatement of fact, it functions very much like a promise. That being so, should it not have to meet the contract rules? Specifically, what is to be done with the parol evidence rule and the statute of frauds? *Pinnacle Peak's* answer is that in some cases the parol evidence rule will bar the tort claim and in others it will not. One factor is whether the parties were business people, negotiating formal contracts. Another is the degree of contradiction between the oral promise and the writing. This second factor is discussed briefly in **Note 3**.

FYI: Fraud on the market or indirect reliance. In recent years, lawyers have urged that a kind of indirect reliance should suffice. The point arose in securities litigation. If D misrepresents something about the company that induces many buyers to pay a higher price (or a lower one), but the plaintiff does not know of the representation when he buys, he has not relied in the traditional sense. On the other hand, he might have relied on the integrity of the market, on the idea that others buying and selling were doing so on the basis of honest information. This might suffice under some circumstances under federal securities laws. See *Basic Inc. v. Levinson*, 485 U.S. 224 (1988). The California Court rejected the idea under California securities laws. *Mirkin v. Wasserman*, 858 P.2d 568 (Cal. 1993). For a non-securities situation, see *Nataros v. Fine Arts Gallery of Scottsdale, Inc.*, 612 P.2d 500 (Ariz. Ct. App. 1980).■

Note 4. Economic loss rule. In *Digicorp, Inc. v. Ameritech Corp.*, cited at the end of this Note, Ameritech was in the business of selling telephone services. Digicorp was an authorized distributor. Ameritech induced Digicorp to accept responsibility for all employees of Digicorp's subcontractor and provided that if any of those employees forged signatures of supposed customers, Ameritech could terminate the contract with Digicorp. Digicorp knowingly signed on to this contract, but it did so because Ameritech had withheld important information. Ameritech knew an employee of Digicorp's subcontractor, while working for another Ameritech distributor, had forged customer signatures, but did not disclose this information. After the new contract was signed, Krinsky forged customer contracts on a massive scale and Ameritech terminated Digicorp, who then claimed fraud damages against Ameritech. The court held that (1) the economic loss doctrine applied to fraud cases, (2) subject to a narrow exception where the fraud in inducing the contract is "extraneous" to the contract, not interwoven with it. Here, the court thought that the fraud was "interwoven" with the contract because Digicorp had contractually undertaken to accept the risks of forging employees. Distinguish such cases as *Tietsworth v. Harley-Davidson,* Inc., 677 N.W.2d 233 (Wis. 2004), where the plaintiff allegedly received goods worth less than they would be worth if the seller's representations had been true. In a case like that, the purchaser might be barred from the fraud claim but still recover for breach of warranty, since the economic loss doctrine does not bar contract claims. These and other cases are discussed in DOBBS ON TORTS § 483A (Supp.).

§ 3. DUTY TO DISCLOSE

OLLERMAN V. O'ROURKE CO., 288 N.W.2d 95 (Wis. 1980)

Granted that a defendant is liable for scienter fraud misstatements, and even some negligent and innocent misstatements, the nonfeasance rules seen in Chapter 16 suggest that the defendant would not be responsible to speak up to save the plaintiff from a mistake, so long as the defendant was not responsible for the plaintiff's mistake in the first place. This is in fact the general rule as traditionally understood.

In *Ollerman,* the seller allegedly knew of a well beneath the surface of the land he sold, but never mentioned it to the plaintiff-purchaser. The plaintiff was put to considerable added expense in building on the lot because of the well. The court quickly considered the exceptions to the no-duty rule: (1) there is liability for failure to disclose where the seller actively conceals the defect; (2) where the seller has told a half-truth or made an ambiguous statement; (3) where there is a fiduciary relationship between the parties; and (4) (perhaps) where the facts are peculiarly within the knowledge of the seller and the other cannot discover them for himself. The *Ollerman* case concededly falls within none of these exceptions, but then the court considered whether it fell within the Restatement's formulation of a wider duty – namely, to disclose "basic" facts going to the "essence" of the transaction. Without stopping here, however, the court went on to present a broader holding: the commercial seller of land has a duty to disclose to the consumer-buyer facts known to him that are material (not "basic," going to the "essence.")

Should the duty to disclose extend so far? What if the seller does not know the fact but should have known in the exercise of reasonable care? Does he then become liable for negligent non-disclosure?

Beyond nondisclosure, you can question whether courts should impose liability for conduct that is persuasive or manipulative when the defendant makes no actual misstatement of fact. This is traditionally not sufficient to show misrepresentation unless the manipulative conduct implies a misstatement of fact as well. Fiduciaries might be liable for persuasion against the beneficiary's best interests, however, and the securities and consumer protection statutes often condemn not only fraud and non-disclosure but also "manipulative" devices, the effect of which is to induce action, though not by misrepresentation. Can common law fraud be expanded in this direction? Should it be?